Writing the Nation

A Concise Introduction to American Literature

1865 to Present

Amy Berke, PhD   Robert R. Bleil, PhD   Jordan Cofer, PhD   Doug Davis, PhD

ISBN: 978-1-940771-34-2

Produced by:
University System of Georgia

Published by:
University of North Georgia Press
Dahlonega, Georgia

Cover Design and Layout Design:
Corey Parson

For more information, please visit http://ung.edu/university-press
Or email ungpress@ung.edu

If you need this text in another format, please contact ungpress@ung.edu
or call 706-864-1556

TABLE OF CONTENTS

1

LATE ROMANTICISM (1855-1870)

Robert R. Bleil

1.1 LEARNING OUTCOMES

After completing this chapter, you should be able to:

- Describe the key features of Romanticism.
- Analyze the ways in which the works of Emily Dickinson and Walt Whitman broke from the American literary tradition of Emerson, Hawthorne, and Melville.
- Analyze the impact of the Industrial Revolution and the Civil War on American literature.
- Compare the ways in which Emily Dickinson and Walt Whitman established new voices in American literature.

1.2 INTRODUCTION

Emily Dickinson and Walt Whitman, the authors whose works appear in this chapter, are unlikely protagonists—or leading characters—for a literary movement. Each was an outsider: Dickinson, an unmarried woman who lived a life of quiet seclusion in western Massachusetts, and Whitman, a vagabond who lived a life in search of community. Dickinson and Whitman promoted a spirit of exploration and inventiveness that matched the geographical, industrial, political, and social growth of the United States. From their works, we gain not so much a literary renaissance as we do a sense of artistic innovation that developed alongside these other areas of American life and commerce.

As literary historians like William Charvat have noted, the development of an American literary tradition owes as much to the development of the American publishing industry in the middle decades of the nineteenth century as it does to the prominence of individual authors like Catharine Maria Sedgwick, Washington Irving, Nathaniel Hawthorne, Edgar Allan Poe, Herman Melville, Ralph Waldo Emerson, Henry David Thoreau, and Harriet Beecher Stowe. Sales of these authors' works were dwarfed by the sales of pirated editions of novels by British authors like Walter Scott and Charles Dickens. Nonetheless, the success of these British imports convinced American publishers that the American market was sufficiently robust to demand new works; this demand created an opportunity for American writers to expand their audience, and a flourishing literary culture began to prosper.

American authors still faced steep odds in seeing their works into print, and American literary publishing did not flourish until the completion of the **First Transcontinental Railroad** in 1869 allowed the reliably consistent shipment of individuals and goods across the country. Additional technological improvements, including the widespread adoption of steam-powered machinery and gas-fueled lights, also provide the necessary conditions for the rapid production of printed materials and the means by which these materials could be enjoyed at the conclusion of a day of laboring. Thus, only when the Industrial Age expands the definition of leisure do Americans begin to embrace the culture of print and expand the boundaries of American literature.

The first attempts to define the literary culture of the mid-nineteenth century began in the 1930s and early 1940s as the United States took on a larger role in global politics, and the need for definition gained sharper focus with the publication of F. O. Matthiessen's *The American Renaissance* in 1941. Matthiessen argued that writers like Hawthorne, Melville, Emerson, and Thoreau represented the expansion of a uniquely American style of writing that interacted with, and embraced, the North American landscape in new ways. What Matthiessen called a renaissance, however, was less of a cultural flourishing than the limited success of a few male authors from New England. Despite the real impact of Matthiessen's work in recognizing the presence of significant male American writers, his catalogue still neglected writing of women, African-Americans, and Native Americans whose works would not be widely recognized until the 1970s.

In order to describe the work of these authors, Matthiessen and others turned to literary labels popularized in reference to British authors of the late eighteenth and early nineteenth centuries. **Romanticism**, a literary movement emphasizing the freedom and originality of self-expression that began in Europe at the end of the eighteenth century, also seemed to capture the spirit of nineteenth-century America and was frequently applied to authors of both prose and poetry. In the hands of these authors, the meadows of western Massachusetts replaced the Lake District as the source of inspiration, and the rejection of Puritan morality continued the American emphasis on freedom of expression. When Whitman and Dickinson began writing poetry in the 1850s, the thriving Abolitionist movement added urgency to the need for new voices and rapid change.

When we refer to Whitman and Dickinson as late Romantics, we place them at the end of a period that begins in the 1820s, and we suggest that their works are merely derivative from those that preceded them chronologically. Yet Whitman's and Dickinson's poetry is contemporary with these other works, and it seems more fruitful to consider the differences in genre than the differences in chronology. Whitman and Dickinson achieved their fame by changing American poetry from patriotic and historical ballads to **free verse**—poetry that lacks both **rhyme** and regular **meter**—and musically inspired celebrations of the individual in the American landscape.

Whitman and Dickinson are the most famous of the Late Romantics, and their work inspired successive generations of American authors. From these poets, Mark Twain, Stephen Crane, and Charles Chesnutt found the freedom to use a variety of American dialects in their work, the realists of the late nineteenth and early twentieth centuries discovered the richness of the American landscape, and the Modernist poets located a source of new poetical forms to meet the needs of the adolescent Republic that came of age in the decades immediately following the **Civil War**.

That national coming of age, in the years of Reconstruction, Western Expansion, Manifest Destiny, industrial might, and rapid immigration, also marks the traditional beginning of courses like this one. The Civil War, while not a precise dividing line, is regarded as the most reliable current method for marking the split between the first and second half of the literary history of the United States. Teachers and critics quickly realized, however, that the continued growth of the literary and cultural productions of the United States required more precise divisions than the chronological division into pre-bellum and post-bellum periods can provide. This collection of readings follows those new divisions, with chapters on Late Romanticism, Realism, Naturalism, Pre-Modernism, Modernism, and post-1945 American Literature, but the boundaries between these divisions remain fluid.

The readings that follow are arranged loosely by chronology, and the author-editors of this collection have tried to provide useful headnotes to the sections and the individual authors, but do not be afraid to draw connections beyond the loose boundaries and invent new terms that better describe these works. As American literature continues to grow, we create new categories that better describe our shared experience.

1.3 WALT WHITMAN

(1819 - 1892)

The second of nine children and born in 1819 to a Long Island farmer and carpenter, Walt Whitman is both the journeyman poet of American-ness and its champion. A journalist and newspaper editor throughout his life, Whitman worked as a law clerk, a schoolteacher, a printer, a civil servant, and a hospital aide, but he was always writing; from his teenage years until his death, his byline was on constant view. Contemporary reports suggest that Whitman was an industrious worker but that he was often accused of idleness because his habit of long midday walks contrasted sharply with nineteenth-century attitudes toward work. In

Image 1.1 | Walt Whitman, 1887.
Photographer | George C. Cox
Source | Wikimedia Commons
License | Public Domain

"Song of Myself," Whitman addressed these critics directly by writing, "I loafe and invite my soul,/ I lean and loafe at my ease observing a spear of summer grass" (4-5). For Whitman, too much industry dulled the ability to celebrate the ordinary. In the preface to the first edition of *Leaves of Grass* in 1855, Whitman expounds on his love for the common: "Other states indicate themselves in their deputies...but the genius of the United States is not best or most in its executives or legislators, nor in its ambassadors or authors or colleges or churches or parlors, nor even in its newspapers or inventors...but always most in the common people."[1] Whitman's love for the common people that he encountered and observed in the urban centers of the north is expressed in all of his poetry; if his British contemporary Alfred Lord Tennyson is the national poet of mourning, then Whitman is the national poet of celebration.

Many readers feel confused and disoriented when reading Whitman for the first time. Without using the aid of rhyme and meter as a guide, Whitman's poetry may initially appear disjointed and meandering, but at the same time readers often take great comfort in the simplicity of the language, the clarity of the images, and the deep **cadences,** or rhythms, of the verse. Such contradictions are at the heart of Whitman's work. Much of Whitman's success and endurance as a poet comes from his ability to marry embedded cultural forms to the needs of a growing and rapidly modernizing nation. Whitman first came to wide public attention with the publication of the first edition of *Leaves of Grass* in 1855 when he was just twenty-five years old. Grand in scope if not in size, the first edition established Whitman as a poet who loved wordplay and common images; by the time of his death in 1892, Whitman had expanded the initial collection of just twelve poems over the course of six editions to one that ultimately included more than 400 poems. The

---

1   http://www.whitmanarchive.org/published/LG/figures/ppp.00271.010.jpg

selection included here largely samples Whitman's early poetry up through the Civil War. In the selections from *Song of Myself* and "Crossing Brooklyn Ferry," we see Whitman at his most iconic: sweeping views of everyday life that freely mingle high and low culture. Yet the poet of the common man did not spend all of his days gazing at his fellow Americans. In the final selection from Whitman, we see Whitman rising as a national poet with "O Captain! My Captain!" one of two poems on the death of Abraham Lincoln. An urban poet who lived almost his entire life in New York, New Jersey, and Washington, DC, the enduring appeal of his works testifies to his ability to connect the great and the common through language.

1.3.1 *Song of Myself*

1

I CELEBRATE myself, and sing myself,
And what I assume you shall assume,
For every atom belonging to me as good belongs to you.
I loafe and invite my soul,
I lean and loafe at my ease observing a spear of summer grass.
My tongue, every atom of my blood, form'd from this soil, this air,
Born here of parents born here from parents the same, and their parents the same,
I, now thirty-seven years old in perfect health begin,
Hoping to cease not till death.
Creeds and schools in abeyance,
Retiring back a while sufficed at what they are, but never forgotten,
I harbor for good or bad, I permit to speak at every hazard,
Nature without check with original energy.

2

Houses and rooms are full of perfumes, the shelves are crowded with perfumes,
I breathe the fragrance myself and know it and like it,
The distillation would intoxicate me also, but I shall not let it.
The atmosphere is not a perfume, it has no taste of the distillation, it is odorless,
It is for my mouth forever, I am in love with it,
I will go to the bank by the wood and become undisguised and naked,
I am mad for it to be in contact with me.
The smoke of my own breath,
Echoes, ripples, buzz'd whispers, love-root, silk-thread, crotch and vine,
My respiration and inspiration, the beating of my heart, the passing of blood and
  air through my lungs,
The sniff of green leaves and dry leaves, and of the shore and dark-color'd sea-
  rocks, and of hay in the barn,
The sound of the belch'd words of my voice loos'd to the eddies of the wind,
A few light kisses, a few embraces, a reaching around of arms,
The play of shine and shade on the trees as the supple boughs wag,

The delight alone or in the rush of the streets, or along the fields and hill-sides,
The feeling of health, the full-noon trill, the song of me rising from bed and
    meeting the sun.
Have you reckon'd a thousand acres much? have you reckon'd the earth much?
Have you practis'd so long to learn to read?
Have you felt so proud to get at the meaning of poems?
Stop this day and night with me and you shall possess the origin of all poems,
You shall possess the good of the earth and sun, (there are millions of suns left,)
You shall no longer take things at second or third hand, nor look through the eyes
    of the dead, nor feed on the spectres in books,
You shall not look through my eyes either, nor take things from me,
You shall listen to all sides and filter them from your self.

3

I have heard what the talkers were talking, the talk of the beginning and the end,
But I do not talk of the beginning or the end.
There was never any more inception than there is now,
Nor any more youth or age than there is now,
And will never be any more perfection than there is now,
Nor any more heaven or hell than there is now.
Urge and urge and urge,
Always the procreant urge of the world.
Out of the dimness opposite equals advance, always substance and increase, always sex,
Always a knit of identity, always distinction, always a breed of life.
To elaborate is no avail, learn'd and unlearn'd feel that it is so.
Sure as the most certain sure, plumb in the uprights, well entretied, braced in the
    beams,
Stout as a horse, affectionate, haughty, electrical,
I and this mystery here we stand.
Clear and sweet is my soul, and clear and sweet is all that is not my soul.
Lack one lacks both, and the unseen is proved by the seen,
Till that becomes unseen and receives proof in its turn.
Showing the best and dividing it from the worst age vexes age,
Knowing the perfect fitness and equanimity of things, while they discuss I am
    silent, and go bathe and admire myself.
Welcome is every organ and attribute of me, and of any man hearty and clean,
Not an inch nor a particle of an inch is vile, and none shall be less familiar than the rest.
I am satisfied—I see, dance, laugh, sing;
As the hugging and loving bed-fellow sleeps at my side through the night, and
    withdraws at the peep of the day with stealthy tread,
Leaving me baskets cover'd with white towels swelling the house with their plenty,
Shall I postpone my acceptation and realization and scream at my eyes,

That they turn from gazing after and down the road,
And forthwith cipher and show me to a cent,
Exactly the value of one and exactly the value of two, and which is ahead?

4

Trippers and askers surround me,
People I meet, the effect upon me of my early life or the ward and city I live in, or
    the nation,
The latest dates, discoveries, inventions, societies, authors old and new,
My dinner, dress, associates, looks, compliments, dues,
The real or fancied indifference of some man or woman I love,
The sickness of one of my folks or of myself, or ill-doing or loss or lack of money,
    or depressions or exaltations,
Battles, the horrors of fratricidal war, the fever of doubtful news, the fitful events;
These come to me days and nights and go from me again,
But they are not the Me myself.
Apart from the pulling and hauling stands what I am,
Stands amused, complacent, compassionating, idle, unitary,
Looks down, is erect, or bends an arm on an impalpable certain rest,
Looking with side-curved head curious what will come next,
Both in and out of the game and watching and wondering at it.
Backward I see in my own days where I sweated through fog with linguists and
    contenders,
I have no mockings or arguments, I witness and wait.

5

I believe in you my soul, the other I am must not abase itself to you,
And you must not be abased to the other.
Loafe with me on the grass, loose the stop from your throat,
Not words, not music or rhyme I want, not custom or lecture, not even the best,
Only the lull I like, the hum of your valved voice.
I mind how once we lay such a transparent summer morning,
How you settled your head athwart my hips and gently turn'd over upon me,
And parted the shirt from my bosom-bone, and plunged your tongue to my bare-
    stript heart,
And reach'd till you felt my beard, and reach'd till you held my feet.
Swiftly arose and spread around me the peace and knowledge that pass all the
    argument of the earth,
And I know that the hand of God is the promise of my own,
And I know that the spirit of God is the brother of my own,
And that all the men ever born are also my brothers, and the women my sisters
    and lovers,
And that a kelson of the creation is love,

And limitless are leaves stiff or drooping in the fields,
And brown ants in the little wells beneath them,
And mossy scabs of the worm fence, heap'd stones, elder, mullein and poke-weed.

6

A child said *What is the grass?* fetching it to me with full hands,
How could I answer the child? I do not know what it is any more than he.
I guess it must be the flag of my disposition, out of hopeful green stuff woven.
Or I guess it is the handkerchief of the Lord,
A scented gift and remembrancer designedly dropt,
Bearing the owner's name someway in the corners, that we may see and remark,
     and say *Whose?*
Or I guess the grass is itself a child, the produced babe of the vegetation.
Or I guess it is a uniform hieroglyphic,
And it means, Sprouting alike in broad zones and narrow zones,
Growing among black folks as among white,
Kanuck, Tuckahoe, Congressman, Cuff, I give them the same, I receive them the same.
And now it seems to me the beautiful uncut hair of graves.
Tenderly will I use you curling grass,
It may be you transpire from the breasts of young men,
It may be if I had known them I would have loved them,
It may be you are from old people, or from offspring taken soon out of their
     mothers' laps,
And here you are the mothers' laps.
This grass is very dark to be from the white heads of old mothers,
Darker than the colourless beards of old men,
Dark to come from under the faint red roofs of mouths.
O I perceive after all so many uttering tongues,
And I perceive they do not come from the roofs of mouths for nothing.
I wish I could translate the hints about the dead young men and women,
And the hints about old men and mothers, and the offspring taken soon out of
     their laps.
What do you think has become of the young and old men?
And what do you think has become of the women and children?
They are alive and well somewhere,
The smallest sprout shows there is really no death,
And if ever there was it led forward life, and does not wait at the end to arrest it,
And ceas'd the moment life appear'd.
All goes onward and outward, nothing collapses,
And to die is different from what any one supposed, and luckier.

7

Has any one supposed it lucky to be born?

I hasten to inform him or her it is just as lucky to die, and I know it.
I pass death with the dying and birth with the new-wash'd babe, and am not
    contain'd between my hat and boots,
And peruse manifold objects, no two alike and every one good,
The earth good and the stars good, and their adjuncts all good.
I am not an earth nor an adjunct of an earth,
I am the mate and companion of people, all just as immortal and fathomless as myself,
(They do not know how immortal, but I know.)
Every kind for itself and its own, for me mine male and female,
For me those that have been boys and that love women,
For me the man that is proud and feels how it stings to be slighted,
For me the sweet-heart and the old maid, for me mothers and the mothers of mothers,
For me lips that have smiled, eyes that have shed tears,
For me children and the begetters of children.
Undrape! you are not guilty to me, nor stale nor discarded,
I see through the broadcloth and gingham whether or no,
And am around, tenacious, acquisitive, tireless, and cannot be shaken away.

8

The little one sleeps in its cradle,
I lift the gauze and look a long time, and silently brush away flies with my hand.
The youngster and the red-faced girl turn aside up the bushy hill,
I peeringly view them from the top.
The suicide sprawls on the bloody floor of the bedroom,
I witness the corpse with its dabbled hair, I note where the pistol has fallen.
The blab of the pave, tires of carts, sluff of boot-soles, talk of the promenaders,
The heavy omnibus, the driver with his interrogating thumb, the clank of the
    shod horses on the granite floor,
The snow-sleighs, clinking, shouted jokes, pelts of snow-balls,
The hurrahs for popular favorites, the fury of rous'd mobs,
The flap of the curtain'd litter, a sick man inside borne to the hospital,
The meeting of enemies, the sudden oath, the blows and fall,
The excited crowd, the policeman with his star quickly working his passage to the
    centre of the crowd,
The impassive stones that receive and return so many echoes,
What groans of over-fed or half-starv'd who fall sunstruck or in fits,
What exclamations of women taken suddenly who hurry home and give birth to
    babes,
What living and buried speech is always vibrating here, what howls restrain'd by
    decorum,
Arrests of criminals, slights, adulterous offers made, acceptances, rejections with
    convex lips,
I mind them or the show or resonance of them—I come and I depart.

9

The big doors of the country barn stand open and ready,
The dried grass of the harvest-time loads the slow-drawn wagon,
The clear light plays on the brown gray and green intertinged,
The armfuls are pack'd to the sagging mow.
I am there, I help, I came stretch'd atop of the load,
I felt its soft jolts, one leg reclined on the other,
I jump from the cross-beams and seize the clover and timothy,
And roll head over heels and tangle my hair full of wisps.

10

Alone far in the wilds and mountains I hunt,
Wandering amazed at my own lightness and glee,
In the late afternoon choosing a safe spot to pass the night,
Kindling a fire and broiling the fresh-kill'd game,
Falling asleep on the gather'd leaves with my dog and gun by my side.
The Yankee clipper is under her sky-sails, she cuts the sparkle and scud,
My eyes settle the land, I bend at her prow or shout joyously from the deck.
The boatmen and clam-diggers arose early and stopt for me,
I tuck'd my trowser-ends in my boots and went and had a good time;
You should have been with us that day round the chowder-kettle.
I saw the marriage of the trapper in the open air in the far west, the bride was a
        red girl,
Her father and his friends sat near cross-legged and dumbly smoking, they had
        moccasins to their feet and large thick blankets hanging from their shoulders,
On a bank lounged the trapper, he was drest mostly in skins, his luxuriant beard
        and curls protected his neck, he held his bride by the hand,
She had long eyelashes, her head was bare, her coarse straight locks descended
        upon her voluptuous limbs and reach'd to her feet.
The runaway slave came to my house and stopt outside,
I heard his motions crackling the twigs of the woodpile,
Through the swung half-door of the kitchen I saw him limpsy and weak,
And went where he sat on a log and led him in and assured him,
And brought water and fill'd a tub for his sweated body and bruis'd feet,
And gave him a room that enter'd from my own, and gave him some coarse clean clothes,
And remember perfectly well his revolving eyes and his awkwardness,
And remember putting plasters on the galls of his neck and ankles;
He staid with me a week before he was recuperated and pass'd north,
I had him sit next me at table, my fire-lock lean'd in the corner.

11

Twenty-eight young men bathe by the shore,
Twenty-eight young men and all so friendly;

Twenty-eight years of womanly life and all so lonesome.
She owns the fine house by the rise of the bank,
She hides handsome and richly drest aft the blinds of the window.
Which of the young men does she like the best?
Ah the homeliest of them is beautiful to her.
Where are you off to, lady? for I see you,
You splash in the water there, yet stay stock still in your room.
Dancing and laughing along the beach came the twenty-ninth bather,
The rest did not see her, but she saw them and loved them.
The beards of the young men glisten'd with wet, it ran from their long hair,
Little streams pass'd all over their bodies.
An unseen hand also pass'd over their bodies,
It descended tremblingly from their temples and ribs.
The young men float on their backs, their white bellies bulge to the sun, they do
    not ask who seizes fast to them,
They do not know who puffs and declines with pendant and bending arch,
They do not think whom they souse with spray.

12

The butcher-boy puts off his killing-clothes, or sharpens his knife at the stall in
    the market,
I loiter enjoying his repartee and his shuffle and break-down.
Blacksmiths with grimed and hairy chests environ the anvil,
Each has his main-sledge, they are all out, there is a great heat in the fire.
From the cinder-strew'd threshold I follow their movements,
The lithe sheer of their waists plays even with their massive arms,
Overhand the hammers swing, overhand so slow, overhand so sure,
They do not hasten, each man hits in his place.

13

The negro holds firmly the reins of his four horses, the block swags underneath
    on its tied-over chain,
The negro that drives the long dray of the stone-yard, steady and tall he stands
    pois'd on one leg on the string-piece,
His blue shirt exposes his ample neck and breast and loosens over his hip-band,
His glance is calm and commanding, he tosses the slouch of his hat away from his
    forehead,
The sun falls on his crispy hair and mustache, falls on the black of his polish'd
    and perfect limbs.
I behold the picturesque giant and love him, and I do not stop there,
I go with the team also.
In me the caresser of life wherever moving, backward as well as forward sluing,
To niches aside and junior bending, not a person or object missing,

Absorbing all to myself and for this song.
Oxen that rattle the yoke and chain or halt in the leafy shade, what is that you
    express in your eyes?
It seems to me more than all the print I have read in my life.
My tread scares the wood-drake and wood-duck on my distant and day-long ramble,
They rise together, they slowly circle around.
I believe in those wing'd purposes,
And acknowledge red, yellow, white, playing within me,
And consider green and violet and the tufted crown intentional,
And do not call the tortoise unworthy because she is not something else,
And the jay in the woods never studied the gamut, yet trills pretty well to me,
And the look of the bay mare shames silliness out of me.

14

The wild gander leads his flock through the cool night,
Ya-honk he says, and sounds it down to me like an invitation,
The pert may suppose it meaningless, but I listening close,
Find its purpose and place up there toward the wintry sky.
The sharp-hoof'd moose of the north, the cat on the housesill, the chickadee, the
    prairie-dog,
The litter of the grunting sow as they tug at her teats,
The brood of the turkey-hen and she with her half-spread wings,
I see in them and myself the same old law.
The press of my foot to the earth springs a hundred affections,
They scorn the best I can do to relate them.
I am enamour'd of growing out-doors,
Of men that live among cattle or taste of the ocean or woods,
Of the builders and steerers of ships and the wielders of axes and mauls, and the
    drivers of horses,
I can eat and sleep with them week in and week out.
What is commonest, cheapest, nearest, easiest, is Me,
Me going in for my chances, spending for vast returns,
Adorning myself to bestow myself on the first that will take me,
Not asking the sky to come down to my good will,
Scattering it freely forever.

15

The pure contralto sings in the organ loft,
The carpenter dresses his plank, the tongue of his foreplane whistles its wild
    ascending lisp,
The married and unmarried children ride home to their Thanksgiving dinner,
The pilot seizes the king-pin, he heaves down with a strong arm,
The mate stands braced in the whale-boat, lance and harpoon are ready,

The duck-shooter walks by silent and cautious stretches,
The deacons are ordain'd with cross'd hands at the altar,
The spinning-girl retreats and advances to the hum of the big wheel,
The farmer stops by the bars as he walks on a First-day loafe and looks at the oats
      and rye,
The lunatic is carried at last to the asylum a confirm'd case,
(He will never sleep any more as he did in the cot in his mother's bedroom;)
The jour printer with gray head and gaunt jaws works at his case,
He turns his quid of tobacco while his eyes blurr with the manuscript;
The malform'd limbs are tied to the surgeon's table,
What is removed drops horribly in a pail;
The quadroon girl is sold at the auction-stand, the drunkard nods by the bar-room
      stove,
The machinist rolls up his sleeves, the policeman travels his beat, the gate-keeper
      marks who pass,
The young fellow drives the express-wagon, (I love him, though I do not know him;)
The half-breed straps on his light boots to compete in the race,
The western turkey-shooting draws old and young, some lean on their rifles,
      some sit on logs,
Out from the crowd steps the marksman, takes his position, levels his piece;
The groups of newly-come immigrants cover the wharf or levee,
As the woolly-pates hoe in the sugar-field, the overseer views them from his saddle,
The bugle calls in the ball-room, the gentlemen run for their partners, the
      dancers bow to each other,
The youth lies awake in the cedar-roof'd garret and harks to the musical rain,
The Wolverine sets traps on the creek that helps fill the Huron,
The squaw wrapt in her yellow-hemm'd cloth is offering moccasins and bead-
      bags for sale,
The connoisseur peers along the exhibition-gallery with half-shut eyes bent sideways,
As the deck-hands make fast the steamboat the plank is thrown for the shore-
      going passengers,
The young sister holds out the skein while the elder sister winds it off in a ball,
      and stops now and then for the knots,
The one-year wife is recovering and happy having a week ago borne her first child,
The clean-hair'd Yankee girl works with her sewing-machine or in the factory or
      mill,
The paving-man leans on his two-handed rammer, the reporter's lead flies swiftly
      over the note-book, the signpainter is lettering with blue and gold,
The canal boy trots on the tow-path, the book-keeper counts at his desk, the
      shoemaker waxes his thread,
The conductor beats time for the band and all the performers follow him,
The child is baptized, the convert is making his first professions,
The regatta is spread on the bay, the race is begun, (how the white sails sparkle!)

The drover watching his drove sings out to them that would stray,
The pedler sweats with his pack on his back, (the purchaser higgling about the
    odd cent;)
The bride unrumples her white dress, the minute-hand of the clock moves slowly,
The opium-eater reclines with rigid head and just-open'd lips,
The prostitute draggles her shawl, her bonnet bobs on her tipsy and pimpled neck,
The crowd laugh at her blackguard oaths, the men jeer and wink to each other,
(Miserable! I do not laugh at your oaths nor jeer you;)
The President holding a cabinet council is surrounded by the great Secretaries,
On the piazza walk three matrons stately and friendly with twined arms,
The crew of the fish-smack pack repeated layers of halibut in the hold,
The Missourian crosses the plains toting his wares and his cattle,
As the fare-collector goes through the train he gives notice by the jingling of loose change,
The floor-men are laying the floor, the tinners are tinning the roof, the masons
    are calling for mortar,
In single file each shouldering his hod pass onward the laborers;
Seasons pursuing each other the indescribable crowd is gather'd, it is the fourth
    of Seventh-month, (what salutes of cannon and small arms!)
Seasons pursuing each other the plougher ploughs, the mower mows, and the
    winter-grain falls in the ground;
Off on the lakes the pike-fisher watches and waits by the hole in the frozen surface,
The stumps stand thick round the clearing, the squatter strikes deep with his axe,
Flatboatmen make fast towards dusk near the cotton-wood or pecan-trees,
Coon-seekers go through the regions of the Red river or through those drain'd by
    the Tennessee, or through those of the Arkansas,
Torches shine in the dark that hangs on the Chattahooche or Altamahaw,
Patriarchs sit at supper with sons and grandsons and great-grandsons around them,
In walls of adobie, in canvas tents, rest hunters and trappers after their day's sport,
The city sleeps and the country sleeps,
The living sleep for their time, the dead sleep for their time,
The old husband sleeps by his wife and the young husband sleeps by his wife;
And these tend inward to me, and I tend outward to them,
And such as it is to be of these more or less I am,
And of these one and all I weave the song of myself.

16

I am of old and young, of the foolish as much as the wise,
Regardless of others, ever regardful of others,
Maternal as well as paternal, a child as well as a man,
Stuff'd with the stuff that is coarse and stuff'd with the stuff that is fine,
One of the Nation of many nations, the smallest the same and the largest the same,
A Southerner soon as a Northerner, a planter nonchalant and hospitable down by
    the Oconee I live,

A Yankee bound my own way ready for trade, my joints the limberest joints on
      earth and the sternest joints on earth,
A Kentuckian walking the vale of the Elkhorn in my deer-skin leggings, a
      Louisianian or Georgian,
A boatman over lakes or bays or along coasts, a Hoosier, Badger, Buck-eye;
At home on Kanadian snow-shoes or up in the bush, or with fishermen off
      Newfoundland,
At home in the fleet of ice-boats, sailing with the rest and tacking,
At home on the hills of Vermont or in the woods of Maine, or the Texan ranch,
Comrade of Californians, comrade of free North-Westerners, (loving their big
      proportions,)
Comrade of raftsmen and coalmen, comrade of all who shake hands and welcome
      to drink and meat,
A learner with the simplest, a teacher of the thoughtfullest,
A novice beginning yet experient of myriads of seasons,
Of every hue and caste am I, of every rank and religion,
A farmer, mechanic, artist, gentleman, sailor, quaker,
Prisoner, fancy-man, rowdy, lawyer, physician, priest.
I resist any thing better than my own diversity,
Breathe the air but leave plenty after me,
And am not stuck up, and am in my place.
(The moth and the fish-eggs are in their place,
The bright suns I see and the dark suns I cannot see are in their place,
The palpable is in its place and the impalpable is in its place.)

17

These are really the thoughts of all men in all ages and lands, they are not original
      with me,
If they are not yours as much as mine they are nothing, or next to nothing,
If they are not the riddle and the untying of the riddle they are nothing,
If they are not just as close as they are distant they are nothing.
This is the grass that grows wherever the land is and the water is,
This the common air that bathes the globe.

18

With music strong I come, with my cornets and my drums,
I play not marches for accepted victors only, I play marches for conquer'd and
      slain persons.
Have you heard that it was good to gain the day?
I also say it is good to fall, battles are lost in the same spirit in which they are won.
I beat and pound for the dead,
I blow through my embouchures my loudest and gayest for them.
Vivas to those who have fail'd!

And to those whose war-vessels sank in the sea!
And to those themselves who sank in the sea!
And to all generals that lost engagements, and all overcome heroes!
And the numberless unknown heroes equal to the greatest heroes known!

19

This is the meal equally set, this the meat for natural hunger,
It is for the wicked just the same as the righteous, I make appointments with all,
I will not have a single person slighted or left away,
The kept-woman, sponger, thief, are hereby invited,
The heavy-lipp'd slave is invited, the venerealee is invited;
There shall be no difference between them and the rest.
This is the press of a bashful hand, this the float and odor of hair,
This the touch of my lips to yours, this the murmur of yearning,
This the far-off depth and height reflecting my own face,
This the thoughtful merge of myself, and the outlet again.
Do you guess I have some intricate purpose?
Well I have, for the Fourth-month showers have, and the mica on the side of a rock has.
Do you take it I would astonish?
Does the daylight astonish? does the early redstart twittering through the woods?
Do I astonish more than they?
This hour I tell things in confidence,
I might not tell everybody, but I will tell you.

20

Who goes there? hankering, gross, mystical, nude;
How is it I extract strength from the beef I eat?
What is a man anyhow? what am I? what are you?
All I mark as my own you shall offset it with your own,
Else it were time lost listening to me.
I do not snivel that snivel the world over,
That months are vacuums and the ground but wallow and filth.
Whimpering and truckling fold with powders for invalids, conformity goes to the
    fourth-remov'd,
I wear my hat as I please indoors or out.
Why should I pray? why should I venerate and be ceremonious?
Having pried through the strata, analyzed to a hair, counsel'd with doctors and
    calculated close,
I find no sweeter fat than sticks to my own bones.
In all people I see myself, none more and not one a barley-corn less,
And the good or bad I say of myself I say of them.
I know I am solid and sound,
To me the converging objects of the universe perpetually flow,

All are written to me, and I must get what the writing means.
I know I am deathless,
I know this orbit of mine cannot be swept by a carpenter's compass,
I know I shall not pass like a child's carlacue cut with a burnt stick at night.
I know I am august,
I do not trouble my spirit to vindicate itself or be understood,
I see that the elementary laws never apologize,
(I reckon I behave no prouder than the level I plant my house by, after all.)
I exist as I am, that is enough,
If no other in the world be aware I sit content,
And if each and all be aware I sit content.
One world is aware and by far the largest to me, and that is myself,
And whether I come to my own to-day or in ten thousand or ten million years,
I can cheerfully take it now, or with equal cheerfulness I can wait.
My foothold is tenon'd and mortis'd in granite,
I laugh at what you call dissolution,
And I know the amplitude of time.

21

I am the poet of the Body and I am the poet of the Soul,
The pleasures of heaven are with me and the pains of hell are with me,
The first I graft and increase upon myself, the latter I translate into a new tongue.
I am the poet of the woman the same as the man,
And I say it is as great to be a woman as to be a man,
And I say there is nothing greater than the mother of men.
I chant the chant of dilation or pride,
We have had ducking and deprecating about enough,
I show that size is only development.
Have you outstript the rest? are you the President?
It is a trifle, they will more than arrive there every one, and still pass on.
I am he that walks with the tender and growing night,
I call to the earth and sea half-held by the night.
Press close bare-bosom'd night—press close magnetic nourishing night!
Night of south winds—night of the large few stars!
Still nodding night—mad naked summer night.
Smile O voluptuous cool-breath'd earth!
Earth of the slumbering and liquid trees!
Earth of departed sunset—earth of the mountains misty-topt!
Earth of the vitreous pour of the full moon just tinged with blue!
Earth of shine and dark mottling the tide of the river!
Earth of the limpid gray of clouds brighter and clearer for my sake!
Far-swooping elbow'd earth—rich apple-blossom'd earth!
Smile, for your lover comes.

Prodigal, you have given me love—therefore I to you give love!
O unspeakable passionate love.

22

You sea! I resign myself to you also—I guess what you mean,
I behold from the beach your crooked inviting fingers,
I believe you refuse to go back without feeling of me,
We must have a turn together, I undress, hurry me out of sight of the land,
Cushion me soft, rock me in billowy drowse,
Dash me with amorous wet, I can repay you.
Sea of stretch'd ground-swells,
Sea breathing broad and convulsive breaths,
Sea of the brine of life and of unshovell'd yet always-ready graves,
Howler and scooper of storms, capricious and dainty sea,
I am integral with you, I too am of one phase and of all phases.
Partaker of influx and efflux, I, extoller of hate and conciliation,
Extoller of amies and those that sleep in each others' arms.
I am he attesting sympathy,
(Shall I make my list of things in the house and skip the house that supports them?)
I am not the poet of goodness only, I do not decline to be the poet of wickedness also.
What blurt is this about virtue and about vice?
Evil propels me and reform of evil propels me, I stand indifferent,
My gait is no fault-finder's or rejecter's gait,
I moisten the roots of all that has grown.
Did you fear some scrofula out of the unflagging pregnancy?
Did you guess the celestial laws are yet to be work'd over and rectified?
I find one side a balance and the antipodal side a balance,
Soft doctrine as steady help as stable doctrine,
Thoughts and deeds of the present our rouse and early start.
This minute that comes to me over the past decillions,
There is no better than it and now.
What behaved well in the past or behaves well to-day is not such a wonder,
The wonder is always and always how there can be a mean man or an infidel.

23

Endless unfolding of words of ages!
And mine a word of the modern, the word En-Masse.
A word of the faith that never balks,
Here or henceforward it is all the same to me, I accept Time absolutely.
It alone is without flaw, it alone rounds and completes all,
That mystic baffling wonder alone completes all.
I accept Reality and dare not question it,
Materialism first and last imbuing.

Hurrah for positive science! long live exact demonstration!

Fetch stonecrop mixt with cedar and branches of lilac,

This is the lexicographer, this the chemist, this made a grammar of the old cartouches,

These mariners put the ship through dangerous unknown seas,

This is the geologist, this works with the scalpel, and this is a mathematician.

Gentlemen, to you the first honors always!

Your facts are useful, and yet they are not my dwelling,

I but enter by them to an area of my dwelling.

Less the reminders of properties told my words,

And more the reminders they of life untold, and of freedom and extrication,

And make short account of neuters and geldings, and favor men and women fully equipt,

And beat the gong of revolt, and stop with fugitives and
    them that plot and conspire.

24

Walt Whitman, a kosmos, of Manhattan the son,

Turbulent, fleshy, sensual, eating, drinking and breeding.

No sentimentalist, no stander above men and women or apart from them,

No more modest than immodest.

Unscrew the locks from the doors!

Unscrew the doors themselves from their jambs!

Whoever degrades another degrades me,

And whatever is done or said returns at last to me.

Through me the afflatus surging and surging, through me the current and index.

I speak the pass-word primeval, I give the sign of democracy,

By God! I will accept nothing which all cannot have their counterpart of on the
    same terms.

Through me many long dumb voices,

Voices of the interminable generation of prisoners and slaves,

Voices of the diseas'd and despairing and of thieves and dwarfs,

Voices of cycles of preparation and accretion,

And of the threads that connect the stars, and of wombs and of the father-stuff,

And of the rights of them the others are down upon,

Of the deform'd, trivial, flat, foolish, despised,

Fog in the air, beetles rolling balls of dung.

Through me forbidden voices,

Voices of sexes and lusts, voices veil'd and I remove the veil,

Voices indecent by me clarified and transfigur'd.

I do not press my fingers across my mouth,

I keep as delicate around the bowels as around the head and heart,

Copulation is no more rank to me than death is.

I believe in the flesh and the appetites,

Seeing, hearing, feeling, are miracles, and each part and tag of me is a miracle.

Divine am I inside and out, and I make holy whatever I touch or am touch'd from,
The scent of these arm-pits aroma finer than prayer,
This head more than churches, bibles, and all the creeds.
If I worship one thing more than another it shall be the spread of my own body, or any part of it,
Translucent mould of me it shall be you!
Shaded ledges and rests it shall be you!
Firm masculine colter it shall be you!
Whatever goes to the tilth of me it shall be you!
You my rich blood! your milky stream pale strippings of my life!
Breast that presses against other breasts it shall be you!
My brain it shall be your occult convolutions!
Root of wash'd sweet-flag! timorous pond-snipe! nest of guarded duplicate eggs! it shall be you!
Mix'd tussled hay of head, beard, brawn, it shall be you!
Trickling sap of maple, fibre of manly wheat, it shall be you!
Sun so generous it shall be you!
Vapors lighting and shading my face it shall be you!
You sweaty brooks and dews it shall be you!
Winds whose soft-tickling genitals rub against me it shall be you!
Broad muscular fields, branches of live oak, loving lounger in my winding paths, it shall be you!
Hands I have taken, face I have kiss'd, mortal I have ever touch'd, it shall be you.
I dote on myself, there is that lot of me and all so luscious,
Each moment and whatever happens thrills me with joy,
I cannot tell how my ankles bend, nor whence the cause of my faintest wish,
Nor the cause of the friendship I emit, nor the cause of the friendship I take again.
That I walk up my stoop, I pause to consider if it really be,
A morning-glory at my window satisfies me more than the metaphysics of books.
To behold the day-break!
The little light fades the immense and diaphanous shadows,
The air tastes good to my palate.
Hefts of the moving world at innocent gambols silently rising, freshly exuding,
Scooting obliquely high and low.
Something I cannot see puts upward libidinous prongs,
Seas of bright juice suffuse heaven.
The earth by the sky staid with, the daily close of their junction,
The heav'd challenge from the east that moment over my head,
The mocking taunt, See then whether you shall be master!

25

Dazzling and tremendous how quick the sun-rise would kill me,
If I could not now and always send sun-rise out of me.

We also ascend dazzling and tremendous as the sun,
We found our own O my soul in the calm and cool of the day-break.
My voice goes after what my eyes cannot reach,
With the twirl of my tongue I encompass worlds and volumes of worlds.
Speech is the twin of my vision, it is unequal to measure itself,
It provokes me forever, it says sarcastically,
Walt you contain enough, why don't you let it out then?
Come now I will not be tantalized, you conceive too much of articulation,
Do you not know O speech how the buds beneath you are folded?
Waiting in gloom, protected by frost,
The dirt receding before my prophetical screams,
I underlying causes to balance them at last,
My knowledge my live parts, it keeping tally with the meaning of all things,
Happiness, (which whoever hears me let him or her set out in search of this day.)
My final merit I refuse you, I refuse putting from me what I really am,
Encompass worlds, but never try to encompass me,
I crowd your sleekest and best by simply looking toward you.
Writing and talk do not prove me,
I carry the plenum of proof and every thing else in my face,
With the hush of my lips I wholly confound the skeptic.

26

Now I will do nothing but listen,
To accrue what I hear into this song, to let sounds contribute toward it.
I hear bravuras of birds, bustle of growing wheat, gossip of flames, clack of sticks
    cooking my meals.
I hear the sound I love, the sound of the human voice,
I hear all sounds running together, combined, fused or following,
Sounds of the city and sounds out of the city, sounds of the day and night,
Talkative young ones to those that like them, the loud laugh of work-people at
    their meals,
The angry base of disjointed friendship, the faint tones of the sick,
The judge with hands tight to the desk, his pallid lips pronouncing a death-sentence,
The heave'e'yo of stevedores unlading ships by the wharves, the refrain of the
    anchor-lifters,
The ring of alarm-bells, the cry of fire, the whirr of swift-streaking engines and
    hose-carts with premonitory tinkles and color'd lights,
The steam-whistle, the solid roll of the train of approaching cars,
The slow march play'd at the head of the association marching two and two,
(They go to guard some corpse, the flag-tops are draped with black muslin.)
I hear the violoncello, ('tis the young man's heart's complaint,)
I hear the key'd cornet, it glides quickly in through my ears,
It shakes mad-sweet pangs through my belly and breast.

I hear the chorus, it is a grand opera,
Ah this indeed is music—this suits me.
A tenor large and fresh as the creation fills me,
The orbic flex of his mouth is pouring and filling me full.
I hear the train'd soprano (what work with hers is this?)
The orchestra whirls me wider than Uranus flies,
It wrenches such ardors from me I did not know I possess'd them,
It sails me, I dab with bare feet, they are lick'd by the indolent waves,
I am cut by bitter and angry hail, I lose my breath,
Steep'd amid honey'd morphine, my windpipe throttled in fakes of death,
At length let up again to feel the puzzle of puzzles,
And that we call Being.

27

To be in any form, what is that?
(Round and round we go, all of us, and ever come back thither,)
If nothing lay more develop'd the quahaug in its callous shell were enough.
Mine is no callous shell,
I have instant conductors all over me whether I pass or stop,
They seize every object and lead it harmlessly through me.
I merely stir, press, feel with my fingers, and am happy,
To touch my person to some one else's is about as much as I can stand.

28

Is this then a touch? quivering me to a new identity,
Flames and ether making a rush for my veins,
Treacherous tip of me reaching and crowding to help them,
My flesh and blood playing out lightning to strike what is hardly different from myself,
On all sides prurient provokers stiffening my limbs,
Straining the udder of my heart for its withheld drip,
Behaving licentious toward me, taking no denial,
Depriving me of my best as for a purpose,
Unbuttoning my clothes, holding me by the bare waist,
Deluding my confusion with the calm of the sunlight and pasture-fields,
Immodestly sliding the fellow-senses away,
They bribed to swap off with touch and go and graze at the edges of me,
No consideration, no regard for my draining strength or my anger,
Fetching the rest of the herd around to enjoy them a while,
Then all uniting to stand on a headland and worry me.
The sentries desert every other part of me,
They have left me helpless to a red marauder,
They all come to the headland to witness and assist against me.
I am given up by traitors,

I talk wildly, I have lost my wits, I and nobody else am the greatest traitor,
I went myself first to the headland, my own hands carried me there.
You villain touch! what are you doing? my breath is tight in its throat,
Unclench your floodgates, you are too much for me.

29

Blind loving wrestling touch, sheath'd hooded sharp-tooth'd touch!
Did it make you ache so, leaving me?
Parting track'd by arriving, perpetual payment of perpetual loan,
Rich showering rain, and recompense richer afterward.
Sprouts take and accumulate, stand by the curb prolific and vital,
Landscapes projected masculine, full-sized and golden.

30

All truths wait in all things,
They neither hasten their own delivery nor resist it,
They do not need the obstetric forceps of the surgeon,
The insignificant is as big to me as any,
(What is less or more than a touch?)
Logic and sermons never convince,
The damp of the night drives deeper into my soul.
(Only what proves itself to every man and woman is so,
Only what nobody denies is so.)
A minute and a drop of me settle my brain,
I believe the soggy clods shall become lovers and lamps,
And a compend of compends is the meat of a man or woman,
And a summit and flower there is the feeling they have for each other,
And they are to branch boundlessly out of that lesson until it becomes omnific,
And until one and all shall delight us, and we them.

31

I believe a leaf of grass is no less than the journey-work of the stars,
And the pismire is equally perfect, and a grain of sand, and the egg of the wren,
And the tree-toad is a chef-d'oeuvre for the highest,
And the running blackberry would adorn the parlors of heaven,
And the narrowest hinge in my hand puts to scorn all machinery,
And the cow crunching with depress'd head surpasses any statue,
And a mouse is miracle enough to stagger sextillions of infidels.
I find I incorporate gneiss, coal, long-threaded moss, fruits, grains, esculent roots,
And am stucco'd with quadrupeds and birds all over,
And have distanced what is behind me for good reasons,
But call any thing back again when I desire it.
In vain the speeding or shyness,

In vain the plutonic rocks send their old heat against my approach,
In vain the mastodon retreats beneath its own powder'd bones,
In vain objects stand leagues off and assume manifold shapes,
In vain the ocean setting in hollows and the great monsters lying low,
In vain the buzzard houses herself with the sky,
In vain the snake slides through the creepers and logs,
In vain the elk takes to the inner passes of the woods,
In vain the razor-bill'd auk sails far north to Labrador,
I follow quickly, I ascend to the nest in the fissure of the cliff.

32

I think I could turn and live with animals, they're so placid and self-contain'd,
I stand and look at them long and long.
They do not sweat and whine about their condition,
They do not lie awake in the dark and weep for their sins,
They do not make me sick discussing their duty to God,
Not one is dissatisfied, not one is demented with the mania of owning things,
Not one kneels to another, nor to his kind that lived thousands of years ago,
Not one is respectable or unhappy over the whole earth.
So they show their relations to me and I accept them,
They bring me tokens of myself, they evince them plainly in their possession.
I wonder where they get those tokens,
Did I pass that way huge times ago and negligently drop them?
Myself moving forward then and now and forever,
Gathering and showing more always and with velocity,
Infinite and omnigenous, and the like of these among them,
Not too exclusive toward the reachers of my remembrancers,
Picking out here one that I love, and now go with him on brotherly terms.
A gigantic beauty of a stallion, fresh and responsive to my caresses,
Head high in the forehead, wide between the ears,
Limbs glossy and supple, tail dusting the ground,
Eyes full of sparkling wickedness, ears finely cut, flexibly moving.
His nostrils dilate as my heels embrace him,
His well-built limbs tremble with pleasure as we race around and return.
I but use you a minute, then I resign you, stallion,
Why do I need your paces when I myself out-gallop them?
Even as I stand or sit passing faster than you.

33

Space and Time! now I see it is true, what I guess'd at,
What I guess'd when I loaf'd on the grass,
What I guess'd while I lay alone in my bed,
And again as I walk'd the beach under the paling stars of the morning.

My ties and ballasts leave me, my elbows rest in sea-gaps,
I skirt sierras, my palms cover continents,
I am afoot with my vision.
By the city's quadrangular houses—in log huts, camping with lumbermen,
Along the ruts of the turnpike, along the dry gulch and rivulet bed,
Weeding my onion-patch or hoeing rows of carrots and parsnips, crossing
     savannas, trailing in forests,
Prospecting, gold-digging, girdling the trees of a new purchase,
Scorch'd ankle-deep by the hot sand, hauling my boat down the shallow river,
Where the panther walks to and fro on a limb overhead, where the buck turns
     furiously at the hunter,
Where the rattlesnake suns his flabby length on a rock, where the otter is feeding
     on fish,
Where the alligator in his tough pimples sleeps by the bayou,
Where the black bear is searching for roots or honey, where the beaver pats the
     mud with his paddle-shaped tail;
Over the growing sugar, over the yellow-flower'd cotton plant, over the rice in its
     low moist field,
Over the sharp-peak'd farm house, with its scallop'd scum and slender shoots
     from the gutters,
Over the western persimmon, over the long-leav'd corn, over the delicate blue-
     flower flax,
Over the white and brown buckwheat, a hummer and buzzer there with the rest,
Over the dusky green of the rye as it ripples and shades in the breeze;
Scaling mountains, pulling myself cautiously up, holding on by low scragged limbs,
Walking the path worn in the grass and beat through the leaves of the brush,
Where the quail is whistling betwixt the woods and the wheatlot,
Where the bat flies in the Seventh-month eve, where the great gold-bug drops
     through the dark,
Where the brook puts out of the roots of the old tree and flows to the meadow,
Where cattle stand and shake away flies with the tremulous shuddering of their hides,
Where the cheese-cloth hangs in the kitchen, where andirons straddle the hearth-
     slab, where cobwebs fall in festoons from the rafters;
Where trip-hammers crash, where the press is whirling its cylinders,
Where the human heart beats with terrible throes under its ribs,
Where the pear-shaped balloon is floating aloft, (floating in it myself and looking
     composedly down,)
Where the life-car is drawn on the slip-noose, where the heat hatches pale-green
     eggs in the dented sand,
Where the she-whale swims with her calf and never forsakes it,
Where the steam-ship trails hind-ways its long pennant of smoke,
Where the fin of the shark cuts like a black chip out of the water,
Where the half-burn'd brig is riding on unknown currents,

Where shells grow to her slimy deck, where the dead are corrupting below;
Where the dense-starr'd flag is borne at the head of the regiments,
Approaching Manhattan up by the long-stretching island,
Under Niagara, the cataract falling like a veil over my countenance,
Upon a door-step, upon the horse-block of hard wood outside,
Upon the race-course, or enjoying picnics or jigs or a good game of base-ball,
At he-festivals, with blackguard gibes, ironical license, bull-dances, drinking,
    laughter,
At the cider-mill tasting the sweets of the brown mash, sucking the juice through
    a straw,
At apple-peelings wanting kisses for all the red fruit I find,
At musters, beach-parties, friendly bees, huskings, house-raisings;
Where the mocking-bird sounds his delicious gurgles, cackles, screams, weeps,
Where the hay-rick stands in the barn-yard, where the dry-stalks are scatter'd,
    where the brood-cow waits in the hovel,
Where the bull advances to do his masculine work, where the stud to the mare,
    where the cock is treading the hen,
Where the heifers browse, where geese nip their food with short jerks,
Where sun-down shadows lengthen over the limitless and lonesome prairie,
Where herds of buffalo make a crawling spread of the square miles far and near,
Where the humming-bird shimmers, where the neck of the long-lived swan is
    curving and winding,
Where the laughing-gull scoots by the shore, where she laughs her near-human laugh,
Where bee-hives range on a gray bench in the garden half hid by the high weeds,
Where band-neck'd partridges roost in a ring on the ground with their heads out,
Where burial coaches enter the arch'd gates of a cemetery,
Where winter wolves bark amid wastes of snow and icicled trees,
Where the yellow-crown'd heron comes to the edge of the marsh at night and
    feeds upon small crabs,
Where the splash of swimmers and divers cools the warm noon,
Where the katy-did works her chromatic reed on the walnut-tree over the wall,
Through patches of citrons and cucumbers with silver-wired leaves,
Through the salt-lick or orange glade, or under conical firs,
Through the gymnasium, through the curtain'd saloon, through the office or
    public hall;
Pleas'd with the native and pleas'd with the foreign, pleas'd with the new and old,
Pleas'd with the homely woman as well as the handsome,
Pleas'd with the quakeress as she puts off her bonnet and talks melodiously,
Pleas'd with the tune of the choir of the whitewash'd church,
Pleas'd with the earnest words of the sweating Methodist preacher, impress'd
    seriously at the camp-meeting;
Looking in at the shop-windows of Broadway the whole forenoon, flatting the
    flesh of my nose on the thick plate glass,

Wandering the same afternoon with my face turn'd up to the clouds, or down a
    lane or along the beach,
My right and left arms round the sides of two friends, and I in the middle;
Coming home with the silent and dark-cheek'd bush-boy, (behind me he rides at
    the drape of the day,)
Far from the settlements studying the print of animals' feet, or the moccasin print,
By the cot in the hospital reaching lemonade to a feverish patient,
Nigh the coffin'd corpse when all is still, examining with a candle;
Voyaging to every port to dicker and adventure,
Hurrying with the modern crowd as eager and flickle as any,
Hot toward one I hate, ready in my madness to knife him,
Solitary at midnight in my back yard, my thoughts gone from me a long while,
Walking the old hills of Judaea with the beautiful gentle God by my side,
Speeding through space, speeding through heaven and the stars,
Speeding amid the seven satellites and the broad ring, and the diameter of eighty
    thousand miles,
Speeding with tail'd meteors, throwing fire-balls like the rest,
Carrying the crescent child that carries its own full mother in its belly,
Storming, enjoying, planning, loving, cautioning,
Backing and filling, appearing and disappearing,
I tread day and night such roads.
I visit the orchards of spheres and look at the product,
And look at quintillions ripen'd and look at quintillions green.
I fly those flights of a fluid and swallowing soul,
My course runs below the soundings of plummets.
I help myself to material and immaterial,
No guard can shut me off, no law prevent me.
I anchor my ship for a little while only,
My messengers continually cruise away or bring their returns to me.
I go hunting polar furs and the seal, leaping chasms with a pike-pointed staff,
    clinging to topples of brittle and blue.
I ascend to the foretruck,
I take my place late at night in the crow's-nest,
We sail the arctic sea, it is plenty light enough,
Through the clear atmosphere I stretch around on the wonderful beauty,
The enormous masses of ice pass me and I pass them, the scenery is plain in all
    directions,
The white-topt mountains show in the distance, I fling out my fancies toward them,
We are approaching some great battle-field in which we are soon to be engaged,
We pass the colossal outposts of the encampment, we pass with still feet and caution,
Or we are entering by the suburbs some vast and ruin'd city,
The blocks and fallen architecture more than all the living cities of the globe.
I am a free companion, I bivouac by invading watchfires,

I turn the bridegroom out of bed and stay with the bride myself,
I tighten her all night to my thighs and lips.
My voice is the wife's voice, the screech by the rail of the stairs,
They fetch my man's body up dripping and drown'd.
I understand the large hearts of heroes,
The courage of present times and all times,
How the skipper saw the crowded and rudderless wreck of the steamship, and
　　Death chasing it up and down the storm,
How he knuckled tight and gave not back an inch, and was faithful of days and
　　faithful of nights,
And chalk'd in large letters on a board, *Be of good cheer, we will not desert you;*
How he follow'd with them and tack'd with them three days and would not give it up,
How he saved the drifting company at last,
How the lank loose-gown'd women look'd when boated from the side of their
　　prepared graves,
How the silent old-faced infants and the lifted sick, and the sharp-lipp'd
　　unshaved men;
All this I swallow, it tastes good, I like it well, it becomes mine,
I am the man, I suffer'd, I was there.
The disdain and calmness of martyrs,
The mother of old, condemn'd for a witch, burnt with dry wood, her children
　　gazing on,
The hounded slave that flags in the race, leans by the fence, blowing, cover'd with
　　sweat,
The twinges that sting like needles his legs and neck, the murderous buckshot
　　and the bullets,
All these I feel or am.
I am the hounded slave, I wince at the bite of the dogs,
Hell and despair are upon me, crack and again crack the marksmen,
I clutch the rails of the fence, my gore dribs, thinn'd with the ooze of my skin,
I fall on the weeds and stones,
The riders spur their unwilling horses, haul close,
Taunt my dizzy ears and beat me violently over the head with whip-stocks.
Agonies are one of my changes of garments,
I do not ask the wounded person how he feels, I myself become the wounded person,
My hurts turn livid upon me as I lean on a cane and observe.
I am the mash'd fireman with breast-bone broken,
Tumbling walls buried me in their debris,
Heat and smoke I inspired, I heard the yelling shouts of my comrades,
I heard the distant click of their picks and shovels,
They have clear'd the beams away, they tenderly life me forth.
I lie in the night air in my red shirt, the pervading hush is for my sake,
Painless after all I lie exhausted but not so unhappy,

White and beautiful are the faces around me, the heads are bared of their fire-caps,
The kneeling crowd fades with the light of the torches.
Distant and dead resuscitate,
They show as the dial or move as the hands of me, I am the clock myself.
I am an old artillerist, I tell of my fort's bombardment,
I am there again.
Again the long roll of the drummers,
Again the attacking cannon, mortars,
Again to my listeing ears the cannon responsive.
I take part, I see and hear the whole,
The cries, curses, roar, the plaudits for well-aim'd shots,
The ambulanza slowly passing trailing its red drip,
Workmen searching after damages, making indispensable repairs,
The fall of grenades through the rent roof, the fan-shaped explosion,
The whizz of limbs, heads, stone, wood, iron, high in the air.
Again gurgles the mouth of my dying general, he furiously waves with his hand,
He gasps through the clot *Mind not me—mind—the entrenchments.*

34

Now I tell what I knew in Texas in my early youth,
(I tell not the fall of Alamo,
Not one escaped to tell the fall of Alamo,
The hundred and fifty are dumb yet at Alamo,)
'Tis the tale of the murder in cold blood of four hundred and twelve young men.
Retreating they had form'd in a hollow square with their baggage for breastworks,
Nine hundred lives out of the surrounding enemy's, nine times their number, was
    the price they took in advance,
Their colonel was wounded and their ammunition gone,
They treated for an honorable capitulation, receiv'd writing and seal, gave up
    their arms and march'd back prisoners of war.
They were the glory of the race of rangers,
Matchless with horse, rifle, song, supper, courtship,
Large, turbulent, generous, handsome, proud, and affectionate,
Bearded, sunburnt, drest in the free costume of hunters,
Not a single one over thirty years of age.
The second First-day morning they were brought out in squads and massacred, it
    was beautiful early summer,
The work commenced about five o'clock and was over by eight.
None obey'd the command to kneel,
Some made a mad and helpless rush, some stood stark and straight,
A few fell at once, shot in the temple or heart, the living and dead lay together,
The maim'd and mangled dug in the dirt, the new-comers saw them there,
Some half-kill'd attempted to crawl away,

These were despatch'd with bayonets or batter'd with the blunts of muskets.
A youth not seventeen years old seiz'd his assassin till two more came to release him,
The three were all torn and cover'd with the boy's blood.
At eleven o'clock began the burning of the bodies;
That is the tale of the murder of the four hundred and twelve young men.

35

Would you hear of an old-time sea-fight?
Would you learn who won by the light of the moon and stars?
List to the yarn, as my grandmother's father the sailor told it to me.
Our foe was no skulk in his ship I tell you, (said he,)
His was the surly English pluck, and there is no tougher or truer, and never was,
    and never will be;
Along the lower'd eve he came horribly raking us.
We closed with him, the yards entangled, the cannon touch'd,
My captain lash'd fast with his own hands.
We had receiv'd some eighteen pound shots under the water,
On our lower-gun-deck two large pieces had burst at the first fire, killing all
    around and blowing up overhead.
Fighting at sun-down, fighting at dark,
Ten o'clock at night, the full moon well up, our leaks on the gain, and five feet of
    water reported,
The master-at-arms loosing the prisoners confined in the after-hold to give them
    a chance for themselves.
The transit to and from the magazine is now stopt by the sentinels,
They see so many strange faces they do not know whom to trust.
Our frigate takes fire,
The other asks if we demand quarter?
If our colors are struck and the fighting done?
Now I laugh content, for I hear the voice of my little captain,
We have not struck, he composedly cries, *we have just begun our part of the fighting.*
Only three guns are in use,
One is directed by the captain himself against the enemy's main-mast,
Two well serv'd with grape and canister silence his musketry and clear his decks.
The tops alone second the fire of this little battery, especially the main-top,
They hold out bravely during the whole of the action.
Not a moment's cease,
The leaks gain fast on the pumps, the fire eats toward the powder-magazine.
One of the pumps has been shot away, it is generally thought we are sinking.
Serene stands the little captain,
He is not hurried, his voice is neither high nor low,
His eyes give more light to us than our battle-lanterns.
Toward twelve there in the beams of the moon they surrender to us.

36

Stretch'd and still lies the midnight,

Two great hulls motionless on the breast of the darkness,

Our vessel riddled and slowly sinking, preparations to pass to the one we have
conquer'd,

The captain on the quarter-deck coldly giving his orders through a countenance
white as a sheet,

Near by the corpse of the child that serv'd in the cabin,

The dead face of an old salt with long white hair and carefully curl'd whiskers,

The flames spite of all that can be done flickering aloft and below,

The husky voices of the two or three officers yet fit for duty,

Formless stacks of bodies and bodies by themselves, dabs of flesh upon the masts
and spars,

Cut of cordage, dangle of rigging, slight shock of the soothe of waves,

Black and impassive guns, litter of powder-parcels, strong scent,

A few large stars overhead, silent and mournful shining,

Delicate sniffs of sea-breeze, smells of sedgy grass and fields by the shore, death-
messages given in charge to survivors,

The hiss of the surgeon's knife, the gnawing teeth of his saw,

Wheeze, cluck, swash of falling blood, short wild scream, and long, dull, tapering groan,

These so, these irretrievable.

37

You laggards there on guard! look to your arms!

In at the conquer'd doors they crowd! I am possess'd!

Embody all presences outlaw'd or suffering,

See myself in prison shaped like another man,

And feel the dull unintermitted pain,

For me the keepers of convicts shoulder their carbines and keep watch,

It is I let out in the morning and barr'd at night.

Not a mutineer walks handcuff'd to jail but I am handcuff'd to him and walk by his side,

(I am less the jolly one there, and more the silent one with sweat on my twitching lips.)

Not a youngster is taken for larceny but I go up too, and am tried and sentenced.

Not a cholera patient lies at the last gasp but I also lie at the last gasp,

My face is ash-color'd, my sinews gnarl, away from me people retreat.

Askers embody themselves in me and I am embodied in them,

I project my hat, sit shame-faced, and beg.

38

Enough! enough! enough!

Somehow I have been stunn'd. Stand back!

Give me a little time beyond my cuff'd head, slumbers, dreams, gaping,

I discover myself on the verse of a usual mistake.

That I could forget the mockers and insults!
That I could forget the trickling tears and the blows of the bludgeons and hammers!
That I could look with a separate look on my own crucifixion and bloody crowning!
I remember now,
I resume the overstaid fraction,
The grave of rock multiplies what has been confided to it, or to any graves,
Corpses rise, gashes heal, fastenings roll from me.
I troop forth replenish'd with supreme power, one of an average unending procession,
Inland and sea-coast we go, and pass all boundary lines,
Our swift ordinances on their way over the whole earth,
The blossoms we wear in our hats the growth of thousands of years.
Eleves, I salute you! come forward!
Continue your annotations, continue your questionings.

39

The friendly and flowing savage, who is he?
Is he waiting for civilization, or past it and mastering it?
Is he some Southwesterner rais'd out-doors? is he Kanadian?
Is he from the Mississippi country? Iowa, Oregon, California?
The mountains? prairie-life, bush-life? or sailor from the sea?
Wherever he goes men and women accept and desire him,
They desire he should like them, touch them, speak to them, stay with them.
Behavior lawless as snow-flakes, words simple as grass, uncomb'd head, laughter, and naivetè,
Slow-stepping feet, common features, common modes and emanations,
They descend in new forms from the tips of his fingers,
They are wafted with the odor of his body or breath, they fly out of the glance of his eyes.

40

Flaunt of the sunshine I need not your bask—lie over!
You light surfaces only, I force surfaces and depths also.
Earth! you seem to look for something at my hands,
Say, old top-knot, what do you want?
Man or woman, I might tell how I like you, but cannot,
And might tell what it is in me and what it is in you, but cannot,
And might tell that pining I have, that pulse of my nights and days.
Behold, I do not give lectures or a little charity,
When I give I give myself.
You there, impotent, loose in the knees,
Open your scarf'd chops till I blow grit within you,
Spread your palms and life the flaps of your pockets,
I am not to be denied, I compel, I have stores plenty and to spare,
And any thing I have I bestow.

I do not ask who you are, that is not important to me,
You can do nothing and be nothing but what I will infold you.
To cotton-field drudge or cleaner of privies I lean,
On his right cheek I put the family kiss,
And in my soul I swear I never will deny him.
On women fit for conception I start bigger and nimbler babes,
(This day I am jetting the stuff of far more arrogant republics.)
To any one dying, thither I speed and twist the knob of the door,
Turn the bed-clothes toward the foot of the bed,
Let the physician and the priest go home.
I seize the descending man and raise him with resistless will,
O despairer, here is my neck,
By God, you shall not go down! hang your whole weight upon me.
I dilate you with tremendous breath, I buoy you up,
Every room of the house do I fill with an arm'd force,
Lovers of me, bafflers of graves.
Sleep—I and they keep guard all night,
Not doubt, not disease shall dare to lay finger upon you,
I have embraced you, and henceforth possess you to myself,
And when you rise in the morning you will find what I tell you is so.

41

I am he bringing help for the sick as they pant on their backs,
And for strong upright men I bring yet more needed help.
I heard what was said of the universe,
Heard it and heard it of several thousand years;
It is middling well as far as it goes—but is that all?
Magnifying and applying come I,
Outbidding at the start the old cautious hucksters,
Taking myself the exact dimensions of Jehovah,
Lithographing Kronos, Zeus his son, and Hercules his grandson,
Buying drafts of Osiris, Isis, Belus, Brahma, Buddha,
In my portfolio placing Manito loose, Allah on a leaf, the crucifix engraved,
With Odin and the hideous-faced Mexitli and every idol and image,
Taking them all for what they are worth and not a cent more,
Admitting they were alive and did the work of their days,
(They bore mites as for unfledg'd birds who have now to rise and fly and sing for
    themselves,)
Accepting the rough deific sketches to fill out better in myself, bestowing them
    freely on each man and woman I see,
Discovering as much or more in a framer framing a house,
Putting higher claims for him there with his roll'd-up sleeves driving the mallet
    and chisel,

Not objecting to special revelations, considering a curl of smoke or a hair on the
    back of my hand just as curious as any revelation,
Lads ahold of fire-engines and hook-and-ladder ropes no less to me than the gods
    of the antique wars,
Minding their voices peal through the crash of destruction,
Their brawny limbs passing safe over charr'd laths, their white foreheads whole
    and unhurt out of the flames;
By the mechanic's wife with her babe at her nipple interceding for every person born,
Three scythes at harvest whizzing in a row from three lusty angels with shirts
    bagg'd out at their waists,
The snag-tooth'd hostler with red hair redeeming sins past and to come,
Selling all he possesses, traveling on foot to fee lawyers for his brother and sit by
    him while he is tried for forgery;
What was strewn in the amplest strewing the square rod about me, and not filling
    the square rod then,
The bull and the bug never worshipp'd half enough,
Dung and dirt more admirable than was dream'd,
The supernatural of no account, myself waiting my time to be one of the supremes,
The day getting ready for me when I shall do as much good as the best, and be as
    prodigious;
By my life-lumps! becoming already a creator,
Putting myself here and now to the ambush'd womb of the shadows.

42

A call in the midst of the crowd,
My own voice, orotund sweeping and final.
Come my children,
Come my boys and girls, my women, household and intimates,
Now the performer launches his nerve, he has pass'd his prelude on the reeds within.
Easily written loose-finger'd chords—I feel the thrum of your climax and close.
My head slues round on my neck,
Music rolls, but not from the organ,
Folks are around me, but they are no household of mine.
Ever the hard unsunk ground,
Ever the eaters and drinkers, ever the upward and downward sun, ever the air
    and the ceaseless tides,
Ever myself and my neighbors, refreshing, wicked, real,
Ever the old inexplicable query, ever that thorn'd thumb, that breath of itches and
    thirsts,
Ever the vexer's *hoot! hoot!* till we find where the sly one hides and bring him forth,
Ever love, ever the sobbing liquid of life,
Ever the bandage under the chin, ever the trestles of death.
Here and there with dimes on the eyes walking,

To feed the greed of the belly the brains liberally spooning,
Tickets buying, taking, selling, but in to the feast never once going,
Many sweating, ploughing, thrashing, and then the chaff for payment receiving,
A few idly owning, and they the wheat continually claiming.
This is the city and I am one of the citizens,
Whatever interests the rest interests me, politics, wars, markets, newspapers, schools,
The mayor and councils, banks, tariffs, steamships, factories, stocks, stores, real estate and personal estate.
The little plentiful manikins skipping around in collars and tail'd coats,
I am aware who they are, (they are positively not worms or fleas,)
I acknowledge the duplicates of myself, the weakest and shallowest is deathless with me,
What I do and say the same waits for them,
Every thought that flounders in me the same flounders in them.
I know perfectly well my own egotism,
Know my omnivorous lines and must not write any less,
And would fetch you whoever you are flush with myself.
Not words of routine this song of mine,
But abruptly to question, to leap beyond yet nearer bring;
This printed and bound book—but the printer and the printing-office boy?
The well-taken photographs—but your wife or friend close and solid in your arms?
The black ship mail'd with iron, her mighty guns in her turrets—but the pluck of the captain and engineers?
In the houses the dishes and fare and furniture—but the host and hostess, and the look out of their eyes?
The sky up there—yet here or next door, or across the way?
The saints and sages in history—but you yourself?
Sermons, creeds, theology—but the fathomless human brain,
And what is reason? and what is love? and what is life?

43

I do not despise you priests, all time, the world over,
My faith is the greatest of faiths and the least of faiths,
Enclosing worship ancient and modern and all between ancient and modern,
Believing I shall come again upon the earth after five thousand years,
Waiting responses from oracles, honoring the gods, saluting the sun,
Making a fetich of the first rock or stump, powowing with sticks in the circle of obis,
Helping the llama or brahmin as he trims the lamps of the idols,
Dancing yet through the streets in a phallic procession, rapt and austere in the woods a gymnosophist,
Drinking mead from the skull-cup, to Shastas and Vedas admirant, minding the Koran,

Walking the teokallis, spotted with gore from the stone and knife, beating the
    serpent-skin drum,
Accepting the Gospels, accepting him that was crucified, knowing assuredly that
    he is divine,
To the mass kneeling or the puritan's prayer rising, or sitting patiently in a pew,
Ranting and frothing in my insane crisis, or waiting dead-like till my spirit arouses me,
Looking forth on pavement and land, or outside of pavement and land,
Belonging to the winders of the circuit of circuits.

One of that centripetal and centrifugal gang I turn and talk like a man leaving
    charges before a journey.

Down-hearted doubters dull and excluded,
Frivolous, sullen, moping, angry, affected, dishearten'd, atheistical,
I know every one of you, I know the sea of torment, doubt, despair and unbelief.

How the flukes splash!
How they contort rapid as lightning, with spasms and spouts of blood!

Be at peace bloody flukes of doubters and sullen mopers,
I take my place among you as much as among any,
The past is the push of you, me, all, precisely the same,
And what is yet untried and afterward is for you, me, all precisely the same.

I do not know what is untried and afterward,
But I know it will in its turn prove sufficient, and cannot fail.

Each who passes is consider'd, each who stops is consider'd, not a single one can it fail.
It cannot fail the young man who died and was buried,
Nor the young woman who died and was put by his side,
Nor the little child that peep'd in at the door, and then drew back and was never
    seen again,
Nor the old man who has lived without purpose, and feels it with bitterness worse
    than gall,
Nor him in the poor house tubercled by rum and the bad disorder,
Nor the numberless slaughter'd and wreck'd, nor the brutish koboo call'd the
    ordure of humanity,
Nor the sacs merely floating with open mouths for food to slip in,
Nor any thing in the earth, or down in the oldest graves of the earth,
Nor any thing in the myriads of spheres, nor the myriads of myriads that inhabit them,
Nor the present, nor the least wisp that is known.

44

It is time to explain myself—let us stand up.

What is known I strip away,
I launch all men and women forward with me into the Unknown.

The clock indicates the moment—but what does eternity indicate?

We have thus far exhausted trillions of winters and summers,
There are trillions ahead, and trillions ahead of them.

Births have brought us richness and variety,
And other births will bring us richness and variety.
I do not call one greater and one smaller,
That which fills its period and place is equal to any.
Were mankind murderous or jealous upon you, my brother, my sister?
I am sorry for you, they are not murderous or jealous upon me,
All has been gentle with me, I keep no account with lamentation,
(What have I to do with lamentation?)
I am an acme of things accomplish'd, and I an encloser of things to be.
My feet strike an apex of the apices of the stairs,
On every step bunches of ages, and larger bunches between the steps,
All below duly travel'd, and still I mount and mount.
Rise after rise bow the phantoms behind me,
Afar down I see the huge first Nothing, I know I was even there,
I waited unseen and always, and slept through the lethargic mist,
And took my time, and took no hurt from the fetid carbon.
Long I was hugg'd close—long and long.
Immense have been the preparations for me,
Faithful and friendly the arms that have help'd me.
Cycles ferried my cradle, rowing and rowing like cheerful boatmen,
For room to me stars kept aside in their own rings,
They sent influences to look after what was to hold me.
Before I was born out of my mother generations guided me,
My embryo has never been torpid, nothing could overlay it.
For it the nebula cohered to an orb,
The long slow strata piled to rest it on,
Vast vegetables gave it sustenance,
Monstrous sauroids transported it in their mouths and deposited it with care.
All forces have been steadily employ'd to complete and delight me,
Now on this spot I stand with my robust soul.

45

O span of youth! ever-push'd elasticity!
O manhood, balanced, florid and full.
My lovers suffocate me,
Crowding my lips, thick in the pores of my skin,
Jostling me through streets and public halls, coming naked to me at night,
Crying by day *Ahoy!* from the rocks of the river, swinging and chirping over my head,
Calling my name from flower-beds, vines, tangled underbrush,
Lighting on every moment of my life,
Bussing my body with soft balsamic busses,
Noiselessly passing handfuls out of their hearts and giving them to be mine.
Old age superbly rising! O welcome, ineffable grace of dying days!

Every condition promulges not only itself, it promulges what grows after and out
    of itself,
And the dark hush promulges as much as any.
I open my scuttle at night and see the far-sprinkled systems,
And all I see multiplied as high as I can cipher edge but the rim of the farther systems.
Wider and wider they spread, expanding, always expanding,
Outward and outward and forever outward.
My sun has his sun and round him obediently wheels,
He joins with his partners a group of superior circuit,
And greater sets follow, making specks of the greatest inside them.
There is no stoppage and never can be stoppage,
If I, you, and the worlds, and all beneath or upon their surfaces, were this
    moment reduced back to a pallid float, it would not avail in the long run,
We should surely bring up again where we now stand,
And surely go as much farther, and then farther and farther.
A few quadrillions of eras, a few octillions of cubic leagues, do not hazard the
    span or make it impatient,
They are but parts, any thing is but a part.
See ever so far, there is limitless space outside of that,
Count ever so much, there is limitless time around that.
My rendezvous is appointed, it is certain,
The Lord will be there and wait till I come on perfect terms,
The great Camerado, the lover true for whom I pine will be there.

46

I know I have the best of time and space, and was never measured and never will
    be measured.
I tramp a perpetual journey, (come listen all!)
My signs are a rain-proof coat, good shoes, and a staff cut from the woods,
No friend of mine takes his ease in my chair,
I have no chair, no church, no philosophy,
I lead no man to a dinner-table, library, exchange,
But each man and each woman of you I lead upon a knoll,
My left hand hooking you round the waist,
My right hand pointing to landscapes of continents and the public road.
Not I, not any one else can travel that road for you,
You must travel it for yourself.
It is not far, it is within reach,
Perhaps you have been on it since you were born and did not know,
Perhaps it is everywhere on water and on land.
Shoulder your duds dear son, and I will mine, and let us hasten forth,
Wonderful cities and free nations we shall fetch as we go.
If you tire, give me both burdens, and rest the chuff of your hand on my hip,

And in due time you shall repay the same service to me,

For after we start we never lie by again.

This day before dawn I ascended a hill and look'd at the crowded heaven,

And I said to my spirit *When we become the enfolders of those orbs, and the pleasure*
      and knowledge of every thing in them, shall we be fill'd and satisfied then?

And my spirit said *No, we but level that lift to pass and continue beyond.*

You are also asking me questions and I hear you,

I answer that I cannot answer, you must find out for yourself.

Sit a while dear son,

Here are biscuits to eat and here is milk to drink,

But as soon as you sleep and renew yourself in sweet clothes, I kiss you with a
      good-by kiss and open the gate for your egress hence.

Long enough have you dream'd contemptible dreams,

Now I wash the gum from your eyes,

You must habit yourself to the dazzle of the light and of every moment of your life.

Long have you timidly waded holding a plank by the shore,

Now I will you to be a bold swimmer,

To jump off in the midst of the sea, rise again, nod to me, shout, and laughingly
      dash with your hair.

47

I am the teacher of athletes,

He that by me spreads a wider breast than my own proves the width of my own,

He most honors my style who learns under it to destroy the teacher.

The boy I love, the same becomes a man not through derived power, but in his
      own right,

Wicked rather than virtuous out of conformity or fear,

Fond of his sweetheart, relishing well his steak,

Unrequited love or a slight cutting him worse than sharp steel cuts,

First-rate to ride, to fight, to hit the bull's eye, to sail a skiff, to sing a song or play
      on the banjo,

Preferring scars and the beard and faces pitted with small-pox over all latherers,

And those well-tann'd to those that keep out of the sun.

I teach straying from me, yet who can stray from me?

I follow you whoever you are from the present hour,

My words itch at your ears till you understand them.

I do not say these things for a dollar or to fill up the time while I wait for a boat,

(It is you talking just as much as myself, I act as the tongue of you,

Tied in your mouth, in mine it begins to be loosen'd.)

I swear I will never again mention love or death inside a house,

And I swear I will never translate myself at all, only to him or her who privately
      stays with me in the open air.

If you would understand me go to the heights or water-shore,

The nearest gnat is an explanation, and a drop or motion of waves a key,
The maul, the oar, the hand-saw, second my words.
No shutter'd room or school can commune with me,
But roughs and little children better than they.
The young mechanic is closest to me, he knows me well,
The woodman that takes his axe and jug with him shall take me with him all day,
The farm-boy ploughing in the field feels good at the sound of my voice,
In vessels that sail my words sail, I go with fishermen and seamen and love them.
The soldier camp'd or upon the march is mine,
On the night ere the pending battle many seek me, and I do not fail them,
On that solemn night (it may be their last) those that know me seek me.
My face rubs to the hunter's face when he lies down alone in his blanket,
The driver thinking of me does not mind the jolt of his wagon,
The young mother and old mother comprehend me,
The girl and the wife rest the needle a moment and forget where they are,
They and all would resume what I have told them.

48

I have said that the soul is not more than the body,
And I have said that the body is not more than the soul,
And nothing, not God, is greater to one than one's self is,
And whoever walks a furlong without sympathy walks to his own funeral drest in
    his shroud,
And I or you pocketless of a dime may purchase the pick of the earth,
And to glance with an eye or show a bean in its pod confounds the learning of all times,
And there is no trade or employment but the young man following it may become a hero,
And there is no object so soft but it makes a hub for the wheel'd universe,
And I say to any man or woman, Let your soul stand cool and composed before a
    million universes.
And I say to mankind, Be not curious about God,
For I who am curious about each am not curious about God,
(No array of terms can say how much I am at peace about God and about death.)
I hear and behold God in every object, yet understand God not in the least,
Nor do I understand who there can be more wonderful than myself.
Why should I wish to see God better than this day?
I see something of God each hour of the twenty-four, and each moment then,
In the faces of men and women I see God, and in my own face in the glass,
I find letters from God dropt in the street, and every one is sign'd by God's name,
And I leave them where they are, for I know that wheresoe'er I go,
Others will punctually come for ever and ever.

49

And as to you Death, and you bitter hug of mortality, it is idle to try to alarm me.
To his work without flinching the accoucheur comes,

I see the elder-hand pressing receiving supporting,
I recline by the sills of the exquisite flexible doors,
And mark the outlet, and mark the relief and escape.
And as to you Corpse I think you are good manure, but that does not offend me,
I smell the white roses sweet-scented and growing,
I reach to the leafy lips, I reach to the polish'd breasts of melons.
And as to you Life I reckon you are the leavings of many deaths,
(No doubt I have died myself ten thousand times before.)
I hear you whispering there O stars of heaven,
O suns—O grass of graves—O perpetual transfers and promotions,
If you do not say any thing how can I say any thing?
Of the turbid pool that lies in the autumn forest,
Of the moon that descends the steeps of the soughing twilight,
Toss, sparkles of day and dusk—toss on the black stems that decay in the muck,
Toss to the moaning gibberish of the dry limbs.
I ascend from the moon, I ascend from the night,
I perceive that the ghastly glimmer is noonday sunbeams reflected,
And debouch to the steady and central from the offspring great or small.

50

There is that in me—I do not know what it is—but I know it is in me.
Wrench'd and sweaty—calm and cool then my body becomes,
I sleep—I sleep long.
I do not know it—it is without name—it is a word unsaid,
It is not in any dictionary, utterance, symbol.
Something it swings on more than the earth I swing on,
To it the creation is the friend whose embracing awakes me.
Perhaps I might tell more. Outlines! I plead for my brothers and sisters.
Do you see O my brothers and sisters?
It is not chaos or death—it is form, union, plan—it is eternal life—it is Happiness.

51

The past and present wilt—I have fill'd them, emptied them,
And proceed to fill my next fold of the future.
Listener up there! what have you to confide to me?
Look in my face while I snuff the sidle of evening,
(Talk honestly, no one else hears you, and I stay only a minute longer.)
Do I contradict myself?
Very well then I contradict myself,
(I am large, I contain multitudes.)
I concentrate toward them that are nigh, I wait on the door-slab.
Who has done his day's work? who will soonest be through with his supper?
Who wishes to walk with me?
Will you speak before I am gone? will you prove already too late?

52

The spotted hawk swoops by and accuses me, he complains of my gab and my
    loitering.
I too am not a bit tamed, I too am untranslatable,
I sound my barbaric yawp over the roofs of the world.
The last scud of day holds back for me,
It flings my likeness after the rest and true as any on the shadow'd wilds,
It coaxes me to the vapor and the dusk.
I depart as air, I shake my white locks at the runaway sun,
I effuse my flesh in eddies, and drift it in lacy jags.
I bequeath myself to the dirt to grow from the grass I love,
If you want me again look for me under your boot-soles.
You will hardly know who I am or what I mean,
But I shall be good health to you nevertheless,
And filter and fibre your blood.
Failing to fetch me at first keep encouraged,
Missing me one place search another,
I stop somewhere waiting for you.

1.3.2 "Oh Captain! My Captain!"

O Captain! my Captain! our fearful trip is done,
The ship has weather'd every rack, the prize we sought is won,
The port is near, the bells I hear, the people all exulting,
While follow eyes the steady keel, the vessel grim and daring;
        But O heart! heart! heart!
         O the bleeding drops of red,
           Where on the deck my Captain lies,
            Fallen cold and dead.

O Captain! my Captain! rise up and hear the bells;
Rise up—for you the flag is flung—for you the bugle trills,
For you bouquets and ribbon'd wreaths—for you the shores a-crowding,
For you they call, the swaying mass, their eager faces turning;
        Here Captain! dear father!
         This arm beneath your head!
          It is some dream that on the deck,
           You've fallen cold and dead.

My Captain does not answer, his lips are pale and still,
My father does not feel my arm, he has no pulse nor will,
The ship is anchor'd safe and sound, its voyage closed and done,
From fearful trip the victor ship comes in with object won;
        Exult O shores, and ring O bells!

But I with mournful tread,
    Walk the deck my Captain lies,
        Fallen cold and dead.

1.3.3 "CROSSING BROOKLYN FERRY"

1

Flood-tide below me! I see you face to face!
Clouds of the west—sun there half an hour high—I see you also face to face.

Crowds of men and women attired in the usual costumes, how curious you are to me!
On the ferry-boats the hundreds and hundreds that cross, returning home, are
    more curious to me than you suppose,
And you that shall cross from shore to shore years hence are more to me, and
    more in my meditations, than you might suppose.

2

The impalpable sustenance of me from all things at all hours of the day,
The simple, compact, well-join'd scheme, myself disintegrated, every one
    disintegrated yet part of the scheme,
The similitudes of the past and those of the future,
The glories strung like beads on my smallest sights and hearings, on the walk in
    the street and the passage over the river,
The current rushing so swiftly and swimming with me far away,
The others that are to follow me, the ties between me and them,
The certainty of others, the life, love, sight, hearing of others.

Others will enter the gates of the ferry and cross from shore to shore,
Others will watch the run of the flood-tide,
Others will see the shipping of Manhattan north and west, and the heights of
    Brooklyn to the south and east,
Others will see the islands large and small;
Fifty years hence, others will see them as they cross, the sun half an hour high,
A hundred years hence, or ever so many hundred years hence, others will see them,
Will enjoy the sunset, the pouring-in of the flood-tide, the falling-back to the sea
    of the ebb-tide.

3

It avails not, time nor place—distance avails not,
I am with you, you men and women of a generation, or ever so many generations
    hence,
Just as you feel when you look on the river and sky, so I felt,
Just as any of you is one of a living crowd, I was one of a crowd,

Just as you are refresh'd by the gladness of the river and the bright flow, I was refresh'd,
Just as you stand and lean on the rail, yet hurry with the swift current, I stood yet
    was hurried,
Just as you look on the numberless masts of ships and the thick-stemm'd pipes of
    steamboats, I look'd.

I too many and many a time cross'd the river of old,
Watched the Twelfth-month sea-gulls, saw them high in the air floating with
    motionless wings, oscillating their bodies,
Saw how the glistening yellow lit up parts of their bodies and left the rest in
    strong shadow,
Saw the slow-wheeling circles and the gradual edging toward the south,
Saw the reflection of the summer sky in the water,
Had my eyes dazzled by the shimmering track of beams,
Look'd at the fine centrifugal spokes of light round the shape of my head in the
    sunlit water,
Look'd on the haze on the hills southward and south-westward,
Look'd on the vapor as it flew in fleeces tinged with violet,
Look'd toward the lower bay to notice the vessels arriving,
Saw their approach, saw aboard those that were near me,
Saw the white sails of schooners and sloops, saw the ships at anchor,
The sailors at work in the rigging or out astride the spars,
The round masts, the swinging motion of the hulls, the slender serpentine pennants,
The large and small steamers in motion, the pilots in their pilot-houses,
The white wake left by the passage, the quick tremulous whirl of the wheels,
The flags of all nations, the falling of them at sunset,
The scallop-edged waves in the twilight, the ladled cups, the frolicsome crests and
    glistening,
The stretch afar growing dimmer and dimmer, the gray walls of the granite
    storehouses by the docks,
On the river the shadowy group, the big steam-tug closely flank'd on each side by
    the barges, the hay-boat, the belated lighter,
On the neighboring shore the fires from the foundry chimneys burning high and
    glaringly into the night,
Casting their flicker of black contrasted with wild red and yellow light over the
    tops of houses, and down into the clefts of streets.

4
These and all else were to me the same as they are to you,
I loved well those cities, loved well the stately and rapid river,
The men and women I saw were all near to me,
Others the same—others who look back on me because I look'd forward to them,
(The time will come, though I stop here to-day and to-night.)

5

What is it then between us?
What is the count of the scores or hundreds of years between us?

Whatever it is, it avails not—distance avails not, and place avails not,
I too lived, Brooklyn of ample hills was mine,
I too walk'd the streets of Manhattan island, and bathed in the waters around it,
I too felt the curious abrupt questionings stir within me,
In the day among crowds of people sometimes they came upon me,
In my walks home late at night or as I lay in my bed they came upon me,
I too had been struck from the float forever held in solution,
I too had receiv'd identity by my body,
That I was I knew was of my body, and what I should be I knew I should be of my body.

6

It is not upon you alone the dark patches fall,
The dark threw its patches down upon me also,
The best I had done seem'd to me blank and suspicious,
My great thoughts as I supposed them, were they not in reality meagre?
Nor is it you alone who know what it is to be evil,
I am he who knew what it was to be evil,
I too knitted the old knot of contrariety,
Blabb'd, blush'd, resented, lied, stole, grudg'd,
Had guile, anger, lust, hot wishes I dared not speak,
Was wayward, vain, greedy, shallow, sly, cowardly, malignant,
The wolf, the snake, the hog, not wanting in me,
The cheating look, the frivolous word, the adulterous wish, not wanting,
Refusals, hates, postponements, meanness, laziness, none of these wanting,
Was one with the rest, the days and haps of the rest,
Was call'd by my nighest name by clear loud voices of young men as they saw me
    approaching or passing,
Felt their arms on my neck as I stood, or the negligent leaning of their flesh
    against me as I sat,
Saw many I loved in the street or ferry-boat or public assembly, yet never told
    them a word,
Lived the same life with the rest, the same old laughing, gnawing, sleeping,

Play'd the part that still looks back on the actor or actress,
The same old role, the role that is what we make it, as great as we like,
Or as small as we like, or both great and small.

7

Closer yet I approach you,
What thought you have of me now, I had as much of you—I laid in my stores in
    advance,
I consider'd long and seriously of you before you were born.

Who was to know what should come home to me?
Who knows but I am enjoying this?
Who knows, for all the distance, but I am as good as looking at you now, for all
    you cannot see me?

8

Ah, what can ever be more stately and admirable to me than mast-hemm'd
    Manhattan?
River and sunset and scallop-edg'd waves of flood-tide?
The sea-gulls oscillating their bodies, the hay-boat in the twilight, and the belated
    lighter?

What gods can exceed these that clasp me by the hand, and with voices I love call
    me promptly and loudly by my nighest name as I approach?
What is more subtle than this which ties me to the woman or man that looks in
    my face?
Which fuses me into you now, and pours my meaning into you?

We understand then do we not?
What I promis'd without mentioning it, have you not accepted?
What the study could not teach—what the preaching could not accomplish is
    accomplish'd, is it not?

9

Flow on, river! flow with the flood-tide, and ebb with the ebb-tide!
Frolic on, crested and scallop-edg'd waves!
Gorgeous clouds of the sunset! drench with your splendor me, or the men and
    women generations after me!
Cross from shore to shore, countless crowds of passengers!
Stand up, tall masts of Mannahatta! stand up, beautiful hills of Brooklyn!
Throb, baffled and curious brain! throw out questions and answers!
Suspend here and everywhere, eternal float of solution!
Gaze, loving and thirsting eyes, in the house or street or public assembly!

Sound out, voices of young men! loudly and musically call me by my nighest name!
Live, old life! play the part that looks back on the actor or actress!
Play the old role, the role that is great or small according as one makes it!

Consider, you who peruse me, whether I may not in unknown ways be looking
　　upon you;
Be firm, rail over the river, to support those who lean idly, yet haste with the
　　hasting current;
Fly on, sea-birds! fly sideways, or wheel in large circles high in the air;
Receive the summer sky, you water, and faithfully hold it till all downcast eyes
　　have time to take it from you!
Diverge, fine spokes of light, from the shape of my head, or any one's head, in the
　　sunlit water!
Come on, ships from the lower bay! pass up or down, white-sail'd schooners,
　　sloops, lighters!
Flaunt away, flags of all nations! be duly lower'd at sunset!
Burn high your fires, foundry chimneys! cast black shadows at nightfall! cast red
　　and yellow light over the tops of the houses!

Appearances, now or henceforth, indicate what you are,
You necessary film, continue to envelop the soul,
About my body for me, and your body for you, be hung out divinest aromas,
Thrive, cities—bring your freight, bring your shows, ample and sufficient rivers,
Expand, being than which none else is perhaps more spiritual,
Keep your places, objects than which none else is more lasting.

You have waited, you always wait, you dumb, beautiful ministers,
We receive you with free sense at last, and are insatiate henceforward,
Not you any more shall be able to foil us, or withhold yourselves from us,
We use you, and do not cast you aside—we plant you permanently within us,
We fathom you not—we love you—there is perfection in you also,
You furnish your parts toward eternity,
Great or small, you furnish your parts toward the soul.

1.3.4 Reading and Review Questions

1. How does Whitman's use of free verse challenge readers? What features
   and/or elements of Whitman's poetry help us to understand how to read it?

2. How does Whitman's use of natural elements compare to his use of man-
   made or urban elements in his poetry?

3. How would you describe the voice of Whitman's poetry?

4. How does Whitman's poetry engage with the Civil War?

1.4 EMILY DICKINSON

(1830 - 1886)

Born into an influential and socially prominent New England family in 1830, Emily Dickinson benefited from a level of education and mobility that most of her contemporaries, female and male, could not comprehend. The middle child of Edward Dickinson and Emily Norcross, Dickinson, along with her older brother Austin and younger sister Lavinia, received both an extensive formal education and the informal education that came by way of countless visitors to the family homestead during Edward Dickinson's political career. Contrary to popular depictions of her life, Dickinson did travel outside of Amherst but

Image 1.2 | Emily Dickinson, 1848
Photographer | Unknown
Source | Wikimedia Commons
License | Public Domain

ultimately chose to remain at home in the close company of family and friends. An intensely private person, Dickinson exerted almost singular control over the distribution of her poetry during her lifetime. That control, coupled with early portrayals of her as reclusive, has led many readers to assume that Dickinson was a fragile and timid figure whose formal, mysterious, concise, and clever poetry revealed the mind of a writer trapped in the rigid gender confines of the nineteenth century. More recent scholarship demonstrates not only the fallacy of Dickinson's depiction as the ghostly "Belle of Amherst," but also reveals the technical complexity of her poetry that predates the Modernism of T. S. Eliot, Ezra Pound, William Carlos Williams, and Marianne Moore by almost three-quarters of a century. In the selections that follow, Dickinson's poetry displays both her technical proficiency and her embrace of techniques that were new to the nineteenth century. Like her contemporary Walt Whitman, Dickinson used poetry to show her readers familiar landscapes from a fresh perspective.

The selections that follow, from Dickinson's most prolific years (1861-1865), illustrate the poet's mastery of the **lyric**—a short poem that often expresses a single theme such as the speaker's mood or feeling. "I taste a liquor never brewed –," our first selection, celebrates the poet's relationship to the natural world in both its wordplay (note the use of liquor in line one to indicate both an alcoholic beverage in the first stanza and a rich nectar in the third) and its natural **imagery**. Here, as in many of her poems, Dickinson's vibrant language demonstrates a vital spark in contrast to her reclusive image. Our second selection, "The Soul selects her own Society –," shows Dickinson using well-known images of power and authority to celebrate the independence of the soul in the face of expectations. In both of these first two poems, readers will note the celebrations of the individual will that engages fully with life without becoming either intoxicated or enslaved. The third selection, "Because I could not stop for Death –," one of the most famous poems in the Dickinson canon, forms an important bookend to our second selection in that both poems show Dickinson's precise control over the speaker's relationship to not only the natural world but also the divine. While death cannot be avoided, neither is it to be feared; the speaker of this poem reminds readers that the omnipresence of death does not mean that death is immanent. This idea of death as always present and potential comes full circle in the final selection in this unit, "My Life had stood – a Loaded Gun –." Here Dickinson plays with our preconceptions not only of death, but also of energy which appears always to be waiting for someone to unleash it. Considered carefully, these four poems demonstrate the range of Dickinson's reach as a poet. In these lyrics, mortality and desire combine in precise lyrics that awaken both our imagination and our awareness of the natural world.

1.4.1 "I TASTE A LIQUOR NEVER BREWED"

I taste a liquor never brewed,
From tankards scooped in pearl;
Not all the vats upon the Rhine
Yield such an alcohol!

Inebriate of air am I,
And debauchee of dew,
Reeling, through endless summer days,
From inns of molten blue.

When landlords turn the drunken bee
Out of the foxglove's door,
When butterflies renounce their drams,
I shall but drink the more!

Till seraphs swing their snowy hats,
And saints to windows run,
To see the little tippler
Leaning against the sun!

1.4.2 "THE SOUL SELECTS HER OWN SOCIETY"

The soul selects her own society,
Then shuts the door;
On her divine majority
Obtrude no more.

Unmoved, she notes the chariot's pausing
At her low gate;

Unmoved, an emperor is kneeling
Upon her mat.

I've known her from an ample nation
Choose one;
Then close the valves of her attention
Like stone.

1.4.3 "BECAUSE I COULD NOT STOP FOR DEATH"

Because I could not stop for Death,
He kindly stopped for me;
The carriage held but just ourselves
And Immortality.

We slowly drove, he knew no haste,
And I had put away
My labor, and my leisure too,
For his civility.

We passed the school where children played,
Their lessons scarcely done;
We passed the fields of gazing grain,
We passed the setting sun.

1.4.4 "MY LIFE HAD STOOD—A LOADED GUN"

My Life had stood—a Loaded Gun— In Corners—till a Day
The Owner passed—identified— And carried Me away—

And now We roam in Sovereign Woods— And now We hunt the Doe—
And every time I speak for Him— The Mountains straight reply—

And do I smile, such cordial light
Upon the Valley glow— It is as a Vesuvian face
Had let its pleasure through—

And when at Night—Our good Day done— I guard My Master's Head—
'Tis better than the Eider-Duck's
Deep Pillow—to have shared—

To foe of His—I'm deadly foe— None stir the second time—
On whom I lay a Yellow Eye— Or an emphatic Thumb—

Though I than He—may longer live
He longer must—than I—
For I have but the power to kill, Without—the power to die—

1.4.4 Reading and Review Questions

1. Many of Dickinson's poems are rhythmically similar to popular nineteenth-century songs. How do those similarities help us to understand Dickinson's poetry?

2. Death and isolation are common themes in Dickinson's poetry, yet her poems rarely seem melancholy. What elements prevent her poems from becoming too solemn?

3. How do Dickinson's poems support or challenge what we think we know about gender roles in the nineteenth century?

4. Compare and contract Dickinson's isolation with Whitman's aggressively public persona.

1.5 KEY TERMS

- Cadence
- Civil War
- Emily Dickinson
- First Transcontinental Railroad
- Free Verse

- Imagery
- Lyric
- Meter
- Rhyme
- Romanticism
- Walt Whitman

2 Realism (1865-1890)
Amy Berke, Jordan Cofer, and Doug Davis

2.1 LEARNING OUTCOMES

After completing this chapter, you should be able to:

- Describe the post-Civil War context of American culture at the time Realistic writing came into prominence.

- List the features of American Literary Realism.

- List the features of the two sub-movements that preceded Realism: Local Color and Regionalism.

- Identify stylistic elements of Local Color, Regionalism, and Realism in literary selections.

- Identify major distinctions and differences among the literary styles of Local Color, Regionalism, and Realism.

- Analyze the ways in which women's literature develops in this period.

- Analyze themes in an early work by an African-American writer.

2.2 INTRODUCTION

After the Civil War and toward the end of the nineteenth century, America experienced significant change. With the closing of the Western frontier and increasing urbanization and **industrialization**, and with the completion of the First Transcontinental Railroad and the advent of new communication technologies such as the telegraph, America began to emerge as a more unified nation as it moved into the **Industrial Age**. As **immigration** from both Europe and Asia peaked during the last half of the nineteenth century, immigrants provided cheap labor to rising urban centers in the Northeast and eventually in the Midwest. There was a subsequent rise in the middle class for the first time in America, as the economic landscape of the country began to change. The country's social, political, and cultural landscape began to change as well. Women argued for the right to vote, to own property, and to earn their own living, and, as African-Americans began to rise to social and political prominence, they called for social equality and the right to vote as well. Workers in factories and businesses began to lobby for better working conditions, organizing to create unions. Free public schools opened throughout the nation, and, by the turn of the century, the majority of children in the United States attended school. Throughout the latter part of the nineteenth century, activists and reformers worked to battle injustice and social ills. Within this heady mix of political, economic, social, and cultural change, American writers began to look more to contemporary society and social issues for their writing material, rather than to the distant or fictional past.

The first members of the new generation of writers sought to create a new American literature, one that distinctly reflected American life and values and did not mimic British literary customs. At the same time, these writers turned to the past, toward writers such as Nathaniel Hawthorne and James Fenimore Cooper, and reacted against their predecessors' allegiance to the Romantic style of writing which favored the ideal over the real representation of life in fiction. William Dean Howells, Mark Twain, and Henry James wrote prolifically about the Realistic method, where writers created characters and plot based on average people experiencing the common concerns of everyday life, and they also produced their own literary masterpieces using this style.

All writers in the Realistic mode shared a commitment to referential narrative. Their readers expected to meet characters that resembled ordinary people, often of the middle class, living in ordinary circumstances, who experienced plausible real-life struggles and who often, as in life, were unable to find resolution to their conflicts. Realists developed these characters by using ordinary speech in dialogue, commensurate to the character's social class. Often in Realistic stories, characterization and plot became intertwined, as the plot was formed from the exploration of a character working through or reacting to a particular issue or struggle. In other words, character often drove the plot of the story. Characters in Realistic fiction were three-dimensional, and their inner lives were often revealed through an objective, omniscient narrator.

Realists set their fiction in places that actually existed, and they were interested in recent or contemporary life, not in history or legend. Setting in Realistic fiction was important but was not limited to a particular place or region. Realists believed in the accuracy of detail, and, for them, accuracy helped build the "truth" conveyed in the work. The implied assumption for these writers is that "reality" is verifiable, is separate from human perception of it, and can be agreed upon collectively. Finally, Realistic writers believed that the function of the author is to *show*, not simply *tell*. The story should be allowed to tell itself with a decided lack of authorial intrusion. Realistic writers attempted to avoid sentimentality or any kind of forced or heavy-handed emotional appeal. The three most prominent theorists and practitioners of American Literary Realism are Mark Twain, often called the comic Realist; William Dean Howells, often termed the social Realist; and Henry James, often characterized as the psychological Realist.

Two earlier literary styles contributed to the emergence of Realism: **Local Color** and **Regionalism**. These two sub-movements cannot be completely separated from one another or from Realism itself, since all three styles have intersecting points. However, there are distinct features of each style that bear comparison.

2.2.1 Local Color (1865-1885)

After the Civil War, as the country became more unified, regions of the country that were previously "closed" politically or isolated geographically became interesting to the populace at large. Readers craved stories about eccentric, peculiar characters living in isolated locales. Local Color writing therefore involves a detailed setting forth of the characteristics of a particular locality, enabling the reader to "see" the setting. The writer typically is concerned with habits, customs, religious practices, dress, fashion, favorite foods, language, dialect, common expressions, peculiarities, and surrounding flora and fauna of a particular locale. Local Color pieces were sometimes told from the perspective of an outsider (such as travelers or journalists) looking into a particular rural, isolated locale that had been generally closed off from the contemporary world. In some stories, the local inhabitants would examine their own environments, nostalgically trying to preserve in writing the "ways things were" in the "good old days." The Local Color story often involved a worldly "stranger" coming into a rather closed off locale populated with common folk. From there the story took a variety of turns, but often the stranger, who believed he was superior to the country bumpkins, was fooled or tricked in some way. Nostalgia and sentimentality, and even elements of the Romantic style of the earlier part of the century, may infuse a Local Color story. Often, the story is humorous, with a local trickster figure outwitting the more urbane outsider or interloper. In Local Color stories about the Old South, for example, nostalgia for a bygone era may be prevalent. The "plantation myth" popularized by Thomas Nelson Page, for instance, might offer a highly filtered and altered view of plantation life as idyllic, for both master and slave. Local Color stories about the West, such as Mark Twain's "The Jumping Frog of Calaveras County," might offer raucous stories with stock characters of gamblers or miners who outwit the interloper from the city, who flaunts his intellectual superiority over the locals. An early African-American writer, Charles Chesnutt, used the Local Color style of writing to deconstruct the plantation myth by showing the innate dignity, intelligence, and power of slaves or former slaves who outwit the white racist landowners.

Local Color writing can be seen as a transitional type of writing that took American literature away from the Romantic style and more firmly into the Realistic style. The characters are more realistically drawn, with very human, sometimes ignoble, traits: they swear, speak in regional dialect, swat flies away from their faces, and make mistakes; they are both comic and pitiable. The setting is realistically drawn as well: a real-life location, with accurate depictions of setting, people, and local customs. Local Color writing, however, does not reach the more stylistically and thematically complicated dimensions of Realistic writing. Local Color works tend to be somewhat sentimental stories with happy endings or at least endings where good prevails over evil. Characters are often flat or two-dimensional who are either good or bad. Outlandish and improbable events often happen during the course of the story, and characters sometimes undergo dramatic and unbelievable changes in characterization. Local Color did, however, begin a trend in American literature that allowed for a more authentic American style and storyline about characters who speak like Americans, not the British aristocracy, real-life American places, and more down-to-earth, recognizably human characters.

2.2.2 Regionalism (1875-1895)

Regionalism can be seen as a more sophisticated form of Local Color, with the author using one main character (the protagonist) to offer a specific point of view in the story. Regionalist writers often employ Local Color elements in their fiction. After all, they are concerned with the characteristics of a particular locale or region. However, regionalist writers tell the story empathetically, from the protagonist's perspective. That is, the Regional writer attempts to render a convincing surface of a particular time and place, but investigates the psychological character traits from a more universal perspective. Characters tend to be more three-dimensional and the plot less formulaic or predictable. Often what prevents Regional writers from squarely falling into the category of "Realist" is their tendency toward nostalgia, sentimentality, authorial intrusion, or a rather contrived or happy ending.

In Sarah Orne Jewett's "A White Heron," for example, the story has a number of features of Local Color stories: characters speak in a New England dialect, the landscape is described in detail, the customs and rituals of farming class families are described, and an outsider—the young male ornithologist—comes to this secluded region with a sense of superiority and is thwarted in his endeavors by young Sylvy who refuses to give up the secret location of the heron. However, the story is told from the perspective of Sylvy, and readers gain insight into her inner conflict as she attempts to make a difficult decision. We gain awareness of Sylvy's complexity as a character, a young girl who is faced with making an adult decision, a choice that will force her to grow up and face the world from a more mature stance. Jewett does, at times, allow the narrator to intrude in order to encourage readers to feel sympathy for Sylvy. Therefore, the story does not exhibit the narrative objectivity of a Realistic story.

Regionalism has often been used as a term to describe many works by women writers during the late nineteenth century; however, it is a term which, unfortunately, has confined these women writers' contribution to American literature to a particular style. Sarah Orne Jewett and Mary Wilkins Freeman, for example, certainly wrote about the New England region, but their larger focus was on ordinary women in domestic spaces who seek self-agency in a male-dominated culture. Kate Chopin set most of her works among the **Creole** and **Acadian** social classes of the Louisiana Bayou region, yet the larger themes of her works offer examinations of women who long for passionate and personal fulfillment and for the ability to live authentic, self-directed lives. Like the established theorists of Realism—Howells, Twain, and James—women writers of the time, including Charlotte Perkins Gilman and Ellen Glasgow, who are generally not thought of as Regional writers, produced work which often defied strict labeling and which contributed to the beginning of a **feminist** tradition in American literature. While literary labels help frame the style and method of stories written in the late nineteenth century, most literary works—especially those that have withstood the test of time—defy reductionism.

2.3 MARK TWAIN

(1835 - 1910)

Image 2.1 | Mark Twain, 1907
Photographer | A. F. Bradley
Source | Wikimedia Commons
License | Public Domain

Mark Twain is the pen name of author Samuel Langhorne Clemmons. Twain was born in Florida, Missouri, but grew up in Hannibal, Missouri, near the banks of the Mississippi River. This location was a major influence on his work and severed as the setting for many of his stories. Although Twain originally apprenticed as a printer, he spent eighteen months on the Mississippi River training as a riverboat pilot (the name Mark Twain is a reference to a nautical term). By the start of the Civil War (1861), traffic on the Mississippi River had slowed considerably, which led Twain to abandon his dreams of piloting a riverboat. Twain claims to have spent two weeks in the Marion Rangers, a poorly organized local confederate militia, after leaving his job on a riverboat. In 1861, Twain's brother Orion was appointed by President Lincoln to serve as the Secretary of Nevada, and Twain initially accompanied him out West, serving as the Assistant Secretary of Nevada. Twain's adventures out West would become the material for his successful book, *Roughing It!*, published in 1872, following on the heels of the success of his international travelogue, *Innocents Abroad* (1869). While living out West, Twain made a name for himself as a journalist, eventually serving as the editor of the *Virginia City Daily Territorial Enterprise*. The multi-talented Twain rose to prominence as a writer, journalist, humorist, memoirist, novelist, and public speaker.

Twain was one of the most influential and important figures of **American Literary Realism**, achieving fame during his lifetime. Twain was hailed as America's most famous writer, and is the author of several classic books such as *The Adventure of Tom Sawyer* (1876), *The Adventures of Huckleberry Finn* (1884), *Roughing It!*, *Innocents Abroad*, *Life on the Mississippi* (1883), and *A Connecticut Yankee in King Arthur's Court* (1889). Twain is known for his use of dialect, regional humor, and **satire**, as well as the repeated theme of having jokes at the expense of an outsider (or work featuring an outsider who comes to fleece locals).

In his famous "The Celebrated Jumping Frog of Calaveras County," which has also been published under its original title "Jim Smiley and His Jumping Frog" and "The Notorious Jumping Frog of Calaveras County," Twain experiments with early versions of **meta-fiction**, embedding a story within a story. Furthermore, the story relies on local color humor and regional dialect ("Why blame my cats") as well as featuring an outsider entering a new place, a staple in Twain's work. In *Roughing It!*, which details Twain's travels out West from 1861-1867, Twain details many adventures visiting with outlaws and other strange characters, as well as encounters with notable figures of the age, such as Brigham Young and Horace Greeley. Furthermore, *Roughing It!* provided descriptions of the frontier from Nevada to San Francisco to Hawaii to an audience largely unfamiliar with the area. Although he claimed it to be a work of non-fiction, *Roughing It!* features many fantastic stories of Twain's travels in the West, several of which were exaggerated or untrue. In "The War Prayer," a satire of the Spanish-American War (1898), Twain proves to be a master of irony. The story, which was originally rejected during Twain's lifetime, begins as a prayer for American soldiers and, as it continues, highlights many of the horrors of war.

2.3.1 "The Celebrated Jumping Frog of Calaveras County"

In compliance with the request of a friend of mine, who wrote me from the East, I called on good-natured, garrulous old Simon Wheeler, and inquired after my friend's friend, Leonidas W. Smiley, as reques.ted to do, and I hereunto append the result. I have a lurking suspicion that *Leonidas W.* Smiley is a myth; that my friend never knew such a personage; and that he only conjectured that if I asked old Wheeler about him, it would remind him of his infamous *Jim* Smiley, and he would go to work and bore me to death with some exasperating reminiscence of him as long and as tedious as it should be useless to me. If that was the design it succeeded.

I found Simon Wheeler dozing comfortably by the bar-room stove of the dilapidated tavern in the decayed mining camp of Engel's, and noticed that he was fat and bald-headed, and had an expression of winning gentleness and simplicity upon his tranquil countenance. He roused up and gave me good-day. I told him a friend of mine had commissioned me to make some inquires about a cherished companion of his boyhood named *Leonidas W.* Smiley—*Rev. Leonidas W.* Smiley, a young minister of the Gospel, who be had heard was at one time a resident of Angel's Camp. I added that if Mr. Wheeler could tell me anything about this Rev. Leonidas W. Smiley, I would feel under many obligations to him.

Simon Wheeler backed me into a corner and blockaded me there with his chair, and then sat down and reeled off the monotonous narrative which follows this paragraph. He never smiled, he never frowned, he never changed his voice from the gentle-flowing key to which he tuned his initial sentence, be never betrayed the slightest suspicion of enthusiasm; but all through the interminable narrative there ran a vein of impressive earnestness and sincerity, which showed me plainly, that, so far from his imagining that there was anything ridiculous or funny about his story, he regarded it as a really important matter, and admired its two heroes as men of transcendant genius in *finesse*. I let him go on in his own way, and never interrupted him once.

"Rev. Leonidas W. H'm, Reverend Le—well, there was a feller here once by the name of *Jim* Smiley, in the winter of '49- or maybe it was the spring of '50—I don't recollect exactly, somehow, though what makes me think it was one or the other is because remember the big flume warn't finished when he first come to the camp; but any way he was the curiosest man about always betting on anything that turned up you ever see, if he could get anybody to bet on the other side; and if he couldn't he'd change sides. Any way that suited the other man would suit *him*—any way just so's he got a bet, *he* was satisfied. But still he was lucky, uncommon lucky; he most always come out winner. He was always ready and laying for a chance; there couldn't be no solit'ry thing mentioned but that feller'd offer to bet on it, and take any side you please as I was just telling you. If there was a horse-race, you'd find him flush or you'd find him busted at the end of it; if there was a dog-fight, he'd bet on it; if there was a cat-fight he'd bet on it; if there was a chicken-fight he'd bet on it; why, if there was two birds sitting on a fence, he would bet you which one would fly first; or if there was a camp-meeting, he would be there reg'lar to bet on Parson Walker, which ·he judged to be the best exhorter about here, and so he was too, and a good man.   If he even see a straddle-bug start to go anywheres, he would bet you how long it would take him to get to—to wherever he was going to, and if you took him up he would foller that straddle-bug to Mexico but what he would find out where he was bound for and how long he was on the road. Lots of the boys here has seen that Smiley, and can tell you about him. Why, it never made no difference to *him*—he'd bet on *any* thing—the dangdest feller. Parson Walker's wife laid very sick once, for a good while, and it seemed as if they warn't going to save her; but one morning he come in, and Smiley up and asked him how she was, and he said she was considerable better—thank the Lord for his inf'nit mercy—and coming on so smart that with the blessing of Prov'dence she'd get well yet; and Smiley, before he thought, says, "Well, I'll resk two-and-a-half she don't anyway."

Thish-yer Smiley had a mare—the boys called her· the fifteen minute nag, but that was only in fun, you know, because of course she was faster than that—and he used to win money on that horse, for all she was so slow and always had the asthma, or the distemper, or the consumption, or something of that kind. They used to give her two or three hundred yards' start, and then pass her under way; but always at the fag end of the race she'd get excited and desperate-like, and come cavorting and straddling up and scattering her legs around limber, sometimes in the air, and sometimes out to one side amongst the fences, and kicking up m-o-r-e dust and raising m-o-r-e racket with her coughing and sneezing and blowing her nose—and *always* fetch up at the stand just about a neck ahead, as near as you could cipher it down.

And he had a little small bull-pup that to look at him you'd think he warn't worth a cent but to set around and look ornery and lay for a chance to steal something. But as soon as money was up on him he was a different dog; his under jaw began to stick out like the fo'castle of a steamboat, and his teeth would uncover and shine like the furnaces. And a dog might tackle him and bullyrag him, and bite him, and throw him over his shoulder two or three times, and Andrew Jackson—which was the name of the pup—Andrew Jackson would never let on but what he was satisfied, and hadn't expected nothing else—and the bets being doubled and doubled on the other side all the time, till the money was all up; and then all of a sudden he would grab that other dog jest by the j'int of his hind leg and freeze to it—not chaw, you understand, but only just grip and hang on till they throwed up the sponge, if it was a year. Smiley always come out winner on that pup, till he harnessed a dog once that did'nt have no hind legs, because they'd been sawed off in a circular saw, and when the thing had gone along far enough, and the money was all up, and he come to make a snatch for his pet holt, he see in a minute how he'd been imposed on, and how the other dog had him in the door, so to speak, and he 'peared surprised, and then he looked sorter discouraged-like, and didn't try no more to win the fight, and so he got shucked out bad. He give Smiley a look, as much as to say his heart was broke, and it was *his* fault, for putting up a dog that hadn't no hind legs for him to take holt of, which was his main dependence in a fight, and then he limped off a piece and laid down and died. It was a good pup was that Andrew Jackson, and would have made a name for hisself if he'd lived, for the stuff was in him and he had genius—I know it, because he hadn't no opportunities to speak of, and it don't stand to reason that a dog could make such a fight as he could under them circumstances if he hadn't no talent.   It always makes me feel sorry when I think of that last fight of his'n, and the way it turned out.

Well, thish-yer Smiley had rat-tarriers, and chicken cocks, and tom-cats and all them kind of things, till you couldn't rest, and you couldn't fetch nothing f or him to bet on but he'd match you. He ketched a frog one day, and took him home, and said be cal'lated to educate him; and so he never done nothing for three months but set in his back yard and learn that frog to jump. And you bet you he *did* learn him, too. He'd give him a little punch behind, and the next minute you'd see that frog whirling in the air like a doughnut-see him turn one summerset, or maybe a couple, if he got a good start, and come down flat-footed and all right, like a cat. He got him up so in the matter of catching flies, and kep' him in practice so constant, that he'd nail a fly every time as fur as he could see him. Smiley said all a frog wanted was education and he could do 'most anything—and I believe him. Why, I've seen him set Dan'l Webster down here on this floor—Dan'l Webster was the name of the frog—and sing out, "Flies Dan'l, flies!" and quicker'n you could wink he'd spring straight up and snake a fly off'n the counter there, and flop down on the floor ag'in as solid as a gob of mud, and fall to scratching the side of his head with his hind foot as indifferent as if he hadn't no idea he'd been doin' any more'n any frog might do. You never see a frog so modest and straightfor'ard as he was, for all he was so gifted. And when it come to fair and square jumping on a dead level, he could get over more ground at one straddle than any animal of his breed you ever see. Jumping on a dead level was his strong suit, you understand; and when it come to that, Smiley would ante up money on him as long as he had a red. Smiley was monstrous proud of his frog, and well he might be, for fellers that had travelled and been everywhere, all said he laid over any frog that ever *they* see.

Well, Smiley kep' the beast in a little lattice box, and he used to fetch him down town sometimes and lay for a bet. One day, a feller—a stranger in the camp, he was—come acrost him with his box, and says:

"What might it be that you've got in the box?"

And Smiley says, sorter indifferent-like, "It might be a parrot, or it might be a canary, maybe, but it ain't—it's only just a frog."

And the feller took it, and looked at it careful, and turned it round this way and that, and says, "H'm—so 'tis. Well, what's *he* good for?"

"Well," Smiley, says, easy and careless, "he's good enough for one thing, I should judge—he can outjump any frog in Calaveras county."

The feller took the box again, and took another long, particular look, and gave it back to Smiley, and says, very deliberate, "Well," he says, "I don't see no p'ints about that frog that's any better'n any other frog."

"Maybe you don't," Smiley says. "Maybe you understand frogs and maybe you don't understand 'em; maybe you've had experience, and maybe you ain't only a amature, as it were. Anyways, I've got my opinion and I'll resk forty dollars that he can outjump any frog in Calaveras county."

And the feller studied a minute, and then says, kinder sad like, "Well, I'm only a stranger here, and I aint got no frog; but if I had a frog, I'd bet you."

And then Smiley says, "That's all right—that's all right—if you'll hold my box a minute, I'll go and get you a frog." And so the feller took the box, and put up his forty dollars along with Smiley's, and set down to wait. So he sat there a good while thinking and thinking to hisself, and then he got the frog out and prized his mouth open and took a teaspoon and filled him full of quail shot—filled him pretty near up to his chin—and set him on the floor. Smiley he went to the swamp and slopped around in the mud for along time, and finally he ketched a frog, and fetched him in, and gave him to this feller and says:

"Now, if you're ready, set him alongside of Dan'l, with his fore-paws just even with Dan'l's, and I'll give the word." Then he says, "One—two—three—*git* !" and him and the feller touched up the frogs from behind, and the new frog hopped off lively, but Dan'l gave a heave, and hysted up his shoulders—so—like a Frenchman, but it warn't no use—he couldn't budge; he was planted as solid as a church, and he couldn't no more stir than if he was anchored out. Smiley was a good deal surprised, and he was disgusted too, but he didn't have no idea what the matter was, of course.

The feller took the money and started away; and when he was going out at the door, he sorter jerked his thumb over his shoulder—so—at Dan'l, and says again, very deliberate, "Well," he says, "*I* don't see no p'ints about that frog that's any better'n any other frog."

Smiley he stood scratching his head and looking down at Dan'l a long time, and at last he says, "I do wonder what in the nation that frog throw'd off for—I wonder if there ain't something the matter with him—he 'pears to look mighty _baggy, somehow." And he ketched Dan'l by the nap of the neck, and hefted him, and says, "Why, blame my cats if he don't weigh five pound!" and turned him upside down and he belched out a double handful of shot. And then he see how it was, and he was the maddest man—he set the frog down and took out after that feller, but he never ketched him. And—"

[Here Simon Wheeler heard his name called from the front yard, and got up to see what was wanted.] And turning to me as he moved away, he said: "Just set where yon are, stranger, and rest easy—I ain't going to be gone a second."

But, by your leave, I did not think that a continuation of the history of the enterprising vagabond *Jim* Smiley would be likely to afford me much information concerning the *Rev. Leonidas W.* Smiley, and so I started away.

At the door I met the sociable Wheeler returning, and he button-holed me and re-commenced:

"Well, thish-yer Smiley had a yaller one-eyed cow that didn't have no tail, only jest a short stump like a bannanner, and—"

However, lacking both time and inclination, I did not wait to hear about the afflicted cow, but took my leave.

2.3.2 Selections From *Roughing It*

CHAPTER VII

IT did seem strange enough to see a town again after what appeared to us such a long acquaintance with deep, still, almost lifeless and houseless solitude! We tumbled out into the busy street feeling like meteoric people crumbled off the corner of some other world, and wakened up suddenly in this. For an hour we took as much interest in Overland City as if we had never seen a town before. The reason we had an hour to spare was because we had to change our stage (for a less sumptuous affair, called a "mud-wagon") and transfer our freight of mails.

Presently we got under way again. We came to the shallow, yellow, muddy South Platte, with its low banks and its scattering flat sand-bars and pigmy islands—a melancholy stream straggling through the centre of the enormous flat plain, and only saved from being impossible to find with the naked eye by its sentinel rank of scattering trees standing on either bank. The Platte was "up," they said—which made me wish I could see it when it was down, if it could look any sicker and sorrier. They said it was a dangerous stream to cross, now, because its quicksands were liable to swallow up horses, coach and passengers if an attempt was made to ford it. But the mails had to go, and we made the attempt. Once or twice in midstream the wheels sunk into the yielding sands so threateningly that we half believed we had dreaded and avoided the sea all our lives to be shipwrecked in a "mud-wagon" in the middle of a desert at last. But we dragged through and sped away toward the setting sun.

Next morning, just before dawn, when about five hundred and fifty miles from St. Joseph, our mud-wagon broke down. We were to be delayed five or six hours, and therefore we took horses, by invitation, and joined a party who were just starting on a buffalo hunt. It was noble sport galloping over the plain in the dewy freshness of the morning, but our part of the hunt ended in disaster and disgrace, for a wounded buffalo bull chased the passenger Bemis nearly two miles, and then he forsook his horse and took to a lone tree. He was very sullen about the matter for some twenty-four hours, but at last he began to soften little by little, and finally he said:

"Well, it was not funny, and there was no sense in those gawks making themselves so facetious over it. I tell you I was angry in earnest for awhile. I should have shot that long gangly lubber they called Hank, if I could have done it without crippling six or seven other people—but of course I couldn't, the old 'Allen's' so confounded comprehensive. I wish those loafers had been up in the tree; they wouldn't have wanted to laugh so. If I had had a horse worth a cent—but no, the minute he saw that buffalo bull wheel on him and give a bellow, he raised straight up in the air and stood on his heels. The saddle began to slip, and I took him round the neck and laid close to him, and began to pray. Then he came down and stood up on the other end awhile, and the bull actually stopped pawing sand and bellowing to contemplate the inhuman spectacle. Then the bull made a pass at him and uttered a bellow that sounded perfectly frightful, it was so close to me, and that seemed to literally prostrate my horse's reason, and make a raving distracted maniac of him, and I wish I may die if he didn't stand on his head for a quarter of a minute and shed tears. He was absolutely out of his mind—he was, as sure as truth itself, and he really didn't know what he was doing. Then the bull came charging at us, and my horse dropped down on all fours and took a fresh start—and then for the next ten minutes he would actually throw one hand-spring after another so fast that the bull began to get unsettled, too, and didn't know where to start in—and so he stood there sneezing, and shovelling dust over his back, and bellowing every now and then, and thinking he had got a fifteen-hundred dollar circus horse for breakfast, certain. Well, I was first out on his neck—the horse's, not the bull's—and then underneath, and next on his rump, and sometimes head up, and sometimes heels—but I tell you it seemed solemn and awful to be ripping and tearing and carrying on so in the presence of death, as you might say. Pretty soon the bull made a snatch for us and brought away some of my horse's tail (I suppose, but do not know, being pretty busy at the time), but *something* made him hungry for solitude and suggested to him to get up and hunt for it. And then you ought to have seen that spider-legged old skeleton go! and you ought to have seen the bull cut out after him, too—head down, tongue out, tail up, bellowing like everything, and actually mowing down the weeds, and tearing up the earth, and boosting up the sand like a whirlwind! By George, it was a hot race! I and the saddle were back on the rump, and I had the bridle in my teeth and holding on to the pommel with both hands. First we left the dogs behind; then we passed a jackass rabbit; then we overtook a cayote, and were gaining on an antelope when the rotten girth let go and threw me about thirty yards off to the left, and as the saddle went down over the horse's rump he gave it a lift with his heels that sent it more than four hundred yards up in the air, I wish I may die in a minute if he didn't. I fell at the foot of the only solitary tree there was in nine counties adjacent (as any creature could see with the naked eye), and the next second I had hold of the bark with four sets of nails and my teeth, and the next second after that I was astraddle of the main limb and blaspheming my luck in a way that made my breath smell of brimstone. I *had* the bull, now, if he did not think of *one* thing. But that one thing I dreaded. I dreaded it very seriously. There was a possibility that the bull might not think of it, but there were greater chances that he would. I made up my mind what I would do in case he did. It was a little over forty feet to the ground from where I sat. I cautiously unwound the lariat from the pommel of my saddle—"

"Your *saddle?* Did you take your saddle up in the tree with you?"

"Take it up in the tree with me? Why, how you talk. Of course I didn't. No man could do that. It *fell* in the tree when it came down."

"Oh—exactly."

"Certainly. I unwound the lariat, and fastened one end of it to the limb. It was the very best green raw-hide, and capable of sustaining tons. I made a slip-noose in the other end, and then hung it down to see the length. It reached down twenty-two feet—half way to the ground. I then loaded every barrel of the Allen with a double charge. I felt satisfied. I said to myself, if he never thinks of that one thing that I dread, all right—but if he does, all right anyhow—I am fixed for him. But don't you know that the very thing a man dreads is the thing that always happens? Indeed it is so. I watched the bull, now, with anxiety—anxiety which no one can conceive of who has not been in such a situation and felt that at any moment death might come. Presently a thought came into the bull's eye. I knew it! said I—if my nerve fails now, I am lost. Sure enough, it was just as I had dreaded, he started in to climb the tree—"

"What, the bull?"

"Of course—who else?"

"But a bull can't climb a tree."

"He can't, can't he? Since you know so much about it, did you ever see a bull try?"

"No! I never dreamt of such a thing."

"Well, then, what is the use of your talking that way, then? Because you never saw a thing done, is that any reason why it can't be done?"

"Well, all right—go on. What did you do?"

"The bull started up, and got along well for about ten feet, then slipped and slid back. I breathed easier. He tried it again—got up a little higher—slipped again. But he came at it once more, and this time he was careful. He got gradually higher and higher, and my spirits went down more and more. Up he came—an inch at a time—with his eyes hot, and his tongue hanging out. Higher and higher— hitched his foot over the stump of a limb, and looked up, as much as to say, 'You are my meat, friend.' Up again—higher and higher, and getting more excited the closer he got. He was within ten feet of me! I took a long breath,—and then said I, 'It is now or never.' I had the coil of the lariat all ready; I paid it out slowly, till it hung right over his head; all of a sudden I let go of the slack, and the slip-noose fell fairly round his neck! Quicker than lightning I out with the Allen and let him have it in the face. It was an awful roar, and must have scared the bull out of his senses. When the smoke cleared away, there he was, dangling in the air, twenty foot from the ground, and going out of one convulsion into another faster than you could count! I didn't stop to count, anyhow—I shinned down the tree and shot for home."

"Bemis, is all that true, just as you have stated it?"

"I wish I may rot in my tracks and die the death of a dog if it isn't."

"Well, we can't refuse to believe it, and we don't. But if there were some proofs—"

"Proofs! Did I bring back my lariat?"

"No."

"Did I bring back my horse?"

"No."

"Did you ever see the bull again?"

"No."

"Well, then, what more do you want? I never saw anybody as particular as you are about a little thing like that."

I made up my mind that if this man was not a liar he only missed it by the skin of his teeth. This episode reminds me of an incident of my brief sojourn in Siam, years afterward. The European citizens of a town in the neighborhood of Bangkok had a prodigy among them by the name of Eckert, an Englishman—a person famous for the number, ingenuity and imposing magnitude of his lies. They were always repeating his most celebrated falsehoods, and always trying to "draw him out" before strangers; but they seldom succeeded. Twice he was invited to the house where I was visiting, but nothing could seduce him into a specimen lie. One day a planter named

Bascom, an influential man, and a proud and sometimes irascible one, invited me to ride over with him and call on Eckert. As we jogged along, said he:

"Now, do you know where the fault lies? It lies in putting Eckert on his guard. The minute the boys go to pumping at Eckert he knows perfectly well what they are after, and of course he shuts up his shell. Anybody might know he would. But when we get there, we must play him finer than that. Let him shape the conversation to suit himself—let him drop it or change it whenever he wants to. Let him see that nobody is trying to draw him out. Just let him have his own way. He will soon forget himself and begin to grind out lies like a mill. Don't get impatient—just keep quiet, and let me play him. I will make him lie. It does seem to me that the boys must be blind to overlook such an obvious and simple trick as that."

Eckert received us heartily—a pleasant-spoken, gentle-mannered creature. We sat in the veranda an hour, sipping English ale, and talking about the king, and the sacred white elephant, the Sleeping Idol, and all manner of things; and I noticed that my comrade never led the conversation himself or shaped it, but simply followed Eckert's lead, and betrayed no solicitude and no anxiety about anything. The effect was shortly perceptible. Eckert began to grow communicative; he grew more and more at his ease, and more and more talkative and sociable. Another hour passed in the same way, and then all of a sudden Eckert said:

"Oh, by the way! I came near forgetting. I have got a thing here to astonish you. Such a thing as neither you nor any other man ever heard of—I've got a cat that will eat cocoanut! Common green cocoanut—and not only eat the meat, but drink the milk. It is so—I'll swear to it."

A quick glance from Bascom—a glance that I understood—then:

"Why, bless my soul, I never heard of such a thing. Man, it is impossible."

"I knew you would say it. I'll fetch the cat."

He went in the house. Bascom said:

"There—what did I tell you? Now, that is the way to handle Eckert. You see, I have petted him along patiently, and put his suspicions to sleep. I am glad we came. You tell the boys about it when you go back. Cat eat a cocoanut—oh, my! Now, that is just his way, exactly—he will tell the absurdest lie, and trust to luck to get out of it again. Cat eat a cocoanut—the innocent fool!"

Eckert approached with his cat, sure enough. Bascom smiled. Said he:

"I'll hold the cat—you bring a cocoanut."

Eckert split one open, and chopped up some pieces. Bascom smuggled a wink to me, and proffered a slice of the fruit to puss. She snatched it, swallowed it ravenously, and asked for more!

We rode our two miles in silence, and wide apart. At least I was silent, though Bascom cuffed his horse and cursed him a good deal, notwithstanding the horse was behaving well enough. When I branched off homeward, Bascom said:

"Keep the horse till morning. And—you need not speak of this—foolishness to the boys."

CHAPTER XIV

Mr. Street was very busy with his telegraphic matters —and considering that he had eight or nine hundred miles of rugged, snowy, uninhabited mountains, and waterless, treeless, melancholy deserts to traverse with his wire, it was natural and needful that he should be as busy as possible. He could not go comfortably along and cut his poles by the roadside, either, but they had to be hauled by ox teams across those exhausting deserts—and it was two days' journey from water to water, in one or two of them. Mr. Street's contract was a vast work, every way one looked at it; and yet to comprehend what the vague words "eight hundred miles of rugged mountains and dismal deserts" mean, one must go over the ground in person—pen and ink descriptions cannot convey the dreary reality to the reader. And after all, Mr. S.'s mightiest difficulty turned out to be one which he had never taken into the account at all. Unto Mormons he had sub-let the hardest and heaviest half of his great undertaking, and all of a sudden they concluded that they were going to make little or nothing, and so they tranquilly threw their poles overboard in mountain or desert, just as it happened when they took the notion, and drove home and went about their customary business! They were under written contract to Mr. Street, but they did not care anything for that. They said they would "admire" to see a "Gentile" force a Mormon to fulfil a losing contract in Utah! And they made themselves very merry over the matter. Street said—for it was he that told us these things:

"I was in dismay. I was under heavy bonds to complete my contract in a given time, and this disaster looked very much like ruin. It was an astounding thing; it was such a wholly unlooked-for difficulty, that I was entirely nonplussed. I am a business man—have always been a business man—do not know anything *but* business—and so you can imagine how like being struck by lightning it was to find myself in a country where *written contracts were worthless!*—that main security, that sheet-anchor, that absolute necessity, of business. My confidence left me. There was no use in making new contracts—that was plain. I talked with first one prominent citizen and then another. They all sympathized with me, first rate, but they did not know how to help me. But at last a Gentile said, 'Go to Brigham Young!—these small fry cannot do you any good.' I did not think much of the idea, for if the *law* could not help me, what could an individual do who had not even anything to do with either making the laws or executing them? He might be a very good patriarch of a church and preacher in its tabernacle, but something sterner than religion and moral suasion was needed to handle a hundred refractory, half-civilized sub-contractors. But what was a man to do? I thought if Mr. Young could not do anything else, he might probably be able to give me some advice and a valuable hint or two, and so I went straight to him and laid the whole case before him. He said very little, but he showed strong interest all the way through. He examined all the papers in detail, and whenever there seemed anything like a hitch, either in the papers or my statement, he would go back and take up the thread and follow it patiently out to an intelligent and satisfactory result. Then he made a list of the contractors' names. Finally he said:

"'Mr. Street, this is all perfectly plain. These contracts are strictly and legally drawn, and are duly signed and certified. These men manifestly entered into them with their eyes open. I see no fault or flaw anywhere.' Then Mr. Young turned to a man waiting at the other end of the room and said: 'Take this list of names to So-and-so, and tell him to have these men here at such-and-such an hour.'

"They were there, to the minute. So was I. Mr. Young asked them a number of questions, and their answers made my statement good. Then he said to them:

"'You signed these contracts and assumed these obligations of your own free will and accord?' 'Yes.' 'Then carry them out to the letter, if it makes paupers of you! Go!' And they *did* go, too! They are strung across the deserts now, working like bees. And I never hear a word out of them. There is a batch of governors, and judges, and other officials here, shipped from Washington, and they maintain the semblance of a republican form of government—but the petrified truth is that Utah is an absolute monarchy and Brigham Young is king!"

Mr. Street was a fine man, and I believe his story. I knew him well during several years afterward in San Francisco.

Our stay in Salt Lake City amounted to only two days, and therefore we had no time to make the customary inquisition into the workings of polygamy and get up the usual statistics and deductions preparatory to calling the attention of the nation at large once more to the matter. I had the will to do it. With the gushing self-sufficiency of youth I was feverish to plunge in headlong and achieve a great reform here—until I saw the Mormon women. Then I was touched. My heart was wiser than my head. It warmed toward these poor, ungainly and pathetically "homely" creatures, and as I turned to hide the generous moisture in my eyes, I said, "No—the man that marries one of them has done an act of Christian charity which entitles him to the kindly applause of mankind, not their harsh censure—and the man that marries sixty of them has done a deed of open-handed generosity so sublime that the nations should stand uncovered in his presence and worship in silence."

2.3.3 "The War Prayer"

It was a time of great and exalting excitement.

The country was up in arms, the war was on, in every breast burned the holy fire of patriotism; the drums were beating, the bands playing, the toy pistols popping, the bunched firecrackers hissing and spluttering; on every hand and far down the receding and fading spread of roofs and balconies a fluttering wilderness of flags flashed in the sun; daily the young volunteers marched down the wide avenue gay and fine in their new uniforms, the proud fathers and mothers and sisters and sweethearts cheering them with voices choked with happy emotion as they swung by; nightly the packed mass meetings listened, panting, to patriot oratory which stirred the deepest deeps of their hearts, and which they interrupted at briefest intervals with cyclones of applause, the tears running down their cheeks the while; in the churches the pastors preached devotion to flag and country, and invoked the God of Battles beseeching His aid in our good cause in outpourings of fervid eloquence which moved every listener. It was indeed a glad and gracious time, and the half dozen rash spirits that ventured to disapprove of the war and cast a doubt upon its righteousness straightway got such a stern and angry warning that for their personal safety's sake they quickly shrank out of sight and offended no more in that way.

Sunday morning came—next day the battalions would leave for the front; the church was filled; the volunteers were there, their young faces alight with martial dreams—visions of the stern advance, the gathering momentum, the rushing charge, the flashing sabers, the flight of the foe, the tumult, the enveloping smoke, the fierce pursuit, the surrender! Then home from the war, bronzed heroes, welcomed, adored, submerged in golden seas of glory! With the volunteers sat their dear ones, proud, happy, and envied by the neighbors and friends who had no sons and brothers to send forth to the field of honor, there to win for the flag, or, failing, die the noblest of noble deaths. The service proceeded; a war chapter from the Old Testament was read; the first prayer was said; it was followed by an organ burst that shook the building, and with one impulse the house rose, with glowing eyes and beating hearts, and poured out that tremendous invocation

God the all-terrible!
Thou who ordainest!
Thunder thy clarion
and lightning thy sword!

Then came the "long" prayer. None could remember the like of it for passionate pleading and moving and beautiful language. The burden of its supplication was, that an ever-merciful and benignant Father of us all would watch over our noble young soldiers, and aid, comfort, and encourage them in their patriotic work; bless them, shield them in the day of battle and the hour of peril, bear them in His mighty hand, make them strong and confident, invincible in the bloody onset; help them to crush the foe, grant to them and to their flag and country imperishable honor and glory—

An aged stranger entered and moved with slow and noiseless step up the main aisle, his eyes fixed upon the minister, his long body clothed in a robe that reached to his feet, his head bare, his white hair descending in a frothy cataract to his shoulders, his seamy face unnaturally pale, pale even to ghastliness. With all eyes following him and wondering, he made his silent way; without pausing, he ascended to the preacher's side and stood there waiting. With shut lids the preacher, unconscious of his presence, continued with his moving prayer, and at last finished it with the words, uttered in fervent appeal, "Bless our arms, grant us the victory, O Lord our God, Father and Protector of our land and flag!"

The stranger touched his arm, motioned him to step aside—which the startled minister did—and took his place. During some moments he surveyed the spellbound audience with solemn eyes, in which burned an uncanny light; then in a deep voice he said:

"I come from the Throne—bearing a message from Almighty God!" The words smote the house with a shock; if the stranger perceived it he gave no attention. "He has heard the prayer of His servant your shepherd, and will grant it if such shall be your desire after I, His messenger, shall have explained to you its import—that is to say, its full import. For it is like unto many of the prayers of men, in that it asks for more than he who utters it is aware of—except he pause and think.

"God's servant and yours has prayed his prayer. Has he paused and taken thought? Is it one prayer? No, it is two—one uttered, the other not. Both have reached the ear of Him Who heareth all supplications, the spoken and the unspoken. Ponder this—keep it in mind. If you would beseech a blessing upon yourself, beware! lest without intent you invoke a curse upon a neighbor at the same time. If you pray for the blessing of rain upon your crop which needs it, by that act you are possibly praying for a curse upon some neighbor's crop which may not need rain and can be injured by it.

"You have heard your servant's prayer—the uttered part of it. I am commissioned of God to put into words the other part of it—that part which the pastor—and also you in your hearts—fervently prayed silently. And ignorantly and unthinkingly? God grant that it was so! You heard these words: 'Grant us the victory, O Lord our God!' That is sufficient. The whole of the uttered prayer is compact into those pregnant words. Elaborations were not necessary. When you have prayed for victory you have prayed for many unmentioned results which follow victory—*must* follow it, cannot help but follow it. Upon the listening spirit of God fell also the unspoken part of the prayer. He commandeth me to put it into words. Listen!

"O Lord our Father, our young patriots, idols of our hearts, go forth to battle—be Thou near them! With them—in spirit—we also go forth from the sweet peace of our beloved firesides to smite the foe. O Lord our God, help us to tear their soldiers to bloody shreds with our shells; help us to cover their smiling fields with the pale forms of their patriot dead; help us to drown the thunder of the guns with the shrieks of their wounded, writhing in pain; help us to lay waste their humble homes with a hurricane of fire; help us to wring the hearts of their unoffending widows with unavailing grief; help us to turn them out roofless with little children to wander unfriended the wastes of their desolated land in rags and hunger and thirst, sports of the sun flames of summer and the icy winds of winter, broken in spirit, worn with travail, imploring Thee for the refuge of the grave and denied it—for our sakes who adore Thee, Lord, blast their hopes, blight their lives, protract their bitter pilgrimage, make heavy their steps, water their way with their tears, stain the white snow with the blood of their wounded feet! We ask it, in the spirit of love, of Him Who is the Source of Love, and Who is the ever-faithful refuge and friend of all that are sore beset and seek His aid with humble and contrite hearts. Amen.

(*After a pause.*) "Ye have prayed it; if ye still desire it, speak! The messenger of the Most High waits!"

It was believed afterward that the man was a lunatic, because there was no sense in what he said.

2.3.4 Reading and Review Questions

1. In "The Celebrated Jumping Frog of Calaveras County," what is Jim Smiley's talent? Why does he lose it?

2. Would you consider Mark Twain an experimental writer? How are his stories different from other authors of his time period?

3. In Twain's "War Prayer," how do the town's people react to the prophet? Is his message clear? How is this a controversial story?

2.4 WILLIAM DEAN HOWELLS

(1837 - 1920)

Image 2.2 | William Dean Howells, 1906
Photographer | Van der Weyde
Source | Wikimedia Commons
License | Public Domain

William Dean Howells was born in Martinsville, Ohio, in 1837. Howells's father was a newspaper editor, and Howells learned the skills of a writer and editor under his father's guidance. Howells continued to work in publishing until he secured a position with *The Atlantic Monthly* in Massachusetts in 1866, where he served as Assistant Editor. In 1871, Howells was promoted to Editor of the magazine, and he continued working in that position until 1881. Howells, along with Mark Twain and Henry James, became one of the main advocates and theorists of American Literary Realism, a style of writing that reacted against the previous Romantic era's perceived literary excesses. Instead, the Realists praised the American novel that presented characters, setting, and action as "true to life." Howells's scope of influence on a generation of American writers can be seen in his endorsement of Henry James, Mark Twain, Sarah Orne Jewett, Mary E. Wilkins Freeman, Charles Chesnutt, Hamlin Garland, Frank Norris, and Stephen Crane, to name but a few. Howells eventually became known as the "Dean of American Letters" and today is considered the father of American Literary Realism. Howells produced his own creative work during his lifetime and is best remembered for two fine novels in the Realist tradition: *A Modern Instance* (1882) and *The Rise of Silas Lapham* (1885), as well as a host of short stories and theoretical works on Realism. Howells lived a long, productive life, dying in 1920 at the age of 83.

With Mark Twain and Henry James, Howells wrote and spoke prolifically about Realism and its superiority over the earlier Romantic style practiced by authors such as James Fenimore Cooper. In *Criticism and Fiction* (1891), Howells set forth his views on Realism, arguing that fiction should be "life-like" and "true to human experience." Howells, along with Twain in particular, rejected the idealistic, the fantastic, the heroic, and the exaggerated, preferring instead simplicity and honesty in fiction writing. Although there were some elements of reality that Howells preferred authors avoid, particularly the salacious and the sensational, Howells consistently privileged realism over idealism in his theory of writing fiction. Howells's own literary work espoused these principles. *A Modern Instance* (1882) and *The Rise of Silas Lapham* (1885), two of his most famous novels, both deal with ordinary middle class people facing plausible personal conflicts in a contemporary setting. The characters are multi-faceted and dimensional, and the resolutions for the main characters are left open, as is often the case in "real life." In his famous short story "Editha," Howells explores a young woman's patriotic impulses in contrast to the reality of war. He sets the story on the eve of the Spanish-American War, when nationalism was soaring and the desire for war with Spain was strong. Editha, a young woman who lives in the "ideal," is caught up in the patriotic fervor, taking her understanding of the heroic from Romantic ideas that glorify war. She insists her fiancé George enlist in the army, imagining him as a heroic warrior leaving to fight for her. The story contrasts Editha's naïve understanding of war with the grim reality of what war means for George.

2.4.1 "Editha"

The air was thick with the war feeling, like the electricity of a storm which had not yet burst. Editha sat looking out into the hot spring afternoon, with her lips parted, and panting with the intensity of the question whether she could let him go. She had decided that she could not let him stay, when she saw him at the end of the still leafless avenue, making slowly up towards the house, with his head down and his figure relaxed. She ran impatiently out on the veranda, to the edge of the steps, and imperatively demanded greater haste of him with her will before she called him aloud to him: "George!"

He had quickened his pace in mystical response to her mystical urgence, before he could have heard her; now he looked up and answered, "Well?"

"Oh, how united we are!" she exulted, and then she swooped down the steps to him, "What is it?" she cried.

"It's war," he said. and he pulled her up to him and kissed her.

She kissed him back intensely, but irrelevantly, as to their passion, and uttered from deep in her throat. "How glorious!"

"It's war," he repeated, without consenting to her sense of it; and she did not know just what to think at first. She never knew what to think of him; that made his mystery, his charm. All through their courtship, which was contemporaneous with the growth of the war feeling, she had been puzzled by his want of seriousness about it. He seemed to despise it even more than he abhorred it. She could have understood his abhorring any sort of bloodshed; that would have been a survival of his old life when he thought he would be a minister, and before he changed and took up the law. But making light of a cause so high and noble seemed to show a want of earnestness at the core of his being. Not but that she felt herself able to cope with a congenital defect of that sort, and make his love for her save him from himself. Now perhaps the miracle was already wrought in him. In the presence of the tremendous fact that he announced, all triviality seemed to have gone out of him; she began to feel that. He sank down on the top step, and wiped his forehead with his handkerchief, while she poured out upon him her question of the origin and authenticity of his news.

All the while, in her duplex emotioning, she was aware that now at the very beginning she must put a guard upon herself against urging him, by any word or act, to take the part that her whole soul willed him to take, for the completion of her ideal of him. He was very nearly perfect as he was, and he must be allowed to perfect himself. But he was peculiar, and he might very well be reasoned out of his peculiarity. Before her reasoning went her emotioning: her nature pulling upon his nature, her womanhood upon his manhood, without her knowing the means she was using to the end she was willing. She had always supposed that the man who won her would have done something to win her; she did not know what, but something. George Gearson had simply asked her for her love, on the way home from a concert, and she gave her love to him, without, as it were, thinking. But now, it flashed upon her, if he could do something worthy to have won her—be a hero, her hero—it would be even better than if he had done it before asking her; it would be grander. Besides, she had believed in the war from the beginning.

"But don't you see, dearest," she said, "that it wouldn't have come to this if it hadn't been in the order of Providence? And I call any war glorious that is for the liberation of people who have been struggling for years against the cruelest oppression. Don't you think so, too?"

"I suppose so," he returned, languidly. "But war! Is it glorious to break the peace of the world?"

"That ignoble peace! It was no peace at all, with that crime and shame at our very gates." She was conscious of parroting the current phrases of the newspapers, but it was no time to pick and choose her words. She must sacrifice anything to the high ideal she had for him, and after a good deal of rapid argument she ended with the climax: "But now it doesn't matter about the how or why. Since the war has come, all that is gone. There are no two sides any more. There is nothing now but our country."

He sat with his eyes closed and his head leant back against the veranda, and he remarked, with a vague smile, as if musing aloud, "Our country—right or wrong."

"Yes, right or wrong!" she returned, fervidly. "I'll go and get you some lemonade." She rose rustling, and whisked away; when she came back with two tall glasses of clouded liquid on a tray, and the ice clucking in them, he still sat as she had left him, and she said, as if there had been no interruption: "But there is no question of wrong in this case. I call it a sacred war. A war for liberty and humanity, if ever there was one. And I know you will see it just as I do, yet."

He took half the lemonade at a gulp, and he answered as he set the glass down: "I know you always have the highest ideal. When I differ from you I ought to doubt myself."

A generous sob rose in Editha's throat for the humility of a man, so very nearly perfect, who was willing to put himself below her.

Besides, she felt, more subliminally, that he was never so near slipping through her fingers as when he took that meek way.

"You shall not say that! Only, for once I happen to be right." She seized his hand in her two hands, and poured her soul from her eyes into his. "Don't you think so?" she entreated him.

He released his hand and drank the rest of his lemonade, and she added, "Have mine, too," but he shook his head in answering, "I've no business to think so, unless I act so, too."

Her heart stopped a beat before it pulsed on with leaps that she felt in her neck. She had noticed that strange thing in men: they seemed to feel bound to do what they believed, and not think a thing was finished when they said it, as girls did. She knew what was in his mind, but she pretended not, and she said, "Oh, I am not sure," and then faltered.

He went on as if to himself, without apparently heeding her: "There's only one way of proving one's faith in a thing like this."

She could not say that she understood, but she did understand.

He went on again. "If I believed—if I felt as you do about this war—Do you wish me to feel as you do?"

Now she was really not sure; so she said: "George, I don't know what you mean."

He seemed to muse away from her as before. "There is a sort of fascination in it. I suppose that at the bottom of his heart every man would like at times to have his courage tested, to see how he would act."

"How can you talk in that ghastly way?"

"It is rather morbid. Still, that's what it comes to, unless you're swept away by ambition or driven by conviction. I haven't the conviction or the ambition, and the other thing is what it comes to with me. I ought to have been a preacher, after all; then I couldn't have asked it of myself, as I must, now I'm a lawyer. And you believe it's a holy war, Editha?" he suddenly addressed her. "Oh, I know you do! But you wish me to believe so, too?"

She hardly knew whether he was mocking or not, in the ironical way he always had with her plainer mind. But the only thing was to be outspoken with him.

"George, I wish you to believe whatever you think is true, at any and every cost. If I've tried to talk you into anything, I take it all back."

"Oh, I know that, Editha. I know how sincere you are, and how—I wish I had your undoubting spirit! I'll think it over; I'd like to believe as you do. But I don't, now; I don't, indeed. It isn't this war alone; though this seems peculiarly wanton and needless; but it's every war—so stupid; it makes me sick. Why shouldn't this thing have been settled reasonably?"

"Because," she said, very throatily again, "God meant it to be war."

"You think it was God? Yes, I suppose that is what people will say."

"Do you suppose it would have been war if God hadn't meant it?"

"I don't know. Sometimes it seems as if God had put this world into men's keeping to work it as they pleased."

"Now, George, that is blasphemy."

"Well, I won't blaspheme. I'll try to believe in your pocket Providence," he said, and then he rose to go.

"Why don't you stay to dinner?" Dinner at Balcom's Works was at one o'clock.

"I'll come back to supper, if you'll let me. Perhaps I shall bring you a convert."

"Well, you may come back, on that condition."

"All right. If I don't come, you'll understand."

He went away without kissing her, and she felt it a suspension of their engagement. It all interested her intensely; she was undergoing a tremendous experience, and she was being equal to it. While she stood looking after him, her mother came out through one of the long windows onto the veranda, with a catlike softness and vagueness.

"Why didn't he stay to dinner?"

"Because—because—war has been declared," Editha pronounced, without turning.

Her mother said, "Oh, my!" and then said nothing more until she had sat down in one of the large Shaker chairs and rocked herself for some time. Then she closed whatever tacit passage of thought there had been in her mind with the spoken words: "Well, I hope he won't go."

"And I hope he will," the girl said, and confronted her mother with a stormy exaltation that would have frightened any creature less unimpressionable than a cat.

Her mother rocked herself again for an interval of cogitation. What she arrived at in speech was: "Well, I guess you've done a wicked thing, Editha Balcom."

The girl said, as she passed indoors through the same window her mother had come out by: "I haven't done anything—yet."

In her room, she put together all her letters and gifts from Gearson, down to the withered petals of the first flower he had offered, with that timidity of his veiled in that irony of his. In the heart of the packet she enshrined her engagement ring which she had restored to the pretty box he had brought it her in. Then she sat down, if not calmly yet strongly, and wrote:

"George:—I understood when you left me. But I think we had better emphasize your meaning that if we cannot be one in everything we had better be one in nothing. So I am sending these things for your keeping till you have made up your mind.

"I shall always love you, and therefore I shall never marry any one else. But the man I marry must love his country first of all, and be able to say to me,

"'I could not love thee, dear, so much,

Loved I not honor more.'

"There is no honor above America with me. In this great hour there is no other honor.

"Your heart will make my words clear to you. I had never expected to say so much, but it has come upon me that I must say the utmost. Editha."

She thought she had worded her letter well, worded it in a way that could not be bettered; all had been implied and nothing expressed.

She had it ready to send with the packet she had tied with red, white, and blue ribbon, when it occurred to her that she was not just to him, that she was not giving him a fair chance. He had said he would go and think it over, and she was not waiting. She was pushing, threatening, compelling. That was not a woman's part. She must leave him free, free, free. She could not accept for her country or herself a forced sacrifice.

In writing her letter she had satisfied the impulse from which it sprang; she could well afford to wait till he had thought it over. She put the packet and the letter by, and rested serene in the consciousness of having done what was laid upon her by her love itself to do, and yet used patience, mercy, justice.

She had her reward. Gearson did not come to tea, but she had given him till morning, when, late at night there came up from the village the sound of a fife and drum, with a tumult of voices, in shouting, singing, and laughing. The noise drew nearer and nearer; it reached the street end of the avenue; there it silenced itself, and one voice, the voice she knew best, rose over the silence. It fell; the air was filled with cheers; the fife and drum struck up, with the shouting, singing, and laughing again, but now retreating; and a single figure came hurrying up the avenue.

She ran down to meet her lover and clung to him. He was very gay, and he put his arm round her with a boisterous laugh. "Well, you must call me Captain now; or Cap, if you prefer; that's what the boys call me. Yes, we've had a meeting at the town-hall, and everybody has volunteered; and they selected me for captain, and I'm going to the war, the big war, the glorious war, the holy war ordained by the pocket Providence that blesses butchery. Come along; let's tell the whole family about it. Call them from their downy beds, father, mother, Aunt Hitty, and all the folks!"

But when they mounted the veranda steps he did not wait for a larger audience; he poured the story out upon Editha alone.

"There was a lot of speaking, and then some of the fools set up a shout for me. It was all going one way, and I thought it would be a good joke to sprinkle a little cold water on them. But you can't do that with a crowd that adores you. The first thing I knew I was sprinkling hell-fire on them. 'Cry havoc, and let slip the dogs of war.' That was the style. Now that it had come to the fight, there were no two parties; there was one country, and the thing was to fight to a finish as quick as possible. I suggested volunteering then and there, and I wrote my name first of all on the roster. Then they elected me—that's all. I wish I had some ice-water."

She left him walking up and down the veranda, while she ran for the ice-pitcher and a goblet, and when she came back he was still walking up and down, shouting the story he had told her to her father and mother, who had come out more sketchily dressed than they commonly were by day. He drank goblet after goblet of the ice-water without noticing who was giving it, and kept on talking, and laughing through his talk wildly. "It's astonishing," he said, "how well the worse reason looks when you try to make it appear the better. Why, I believe I was the first convert to the war in that crowd to-night! I never thought I should like to kill a man; but now I shouldn't care; and the smokeless powder lets you see the man drop that you kill. It's all for the country! What a thing it is to have a country that can't be wrong, but if it is, is right, anyway!"

Editha had a great, vital thought, an inspiration. She set down the ice-pitcher on the veranda floor, and ran up-stairs and got the letter she had written him. When at last he noisily bade her father and mother, "Well, good-night. I forgot I woke you up; I sha'n't want any sleep myself," she followed him down the avenue to the gate. There, after the whirling words that seemed to fly away from her thoughts and refuse to serve them, she made a last effort to solemnize the moment that seemed so crazy, and pressed the letter she had written upon him.

"What's this?" he said. "Want me to mail it?"

"No, no. It's for you. I wrote it after you went this morning. Keep it—keep it—and read it sometime—" She thought, and then her inspiration came: "Read it if ever you doubt what you've done, or fear that I regret your having done it. Read it after you've started."

They strained each other in embraces that seemed as ineffective as their words, and he kissed her face with quick, hot breaths that were so unlike him, that made her feel as if she had lost her old lover and found a stranger in his place. The stranger said: "What a gorgeous flower you are, with your red hair, and your blue eyes that look black now, and your face with the color painted out by the white moonshine! Let me hold you under the chin, to see whether I love blood, you tiger-lily!" Then he laughed Gearson's laugh, and released her, scared and giddy. Within her wilfulness she had been frightened by a sense of subtler force in him, and mystically mastered as she had never been before.

She ran all the way back to the house, and mounted the steps panting. Her mother and father were talking of the great affair. Her mother said: "Wa'n't Mr. Gearson in rather of an excited state of mind? Didn't you think he acted curious?"

"Well, not for a man who'd just been elected captain and had set 'em up for the whole of Company A," her father chuckled back.

"What in the world do you mean, Mr. Balcom? Oh! There's Editha!" She offered to follow the girl indoors.

"Don't come, mother!" Editha called, vanishing.

Mrs. Balcom remained to reproach her husband. "I don't see much of anything to laugh at."

"Well, it's catching. Caught it from Gearson. I guess it won't be much of a war, and I guess Gearson don't think so either. The other fellows will back down as soon as they see we mean it. I wouldn't lose any sleep over it. I'm going back to bed, myself."

Gearson came again next afternoon, looking pale and rather sick, but quite himself, even to his languid irony. "I guess I'd better tell you, Editha, that I consecrated myself to your god of battles last night by pouring too many libations to him down my own throat. But I'm all right now. One has to carry off the excitement, somehow."

"Promise me," she commanded, "that you'll never touch it again!"

"What! Not let the cannikin clink? Not let the soldier drink? Well, I promise."

"You don't belong to yourself now; you don't even belong to me. You belong to your country, and you have a sacred charge to keep yourself strong and well for your country's sake. I have been thinking, thinking all night and all day long."

"You look as if you had been crying a little, too," he said, with his queer smile.

"That's all past. I've been thinking, and worshipping you. Don't you suppose I know all that you've been through, to come to this? I've followed you every step from your old theories and opinions."

"Well, you've had a long row to hoe."

"And I know you've done this from the highest motives—"

"Oh, there won't be much pettifogging to do till this cruel war is—"

"And you haven't simply done it for my sake. I couldn't respect you if you had."

"Well, then we'll say I haven't. A man that hasn't got his own respect intact wants the respect of all the other people he can corner. But we won't go into that. I'm in for the thing now, and we've got to face our future. My idea is that this isn't going to be a very protracted struggle; we shall just scare the enemy to death before it comes to a fight at all. But we must provide for contingencies, Editha. If anything happens to me—"

"Oh, George!" She clung to him, sobbing.

"I don't want you to feel foolishly bound to my memory. I should hate that, wherever I happened to be."

"I am yours, for time and eternity—time and eternity." She liked the words; they satisfied her famine for phrases.

"Well, say eternity; that's all right; but time's another thing; and I'm talking about time. But there is something! My mother! If anything happens—"

She winced, and he laughed. "You're not the bold soldier-girl of yesterday!" Then he sobered. "If anything happens, I want you to help my mother out. She won't like my doing this thing. She brought me up to think war a fool thing as well as a bad thing. My father was in the Civil War; all through it; lost his arm in it." She thrilled with the sense of the arm round her; what if that should be lost? He laughed as if divining her: "Oh, it doesn't run in the family, as far as I know!" Then he added gravely: "He came home with misgivings about war, and they grew on him. I guess he and mother agreed between them that I was to be brought up in his final mind about it; but that was before my time. I only knew him from my mother's report of him and his opinions; I don't know whether they were hers first; but they were hers last. This will be a blow to her. I shall have to write and tell her—"

He stopped, and she asked: "Would you like me to write, too, George?"

"I don't believe that would do. No, I'll do the writing. She'll understand a little if I say that I thought the way to minimize it was to make war on the largest possible scale at once—that I felt I must have been helping on the war somehow if I hadn't helped keep it from coming, and I knew I hadn't; when it came, I had no right to stay out of it."

Whether his sophistries satisfied him or not, they satisfied her. She clung to his breast, and whispered, with closed eyes and quivering lips: "Yes, yes, yes!"

"But if anything should happen, you might go to her and see what you could do for her. You know? It's rather far off; she can't leave her chair—"

"Oh, I'll go, if it's the ends of the earth! But nothing will happen! Nothing can! I—"

She felt her lifted with his rising, and Gearson was saying, with his arm still round her, to her father: "Well, we're off at once, Mr. Balcom. We're to be formally accepted at the capital, and then bunched up with the rest somehow, and sent into camp somewhere, and got to the front as soon as possible. We all want to be in the van, of course; we're the first company to report to the Governor. I came to tell Editha, but I hadn't got round to it."

She saw him again for a moment at the capital, in the station, just before the train started southward with his regiment. He looked well, in his uniform, and very soldier-ly, but somehow girlish, too, with his clean-shaven face and slim figure. The manly eyes and the strong voice satisfied her, and his preoccupation with some unexpected details of duty flattered her. Other girls were weeping and bemoaning themselves, but she felt a sort of noble distinction in the abstraction, the almost unconsciousness, with which they parted. Only at the last moment he said: "Don't forget my mother. It mayn't be such a walk-over as I supposed," and he laughed at the notion.

He waved his hand to her as the train moved off—she knew it among a score of hands that were waved to other girls from the platform of the car, for it held a letter which she knew was hers. Then he went inside the car to read it, doubtless, and she did not see him again. But she felt safe for him through the strength of what she called her love. What she called her God, always speaking the name in a deep voice and with the implication of a mutual understanding, would watch over him and keep him and bring him back to her. If with an empty sleeve, then he should have three arms instead of two, for both of hers should be his for life. She did not see, though, why she should always be thinking of the arm his father had lost.

There were not many letters from him, but they were such as she could have wished, and she put her whole strength into making hers such as she imagined he could have wished, glorifying and supporting him. She wrote to his mother glori-fying him as their hero, but the brief answer she got was merely to the effect that Mrs. Gearson was not well enough to write herself, and thanking her for her letter by the hand of someone who called herself "Yrs truly, Mrs. W. J. Andrews."

Editha determined not to be hurt, but to write again quite as if the answer had been all she expected. Before it seemed as if she could have written, there came news of the first skirmish, and in the list of the killed, which was telegraphed as a trifling loss on our side, was Gearson's name. There was a frantic time of trying to make out that it might be, must be, some other Gearson; but the name and the company and the regiment and the State were too definitely given.

Then there was a lapse into depths out of which it seemed as if she never could rise again; then a lift into clouds far above all grief, black clouds, that blotted out the sun, but where she soared with him, with George—George! She had the fever that she expected of herself, but she did not die in it; she was not even delirious, and it did not last long. When she was well enough to leave her bed, her one thought was of George's mother, of his strangely worded wish that she should go to her and see what she could do for her. In the exaltation of the duty laid upon her—it buoyed her up instead of burdening her—she rapidly recovered.

Her father went with her on the long railroad journey from northern New York to western Iowa; he had business out at Davenport, and he said he could just as well go then as any other time; and he went with her to the little country town where George's mother lived in a little house on the edge of the illimitable corn-fields, under trees pushed to a top of the rolling prairie. George's father had settled there after the Civil War, as so many other old soldiers had done; but they were Eastern people, and Editha fancied touches of the East in the June rose overhanging the front door, and the garden with early summer flowers stretching from the gate of the paling fence.

It was very low inside the house, and so dim, with the closed blinds, that they could scarcely see one another: Editha tall and black in her crapes which filled the air with the smell of their dyes; her father standing decorously apart with his hat on his forearm, as at funerals; a woman rested in a deep arm-chair, and the woman who had let the strangers in stood behind the chair.

The seated woman turned her head round and up, and asked the woman behind her chair: "Who did you say?"

Editha, if she had done what she expected of herself, would have gone down on her knees at the feet of the seated figure and said, "I am George's Editha," for answer.

But instead of her own voice she heard that other woman's voice, saying: "Well, I don't know as I did get the name just right. I guess I'll have to make a little more light in here," and she went and pushed two of the shutters ajar.

Then Editha's father said, in his public will-now-address-a-few-remarks tone: "My name is Balcom, ma'am—Junius H. Balcom, of Balcom's Works, New York; my daughter—"

"Oh!" the seated woman broke in, with a powerful voice, the voice that always surprised Editha from Gearson's slender frame. "Let me see you. Stand round where the light can strike on your face," and Editha dumbly obeyed. "So, you're Editha Balcom," she sighed.

"Yes," Editha said, more like a culprit than a comforter.

"What did you come for?" Mrs. Gearson asked.

Editha's face quivered and her knees shook. "I came—because—because George—" She could go no further.

"Yes," the mother said, "he told me he had asked you to come if he got killed. You didn't expect that, I suppose, when you sent him."

"I would rather have died myself than done it!" Editha said, with more truth in her deep voice than she ordinarily found in it. "I tried to leave him free—"

"Yes, that letter of yours, that came back with his other things, left him free."

Editha saw now where George's irony came from.

"It was not to be read before—unless—until—I told him so," she faltered.

"Of course, he wouldn't read a letter of yours, under the circumstances, till he thought you wanted him to. Been sick?" the woman abruptly demanded.

"Very sick," Editha said, with self-pity.

"Daughter's life," her father interposed, "was almost despaired of, at one time."

Mrs. Gearson gave him no heed. "I suppose you would have been glad to die, such a brave person as you! I don't believe he was glad to die. He was always a timid boy, that way; he was afraid of a good many things; but if he was afraid he did what he made up his mind to. I suppose he made up his mind to go, but I knew what it cost him by what it cost me when I heard of it. I had been through one war before. When you sent him you didn't expect he would get killed."

The voice seemed to compassionate Editha, and it was time. "No," she huskily murmured.

"No, girls don't; women don't, when they give their men up to their country. They think they'll come marching back, somehow, just as gay as they went, or if it's an empty sleeve, or even an empty pantaloon, it's all the more glory, and they're so much the prouder of them, poor things!"

The tears began to run down Editha's face; she had not wept till then; but it was now such a relief to be understood that the tears came.

"No, you didn't expect him to get killed," Mrs. Gearson repeated, in a voice which was startlingly like George's again. "You just expected him to kill some one else, some of those foreigners, that weren't there because they had any say about it, but because they had to be there, poor wretches—conscripts, or whatever they call 'em. You thought it would be all right for my George, your George, to kill the sons of those miserable mothers and the husbands of those girls that you would never see the faces of." The woman lifted her powerful voice in a psalmlike note. "I thank my God he didn't live to do it! I thank my God they killed him first, and that he ain't livin' with their blood on his hands!" She dropped her eyes, which she had raised with her voice, and glared at Editha. "What you got that black on for?" She lifted herself by her powerful arms so high that her helpless body seemed to hang limp its full length. "Take it off, take it off, before I tear it from your back!"

The lady who was passing the summer near Balcom's Works was sketching Editha's beauty, which lent itself wonderfully to the effects of a colorist. It had come to that confidence which is rather apt to grow between artist and sitter, and Editha had told her everything.

"To think of your having such a tragedy in your life!" the lady said. She added: "I suppose there are people who feel that way about war. But when you consider the good this war has done—how much it has done for the country! I can't understand such people, for my part. And when you had come all the way out there to console her—got up out of a sick-bed! Well!"

"I think," Editha said, magnanimously, "she wasn't quite in her right mind; and so did papa."

"Yes," the lady said, looking at Editha's lips in nature and then at her lips in art, and giving an empirical touch to them in the picture. "But how dreadful of her! How perfectly—excuse me—how vulgar!"

A light broke upon Editha in the darkness which she felt had been without a gleam of brightness for weeks and months. The mystery that had bewildered her was solved by the word; and from that moment she rose from grovelling in shame and self-pity, and began to live again in the ideal.

2.4.2 Reading and Review Questions

1. Examine the tension between the "ideal" and the "real" in "Editha." Which mode of representation is depicted as superior to the other? Why?

2. What strategies does Editha use to convince George to go to war? Why does she use these particular strategies? Are the principles she espouses truly hers? Or is she manipulating him using catch phrases from the time period?

3. What motivates George to finally enlist?

4. Characterize Editha's feelings about George's death.

5. Contrast Editha with George's mother.

6. At the end of "Editha," how does the word "vulgar" expressed by the artist help Editha return to living again in the ideal?

2.5 AMBROSE BIERCE

(1842–circa 1914)

Ambrose Bierce was born in a rural area of Meigs County, Ohio, in 1842. Although poor, Bierce's father owned a collection of books and instilled in his son an appreciation for the written word. Bierce left home in his teens, eager to make his way in the world, living with relatives and attempting formal education. He eventually joined the Union Army at the onset of the Civil War, serving in the 9th Indiana Infantry Regiment, eventually as a lieutenant. He survived some of the most brutal battles of the Civil War, including Shiloh and Chickamauga. After the war, Bierce settled out West in San Francisco, married, and had three children. Bierce began

Image 2.3 | Ambrose Bierce, 1892
Photographer | Unknown
Source | Wikimedia Commons
License | Public Domain

to write and publish a number of short stories while working at several well-known West Coast literary magazines. In 1892, he published *Tales of Soldiers and Civil-*

ians, a collection of his war stories, many of which are considered his best works today. After suffering a number of personal losses, including the death of two of his children and a divorce from his wife, who died soon thereafter, Bierce left the States to travel to Mexico. While many fictitious stories relaying the events of his last days persist, there is no conclusive proof of his fate. He was never heard from again after late 1913.

Bierce was an **iconoclast**, a writer who was fiercely independent and who, using the power of his pen, cynically derided current trends in literature. He was sometimes referred to as "Bitter Bierce," and his *Devil's Dictionary* (1911), compiled during most of his writing career, offered dark, satiric definitions of common words. While Bierce was praised by William Dean Howells as an important new writer on the literary scene in the 1890s, Bierce in his journalistic pieces for West Coast literary magazines could be brutal in his assessment of Howells and James, mocking them for their views on Realism, a mode which he considered too tame to tackle the breadth and depth of human experience. Not surprisingly, it is difficult to categorize Bierce's work, particularly his war stories. His fiction is aligned, at least in principle, with Realist features such as the depiction of life-like characters and authentic details of setting. However, in Bierce's war stories, the landscape often transforms beyond the objectively realistic, as Bierce probes the subjective reality of those who experience the nightmarish events most traumatically; the result is that the story moves into the realm of the fantastic or the grotesque, particularly in two of his most famous war stories, "An Occurrence at Owl Creek Bridge" and "Chickamauga," where Bierce lays bare the human cost of war. In "Owl Creek Bridge" and "Chickamauga," the central civilian characters, a Southern planter and a young Southern boy, respectively, both seem to believe that they can participate in or "play" at war and remain unscathed. Whether as a result of impaired senses, naïvete, inexperience, or cultural conditioning, the characters are unable to read accurately the horror of war or to comprehend their own personal peril in "playing" war—until, that is, the horror of the moment is brought home to them: facing their own imminent death or the brutal death of a loved one.

2.5.1 "Chickamauga"

One sunny autumn afternoon a child strayed away from its rude home in a small field and entered a forest unobserved. It was happy in a new sense of freedom from control, happy in the opportunity of exploration and adventure; for this child's spirit, in bodies of its ancestors, had for thousands of years been trained to memorable feats of discovery and conquest—victories in battles whose critical moments were centuries, whose victors' camps were cities of hewn stone. From the cradle of its race it had conquered its way through two continents and passing a great sea had penetrated a third, there to be born to war and dominion as a heritage.

The child was a boy aged about six years, the son of a poor planter. In his younger manhood the father had been a soldier, had fought against naked savages and followed the flag of his country into the capital of a civilized race to the far South. In the peaceful life of a planter the warrior-fire survived; once kindled, it is never extinguished. The man loved military books and pictures and the boy had understood enough to make himself a wooden sword, though even the eye of his father would hardly have known it for what it was. This weapon he now bore bravely, as became the son of an heroic race, and pausing now and again in the sunny space of the forest assumed, with some exaggeration, the postures of aggression and defense that he had been taught by the engraver's art. Made reckless by the ease with which he overcame invisible foes attempting to stay his advance, he committed the common enough military error of pushing the pursuit to a dangerous extreme, until he found himself upon the margin of a wide but shallow brook, whose rapid waters barred his direct advance against the flying foe that had crossed with illogical ease. But the intrepid victor was not to be baffled; the spirit of the race which had passed the great sea burned unconquerable in that small breast and would not be denied. Finding a place where some bowlders in the bed of the stream lay but a step or a leap apart, he made his way across and fell again upon the rear-guard of his imaginary foe, putting all to the sword.

Now that the battle had been won, prudence required that he withdraw to his base of operations. Alas; like many a mightier conqueror, and like one, the mightiest, he could not curb the lust for war, Nor learn that tempted Fate will leave the loftiest star.

Advancing from the bank of the creek he suddenly found himself confronted with a new and more formidable enemy: in the path that he was following, sat, bolt upright, with ears erect and paws suspended before it, a rabbit! With a startled cry the child turned and fled, he knew not in what direction, calling with inarticulate cries for his mother, weeping, stumbling, his tender skin cruelly torn by brambles, his little heart beating hard with terror—breathless, blind with tears—lost in the forest! Then, for more than an hour, he wandered with erring feet through the tangled undergrowth, till at last, overcome by fatigue, he lay down in a narrow space between two rocks, within a few yards of the stream and still grasping his toy sword, no longer a weapon but a companion, sobbed himself to sleep. The wood birds sang merrily above his head; the squirrels, whisking their bravery of tail, ran barking from tree to tree, unconscious of the pity of it, and somewhere far away was a strange, muffled thunder, as if the partridges were drumming in celebration of nature's victory over the son of her immemorial enslavers. And back at the little plantation, where white men and black were hastily searching the fields and hedges in alarm, a mother's heart was breaking for her missing child.

Hours passed, and then the little sleeper rose to his feet. The chill of the evening was in his limbs, the fear of the gloom in his heart. But he had rested, and he no longer wept. With some blind instinct which impelled to action he struggled through the undergrowth about him and came to a more open ground—on his right the brook, to the left a gentle acclivity studded with infrequent trees; over all, the gathering gloom of twilight. A thin, ghostly mist rose along the water. It frightened and repelled him; instead of recrossing, in the direction whence he had come, he turned his back upon it, and went forward toward the dark inclosing wood. Suddenly he saw before him a strange moving object which he took to be some large animal—a dog, a pig—he could not name it; perhaps it was a bear. He had seen pictures of bears, but knew of nothing to their discredit and had vaguely wished to meet one. But something in form or movement of this object—something in the awkwardness of its approach—told him that it was not a bear, and curiosity was stayed by fear. He stood still and as it came slowly on gained courage every moment, for he saw that at least it had not the long, menacing ears of the rabbit. Possibly his impressionable mind was half conscious of something familiar in its shambling, awkward gait. Before it had approached near enough to resolve his doubts he saw that it was followed by another and another. To right and to left were many more; the whole open space about him was alive with them—all moving toward the brook.

They were men. They crept upon their hands and knees. They used their hands only, dragging their legs. They used their knees only, their arms hanging idle at their sides. They strove to rise to their feet, but fell prone in the attempt. They did nothing naturally, and nothing alike, save only to advance foot by foot in the same direction. Singly, in pairs and in little groups, they came on through the gloom, some halting now and again while others crept slowly past them, then resuming their movement. They came by dozens and by hundreds; as far on either hand as one could see in the deepening gloom they extended and the black wood behind them appeared to be inexhaustible. The very ground seemed in motion toward the creek. Occasionally one who had paused did not again go on, but lay motionless. He was dead. Some, pausing, made strange gestures with their hands, erected their arms and lowered them again, clasped their heads; spread their palms upward, as men are sometimes seen to do in public prayer.

Not all of this did the child note; it is what would have been noted by an elder observer; he saw little but that these were men, yet crept like babes. Being men, they were not terrible, though unfamiliarly clad. He moved among them freely, going from one to another and peering into their faces with childish curiosity. All their faces were singularly white and many were streaked and gouted with red. Something in this—something too, perhaps, in their grotesque attitudes and movements—reminded him of the painted clown whom he had seen last summer in the circus, and he laughed as he watched them. But on and ever on they crept, these maimed and bleeding men, as heedless as he of the dramatic contrast between his laughter and their own ghastly gravity. To him it was a merry spectacle. He had seen his father's negroes creep upon their hands and knees for his amusement—had ridden them so, "making believe" they were his horses. He now approached one of these crawling figures from behind and with an agile movement mounted it astride. The man sank upon his breast, recovered, flung the small boy fiercely to the ground as an unbroken colt might have done, then turned upon him a face that lacked a lower jaw—from the upper teeth to the throat was a great red gap fringed with hanging shreds of flesh and splinters of bone. The unnatural prominence of nose, the absence of chin, the fierce eyes, gave this man the appearance of a great bird of prey crimsoned in throat and breast by the blood of its quarry. The man rose to his knees, the child to his feet. The man shook his fist at the child; the child, terrified at last, ran to a tree near by, got upon the farther side of it and took a more serious view of the situation. And so the clumsy multitude dragged itself slowly and painfully along in hideous pantomime—moved forward down the slope like a swarm of great black beetles, with never a sound of going—in silence profound, absolute.

Instead of darkening, the haunted landscape began to brighten. Through the belt of trees beyond the brook shone a strange red light, the trunks and branches of the trees making a black lacework against it. It struck the creeping figures and gave them monstrous shadows, which caricatured their movements on the lit grass. It fell upon their faces, touching their whiteness with a ruddy tinge, accentuating the stains with which so many of them were freaked and maculated. It sparkled on buttons and bits of metal in their clothing. Instinctively the child turned toward the growing splendor and moved down the slope with his horrible companions; in a few moments had passed the foremost of the throng—not much of a feat, considering his advantages. He placed himself in the lead, his wooden sword still in hand, and solemnly directed the march, conforming his pace to theirs and occasionally turning as if to see that his forces did not straggle. Surely such a leader never before had such a following.

Scattered about upon the ground now slowly narrowing by the encroachment of this awful march to water, were certain articles to which, in the leader's mind, were coupled no significant associations: an occasional blanket, tightly rolled lengthwise, doubled and the ends bound together with a string; a heavy knapsack here, and there a broken rifle—such things, in short, as are found in the rear of retreating troops, the "spoor" of men flying from their hunters. Everywhere near the creek, which here had a margin of lowland, the earth was trodden into mud by the feet of men and horses. An observer of better experience in the use of his eyes would have noticed that these footprints pointed in both directions; the ground had been twice passed over—in advance and in retreat. A few hours before, these desperate, stricken men, with their more fortunate and now distant comrades, had penetrated the forest in thousands. Their successive battalions, breaking into swarms and re-forming in lines, had passed the child on every side—had almost trodden on him as he slept. The rustle and murmur of their march had not awakened him. Almost within a stone's throw of where he lay they had fought a battle; but all unheard by him were the roar of the musketry, the shock of the cannon, "the thunder of the captains and the shouting." He had slept through it all, grasping his little wooden sword with perhaps a tighter clutch in unconscious sympathy with his martial environment, but as heedless of the grandeur of the struggle as the dead who had died to make the glory.

The fire beyond the belt of woods on the farther side of the creek, reflected to earth from the canopy of its own smoke, was now suffusing the whole landscape. It transformed the sinuous line of mist to the vapor of gold. The water gleamed with dashes of red, and red, too, were many of the stones protruding above the surface. But that was blood; the less desperately wounded had stained them in crossing. On them, too, the child now crossed with eager steps; he was going to the fire. As he stood upon the farther bank he turned about to look at the companions of his march. The advance was arriving at the creek. The stronger had already drawn themselves to the brink and plunged their faces into the flood. Three or four who lay without motion appeared to have no heads. At this the child's eyes expanded with wonder; even his hospitable understanding could not accept a phenomenon implying such vitality as that. After slaking their thirst these men had not had the strength to back away from the water, nor to keep their heads above it. They were drowned. In rear of these, the open spaces of the forest showed the leader as many formless figures of his grim command as at first; but not nearly so many were in motion. He waved his cap for their encouragement and smilingly pointed with his weapon in the direction of the guiding light—a pillar of fire to this strange exodus.

Confident of the fidelity of his forces, he now entered the belt of woods, passed through it easily in the red illumination, climbed a fence, ran across a field, turning now and again to coquet with his responsive shadow, and so approached the blazing ruin of a dwelling. Desolation everywhere! In all the wide glare not a living thing was visible. He cared nothing for that; the spectacle pleased, and he danced with glee in imitation of the wavering flames. He ran about, collecting fuel, but every object that he found was too heavy for him to cast in from the distance to which the heat limited his approach. In despair he flung in his sword—a surrender to the superior forces of nature. His military career was at an end.

Shifting his position, his eyes fell upon some outbuildings which had an oddly familiar appearance, as if he had dreamed of them. He stood considering them with wonder, when suddenly the entire plantation, with its inclosing forest, seemed to turn as if upon a pivot. His little world swung half around; the points of the compass were reversed. He recognized the blazing building as his own home!

For a moment he stood stupefied by the power of the revelation, then ran with stumbling feet, making a half-circuit of the ruin. There, conspicuous in the light of the conflagration, lay the dead body of a woman—the white face turned upward, the hands thrown out and clutched full of grass, the clothing deranged, the long dark hair in tangles and full of clotted blood. The greater part of the forehead was torn away, and from the jagged hole the brain protruded, overflowing the temple, a frothy mass of gray, crowned with clusters of crimson bubbles—the work of a shell.

The child moved his little hands, making wild, uncertain gestures. He uttered a series of inarticulate and indescribable cries—something between the chattering of an ape and the gobbling of a turkey—a startling, soulless, unholy sound, the language of a devil. The child was a deaf mute.

Then he stood motionless, with quivering lips, looking down upon the wreck.

2.5.2 "Occurence at Owl Creek Bridge"

I

A man stood upon a railroad bridge in northern Alabama, looking down into the swift water twenty feet below. The man's hands were behind his back, the wrists bound with a cord. A rope closely encircled his neck. It was attached to a stout cross-timber above his head and the slack fell to the level of his knees. Some loose boards laid upon the sleepers supporting the metals of the railway supplied a footing for him and his executioners—two private soldiers of the Federal army, directed by a sergeant who in civil life may have been a deputy sheriff. At a short remove upon the same temporary platform was an officer in the uniform of his rank, armed. He was a captain. A sentinel at each end of the bridge stood with his rifle in the position known as "support," that is to say, vertical in front of the left shoulder, the hammer resting on the forearm thrown straight across the chest—a formal and unnatural position, enforcing an erect carriage of the body. It did not appear to be the duty of these two men to know what was occurring at the centre of the bridge; they merely blockaded the two ends of the foot planking that traversed it.

Beyond one of the sentinels nobody was in sight; the railroad ran straight away into a forest for a hundred yards, then, curving, was lost to view. Doubtless there was an outpost farther along. The other bank of the stream was open ground—a gentle acclivity topped with a stockade of vertical tree trunks, loop-holed for rifles, with a single embrasure through which protruded the muzzle of a brass cannon commanding the bridge. Mid-way of the slope between bridge and fort were the spectators—a single company of infantry in line, at "parade rest," the butts of the rifles on the ground, the barrels inclining slightly backward against the right shoulder, the hands crossed upon the stock. A lieutenant stood at the right of the line, the point of his sword upon the ground, his left hand resting upon his right. Excepting the group of four at the centre of the bridge, not a man moved. The company faced the bridge, staring stonily, motionless. The sentinels, facing the banks of the stream, might have been statues to adorn the bridge. The captain stood with folded arms, silent, observing the work of his subordinates, but making no sign. Death is a dignitary who when he comes announced is to be received with formal manifestations of respect, even by those most familiar with him. In the code of military etiquette silence and fixity are forms of deference.

The man who was engaged in being hanged was apparently about thirty-five years of age. He was a civilian, if one might judge from his habit, which was that of a planter. His features were good—a straight nose, firm mouth, broad forehead, from which his long, dark hair was combed straight back, falling behind his ears to the collar of his well-fitting frock-coat. He wore a mustache and pointed beard, but no whiskers; his eyes were large and dark gray, and had a kindly expression which one would hardly have expected in one whose neck was in the hemp. Evidently this was no vulgar assassin. The liberal military code makes provision for hanging many kinds of persons, and gentlemen are not excluded.

The preparations being complete, the two private soldiers stepped aside and each drew away the plank upon which he had been standing. The sergeant turned to the captain, saluted and placed himself immediately behind that officer, who in turn moved apart one pace. These movements left the condemned man and the sergeant standing on the two ends of the same plank, which spanned three of the cross-ties of the bridge. The end upon which the civilian stood almost, but not quite, reached a fourth. This plank had been held in place by the weight of the captain; it was now held by that of the sergeant. At a signal from the former the latter would step aside, the plank would tilt and the condemned man go down between two ties. The arrangement commended itself to his judgment as simple and effective. His face had not been covered nor his eyes bandaged. He looked a moment at his "unsteadfast footing," then let his gaze wander to the swirling water of the stream racing madly beneath his feet. A piece of dancing driftwood caught his attention and his eyes followed it down the current. How slowly it appeared to move! What a sluggish stream!

He closed his eyes in order to fix his last thoughts upon his wife and children. The water, touched to gold by the early sun, the brooding mists under the banks at some distance down the stream, the fort, the soldiers, the piece of drift—all had distracted him. And now he became conscious of a new disturbance. Striking through the thought of his dear ones was a sound which he could neither ignore nor understand, a sharp, distinct, metallic percussion like the stroke of a blacksmith's hammer upon the anvil; it had the same ringing quality. He wondered what it was, and whether immeasurably distant or near by—it seemed both. Its recurrence was regular, but as slow as the tolling of a death knell. He awaited each stroke with impatience and—he knew not why—apprehension. The intervals of silence grew progressively longer; the delays became maddening. With their greater infrequency the sounds increased in strength and sharpness. They hurt his ear like the thrust of a knife; he feared he would shriek. What he heard was the ticking of his watch.

He unclosed his eyes and saw again the water below him. "If I could free my hands," he thought, "I might throw off the noose and spring into the stream. By diving I could evade the bullets and, swimming vigorously, reach the bank, take to the woods and get away home. My home, thank God, is as yet outside their lines; my wife and little ones are still beyond the invader's farthest advance."

As these thoughts, which have here to be set down in words, were flashed into the doomed man's brain rather than evolved from it the captain nodded to the sergeant. The sergeant stepped aside.

II

Peyton Farquhar was a well-to-do planter, of an old and highly respected Alabama family. Being a slave owner and like other slave owners a politician he was naturally an original secessionist and ardently devoted to the Southern cause. Circumstances of an imperious nature, which it is unnecessary to relate here, had prevented him from taking service with the gallant army that had fought the disastrous campaigns ending with the fall of Corinth, and he chafed under the inglorious restraint, longing for the release of his energies, the larger life of the soldier, the opportunity for distinction. That opportunity, he felt, would come, as it comes to all in war time. Meanwhile he did what he could. No service was too humble for him to perform in aid of the South, no adventure too perilous for him to undertake if consistent with the character of a civilian who was at heart a soldier, and who in good faith and without too much qualification assented to at least a part of the frankly villainous dictum that all is fair in love and war.

One evening while Farquhar and his wife were sitting on a rustic bench near the entrance to his grounds, a gray-clad soldier rode up to the gate and asked for a drink of water. Mrs. Farquhar was only too happy to serve him with her own white hands. While she was fetching the water her husband approached the dusty horseman and inquired eagerly for news from the front.

"The Yanks are repairing the railroads," said the man, "and are getting ready for another advance. They have reached the Owl Creek bridge, put it in order and built a stockade on the north bank. The commandant has issued an order, which is posted everywhere, declaring that any civilian caught interfering with the railroad, its bridges, tunnels or trains will be summarily hanged. I saw the order."

"How far is it to the Owl Creek bridge?" Farquhar asked.

"About thirty miles."

"Is there no force on this side the creek?"

"Only a picket post half a mile out, on the railroad, and a single sentinel at this end of the bridge."

"Suppose a man—a civilian and student of hanging—should elude the picket post and perhaps get the better of the sentinel," said Farquhar, smiling, "what could he accomplish?"

The soldier reflected. "I was there a month ago," he replied. "I observed that the flood of last winter had lodged a great quantity of driftwood against the wooden pier at this end of the bridge. It is now dry and would burn like tow."

The lady had now brought the water, which the soldier drank. He thanked her ceremoniously, bowed to her husband and rode away. An hour later, after nightfall, he repassed the plantation, going northward in the direction from which he had come. He was a Federal scout.

III

As Peyton Farquhar fell straight downward through the bridge he lost consciousness and was as one already dead. From this state he was awakened—ages later, it seemed to him—by the pain of a sharp pressure upon his throat, followed by a sense of suffocation. Keen, poignant agonies seemed to shoot from his neck downward through every fibre of his body and limbs. These pains appeared to flash along well-defined lines of ramification and to beat with an inconceivably rapid periodicity. They seemed like streams of pulsating fire heating him to an intolerable temperature. As to his head, he was conscious of nothing but a feeling of fulness—

of congestion. These sensations were unaccompanied by thought. The intellectual part of his nature was already effaced; he had power only to feel, and feeling was torment. He was conscious of motion. Encompassed in a luminous cloud, of which he was now merely the fiery heart, without material substance, he swung through unthinkable arcs of oscillation, like a vast pendulum. Then all at once, with terrible suddenness, the light about him shot upward with the noise of a loud plash; a frightful roaring was in his ears, and all was cold and dark. The power of thought was restored; he knew that the rope had broken and he had fallen into the stream. There was no additional strangulation; the noose about his neck was already suffocating him and kept the water from his lungs. To die of hanging at the bottom of a river!—the idea seemed to him ludicrous. He opened his eyes in the darkness and saw above him a gleam of light, but how distant, how inaccessible! He was still sinking, for the light became fainter and fainter until it was a mere glimmer. Then it began to grow and brighten, and he knew that he was rising toward the surface—knew it with reluctance, for he was now very comfortable. "To be hanged and drowned," he thought, "that is not so bad; but I do not wish to be shot. No; I will not be shot; that is not fair."

He was not conscious of an effort, but a sharp pain in his wrist apprised him that he was trying to free his hands. He gave the struggle his attention, as an idler might observe the feat of a juggler, without interest in the outcome. What splendid effort!—what magnificent, what superhuman strength! Ah, that was a fine endeavor! Bravo! The cord fell away; his arms parted and floated upward, the hands dimly seen on each side in the growing light. He watched them with a new interest as first one and then the other pounced upon the noose at his neck. They tore it away and thrust it fiercely aside, its undulations resembling those of a water-snake. "Put it back, put it back!" He thought he shouted these words to his hands, for the undoing of the noose had been succeeded by the direst pang that he had yet experienced. His neck ached horribly; his brain was on fire; his heart, which had been fluttering faintly, gave a great leap, trying to force itself out at his mouth. His whole body was racked and wrenched with an insupportable anguish! But his disobedient hands gave no heed to the command. They beat the water vigorously with quick, downward strokes, forcing him to the surface. He felt his head emerge; his eyes were blinded by the sunlight; his chest expanded convulsively, and with a supreme and crowning agony his lungs engulfed a great draught of air, which instantly he expelled in a shriek!

He was now in full possession of his physical senses. They were, indeed, preternaturally keen and alert. Something in the awful disturbance of his organic system had so exalted and refined them that they made record of things never before perceived. He felt the ripples upon his face and heard their separate sounds as they struck. He looked at the forest on the bank of the stream, saw the individual trees, the leaves and the veining of each leaf—saw the very insects upon them: the locusts, the brilliant-bodied flies, the gray spiders stretching their webs from twig to twig. He noted the prismatic colors in all the dewdrops upon a million blades of grass. The humming of the gnats that danced above the eddies of the stream, the beating of the dragon-flies' wings, the strokes of the water-spiders' legs, like oars which had lifted their boat—all these made audible music. A fish slid along beneath his eyes and he heard the rush of its body parting the water.

He had come to the surface facing down the stream; in a moment the visible world seemed to wheel slowly round, himself the pivotal point, and he saw the bridge, the fort, the soldiers upon the bridge, the captain, the sergeant, the two privates, his executioners. They were in silhouette against the blue sky. They shouted and gesticulated, pointing at him. The captain had drawn his pistol, but did not fire; the others were unarmed. Their movements were grotesque and horrible, their forms gigantic.

Suddenly he heard a sharp report and something struck the water smartly within a few inches of his head, spattering his face with spray. He heard a second report, and saw one of the sentinels with his rifle at his shoulder, a light cloud of blue smoke rising from the muzzle. The man in the water saw the eye of the man on the bridge gazing into his own through the sights of the rifle. He observed that it was a gray eye and remembered having read that gray eyes were keenest, and that all famous markmen had them. Nevertheless, this one had missed.

A counter-swirl had caught Farquhar and turned him half round; he was again looking into the forest on the bank opposite the fort. The sound of a clear, high voice in a monotonous singsong now rang out behind him and came across the water with a distinctness that pierced and subdued all other sounds, even the beating of the ripples in his ears. Although no soldier, he had frequented camps enough to know the dread significance of that deliberate, drawling, aspirated chant; the lieutenant on shore was taking a part in the morning's work. How coldly and pitilessly—with what an even, calm intonation, presaging, and enforcing tranquillity in the men—with what accurately measured intervals fell those cruel words:

"Attention, company! . . . Shoulder arms! . . . Ready! . . . Aim! . . . Fire!"

Farquhar dived—dived as deeply as he could. The water roared in his ears like the voice of Niagara, yet he heard the dulled thunder of the volley and, rising again toward the surface, met shining bits of metal, singularly flattened, oscillating slowly downward. Some of them touched him on the face and hands, then fell away, continuing their descent. One lodged between his collar and neck; it was uncomfortably warm and he snatched it out.

As he rose to the surface, gasping for breath, he saw that he had been a long time under water; he was perceptibly farther down stream—nearer to safety. The soldiers had almost finished reloading; the metal ramrods flashed all at once in the sunshine as they were drawn from the barrels, turned in the air, and thrust into their sockets. The two sentinels fired again, independently and ineffectually.

The hunted man saw all this over his shoulder; he was now swimming vigorously with the current. His brain was as energetic as his arms and legs; he thought with the rapidity of lightning.

"The officer," he reasoned, "will not make that martinet's error a second time. It is as easy to dodge a volley as a single shot. He has probably already given the command to fire at will. God help me, I cannot dodge them all!"

An appalling plash within two yards of him was followed by a loud, rushing sound, *diminuendo*, which seemed to travel back through the air to the fort and died in an explosion which stirred the very river to its deeps! A rising sheet of water curved over him, fell down upon him, blinded him, strangled him! The cannon had taken a hand in the game. As he shook his head free from the commotion of the smitten water he heard the deflected shot humming through the air ahead, and in an instant it was cracking and smashing the branches in the forest beyond.

"They will not do that again," he thought; "the next time they will use a charge of grape. I must keep my eye upon the gun; the smoke will apprise me—the report arrives too late; it lags behind the missile. That is a good gun."

Suddenly he felt himself whirled round and round—spinning like a top. The water, the banks, the forests, the now distant bridge, fort and men—all were commingled and blurred. Objects were represented by their colors only; circular horizontal streaks of color—that was all he saw. He had been caught in a vortex and was being whirled on with a velocity of advance and gyration that made him giddy and sick. In a few moments he was flung upon the gravel at the foot of the left bank of the stream—the southern bank—and behind a projecting point which concealed him from his enemies. The sudden arrest of his motion, the abrasion of one of his hands on the gravel, restored him, and he wept with delight. He dug his fingers into the sand, threw it over himself in handfuls and audibly blessed it. It looked like diamonds, rubies, emeralds; he could think of nothing beautiful which it did not resemble. The trees upon the bank were giant garden plants; he noted a definite order in their arrangement, inhaled the fragrance of their blooms. A strange, roseate light shone through the spaces among their trunks and the wind made in their branches the music of æolian harps. He had no wish to perfect his escape—was content to remain in that enchanting spot until retaken.

A whiz and rattle of grapeshot among the branches high above his head roused him from his dream. The baffled cannoneer had fired him a random farewell. He sprang to his feet, rushed up the sloping bank, and plunged into the forest.

All that day he traveled, laying his course by the rounding sun. The forest seemed interminable; nowhere did he discover a break in it, not even a woodman's road. He had not known that he lived in so wild a region. There was something uncanny in the revelation.

By nightfall he was fatigued, footsore, famishing. The thought of his wife and children urged him on. At last he found a road which led him in what he knew to be the right direction. It was as wide and straight as a city street, yet it seemed untraveled. No fields bordered it, no dwelling anywhere. Not so much as the barking of a dog suggested human habitation. The black bodies of the trees formed a straight wall on both sides, terminating on the horizon in a point, like a diagram in a lesson in perspective. Over-head, as he looked up through this rift in the wood, shone great golden stars looking unfamiliar and grouped in strange constellations. He was sure they were arranged in some order which had a secret and malign significance. The wood on either side was full of singular noises, among which—once, twice, and again—he distinctly heard whispers in an unknown tongue.

His neck was in pain and lifting his hand to it he found it horribly swollen. He knew that it had a circle of black where the rope had bruised it. His eyes felt congested; he could no longer close them. His tongue was swollen with thirst; he relieved its fever by thrusting it forward from between his teeth into the cold air. How softly the turf had carpeted the untraveled avenue—he could no longer feel the roadway beneath his feet!

Doubtless, despite his suffering, he had fallen asleep while walking, for now he sees another scene—perhaps he has merely recovered from a delirium. He stands at the gate of his own home. All is as he left it, and all bright and beautiful in the morning sunshine. He must have traveled the entire night. As he pushes open the gate and passes up the wide white walk, he sees a flutter of female garments; his wife, looking fresh and cool and sweet, steps down from the veranda to meet him. At the bottom of the steps she stands waiting, with a smile of ineffable joy, an attitude of matchless grace and dignity. Ah, how beautiful she is! He springs forward with extended arms. As he is about to clasp her he feels a stunning blow upon the back of the neck; a blinding white light blazes all about him with a sound like the shock of a cannon—then all is darkness and silence!

Peyton Farquhar was dead; his body, with a broken neck, swung gently from side to side beneath the timbers of the Owl Creek bridge.

2.5.3 Reading and Review Questions

1. In "Chickamauga," what is the effect, at the end, of realizing that the story has been filtered through the eyes of a child who is deaf and mute?

2. In "Chickamauga," how are ideas about war, glory, and the heroic absorbed by father and son in the story? Observe the use of words at the beginning of the story that are associated with war and warriors ("warrior-fire," "adventure," "memorable feats of discovery and conquest," "intrepid victor," "unconquerable," "lust for war"). By the end of the story, how does the vocabulary associated with war and warriors change?

3. In "Chickamauga," contrast the young boy's viewing the scene of wounded and dying soldiers retreating from battle and his viewing the scene of his destroyed home and dead mother. What does such a shift in perspective convey in terms of how those unfamiliar with war might view it?

4. Explain the story's title "Chickamauga," given the fact that the battle is never mentioned in the story.

5. In "An Occurrence at Owl Creek Bridge," examine the measuring and passing of time in the story. What is the significance of these references to time?

6. Compare the two stories in terms of the idea of the hero. Is the idea of a hero subverted in either or both stories? If so, how?

2.6 HENRY JAMES

(1843 - 1916)

Henry James was born in New York City in 1843 to a wealthy family. James's father, Henry James, Sr., was a theologian and philosopher who provided James and his siblings with a life rich in travel and exposure to different cultures and languages. Having lived abroad for several years, the James family returned to America prior to the start of the Civil War, settling in Newport, Rhode Island, and later in Cambridge, Massachusetts. Unable to serve in the Union Army during the Civil War as a result of a physical disability, James attended Harvard Law School before deciding to embark on a life of traveling and writing, eventually locating to London in 1876. James's short works soon

Image 2.4 | Henry James, 1910
Publisher | Bain News Service
Source | Wikimedia Commons
License | Public Domain

came to the attention of William Dean Howells, then assistant editor at the *Atlantic Monthly* in Boston, and James and Howells eventually became proponents and literary theorists for the Realism movement in literature that had reached American shores. Although gregarious and well-connected to leading artists and intellectuals of his age, James never married, preferring to live alone and to focus his personal time on reading and writing. While James spent a number of years traveling between England and America, he lived most of his adult life in England, eventually receiving British citizenship in 1915, one year before he died.

James was one of the leading proponents of American Literary Realism, along with William Dean Howells and Mark Twain. James's *The Art of Fiction* (1884) sets forth many of James's ideas about the nature and importance of Realistic fiction. Often described as a psychological Realist, James went further than Howells and Twain in terms of experimentation with point of view, particularly in employing unreliable narrators and interior monologues. His notable novel-length works, including *Daisy Miller* (1878), *The Portrait of a Lady* (1881), *The Bostonians* (1886), *What Maisie Knew* (1897), *The Turn of the Screw* (1898), and *The Ambassadors* (1903), examine a variety of themes, such as the plight of strong-willed or precocious young women or children at odds with the pressures of conventional society, tensions arising from transatlantic travel and living abroad where Americans experience clashes between American and European cultures, and emotional devastation resulting from a life not fully lived.

James's *Daisy Miller, A Study* (1878) is a novella that focuses on a young independent-minded American girl traveling abroad with her mother and brother in Europe who meets an American living abroad, Frederick Winterbourne. Her interactions with Winterbourne provide an examination of ways in which Daisy is viewed by those acclimated to European manners and unwritten rules of etiquette and behavior for young women. Winterbourne's obsessive desire to understand whether or not Daisy is "innocent" provides much of the plot of the story. He cannot determine, for example, whether she is a playful young girl, simply ignorant of the cultural conventions of place and time, or whether she is more worldly and manipulative than meets the eye. Winterbourne himself becomes a psychological study: is his preoccupation with Daisy's innocence a reflection of his own inhibitions? Is he living essentially a half-life, unable or unwilling to commit fully to another person? Is he paralyzed in a complex web of social or psychological fears? In characteristic Realist style, James offers no resolution at the end of the story, allowing questions about Daisy's character and Winterbourne's future to go unanswered.

2.6.1 *Daisy Miller: A Study*

PART I

At the little town of Vevey, in Switzerland, there is a particularly comfortable hotel. There are, indeed, many hotels, for the entertainment of tourists is the business of the place, which, as many travelers will remember, is seated upon the edge of a remarkably blue lake—a lake that it behooves every tourist to visit. The shore of the lake presents an unbroken array of establishments of this order, of every category, from the "grand hotel" of the newest fashion, with a chalk-white front, a hundred balconies, and a dozen flags flying from its roof, to the little Swiss pension of an elder day, with its name inscribed in German-looking lettering upon a pink or yellow wall and an awkward summerhouse in the angle of the garden. One of the hotels at Vevey, however, is famous, even classical, being distinguished from many of its upstart neighbors by an air both of luxury and of maturity. In this region, in the month of June, American travelers are extremely numerous; it may be said, indeed, that Vevey assumes at this period some of the characteristics of an American watering place. There are sights and sounds which evoke a vision, an echo, of Newport and Saratoga. There is a flitting hither and thither of "stylish" young girls, a rustling of muslin flounces, a rattle of dance music in the morning hours, a sound of high-pitched voices at all times. You receive an impression of these things at the excellent inn of the "Trois Couronnes" and are transported in fancy to the Ocean House or to Congress Hall. But at the "Trois Couronnes," it must be added, there are other features that are much at variance with these suggestions: neat German waiters, who look like secretaries of legation; Russian princesses sitting in the garden; little Polish boys walking about held by the hand, with their governors; a view of the sunny crest of the Dent du Midi and the picturesque towers of the Castle of Chillon.

I hardly know whether it was the analogies or the differences that were uppermost in the mind of a young American, who, two or three years ago, sat in the garden of the "Trois Couronnes," looking about him, rather idly, at some of the graceful objects I have mentioned. It was a beautiful summer morning, and in whatever fashion the young American looked at things, they must have seemed to him charming. He had come from Geneva the day before by the little steamer, to see his aunt, who was staying at the hotel—Geneva having been for a long time his place of residence. But his aunt had a headache—his aunt had almost always a headache—and now she was shut up in her room, smelling camphor, so that he was at liberty to wander about. He was some seven-and-twenty years of age; when his friends spoke of him, they usually said that he was at Geneva "studying." When his enemies spoke of him, they said—but, after all, he had no enemies; he was an extremely amiable fellow, and universally liked. What I should say is, simply, that when certain persons spoke of him they affirmed that the reason of his spending so much time at Geneva was that he was extremely devoted to a lady who lived there—a foreign lady—a person older than himself. Very few Americans—indeed, I think none—had ever seen this lady, about whom there were some singular stories. But Winterbourne had an old attachment for the little metropolis of Calvinism; he had been put to school there as a boy, and he had afterward gone to college there— circumstances which had led to his forming a great many youthful friendships. Many of these he had kept, and they were a source of great satisfaction to him.

After knocking at his aunt's door and learning that she was indisposed, he had taken a walk about the town, and then he had come in to his breakfast. He had now finished his breakfast; but he was drinking a small cup of coffee, which had been served to him on a little table in the garden by one of the waiters who looked like an attache. At last he finished his coffee and lit a cigarette. Presently a small boy came walking along the path—an urchin of nine or ten. The child, who was diminutive for his years, had an aged expression of countenance, a pale complexion, and sharp little features. He was dressed in knickerbockers, with red stockings, which displayed his poor little spindle-shanks; he also wore a brilliant red cravat. He carried in his hand a long alpenstock, the sharp point of which he thrust into everything that he approached—the flowerbeds, the garden benches, the trains of the ladies' dresses. In front of Winterbourne he paused, looking at him with a pair of bright, penetrating little eyes.

"Will you give me a lump of sugar?" he asked in a sharp, hard little voice—a voice immature and yet, somehow, not young.

Winterbourne glanced at the small table near him, on which his coffee service rested, and saw that several morsels of sugar remained. "Yes, you may take one," he answered; "but I don't think sugar is good for little boys."

This little boy stepped forward and carefully selected three of the coveted fragments, two of which he buried in the pocket of his knickerbockers, depositing the other as promptly in another place. He poked his alpenstock, lance-fashion, into Winterbourne's bench and tried to crack the lump of sugar with his teeth.

"Oh, blazes; it's har-r-d!" he exclaimed, pronouncing the adjective in a peculiar manner.

Winterbourne had immediately perceived that he might have the honor of claiming him as a fellow countryman. "Take care you don't hurt your teeth," he said, paternally.

"I haven't got any teeth to hurt. They have all come out. I have only got seven teeth. My mother counted them last night, and one came out right afterward. She said she'd slap me if any more came out. I can't help it. It's this old Europe. It's the climate that makes them come out. In America they didn't come out. It's these hotels."

Winterbourne was much amused. "If you eat three lumps of sugar, your mother will certainly slap you," he said.

"She's got to give me some candy, then," rejoined his young interlocutor. "I can't get any candy here—any American candy. American candy's the best candy."

"And are American little boys the best little boys?" asked Winterbourne.

"I don't know. I'm an American boy," said the child.

"I see you are one of the best!" laughed Winterbourne.

"Are you an American man?" pursued this vivacious infant. And then, on Winterbourne's affirmative reply—"American men are the best," he declared.

His companion thanked him for the compliment, and the child, who had now got astride of his alpenstock, stood looking about him, while he attacked a second lump of sugar. Winterbourne wondered if he himself had been like this in his infancy, for he had been brought to Europe at about this age.

"Here comes my sister!" cried the child in a moment. "She's an American girl."

Winterbourne looked along the path and saw a beautiful young lady advancing. "American girls are the best girls," he said cheerfully to his young companion.

"My sister ain't the best!" the child declared. "She's always blowing at me."

"I imagine that is your fault, not hers," said Winterbourne. The young lady meanwhile had drawn near. She was dressed in white muslin, with a hundred frills and flounces, and knots of pale-colored ribbon. She was bareheaded, but she balanced in her hand a large parasol, with a deep border of embroidery; and she was strikingly, admirably pretty. "How pretty they are!" thought Winterbourne, straightening himself in his seat, as if he were prepared to rise.

The young lady paused in front of his bench, near the parapet of the garden, which overlooked the lake. The little boy had now converted his alpenstock into a vaulting pole, by the aid of which he was springing about in the gravel and kicking it up not a little.

"Randolph," said the young lady, "what ARE you doing?"

"I'm going up the Alps," replied Randolph. "This is the way!" And he gave another little jump, scattering the pebbles about Winterbourne's ears.

"That's the way they come down," said Winterbourne.

"He's an American man!" cried Randolph, in his little hard voice.

The young lady gave no heed to this announcement, but looked straight at her brother. "Well, I guess you had better be quiet," she simply observed.

It seemed to Winterbourne that he had been in a manner presented. He got up and stepped slowly toward the young girl, throwing away his cigarette. "This little boy and I have made acquaintance," he said, with great civility. In Geneva, as he had been perfectly aware, a young man was not at liberty to speak to a young unmarried lady except under certain rarely occurring conditions; but here at Vevey, what conditions could be better than these?—a pretty American girl coming and standing in front of you in a garden. This pretty American girl, however, on hearing Winterbourne's observation, simply glanced at him; she then turned her head and looked over the parapet, at the lake and the opposite mountains. He wondered whether he had gone too far, but he decided that he must advance farther, rather than retreat. While he was thinking of something else to say, the young lady turned to the little boy again.

"I should like to know where you got that pole," she said.

"I bought it," responded Randolph.

"You don't mean to say you're going to take it to Italy?"

"Yes, I am going to take it to Italy," the child declared.

The young girl glanced over the front of her dress and smoothed out a knot or two of ribbon. Then she rested her eyes upon the prospect again. "Well, I guess you had better leave it somewhere," she said after a moment.

"Are you going to Italy?" Winterbourne inquired in a tone of great respect.

The young lady glanced at him again. "Yes, sir," she replied. And she said nothing more.

"Are you—a—going over the Simplon?" Winterbourne pursued, a little embarrassed.

"I don't know," she said. "I suppose it's some mountain. Randolph, what mountain are we going over?"

"Going where?" the child demanded.

"To Italy," Winterbourne explained.

"I don't know," said Randolph. "I don't want to go to Italy. I want to go to America."

"Oh, Italy is a beautiful place!" rejoined the young man.

"Can you get candy there?" Randolph loudly inquired.

"I hope not," said his sister. "I guess you have had enough candy, and mother thinks so too."

"I haven't had any for ever so long—for a hundred weeks!" cried the boy, still jumping about.

The young lady inspected her flounces and smoothed her ribbons again; and Winterbourne presently risked an observation upon the beauty of the view. He was ceasing to be embarrassed, for he had begun to perceive that she was not in the least embarrassed herself. There had not been the slightest alteration in her charming complexion; she was evidently neither offended nor flattered. If she looked another way when he spoke to her, and seemed not particularly to hear him, this was simply her habit, her manner. Yet, as he talked a little more and pointed out some of the objects of interest in the view, with which she appeared quite unacquainted, she gradually gave him more of the benefit of her glance; and then he saw that this glance was perfectly direct and unshrinking. It was not, however, what would have been called an immodest glance, for the young girl's eyes were singularly honest and fresh. They were wonderfully pretty eyes; and, indeed, Winterbourne had not seen for a long time anything prettier than his fair countrywoman's various features—her complexion, her nose, her ears, her teeth. He had a great relish for feminine beauty; he was addicted to observing and analyzing it; and as regards this young lady's face he made several observations. It was not at all insipid, but it was not exactly expressive; and though it was eminently delicate, Winterbourne mentally accused it—very forgivingly—of a want of finish. He thought it very possible that Master Randolph's sister was a coquette; he was sure she had a spirit of her own; but in her bright, sweet, superficial little visage there was no mockery, no irony. Before long it became obvious that she was much disposed toward conversation. She told him that they were going to Rome for the winter—she and her mother and Randolph. She asked him if he was a "real American"; she shouldn't have taken him for one; he seemed more like a German—this was said after a little hesitation—especially when he spoke. Winterbourne, laughing, answered that he had met Germans who spoke like Americans, but that he had not, so far as he remembered, met an American who spoke like a German. Then he asked her if she should not be more comfortable in sitting upon the bench which he had just quitted. She answered that she liked standing up and walking about; but she presently sat down. She told him she was from New York State—"if you know where that is." Winterbourne learned more about her by catching hold of her small, slippery brother and making him stand a few minutes by his side.

"Tell me your name, my boy," he said.

"Randolph C. Miller," said the boy sharply. "And I'll tell you her name;" and he leveled his alpenstock at his sister.

"You had better wait till you are asked!" said this young lady calmly.

"I should like very much to know your name," said Winterbourne.

"Her name is Daisy Miller!" cried the child. "But that isn't her real name; that isn't her name on her cards."

"It's a pity you haven't got one of my cards!" said Miss Miller.

"Her real name is Annie P. Miller," the boy went on.

"Ask him HIS name," said his sister, indicating Winterbourne.

But on this point Randolph seemed perfectly indifferent; he continued to supply information with regard to his own family. "My father's name is Ezra B. Miller," he announced. "My father ain't in Europe; my father's in a better place than Europe."

Winterbourne imagined for a moment that this was the manner in which the child had been taught to intimate that Mr. Miller had been removed to the sphere of celestial reward. But Randolph immediately added, "My father's in Schenectady. He's got a big business. My father's rich, you bet!"

"Well!" ejaculated Miss Miller, lowering her parasol and looking at the embroidered border. Winterbourne presently released the child, who departed, dragging his alpenstock along the path. "He doesn't like Europe," said the young girl. "He wants to go back."

"To Schenectady, you mean?"

"Yes; he wants to go right home. He hasn't got any boys here. There is one boy here, but he always goes round with a teacher; they won't let him play."

"And your brother hasn't any teacher?" Winterbourne inquired.

"Mother thought of getting him one, to travel round with us. There was a lady told her of a very good teacher; an American lady—perhaps you know her—Mrs. Sanders. I think she came from Boston. She told her of this teacher, and we thought of getting him to travel round with us. But Randolph said he didn't want a teacher traveling round with us. He said he wouldn't have lessons when he was in the cars. And we ARE in the cars about half the time. There was an English lady we met in the cars—I think her name was Miss Featherstone; perhaps you know her. She wanted to know why I didn't give Randolph lessons—give him 'instruction,' she called it. I guess he could give me more instruction than I could give him. He's very smart."

"Yes," said Winterbourne; "he seems very smart."

"Mother's going to get a teacher for him as soon as we get to Italy. Can you get good teachers in Italy?"

"Very good, I should think," said Winterbourne.

"Or else she's going to find some school. He ought to learn some more. He's only nine. He's going to college." And in this way Miss Miller continued to converse upon the affairs of her family and upon other topics. She sat there with her extremely pretty hands, ornamented with very brilliant rings, folded in her lap, and with her pretty eyes now resting upon those of Winterbourne, now wandering over the garden, the people who passed by, and the beautiful view. She talked to Winterbourne as if she had known him a long time. He found it very pleasant. It was many years since he had heard a young girl talk so much. It might have been said of this unknown young lady, who had come and sat down beside him upon a bench, that she chattered. She was very quiet; she sat in a charming, tranquil attitude; but her lips and her eyes were constantly moving. She had a soft, slender, agreeable voice, and her tone was decidedly sociable. She gave Winterbourne a history of her movements and intentions and those of her mother and brother, in Europe, and enumerated, in particular, the various hotels at which they had stopped. "That English lady in the cars," she said—"Miss Featherstone—asked me if we didn't all live in hotels in America. I told her I had never been in so many hotels in my life as since I came to Europe. I have never seen so many—it's nothing but hotels." But Miss Miller did not make this remark with a querulous accent; she appeared to be in the best humor with everything. She declared that the hotels were very good, when once you got used to their ways, and that Europe was perfectly sweet. She was not disappointed—not a bit. Perhaps it was because she had heard so much about it before. She had ever so many intimate friends that had been there ever so many times. And then she had had ever so many dresses and things from Paris. Whenever she put on a Paris dress she felt as if she were in Europe.

"It was a kind of a wishing cap," said Winterbourne.

"Yes," said Miss Miller without examining this analogy; "it always made me wish I was here. But I needn't have done that for dresses. I am sure they send all the pretty ones to America; you see the most frightful things here. The only thing I don't like," she proceeded, "is the society. There isn't any society; or, if there is, I don't know where it keeps itself. Do you? I suppose there is some society somewhere, but I haven't seen anything of it. I'm very fond of society, and I have always had a great deal of it. I don't mean only in Schenectady, but in New York. I used to go to New York every winter. In New York I had lots of society. Last winter I had seventeen dinners given me; and three of them were by gentlemen," added Daisy Miller. "I have more friends in New York than in Schenectady—more gentleman friends; and more young lady friends too," she resumed in a moment. She paused again for an instant; she was looking at Winterbourne with all her prettiness in her lively eyes and in her light, slightly monotonous smile. "I have always had," she said, "a great deal of gentlemen's society."

Poor Winterbourne was amused, perplexed, and decidedly charmed. He had never yet heard a young girl express herself in just this fashion; never, at least, save in cases where to say such things seemed a kind of demonstrative evidence of a certain laxity of deportment. And yet was he to accuse Miss Daisy Miller of actual or potential inconduite, as they said at Geneva? He felt that he had lived at Geneva so long that he had lost a good deal; he had become dishabituated to the American tone. Never, indeed, since he had grown old enough to appreciate things, had he encountered a young American girl of so pronounced a type as this. Certainly she was very charming, but how deucedly sociable! Was she simply a pretty girl from New York State? Were they all like that, the pretty girls who had a good deal of gentlemen's society? Or was she also a designing, an audacious, an unscrupulous young person? Winterbourne had lost his instinct in this matter, and his reason could not help him. Miss Daisy Miller looked extremely innocent. Some people had told him that, after all, American girls were exceedingly innocent; and others had told him that, after all, they were not. He was inclined to think Miss Daisy Miller was a flirt—a pretty American flirt. He had never, as yet, had any relations with young ladies of this category. He had known, here in Europe, two or three women—persons older than Miss Daisy Miller, and provided, for respectability's sake, with husbands—who were great coquettes—dangerous, terrible women, with whom one's relations were liable to take a serious turn. But this young girl was not a coquette in that sense; she was very unsophisticated; she was only a pretty American flirt. Winterbourne was almost grateful for having found the formula that applied to Miss Daisy Miller. He leaned back in his seat; he remarked to himself that she had the most charming nose he had ever seen; he wondered what were the regular conditions and limitations of one's intercourse with a pretty American flirt. It presently became apparent that he was on the way to learn.

"Have you been to that old castle?" asked the young girl, pointing with her parasol to the far-gleaming walls of the Chateau de Chillon.

"Yes, formerly, more than once," said Winterbourne. "You too, I suppose, have seen it?"

"No; we haven't been there. I want to go there dreadfully. Of course I mean to go there. I wouldn't go away from here without having seen that old castle."

"It's a very pretty excursion," said Winterbourne, "and very easy to make. You can drive, you know, or you can go by the little steamer."

"You can go in the cars," said Miss Miller.

"Yes; you can go in the cars," Winterbourne assented.

"Our courier says they take you right up to the castle," the young girl continued. "We were going last week, but my mother gave out. She suffers dreadfully from dyspepsia. She said she couldn't go. Randolph wouldn't go either; he says he doesn't think much of old castles. But I guess we'll go this week, if we can get Randolph."

"Your brother is not interested in ancient monuments?" Winterbourne inquired, smiling.

"He says he don't care much about old castles. He's only nine. He wants to stay at the hotel. Mother's afraid to leave him alone, and the courier won't stay with him; so we haven't been to many places. But it will be too bad if we don't go up there." And Miss Miller pointed again at the Chateau de Chillon.

"I should think it might be arranged," said Winterbourne. "Couldn't you get some one to stay for the afternoon with Randolph?"

Miss Miller looked at him a moment, and then, very placidly, "I wish YOU would stay with him!" she said.

Winterbourne hesitated a moment. "I should much rather go to Chillon with you."

"With me?" asked the young girl with the same placidity.

She didn't rise, blushing, as a young girl at Geneva would have done; and yet Winterbourne, conscious that he had been very bold, thought it possible she was offended. "With your mother," he answered very respectfully.

But it seemed that both his audacity and his respect were lost upon Miss Daisy Miller. "I guess my mother won't go, after all," she said. "She don't like to ride round in the afternoon. But did you really mean what you said just now—that you would like to go up there?"

"Most earnestly," Winterbourne declared.

"Then we may arrange it. If mother will stay with Randolph, I guess Eugenio will."

"Eugenio?" the young man inquired.

"Eugenio's our courier. He doesn't like to stay with Randolph; he's the most fastidious man I ever saw. But he's a splendid courier. I guess he'll stay at home with Randolph if mother does, and then we can go to the castle."

Winterbourne reflected for an instant as lucidly as possible—"we" could only mean Miss Daisy Miller and himself. This program seemed almost too agreeable for credence; he felt as if he ought to kiss the young lady's hand. Possibly he would have done so and quite spoiled the project, but at this moment another person, presumably Eugenio, appeared. A tall, handsome man, with superb whiskers, wearing a velvet morning coat and a brilliant watch chain, approached Miss Miller, looking sharply at her companion. "Oh, Eugenio!" said Miss Miller with the friendliest accent.

Eugenio had looked at Winterbourne from head to foot; he now bowed gravely to the young lady. "I have the honor to inform mademoiselle that luncheon is upon the table."

Miss Miller slowly rose. "See here, Eugenio!" she said; "I'm going to that old castle, anyway."

"To the Chateau de Chillon, mademoiselle?" the courier inquired. "Mademoiselle has made arrangements?" he added in a tone which struck Winterbourne as very impertinent.

Eugenio's tone apparently threw, even to Miss Miller's own apprehension, a slightly ironical light upon the young girl's situation. She turned to Winterbourne, blushing a little—a very little. "You won't back out?" she said.

"I shall not be happy till we go!" he protested.

"And you are staying in this hotel?" she went on. "And you are really an American?"

The courier stood looking at Winterbourne offensively. The young man, at least, thought his manner of looking an offense to Miss Miller; it conveyed an imputation that she "picked up" acquaintances. "I shall have the honor of presenting to you a person who will tell you all about me," he said, smiling and referring to his aunt.

"Oh, well, we'll go some day," said Miss Miller. And she gave him a smile and turned away. She put up her parasol and walked back to the inn beside Eugenio. Winterbourne stood looking after her; and as she moved away, drawing her muslin furbelows over the gravel, said to himself that she had the tournure of a princess.

He had, however, engaged to do more than proved feasible, in promising to present his aunt, Mrs. Costello, to Miss Daisy Miller. As soon as the former lady had got better of her headache, he waited upon her in her apartment; and, after the proper inquiries in regard to her health, he asked her if she had observed in the hotel an American family—a mamma, a daughter, and a little boy.

"And a courier?" said Mrs. Costello. "Oh yes, I have observed them. Seen them—heard them—and kept out of their way." Mrs. Costello was a widow with a fortune; a person of much distinction, who frequently intimated that, if she were not so dreadfully liable to sick headaches, she would probably have left a deeper impress upon her time. She had a long, pale face, a high nose, and a great deal of very striking white hair, which she wore in large puffs and rouleaux over the top of her head. She had two sons married in New York and another who was now in Europe. This young man was amusing himself at Hamburg, and, though he was on his travels, was rarely perceived to visit any particular city at the moment selected by his mother for her own appearance there. Her nephew, who had come up to Vevey expressly to see her, was therefore more attentive than those who, as she said, were nearer to her. He had imbibed at Geneva the idea that one must always be attentive to one's aunt. Mrs. Costello had not seen him for many years, and she was greatly pleased with him, manifesting her approbation by initiating him into many of the secrets of that social sway which, as she gave him to understand, she exerted in the American capital. She admitted that she was very exclusive; but, if he were acquainted with New York, he would see that one had to be. And her picture of the minutely hierarchical constitution of the society of that city, which she presented to him in many different lights, was, to Winterbourne's imagination, almost oppressively striking.

He immediately perceived, from her tone, that Miss Daisy Miller's place in the social scale was low. "I am afraid you don't approve of them," he said.

"They are very common," Mrs. Costello declared. "They are the sort of Americans that one does one's duty by not—not accepting."

"Ah, you don't accept them?" said the young man.

"I can't, my dear Frederick. I would if I could, but I can't."

"The young girl is very pretty," said Winterbourne in a moment.

"Of course she's pretty. But she is very common."

"I see what you mean, of course," said Winterbourne after another pause.

"She has that charming look that they all have," his aunt resumed. "I can't think where they pick it up; and she dresses in perfection—no, you don't know how well she dresses. I can't think where they get their taste."

"But, my dear aunt, she is not, after all, a Comanche savage."

"She is a young lady," said Mrs. Costello, "who has an intimacy with her mamma's courier."

"An intimacy with the courier?" the young man demanded.

"Oh, the mother is just as bad! They treat the courier like a familiar friend—like a gentleman. I shouldn't wonder if he dines with them. Very likely they have never seen a man with such good manners, such fine clothes, so like a gentleman. He probably corresponds to the young lady's idea of a count. He sits with them in the garden in the evening. I think he smokes."

Winterbourne listened with interest to these disclosures; they helped him to make up his mind about Miss Daisy. Evidently she was rather wild. "Well," he said, "I am not a courier, and yet she was very charming to me."

"You had better have said at first," said Mrs. Costello with dignity, "that you had made her acquaintance."

"We simply met in the garden, and we talked a bit."

"Tout bonnement! And pray what did you say?"

"I said I should take the liberty of introducing her to my admirable aunt."

"I am much obliged to you."

"It was to guarantee my respectability," said Winterbourne.

"And pray who is to guarantee hers?"

"Ah, you are cruel!" said the young man. "She's a very nice young girl."

"You don't say that as if you believed it," Mrs. Costello observed.

"She is completely uncultivated," Winterbourne went on. "But she is wonderfully pretty, and, in short, she is very nice. To prove that I believe it, I am going to take her to the Chateau de Chillon."

"You two are going off there together? I should say it proved just the contrary. How long had you known her, may I ask, when this interesting project was formed? You haven't been twenty-four hours in the house."

"I have known her half an hour!" said Winterbourne, smiling.

"Dear me!" cried Mrs. Costello. "What a dreadful girl!"

Her nephew was silent for some moments. "You really think, then," he began earnestly, and with a desire for trustworthy information—"you really think that—" But he paused again.

"Think what, sir?" said his aunt.

"That she is the sort of young lady who expects a man, sooner or later, to carry her off?"

"I haven't the least idea what such young ladies expect a man to do. But I really think that you had better not meddle with little American girls that are uncultivated, as you call them. You have lived too long out of the country. You will be sure to make some great mistake. You are too innocent."

"My dear aunt, I am not so innocent," said Winterbourne, smiling and curling his mustache.

"You are guilty too, then!"

Winterbourne continued to curl his mustache meditatively. "You won't let the poor girl know you then?" he asked at last.

"Is it literally true that she is going to the Chateau de Chillon with you?"

"I think that she fully intends it."

"Then, my dear Frederick," said Mrs. Costello, "I must decline the honor of her acquaintance. I am an old woman, but I am not too old, thank Heaven, to be shocked!"

"But don't they all do these things—the young girls in America?" Winterbourne inquired.

Mrs. Costello stared a moment. "I should like to see my granddaughters do them!" she declared grimly.

This seemed to throw some light upon the matter, for Winterbourne remembered to have heard that his pretty cousins in New York were "tremendous flirts." If, therefore, Miss Daisy Miller exceeded the liberal margin allowed to these young ladies, it was probable that anything might be expected of her. Winterbourne was impatient to see her again, and he was vexed with himself that, by instinct, he should not appreciate her justly.

Though he was impatient to see her, he hardly knew what he should say to her about his aunt's refusal to become acquainted with her; but he discovered, promptly enough, that with Miss Daisy Miller there was no great need of walking on tiptoe. He found her that evening in the garden, wandering about in the warm starlight like an indolent sylph, and swinging to and fro the largest fan he had ever beheld. It was ten o'clock. He had dined with his aunt, had been sitting with her since dinner, and had just taken leave of her till the morrow. Miss Daisy Miller seemed very glad to see him; she declared it was the longest evening she had ever passed.

"Have you been all alone?" he asked.

"I have been walking round with mother. But mother gets tired walking round," she answered.

"Has she gone to bed?"

"No; she doesn't like to go to bed," said the young girl. "She doesn't sleep—not three hours. She says she doesn't know how she lives. She's dreadfully nervous. I guess she sleeps more than she thinks. She's gone somewhere after Randolph; she wants to try to get him to go to bed. He doesn't like to go to bed."

"Let us hope she will persuade him," observed Winterbourne.

"She will talk to him all she can; but he doesn't like her to talk to him," said Miss Daisy, opening her fan. "She's going to try to get Eugenio to talk to him. But he isn't afraid of Eugenio. Eugenio's a splendid courier, but he can't make much impression on Randolph! I don't believe he'll go to bed before eleven." It appeared that Randolph's vigil was in fact triumphantly prolonged, for Winterbourne strolled about with the young girl for some time without meeting her mother. "I have been looking round for that lady you want to introduce me to," his companion resumed. "She's your aunt." Then, on Winterbourne's admitting the fact and expressing some curiosity as to how she had learned it, she said she had heard all about Mrs. Costello from the chambermaid. She was very quiet and very comme il faut; she wore white puffs; she spoke to no one, and she never dined at the table d'hote. Every two days she had a headache. "I think that's a lovely description, headache and all!" said Miss Daisy, chattering along in her thin, gay voice. "I want to know her ever so much. I know just what YOUR aunt would be; I know I should like her. She would be very exclusive. I like a lady to be exclusive; I'm dying to be exclusive myself. Well, we ARE exclusive, mother and I. We don't speak to everyone—or they don't speak to us. I suppose it's about the same thing. Anyway, I shall be ever so glad to know your aunt."

Winterbourne was embarrassed. "She would be most happy," he said; "but I am afraid those headaches will interfere."

The young girl looked at him through the dusk. "But I suppose she doesn't have a headache every day," she said sympathetically.

Winterbourne was silent a moment. "She tells me she does," he answered at last, not knowing what to say.

Miss Daisy Miller stopped and stood looking at him. Her prettiness was still visible in the darkness; she was opening and closing her enormous fan. "She doesn't want to know me!" she said suddenly. "Why don't you say so? You needn't be afraid. I'm not afraid!" And she gave a little laugh.

Winterbourne fancied there was a tremor in her voice; he was touched, shocked, mortified by it. "My dear young lady," he protested, "she knows no one. It's her wretched health."

The young girl walked on a few steps, laughing still. "You needn't be afraid," she repeated. "Why should she want to know me?" Then she paused again; she was close to the parapet of the garden, and in front of her was the starlit lake. There was a vague sheen upon its surface, and in the distance were dimly seen mountain forms. Daisy Miller looked out upon the mysterious prospect and then she gave another little laugh. "Gracious! she IS exclusive!" she said. Winterbourne wondered whether she was seriously wounded, and for a moment almost wished that her sense of injury might be such as to make it becoming in him to attempt to reassure and comfort her. He had a pleasant sense that she would be very approachable for consolatory purposes. He felt then, for the instant, quite ready to sacrifice his aunt, conversationally; to admit that she was a proud, rude woman, and to declare that they needn't mind her. But before he had time to commit himself to this perilous mixture of gallantry and impiety, the young lady, resuming her walk, gave an exclamation in quite another tone. "Well, here's Mother! I guess she hasn't got Randolph to go to bed." The figure of a lady appeared at a distance, very indistinct in the darkness, and advancing with a slow and wavering movement. Suddenly it seemed to pause.

"Are you sure it is your mother? Can you distinguish her in this thick dusk?" Winterbourne asked.

"Well!" cried Miss Daisy Miller with a laugh; "I guess I know my own mother. And when she has got on my shawl, too! She is always wearing my things."

The lady in question, ceasing to advance, hovered vaguely about the spot at which she had checked her steps.

"I am afraid your mother doesn't see you," said Winterbourne. "Or perhaps," he added, thinking, with Miss Miller, the joke permissible—"perhaps she feels guilty about your shawl."

"Oh, it's a fearful old thing!" the young girl replied serenely. "I told her she could wear it. She won't come here because she sees you."

"Ah, then," said Winterbourne, "I had better leave you."

"Oh, no; come on!" urged Miss Daisy Miller.

"I'm afraid your mother doesn't approve of my walking with you."

Miss Miller gave him a serious glance. "It isn't for me; it's for you—that is, it's for HER. Well, I don't know who it's for! But mother doesn't like any of my gentlemen friends. She's right down timid. She always makes a fuss if I introduce a gentleman. But I DO introduce them—almost always. If I didn't introduce my gentlemen friends to Mother," the young girl added in her little soft, flat monotone, "I shouldn't think I was natural."

"To introduce me," said Winterbourne, "you must know my name." And he proceeded to pronounce it.

"Oh, dear, I can't say all that!" said his companion with a laugh. But by this time they had come up to Mrs. Miller, who, as they drew near, walked to the parapet of the garden and leaned upon it, looking intently at the lake and turning her back to them. "Mother!" said the young girl in a tone of decision. Upon this the elder lady turned round. "Mr. Winterbourne," said Miss Daisy Miller, introducing the young man very frankly and prettily. "Common," she was, as Mrs. Costello had pronounced her; yet it was a wonder to Winterbourne that, with her commonness, she had a singularly delicate grace.

Her mother was a small, spare, light person, with a wandering eye, a very exiguous nose, and a large forehead, decorated with a certain amount of thin, much frizzled hair. Like her daughter, Mrs. Miller was dressed with extreme elegance; she had enormous diamonds in her ears. So far as Winterbourne could observe, she gave him no greeting—she certainly was not looking at him. Daisy was near her, pulling her shawl straight. "What are you doing, poking round here?" this young lady inquired, but by no means with that harshness of accent which her choice of words may imply.

"I don't know," said her mother, turning toward the lake again.

"I shouldn't think you'd want that shawl!" Daisy exclaimed.

"Well I do!" her mother answered with a little laugh.

"Did you get Randolph to go to bed?" asked the young girl.

"No; I couldn't induce him," said Mrs. Miller very gently. "He wants to talk to the waiter. He likes to talk to that waiter."

"I was telling Mr. Winterbourne," the young girl went on; and to the young man's ear her tone might have indicated that she had been uttering his name all her life.

"Oh, yes!" said Winterbourne; "I have the pleasure of knowing your son."

Randolph's mamma was silent; she turned her attention to the lake. But at last she spoke. "Well, I don't see how he lives!"

"Anyhow, it isn't so bad as it was at Dover," said Daisy Miller.

"And what occurred at Dover?" Winterbourne asked.

"He wouldn't go to bed at all. I guess he sat up all night in the public parlor. He wasn't in bed at twelve o'clock: I know that."

"It was half-past twelve," declared Mrs. Miller with mild emphasis.

"Does he sleep much during the day?" Winterbourne demanded.

"I guess he doesn't sleep much," Daisy rejoined.

"I wish he would!" said her mother. "It seems as if he couldn't."

"I think he's real tiresome," Daisy pursued.

Then, for some moments, there was silence. "Well, Daisy Miller," said the elder lady, presently, "I shouldn't think you'd want to talk against your own brother!"

"Well, he IS tiresome, Mother," said Daisy, quite without the asperity of a retort.

"He's only nine," urged Mrs. Miller.

"Well, he wouldn't go to that castle," said the young girl. "I'm going there with Mr. Winterbourne."

To this announcement, very placidly made, Daisy's mamma offered no response. Winterbourne took for granted that she deeply disapproved of the projected excursion; but he said to himself that she was a simple, easily managed person, and that a few deferential protestations would take the edge from her displeasure. "Yes," he began; "your daughter has kindly allowed me the honor of being her guide."

Mrs. Miller's wandering eyes attached themselves, with a sort of appealing air, to Daisy, who, however, strolled a few steps farther, gently humming to herself. "I presume you will go in the cars," said her mother.

"Yes, or in the boat," said Winterbourne.

"Well, of course, I don't know," Mrs. Miller rejoined. "I have never been to that castle."

"It is a pity you shouldn't go," said Winterbourne, beginning to feel reassured as to her opposition. And yet he was quite prepared to find that, as a matter of course, she meant to accompany her daughter.

"We've been thinking ever so much about going," she pursued; "but it seems as if we couldn't. Of course Daisy—she wants to go round. But there's a lady here—I don't know her name—she says she shouldn't think we'd want to go to see castles HERE; she should think we'd want to wait till we got to Italy. It seems as if there would be so many there," continued Mrs. Miller with an air of increasing confidence. "Of course we only want to see the principal ones. We visited several in England," she presently added.

"Ah yes! in England there are beautiful castles," said Winterbourne. "But Chillon here, is very well worth seeing."

"Well, if Daisy feels up to it—" said Mrs. Miller, in a tone impregnated with a sense of the magnitude of the enterprise. "It seems as if there was nothing she wouldn't undertake."

"Oh, I think she'll enjoy it!" Winterbourne declared. And he desired more and more to make it a certainty that he was to have the privilege of a tete-a-tete with the young lady, who was still strolling along in front of them, softly vocalizing. "You are not disposed, madam," he inquired, "to undertake it yourself?"

Daisy's mother looked at him an instant askance, and then walked forward in silence. Then—"I guess she had better go alone," she said simply. Winterbourne observed to himself that this was a very different type of maternity from that of the vigilant matrons who massed themselves in the forefront of social intercourse in the dark old city at the other end of the lake. But his meditations were interrupted by hearing his name very distinctly pronounced by Mrs. Miller's unprotected daughter.

"Mr. Winterbourne!" murmured Daisy.

"Mademoiselle!" said the young man.

"Don't you want to take me out in a boat?"

"At present?" he asked.

"Of course!" said Daisy.

"Well, Annie Miller!" exclaimed her mother.

"I beg you, madam, to let her go," said Winterbourne ardently; for he had never yet enjoyed the sensation of guiding through the summer starlight a skiff freighted with a fresh and beautiful young girl.

"I shouldn't think she'd want to," said her mother. "I should think she'd rather go indoors."

"I'm sure Mr. Winterbourne wants to take me," Daisy declared. "He's so awfully devoted!"

"I will row you over to Chillon in the starlight."

"I don't believe it!" said Daisy.

"Well!" ejaculated the elder lady again.

"You haven't spoken to me for half an hour," her daughter went on.

"I have been having some very pleasant conversation with your mother," said Winterbourne.

"Well, I want you to take me out in a boat!" Daisy repeated. They had all stopped, and she had turned round and was looking at Winterbourne. Her face wore a charming smile, her pretty eyes were gleaming, she was swinging her great fan about. No; it's impossible to be prettier than that, thought Winterbourne.

"There are half a dozen boats moored at that landing place," he said, pointing to certain steps which descended from the garden to the lake. "If you will do me the honor to accept my arm, we will go and select one of them."

Daisy stood there smiling; she threw back her head and gave a little, light laugh. "I like a gentleman to be formal!" she declared.

"I assure you it's a formal offer."

"I was bound I would make you say something," Daisy went on.

"You see, it's not very difficult," said Winterbourne. "But I am afraid you are chaffing me."

"I think not, sir," remarked Mrs. Miller very gently.

"Do, then, let me give you a row," he said to the young girl.

"It's quite lovely, the way you say that!" cried Daisy.

"It will be still more lovely to do it."

"Yes, it would be lovely!" said Daisy. But she made no movement to accompany him; she only stood there laughing.

"I should think you had better find out what time it is," interposed her mother.

"It is eleven o'clock, madam," said a voice, with a foreign accent, out of the neighboring darkness; and Winterbourne, turning, perceived the florid personage who was in attendance upon the two ladies. He had apparently just approached.

"Oh, Eugenio," said Daisy, "I am going out in a boat!"

Eugenio bowed. "At eleven o'clock, mademoiselle?"

"I am going with Mr. Winterbourne—this very minute."

"Do tell her she can't," said Mrs. Miller to the courier.

"I think you had better not go out in a boat, mademoiselle," Eugenio declared.

Winterbourne wished to Heaven this pretty girl were not so familiar with her courier; but he said nothing.

"I suppose you don't think it's proper!" Daisy exclaimed. "Eugenio doesn't think anything's proper."

"I am at your service," said Winterbourne.

"Does mademoiselle propose to go alone?" asked Eugenio of Mrs. Miller.

"Oh, no; with this gentleman!" answered Daisy's mamma.

The courier looked for a moment at Winterbourne—the latter thought he was smiling—and then, solemnly, with a bow, "As mademoiselle pleases!" he said.

"Oh, I hoped you would make a fuss!" said Daisy. "I don't care to go now."

"I myself shall make a fuss if you don't go," said Winterbourne.

"That's all I want—a little fuss!" And the young girl began to laugh again.

"Mr. Randolph has gone to bed!" the courier announced frigidly.

"Oh, Daisy; now we can go!" said Mrs. Miller.

Daisy turned away from Winterbourne, looking at him, smiling and fanning herself. "Good night," she said; "I hope you are disappointed, or disgusted, or something!"

He looked at her, taking the hand she offered him. "I am puzzled," he answered.

"Well, I hope it won't keep you awake!" she said very smartly; and, under the escort of the privileged Eugenio, the two ladies passed toward the house.

Winterbourne stood looking after them; he was indeed puzzled. He lingered beside the lake for a quarter of an hour, turning over the mystery of the young girl's sudden familiarities and caprices. But the only very definite conclusion he came to was that he should enjoy deucedly "going off" with her somewhere.

Two days afterward he went off with her to the Castle of Chillon. He waited for her in the large hall of the hotel, where the couriers, the servants, the foreign tourists, were lounging about and staring. It was not the place he should have chosen, but she had appointed it. She came tripping downstairs, buttoning her long gloves, squeezing her folded parasol against her pretty figure, dressed in the perfection of a soberly elegant traveling costume. Winterbourne was a man of imagination and, as our ancestors used to say, sensibility; as he looked at her dress and, on the great staircase, her little rapid, confiding step, he felt as if there were something romantic going forward. He could have believed he was going to elope with her. He passed out with her among all the idle people that were assembled there; they were all looking at her very hard; she had begun to chatter as soon as she joined him. Winterbourne's preference had been that they should be conveyed to Chillon in a carriage; but she expressed a lively wish to go in the little steamer; she declared that she had a passion for steamboats. There was always such a lovely breeze upon the water, and you saw such lots of people. The sail was not long, but Winterbourne's companion found time to say a great many things. To the young man himself their little excursion was so much of an escapade—an adventure—that, even allowing for her habitual sense of freedom, he had some expectation of seeing her regard it in the same way. But it must be confessed that, in this particular, he was disappointed. Daisy Miller was extremely animated, she was in charming spirits; but she was apparently not at all excited; she was not fluttered; she avoided neither his eyes nor those of anyone else; she blushed neither when she looked at him nor when she felt that people were looking at her. People continued to look at her a great deal, and Winterbourne took much satisfaction in his pretty companion's distinguished air. He had been a little afraid that she would talk loud, laugh overmuch, and even, perhaps, desire to move about the boat a good deal. But he quite forgot his fears; he sat smiling, with his eyes upon her face, while, without moving from her place, she delivered herself of a great number of original reflections. It was the most charming garrulity he had ever heard. He had assented to the idea that she was "common"; but was she so, after all, or was he simply getting used to her commonness? Her conversation was chiefly of what metaphysicians term the objective cast, but every now and then it took a subjective turn.

"What on EARTH are you so grave about?" she suddenly demanded, fixing her agreeable eyes upon Winterbourne's.

"Am I grave?" he asked. "I had an idea I was grinning from ear to ear."

"You look as if you were taking me to a funeral. If that's a grin, your ears are very near together."

"Should you like me to dance a hornpipe on the deck?"

"Pray do, and I'll carry round your hat. It will pay the expenses of our journey."

"I never was better pleased in my life," murmured Winterbourne.

She looked at him a moment and then burst into a little laugh. "I like to make you say those things! You're a queer mixture!"

In the castle, after they had landed, the subjective element decidedly prevailed. Daisy tripped about the vaulted chambers, rustled her skirts in the corkscrew staircases, flirted back with a pretty little cry and a shudder from the edge of the oubliettes, and turned a singularly well-shaped ear to everything that Winterbourne told her about the place. But he saw that she cared very little for feudal antiquities and that the dusky traditions of Chillon made but a slight impression upon her. They had the good fortune to have been able to walk about without other companionship than that of the custodian; and Winterbourne arranged with this functionary that they should not be hurried—that they should linger and pause wherever they chose. The custodian interpreted the bargain generously—Winterbourne, on his side, had been generous—and ended by leaving them quite to themselves. Miss Miller's observations were not remarkable for logical consistency; for anything she wanted to say she was sure to find a pretext. She found a great many pretexts in the rugged embrasures of Chillon for asking Winterbourne sudden questions about himself—his family, his previous history, his tastes, his habits, his intentions—and for supplying information upon corresponding points in her own personality. Of her own tastes, habits, and intentions Miss Miller was prepared to give the most definite, and indeed the most favorable account.

"Well, I hope you know enough!" she said to her companion, after he had told her the history of the unhappy Bonivard. "I never saw a man that knew so much!" The history of Bonivard had evidently, as they say, gone into one ear and out of the other. But Daisy went on to say that she wished Winterbourne would travel with them and "go round" with them; they might know something, in that case. "Don't you want to come and teach Randolph?" she asked. Winterbourne said that nothing could possibly please him so much, but that he had unfortunately other occupations. "Other occupations? I don't believe it!" said Miss Daisy. "What do you mean? You are not in business." The young man admitted that he was not in business; but he had engagements which, even within a day or two, would force him to go back to Geneva. "Oh, bother!" she said; "I don't believe it!" and she began to talk about something else. But a few moments later, when he was pointing out to her the pretty design of an antique fireplace, she broke out irrelevantly, "You don't mean to say you are going back to Geneva?"

"It is a melancholy fact that I shall have to return to Geneva tomorrow."

"Well, Mr. Winterbourne," said Daisy, "I think you're horrid!"

"Oh, don't say such dreadful things!" said Winterbourne—"just at the last!"

"The last!" cried the young girl; "I call it the first. I have half a mind to leave you here and go straight back to the hotel alone." And for the next ten minutes she did nothing but call him horrid. Poor Winterbourne was fairly bewildered; no young lady had as yet done him the honor to be so agitated by the announcement of his movements. His companion, after this, ceased to pay any attention to the curiosities of Chillon or the beauties of the lake; she opened fire upon the mysterious charmer in Geneva whom she appeared to have instantly taken it for granted that he was hurrying back to see. How did Miss Daisy Miller know that there was a charmer in Geneva? Winterbourne, who denied the existence of such a person, was quite unable to discover, and he was divided between amazement at the rapidity of her induction and amusement at the frankness of her persiflage. She seemed to him, in all this, an extraordinary mixture of innocence and crudity. "Does she never allow you more than three days at a time?" asked Daisy ironically. "Doesn't she give you a vacation in summer? There's no one so hard worked but they can get leave to go off somewhere at this season. I suppose, if you stay another day, she'll come after you in the boat. Do wait over till Friday, and I will go down to the landing to see her arrive!" Winterbourne began to think he had been wrong to feel disappointed in the temper in which the young lady had embarked. If he had missed the personal accent, the personal accent was now making its appearance. It sounded very distinctly, at last, in her telling him she would stop "teasing" him if he would promise her solemnly to come down to Rome in the winter.

"That's not a difficult promise to make," said Winterbourne. "My aunt has taken an apartment in Rome for the winter and has already asked me to come and see her."

"I don't want you to come for your aunt," said Daisy; "I want you to come for me." And this was the only allusion that the young man was ever to hear her make to his invidious kinswoman. He declared that, at any rate, he would certainly come. After this Daisy stopped teasing. Winterbourne took a carriage, and they drove back to Vevey in the dusk; the young girl was very quiet.

In the evening Winterbourne mentioned to Mrs. Costello that he had spent the afternoon at Chillon with Miss Daisy Miller.

"The Americans—of the courier?" asked this lady.

"Ah, happily," said Winterbourne, "the courier stayed at home."

"She went with you all alone?"

"All alone."

Mrs. Costello sniffed a little at her smelling bottle. "And that," she exclaimed, "is the young person whom you wanted me to know!"

PART II

Winterbourne, who had returned to Geneva the day after his excursion to Chillon, went to Rome toward the end of January. His aunt had been established there for several weeks, and he had received a couple of letters from her. "Those people you were so devoted to last summer at Vevey have turned up here, courier and all," she wrote. "They seem to have made several acquaintances, but the courier continues to be the most intime. The young lady, however, is also very intimate with some third-rate Italians, with whom she rackets about in a way that makes much talk. Bring me that pretty novel of Cherbuliez's—Paule Mere—and don't come later than the 23rd."

In the natural course of events, Winterbourne, on arriving in Rome, would presently have ascertained Mrs. Miller's address at the American banker's and have gone to pay his compliments to Miss Daisy. "After what happened at Vevey, I think I may certainly call upon them," he said to Mrs. Costello.

"If, after what happens—at Vevey and everywhere—you desire to keep up the acquaintance, you are very welcome. Of course a man may know everyone. Men are welcome to the privilege!"

"Pray what is it that happens—here, for instance?" Winterbourne demanded.

"The girl goes about alone with her foreigners. As to what happens further, you must apply elsewhere for information. She has picked up half a dozen of the regular Roman fortune hunters, and she takes them about to people's houses. When she comes to a party she brings with her a gentleman with a good deal of manner and a wonderful mustache."

"And where is the mother?"

"I haven't the least idea. They are very dreadful people."

Winterbourne meditated a moment. "They are very ignorant—very innocent only. Depend upon it they are not bad."

"They are hopelessly vulgar," said Mrs. Costello. "Whether or no being hopelessly vulgar is being 'bad' is a question for the metaphysicians. They are bad enough to dislike, at any rate; and for this short life that is quite enough."

The news that Daisy Miller was surrounded by half a dozen wonderful mustaches checked Winterbourne's impulse to go straightway to see her. He had, perhaps, not definitely flattered himself that he had made an ineffaceable impression upon her heart, but he was annoyed at hearing of a state of affairs so little in harmony with an image that had lately flitted in and out of his own meditations; the image of a very pretty girl looking out of an old Roman window and asking herself urgently when Mr. Winterbourne would arrive. If, however, he determined to wait a little before reminding Miss Miller of his claims to her consideration, he went very soon to call upon two or three other friends. One of these friends was an American lady who had spent several winters at Geneva, where she had placed her children at school. She was a very accomplished woman, and she lived in the Via Gregoriana. Winterbourne found her in a little crimson drawing room on a third floor; the room was filled with southern sunshine. He had not been there ten minutes when the servant came in, announcing "Madame Mila!" This announcement was presently followed by the entrance of little Randolph Miller, who stopped in the middle of the room and stood staring at Winterbourne. An instant later his pretty sister crossed the threshold; and then, after a considerable interval, Mrs. Miller slowly advanced.

"I know you!" said Randolph.

"I'm sure you know a great many things," exclaimed Winterbourne, taking him by the hand. "How is your education coming on?"

Daisy was exchanging greetings very prettily with her hostess, but when she heard Winterbourne's voice she quickly turned her head. "Well, I declare!" she said.

"I told you I should come, you know," Winterbourne rejoined, smiling.

"Well, I didn't believe it," said Miss Daisy.

"I am much obliged to you," laughed the young man.

"You might have come to see me!" said Daisy.

"I arrived only yesterday."

"I don't believe that!" the young girl declared.

Winterbourne turned with a protesting smile to her mother, but this lady evaded his glance, and, seating herself, fixed her eyes upon her son. "We've got a bigger place than this," said Randolph. "It's all gold on the walls."

Mrs. Miller turned uneasily in her chair. "I told you if I were to bring you, you would say something!" she murmured.

"I told YOU!" Randolph exclaimed. "I tell YOU, sir!" he added jocosely, giving Winterbourne a thump on the knee. "It IS bigger, too!"

Daisy had entered upon a lively conversation with her hostess; Winterbourne judged it becoming to address a few words to her mother. "I hope you have been well since we parted at Vevey," he said.

Mrs. Miller now certainly looked at him—at his chin. "Not very well, sir," she answered.

"She's got the dyspepsia," said Randolph. "I've got it too. Father's got it. I've got it most!"

This announcement, instead of embarrassing Mrs. Miller, seemed to relieve her. "I suffer from the liver," she said. "I think it's this climate; it's less bracing than Schenectady, especially in the winter season. I don't know whether you know we reside at Schenectady. I was saying to Daisy that I certainly hadn't found any one like Dr. Davis, and I didn't believe I should. Oh, at Schenectady he stands first; they think everything of him. He has so much to do, and yet there was nothing he wouldn't do for me. He said he never saw anything like my dyspepsia, but he was bound to cure it. I'm sure there was nothing he wouldn't try. He was just going to try something new when we came off. Mr. Miller wanted Daisy to see Europe for herself. But I wrote to Mr. Miller that it seems as if I couldn't get on without Dr. Davis. At Schenectady he stands at the very top; and there's a great deal of sickness there, too. It affects my sleep."

Winterbourne had a good deal of pathological gossip with Dr. Davis's patient, during which Daisy chattered unremittingly to her own companion. The young man asked Mrs. Miller how she was pleased with Rome. "Well, I must say I am disappointed," she answered. "We had heard so much about it; I suppose we had heard too much. But we couldn't help that. We had been led to expect something different."

"Ah, wait a little, and you will become very fond of it," said Winterbourne.

"I hate it worse and worse every day!" cried Randolph.

"You are like the infant Hannibal," said Winterbourne.

"No, I ain't!" Randolph declared at a venture.

"You are not much like an infant," said his mother. "But we have seen places," she resumed, "that I should put a long way before Rome." And in reply to Winterbourne's interrogation, "There's Zurich," she concluded, "I think Zurich is lovely; and we hadn't heard half so much about it."

"The best place we've seen is the City of Richmond!" said Randolph.

"He means the ship," his mother explained. "We crossed in that ship. Randolph had a good time on the City of Richmond."

"It's the best place I've seen," the child repeated. "Only it was turned the wrong way."

"Well, we've got to turn the right way some time," said Mrs. Miller with a little laugh. Winterbourne expressed the hope that her daughter at least found some gratification in Rome, and she declared that Daisy was quite carried away. "It's on account of the society—the society's splendid. She goes round everywhere; she has made a great number of acquaintances. Of course she goes round more than I do. I must say they have been very sociable; they have taken her right in. And then she knows a great many gentlemen. Oh, she thinks there's nothing like Rome. Of course, it's a great deal pleasanter for a young lady if she knows plenty of gentlemen."

By this time Daisy had turned her attention again to Winterbourne. "I've been telling Mrs. Walker how mean you were!" the young girl announced.

"And what is the evidence you have offered?" asked Winterbourne, rather annoyed at Miss Miller's want of appreciation of the zeal of an admirer who on his way down to Rome had stopped neither at Bologna nor at Florence, simply because of a certain sentimental impatience. He remembered that a cynical compatriot had once told him that American women—the pretty ones, and this gave a largeness to the axiom—were at once the most exacting in the world and the least endowed with a sense of indebtedness.

"Why, you were awfully mean at Vevey," said Daisy. "You wouldn't do anything. You wouldn't stay there when I asked you."

"My dearest young lady," cried Winterbourne, with eloquence, "have I come all the way to Rome to encounter your reproaches?"

"Just hear him say that!" said Daisy to her hostess, giving a twist to a bow on this lady's dress. "Did you ever hear anything so quaint?"

"So quaint, my dear?" murmured Mrs. Walker in the tone of a partisan of Winterbourne.

"Well, I don't know," said Daisy, fingering Mrs. Walker's ribbons. "Mrs. Walker, I want to tell you something."

"Mother-r," interposed Randolph, with his rough ends to his words, "I tell you you've got to go. Eugenio'll raise—something!"

"I'm not afraid of Eugenio," said Daisy with a toss of her head. "Look here, Mrs. Walker," she went on, "you know I'm coming to your party."

"I am delighted to hear it."

"I've got a lovely dress!"

"I am very sure of that."

"But I want to ask a favor—permission to bring a friend."

"I shall be happy to see any of your friends," said Mrs. Walker, turning with a smile to Mrs. Miller.

"Oh, they are not my friends," answered Daisy's mamma, smiling shyly in her own fashion. "I never spoke to them."

"It's an intimate friend of mine—Mr. Giovanelli," said Daisy without a tremor in her clear little voice or a shadow on her brilliant little face.

Mrs. Walker was silent a moment; she gave a rapid glance at Winterbourne. "I shall be glad to see Mr. Giovanelli," she then said.

"He's an Italian," Daisy pursued with the prettiest serenity. "He's a great friend of mine; he's the handsomest man in the world—except Mr. Winterbourne! He knows plenty of Italians, but he wants to know some Americans. He thinks ever so much of Americans. He's tremendously clever. He's perfectly lovely!"

It was settled that this brilliant personage should be brought to Mrs. Walker's party, and then Mrs. Miller prepared to take her leave. "I guess we'll go back to the hotel," she said.

"You may go back to the hotel, Mother, but I'm going to take a walk," said Daisy.

"She's going to walk with Mr. Giovanelli," Randolph proclaimed.

"I am going to the Pincio," said Daisy, smiling.

"Alone, my dear—at this hour?" Mrs. Walker asked. The afternoon was drawing to a close—it was the hour for the throng of carriages and of contemplative pedestrians. "I don't think it's safe, my dear," said Mrs. Walker.

"Neither do I," subjoined Mrs. Miller. "You'll get the fever, as sure as you live. Remember what Dr. Davis told you!"

"Give her some medicine before she goes," said Randolph.

The company had risen to its feet; Daisy, still showing her pretty teeth, bent over and kissed her hostess. "Mrs. Walker, you are too perfect," she said. "I'm not going alone; I am going to meet a friend."

"Your friend won't keep you from getting the fever," Mrs. Miller observed.

"Is it Mr. Giovanelli?" asked the hostess.

Winterbourne was watching the young girl; at this question his attention quickened. She stood there, smiling and smoothing her bonnet ribbons; she glanced at Winterbourne. Then, while she glanced and smiled, she answered, without a shade of hesitation, "Mr. Giovanelli—the beautiful Giovanelli."

"My dear young friend," said Mrs. Walker, taking her hand pleadingly, "don't walk off to the Pincio at this hour to meet a beautiful Italian."

"Well, he speaks English," said Mrs. Miller.

"Gracious me!" Daisy exclaimed, "I don't to do anything improper. There's an easy way to settle it." She continued to glance at Winterbourne. "The Pincio is only a hundred yards distant; and if Mr. Winterbourne were as polite as he pretends, he would offer to walk with me!"

Winterbourne's politeness hastened to affirm itself, and the young girl gave him gracious leave to accompany her. They passed downstairs before her mother, and at the door Winterbourne perceived Mrs. Miller's carriage drawn up, with the ornamental courier whose acquaintance he had made at Vevey seated within. "Goodbye, Eugenio!" cried Daisy; "I'm going to take a walk." The distance from the Via Gregoriana to the beautiful garden at the other end of the Pincian Hill is, in fact, rapidly traversed. As the day was splendid, however, and the concourse of vehicles, walkers, and loungers numerous, the young Americans found their progress much delayed. This fact was highly agreeable to Winterbourne, in spite of his consciousness of his singular situation. The slow-moving, idly gazing Roman crowd bestowed much attention upon the extremely pretty young foreign lady who was passing through it upon his arm; and he wondered what on earth had been in Daisy's mind when she proposed to expose herself, unattended, to its appreciation. His own mission, to her sense, apparently, was to consign her to the hands of Mr. Giovanelli; but Winterbourne, at once annoyed and gratified, resolved that he would do no such thing.

"Why haven't you been to see me?" asked Daisy. "You can't get out of that."

"I have had the honor of telling you that I have only just stepped out of the train."

"You must have stayed in the train a good while after it stopped!" cried the young girl with her little laugh. "I suppose you were asleep. You have had time to go to see Mrs. Walker."

"I knew Mrs. Walker—" Winterbourne began to explain.

"I know where you knew her. You knew her at Geneva. She told me so. Well, you knew me at Vevey. That's just as good. So you ought to have come." She asked him no other question than this; she began to prattle about her own affairs. "We've got splendid rooms at the hotel; Eugenio says they're the best rooms in Rome. We are going to stay all winter, if we don't die of the fever; and I guess we'll stay then. It's a great deal nicer than I thought; I thought it would be fearfully quiet; I was sure it would be awfully poky. I was sure we should be going round all the time with one of those dreadful old men that explain about the pictures and things. But we only had about a week of that, and now I'm enjoying myself. I know ever so many people, and they are all so charming. The society's extremely select. There are all kinds—English, and Germans, and Italians. I think I like the English best. I like their style of conversation. But there are some lovely Americans. I never saw anything so hospitable. There's something or other every day. There's not much dancing; but I must say I never thought dancing was everything. I was always fond of conversation. I guess I shall have plenty at Mrs. Walker's, her rooms are so small." When they had passed the gate of the Pincian Gardens, Miss Miller began to wonder where Mr. Giovanelli might be. "We had better go straight to that place in front," she said, "where you look at the view."

"I certainly shall not help you to find him," Winterbourne declared.

"Then I shall find him without you," cried Miss Daisy.

"You certainly won't leave me!" cried Winterbourne.

She burst into her little laugh. "Are you afraid you'll get lost—or run over? But there's Giovanelli, leaning against that tree. He's staring at the women in the carriages: did you ever see anything so cool?"

Winterbourne perceived at some distance a little man standing with folded arms nursing his cane. He had a handsome face, an artfully poised hat, a glass in one eye, and a nosegay in his buttonhole. Winterbourne looked at him a moment and then said, "Do you mean to speak to that man?"

"Do I mean to speak to him? Why, you don't suppose I mean to communicate by signs?"

"Pray understand, then," said Winterbourne, "that I intend to remain with you."

Daisy stopped and looked at him, without a sign of troubled consciousness in her face, with nothing but the presence of her charming eyes and her happy dimples. "Well, she's a cool one!" thought the young man.

"I don't like the way you say that," said Daisy. "It's too imperious."

"I beg your pardon if I say it wrong. The main point is to give you an idea of my meaning."

The young girl looked at him more gravely, but with eyes that were prettier than ever. "I have never allowed a gentleman to dictate to me, or to interfere with anything I do."

"I think you have made a mistake," said Winterbourne. "You should sometimes listen to a gentleman—the right one."

Daisy began to laugh again. "I do nothing but listen to gentlemen!" she exclaimed. "Tell me if Mr. Giovanelli is the right one?"

The gentleman with the nosegay in his bosom had now perceived our two friends, and was approaching the young girl with obsequious rapidity. He bowed to Winterbourne as well as to the latter's companion; he had a brilliant smile, an intelligent eye; Winterbourne thought him not a bad-looking fellow. But he nevertheless said to Daisy, "No, he's not the right one."

Daisy evidently had a natural talent for performing introductions; she mentioned the name of each of her companions to the other. She strolled alone with one of them on each side of her; Mr. Giovanelli, who spoke English very cleverly—Winterbourne afterward learned that he had practiced the idiom upon a great many American heiresses—addressed her a great deal of very polite nonsense; he was extremely urbane, and the young American, who said nothing, reflected upon that profundity of Italian cleverness which enables people to appear more gracious in proportion as they are more acutely disappointed. Giovanelli, of course, had counted upon something more intimate; he had not bargained for a party of three. But he kept his temper in a manner which suggested far-stretching intentions. Winterbourne flattered himself that he had taken his measure. "He is not a gentleman," said the young American; "he is only a clever imitation of one. He is a music master, or a penny-a-liner, or a third-rate artist. D___n his good looks!" Mr. Giovanelli had certainly a very pretty face; but Winterbourne felt a superior indignation at his own lovely fellow countrywoman's not knowing the difference between a spurious gentleman and a real one. Giovanelli chattered and jested and made himself wonderfully agreeable. It was true that, if he was an imitation, the imitation was brilliant. "Nevertheless," Winterbourne said to himself, "a nice girl ought to know!" And then he came back to the question whether this was, in fact, a nice girl. Would a nice girl, even allowing for her being a little American flirt, make a rendezvous with a presumably low-lived foreigner? The rendezvous in this case, indeed, had been in broad daylight and in the most crowded corner of Rome, but was it not impossible to regard the choice of these circumstances as a proof of extreme cynicism? Singular though it may seem, Winterbourne was vexed that the young girl, in joining her amoroso, should not appear more impatient of his own company, and he was vexed because of his inclination. It was impossible to regard her as a perfectly well-conducted young lady; she was wanting in a certain indispensable delicacy. It would therefore simplify matters greatly to be able to treat her as the object of one of those sentiments which are called by romancers "lawless passions." That she should seem to wish to get rid of him would help him to think more lightly of her, and to be able to think more lightly of her would make her much less perplexing. But Daisy, on this occasion, continued to present herself as an inscrutable combination of audacity and innocence.

She had been walking some quarter of an hour, attended by her two cavaliers, and responding in a tone of very childish gaiety, as it seemed to Winterbourne, to the pretty speeches of Mr. Giovanelli, when a carriage that had detached itself from the revolving train drew up beside the path. At the same moment Winterbourne perceived that his friend Mrs. Walker—the lady whose house he had lately left— was seated in the vehicle and was beckoning to him. Leaving Miss Miller's side, he hastened to obey her summons. Mrs. Walker was flushed; she wore an excited air. "It is really too dreadful," she said. "That girl must not do this sort of thing. She must not walk here with you two men. Fifty people have noticed her."

Winterbourne raised his eyebrows. "I think it's a pity to make too much fuss about it."

"It's a pity to let the girl ruin herself!"

"She is very innocent," said Winterbourne.

"She's very crazy!" cried Mrs. Walker. "Did you ever see anything so imbecile as her mother? After you had all left me just now, I could not sit still for thinking of it. It seemed too pitiful, not even to attempt to save her. I ordered the carriage and put on my bonnet, and came here as quickly as possible. Thank Heaven I have found you!"

"What do you propose to do with us?" asked Winterbourne, smiling.

"To ask her to get in, to drive her about here for half an hour, so that the world may see she is not running absolutely wild, and then to take her safely home."

"I don't think it's a very happy thought," said Winterbourne; "but you can try."

Mrs. Walker tried. The young man went in pursuit of Miss Miller, who had simply nodded and smiled at his interlocutor in the carriage and had gone her way with her companion. Daisy, on learning that Mrs. Walker wished to speak to her, retraced her steps with a perfect good grace and with Mr. Giovanelli at her side. She declared that she was delighted to have a chance to present this gentleman to Mrs. Walker. She immediately achieved the introduction, and declared that she had never in her life seen anything so lovely as Mrs. Walker's carriage rug.

"I am glad you admire it," said this lady, smiling sweetly. "Will you get in and let me put it over you?"

"Oh, no, thank you," said Daisy. "I shall admire it much more as I see you driving round with it."

"Do get in and drive with me!" said Mrs. Walker.

"That would be charming, but it's so enchanting just as I am!" and Daisy gave a brilliant glance at the gentlemen on either side of her.

"It may be enchanting, dear child, but it is not the custom here," urged Mrs. Walker, leaning forward in her victoria, with her hands devoutly clasped.

"Well, it ought to be, then!" said Daisy. "If I didn't walk I should expire."

"You should walk with your mother, dear," cried the lady from Geneva, losing patience.

"With my mother dear!" exclaimed the young girl. Winterbourne saw that she scented interference. "My mother never walked ten steps in her life. And then, you know," she added with a laugh, "I am more than five years old."

"You are old enough to be more reasonable. You are old enough, dear Miss Miller, to be talked about."

Daisy looked at Mrs. Walker, smiling intensely. "Talked about? What do you mean?"

"Come into my carriage, and I will tell you."

Daisy turned her quickened glance again from one of the gentlemen beside her to the other. Mr. Giovanelli was bowing to and fro, rubbing down his gloves and laughing very agreeably; Winterbourne thought it a most unpleasant scene. "I don't think I want to know what you mean," said Daisy presently. "I don't think I should like it."

Winterbourne wished that Mrs. Walker would tuck in her carriage rug and drive away, but this lady did not enjoy being defied, as she afterward told him. "Should you prefer being thought a very reckless girl?" she demanded.

"Gracious!" exclaimed Daisy. She looked again at Mr. Giovanelli, then she turned to Winterbourne. There was a little pink flush in her cheek; she was tremendously pretty. "Does Mr. Winterbourne think," she asked slowly, smiling, throwing back her head, and glancing at him from head to foot, "that, to save my reputation, I ought to get into the carriage?"

Winterbourne colored; for an instant he hesitated greatly. It seemed so strange to hear her speak that way of her "reputation." But he himself, in fact, must speak in accordance with gallantry. The finest gallantry, here, was simply to tell her the truth; and the truth, for Winterbourne, as the few indications I have been able to give have made him known to the reader, was that Daisy Miller should take Mrs. Walker's advice. He looked at her exquisite prettiness, and then he said, very gently, "I think you should get into the carriage."

Daisy gave a violent laugh. "I never heard anything so stiff! If this is improper, Mrs. Walker," she pursued, "then I am all improper, and you must give me up. Goodbye; I hope you'll have a lovely ride!" and, with Mr. Giovanelli, who made a triumphantly obsequious salute, she turned away.

Mrs. Walker sat looking after her, and there were tears in Mrs. Walker's eyes. "Get in here, sir," she said to Winterbourne, indicating the place beside her. The young man answered that he felt bound to accompany Miss Miller, whereupon Mrs. Walker declared that if he refused her this favor she would never speak to him again. She was evidently in earnest. Winterbourne overtook Daisy and her companion, and, offering the young girl his hand, told her that Mrs. Walker had made an imperious claim upon his society. He expected that in answer she would say something rather free, something to commit herself still further to that "recklessness" from which Mrs. Walker had so charitably endeavored to dissuade her. But she only shook his hand, hardly looking at him, while Mr. Giovanelli bade him farewell with a too emphatic flourish of the hat.

Winterbourne was not in the best possible humor as he took his seat in Mrs. Walker's victoria. "That was not clever of you," he said candidly, while the vehicle mingled again with the throng of carriages.

"In such a case," his companion answered, "I don't wish to be clever; I wish to be EARNEST!"

"Well, your earnestness has only offended her and put her off."

"It has happened very well," said Mrs. Walker. "If she is so perfectly determined to compromise herself, the sooner one knows it the better; one can act accordingly."

"I suspect she meant no harm," Winterbourne rejoined.

"So I thought a month ago. But she has been going too far."

"What has she been doing?"

"Everything that is not done here. Flirting with any man she could pick up; sitting in corners with mysterious Italians; dancing all the evening with the same partners; receiving visits at eleven o'clock at night. Her mother goes away when visitors come."

"But her brother," said Winterbourne, laughing, "sits up till midnight."

"He must be edified by what he sees. I'm told that at their hotel everyone is talking about her, and that a smile goes round among all the servants when a gentleman comes and asks for Miss Miller."

"The servants be hanged!" said Winterbourne angrily. "The poor girl's only fault," he presently added, "is that she is very uncultivated."

"She is naturally indelicate," Mrs. Walker declared.

"Take that example this morning. How long had you known her at Vevey?"

"A couple of days."

"Fancy, then, her making it a personal matter that you should have left the place!"

Winterbourne was silent for some moments; then he said, "I suspect, Mrs. Walker, that you and I have lived too long at Geneva!" And he added a request that she should inform him with what particular design she had made him enter her carriage.

"I wished to beg you to cease your relations with Miss Miller—not to flirt with her—to give her no further opportunity to expose herself—to let her alone, in short."

"I'm afraid I can't do that," said Winterbourne. "I like her extremely."

"All the more reason that you shouldn't help her to make a scandal."

"There shall be nothing scandalous in my attentions to her."

"There certainly will be in the way she takes them. But I have said what I had on my conscience," Mrs. Walker pursued. "If you wish to rejoin the young lady I will put you down. Here, by the way, you have a chance."

The carriage was traversing that part of the Pincian Garden that overhangs the wall of Rome and overlooks the beautiful Villa Borghese. It is bordered by a large parapet, near which there are several seats. One of the seats at a distance was occupied by a gentleman and a lady, toward whom Mrs. Walker gave a toss of her head. At the same moment these persons rose and walked toward the parapet. Winterbourne had asked the coachman to stop; he now descended from the carriage. His companion looked at him a moment in silence; then, while he raised his hat, she drove majestically away. Winterbourne stood there; he had turned his eyes toward Daisy and her cavalier. They evidently saw no one; they were too deeply occupied with each other. When they reached the low garden wall, they stood a moment looking off at the great flat-topped pine clusters of the Villa Borghese; then Giovanelli seated himself, familiarly, upon the broad ledge of the wall. The western sun in the opposite sky sent out a brilliant shaft through a couple of cloud bars, whereupon Daisy's companion took her parasol out of her hands and opened it. She came a little nearer, and he held the parasol over her; then, still holding it, he let it rest upon her shoulder, so that both of their heads were hidden from Winterbourne. This young man lingered a moment, then he began to walk. But he walked—not toward the couple with the parasol; toward the residence of his aunt, Mrs. Costello.

He flattered himself on the following day that there was no smiling among the servants when he, at least, asked for Mrs. Miller at her hotel. This lady and her daughter, however, were not at home; and on the next day after, repeating his visit, Winterbourne again had the misfortune not to find them. Mrs. Walker's party took place on the evening of the third day, and, in spite of the frigidity of his last interview with the hostess, Winterbourne was among the guests. Mrs. Walker was one of those American ladies who, while residing abroad, make a point, in their own phrase, of studying European society, and she had on this occasion collected several specimens of her diversely born fellow mortals to serve, as it were, as textbooks. When Winterbourne arrived, Daisy Miller was not there, but in a few moments he saw her mother come in alone, very shyly and ruefully. Mrs. Miller's hair above her exposed-looking temples was more frizzled than ever. As she approached Mrs. Walker, Winterbourne also drew near.

"You see, I've come all alone," said poor Mrs. Miller. "I'm so frightened; I don't know what to do. It's the first time I've ever been to a party alone, especially in this country. I wanted to bring Randolph or Eugenio, or someone, but Daisy just pushed me off by myself. I ain't used to going round alone."

"And does not your daughter intend to favor us with her society?" demanded Mrs. Walker impressively.

"Well, Daisy's all dressed," said Mrs. Miller with that accent of the dispassionate, if not of the philosophic, historian with which she always recorded the current incidents of her daughter's career. "She got dressed on purpose before dinner. But she's got a friend of hers there; that gentleman—the Italian—that she wanted to bring. They've got going at the piano; it seems as if they couldn't leave off. Mr. Giovanelli sings splendidly. But I guess they'll come before very long," concluded Mrs. Miller hopefully.

"I'm sorry she should come in that way," said Mrs. Walker.

"Well, I told her that there was no use in her getting dressed before dinner if she was going to wait three hours," responded Daisy's mamma. "I didn't see the use of her putting on such a dress as that to sit round with Mr. Giovanelli."

"This is most horrible!" said Mrs. Walker, turning away and addressing herself to Winterbourne. "Elle s'affiche. It's her revenge for my having ventured to remonstrate with her. When she comes, I shall not speak to her."

Daisy came after eleven o'clock; but she was not, on such an occasion, a young lady to wait to be spoken to. She rustled forward in radiant loveliness, smiling and chattering, carrying a large bouquet, and attended by Mr. Giovanelli. Everyone stopped talking and turned and looked at her. She came straight to Mrs. Walker. "I'm afraid you thought I never was coming, so I sent mother off to tell you. I wanted to make Mr. Giovanelli practice some things before he came; you know he sings beautifully, and I want you to ask him to sing. This is Mr. Giovanelli; you know I introduced him to you; he's got the most lovely voice, and he knows the most charming set of songs. I made him go over them this evening on purpose; we had the greatest time at the hotel." Of all this Daisy delivered herself with the sweetest, brightest audibleness, looking now at her hostess and now round the room, while she gave a series of little pats, round her shoulders, to the edges of her dress. "Is there anyone I know?" she asked.

"I think every one knows you!" said Mrs. Walker pregnantly, and she gave a very cursory greeting to Mr. Giovanelli. This gentleman bore himself gallantly. He smiled and bowed and showed his white teeth; he curled his mustaches and rolled his eyes and performed all the proper functions of a handsome Italian at an evening party. He sang very prettily half a dozen songs, though Mrs. Walker afterward declared that she had been quite unable to find out who asked him. It was apparently not Daisy who had given him his orders. Daisy sat at a distance from the piano, and though she had publicly, as it were, professed a high admiration for his singing, talked, not inaudibly, while it was going on.

"It's a pity these rooms are so small; we can't dance," she said to Winterbourne, as if she had seen him five minutes before.

"I am not sorry we can't dance," Winterbourne answered; "I don't dance."

"Of course you don't dance; you're too stiff," said Miss Daisy. "I hope you enjoyed your drive with Mrs. Walker!"

"No. I didn't enjoy it; I preferred walking with you."

"We paired off: that was much better," said Daisy. "But did you ever hear anything so cool as Mrs. Walker's wanting me to get into her carriage and drop poor Mr. Giovanelli, and under the pretext that it was proper? People have different ideas! It would have been most unkind; he had been talking about that walk for ten days."

"He should not have talked about it at all," said Winterbourne; "he would never have proposed to a young lady of this country to walk about the streets with him."

"About the streets?" cried Daisy with her pretty stare. "Where, then, would he have proposed to her to walk? The Pincio is not the streets, either; and I, thank goodness, am not a young lady of this country. The young ladies of this country have a dreadfully poky time of it, so far as I can learn; I don't see why I should change my habits for THEM."

"I am afraid your habits are those of a flirt," said Winterbourne gravely.

"Of course they are," she cried, giving him her little smiling stare again. "I'm a fearful, frightful flirt! Did you ever hear of a nice girl that was not? But I suppose you will tell me now that I am not a nice girl."

"You're a very nice girl; but I wish you would flirt with me, and me only," said Winterbourne.

"Ah! thank you—thank you very much; you are the last man I should think of flirting with. As I have had the pleasure of informing you, you are too stiff."

"You say that too often," said Winterbourne.

Daisy gave a delighted laugh. "If I could have the sweet hope of making you angry, I should say it again."

"Don't do that; when I am angry I'm stiffer than ever. But if you won't flirt with me, do cease, at least, to flirt with your friend at the piano; they don't understand that sort of thing here."

"I thought they understood nothing else!" exclaimed Daisy.

"Not in young unmarried women."

"It seems to me much more proper in young unmarried women than in old married ones," Daisy declared.

"Well," said Winterbourne, "when you deal with natives you must go by the custom of the place. Flirting is a purely American custom; it doesn't exist here. So when you show yourself in public with Mr. Giovanelli, and without your mother—"

"Gracious! poor Mother!" interposed Daisy.

"Though you may be flirting, Mr. Giovanelli is not; he means something else."

"He isn't preaching, at any rate," said Daisy with vivacity. "And if you want very much to know, we are neither of us flirting; we are too good friends for that: we are very intimate friends."

"Ah!" rejoined Winterbourne, "if you are in love with each other, it is another affair."

She had allowed him up to this point to talk so frankly that he had no expectation of shocking her by this ejaculation; but she immediately got up, blushing visibly, and leaving him to exclaim mentally that little American flirts were the queerest creatures in the world. "Mr. Giovanelli, at least," she said, giving her interlocutor a single glance, "never says such very disagreeable things to me."

Winterbourne was bewildered; he stood, staring. Mr. Giovanelli had finished singing. He left the piano and came over to Daisy. "Won't you come into the other room and have some tea?" he asked, bending before her with his ornamental smile.

Daisy turned to Winterbourne, beginning to smile again. He was still more perplexed, for this inconsequent smile made nothing clear, though it seemed to prove, indeed, that she had a sweetness and softness that reverted instinctively to the pardon of offenses. "It has never occurred to Mr. Winterbourne to offer me any tea," she said with her little tormenting manner.

"I have offered you advice," Winterbourne rejoined.

"I prefer weak tea!" cried Daisy, and she went off with the brilliant Giovanelli. She sat with him in the adjoining room, in the embrasure of the window, for the rest of the evening. There was an interesting performance at the piano, but neither of these young people gave heed to it. When Daisy came to take leave of Mrs. Walker, this lady conscientiously repaired the weakness of which she had been guilty at the moment of the young girl's arrival. She turned her back straight upon Miss Miller and left her to depart with what grace she might. Winterbourne was standing near the door; he saw it all. Daisy turned very pale and looked at her mother, but Mrs. Miller was humbly unconscious of any violation of the usual social forms. She appeared, indeed, to have felt an incongruous impulse to draw attention to her own striking observance of them. "Good night, Mrs. Walker," she said; "we've had a beautiful evening. You see, if I let Daisy come to parties without me, I don't want her to go away without me." Daisy turned away, looking with a pale, grave face at the circle near the door; Winterbourne saw that, for the first moment, she was too much shocked and puzzled even for indignation. He on his side was greatly touched.

"That was very cruel," he said to Mrs. Walker.

"She never enters my drawing room again!" replied his hostess.

Since Winterbourne was not to meet her in Mrs. Walker's drawing room, he went as often as possible to Mrs. Miller's hotel. The ladies were rarely at home, but when he found them, the devoted Giovanelli was always present. Very often the brilliant little Roman was in the drawing room with Daisy alone, Mrs. Miller being apparently constantly of the opinion that discretion is the better part of surveillance. Winterbourne noted, at first with surprise, that Daisy on these occasions was never embarrassed or annoyed by his own entrance; but he very presently began to feel that she had no more surprises for him; the unexpected in her behavior was the only thing to expect. She showed no displeasure at her tete-a-tete with Giovanelli being interrupted; she could chatter as freshly and freely with two gentlemen as with one; there was always, in her conversation, the same odd mixture of audacity and puerility. Winterbourne remarked to himself that if she was seriously interested in Giovanelli, it was very singular that she should not take more trouble to preserve the sanctity of their interviews; and he liked her the more for her innocent-looking indifference and her apparently inexhaustible good humor. He could hardly have said why, but she seemed to him a girl who would never be jealous. At the risk of exciting a somewhat derisive smile on the reader's part, I may affirm that with regard to the women who had hitherto interested him, it very often seemed to Winterbourne among the possibilities that, given certain contingencies, he should be afraid—literally afraid—of these ladies; he had a pleasant sense that he should never be afraid of Daisy Miller. It must be added that this sentiment was not altogether flattering to Daisy; it was part of his conviction, or rather of his apprehension, that she would prove a very light young person.

But she was evidently very much interested in Giovanelli. She looked at him whenever he spoke; she was perpetually telling him to do this and to do that; she was constantly "chaffing" and abusing him. She appeared completely to have forgotten that Winterbourne had said anything to displease her at Mrs. Walker's little party. One Sunday afternoon, having gone to St. Peter's with his aunt, Winterbourne perceived Daisy strolling about the great church in company with the inevitable Giovanelli. Presently he pointed out the young girl and her cavalier to Mrs. Costello. This lady looked at them a moment through her eyeglass, and then she said:

"That's what makes you so pensive in these days, eh?"

"I had not the least idea I was pensive," said the young man.

"You are very much preoccupied; you are thinking of something."

"And what is it," he asked, "that you accuse me of thinking of?"

"Of that young lady's—Miss Baker's, Miss Chandler's—what's her name?—Miss Miller's intrigue with that little barber's block."

"Do you call it an intrigue," Winterbourne asked—"an affair that goes on with such peculiar publicity?"

"That's their folly," said Mrs. Costello; "it's not their merit."

"No," rejoined Winterbourne, with something of that pensiveness to which his aunt had alluded. "I don't believe that there is anything to be called an intrigue."

"I have heard a dozen people speak of it; they say she is quite carried away by him."

"They are certainly very intimate," said Winterbourne.

Mrs. Costello inspected the young couple again with her optical instrument. "He is very handsome. One easily sees how it is. She thinks him the most elegant man in the world, the finest gentleman. She has never seen anything like him; he is better, even, than the courier. It was the courier probably who introduced him; and if he succeeds in marrying the young lady, the courier will come in for a magnificent commission."

"I don't believe she thinks of marrying him," said Winterbourne, "and I don't believe he hopes to marry her."

"You may be very sure she thinks of nothing. She goes on from day to day, from hour to hour, as they did in the Golden Age. I can imagine nothing more vulgar. And at the same time," added Mrs. Costello, "depend upon it that she may tell you any moment that she is 'engaged.'"

"I think that is more than Giovanelli expects," said Winterbourne.

"Who is Giovanelli?"

"The little Italian. I have asked questions about him and learned something. He is apparently a perfectly respectable little man. I believe he is, in a small way, a cavaliere avvocato. But he doesn't move in what are called the first circles. I think it is really not absolutely impossible that the courier introduced him. He is evidently immensely charmed with Miss Miller. If she thinks him the finest gentleman in the world, he, on his side, has never found himself in personal contact with such splendor, such opulence, such expensiveness as this young lady's. And then she must seem to him wonderfully pretty and interesting. I rather doubt that he dreams of marrying her. That must appear to him too impossible a piece of luck. He has nothing but his handsome face to offer, and there is a substantial Mr. Miller in that mysterious land of dollars. Giovanelli knows that he hasn't a title to offer. If he were only a count or a marchese! He must wonder at his luck, at the way they have taken him up."

"He accounts for it by his handsome face and thinks Miss Miller a young lady qui se passe ses fantaisies!" said Mrs. Costello.

"It is very true," Winterbourne pursued, "that Daisy and her mamma have not yet risen to that stage of—what shall I call it?—of culture at which the idea of catching a count or a marchese begins. I believe that they are intellectually incapable of that conception."

"Ah! but the avvocato can't believe it," said Mrs. Costello.

Of the observation excited by Daisy's "intrigue," Winterbourne gathered that day at St. Peter's sufficient evidence. A dozen of the American colonists in Rome came to talk with Mrs. Costello, who sat on a little portable stool at the base of one of the great pilasters. The vesper service was going forward in splendid chants and organ tones in the adjacent choir, and meanwhile, between Mrs. Costello and her friends, there was a great deal said about poor little Miss Miller's going really "too far." Winterbourne was not pleased with what he heard, but when, coming out upon the great steps of the church, he saw Daisy, who had emerged before him, get into an open cab with her accomplice and roll away through the cynical streets of Rome, he could not deny to himself that she was going very far indeed. He felt very sorry for her—not exactly that he believed that she had completely lost her head, but because it was painful to hear so much that was pretty, and undefended, and natural assigned to a vulgar place among the categories of disorder. He made an attempt after this to give a hint to Mrs. Miller. He met one day in the Corso a friend, a tourist like himself, who had just come out of the Doria Palace, where he had been walking through the beautiful gallery. His friend talked for a moment about the superb portrait of Innocent X by Velasquez which hangs in one of the cabinets of the palace, and then said, "And in the same cabinet, by the way, I had the pleasure of contemplating a picture of a different kind—that pretty American girl whom you pointed out to me last week." In answer to Winterbourne's inquiries, his friend narrated that the pretty American girl—prettier than ever—was seated with a companion in the secluded nook in which the great papal portrait was enshrined.

"Who was her companion?" asked Winterbourne.

"A little Italian with a bouquet in his buttonhole. The girl is delightfully pretty, but I thought I understood from you the other day that she was a young lady du meilleur monde."

"So she is!" answered Winterbourne; and having assured himself that his informant had seen Daisy and her companion but five minutes before, he jumped into a cab and went to call on Mrs. Miller. She was at home; but she apologized to him for receiving him in Daisy's absence.

"She's gone out somewhere with Mr. Giovanelli," said Mrs. Miller. "She's always going round with Mr. Giovanelli."

"I have noticed that they are very intimate," Winterbourne observed.

"Oh, it seems as if they couldn't live without each other!" said Mrs. Miller. "Well, he's a real gentleman, anyhow. I keep telling Daisy she's engaged!"

"And what does Daisy say?"

"Oh, she says she isn't engaged. But she might as well be!" this impartial parent resumed; "she goes on as if she was. But I've made Mr. Giovanelli promise to tell me, if SHE doesn't. I should want to write to Mr. Miller about it—shouldn't you?"

Winterbourne replied that he certainly should; and the state of mind of Daisy's mamma struck him as so unprecedented in the annals of parental vigilance that he gave up as utterly irrelevant the attempt to place her upon her guard.

After this Daisy was never at home, and Winterbourne ceased to meet her at the houses of their common acquaintances, because, as he perceived, these shrewd people had quite made up their minds that she was going too far. They ceased to invite her; and they intimated that they desired to express to observant Europeans the great truth that, though Miss Daisy Miller was a young American lady, her behavior was not representative—was regarded by her compatriots as abnormal. Winterbourne wondered how she felt about all the cold shoulders that were turned toward her, and sometimes it annoyed him to suspect that she did not feel at all. He said to himself that she was too light and childish, too uncultivated and unreasoning, too provincial, to have reflected upon her ostracism, or even to have perceived it. Then at other moments he believed that she carried about in her elegant and irresponsible little organism a defiant, passionate, perfectly observant consciousness of the impression she produced. He asked himself whether Daisy's defiance came from the consciousness of innocence, or from her being, essentially, a young person of the reckless class. It must be admitted that holding one's self to a belief in Daisy's "innocence" came to seem to Winterbourne more and more a matter of fine-spun gallantry. As I have already had occasion to relate, he was angry at finding himself reduced to chopping logic about this young lady; he was vexed at his want of instinctive certitude as to how far her eccentricities were generic, national, and how far they were personal. From either view of them he had somehow missed her, and now it was too late. She was "carried away" by Mr. Giovanelli.

A few days after his brief interview with her mother, he encountered her in that beautiful abode of flowering desolation known as the Palace of the Caesars. The early Roman spring had filled the air with bloom and perfume, and the rugged surface of the Palatine was muffled with tender verdure. Daisy was strolling along the top of one of those great mounds of ruin that are embanked with mossy marble and paved with monumental inscriptions. It seemed to him that Rome had never been so lovely as just then. He stood, looking off at the enchanting harmony of line and color that remotely encircles the city, inhaling the softly humid odors, and feeling the freshness of the year and the antiquity of the place reaffirm themselves in mysterious interfusion. It seemed to him also that Daisy had never looked so pretty, but this had been an observation of his whenever he met her. Giovanelli was at her side, and Giovanelli, too, wore an aspect of even unwonted brilliancy.

"Well," said Daisy, "I should think you would be lonesome!"

"Lonesome?" asked Winterbourne.

"You are always going round by yourself. Can't you get anyone to walk with you?"

"I am not so fortunate," said Winterbourne, "as your companion."

Giovanelli, from the first, had treated Winterbourne with distinguished politeness. He listened with a deferential air to his remarks; he laughed punctiliously at his pleasantries; he seemed disposed to testify to his belief that Winterbourne was a superior young man. He carried himself in no degree like a jealous wooer; he had obviously a great deal of tact; he had no objection to your expecting a little humility of him. It even seemed to Winterbourne at times that Giovanelli would find a certain mental relief in being able to have a private understanding with him—to say to him, as an intelligent man, that, bless you, HE knew how extraordinary was this young lady, and didn't flatter himself with delusive—or at least TOO delusive—hopes of matrimony and dollars. On this occasion he strolled away from his companion to pluck a sprig of almond blossom, which he carefully arranged in his buttonhole.

"I know why you say that," said Daisy, watching Giovanelli. "Because you think I go round too much with HIM." And she nodded at her attendant.

"Every one thinks so—if you care to know," said Winterbourne.

"Of course I care to know!" Daisy exclaimed seriously. "But I don't believe it. They are only pretending to be shocked. They don't really care a straw what I do. Besides, I don't go round so much."

"I think you will find they do care. They will show it disagreeably."

Daisy looked at him a moment. "How disagreeably?"

"Haven't you noticed anything?" Winterbourne asked.

"I have noticed you. But I noticed you were as stiff as an umbrella the first time I saw you."

"You will find I am not so stiff as several others," said Winterbourne, smiling.

"How shall I find it?"

"By going to see the others."

"What will they do to me?"

"They will give you the cold shoulder. Do you know what that means?"

Daisy was looking at him intently; she began to color. "Do you mean as Mrs. Walker did the other night?"

"Exactly!" said Winterbourne.

She looked away at Giovanelli, who was decorating himself with his almond blossom. Then looking back at Winterbourne, "I shouldn't think you would let people be so unkind!" she said.

"How can I help it?" he asked.

"I should think you would say something."

"I do say something;" and he paused a moment. "I say that your mother tells me that she believes you are engaged."

"Well, she does," said Daisy very simply.

Winterbourne began to laugh. "And does Randolph believe it?" he asked.

"I guess Randolph doesn't believe anything," said Daisy. Randolph's skepticism excited Winterbourne to further hilarity, and he observed that Giovanelli was coming back to them. Daisy, observing it too, addressed herself again to her countryman. "Since you have mentioned it," she said, "I AM engaged."

Winterbourne looked at her; he had stopped laughing. "You don't believe!" she added.

He was silent a moment; and then, "Yes, I believe it," he said.

"Oh, no, you don't!" she answered. "Well, then—I am not!"

The young girl and her cicerone were on their way to the gate of the enclosure, so that Winterbourne, who had but lately entered, presently took leave of them. A week afterward he went to dine at a beautiful villa on the Caelian Hill, and, on arriving, dismissed his hired vehicle. The evening was charming, and he promised himself the satisfaction of walking home beneath the Arch of Constantine and past the vaguely lighted monuments of the Forum. There was a waning moon in the sky, and her radiance was not brilliant, but she was veiled in a thin cloud curtain which seemed to diffuse and equalize it. When, on his return from the villa (it was eleven o'clock), Winterbourne approached the dusky circle of the Colosseum, it recurred to him, as a lover of the picturesque, that the interior, in the pale moonshine, would be well worth a glance. He turned aside and walked to one of the empty arches, near which, as he observed, an open carriage—one of the little Roman streetcabs—was stationed. Then he passed in, among the cavernous shadows of the great structure, and emerged upon the clear and silent arena. The place had never seemed to him more impressive. One-half of the gigantic circus was in deep shade, the other was sleeping in the luminous dusk. As he stood there he began to murmur Byron's famous lines, out of "Manfred," but before he had finished his quotation he remembered that if nocturnal meditations in the Colosseum are recommended by the poets, they are deprecated by the doctors. The historic atmosphere was there, certainly; but the historic atmosphere, scientifically considered, was no better than a villainous miasma. Winterbourne walked to the middle of the arena, to take a more general glance, intending thereafter to make a hasty retreat. The great cross in the center was covered with shadow; it was only as he drew near it that he made it out distinctly. Then he saw that two persons were stationed upon the low steps which formed its base. One of these was a woman, seated; her companion was standing in front of her.

Presently the sound of the woman's voice came to him distinctly in the warm night air. "Well, he looks at us as one of the old lions or tigers may have looked at the Christian martyrs!" These were the words he heard, in the familiar accent of Miss Daisy Miller.

"Let us hope he is not very hungry," responded the ingenious Giovanelli. "He will have to take me first; you will serve for dessert!"

Winterbourne stopped, with a sort of horror, and, it must be added, with a sort of relief. It was as if a sudden illumination had been flashed upon the ambiguity of Daisy's behavior, and the riddle had become easy to read. She was a young lady whom a gentleman need no longer be at pains to respect. He stood there, looking at her—looking at her companion and not reflecting that though he saw them vaguely, he himself must have been more brightly visible. He felt angry with himself that he had bothered so much about the right way of regarding Miss Daisy Miller. Then, as he was going to advance again, he checked himself, not from the fear that he was doing her injustice, but from a sense of the danger of appearing unbecomingly exhilarated by this sudden revulsion from cautious criticism. He turned away toward the entrance of the place, but, as he did so, he heard Daisy speak again.

"Why, it was Mr. Winterbourne! He saw me, and he cuts me!"

What a clever little reprobate she was, and how smartly she played at injured innocence! But he wouldn't cut her. Winterbourne came forward again and went toward the great cross. Daisy had got up; Giovanelli lifted his hat. Winterbourne had now begun to think simply of the craziness, from a sanitary point of view, of a delicate young girl lounging away the evening in this nest of malaria. What if she WERE a clever little reprobate? that was no reason for her dying of the perniciosa. "How long have you been here?" he asked almost brutally.

Daisy, lovely in the flattering moonlight, looked at him a moment. Then—"All the evening," she answered, gently.

"I never saw anything so pretty."

"I am afraid," said Winterbourne, "that you will not think Roman fever very pretty. This is the way people catch it. I wonder," he added, turning to Giovanelli, "that you, a native Roman, should countenance such a terrible indiscretion."

"Ah," said the handsome native, "for myself I am not afraid."

"Neither am I—for you! I am speaking for this young lady."

Giovanelli lifted his well-shaped eyebrows and showed his brilliant teeth. But he took Winterbourne's rebuke with docility. "I told the signorina it was a grave indiscretion, but when was the signorina ever prudent?"

"I never was sick, and I don't mean to be!" the signorina declared. "I don't look like much, but I'm healthy! I was bound to see the Colosseum by moonlight; I shouldn't have wanted to go home without that; and we have had the most beautiful time, haven't we, Mr. Giovanelli? If there has been any danger, Eugenio can give me some pills. He has got some splendid pills."

"I should advise you," said Winterbourne, "to drive home as fast as possible and take one!"

"What you say is very wise," Giovanelli rejoined. "I will go and make sure the carriage is at hand." And he went forward rapidly.

Daisy followed with Winterbourne. He kept looking at her; she seemed not in the least embarrassed. Winterbourne said nothing; Daisy chattered about the beauty of the place. "Well, I HAVE seen the Colosseum by moonlight!" she exclaimed. "That's one good thing." Then, noticing Winterbourne's silence, she asked him why he didn't speak. He made no answer; he only began to laugh. They passed under one of the dark archways; Giovanelli was in front with the carriage. Here Daisy stopped a moment, looking at the young American. "DID you believe I was engaged, the other day?" she asked.

"It doesn't matter what I believed the other day," said Winterbourne, still laughing.

"Well, what do you believe now?"

"I believe that it makes very little difference whether you are engaged or not!"

He felt the young girl's pretty eyes fixed upon him through the thick gloom of the archway; she was apparently going to answer. But Giovanelli hurried her forward. "Quick! quick!" he said; "if we get in by midnight we are quite safe."

Daisy took her seat in the carriage, and the fortunate Italian placed himself beside her. "Don't forget Eugenio's pills!" said Winterbourne as he lifted his hat.

"I don't care," said Daisy in a little strange tone, "whether I have Roman fever or not!" Upon this the cab driver cracked his whip, and they rolled away over the desultory patches of the antique pavement.

Winterbourne, to do him justice, as it were, mentioned to no one that he had encountered Miss Miller, at midnight, in the Colosseum with a gentleman; but nevertheless, a couple of days later, the fact of her having been there under these circumstances was known to every member of the little American circle, and commented accordingly. Winterbourne reflected that they had of course known it at the hotel, and that, after Daisy's return, there had been an exchange of remarks between the porter and the cab driver. But the young man was conscious, at the same moment, that it had ceased to be a matter of serious regret to him that the little American flirt should be "talked about" by low-minded menials. These people, a day or two later, had serious information to give: the little American flirt was alarmingly ill. Winterbourne, when the rumor came to him, immediately went to the hotel for more news. He found that two or three charitable friends had preceded him, and that they were being entertained in Mrs. Miller's salon by Randolph.

"It's going round at night," said Randolph—"that's what made her sick. She's always going round at night. I shouldn't think she'd want to, it's so plaguy dark. You can't see anything here at night, except when there's a moon. In America there's always a moon!" Mrs. Miller was invisible; she was now, at least, giving her daughter the advantage of her society. It was evident that Daisy was dangerously ill.

Winterbourne went often to ask for news of her, and once he saw Mrs. Miller, who, though deeply alarmed, was, rather to his surprise, perfectly composed, and, as it appeared, a most efficient and judicious nurse. She talked a good deal about Dr. Davis, but Winterbourne paid her the compliment of saying to himself that she was not, after all, such a monstrous goose. "Daisy spoke of you the other day," she said to him. "Half the time she doesn't know what she's saying, but that time I think she did. She gave me a message she told me to tell you. She told me to tell you that she never was engaged to that handsome Italian. I am sure I am very glad; Mr. Giovanelli hasn't been near us since she was taken ill. I thought he was so much of a gentleman; but I don't call that very polite! A lady told me that he was afraid I was angry with him for taking Daisy round at night. Well, so I am, but I suppose he knows I'm a lady. I would scorn to scold him. Anyway, she says she's not engaged. I don't know why she wanted you to know, but she said to me three times, 'Mind you tell Mr. Winterbourne.' And then she told me to ask if you remembered the time you went to that castle in Switzerland. But I said I wouldn't give any such messages as that. Only, if she is not engaged, I'm sure I'm glad to know it."

But, as Winterbourne had said, it mattered very little. A week after this, the poor girl died; it had been a terrible case of the fever. Daisy's grave was in the little Protestant cemetery, in an angle of the wall of imperial Rome, beneath the cypresses and the thick spring flowers. Winterbourne stood there beside it, with a number of other mourners, a number larger than the scandal excited by the young lady's career would have led you to expect. Near him stood Giovanelli, who came nearer still before Winterbourne turned away. Giovanelli was very pale: on this occasion he had no flower in his buttonhole; he seemed to wish to say something. At last he said, "She was the most beautiful young lady I ever saw, and the most amiable;" and then he added in a moment, "and she was the most innocent."

Winterbourne looked at him and presently repeated his words, "And the most innocent?"

"The most innocent!"

Winterbourne felt sore and angry. "Why the devil," he asked, "did you take her to that fatal place?"

Mr. Giovanelli's urbanity was apparently imperturbable. He looked on the ground a moment, and then he said, "For myself I had no fear; and she wanted to go."

"That was no reason!" Winterbourne declared.

The subtle Roman again dropped his eyes. "If she had lived, I should have got nothing. She would never have married me, I am sure."

"She would never have married you?"

"For a moment I hoped so. But no. I am sure."

Winterbourne listened to him: he stood staring at the raw protuberance among the April daisies. When he turned away again, Mr. Giovanelli, with his light, slow step, had retired.

Winterbourne almost immediately left Rome; but the following summer he again met his aunt, Mrs. Costello at Vevey. Mrs. Costello was fond of Vevey. In the interval Winterbourne had often thought of Daisy Miller and her mystifying manners. One day he spoke of her to his aunt—said it was on his conscience that he had done her injustice.

"I am sure I don't know," said Mrs. Costello. "How did your injustice affect her?"

"She sent me a message before her death which I didn't understand at the time; but I have understood it since. She would have appreciated one's esteem."

"Is that a modest way," asked Mrs. Costello, "of saying that she would have reciprocated one's affection?"

Winterbourne offered no answer to this question; but he presently said, "You were right in that remark that you made last summer. I was booked to make a mistake. I have lived too long in foreign parts."

Nevertheless, he went back to live at Geneva, whence there continue to come the most contradictory accounts of his motives of sojourn: a report that he is "studying" hard—an intimation that he is much interested in a very clever foreign lady.

2.6.2 Reading and Review Questions

1. What features of Realism do you see in *Daisy Miller?*

2. How does James use point of view in the novella? For example, who is the narrator in the story? What effect does the narrative voice have in conveying the story as gossip?

3. Is Daisy Miller truly an innocent? Is she a victim of a cynical, hypocritical culture? Or does she bring about her own fate?

4. How is Winterbourne, also an American abroad, different from Daisy? Through what lens does he view Daisy?

5. Why does Winterbourne obsess over whether Daisy is "innocent" or not? What is Winterbourne seeking in Daisy?

6. What does the expression "Roman fever" mean in the context of the story? While the expression refers literally to malaria, what other figurative associations might the expression convey?

2.7 SARAH ORNE JEWETT

(1849 - 1909)

Born in 1849 in the coastal town of South Berwick, Maine, Sarah Orne Jewett grew up accompanying her father, a doctor, on rounds across the rural countryside. She was educated at South Berwick Academy, graduating in 1866. In spite of obstacles she would have faced as a woman seeking a medical education in the nineteenth century, Jewett harbored ambitions of becoming a doctor herself, but ill health prevented her from moving forward with the plan. Instead, she continued to educate herself by reading widely in her father's private library, eventually deciding upon a life of writing. She published a short story at age nineteen in *The Atlantic Monthly*, and her work was promoted

Image 2.5 | Sarah Orne Jewett, 1894
Publisher | Houghton Mifflin
Source | Wikimedia Commons
License | Public Domain

by William Dean Howells, assistant editor at the magazine, who praised Jewett's ability to capture the distinctive voice of ordinary people in the New England region. As her reputation grew, she regularly traveled to Boston, where she enjoyed the company of other writers. Jewett never married but later in life befriended the widow of James Thomas Fields, Howells's predecessor at *The Atlantic Monthly*. Annie Adams Fields and Sarah Orne Jewett were companions for the rest of Jewett's life. Jewett died in 1909 after a long illness.

Jewett's most notable works are her novels and short stories that explore characters firmly rooted in the New England region, particularly *A Country Doctor* (1884); *A White Heron* (1886), a short story collection; and *The Country of the Pointed Firs* (1896). Jewett has been described as both a local colorist and a regionalist, and even as an early realist. The difficulty in labeling her work points to limits of categorizing literature using terms for distinct literary movements that developed at times parallel to one another and at other instances overlapped. Most literary critics, though, are comfortable describing Jewett's work as representative of American Literary Regionalism. Similar to fellow New England writer Mary E. Wilkins Freeman's fiction, Jewett's work does exhibit features of Local Color—the important sense of locale in terms of geography and landscape, as well as the speech patterns and customs of the inhabitants. However, beyond the particulars of place, these stories focus on characterization, particularly in ways that plot or action in the story is filtered through the consciousness of a central protagonist, most often a young girl or a woman. In Jewett's work, as in Freeman's, there is evidence of three dimensional characters who must work through an internal conflict, and this dimensional characterization predicts the kind of psychological complexity of character that becomes even more refined and sophisticated in works by Realistic writers such as Howells and James. Additionally, her work, with its focus on the lives of women and the limitations placed on them by the cultural and historical moment, predicts an early feminist realism. In one of her most important short stories, *A White Heron*, Sylvy's internal conflict—whether or not to give away the location of the heron's nest to the handsome male stranger—forms the basis of the plot of the story. Sylvy's allegiance is challenged, then, in terms of whether she will protect the wild bird or please the young man. However, Sylvy must also decide a larger issue than whether she will be loyal to the bird or the ornithologist (and all each represents symbolically). She must determine who she is and whether she can be loyal to this new sense of self.

2.7.1 "A White Heron"

I

The woods were already filled with shadows one June evening, just before eight o'clock, though a bright sunset still glimmered faintly among the trunks of the trees. A little girl was driving home her cow, a plodding, dilatory, provoking creature in her behavior, but a valued companion for all that. They were going away from whatever light there was, and striking deep into the woods, but their feet were familiar with the path, and it was no matter whether their eyes could see it or not.

There was hardly a night the summer through when the old cow could be found waiting at the pasture bars; on the contrary, it was her greatest pleasure to hide herself away among the huckleberry bushes, and though she wore a loud bell she had made the discovery that if one stood perfectly still it would not ring. So Sylvia had to hunt for her until she found her, and call Co' ! Co' ! with never an answering Moo, until her childish patience was quite spent. If the creature had not given good milk and plenty of it, the case would have seemed very different to her owners. Besides, Sylvia had all the time there was, and very little use to make of it. Sometimes in pleasant weather it was a consolation to look upon the cow's pranks as an intelligent attempt to play hide and seek, and as the child had no playmates she lent herself to this amusement with a good deal of zest. Though this chase had been so long that the wary animal herself had given an unusual signal of her whereabouts, Sylvia had only laughed when she came upon Mistress Moolly at the swamp-side, and urged her affectionately homeward with a twig of birch leaves. The old cow was not inclined to wander farther, she even turned in the right direction for once as they left the pasture, and stepped along the road at a good pace. She was quite ready to be milked now, and seldom stopped to browse. Sylvia wondered what her grandmother would say because they were so late. It was a great while since she had left home at half-past five o'clock, but everybody knew the difficulty of making this errand a short one. Mrs. Tilley had chased the hornéd torment too many summer evenings herself to blame any one else for lingering, and was only thankful as she waited that she had Sylvia, nowadays, to give such valuable assistance. The good woman suspected that Sylvia loitered occasionally on her own account;

there never was such a child for straying about out-of-doors since the world was made! Everybody said that it was a good change for a little maid who had tried to grow for eight years in a crowded manufacturing town, but, as for Sylvia herself, it seemed as if she never had been alive at all before she came to live at the farm. She thought often with wistful compassion of a wretched geranium that belonged to a town neighbor.

"'Afraid of folks,'" old Mrs. Tilley said to herself, with a smile, after she had made the unlikely choice of Sylvia from her daughter's houseful of children, and was returning to the farm. "'Afraid of folks,' they said! I guess she won't be troubled no great with 'em up to the old place!" When they reached the door of the lonely house and stopped to unlock it, and the cat came to purr loudly, and rub against them, a deserted pussy, indeed, but fat with young robins, Sylvia whispered that this was a beautiful place to live in, and she never should wish to go home.

The companions followed the shady wood-road, the cow taking slow steps and the child very fast ones. The cow stopped long at the brook to drink, as if the pasture were not half a swamp, and Sylvia stood still and waited, letting her bare feet cool themselves in the shoal water, while the great twilight moths struck softly against her. She waded on through the brook as the cow moved away, and listened to the thrushes with a heart that beat fast with pleasure. There was a stirring in the great boughs overhead. They were full of little birds and beasts that seemed to be wide awake, and going about their world, or else saying good-night to each other in sleepy twitters. Sylvia herself felt sleepy as she walked along. However, it was not much farther to the house, and the air was soft and sweet. She was not often in the woods so late as this, and it made her feel as if she were a part of the gray shadows and the moving leaves. She was just thinking how long it seemed since she first came to the farm a year ago, and wondering if everything went on in the noisy town just the same as when she was there, the thought of the great red-faced boy who used to chase and frighten her made her hurry along the path to escape from the shadow of the trees.

Suddenly this little woods-girl is horror-stricken to hear a clear whistle not very far away. Not a bird's-whistle, which would have a sort of friendliness, but a boy's whistle, determined, and somewhat aggressive. Sylvia left the cow to whatever sad fate might await her, and stepped discreetly aside into the bushes, but she was just too late. The enemy had discovered her, and called out in a very cheerful and persuasive tone, "Halloa, little girl, how far is it to the road?" and trembling Sylvia answered almost inaudibly, "A good ways."

She did not dare to look boldly at the tall young man, who carried a gun over his shoulder, but she came out of her bush and again followed the cow, while he walked alongside.

"I have been hunting for some birds," the stranger said kindly, "and I have lost my way, and need a friend very much. Don't be afraid," he added gallantly. "Speak up and tell me what your name is, and whether you think I can spend the night at your house, and go out gunning early in the morning."

Sylvia was more alarmed than before. Would not her grandmother consider her much to blame? But who could have foreseen such an accident as this? It did not seem to be her fault, and she hung her head as if the stem of it were broken, but managed to answer "Sylvy," with much effort when her companion again asked her name.

Mrs. Tilley was standing in the doorway when the trio came into view. The cow gave a loud moo by way of explanation.

"Yes, you'd better speak up for yourself, you old trial! Where'd she tucked herself away this time, Sylvy?" But Sylvia kept an awed silence; she knew by instinct that her grandmother did not comprehend the gravity of the situation. She must be mistaking the stranger for one of the farmer-lads of the region.

The young man stood his gun beside the door, and dropped a lumpy game-bag beside it; then he bade Mrs. Tilley good-evening, and repeated his wayfarer's story, and asked if he could have a night's lodging.

"Put me anywhere you like," he said. "I must be off early in the morning, before day; but I am very hungry, indeed. You can give me some milk at any rate, that's plain."

"Dear sakes, yes," responded the hostess, whose long slumbering hospitality seemed to be easily awakened. "You might fare better if you went out to the main road a mile or so, but you're welcome to what we've got. I'll milk right off, and you make yourself at home. You can sleep on husks or feathers," she proffered graciously. "I raised them all myself. There's good pasturing for geese just below here towards the ma'sh. Now step round and set a plate for the gentleman, Sylvy!" And Sylvia promptly stepped. She was glad to have something to do, and she was hungry herself.

It was a surprise to find so clean and comfortable a little dwelling in this New England wilderness. The young man had known the horrors of its most primitive housekeeping, and the dreary squalor of that level of society which does not rebel at the companionship of hens. This was the best thrift of an old-fashioned farmstead, though on such a small scale that it seemed like a hermitage. He listened eagerly to the old woman's quaint talk, he watched Sylvia's pale face and shining gray eyes with ever growing enthusiasm, and insisted that this was the best supper he had eaten for a month, and afterward the new-made friends sat down in the door-way together while the moon came up.

Soon it would be berry-time, and Sylvia was a great help at picking. The cow was a good milker, though a plaguy thing to keep track of, the hostess gossiped frankly, adding presently that she had buried four children, so Sylvia's mother, and a son (who might be dead) in California were all the children she had left. "Dan, my boy, was a great hand to go gunning," she explained sadly. "I never wanted for pa'tridges or gray squer'ls while he was to home. He's been a great wand'rer, I expect, and he's no hand to write letters. There, I don't blame him, I'd ha' seen the world myself if it had been so I could.

"Sylvy takes after him," the grandmother continued affectionately, after a minute's pause. "There ain't a foot o' ground she don't know her way over, and the wild creaturs counts her one o' themselves. Squer'ls she'll tame to come an' feed right out o' her hands, and all sorts o' birds. Last winter she got the jay-birds to bange-ing here, and I believe she'd 'a' scanted herself of her own meals to have plenty to throw out amongst 'em, if I hadn't kep' watch. Anything but crows, I tell her, I'm willin' to help support—though Dan he had a tamed one o' them that did seem to have reason same as folks. It was round here a good spell after he went away. Dan an' his father they didn't hitch,—but he never held up his head ag'in after Dan had dared him an' gone off."

The guest did not notice this hint of family sorrows in his eager interest in something else.

"So Sylvy knows all about birds, does she?" he exclaimed, as he looked round at the little girl who sat, very demure but increasingly sleepy, in the moonlight. "I am making a collection of birds myself. I have been at it ever since I was a boy." (Mrs. Tilley smiled.) "There are two or three very rare ones I have been hunting for these five years. I mean to get them on my own ground if they can be found."

"Do you cage 'em up?" asked Mrs. Tilley doubtfully, in response to this enthu-siastic announcement.

"Oh no, they're stuffed and preserved, dozens and dozens of them," said the ornithologist, "and I have shot or snared every one myself. I caught a glimpse of a white heron a few miles from here on Saturday, and I have followed it in this direc-tion. They have never been found in this district at all. The little white heron, it is," and he turned again to look at Sylvia with the hope of discovering that the rare bird was one of her acquaintances.

But Sylvia was watching a hop-toad in the narrow footpath.

"You would know the heron if you saw it," the stranger continued eagerly. "A queer tall white bird with soft feathers and long thin legs. And it would have a nest perhaps in the top of a high tree, made of sticks, something like a hawk's nest."

Sylvia's heart gave a wild beat; she knew that strange white bird, and had once stolen softly near where it stood in some bright green swamp grass, away over at the other side of the woods. There was an open place where the sunshine al-ways seemed strangely yellow and hot, where tall, nodding rushes grew, and her grandmother had warned her that she might sink in the soft black mud underneath and never be heard of more. Not far beyond were the salt marshes just this side the sea itself, which Sylvia wondered and dreamed much about, but never had seen, whose great voice could sometimes be heard above the noise of the woods on stormy nights.

"I can't think of anything I should like so much as to find that heron's nest," the handsome stranger was saying. "I would give ten dollars to anybody who could show it to me," he added desperately, "and I mean to spend my whole vacation hunting for it if need be. Perhaps it was only migrating, or had been chased out of its own region by some bird of prey."

Mrs. Tilley gave amazed attention to all this, but Sylvia still watched the toad, not divining, as she might have done at some calmer time, that the creature wished to get to its hole under the door-step, and was much hindered by the unusual spectators at that hour of the evening. No amount of thought, that night, could decide how many wished-for treasures the ten dollars, so lightly spoken of, would buy.

The next day the young sportsman hovered about the woods, and Sylvia kept him company, having lost her first fear of the friendly lad, who proved to be most kind and sympathetic. He told her many things about the birds and what they knew and where they lived and what they did with themselves. And he gave her a jack-knife, which she thought as great a treasure as if she were a desert-islander. All day long he did not once make her troubled or afraid except when he brought down some unsuspecting singing creature from its bough. Sylvia would have liked him vastly better without his gun; she could not understand why he killed the very birds he seemed to like so much. But as the day waned, Sylvia still watched the young man with loving admiration. She had never seen anybody so charming and delightful; the woman's heart, asleep in the child, was vaguely thrilled by a dream of love. Some premonition of that great power stirred and swayed these young creatures who traversed the solemn woodlands with soft-footed silent care. They stopped to listen to a bird's song; they pressed forward again eagerly, parting the branches—speaking to each other rarely and in whispers; the young man going first and Sylvia following, fascinated, a few steps behind, with her gray eyes dark with excitement.

She grieved because the longed-for white heron was elusive, but she did not lead the guest, she only followed, and there was no such thing as speaking first. The sound of her own unquestioned voice would have terrified her—it was hard enough to answer yes or no when there was need of that. At last evening began to fall, and they drove the cow home together, and Sylvia smiled with pleasure when they came to the place where she heard the whistle and was afraid only the night before.

II

Half a mile from home, at the farther edge of the woods, where the land was highest, a great pine-tree stood, the last of its generation. Whether it was left for a boundary mark, or for what reason, no one could say; the woodchoppers who had felled its mates were dead and gone long ago, and a whole forest of sturdy trees, pines and oaks and maples, had grown again. But the stately head of this old pine towered above them all and made a landmark for sea and shore miles and miles away. Sylvia knew it well. She had always believed that whoever climbed to the top of it could see the ocean; and the little girl had often laid her hand on the great rough trunk and looked up wistfully at those dark boughs that the wind always stirred, no matter how hot and still the air might be below. Now she thought of the tree with a new excitement, for why, if one climbed it at break of day, could not one see all the world, and easily discover from whence the white heron flew, and mark the place, and find the hidden nest?

What a spirit of adventure, what wild ambition! What fancied triumph and delight and glory for the later morning when she could make known the secret! It was almost too real and too great for the childish heart to bear.

All night the door of the little house stood open and the whippoorwills came and sang upon the very step. The young sportsman and his old hostess were sound asleep, but Sylvia's great design kept her broad awake and watching. She forgot to think of sleep. The short summer night seemed as long as the winter darkness, and at last when the whippoorwills ceased, and she was afraid the morning would after all come too soon, she stole out of the house and followed the pasture path through the woods, hastening toward the open ground beyond, listening with a sense of comfort and companionship to the drowsy twitter of a half-awakened bird, whose perch she had jarred in passing. Alas, if the great wave of human interest which flooded for the first time this dull little life should sweep away the satisfactions of an existence heart to heart with nature and the dumb life of the forest!

There was the huge tree asleep yet in the paling moonlight, and small and silly Sylvia began with utmost bravery to mount to the top of it, with tingling, eager blood coursing the channels of her whole frame, with her bare feet and fingers, that pinched and held like bird's claws to the monstrous ladder reaching up, up, almost to the sky itself. First she must mount the white oak tree that grew alongside, where she was almost lost among the dark branches and the green leaves heavy and wet with dew; a bird fluttered off its nest, and a red squirrel ran to and fro and scolded pettishly at the harmless housebreaker. Sylvia felt her way easily. She had often climbed there, and knew that higher still one of the oak's upper branches chafed against the pine trunk, just where its lower boughs were set close together. There, when she made the dangerous pass from one tree to the other, the great enterprise would really begin.

She crept out along the swaying oak limb at last, and took the daring step across into the old pine-tree. The way was harder than she thought; she must reach far and hold fast, the sharp dry twigs caught and held her and scratched her like angry talons, the pitch made her thin little fingers clumsy and stiff as she went round and round the tree's great stem, higher and higher upward. The sparrows and robins in the woods below were beginning to wake and twitter to the dawn, yet it seemed much lighter there aloft in the pine-tree, and the child knew she must hurry if her project were to be of any use.

The tree seemed to lengthen itself out as she went up, and to reach farther and farther upward. It was like a great main-mast to the voyaging earth; it must truly have been amazed that morning through all its ponderous frame as it felt this determined spark of human spirit wending its way from higher branch to branch. Who knows how steadily the least twigs held themselves to advantage this light, weak creature on her way! The old pine must have loved his new dependent. More than all the hawks, and bats, and moths, and even the sweet voiced thrushes, was the brave, beating heart of the solitary gray-eyed child. And the tree stood still and frowned away the winds that June morning while the dawn grew bright in the east.

Sylvia's face was like a pale star, if one had seen it from the ground, when the last thorny bough was past, and she stood trembling and tired but wholly triumphant, high in the tree-top. Yes, there was the sea with the dawning sun making a golden dazzle over it, and toward that glorious east flew two hawks with slow-moving pinions. How low they looked in the air from that height when one had only seen them before far up, and dark against the blue sky. Their gray feathers were as soft as moths; they seemed only a little way from the tree, and Sylvia felt as if she too could go flying away among the clouds. Westward, the woodlands and farms reached miles and miles into the distance; here and there were church steeples, and white villages, truly it was a vast and awesome world

The birds sang louder and louder. At last the sun came up bewilderingly bright. Sylvia could see the white sails of ships out at sea, and the clouds that were purple and rose-colored and yellow at first began to fade away. Where was the white heron's nest in the sea of green branches, and was this wonderful sight and pageant of the world the only reward for having climbed to such a giddy height? Now look down again, Sylvia, where the green marsh is set among the shining birches and dark hemlocks; there where you saw the white heron once you will see him again; look, look! a white spot of him like a single floating feather comes up from the dead hemlock and grows larger, and rises, and comes close at last, and goes by the landmark pine with steady sweep of wing and outstretched slender neck and crested head. And wait! wait! do not move a foot or a finger, little girl, do not send an arrow of light and consciousness from your two eager eyes, for the heron has perched on a pine bough not far beyond yours, and cries back to his mate on the nest and plumes his feathers for the new day!

The child gives a long sigh a minute later when a company of shouting cat-birds comes also to the tree, and vexed by their fluttering and lawlessness the solemn heron goes away. She knows his secret now, the wild, light, slender bird that floats and wavers, and goes back like an arrow presently to his home in the green world beneath. Then Sylvia, well satisfied, makes her perilous way down again, not daring to look far below the branch she stands on, ready to cry sometimes because her fingers ache and her lamed feet slip. Wondering over and over again what the stranger would say to her, and what he would think when she told him how to find his way straight to the heron's nest.

"Sylvy, Sylvy!" called the busy old grandmother again and again, but nobody answered, and the small husk bed was empty and Sylvia had disappeared.

The guest waked from a dream, and remembering his day's pleasure hurried to dress himself that it might sooner begin. He was sure from the way the shy little girl looked once or twice yesterday that she had at least seen the white heron, and now she must really be made to tell. Here she comes now, paler than ever, and her worn old frock is torn and tattered, and smeared with pine pitch. The grandmother and the sportsman stand in the door together and question her, and the splendid moment has come to speak of the dead hemlock-tree by the green marsh.

But Sylvia does not speak after all, though the old grandmother fretfully rebukes her, and the young man's kind, appealing eyes are looking straight in her own. He can make them rich with money; he has promised it, and they are poor now. He is so well worth making happy, and he waits to hear the story she can tell.

No, she must keep silence! What is it that suddenly forbids her and makes her dumb? Has she been nine years growing and now, when the great world for the first time puts out a hand to her, must she thrust it aside for a bird's sake? The murmur of the pine's green branches is in her ears, she remembers how the white heron came flying through the golden air and how they watched the sea and the morning together, and Sylvia cannot speak; she cannot tell the heron's secret and give its life away.

Dear loyalty, that suffered a sharp pang as the guest went away disappointed later in the day, that could have served and followed him and loved him as a dog loves! Many a night Sylvia heard the echo of his whistle haunting the pasture path as she came home with the loitering cow. She forgot even her sorrow at the sharp report of his gun and the sight of thrushes and sparrows dropping silent to the ground, their songs hushed and their pretty feathers stained and wet with blood. Were the birds better friends than their hunter might have been,—who can tell? Whatever treasures were lost to her, woodlands and summer-time, remember! Bring your gifts and graces and tell your secrets to this lonely country child!

2.7.2 Reading and Review Questions

1. What overlapping features of Local Color, Regionalism, and Realism can been seen in *A White Heron*?

2. What is the symbolic value in various elements of nature in the story, for example, of the tree, the cow, the heron, the sea, or even Sylvy (whose name means "the forest" or "woods")?

3. How does the story convey a feminist or proto-feminist theme?

4. Is Sylvy saving only the heron when she keeps the heron's location secret? Explain.

5. Even though Sylvy is only nine years old, how does Jewett explore the concept of heterosexual love in the story? How is the possibility of future love between Sylvy and the ornithologist portrayed?

6. What contrasts between the country and city are examined in terms of Sylvy's characterization?

2.8 KATE CHOPIN

(1850 - 1904)

Image 2.6 | Kate Chopin, 1894
Photographer | Unknown
Source | Wikimedia Commons
License | Public Domain

Katherine O'Flaherty Chopin was born in 1850 in St. Louis, Missouri, to an affluent family. She was formally educated in a Catholic school for girls. At age twenty, she married Oscar Chopin and moved with him to New Orleans. The couple eventually relocated to Cloutierville in 1879, an area where many members of the Creole community lived. The Chopins lived, worked, and raised their six children together until Oscar died unexpectedly in 1882, leaving his wife in serious debt. Chopin worked and sold the family business to pay off the debt, eventually moving back to St. Louis to be near her mother, who died soon after Chopin returned. After experiencing these losses, Chopin turned to reading and writing to deal with her grief. Her experiences in New Orleans and Cloutierville provided rich writing material, and during the 1890s, she enjoyed success as a writer, publishing a number of stories in the Local Color tradition. By 1899, her style had evolved, and her important work *The Awakening,* published that year, shocked the Victorian audience of the time in its frank depiction of a woman's sexuality. Unprepared for the negative critical reception that ensued, Chopin retreated from the publishing world. She died unexpectedly a few years later in 1904, from a brain hemorrhage.

In her lifetime, Chopin was known primarily as a Local Color writer who produced a number of important short stories, many of which were collected in *Bayou Folk* in 1894. Her ground-breaking novel *The Awakening* published in 1899 was ahead of its time in the examination of the rigid cultural and legal boundaries placed on women which limited or prevented them from living authentic, fully self-directed lives. The novel offers a sensuous portrait of a young married woman and mother, Edna Pontellier, who awakens to herself as a dimensional human being with sexual longings and a strong will to live an authentic life, not the repressed half-life she is assigned by tradition and culture, through the institutions of marriage and motherhood, to "perform."

Though today it is viewed as an important early feminist work, the novel shocked and offended the turn of the century reading audience. It was all but forgotten until interest in the novel and in Chopin's work in general was revived in the 1960s. During this revival, an unpublished short story was discovered, "The Storm," written in 1898 but not published until 1969. The story, which offers an erotic depiction of sex between a man and a woman who are not married to each other, would have been unpublishable by most, if not all, major literary magazines in late nineteenth-century America. The story's title indicates that it was intended as a sequel to "At the 'Cadian Ball," first published in 1892 and reprinted in *Bayou Folk*. Read together, the linked stories concern two couples, one from the upper class Creoles (Alcée and Clarisse), and the other from the less prominent Acadians or Cajuns (Calixta and Bobinôt). What begins as a strong flirtation in the first story between Calixta and Alcée, both single at the time and from different social classes, culminates in torrid lovemaking years later in the second story, years after Calixta had married Bobinôt and Alcée had married Clarisse. Beyond the candid, natural depiction of sexual intimacy between the lovers during a stormy afternoon, including the scenes of a woman clearly enjoying an afternoon of passion, the story offers a non-judgmental ending: no one appears to be hurt by the affair; in fact, after the storm passes, Alcée and Calixta go their separate ways, and everyone, the reader is told, is quite happy.

2.8.1 "At The 'Cadian Ball"

Bobinôt, that big, brown, good-natured Bobinôt, had no intention of going to the ball, even though he knew Calixta would be there. For what came of those balls but heartache, and a sickening disinclination for work the whole week through, till Saturday night came again and his tortures began afresh? Why could he not love Ozéina, who would marry him to-morrow; or Fronie, or any one of a dozen others, rather than that little Spanish vixen? Calixta's slender foot had never touched Cuban soil; but her mother's had, and the Spanish was in her blood all the same. For that reason the prairie people forgave her much that they would not have overlooked in their own daughters or sisters.

Her eyes, Bobinôt thought of her eyes, and weakened, the bluest, the drowsiest, most tantalizing that ever looked into a man's, he thought of her flaxen hair that kinked worse than a mulatto's close to her head; that broad, smiling mouth and tip-tilted nose, that full figure; that voice like a rich contralto song, with cadences in it that must have been taught by Satan, for there was no one else to teach her tricks on that 'Cadian prairie. Bobinôt thought of them all as he plowed his rows of cane.

There had even been a breath of scandal whispered about her a year ago, when she went to Assumption, but why talk of it? No one did now. "C'est Espagnol, ça," most of them said with lenient shoulder-shrugs. "Bon chien tient de race," the old men mumbled over their pipes, stirred by recollections. Nothing was made of it, except that Fronie threw it up to Calixta when the two quarreled and fought on the church steps after mass one Sunday, about a lover. Calixta swore roundly in fine 'Cadian French and with true Spanish spirit, and slapped Fronie's face. Fronie had slapped her back; "Tiens, bocotte, va!" "Espèce de lionèse; prends ça, et ça!" till the curé himself was obliged to hasten and make peace between them. Bobinôt thought of it all, and would not go to the ball.

But in the afternoon, over at Friedheimer's store, where he was buying a trace-chain, he heard some one say that Alcée Laballèire would be there. Then wild horses could not have kept him away. He knew how it would be or rather he did not know how it would be if the handsome young planter came over to the ball as he sometimes did. If Alcée happened to be in a serious mood, he might only go to the card-room and play a round or two; or he might stand out on the galleries talking crops and politics with the old people. But there was no telling. A drink or two could put the devil in his head,—that was what Bobinôt said to himself, as he wiped the sweat from his brow with his red bandanna; a gleam from Calixta's eyes, a flash of her ankle, a twirl of her skirts could do the same. Yes, Bobinôt would go to the ball.

***

That was the year Alcée Laballière put nine hundred acres in rice. It was putting a good deal of money into the ground, but the returns promised to be glorious. Old Madame Laballière, sailing about the spacious galleries in her white *volante*, figured it all out in her head. Clarisse, her goddaughter helped her a little, and together they built more air-castles than enough. Alcée worked like a mule that time; and if he did not kill himself, it was because his constitution was an iron one. It was an every-day affair for him to come in from the field well-nigh exhausted, and wet to the waist. He did not mind if there were visitors; he left them to his mother and Clarisse. There were often guests: young men and women who came up from the city, which was but a few hours away, to visit his beautiful kinswoman. She was worth going a good deal farther than that to see. Dainty as a lily; hardy as a sunflower; slim, tall, graceful, like one of the reeds that grew in the marsh. Cold and kind and cruel by turn, and everything that was aggravating to Alcée.

He would have liked to sweep the place of those visitors, often. Of the men, above all, with their ways and their manners; their swaying of fans like women, and dandling about hammocks. He could have pitched them over the levee into the river, if it hadn't meant murder. That was Alcée. But he must have been crazy the day he came in from the rice-field, and, toil-stained as he was, clasped Clarisse by the arms and panted a volley of hot, blistering love-words into her face. No man had ever spoken love to her like that.

"Monsieur!" she exclaimed, looking him full in the eyes, without a quiver. Alcée's hands dropped and his glance wavered before the chill of her calm, clear eyes.

"*Par exemple!*" she muttered disdainfully, as she turned from him, deftly adjusting the careful toilet that he had so brutally disarranged.

That happened a day or two before the cyclone came that cut into the rice like fine steel. It was an awful thing, coming so swiftly, without a moment's warning in which to light a holy candle or set a piece of blessed palm burning. Old madame wept openly and said her beads, just as her son Didier, the New Orleans one, would have done. If such a thing had happened to Alphonse, the Laballière planting cotton up in Natchitoches, he would have raved and stormed like a second cyclone, and made his surroundings unbearable for a day or two. But Alcée took the misfortune differently. He looked ill and gray after it, and said nothing. His speechlessness was frightful. Clarisse's heart melted with tenderness; but when she offered her soft, purring words of condolence, he accepted them with mute indifference. Then she and her nénaine wept afresh in each other's arms.

A night or two later, when Clarisse went to her window to kneel there in the moonlight and say her prayers before retiring, she saw that Bruce, Alcée's negro servant, had led his master's saddle-horse noiselessly along the edge of the sward that bordered the gravel-path, and stood holding him near by. Presently, she heard Alcée quit his room, which was beneath her own, and traverse the lower portico. As he emerged from the shadow and crossed the strip of moonlight, she perceived that he carried a pair of well-filled saddle-bags which he at once flung across the animal's back. He then lost no time in mounting, and after a brief exchange of words with Bruce, went cantering away, taking no precaution to avoid the noisy gravel as the negro had done.

Clarisse had never suspected that it might be Alcée's custom to sally forth from the plantation secretly, and at such an hour; for it was nearly midnight. And had it not been for the telltale saddle-bags, she would only have crept to bed, to wonder, to fret and dream unpleasant dreams. But her impatience and anxiety would not be held in check. Hastily unbolting the shutters of her door that opened upon the gallery, she stepped outside and called softly to the old negro.

"Gre't Peter! Miss Clarisse. I was n' sho it was a ghos' o' w'at, stan'in' up dah, plumb in de night, dataway."

He mounted halfway up the long, broad flight of stairs. She was standing at the top.

"Bruce, w'ere has Monsieur Alcée gone?" she asked.

"W'y, he gone 'bout he business, I reckin," replied Bruce, striving to be non-committal at the outset.

"W'ere has Monsieur Alcée gone?" she reiterated, stamping her bare foot. "I won't stan' any nonsense or any lies; mine, Bruce."

"I don' ric'lic ez I eva tole you lie yit, Miss Clarisse. Mista Alcée, he all broke up, sho."

"W'ere - has - he gone? Ah, Sainte Vierge! faut de la patience! butor, va!"

"W'en I was in he room, a-breshin' off he clo'es to-day," the darkey began, set-tling himself against the stair-rail, "he look dat speechless an' down, I say, 'You 'pear tu me like some pussun w'at gwine have a spell o' sickness, Mista Alcée.' He say, 'You reckin?' 'I dat he git up, go look hisse'f stiddy in de glass. Den he go to de chimbly an' jerk up de quinine bottle an po' a gre't hoss-dose on to he han'. An' he swalla dat mess in a wink, an' wash hit down wid a big dram o' w'iskey w'at he keep in he room, aginst he come all soppin' wet outen de fiel'.

"He 'lows, 'No, I ain' gwine be sick, Bruce.' Den he square off. He say, 'I kin mak out to stan' up an' gi' an' take wid any man I knows, lessen hit 's John L. Sulvun. But w'en God A'mighty an' a 'omen jines fo'ces agin me, dat 's one too many fur me.' I tell 'im, 'Jis so,' while' I 'se makin' out to bresh a spot off w'at ain' dah, on he coat colla. I tell 'im, 'You wants li'le res', suh.' He say, 'No, I wants li'le fling; dat w'at I wants; an I gwine git it. Pitch me a fis'ful o' clo'es in dem 'ar saddle-bags.' Dat w'at he say. Don't you bodda, missy. He jis' gone a-caperin' yonda to de Cajun ball. Uh - uh - de skeeters is fair' a-swarmin' like bees roun' yo' foots!"

The mosquitoes were indeed attacking Clarisse's white feet savagely. She had unconsciously been alternately rubbing one foot over the other during the darkey's recital.

"The 'Cadian ball," she repeated contemptuously. "Humph! *Par exemple*! Nice conduc' for a Laballière. An' he needs a saddle-bag, fill' with clothes, to go to the 'Cadian ball!"

"Oh, Miss Clarisse; you go on to bed, chile; git yo' soun' sleep. He 'low he come back in couple weeks o' so. I kiarn be repeatin' lot o' truck w'at young mans say, out heah face o' a young gal."

Clarisse said no more, but turned and abruptly reentered the house.

"You done talk too much wid yo' mouf already, you ole fool nigga, you," muttered Bruce to himself as he walked away.

***

Alcée reached the ball very late, of course—too late for the chicken gumbo which had been served at midnight.

The big, low-ceiled room—they called it a hall—was packed with men and women dancing to the music of three fiddles. There were broad galleries all around it. There was a room at one side where sober-faced men were playing cards. Another, in which babies were sleeping, was called *le parc aux petits*. Any one who is white may go to a 'Cadian ball, but he must pay for his lemonade, his coffee and chicken gumbo. And he must behave himself like a 'Cadian. Grosboeuf was giving this ball. He had been giving them since he was a young man, and he was a middle-aged one, now. In that time he could recall but one disturbance, and that was caused by American railroaders, who were not in touch with their surroundings and had no business there. "Ces maudits gens du raiderode," Grosboeuf called them.

Alcée Laballière's presence at the ball caused a flutter even among the men, who could not but admire his "nerve" after such misfortune befalling him. To be sure, they knew the Laballières were rich—that there were resources East, and more again in the city. But they felt it took a *brave homme* to stand a blow like that philosophically. One old gentleman, who was in the habit of reading a Paris newspaper and knew things, chuckled gleefully to everybody that Alcée's conduct was altogether *chic, mais chic*. That he had more panache than Boulanger. Well, perhaps he had.

But what he did not show outwardly was that he was in a mood for ugly things to-night. Poor Bobinôt alone felt it vaguely. He discerned a gleam of it in Alcée's handsome eyes, as the young planter stood in the doorway, looking with rather feverish glance upon the assembly, while he laughed and talked with a 'Cadian farmer who was beside him.

Bobinôt himself was dull-looking and clumsy. Most of the men were. But the young women were very beautiful. The eyes that glanced into Alcée's as they passed him were big, dark, soft as those of the young heifers standing out in the cool prairie grass.

But the belle was Calixta. Her white dress was not nearly so handsome or well made as Fronie's (she and Fronie had quite forgotten the battle on the church steps, and were friends again), nor were her slippers so stylish as those of Ozéina; and she fanned herself with a handkerchief, since she had broken her red fan at the last ball, and her aunts and uncles were not willing to give her another. But all the men agreed she was at her best to-night. Such animation! and abandon! such flashes of wit!

"Hé, Bobinôt! *Mais* w'at's the matta? W'at you standin' *planté là* like ole Ma'ame Tina's cow in the bog, you?"

That was good. That was an excellent thrust at Bobinôt, who had forgotten the figure of the dance with his mind bent on other things, and it started a clamor of laughter at his expense. He joined good-naturedly. It was better to receive even such notice as that from Calixta than none at all. But Madame Suzonne, sitting in a corner, whispered to her neighbor that if Ozéina were to conduct herself in a like manner, she should immediately be taken out to the mule-cart and driven home. The women did not always approve of Calixta.

Now and then were short lulls in the dance, when couples flocked out upon the galleries for a brief respite and fresh air. The moon had gone down pale in the west, and in the east was yet no promise of day. After such an interval, when the dancers again assembled to resume the interrupted quadrille, Calixta was not among them.

She was sitting upon a bench out in the shadow, with Alcée beside her. They were acting like fools. He had attempted to take a little gold ring from her finger; just for the fun of it, for there was nothing he could have done with the ring but replace it again. But she clinched her hand tight. He pretended that it was a very difficult matter to open it. Then he kept the hand in his. They seemed to forget about it. He played with her ear-ring, a thin crescent of gold hanging from her small brown ear. He caught a wisp of the kinky hair that had escaped its fastening, and rubbed the ends of it against his shaven cheek.

"You know, last year in Assumption, Calixta?" They belonged to the younger generation, so preferred to speak English.

"Don't come say Assumption to me, M'sieur Alcée. I done yeard Assumption till I 'm plumb sick."

"Yes, I know. The idiots! Because you were in Assumption, and I happened to go to Assumption, they must have it that we went together. But it was nice hein, Calixta?—in Assumption?"

They saw Bobinôt emerge from the hall and stand a moment outside the lighted doorway, peering uneasily and searchingly into the darkness. He did not see them, and went slowly back.

"There is Bobinôt looking for you. You are going to set poor Bobinôt crazy. You'll marry him some day; hein, Calixta?"

"I don't say no, me," she replied, striving to withdraw her hand, which he held more firmly for the attempt.

"But come, Calixta; you know you said you would go back to Assumption, just to spite them."

"No, I neva said that, me. You mus' dreamt that."

"Oh, I thought you did. You know I 'm going down to the city."

"W'en?"

"To-night."

"Betta make has'e, then; it 's mos' day."

"Well, to-morrow 'll do."

"W'at you goin' do, yonda?"

"I don't know. Drown myself in the lake, maybe; unless you go down there to visit your uncle."

Calixta's senses were reeling; and they well-nigh left her when she felt Alcée's lips brush her ear like the touch of a rose.

"Mista Alcée! Is dat Mista Alcée?" the thick voice of a negro was asking; he stood on the ground, holding to the banister-rails near which the couple sat.

"W'at do you want now?" cried Alcée impatiently. "Can't I have a moment of peace?"

"I ben huntin' you high an' low, suh," answered the man. "Dey - dey some one in de road, onda de mulbare-tree, want see you a minute."

"I would n't go out to the road to see the Angel Gabriel. And if you come back here with any more talk, I 'll have to break your neck." The negro turned mumbling away.

Alcée and Calixta laughed softly about it. Her boisterousness was all gone. They talked low, and laughed softly, as lovers do.

"Alcée! Alcée Laballière!"

It was not the negro's voice this time; but one that went through Alcée's body like an electric shock, bringing him to his feet.

Clarisse was standing there in her riding-habit, where the negro had stood. For an instant confusion reigned in Alcée's thoughts, as with one who awakes suddenly from a dream. But he felt that something of serious import had brought his cousin to the ball in the dead of night.

"W'at does this mean, Clarisse?" he asked.

"It means something has happen' at home. You mus' come."

"Happened to maman?" he questioned, in alarm.

"No; nénaine is well, and asleep. It is something else. Not to frighten you. But you mus' come. Come with me, Alcée."

There was no need for the imploring note. He would have followed the voice anywhere.

She had now recognized the girl sitting back on the bench.

"Ah, c'est vous, Calixta? Comment ça va, mon enfant?"

"Tcha va b'en; et vous, mam'zélle?"

Alcée swung himself over the low rail and started to follow Clarisse, without a word, without a glance back at the girl. He had forgotten he was leaving her there. But Clarisse whispered something to him, and he turned back to say "Good-night, Calixta," and offer his hand to press through the railing. She pretended not to see it.

***

"How come that? You settin' yere by yo'se'f, Calixta?" It was Bobinôt who had found her there alone. The dancers had not yet come out. She looked ghastly in the faint, gray light struggling out of the east.

"Yes, that 's me. Go yonda in *the parc aux petits* an' ask Aunt Olisse fu' my hat. She knows w'ere 't is. I want to go home, me."

"How you came?"

"I come afoot, with the Cateaus. But I 'm goin' now. I ent goin' wait fu' 'em. I 'm plumb wo' out, me."

"Kin I go with you, Calixta?"

"I don' care."

They went together across the open prairie and along the edge of the fields, stumbling in the uncertain light. He told her to lift her dress that was getting wet and bedraggled; for she was pulling at the weeds and grasses with her hands.

"I don' care; it 's got to go in the tub, anyway. You been sayin' all along you want to marry me, Bobinôt. Well, if you want, yet, I don' care, me."

The glow of a sudden and overwhelming happiness shone out in the brown, rugged face of the young Acadian. He could not speak, for very joy. It choked him.

"Oh well, if you don' want," snapped Calixta, flippantly, pretending to be piqued at his silence.

"*Bon Dieu*! You know that makes me crazy, w'at you sayin'. You mean that, Calixta? You ent goin' turn roun' agin?"

"I neva tole you that much yet, Bobinôt. I mean that. *Tiens*," and she held out her hand in the business-like manner of a man who clinches a bargain with a hand-clasp. Bobinôt grew bold with happiness and asked Calixta to kiss him. She turned her face, that was almost ugly after the night's dissipation, and looked steadily into his.

"I don' want to kiss you, Bobinôt," she said, turning away again, "not to-day. Some other time. *Bonté divine*! ent you satisfy, yet!"

"Oh, I 'm satisfy, Calixta," he said.

***

Riding through a patch of wood, Clarisse's saddle became ungirted, and she and Alcée dismounted to readjust it.

For the twentieth time he asked her what had happened at home.

"But, Clarisse, w'at is it? Is it a misfortune?"

"Ah Dieu sait! It 's only something that happen' to me."

"To you!"

"I saw you go away las night, Alcée, with those saddle-bags," she said, halting-ly, striving to arrange something about the saddle, "an' I made Bruce tell me. He said you had gone to the ball, an' wouldn' be home for weeks an' weeks. I thought, Alcée—maybe you were going to—to Assumption. I got wild. An' then I knew if you didn't come back, now, to-night, I could n't stan' it,again."

She had her face hidden in her arm that she was resting against the saddle when she said that.

He began to wonder if this meant love. But she had to tell him so, before he believed it. And when she told him, he thought the face of the Universe was changed—just like Bobinôt. Was it last week the cyclone had well-nigh ruined him? The cyclone seemed a huge joke, now. It was he, then, who, an hour ago was kissing little Calixta's ear and whispering nonsense into it. Calixta was like a myth, now. The one, only, great reality in the world was Clarisse standing before him, telling him that she loved him.

In the distance they heard the rapid discharge of pistol-shots; but it did not dis-turb them. They knew it was only the negro musicians who had gone into the yard to fire their pistols into the air, as the custom is, and to announce "*le bal est fini.*"

2.8.2 "The Storm"

I

The leaves were so still that even Bibi thought it was going to rain. Bobinôt, who was accustomed to converse on terms of perfect equality with his little son, called the child's attention to certain sombre clouds that were rolling with sinister intention from the west, accompanied by a sullen, threatening roar. They were at Friedheimer's store and decided to remain there till the storm had passed. They sat within the door on two empty kegs. Bibi was four years old and looked very wise.

"Mama'll be 'fraid, yes, he suggested with blinking eyes.

"She'll shut the house. Maybe she got Sylvie helpin' her this evenin'," Bobinôt responded reassuringly.

"No; she ent got Sylvie. Sylvie was helpin' her yistiday,' piped Bibi.

Bobinôt arose and going across to the counter purchased a can of shrimps, of which Calixta was very fond. Then he returned to his perch on the keg and sat stol-idly holding the can of shrimps while the storm burst. It shook the wooden store and seemed to be ripping great furrows in the distant field. Bibi laid his little hand on his father's knee and was not afraid.

II

Calixta, at home, felt no uneasiness for their safety. She sat at a side window sewing furiously on a sewing machine. She was greatly occupied and did not notice the approaching storm. But she felt very warm and often stopped to mop her face on which the perspiration gathered in beads. She unfastened her white sacque at the throat. It began to grow dark, and suddenly realizing the situation she got up hurriedly and went about closing windows and doors.

Out on the small front gallery she had hung Bobinôt's Sunday clothes to dry and she hastened out to gather them before the rain fell. As she stepped outside, Alcée Laballière rode in at the gate. She had not seen him very often since her marriage, and never alone. She stood there with Bobinôt's coat in her hands, and the big rain drops began to fall. Alcée rode his horse under the shelter of a side projection where the chickens had huddled and there were plows and a harrow piled up in the corner.

"May I come and wait on your gallery till the storm is over, Calixta?" he asked.

Come 'long in, M'sieur Alcée."

His voice and her own startled her as if from a trance, and she seized Bobinôt's vest. Alcée, mounting to the porch, grabbed the trousers and snatched Bibi's braided jacket that was about to be carried away by a sudden gust of wind. He expressed an intention to remain outside, but it was soon apparent that he might as well have been out in the open: the water beat in upon the boards in driving sheets, and he went inside, closing the door after him. It was even necessary to put something beneath the door to keep the water out.

"My! what a rain! It's good two years sence it rain' like that," exclaimed Calixta as she rolled up a piece of bagging and Alcée helped her to thrust it beneath the crack.

She was a little fuller of figure than five years before when she married; but she had lost nothing of her vivacity. Her blue eyes still retained their melting quality; and her yellow hair, dishevelled by the wind and rain, kinked more stubbornly than ever about her ears and temples.

The rain beat upon the low, shingled roof with a force and clatter that threatened to break an entrance and deluge them there. They were in the dining room the sitting room the general utility room. Adjoining was her bed room, with Bibi's couch along side her own. The door stood open, and the room with its white, monumental bed, its closed shutters, looked dim and mysterious.

Alcée flung himself into a rocker and Calixta nervously began to gather up from the floor the lengths of a cotton sheet which she had been sewing.

If this keeps up, Dieu sait if the levees goin' to stan it!" she exclaimed.

"What have you got to do with the levees?"

"I got enough to do! An' there's Bobinôt with Bibi out in that storm if he only didn' left Friedheimer's!"

"Let us hope, Calixta, that Bobinôt's got sense enough to come in out of a cyclone."

She went and stood at the window with a greatly disturbed look on her face. She wiped the frame that was clouded with moisture. It was stiflingly hot. Alcée got up and joined her at the window, looking over her shoulder. The rain was coming down in sheets obscuring the view of far-off cabins and enveloping the distant wood in a gray mist. The playing of the lightning was incessant. A bolt struck a tall chinaberry tree at the edge of the field. It filled all visible space with a blinding glare and the crash seemed to invade the very boards they stood upon.

Calixta put her hands to her eyes, and with a cry, staggered backward. Alcée's arm encircled her, and for an instant he drew her close and spasmodically to him.

"Bonté!" she cried, releasing herself from his encircling arm and retreating from the window, "the house'll go next! If I only knew w'ere Bibi was!" She would not compose herself; she would not be seated. Alcée clasped her shoulders and looked into her face. The contact of her warm, palpitating body when he had unthinkingly drawn her into his arms, had aroused all the old-time infatuation and desire for her flesh.

"Calixta," he said, "don't be frightened. Nothing can happen. The house is too low to be struck, with so many tall trees standing about. There! aren't you going to be quiet? say, aren't you?" He pushed her hair back from her face that was warm and steaming. Her lips were as red and moist as pomegranate seed. Her white neck and a glimpse of her full, firm bosom disturbed him powerfully. As she glanced up at him the fear in her liquid blue eyes had given place to a drowsy gleam that unconsciously betrayed a sensuous desire. He looked down into her eyes and there was nothing for him to do but to gather her lips in a kiss. It reminded him of Assumption.

"Do you remember in Assumption, Calixta?" he asked in a low voice broken by passion. Oh! she remembered; for in Assumption he had kissed her and kissed and kissed her; until his senses would well nigh fail, and to save her he would resort to a desperate flight. If she was not an immaculate dove in those days, she was still inviolate; a passionate creature whose very defenselessness had made her defense, against which his honor forbade him to prevail. Now well, now her lips seemed in a manner free to be tasted, as well as her round, white throat and her whiter breasts.

They did not heed the crashing torrents, and the roar of the elements made her laugh as she lay in his arms. She was a revelation in that dim, mysterious chamber; as white as the couch she lay upon. Her firm, elastic flesh that was knowing for the first time its birthright, was like a creamy lily that the sun invites to contribute its breath and perfume to the undying life of the world.

The generous abundance of her passion, without guile or trickery, was like a white flame which penetrated and found response in depths of his own sensuous nature that had never yet been reached.

When he touched her breasts they gave themselves up in quivering ecstasy, inviting his lips. Her mouth was a fountain of delight. And when he possessed her, they seemed to swoon together at the very borderland of life's mystery.

He stayed cushioned upon her, breathless, dazed, enervated, with his heart beating like a hammer upon her. With one hand she clasped his head, her lips lightly touching his forehead. The other hand stroked with a soothing rhythm his muscular shoulders.

The growl of the thunder was distant and passing away. The rain beat softly upon the shingles, inviting them to drowsiness and sleep. But they dared not yield.

III

The rain was over; and the sun was turning the glistening green world into a palace of gems. Calixta, on the gallery, watched Alcée ride away. He turned and smiled at her with a beaming face; and she lifted her pretty chin in the air and laughed aloud.

Bobinôt and Bibi, trudging home, stopped without at the cistern to make themselves presentable.

"My! Bibi, w'at will yo' mama say! You ought to be ashame'. You oughta' put on those good pants. Look at 'em! An' that mud on yo' collar! How you got that mud on yo' collar, Bibi? I never saw such a boy!" Bibi was the picture of pathetic resignation. Bobinôt was the embodiment of serious solicitude as he strove to remove from his own person and his son's the signs of their tramp over heavy roads and through wet fields. He scraped the mud off Bibi's bare legs and feet with a stick and carefully removed all traces from his heavy brogans. Then, prepared for the worst the meeting with an over-scrupulous housewife, they entered cautiously at the back door.

Calixta was preparing supper. She had set the table and was dripping coffee at the hearth. She sprang up as they came in.

"Oh, Bobinôt! You back! My! But I was uneasy. W'ere you been during the rain? An' Bibi? he ain't wet? he ain't hurt?" She had clasped Bibi and was kissing him effusively. Bobinôt's explanations and apologies which he had been composing all along the way, died on his lips as Calixta felt him to see if he were dry, and seemed to express nothing but satisfaction at their safe return.

"I brought you some shrimps, Calixta," offered Bobinôt, hauling the can from his ample side pocket and laying it on the table.

"Shrimps! Oh, Bobinôt! you too good fo' anything!" and she gave him a smacking kiss on the cheek that resounded, "J'vous rponds, we'll have a feas' to-night! umph-umph!"

Bobinôt and Bibi began to relax and enjoy themselves, and when the three seated themselves at table they laughed much and so loud that anyone might have heard them as far away as Laballière's.

IV

Alcée Laballière wrote to his wife, Clarisse, that night. It was a loving letter, full of tender solicitude. He told her not to hurry back, but if she and the babies liked it at Biloxi, to stay a month longer. He was getting on nicely; and though he missed them, he was willing to bear the separation a while longer realizing that their health and pleasure were the first things to be considered.

V

As for Clarisse, she was charmed upon receiving her husband's letter. She and the babies were doing well. The society was agreeable; many of her old friends and acquaintances were at the bay. And the first free breath since her marriage seemed to restore the pleasant liberty of her maiden days. Devoted as she was to her husband, their intimate conjugal life was something which she was more than willing to forego for a while.

So the storm passed and every one was happy.

2.8.3 Reading and Review Questions

1. How do either (or both) stories represent elements of Realistic or Naturalistic fiction?

2. In "At the 'Cadian Ball," what is the relationship between social classes presented in the story (Creoles and Acadians)?

3. In "The Storm," what does the title suggest in terms of figurative meaning?

4. In "The Storm," is it reasonable to accept that at the end "everyone was happy"? Or are consequences possible—or inevitable—beyond the ending of the story?

5. What does a reading of the stories in sequence provide readers in terms of interpretation of "The Storm" that a reading of the second story alone might not?

6. Examine the role social class plays in both stories.

2.9 MARY E. WILKINS FREEMAN

(1852 - 1930)

Mary E. Wilkins Freeman was born in 1852 in Randolph, Massachusetts. After high school, Freeman attended Mount Holyoke Female Seminary and later completed her studies at West Brattleboro Seminary while she pursued writing as a career. By her mid-thirties, Freeman's parents had died, and she was alone with only a small inheritance. She lived with family friends and continued her writing, eventually supporting herself by publishing important works recognized and praised by William Dean Howells, Henry James, and other major writers of the day. While she wrote a number of novels, she is best known for her short stories, especially those that focused on the New England region. How-

Image 2.7 | Mary E. Wilkins Freeman, 1900
Photographer | Floride Green
Source | Wikimedia Commons
License | Public Domain

ever, Freeman expanded her scope and produced a variety of fictional genres, including mysteries and ghost stories. *A New England Nun and Other Stories* (1891) stands as her most critically acclaimed achievement, a collection of regional stories focusing primarily on women and New England life. At forty-nine, Freeman married a physician, Dr. Charles Freeman from New Jersey. However, the marriage was marred by her husband's alcoholism, and she eventually separated from him. He was ultimately committed to the New Jersey State Hospital for the mentally ill. She died in 1930 at the age of seventy-eight after suffering a heart attack.

While Freeman was a prolific writer, she is best remembered for two important collections of short stories, *A Humble Romance and Other Stories* (1887) and *A New England Nun and Other Stories* (1891). The stories in these collections concern rural New England life and focus, in particular, on the domestic concerns of women. Like Sarah Orne Jewett, Freeman has been labeled a local colorist. However, the fiction of Jewett and Freeman generally is considered more representative of American Literary Regionalism, especially since both authors develop in their work dimensional characters whose internal conflicts are explored. Freeman's focus in "A New England Nun" and "The Revolt of Mother" is on women's redefining their place in the domestic sphere. In "A New England Nun," Louisa rejects having her domestic world invaded or controlled by a male presence. She preserves dominion over her small home, gently suggesting to her betrothed Joe Daggett that they may not be a good match after all. Her choice is courageous—she forgoes the role of wife and mother that her culture pressures her to accept—and the peace, solitude, and self-determination that she claims in return are worth the price of her rebellion against cultural norms. In "The Revolt of Mother," Sarah Penn is a New England woman who has accepted the traditional role of wife and mother for herself; nevertheless, like Louisa, she revolts against established cultural expectations for women. Sarah refuses to accept her husband's dismissive attitude when she argues that the farming family needs a new house. Instead, she enacts a revolt where she, through action likened to a military general storming a fortress, makes the statement that her work on the family farm within the domestic sphere is just as important as her husband's work as a farmer. Freeman's fiction, as does Jewett's, often moves beyond simply regional concerns to explore wider issues of women's roles in late nineteenth-century America, thus approaching an early feminist realism.

2.9.1 "A New England Nun"

It was late in the afternoon, and the light was waning. There was a difference in the look of the tree shadows out in the yard. Somewhere in the distance cows were lowing, and a little bell was tinkling; now and then a farm-wagon tilted by, and the dust flew; some blue-shirted laborers with shovels over their shoulders plodded past; little swarms of flies were dancing up and down before the peoples' faces in the soft air. There seemed to be a gentle stir arising over everything, for the mere sake of subsidences very premonition of rest and hush and night.

This soft diurnal commotion was over Louisa Ellis also. She had been peacefully sewing at her sitting-room window all the afternoon. Now she quilted her needle carefully into her work, which she folded precisely, and laid in a basket with her thimble and thread and scissors. Louisa Ellis could not remember that ever in her life she had mislaid one of these little feminine appurtenances, which had become, from long use and constant association, a very part of her personality.

Louisa tied a green apron round her waist, and got out a flat straw hat with a green ribbon. Then she went into the garden with a little blue crockery bowl, to pick some currants for her tea. After the currants were picked she sat on the back door-step and stemmed them, collecting the stems carefully in her apron, and afterwards throwing them into the hen-coop. She looked sharply at the grass beside the step to see if any bad fallen there.

Louisa was slow and still in her movements; it took her a long time to prepare her tea; but when ready it was set forth with as much grace as if she bad been a veritable guest to her own self. The little square table stood exactly in the centre of the kitchen, and was covered with a starched linen cloth whose border pattern of flowers glistened. Louisa had a damask napkin on her tea-tray, where were arranged a cut—lass tumbler full of teaspoons, a silver cream-pitcher, a china sugar-bowl, and one pink china cup and saucer. Louisa used china every day-something which none of her neighbors did. They whispered about it among themselves. Their daily tables were laid with common crockery, their sets of best china stayed in the parlor closet, and Louisa Ellis was no richer nor better bred than they. Still she would use the china. She had for her supper a glass dish full of sugared currants, a plate of little cakes, and one of little white biscuits. Also a leaf or two of lettuce, which she cut up daintily. Louisa was very fond of lettuce, which she raised to perfection in her little garden. She ate quite heartily, though, in a delicate, pecking, way; it seemed almost surprising that any considerable bulk of the food should vanish.

After tea she filled a plate with nicely baked thin corn- cakes, and carried them out into the back-yard.

"Caesar!" she called. "Caesar! Caesar!"

There was a little rush, and the clank of a chain, and a large yellow-and-white dog appeared at the door of his tiny hut, which was half hidden among the tall grasses and flowers. Louisa patted him and gave him the corn-cakes. Then she returned to the house and washed the tea-things, polishing the china carefully. The twilight had deepened; the chorus of the frogs floated in at the open window wonderfully loud and shrill, and once in a while a long sharp drone from a tree-toad pierced it. Louisa took off her green gingham apron, disclosing a shorter one of pink and white print. She lighted her lamp, and sat down again with her sewing.

In about half an hour Joe Dagget came. She heard his heavy step on the walk, and rose and took off her pink-and- white apron. Under that was still another-white linen with a little cambric edging on the bottom; that was Louisa's company apron. She never wore it without her calico sewing apron over it unless she had a guest. She had barely folded the pink and white one with methodical haste and laid it in a table-drawer when the door opened and Joe Dagget entered.

He seemed to fill up the whole room. A little yellow canary that had been asleep in his green cage at the south window woke up and fluttered wildly, beating his little yellow wings against the wires. He always did so when Joe Dagget came into the room.

"Good-evening," said Louisa. She extended her hand with a kind of solemn cordiality.

"Good-evening, Louisa," returned the man, in a loud voice.

She placed a chair for him, and they sat facing each other, with the table between them. He sat bolt-upright, toeing out his heavy feet squarely, glancing with a good-humored uneasiness around the room. She sat gently erect, folding her slender hands in her white-linen lap.

"Been a pleasant day," remarked Dagget.

"Real pleasant," Louisa assented, softly.

"Have you been haying?" she asked, after a little while.

"Yes, I've been baying all day, down in the ten-acre lot. Pretty hot work."

"It must be."

"Yes, it's pretty hot work in the sun."

"Is your mother well to-day?"

"Yes, mother's pretty well."

"I suppose Lily Dyer's with her now?"

Dagget colored. "Yes, she's with her," he answered, slowly.

He was not very young, but there was a boyish look about his large face. Louisa was not quite as old as he, her face was fairer and smoother, but she gave people the impression of being older.

"I suppose she's a good deal of help to your mother," she said, further.

"I guess she is; I don't know how mother'd get along without her," said Dagget, with a sort of embarrassed warmth.

"She looks like a real capable girl. She's pretty-looking too," remarked Louisa.

"Yes, she is pretty fair looking."

Presently Dagget began fingering the books on the table. There was a square red autograph album, and a Young Lady's Gift-Book which had belonged to Louisa's mother. He took them up one after the other and opened them then laid them down again, the album on the Gift-Book.

Louisa kept eying them with mild uneasiness. Finally she rose and changed the position of the books, putting the album underneath. That was the way they had been arranged in the first place.

Dagget gave an awkward little laugh. " Now what difference did it make which book was on top?" said he.

Louisa looked at him with a deprecating smile. " I always keep them that way," murmured she.

"You do beat everything," said Dagget, trying to laugh again. His large face was flushed.

He remained about an hour longer, then rose to take leave. Going out, he stumbled over a rug, and trying to recover himself, hit Louisa's work-basket on the table, and knocked it on the floor.

He looked at Louisa, then at the rolling spools; he ducked himself awkwardly toward them, but she stopped him. " Never mind," said she   I'll pick them up after you're gone."

She spoke with a mild stiffness. Either she was a little disturbed, or his nervousness affected her, and made her seem constrained in her effort to reassure him.

When Joe Dagget was outside he drew in the sweet evening air with a sigh, and felt much as an innocent and perfectly well-intentioned bear might after his exit from a china shop.

Louisa, on her part, felt much as the kind-hearted, long- suffering owner of the china shop might have done after the exit of the bear.

She tied on the pink, then the green apron, picked up all the scattered treasures and replaced them in her work- basket, and straightened the rug. Then she set the lamp on the floor, and began sharply examining the carpet. She even rubbed her fingers over it, and looked at them.

"He's tracked in a good deal of dust," she murmured. "I thought he must have."

Louisa got a dust-pan and brush, and swept Joe Dagget's track carefully.

If he could have known it, it would have increased his perplexity and Uneasiness, although it would not have disturbed his loyalty in the least. He came twice a week to see Louisa Ellis, and every time, sitting there in her delicately sweet room, he felt as if surrounded by a hedge of lace. He was afraid to stir lest he should put a clumsy foot or hand through the fairy web, and he had always the consciousness that Louisa was watching fearfully lest he should.

Still the lace and Louisa commanded perforce his perfect respect and patience and loyalty. They were to be married in a month, after a singular courtship which had lasted for a matter of fifteen years. For fourteen out of the fifteen years the two had not once seen each other, and they bad seldom exchanged letters. Joe had been all those years in Australia, where he had gone to make his fortune, and where be had stayed until be made it. He would have stayed fifty years if it had taken so long, and come home feeble and tottering, or never come home at all, to marry Louisa.

But the fortune had been made in the fourteen years, and he had come home now to marry the woman who had been patiently and unquestioningly waiting for him all that time.

Shortly after they were engaged he had announced to Louisa his determination to strike out into new fields, and secure a competency before they should be married. She had listened and assented with the sweet serenity which never failed her, not even when her lover set forth on that long and uncertain journey. Joe, buoyed up as he was by his sturdy determination, broke down a little at the last, but Louisa kissed him with a mild blush, and said good-by.

"It won't be for long," poor Joe had said, huskily; but it was for fourteen years.

In that length of time much had happened. Louisa's mother and brother had died, and she was all alone in the world. But greatest happening of all-a subtle happening which both were too simple to understand-Louisa's feet had turned into a path, smooth maybe under a calm, serene sky, but so straight and unswerving that it could only meet a check at her grave, and so narrow that there was no room for any one at her side.

Louisa's first emotion when Joe Dagget came home (he had not apprised her of his coming) was consternation, although she would not admit it to herself, and he never dreamed of it. Fifteen years ago she had been in love with him-at least she considered herself to be. Just at that time, gently acquiescing with and falling into the natural drift of girlhood, she had seen marriage ahead as a reasonable feature and a probable desirability of life. She had listened with came docility to her mother's views upon the subject. Her mother was remarkable for her cool sense and sweet, even temperament. She talked wisely to her daughter when Joe Dagget presented himself, and Louisa accepted him with no hesitation. He was the first lover she had ever had.

She had been faithful to him all these years. She had never dreamed of the possibility of marrying any one else. Her life, especially for the last seven years, had been full of a pleasant peace, she had never felt discontented nor impatient over her lover's absence; still she had always looked forward to his return and their marriage as the inevitable conclusion of things. However she had fallen into a way of placing it so far in the future that it was almost equal to placing it over the boundaries of another life.

When Joe came she had been expecting him, and expecting to be married for fourteen years, but she was as much surprised and taken aback as if she had never thought of it.

Joe's consternation came later. He eyed Louisa with an instant confirmation of his old admiration. She had changed but little. She still kept her pretty manner and soft grace, and was, he considered, every whit as attractive as ever. As for himself, his stent was done; he had turned his face away from fortune-seeking, and the old winds of romance whistled as loud and sweet as ever through his ears. All the song which he had been wont to hear in them was Louisa; he had for a long time a loyal belief that he heard it still, but finally it seemed to him that although the winds sang always that one song, it had another name. But for Louisa the wind had never more than murmured; now it hid gone down, and everything was still. She listened for a little while with half-wistful attention then she turned quietly away and went to work on her wedding clothes.

Joe had made some extensive and quite magnificent alterations in his house. It was the old homestead; the newly-married couple would live there, for Joe could not desert his mother, who refused to leave her old home. So Louisa must leave hers. Every morning rising and going about among her neat maidenly possessions, she felt as one looking her last upon the faces of dear friends. It was true that in a measure she could take them with her, but, robbed of their old environments, they would appear in such new guises that they would almost cease to be themselves. Then there were some peculiar features of her happy solitary life which she would probably be obliged to relinquish altogether. Sterner tasks than these graceful but half-needless ones would probably devolve upon her. There would be a large house to care for; there would be company to entertain; there would be Joe's rigorous and feeble old mother to wait upon; and it would be contrary to all thrifty village traditions for her to keep more than one servant. Louisa had a little still, and she used to occupy herself pleasantly in summer weather with distilling the sweet and aromatic essences from roses and peppermint and spear- mint. By-and-by her still must be laid away. Her store of essences was already considerable, and there would be no time for her to distil for the mere pleasure of it. Then Joe's mother would think it foolishness; she had already hinted her opinion in the matter. Louisa dearly loved to sew a linen scam, not always for use, but for the simple, mild pleasure which she took in it. She would have been loath to confess how more than once she had ripped a seam for the mere delight of sewing it together again. Sitting at her window during long sweet afternoons, drawing her needle gently through the dainty fabric, she was peace itself. But there was small chance of such foolish comfort in the future. Joe's mother, domineering, shrewd old matron that she was even in her old age, and very likely even Joe himself, with his honest masculine rudeness, would laugh and frown down all these pretty but senseless old maiden ways.

Louisa had almost the enthusiasm of an artist over the mere order and cleanliness of her solitary home. She had throbs of genuine triumph at the sight of the windowpanes which she had polished until they shone like jewels. She gloated gently over her orderly bureau-drawers, with their exquisitely folded contents redolent with lavender and sweet clover and very purity. Could she be sure of the endurance of even this? She had visions, so startling that she half repudiated them as indelicate, of coarse masculine belongings strewn about in endless litter; of dust and disorder arising necessarily from a coarse masculine presence in the midst of all this delicate harmony. Among her forebodings of disturbance, not the least was with regard to Caesar. Caesar was a veritable hermit of a dog. For the greater part of his life he had dwelt in his secluded hut, shut out from the society of his kind and all innocent canine joys. Never had Caesar since his early youth watched at a woodchuck's hole; never had he known the delights of a stray bone at a neighbor's kitchen door. And it was all on account of a sin committed when hardly out of his puppyhood. No one knew the possible depth of remorse of which this mild-visaged, altogether innocent-looking old dog might be capable - but whether or not he had encountered remorse, he had encountered a full measure of righteous retribution. Old Caesar seldom lifted up his voice in a growl or a bark; he was fat and sleepy; there were yellow rings which looked like spectacles around his dim old eyes; but there was a neighbor who bore on his hand the imprint of several of Caesar's sharp white youthful teeth, and for that be had lived at the end of a chain, all alone in a little but, for fourteen years. The neighbor, who was choleric and smarting with the pain of his wound, had demanded either Caesar's death or complete ostracism. So Louisa's brother, to whom the dog had belonged, had built him his little kennel and tied him up. It was now fourteen years since, in a flood of youthful spirits, he had inflicted that memorable bite, and with the exception of short excursions, always at the end of the chain, under the strict guardianship of his master or Louisa, the old dog had remained a close prisoner. It is doubtful if, with his limited ambition, he took much pride in the fact, but it is certain that lie was possessed of considerable cheap fame, He was regarded by all the children in the village and by many adults as a very monster of ferocity. St. George's dragon could hardly have surpassed in evil repute Louisa Ellis's old yellow dog. Mothers cleared their children with solemn emphasis not to go too near to him, and the children listened and believed greedily, with a fascinated appetite for terror, and ran by Louisa's house stealthily, with many sidelong and backward glances at the terrible dog. If perchance he sounded a hoarse bark, there was a panic. Wayfarers chancing into Louisa's yard eyed him with respect, and inquired if the chain were stout. Caesar at large might have seemed a very ordinary dog, and excited no comment whatever - chained, his reputation overshadowed him, so that he lost his own proper outlines and looked darkly vague and enormous. Joe Dagget, however, with his good-humored sense and shrewdness, saw him as he was. He strode valiantly up to him and patted him on the bead, in spite of Louisa's soft clamor of warning, and even attempted to set him loose. Louisa grew so alarmed that he desisted, but kept announcing his opinion in the matter quite forcibly at intervals. "There ain't a better-natured dog in town," be would say, " and it's down-right cruel to keep him tied up there. Some day I'm going to take him out."

Louisa had very little hope that be would not, one of these days, when their interests and possessions should be more completely fused in one. She pictured to herself Caesar on the rampage through the quiet and unguarded village. She saw innocent children bleeding in his path. She was herself very fond of the old dog, because he had belonged to her dead brother, and he was always very gentle with her; still she had great faith in his ferocity. She always warned people not to go too near him. She fed him on ascetic fare of corn-mush and cakes, and never fired his dangerous temper with heating and sanguinary diet of flesh and bones. Louisa looked at the old dog munching his simple fare, and thought of her approaching marriage and trembled. Still no anticipation of disorder and confusion in lieu of sweet peace and harmony, no forebodings of Caesar on the rampage, no wild fluttering of her little yellow canary, were sufficient to turn her a hairsbreadth. Joe Dagget had been fond of her and working for her all these years. It was not for her, whatever came to pass, to prove untrue and break his heart. She put the exquisite little studies into her wedding-garments, and the time went on until it was only a week before her wedding-day. It was a Tuesday evening, and the wedding was to be a week from Wednesday.

There was a full moon that night. About nine o'clock Louisa strolled down the road a little way. There were harvest-fields on either hand, bordered by low stone walls. Luxuriant clumps of bushes grew beside the wall, and trees—wild cherry and old apple-trees-at intervals. Presently Louisa sat down on the wall and looked about her with mildly sorrowful reflectiveness. Tall shrubs of blueberry and meadow-sweet, all woven together and tangled with blackberry vines and horsebriers, shut her in on either side. She had a little clear space between them. Opposite her, on the other side of the road, was a spreading tree; the moon shone between its boughs, and the leaves twinkled like silver. The road was bespread with a beautiful shifting dapple of silver and shadow; the air was full of a mysterious sweetness. "I wonder if it's wild grapes?" murmured Louisa. She sat there some time. She was just thinking of rising, when she beard footsteps and low voices, and remained quiet. It was a lonely place, and she felt a little timid. She thought she would keep still in the shadow and let the persons, whoever they might be, pass her.

But just before they reached her the voices ceased, and the footsteps. She understood that. their owners had also found seats upon the stone wall. She was wondering if she could not steal away unobserved, when the voice broke the stillness. It was Joe Dagget's. She sat still and listened.

The voice was announced by a loud sigh, which was as familiar as itself. "Well," said Dagget, "you've made up your mind, then, I suppose ?"

"Yes," returned another voice; "I'm going, day after tomorrow."

"That's Lily Dyer," thought Louisa to herself. The voice embodied itself in her mind. She saw a girl tall and full-figured, with a firm, fair face, looking fairer and firmer in the moonlight, her strong yellow hair braided in a close knot. A girl full of a calm rustic strength and bloom, with a masterful way which might have beseemed a princess. Lily Dyer was a favorite with the village folk; she had just the qualities to arouse the admiration. She was good and handsome and smart. Louisa had often heard her praises sounded.

"Well," said Joe Dagget, "I ain't got a word to say."

"I don't know what you could say," returned Lily Dver.

"Not a word to say," repeated Joe, drawing out the words heavily. Then there was a silence. " I ain't sorry," he began at last, "that that happened yesterday—that we kind of let on how we felt to each other. I guess it's just as well we knew. Of course I can't do anything any different. I'm going right on an' get married next week. I ain't going back on a woman that's waited for me fourteen years, an' break her heart."

"If you should jilt her to-morrow, I wouldn't have you," spoke up the girl, with sudden vehemence.

"Well, I ain't going to give you the chance," said he; "but I don't believe you would, either."

"You'd see I wouldn't. Honor's honor, an' right's right. An' I'd never think anything of any man that went against 'em for me or any other girl - you'd find that out, Joe Dagget."

"Well, you'll find out fast enough that I ain't going against 'em for you or any other girl," returned he. Their voices sounded almost as if they were angry with each other. Louisa was listening eagerly.

"I'm sorry you feel as if you must go away," said Joe, "but I don't know but it's best."

"Of course it's best. I hope you and I have got common-sense."

"Well, I suppose you're right." Suddenly Joe's voice got an undertone of tenderness. "Say, Lily," said he, "I'll get along well enough myself, but I can't bear to think—You don't suppose you're going to fret much over it?"

"I guess you'll find out I sha'n't fret much over a married man."

"Well, I hope you won't-I hope you won't, Lily. God knows I do. And - I hope - one of these days - you'll -come across somebody else—"

"I don't see any reason why I shouldn't." Suddenly her tone changed. She spoke in a sweet, clear voice, so loud that she could have been heard across the street. "No, Joe Dagget," said she, "I'll never marry any other man as long as I live. I've got good sense, an' I ain't going to break my heart nor make a fool of myself; but I'm never going to be married, you can be sure of that. I ain't that sort of a girl to feel this way twice."

Louisa heard an exclamation and a soft commotion behind the bushes; then Lily spoke again-the voice sounded as if she had risen. "This must be put a stop to," said she. "We've stayed here long enough. I'm going home."

Louisa sat there in a daze, listening to their retreating steps. After a while she got up and slunk softly home herself. The next day she did her housework methodically; that was as much a matter of course as breathing; but she did not sew on her wedding-clothes. She sat at her window and meditated. In the evening Joe came. Louisa Ellis had never known that she had any diplomacy in her, but when she came to look for it that night she found it, although meek of its kind, among her little feminine weapons. Even now she could hardly believe that she had heard aright, and that she would not do Joe a terrible injury should she break her troth-plight. She wanted to sound him without betraying too soon her own inclinations in the matter. She did it successfully, and they finally came to an understanding - but it was a difficult thing, for he was as afraid of betraying himself as she.

She never mentioned Lily Dyer. She simply said that while she had no cause of complaint against him, she had lived so long in one way that she shrank from making a change.

"Well, I never shrank, Louisa," said Dagget. "I'm going to be honest enough to say that I think maybe it's better this way; but if you'd wanted to keep on, I'd have stuck to you till my dying day. I hope you know that."

"Yes, I do," said she.

That night she and Joe parted more tenderly than they had done for a long time. Standing in the door, holding each other's hands, a last great wave of regretful memory swept over them.

"Well, this ain't the way we've thought it was all going to end, is it, Louisa?" said Joe.

She shook her head. There was a little quiver on her placid face.

"You let me know if there's ever anything I can do for you," said he. "I ain't ever going to forget you, Louisa." Then he kissed her, and went down the path.

Louisa, all alone by herself that night, wept a little, she hardly knew why, but the next morning, on waking, she felt like a queen who, after fearing lest her domain be wrested away from her, sees it firmly insured in her possession. Now the tall weeds and grasses might cluster around Caesar's little hermit hut, the snow might fall on its roof year in and year out, but he never would go on a rampage through the unguarded village. Now the little canary might turn itself into a peaceful yellow ball night after night, and have no need to wake and flutter with wild terror against its bars. Louisa could sew linen seams, and distil roses, and dust and polish and fold away in lavender, as long as she listed. That afternoon she sat with her needle-work at the window, and felt fairly steeped in peace. Lily Dyer, tall and erect and blooming, went past; but she felt no qualm. If Louisa Ellis had sold her birthright she did not know it, the taste of the pottage was so delicious, and had been her sole satisfaction for so long. Serenity and placid narrowness had become to her as the birthright itself. She gazed ahead through a long reach of future days strung together like pearls in a rosary, every one like the others, and all smooth and flawless and innocent, and her heart went up in thankfulness. Outside was the fervid sunnier afternoon; the air was filled with the sounds of the busy harvest of men and birds and bees; there were halloos, metallic clattering, sweet calls, and long hummings. Louisa sat, prayerfully numbering her days, like an uncloistered nun.

2.9.2 "The Revolt of 'Mother'"

"Father!"

"What is it?"

"What are them men diggin' over there in the field for?"

There was a sudden dropping and enlarging of the lower part of the old man's face, as if some heavy weight had settled therein; he shut his mouth tight, and went on harnessing the great bay mare. He hustled the collar on to her neck with a jerk.

"Father!"

The old man slapped the saddle upon the mare's back.

"Look here, father, I want to know what them men are diggin' over in the field for, an' I'm goin' to know."

"I wish you'd go into the house, mother, an' 'tend to your own affairs," the old man said then. He ran his words together, and his speech was almost as inarticulate as a growl.

But the woman understood; it was her most native tongue. "I ain't goin' into the house till you tell me what them men are doin' over there in the field," said she.

Then she stood waiting. She was a small woman, short and straight-waisted like a child in her brown cotton gown. Her forehead was mild and benevolent between the smooth curves of gray hair; there were meek downward lines about her nose and mouth; but her eyes, fixed upon the old man, looked as if the meekness had been the result of her own will, never of the will of another.

They were in the barn, standing before the wide open doors. The spring air, full of the smell of growing grass and unseen blossoms, came in their faces. The deep yard in front was littered with farm wagons and piles of wood; on the edges, close to the fence and the house, the grass was a vivid green, and there were some dandelions.

The old man glanced doggedly at his wife as he tightened the last buckles on the harness. She looked as immovable to him as one of the rocks in his pasture-land, bound to the earth with generations of blackberry vines. He slapped the reins over the horse, and started forth from the barn.

"*Father!*" said she.

The old man pulled up. "What is it?"

"I want to know what them men are diggin' over there in that field for."

"They're diggin' a cellar, I s'pose, if you've got to know."

"A cellar for what?"

"A barn."

"A barn? You ain't goin' to build a barn over there where we was goin' to have a house, father?"

The old man said not another word. He hurried the horse into the farm wagon, and clattered out of the yard, jouncing as sturdily on his seat as a boy.

The woman stood a moment looking after him, then she went out of the barn across a corner of the yard to the house. The house, standing at right angles with the great barn and a long reach of sheds and out-buildings, was infinitesimal compared with them. It was scarcely as commodious for people as the little boxes under the barn eaves were for doves.

A pretty girl's face, pink and delicate as a flower, was looking out of one of the house windows. She was watching three men who were digging over in the field which bounded the yard near the road line. She turned quietly when the woman entered.

"What are they diggin' for, mother?" said she. "Did he tell you?"

"They're diggin' for—a cellar for a new barn."

"Oh, mother, he ain't goin' to build another barn?"

"That's what he says."

A boy stood before the kitchen glass combing his hair. He combed slowly and painstakingly, arranging his brown hair in a smooth hillock over his forehead. He did not seem to pay any attention to the conversation.

"Sammy, did you know father was goin' to build a new barn?" asked the girl.

The boy combed assiduously.

"Sammy!"

He turned, and showed a face like his father's under his smooth crest of hair. "Yes, I s'pose I did," he said, reluctantly.

"How long have you known it?" asked his mother.

"'Bout three months, I guess."

"Why didn't you tell of it?"

"Didn't think 'twould do no good."

"I don't see what father wants another barn for," said the girl, in her sweet, slow voice. She turned again to the window, and stared out at the digging men in the field. Her tender, sweet face was full of a gentle distress. Her forehead was as bald and innocent as a baby's, with the light hair strained back from it in a row of curl-papers. She was quite large, but her soft curves did not look as if they covered muscles.

Her mother looked sternly at the boy. "Is he goin' to buy more cows?" said she.

The boy did not reply; he was tying his shoes.

"Sammy, I want you to tell me if he's goin' to buy more cows."

"I s'pose he is."

"How many?"

"Four, I guess."

His mother said nothing more. She went into the pantry, and there was a clatter of dishes. The boy got his cap from a nail behind the door, took an old arithmetic from the shelf, and started for school. He was lightly built, but clumsy. He went out of the yard with a curious spring in the hips, that made his loose home-made jacket tilt up in the rear.

The girl went to the sink, and began to wash the dishes that were piled up there. Her mother came promptly out of the pantry, and shoved her aside. "You wipe 'em," said she; "I'll wash. There's a good many this mornin'."

The mother plunged her hands vigorously into the water, the girl wiped the plates slowly and dreamily. "Mother," said she, "don't you think it's too bad father's goin' to build that new barn, much as we need a decent house to live in?"

Her mother scrubbed a dish fiercely. "You ain't found out yet we're women-folks, Nanny Penn," said she. "You ain't seen enough of men-folks yet to. One of these days you'll find it out, an' then you'll know that we know only what men-folks think we do, so far as any use of it goes, an' how we'd ought to reckon men-folks in with Providence, an' not complain of what they do any more than we do of the weather."

"I don't care; I don't believe George is anything like that, anyhow," said Nanny. Her delicate face flushed pink, her lips pouted softly, as if she were going to cry.

"You wait an' see. I guess George Eastman ain't no better than other men. You hadn't ought to judge father, though. He can't help it, 'cause he don't look at things jest the way we do. An' we've been pretty comfortable here, after all. The roof don't leak—ain't never but once—that's one thing. Father's kept it shingled right up."

"I do wish we had a parlor."

"I guess it won't hurt George Eastman any to come to see you in a nice clean kitchen. I guess a good many girls don't have as good a place as this. Nobody's ever heard me complain."

"I ain't complained either, mother."

"Well, I don't think you'd better, a good father an' a good home as you've got. S'pose your father made you go out an' work for your livin'? Lots of girls have to that ain't no stronger an' better able to than you be."

Sarah Penn washed the frying-pan with a conclusive air. She scrubbed the outside of it as faithfully as the inside. She was a masterly keeper of her box of a house. Her one living-room never seemed to have in it any of the dust which the friction of life with inanimate matter produces. She swept, and there seemed to be no dirt to go before the broom; she cleaned, and one could see no difference. She was like an artist so perfect that he has apparently no art. To-day she got out a mixing bowl and a board, and rolled some pies, and there was no more flour upon her than upon her daughter who was doing finer work. Nanny was to be married in the fall, and she was sewing on some white cambric and embroidery. She sewed industriously while her mother cooked, her soft milk-white hands and wrists showed whiter than her delicate work.

"We must have the stove moved out in the shed before long," said Mrs. Penn. "Talk about not havin' things, it's been a real blessin' to be able to put a stove up in that shed in hot weather. Father did one good thing when he fixed that stove-pipe out there."

Sarah Penn's face as she rolled her pies had that expression of meek vigor which might have characterized one of the New Testament saints. She was making mince-pies. Her husband, Adoniram Penn, liked them better than any other kind. She baked twice a week. Adoniram often liked a piece of pie between meals. She hurried this morning. It had been later than usual when she began, and she wanted to have a pie baked for dinner. However deep a resentment she might be forced to hold against her husband, she would never fail in sedulous attention to his wants.

Nobility of character manifests itself at loop-holes when it is not provided with large doors. Sarah Penn's showed itself to-day in flaky dishes of pastry. So she made the pies faithfully, while across the table she could see, when she glanced up from her work, the sight that rankled in her patient and steadfast soul—the digging of the cellar of the new barn in the place where Adoniram forty years ago had promised her their new house should stand.

The pies were done for dinner. Adoniram and Sammy were home a few minutes after twelve o'clock. The dinner was eaten with serious haste. There was never much conversation at the table in the Penn family. Adoniram asked a blessing, and they ate promptly, then rose up and went about their work.

Sammy went back to school, taking soft sly lopes out of the yard like a rabbit. He wanted a game of marbles before school, and feared his father would give him some chores to do. Adoniram hastened to the door and called after him, but he was out of sight.

"I don't see what you let him go for, mother," said he. "I wanted him to help me unload that wood."

Adoniram went to work out in the yard unloading wood from the wagon. Sarah put away the dinner dishes, while Nanny took down her curl-papers and changed her dress. She was going down to the store to buy some more embroidery and thread.

When Nanny was gone, Mrs. Penn went to the door. "Father!" she called.

"Well, what is it!"

"I want to see you jest a minute, father."

"I can't leave this wood nohow. I've got to git it unloaded an' go for a load of gravel afore two o'clock. Sammy had ought to helped me. You hadn't ought to let him go to school so early."

"I want to see you jest a minute."

"I tell ye I can't, nohow, mother."

"Father, you come here." Sarah Penn stood in the door like a queen; she held her head as if it bore a crown; there was that patience which makes authority royal in her voice. Adoniram went.

Mrs. Penn led the way into the kitchen, and pointed to a chair. "Sit down, father," said she; "I've got somethin' I want to say to you."

He sat down heavily; his face was quite stolid, but he looked at her with restive eyes. "Well, what is it, mother?"

"I want to know what you're buildin' that new barn for, father?"

"I ain't got nothin' to say about it."

"It can't be you think you need another barn?"

"I tell ye I ain't got nothin' to say about it, mother; an' I ain't goin' to say nothin'."

"Be you goin' to buy more cows?"

Adoniram did not reply; he shut his mouth tight.

"I know you be, as well as I want to. Now, father, look here"—Sarah Penn had not sat down; she stood before her husband in the humble fashion of a Scripture woman—"I'm goin' to talk real plain to you; I never have sence I married you, but I'm goin' to now. I ain't never complained, an' I ain't goin' to complain now, but I'm goin' to talk plain. You see this room here, father; you look at it well. You see there ain't no carpet on the floor, an' you see the paper is all dirty, an' droppin' off the walls. We ain't had no new paper on it for ten year, an' then I put it on myself, an' it didn't cost but ninepence a roll. You see this room, father; it's all the one I've had to work in an' eat in an' sit in sence we was married. There ain't another woman in the whole town whose husband ain't got half the means you have but what's got better. It's all the room Nanny's got to have her company in; an' there ain't one of her mates but what's got better, an' their fathers not so able as hers is. It's all the room she'll have to be married in. What would you have thought, father, if we had had our weddin' in a room no better than this? I was married in my mother's parlor, with a carpet on the floor, an' stuffed furniture, an' a mahogany card-table. An' this is all the room my daughter will have to be married in. Look here, father!"

Sarah Penn went across the room as though it were a tragic stage. She flung open a door and disclosed a tiny bedroom, only large enough for a bed and bureau, with a path between. "There, father," said she—"there's all the room I've had to sleep in forty year. All my children were born there—the two that died, an' the two that's livin'. I was sick with a fever there."

She stepped to another door and opened it. It led into the small, ill-lighted pantry. "Here," said she, "is all the buttery I've got—every place I've got for my dishes, to set away my victuals in, an' to keep my milk-pans in. Father, I've been takin' care of the milk of six cows in this place, an' now you're goin' to build a new barn, an' keep more cows, an' give me more to do in it."

She threw open another door. A narrow crooked flight of stairs wound upward from it. "There, father," said she, "I want you to look at the stairs that go up to them two unfinished chambers that are all the places our son an' daughter have had to sleep in all their lives. There ain't a prettier girl in town nor a more ladylike one than Nanny, an' that's the place she has to sleep in. It ain't so good as your horse's stall; it ain't so warm an' tight."

Sarah Penn went back and stood before her husband. "Now, father," said she, "I want to know if you think you're doin' right an' accordin' to what you profess. Here, when we was married, forty year ago, you promised me faithful that we should have a new house built in that lot over in the field before the year was out. You said you had money enough, an' you wouldn't ask me to live in no such place as this. It is forty year now, an' you've been makin' more money, an' I've been savin' of it for you ever since, an' you ain't built no house yet. You've built sheds an' cow-houses an' one new barn, an' now you're goin' to build another. Father, I want to know if you think it's right. You're lodgin' your dumb beasts better than you are your own flesh an' blood. I want to know if you think it's right."

"I ain't got nothin' to say."

"You can't say nothin' without ownin' it ain't right, father. An' there's another thing—I ain't complained; I've got along forty year, an' I s'pose I should forty more, if it wa'n't for that—if we don't have another house. Nanny she can't live with us after she's married. She'll have to go somewheres else to live away from us, an' it don't seem as if I could have it so, noways, father. She wa'n't ever strong. She's got considerable color, but there wa'n't never any backbone to her. I've always took the heft of everything off her, an' she ain't fit to keep house an' do everything herself. She'll be all worn out inside of a year. Think of her doin' all the washin' an' ironin' an' bakin' with them soft white hands an' arms, an' sweepin'! I can't have it so, noways, father."

Mrs. Penn's face was burning; her mild eyes gleamed. She had pleaded her little cause like a Webster; she had ranged from severity to pathos; but her opponent employed that obstinate silence which makes eloquence futile with mocking echoes. Adoniram arose clumsily.

"Father, ain't you got nothin' to say?" said Mrs. Penn.

"I've got to go off after that load of gravel. I can't stan' here talkin' all day."

"Father, won't you think it over, an' have a house built there instead of a barn?"

"I ain't got nothin' to say."

Adoniram shuffled out. Mrs. Penn went into her bedroom. When she came out, her eyes were red. She had a roll of unbleached cotton cloth. She spread it out on the kitchen table, and began cutting out some shirts for her husband. The men over in the field had a team to help them this afternoon; she could hear their halloos. She had a scanty pattern for the shirts; she had to plan and piece the sleeves.

Nanny came home with her embroidery, and sat down with her needlework. She had taken down her curl-papers, and there was a soft roll of fair hair like an aureole over her forehead; her face was as delicately fine and clear as porcelain. Suddenly she looked up, and the tender red flamed all over her face and neck. "Mother," said she.

"What say?"

"I've been thinking—I don't see how we're goin' to have any—wedding in this room. I'd be ashamed to have his folks come if we didn't have anybody else."

"Mebbe we can have some new paper before then; I can put it on. I guess you won't have no call to be ashamed of your belongin's."

"We might have the wedding in the new barn," said Nanny, with gentle pettishness. "Why, mother, what makes you look so?"

Mrs. Penn had started, and was staring at her with a curious expression. She turned again to her work, and spread out a pattern carefully on the cloth. "Nothin'," said she.

Presently Adoniram clattered out of the yard in his two-wheeled dump cart, standing as proudly upright as a Roman charioteer. Mrs. Penn opened the door and stood there a minute looking out; the halloos of the men sounded louder.

It seemed to her all through the spring months that she heard nothing but the halloos and the noises of saws and hammers. The new barn grew fast. It was a fine edifice for this little village. Men came on pleasant Sundays, in their meeting suits and clean shirt bosoms, and stood around it admiringly. Mrs. Penn did not speak of it, and Adoniram did not mention it to her, although sometimes, upon a return from inspecting it, he bore himself with injured dignity.

"It's a strange thing how your mother feels about the new barn," he said, confidentially, to Sammy one day.

Sammy only grunted after an odd fashion for a boy; he had learned it from his father.

The barn was all completed ready for use by the third week in July. Adoniram had planned to move his stock in on Wednesday; on Tuesday he received a letter which changed his plans. He came in with it early in the morning. "Sammy's been to the post-office," said he, "an' I've got a letter from Hiram." Hiram was Mrs. Penn's brother, who lived in Vermont.

"Well," said Mrs. Penn, "what does he say about the folks?"

"I guess they're all right. He says he thinks if I come up country right off there's a chance to buy jest the kind of a horse I want." He stared reflectively out of the window at the new barn.

Mrs. Penn was making pies. She went on clapping the rolling-pin into the crust, although she was very pale, and her heart beat loudly.

"I dun' know but what I'd better go," said Adoniram. "I hate to go off jest now, right in the midst of hayin', but the ten-acre lot's cut, an' I guess Rufus an' the others can git along without me three or four days. I can't get a horse round here to suit me, nohow, an' I've got to have another for all that wood-haulin' in the fall. I told Hiram to watch out, an' if he got wind of a good horse to let me know. I guess I'd better go."

"I'll get out your clean shirt an' collar," said Mrs. Penn calmly.

She laid out Adoniram's Sunday suit and his clean clothes on the bed in the little bedroom. She got his shaving-water and razor ready. At last she buttoned on his collar and fastened his black cravat.

Adoniram never wore his collar and cravat except on extra occasions. He held his head high, with a rasped dignity. When he was all ready, with his coat and hat brushed, and a lunch of pie and cheese in a paper bag, he hesitated on the threshold of the door. He looked at his wife, and his manner was defiantly apologetic. "*If* them cows come to-day, Sammy can drive 'em into the new barn," said he; "an' when they bring the hay up, they can pitch it in there."

"Well," replied Mrs. Penn.

Adoniram set his shaven face ahead and started. When he had cleared the door-step, he turned and looked back with a kind of nervous solemnity. "I shall be back by Saturday if nothin' happens," said he.

"Do be careful, father," returned his wife.

She stood in the door with Nanny at her elbow and watched him out of sight. Her eyes had a strange, doubtful expression in them; her peaceful forehead was contracted. She went in, and about her baking again. Nanny sat sewing. Her wedding-day was drawing nearer, and she was getting pale and thin with her steady sewing. Her mother kept glancing at her.

"Have you got that pain in your side this mornin'?" she asked.

"A little."

Mrs. Penn's face, as she worked, changed, her perplexed forehead smoothed, her eyes were steady, her lips firmly set. She formed a maxim for herself, although incoherently with her unlettered thoughts. "Unsolicited opportunities are the guide-posts of the Lord to the new roads of life," she repeated in effect, and she made up her mind to her course of action.

"S'posin' I *had* wrote to Hiram," she muttered once, when she was in the pantry—"s'posin' I had wrote, an' asked him if he knew of any horse? But I didn't, an' father's goin' wa'n't none of my doin'. It looks like a providence." Her voice rang out quite loud at the last.

"What you talkin' about, mother?" called Nanny.

"Nothin'."

Mrs. Penn hurried her baking; at eleven o'clock it was all done. The load of hay from the west field came slowly down the cart track, and drew up at the new barn. Mrs. Penn ran out. "Stop!" she screamed—"stop!"

The men stopped and looked; Sammy upreared from the top of the load, and stared at his mother.

"Stop!" she cried out again. "Don't you put the hay in that barn; put it in the old one."

"Why, he said to put it in here," returned one of the haymakers, wonderingly. He was a young man, a neighbor's son, whom Adoniram hired by the year to help on the farm.

"Don't you put the hay in the new barn; there's room enough in the old one, ain't there?" said Mrs. Penn.

"Room enough," returned the hired man, in his thick, rustic tones. "Didn't need the new barn, nohow, far as room's concerned. Well, I s'pose he changed his mind." He took hold of the horses' bridles.

Mrs. Penn went back to the house. Soon the kitchen windows were darkened, and a fragrance like warm honey came into the room.

Nanny laid down her work. "I thought father wanted them to put the hay into the new barn?" she said, wonderingly.

"It's all right," replied her mother.

Sammy slid down from the load of hay, and came in to see if dinner was ready.

"I ain't goin' to get a regular dinner to-day, as long as father's gone," said his mother. "I've let the fire go out. You can have some bread an' milk an' pie. I thought we could get along." She set out some bowls of milk, some bread, and a pie on the kitchen table. "You'd better eat your dinner now," said she. "You might jest as well get through with it. I want you to help me afterward."

Nanny and Sammy stared at each other. There was something strange in their mother's manner. Mrs. Penn did not eat anything herself. She went into the pantry, and they heard her moving dishes while they ate. Presently she came out with a pile of plates. She got the clothes-basket out of the shed, and packed them in it. Nanny and Sammy watched. She brought out cups and saucers, and put them in with the plates.

"What you goin' to do, mother?" inquired Nanny, in a timid voice. A sense of something unusual made her tremble, as if it were a ghost. Sammy rolled his eyes over his pie.

"You'll see what I'm goin' to do," replied Mrs. Penn. "If you're through, Nanny, I want you to go up-stairs an' pack up your things; an' I want you, Sammy, to help me take down the bed in the bedroom."

"Oh, mother, what for?" gasped Nanny.

"You'll see."

During the next few hours a feat was performed by this simple, pious New England mother which was equal in its way to Wolfe's storming of the Heights of Abraham. It took no more genius and audacity of bravery for Wolfe to cheer his wondering soldiers up those steep precipices, under the sleeping eyes of the enemy, than for Sarah Penn, at the head of her children, to move all their little household goods into the new barn while her husband was away.

Nanny and Sammy followed their mother's instructions without a murmur; indeed, they were overawed. There is a certain uncanny and superhuman quality about all such purely original undertakings as their mother's was to them. Nanny went back and forth with her light loads, and Sammy tugged with sober energy.

At five o'clock in the afternoon the little house in which the Penns had lived for forty years had emptied itself into the new barn.

Every builder builds somewhat for unknown purposes, and is in a measure a prophet. The architect of Adoniram Penn's barn, while he designed it for the comfort of four-footed animals, had planned better than he knew for the comfort of humans. Sarah Penn saw at a glance its possibilities. Those great box-stalls, with quilts hung before them, would make better bedrooms than the one she had occupied for forty years, and there was a tight carriage-room. The harness-room, with its chimney and shelves, would make a kitchen of her dreams. The great middle space would make a parlor, by-and-by, fit for a palace. Up stairs there was as much room as down. With partitions and windows, what a house would there be! Sarah looked at the row of stanchions before the allotted space for cows, and reflected that she would have her front entry there.

At six o'clock the stove was up in the harness-room, the kettle was boiling, and the table set for tea. It looked almost as home-like as the abandoned house across the yard had ever done. The young hired man milked, and Sarah directed him calmly to bring the milk to the new barn. He came gaping, dropping little blots of foam from the brimming pails on the grass. Before the next morning he had spread the story of Adoniram Penn's wife moving into the new barn all over the little village. Men assembled in the store and talked it over, women with shawls over their heads scuttled into each other's houses before their work was done. Any deviation from the ordinary course of life in this quiet town was enough to stop all progress in it. Everybody paused to look at the staid, independent figure on the side track. There was a difference of opinion with regard to her. Some held her to be insane; some, of a lawless and rebellious spirit.

Friday the minister went to see her. It was in the forenoon, and she was at the barn door shelling pease for dinner. She looked up and returned his salutation with dignity, then she went on with her work. She did not invite him in. The saintly expression of her face remained fixed, but there was an angry flush over it.

The minister stood awkwardly before her, and talked. She handled the pease as if they were bullets. At last she looked up, and her eyes showed the spirit that her meek front had covered for a lifetime.

"There ain't no use talkin', Mr. Hersey," said she. "I've thought it all over an' over, an' I believe I'm doin' what's right. I've made it the subject of prayer, an' it's betwixt me an' the Lord an' Adoniram. There ain't no call for nobody else to worry about it."

"Well, of course, if you have brought it to the Lord in prayer, and feel satisfied that you are doing right, Mrs. Penn," said the minister, helplessly. His thin gray-bearded face was pathetic. He was a sickly man; his youthful confidence had cooled; he had to scourge himself up to some of his pastoral duties as relentlessly as a Catholic ascetic, and then he was prostrated by the smart.

"I think it's right jest as much as I think it was right for our forefathers to come over from the old country 'cause they didn't have what belonged to 'em," said Mrs. Penn. She arose. The barn threshold might have been Plymouth Rock from her bearing. "I don't doubt you mean well, Mr. Hersey," said she, "but there are things people hadn't ought to interfere with. I've been a member of the church for over forty year. I've got my own mind an' my own feet, an' I'm goin' to think my own thoughts an' go my own ways, an' nobody but the Lord is goin' to dictate to me unless I've a mind to have him. Won't you come in an' set down? How is Mis' Hersey?"

"She is well, I thank you," replied the minister. He added some more perplexed apologetic remarks; then he retreated.

He could expound the intricacies of every character study in the Scriptures, he was competent to grasp the Pilgrim Fathers and all historical innovators, but Sarah Penn was beyond him. He could deal with primal cases, but parallel ones worsted him. But, after all, although it was aside from his province, he wondered more how Adoniram Penn would deal with his wife than how the Lord would. Everybody shared the wonder. When Adoniram's four new cows arrived, Sarah ordered three to be put in the old barn, the other in the house shed where the cooking-stove had stood. That added to the excitement. It was whispered that all four cows were domiciled in the house.

Toward sunset on Saturday, when Adoniram was expected home, there was a knot of men in the road near the new barn. The hired man had milked, but he still hung around the premises. Sarah Penn had supper all ready. There were brown-bread and baked beans and a custard pie; it was the supper that Adoniram loved on a Saturday night. She had on a clean calico, and she bore herself imperturbably. Nanny and Sammy kept close at her heels. Their eyes were large, and Nanny was full of nervous tremors. Still there was to them more pleasant excitement than anything else. An inborn confidence in their mother over their father asserted itself.

Sammy looked out of the harness-room window. "There he is," he announced, in an awed whisper. He and Nanny peeped around the casing. Mrs. Penn kept on about her work. The children watched Adoniram leave the new horse standing in the drive while he went to the house door. It was fastened. Then he went around to the shed. That door was seldom locked, even when the family was away. The thought how her father would be confronted by the cow flashed upon Nanny. There was a hysterical sob in her throat. Adoniram emerged from the shed and stood looking about in a dazed fashion. His lips moved; he was saying something, but they could not hear what it was. The hired man was peeping around a corner of the old barn, but nobody saw him.

Adoniram took the new horse by the bridle and led him across the yard to the new barn. Nanny and Sammy slunk close to their mother. The barn doors rolled back, and there stood Adoniram, with the long mild face of the great Canadian farm horse looking over his shoulder.

Nanny kept behind her mother, but Sammy stepped suddenly forward, and stood in front of her.

Adoniram stared at the group. "What on airth you all down here for?" said he. "What's the matter over to the house?"

"We've come here to live, father," said Sammy. His shrill voice quavered out bravely.

"What"—Adoniram sniffed—"what is it smells like cookin'?" said he. He stepped forward and looked in the open door of the harness-room. Then he turned to his wife. His old bristling face was pale and frightened. "What on airth does this mean, mother?" he gasped.

"You come in here, father," said Sarah. She led the way into the harness-room and shut the door. "Now, father," said she, "you needn't be scared. I ain't crazy. There ain't nothin' to be upset over. But we've come here to live, an' we're goin' to live here. We've got jest as good a right here as new horses an' cows. The house wa'n't fit for us to live in any longer, an' I made up my mind I wa'n't goin' to stay there. I've done my duty by you forty year, an' I'm goin' to do it now; but I'm goin' to live here. You've got to put in some windows and partitions; an' you'll have to buy some furniture."

"Why, mother!" the old man gasped.

"You'd better take your coat off an' get washed—there's the wash-basin—an' then we'll have supper."

"Why, mother!"

Sammy went past the window, leading the new horse to the old barn. The old man saw him, and shook his head speechlessly. He tried to take off his coat, but his arms seemed to lack the power. His wife helped him. She poured some water into the tin basin, and put in a piece of soap. She got the comb and brush, and smoothed his thin gray hair after he had washed. Then she put the beans, hot bread, and tea on the table. Sammy came in, and the family drew up. Adoniram sat looking dazedly at his plate, and they waited.

"Ain't you goin' to ask a blessin', father?" said Sarah.

And the old man bent his head and mumbled.

All through the meal he stopped eating at intervals, and stared furtively at his wife; but he ate well. The home food tasted good to him, and his old frame was too sturdily healthy to be affected by his mind. But after supper he went out, and sat down on the step of the smaller door at the right of the barn, through which he had meant his Jerseys to pass in stately file, but which Sarah designed for her front house door, and he leaned his head on his hands.

After the supper dishes were cleared away and the milk-pans washed, Sarah went out to him. The twilight was deepening. There was a clear green glow in the sky. Before them stretched the smooth level of field; in the distance was a cluster of hay-stacks like the huts of a village; the air was very cool and calm and sweet. The landscape might have been an ideal one of peace.

Sarah bent over and touched her husband on one of his thin, sinewy shoulders. "Father!"

The old man's shoulders heaved: he was weeping.

"Why, don't do so, father," said Sarah.

"I'll—put up the—partitions, an'—everything you—want, mother."

Sarah put her apron up to her face; she was overcome by her own triumph.

Adoniram was like a fortress whose walls had no active resistance, and went down the instant the right besieging tools were used. "Why, mother," he said, hoarsely, "I hadn't no idee you was so set on't as all this comes to."

2.9.3 Reading and Review Questions

1. In Freeman's "A New England Nun," analyze the confinement or restraint of the bird and the dog in the story and examine how such images contribute to the story's theme.

2. In "A New England Nun," compare Louisa Ellis and Lily Dyer. How are they similar or different?

3. Examine the concept of "order" in Freeman's "A New England Nun." Why is Louisa so concerned with order?

4. In "A New England Nun," why is Louisa likened to an "artist" and later a "queen" in the story?

5. In Freeman's "Revolt of Mother," examine the term "revolt" in the title. What does it mean in terms of the story's theme?

6. Examine the central conflict in "Revolt of Mother." Who is revolting, and what is he or she rebelling against both literally and symbolically?

7. What happens to Adoniram when he changes his mind at the end of the story? What kind of conversion does he experience?

2.10 CHARLES WADDELL CHESNUTT

(1858 - 1932)

Charles Waddell Chesnutt was born in 1858 in Cleveland, Ohio, to parents who were free African-Americans. The family moved to Fayetteville, North Carolina, when Chesnutt was a young boy, and there Chesnutt attended school, eventually becoming a teacher and later a principal. Chesnutt's parents were mixed race, and Chesnutt himself could have identified as white but chose to identify as African-American. After he married, he and his wife returned to Cleveland where Chesnutt passed the bar exam in 1887 and opened a court reporting firm, providing a prosperous life for his wife and four children. In Cleveland, Chesnutt began submitting his stories for publication and soon enjoyed success publishing a number of his stories

Image 2.8 | Charles Waddell Chesnutt, circa 1898
Photographer | Unknown
Source | Wikimedia Commons
License | Public Domain

in prominent literary magazines, gaining the attention of William Dean Howells, Mark Twain, and other writers in the Realist literary movement. While Chesnutt was never able to support himself and his family with earnings from his writing, he continued to write and publish through the turn of the century. Later in his life, he devoted time and energy to political activism, serving on the General Committee for the **National Association for the Advancement of Colored People (NAACP)**, a civil rights organization formed in 1909.

Chesnutt was one of the first successful African-American writers producing fiction during the period of American Literary Realism. Chesnutt capitalized on the popularity of Local Color fiction after the Civil War and crafted stories about the Old South, depicting, for example, slaves living on plantations interacting with white plantation owners. Some of his first short stories, including the often-anthologized "The Goophered Grapevine" (1887), began appearing in literary magazines in 1887 and then were collected in *The Conjure Woman* (1899). In these stories about folk culture and voodoo practices in the slave community and later in the freed African-American community during Reconstruction, Chesnutt cleverly borrows the plantation tradition popular in Local Color fiction as a form which he then subverts by depicting African-American characters with innate humanity, intelligence, shrewdness, and an ability to outwit those in power. In a second collection of stories, The Wife of His Youth and Other Stories (1899), Chesnutt works with similar themes, exploring in "The Passing of Grandison," for example, issues of "**passing**," or the process by which light-skinned African-Americans could pass as whites. In this story, Chesnutt uses the term in a broader context by presenting a supposedly humble, untutored slave named Grandison whose apparent dedication to the plantation's master, Colonel Owens, is quite possibly an act of passing; in other words, Grandison wears the mask of submission as a slave in order to trick Colonel Owens into believing that Grandison is no threat to the hierarchical order of the plantation so that eventually his planning to escape with his family goes unnoticed. As the ending of the story indicates, Grandison is, in fact, a much more dimensional, complex, determined, and daring person than the Colonel can see or even imagine.

2.10.1 "The Passing of Grandison"

I

When it is said that it was done to please a woman, there ought perhaps to be enough said to explain anything; for what a man will not do to please a woman is yet to be discovered. Nevertheless, it might be well to state a few preliminary facts to make it clear why young Dick Owens tried to run one of his father's negro men off to Canada.

In the early fifties, when the growth of anti-slavery sentiment and the constant drain of fugitive slaves into the North had so alarmed the slaveholders of the border States as to lead to the passage of the Fugitive Slave Law, a young white man from Ohio, moved by compassion for the sufferings of a certain bondman who happened to have a "hard master," essayed to help the slave to freedom. The attempt was discovered and frustrated; the abductor was tried and convicted for slave-stealing, and sentenced to a term of imprisonment in the penitentiary. His death, after the expiration of only a small part of the sentence, from cholera contracted while nursing stricken fellow prisoners, lent to the case a melancholy interest that made it famous in anti-slavery annals.

Dick Owens had attended the trial. He was a youth of about twenty-two, intelligent, handsome, and amiable, but extremely indolent, in a graceful and gentlemanly way; or, as old Judge Fenderson put it more than once, he was lazy as the Devil,—a mere figure of speech, of course, and not one that did justice to the Enemy of Mankind. When asked why he never did anything serious, Dick would good-naturedly reply, with a well-modulated drawl, that he didn't have to. His father was rich; there was but one other child, an unmarried daughter, who because of poor health would probably never marry, and Dick was therefore heir presumptive to a large estate. Wealth or social position he did not need to seek, for he was born to both. Charity Lomax had shamed him into studying law, but notwithstanding an hour or so a day spent at old Judge Fenderson's office, he did not make remarkable headway in his legal studies.

"What Dick needs," said the judge, who was fond of tropes, as became a scholar, and of horses, as was befitting a Kentuckian, "is the whip of necessity, or the spur of ambition. If he had either, he would soon need the snaffle to hold him back."

But all Dick required, in fact, to prompt him to the most remarkable thing he accomplished before he was twenty-five, was a mere suggestion from Charity

Lomax. The story was never really known to but two persons until after the war, when it came out because it was a good story and there was no particular reason for its concealment.

Young Owens had attended the trial of this slave-stealer, or martyr,—either or both,—and, when it was over, had gone to call on Charity Lomax, and, while they sat on the veranda after sundown, had told her all about the trial. He was a good talker, as his career in later years disclosed, and described the proceedings very graphically.

"I confess," he admitted, "that while my principles were against the prisoner, my sympathies were on his side. It appeared that he was of good family, and that he had an old father and mother, respectable people, dependent upon him for support and comfort in their declining years. He had been led into the matter by pity for a negro whose master ought to have been run out of the county long ago for abusing his slaves. If it had been merely a question of old Sam Briggs's negro, nobody would have cared anything about it. But father and the rest of them stood on the principle of the thing, and told the judge so, and the fellow was sentenced to three years in the penitentiary."

Miss Lomax had listened with lively interest.

"I've always hated old Sam Briggs," she said emphatically, "ever since the time he broke a negro's leg with a piece of cordwood. When I hear of a cruel deed it makes the Quaker blood that came from my grandmother assert itself. Personally I wish that all Sam Briggs's negroes would run away. As for the young man, I regard him as a hero. He dared something for humanity. I could love a man who would take such chances for the sake of others."

"Could you love me, Charity, if I did something heroic?"

"You never will, Dick. You're too lazy for any use. You'll never do anything harder than playing cards or fox-hunting."

"Oh, come now, sweetheart! I've been courting you for a year, and it's the hardest work imaginable. Are you never going to love me?" he pleaded.

His hand sought hers, but she drew it back beyond his reach.

"I'll never love you, Dick Owens, until you have done something. When that time comes, I'll think about it." wait. One must read two years to become a lawyer, and work five more to make a reputation. We shall both be gray by then."

"Oh, I don't know," she rejoined. "It does n't require a lifetime for a man to prove that he is a man. This one did something, or at least tried to."

"Well, I'm willing to attempt as much as any other man. What do you want me to do, sweetheart? Give me a test."

"Oh, dear me!" said Charity, "I don't care what you do, so you do something. Really, come to think of it, why should I care whether you do anything or not?"

"I'm sure I don't know why you should, Charity," rejoined Dick humbly, "for I'm aware that I 'm not worthy of it."

"Except that I do hate," she added, relenting slightly, "to see a really clever man so utterly lazy and good for nothing."

"Thank you, my dear; a word of praise from you has sharpened my wits already. I have an idea! Will you love me if I run a negro off to Canada?"

"What nonsense!" said Charity scornfully. "You must be losing your wits. Steal another man's slave, indeed, while your father owns a hundred!"

"Oh, there'll be no trouble about that," responded Dick lightly; "I'll run off one of the old man's; we 've got too many anyway. It may not be quite as difficult as the other man found it, but it will be just as unlawful, and will demonstrate what I am capable of."

"Seeing 's believing," replied Charity. "Of course, what you are talking about now is merely absurd. I'm going away for three weeks, to visit my aunt in Tennessee. If you're able to tell me, when I return, that you 've done something to prove your quality, I'll—well, you may come and tell me about it."

II

Young Owens got up about nine o'clock next morning, and while making his toilet put some questions to his personal attendant, a rather bright looking young mulatto of about his own age.

"Tom," said Dick.

"Yas, Mars Dick," responded the servant.

"I 'm going on a trip North. Would you like to go with me?"

Now, if there was anything that Tom would have liked to make, it was a trip North. It was something he had long contemplated in the abstract, but had never been able to muster up sufficient courage to attempt in the concrete. He was prudent enough, however, to dissemble his feelings.

"I would n't min' it, Mars Dick, ez long ez you'd take keer er me an' fetch me home all right."

Tom's eyes belied his words, however, and his young master felt well assured that Tom needed only a good opportunity to make him run away. Having a comfortable home, and a dismal prospect in case of failure, Tom was not likely to take any desperate chances; but young Owens was satisfied that in a free State but little persuasion would be required to lead Tom astray. With a very logical and characteristic desire to gain his end with the least necessary expenditure of effort, he decided to take Tom with him, if his father did not object.

Colonel Owens had left the house when Dick went to breakfast, so Dick did not see his father till luncheon.

"Father," he remarked casually to the colonel, over the fried chicken, "I'm feeling a trifle run down. I imagine my health would be improved somewhat by a little travel and change of scene."

"Why don't you take a trip North?" suggested his father. The colonel added to paternal affection a considerable respect for his son as the heir of a large estate. He himself had been "raised" in comparative poverty, and had laid the foundations of his fortune by hard work; and while he despised the ladder by which he had climbed, he could not entirely forget it, and unconsciously manifested, in his intercourse with his son, some of the poor man's deference toward the wealthy and well-born.

"I think I'll adopt your suggestion, sir," replied the son, "and run up to New York; and after I've been there awhile I may go on to Boston for a week or so. I've never been there, you know."

"There are some matters you can talk over with my factor in New York," rejoined the colonel, "and while you are up there among the Yankees, I hope you'll keep your eyes and ears open to find out what the rascally abolitionists are saying and doing. They're becoming altogether too active for our comfort, and entirely too many ungrateful niggers are running away. I hope the conviction of that fellow yesterday may discourage the rest of the breed. I'd just like to catch any one trying to run off one of my darkeys. He'd get short shrift; I don't think any Court would have a chance to try him."

"They are a pestiferous lot," assented Dick, "and dangerous to our institutions. But say, father, if I go North I shall want to take Tom with me."

Now, the colonel, while a very indulgent father, had pronounced views on the subject of negroes, having studied them, as he often said, for a great many years, and, as he asserted oftener still, understanding them perfectly. It is scarcely worth while to say, either, that he valued more highly than if he had inherited them the slaves he had toiled and schemed for.

"I don't think it safe to take Tom up North," he declared, with promptness and decision. "He's a good enough boy, but too smart to trust among those low-down abolitionists. I strongly suspect him of having learned to read, though I can't imagine how. I saw him with a newspaper the other day, and while he pretended to be looking at a woodcut, I'm almost sure he was reading the paper. I think it by no means safe to take him."

Dick did not insist, because he knew it was useless. The colonel would have obliged his son in any other matter, but his negroes were the outward and visible sign of his wealth and station, and therefore sacred to him.

"Whom do you think it safe to take?" asked Dick. "I suppose I'll have to have a body-servant."

"What's the matter with Grandison?" suggested the colonel. "He's handy enough, and I reckon we can trust him. He's too fond of good eating, to risk losing his regular meals; besides, he's sweet on your mother's maid, Betty, and I've promised to let 'em get married before long. I'll have Grandison up, and we'll talk to him. Here, you boy Jack," called the colonel to a yellow youth in the next room who was catching flies and pulling their wings off to pass the time, "go down to the barn and tell Grandison to come here."

"Grandison," said the colonel, when the negro stood before him, hat in hand.

"Yas, marster."

"Have n't I always treated you right?"

"Yas, marster."

"Haven't you always got all you wanted to eat?"

"Yas, marster."

"And as much whiskey and tobacco as was good for you, Grandison?"

"Y-a-s, marster."

"I should just like to know, Grandison, whether you don't think yourself a great deal better off than those poor free negroes down by the plank road, with no kind master to look after them and no mistress to give them medicine when they're sick and—and"—

"Well, I sh'd jes' reckon I is better off, suh, dan dem low-down free niggers, suh! Ef anybody ax 'em who dey b'long ter, dey has ter say nobody, er e'se lie erbout it. Anybody ax me who I b'longs ter, I ain' got no 'casion ter be shame' ter tell 'em, no, suh, 'deed I ain', suh!"

The colonel was beaming. This was true gratitude, and his feudal heart thrilled at such appreciative homage. What cold-blooded, heartless monsters they were who would break up this blissful relationship of kindly protection on the one hand, of wise subordination and loyal dependence on the other! The colonel always became indignant at the mere thought of such wickedness.

"Grandison," the colonel continued, "your young master Dick is going North for a few weeks, and I am thinking of letting him take you along. I shall send you on this trip, Grandison, in order that you may take care of your young master. He will need some one to wait on him, and no one can ever do it so well as one of the boys brought up with him on the old plantation. I am going to trust him in your hands, and I'm sure you'll do your duty faithfully, and bring him back home safe and sound—to old Kentucky."

Grandison grinned. "Oh yas, marster, I'll take keer er young Mars Dick."

"I want to warn you, though, Grandison," continued the colonel impressively, "against these cussed abolitionists, who try to entice servants from their comfortable homes and their indulgent masters, from the blue skies, the green fields, and the warm sunlight of their southern home, and send them away off yonder to Canada, a dreary country, where the woods are full of wildcats and wolves and bears, where the snow lies up to the eaves of the houses for six months of the year, and the cold is so severe that it freezes your breath and curdles your blood; and where, when runaway niggers get sick and can't work, they are turned out to starve and die, unloved and uncared for. I reckon, Grandison, that you have too much sense to permit yourself to be led astray by any such foolish and wicked people."

"'Deed, suh, I would n' 'low none er dem cussed, low-down abolitioners ter come nigh me, suh, I'd—I'd—would I be 'lowed ter hit 'em, suh?"

"Certainly, Grandison," replied the colonel, chuckling, "hit 'em as hard as you can. I reckon they 'd rather like it. Begad, I believe they would! It would serve 'em right to be hit by a nigger!"

"Er ef I did n't hit 'em, suh," continued Grandison reflectively, "I'd tell Mars Dick, en he 'd fix 'em. He'd smash de face off'n 'em, suh, I jes' knows he would."

"Oh yes, Grandison, your young master will protect you. You need fear no harm while he is near."

"Dey won't try ter steal me, will dey, marster?" asked the negro, with sudden alarm.

"I don't know, Grandison," replied the colonel, lighting a fresh cigar.

"They're a desperate set of lunatics, and there 's no telling what they may resort to. But if you stick close to your young master, and remember always that he is your best friend, and understands your real needs, and has your true interests at heart, and if you will be careful to avoid strangers who try to talk to you, you 'll stand a fair chance of getting back to your home and your friends. And if you please your master Dick, he 'll buy you a present, and a string of beads for Betty to wear when you and she get married in the fall."

"Thanky, marster, thanky, suh," replied Grandison, oozing gratitude at every pore; "you is a good marster, to be sho', suh; yas, 'deed you is. You kin jes' bet me and Mars Dick gwine git 'long jes' lack I wuz own boy ter Mars Dick. En it won't be my fault ef he don' want me fer his boy all de time, w'en we come back home ag'in."

"All right, Grandison, you may go now. You need n't work any more today, and here's a piece of tobacco for you off my own plug."

"Thanky, marster, thanky, marster! You is de bes' marster any nigger ever had in dis worl'." And Grandison bowed and scraped and disappeared round the corner, his jaws closing around a large section of the colonel's best tobacco.

"You may take Grandison," said the colonel to his son. "I allow he's abolitionist-proof."

III

Richard Owens, Esq., and servant, from Kentucky, registered at the fashionable New York hostelry for Southerners in those days, a hotel where an atmosphere congenial to Southern institutions was sedulously maintained. But there were negro waiters in the dining-room, and mulatto bell-boys, and Dick had no doubt that Grandison, with the native gregariousness and garrulousness of his race, would foregather and palaver with them sooner or later, and Dick hoped that they would speedily inoculate him with the virus of freedom. For it was not Dick's intention to say anything to his servant about his plan to free him, for obvious reasons. To mention one of them, if Grandison should go away, and by legal process be recaptured, his young master's part in the matter would doubtless become known, which would be embarrassing to Dick, to say the least. If, on the other hand, he should merely give Grandison sufficient latitude, he had no doubt he would eventually lose him. For while not exactly skeptical about Grandison's perfervid loyalty, Dick had been a somewhat keen observer of human nature, in his own indolent way, and based his expectations upon the force of the example and argument that his servant could scarcely fail to encounter. Grandison should have a fair chance to become free by his own initiative; if it should become necessary to adopt other measures to get rid of him, it would be time enough to act when the necessity arose; and Dick Owens was not the youth to take needless trouble.

The young master renewed some acquaintances and made others, and spent a week or two very pleasantly in the best society of the metropolis, easily accessible to a wealthy, well-bred young Southerner, with proper introductions. Young women smiled on him, and young men of convivial habits pressed their hospitalities; but the memory of Charity's sweet, strong face and clear blue eyes made him proof against the blandishments of the one sex and the persuasions of the other. Meanwhile he kept Grandison supplied with pocket-money, and left him mainly to his own devices. Every night when Dick came in he hoped he might have to wait upon himself, and every morning he looked forward with pleasure to the prospect of making his toilet unaided. His hopes, however, were doomed to disappointment, for every night when he came in Grandison was on hand with a bootjack, and a nightcap mixed for his young master as the colonel had taught him to mix it, and every morning Grandison appeared with his master's boots blacked and his clothes brushed, and laid his linen out for the day.

"Grandison," said Dick one morning, after finishing his toilet, "this is the chance of your life to go around among your own people and see how they live. Have you met any of them?"

"Yas, suh, I's seen some of 'em. But I don' keer nuffin fer 'em, suh, Dey're diffe'nt f'm de niggers down ou' way. Dey 'lows dey 're free, but dey ain' got sense 'nuff ter know dey ain' half as well off as dey would be down Souf, whar dey 'd be 'preciated."

When two weeks had passed without any apparent effect of evil example upon Grandison, Dick resolved to go on to Boston, where he thought the atmosphere might prove more favorable to his ends. After he had been at the Revere House for a day or two without losing Grandison, he decided upon slightly different tactics.

Having ascertained from a city directory the addresses of several wellknown abolitionists, he wrote them each a letter something like this:—DEAR FRIEND AND BROTHER:—A wicked slaveholder from Kentucky, stopping at the Revere House, has dared to insult the liberty-loving people of Boston by bringing his slave into their midst. Shall this be tolerated? Or shall steps be taken in the name of liberty to rescue a fellow-man from bondage? For obvious reasons I can only sign myself, A FRIEND OF HUMANITY.

That his letter might have an opportunity to prove effective, Dick made it a point to send Grandison away from the hotel on various errands. On one of these occasions Dick watched him for quite a distance down the street. Grandison had scarcely left the hotel when a long-haired, sharp-featured man came out behind him, followed him, soon overtook him, and kept along beside him until they turned the next corner. Dick's hopes were roused by this spectacle, but sank correspondingly when Grandison returned to the hotel. As Grandison said nothing about the encounter, Dick hoped there might be some self-consciousness behind this unexpected reticence, the results of which might develop later on.

But Grandison was on hand again when his master came back to the hotel at night, and was in attendance again in the morning, with hot water, to assist at his master's toilet. Dick sent him on further errands from day to day, and upon one occasion came squarely up to him—inadvertently of course—while Grandison was engaged in conversation with a young white man in clerical garb. When Grandison saw Dick approaching, he edged away from the preacher and hastened toward his master, with a very evident expression of relief upon his countenance.

"Mars Dick," he said, "dese yer abolitioners is jes' pesterin' de life out er me tryin' ter git me ter run away. I don' pay no 'tention ter 'em, but dey riles me so sometimes dat I'm feared I'll hit some of 'em some er dese days, an' dat mought git me inter trouble. I ain' said nuffin' ter you 'bout it, Mars Dick, fer I did n' wanter 'sturb yo' min'; but I don' like it, suh; no, suh, I don'! Is we gwine back home 'fo' long, Mars Dick?"

"We'll be going back soon enough," replied Dick somewhat shortly, while he inwardly cursed the stupidity of a slave who could be free and would not, and registered a secret vow that if he were unable to get rid of Grandison without assassinating him, and were therefore compelled to take him back to Kentucky, he would see that Grandison got a taste of an article of slavery that would make him regret his wasted opportunities. Meanwhile he determined to tempt his servant yet more strongly.

"Grandison," he said next morning, "I'm going away for a day or two, but I shall leave you here. I shall lock up a hundred dollars in this drawer and give you the key. If you need any of it, use it and enjoy yourself,—spend it all if you like,—for this is probably the last chance you'll have for some time to be in a free State, and you 'd better enjoy your liberty while you may."

When he came back a couple of days later and found the faithful Grandison at his post, and the hundred dollars intact, Dick felt seriously annoyed. His vexation was increased by the fact that he could not express his feelings adequately. He did not even scold Grandison; how could he, indeed, find fault with one who so sensibly recognized his true place in the economy of civilization, and kept it with such touching fidelity?

"I can't say a thing to him," groaned Dick. "He deserves a leather medal, made out of his own hide tanned. I reckon I'll write to father and let him know what a model servant he has given me."

He wrote his father a letter which made the colonel swell with pride and pleasure. "I really think," the colonel observed to one of his friends, "that Dick ought to have the nigger interviewed by the Boston papers, so that they may see how contented and happy our darkeys really are."

Dick also wrote a long letter to Charity Lomax, in which he said, among many other things, that if she knew how hard he was working, and under what difficulties, to accomplish something serious for her sake, she would no longer keep him in suspense, but overwhelm him with love and admiration.

Having thus exhausted without result the more obvious methods of getting rid of Grandison, and diplomacy having also proved a failure, Dick was forced to consider more radical measures. Of course he might run away himself, and abandon Grandison, but this would be merely to leave him in the United States, where he was still a slave, and where, with his notions of loyalty, he would speedily be reclaimed. It was necessary, in order to accomplish the purpose of his trip to the North, to leave Grandison permanently in Canada, where he would be legally free.

"I might extend my trip to Canada," he reflected, "but that would be too palpable. I have it! I'll visit Niagara Falls on the way home, and lose him on the Canada side. When he once realizes that he is actually free, I'll warrant that he'll stay."

So the next day saw them westward bound, and in due course of time, by the somewhat slow conveyances of the period, they found themselves at Niagara. Dick walked and drove about the Falls for several days, taking Grandison along with him on most occasions. One morning they stood on the Canadian side, watching the wild whirl of the waters below them.

"Grandison," said Dick, raising his voice above the roar of the cataract, "do you know where you are now?"

"I's wid you, Mars Dick; dat's all I keers."

"You are now in Canada, Grandison, where your people go when they run away from their masters. If you wished, Grandison, you might walk away from me this very minute, and I could not lay my hand upon you to take you back."

Grandison looked around uneasily.

"Let's go back ober de ribber, Mars Dick. I's feared I'll lose you ovuh heah, an' den I won' hab no marster, an' won't nebber be able to git back home no mo'."

Discouraged, but not yet hopeless, Dick said, a few minutes later,—

"Grandison, I 'm going up the road a bit, to the inn over yonder. You stay here until I return. I'll not be gone a great while."

Grandison's eyes opened wide and he looked somewhat fearful.

"Is dey any er dem dadblasted abolitioners roun' heah, Mars Dick?"

"I don't imagine that there are," replied his master, hoping there might be.

"But I 'm not afraid of yourrunning away, Grandison. I only wish I were," he added to himself.

Dick walked leisurely down the road to where the whitewashed inn, built of stone, with true British solidity, loomed up through the trees by the roadside. Arrived there he ordered a glass of ale and a sandwich, and took a seat at a table by a window, from which he could see Grandison in the distance. For a while he hoped that the seed he had sown might have fallen on fertile ground, and that Grandison, relieved from the restraining power of a master's eye, and finding himself in a free country, might get up and walk away; but the hope was vain, for Grandison remained faithfully at his post, awaiting his master's return. He had seated himself on a broad flat stone, and, turning his eyes away from the grand and awe-inspiring spectacle that lay close at hand, was looking anxiously toward the inn where his master sat cursing his ill-timed fidelity.

By and by a girl came into the room to serve his order, and Dick very naturally glanced at her; and as she was young and pretty and remained in attendance, it was some minutes before he looked for Grandison. When he did so his faithful servant had disappeared.

To pay his reckoning and go away without the change was a matter quickly accomplished. Retracing his footsteps toward the Falls, he saw, to his great disgust, as he approached the spot where he had left Grandison, the familiar form of his servant stretched out on the ground, his face to the sun, his mouth open, sleeping the time away, oblivious alike to the grandeur of the scenery, the thunderous roar of the cataract, or the insidious voice of sentiment.

"Grandison," soliloquized his master, as he stood gazing down at his ebony encumbrance, "I do not deserve to be an American citizen; I ought not to have the advantages I possess over you; and I certainly am not worthy of Charity Lomax, if I am not smart enough to get rid of you. I have an idea! You shall yet be free, and I will be the instrument of your deliverance. Sleep on, faithful and affectionate servitor, and dream of the blue grass and the bright skies of old Kentucky, for it is only in your dreams that you will ever see them again!"

Dick retraced his footsteps towards the inn. The young woman chanced to look out of the window and saw the handsome young gentleman she had waited on a few minutes before, standing in the road a short distance away, apparently engaged in earnest conversation with a colored man employed as hostler for the inn. She thought she saw something pass from the white man to the other, but at that moment her duties called her away from the window, and when she looked out again the young gentleman had disappeared, and the hostler, with two other young men of the neighborhood, one white and one colored, were walking rapidly towards the Falls.

IV

Dick made the journey homeward alone, and as rapidly as the conveyances of the day would permit. As he drew near home his conduct in going back without Grandison took on a more serious aspect than it had borne at any previous time, and although he had prepared the colonel by a letter sent several days ahead, there was still the prospect of a bad quarter of an hour with him; not, indeed, that his father would upbraid him, but he was likely to make searching inquiries. And notwithstanding the vein of quiet recklessness that had carried Dick through his preposterous scheme, he was a very poor liar, having rarely had occasion or inclination to tell anything but the truth. Any reluctance to meet his father was more than offset, however, by a stronger force drawing him homeward, for Charity Lomax must long since have returned from her visit to her aunt in Tennessee.

Dick got off easier than he had expected. He told a straight story, and a truthful one, so far as it went.

The colonel raged at first, but rage soon subsided into anger, and anger moderated into annoyance, and annoyance into a sort of garrulous sense of injury. The colonel thought he had been hardly used; he had trusted this negro, and he had broken faith. Yet, after all, he did not blame Grandison so much as he did the abolitionists, who were undoubtedly at the bottom of it. As for Charity Lomax, Dick told her, privately of course, that he had run his father's man, Grandison, off to Canada, and left him there.

"Oh, Dick," she had said with shuddering alarm, "what have you done? If they knew it they'd send you to the penitentiary, like they did that Yankee."

"But they don't know it," he had replied seriously; adding, with an injured tone, "you don't seem to appreciate my heroism like you did that of the Yankee; perhaps it's because I was n't caught and sent to the penitentiary. I thought you wanted me to do it."

"Why, Dick Owens!" she exclaimed. "You know I never dreamed of any such outrageous proceeding.

"But I presume I'll have to marry you," she concluded, after some insistence on Dick's part, "if only to take care of you. You are too reckless for anything; and a man who goes chasing all over the North, being entertained by New York and Boston society and having negroes to throw away, needs some one to look after him."

"It's a most remarkable thing," replied Dick fervently, "that your views correspond exactly with my profoundest convictions. It proves beyond question that we were made for one another."

They were married three weeks later. As each of them had just returned from a journey, they spent their honeymoon at home.

A week after the wedding they were seated, one afternoon, on the piazza of the colonel's house, where Dick had taken his bride, when a negro from the yard ran down the lane and threw open the big gate for the colonel's buggy to enter. The colonel was not alone. Beside him, ragged and travel-stained, bowed with weariness, and upon his face a haggard look that told of hardship and privation, sat the lost Grandison.

The colonel alighted at the steps.

"Take the lines, Tom," he said to the man who had opened the gate, "and drive round to the barn. Help Grandison down,—poor devil, he's so stiff he can hardly move!—and get a tub of water and wash him and rub him down, and feed him, and give him a big drink of whiskey, and then let him come round and see his young master and his new mistress."

The colonel's face wore an expression compounded of joy and indignation,—joy at the restoration of a valuable piece of property; indignation for reasons he proceeded to state.

"It's astounding, the depths of depravity the human heart is capable of! I was coming along the road three miles away, when I heard some one call me from the roadside. I pulled up the mare, and who should come out of the woods but Grandison. The poor nigger could hardly crawl along, with the help of a broken limb. I was never more astonished in my life. You could have knocked me down with a feather. He seemed pretty far gone,—he could hardly talk above a whisper,—and I had to give him a mouthful of whiskey to brace him up so he could tell his story. It's just as I thought from the beginning, Dick; Grandison had no notion of running away; he knew when he was well off, and where his friends were. All the persuasions of abolition liars and runaway niggers did not move him. But the desperation of those fanatics knew no bounds; their guilty consciences gave them no rest. They got the notion somehow that Grandison belonged to a nigger-catcher, and had been brought North as a spy to help capture ungrateful runaway servants. They actually kidnaped him—just think of it!—and gagged him and bound him and threw him rudely into a wagon, and carried him into the gloomy depths of a Canadian forest, and locked him in a lonely hut, and fed him on bread and water for three weeks. One of the scoundrels wanted to kill him, and persuaded the others that it ought to be done; but they got to quarreling about how they should do it, and before they had their minds made up Grandison escaped, and, keeping his back steadily to the North Star, made his way, after suffering incredible hardships, back to the old plantation, back to his master, his friends, and his home. Why, it's as good as one of Scott's novels! Mr. Simms or some other one of our Southern authors ought to write it up."

"Don't you think, sir," suggested Dick, who had calmly smoked his cigar throughout the colonel's animated recital, "that that kidnaping yarn sounds a little improbable? Is n't there some more likely explanation?"

"Nonsense, Dick; it's the gospel truth! Those infernal abolitionists are capable of anything—everything! Just think of their locking the poor, faithful nigger up, beating him, kicking him, depriving him of his liberty, keeping him on bread and water for three long, lonesome weeks, and he all the time pining for the old plantation!"

There were almost tears in the colonel's eyes at the picture of Grandison's sufferings that he conjured up. Dick still professed to be slightly skeptical, and met Charity's severely questioning eye with bland unconsciousness.

The colonel killed the fatted calf for Grandison, and for two or three weeks the returned wanderer's life was a slave's dream of pleasure. His fame spread throughout the county, and the colonel gave him a permanent place among the house servants, where he could always have him conveniently at hand to relate his adventures to admiring visitors.

About three weeks after Grandison's return the colonel's faith in sable humanity was rudely shaken, and its foundations almost broken up. He came near losing his belief in the fidelity of the negro to his master,—the servile virtue most highly prized and most sedulously cultivated by the colonel and his kind. One Monday morning Grandison was missing. And not only Grandison, but his wife, Betty the maid; his mother, aunt Eunice; his father, uncle Ike; his brothers, Tom and John, and his little sister Elsie, were likewise absent from the plantation; and a hurried search and inquiry in the neighborhood resulted in no information as to their whereabouts. So much valuable property could not be lost without an effort to recover it, and the wholesale nature of the transaction carried consternation to the hearts of those whose ledgers were chiefly bound in black. Extremely energetic measures were taken by the colonel and his friends. The fugitives were traced, and followed from point to point, on their northward run through Ohio. Several times the hunters were close upon their heels, but the magnitude of the escaping party begot unusual vigilance on the part of those who sympathized with the fugitives, and strangely enough, the underground railroad seemed to have had its tracks cleared and signals set for this particular train. Once, twice, the colonel thought he had them, but they slipped through his fingers. One last glimpse he caught of his vanishing property, as he stood, accompanied by a United States marshal, on a wharf at a port on the south shore of Lake Erie. On the stern of a small steamboat which was receding rapidly from the wharf, with her nose pointing toward Canada, there stood a group of familiar dark faces, and the look they cast backward was not one of longing for the fleshpots of Egypt. The colonel saw Grandison point him out to one of the crew of the vessel, who waved his hand derisively toward the colonel. The latter shook his fist impotently—and the incident was closed.

2.10.2 Reading and Review Questions

1. What elements of Local Color do you see in "The Passing of Grandison"? How does the story exhibit features of Realism?

2. Examine ways in which people may not be what they seem in the story. To what extent are any of the characters wearing "masks" or veiling their identities?

3. What is Chesnutt's view toward the Old South in the story?

4. How is "passing" depicted in the story? What meanings might the word have in light of the ending of the story?

5. Examine the idea of the hero in the story, paying particular attention to Charity Lomax's charge to Dick Owns to do something heroic.

6. Examine the layers of trickery in the story. Who wins, and who loses? Why?

2.11 CHARLOTTE PERKINS GILMAN

(1860 - 1935)

Image 2.9 | Charlotte Perkins Gilman, circa 1900
Photographer | C .F. Lummis
Source | Wikimedia Commons
License | Public Domain

As she writes in her autobiography, Charlotte Perkins Gilman had one overriding goal in her life: "the improvement of the human race." The niece of both the abolitionist Harriet Beecher Stowe and the suffragist Isabella Beecher Hooker, Gilman was one of the most important feminist writers, editors, and activists of the late nineteenth and early twentieth centuries. She led an unconventional life that directly inspired her poetry, fiction, and nonfiction alike. At the age of thirty-four, she divorced a husband who sought to "domesticate" her, leaving both him and her daughter to pursue an independent career authoring works of poetry, fiction, and social criticism; editing and publishing her own feminist magazine, *Forerunner*; and lecturing for the **American Woman Suffrage Association** and other organizations on the need for social reform to ensure equality between men and women. In the 1890s, Gilman published three works that solidified her reputation as both a major American writer and a groundbreaking feminist theorist: a well-received collection of feminist poems, *In This Our World* (1893); the groundbreaking work of social theory, *Women and Economics: A Study of the Economic Relation between Men and Women* *as a Factor in Social Evolution* (1898), in which she criticized the economic dependency of women upon men; and the shocking short story included in this chapter, "The Yellow Wall-Paper" (1892). Gilman remarried in 1900 and over the course of the first three decades of the twentieth century continued to edit, lecture, and publish works that advocated for the progressive reform of society. In her utopian novel *Herland* (1915), for example, she imagines a peaceful and ecologically sustainable society comprised solely of women who use technology and not men to reproduce.

While presented in the guise of a gothic tale of terror, "The Yellow Wall-Paper" is a fine example of political realism. Through this terrifying story of a woman locked in an ancient manor and haunted by a shadowy figure, Gilman shows that the real relationship between married men and women in her time is not one of equality but of domination and dependency. Gilman based the story on her own life. After giving birth to her daughter, Gilman fell into a state of depression and was sent to a clinic for treatment. Her doctor, a world-famous neurologist, advised her to quit all creative and intellectual activity and instead dedicate herself wholly to a private domestic routine. However, this so-called "**rest-cure**" only further deepened Gilman's depression and so she sought—and found—a cure for herself in her true callings: the literary and political work to which she dedicated the rest of her life.

2.11.1 "The Yellow Wall-Paper"

It is very seldom that mere ordinary people like John and myself secure ancestral halls for the summer.

A colonial mansion, a hereditary estate, I would say a haunted house, and reach the height of romantic felicity—but that would be asking too much of fate!

Still I will proudly declare that there is something queer about it.

Else, why should it be let so cheaply? And why have stood so long untenanted?

John laughs at me, of course, but one expects that in marriage.

John is practical in the extreme. He has no patience with faith, an intense horror of superstition, and he scoffs openly at any talk of things not to be felt and seen and put down in figures.

John is a physician, and PERHAPS—(I would not say it to a living soul, of course, but this is dead paper and a great relief to my mind)—PERHAPS that is one reason I do not get well faster.

You see he does not believe I am sick!

And what can one do?

If a physician of high standing, and one's own husband, assures friends and relatives that there is really nothing the matter with one but temporary nervous depression—a slight hysterical tendency—what is one to do?

My brother is also a physician, and also of high standing, and he says the same thing.

So I take phosphates or phosphites—whichever it is, and tonics, and journeys, and air, and exercise, and am absolutely forbidden to "work" until I am well again.

Personally, I disagree with their ideas.

Personally, I believe that congenial work, with excitement and change, would do me good.

But what is one to do?

I did write for a while in spite of them; but it DOES exhaust me a good deal—having to be so sly about it, or else meet with heavy opposition.

I sometimes fancy that in my condition if I had less opposition and more society and stimulus—but John says the very worst thing I can do is to think about my condition, and I confess it always makes me feel bad.

So I will let it alone and talk about the house.

The most beautiful place! It is quite alone, standing well back from the road, quite three miles from the village. It makes me think of English places that you read about, for there are hedges and walls and gates that lock, and lots of separate little houses for the gardeners and people.

There is a DELICIOUS garden! I never saw such a garden—large and shady, full of box-bordered paths, and lined with long grape-covered arbors with seats under them.

There were greenhouses, too, but they are all broken now.

There was some legal trouble, I believe, something about the heirs and coheirs; anyhow, the place has been empty for years.

That spoils my ghostliness, I am afraid, but I don't care—there is something strange about the house—I can feel it.

I even said so to John one moonlight evening, but he said what I felt was a DRAUGHT, and shut the window.

I get unreasonably angry with John sometimes. I'm sure I never used to be so sensitive. I think it is due to this nervous condition.

But John says if I feel so, I shall neglect proper self-control; so I take pains to control myself—before him, at least, and that makes me very tired.

I don't like our room a bit. I wanted one downstairs that opened on the piazza and had roses all over the window, and such pretty old-fashioned chintz hangings! but John would not hear of it.

He said there was only one window and not room for two beds, and no near room for him if he took another.

He is very careful and loving, and hardly lets me stir without special direction.

I have a schedule prescription for each hour in the day; he takes all care from me, and so I feel basely ungrateful not to value it more.

He said we came here solely on my account, that I was to have perfect rest and all the air I could get. "Your exercise depends on your strength, my dear," said he, "and your food somewhat on your appetite; but air you can absorb all the time." So we took the nursery at the top of the house.

It is a big, airy room, the whole floor nearly, with windows that look all ways, and air and sunshine galore. It was nursery first and then playroom and gymnasium, I should judge; for the windows are barred for little children, and there are rings and things in the walls.

The paint and paper look as if a boys' school had used it. It is stripped off—the paper—in great patches all around the head of my bed, about as far as I can reach, and in a great place on the other side of the room low down. I never saw a worse paper in my life.

One of those sprawling flamboyant patterns committing every artistic sin.

It is dull enough to confuse the eye in following, pronounced enough to constantly irritate and provoke study, and when you follow the lame uncertain curves for a little distance they suddenly commit suicide—plunge off at outrageous angles, destroy themselves in unheard of contradictions.

The color is repellent, almost revolting; a smouldering unclean yellow, strangely faded by the slow-turning sunlight.

It is a dull yet lurid orange in some places, a sickly sulphur tint in others.

No wonder the children hated it! I should hate it myself if I had to live in this room long.

There comes John, and I must put this away,—he hates to have me write a word.

We have been here two weeks, and I haven't felt like writing before, since that first day.

I am sitting by the window now, up in this atrocious nursery, and there is nothing to hinder my writing as much as I please, save lack of strength.

John is away all day, and even some nights when his cases are serious.

I am glad my case is not serious!

But these nervous troubles are dreadfully depressing.

John does not know how much I really suffer. He knows there is no REASON to suffer, and that satisfies him.

Of course it is only nervousness. It does weigh on me so not to do my duty in any way!

I meant to be such a help to John, such a real rest and comfort, and here I am a comparative burden already!

Nobody would believe what an effort it is to do what little I am able,—to dress and entertain, and order things.

It is fortunate Mary is so good with the baby. Such a dear baby!

And yet I CANNOT be with him, it makes me so nervous.

I suppose John never was nervous in his life. He laughs at me so about this wall-paper!

At first he meant to repaper the room, but afterwards he said that I was letting it get the better of me, and that nothing was worse for a nervous patient than to give way to such fancies.

He said that after the wall-paper was changed it would be the heavy bedstead, and then the barred windows, and then that gate at the head of the stairs, and so on.

"You know the place is doing you good," he said, "and really, dear, I don't care to renovate the house just for a three months' rental."

"Then do let us go downstairs," I said, "there are such pretty rooms there."

Then he took me in his arms and called me a blessed little goose, and said he would go down to the cellar, if I wished, and have it whitewashed into the bargain.

But he is right enough about the beds and windows and things.

It is an airy and comfortable room as any one need wish, and, of course, I would not be so silly as to make him uncomfortable just for a whim.

I'm really getting quite fond of the big room, all but that horrid paper.

Out of one window I can see the garden, those mysterious deepshaded arbors, the riotous old-fashioned flowers, and bushes and gnarly trees.

Out of another I get a lovely view of the bay and a little private wharf belonging to the estate. There is a beautiful shaded lane that runs down there from the house. I always fancy I see people walking in these numerous paths and arbors, but John has cautioned me not to give way to fancy in the least. He says that with my imaginative power and habit of story-making, a nervous weakness like mine is sure to lead to all manner of excited fancies, and that I ought to use my will and good sense to check the tendency. So I try.

I think sometimes that if I were only well enough to write a little it would relieve the press of ideas and rest me.

But I find I get pretty tired when I try.

It is so discouraging not to have any advice and companionship about my work. When I get really well, John says we will ask Cousin Henry and Julia down for a long visit; but he says he would as soon put fireworks in my pillow-case as to let me have those stimulating people about now.

I wish I could get well faster.

But I must not think about that. This paper looks to me as if it KNEW what a vicious influence it had!

There is a recurrent spot where the pattern lolls like a broken neck and two bulbous eyes stare at you upside down.

I get positively angry with the impertinence of it and the everlastingness. Up and down and sideways they crawl, and those absurd, unblinking eyes are everywhere. There is one place where two breadths didn't match, and the eyes go all up and down the line, one a little higher than the other.

I never saw so much expression in an inanimate thing before, and we all know how much expression they have! I used to lie awake as a child and get more entertainment and terror out of blank walls and plain furniture than most children could find in a toy store.

I remember what a kindly wink the knobs of our big, old bureau used to have, and there was one chair that always seemed like a strong friend.

I used to feel that if any of the other things looked too fierce I could always hop into that chair and be safe.

The furniture in this room is no worse than inharmonious, however, for we had to bring it all from downstairs. I suppose when this was used as a playroom they had to take the nursery things out, and no wonder! I never saw such ravages as the children have made here.

The wall-paper, as I said before, is torn off in spots, and it sticketh closer than a brother—they must have had perseverance as well as hatred.

Then the floor is scratched and gouged and splintered, the plaster itself is dug out here and there, and this great heavy bed which is all we found in the room, looks as if it had been through the wars.

But I don't mind it a bit—only the paper.

There comes John's sister. Such a dear girl as she is, and so careful of me! I must not let her find me writing.

She is a perfect and enthusiastic housekeeper, and hopes for no better profession. I verily believe she thinks it is the writing which made me sick!

But I can write when she is out, and see her a long way off from these windows.

There is one that commands the road, a lovely shaded winding road, and one that just looks off over the country. A lovely country, too, full of great elms and velvet meadows.

This wall-paper has a kind of sub-pattern in a different shade, a particularly irritating one, for you can only see it in certain lights, and not clearly then.

But in the places where it isn't faded and where the sun is just so—I can see a strange, provoking, formless sort of figure, that seems to skulk about behind that silly and conspicuous front design.

There's sister on the stairs!

Well, the Fourth of July is over! The people are gone and I am tired out. John thought it might do me good to see a little company, so we just had mother and Nellie and the children down for a week.

Of course I didn't do a thing. Jennie sees to everything now.

But it tired me all the same.

John says if I don't pick up faster he shall send me to Weir Mitchell in the fall.

But I don't want to go there at all. I had a friend who was in his hands once, and she says he is just like John and my brother, only more so!

Besides, it is such an undertaking to go so far.

I don't feel as if it was worth while to turn my hand over for anything, and I'm getting dreadfully fretful and querulous.

I cry at nothing, and cry most of the time.

Of course I don't when John is here, or anybody else, but when I am alone.

And I am alone a good deal just now. John is kept in town very often by serious cases, and Jennie is good and lets me alone when I want her to.

So I walk a little in the garden or down that lovely lane, sit on the porch under the roses, and lie down up here a good deal.

I'm getting really fond of the room in spite of the wall-paper. Perhaps BE-CAUSE of the wall-paper.

It dwells in my mind so!

I lie here on this great immovable bed—it is nailed down, I believe—and follow that pattern about by the hour. It is as good as gymnastics, I assure you. I start, we'll say, at the bottom, down in the corner over there where it has not been touched, and I determine for the thousandth time that I WILL follow that pointless pattern to some sort of a conclusion.

I know a little of the principle of design, and I know this thing was not arranged on any laws of radiation, or alternation, or repetition, or symmetry, or anything else that I ever heard of.

It is repeated, of course, by the breadths, but not otherwise.

Looked at in one way each breadth stands alone, the bloated curves and flourishes—a kind of "debased Romanesque" with delirium tremens—go waddling up and down in isolated columns of fatuity.

But, on the other hand, they connect diagonally, and the sprawling outlines run off in great slanting waves of optic horror, like a lot of wallowing seaweeds in full chase.

The whole thing goes horizontally, too, at least it seems so, and I exhaust myself in trying to distinguish the order of its going in that direction.

They have used a horizontal breadth for a frieze, and that adds wonderfully to the confusion.

There is one end of the room where it is almost intact, and there, when the crosslights fade and the low sun shines directly upon it, I can almost fancy radiation after all,—the interminable grotesques seem to form around a common centre and rush off in headlong plunges of equal distraction.

It makes me tired to follow it. I will take a nap I guess.

I don't know why I should write this.

I don't want to.

I don't feel able.

And I know John would think it absurd. But I MUST say what I feel and think in some way—it is such a relief!

But the effort is getting to be greater than the relief.

Half the time now I am awfully lazy, and lie down ever so much.

John says I musn't lose my strength, and has me take cod liver oil and lots of tonics and things, to say nothing of ale and wine and rare meat.

Dear John! He loves me very dearly, and hates to have me sick. I tried to have a real earnest reasonable talk with him the other day, and tell him how I wish he would let me go and make a visit to Cousin Henry and Julia.

But he said I wasn't able to go, nor able to stand it after I got there; and I did not make out a very good case for myself, for I was crying before I had finished.

It is getting to be a great effort for me to think straight. Just this nervous weakness I suppose.

And dear John gathered me up in his arms, and just carried me upstairs and laid me on the bed, and sat by me and read to me till it tired my head.

He said I was his darling and his comfort and all he had, and that I must take care of myself for his sake, and keep well.

He says no one but myself can help me out of it, that I must use my will and self-control and not let any silly fancies run away with me.

There's one comfort, the baby is well and happy, and does not have to occupy this nursery with the horrid wall-paper.

If we had not used it, that blessed child would have! What a fortunate escape! Why, I wouldn't have a child of mine, an impressionable little thing, live in such a room for worlds.

I never thought of it before, but it is lucky that John kept me here after all, I can stand it so much easier than a baby, you see.

Of course I never mention it to them any more—I am too wise,—but I keep watch of it all the same.

There are things in that paper that nobody knows but me, or ever will.

Behind that outside pattern the dim shapes get clearer every day.

It is always the same shape, only very numerous.

And it is like a woman stooping down and creeping about behind that pattern. I don't like it a bit. I wonder—I begin to think—I wish John would take me away from here!

It is so hard to talk with John about my case, because he is so wise, and because he loves me so.

But I tried it last night.

It was moonlight. The moon shines in all around just as the sun does.

I hate to see it sometimes, it creeps so slowly, and always comes in by one window or another.

John was asleep and I hated to waken him, so I kept still and watched the moonlight on that undulating wall-paper till I felt creepy.

The faint figure behind seemed to shake the pattern, just as if she wanted to get out.

I got up softly and went to feel and see if the paper DID move, and when I came back John was awake.

"What is it, little girl?" he said. "Don't go walking about like that—you'll get cold."

I though it was a good time to talk, so I told him that I really was not gaining here, and that I wished he would take me away.

"Why darling!" said he, "our lease will be up in three weeks, and I can't see how to leave before.

"The repairs are not done at home, and I cannot possibly leave town just now. Of course if you were in any danger, I could and would, but you really are better, dear, whether you can see it or not. I am a doctor, dear, and I know. You are gaining flesh and color, your appetite is better, I feel really much easier about you."

"I don't weigh a bit more," said I, "nor as much; and my appetite may be better in the evening when you are here, but it is worse in the morning when you are away!"

"Bless her little heart!" said he with a big hug, "she shall be as sick as she pleases! But now let's improve the shining hours by going to sleep, and talk about it in the morning!"

"And you won't go away?" I asked gloomily.

"Why, how can I, dear? It is only three weeks more and then we will take a nice little trip of a few days while Jennie is getting the house ready. Really dear you are better!"

"Better in body perhaps—" I began, and stopped short, for he sat up straight and looked at me with such a stern, reproachful look that I could not say another word.

"My darling," said he, "I beg of you, for my sake and for our child's sake, as well as for your own, that you will never for one instant let that idea enter your mind! There is nothing so dangerous, so fascinating, to a temperament like yours. It is a false and foolish fancy. Can you not trust me as a physician when I tell you so?"

So of course I said no more on that score, and we went to sleep before long. He thought I was asleep first, but I wasn't, and lay there for hours trying to decide whether that front pattern and the back pattern really did move together or separately.

On a pattern like this, by daylight, there is a lack of sequence, a defiance of law, that is a constant irritant to a normal mind.

The color is hideous enough, and unreliable enough, and infuriating enough, but the pattern is torturing.

You think you have mastered it, but just as you get well underway in following, it turns a back-somersault and there you are. It slaps you in the face, knocks you down, and tramples upon you. It is like a bad dream.

The outside pattern is a florid arabesque, reminding one of a fungus. If you can imagine a toadstool in joints, an interminable string of toadstools, budding and sprouting in endless convolutions—why, that is something like it.

That is, sometimes!

There is one marked peculiarity about this paper, a thing nobody seems to notice but myself, and that is that it changes as the light changes.

When the sun shoots in through the east window—I always watch for that first long, straight ray—it changes so quickly that I never can quite believe it.

That is why I watch it always.

By moonlight—the moon shines in all night when there is a moon—I wouldn't know it was the same paper.

At night in any kind of light, in twilight, candle light, lamplight, and worst of all by moonlight, it becomes bars! The outside pattern I mean, and the woman behind it is as plain as can be.

I didn't realize for a long time what the thing was that showed behind, that dim sub-pattern, but now I am quite sure it is a woman.

By daylight she is subdued, quiet. I fancy it is the pattern that keeps her so still. It is so puzzling. It keeps me quiet by the hour.

I lie down ever so much now. John says it is good for me, and to sleep all I can.

Indeed he started the habit by making me lie down for an hour after each meal.

It is a very bad habit I am convinced, for you see I don't sleep.

And that cultivates deceit, for I don't tell them I'm awake—O no!

The fact is I am getting a little afraid of John.

He seems very queer sometimes, and even Jennie has an inexplicable look.

It strikes me occasionally, just as a scientific hypothesis,—that perhaps it is the paper!

I have watched John when he did not know I was looking, and come into the room suddenly on the most innocent excuses, and I've caught him several times LOOKING AT THE PAPER! And Jennie too. I caught Jennie with her hand on it once.

She didn't know I was in the room, and when I asked her in a quiet, a very quiet voice, with the most restrained manner possible, what she was doing with the paper—she turned around as if she had been caught stealing, and looked quite angry—asked me why I should frighten her so!

Then she said that the paper stained everything it touched, that she had found yellow smooches on all my clothes and John's, and she wished we would be more careful!

Did not that sound innocent? But I know she was studying that pattern, and I am determined that nobody shall find it out but myself!

Life is very much more exciting now than it used to be. You see I have something more to expect, to look forward to, to watch. I really do eat better, and am more quiet than I was.

John is so pleased to see me improve! He laughed a little the other day, and said I seemed to be flourishing in spite of my wall-paper.

I turned it off with a laugh. I had no intention of telling him it was

BECAUSE of the wall-paper—he would make fun of me. He might even want to take me away.

I don't want to leave now until I have found it out. There is a week more, and I think that will be enough.

I'm feeling ever so much better! I don't sleep much at night, for it is so interesting to watch developments; but I sleep a good deal in the daytime.

In the daytime it is tiresome and perplexing.

There are always new shoots on the fungus, and new shades of yellow all over it. I cannot keep count of them, though I have tried conscientiously.

It is the strangest yellow, that wall-paper! It makes me think of all the yellow things I ever saw—not beautiful ones like buttercups, but old foul, bad yellow things.

But there is something else about that paper—the smell! I noticed it the moment we came into the room, but with so much air and sun it was not bad. Now we have had a week of fog and rain, and whether the windows are open or not, the smell is here.

It creeps all over the house.

I find it hovering in the dining-room, skulking in the parlor, hiding in the hall, lying in wait for me on the stairs.

It gets into my hair.

Even when I go to ride, if I turn my head suddenly and surprise it—there is that smell!

Such a peculiar odor, too! I have spent hours in trying to analyze it, to find what it smelled like.

It is not bad—at first, and very gentle, but quite the subtlest, most enduring odor I ever met.

In this damp weather it is awful, I wake up in the night and find it hanging over me.

It used to disturb me at first. I thought seriously of burning the house—to reach the smell.

But now I am used to it. The only thing I can think of that it is like is the COLOR of the paper! A yellow smell.

There is a very funny mark on this wall, low down, near the mopboard. A streak that runs round the room. It goes behind every piece of furniture, except the bed, a long, straight, even SMOOCH, as if it had been rubbed over and over.

I wonder how it was done and who did it, and what they did it for. Round and round and round—round and round and round—it makes me dizzy!

I really have discovered something at last.

Through watching so much at night, when it changes so, I have finally found out.

The front pattern DOES move—and no wonder! The woman behind shakes it!

Sometimes I think there are a great many women behind, and sometimes only one, and she crawls around fast, and her crawling shakes it all over.

Then in the very bright spots she keeps still, and in the very shady spots she just takes hold of the bars and shakes them hard.

And she is all the time trying to climb through. But nobody could climb through that pattern—it strangles so; I think that is why it has so many heads.

They get through, and then the pattern strangles them off and turns them up-side down, and makes their eyes white!

If those heads were covered or taken off it would not be half so bad.

I think that woman gets out in the daytime!

And I'll tell you why—privately—I've seen her!

I can see her out of every one of my windows!

It is the same woman, I know, for she is always creeping, and most women do not creep by daylight.

I see her on that long road under the trees, creeping along, and when a carriage comes she hides under the blackberry vines.

I don't blame her a bit. It must be very humiliating to be caught creeping by daylight!

I always lock the door when I creep by daylight. I can't do it at night, for I know John would suspect something at once.

And John is so queer now, that I don't want to irritate him. I wish he would take another room! Besides, I don't want anybody to get that woman out at night but myself.

I often wonder if I could see her out of all the windows at once.

But, turn as fast as I can, I can only see out of one at one time.

And though I always see her, she MAY be able to creep faster than I can turn!

I have watched her sometimes away off in the open country, creeping as fast as a cloud shadow in a high wind.

If only that top pattern could be gotten off from the under one! I mean to try it, little by little.

I have found out another funny thing, but I shan't tell it this time! It does not do to trust people too much.

There are only two more days to get this paper off, and I believe John is beginning to notice. I don't like the look in his eyes.

And I heard him ask Jennie a lot of professional questions about me. She had a very good report to give.

She said I slept a good deal in the daytime.

John knows I don't sleep very well at night, for all I'm so quiet!

He asked me all sorts of questions, too, and pretended to be very loving and kind.

As if I couldn't see through him!

Still, I don't wonder he acts so, sleeping under this paper for three months.

It only interests me, but I feel sure John and Jennie are secretly affected by it.

Hurrah! This is the last day, but it is enough. John is to stay in town over night, and won't be out until this evening.

Jennie wanted to sleep with me—the sly thing! but I told her I should undoubtedly rest better for a night all alone.

That was clever, for really I wasn't alone a bit! As soon as it was moonlight and that poor thing began to crawl and shake the pattern, I got up and ran to help her.

I pulled and she shook, I shook and she pulled, and before morning we had peeled off yards of that paper.

A strip about as high as my head and half around the room.

And then when the sun came and that awful pattern began to laugh at me, I declared I would finish it to-day!

We go away to-morrow, and they are moving all my furniture down again to leave things as they were before.

Jennie looked at the wall in amazement, but I told her merrily that I did it out of pure spite at the vicious thing.

She laughed and said she wouldn't mind doing it herself, but I must not get tired.

How she betrayed herself that time!

But I am here, and no person touches this paper but me—not ALIVE!

She tried to get me out of the room—it was too patent! But I said it was so quiet and empty and clean now that I believed I would lie down again and sleep all I could; and not to wake me even for dinner—I would call when I woke.

So now she is gone, and the servants are gone, and the things are gone, and there is nothing left but that great bedstead nailed down, with the canvas mattress we found on it.

We shall sleep downstairs to-night, and take the boat home to-morrow.

I quite enjoy the room, now it is bare again.

How those children did tear about here!

This bedstead is fairly gnawed!

But I must get to work.

I have locked the door and thrown the key down into the front path.

I don't want to go out, and I don't want to have anybody come in, till John comes.

I want to astonish him.

I've got a rope up here that even Jennie did not find. If that woman does get out, and tries to get away, I can tie her!

But I forgot I could not reach far without anything to stand on!

This bed will NOT move!

I tried to lift and push it until I was lame, and then I got so angry I bit off a little piece at one corner—but it hurt my teeth.

Then I peeled off all the paper I could reach standing on the floor. It sticks horribly and the pattern just enjoys it! All those strangled heads and bulbous eyes and waddling fungus growths just shriek with derision!

I am getting angry enough to do something desperate. To jump out of the window would be admirable exercise, but the bars are too strong even to try.

Besides I wouldn't do it. Of course not. I know well enough that a step like that is improper and might be misconstrued.

I don't like to LOOK out of the windows even—there are so many of those creeping women, and they creep so fast.

I wonder if they all come out of that wall-paper as I did?

But I am securely fastened now by my well-hidden rope—you don't get ME out in the road there!

I suppose I shall have to get back behind the pattern when it comes night, and that is hard!

It is so pleasant to be out in this great room and creep around as I please!

I don't want to go outside. I won't, even if Jennie asks me to.

For outside you have to creep on the ground, and everything is green instead of yellow.

But here I can creep smoothly on the floor, and my shoulder just fits in that long smooch around the wall, so I cannot lose my way.

Why there's John at the door!

It is no use, young man, you can't open it!

How he does call and pound!

Now he's crying for an axe.

It would be a shame to break down that beautiful door!

"John dear!" said I in the gentlest voice, "the key is down by the front steps, under a plantain leaf!"

That silenced him for a few moments.

Then he said—very quietly indeed, "Open the door, my darling!"

"I can't," said I. "The key is down by the front door under a plantain leaf!"

And then I said it again, several times, very gently and slowly, and said it so often that he had to go and see, and he got it of course, and came in. He stopped short by the door.

"What is the matter?" he cried. "For God's sake, what are you doing!"

I kept on creeping just the same, but I looked at him over my shoulder.

"I've got out at last," said I, "in spite of you and Jane. And I've pulled off most of the paper, so you can't put me back!"

Now why should that man have fainted? But he did, and right across my path by the wall, so that I had to creep over him every time!

2.11.2 Reading and Review Questions

1. As you read "The Yellow Wall-Paper," you will be tempted to diagnose the narrator as suffering from postpartum depression. However, does the source of the narrator's lingering illness reside entirely in her body? Consider other causes for her on-going malaise. Why isn't she getting better?

2. Consider how the narrator's loving doctor-husband John talks to and controls her. What does John allow—and, more importantly, forbid—his sick wife to think and do?

3. The narrator of this story is unreliable as she is suffering from mental illness, which leads her to misinterpret the nature of her confinement. For instance, the narrator presumes that she is confined within a child's former playroom. Close-read the details of the story's setting, contrasting the narrator's interpretation of the details of her room—the bars on the windows, for instance—with your own sense of what these things mean.

2.12 CHAPTER TWO KEY TERMS

- Acadian
- Ambrose Bierce
- American Literary Realism
- Charles Waddell Chesnutt
- Charlotte Perkins Gilman
- Creole
- Feminism/Feminism
- Henry James
- Iconoclast
- Immigration
- Industrial Age
- Industrialization
- Kate Chopin
- Local Color
- Mark Twain
- Mary E. Wilkins Freeman
- Meta-fiction
- NAACP
- Passing
- Realism
- Realists
- Regionalism
- Rest-Cure
- Sarah Orne Jewett
- Satire
- The Woman Suffrage Movement
- William Dean Howells

Naturalism (1890-1914)

Amy Berke and Doug Davis

3.1 LEARNING OUTCOMES

After completing this chapter, you should be able to:
- Describe the influence of Darwin's theory of evolution and Zola's theory of literary naturalism on American Naturalist writers.

- List the features of American Literary Naturalism.

- Identify stylistic elements of Naturalism in literary selections.

- Identify prominent similarities and differences among the literary works by Naturalist writers.

3.2 INTRODUCTION

The generation of writers that followed William Dean Howells broke with their past, as did the Realists when they rejected Romanticism as a literary style. Frank Norris, Stephen Crane, Jack London, Theodore Dreiser, Harold Frederic, Hamlin Garland, Ellen Glasgow and Kate Chopin, to name a few, rejected the limitations of Realism in terms of subject matter. While they all, to some extent, embraced the Realist style of writing with its attention to detail and authenticity, they rejected Realism's tendency not to offend the sensibilities of readers in the genteel classes. The new writers were not afraid of provocative subject matters and wrote about the human condition in starker, grimmer contexts. They all, to some extent, were influenced by not only scientific ideas of the day, including **Charles Darwin's** views on evolution, but also European writers experimenting with this new style: **Naturalism**. Émile **Zola**, a prominent French novelist, had articulated a theory of Naturalism in *Le Roman Expérimental* (1880). Zola had argued for a kind of intense Realism, one that did not look away from any aspects of life, including the base, dirty, or ugly. Also influenced by Darwin, Zola saw the human in animal terms, and he argued that a novel written about the human animal could be set up as a kind of scientific experiment, where, once the ingredients were added, the story would unfold with scientific accuracy. He was particularly interested in how hereditary traits under the influence of a particular social environment might determine how a human behaves. The American writers Norris, Crane, and London, similarly characterize humans as part of the evolutionary landscape, as beings influenced—and even determined—by forces of heredity and environment beyond their understanding or control.

With Darwin's and Zola's influence apparent, the naturalists sought to push Realism even further, or as Frank Norris argued in his essay "A Plea for Romantic Fiction," to go beyond the "meticulous presentation of teacups, rag carpets, wall paper, and hair-cloth sofas"—or beyond Realism as mere photographic accuracy—and to embrace a kind of writing that explores the "unplumbed depths of the human heart, and the mystery of sex, and the black, unsearched penetralia of the souls of men." Norris is calling for a grittier approach in examining the human being as essentially an upright animal, a kind of walking complex combination of inherited traits, attributes, and habits deeply affected by social and economic forces.

Naturalistic works went where Realistic works did not go, dealing with taboo subjects for the time, subjects such as prostitution, alcoholism, domestic violence, violent deaths, crime, madness, and degeneration. Sometimes defined as pessimistic materialistic determinism, Naturalism sought to look at human nature in a scientific light, and the author often took on the role of scientist, coolly observing the human animal in a variety of plights, at the mercy of forces beyond his control or understanding, compelled by instinct and determined by cause and effect to behave in certain, often self-destructive, ways as a result of heredity and environment. In such works, the plot plays out on the material evolutionary plain, where a benevolent deity or any supernatural form is absent and idealistic concepts, such as justice, liberty, innate goodness, and morality, are shown as illusions, as simple fabrications of the human animal trying to elevate himself above the other animals.

In the Naturalistic works, nature is depicted as indifferent, sometimes even hostile, to humans, and humans are often depicted as small, insignificant, nameless losers in battles against an all-powerful nature. Characters may dream of heroic actions in the midst of a battle to survive extreme conditions, but they are most often trapped by circumstances, unable to summon the will to change their determined outcome. Characters rarely exhibit free will at all; they often stumble through events, victims of their own vices, weaknesses, hereditary traits, and grim social or natural environments. A male character in a Naturalistic novel is often characterized as part "brute," and he typically exhibits strong impulses, compulsions, or instinctive drives, as he attempts to satiate his greed, his sexual urges, his decadent lusts, or his desire for power or dominance. Female characters also typically exhibit subconscious drives, acting without knowing why, unable to change course.

Naturalistic works are not defined by a region; the characters' action may take place in the frozen Alaska wilderness, on the raging sea, or within the slums of a city. Stylistically, Naturalistic novels are written from an almost journalistic perspective, with narrative distance from action and the characters. Often characters are not given names as a way to reinforce their cosmic insignificance. The plot of the story often follows the steady decline of a character into degeneration or death (known as the "**plot of decline**").

3.3 FRANK NORRIS

(1870 - 1902)

Norris grew up in an affluent household in Chicago before moving to San Francisco at the age of fourteen. His father's jewelry and real estate businesses provided for his education in the fine arts while his mother's interest in romantic literature introduced him to authors such as Sir Walter Scott, whose novel of medieval chivalry, *Ivanhoe*, heavily influenced the young Norris. At the age of seventeen, Norris left his family for Paris to study painting, revel in the city's delights, and pen romantic tales of medieval knights that he mailed to his younger brother. Returning home, Norris attended the University of California at Berkeley before transferring to Harvard to study creative writing. Although he never received a degree, Norris's time at Harvard was crucial to his development as an author. While there, he followed

Image 3.1 | Frank Norris, 1911
Photographer | Unknown
Source | Wikimedia Commons
License | Public Domain

the advice of his professors and developed a more realistic style while beginning the novels *McTeague (1899)*, *Blix* (1900), and *Vandover and the Brute* (1914). He also came, in this period, to greatly admire the French novelist Émile Zola, whose emphasis on the power of nature and the environment over individual characters inspired the composition of *McTeague* in particular. Returning to San Francisco, Norris wrote over 150 articles as a journalist, traveling to remote nations such as South Africa and Cuba as a war reporter for *McClure's Magazine*. He then moved to New York to work in publishing, where he is credited with discovering Theodore Dreiser's *Sister Carrie* (1900) for Doubleday & McClure Company. Before his untimely death from illness at the age of thirty-two, Norris published less than half a dozen novels, most notably the first two novels in his unfinished "Epic of Wheat" trilogy, *The Octopus: A Story of California* (1901) and (posthumously) *The Pit* (1903), both of which explore the brutality of the business world.

Like fellow naturalist Jack London, Norris was more interested in the raw, violent human animal than in the polite, civilized human being. In his most memorable stories, he sought to combine the scientific sensibilities of naturalism with the melodrama of romantic fiction. Norris produced a theory of naturalism in his critical essays, seeking to distinguish it from both American realism, which he condemned as too focused on the manners of middle-class society, and historical "cut and thrust" romances, which he saw as merely escapist entertainment. In the essay included here, "A Plea for Romantic Fiction," Norris describes the Romance genre itself as a woman entering a house, imagining the intense, instructive dramas she would uncover if she were to abandon medieval swordplay and instead visit an average middle-class American home.

Norris puts his theory of naturalism into practice in his novel *McTeague*, crafting a titular protagonist—a "poor crude dentist of Polk Street, stupid, ignorant, vulgar" with "enormous bones and corded muscles"—who is more animal than man. The novel traces the upward trajectory of McTeague, from the grim poverty of life in the mining camp to the middle class life of a practicing dentist in San Francisco. However, McTeague, for all his apparent human striving, ultimately ends up where he started: in a mining camp, poor, uneducated, alone, and in trouble. He ends up a victim of instinctive, hereditary, and environmental influences and forces beyond his knowledge or his control.

3.3.1 "A Plea For Romantic Fiction"

Let us at the start make a distinction. Observe that one speaks of romanticism and not sentimentalism. One claims that the latter is as distinct from the former as is that other form of art which is called Realism. Romance has been often put upon and overburdened by being forced to bear the onus of abuse that by right should fall to sentiment; but the two should be kept very distinct, for a very high and illustrious place will be claimed for romance, while sentiment will be handed down the scullery stairs.

Many people to-day are composing mere sentimentalism, and calling it and causing it to be called romance; so with those who are too busy to think much upon these subjects, but who none the less love honest literature, Romance, too, has fallen into disrepute. Consider now the cut-and-thrust stories. They are all labeled Romances, and it is very easy to get the impression that Romance must be an affair of cloaks and daggers, or moonlight and golden hair. But this is not so at all. The true Romance is a more serious business than this. It is not merely a conjurer's trick-box, full of flimsy quackeries, tinsel and claptraps, meant only to amuse, and relying upon deception to do even that. Is it not something better than this? Can we not see in it an instrument, keen, finely tempered, flawless an instrument with which we may go straight through the clothes and tissues and wrappings of flesh down deep into the red, living heart of things?

Is all this too subtle, too merely speculative and intrinsic, too *precieuse* and nice and "literary"? Devoutly one hopes the contrary. So much is made of so-called Romanticism in present-day fiction that the subject seems worthy of discussion, and a protest against the misuse of a really noble and honest formula of literature appeals to be timely—misuse, that is, in the sense of limited use. Let us suppose for the moment that a romance can be made out of a cut-and-thrust business. Good Heavens, are there no other things that are romantic, even in this—falsely, falsely called—humdrum world of to-day? Why should it be that so soon as the novelist addresses himself—seriously—to the consideration of contemporary life he must abandon Romance and take up that harsh, loveless, colourless, blunt tool called Realism?

Now, let us understand at once what is meant by Romance and what by Realism. Romance, I take it, is the kind of fiction that takes cognizance of variations from the type of normal life. Realism is the kind of fiction that confines itself to the type of normal life. According to this definition, then, Romance may even treat of the sordid, the unlovely—as for instance, the novels of M. Zola. (Zola has been dubbed a Realist, but he is, on the contrary, the very head of the Romanticists.) Also, Realism, used as it sometimes is as a term of reproach, need not be in the remotest sense or degree offensive, but on the other hand respectable as a church and proper as a deacon—as, for instance, the novels of Mr. Howells.

The reason why one claims so much for Romance, and quarrels so pointedly with Realism, is that Realism stultifies itself. It notes only the surface of things. For it, Beauty is not even skin deep, but only a geometrical plane, without dimensions and depth, a mere outside. Realism is very excellent so far as it goes, but it goes no further than the Realist himself can actually see, or actually hear. Realism is minute! it is the drama of a broken teacup, the tragedy of a walk down the block, the excitement of an afternoon call, the adventure of an invitation to dinner. It is the visit to my neighbour's house, a formal visit, from which I may draw no conclusions. I see my neighbour and his friends—very, oh, such very! probable people—and that is all. Realism bows upon the doormat and goes away and says to me, as we link arms on the sidewalk: "That is life." And I say it is not. It is not, as you would very well see if you took Romance with you to call upon your neighbour.

Lately you have been taking Romance a weary journey across the water—ages and the flood of years—and haling her into the fusby, musty, worm-eaten, moth-riddled, rust-corroded "Grandes Salles" of the Middle Ages and the Renaissance, and she has found the drama of a bygone age for you there. But would you take her across the street to your neighbour's front parlour (with the bisque fisher-boy on the mantel and the photograph of Niagara Falls on glass hanging in the front window); would you introduce her there? Not you. Would you take a walk with her on Fifth Avenue, or Beacon Street, or Michigan Avenue? No, indeed. Would you choose her for a companion of a morning spent in Wall Street, or an afternoon in the Waldorf-Astoria? You just guess you would not.

She would be out of place, you say—inappropriate. She might be awkward in my neighbour's front parlour, and knock over the little bisque fisher-boy. Well, she might. If she did, you might find underneath the base of the statuette, hidden away, tucked away—what? God knows. But something that would be a complete revelation of my neighbour's secretest life.

So you think Romance would stop in the front parlour and discuss medicated flannels and mineral waters with the ladies? Not for more than five minutes. She would be off upstairs with you, prying, peeping, peering into the closets of the bedroom, into the nursery, into the sitting-room; yes, and into that little iron box screwed to the lower shelf of the closet in the library; and into those compartments and pigeon-holes of the *secretaire* in the study. She would find a heartache (maybe) between the pillows of the mistress's bed, and a memory carefully secreted in the master's deed-box. She would come upon a great hope amid the books and papers of the study-table of the young man's room, and—perhaps—who knows an—affair, or, great Heavens, an intrigue, in the scented ribbons and gloves and hairpins of the young lady's bureau. And she would pick here a little and there a little, making up a bag of hopes and fears and a package of joys and sorrows—great ones, mind you—and then come down to the front door, and, stepping out into the street, hand you the bags and package and say to you—"That is Life!" Romance does very well in the castles of the Middle Ages and the Renaissance chateaux, and she has the *entree* there and is very well received. That is all well and good. But let us protest against limiting her to such places and such times. You will find her, I grant you, in the chatelaine's chamber and the dungeon of the man-at-arms; but, if you choose to look for her, you will find her equally at home in the brownstone house on the corner and in the office-building downtown. And this very day, in this very hour, she is sitting among the rags and wretchedness, the dirt and despair of the tenements of the East Side of New York.

"What?" I hear you say, "look for Romance—the lady of the silken robes and golden crown, our beautiful, chaste maiden of soft voice and gentle eyes—look for her among the vicious ruffians, male and female, of Allen Street and Mulberry Bend?" I tell you she is there, and to your shame be it said you will not know her in those surroundings. You, the aristocrats, who demand the fine linen and the purple in your fiction; you, the sensitive, the delicate, who will associate with your

Romance only so long as she wears a silken gown. You will not follow her to the slums, for you believe that Romance should only amuse and entertain you, singing you sweet songs and touching the harp of silver strings with rosy-tipped fingers. If haply she should call to you from the squalour of a dive, or the awful degradation of a disorderly house, crying: "Look! listen! This, too, is life. These, too, are my children! Look at them, know them and, knowing, help!" Should she call thus you would stop your ears! you would avert your eyes and you would answer, "Come from there, Romance. Your place is not there!" And you would make of her a harlequin, a tumbler, a sword-dancer, when, as a matter of fact, she should be by right divine a teacher sent from God.

She will not often wear the robe of silk, the gold crown, the jeweled shoon; will not always sweep the silver harp. An iron note is hers if so she choose, and coarse garments, and stained hands; and, meeting her thus, it is for you to know her as she passes—know her for the same young queen of the blue mantle and lilies. She can teach you if you will be humble to learn—teach you by showing. God help you if at last you take from Romance her mission of teaching; if you do not believe that she has a purpose—a nobler purpose and a mightier than mere amusement, mere entertainment. Let Realism do the entertaining with its meticulous presentation of teacups, rag carpets, wall-paper and haircloth sofas, stopping with these, going no deeper than it sees, choosing the ordinary, the untroubled, the commonplace.

But to Romance belongs the wide world for range, and the unplumbed depths of the human heart, and the mystery of sex, and the problems of life, and the black, unsearched penetralia of the soul of man. You, the indolent, must not always be amused. What matter the silken clothes, what matter the prince's houses? Romance, too, is a teacher, and if—throwing aside the purple—she wears the camel's-hair and feeds upon the locusts, it is to cry aloud unto the people, "Prepare ye the way of the Lord; make straight his path."

3.3.2 Selections from *McTeague*

CHAPTER 1

It was Sunday, and, according to his custom on that day, McTeague took his dinner at two in the afternoon at the car conductors' coffee-joint on Polk Street. He had a thick gray soup; heavy, underdone meat, very hot, on a cold plate; two kinds of vegetables; and a sort of suet pudding, full of strong butter and sugar. On his way back to his office, one block above, he stopped at Joe Frenna's saloon and bought a pitcher of steam beer. It was his habit to leave the pitcher there on his way to dinner.

Once in his office, or, as he called it on his signboard, "Dental Parlors," he took off his coat and shoes, unbuttoned his vest, and, having crammed his little stove full of coke, lay back in his operating chair at the bay window, reading the paper, drinking his beer, and smoking his huge porcelain pipe while his food digested; crop-full, stupid, and warm. By and by, gorged with steam beer, and overcome by the heat of the room, the cheap tobacco, and the effects of his heavy meal, he dropped off to sleep. Late in the afternoon his canary bird, in its gilt cage just over his head, began to sing. He woke slowly, finished the rest of his beer—very flat and stale by this time—and taking down his concertina from the bookcase, where in week days it kept the company of seven volumes of "Allen's Practical Dentist," played upon it some half-dozen very mournful airs.

McTeague looked forward to these Sunday afternoons as a period of relaxation and enjoyment. He invariably spent them in the same fashion. These were his only pleasures—to eat, to smoke, to sleep, and to play upon his concertina.

The six lugubrious airs that he knew, always carried him back to the time when he was a car-boy at the Big Dipper Mine in Placer County, ten years before. He remembered the years he had spent there trundling the heavy cars of ore in and out of the tunnel under the direction of his father. For thirteen days of each fortnight his father was a steady, hard-working shift-boss of the mine. Every other Sunday he became an irresponsible animal, a beast, a brute, crazy with alcohol.

McTeague remembered his mother, too, who, with the help of the Chinaman, cooked for forty miners. She was an overworked drudge, fiery and energetic for all that, filled with the one idea of having her son rise in life and enter a profession. The chance had come at last when the father died, corroded with alcohol, collapsing in a few hours. Two or three years later a travelling dentist visited the mine and put up his tent near the bunk-house. He was more or less of a charlatan, but he fired Mrs. McTeague's ambition, and young McTeague went away with him to learn his profession. He had learnt it after a fashion, mostly by watching the charlatan operate. He had read many of the necessary books, but he was too hopelessly stupid to get much benefit from them.

Then one day at San Francisco had come the news of his mother's death; she had left him some money—not much, but enough to set him up in business; so he had cut loose from the charlatan and had opened his "Dental Parlors" on Polk Street, an "accommodation street" of small shops in the residence quarter of the town. Here he had slowly collected a clientele of butcher boys, shop girls, drug clerks, and car conductors. He made but few acquaintances. Polk Street called him the "Doctor" and spoke of his enormous strength. For McTeague was a young giant, carrying his huge shock of blond hair six feet three inches from the ground; moving his immense limbs, heavy with ropes of muscle, slowly, ponderously. His hands were enormous, red, and covered with a fell of stiff yellow hair; they were hard as wooden mallets, strong as vises, the hands of the old-time car-boy. Often he dispensed with forceps and extracted a refractory tooth with his thumb and finger. His head was square-cut, angular; the jaw salient, like that of the carnivora.

McTeague's mind was as his body, heavy, slow to act, sluggish. Yet there was nothing vicious about the man. Altogether he suggested the draught horse, immensely strong, stupid, docile, obedient.

When he opened his "Dental Parlors," he felt that his life was a success, that he could hope for nothing better. In spite of the name, there was but one room. It was a corner room on the second floor over the branch post-office, and faced the street. McTeague made it do for a bedroom as well, sleeping on the big bed-lounge against the wall opposite the window. There was a washstand behind the screen in the corner where he manufactured his moulds. In the round bay window were his operating chair, his dental engine, and the movable rack on which he laid out his instruments. Three chairs, a bargain at the second-hand store, ranged themselves against the wall with military precision underneath a steel engraving of the court of Lorenzo de' Medici, which he had bought because there were a great many figures in it for the money. Over the bed-lounge hung a rifle manufacturer's advertisement calendar which he never used. The other ornaments were a small marble-topped centre table covered with back numbers of "The American System of Dentistry," a stone pug dog sitting before the little stove, and a thermometer. A stand of shelves occupied one corner, filled with the seven volumes of "Allen's Practical Dentist." On the top shelf McTeague kept his concertina and a bag of bird seed for the canary. The whole place exhaled a mingled odor of bedding, creosote, and ether.

But for one thing, McTeague would have been perfectly contented. Just outside his window was his signboard—a modest affair—that read: "Doctor McTeague. Dental Parlors. Gas Given"; but that was all. It was his ambition, his dream, to have projecting from that corner window a huge gilded tooth, a molar with enormous prongs, something gorgeous and attractive. He would have it some day, on that he was resolved; but as yet such a thing was far beyond his means.

When he had finished the last of his beer, McTeague slowly wiped his lips and huge yellow mustache with the side of his hand. Bull-like, he heaved himself laboriously up, and, going to the window, stood looking down into the street.

The street never failed to interest him. It was one of those cross streets peculiar to Western cities, situated in the heart of the residence quarter, but occupied by small tradespeople who lived in the rooms above their shops. There were corner drug stores with huge jars of red, yellow, and green liquids in their windows, very brave and gay; stationers' stores, where illustrated weeklies were tacked upon bulletin boards; barber shops with cigar stands in their vestibules; sad-looking plumbers' offices; cheap restaurants, in whose windows one saw piles of unopened oysters weighted down by cubes of ice, and china pigs and cows knee deep in layers of white beans. At one end of the street McTeague could see the huge power-house of the cable line. Immediately opposite him was a great market; while farther on, over the chimney stacks of the intervening houses, the glass roof of some huge public baths glittered like crystal in the afternoon sun. Underneath him the branch post-office was opening its doors, as was its custom between two and three o'clock on Sunday afternoons. An acrid odor of ink rose upward to him. Occasionally a cable car passed, trundling heavily, with a strident whirring of jostled glass windows.

On week days the street was very lively. It woke to its work about seven o'clock, at the time when the newsboys made their appearance together with the day laborers. The laborers went trudging past in a straggling file—plumbers' apprentices, their pockets stuffed with sections of lead pipe, tweezers, and pliers; carpenters, carrying nothing but their little pasteboard lunch baskets painted to imitate leather; gangs of street workers, their overalls soiled with yellow clay, their picks and long-handled shovels over their shoulders; plasterers, spotted with lime from head to foot. This little army of workers, tramping steadily in one direction, met and mingled with other toilers of a different description—conductors and "swing men" of the cable company going on duty; heavy-eyed night clerks from the drug stores on their way home to sleep; roundsmen returning to the precinct police station to make their night report, and Chinese market gardeners teetering past under their heavy baskets. The cable cars began to fill up; all along the street could be seen the shopkeepers taking down their shutters.

Between seven and eight the street breakfasted. Now and then a waiter from one of the cheap restaurants crossed from one sidewalk to the other, balancing on one palm a tray covered with a napkin. Everywhere was the smell of coffee and of frying steaks. A little later, following in the path of the day laborers, came the clerks and shop girls, dressed with a certain cheap smartness, always in a hurry, glancing apprehensively at the power-house clock. Their employers followed an hour or so later—on the cable cars for the most part whiskered gentlemen with huge stomachs, reading the morning papers with great gravity; bank cashiers and insurance clerks with flowers in their buttonholes.

At the same time the school children invaded the street, filling the air with a clamor of shrill voices, stopping at the stationers' shops, or idling a moment in the doorways of the candy stores. For over half an hour they held possession of the sidewalks, then suddenly disappeared, leaving behind one or two stragglers who hurried along with great strides of their little thin legs, very anxious and preoccupied.

Towards eleven o'clock the ladies from the great avenue a block above Polk Street made their appearance, promenading the sidewalks leisurely, deliberately. They were at their morning's marketing. They were handsome women, beautifully dressed. They knew by name their butchers and grocers and vegetable men. From his window McTeague saw them in front of the stalls, gloved and veiled and daintily shod, the subservient provision men at their elbows, scribbling hastily in the order books. They all seemed to know one another, these grand ladies from the fashionable avenue. Meetings took place here and there; a conversation was begun; others arrived; groups were formed; little impromptu receptions were held before the chopping blocks of butchers' stalls, or on the sidewalk, around boxes of berries and fruit.

From noon to evening the population of the street was of a mixed character. The street was busiest at that time; a vast and prolonged murmur arose—the mingled shuffling of feet, the rattle of wheels, the heavy trundling of cable cars. At four o'clock the school children once more swarmed the sidewalks, again disappearing with surprising suddenness. At six the great homeward march commenced; the cars were crowded, the laborers thronged the sidewalks, the newsboys chanted the evening papers. Then all at once the street fell quiet; hardly a soul was in sight; the sidewalks were deserted. It was supper hour. Evening began; and one by one a multitude of lights, from the demoniac glare of the druggists' windows to the dazzling blue whiteness of the electric globes, grew thick from street corner to street corner. Once more the street was crowded. Now there was no thought but for amusement. The cable cars were loaded with theatre-goers—men in high hats and young girls in furred opera cloaks. On the sidewalks were groups and couples—the plumbers' apprentices, the girls of the ribbon counters, the little families that lived on the second stories over their shops, the dressmakers, the small doctors, the harness-makers—all the various inhabitants of the street were abroad, strolling idly from shop window to shop window, taking the air after the day's work. Groups of girls collected on the corners, talking and laughing very loud, making remarks upon the young men that passed them. The tamale men appeared. A band of Salvationists began to sing before a saloon.

Then, little by little, Polk Street dropped back to solitude. Eleven o'clock struck from the power-house clock. Lights were extinguished. At one o'clock the cable stopped, leaving an abrupt silence in the air. All at once it seemed very still. The ugly noises were the occasional footfalls of a policeman and the persistent calling of ducks and geese in the closed market. The street was asleep.

Day after day, McTeague saw the same panorama unroll itself. The bay window of his "Dental Parlors" was for him a point of vantage from which he watched the world go past.

On Sundays, however, all was changed. As he stood in the bay window, after finishing his beer, wiping his lips, and looking out into the street, McTeague was conscious of the difference. Nearly all the stores were closed. No wagons passed. A few people hurried up and down the sidewalks, dressed in cheap Sunday finery. A cable car went by; on the outside seats were a party of returning picnickers. The mother, the father, a young man, and a young girl, and three children. The two older people held empty lunch baskets in their laps, while the bands of the children's hats were stuck full of oak leaves. The girl carried a huge bunch of wilting poppies and wild flowers.

As the car approached McTeague's window the young man got up and swung himself off the platform, waving goodbye to the party. Suddenly McTeague recognized him.

"There's Marcus Schouler," he muttered behind his mustache.

Marcus Schouler was the dentist's one intimate friend. The acquaintance had begun at the car conductors' coffee-joint, where the two occupied the same table and met at every meal. Then they made the discovery that they both lived in the same flat, Marcus occupying a room on the floor above McTeague. On different occasions McTeague had treated Marcus for an ulcerated tooth and had refused to accept payment. Soon it came to be an understood thing between them. They were "pals."

McTeague, listening, heard Marcus go up-stairs to his room above. In a few minutes his door opened again. McTeague knew that he had come out into the hall and was leaning over the banisters.

"Oh, Mac!" he called. McTeague came to his door.

"Hullo! 'sthat you, Mark?" "Sure," answered Marcus. "Come on up."

"You come on down."

"No, come on up."

"Oh, you come on down."

"Oh, you lazy duck!" retorted Marcus, coming down the stairs.

"Been out to the Cliff House on a picnic," he explained as he sat down on the bed-lounge, "with my uncle and his people—the Sieppes, you know. By damn! it was hot," he suddenly vociferated. "Just look at that! Just look at that!" he cried, dragging at his limp collar. "That's the third one since morning; it is—it is, for a fact—and you got your stove going." He began to tell about the picnic, talking very loud and fast, gesturing furiously, very excited over trivial details. Marcus could not talk without getting excited.

"You ought t'have seen, y'ought t'have seen. I tell you, it was outa sight. It was; it was, for a fact."

"Yes, yes," answered McTeague, bewildered, trying to follow. "Yes, that's so."

In recounting a certain dispute with an awkward bicyclist, in which it appeared he had become involved, Marcus quivered with rage. "'Say that again,' says I to um. 'Just say that once more, and'"—here a rolling explosion of oaths—"'you'll go back to the city in the Morgue wagon. Ain't I got a right to cross a street even, I'd like to know, without being run down—what?' I say it's outrageous. I'd a knifed him in another minute. It was an outrage. I say it was an *outrage*."

"Sure it was," McTeague hastened to reply. "Sure, sure."

"Oh, and we had an accident," shouted the other, suddenly off on another tack. "It was awful. Trina was in the swing there—that's my cousin Trina, you know who I mean—and she fell out. By damn! I thought she'd killed herself; struck her face on a rock and knocked out a front tooth. It's a wonder she didn't kill herself. It IS a wonder; it is, for a fact. Ain't it, now? Huh? Ain't it? Y'ought t'have seen."

McTeague had a vague idea that Marcus Schouler was stuck on his cousin Trina. They "kept company" a good deal; Marcus took dinner with the Sieppes every Saturday evening at their home at B Street station, across the bay, and Sunday afternoons he and the family usually made little excursions into the suburbs. McTeague began to wonder dimly how it was that on this occasion Marcus had not gone home with his cousin. As sometimes happens, Marcus furnished the explanation upon the instant.

"I promised a duck up here on the avenue I'd call for his dog at four this afternoon."

Marcus was Old Grannis's assistant in a little dog hospital that the latter had opened in a sort of alley just off Polk Street, some four blocks above Old Grannis lived in one of the back rooms of McTeague's flat. He was an Englishman and an expert dog surgeon, but Marcus Schouler was a bungler in the profession. His father had been a veterinary surgeon who had kept a livery stable near by, on California Street, and Marcus's knowledge of the diseases of domestic animals had been picked up in a haphazard way, much after the manner of McTeague's education. Somehow he managed to impress Old Grannis, a gentle, simple-minded old man, with a sense of his fitness, bewildering him with a torrent of empty phrases that he delivered with fierce gestures and with a manner of the greatest conviction.

"You'd better come along with me, Mac," observed Marcus. "We'll get the duck's dog, and then we'll take a little walk, huh? You got nothun to do. Come along."

McTeague went out with him, and the two friends proceeded up to the avenue to the house where the dog was to be found. It was a huge mansion-like place, set in an enormous garden that occupied a whole third of the block; and while Marcus tramped up the front steps and rang the doorbell boldly, to show his independence, McTeague remained below on the sidewalk, gazing stupidly at the curtained windows, the marble steps, and the bronze griffins, troubled and a little confused by all this massive luxury.

After they had taken the dog to the hospital and had left him to whimper behind the wire netting, they returned to Polk Street and had a glass of beer in the back room of Joe Frenna's corner grocery.

Ever since they had left the huge mansion on the avenue, Marcus had been attacking the capitalists, a class which he pretended to execrate. It was a pose which he often assumed, certain of impressing the dentist. Marcus had picked up a few half-truths of political economy—it was impossible to say where—and as soon as the two had settled themselves to their beer in Frenna's back room he took up the theme of the labor question. He discussed it at the top of his voice, vociferating, shaking his fists, exciting himself with his own noise. He was continually making use of the stock phrases of the professional politician—phrases he had caught at some of the ward "rallies" and "ratification meetings." These rolled off his tongue with incredible emphasis, appearing at every turn of his conversation—"Outraged constituencies," "cause of labor," "wage earners," "opinions biased by personal interests," "eyes blinded by party prejudice." McTeague listened to him, awestruck.

"There's where the evil lies," Marcus would cry.

"The masses must learn self-control; it stands to reason. Look at the figures, look at the figures. Decrease the number of wage earners and you increase wages, don't you? don't you?"

Absolutely stupid, and understanding never a word, McTeague would answer:

"Yes, yes, that's it—self-control—that's the word."

"It's the capitalists that's ruining the cause of labor," shouted Marcus, banging the table with his fist till the beer glasses danced; "white-livered drones, traitors, with their livers white as snow, eatun the bread of widows and orphuns; there's where the evil lies."

Stupefied with his clamor, McTeague answered, wagging his head:

"Yes, that's it; I think it's their livers."

Suddenly Marcus fell calm again, forgetting his pose all in an instant.

"Say, Mac, I told my cousin Trina to come round and see you about that tooth of her's. She'll be in to-morrow, I guess."

CHAPTER 2

After his breakfast the following Monday morning, McTeague looked over the appointments he had written down in the book-slate that hung against the screen.

His writing was immense, very clumsy, and very round, with huge, full- bellied l's and h's. He saw that he had made an appointment at one o'clock for Miss Baker, the retired dressmaker, a little old maid who had a tiny room a few doors down the hall. It adjoined that of Old Grannis.

Quite an affair had arisen from this circumstance. Miss Baker and Old Grannis were both over sixty, and yet it was current talk amongst the lodgers of the flat that the two were in love with each other . Singularly enough, they were not even acquaintances; never a word had passed between them. At intervals they met on the stairway; he on his way to his little dog hospital, she returning from a bit of marketing in the street. At such times they passed each other with averted eyes, pretending a certain pre- occupation, suddenly seized with a great embarrassment, the timidity of a second childhood. He went on about his business, disturbed and thoughtful. She hurried up to her tiny room, her curious little false curls shaking with her agitation, the faintest suggestion of a flush coming and going in her with- ered cheeks. The emotion of one of these chance meetings remained with them during all the rest of the day.

Was it the first romance in the lives of each? Did Old Grannis ever remember a certain face amongst those that he had known when he was young Grannis—the face of some pale- haired girl, such as one sees in the old cathedral towns of En- gland? Did Miss Baker still treasure up in a seldom opened drawer or box some faded daguerreotype, some strange old-fashioned likeness, with its curling hair and high stock? It was impossible to say.

Maria Macapa, the Mexican woman who took care of the lodgers' rooms, had been the first to call the flat's attention to the affair, spreading the news of it from room to room, from floor to floor. Of late she had made a great discovery; all the women folk of the flat were yet vibrant with it. Old Grannis came home from his work at four o'clock, and between that time and six Miss Baker would sit in her room, her hands idle in her lap, doing nothing, listening, waiting. Old Grannis did the same, drawing his arm-chair near to the wall, knowing that Miss Baker was upon the other side, conscious, perhaps, that she was thinking of him; and there the two would sit through the hours of the afternoon, listening and waiting, they did not know exactly for what, but near to each other, separated only by the thin partition of their rooms. They had come to know each other's habits. Old Grannis knew that at quarter of five precisely Miss Baker made a cup of tea over the oil stove on the stand between the bureau and the window. Miss Baker felt instinctive- ly the exact moment when Old Grannis took down his little binding apparatus from the second shelf of his clothes closet and began his favorite occupation of binding pamphlets—pamphlets that he never read, for all that.

In his "Parlors" McTeague began his week's work. He glanced in the glass sau- cer in which he kept his sponge-gold, and noticing that he had used up all his pel- lets, set about making some more. In examining Miss Baker's teeth at the prelim- inary sitting he had found a cavity in one of the incisors. Miss Baker had decided to have it filled with gold. McTeague remembered now that it was what is called a "proximate case," where there is not sufficient room to fill with large pieces of gold. He told himself that he should have to use "mats" in the filling. He made some dozen of these "mats" from his tape of non-cohesive gold, cutting it transversely into small pieces that could be inserted edgewise between the teeth and consolidated by packing. After he had made his "mats" he continued with the other kind of gold fillings, such as he would have occasion to use during the week; "blocks" to be used in large proximal cavities, made by folding the tape on itself a number of times and then shaping it with the soldering pliers; "cylinders" for commencing fillings, which he formed by rolling the tape around a needle called a "broach," cutting it afterwards into different lengths. He worked slowly, mechanically, turning the foil between his fingers with the manual dexterity that one sometimes sees in stupid persons. His head was quite empty of all thought, and he did not whistle over his work as another man might have done. The canary made up for his silence, trilling and chittering continually, splashing about in its morning bath, keeping up an incessant noise and movement that would have been maddening to any one but McTeague, who seemed to have no nerves at all.

After he had finished his fillings, he made a hook broach from a bit of piano wire to replace an old one that he had lost. It was time for his dinner then, and when he returned from the car conductors' coffee-joint, he found Miss Baker waiting for him.

The ancient little dressmaker was at all times willing to talk of Old Grannis to anybody that would listen, quite unconscious of the gossip of the flat. McTeague found her all a-flutter with excitement. Something extraordinary had happened. She had found out that the wall-paper in Old Grannis's room was the same as that in hers.

"It has led me to thinking, Doctor McTeague," she exclaimed, shaking her little false curls at him. "You know my room is so small, anyhow, and the wall-paper being the same—the pattern from my room continues right into his—I declare, I believe at one time that was all one room. Think of it, do you suppose it was? It almost amounts to our occupying the same room. I don't know—why, really—do you think I should speak to the landlady about it? He bound pamphlets last night until half-past nine. They say that he's the younger son of a baronet; that there are reasons for his not coming to the title; his stepfather wronged him cruelly."

No one had ever said such a thing. It was preposterous to imagine any mystery connected with Old Grannis. Miss Baker had chosen to invent the little fiction, had created the title and the unjust stepfather from some dim memories of the novels of her girlhood.

She took her place in the operating chair. McTeague began the filling. There was a long silence. It was impossible for McTeague to work and talk at the same time.

He was just burnishing the last "mat" in Miss Baker's tooth, when the door of the "Parlors" opened, jangling the bell which he had hung over it, and which was absolutely unnecessary. McTeague turned, one foot on the pedal of his dental engine, the corundum disk whirling between his fingers.

It was Marcus Schouler who came in, ushering a young girl of about twenty.

"Hello, Mac," exclaimed Marcus; "busy? Brought my cousin round about that broken tooth."

McTeague nodded his head gravely.

"In a minute," he answered.

Marcus and his cousin Trina sat down in the rigid chairs underneath the steel engraving of the Court of Lorenzo de' Medici. They began talking in low tones. The girl looked about the room, noticing the stone pug dog, the rifle manufacturer's calendar, the canary in its little gilt prison, and the tumbled blankets on the unmade bed-lounge against the wall. Marcus began telling her about McTeague. "We're pals," he explained, just above a whisper. "Ah, Mac's all right, you bet. Say, Trina, he's the strongest duck you ever saw. What do you suppose? He can pull out your teeth with his fingers; yes, he can. What do you think of that? With his fingers, mind you; he can, for a fact. Get on to the size of him, anyhow. Ah, Mac's all right!"

Maria Macapa had come into the room while he had been speaking. She was making up McTeague's bed. Suddenly Marcus exclaimed under his breath: "Now we'll have some fun. It's the girl that takes care of the rooms. She's a greaser, and she's queer in the head. She ain't regularly crazy, but I don't know, she's queer. Y'ought to hear her go on about a gold dinner service she says her folks used to own. Ask her what her name is and see what she'll say." Trina shrank back, a little frightened.

"No, you ask," she whispered.

"Ah, go on; what you 'fraid of?" urged Marcus.

Trina shook her head energetically, shutting her lips together.

"Well, listen here," answered Marcus, nudging her; then raising his voice, he said:

"How do, Maria?" Maria nodded to him over her shoulder as she bent over the lounge.

"Workun hard nowadays, Maria?"

"Pretty hard."

"Didunt always have to work for your living, though, did you, when you ate offa gold dishes?" Maria didn't answer, except by putting her chin in the air and shutting her eyes, as though to say she knew a long story about that if she had a mind to talk. All Marcus's efforts to draw her out on the subject were unavailing. She only responded by movements of her head.

"Can't always start her going," Marcus told his cousin.

"What does she do, though, when you ask her about her name?"

"Oh, sure," said Marcus, who had forgotten. "Say, Maria, what's your name?"

"Huh?" asked Maria, straightening up, her hands on he hips.

"Tell us your name," repeated Marcus.

"Name is Maria—Miranda—Macapa." Then, after a pause, she added, as though she had but that moment thought of it, "Had a flying squirrel an' let him go."

Invariably Maria Macapa made this answer. It was not always she would talk about the famous service of gold plate, but a question as to her name never failed to elicit the same strange answer, delivered in a rapid undertone: "Name is Maria—Miranda—Macapa." Then, as if struck with an after thought, "Had a flying squirrel an' let him go."

Why Maria should associate the release of the mythical squirrel with her name could not be said. About Maria the flat knew absolutely nothing further than that she was Spanish-American. Miss Baker was the oldest lodger in the flat, and Maria was a fixture there as maid of all work when she had come. There was a legend to the effect that Maria's people had been at one time immensely wealthy in Central America.

Maria turned again to her work. Trina and Marcus watched her curiously. There was a silence. The corundum burr in McTeague's engine hummed in a prolonged monotone. The canary bird chittered occasionally. The room was warm, and the breathing of the five people in the narrow space made the air close and thick. At long intervals an acrid odor of ink floated up from the branch post-office immediately below.

Maria Macapa finished her work and started to leave. As she passed near Marcus and his cousin she stopped, and drew a bunch of blue tickets furtively from her pocket. "Buy a ticket in the lottery?" she inquired, looking at the girl. "Just a dollar."

"Go along with you, Maria," said Marcus, who had but thirty cents in his pocket. "Go along; it's against the law."

"Buy a ticket," urged Maria, thrusting the bundle toward Trina. "Try your luck. The butcher on the next block won twenty dollars the last drawing."

Very uneasy, Trina bought a ticket for the sake of being rid of her. Maria disappeared.

"Ain't she a queer bird?" muttered Marcus. He was much embarrassed and disturbed because he had not bought the ticket for Trina.

But there was a sudden movement. McTeague had just finished with Miss Baker.

"You should notice," the dressmaker said to the dentist, in a low voice, "he always leaves the door a little ajar in the afternoon." When she had gone out, Marcus Schouler brought Trina forward.

"Say, Mac, this is my cousin, Trina Sieppe." The two shook hands dumbly, McTeague slowly nodding his huge head with its great shock of yellow hair. Trina was very small and prettily made. Her face was round and rather pale; her eyes long and narrow and blue, like the half-open eyes of a little baby; her lips and the lobes of her tiny ears were pale, a little suggestive of anaemia; while across the bridge of her nose ran an adorable little line of freckles. But it was to her hair that one's attention was most attracted. Heaps and heaps of blue-black coils and braids, a royal crown of swarthy bands, a veritable sable tiara, heavy, abundant, odorous. All the vitality that should have given color to her face seemed to have been absorbed by this marvellous hair. It was the coiffure of a queen that shadowed the pale temples of this little bourgeoise. So heavy was it that it tipped her head backward, and the position thrust her chin out a little. It was a charming poise, innocent, confiding, almost infantile.

She was dressed all in black, very modest and plain. The effect of her pale face in all this contrasting black was almost monastic.

"Well," exclaimed Marcus suddenly, "I got to go. Must get back to work. Don't hurt her too much, Mac. S'long, Trina."

McTeague and Trina were left alone. He was embarrassed, troubled. These young girls disturbed and perplexed him. He did not like them, obstinately cherishing that intuitive suspicion of all things feminine—the perverse dislike of an overgrown boy. On the other hand, she was perfectly at her ease; doubtless the woman in her was not yet awakened; she was yet, as one might say, without sex. She was almost like a boy, frank, candid, unreserved.

She took her place in the operating chair and told him what was the matter, looking squarely into his face. She had fallen out of a swing the afternoon of the preceding day; one of her teeth had been knocked loose and the other altogether broken out.

McTeague listened to her with apparent stolidity, nodding his head from time to time as she spoke. The keenness of his dislike of her as a woman began to be blunted. He thought she was rather pretty, that he even liked her because she was so small, so prettily made, so good natured and straightforward.

"Let's have a look at your teeth," he said, picking up his mirror. "You better take your hat off." She leaned back in her chair and opened her mouth, showing the rows of little round teeth, as white and even as the kernels on an ear of green corn, except where an ugly gap came at the side.

McTeague put the mirror into her mouth, touching one and another of her teeth with the handle of an excavator. By and by he straightened up, wiping the moisture from the mirror on his coat-sleeve.

"Well, Doctor," said the girl, anxiously, "it's a dreadful disfigurement, isn't it?" adding, "What can you do about it?" "Well," answered McTeague, slowly, looking vaguely about on the floor of the room, "the roots of the broken tooth are still in the gum; they'll have to come out, and I guess I'll have to pull that other bicuspid. Let me look again. Yes," he went on in a moment, peering into her mouth with the mirror, "I guess that'll have to come out, too." The tooth was loose, discolored, and evidently dead. "It's a curious case," McTeague went on. "I don't know as I ever had a tooth like that before. It's what's called necrosis. It don't often happen. It'll have to come out sure."

Then a discussion was opened on the subject, Trina sitting up in the chair, holding her hat in her lap; McTeague leaning against the window frame his hands in his pockets, his eyes wandering about on the floor. Trina did not want the other tooth removed; one hole like that was bad enough; but two—ah, no, it was not to be thought of.

But McTeague reasoned with her, tried in vain to make her understand that there was no vascular connection between the root and the gum. Trina was blindly persistent, with the persistency of a girl who has made up her mind.

McTeague began to like her better and better, and after a while commenced himself to feel that it would be a pity to disfigure such a pretty mouth. He became interested; perhaps he could do something, something in the way of a crown or bridge. "Let's look at that again," he said, picking up his mirror. He began to study the situation very carefully, really desiring to remedy the blemish.

It was the first bicuspid that was missing, and though part of the root of the second (the loose one) would remain after its extraction, he was sure it would not be strong enough to sustain a crown. All at once he grew obstinate, resolving, with all the strength of a crude and primitive man, to conquer the difficulty in spite of everything. He turned over in his mind the technicalities of the case. No, evidently the root was not strong enough to sustain a crown; besides that, it was placed a little irregularly in the arch. But, fortunately, there were cavities in the two teeth on either side of the gap—one in the first molar and one in the palatine surface of the cuspid; might he not drill a socket in the remaining root and sockets in the molar and cuspid, and, partly by bridging, partly by crowning, fill in the gap? He made up his mind to do it.

Why he should pledge himself to this hazardous case McTeague was puzzled to know. With most of his clients he would have contented himself with the extraction of the loose tooth and the roots of the broken one. Why should he risk his reputation in this case? He could not say why.

It was the most difficult operation he had ever performed. He bungled it considerably, but in the end he succeeded passably well. He extracted the loose tooth with his bayonet forceps and prepared the roots of the broken one as if for filling, fitting into them a flattened piece of platinum wire to serve as a dowel. But this was only the beginning; altogether it was a fortnight's work. Trina came nearly every other day, and passed two, and even three, hours in the chair.

By degrees McTeague's first awkwardness and suspicion vanished entirely. The two became good friends. McTeague even arrived at that point where he could work and talk to her at the same time—a thing that had never before been possible for him.

Never until then had McTeague become so well acquainted with a girl of Trina's age. The younger women of Polk Street—the shop girls, the young women of the soda fountains, the waitresses in the cheap restaurants—preferred another dentist, a young fellow just graduated from the college, a poser, a rider of bicycles, a man about town, who wore astonishing waistcoats and bet money on greyhound coursing. Trina was McTeague's first experience. With her the feminine element suddenly entered his little world. It was not only her that he saw and felt, it was the woman, the whole sex, an entire new humanity, strange and alluring, that he seemed to have discovered. How had he ignored it so long? It was dazzling, delicious, charming beyond all words. His narrow point of view was at once enlarged and confused, and all at once he saw that there was something else in life besides concertinas and steam beer. Everything had to be made over again. His whole rude idea of life had to be changed. The male virile desire in him tardily awakened, aroused itself, strong and brutal. It was resistless, untrained, a thing not to be held in leash an instant.

Little by little, by gradual, almost imperceptible degrees, the thought of Trina Sieppe occupied his mind from day to day, from hour to hour. He found himself thinking of her constantly; at every instant he saw her round, pale face; her narrow, milk-blue eyes; her little out-thrust chin; her heavy, huge tiara of black hair.

At night he lay awake for hours under the thick blankets of the bed-lounge, staring upward into the darkness, tormented with the idea of her, exasperated at the delicate, subtle mesh in which he found himself entangled. During the forenoons, while he went about his work, he thought of her. As he made his plaster- of-paris moulds at the washstand in the corner behind the screen he turned over in his mind all that had happened, all that had been said at the previous sitting. Her little tooth that he had extracted he kept wrapped in a bit of newspaper in his vest pocket. Often he took it out and held it in the palm of his immense, horny hand, seized with some strange elephantine sentiment, wagging his head at it, heaving tremendous sighs. What a folly!

At two o'clock on Tuesdays, Thursdays, and Saturdays Trina arrived and took her place in the operating chair. While at his work McTeague was every minute obliged to bend closely over her; his hands touched her face, her cheeks, her adorable little chin; her lips pressed against his fingers. She breathed warmly on his forehead and on his eyelids, while the odor of her hair, a charming feminine perfume, sweet, heavy, enervating, came to his nostrils, so penetrating, so delicious, that his flesh pricked and tingled with it; a veritable sensation of faintness passed over this huge, callous fellow, with his enormous bones and corded muscles. He drew a short breath through his nose; his jaws suddenly gripped together vise-like.

But this was only at times—a strange, vexing spasm, that subsided almost immediately. For the most part, McTeague enjoyed the pleasure of these sittings with Trina with a certain strong calmness, blindly happy that she was there. This poor crude dentist of Polk Street, stupid, ignorant, vulgar, with his sham education and plebeian tastes, whose only relaxations were to eat, to drink steam beer, and to play upon his concertina, was living through his first romance, his first idyl. It was delightful. The long hours he passed alone with Trina in the "Dental Parlors," silent, only for the scraping of the instruments and the pouring of bud-burrs in the engine, in the foul atmosphere, overheated by the little stove and heavy with the smell of ether, creosote, and stale bedding, had all the charm of secret appointments and stolen meetings under the moon.

By degrees the operation progressed. One day, just after McTeague had put in the temporary gutta-percha fillings and nothing more could be done at that sitting, Trina asked him to examine the rest of her teeth. They were perfect, with one exception—a spot of white caries on the lateral surface of an incisor. McTeague filled it with gold, enlarging the cavity with hard-bits and hoe-excavators, and burring in afterward with half-cone burrs. The cavity was deep, and Trina began to wince and moan. To hurt Trina was a positive anguish for McTeague, yet an anguish which he was obliged to endure at every hour of the sitting. It was harrowing—he sweated under it—to be forced to torture her, of all women in the world; could anything be worse than that?

"Hurt?" he inquired, anxiously.

She answered by frowning, with a sharp intake of breath, putting her fingers over her closed lips and nodding her head. McTeague sprayed the tooth with glycerite of tannin, but without effect. Rather than hurt her he found himself forced to the use of anaesthesia, which he hated. He had a notion that the nitrous oxide gas was dangerous, so on this occasion, as on all others, used ether.

He put the sponge a half dozen times to Trina's face, more nervous than he had ever been before, watching the symptoms closely. Her breathing became short and irregular; there was a slight twitching of the muscles. When her thumbs turned inward toward the palms, he took the sponge away. She passed off very quickly, and, with a long sigh, sank back into the chair.

McTeague straightened up, putting the sponge upon the rack behind him, his eyes fixed upon Trina's face. For some time he stood watching her as she lay there, unconscious and helpless, and very pretty. He was alone with her, and she was absolutely without defense.

Suddenly the animal in the man stirred and woke; the evil instincts that in him were so close to the surface leaped to life, shouting and clamoring.

It was a crisis—a crisis that had arisen all in an instant; a crisis for which he was totally unprepared. Blindly, and without knowing why, McTeague fought against it, moved by an unreasoned instinct of resistance. Within him, a certain second self, another better McTeague rose with the brute; both were strong, with the huge crude strength of the man himself. The two were at grapples. There in that cheap and shabby "Dental Parlor" a dreaded struggle began. It was the old battle, old as the world, wide as the world—the sudden panther leap of the animal, lips drawn, fangs aflash, hideous, monstrous, not to be resisted, and the simultaneous arousing of the other man, the better self that cries, "Down, down," without knowing why; that grips the monster; that fights to strangle it, to thrust it down and back.

Dizzied and bewildered with the shock, the like of which he had never known before, McTeague turned from Trina, gazing bewilderedly about the room. The struggle was bitter; his teeth ground themselves together with a little rasping sound; the blood sang in his ears; his face flushed scarlet; his hands twisted themselves together like the knotting of cables. The fury in him was as the fury of a young bull in the heat of high summer. But for all that he shook his huge head from time to time, muttering: "No, by God! No, by God!"

Dimly he seemed to realize that should he yield now he would never be able to care for Trina again. She would never be the same to him, never so radiant, so sweet, so adorable; her charm for him would vanish in an instant. Across her forehead, her little pale forehead, under the shadow of her royal hair, he would surely see the smudge of a foul ordure, the footprint of the monster. It would be a sacrilege, an abomination. He recoiled from it, banding all his strength to the issue.

"No, by God! No, by God!"

He turned to his work, as if seeking a refuge in it. But as he drew near to her again, the charm of her innocence and helplessness came over him afresh. It was a final protest against his resolution. Suddenly he leaned over and kissed her, grossly, full on the mouth. The thing was done before he knew it. Terrified at his weakness at the very moment he believed himself strong, he threw himself once more into his work with desperate energy. By the time he was fastening the sheet of rubber upon the tooth, he had himself once more in hand. He was disturbed, still trembling, still vibrating with the throes of the crisis, but he was the master; the animal was downed, was cowed for this time, at least.

But for all that, the brute was there. Long dormant, it was now at last alive, awake. From now on he would feel its presence continually; would feel it tugging at its chain, watching its opportunity. Ah, the pity of it! Why could he not always love her purely, cleanly? What was this perverse, vicious thing that lived within him, knitted to his flesh?

Below the fine fabric of all that was good in him ran the foul stream of hereditary evil, like a sewer. The vices and sins of his father and of his father's father, to the third and fourth and five hundredth generation, tainted him. The evil of an entire race flowed in his veins. Why should it be? He did not desire it. Was he to blame?

But McTeague could not understand this thing. It had faced him, as sooner or later it faces every child of man; but its significance was not for him. To reason with it was beyond him. He could only oppose to it an instinctive stubborn resistance, blind, inert.

McTeague went on with his work. As he was rapping in the little blocks and cylinders with the mallet, Trina slowly came back to herself with a long sigh. She still felt a little confused, and lay quiet in the chair. There was a long silence, broken only by the uneven tapping of the hardwood mallet. By and by she said, "I never felt a thing," and then she smiled at him very prettily beneath the rubber dam. McTeague turned to her suddenly, his mallet in one hand, his pliers holding a pellet of sponge-gold in the other. All at once he said, with the unreasoned simplicity and directness of a child: "Listen here, Miss Trina, I like you better than any one else; what's the matter with us getting married?"

Trina sat up in the chair quickly, and then drew back from him, frightened and bewildered.

"Will you? Will you?" said McTeague. "Say, Miss Trina, will you?"

"What is it? What do you mean?" she cried, confusedly, her words muffled beneath the rubber.

"Will you?" repeated McTeague. "No, no," she exclaimed, refusing without knowing why, suddenly seized with a fear of him, the intuitive feminine fear of the male. McTeague could only repeat the same thing over and over again. Trina, more and more frightened at his huge hands—the hands of the old-time car-boy—his immense square-cut head and his enormous brute strength, cried out: "No, no," behind the rubber dam, shaking her head violently, holding out her hands, and shrinking down before him in the operating chair. McTeague came nearer to her, repeating the same question. "No, no," she cried, terrified. Then, as she exclaimed, "Oh, I am sick," was suddenly taken with a fit of vomiting. It was the not unusual after effect of the ether, aided now by her excitement and nervousness. McTeague was checked. He poured some bromide of potassium into a graduated glass and held it to her lips.

"Here, swallow this," he said.

CHAPTER 3

Once every two months Maria Macapa set the entire flat in commotion. She roamed the building from garret to cellar, searching each corner, ferreting through every old box and trunk and barrel, groping about on the top shelves of closets, peering into rag-bags, exasperating the lodgers with her persistence and importunity. She was collecting junks, bits of iron, stone jugs, glass bottles, old sacks, and cast-off garments. It was one of her perquisites. She sold the junk to Zerkow, the rags-bottles-sacks man, who lived in a filthy den in the alley just back of the flat, and who sometimes paid her as much as three cents a pound. The stone jugs, however, were worth a nickel. The money that Zerkow paid her, Maria spent on shirt waists and dotted blue neckties, trying to dress like the girls who tended the soda-water fountain in the candy store on the corner. She was sick with envy of these young women. They were in the world, they were elegant, they were debonair, they had their "young men."

On this occasion she presented herself at the door of Old Grannis's room late in the afternoon. His door stood a little open. That of Miss Baker was ajar a few inches. The two old people were "keeping company" after their fashion.

"Got any junk, Mister Grannis?" inquired Maria, standing in the door, a very dirty, half-filled pillowcase over one arm.

"No, nothing—nothing that I can think of, Maria," replied Old Grannis, terribly vexed at the interruption, yet not wishing to be unkind. "Nothing I think of. Yet, however—perhaps—if you wish to look."

He sat in the middle of the room before a small pine table. His little binding apparatus was before him. In his fingers was a huge upholsterer's needle threaded with twine, a brad-awl lay at his elbow, on the floor beside him was a great pile of pamphlets, the pages uncut. Old Grannis bought the "Nation" and the "Breeder and Sportsman." In the latter he occasionally found articles on dogs which interested him. The former he seldom read. He could not afford to subscribe regularly to either of the publications, but purchased their back numbers by the score, almost solely for the pleasure he took in binding them.

"What you alus sewing up them books for, Mister Grannis?" asked Maria, as she began rummaging about in Old Grannis's closet shelves. "There's just hundreds of 'em in here on yer shelves; they ain't no good to you."

"Well, well," answered Old Grannis, timidly, rubbing his chin, "I—I'm sure I can't quite say; a little habit, you know; a diversion, a—a—it occupies one, you know. I don't smoke; it takes the place of a pipe, perhaps."

"Here's this old yellow pitcher," said Maria, coming out of the closet with it in her hand. "The handle's cracked; you don't want it; better give me it."

Old Grannis did want the pitcher; true, he never used it now, but he had kept it a long time, and somehow he held to it as old people hold to trivial, worthless things that they have had for many years.

"Oh, that pitcher—well, Maria, I—I don't know. I'm afraid—you see, that pitcher—"

"Ah, go 'long," interrupted Maria Macapa, "what's the good of it?"

"If you insist, Maria, but I would much rather—" he rubbed his chin, perplexed and annoyed, hating to refuse, and wishing that Maria were gone.

"Why, what's the good of it?" persisted Maria. He could give no sufficient answer. "That's all right," she asserted, carrying the pitcher out.

"Ah—Maria—I say, you—you might leave the door—ah, don't quite shut it—it's a bit close in here at times." Maria grinned, and swung the door wide. Old Grannis was horribly embarrassed; positively, Maria was becoming unbearable.

"Got any junk?" cried Maria at Miss Baker's door. The little old lady was sitting close to the wall in her rocking-chair; her hands resting idly in her lap.

"Now, Maria," she said plaintively, "you are always after junk; you know I never have anything laying 'round like that."

It was true. The retired dressmaker's tiny room was a marvel of neatness, from the little red table, with its three Gorham spoons laid in exact parallels, to the decorous geraniums and mignonettes growing in the starch box at the window, underneath the fish globe with its one venerable gold fish. That day Miss Baker had been doing a bit of washing; two pocket handkerchiefs, still moist, adhered to the window panes, drying in the sun.

"Oh, I guess you got something you don't want," Maria went on, peering into the corners of the room. "Look-a-here what Mister Grannis gi' me," and she held out the yellow pitcher. Instantly Miss Baker was in a quiver of confusion. Every word spoken aloud could be perfectly heard in the next room. What a stupid drab was this Maria! Could anything be more trying than this position?

"Ain't that right, Mister Grannis?" called Maria; "didn't you gi' me this pitcher?" Old Grannis affected not to hear; perspiration stood on his forehead; his timidity overcame him as if he were a ten-year-old schoolboy. He half rose from his chair, his fingers dancing nervously upon his chin.

Maria opened Miss Baker's closet unconcernedly. "What's the matter with these old shoes?" she exclaimed, turning about with a pair of half-worn silk gaiters in her hand. They were by no means old enough to throw away, but Miss Baker was almost beside herself. There was no telling what might happen next. Her only thought was to be rid of Maria.

"Yes, yes, anything. You can have them; but go, go. There's nothing else, not a thing."

Maria went out into the hall, leaving Miss Baker's door wide open, as if maliciously. She had left the dirty pillow-case on the floor in the hall, and she stood outside, between the two open doors, stowing away the old pitcher and the half- worn silk shoes. She made remarks at the top of her voice, calling now to Miss Baker, now to Old Grannis. In a way she brought the two old people face to face. Each time they were forced to answer her questions it was as if they were talking directly to each other.

"These here are first-rate shoes, Miss Baker. Look here, Mister Grannis, get on to the shoes Miss Baker gi' me. You ain't got a pair you don't want, have you? You two people have less junk than any one else in the flat. How do you manage, Mister Grannis? You old bachelors are just like old maids, just as neat as pins. You two are just alike—you and Mister Grannis—ain't you, Miss Baker?"

Nothing could have been more horribly constrained, more awkward. The two old people suffered veritable torture. When Maria had gone, each heaved a sigh of unspeakable relief. Softly they pushed to their doors, leaving open a space of half a dozen inches. Old Grannis went back to his binding. Miss Baker brewed a cup of tea to quiet her nerves. Each tried to regain their composure, but in vain. Old Grannis's fingers trembled so that he pricked them with his needle. Miss Baker dropped her spoon twice. Their nervousness would not wear off. They were perturbed, upset. In a word, the afternoon was spoiled.

Maria went on about the flat from room to room. She had already paid Marcus Schouler a visit early that morning before he had gone out. Marcus had sworn at her, excitedly vociferating; "No, by damn! No, he hadn't a thing for her; he hadn't, for a fact. It was a positive persecution. Every day his privacy was invaded. He would complain to the landlady, he would. He'd move out of the place." In the end he had given Maria seven empty whiskey flasks, an iron grate, and ten cents—the latter because he said she wore her hair like a girl he used to know.

After coming from Miss Baker's room Maria knocked at McTeague's door. The dentist was lying on the bed-lounge in his stocking feet, doing nothing apparently, gazing up at the ceiling, lost in thought.

Since he had spoken to Trina Sieppe, asking her so abruptly to marry him, McTeague had passed a week of torment. For him there was no going back. It was Trina now, and none other. It was all one with him that his best friend, Marcus, might be in love with the same girl. He must have Trina in spite of everything; he would have her even in spite of herself. He did not stop to reflect about the matter; he followed his desire blindly, recklessly, furious and raging at every obstacle. And she had cried "No, no!" back at him; he could not forget that. She, so small and pale and delicate, had held him at bay, who was so huge, so immensely strong.

Besides that, all the charm of their intimacy was gone. After that unhappy sitting, Trina was no longer frank and straight-forward. Now she was circumspect, reserved, distant. He could no longer open his mouth; words failed him. At one sitting in particular they had said but good- day and good-by to each other. He felt that he was clumsy and ungainly. He told himself that she despised him.

But the memory of her was with him constantly. Night after night he lay broad awake thinking of Trina, wondering about her, racked with the infinite desire of her. His head burnt and throbbed. The palms of his hands were dry. He dozed and woke, and walked aimlessly about the dark room, bruising himself against the three chairs drawn up "at attention" under the steel engraving, and stumbling over the stone pug dog that sat in front of the little stove.

Besides this, the jealousy of Marcus Schouler harassed him. Maria Macapa, coming into his "Parlor" to ask for junk, found him flung at length upon the bed-lounge, gnawing at his fingers in an excess of silent fury. At lunch that day Marcus had told him of an excursion that was planned for the next Sunday afternoon. Mr. Sieppe, Trina's father, belonged to a rifle club that was to hold a meet at Schuetzen Park across the bay. All the Sieppes were going; there was to be a basket picnic.

Marcus, as usual, was invited to be one of the party. McTeague was in agony. It was his first experience, and he suffered all the worse for it because he was totally unprepared. What miserable complication was this in which he found himself involved? It seemed so simple to him since he loved Trina to take her straight to himself, stopping at nothing, asking no questions, to have her, and by main strength to carry her far away somewhere, he did not know exactly where, to some vague country, some undiscovered place where every day was Sunday.

"Got any junk?"

"Huh? What? What is it?" exclaimed McTeague, suddenly rousing up from the lounge. Often Maria did very well in the "Dental Parlors." McTeague was continually breaking things which he was too stupid to have mended; for him anything that was broken was lost. Now it was a cuspidor, now a fire-shovel for the little stove, now a China shaving mug.

"Got any junk?"

"I don't know—I don't remember," muttered McTeague. Maria roamed about the room, McTeague following her in his huge stockinged feet. All at once she pounced upon a sheaf of old hand instruments in a coverless cigar-box, pluggers, hard bits, and excavators. Maria had long coveted such a find in McTeague's "Parlor," knowing it should be somewhere about. The instruments were of the finest tempered steel and really valuable.

"Say, Doctor, I can have these, can't I?" exclaimed Maria. "You got no more use for them." McTeague was not at all sure of this. There were many in the sheaf that might be repaired, reshaped.

"No, no," he said, wagging his head. But Maria Macapa, knowing with whom she had to deal, at once let loose a torrent of words. She made the dentist believe that he had no right to withhold them, that he had promised to save them for her. She affected a great indignation, pursing her lips and putting her chin in the air as though wounded in some finer sense, changing so rapidly from one mood to another, filling the room with such shrill clamor, that McTeague was dazed and benumbed.

"Yes, all right, all right," he said, trying to make himself heard. "It WOULD be mean. I don't want 'em." As he turned from her to pick up the box, Maria took advantage of the moment to steal three "mats" of sponge-gold out of the glass saucer. Often she stole McTeague's gold, almost under his very eyes; indeed, it was so easy to do so that there was but little pleasure in the theft. Then Maria took herself off. McTeague returned to the sofa and flung himself upon it face downward.

A little before supper time Maria completed her search. The flat was cleaned of its junk from top to bottom. The dirty pillow-case was full to bursting. She took advantage of the supper hour to carry her bundle around the corner and up into the alley where Zerkow lived.

When Maria entered his shop, Zerkow had just come in from his daily rounds. His decrepit wagon stood in front of his door like a stranded wreck; the miserable horse, with its lamentable swollen joints, fed greedily upon an armful of spoiled hay in a shed at the back.

The interior of the junk shop was dark and damp, and foul with all manner of choking odors. On the walls, on the floor, and hanging from the rafters was a world of debris, dust-blackened, rust-corroded. Everything was there, every trade was represented, every class of society; things of iron and cloth and wood; all the detritus that a great city sloughs off in its daily life. Zerkow's junk shop was the last abiding-place, the almshouse, of such articles as had outlived their usefulness.

Maria found Zerkow himself in the back room, cooking some sort of a meal over an alcohol stove. Zerkow was a Polish Jew—curiously enough his hair was fiery red. He was a dry, shrivelled old man of sixty odd. He had the thin, eager, cat-like lips of the covetous; eyes that had grown keen as those of a lynx from long searching amidst muck and debris; and claw-like, prehensile fingers—the fingers of a man who accumulates, but never disburses. It was impossible to look at Zerkow and not know instantly that greed—inordinate, insatiable greed—was the dominant passion of the man. He was the Man with the Rake, groping hourly in the muck-heap of the city for gold, for gold, for gold. It was his dream, his passion; at every instant he seemed to feel the generous solid weight of the crude fat metal in his palms. The glint of it was constantly in his eyes; the jangle of it sang forever in his ears as the jangling of cymbals.

"Who is it? Who is it?" exclaimed Zerkow, as he heard Maria's footsteps in the outer room. His voice was faint, husky, reduced almost to a whisper by his prolonged habit of street crying.

"Oh, it's you again, is it?" he added, peering through the gloom of the shop. "Let's see; you've been here before, ain't you? You're the Mexican woman from Polk Street. Macapa's your name, hey?"

Maria nodded. "Had a flying squirrel an' let him go," she muttered, absently. Zerkow was puzzled; he looked at her sharply for a moment, then dismissed the matter with a movement of his head.

"Well, what you got for me?" he said. He left his supper to grow cold, absorbed at once in the affair.

Then a long wrangle began. Every bit of junk in Maria's pillow-case was discussed and weighed and disputed. They clamored into each other's faces over Old Grannis's cracked pitcher, over Miss Baker's silk gaiters, over Marcus Schouler's whiskey flasks, reaching the climax of disagreement when it came to McTeague's instruments.

"Ah, no, no!" shouted Maria. "Fifteen cents for the lot! I might as well make you a Christmas present! Besides, I got some gold fillings off him; look at um."

Zerkow drew a quick breath as the three pellets suddenly flashed in Maria's palm. There it was, the virgin metal, the pure, unalloyed ore, his dream, his consuming desire. His fingers twitched and hooked themselves into his palms, his thin lips drew tight across his teeth.

"Ah, you got some gold," he muttered, reaching for it.

Maria shut her fist over the pellets. "The gold goes with the others," she declared. "You'll gi' me a fair price for the lot, or I'll take um back."

In the end a bargain was struck that satisfied Maria. Zerkow was not one who would let gold go out of his house. He counted out to her the price of all her junk, grudging each piece of money as if it had been the blood of his veins. The affair was concluded.

But Zerkow still had something to say. As Maria folded up the pillow-case and rose to go, the old Jew said:

"Well, see here a minute, we'll—you'll have a drink before you go, won't you? Just to show that it's all right between us." Maria sat down again.

"Yes, I guess I'll have a drink," she answered.

Zerkow took down a whiskey bottle and a red glass tumbler with a broken base from a cupboard on the wall. The two drank together, Zerkow from the bottle, Maria from the broken tumbler. They wiped their lips slowly, drawing breath again. There was a moment's silence.

"Say," said Zerkow at last, "how about those gold dishes you told me about the last time you were here?"

"What gold dishes?" inquired Maria, puzzled.

"Ah, you know," returned the other. "The plate your father owned in Central America a long time ago. Don't you know, it rang like so many bells? Red gold, you know, like oranges?"

"Ah," said Maria, putting her chin in the air as if she knew a long story about that if she had a mind to tell it. "Ah, yes, that gold service."

"Tell us about it again," said Zerkow, his bloodless lower lip moving against the upper, his claw-like fingers feeling about his mouth and chin.

"Tell us about it; go on."

He was breathing short, his limbs trembled a little. It was as if some hungry beast of prey had scented a quarry. Maria still refused, putting up her head, insisting that she had to be going.

"Let's have it," insisted the Jew. "Take another drink." Maria took another swallow of the whiskey. "Now, go on," repeated Zerkow; "let's have the story." Maria squared her elbows on the deal table, looking straight in front of her with eyes that saw nothing.

"Well, it was this way," she began. "It was when I was little. My folks must have been rich, oh, rich into the millions—coffee, I guess—and there was a large house, but I can only remember the plate. Oh, that service of plate! It was wonderful. There were more than a hundred pieces, and every one of them gold. You should have seen the sight when the leather trunk was opened. It fair dazzled your eyes. It was a yellow blaze like a fire, like a sunset; such a glory, all piled up together, one piece over the other. Why, if the room was dark you'd think you could see just the same with all that glitter there. There wa'n't a piece that was so much as scratched; every one was like a mirror, smooth and bright, just like a little pool when the sun shines into it. There was dinner dishes and soup tureens and pitchers; and great, big platters as long as that and wide too; and cream-jugs and bowls with carved handles, all vines and things; and drinking mugs, every one a different shape; and dishes for gravy and sauces; and then a great, big punch-bowl with a ladle, and the bowl was all carved out with figures and bunches of grapes. Why, just only that punch-bowl was worth a fortune, I guess. When all that plate was set out on a table, it was a sight for a king to look at. Such a service as that was! Each piece was heavy, oh, so heavy! and thick, you know; thick, fat gold, nothing but gold—red, shining, pure gold, orange red—and when you struck it with your knuckle, ah, you should have heard! No church bell ever rang sweeter or clearer. It was soft gold, too; you could bite into it, and leave the dent of your teeth. Oh, that gold plate! I can see it just as plain—solid, solid, heavy, rich, pure gold; nothing but gold, gold, heaps and heaps of it. What a service that was!"

Maria paused, shaking her head, thinking over the vanished splendor. Illiterate enough, unimaginative enough on all other subjects, her distorted wits called up this picture with marvellous distinctness. It was plain she saw the plate clearly. Her description was accurate, was almost eloquent.

Did that wonderful service of gold plate ever exist outside of her diseased imagination? Was Maria actually remembering some reality of a childhood of barbaric luxury? Were her parents at one time possessed of an incalculable fortune derived from some Central American coffee plantation, a fortune long since confiscated by armies of insurrectionists, or squandered in the support of revolutionary governments?

It was not impossible. Of Maria Macapa's past prior to the time of her appearance at the "flat" absolutely nothing could be learned. She suddenly appeared from the unknown, a strange woman of a mixed race, sane on all subjects but that of the famous service of gold plate; but unusual, complex, mysterious, even at her best.

But what misery Zerkow endured as he listened to her tale! For he chose to believe it, forced himself to believe it, lashed and harassed by a pitiless greed that checked at no tale of treasure, however preposterous. The story ravished him with delight. He was near someone who had possessed this wealth. He saw someone who had seen this pile of gold. He seemed near it; it was there, somewhere close by, under his eyes, under his fingers; it was red, gleaming, ponderous. He gazed about him wildly; nothing, nothing but the sordid junk shop and the rust-corroded tins. What exasperation, what positive misery, to be so near to it and yet to know that it was irrevocably, irretrievably lost! A spasm of anguish passed through him. He gnawed at his bloodless lips, at the hopelessness of it, the rage, the fury of it.

"Go on, go on," he whispered; "let's have it all over again. Polished like a mirror, hey, and heavy? Yes, I know, I know. A punch-bowl worth a fortune. Ah! and you saw it, you had it all!"

Maria rose to go. Zerkow accompanied her to the door, urging another drink upon her.

"Come again, come again," he croaked. "Don't wait till you've got junk; come any time you feel like it, and tell me more about the plate."

He followed her a step down the alley.

"How much do you think it was worth?" he inquired, anxiously.

"Oh, a million dollars," answered Maria, vaguely.

When Maria had gone, Zerkow returned to the back room of the shop, and stood in front of the alcohol stove, looking down into his cold dinner, preoccupied, thoughtful.

"A million dollars," he muttered in his rasping, guttural whisper, his finger-tips wandering over his thin, cat-like lips. "A golden service worth a million dollars; a punch- bowl worth a fortune; red gold plates, heaps and piles. God!"

CHAPTER 4

The days passed. McTeague had finished the operation on Trina's teeth. She did not come any more to the "Parlors." Matters had readjusted themselves a little between the two during the last sittings. Trina yet stood upon her reserve, and McTeague still felt himself shambling and ungainly in her presence; but that constraint and embarrassment that had followed upon McTeague's blundering declaration broke up little by little. In spite of themselves they were gradually resuming the same relative positions they had occupied when they had first met.

But McTeague suffered miserably for all that. He never would have Trina, he saw that clearly. She was too good for him; too delicate, too refined, too prettily made for him, who was so coarse, so enormous, so stupid. She was for someone else—Marcus, no doubt—or at least for some finer- grained man. She should have gone to some other dentist; the young fellow on the corner, for instance, the poser, the rider of bicycles, the courser of grey-hounds. McTeague began to loathe and to envy this fellow. He spied upon him going in and out of his office, and noted his salmon-pink neckties and his astonishing waistcoats.

One Sunday, a few days after Trina's last sitting, McTeague met Marcus Schouler at his table in the car conductors' coffee-joint, next to the harness shop.

"What you got to do this afternoon, Mac?" inquired the other, as they ate their suet pudding.

"Nothing, nothing," replied McTeague, shaking his head. His mouth was full of pudding. It made him warm to eat, and little beads of perspiration stood across the bridge of his nose. He looked forward to an afternoon passed in his operating chair as usual. On leaving his "Parlors" he had put ten cents into his pitcher and had left it at Frenna's to be filled.

"What do you say we take a walk, huh?" said Marcus. "Ah, that's the thing—a walk, a long walk, by damn! It'll be outa sight. I got to take three or four of the dogs out for exercise, anyhow. Old Grannis thinks they need ut. We'll walk out to the Presidio."

Of late it had become the custom of the two friends to take long walks from time to time. On holidays and on those Sunday afternoons when Marcus was not absent with the Sieppes they went out together, sometimes to the park, sometimes to the Presidio, sometimes even across the bay. They took a great pleasure in each other's company, but silently and with reservation, having the masculine horror of any demonstration of friendship.

They walked for upwards of five hours that afternoon, out the length of California Street, and across the Presidio Reservation to the Golden Gate. Then they turned, and, following the line of the shore, brought up at the Cliff House. Here they halted for beer, Marcus swearing that his mouth was as dry as a hay-bin. Before starting on their walk they had gone around to the little dog hospital, and Marcus had let out four of the convalescents, crazed with joy at the release.

"Look at that dog," he cried to McTeague, showing him a finely-bred Irish setter. "That's the dog that belonged to the duck on the avenue, the dog we called for that day. I've bought 'um. The duck thought he had the distemper, and just threw 'um away. Nothun wrong with 'um but a little catarrh. Ain't he a bird? Say, ain't he a bird? Look at his flag; it's perfect; and see how he carries his tail on a line with his back. See how stiff and white his whiskers are. Oh, by damn! you can't fool me on a dog. That dog's a winner."

At the Cliff House the two sat down to their beer in a quiet corner of the billiard-room. There were but two players. Somewhere in another part of the building a mammoth music- box was jangling out a quickstep. From outside came the long, rhythmical rush of the surf and the sonorous barking of the seals upon the seal rocks. The four dogs curled themselves down upon the sanded floor.

"Here's how," said Marcus, half emptying his glass. "Ah-h!" he added, with a long breath, "that's good; it is, for a fact."

For the last hour of their walk Marcus had done nearly all the talking. McTeague merely answering him by uncertain movements of the head. For that matter, the dentist had been silent and preoccupied throughout the whole afternoon. At length Marcus noticed it. As he set down his glass with a bang he suddenly exclaimed:

"What's the matter with you these days, Mac? You got a bean about somethun, hey? Spit ut out."

"No, no," replied McTeague, looking about on the floor, rolling his eyes; "nothing, no, no."

"Ah, rats!" returned the other. McTeague kept silence. The two billiard players departed. The huge music-box struck into a fresh tune.

"Huh!" exclaimed Marcus, with a short laugh, "guess you're in love."

McTeague gasped, and shuffled his enormous feet under the table.

"Well, somethun's bitun you, anyhow," pursued Marcus. "Maybe I can help you. We're pals, you know. Better tell me what's up; guess we can straighten ut out. Ah, go on; spit ut out."

The situation was abominable. McTeague could not rise to it. Marcus was his best friend, his only friend. They were "pals" and McTeague was very fond of him. Yet they were both in love, presumably, with the same girl, and now Marcus would try and force the secret out of him; would rush blindly at the rock upon which the two must split, stirred by the very best of motives, wishing only to be of service. Besides this, there was nobody to whom McTeague would have better preferred to tell his troubles than to Marcus, and yet about this trouble, the greatest trouble of his life, he must keep silent; must refrain from speaking of it to Marcus above everybody.

McTeague began dimly to feel that life was too much for him. How had it all come about? A month ago he was perfectly content; he was calm and peaceful, taking his little pleasures as he found them. His life had shaped itself; was, no doubt, to continue always along these same lines. A woman had entered his small world and instantly there was discord. The disturbing element had appeared. Wherever the woman had put her foot a score of distressing complications had sprung up, like the sudden growth of strange and puzzling flowers.

"Say, Mac, go on; let's have ut straight," urged Marcus, leaning toward him. "Has any duck been doing you dirt?" he cried, his face crimson on the instant.

"No," said McTeague, helplessly.

"Come along, old man," persisted Marcus; "let's have ut. What is the row? I'll do all I can to help you."

It was more than McTeague could bear. The situation had got beyond him. Stupidly he spoke, his hands deep in his pockets, his head rolled forward.

"It's—it's Miss Sieppe," he said.

"Trina, my cousin? How do you mean?" inquired Marcus sharply.

"I—I—I don' know," stammered McTeague, hopelessly confounded.

"You mean," cried Marcus, suddenly enlightened, "that you are—that you, too."

McTeague stirred in his chair, looking at the walls of the room, avoiding the other's glance. He nodded his head, then suddenly broke out:

"I can't help it. It ain't my fault, is it?"

Marcus was struck dumb; he dropped back in his chair breathless. Suddenly McTeague found his tongue.

"I tell you, Mark, I can't help it. I don't know how it happened. It came on so slow that I was, that—that—that it was done before I knew it, before I could help myself. I know we're pals, us two, and I knew how—how you and Miss Sieppe were. I know now, I knew then; but that wouldn't have made any difference. Before I knew it—it—it—there I was. I can't help it. I wouldn't 'a' had ut happen for anything, if I could 'a' stopped it, but I don' know, it's something that's just stronger than you are, that's all. She came there—Miss Sieppe came to the parlors there three or four times a week, and she was the first girl I had ever known,—and you don' know! Why, I was so close to her I touched her face every minute, and her mouth, and smelt her hair and her breath—oh, you don't know anything about it. I can't give you any idea. I don' know exactly myself; I only know how I'm fixed. I—I—it's been done; it's too late, there's no going back. Why, I can't think of anything else night and day. It's everything. It's—it's—oh, it's everything! I—I—why, Mark, it's everything—I can't explain." He made a helpless movement with both hands.

Never had McTeague been so excited; never had he made so long a speech. His arms moved in fierce, uncertain gestures, his face flushed, his enormous jaws shut together with a sharp click at every pause. It was like some colossal brute trapped in a delicate, invisible mesh, raging, exasperated, powerless to extricate himself.

Marcus Schouler said nothing. There was a long silence. Marcus got up and walked to the window and stood looking out, but seeing nothing. "Well, who would have thought of this?" he muttered under his breath. Here was a fix. Marcus cared for Trina. There was no doubt in his mind about that. He looked forward eagerly to the Sunday afternoon excursions. He liked to be with Trina. He, too, felt the charm of the little girl—the charm of the small, pale forehead; the little chin thrust out as if in confidence and innocence; the heavy, odorous crown of black hair. He liked her immensely. Some day he would speak; he would ask her to marry him. Marcus put off this matter of marriage to some future period; it would be some time—a year, perhaps, or two. The thing did not take definite shape in his mind. Marcus "kept company" with his cousin Trina, but he knew plenty of other girls. For the matter of that, he liked all girls pretty well. Just now the singleness and strength of McTeague's passion startled him. McTeague would marry Trina that very afternoon if she would have him; but would he—Marcus? No, he would not; if it came to that, no, he would not. Yet he knew he liked Trina. He could say—yes, he could say—he loved her. She was his "girl." The Sieppes acknowledged him as Trina's "young man." Marcus came back to the table and sat down sideways upon it.

"Well, what are we going to do about it, Mac?" he said.

"I don' know," answered McTeague, in great distress. "I don' want anything to—to come between us, Mark."

"Well, nothun will, you bet!" vociferated the other. "No, sir; you bet not, Mac."

Marcus was thinking hard. He could see very clearly that McTeague loved Trina more than he did; that in some strange way this huge, brutal fellow was capable of a greater passion than himself, who was twice as clever. Suddenly Marcus jumped impetuously to a resolution.

"Well, say, Mac," he cried, striking the table with his fist, "go ahead. I guess you—you want her pretty bad. I'll pull out; yes, I will. I'll give her up to you, old man."

The sense of his own magnanimity all at once overcame Marcus. He saw himself as another man, very noble, self- sacrificing; he stood apart and watched this second self with boundless admiration and with infinite pity. He was so good, so magnificent, so heroic, that he almost sobbed. Marcus made a sweeping gesture of resignation, throwing out both his arms, crying:

"Mac, I'll give her up to you. I won't stand between you." There were actually tears in Marcus's eyes as he spoke. There was no doubt he thought himself sincere. At that moment he almost believed he loved Trina conscientiously, that he was sacrificing himself for the sake of his friend. The two stood up and faced each other, gripping hands. It was a great moment; even McTeague felt the drama of it. What a fine thing was this friendship between men! the dentist treats his friend for an ulcerated tooth and refuses payment; the friend reciprocates by giving up his girl. This was nobility. Their mutual affection and esteem suddenly increased enormously. It was Damon and Pythias; it was David and Jonathan; nothing could ever estrange them. Now it was for life or death.

"I'm much obliged," murmured McTeague. He could think of nothing better to say. "I'm much obliged," he repeated; "much obliged, Mark."

"That's all right, that's all right," returned Marcus Schouler, bravely, and it oc-curred to him to add, "You'll be happy together. Tell her for me—tell her—-tell her—" Marcus could not go on. He wrung the dentist's hand silently.

It had not appeared to either of them that Trina might refuse McTeague. McTe-ague's spirits rose at once. In Marcus's withdrawal he fancied he saw an end to all his difficulties. Everything would come right, after all. The strained, exalted state of Marcus's nerves ended by putting him into fine humor as well. His grief suddenly changed to an excess of gaiety. The afternoon was a success. They slapped each other on the back with great blows of the open palms, and they drank each other's health in a third round of beer.

Ten minutes after his renunciation of Trina Sieppe, Marcus astounded McTe-ague with a tremendous feat.

"Looka here, Mac. I know somethun you can't do. I'll bet you two bits I'll stump you." They each put a quarter on the table. "Now watch me," cried Marcus. He caught up a billiard ball from the rack, poised it a moment in front of his face, then with a sudden, horrifying distension of his jaws crammed it into his mouth, and shut his lips over it.

For an instant McTeague was stupefied, his eyes bulging. Then an enormous laugh shook him. He roared and shouted, swaying in his chair, slapping his knee. What a josher was this Marcus! Sure, you never could tell what he would do next. Marcus slipped the ball out, wiped it on the tablecloth, and passed it to McTeague. "Now let's see you do it."

McTeague fell suddenly grave. The matter was serious. He parted his thick mustaches and opened his enormous jaws like an anaconda. The ball disappeared inside his mouth. Marcus applauded vociferously, shouting, "Good work!" McTe-ague reached for the money and put it in his vest pocket, nodding his head with a knowing air.

Then suddenly his face grew purple, his jaws moved convulsively, he pawed at his cheeks with both hands. The billiard ball had slipped into his mouth easily enough; now, however, he could not get it out again.

It was terrible. The dentist rose to his feet, stumbling about among the dogs, his face working, his eyes starting. Try as he would, he could not stretch his jaws wide enough to slip the ball out. Marcus lost his wits, swearing at the top of his voice. McTeague sweated with terror; inarticulate sounds came from his crammed mouth; he waved his arms wildly; all the four dogs caught the excitement and be-gan to bark. A waiter rushed in, the two billiard players returned, a little crowd formed. There was a veritable scene.

All at once the ball slipped out of McTeague's jaws as easily as it had gone in. What a relief! He dropped into a chair, wiping his forehead, gasping for breath.

On the strength of the occasion Marcus Schouler invited the entire group to drink with him.

By the time the affair was over and the group dispersed it was after five. Mar-cus and McTeague decided they would ride home on the cars. But they soon found this impossible. The dogs would not follow. Only Alexander, Marcus's new setter, kept his place at the rear of the car. The other three lost their senses immediately, running wildly about the streets with their heads in the air, or suddenly starting off at a furious gallop directly away from the car. Marcus whistled and shouted and lathered with rage in vain. The two friends were obliged to walk. When they finally reached Polk Street, Marcus shut up the three dogs in the hospital. Alexander he brought back to the flat with him.

There was a minute back yard in the rear, where Marcus had made a kennel for Alexander out of an old water barrel. Before he thought of his own supper Marcus put Alexander to bed and fed him a couple of dog biscuits. McTeague had followed him to the yard to keep him company. Alexander settled to his supper at once, chewing vigorously at the biscuit, his head on one side.

"What you going to do about this—about that—about—about my cousin now, Mac?" inquired Marcus.

McTeague shook his head helplessly. It was dark by now and cold. The little back yard was grimy and full of odors. McTeague was tired with their long walk. All his uneasiness about his affair with Trina had returned. No, surely she was not for him. Marcus or some other man would win her in the end. What could she ever see to desire in him—in him, a clumsy giant, with hands like wooden mallets? She had told him once that she would not marry him. Was that not final?

"I don' know what to do, Mark," he said.

"Well, you must make up to her now," answered Marcus. "Go and call on her."

McTeague started. He had not thought of calling on her. The idea frightened him a little.

"Of course," persisted Marcus, "that's the proper caper. What did you expect? Did you think you was never going to see her again?"

"I don' know, I don' know," responded the dentist, looking stupidly at the dog.

"You know where they live," continued Marcus Schouler. "Over at B Street station, across the bay. I'll take you over there whenever you want to go. I tell you what, we'll go over there Washington's Birthday. That's this next Wednesday; sure, they'll be glad to see you." It was good of Marcus. All at once McTeague rose to an appreciation of what his friend was doing for him. He stammered:

"Say, Mark—you're—you're all right, anyhow."

"Why, pshaw!" said Marcus. "That's all right, old man. I'd like to see you two fixed, that's all. We'll go over Wednesday, sure."

They turned back to the house. Alexander left off eating and watched them go away, first with one eye, then with the other. But he was too self-respecting to whimper. However, by the time the two friends had reached the second landing on the back stairs a terrible commotion was under way in the little yard. They rushed to an open window at the end of the hall and looked down.

A thin board fence separated the flat's back yard from that used by the branch post-office. In the latter place lived a collie dog. He and Alexander had smelt each other out, blowing through the cracks of the fence at each other. Suddenly the quarrel had exploded on either side of the fence. The dogs raged at each other, snarling and barking, frantic with hate. Their teeth gleamed. They tore at the fence with their front paws. They filled the whole night with their clamor.

"By damn!" cried Marcus, "they don't love each other. Just listen; wouldn't that make a fight if the two got together? Have to try it some day."

CHAPTER 5

Wednesday morning, Washington's Birthday, McTeague rose very early and shaved himself. Besides the six mournful concertina airs, the dentist knew one song. Whenever he shaved, he sung this song; never at any other time. His voice was a bellowing roar, enough to make the window sashes rattle. Just now he woke up all the lodgers in his hall with it. It was a lamentable wail:

"No one to love, none to caress, Left all alone in this world's wilderness."

As he paused to strop his razor, Marcus came into his room, half-dressed, a startling phantom in red flannels.

Marcus often ran back and forth between his room and the dentist's "Parlors" in all sorts of undress. Old Miss Baker had seen him thus several times through her half-open door, as she sat in her room listening and waiting. The old dressmaker was shocked out of all expression. She was outraged, offended, pursing her lips, putting up her head. She talked of complaining to the landlady. "And Mr. Grannis right next door, too. You can understand how trying it is for both of us." She would come out in the hall after one of these apparitions, her little false curls shaking, talking loud and shrill to any one in reach of her voice.

"Well," Marcus would shout, "shut your door, then, if you don't want to see. Look out, now, here I come again. Not even a porous plaster on me this time."

On this Wednesday morning Marcus called McTeague out into the hall, to the head of the stairs that led down to the street door.

"Come and listen to Maria, Mac," said he.

Maria sat on the next to the lowest step, her chin propped by her two fists. The red-headed Polish Jew, the ragman Zerkow, stood in the doorway. He was talking eagerly.

"Now, just once more, Maria," he was saying. "Tell it to us just once more." Maria's voice came up the stairway in a monotone. Marcus and McTeague caught a phrase from time to time.

"There were more than a hundred pieces, and every one of them gold—just that punch-bowl was worth a fortune-thick, fat, red gold."

"Get onto to that, will you?" observed Marcus. "The old skin has got her started on the plate. Ain't they a pair for you?"

"And it rang like bells, didn't it?" prompted Zerkow.

"Sweeter'n church bells, and clearer."

"Ah, sweeter'n bells. Wasn't that punch-bowl awful heavy?"

"All you could do to lift it."

"I know. Oh, I know," answered Zerkow, clawing at his lips. "Where did it all go to? Where did it go?"

Maria shook her head.

"It's gone, anyhow."

"Ah, gone, gone! Think of it! The punch-bowl gone, and the engraved ladle, and the plates and goblets. What a sight it must have been all heaped together!"

"It was a wonderful sight."

"Yes, wonderful; it must have been."

On the lower steps of that cheap flat, the Mexican woman and the red-haired Polish Jew mused long over that vanished, half-mythical gold plate.

Marcus and the dentist spent Washington's Birthday across the bay. The journey over was one long agony to McTeague. He shook with a formless, uncertain dread; a dozen times he would have turned back had not Marcus been with him. The stolid giant was as nervous as a schoolboy. He fancied that his call upon Miss Sieppe was an outrageous affront. She would freeze him with a stare; he would be shown the door, would be ejected, disgraced.

As they got off the local train at B Street station they suddenly collided with the whole tribe of Sieppes—the mother, father, three children, and Trina—equipped for one of their eternal picnics. They were to go to Schuetzen Park, within walking distance of the station. They were grouped about four lunch baskets. One of the children, a little boy, held a black greyhound by a rope around its neck. Trina wore a blue cloth skirt, a striped shirt waist, and a white sailor; about her round waist was a belt of imitation alligator skin.

At once Mrs. Sieppe began to talk to Marcus. He had written of their coming, but the picnic had been decided upon after the arrival of his letter. Mrs. Sieppe explained this to him. She was an immense old lady with a pink face and wonderful hair, absolutely white. The Sieppes were a German-Swiss family.

"We go to der park, Schuetzen Park, mit alle dem childern, a little eggs-kursion, eh not soh? We breathe der freshes air, a celubration, a pignic bei der seashore on. Ach, dot wull be soh gay, ah?"

"You bet it will. It'll be outa sight," cried Marcus, enthusiastic in an instant. "This is m' friend Doctor McTeague I wrote you about, Mrs. Sieppe."

"Ach, der doktor," cried Mrs. Sieppe.

McTeague was presented, shaking hands gravely as Marcus shouldered him from one to the other.

Mr. Sieppe was a little man of a military aspect, full of importance, taking himself very seriously. He was a member of a rifle team. Over his shoulder was slung a Springfield rifle, while his breast was decorated by five bronze medals.

Trina was delighted. McTeague was dumfounded. She appeared positively glad to see him.

"How do you do, Doctor McTeague," she said, smiling at him and shaking his hand. "It's nice to see you again. Look, see how fine my filling is." She lifted a corner of her lip and showed him the clumsy gold bridge.

Meanwhile, Mr. Sieppe toiled and perspired. Upon him devolved the responsibility of the excursion. He seemed to consider it a matter of vast importance, a veritable expedition.

"Owgooste!" he shouted to the little boy with the black greyhound, "you will der hound und basket number three carry. Der tervins," he added, calling to the two smallest boys, who were dressed exactly alike, "will releef one unudder mit der camp-stuhl und basket number four. Dat is comprehend, hay? When we make der start, you childern will in der advance march. Dat is your orders. But we do not start," he exclaimed, excitedly; "we remain. Ach Gott, Selina, who does not arrive."

Selina, it appeared, was a niece of Mrs. Sieppe's. They were on the point of starting without her, when she suddenly arrived, very much out of breath. She was a slender, unhealthy looking girl, who overworked herself giving lessons in hand-painting at twenty-five cents an hour. McTeague was presented. They all began to talk at once, filling the little station-house with a confusion of tongues.

"Attention!" cried Mr. Sieppe, his gold-headed cane in one hand, his Springfield in the other. "Attention! We depart." The four little boys moved off ahead; the greyhound suddenly began to bark, and tug at his leash. The others picked up their bundles.

"Vorwarts!" shouted Mr. Sieppe, waving his rifle and assuming the attitude of a lieutenant of infantry leading a charge. The party set off down the railroad track.

Mrs. Sieppe walked with her husband, who constantly left her side to shout an order up and down the line. Marcus followed with Selina. McTeague found himself with Trina at the end of the procession.

"We go off on these picnics almost every week," said Trina, by way of a beginning, "and almost every holiday, too. It is a custom."

"Yes, yes, a custom," answered McTeague, nodding; "a custom—that's the word."

"Don't you think picnics are fine fun, Doctor McTeague?" she continued. "You take your lunch; you leave the dirty city all day; you race about in the open air, and when lunchtime comes, oh, aren't you hungry? And the woods and the grass smell so fine!"

"I don' know, Miss Sieppe," he answered, keeping his eyes fixed on the ground between the rails.

"I never went on a picnic."

"Never went on a picnic?" she cried, astonished.

"Oh, you'll see what fun we'll have. In the morning father and the children dig clams in the mud by the shore, an' we bake them, and—oh, there's thousands of things to do."

"Once I went sailing on the bay," said McTeague. "It was in a tugboat; we fished off the heads. I caught three codfishes."

"I'm afraid to go out on the bay," answered Trina, shaking her head, "sailboats tip over so easy. A cousin of mine, Selina's brother, was drowned one Decoration Day. They never found his body. Can you swim, Doctor McTeague?"

"I used to at the mine."

"At the mine? Oh, yes, I remember, Marcus told me you were a miner once."

"I was a car-boy; all the car-boys used to swim in the reservoir by the ditch every Thursday evening. One of them was bit by a rattlesnake once while he was dressing. He was a Frenchman, named Andrew. He swelled up and began to twitch."

"Oh, how I hate snakes! They're so crawly and graceful—but, just the same, I like to watch them. You know that drug store over in town that has a showcase full of live ones?"

"We killed the rattler with a cart whip."

"How far do you think you could swim? Did you ever try? D'you think you could swim a mile?"

"A mile? I don't know. I never tried. I guess I could."

"I can swim a little. Sometimes we all go out to the Crystal Baths."

"The Crystal Baths, huh? Can you swim across the tank?"

"Oh, I can swim all right as long as papa holds my chin up. Soon as he takes his hand away, down I go. Don't you hate to get water in your ears?"

"Bathing's good for you."

"If the water's too warm, it isn't. It weakens you."

Mr. Sieppe came running down the tracks, waving his cane.

"To one side," he shouted, motioning them off the track; "der drain gomes." A local passenger train was just passing B Street station, some quarter of a mile behind them. The party stood to one side to let it pass. Marcus put a nickel and two crossed pins upon the rail, and waved his hat to the passengers as the train roared past. The children shouted shrilly. When the train was gone, they all rushed to see the nickel and the crossed pins. The nickel had been jolted off, but the pins had been flattened out so that they bore a faint resemblance to opened scissors. A great contention arose among the children for the possession of these "scissors." Mr. Sieppe was obliged to intervene. He reflected gravely. It was a matter of tremendous moment. The whole party halted, awaiting his decision.

"Attend now," he suddenly exclaimed. "It will not be soh soon. At der end of der day, ven we shall have home gecommen, den wull it pe adjudge, eh? A *reward* of merit to him who der bes' pehaves. It is an order. Vorwarts!"

"That was a Sacramento train," said Marcus to Selina as they started off; "it was, for a fact."

"I know a girl in Sacramento," Trina told McTeague. "She's forewoman in a glove store, and she's got consumption."

"I was in Sacramento once," observed McTeague, "nearly eight years ago."

"Is it a nice place—as nice as San Francisco?"

"It's hot. I practised there for a while."

"I like San Francisco," said Trina, looking across the bay to where the city piled itself upon its hills.

"So do I," answered McTeague. "Do you like it better than living over here?"

"Oh, sure, I wish we lived in the city. If you want to go across for anything it takes up the whole day."

"Yes, yes, the whole day—almost."

"Do you know many people in the city? Do you know anybody named Oelbermann? That's my uncle. He has a wholesale toy store in the Mission. They say he's awful rich."

"No, I don' know him."

"His stepdaughter wants to be a nun. Just fancy! And Mr. Oelbermann won't have it. He says it would be just like burying his child. Yes, she wants to enter the convent of the Sacred Heart. Are you a Catholic, Doctor McTeague?"

"No. No, I—"

"Papa is a Catholic. He goes to Mass on the feast days once in a while. But mamma's Lutheran."

"The Catholics are trying to get control of the schools," observed McTeague, suddenly remembering one of Marcus's political tirades.

"That's what cousin Mark says. We are going to send the twins to the kindergarten next month."

"What's the kindergarten?"

"Oh, they teach them to make things out of straw and toothpicks—kind of a play place to keep them off the street."

"There's one up on Sacramento Street, not far from Polk Street. I saw the sign."

"I know where. Why, Selina used to play the piano there."

"Does she play the piano?"

"Oh, you ought to hear her. She plays fine. Selina's very accomplished. She paints, too."

"I can play on the concertina."

"Oh, can you? I wish you'd brought it along. Next time you will. I hope you'll come often on our picnics. You'll see what fun we'll have."

"Fine day for a picnic, ain't it? There ain't a cloud."

"That's so," exclaimed Trina, looking up, "not a single cloud. Oh, yes; there is one, just over Telegraph Hill."

"That's smoke."

"No, it's a cloud. Smoke isn't white that way."

"'Tis a cloud."

"I knew I was right. I never say a thing unless I'm pretty sure."

"It looks like a dog's head."

"Don't it? Isn't Marcus fond of dogs?" "He got a new dog last week—a setter."

"Did he?"

"Yes. He and I took a lot of dogs from his hospital out for a walk to the Cliff House last Sunday, but we had to walk all the way home, because they wouldn't follow. You've been out to the Cliff House?"

"Not for a long time. We had a picnic there one Fourth of July, but it rained. Don't you love the ocean?"

"Yes—yes, I like it pretty well."

"Oh, I'd like to go off in one of those big sailing ships. Just away, and away, and away, anywhere. They're different from a little yacht. I'd love to travel."

"Sure; so would I."

"Papa and mamma came over in a sailing ship. They were twenty-one days. Mamma's uncle used to be a sailor. He was captain of a steamer on Lake Geneva, in Switzerland."

"Halt!" shouted Mr. Sieppe, brandishing his rifle. They had arrived at the gates of the park. All at once McTeague turned cold. He had only a quarter in his pocket. What was he expected to do—pay for the whole party, or for Trina and himself, or merely buy his own ticket? And even in this latter case would a quarter be enough? He lost his wits, rolling his eyes helplessly. Then it occurred to him to feign a great abstraction, pretending not to know that the time was come to pay. He looked intently up and down the tracks; perhaps a train was coming. "Here we are," cried Trina, as they came up to the rest of the party, crowded about the entrance. "Yes, yes," observed McTeague, his head in the air.

"Gi' me four bits, Mac," said Marcus, coming up. "Here's where we shell out."

"I—I—I only got a quarter," mumbled the dentist, miserably. He felt that he had ruined himself forever with Trina. What was the use of trying to win her? Destiny was against him. "I only got a quarter," he stammered. He was on the point of adding that he would not go in the park. That seemed to be the only alternative.

"Oh, all right!" said Marcus, easily. "I'll pay for you, and you can square with me when we go home."

They filed into the park, Mr. Sieppe counting them off as they entered.

"Ah," said Trina, with a long breath, as she and McTeague pushed through the wicket, "here we are once more, Doctor." She had not appeared to notice McTeague's embarrassment. The difficulty had been tided over somehow. Once more McTeague felt himself saved.

"To der beach!" shouted Mr. Sieppe. They had checked their baskets at the peanut stand. The whole party trooped down to the seashore. The greyhound was turned loose. The children raced on ahead.

From one of the larger parcels Mrs. Sieppe had drawn forth a small tin steamboat—August's birthday present—a gaudy little toy which could be steamed up and navigated by means of an alcohol lamp. Her trial trip was to be made this morning.

"Gi' me it, gi' me it," shouted August, dancing around his father.

"Not soh, not soh," cried Mr. Sieppe, bearing it aloft. "I must first der eggsperimunt make."

"No, no!" wailed August. "I want to play with ut."

"Obey!" thundered Mr. Sieppe. August subsided. A little jetty ran part of the way into the water. Here, after a careful study of the directions printed on the cover of the box, Mr. Sieppe began to fire the little boat.

"I want to put ut in the wa-ater," cried August. "Stand back!" shouted his parent. "You do not know so well as me; dere is dandger. Mitout attention he will eggsplode."

"I want to play with ut," protested August, beginning to cry.

"Ach, soh; you cry, bube!" vociferated Mr. Sieppe. "Mommer," addressing Mrs. Sieppe, "he will soh soon be ge-whipt, eh?"

"I want my boa-wut," screamed August, dancing.

"Silence!" roared Mr. Sieppe. The little boat began to hiss and smoke.

"Soh," observed the father, "he gommence. Attention! I put him in der water." He was very excited. The perspiration dripped from the back of his neck. The little boat was launched. It hissed more furiously than ever. Clouds of steam rolled from it, but it refused to move.

"You don't know how she wo-rks," sobbed August.

"I know more soh mudge as der grossest liddle fool as you," cried Mr. Sieppe, fiercely, his face purple.

"You must give it sh—shove!" exclaimed the boy.

"Den he eggsplode, idiot!" shouted his father. All at once the boiler of the steamer blew up with a sharp crack. The little tin toy turned over and sank out of sight before any one could interfere.

"Ah—h! Yah! Yah!" yelled August. "It's go-one!" Instantly Mr. Sieppe boxed his ears. There was a lamentable scene. August rent the air with his outcries; his father shook him till his boots danced on the jetty, shouting into his face:

"Ach, idiot! Ach, imbecile! Ach, miserable! I tol' you he eggsplode. Stop your cry. Stop! It is an order. Do you wish I drow you in der water, eh? Speak. Silence, bube! Mommer, where ist mein stick? He will der grossest whippun ever of his life receive."

Little by little the boy subsided, swallowing his sobs, knuckling his eyes, gazing ruefully at the spot where the boat had sunk. "Dot is better soh," commented Mr. Sieppe, finally releasing him. "Next dime berhaps you will your fat'er better pelief. Now, no more. We will der glams ge- dig, Mommer, a fire. Ach, himmel! we have der pfeffer forgotten."

The work of clam digging began at once, the little boys taking off their shoes and stockings. At first August refused to be comforted, and it was not until his father drove him into the water with his gold-headed cane that he consented to join the others.

What a day that was for McTeague! What a never-to-be- forgotten day! He was with Trina constantly. They laughed together—she demurely, her lips closed tight, her little chin thrust out, her small pale nose, with its adorable little freckles, wrinkling; he roared with all the force of his lungs, his enormous mouth distended, striking sledge- hammer blows upon his knee with his clenched fist.

The lunch was delicious. Trina and her mother made a clam chowder that melt- ed in one's mouth. The lunch baskets were emptied. The party were fully two hours eating. There were huge loaves of rye bread full of grains of chickweed. There were weiner-wurst and frankfurter sausages. There was unsalted butter. There were pretzels. There was cold underdone chicken, which one ate in slices, plastered with a wonderful kind of mustard that did not sting. There were dried apples, that gave Mr. Sieppe the hiccoughs. There were a dozen bottles of beer, and, last of all, a crowning achievement, a marvellous Gotha truffle. After lunch came tobacco. Stuffed to the eyes, McTeague drowsed over his pipe, prone on his back in the sun, while Trina, Mrs. Sieppe, and Selina washed the dishes. In the afternoon Mr. Sieppe disappeared. They heard the reports of his rifle on the range. The others swarmed over the park, now around the swings, now in the Casino, now in the museum, now invading the merry-go-round.

At half-past five o'clock Mr. Sieppe marshalled the party together. It was time to return home.

The family insisted that Marcus and McTeague should take supper with them at their home and should stay over night. Mrs. Sieppe argued they could get no decent supper if they went back to the city at that hour; that they could catch an early morning boat and reach their business in good time. The two friends accepted.

The Sieppes lived in a little box of a house at the foot of B Street, the first house to the right as one went up from the station. It was two stories high, with a funny red mansard roof of oval slates. The interior was cut up into innumerable tiny rooms, some of them so small as to be hardly better than sleeping closets. In the back yard was a contrivance for pumping water from the cistern that interested McTeague at once. It was a dog-wheel, a huge revolving box in which the unhappy black greyhound spent most of his waking hours. It was his kennel; he slept in it. From time to time during the day Mrs. Sieppe appeared on the back doorstep, crying shrilly, "Hoop, hoop!" She threw lumps of coal at him, waking him to his work.

They were all very tired, and went to bed early. After great discussion it was decided that Marcus would sleep upon the lounge in the front parlor. Trina would sleep with August, giving up her room to McTeague. Selina went to her home, a block or so above the Sieppes's. At nine o'clock Mr. Sieppe showed McTeague to his room and left him to himself with a newly lighted candle.

For a long time after Mr. Sieppe had gone McTeague stood motionless in the middle of the room, his elbows pressed close to his sides, looking obliquely from the corners of his eyes. He hardly dared to move. He was in Trina's room.

It was an ordinary little room. A clean white matting was on the floor; gray paper, spotted with pink and green flowers, covered the walls. In one corner, under a white netting, was a little bed, the woodwork gayly painted with knots of bright flowers. Near it, against the wall, was a black walnut bureau. A work-table with spiral legs stood by the window, which was hung with a green and gold window curtain. Opposite the window the closet door stood ajar, while in the corner across from the bed was a tiny washstand with two clean towels.

And that was all. But it was Trina's room. McTeague was in his lady's bower; it seemed to him a little nest, intimate, discreet. He felt hideously out of place. He was an intruder; he, with his enormous feet, his colossal bones, his crude, brutal gestures. The mere weight of his limbs, he was sure, would crush the little bed-stead like an eggshell.

Then, as this first sensation wore off, he began to feel the charm of the little chamber. It was as though Trina were close by, but invisible. McTeague felt all the delight of her presence without the embarrassment that usually accompanied it. He was near to her—nearer than he had ever been before. He saw into her daily life, her little ways and manners, her habits, her very thoughts. And was there not in the air of that room a certain faint perfume that he knew, that recalled her to his mind with marvellous vividness?

As he put the candle down upon the bureau he saw her hair-brush lying there. Instantly he picked it up, and, without knowing why, held it to his face. With what a delicious odor was it redolent! That heavy, enervating odor of her hair—her wonderful, royal hair! The smell of that little hairbrush was talismanic. He had but to close his eyes to see her as distinctly as in a mirror. He saw her tiny, round figure, dressed all in black—for, curiously enough, it was his very first impression of Trina that came back to him now—not the Trina of the later occasions, not the Trina of the blue cloth skirt and white sailor. He saw her as he had seen her the day that Marcus had introduced them: saw her pale, round face; her narrow, half-open eyes, blue like the eyes of a baby; her tiny, pale ears, suggestive of anaemia; the freckles across the bridge of her nose; her pale lips; the tiara of royal black hair; and, above all, the delicious poise of the head, tipped back as though by the weight of all that hair—the poise that thrust out her chin a little, with the movement that was so confiding, so innocent, so nearly infantile.

McTeague went softly about the room from one object to another, beholding Trina in everything he touched or looked at. He came at last to the closet door. It was ajar. He opened it wide, and paused upon the threshold.

Trina's clothes were hanging there—skirts and waists, jackets, and stiff white petticoats. What a vision! For an instant McTeague caught his breath, spellbound. If he had suddenly discovered Trina herself there, smiling at him, holding out her hands, he could hardly have been more overcome. Instantly he recognized the black dress she had worn on that famous first day. There it was, the little jacket she had carried over her arm the day he had terrified her with his blundering declaration, and still others, and others—a whole group of Trinas faced him there. He went farther into the closet, touching the clothes gingerly, stroking them softly with his huge leathern palms. As he stirred them a delicate perfume disengaged itself from the folds. Ah, that exquisite feminine odor! It was not only her hair now, it was Trina herself—her mouth, her hands, her neck; the indescribably sweet, fleshly aroma that was a part of her, pure and clean, and redolent of youth and freshness. All at once, seized with an unreasoned impulse, McTeague opened his huge arms and gathered the little garments close to him, plunging his face deep amongst them, savoring their delicious odor with long breaths of luxury and supreme content.

***

The picnic at Schuetzen Park decided matters. McTeague began to call on Trina regularly Sunday and Wednesday afternoons. He took Marcus Schouler's place. Sometimes Marcus accompanied him, but it was generally to meet Selina by appointment at the Sieppes's house.

But Marcus made the most of his renunciation of his cousin. He remembered his pose from time to time. He made McTeague unhappy and bewildered by wringing his hand, by venting sighs that seemed to tear his heart out, or by giving evidences of an infinite melancholy. "What is my life!" he would exclaim. "What is left for me? Nothing, by damn!" And when McTeague would attempt remonstrance, he would cry: "Never mind, old man. Never mind me. Go, be happy. I forgive you."

Forgive what? McTeague was all at sea, was harassed with the thought of some shadowy, irreparable injury he had done his friend.

"Oh, don't think of me!" Marcus would exclaim at other times, even when Trina was by. "Don't think of me; I don't count any more. I ain't in it." Marcus seemed to take great pleasure in contemplating the wreck of his life. There is no doubt he enjoyed himself hugely during these days.

The Sieppes were at first puzzled as well over this change of front.

"Trina has den a new younge man," cried Mr. Sieppe. "First Schouler, now der doktor, eh? What die tevil, I say!"

Weeks passed, February went, March came in very rainy, putting a stop to all their picnics and Sunday excursions.

One Wednesday afternoon in the second week in March McTeague came over to call on Trina, bringing his concertina with him, as was his custom nowadays. As he got off the train at the station he was surprised to find Trina waiting for him.

"This is the first day it hasn't rained in weeks," she explained, "an' I thought it would be nice to walk."

"Sure, sure," assented McTeague.

B Street station was nothing more than a little shed. There was no ticket office, nothing but a couple of whittled and carven benches. It was built close to the railroad tracks, just across which was the dirty, muddy shore of San Francisco Bay. About a quarter of a mile back from the station was the edge of the town of Oakland. Between the station and the first houses of the town lay immense salt flats, here and there broken by winding streams of black water. They were covered with a growth of wiry grass, strangely discolored in places by enormous stains of orange yellow.

Near the station a bit of fence painted with a cigar advertisement reeled over into the mud, while under its lee lay an abandoned gravel wagon with dished wheels. The station was connected with the town by the extension of B Street, which struck across the flats geometrically straight, a file of tall poles with intervening wires marching along with it. At the station these were headed by an iron electric-light pole that, with its supports and outriggers, looked for all the world like an immense grasshopper on its hind legs.

Across the flats, at the fringe of the town, were the dump heaps, the figures of a few Chinese rag-pickers moving over them. Far to the left the view was shut off by the immense red-brown drum of the gas-works; to the right it was bounded by the chimneys and workshops of an iron foundry.

Across the railroad tracks, to seaward, one saw the long stretch of black mud bank left bare by the tide, which was far out, nearly half a mile. Clouds of sea-gulls were forever rising and settling upon this mud bank; a wrecked and abandoned wharf crawled over it on tottering legs; close in an old sailboat lay canted on her bilge.

But farther on, across the yellow waters of the bay, beyond Goat Island, lay San Francisco, a blue line of hills, rugged with roofs and spires. Far to the westward opened the Golden Gate, a bleak cutting in the sand-hills, through which one caught a glimpse of the open Pacific.

The station at B Street was solitary; no trains passed at this hour; except the distant rag-pickers, not a soul was in sight. The wind blew strong, carrying with it the mingled smell of salt, of tar, of dead seaweed, and of bilge. The sky hung low and brown; at long intervals a few drops of rain fell.

Near the station Trina and McTeague sat on the roadbed of the tracks, at the edge of the mud bank, making the most out of the landscape, enjoying the open air, the salt marshes, and the sight of the distant water. From time to time McTeague played his six mournful airs upon his concertina.

After a while they began walking up and down the tracks, McTeague talking about his profession, Trina listening, very interested and absorbed, trying to understand.

"For pulling the roots of the upper molars we use the cow- horn forceps," continued the dentist, monotonously. "We get the inside beak over the palatal roots and the cow-horn beak over the buccal roots—that's the roots on the outside, you see. Then we close the forceps, and that breaks right through the alveolus—that's the part of the socket in the jaw, you understand."

At another moment he told her of his one unsatisfied desire. "Some day I'm going to have a big gilded tooth outside my window for a sign. Those big gold teeth are beautiful, beautiful—only they cost so much, I can't afford one just now."

"Oh, it's raining," suddenly exclaimed Trina, holding out her palm. They turned back and reached the station in a drizzle. The afternoon was closing in dark and rainy. The tide was coming back, talking and lapping for miles along the mud bank. Far off across the flats, at the edge of the town, an electric car went by, stringing out a long row of diamond sparks on the overhead wires.

"Say, Miss Trina," said McTeague, after a while, "what's the good of waiting any longer? Why can't us two get married?"

Trina still shook her head, saying "No" instinctively, in spite of herself.

"Why not?" persisted McTeague. "Don't you like me well enough?"

"Yes."

"Then why not?"

"Because."

"Ah, come on," he said, but Trina still shook her head.

"Ah, come on," urged McTeague. He could think of nothing else to say, repeating the same phrase over and over again to all her refusals.

"Ah, come on! Ah, come on!"

Suddenly he took her in his enormous arms, crushing down her struggle with his immense strength. Then Trina gave up, all in an instant, turning her head to his. They kissed each other, grossly, full in the mouth.

A roar and a jarring of the earth suddenly grew near and passed them in a reek of steam and hot air. It was the Overland, with its flaming headlight, on its way across the continent.

The passage of the train startled them both. Trina struggled to free herself from McTeague. "Oh, please! please!" she pleaded, on the point of tears. McTeague released her, but in that moment a slight, a barely perceptible, revulsion of feeling had taken place in him. The instant that Trina gave up, the instant she allowed him to kiss her, he thought less of her. She was not so desirable, after all. But this reaction was so faint, so subtle, so intangible, that in another moment he had doubted its occurrence. Yet afterward it returned. Was there not something gone from Trina now? Was he not disappointed in her for doing that very thing for which he had longed? Was Trina the submissive, the compliant, the attainable just the same, just as delicate and adorable as Trina the inaccessible? Perhaps he dimly saw that this must be so, that it belonged to the changeless order of things—the man desiring the woman only for what she withholds; the woman worshipping the man for that which she yields up to him. With each concession gained the man's desire cools; with every surrender made the woman's adoration increases. But why should it be so?

Trina wrenched herself free and drew back from McTeague, her little chin quivering; her face, even to the lobes of her pale ears, flushed scarlet; her narrow blue eyes brimming. Suddenly she put her head between her hands and began to sob.

"Say, say, Miss Trina, listen—listen here, Miss Trina," cried McTeague, coming forward a step.

"Oh, don't!" she gasped, shrinking. "I must go home," she cried, springing to her feet. "It's late. I must. I must. Don't come with me, please. Oh, I'm so—so,"—she could not find any words. "Let me go alone," she went on. "You may—you come Sunday. Good-by."

"Good-by," said McTeague, his head in a whirl at this sudden, unaccountable change. "Can't I kiss you again?" But Trina was firm now. When it came to his pleading—a mere matter of words—she was strong enough.

"No, no, you must not!" she exclaimed, with energy. She was gone in another instant. The dentist, stunned, bewildered, gazed stupidly after her as she ran up the extension of B Street through the rain.

But suddenly a great joy took possession of him. He had won her. Trina was to be for him, after all. An enormous smile distended his thick lips; his eyes grew wide, and flashed; and he drew his breath quickly, striking his mallet-like fist upon his knee, and exclaiming under his breath:

"I got her, by God! I got her, by God!" At the same time he thought better of himself; his self-respect increased enormously. The man that could win Trina Sieppe was a man of extraordinary ability.

Trina burst in upon her mother while the latter was setting a mousetrap in the kitchen.

"Oh, mamma!"

"Eh? Trina? Ach, what has happun?"

Trina told her in a breath.

"Soh soon?" was Mrs. Sieppe's first comment. "Eh, well, what you cry for, then?"

"I don't know," wailed Trina, plucking at the end of her handkerchief.

"You loaf der younge doktor?"

"I don't know."

"Well, what for you kiss him?"

"I don't know."

"You don' know, you don' know? Where haf your sensus gone, Trina? You kiss der doktor. You cry, and you don' know. Is ut Marcus den?"

"No, it's not Cousin Mark."

"Den ut must be der doktor."

Trina made no answer.

"Eh?"

"I—I guess so."

"You loaf him?"

"I don't know."

Mrs. Sieppe set down the mousetrap with such violence that it sprung with a sharp snap.

CHAPTER 6

No, Trina did not know. "Do I love him? Do I love him?" A thousand times she put the question to herself during the next two or three days. At night she hardly slept, but lay broad awake for hours in her little, gayly painted bed, with its white netting, torturing herself with doubts and questions. At times she remembered the scene in the station with a veritable agony of shame, and at other times she was ashamed to recall it with a thrill of joy. Nothing could have been more sudden, more unexpected, than that surrender of herself. For over a year she had thought that Marcus would some day be her husband. They would be married, she supposed, some time in the future, she did not know exactly when; the matter did not take definite shape in her mind. She liked Cousin Mark very well. And then suddenly this cross-current had set in; this blond giant had appeared, this huge, stolid fellow, with his immense, crude strength. She had not loved him at first, that was certain. The day he had spoken to her in his "Parlors" she had only been terrified. If he had confined himself to merely speaking, as did Marcus, to pleading with her, to wooing her at a distance, forestalling her wishes, showing her little attentions, sending her boxes of candy, she could have easily withstood him. But he had only to take her in his arms, to crush down her struggle with his enormous strength, to subdue her, conquer her by sheer brute force, and she gave up in an instant.

But why—why had she done so? Why did she feel the desire, the necessity of being conquered by a superior strength? Why did it please her? Why had it suddenly thrilled her from head to foot with a quick, terrifying gust of passion, the like of which she had never known? Never at his best had Marcus made her feel like that, and yet she had always thought she cared for Cousin Mark more than for any one else.

When McTeague had all at once caught her in his huge arms, something had leaped to life in her—something that had hitherto lain dormant, something strong and overpowering. It frightened her now as she thought of it, this second self that had wakened within her, and that shouted and clamored for recognition. And yet, was it to be feared? Was it something to be ashamed of? Was it not, after all, natural, clean, spontaneous? Trina knew that she was a pure girl; knew that this sudden commotion within her carried with it no suggestion of vice.

Dimly, as figures seen in a waking dream, these ideas floated through Trina's mind. It was quite beyond her to realize them clearly; she could not know what they meant. Until that rainy day by the shore of the bay Trina had lived her life with as little self-consciousness as a tree. She was frank, straightforward, a healthy, natural human being, without sex as yet. She was almost like a boy. At once there had been a mysterious disturbance. The woman within her suddenly awoke.

Did she love McTeague? Difficult question. Did she choose him for better or for worse, deliberately, of her own free will, or was Trina herself allowed even a choice in the taking of that step that was to make or mar her life? The Woman is awakened, and, starting from her sleep, catches blindly at what first her newly opened eyes light upon. It is a spell, a witchery, ruled by chance alone, inexplicable—a fairy queen enamored of a clown with ass's ears.

McTeague had awakened the Woman, and, whether she would or no, she was his now irrevocably; struggle against it as she would, she belonged to him, body and soul, for life or for death. She had not sought it, she had not desired it. The spell was laid upon her. Was it a blessing? Was it a curse? It was all one; she was his, indissolubly, for evil or for good.

And he? The very act of submission that bound the woman to him forever had made her seem less desirable in his eyes. Their undoing had already begun. Yet neither of them was to blame. From the first they had not sought each other. Chance had brought them face to face, and mysterious instincts as ungovernable as the winds of heaven were at work knitting their lives together. Neither of them had asked that this thing should be—that their destinies, their very souls, should be the sport of chance. If they could have known, they would have shunned the fearful risk. But they were allowed no voice in the matter. Why should it all be?

It had been on a Wednesday that the scene in the B Street station had taken place. Throughout the rest of the week, at every hour of the day, Trina asked herself the same question: "Do I love him? Do I really love him? Is this what love is like?" As she recalled McTeague—recalled his huge, square-cut head, his salient jaw, his shock of yellow hair, his heavy, lumbering body, his slow wits—she found little to admire in him beyond his physical strength, and at such moments she shook her head decisively. "No, surely she did not love him." Sunday afternoon, however, McTeague called. Trina had prepared a little speech for him. She was to tell him that she did not know what had been the matter with her that Wednesday afternoon; that she had acted like a bad girl; that she did not love him well enough to marry him; that she had told him as much once before.

McTeague saw her alone in the little front parlor. The instant she appeared he came straight towards her. She saw what he was bent upon doing. "Wait a minute," she cried, putting out her hands. "Wait. You don't understand. I have got something to say to you." She might as well have talked to the wind. McTeague put aside her hands with a single gesture, and gripped her to him in a bearlike embrace that all but smothered her. Trina was but a reed before that giant strength. McTeague turned her face to his and kissed her again upon the mouth. Where was all Trina's resolve then? Where was her carefully prepared little speech? Where was all her hesitation and torturing doubts of the last few days? She clasped McTeague's huge red neck with both her slender arms; she raised her adorable little chin and kissed him in return, exclaiming: "Oh, I do love you! I do love you!" Never afterward were the two so happy as at that moment.

A little later in that same week, when Marcus and McTeague were taking lunch at the car conductors' coffee-joint, the former suddenly exclaimed:

"Say, Mac, now that you've got Trina, you ought to do more for her. By damn! you ought to, for a fact. Why don't you take her out somewhere—to the theatre, or somewhere? You ain't on to your job."

Naturally, McTeague had told Marcus of his success with Trina. Marcus had taken on a grand air.

"You've got her, have you? Well, I'm glad of it, old man. I am, for a fact. I know you'll be happy with her. I know how I would have been. I forgive you; yes, I forgive you, freely."

McTeague had not thought of taking Trina to the theatre.

"You think I ought to, Mark?" he inquired, hesitating. Marcus answered, with his mouth full of suet pudding:

"Why, of course. That's the proper caper."

"Well—well, that's so. The theatre—that's the word."

"Take her to the variety show at the Orpheum. There's a good show there this week; you'll have to take Mrs. Sieppe, too, of course," he added. Marcus was not sure of himself as regarded certain proprieties, nor, for that matter, were any of the people of the little world of Polk Street. The shop girls, the plumbers' apprentices, the small tradespeople, and their like, whose social position was not clearly defined, could never be sure how far they could go and yet preserve their "respectability." When they wished to be "proper," they invariably overdid the thing. It was not as if they belonged to the "tough" element, who had no appearances to keep up. Polk Street rubbed elbows with the "avenue" one block above. There were certain limits which its dwellers could not overstep; but unfortunately for them, these limits were poorly defined. They could never be sure of themselves. At an unguarded moment they might be taken for "toughs," so they generally erred in the other direction, and were absurdly formal. No people have a keener eye for the amenities than those whose social position is not assured.

"Oh, sure, you'll have to take her mother," insisted Marcus. "It wouldn't be the proper racket if you didn't."

McTeague undertook the affair. It was an ordeal. Never in his life had he been so perturbed, so horribly anxious. He called upon Trina the following Wednesday and made arrangements. Mrs. Sieppe asked if little August might be included. It would console him for the loss of his steamboat.

"Sure, sure," said McTeague. "August too—everybody," he added, vaguely.

"We always have to leave so early," complained Trina, "in order to catch the last boat. Just when it's becoming interesting."

At this McTeague, acting upon a suggestion of Marcus Schouler's, insisted they should stay at the flat over night. Marcus and the dentist would give up their rooms to them and sleep at the dog hospital. There was a bed there in the sick ward that old Grannis sometimes occupied when a bad case needed watching. All at once McTeague had an idea, a veritable inspiration.

"And we'll—we'll—we'll have—what's the matter with having something to eat afterward in my "Parlors?"

"Vairy goot," commented Mrs. Sieppe. "Bier, eh? And some damales."

"Oh, I love tamales!" exclaimed Trina, clasping her hands.

McTeague returned to the city, rehearsing his instructions over and over. The theatre party began to assume tremendous proportions. First of all, he was to get the seats, the third or fourth row from the front, on the left-hand side, so as to be out of the hearing of the drums in the orchestra; he must make arrangements about the rooms with Marcus, must get in the beer, but not the tamales; must buy for himself a white lawn tie—so Marcus directed; must look to it that Maria Maca-pa put his room in perfect order; and, finally, must meet the Sieppes at the ferry slip at half- past seven the following Monday night.

The real labor of the affair began with the buying of the tickets. At the theatre McTeague got into wrong entrances; was sent from one wicket to another; was bewildered, confused; misunderstood directions; was at one moment suddenly convinced that he had not enough money with him, and started to return home. Finally he found himself at the box-office wicket.

"Is it here you buy your seats?"

"How many?"

"Is it here—" "What night do you want 'em? Yes, sir, here's the place."

McTeague gravely delivered himself of the formula he had been reciting for the last dozen hours.

"I want four seats for Monday night in the fourth row from the front, and on the right-hand side."

"Right hand as you face the house or as you face the stage?" McTeague was dumfounded.

"I want to be on the right-hand side," he insisted, stolidly; adding, "in order to be away from the drums."

"Well, the drums are on the right of the orchestra as you face the stage," shout-ed the other impatiently; "you want to the left, then, as you face the house."

"I want to be on the right-hand side," persisted the dentist.

Without a word the seller threw out four tickets with a magnificent, supercil-ious gesture.

"There's four seats on the right-hand side, then, and you're right up against the drums."

"But I don't want to be near the drums," protested McTeague, beginning to perspire.

"Do you know what you want at all?" said the ticket seller with calmness, thrusting his head at McTeague. The dentist knew that he had hurt this young man's feelings.

"I want—I want," he stammered. The seller slammed down a plan of the house in front of him and began to explain excitedly. It was the one thing lacking to complete McTeague's confusion.

"There are your seats," finished the seller, shoving the tickets into McTeague's hands. "They are the fourth row from the front, and away from the drums. Now are you satisfied?"

"Are they on the right-hand side? I want on the right—no, I want on the left. I want—I don' know, I don' know."

The seller roared. McTeague moved slowly away, gazing stupidly at the blue slips of pasteboard. Two girls took his place at the wicket. In another moment McTeague came back, peering over the girls' shoulders and calling to the seller:

"Are these for Monday night?"

The other disdained reply. McTeague retreated again timidly, thrusting the tickets into his immense wallet. For a moment he stood thoughtful on the steps of the entrance. Then all at once he became enraged, he did not know exactly why; somehow he felt himself slighted. Once more he came back to the wicket.

"You can't make small of me," he shouted over the girls' shoulders; "you—you can't make small of me. I'll thump you in the head, you little—you little—you little—little—little pup." The ticket seller shrugged his shoulders wearily. "A dollar and a half," he said to the two girls.

McTeague glared at him and breathed loudly. Finally he decided to let the matter drop. He moved away, but on the steps was once more seized with a sense of injury and outraged dignity.

"You can't make small of me," he called back a last time, wagging his head and shaking his fist. "I will—I will—I will—yes, I will." He went off muttering.

At last Monday night came. McTeague met the Sieppes at the ferry, dressed in a black Prince Albert coat and his best slate-blue trousers, and wearing the made-up lawn necktie that Marcus had selected for him. Trina was very pretty in the black dress that McTeague knew so well. She wore a pair of new gloves. Mrs. Sieppe had on lisle-thread mits, and carried two bananas and an orange in a net reticule. "For Owgooste," she confided to him. Owgooste was in a Fauntleroy "costume" very much too small for him. Already he had been crying.

"Woult you pelief, Doktor, dot bube has torn his stockun alreatty? Walk in der front, you; stop cryun. Where is dot berliceman?"

At the door of the theatre McTeague was suddenly seized with a panic terror. He had lost the tickets. He tore through his pockets, ransacked his wallet. They were nowhere to be found. All at once he remembered, and with a gasp of relief removed his hat and took them out from beneath the sweatband.

The party entered and took their places. It was absurdly early. The lights were all darkened, the ushers stood under the galleries in groups, the empty auditorium echoing with their noisy talk. Occasionally a waiter with his tray and clean white apron sauntered up and doun the aisle. Directly in front of them was the great iron curtain of the stage, painted with all manner of advertisements. From behind this came a noise of hammering and of occasional loud voices.

While waiting they studied their programmes. First was an overture by the orchestra, after which came "The Gleasons, in their mirth-moving musical farce, entitled 'McMonnigal's Court-ship.'" This was to be followed by "The Lamont Sisters, Winnie and Violet, serio-comiques and skirt dancers." And after this came a great array of other "artists" and "specialty performers," musical wonders, acrobats, lightning artists, ventriloquists, and last of all, "The feature of the evening, the crowning scientific achievement of the nineteenth century, the kinetoscope." McTeague was excited, dazzled. In five years he had not been twice to the theatre. Now he beheld himself inviting his "girl" and her mother to accompany him. He began to feel that he was a man of the world. He ordered a cigar.

Meanwhile the house was filling up. A few side brackets were turned on. The ushers ran up and down the aisles, stubs of tickets between their thumb and finger, and from every part of the auditorium could be heard the sharp clap- clapping of the seats as the ushers flipped them down. A buzz of talk arose. In the gallery a street gamin whistled shrilly, and called to some friends on the other side of the house.

"Are they go-wun to begin pretty soon, ma?" whined Owgooste for the fifth or sixth time; adding, "Say, ma, can't I have some candy?" A cadaverous little boy had appeared in their aisle, chanting, "Candies, French mixed candies, popcorn, peanuts and candy." The orchestra entered, each man crawling out from an opening under the stage, hardly larger than the gate of a rabbit hutch. At every instant now the crowd increased; there were but few seats that were not taken. The waiters hurried up and down the aisles, their trays laden with beer glasses. A smell of cigar-smoke filled the air, and soon a faint blue haze rose from all corners of the house.

"Ma, when are they go-wun to begin?" cried Owgooste. As he spoke the iron advertisement curtain rose, disclosing the curtain proper underneath. This latter curtain was quite an affair. Upon it was painted a wonderful picture. A flight of marble steps led down to a stream of water; two white swans, their necks arched like the capital letter S, floated about. At the head of the marble steps were two vases filled with red and yellow flowers, while at the foot was moored a gondola. This gondola was full of red velvet rugs that hung over the side and trailed in the water. In the prow of the gondola a young man in vermilion tights held a mandolin in his left hand, and gave his right to a girl in white satin. A King Charles spaniel, dragging a leading- string in the shape of a huge pink sash, followed the girl. Seven scarlet roses were scattered upon the two lowest steps, and eight floated in the water.

"Ain't that pretty, Mac?" exclaimed Trina, turning to the dentist.

"Ma, ain't they go-wun to begin now-wow?" whined Owgooste. Suddenly the lights all over the house blazed up. "Ah!" said everybody all at once.

"Ain't ut crowdut?" murmured Mr. Sieppe. Every seat was taken; many were even standing up.

"I always like it better when there is a crowd," said Trina. She was in great spirits that evening. Her round, pale face was positively pink.

The orchestra banged away at the overture, suddenly finishing with a great flourish of violins. A short pause followed. Then the orchestra played a quick-step strain, and the curtain rose on an interior furnished with two red chairs and a green sofa. A girl in a short blue dress and black stockings entered in a hurry and began to dust the two chairs. She was in a great temper, talking very fast, disclaiming against the "new lodger." It appeared that this latter never paid his rent; that he was given to late hours. Then she came down to the footlights and began to sing in a tremendous voice, hoarse and flat, almost like a man's. The chorus, of a feeble originality, ran:

"Oh, how happy I will be,
When my darling's face I'll see;
Oh, tell him for to meet me in the moonlight,
Down where the golden lilies bloom."

The orchestra played the tune of this chorus a second time, with certain variations, while the girl danced to it. She sidled to one side of the stage and kicked, then sidled to the other and kicked again. As she finished with the song, a man, evidently the lodger in question, came in. Instantly McTeague exploded in a roar of laughter. The man was intoxicated, his hat was knocked in, one end of his collar was unfastened and stuck up into his face, his watch-chain dangled from his pocket, and a yellow satin slipper was tied to a button-hole of his vest; his nose was vermilion, one eye was black and blue. After a short dialogue with the girl, a third actor appeared. He was dressed like a little boy, the girl's younger brother. He wore an immense turned-down collar, and was continually doing handsprings and wonderful back somersaults. The "act" devolved upon these three people; the lodger making love to the girl in the short blue dress, the boy playing all manner of tricks upon him, giving him tremendous digs in the ribs or slaps upon the back that made him cough, pulling chairs from under him, running on all fours between his legs and upsetting him, knocking him over at inopportune moments. Every one of his falls was accentuated by a bang upon the bass drum. The whole humor of the "act" seemed to consist in the tripping up of the intoxicated lodger.

This horse-play delighted McTeague beyond measure. He roared and shouted every time the lodger went down, slapping his knee, wagging his head. Owgooste crowed shrilly, clapping his hands and continually asking, "What did he say, ma? What did he say?" Mrs. Sieppe laughed immoderately, her huge fat body shaking like a mountain of jelly. She exclaimed from time to time, "Ach, Gott, dot fool!" Even Trina was moved, laughing demurely, her lips closed, putting one hand with its new glove to her mouth.

The performance went on. Now it was the "musical marvels," two men extravagantly made up as negro minstrels, with immense shoes and plaid vests. They seemed to be able to wrestle a tune out of almost anything—glass bottles, cigar-box fiddles, strings of sleigh-bells, even graduated brass tubes, which they rubbed with resined fingers. McTeague was stupefied with admiration.

"That's what you call musicians," he announced gravely. "Home, Sweet Home," played upon a trombone. Think of that! Art could go no farther.

The acrobats left him breathless. They were dazzling young men with beautifully parted hair, continually making graceful gestures to the audience. In one of them the dentist fancied he saw a strong resemblance to the boy who had tormented the intoxicated lodger and who had turned such marvellous somersaults. Trina could not bear to watch their antics. She turned away her head with a little shudder. "It always makes me sick," she explained.

The beautiful young lady, "The Society Contralto," in evening dress, who sang the sentimental songs, and carried the sheets of music at which she never looked, pleased McTeague less. Trina, however, was captivated. She grew pensive over

"You do not love me—no;
Bid me good-by and go;"

and split her new gloves in her enthusiasm when it was finished.

"Don't you love sad music, Mac?" she murmured.

Then came the two comedians. They talked with fearful rapidity; their wit and repartee seemed inexhaustible.

"As I was going down the street yesterday—"

"Ah! as YOU were going down the street—all right."

"I saw a girl at a window—"

"YOU saw a girl at a window."

"And this girl she was a corker—"

"Ah! as YOU were going down the street yesterday *you* saw a girl at a window, and this girl she was a corker. All right, go on."

The other comedian went on. The joke was suddenly evolved. A certain phrase led to a song, which was sung with lightning rapidity, each performer making precisely the same gestures at precisely the same instant. They were irresistible. McTeague, though he caught but a third of the jokes, could have listened all night.

After the comedians had gone out, the iron advertisement curtain was let down.

"What comes now?" said McTeague, bewildered.

"It's the intermission of fifteen minutes now."

The musicians disappeared through the rabbit hutch, and the audience stirred and stretched itself. Most of the young men left their seats.

During this intermission McTeague and his party had "refreshments." Mrs. Sieppe and Trina had Queen Charlottes, McTeague drank a glass of beer, Owgooste ate the orange and one of the bananas. He begged for a glass of lemonade, which was finally given him.

"Joost to geep um quiet," observed Mrs. Sieppe.

But almost immediately after drinking his lemonade Owgooste was seized with a sudden restlessness. He twisted and wriggled in his seat, swinging his legs violently, looking about him with eyes full of a vague distress. At length, just as the musicians were returning, he stood up and whispered energetically in his mother's ear. Mrs. Sieppe was exasperated at once. "No, no," she cried, reseating him brusquely.

The performance was resumed. A lightning artist appeared, drawing caricatures and portraits with incredible swiftness. He even went so far as to ask for subjects from the audience, and the names of prominent men were shouted to him from the gallery. He drew portraits of the President, of Grant, of Washington, of Napoleon Bonaparte, of Bismarck, of Garibaldi, of P. T. Barnum.

And so the evening passed. The hall grew very hot, and the smoke of innumerable cigars made the eyes smart. A thick blue mist hung low over the heads of the audience. The air was full of varied smells—the smell of stale cigars, of flat beer, of orange peel, of gas, of sachet powders, and of cheap perfumery.

One "artist" after another came upon the stage. McTeague's attention never wandered for a minute. Trina and her mother enjoyed themselves hugely. At every moment they made comments to one another, their eyes never leaving the stage.

"Ain't dot fool joost too funny?"

"That's a pretty song. Don't you like that kind of a song?"

"Wonderful! It's wonderful! Yes, yes, wonderful! That's the word."

Owgooste, however, lost interest. He stood up in his place, his back to the stage, chewing a piece of orange peel and watching a little girl in her father's lap across the aisle, his eyes fixed in a glassy, ox-like stare. But he was uneasy. He danced from one foot to the other, and at intervals appealed in hoarse whispers to his mother, who disdained an answer.

"Ma, say, ma-ah," he whined, abstractedly chewing his orange peel, staring at the little girl.

"Ma-ah, say, ma." At times his monotonous plaint reached his mother's consciousness. She suddenly realized what this was that was annoying her.

"Owgooste, will you sit down?" She caught him up all at once, and jammed him down into his place.

"Be quiet, den; loog; listun at der yunge girls."

Three young women and a young man who played a zither occupied the stage. They were dressed in Tyrolese costume; they were yodlers, and sang in German about "mountain tops" and "bold hunters" and the like. The yodling chorus was a marvel of flute-like modulations. The girls were really pretty, and were not made up in the least. Their "turn" had a great success. Mrs. Sieppe was entranced. Instantly she remembered her girlhood and her native Swiss village.

"Ach, dot is heavunly; joost like der old country. Mein gran'mutter used to be one of der mos' famous yodlers. When I was leedle, I haf seen dem joost like dat."

"Ma-ah," began Owgooste fretfully, as soon as the yodlers had departed. He could not keep still an instant; he twisted from side to side, swinging his legs with incredible swiftness.

"Ma-ah, I want to go ho-ome."

"Pehave!" exclaimed his mother, shaking him by the arm; "loog, der leedle girl is watchun you. Dis is der last dime I take you to der blay, you see."

"I don't ca-are; I'm sleepy." At length, to their great relief, he went to sleep, his head against his mother's arm.

The kinetoscope fairly took their breaths away.

"What will they do next?" observed Trina, in amazement. "Ain't that wonderful, Mac?"

McTeague was awe-struck. "Look at that horse move his head," he cried excitedly, quite carried away. "Look at that cable car coming—and the man going across the street. See, here comes a truck. Well, I never in all my life! What would Marcus say to this?"

"It's all a drick!" exclaimed Mrs. Sieppe, with sudden conviction. "I ain't no fool; dot's nothun but a drick."

"Well, of course, mamma," exclaimed Trina, "it's—"

But Mrs. Sieppe put her head in the air.

"I'm too old to be fooled," she persisted. "It's a drick." Nothing more could be got out of her than this.

The party stayed to the very end of the show, though the kinetoscope was the last number but one on the programme, and fully half the audience left immediately afterward. However, while the unfortunate Irish comedian went through his "act" to the backs of the departing people, Mrs. Sieppe woke Owgooste, very cross and sleepy, and began getting her "things together." As soon as he was awake Owgooste began fidgeting again.

"Save der brogramme, Trina," whispered Mrs. Sieppe. "Take ut home to popper. Where is der hat of Owgooste? Haf you got mein handkerchief, Trina?"

But at this moment a dreadful accident happened to Owgooste; his distress reached its climax; his fortitude collapsed. What a misery! It was a veritable catastrophe, deplorable, lamentable, a thing beyond words! For a moment he gazed wildly about him, helpless and petrified with astonishment and terror. Then his grief found utterance, and the closing strains of the orchestra were mingled with a prolonged wail of infinite sadness. "Owgooste, what is ut?" cried his mother eyeing him with dawning suspicion; then suddenly, "What haf you done? You haf ruin your new Vauntleroy gostume!" Her face blazed; without more ado she smacked him soundly. Then it was that Owgooste touched the limit of his misery, his unhappiness, his horrible discomfort; his utter wretchedness was complete. He filled the air with his doleful outcries. The more he was smacked and shaken, the louder he wept. "What—what is the matter?" inquired McTeague. Trina's face was scarlet. "Nothing, nothing," she exclaimed hastily, looking away. "Come, we must be going. It's about over." The end of the show and the breaking up of the audience tided over the embarrassment of the moment.

The party filed out at the tail end of the audience. Already the lights were being extinguished and the ushers spreading druggeting over the upholstered seats.

McTeague and the Sieppes took an uptown car that would bring them near Polk Street. The car was crowded; McTeague and Owgooste were obliged to stand. The little boy fretted to be taken in his mother's lap, but Mrs. Sieppe emphatically refused.

On their way home they discussed the performance.

"I—I like best der yodlers."

"Ah, the soloist was the best—the lady who sang those sad songs."

"Wasn't—wasn't that magic lantern wonderful, where the figures moved? Wonderful—ah, wonderful! And wasn't that first act funny, where the fellow fell down all the time? And that musical act, and the fellow with the burnt-cork face who played 'Nearer, My God, to Thee' on the beer bottles."

They got off at Polk Street and walked up a block to the flat. The street was dark and empty; opposite the flat, in the back of the deserted market, the ducks and geese were calling persistently.

As they were buying their tamales from the half-breed Mexican at the street corner, McTeague observed:

"Marcus ain't gone to bed yet. See, there's a light in his window. There!" he exclaimed at once, "I forgot the doorkey. Well, Marcus can let us in."

Hardly had he rung the bell at the street door of the flat when the bolt was shot back. In the hall at the top of the long, narrow staircase there was the sound of a great scurrying. Maria Macapa stood there, her hand upon the rope that drew the bolt; Marcus was at her side; Old Grannis was in the background, looking over their shoulders; while little Miss Baker leant over the banisters, a strange man in a drab overcoat at her side. As McTeague's party stepped into the doorway a half-dozen voices cried:

"Yes, it's them."

"Is that you, Mac?"

"Is that you, Miss Sieppe?"

"Is your name Trina Sieppe?"

Then, shriller than all the rest, Maria Macapa screamed:

"Oh, Miss Sieppe, come up here quick. Your lottery ticket has won five thousand dollars!"

CHAPTER 7

"What nonsense!" answered Trina.

"Ach Gott! What is ut?" cried Mrs. Sieppe, misunderstanding, supposing a calamity.

"What—what—what," stammered the dentist, confused by the lights, the crowded stairway, the medley of voices. The party reached the landing. The others surrounded them. Marcus alone seemed to rise to the occasion.

"Le' me be the first to congratulate you," he cried, catching Trina's hand. Every one was talking at once.

"Miss Sieppe, Miss Sieppe, your ticket has won five thousand dollars," cried Maria. "Don't you remember the lottery ticket I sold you in Doctor McTeague's office?"

"Trina!" almost screamed her mother. "Five tausend thalers! five tausend thalers! If popper were only here!"

"What is it—what is it?" exclaimed McTeague, rolling his eyes.

"What are you going to do with it, Trina?" inquired Marcus.

"You're a rich woman, my dear," said Miss Baker, her little false curls quivering with excitement, "and I'm glad for your sake. Let me kiss you. To think I was in the room when you bought the ticket!"

"Oh, oh!" interrupted Trina, shaking her head, "there is a mistake. There must be. Why—why should I win five thousand dollars? It's nonsense!"

"No mistake, no mistake," screamed Maria. "Your number was 400,012. Here it is in the paper this evening. I remember it well, because I keep an account."

"But I know you're wrong," answered Trina, beginning to tremble in spite of herself. "Why should I win?"

"Eh? Why shouldn't you?" cried her mother.

In fact, why shouldn't she? The idea suddenly occurred to Trina. After all, it was not a question of effort or merit on her part. Why should she suppose a mistake? What if it were true, this wonderful fillip of fortune striking in there like some chance-driven bolt?

"Oh, do you think so?" she gasped.

The stranger in the drab overcoat came forward.

"It's the agent," cried two or three voices, simultaneously.

"I guess you're one of the lucky ones, Miss Sieppe," he said. I suppose you have kept your ticket."

"Yes, yes; four three oughts twelve—I remember."

"That's right," admitted the other. "Present your ticket at the local branch office as soon as possible—the address is printed on the back of the ticket—and you'll receive a check on our bank for five thousand dollars. Your number will have to be verified on our official list, but there's hardly a chance of a mistake. I congratulate you."

All at once a great shrill of gladness surged up in Trina. She was to possess five thousand dollars. She was carried away with the joy of her good fortune, a natural, spontaneous joy—the gaiety of a child with a new and wonderful toy. "

Oh, I've won, I've won, I've won!" she cried, clapping her hands. "Mamma, think of it. I've won five thousand dollars, just by buying a ticket. Mac, what do you say to that? I've got five thousand dollars. August, do you hear what's happened to sister?"

"Kiss your mommer, Trina," suddenly commanded Mrs. Sieppe. "What efer will you do mit all dose money, eh, Trina?"

"Huh!" exclaimed Marcus. "Get married on it for one thing. Thereat they all shouted with laughter. McTeague grinned, and looked about sheepishly. "Talk about luck," muttered Marcus, shaking his head at the dentist; then suddenly he added:

"Well, are we going to stay talking out here in the hall all night? Can't we all come into your 'Parlors,' Mac?"

"Sure, sure," exclaimed McTeague, hastily unlocking his door.

"Efery botty gome," cried Mrs. Sieppe, genially. "Ain't ut so, Doktor?"

"Everybody," repeated the dentist. "There's—there's some beer."

"We'll celebrate, by damn!" exclaimed Marcus. "It ain't every day you win five thousand dollars. It's only Sundays and legal holidays." Again he set the company off into a gale of laughter. Anything was funny at a time like this. In some way every one of them felt elated. The wheel of fortune had come spinning close to them. They were near to this great sum of money. It was as though they too had won.

"Here's right where I sat when I bought that ticket," cried Trina, after they had come into the "Parlors," and Marcus had lit the gas. "Right here in this chair." She sat down in one of the rigid chairs under the steel engraving. "And, Marcus, you sat here—"

"And I was just getting out of the operating chair," interposed Miss Baker.

"Yes, yes. That's so; and you," continued Trina, pointing to Maria, "came up and said, 'Buy a ticket in the lottery; just a dollar.' Oh, I remember it just as plain as though it was yesterday, and I wasn't going to at first—"

"And don't you know I told Maria it was against the law?"

"Yes, I remember, and then I gave her a dollar and put the ticket in my pocketbook. It's in my pocketbook now at home in the top drawer of my bureau—oh, suppose it should be stolen now," she suddenly exclaimed.

"It's worth big money now," asserted Marcus.

"Five thousand dollars. Who would have thought it? It's wonderful." Everybody started and turned. It was McTeague. He stood in the middle of the floor, wagging his huge head. He seemed to have just realized what had happened.

"Yes, sir, five thousand dollars!" exclaimed Marcus, with a sudden unaccountable mirthlessness. "Five thousand dollars! Do you get on to that? Cousin Trina and you will be rich people."

"At six per cent, that's twenty-five dollars a month," hazarded the agent.

"Think of it. Think of it," muttered McTeague. He went aimlessly about the room, his eyes wide, his enormous hands dangling."

A cousin of mine won forty dollars once," observed Miss Baker. "But he spent every cent of it buying more tickets, and never won anything."

Then the reminiscences began. Maria told about the butcher on the next block who had won twenty dollars the last drawing. Mrs. Sieppe knew a gasfitter in Oakland who had won several times; once a hundred dollars. Little Miss Baker announced that she had always believed that lotteries were wrong; but, just the same, five thousand was five thousand.

"It's all right when you win, ain't it, Miss Baker?" observed Marcus, with a certain sarcasm. What was the matter with Marcus? At moments he seemed singularly out of temper.

But the agent was full of stories. He told his experiences, the legends and myths that had grown up around the history of the lottery; he told of the poor newsboy with a dying mother to support who had drawn a prize of fifteen thousand; of the man who was driven to suicide through want, but who held (had he but known it) the number that two days after his death drew the capital prize of thirty thousand dollars; of the little milliner who for ten years had played the lottery without success, and who had one day declared that she would buy but one more ticket and then give up trying, and of how this last ticket had brought her a fortune upon which she could retire; of tickets that had been lost or destroyed, and whose numbers had won fabulous sums at the drawing; of criminals, driven to vice by poverty, and who had reformed after winning competencies; of gamblers who played the lottery as they would play a faro bank, turning in their winnings again as soon as made, buying thousands of tickets all over the country; of superstitions as to terminal and initial numbers, and as to lucky days of purchase; of marvellous coincidences—three capital prizes drawn consecutively by the same town; a ticket bought by a millionaire and given to his boot-black, who won a thousand dollars upon it; the same number winning the same amount an indefinite number of times; and so on to infinity. Invariably it was the needy who won, the destitute and starving woke to wealth and plenty, the virtuous toiler suddenly found his reward in a ticket bought at a hazard; the lottery was a great charity, the friend of the people, a vast beneficent machine that recognized neither rank nor wealth nor station.

The company began to be very gay. Chairs and tables were brought in from the adjoining rooms, and Maria was sent out for more beer and tamales, and also commissioned to buy a bottle of wine and some cake for Miss Baker, who abhorred beer.

The "Dental Parlors" were in great confusion. Empty beer bottles stood on the movable rack where the instruments were kept; plates and napkins were upon the seat of the operating chair and upon the stand of shelves in the corner, side by side with the concertina and the volumes of "Allen's Practical Dentist." The canary woke and chittered crossly, his feathers puffed out; the husks of tamales littered the floor; the stone pug dog sitting before the little stove stared at the unusual scene, his glass eyes starting from their sockets.

They drank and feasted in impromptu fashion. Marcus Schouler assumed the office of master of ceremonies; he was in a lather of excitement, rushing about here and there, opening beer bottles, serving the tamales, slapping McTeague upon the back, laughing and joking continually. He made McTeague sit at the head of the table, with Trina at his right and the agent at his left; he—when he sat down at all—occupied the foot, Maria Macapa at his left, while next to her was Mrs. Sieppe, opposite Miss Baker. Owgooste had been put to bed upon the bed-lounge.

"Where's Old Grannis?" suddenly exclaimed Marcus. Sure enough, where had the old Englishman gone? He had been there at first.

"I called him down with everybody else," cried Maria Macapa, "as soon as I saw in the paper that Miss Sieppe had won. We all came down to Mr. Schouler's room and waited for you to come home. I think he must have gone back to his room. I'll bet you'll find him sewing up his books."

"No, no," observed Miss Baker, "not at this hour."

Evidently the timid old gentleman had taken advantage of the confusion to slip unobtrusively away.

"I'll go bring him down," shouted Marcus; "he's got to join us."

Miss Baker was in great agitation.

"I—I hardly think you'd better," she murmured; "he—he—I don't think he drinks beer."

"He takes his amusement in sewin' up books," cried Maria.

Marcus brought him down, nevertheless, having found him just preparing for bed.

"I—I must apologize," stammered Old Grannis, as he stood in the doorway. "I had not quite expected—I—find—find myself a little unprepared." He was without collar and cravat, owing to Marcus Schouler's precipitate haste. He was annoyed beyond words that Miss Baker saw him thus. Could anything be more embarrassing?

Old Grannis was introduced to Mrs. Sieppe and to Trina as Marcus's employer. They shook hands solemnly.

"I don't believe that he an' Miss Baker have ever been introduced," cried Maria Macapa, shrilly, "an' they've been livin' side by side for years."

The two old people were speechless, avoiding each other's gaze. It had come at last; they were to know each other, to talk together, to touch each other's hands.

Marcus brought Old Grannis around the table to little Miss Baker, dragging him by the coat sleeve, exclaiming: "Well, I thought you two people knew each other long ago. Miss Baker, this is Mr. Grannis; Mr. Grannis, this is Miss Baker." Neither spoke. Like two little children they faced each other, awkward, constrained, tongue-tied with embarrassment. Then Miss Baker put out her hand shyly. Old Grannis touched it for an instant and let it fall.

"Now you know each other," cried Marcus, "and it's about time." For the first time their eyes met; Old Grannis trembled a little, putting his hand uncertainly to his chin. Miss Baker flushed ever so slightly, but Maria Macapa passed suddenly between them, carrying a half empty beer bottle. The two old people fell back from one another, Miss Baker resuming her seat.

"Here's a place for you over here, Mr. Grannis," cried Marcus, making room for him at his side. Old Grannis slipped into the chair, withdrawing at once from the company's notice. He stared fixedly at his plate and did not speak again. Old Miss Baker began to talk volubly across the table to Mrs. Sieppe about hot-house flowers and medicated flannels.

It was in the midst of this little impromptu supper that the engagement of Trina and the dentist was announced. In a pause in the chatter of conversation Mrs. Sieppe leaned forward and, speaking to the agent, said:

"Vell, you know also my daughter Trina get married bretty soon. She and der dentist, Doktor McTeague, eh, yes?"

There was a general exclamation.

"I thought so all along," cried Miss Baker, excitedly. "The first time I saw them together I said, 'What a pair!'"

"Delightful!" exclaimed the agent, "to be married and win a snug little fortune at the same time."

"So—So," murmured Old Grannis, nodding at his plate.

"Good luck to you," cried Maria.

"He's lucky enough already," growled Marcus under his breath, relapsing for a moment into one of those strange moods of sullenness which had marked him throughout the evening.

Trina flushed crimson, drawing shyly nearer her mother. McTeague grinned from ear to ear, looking around from one to another, exclaiming "Huh! Huh!"

But the agent rose to his feet, a newly filled beer glass in his hand. He was a man of the world, this agent. He knew life. He was suave and easy. A diamond was on his little finger.

"Ladies and gentlemen," he began. There was an instant silence. "This is indeed a happy occasion. I—I am glad to be here to-night; to be a witness to such good fortune; to partake in these—in this celebration. Why, I feel almost as glad as if I had held four three oughts twelve myself; as if the five thousand were mine instead of belonging to our charming hostess. The good wishes of my humble self go out to Miss Sieppe in this moment of her good fortune, and I think—in fact, I am sure I can speak for the great institution, the great company I represent. The company congratulates Miss Sieppe. We—they—ah—They wish her every happiness her new fortune can procure her. It has been my duty, my—ah—cheerful duty to call upon the winners of large prizes and to offer the felicitation of the company. I have, in my experience, called upon many such; but never have I seen fortune so happily bestowed as in this case. The company have dowered the prospective bride. I am sure I but echo the sentiments of this assembly when I wish all joy and happiness to this happy pair, happy in the possession of a snug little fortune, and happy—happy in—" he finished with a sudden inspiration—"in the possession of each other; I drink to the health, wealth, and happiness of the future bride and groom. Let us drink standing up." They drank with enthusiasm. Marcus was carried away with the excitement of the moment.

"Outa sight, outa sight," he vociferated, clapping his hands. "Very well said. To the health of the bride. McTeague, McTeague, speech, speech!"

In an instant the whole table was clamoring for the dentist to speak. McTeague was terrified; he gripped the table with both hands, looking wildly about him.

"Speech, speech!" shouted Marcus, running around the table and endeavoring to drag McTeague up.

"No—no—no," muttered the other. "No speech." The company rattled upon the table with their beer glasses, insisting upon a speech. McTeague settled obstinately into his chair, very red in the face, shaking his head energetically.

"Ah, go on!" he exclaimed; "no speech."

"Ah, get up and say somethun, anyhow," persisted Marcus; "you ought to do it. It's the proper caper."

McTeague heaved himself up; there was a burst of applause; he looked slowly about him, then suddenly sat down again, shaking his head hopelessly.

"Oh, go on, Mac," cried Trina.

"Get up, say somethun, anyhow, cried Marcus, tugging at his arm; "you GOT to." Once more McTeague rose to his feet.

"Huh!" he exclaimed, looking steadily at the table. Then he began:

"I don' know what to say—I—I—I ain't never made a speech before; I—I ain't never made a speech before. But I'm glad Trina's won the prize—"

"Yes, I'll bet you are," muttered Marcus.

"I—I—I'm glad Trina's won, and I—I want to—I want to—I want to—want to say that—you're—all—welcome, an' drink hearty, an' I'm much obliged to the agent. Trina and I are goin' to be married, an' I'm glad everybody's here to- night, an' you're—all—welcome, an' drink hearty, an' I hope you'll come again, an' you're always welcome—an'—I—an'—an'—That's—about—all—I—gotta say." He sat down, wiping his forehead, amidst tremendous applause.

Soon after that the company pushed back from the table and relaxed into couples and groups. The men, with the exception of Old Grannis, began to smoke, the smell of their tobacco mingling with the odors of ether, creosote, and stale bedding, which pervaded the "Parlors." Soon the windows had to be lowered from the top. Mrs. Sieppe and old Miss Baker sat together in the bay window exchanging confidences. Miss Baker had turned back the overskirt of her dress; a plate of cake was in her lap; from time to time she sipped her wine with the delicacy of a white cat. The two women were much interested in each other. Miss Baker told Mrs. Sieppe all about Old Grannis, not forgetting the fiction of the title and the unjust stepfather.

"He's quite a personage really," said Miss Baker. Mrs. Sieppe led the conversation around to her children. "Ach, Trina is sudge a goote girl," she said; "always gay, yes, und sing from morgen to night. Und Owgooste, he is soh smart also, yes, eh? He has der genius for machines, always making somethun mit wheels und sbrings."

"Ah, if—if—I had children," murmured the little old maid a trifle wistfully, "one would have been a sailor; he would have begun as a midshipman on my brother's ship; in time he would have been an officer. The other would have been a landscape gardener."

"Oh, Mac!" exclaimed Trina, looking up into the dentist's face, "think of all this money coming to us just at this very moment. Isn't it wonderful? Don't it kind of scare you?"

"Wonderful, wonderful!" muttered McTeague, shaking his head. "Let's buy a lot of tickets," he added, struck with an idea.

"Now, that's how you can always tell a good cigar," observed the agent to Marcus as the two sat smoking at the end of the table. "The light end should be rolled to a point."

"Ah, the Chinese cigar-makers," cried Marcus, in a passion, brandishing his fist. "It's them as is ruining the cause of white labor. They are, they are for a *fact*. Ah, the rat-eaters! Ah, the white-livered curs!"

Over in the corner, by the stand of shelves, Old Grannis was listening to Maria Macapa. The Mexican woman had been violently stirred over Trina's sudden wealth; Maria's mind had gone back to her younger days. She leaned forward, her elbows on her knees, her chin in her hands, her eyes wide and fixed. Old Grannis listened to her attentively.

"There wa'n't a piece that was so much as scratched," Maria was saying. "Every piece was just like a mirror, smooth and bright; oh, bright as a little sun. Such a service as that was—platters and soup tureens and an immense big punch- bowl. Five thousand dollars, what does that amount to? Why, that punch-bowl alone was worth a fortune."

"What a wonderful story!" exclaimed Old Grannis, never for an instant doubting its truth. "And it's all lost now, you say?"

"Lost, lost," repeated Maria.

"Tut, tut! What a pity! What a pity!"

Suddenly the agent rose and broke out with:

"Well, I must be going, if I'm to get any car."

He shook hands with everybody, offered a parting cigar to Marcus, congratulated McTeague and Trina a last time, and bowed himself out.

"What an elegant gentleman," commented Miss Baker.

"Ah," said Marcus, nodding his head, "there's a man of the world for you. Right on to himself, by damn!"

The company broke up.

"Come along, Mac," cried Marcus; "we're to sleep with the dogs to-night, you know."

The two friends said "Good-night" all around and departed for the little dog hospital.

Old Grannis hurried to his room furtively, terrified lest he should again be brought face to face with Miss Baker. He bolted himself in and listened until he heard her foot in the hall and the soft closing of her door. She was there close beside him; as one might say, in the same room; for he, too, had made the discovery as to the similarity of the wallpaper. At long intervals he could hear a faint rustling as she moved about. What an evening that had been for him! He had met her, had spoken to her, had touched her hand; he was in a tremor of excitement. In a like manner the little old dressmaker listened and quivered. HE was there in that same room which they shared in common, separated only by the thinnest board partition. He was thinking of her, she was almost sure of it. They were strangers no longer; they were acquaintances, friends. What an event that evening had been in their lives!

Late as it was, Miss Baker brewed a cup of tea and sat down in her rocking chair close to the partition; she rocked gently, sipping her tea, calming herself after the emotions of that wonderful evening.

Old Grannis heard the clinking of the tea things and smelt the faint odor of the tea. It seemed to him a signal, an invitation. He drew his chair close to his side of the partition, before his work-table. A pile of half-bound "Nations" was in the little binding apparatus; he threaded his huge upholsterer's needle with stout twine and set to work.

It was their tete-a-tete. Instinctively they felt each other's presence, felt each other's thought coming to them through the thin partition. It was charming; they were perfectly happy. There in the stillness that settled over the flat in the half hour after midnight the two old people "kept company," enjoying after their fashion their little romance that had come so late into the lives of each.

On the way to her room in the garret Maria Macapa paused under the single gas-jet that burned at the top of the well of the staircase; she assured herself that she was alone, and then drew from her pocket one of McTeague's "tapes" of non-co-hesive gold. It was the most valuable steal she had ever yet made in the dentist's "Parlors." She told herself that it was worth at least a couple of dollars. Suddenly an idea occurred to her, and she went hastily to a window at the end of the hall, and, shading her face with both hands, looked down into the little alley just back of the flat. On some nights Zerkow, the red-headed Polish Jew, sat up late, taking account of the week's ragpicking. There was a dim light in his window now.

Maria went to her room, threw a shawl around her head, and descended into the little back yard of the flat by the back stairs. As she let herself out of the back gate into the alley, Alexander, Marcus's Irish setter, woke suddenly with a gruff bark. The col-lie who lived on the other side of the fence, in the back yard of the branch post-office, answered with a snarl. Then in an instant the endless feud between the two dogs was resumed. They dragged their respective kennels to the fence, and through the cracks raged at each other in a frenzy of hate; their teeth snapped and gleamed; the hackles on their backs rose and stiffened. Their hideous clamor could have been heard for blocks around. What a massacre should the two ever meet!

Meanwhile, Maria was knocking at Zerkow's miserable hovel.

"Who is it? Who is it?" cried the rag-picker from within, in his hoarse voice, that was half whisper, starting nervously, and sweeping a handful of silver into his drawer.

"It's me, Maria Macapa;" then in a lower voice, and as if speaking to herself, "had a flying squirrel an' let him go."

"Ah, Maria," cried Zerkow, obsequiously opening the door. "Come in, come in, my girl; you're always welcome, even as late as this. No junk, hey? But you're welcome for all that. You'll have a drink, won't you?" He led her into his back room and got down the whiskey bottle and the broken red tumbler.

After the two had drunk together Maria produced the gold "tape." Zerkow's eyes glittered on the instant. The sight of gold invariably sent a qualm all through him; try as he would, he could not repress it. His fingers trembled and clawed at his mouth; his breath grew short.

"Ah, ah, ah!" he exclaimed, "give it here, give it here; give it to me, Maria. That's a good girl, come give it to me."

They haggled as usual over the price, but to-night Maria was too excited over other matters to spend much time in bickering over a few cents.

"Look here, Zerkow," she said as soon as the transfer was made, "I got something to tell you. A little while ago I sold a lottery ticket to a girl at the flat; the drawing was in this evening's papers. How much do you suppose that girl has won?"

"I don't know. How much? How much?"

"Five thousand dollars."

It was as though a knife had been run through the Jew; a spasm of an almost physical pain twisted his face—his entire body. He raised his clenched fists into the air, his eyes shut, his teeth gnawing his lip.

"Five thousand dollars," he whispered; "five thousand dollars. For what? For nothing, for simply buying a ticket; and I have worked so hard for it, so hard, so hard. Five thousand dollars, five thousand dollars. Oh, why couldn't it have come to me?" he cried, his voice choking, the tears starting to his eyes; "why couldn't it have come to me? To come so close, so close, and yet to miss me—me who have worked for it, fought for it, starved for it, am dying for it every day. Think of it, Maria, five thousand dollars, all bright, heavy pieces—"

"Bright as a sunset," interrupted Maria, her chin propped on her hands. "Such a glory, and heavy. Yes, every piece was heavy, and it was all you could do to lift the punch-bowl. Why, that punch-bowl was worth a fortune alone—"

"And it rang when you hit it with your knuckles, didn't it?" prompted Zerkow, eagerly, his lips trembling, his fingers hooking themselves into claws.

"Sweeter'n any church bell," continued Maria.

"Go on, go on, go on," cried Zerkow, drawing his chair closer, and shutting his eyes in ecstasy.

"There were more than a hundred pieces, and every one of them gold—"

"Ah, every one of them gold."

"You should have seen the sight when the leather trunk was opened. There wa'n't a piece that was so much as scratched; every one was like a mirror, smooth and bright, polished so that it looked black—you know how I mean."

"Oh, I know, I know," cried Zerkow, moistening his lips.

Then he plied her with questions—questions that covered every detail of that service of plate. It was soft, wasn't it? You could bite into a plate and leave a dent? The handles of the knives, now, were they gold, too? All the knife was made from one piece of gold, was it? And the forks the same? The interior of the trunk was quilted, of course? Did Maria ever polish the plates herself? When the company ate off this service, it must have made a fine noise—these gold knives and forks clinking together upon these gold plates.

"Now, let's have it all over again, Maria," pleaded Zerkow. "Begin now with 'There were more than a hundred pieces, and every one of them gold.' Go on, begin, begin, begin!"

The red-headed Pole was in a fever of excitement. Maria's recital had become a veritable mania with him. As he listened, with closed eyes and trembling lips, he fancied he could see that wonderful plate before him, there on the table, under his eyes, under his hand, ponderous, massive, gleaming. He tormented Maria into a second repetition of the story—into a third. The more his mind dwelt upon it, the sharper grew his desire. Then, with Maria's refusal to continue the tale, came the reaction. Zerkow awoke as from some ravishing dream. The plate was gone, was irretrievably lost. There was nothing in that miserable room but grimy rags and rust-corroded iron. What torment! what agony! to be so near—so near, to see it in one's distorted fancy as plain as in a mirror. To know every individual piece as an old friend; to feel its weight; to be dazzled by its glitter; to call it one's own, own; to have it to oneself, hugged to the breast; and then to start, to wake, to come down to the horrible reality.

"And you, *you* had it once," gasped Zerkow, clawing at her arm; "you had it once, all your own. Think of it, and now it's gone."

"Gone for good and all."

"Perhaps it's buried near your old place somewhere."

"It's gone—gone—gone," chanted Maria in a monotone.

Zerkow dug his nails into his scalp, tearing at his red hair.

"Yes, yes, it's gone, it's gone—lost forever! Lost forever!"

Marcus and the dentist walked up the silent street and reached the little dog hospital. They had hardly spoken on the way. McTeague's brain was in a whirl; speech failed him. He was busy thinking of the great thing that had happened that night, and was trying to realize what its effect would be upon his life—his life and Trina's. As soon as they had found themselves in the street, Marcus had relapsed at once to a sullen silence, which McTeague was too abstracted to notice.

They entered the tiny office of the hospital with its red carpet, its gas stove, and its colored prints of famous dogs hanging against the walls. In one corner stood the iron bed which they were to occupy.

"You go on an' get to bed, Mac," observed Marcus. "I'll take a look at the dogs before I turn in."

He went outside and passed along into the yard, that was bounded on three sides by pens where the dogs were kept. A bull terrier dying of gastritis recognized him and began to whimper feebly.

Marcus paid no attention to the dogs. For the first time that evening he was alone and could give vent to his thoughts. He took a couple of turns up and down the yard, then suddenly in a low voice exclaimed:

"You fool, you fool, Marcus Schouler! If you'd kept Trina you'd have had that money. You might have had it yourself. You've thrown away your chance in life—to give up the girl, yes—but this," he stamped his foot with rage—"to throw five thousand dollars out of the window—to stuff it into the pockets of someone else, when it might have been yours, when you might have had Trina *and* the money—and all for what? Because we were pals . Oh, 'pals' is all right—but five thousand dollars—to have played it right into his hands—God *damn* the luck!"

CHAPTER 8

The next two months were delightful. Trina and McTeague saw each other regularly, three times a week. The dentist went over to B Street Sunday and Wednesday afternoons as usual; but on Fridays it was Trina who came to the city. She spent the morning between nine and twelve o'clock down town, for the most part in the cheap department stores, doing the weekly shopping for herself and the family. At noon she took an uptown car and met McTeague at the corner of Polk Street. The two lunched together at a small uptown hotel just around the corner on Sutter Street. They were given a little room to themselves. Nothing could have been more delicious. They had but to close the sliding door to shut themselves off from the whole world.

Trina would arrive breathless from her raids upon the bargain counters, her pale cheeks flushed, her hair blown about her face and into the corners of her lips, her mother's net reticule stuffed to bursting. Once in their tiny private room, she would drop into her chair with a little groan.

"Oh, *Mac*, I am so tired; I've just been all *over* town. Oh, it's good to sit down. Just think, I had to stand up in the car all the way, after being on my feet the whole blessed morning. Look here what I've bought. Just things and things. Look, there's some dotted veiling I got for myself; see now, do you think it looks pretty?"—she spread it over her face—"and I got a box of writing paper, and a roll of crepe paper to make a lamp shade for the front parlor; and—what do you suppose—I saw a pair of Nottingham lace curtains for *forty-nine cents*; isn't that cheap? and some chenille portieres for two and a half. Now what have *you* been doing since I last saw you? Did Mr. Heise finally get up enough courage to have his tooth pulled yet?" Trina took off her hat and veil and rearranged her hair before the looking-glass.

"No, no—not yet. I went down to the sign painter's yesterday afternoon to see about that big gold tooth for a sign. It costs too much; I can't get it yet a while. There's two kinds, one German gilt and the other French gilt; but the German gilt is no good."

McTeague sighed, and wagged his head. Even Trina and the five thousand dollars could not make him forget this one unsatisfied longing.

At other times they would talk at length over their plans, while Trina sipped her chocolate and McTeague devoured huge chunks of butterless bread. They were to be married at the end of May, and the dentist already had his eye on a couple of rooms, part of the suite of a bankrupt photographer. They were situated in the flat, just back of his "Parlors," and he believed the photographer would sublet them furnished.

McTeague and Trina had no apprehensions as to their finances. They could be sure, in fact, of a tidy little income. The dentist's practice was fairly good, and they could count upon the interest of Trina's five thousand dollars. To McTeague's mind this interest seemed woefully small. He had had uncertain ideas about that five thousand dollars; had imagined that they would spend it in some lavish fashion; would buy a house, perhaps, or would furnish their new rooms with overwhelming luxury—luxury that implied red velvet carpets and continued feasting. The old-time miner's idea of wealth easily gained and quickly spent persisted in his mind. But when Trina had begun to talk of investments and interests and per cents, he was troubled and not a little disappointed. The lump sum of five thousand dollars was one thing, a miserable little twenty or twenty-five a month was quite another; and then someone else had the money.

"But don't you see, Mac," explained Trina, "it's ours just the same. We could get it back whenever we wanted it; and then it's the reasonable way to do. We mustn't let it turn our heads, Mac, dear, like that man that spent all he won in buying more tickets. How foolish we'd feel after we'd spent it all! We ought to go on just the same as before; as if we hadn't won. We must be sensible about it, mustn't we?"

"Well, well, I guess perhaps that's right," the dentist would answer, looking slowly about on the floor.

Just what should ultimately be done with the money was the subject of endless discussion in the Sieppe family. The savings bank would allow only three per cent., but Trina's parents believed that something better could be got.

"There's Uncle Oelbermann," Trina had suggested, remembering the rich relative who had the wholesale toy store in the Mission.

Mr. Sieppe struck his hand to his forehead. "Ah, an idea," he cried. In the end an agreement was made. The money was invested in Mr. Oelbermann's business. He gave Trina six per cent.

Invested in this fashion, Trina's winning would bring in twenty-five dollars a month. But, besides this, Trina had her own little trade. She made Noah's ark animals for Uncle Oelbermann's store. Trina's ancestors on both sides were German-Swiss, and some long-forgotten forefather of the sixteenth century, some worsted-leggined wood-carver of the Tyrol, had handed down the talent of the national industry, to reappear in this strangely distorted guise.

She made Noah's ark animals, whittling them out of a block of soft wood with a sharp jack-knife, the only instrument she used. Trina was very proud to explain her work to McTeague as he had already explained his own to her.

"You see, I take a block of straight-grained pine and cut out the shape, roughly at first, with the big blade; then I go over it a second time with the little blade, more carefully; then I put in the ears and tail with a drop of glue, and paint it with a 'non-poisonous' paint—Vandyke brown for the horses, foxes, and cows; slate gray for the elephants and camels; burnt umber for the chickens, zebras, and so on; then, last, a dot of Chinese white for the eyes, and there you are, all finished. They sell for nine cents a dozen. Only I can't make the manikins."

"The manikins?"

"The little figures, you know—Noah and his wife, and Shem, and all the others."

It was true. Trina could not whittle them fast enough and cheap enough to compete with the turning lathe, that could throw off whole tribes and peoples of manikins while she was fashioning one family. Everything else, however, she made—the ark itself, all windows and no door; the box in which the whole was packed; even down to pasting on the label, which read, "Made in France." She earned from three to four dollars a week.

The income from these three sources, McTeague's profession, the interest of the five thousand dollars, and Trina's whittling, made a respectable little sum taken altogether. Trina declared they could even lay by something, adding to the five thousand dollars little by little.

It soon became apparent that Trina would be an extraordinarily good house-keeper. Economy was her strong point. A good deal of peasant blood still ran undi-luted in her veins, and she had all the instinct of a hardy and penurious mountain race—the instinct which saves without any thought, without idea of consequence—saving for the sake of saving, hoarding without knowing why. Even McTeague did not know how closely Trina held to her new-found wealth.

But they did not always pass their luncheon hour in this discussion of incomes and economies. As the dentist came to know his little woman better she grew to be more and more of a puzzle and a joy to him. She would suddenly interrupt a grave discourse upon the rents of rooms and the cost of light and fuel with a brusque outburst of affection that set him all a-tremble with delight. All at once she would set down her chocolate, and, leaning across the narrow table, would exclaim:

"Never mind all that! Oh, Mac, do you truly, really love me—love me *big*?"

McTeague would stammer something, gasping, and wagging his head, beside himself for the lack of words.

"Old bear," Trina would answer, grasping him by both huge ears and swaying his head from side to side. "Kiss me, then. Tell me, Mac, did you think any less of me that first time I let you kiss me there in the station? Oh, Mac, dear, what a funny nose you've got, all full of hairs inside; and, Mac, do you know you've got a bald spot—" she dragged his head down towards her—"right on the top of your head." Then she would seriously kiss the bald spot in question, declaring:

"That'll make the hair grow."

Trina took an infinite enjoyment in playing with McTeague's great square-cut head, rumpling his hair till it stood on end, putting her fingers in his eyes, or stretching his ears out straight, and watching the effect with her head on one side. It was like a little child playing with some gigantic, good-natured Saint Bernard.

One particular amusement they never wearied of. The two would lean across the table towards each other, McTeague folding his arms under his breast. Then Trina, resting on her elbows, would part his mustache—the great blond mustache of a viking—with her two hands, pushing it up from his lips, causing his face to as-sume the appearance of a Greek mask. She would curl it around either forefinger, drawing it to a fine end. Then all at once McTeague would make a fearful snorting noise through his nose. Invariably—though she was expecting this, though it was part of the game—Trina would jump with a stifled shriek. McTeague would bellow with laughter till his eyes watered. Then they would recommence upon the instant, Trina protesting with a nervous tremulousness:

"Now—now—now, Mac, *don't*; you *scare* me so."

But these delicious tete-a-tetes with Trina were offset by a certain coolness that Marcus Schouler began to affect towards the dentist. At first McTeague was unaware of it; but by this time even his slow wits began to perceive that his best friend—his "pal"—was not the same to him as formerly. They continued to meet at lunch nearly every day but Friday at the car conductors' coffee-joint. But Marcus was sulky; there could be no doubt about that. He avoided talking to McTeague, read the paper continually, answering the dentist's timid efforts at conversation in gruff monosyllables. Sometimes, even, he turned sideways to the table and talked at great length to Heise the harness-maker, whose table was next to theirs. They took no more long walks together when Marcus went out to exercise the dogs. Nor did Marcus ever again recur to his generosity in renouncing Trina.

One Tuesday, as McTeague took his place at the table in the coffee-joint, he found Marcus already there.

"Hello, Mark," said the dentist, "you here already?"

"Hello," returned the other, indifferently, helping himself to tomato catsup. There was a silence. After a long while Marcus suddenly looked up.

"Say, Mac," he exclaimed, "when you going to pay me that money you owe me?"

McTeague was astonished.

"Huh? What? I don't—do I owe you any money, Mark?"

"Well, you owe me four bits," returned Marcus, doggedly. "I paid for you and Trina that day at the picnic, and you never gave it back."

"Oh—oh!" answered McTeague, in distress. "That's so, that's so. I—you ought to have told me before. Here's your money, and I'm obliged to you."

"It ain't much," observed Marcus, sullenly. "But I need all I can get now-a-days."

"Are you—are you broke?" inquired McTeague.

"And I ain't saying anything about your sleeping at the hospital that night, either," muttered Marcus, as he pocketed the coin.

"Well—well—do you mean—should I have paid for that?"

"Well, you'd 'a' had to sleep *somewheres*, wouldn't you?" flashed out Marcus. "You 'a' had to pay half a dollar for a bed at the flat."

"All right, all right," cried the dentist, hastily, feeling in his pockets. "I don't want you should be out anything on my account, old man. Here, will four bits do?"

"I don't *want* your damn money," shouted Marcus in a sudden rage, throwing back the coin. "I ain't no beggar."

McTeague was miserable. How had he offended his pal?

"Well, I want you should take it, Mark," he said, pushing it towards him.

"I tell you I won't touch your money," exclaimed the other through his clenched teeth, white with passion. "I've been played for a sucker long enough."

"What's the matter with you lately, Mark?" remonstrated McTeague. "You've got a grouch about something. Is there anything I've done?"

"Well, that's all right, that's all right," returned Marcus as he rose from the table. "That's all right. I've been played for a sucker long enough, that's all. I've been played for a sucker long enough." He went away with a parting malevolent glance.

At the corner of Polk Street, between the flat and the car conductors' coffee-joint, was Frenna's. It was a corner grocery; advertisements for cheap butter and eggs, painted in green marking-ink upon wrapping paper, stood about on the sidewalk outside. The doorway was decorated with a huge Milwaukee beer sign.

Back of the store proper was a bar where white sand covered the floor. A few tables and chairs were scattered here and there. The walls were hung with gorgeously-colored tobacco advertisements and colored lithographs of trotting horses. On the wall behind the bar was a model of a full-rigged ship enclosed in a bottle.

It was at this place that the dentist used to leave his pitcher to be filled on Sunday afternoons. Since his engagement to Trina he had discontinued this habit. However, he still dropped into Frenna's one or two nights in the week. He spent a pleasant hour there, smoking his huge porcelain pipe and drinking his beer. He never joined any of the groups of piquet players around the tables. In fact, he hardly spoke to anyone but the bartender and Marcus.

For Frenna's was one of Marcus Schouler's haunts; a great deal of his time was spent there. He involved himself in fearful political and social discussions with Heise the harness-maker, and with one or two old German, habitues of the place. These discussions Marcus carried on, as was his custom, at the top of his voice, gesticulating fiercely, banging the table with his fists, brandishing the plates and glasses, exciting himself with his own clamor.

On a certain Saturday evening, a few days after the scene at the coffee-joint, the dentist bethought him to spend a quiet evening at Frenna's. He had not been there for some time, and, besides that, it occurred to him that the day was his birthday. He would permit himself an extra pipe and a few glasses of beer. When McTeague entered Frenna's back room by the street door, he found Marcus and Heise already installed at one of the tables. Two or three of the old Germans sat opposite them, gulping their beer from time to time. Heise was smoking a cigar, but Marcus had before him his fourth whiskey cocktail. At the moment of McTeague's entrance Marcus had the floor.

"It can't be proven," he was yelling. "I defy any sane politician whose eyes are not blinded by party prejudices, whose opinions are not warped by a personal bias, to substantiate such a statement. Look at your facts, look at your figures. I am a free American citizen, ain't I? I pay my taxes to support a good government, don't I? It's a contract between me and the government, ain't it? Well, then, by damn! if the authorities do not or will not afford me protection for life, liberty, and the pursuit of happiness, then my obligations are at an end; I withhold my taxes. I do—I do—I say I do. What?" He glared about him, seeking opposition.

"That's nonsense," observed Heise, quietly. "Try it once; you'll get jugged." But this observation of the harness-maker's roused Marcus to the last pitch of frenzy.

"Yes, ah, yes!" he shouted, rising to his feet, shaking his finger in the other's face. "Yes, I'd go to jail; but because I—I am crushed by a tyranny, does that make the tyranny right? Does might make right?"

"You must make less noise in here, Mister Schouler," said Frenna, from behind the bar.

"Well, it makes me mad," answered Marcus, subsiding into a growl and resuming his chair. "Hullo, Mac." "Hullo, Mark."

But McTeague's presence made Marcus uneasy, rousing in him at once a sense of wrong. He twisted to and fro in his chair, shrugging first one shoulder and then another. Quarrelsome at all times, the heat of the previous discussion had awakened within him all his natural combativeness. Besides this, he was drinking his fourth cocktail.

McTeague began filling his big porcelain pipe. He lit it, blew a great cloud of smoke into the room, and settled himself comfortably in his chair. The smoke of his cheap tobacco drifted into the faces of the group at the adjoining table, and Marcus strangled and coughed. Instantly his eyes flamed.

"Say, for God's sake," he vociferated, "choke off on that pipe! If you've got to smoke rope like that, smoke it in a crowd of muckers; don't come here amongst gentlemen."

"Shut up, Schouler!" observed Heise in a low voice.

McTeague was stunned by the suddenness of the attack. He took his pipe from his mouth, and stared blankly at Marcus; his lips moved, but he said no word. Marcus turned his back on him, and the dentist resumed his pipe.

But Marcus was far from being appeased. McTeague could not hear the talk that followed between him and the harness- maker, but it seemed to him that Marcus was telling Heise of some injury, some grievance, and that the latter was trying to pacify him. All at once their talk grew louder. Heise laid a retaining hand upon his companion's coat sleeve, but Marcus swung himself around in his chair, and, fixing his eyes on McTeague, cried as if in answer to some protestation on the part of Heise:

"All I know is that I've been soldiered out of five thousand dollars."

McTeague gaped at him, bewildered. He removed his pipe from his mouth a second time, and stared at Marcus with eyes full of trouble and perplexity.

"If I had my rights," cried Marcus, bitterly, "I'd have part of that money. It's my due—it's only justice." The dentist still kept silence.

"If it hadn't been for me," Marcus continued, addressing himself directly to McTeague, "you wouldn't have had a cent of it—no, not a cent. Where's my share, I'd like to know? Where do I come in? No, I ain't in it any more. I've been played for a sucker, an' now that you've got all you can out of me, now that you've done me out of my girl and out of my money, you give me the go-by. Why, where would you have been *to-day* if it hadn't been for me?" Marcus shouted in a sudden exasperation, "You'd a been plugging teeth at two bits an hour. Ain't you got any gratitude? Ain't you got any sense of decency?"

"Ah, hold up, Schouler," grumbled Heise. "You don't want to get into a row."

"No, I don't, Heise," returned Marcus, with a plaintive, aggrieved air. "But it's too much sometimes when you think of it. He stole away my girl's affections, and now that he's rich and prosperous, and has got five thousand dollars that I might have had, he gives me the go-by; he's played me for a sucker. Look here," he cried, turning again to McTeague, "do I get any of that money?"

"It ain't mine to give," answered McTeague. "You're drunk, that's what you are."

"Do I get any of that money?" cried Marcus, persistently.

The dentist shook his head. "No, you don't get any of it."

"Now—*now*," clamored the other, turning to the harness- maker, as though this explained everything. "Look at that, look at that. Well, I've done with you from now on." Marcus had risen to his feet by this time and made as if to leave, but at every instant he came back, shouting his phrases into McTeague's face, moving off again as he spoke the last words, in order to give them better effect.

"This settles it right here. I've done with you. Don't you ever dare speak to me again"—his voice was shaking with fury—"and don't you sit at my table in the restaurant again. I'm sorry I ever lowered myself to keep company with such dirt. Ah, one-horse dentist! Ah, ten-cent zinc- plugger—hoodlum—*mucker*! Get your damn smoke outa my face."

Then matters reached a sudden climax. In his agitation the dentist had been pulling hard on his pipe, and as Marcus for the last time thrust his face close to his own, McTeague, in opening his lips to reply, blew a stifling, acrid cloud directly in Marcus Schouler's eyes. Marcus knocked the pipe from his fingers with a sudden flash of his hand; it spun across the room and broke into a dozen fragments in a far corner.

McTeague rose to his feet, his eyes wide. But as yet he was not angry, only sur- prised, taken all aback by the suddenness of Marcus Schouler's outbreak as well as by its unreasonableness. Why had Marcus broken his pipe? What did it all mean, anyway? As he rose the dentist made a vague motion with his right hand. Did Mar- cus misinterpret it as a gesture of menace? He sprang back as though avoiding a blow. All at once there was a cry. Marcus had made a quick, peculiar motion, swinging his arm upward with a wide and sweeping gesture; his jack-knife lay open in his palm; it shot forward as he flung it, glinted sharply by McTeague's head, and struck quivering into the wall behind.

A sudden chill ran through the room; the others stood transfixed, as at the swift passage of some cold and deadly wind. Death had stooped there for an instant, had stooped and past, leaving a trail of terror and confusion. Then the door leading to the street slammed; Marcus had disappeared.

Thereon a great babel of exclamation arose. The tension of that all but fatal instant snapped, and speech became once more possible.

"He would have knifed you."

"Narrow escape."

"What kind of a man do you call *that*?"

"'Tain't his fault he ain't a murderer."

"I'd have him up for it."

"And they two have been the greatest kind of friends."

"He didn't touch you, did he?"

"No—no—no."

"What a—what a devil! What treachery! A regular greaser trick!"

"Look out he don't stab you in the back. If that's the kind of man he is, you never can tell."

Frenna drew the knife from the wall.

"Guess I'll keep this toad-stabber," he observed. "That fellow won't come round for it in a hurry; goodsized blade, too." The group examined it with intense interest.

"Big enough to let the life out of any man," observed Heise.

"What—what—what did he do it for?" stammered McTeague. "I got no quarrel with him."

He was puzzled and harassed by the strangeness of it all. Marcus would have killed him; had thrown his knife at him in the true, uncanny "greaser" style. It was inexplicable. McTeague sat down again, looking stupidly about on the floor. In a corner of the room his eye encountered his broken pipe, a dozen little fragments of painted porcelain and the stem of cherry wood and amber.

At that sight his tardy wrath, ever lagging behind the original affront, suddenly blazed up. Instantly his huge jaws clicked together.

"He can't make small of ME," he exclaimed, suddenly. "I'll show Marcus Schouler—I'll show him—I'll—"

He got up and clapped on his hat.

"Now, Doctor," remonstrated Heise, standing between him and the door, "don't go make a fool of yourself."

"Let 'um alone," joined in Frenna, catching the dentist by the arm; "he's full, anyhow."

"He broke my pipe," answered McTeague.

It was this that had roused him. The thrown knife, the attempt on his life, was beyond his solution; but the breaking of his pipe he understood clearly enough.

"I'll show him," he exclaimed.

As though they had been little children, McTeague set Frenna and the harness-maker aside, and strode out at the door like a raging elephant. Heise stood rubbing his shoulder.

"Might as well try to stop a locomotive," he muttered. "The man's made of iron."

Meanwhile, McTeague went storming up the street toward the flat, wagging his head and grumbling to himself. Ah, Marcus would break his pipe, would he? Ah, he was a zinc-plugger, was he? He'd show Marcus Schouler. No one should make small of him. He tramped up the stairs to Marcus's room. The door was locked. The dentist put one enormous hand on the knob and pushed the door in, snapping the wood-work, tearing off the lock. Nobody—the room was dark and empty. Never mind, Marcus would have to come home some time that night. McTeague would go down and wait for him in his "Parlors." He was bound to hear him as he came up the stairs.

As McTeague reached his room he stumbled over, in the darkness, a big packing-box that stood in the hallway just outside his door. Puzzled, he stepped over it, and lighting the gas in his room, dragged it inside and examined it.

It was addressed to him. What could it mean? He was expecting nothing. Never since he had first furnished his room had packing-cases been left for him in this fashion. No mistake was possible. There were his name and address unmistakably. "Dr. McTeague, dentist—Polk Street, San Francisco, Cal.," and the red Wells Fargo tag.

Seized with the joyful curiosity of an overgrown boy, he pried off the boards with the corner of his fireshovel. The case was stuffed full of excelsior. On the top lay an envelope addressed to him in Trina's handwriting. He opened it and read, "For my dear Mac's birthday, from Trina;" and below, in a kind of post-script, "The man will be round to-morrow to put it in place." McTeague tore away the excelsior. Suddenly he uttered an exclamation.

It was the Tooth—the famous golden molar with its huge prongs—his sign, his ambition, the one unrealized dream of his life; and it was French gilt, too, not the cheap German gilt that was no good. Ah, what a dear little woman was this Trina, to keep so quiet, to remember his birthday!

"Ain't she—ain't she just a—just a *jewel*," exclaimed McTeague under his breath, "a *jewel*—yes, just a *jewel*; that's the word."

Very carefully he removed the rest of the excelsior, and lifting the ponderous Tooth from its box, set it upon the marble-top centre table. How immense it looked in that little room! The thing was tremendous, overpowering—the tooth of a gigantic fossil, golden and dazzling. Beside it everything seemed dwarfed. Even McTeague himself, big boned and enormous as he was, shrank and dwindled in the presence of the monster. As for an instant he bore it in his hands, it was like a puny Gulliver struggling with the molar of some vast Brobdingnag.

The dentist circled about that golden wonder, gasping with delight and stupefaction, touching it gingerly with his hands as if it were something sacred. At every moment his thought returned to Trina. No, never was there such a little woman as his—the very thing he wanted—how had she remembered? And the money, where had that come from? No one knew better than he how expensive were these signs; not another dentist on Polk Street could afford one. Where, then, had Trina found the money? It came out of her five thousand dollars, no doubt.

But what a wonderful, beautiful tooth it was, to be sure, bright as a mirror, shining there in its coat of French gilt, as if with a light of its own! No danger of that tooth turning black with the weather, as did the cheap German gilt impostures. What would that other dentist, that poser, that rider of bicycles, that courser of greyhounds, say when he should see this marvellous molar run out from McTeague's bay window like a flag of defiance? No doubt he would suffer veritable convulsions of envy; would be positively sick with jealousy. If McTeague could only see his face at the moment!

For a whole hour the dentist sat there in his little "Parlor," gazing ecstatically at his treasure, dazzled, supremely content. The whole room took on a different aspect because of it. The stone pug dog before the little stove reflected it in his protruding eyes; the canary woke and chittered feebly at this new gilt, so much brighter than the bars of its little prison. Lorenzo de' Medici, in the steel engraving, sitting in the heart of his court, seemed to ogle the thing out of the corner of one eye, while the brilliant colors of the unused rifle manufacturer's calendar seemed to fade and pale in the brilliance of this greater glory.

At length, long after midnight, the dentist started to go to bed, undressing himself with his eyes still fixed on the great tooth. All at once he heard Marcus

Schouler's foot on the stairs; he started up with his fists clenched, but immediately dropped back upon the bed-lounge with a gesture of indifference.

He was in no truculent state of mind now. He could not reinstate himself in that mood of wrath wherein he had left the corner grocery. The tooth had changed all that. What was Marcus Schouler's hatred to him, who had Trina's affection? What did he care about a broken pipe now that he had the tooth? Let him go. As Frenna said, he was not worth it. He heard Marcus come out into the hall, shouting aggrievedly to anyone within sound of his voice:

"An' now he breaks into my room—into my room, by damn! How do I know how many things he's stolen? It's come to stealing from me, now, has it?" He went into his room, banging his splintered door.

McTeague looked upward at the ceiling, in the direction of the voice, muttering:

"Ah, go to bed, you."

He went to bed himself, turning out the gas, but leaving the window-curtains up so that he could see the tooth the last thing before he went to sleep and the first thing as he arose in the morning.

But he was restless during the night. Every now and then he was awakened by noises to which he had long since become accustomed. Now it was the cackling of the geese in the deserted market across the street; now it was the stoppage of the cable, the sudden silence coming almost like a shock; and now it was the in-furiated barking of the dogs in the back yard—Alec, the Irish setter, and the collie that belonged to the branch post-office raging at each other through the fence, snarling their endless hatred into each other's faces. As often as he woke, McTeague turned and looked for the tooth, with a sudden suspicion that he had only that moment dreamed the whole business. But he always found it—Trina's gift, his birthday from his little woman—a huge, vague bulk, looming there through the half darkness in the centre of the room, shining dimly out as if with some mysterious light of its own.

CHAPTER 9

Trina and McTeague were married on the first day of June, in the photographer's rooms that the dentist had rented. All through May the Sieppe household had been turned upside down. The little box of a house vibrated with excitement and confusion, for not only were the preparations for Trina's marriage to be made, but also the preliminaries were to be arranged for the hegira of the entire Sieppe family.

They were to move to the southern part of the State the day after Trina's marriage, Mr. Sieppe having bought a third interest in an upholstering business in the suburbs of Los Angeles. It was possible that Marcus Schouler would go with them.

Not Stanley penetrating for the first time into the Dark Continent, not Napoleon leading his army across the Alps, was more weighted with responsibility, more burdened with care, more overcome with the sense of the importance of his undertaking, than was Mr. Sieppe during this period of preparation. From dawn to dark, from dark to early dawn, he toiled and planned and fretted, organizing and reorganizing, projecting and devising. The trunks were lettered, A, B, and C, the packages and smaller bundles numbered. Each member of the family had his especial duty to perform, his particular bundles to oversee. Not a detail was forgotten—fares, prices, and tips were calculated to two places of decimals. Even the amount of food that it would be necessary to carry for the black greyhound was determined. Mrs. Sieppe was to look after the lunch, "der gomisariat." Mr. Sieppe would assume charge of the checks, the money, the tickets, and, of course, general supervision. The twins would be under the command of Owgooste, who, in turn, would report for orders to his father.

Day in and day out these minutiae were rehearsed. The children were drilled in their parts with a military exactitude; obedience and punctuality became cardinal virtues. The vast importance of the undertaking was insisted upon with scrupulous iteration. It was a manoeuvre, an army changing its base of operations, a veritable tribal migration.

On the other hand, Trina's little room was the centre around which revolved another and different order of things. The dressmaker came and went, congratulatory visitors invaded the little front parlor, the chatter of unfamiliar voices resounded from the front steps; bonnet-boxes and yards of dress-goods littered the beds and chairs; wrapping paper, tissue paper, and bits of string strewed the floor; a pair of white satin slippers stood on a corner of the toilet table; lengths of white veiling, like a snow-flurry, buried the little work-table; and a mislaid box of artificial orange blossoms was finally discovered behind the bureau.

The two systems of operation often clashed and tangled. Mrs. Sieppe was found by her harassed husband helping Trina with the waist of her gown when she should have been slicing cold chicken in the kitchen. Mr. Sieppe packed his frock coat, which he would have to wear at the wedding, at the very bottom of "Trunk C." The minister, who called to offer his congratulations and to make arrangements, was mistaken for the expressman.

McTeague came and went furtively, dizzied and made uneasy by all this bustle. He got in the way; he trod upon and tore breadths of silk; he tried to help carry the packing-boxes, and broke the hall gas fixture; he came in upon Trina and the dress-maker at an ill-timed moment, and retiring precipitately, overturned the piles of pictures stacked in the hall.

There was an incessant going and coming at every moment of the day, a great calling up and down stairs, a shouting from room to room, an opening and shutting of doors, and an intermittent sound of hammering from the laundry, where Mr. Sieppe in his shirt sleeves labored among the packing-boxes. The twins clattered about on the carpetless floors of the denuded rooms. Owgooste was smacked from hour to hour, and wept upon the front stairs; the dressmaker called over the banisters for a hot flatiron; expressmen tramped up and down the stairway. Mrs. Sieppe stopped in the preparation of the lunches to call "Hoop, Hoop" to the greyhound, throwing lumps of coal. The dog-wheel creaked, the front door bell rang, delivery wagons rumbled away, windows rattled—the little house was in a positive uproar.

Almost every day of the week now Trina was obliged to run over to town and meet McTeague. No more philandering over their lunch now-a-days. It was business now. They haunted the house-furnishing floors of the great department houses, inspecting and pricing ranges, hardware, china, and the like. They rented the photographer's rooms furnished, and fortunately only the kitchen and dining-room utensils had to be bought.

The money for this as well as for her trousseau came out of Trina's five thousand dollars. For it had been finally decided that two hundred dollars of this amount should be devoted to the establishment of the new household. Now that Trina had made her great winning, Mr. Sieppe no longer saw the necessity of dowering her further, especially when he considered the enormous expense to which he would be put by the voyage of his own family.

It had been a dreadful wrench for Trina to break in upon her precious five thousand. She clung to this sum with a tenacity that was surprising; it had become for her a thing miraculous, a god-from-the-machine, suddenly descending upon the stage of her humble little life; she regarded it as something almost sacred and inviolable. Never, never should a penny of it be spent. Before she could be induced to part with two hundred dollars of it, more than one scene had been enacted between her and her parents.

Did Trina pay for the golden tooth out of this two hundred? Later on, the dentist often asked her about it, but Trina invariably laughed in his face, declaring that it was her secret. McTeague never found out.

One day during this period McTeague told Trina about his affair with Marcus. Instantly she was aroused.

"He threw his knife at you! The coward! He wouldn't of dared stand up to you like a man. Oh, Mac, suppose he *had* hit you?"

"Came within an inch of my head," put in McTeague, proudly.

"Think of it!" she gasped; "and he wanted part of my money. Well, I do like his cheek; part of my five thousand! Why, it's mine, every single penny of it. Marcus hasn't the least bit of right to it. It's mine, mine.—I mean, it's ours, Mac, dear."

The elder Sieppes, however, made excuses for Marcus. He had probably been drinking a good deal and didn't know what he was about. He had a dreadful temper, anyhow. Maybe he only wanted to scare McTeague.

The week before the marriage the two men were reconciled. Mrs. Sieppe brought them together in the front parlor of the B Street house.

"Now, you two fellers, don't be dot foolish. Schake hands und maig ut oop, soh."

Marcus muttered an apology. McTeague, miserably embarrassed, rolled his eyes about the room, murmuring, "That's all right—that's all right—that's all right."

However, when it was proposed that Marcus should be McTeague's best man, he flashed out again with renewed violence. Ah, no! ah, *no!* He'd make up with the dentist now that he was going away, but he'd be damned—yes, he would—before he'd be his best man. That was rubbing it in. Let him get Old Grannis.

"I'm friends with um all right," vociferated Marcus, "but I'll not stand up with um. I'll not be *anybody's* best man, I won't."

The wedding was to be very quiet; Trina preferred it that way. McTeague would invite only Miss Baker and Heise the harness-maker. The Sieppes sent cards to Selina, who was counted on to furnish the music; to Marcus, of course; and to Uncle Oelbermann.

At last the great day, the first of June, arrived. The Sieppes had packed their last box and had strapped the last trunk. Trina's two trunks had already been sent to her new home—the remodelled photographer's rooms. The B Street house was deserted; the whole family came over to the city on the last day of May and stopped over night at one of the cheap downtown hotels. Trina would be married the following evening, and immediately after the wedding supper the Sieppes would leave for the South.

McTeague spent the day in a fever of agitation, frightened out of his wits each time that Old Grannis left his elbow.

Old Grannis was delighted beyond measure at the prospect of acting the part of best man in the ceremony. This wedding in which he was to figure filled his mind with vague ideas and half-formed thoughts. He found himself continually wondering what Miss Baker would think of it. During all that day he was in a reflective mood.

"Marriage is a—a noble institution, is it not, Doctor?" he observed to McTeague. "The—the foundation of society. It is not good that man should be alone. No, no," he added, pensively, "it is not good."

"Huh? Yes, yes," McTeague answered, his eyes in the air, hardly hearing him. "Do you think the rooms are all right? Let's go in and look at them again."

They went down the hall to where the new rooms were situated, and the dentist inspected them for the twentieth time.

The rooms were three in number—first, the sitting-room, which was also the dining-room; then the bedroom, and back of this the tiny kitchen.

The sitting-room was particularly charming. Clean matting covered the floor, and two or three bright colored rugs were scattered here and there. The backs of the chairs were hung with knitted worsted tidies, very gay. The bay window should have been occupied by Trina's sewing machine, but this had been moved to the other side of the room to give place to a little black walnut table with spiral legs, before which the pair were to be married. In one corner stood the parlor melodeon, a family possession of the Sieppes, but given now to Trina as one of her parents' wedding presents. Three pictures hung upon the walls. Two were companion pieces. One of these represented a little boy wearing huge spectacles and trying to smoke an enormous pipe. This was called "I'm Grandpa," the title being printed in large black letters; the companion picture was entitled "I'm Grandma," a little girl in cap and "specs," wearing mitts, and knitting. These pictures were hung on either side of the mantelpiece. The other picture was quite an affair, very large and striking. It was a colored lithograph of two little golden-haired girls in their night-gowns. They were kneeling down and saying their prayers; their eyes—very large and very blue—rolled upward. This picture had for name, "Faith," and was bordered with a red plush mat and a frame of imitation beaten brass.

A door hung with chenille portieres—a bargain at two dollars and a half—admitted one to the bedroom. The bedroom could boast a carpet, three-ply ingrain, the design being bunches of red and green flowers in yellow baskets on a white ground. The wall-paper was admirable—hundreds and hundreds of tiny Japanese mandarins, all identically alike, helping hundreds of almond-eyed ladies into hundreds of impossible junks, while hundreds of bamboo palms overshadowed the pair, and hundreds of long-legged storks trailed contemptuously away from the scene. This room was prolific in pictures. Most of them were framed colored prints from Christmas editions of the London "Graphic" and "Illustrated News," the subject of each picture inevitably involving very alert fox terriers and very pretty moon-faced little girls.

Back of the bedroom was the kitchen, a creation of Trina's, a dream of a kitchen, with its range, its porcelain-lined sink, its copper boiler, and its overpowering array of flashing tinware. Everything was new; everything was complete.

Maria Macapa and a waiter from one of the restaurants in the street were to prepare the wedding supper here. Maria had already put in an appearance. The fire was crackling in the new stove, that smoked badly; a smell of cooking was in the air. She drove McTeague and Old Grannis from the room with great gestures of her bare arms.

This kitchen was the only one of the three rooms they had been obliged to furnish throughout. Most of the sitting- room and bedroom furniture went with the suite; a few pieces they had bought; the remainder Trina had brought over from the B Street house.

The presents had been set out on the extension table in the sitting-room. Besides the parlor melodeon, Trina's parents had given her an ice-water set, and a carving knife and fork with elk-horn handles. Selina had painted a view of the Golden Gate upon a polished slice of redwood that answered the purposes of a paper weight. Marcus Schouler—after impressing upon Trina that his gift was to HER, and not to McTeague—had sent a chatelaine watch of German silver; Uncle Oelbermann's present, however, had been awaited with a good deal of curiosity. What would he send? He was very rich; in a sense Trina was his protege. A couple of days before that upon which the wedding was to take place, two boxes arrived with his card. Trina and McTeague, assisted by Old Grannis, had opened them. The first was a box of all sorts of toys.

"But what—what—I don't make it out," McTeague had exclaimed. "Why should he send us toys? We have no need of toys." Scarlet to her hair, Trina dropped into a chair and laughed till she cried behind her handkerchief.

"We've no use of toys," muttered McTeague, looking at her in perplexity. Old Grannis smiled discreetly, raising a tremulous hand to his chin.

The other box was heavy, bound with withes at the edges, the letters and stamps burnt in.

"I think—I really think it's champagne," said Old Grannis in a whisper. So it was. A full case of Monopole. What a wonder! None of them had seen the like before. Ah, this Uncle Oelbermann! That's what it was to be rich. Not one of the other presents produced so deep an impression as this.

After Old Grannis and the dentist had gone through the rooms, giving a last look around to see that everything was ready, they returned to McTeague's "Parlors." At the door Old Grannis excused himself.

At four o'clock McTeague began to dress, shaving himself first before the hand-glass that was hung against the woodwork of the bay window. While he shaved he sang with strange inappropriateness:

"No one to love, none to Caress, Left all alone in this world's wilderness."

But as he stood before the mirror, intent upon his shaving, there came a roll of wheels over the cobbles in front of the house. He rushed to the window. Trina had arrived with her father and mother. He saw her get out, and as she glanced upward at his window, their eyes met.

Ah, there she was. There she was, his little woman, looking up at him, her adorable little chin thrust upward with that familiar movement of innocence and confidence. The dentist saw again, as if for the first time, her small, pale face looking out from beneath her royal tiara of black hair; he saw again her long, narrow blue eyes; her lips, nose, and tiny ears, pale and bloodless, and suggestive of anaemia, as if all the vitality that should have lent them color had been sucked up into the strands and coils of that wonderful hair.

As their eyes met they waved their hands gayly to each other; then McTeague heard Trina and her mother come up the stairs and go into the bedroom of the photographer's suite, where Trina was to dress.

No, no; surely there could be no longer any hesitation. He knew that he loved her. What was the matter with him, that he should have doubted it for an instant? The great difficulty was that she was too good, too adorable, too sweet, too delicate for him, who was so huge, so clumsy, so brutal.

There was a knock at the door. It was Old Grannis. He was dressed in his one black suit of broadcloth, much wrinkled; his hair was carefully brushed over his bald forehead.

"Miss Trina has come," he announced, "and the minister. You have an hour yet."

The dentist finished dressing. He wore a suit bought for the occasion—a ready made "Prince Albert" coat too short in the sleeves, striped "blue" trousers, and new patent leather shoes—veritable instruments of torture. Around his collar was a wonderful necktie that Trina had given him; it was of salmon-pink satin; in its centre Selina had painted a knot of blue forget-me-nots.

At length, after an interminable period of waiting, Mr. Sieppe appeared at the door.

"Are you reatty?" he asked in a sepulchral whisper. "Gome, den." It was like King Charles summoned to execution. Mr. Sieppe preceded them into the hall, moving at a funereal pace. He paused. Suddenly, in the direction of the sitting-room, came the strains of the parlor melodeon. Mr. Sieppe flung his arm in the air.

"Vowaarts!" he cried.

He left them at the door of the sitting-room, he himself going into the bedroom where Trina was waiting, entering by the hall door. He was in a tremendous state of nervous tension, fearful lest something should go wrong. He had employed the period of waiting in going through his part for the fiftieth time, repeating what he had to say in a low voice. He had even made chalk marks on the matting in the places where he was to take positions.

The dentist and Old Grannis entered the sitting-room; the minister stood behind the little table in the bay window, holding a book, one finger marking the place; he was rigid, erect, impassive. On either side of him, in a semi-circle, stood the invited guests. A little pock-marked gentleman in glasses, no doubt the famous Uncle Oelbermann; Miss Baker, in her black grenadine, false curls, and coral brooch; Marcus Schouler, his arms folded, his brows bent, grand and gloomy; Heise the harness-maker, in yellow gloves, intently studying the pattern of the matting; and Owgooste, in his Fauntleroy "costume," stupefied and a little frightened, rolling his eyes from face to face. Selina sat at the parlor melodeon, fingering the keys, her glance wandering to the chenille portieres. She stopped playing as McTeague and Old Grannis entered and took their places. A profound silence ensued. Uncle Oelbermann's shirt front could be heard creaking as he breathed. The most solemn expression pervaded every face.

All at once the portieres were shaken violently. It was a signal. Selina pulled open the stops and swung into the wedding march.

Trina entered. She was dressed in white silk, a crown of orange blossoms was around her swarthy hair—dressed high for the first time—her veil reached to the floor. Her face was pink, but otherwise she was calm. She looked quietly around the room as she crossed it, until her glance rested on McTeague, smiling at him then very prettily and with perfect self-possession.

She was on her father's arm. The twins, dressed exactly alike, walked in front, each carrying an enormous bouquet of cut flowers in a "lace-paper" holder. Mrs. Sieppe followed in the rear. She was crying; her handkerchief was rolled into a wad. From time to time she looked at the train of Trina's dress through her tears. Mr. Sieppe marched his daughter to the exact middle of the floor, wheeled at right angles, and brought her up to the minister. He stepped back three paces, and stood planted upon one of his chalk marks, his face glistening with perspiration.

Then Trina and the dentist were married. The guests stood in constrained attitudes, looking furtively out of the corners of their eyes. Mr. Sieppe never moved a muscle; Mrs. Sieppe cried into her handkerchief all the time. At the melodeon Selina played "Call Me Thine Own," very softly, the tremulo stop pulled out. She looked over her shoulder from time to time. Between the pauses of the music one could hear the low tones of the minister, the responses of the participants, and the suppressed sounds of Mrs. Sieppe's weeping. Outside the noises of the street rose to the windows in muffled undertones, a cable car rumbled past, a newsboy went by chanting the evening papers; from somewhere in the building itself came a persistent noise of sawing.

Trina and McTeague knelt. The dentist's knees thudded on the floor and he presented to view the soles of his shoes, painfully new and unworn, the leather still yellow, the brass nail heads still glittering. Trina sank at his side very gracefully, setting her dress and train with a little gesture of her free hand. The company bowed their heads, Mr. Sieppe shutting his eyes tight. But Mrs. Sieppe took advantage of the moment to stop crying and make furtive gestures towards Owgooste, signing him to pull down his coat. But Owgooste gave no heed; his eyes were starting from their sockets, his chin had dropped upon his lace collar, and his head turned vaguely from side to side with a continued and maniacal motion.

All at once the ceremony was over before any one expected it. The guests kept their positions for a moment, eyeing one another, each fearing to make the first move, not quite certain as to whether or not everything were finished. But the couple faced the room, Trina throwing back her veil. She—perhaps McTeague as well—felt that there was a certain inadequateness about the ceremony. Was that all there was to it? Did just those few muttered phrases make them man and wife? It had been over in a few moments, but it had bound them for life. Had not something been left out? Was not the whole affair cursory, superficial? It was disappointing.

But Trina had no time to dwell upon this. Marcus Schouler, in the manner of a man of the world, who knew how to act in every situation, stepped forward and, even before Mr. or Mrs. Sieppe, took Trina's hand.

"Let me be the first to congratulate Mrs. McTeague," he said, feeling very noble and heroic. The strain of the previous moments was relaxed immediately, the guests crowded around the pair, shaking hands—a babel of talk arose.

"Owgooste, WILL you pull down your goat, den?"

"Well, my dear, now you're married and happy. When I first saw you two together, I said, 'What a pair!' We're to be neighbors now; you must come up and see me very often and we'll have tea together."

"Did you hear that sawing going on all the time? I declare it regularly got on my nerves."

Trina kissed her father and mother, crying a little herself as she saw the tears in Mrs. Sieppe's eyes.

Marcus came forward a second time, and, with an air of great gravity, kissed his cousin upon the forehead. Heise was introduced to Trina and Uncle Oelbermann to the dentist.

For upwards of half an hour the guests stood about in groups, filling the little sitting-room with a great chatter of talk. Then it was time to make ready for supper.

This was a tremendous task, in which nearly all the guests were obliged to assist. The sitting-room was transformed into a dining-room. The presents were removed from the extension table and the table drawn out to its full length. The cloth was laid, the chairs—rented from the dancing academy hard by—drawn up, the dishes set out, and the two bouquets of cut flowers taken from the twins under their shrill protests, and "arranged" in vases at either end of the table.

There was a great coming and going between the kitchen and the sitting-room. Trina, who was allowed to do nothing, sat in the bay window and fretted, calling to her mother from time to time:

"The napkins are in the right-hand drawer of the pantry."

"Yes, yes, I got um. Where do you geep der zoup blates?"

"The soup plates are here already."

"Say, Cousin Trina, is there a corkscrew? What is home without a corkscrew?"

"In the kitchen-table drawer, in the left-hand corner."

"Are these the forks you want to use, Mrs. McTeague?"

"No, no, there's some silver forks. Mamma knows where."

They were all very gay, laughing over their mistakes, getting in one another's way, rushing into the sitting-room, their hands full of plates or knives or glasses, and darting out again after more. Marcus and Mr. Sieppe took their coats off. Old Grannis and Miss Baker passed each other in the hall in a constrained silence, her grenadine brushing against the elbow of his wrinkled frock coat. Uncle Oelbermann superintended Heise opening the case of champagne with the gravity of a magistrate. Owgooste was assigned the task of filling the new salt and pepper canisters of red and blue glass.

In a wonderfully short time everything was ready. Marcus Schouler resumed his coat, wiping his forehead, and remarking:

"I tell you, I've been doing *chores* for *my* board."

"To der table!" commanded Mr. Sieppe.

The company sat down with a great clatter, Trina at the foot, the dentist at the head, the others arranged themselves in haphazard fashion. But it happened that Marcus Schouler crowded into the seat beside Selina, towards which Old Grannis was directing himself. There was but one other chair vacant, and that at the side of Miss Baker. Old Grannis hesitated, putting his hand to his chin. However, there was no escape. In great trepidation he sat down beside the retired dressmaker. Neither of them spoke. Old Grannis dared not move, but sat rigid, his eyes riveted on his empty soup plate.

All at once there was a report like a pistol. The men started in their places. Mrs. Sieppe uttered a muffled shriek. The waiter from the cheap restaurant, hired as Maria's assistant, rose from a bending posture, a champagne bottle frothing in his hand; he was grinning from ear to ear.

"Don't get scairt," he said, reassuringly, "it ain't loaded."

When all their glasses had been filled, Marcus proposed the health of the bride, "standing up." The guests rose and drank. Hardly one of them had ever tasted champagne before. The moment's silence after the toast was broken by McTeague exclaiming with a long breath of satisfaction: "That's the best beer I ever drank."

There was a roar of laughter. Especially was Marcus tickled over the dentist's blunder; he went off in a very spasm of mirth, banging the table with his fist, laughing until his eyes watered. All through the meal he kept breaking out into cackling imitations of McTeague's words: "That's the best *beer* I ever drank. Oh, Lord, ain't that a break!"

What a wonderful supper that was! There was oyster soup; there were sea bass and barracuda; there was a gigantic roast goose stuffed with chestnuts; there were egg-plant and sweet potatoes—Miss Baker called them "yams." There was calf's head in oil, over which Mr. Sieppe went into ecstasies; there was lobster salad; there were rice pudding, and strawberry ice cream, and wine jelly, and stewed prunes, and cocoanuts, and mixed nuts, and raisins, and fruit, and tea, and coffee, and mineral waters, and lemonade.

For two hours the guests ate; their faces red, their elbows wide, the perspiration beading their foreheads. All around the table one saw the same incessant movement of jaws and heard the same uninterrupted sound of chewing. Three times Heise passed his plate for more roast goose. Mr. Sieppe devoured the calf's head with long breaths of contentment; McTeague ate for the sake of eating, without choice; everything within reach of his hands found its way into his enormous mouth.

There was but little conversation, and that only of the food; one exchanged opinions with one's neighbor as to the soup, the egg-plant, or the stewed prunes. Soon the room became very warm, a faint moisture appeared upon the windows, the air was heavy with the smell of cooked food. At every moment Trina or Mrs. Sieppe urged some one of the company to have his or her plate refilled. They were constantly employed in dishing potatoes or carving the goose or ladling gravy. The hired waiter circled around the room, his limp napkin over his arm, his hands full of plates and dishes. He was a great joker; he had names of his own for different articles of food, that sent gales of laughter around the table. When he spoke of a bunch of parsley as "scenery," Heise all but strangled himself over a mouthful of potato. Out in the kitchen Maria Macapa did the work of three, her face scarlet, her sleeves rolled up; every now and then she uttered shrill but unintelligible outcries, supposedly addressed to the waiter.

"Uncle Oelbermann," said Trina, "let me give you another helping of prunes."

The Sieppes paid great deference to Uncle Oelbermann, as indeed did the whole company. Even Marcus Schouler lowered his voice when he addressed him. At the beginning of the meal he had nudged the harness-maker and had whispered behind his hand, nodding his head toward the wholesale toy dealer, "Got thirty thousand dollars in the bank; has, for a fact."

"Don't have much to say," observed Heise.

"No, no. That's his way; never opens his face."

As the evening wore on, the gas and two lamps were lit. The company were still eating. The men, gorged with food, had unbuttoned their vests. McTeague's cheeks were distended, his eyes wide, his huge, salient jaw moved with a machine- like regularity; at intervals he drew a series of short breaths through his nose. Mrs. Sieppe wiped her forehead with her napkin.

"Hey, dere, poy, gif me some more oaf dat—what you call—'bubble-water.'"

That was how the waiter had spoken of the champagne—"bubble-water." The guests had shouted applause, "Outa sight." He was a heavy josher was that waiter.

Bottle after bottle was opened, the women stopping their ears as the corks were drawn. All of a sudden the dentist uttered an exclamation, clapping his hand to his nose, his face twisting sharply.

"Mac, what is it?" cried Trina in alarm.

"That champagne came to my nose," he cried, his eyes watering. "It stings like everything."

"Great BEER, ain't ut?" shouted Marcus.

"Now, Mark," remonstrated Trina in a low voice. "Now, Mark, you just shut up; that isn't funny any more. I don't want you should make fun of Mac. He called it beer on purpose. I guess HE knows."

Throughout the meal old Miss Baker had occupied herself largely with Owgooste and the twins, who had been given a table by themselves—the black walnut table before which the ceremony had taken place. The little dressmaker was continually turning about in her place, inquiring of the children if they wanted for anything; inquiries they rarely answered other than by stare, fixed, ox-like, expressionless.

Suddenly the little dressmaker turned to Old Grannis and exclaimed:

"I'm so very fond of little children."

"Yes, yes, they're very interesting. I'm very fond of them, too."

The next instant both of the old people were overwhelmed with confusion. What! They had spoken to each other after all these years of silence; they had for the first time addressed remarks to each other.

The old dressmaker was in a torment of embarrassment. How was it she had come to speak? She had neither planned nor wished it. Suddenly the words had escaped her, he had answered, and it was all over—over before they knew it.

Old Grannis's fingers trembled on the table ledge, his heart beat heavily, his breath fell short. He had actually talked to the little dressmaker. That possibility to which he had looked forward, it seemed to him for years—that companionship, that intimacy with his fellow-lodger, that delightful acquaintance which was only to ripen at some far distant time, he could not exactly say when—behold, it had suddenly come to a head, here in this over-crowded, over-heated room, in the midst of all this feeding, surrounded by odors of hot dishes, accompanied by the sounds of incessant mastication. How different he had imagined it would be! They were to be alone—he and Miss Baker—in the evening somewhere, withdrawn from the world, very quiet, very calm and peaceful. Their talk was to be of their lives, their lost illusions, not of other people's children.

The two old people did not speak again. They sat there side by side, nearer than they had ever been before, motionless, abstracted; their thoughts far away from that scene of feasting. They were thinking of each other and they were conscious of it. Timid, with the timidity of their second childhood, constrained and embarrassed by each other's presence, they were, nevertheless, in a little Elysium of their own creating. They walked hand in hand in a delicious garden where it was always autumn; together and alone they entered upon the long retarded romance of their commonplace and uneventful lives.

At last that great supper was over, everything had been eaten; the enormous roast goose had dwindled to a very skeleton. Mr. Sieppe had reduced the calf's head to a mere skull; a row of empty champagne bottles—"dead soldiers," as the facetious waiter had called them—lined the mantelpiece. Nothing of the stewed prunes remained but the juice, which was given to Owgooste and the twins. The platters were as clean as if they had been washed; crumbs of bread, potato parings, nutshells, and bits of cake littered the table; coffee and ice-cream stains and spots of congealed gravy marked the position of each plate. It was a devastation, a pillage; the table presented the appearance of an abandoned battlefield.

"Ouf," cried Mrs. Sieppe, pushing back, "I haf eatun und eatun, ach, Gott, how I haf eatun!"

"Ah, dot kaf's het," murmured her husband, passing his tongue over his lips.

The facetious waiter had disappeared. He and Maria Macapa foregathered in the kitchen. They drew up to the washboard of the sink, feasting off the remnants of the supper, slices of goose, the remains of the lobster salad, and half a bottle of champagne. They were obliged to drink the latter from teacups.

"Here's how," said the waiter gallantly, as he raised his tea-cup, bowing to Maria across the sink. "Hark," he added, "they're singing inside."

The company had left the table and had assembled about the melodeon, where Selina was seated. At first they attempted some of the popular songs of the day, but were obliged to give over as none of them knew any of the words beyond the first line of the chorus. Finally they pitched upon "Nearer, My God, to Thee," as the only song which they all knew. Selina sang the "alto," very much off the key; Marcus intoned the bass, scowling fiercely, his chin drawn into his collar. They sang in very slow time. The song became a dirge, a lamentable, prolonged wail of distress:

"Nee-rah, my Gahd, to Thee, Nee-rah to Thee-ah."

At the end of the song, Uncle Oelbermann put on his hat without a word of warning. Instantly there was a hush. The guests rose.

"Not going so soon, Uncle Oelbermann?" protested Trina, politely. He only nodded. Marcus sprang forward to help him with his overcoat. Mr. Sieppe came up and the two men shook hands.

Then Uncle Oelbermann delivered himself of an oracular phrase. No doubt he had been meditating it during the supper. Addressing Mr. Sieppe, he said:

"You have not lost a daughter, but have gained a son."

These were the only words he had spoken the entire evening. He departed; the company was profoundly impressed.

About twenty minutes later, when Marcus Schouler was entertaining the guests by eating almonds, shells and all, Mr. Sieppe started to his feet, watch in hand.

"Haf-bast elevun," he shouted. "Attention! Der dime haf arrive, shtop eferyting. We depart."

This was a signal for tremendous confusion. Mr. Sieppe immediately threw off his previous air of relaxation, the calf's head was forgotten, he was once again the leader of vast enterprises.

"To me, to me," he cried. "Mommer, der tervins, Owgooste." He marshalled his tribe together, with tremendous commanding gestures. The sleeping twins were suddenly shaken into a dazed consciousness; Owgooste, whom the almond-eating of Marcus Schouler had petrified with admiration, was smacked to a realization of his surroundings.

Old Grannis, with a certain delicacy that was one of his characteristics, felt instinctively that the guests—the mere outsiders—should depart before the family began its leave-taking of Trina. He withdrew unobtrusively, after a hasty good-night to the bride and groom. The rest followed almost immediately.

"Well, Mr. Sieppe," exclaimed Marcus, "we won't see each other for some time." Marcus had given up his first intention of joining in the Sieppe migration. He spoke in a large way of certain affairs that would keep him in San Francisco till the fall. Of late he had entertained ambitions of a ranch life, he would breed cattle, he had a little money and was only looking for some one "to go in with." He dreamed of a cowboy's life and saw himself in an entrancing vision involving silver spurs and untamed bronchos. He told himself that Trina had cast him off, that his best friend had "played him for a sucker," that the "proper caper" was to withdraw from the world entirely.

"If you hear of anybody down there," he went on, speaking to Mr. Sieppe, "that wants to go in for ranching, why just let me know."

"Soh, soh," answered Mr. Sieppe abstractedly, peering about for Owgooste's cap.

Marcus bade the Sieppes farewell. He and Heise went out together. One heard them, as they descended the stairs, discussing the possibility of Frenna's place being still open.

Then Miss Baker departed after kissing Trina on both cheeks. Selina went with her. There was only the family left.

Trina watched them go, one by one, with an increasing feeling of uneasiness and vague apprehension. Soon they would all be gone.

"Well, Trina," exclaimed Mr. Sieppe, "goot-py; perhaps you gome visit us somedime."

Mrs. Sieppe began crying again.

"Ach, Trina, ven shall I efer see you again?"

Tears came to Trina's eyes in spite of herself. She put her arms around her mother.

"Oh, sometime, sometime," she cried. The twins and Owgooste clung to Trina's skirts, fretting and whimpering.

McTeague was miserable. He stood apart from the group, in a corner. None of them seemed to think of him; he was not of them.

"Write to me very often, mamma, and tell me about everything—about August and the twins."

"It is dime," cried Mr. Sieppe, nervously. "Goot-py, Trina. Mommer, Owgooste, say goot-py, den we must go. Goot-py, Trina." He kissed her. Owgooste and the twins were lifted up. "Gome, gome," insisted Mr. Sieppe, moving toward the door.

"Goot-py, Trina," exclaimed Mrs. Sieppe, crying harder than ever. "Doktor—where is der doktor—Doktor, pe goot to her, eh? pe vairy goot, eh, won't you? Zum day, Dokter, you vill haf a daughter, den you know berhaps how I feel, yes."

They were standing at the door by this time. Mr. Sieppe, half way down the stairs, kept calling "Gome, gome, we miss der drain."

Mrs. Sieppe released Trina and started down the hall, the twins and Owgooste following. Trina stood in the doorway, looking after them through her tears. They were going, going. When would she ever see them again? She was to be left alone with this man to whom she had just been married. A sudden vague terror seized her; she left McTeague and ran down the hall and caught her mother around the neck.

"I don't WANT you to go," she whispered in her mother's ear, sobbing. "Oh, mamma, I—I'm 'fraid."

"Ach, Trina, you preak my heart. Don't gry, poor leetle girl." She rocked Trina in her arms as though she were a child again. "Poor leetle scairt girl, don' gry— soh—soh—soh, dere's nuttun to pe 'fraid oaf. Dere, go to your hoasban'. Listen, popper's galling again; go den; goot-by."

She loosened Trina's arms and started down the stairs. Trina leaned over the banisters, straining her eyes after her mother.

"What is ut, Trina?"

"Oh, good-by, good-by."

"Gome, gome, we miss der drain."

"Mamma, oh, mamma!"

"What is ut, Trina?"

"Good-by."

"Goot-py, leetle daughter."

"Good-by, good-by, good-by."

The street door closed. The silence was profound.

For another moment Trina stood leaning over the banisters, looking down into the empty stairway. It was dark. There was nobody. They—her father, her mother, the children—had left her, left her alone. She faced about toward the rooms—faced her husband, faced her new home, the new life that was to begin now.

The hall was empty and deserted. The great flat around her seemed new and huge and strange; she felt horribly alone. Even Maria and the hired waiter were gone. On one of the floors above she heard a baby crying. She stood there an instant in the dark hall, in her wedding finery, looking about her, listening. From the open door of the sitting- room streamed a gold bar of light.

She went down the hall, by the open door of the sitting- room, going on toward the hall door of the bedroom.

As she softly passed the sitting-room she glanced hastily in. The lamps and the gas were burning brightly, the chairs were pushed back from the table just as the guests had left them, and the table itself, abandoned, deserted, presented to view the vague confusion of its dishes, its knives and forks, its empty platters and crumpled napkins. The dentist sat there leaning on his elbows, his back toward her; against the white blur of the table he looked colossal. Above his giant shoulders rose his thick, red neck and mane of yellow hair. The light shone pink through the gristle of his enormous ears.

Trina entered the bedroom, closing the door after her. At the sound, she heard McTeague start and rise.

"Is that you, Trina?"

She did not answer; but paused in the middle of the room, holding her breath, trembling.

The dentist crossed the outside room, parted the chenille portieres, and came in. He came toward her quickly, making as if to take her in his arms. His eyes were alight.

"No, no," cried Trina, shrinking from him. Suddenly seized with the fear of him—the intuitive feminine fear of the male—her whole being quailed before him. She was terrified at his huge, square-cut head; his powerful, salient jaw; his huge, red hands; his enormous, resistless strength.

"No, no—I'm afraid," she cried, drawing back from him to the other side of the room.

"Afraid?" answered the dentist in perplexity. "What are you afraid of, Trina? I'm not going to hurt you. What are you afraid of?"

What, indeed, was Trina afraid of? She could not tell. But what did she know of McTeague, after all? Who was this man that had come into her life, who had taken her from her home and from her parents, and with whom she was now left alone here in this strange, vast flat?

"Oh, I'm afraid. I'm afraid," she cried.

McTeague came nearer, sat down beside her and put one arm around her.

"What are you afraid of, Trina?" he said, reassuringly. "I don't want to frighten you."

She looked at him wildly, her adorable little chin quivering, the tears brimming in her narrow blue eyes. Then her glance took on a certain intentness, and she peered curiously into his face, saying almost in a whisper:

"I'm afraid of *you*."

But the dentist did not heed her. An immense joy seized upon him—the joy of possession. Trina was his very own now. She lay there in the hollow of his arm, helpless and very pretty.

Those instincts that in him were so close to the surface suddenly leaped to life, shouting and clamoring, not to be resisted. He loved her. Ah, did he not love her? The smell of her hair, of her neck, rose to him.

Suddenly he caught her in both his huge arms, crushing down her struggle with his immense strength, kissing her full upon the mouth. Then her great love for McTeague suddenly flashed up in Trina's breast; she gave up to him as she had done before, yielding all at once to that strange desire of being conquered and subdued. She clung to him, her hands clasped behind his neck, whispering in his ear:

"Oh, you must be good to me—very, very good to me, dear—for you're all that I have in the world now."

3.3.3 Reading and Review Questions

1. As you read the first nine chapters of *McTeague*, pay close attention to how Norris describes his antihero protagonist. What environmental forces and natural drives motivate McTeague to descend from his position of working-class respectability to that of fugitive murderer?

2. Norris argues that true naturalistic romance can "teach you by showing." What does *McTeague* teach us about the human condition by showing "the animal in the man"?

3.4 STEPHEN CRANE

(1871 - 1900)

Image 3.2 | Stephen Crane, 1896
Photographer | Unknown
Source | Wikimedia Commons
License | Public Domain

Stephen Crane was born in Newark, New Jersey, in 1871. He was the fourteenth and last child born to a Methodist minister and his devout wife. After the death of his father, Crane attended military school and later college but eventually left to become a writer. He secured work as a freelance journalist, eventually accepting an assignment as a war correspondent in Cuba during the **Spanish-American War**. His first novel, *Maggie: A Girl of the Streets*, published in 1893, offered a raw exploration of a young woman's struggle to thrive in the slums of New York amid poverty and prostitution, and it represented a distinct departure from mainstream Realist works to a new literary style known as Naturalism. Crane next turned his attention to the psychological experience of war in *The Red Badge of Courage* (1895), his second novel. Praised by audiences and critics alike, the novel about a young Union soldier in the Civil War, secured Crane's reputation as an important new writer on the scene and became his signature work. Through his short life, Crane was a prolific writer, producing a significant number of poems, short stories, and journalistic pieces, as well as several other novels. While he never married, Crane established a relationship with Cora Taylor, a free-spirited bohemian from Jacksonville, Florida. The two traveled and lived abroad, eventually settling in England where Crane's health deteriorated from his long struggle with tuberculosis. Crane died at the young age of twenty-eight.

Crane was an innovative author within the generation of writers that followed Howells and other Realists. Always the maverick, Crane did not adhere to any one style. However, most critics today see many of his major works as representative of American Literary Naturalism. Taking issue with Howellsian Realism as too restrictive and genteel and under the influence of Darwin's ideas, Naturalist writers such as Crane, Frank Norris, and Jack London pushed for Realism to go further in scope and subject matter, to tackle grittier subjects such as poverty, crime, violence, and other sociological ills of the increasingly urban landscapes of the late nineteenth century. Naturalist writers also explored humans at odds with the natural world—vast oceans, deserts, and frozen tundra—characterized as indifferent or even hostile to human striving and suffering. In Crane's "The Open Boat," based on a real-life ordeal that Crane endured off the coast of Florida, the shipwreck survivors are depicted not as larger than life figures able to control their destinies through free will but as small insignificant dots on the vast and indifferent sea, unable to understand their plight or control the outcome of their desperate circumstances. While they fight for their lives, the correspondent comes to the stark conclusion that after a brutal and exhausting fight to reach shore and safety, the waves may cause their dinghy to crash on the rocks, raising yet another hurdle to survival for the weakened and injured men, who must now swim to shore among the dangerous rocks in order to save their lives. As mentioned before, ideas such as justice, fairness, and mercy are shown as illusions in the Darwinian environment. The men are at the mercy of natural forces that they can neither understand nor control, and while they may feel some solidarity with one another in the boat, once it swamps each man is alone in his struggle for survival.

3.4.1 "The Open Boat"

None of them knew the color of the sky. Their eyes glanced level, and were fastened upon the waves that swept toward them. These waves were of the hue of slate, save for the tops, which were of foaming white, and all of the men knew the colors of the sea. The horizon narrowed and widened, and dipped and rose, and at all times its edge was jagged with waves that seemed thrust up in points like rocks.

Many a man ought to have a bath-tub larger than the boat which here rode upon the sea. These waves were most wrongfully and barbarously abrupt and tall, and each froth-top was a problem in small boat navigation.

The cook squatted in the bottom and looked with both eyes at the six inches of gunwale which separated him from the ocean. His sleeves were rolled over his fat forearms, and the two flaps of his unbuttoned vest dangled as he bent to bail out the boat. Often he said: "Gawd! That was a narrow clip." As he remarked it he invariably gazed eastward over the broken sea.

The oiler, steering with one of the two oars in the boat, sometimes raised himself suddenly to keep clear of water that swirled in over the stern. It was a thin little oar and it seemed often ready to snap.

The correspondent, pulling at the other oar, watched the waves and wondered why he was there.

The injured captain, lying in the bow, was at this time buried in that profound dejection and indifference which comes, temporarily at least, to even the bravest and most enduring when, willy nilly, the firm fails, the army loses, the ship goes down. The mind of the master of a vessel is rooted deep in the timbers of her, though he command for a day or a decade, and this captain had on him the stern impression of a scene in the grays of dawn of seven turned faces, and later a stump of a top-mast with a white ball on it that slashed to and fro at the waves, went low and lower, and down. Thereafter there was something strange in his voice. Although steady, it was deep with mourning, and of a quality beyond oration or tears.

"Keep'er a little more south, Billie," said he.

"'A little more south,' sir," said the oiler in the stern.

A seat in this boat was not unlike a seat upon a bucking broncho, and, by the same token, a broncho is not much smaller. The craft pranced and reared, and plunged like an animal. As each wave came, and she rose for it, she seemed like a horse making at a fence outrageously high. The manner of her scramble over these walls of water is a mystic thing, and, moreover, at the top of them were ordinarily these problems in white water, the foam racing down from the summit of each wave, requiring a new leap, and a leap from the air. Then, after scornfully bumping a crest, she would slide, and race, and splash down a long incline and arrive bobbing and nodding in front of the next menace.

A singular disadvantage of the sea lies in the fact that after successfully surmounting one wave you discover that there is another behind it just as important and just as nervously anxious to do something effective in the way of swamping boats. In a ten-foot dingey one can get an idea of the resources of the sea in the line of waves that is not probable to the average experience, which is never at sea in a dingey. As each slaty wall of water approached, it shut all else from the view of the men in the boat, and it was not difficult to imagine that this particular wavewas the final outburst of the ocean, the last effort of the grim water. There was a terrible grace in the move of the waves, and they came in silence, save for the snarling of the crests.

In the wan light, the faces of the men must have been gray. Their eyes must have glinted in strange ways as they gazed steadily astern. Viewed from a balcony, the whole thing would doubtlessly have been weirdly picturesque. But the men in the boat had no time to see it, and if they had had leisure there were other things to occupy their minds. The sun swung steadily up the sky, and they knew it was broad day because the color of the sea changed from slate to emerald-green, streaked with amber lights, and the foam was like tumbling snow. The process of the breaking day was unknown to them. They were aware only of this effect upon the color of the waves that rolled toward them.

In disjointed sentences the cook and the correspondent argued as to the difference between a life-saving station and a house of refuge. The cook had said: "There's a house of refuge just north of the Mosquito Inlet Light, and as soon as they see us, they'll come off in their boat and pick us up."

"As soon as who see us?" said the correspondent.

"The crew," said the cook.

"Houses of refuge don't have crews," said the correspondent. "As I understand them, they are only places where clothes and grub are stored for the benefit of ship-wrecked people. They don't carry crews."

"Oh, yes, they do," said the cook.

"No, they don't," said the correspondent.

"Well, we're not there yet, anyhow," said the oiler, in the stern.

"Well," said the cook, "perhaps it's not a house of refuge that I'm thinking of as being near Mosquito Inlet Light. Perhaps it's a life-saving station."

"We're not there yet," said the oiler, in the stern. II.

As the boat bounced from the top of each wave, the wind tore through the hair of the hatless men, and as the craft plopped her stern down again the spray slashed past them. The crest of each of these waves was a hill, from the top of which the men surveyed, for a moment, a broad tumultuous expanse; shining and wind-riven. It was probably splendid. It was probably glorious, this play of the free sea, wild with lights of emerald and white and amber.

"Bully good thing it's an on-shore wind," said the cook. "If not, where would we be? Wouldn't have a show."

"That's right," said the correspondent.

The busy oiler nodded his assent.

Then the captain, in the bow, chuckled in a way that expressed humor, contempt, tragedy, all in one. "Do you think we've got much of a show, now, boys?" said he.

Whereupon the three were silent, save for a trifle of hemming and hawing. To express any particular optimism at this time they felt to be childish and stupid, but they all doubtless possessed this sense of the situation in their mind. A young man thinks doggedly at such times. On the other hand, the ethics of their condition was decidedly against any open suggestion of hopelessness. So they were silent.

"Oh, well," said the captain, soothing his children, "we'll get ashore all right."

But there was that in his tone which made them think, so the oiler quoth: "Yes! If this wind holds!"

The cook was bailing: "Yes! If we don't catch hell in the surf."

Canton flannel gulls flew near and far. Sometimes they sat down on the sea, near patches of brown sea-weed that rolled over the waves with a movement like carpets on line in a gale. The birds sat comfortably in groups, and they were envied by some in the dingey, for the wrath of the sea was no more to them than it was to a covey of prairie chickens a thousand miles inland. Often they came very close and stared at the men with black bead-like eyes. At these times they were uncanny and sinister in their unblinking scrutiny, and the men hooted angrily at them, telling them to be gone. One came, and evidently decided to alight on the top of the captain's head. The bird flew parallel to the boat and did not circle, but made short sidelong jumps in the air in chicken-fashion. His black eyes were wistfully fixed upon the captain's head. "Ugly brute," said the oiler to the bird. "You look as if you were made with a jack-knife." The cook and the correspondent swore darkly at the creature. The captain naturally wished to knock it away with the end of the heavy painter, but he did not dare do it, because anything resembling an emphatic gesture would have capsized this freighted boat, and so with his open hand, the captain gently and carefully waved the gull away. After it had been discouraged from the pursuit the captain breathed easier on account of his hair, and others breathed easier because the bird struck their minds at this time as being somehow grewsome and ominous.

In the meantime the oiler and the correspondent rowed. And also they rowed.

They sat together in the same seat, and each rowed an oar. Then the oiler took both oars; then the correspondent took both oars; then the oiler; then the correspondent. They rowed and they rowed. The very ticklish part of the business was when the time came for the reclining one in the stern to take his turn at the oars. By the very last star of truth, it is easier to steal eggs from under a hen than it was to change seats in the dingey. First the man in the stern slid his hand along the thwart and moved with care, as if he were of Sevres. Then the man in the rowing seat slid his hand along the other thwart. It was all done with the most extraordinary care. As the two sidled past each other, the whole party kept watchful eyes on the coming wave, and the captain cried: "Look out now! Steady there!"

The brown mats of sea-weed that appeared from time to time were like islands, bits of earth. They were travelling, apparently, neither one way nor the other. They were, to all intents stationary. They informed the men in the boat that it was making progress slowly toward the land.

The captain, rearing cautiously in the bow, after the dingey soared on a great swell, said that he had seen the lighthouse at Mosquito Inlet. Presently the cook remarked that he had seen it. The correspondent was at the oars, then, and for some reason he too wished to look at the lighthouse, but his back was toward the far shore and the waves were important, and for some time he could not seize an opportunity to turn his head. But at last there came a wave more gentle than the others, and when at the crest of it he swiftly scoured the western horizon.

"See it?" said the captain.

"No," said the correspondent, slowly, "I didn't see anything."

"Look again," said the captain. He pointed. "It's exactly in that direction."

At the top of another wave, the correspondent did as he was bid, and this time his eyes chanced on a small still thing on the edge of the swaying horizon. It was precisely like the point of a pin. It took an anxious eye to find a lighthouse so tiny.

"Think we'll make it, captain?"

"If this wind holds and the boat don't swamp, we can't do much else," said the captain.

The little boat, lifted by each towering sea, and splashed viciously by the crests, made progress that in the absence of sea-weed was not apparent to those in her. She seemed just a wee thing wallowing, miraculously, top-up, at the mercy of five oceans. Occasionally, a great spread of water, like white flames, swarmed into her.

"Bail her, cook," said the captain, serenely.

"All right, captain," said the cheerful cook. III

IT would be difficult to describe the subtle brotherhood of men that was here established on the seas. No one said that it was so. No one mentioned it. But it dwelt in the boat, and each man felt it warm him. They were a captain, an oiler, a cook, and a correspondent, and they were friends, friends in a more curiously iron-bound degree than may be common. The hurt captain, lying against the water-jar in the bow, spoke always in a low voice and calmly, but he could never command a more ready and swiftly obedient crew than the motley three of the dingey. It was more than a mere recognition of what was best for the common safety. There was surely in it a quality that was personal and heartfelt. And after this devotion to the commander of the boat there was this comradeship that the correspondent, for instance, who had been taught to be cynical of men, knew even at the time was the best experience of his life. But no one said that it was so. No one mentioned it.

"I wish we had a sail," remarked the captain. "We might try my overcoat on the end of an oar and give you two boys a chance to rest." So the cook and the correspondent held the mast and spread wide the overcoat. The oiler steered, and the little boat made good way with her new rig. Sometimes the oiler had to scull sharply to keep a sea from breaking into the boat, but otherwise sailing was a success.

Meanwhile the light-house had been growing slowly larger. It had now almost assumed color, and appeared like a little gray shadow on the sky. The man at the oars could not be prevented from turning his head rather often to try for a glimpse of this little gray shadow.

At last, from the top of each wave the men in the tossing boat could see land. Even as the light-house was an upright shadow on the sky, this land seemed but a long black shadow on the sea. It certainly was thinner than paper. "We must be about opposite New Smyrna," said the cook, who had coasted this shore often in schooners. "Captain, by the way, I believe they abandoned that life-saving station there about a year ago."

"Did they?" said the captain.

The wind slowly died away. The cook and the correspondent were not now obliged to slave in order to hold high the oar. But the waves continued their old impetuous swooping at the dingey, and the little craft, no longer under way, struggled woundily over them. The oiler or the correspondent took the oars again.

Shipwrecks are apropos of nothing. If men could only train for them and have them occur when the men had reached pink condition, there would be less drowning at sea. Of the four in the dingey none had slept any time worth mentioning for two days and two nights previous to embarking in the dingey, and in the excitement of clambering about the deck of a foundering ship they had also forgotten to eat heartily.

For these reasons, and for others, neither the oiler nor the correspondent was fond of rowing at this time. The correspondent wondered ingenuously how in the name of all that was sane could there be people who thought it amusing to row a boat. It was not an amusement; it was a diabolical punishment, and even a genius of mental aberrations could never conclude that it was anything but a horror to the muscles and a crime against the back. He mentioned to the boat in general how the amusement of rowing struck him, and the weary-faced oiler smiled in full sympathy. Previously to the foundering, by the way, the oiler had worked double-watch in the engine-room of the ship.

"Take her easy, now, boys," said the captain. "Don't spend yourselves. If we have to run a surf you'll need all your strength, because we'll sure have to swim for it. Take your time."

Slowly the land arose from the sea. From a black line it became a line of black and a line of white, trees, and sand. Finally, the captain said that he could make out a house on the shore. "That's the house of refuge, sure," said the cook. "They'll see us before long, and come out after us."

The distant light-house reared high. "The keeper ought to be able to make us out now, if he's looking through a glass," said the captain. "He'll notify the life-saving people."

"None of those other boats could have got ashore to give word of the wreck," said the oiler, in a low voice. "Else the life-boat would be out hunting us."

Slowly and beautifully the land loomed out of the sea. The wind came again. It had veered from the northeast to the southeast. Finally, a new sound struck the ears of the men in the boat. It was the low thunder of the surf on the shore. "We'll never be able to make the light-house now," said the captain. "Swing her head a little more north, Billie," said the captain.

"'A little more north,' sir," said the oiler.

Whereupon the little boat turned her nose once more down the wind, and all but the oarsman watched the shore grow. Under the influence of this expansion doubt and direful apprehension was leaving the minds of the men. The management of the boat was still most absorbing, but it could not prevent a quiet cheerfulness. In an hour, perhaps, they would be ashore.

Their back-bones had become thoroughly used to balancing in the boat and they now rode this wild colt of a dingey like circus men. The correspondent thought that he had been drenched to the skin, but happening to feel in the top pocket of his coat, he found therein eight cigars. Four of them were soaked with sea-water; four were perfectly scatheless. After a search, somebody produced three dry matches, and thereupon the four waifs rode in their little boat, and with an assurance of an impending rescue shining in their eyes, puffed at the big cigars and judged well and ill of all men. Everybody took a drink of water. IV

"COOK," remarked the captain, "there don't seem to be any signs of life about your house of refuge."

"No," replied the cook. "Funny they don't see us!"

A broad stretch of lowly coast lay before the eyes of the men. It was of low dunes topped with dark vegetation. The roar of the surf was plain, and sometimes they could see the white lip of a wave as it spun up the beach. A tiny house was blocked out black upon the sky. Southward, the slim light-house lifted its little gray length.

Tide, wind, and waves were swinging the dingey northward. "Funny they don't see us," said the men.

The surf's roar was here dulled, but its tone was, nevertheless, thunderous and mighty. As the boat swam over the great rollers, the men sat listening to this roar. "We'll swamp sure," said everybody.

It is fair to say here that there was not a life-saving station within twenty miles in either direction, but the men did not know this fact and in consequence they made dark and opprobrious remarks concerning the eyesight of the nation's life-savers. Four scowling men sat in the dingey and surpassed records in the invention of epithets.

"Funny they don't see us."

The light-heartedness of a former time had completely faded. To their sharpened minds it was easy to conjure pictures of all kinds of incompetency and blindness and indeed, cowardice. There was the shore of the populous land, and it was bitter and bitter to them that from it came no sign.

"Well," said the captain, ultimately, "I suppose we'll have to make a try for ourselves. If we stay out here too long, we'll none of us have strength left to swim after the boat swamps."

And so the oiler, who was at the oars, turned the boat straight for the shore. There was a sudden tightening of muscles. There was some thinking.

"If we don't all get ashore—" said the captain. "If we don't all get ashore, I suppose you fellows know where to send news of my finish?"

They then briefly exchanged some addresses and admonitions. As for the reflections of the men, there was a great deal of rage in them. Perchance they might be formulated thus: "If I am going to be drowned—if I am going to be drowned—if I am going to be drowned, why, in the name of the seven mad gods who rule the sea, was I allowed to come thus far and contemplate sand and trees? Was I brought here merely to have my nose dragged away as I was about to nibble the sacred cheese of life? It is preposterous. If this old ninny-woman, Fate, cannot do better than this, she should be deprived of the management of men's fortunes. She is an old hen who knows not her intention. If she has decided to drown me, why did she not do it in the beginning and save me all this trouble. The whole affair is absurd. . . . But, no, she cannot mean to drown me. She dare not drown me. She cannot drown me. Not after all this work." Afterward the man might have had an impulse to shake his fist at the clouds: "Just you drown me, now, and then hear what I call you!"

The billows that came at this time were more formidable. They seemed always just about to break and roll over the little boat in a turmoil of foam. There was a preparatory and long growl in the speech of them. No mind unused to the sea would have concluded that the dingey could ascend these sheer heights in time. The shore was still afar. The oiler was a wily surfman. "Boys," he said, swiftly, "she won't live three minutes more and we're too far out to swim. Shall I take her to sea again, captain?"

"Yes! Go ahead!" said the captain.

This oiler, by a series of quick miracles, and fast and steady oarsmanship, turned the boat in the middle of the surf and took her safely to sea again.

There was a considerable silence as the boat bumped over the furrowed sea to deeper water. Then somebody in gloom spoke. "Well, anyhow, they must have seen us from the shore by now."

The gulls went in slanting flight up the wind toward the gray desolate east. A squall, marked by dingy clouds, and clouds brick-red, like smoke from a burning building, appeared from the southeast.

"What do you think of those life-saving people? Ain't they peaches?"

"Funny they haven't seen us."

"Maybe they think we're out here for sport! Maybe they think we're fishin'. Maybe they think we're damned fools."

It was a long afternoon. A changed tide tried to force them southward, but wind and wave said northward. Far ahead, where coast-line, sea, and sky formed their mighty angle, there were little dots which seemed to indicate a city on the shore.

"St. Augustine?"

The captain shook his head. "Too near Mosquito Inlet."

And the oiler rowed, and then the correspondent rowed. Then the oiler rowed. It was a weary business. The human back can become the seat of more aches and pains than are registered in books for the composite anatomy of a regiment. It is a limited area, but it can become the theatre of innumerable muscular conflicts, tangles, wrenches, knots, and other comforts.

"Did you ever like to row, Billie?" asked the correspondent.

"No," said the oiler. "Hang it."

When one exchanged the rowing-seat for a place in the bottom of the boat, he suffered a bodily depression that caused him to be careless of everything save an obligation to wiggle one finger. There was cold sea-water swashing to and fro in the boat, and he lay in it. His head, pillowed on a thwart, was within an inch of the swirl of a wave crest, and sometimes a particularly obstreperous sea came in-board and drenched him once more. But these matters did not annoy him. It is almost certain that if the boat had capsized he would have tumbled comfortably out upon the ocean as if he felt sure it was a great soft mattress.

"Look! There's a man on the shore!"

"Where?"

"There! See 'im? See 'im?"

"Yes, sure! He's walking along."

"Now he's stopped. Look! He's facing us!"

"He's waving at us!"

"So he is! By thunder!"

"Ah, now, we're all right! Now we're all right! There'll be a boat out here for us in half an hour."

"He's going on. He's running. He's going up to that house there."

The remote beach seemed lower than the sea, and it required a searching glance to discern the little black figure. The captain saw a floating stick and they rowed to it. A bath-towel was by some weird chance in the boat, and, tying this on the stick, the captain waved it. The oarsman did not dare turn his head, so he was obliged to ask questions.

"What's he doing now?"

"He's standing still again. He's looking, I think. . . . There he goes again. Toward the house. . . . Now he's stopped again."

"Is he waving at us?"

"No, not now! he was, though."

"Look! There comes another man!"

"He's running."

"Look at him go, would you."

"Why, he's on a bicycle. Now he's met the other man. They're both waving at us. Look!"

"There comes something up the beach."

"What the devil is that thing?"

"Why, it looks like a boat."

"Why, certainly it's a boat."

"No, it's on wheels."

"Yes, so it is. Well, that must be the life-boat. They drag them along shore on a wagon."

"That's the life-boat, sure."

"No, by—, it's—it's an omnibus."

"I tell you it's a life-boat."

"It is not! It's an omnibus. I can see it plain. See? One of these big hotel omnibuses."

"By thunder, you're right. It's an omnibus, sure as fate. What do you suppose they are doing with an omnibus? Maybe they are going around collecting the life-crew, hey?"

"That's it, likely. Look! There's a fellow waving a little black flag. He's standing on the steps of the omnibus. There come those other two fellows. Now they're all talking together. Look at the fellow with the flag. Maybe he ain't waving it."

"That ain't a flag, is it? That's his coat. Why, certainly, that's his coat."

"So it is. It's his coat. He's taken it off and is waving it around his head. But would you look at him swing it."

"Oh, say, there isn't any life-saving station there. That's just a winter resort hotel omnibus that has brought over some of the boarders to see us drown."

"What's that idiot with the coat mean? What's he signaling, anyhow?"

"It looks as if he were trying to tell us to go north. There must be a life-saving station up there."

"No! He thinks we're fishing. Just giving us a merry hand. See? Ah, there, Willie."

"Well, I wish I could make something out of those signals. What do you suppose he means?"

"He don't mean anything. He's just playing."

"Well, if he'd just signal us to try the surf again, or to go to sea and wait, or go north, or go south, or go to hell—there would be some reason in it. But look at him. He just stands there and keeps his coat revolving like a wheel. The ass!"

"There come more people."

"Now there's quite a mob. Look! Isn't that a boat?"

"Where? Oh, I see where you mean. No, that's no boat."

"That fellow is still waving his coat."

"He must think we like to see him do that. Why don't he quit it. It don't mean anything."

"I don't know. I think he is trying to make us go north. It must be that there's a life-saving station there somewhere."

"Say, he ain't tired yet. Look at 'im wave."

"Wonder how long he can keep that up. He's been revolving his coat ever since he caught sight of us. He's an idiot. Why aren't they getting men to bring a boat out. A fishing boat—one of those big yawls—could come out here all right. Why don't he do something?"

"Oh, it's all right, now."

"They'll have a boat out here for us in less than no time, now that they've seen us."

A faint yellow tone came into the sky over the low land. The shadows on the sea slowly deepened. The wind bore coldness with it, and the men began to shiver.

"Holy smoke!" said one, allowing his voice to express his impious mood, "if we keep on monkeying out here! If we've got to flounder out here all night!"

"Oh, we'll never have to stay here all night! Don't you worry. They've seen us now, and it won't be long before they'll come chasing out after us."

The shore grew dusky. The man waving a coat blended gradually into this gloom, and it swallowed in the same manner the omnibus and the group of people. The spray, when it dashed uproariously over the side, made the voyagers shrink and swear like men who were being branded.

"I'd like to catch the chump who waved the coat. I feel like soaking him one, just for luck."

"Why? What did he do?"

"Oh, nothing, but then he seemed so damned cheerful."

In the meantime the oiler rowed, and then the correspondent rowed, and then the oiler rowed. Gray-faced and bowed forward, they mechanically, turn by turn, plied the leaden oars. The form of the light-house had vanished from the southern horizon, but finally a pale star appeared, just lifting from the sea. The streaked saffron in the west passed before the all-merging darkness, and the sea to the east was black. The land had vanished, and was expressed only by the low and drear thunder of the surf.

"If I am going to be drowned—if I am going to be drowned—if I am going to be drowned, why, in the name of the seven mad gods, who rule the sea, was I allowed to come thus far and contemplate sand and trees? Was I brought here merely to have my nose dragged away as I was about to nibble the sacred cheese of life?"

The patient captain, drooped over the water-jar, was sometimes obliged to speak to the oarsman.

"Keep her head up! Keep her head up!"

"'Keep her head up,' sir." The voices were weary and low.

This was surely a quiet evening. All save the oarsman lay heavily and listlessly in the boat's bottom. As for him, his eyes were just capable of noting the tall black waves that swept forward in a most sinister silence, save for an occasional subdued growl of a crest.

The cook's head was on a thwart, and he looked without interest at the water under his nose. He was deep in other scenes. Finally he spoke. "Billie," he murmured, dreamfully, "what kind of pie do you like best?"

"PIE," said the oiler and the correspondent, agitatedly. "Don't talk about those things, blast you!"

"Well," said the cook, "I was just thinking about ham sandwiches, and—"

A night on the sea in an open boat is a long night. As darkness settled finally, the shine of the light, lifting from the sea in the south, changed to full gold. On the northern horizon a new light appeared, a small bluish gleam on the edge of the waters. These two lights were the furniture of the world. Otherwise there was nothing but waves.

Two men huddled in the stern, and distances were so magnificent in the dingey that the rower was enabled to keep his feet partly warmed by thrusting them under his companions. Their legs indeed extended far under the rowing-seat until they touched the feet of the captain forward. Sometimes, despite the efforts of the tired oarsman, a wave came piling into the boat, an icy wave of the night, and the chilling water soaked them anew. They would twist their bodies for a moment and groan, and sleep the dead sleep once more, while the water in the boat gurgled about them as the craft rocked.

The plan of the oiler and the correspondent was for one to row until he lost the ability, and then arouse the other from his sea-water couch in the bottom of the boat.

The oiler plied the oars until his head drooped forward, and the overpowering sleep blinded him. And he rowed yet afterward. Then he touched a man in the bottom of the boat, and called his name. "Will you spell me for a little while?" he said, meekly.

"Sure, Billie," said the correspondent, awakening and dragging himself to a sitting position. They exchanged places carefully, and the oiler, cuddling down to the sea-water at the cook's side, seemed to go to sleep instantly.

The particular violence of the sea had ceased. The waves came without snarling. The obligation of the man at the oars was to keep the boat headed so that the tilt of the rollers would not capsize her, and to preserve her from filling when the crests rushed past. The black waves were silent and hard to be seen in the darkness. Often one was almost upon the boat before the oarsman was aware.

In a low voice the correspondent addressed the captain. He was not sure that the captain was awake, although this iron man seemed to be always awake. "Captain, shall I keep her making for that light north, sir?"

The same steady voice answered him. "Yes. Keep it about two points off the port bow."

The cook had tied a life-belt around himself in order to get even the warmth which this clumsy cork contrivance could donate, and he seemed almost stove-like when a rower, whose teeth invariably chattered wildly as soon as he ceased his labor, dropped down to sleep.

The correspondent, as he rowed, looked down at the two men sleeping under foot. The cook's arm was around the oiler's shoulders, and, with their fragmentary clothing and haggard faces, they were the babes of the sea, a grotesque rendering of the old babes in the wood.

Later he must have grown stupid at his work, for suddenly there was a growling of water, and a crest came with a roar and a swash into the boat, and it was a wonder that it did not set the cook afloat in his life-belt. The cook continued to sleep, but the oiler sat up, blinking his eyes and shaking with the new cold.

"Oh, I'm awful sorry, Billie," said the correspondent, contritely.

"That's all right, old boy," said the oiler, and lay down again and was asleep.

Presently it seemed that even the captain dozed, and the correspondent thought that he was the one man afloat on all the oceans. The wind had a voice as it came over the waves, and it was sadder than the end.

There was a long, loud swishing astern of the boat, and a gleaming trail of phosphorescence, like blue flame, was furrowed on the black waters. It might have been made by a monstrous knife.

Then there came a stillness, while the correspondent breathed with the open mouth and looked at the sea.

Suddenly there was another swish and another long flash of bluish light, and this time it was alongside the boat, and might almost have been reached with an oar. The correspondent saw an enormous fin speed like a shadow through the water, hurling the crystalline spray and leaving the long glowing trail.

The correspondent looked over his shoulder at the captain. His face was hidden, and he seemed to be asleep. He looked at the babes of the sea. They certainly were asleep. So, being bereft of sympathy, he leaned a little way to one side and swore softly into the sea.

But the thing did not then leave the vicinity of the boat. Ahead or astern, on one side or the other, at intervals long or short, fled the long sparkling streak, and there was to be heard the whiroo of the dark fin. The speed and power of the thing was greatly to be admired. It cut the water like a gigantic and keen projectile.

The presence of this biding thing did not affect the man with the same horror that it would if he had been a picnicker. He simply looked at the sea dully and swore in an undertone.

Nevertheless, it is true that he did not wish to be alone with the thing. He wished one of his companions to awaken by chance and keep him company with it. But the captain hung motionless over the water-jar and the oiler and the cook in the bottom of the boat were plunged in slumber.

"IF I am going to be drowned—if I am going to be drowned—if I am going to be drowned, why, in the name of the seven mad gods, who rule the sea, was I allowed to come thus far and contemplate sand and trees?"

During this dismal night, it may be remarked that a man would conclude that it was really the intention of the seven mad gods to drown him, despite the abominable injustice of it. For it was certainly an abominable injustice to drown a man who had worked so hard, so hard. The man felt it would be a crime most unnatural. Other people had drowned at sea since galleys swarmed with painted sails, but still—

When it occurs to a man that nature does not regard him as important, and that she feels she would not maim the universe by disposing of him, he at first wishes to throw bricks at the temple, and he hates deeply the fact that there are no bricks and no temples. Any visible expression of nature would surely be pelleted with his jeers.

Then, if there be no tangible thing to hoot he feels, perhaps, the desire to confront a personification and indulge in pleas, bowed to one knee, and with hands supplicant, saying: "Yes, but I love myself."

A high cold star on a winter's night is the word he feels that she says to him. Thereafter he knows the pathos of his situation.

The men in the dingey had not discussed these matters, but each had, no doubt, reflected upon them in silence and according to his mind. There was seldom any expression upon their faces save the general one of complete weariness. Speech was devoted to the business of the boat.

To chime the notes of his emotion, a verse mysteriously entered the correspondent's head. He had even forgotten that he had forgotten this verse, but it suddenly was in his mind. A soldier of the Legion lay dying in Algiers, There was lack of woman's nursing, there was dearth of woman's tears; But a comrade stood beside him, and he took that comrade's hand And he said: "I shall never see my own, my native land."

In his childhood, the correspondent had been made acquainted with the fact that a soldier of the Legion lay dying in Algiers, but he had never regarded the fact as important. Myriads of his school-fellows had informed him of the soldier's plight, but the dinning had naturally ended by making him perfectly indifferent. He had never considered it his affair that a soldier of the Legion lay dying in Algiers, nor had it appeared to him as a matter for sorrow. It was less to him than breaking of a pencil's point.

Now, however, it quaintly came to him as a human, living thing. It was no longer merely a picture of a few throes in the breast of a poet, meanwhile drinking tea and warming his feet at the grate; it was an actuality—stern, mournful, and fine.

The correspondent plainly saw the soldier. He lay on the sand with his feet out straight and still. While his pale left hand was upon his chest in an attempt to thwart the going of his life, the blood came between his fingers. In the far Algerian distance, a city of low square forms was set against a sky that was faint with the last sunset hues. The correspondent, plying the oars and dreaming of the slow and slower movements of the lips of the soldier, was moved by a profound and perfectly impersonal comprehension. He was sorry for the soldier of the Legion who lay dying in Algiers.

The thing which had followed the boat and waited had evidently grown bored at the delay. There was no longer to be heard the slash of the cut-water, and there was no longer the flame of the long trail. The light in the north still glimmered, but it was apparently no nearer to the boat. Sometimes the boom of the surf rang in the correspondent's ears, and he turned the craft seaward then and rowed harder. Southward, someone had evidently built a watch-fire on the beach. It was too low and too far to be seen, but it made a shimmering, roseate reflection upon the bluff back of it, and this could be discerned from the boat. The wind came stronger, and sometimes a wave suddenly raged out like a mountain-cat and there was to be seen the sheen and sparkle of a broken crest.

The captain, in the bow, moved on his water-jar and sat erect. "Pretty long night," he observed to the correspondent. He looked at the shore. "Those life-saving people take their time."

"Did you see that shark playing around?"

"Yes, I saw him. He was a big fellow, all right."

"Wish I had known you were awake."

Later the correspondent spoke into the bottom of the boat.

"Billie!" There was a slow and gradual disentanglement. "Billie, will you spell me?"

"Sure," said the oiler.

As soon as the correspondent touched the cold comfortable sea-water in the bottom of the boat, and had huddled close to the cook's life-belt he was deep in sleep, despite the fact that his teeth played all the popular airs. This sleep was so good to him that it was but a moment before he heard a voice call his name in a tone that demonstrated the last stages of exhaustion. "Will you spell me?"

"Sure, Billie."

The light in the north had mysteriously vanished, but the correspondent took his course from the wide-awake captain.

Later in the night they took the boat farther out to sea, and the captain directed the cook to take one oar at the stern and keep the boat facing the seas. He was to call out if he should hear the thunder of the surf. This plan enabled the oiler and the correspondent to get respite together. "We'll give those boys a chance to get into shape again," said the captain. They curled down and, after a few preliminary chatterings and trembles, slept once more the dead sleep. Neither knew they had bequeathed to the cook the company of another shark, or perhaps the same shark.

As the boat caroused on the waves, spray occasionally bumped over the side and gave them a fresh soaking, but this had no power to break their repose. The ominous slash of the wind and the water affected them as it would have affected mummies.

"Boys," said the cook, with the notes of every reluctance in his voice, "she's drifted in pretty close. I guess one of you had better take her to sea again." The correspondent, aroused, heard the crash of the toppled crests.

As he was rowing, the captain gave him some whiskey and water, and this steadied the chills out of him. "If I ever get ashore and anybody shows me even a photograph of an oar—"

At last there was a short conversation.

"Billie. . . . Billie, will you spell me?"

"Sure," said the oiler.

WHEN the correspondent again opened his eyes, the sea and the sky were each of the gray hue of the dawning. Later, carmine and gold was painted upon the waters. The morning appeared finally, in its splendor with a sky of pure blue, and the sunlight flamed on the tips of the waves.

On the distant dunes were set many little black cottages, and a tall white windmill reared above them. No man, nor dog, nor bicycle appeared on the beach. The cottages might have formed a deserted village.

The voyagers scanned the shore. A conference was held in the boat. "Well," said the captain, "if no help is coming, we might better try a run through the surf right away. If we stay out here much longer we will be too weak to do anything for ourselves at all." The others silently acquiesced in this reasoning. The boat was headed for the beach. The correspondent wondered if none ever ascended the tall wind-tower, and if then they never looked seaward. This tower was a giant, standing with its back to the plight of the ants. It represented in a degree, to the correspondent, the serenity of nature amid the struggles of the individual—nature in the wind, and nature in the vision of men. She did not seem cruel to him, nor beneficent, nor treacherous, nor wise. But she was indifferent, flatly indifferent. It is, perhaps, plausible that a man in this situation, impressed with the unconcern of the universe, should see the innumerable flaws of his life and have them taste wickedly in his mind and wish for another chance. A distinction between right and wrong seems absurdly clear to him, then, in this new ignorance of the grave-edge, and he understands that if he were given another opportunity he would mend his conduct and his words, and be better and brighter during an introduction, or at a tea.

"Now, boys," said the captain, "she is going to swamp sure. All we can do is to work her in as far as possible, and then when she swamps, pile out and scramble for the beach. Keep cool now and don't jump until she swamps sure."

The oiler took the oars. Over his shoulders he scanned the surf. "Captain," he said, "I think I'd better bring her about, and keep her head-on to the seas and back her in."

"All right, Billie," said the captain. "Back her in." The oiler swung the boat then and, seated in the stern, the cook and the correspondent were obliged to look over their shoulders to contemplate the lonely and indifferent shore.

The monstrous inshore rollers heaved the boat high until the men were again enabled to see the white sheets of water scudding up the slanted beach. "We won't get in very close," said the captain. Each time a man could wrest his attention from the rollers, he turned his glance toward the shore, and in the expression of the eyes during this contemplation there was a singular quality. The correspondent, observing the others, knew that they were not afraid, but the full meaning of their glances was shrouded.

As for himself, he was too tired to grapple fundamentally with the fact. He tried to coerce his mind into thinking of it, but the mind was dominated at this time by the muscles, and the muscles said they did not care. It merely occurred to him that if he should drown it would be a shame.

There were no hurried words, no pallor, no plain agitation. The men simply looked at the shore. "Now, remember to get well clear of the boat when you jump," said the captain.

Seaward the crest of a roller suddenly fell with a thunderous crash, and the long white comber came roaring down upon the boat.

"Steady now," said the captain. The men were silent. They turned their eyes from the shore to the comber and waited. The boat slid up the incline, leaped at the furious top, bounced over it, and swung down the long back of the waves. Some water had been shipped and the cook bailed it out.

But the next crest crashed also. The tumbling boiling flood of white water caught the boat and whirled it almost perpendicular. Water swarmed in from all sides. The correspondent had his hands on the gunwale at this time, and when the water entered at that place he swiftly withdrew his fingers, as if he objected to wetting them.

The little boat, drunken with this weight of water, reeled and snuggled deeper into the sea.

"Bail her out, cook! Bail her out," said the captain.

"All right, captain," said the cook.

"Now, boys, the next one will do for us, sure," said the oiler. "Mind to jump clear of the boat."

The third wave moved forward, huge, furious, implacable. It fairly swallowed the dingey, and almost simultaneously the men tumbled into the sea. A piece of life-belt had lain in the bottom of the boat, and as the correspondent went over-board he held this to his chest with his left hand.

The January water was icy, and he reflected immediately that it was colder than he had expected to find it off the coast of Florida. This appeared to his dazed mind as a fact important enough to be noted at the time. The coldness of the water was sad; it was tragic. This fact was somehow mixed and confused with his opinion of his own situation that it seemed almost a proper reason for tears. The water was cold.

When he came to the surface he was conscious of little but the noisy water. Afterward he saw his companions in the sea. The oiler was ahead in the race. He was swimming strongly and rapidly. Off to the correspondent's left, the cook's great white and corked back bulged out of the water, and in the rear the captain was hanging with his one good hand to the keel of the overturned dingey.

There is a certain immovable quality to a shore, and the correspondent wondered at it amid the confusion of the sea.

It seemed also very attractive, but the correspondent knew that it was a long journey, and he paddled leisurely. The piece of life-preserver lay under him, and sometimes he whirled down the incline of a wave as if he were on a hand-sled.

But finally he arrived at a place in the sea where travel was beset with difficulty. He did not pause swimming to inquire what manner of current had caught him, but there his progress ceased. The shore was set before him like a bit of scenery on a stage, and he looked at it and understood with his eyes each detail of it.

As the cook passed, much farther to the left, the captain was calling to him, "Turn over on your back, cook! Turn over on your back and use the oar."

"All right, sir!" The cook turned on his back, and, paddling with an oar, went ahead as if he were a canoe.

Presently the boat also passed to the left of the correspondent with the captain clinging with one hand to the keel. He would have appeared like a man raising himself to look over a board fence, if it were not for the extraordinary gymnastics of the boat. The correspondent marvelled that the captain could still hold to it.

They passed on, nearer to shore—the oiler, the cook, the captain—and following them went the water-jar, bouncing gayly over the seas.

The correspondent remained in the grip of this strange new enemy—a current. The shore, with its white slope of sand and its green bluff, topped with little silent cottages, was spread like a picture before him. It was very near to him then, but he was impressed as one who in a gallery looks at a scene from Brittany or Algiers.

He thought: "I am going to drown? Can it be possible? Can it be possible? Can it be possible?" Perhaps an individual must consider his own death to be the final phenomenon of nature.

But later a wave perhaps whirled him out of this small deadly current, for he found suddenly that he could again make progress toward the shore. Later still, he was aware that the captain, clinging with one hand to the keel of the dingey, had his face turned away from the shore and toward him, and was calling his name. "Come to the boat! Come to the boat!"

In his struggle to reach the captain and the boat, he reflected that when one gets properly wearied, drowning must really be a comfortable arrangement, a cessation of hostilities accompanied by a large degree of relief, and he was glad of it, for the main thing in his mind for some moments had been horror of the temporary agony. He did not wish to be hurt.

Presently he saw a man running along the shore. He was undressing with most remarkable speed. Coat, trousers, shirt, everything flew magically off him.

"Come to the boat," called the captain.

"All right, captain." As the correspondent paddled, he saw the captain let himself down to bottom and leave the boat. Then the correspondent performed his one little marvel of the voyage. A large wave caught him and flung him with ease and supreme speed completely over the boat and far beyond it. It struck him even then as an event in gymnastics, and a true miracle of the sea. An overturned boat in the surf is not a plaything to a swimming man.

The correspondent arrived in water that reached only to his waist, but his condition did not enable him to stand for more than a moment. Each wave knocked him into a heap, and the under-tow pulled at him.

Then he saw the man who had been running and undressing, and undressing and running, come bounding into the water. He dragged ashore the cook, and then waded toward the captain, but the captain waved him away, and sent him to the correspondent. He was naked, naked as a tree in winter, but a halo was about his head, and he shone like a saint. He gave a strong pull, and a long drag, and a bully heave at the correspondent's hand. The correspondent, schooled in the minor formulae, said: "Thanks, old man." But suddenly the man cried: "What's that?" He pointed a swift finger. The correspondent said: "Go."

In the shallows, face downward, lay the oiler. His forehead touched sand that was periodically, between each wave, clear of the sea.

The correspondent did not know all that transpired afterward. When he achieved safe ground he fell, striking the sand with each particular part of his body. It was as if he had dropped from a roof, but the thud was grateful to him.

It seems that instantly the beach was populated with men with blankets, clothes, and flasks, and women with coffee-pots and all the remedies sacred to their minds. The welcome of the land to the men from the sea was warm and generous, but a still and dripping shape was carried slowly up the beach, and the land's welcome for it could only be the different and sinister hospitality of the grave.

When it came night, the white waves paced to and fro in the moonlight, and the wind brought the sound of the great sea's voice to the men on shore, and they felt that they could then be interpreters.

3.4.2 Reading and Review Questions

1. Trace the features of Naturalism in "The Open Boat."

2. Why is Billie the Oiler the only man named in the "The Open Boat"?

3. In "The Open Boat," why does the correspondent come to the conclusion that being in the open boat and trying to survive the shipwreck, in spite of all the horrors it brings, was the best experience of his life?

4. In "The Open Boat," what does the correspondent mean when he wants to throw bricks at the temple and discovers there are no bricks and no temples?

5. How is nature characterized in "The Open Boat"?

6. What does the last line in "The Open Boat" mean, the last line being when the survivors, after hearing "the great sea's voice," feel that they can be "interpreters."

3.5 JACK LONDON

(1876 - 1916)

"Let us be very humble," Jack London once wrote to no less a reader than American President Teddy Roosevelt. "We who are so very human are very animal." Committed to producing 1000 words a day, London authored before his death at the age of forty over 400 works of non-fiction, twenty novels, and almost 200 short stories in numerous genres ranging from journalistic social criticism to juvenile, adventure, dystopian, and science fiction. As a teenager in Oakland, California, London was a voracious reader but received only a sporadic and mostly informal education. Throughout his youth he supported his family by working in mills and canneries, upon sailing boats, and

Image 3.3 | Jack London, 1903
Publisher | L C Page and Company Boston
Source | Wikimedia Commons
License | Public Domain

even as an oyster pirate. Before he was twenty-two, he had spent time in jail for vagrancy, lectured publicly on socialism, attended one semester at the University of California, and ventured to the Canadian Yukon in search of gold. The prolific and adventurous London soon found great success as a writer, authoring many books while sailing around the world in his private yacht, and eventually becoming America's first millionaire author. From the time of his youth, London was swept up in the intellectual and political movements of his day. He was especially influenced by the writings of **Friedrich Nietzsche**, **Charles Darwin**, and **Karl Marx**. The theme that unites these three great thinkers—and that appealed to London—is struggle: Marx saw history as a struggle between classes; Darwin saw nature as a struggle for survival between species; and Nietzsche saw society as a struggle between brilliant individuals and social institutions. London's jobs and adventures at the bottom of the work force, in the arctic, and at sea combined with the ideas of these thinkers to become the subjects of his popular literature.

A literary naturalist, London is arguably best known today for his stories about dogs, most notably the novels *Call of the Wild* (1903) and *White Fang* (1906), and the story included here, "To Build a Fire" (1908). "To Build a Fire" is an excellent example of literary naturalism, for its plot centers around a man's struggle for survival. Interestingly, London published an earlier draft of this same story in 1902 in the juvenile *Youth's Magazine*, in which he gave his protagonist a name (Tom Vincent) and set him out alone in the Yukon without a dog. However, in the revised and much more famous version of the story you read here, London does not name the man but instead has given him a dog. As man and dog journey together on a frozen trail, London shows how heredity and environment are just as much a part of the human condition as culture and individual character.

3.5.1 "To Build a Fire"

Day had broken cold and grey, exceedingly cold and grey, when the man turned aside from the main Yukon trail and climbed the high earth- bank, where a dim and little-travelled trail led eastward through the fat spruce timberland. It was a steep bank, and he paused for breath at the top, excusing the act to himself by looking at his watch. It was nine o'clock. There was no sun nor hint of sun, though there was not a cloud in the sky. It was a clear day, and yet there seemed an intangible pall over the face of things, a subtle gloom that made the day dark, and that was due to the absence of sun. This fact did not worry the man. He was used to the lack of sun. It had been days since he had seen the sun, and he knew that a few more days must pass before that cheerful orb, due south, would just peep above the sky-line and dip immediately from view.

The man flung a look back along the way he had come. The Yukon lay a mile wide and hidden under three feet of ice. On top of this ice were as many feet of snow. It was all pure white, rolling in gentle undulations where the ice-jams of the freeze-up had formed. North and south, as far as his eye could see, it was un-broken white, save for a dark hair-line that curved and twisted from around the spruce- covered island to the south, and that curved and twisted away into the north, where it disappeared behind another spruce-covered island. This dark hair-line was the trail—the main trail—that led south five hundred miles to the Chilcoot Pass, Dyea, and salt water; and that led north seventy miles to Dawson, and still on to the north a thousand miles to Nulato, and finally to St. Michael on Bering Sea, a thousand miles and half a thousand more.

But all this—the mysterious, far-reaching hairline trail, the absence of sun from the sky, the tremendous cold, and the strangeness and weirdness of it all—made no impression on the man. It was not because he was long used to it. He was a new-comer in the land, a chechaquo, and this was his first winter. The trouble with him was that he was without imagination. He was quick and alert in the things of life, but only in the things, and not in the significances. Fifty degrees below zero meant eighty odd degrees of frost. Such fact impressed him as being cold and un-comfortable, and that was all. It did not lead him to meditate upon his frailty as a creature of temperature, and upon man's frailty in general, able only to live within certain narrow limits of heat and cold; and from there on it did not lead him to the conjectural field of immortality and man's place in the universe. Fifty degrees be-low zero stood for a bite of frost that hurt and that must be guarded against by the use of mittens, ear-flaps, warm moccasins, and thick socks. Fifty degrees below ze-ro was to him just precisely fifty degrees below zero. That there should be anything more to it than that was a thought that never entered his head.

As he turned to go on, he spat speculatively. There was a sharp, explosive crackle that startled him. He spat again. And again, in the air, before it could fall to the snow, the spittle crackled. He knew that at fifty below spittle crackled on the snow, but this spittle had crackled in the air. Undoubtedly it was colder than fifty below—how much colder he did not know. But the temperature did not matter. He was bound for the old claim on the left fork of Henderson Creek, where the boys were already. They had come over across the divide from the Indian Creek country, while he had come the roundabout way to take a look at the possibilities of getting out logs in the spring from the islands in the Yukon. He would be in to camp by six o'clock; a bit after dark, it was true, but the boys would be there, a fire would be going, and a hot supper would be ready. As for lunch, he pressed his hand against the protruding bundle under his jacket. It was also under his shirt, wrapped up in a handkerchief and lying against the naked skin. It was the only way to keep the biscuits from freezing. He smiled agreeably to himself as he thought of those biscuits, each cut open and sopped in bacon grease, and each enclosing a generous slice of fried bacon.

He plunged in among the big spruce trees. The trail was faint. A foot of snow had fallen since the last sled had passed over, and he was glad he was without a sled, travelling light. In fact, he carried nothing but the lunch wrapped in the handkerchief. He was surprised, however, at the cold. It certainly was cold, he concluded, as he rubbed his numbed nose and cheek-bones with his mittened hand. He was a warm- whiskered man, but the hair on his face did not protect the high cheek-bones and the eager nose that thrust itself aggressively into the frosty air.

At the man's heels trotted a dog, a big native husky, the proper wolf-dog, grey-coated and without any visible or temperamental difference from its brother, the wild wolf. The animal was depressed by the tremendous cold. It knew that it was no time for travelling. Its instinct told it a truer tale than was told to the man by the man's judgment. In reality, it was not merely colder than fifty below zero; it was colder than sixty below, than seventy below. It was seventy-five below zero. Since the freezing-point is thirty-two above zero, it meant that one hundred and seven degrees of frost obtained. The dog did not know anything about thermometers. Possibly in its brain there was no sharp consciousness of a condition of very cold such as was in the man's brain. But the brute had its instinct. It experienced a vague but menacing apprehension that subdued it and made it slink along at the man's heels, and that made it question eagerly every unwonted movement of the man as if expecting him to go into camp or to seek shelter somewhere and build a fire. The dog had learned fire, and it wanted fire, or else to burrow under the snow and cuddle its warmth away from the air.

The frozen moisture of its breathing had settled on its fur in a fine powder of frost, and especially were its jowls, muzzle, and eyelashes whitened by its crystalled breath. The man's red beard and moustache were likewise frosted, but more solidly, the deposit taking the form of ice and increasing with every warm, moist breath he exhaled. Also, the man was chewing tobacco, and the muzzle of ice held his lips so rigidly that he was unable to clear his chin when he expelled the juice. The result was that a crystal beard of the colour and solidity of amber was increasing its length on his chin. If he fell down it would shatter itself, like glass, into brittle fragments. But he did not mind the appendage. It was the penalty all tobacco-chewers paid in that country, and he had been out before in two cold snaps. They had not been so cold as this, he knew, but by the spirit thermometer at Sixty Mile he knew they had been registered at fifty below and at fifty-five.

He held on through the level stretch of woods for several miles, crossed a wide flat of nigger-heads, and dropped down a bank to the frozen bed of a small stream. This was Henderson Creek, and he knew he was ten miles from the forks. He looked at his watch. It was ten o'clock. He was making four miles an hour, and he calculated that he would arrive at the forks at half-past twelve. He decided to celebrate that event by eating his lunch there.

The dog dropped in again at his heels, with a tail drooping discouragement, as the man swung along the creek-bed. The furrow of the old sled-trail was plainly visible, but a dozen inches of snow covered the marks of the last runners. In a month no man had come up or down that silent creek. The man held steadily on. He was not much given to thinking, and just then particularly he had nothing to think about save that he would eat lunch at the forks and that at six o'clock he would be in camp with the boys. There was nobody to talk to and, had there been, speech would have been impossible because of the ice-muzzle on his mouth. So he continued monotonously to chew tobacco and to increase the length of his amber beard.

Once in a while the thought reiterated itself that it was very cold and that he had never experienced such cold. As he walked along he rubbed his cheek-bones and nose with the back of his mittened hand. He did this automatically, now and again changing hands. But rub as he would, the instant he stopped his cheekbones went numb, and the following instant the end of his nose went numb. He was sure to frost his cheeks; he knew that, and experienced a pang of regret that he had not devised a nose-strap of the sort Bud wore in cold snaps. Such a strap passed across the cheeks, as well, and saved them. But it didn't matter much, after all. What were frosted cheeks? A bit painful, that was all; they were never serious.

Empty as the man's mind was of thoughts, he was keenly observant, and he noticed the changes in the creek, the curves and bends and timber-jams, and always he sharply noted where he placed his feet. Once, coming around a bend, he shied abruptly, like a startled horse, curved away from the place where he had been walking, and retreated several paces back along the trail. The creek he knew was frozen clear to the bottom—no creek could contain water in that arctic winter—but he knew also that there were springs that bubbled out from the hillsides and ran along under the snow and on top the ice of the creek. He knew that the coldest snaps never froze these springs, and he knew likewise their danger. They were traps. They hid pools of water under the snow that might be three inches deep, or three feet. Sometimes a skin of ice half an inch thick covered them, and in turn was covered by the snow. Sometimes there were alternate layers of water and ice-skin, so that when one broke through he kept on breaking through for a while, sometimes wetting himself to the waist.

That was why he had shied in such panic. He had felt the give under his feet and heard the crackle of a snow-hidden ice-skin. And to get his feet wet in such a temperature meant trouble and danger. At the very least it meant delay, for he would be forced to stop and build a fire, and under its protection to bare his feet while he dried his socks and moccasins. He stood and studied the creek-bed and its banks, and decided that the flow of water came from the right. He reflected awhile, rubbing his nose and cheeks, then skirted to the left, stepping gingerly and testing the footing for each step. Once clear of the danger, he took a fresh chew of tobacco and swung along at his four-mile gait.

In the course of the next two hours he came upon several similar traps. Usually the snow above the hidden pools had a sunken, candied appearance that advertised the danger. Once again, however, he had a close call; and once, suspecting danger, he compelled the dog to go on in front. The dog did not want to go. It hung back until the man shoved it forward, and then it went quickly across the white, unbroken surface. Suddenly it broke through, floundered to one side, and got away to firmer footing. It had wet its forefeet and legs, and almost immediately the water that clung to it turned to ice. It made quick efforts to lick the ice off its legs, then dropped down in the snow and began to bite out the ice that had formed between the toes. This was a matter of instinct. To permit the ice to remain would mean sore feet. It did not know this. It merely obeyed the mysterious prompting that arose from the deep crypts of its being. But the man knew, having achieved a judgment on the subject, and he removed the mitten from his right hand and helped tear out the ice- particles. He did not expose his fingers more than a minute, and was astonished at the swift numbness that smote them. It certainly was cold. He pulled on the mitten hastily, and beat the hand savagely across his chest.

At twelve o'clock the day was at its brightest. Yet the sun was too far south on its winter journey to clear the horizon. The bulge of the earth intervened between it and Henderson Creek, where the man walked under a clear sky at noon and cast no shadow. At half-past twelve, to the minute, he arrived at the forks of the creek. He was pleased at the speed he had made. If he kept it up, he would certainly be with the boys by six. He unbuttoned his jacket and shirt and drew forth his lunch. The action consumed no more than a quarter of a minute, yet in that brief moment the numbness laid hold of the exposed fingers. He did not put the mitten on, but, instead, struck the fingers a dozen sharp smashes against his leg. Then he sat down on a snow-covered log to eat. The sting that followed upon the striking of his fingers against his leg ceased so quickly that he was startled, he had had no chance to take a bite of biscuit. He struck the fingers repeatedly and returned them to the mitten, baring the other hand for the purpose of eating. He tried to take a mouthful, but the ice-muzzle prevented. He had forgotten to build a fire and thaw out. He chuckled at his foolishness, and as he chuckled he noted the numbness creeping into the exposed fingers. Also, he noted that the stinging which had first come to his toes when he sat down was already passing away. He wondered whether the toes were warm or numbed. He moved them inside the moccasins and decided that they were numbed.

He pulled the mitten on hurriedly and stood up. He was a bit frightened. He stamped up and down until the stinging returned into the feet. It certainly was cold, was his thought. That man from Sulphur Creek had spoken the truth when telling how cold it sometimes got in the country. And he had laughed at him at the time! That showed one must not be too sure of things. There was no mistake about it, it was cold. He strode up and down, stamping his feet and threshing his arms, until reassured by the returning warmth. Then he got out matches and proceeded to make a fire. From the undergrowth, where high water of the previous spring had lodged a supply of seasoned twigs, he got his firewood. Working carefully from a small beginning, he soon had a roaring fire, over which he thawed the ice from his face and in the protection of which he ate his biscuits. For the moment the cold of space was outwitted. The dog took satisfaction in the fire, stretching out close enough for warmth and far enough away to escape being singed.

When the man had finished, he filled his pipe and took his comfortable time over a smoke. Then he pulled on his mittens, settled the ear-flaps of his cap firmly about his ears, and took the creek trail up the left fork. The dog was disappointed and yearned back toward the fire. This man did not know cold. Possibly all the generations of his ancestry had been ignorant of cold, of real cold, of cold one hundred and seven degrees below freezing-point. But the dog knew; all its ancestry knew, and it had inherited the knowledge. And it knew that it was not good to walk abroad in such fearful cold. It was the time to lie snug in a hole in the snow and wait for a curtain of cloud to be drawn across the face of outer space whence this cold came. On the other hand, there was keen intimacy between the dog and the man. The one was the toilslave of the other, and the only caresses it had ever received were the caresses of the whip- lash and of harsh and menacing throat-sounds that threatened the whip-lash. So the dog made no effort to communicate its apprehension to the man. It was not concerned in the welfare of the man; it was for its own sake that it yearned back toward the fire. But the man whistled, and spoke to it with the sound of whip-lashes, and the dog swung in at the man's heels and followed after.

The man took a chew of tobacco and proceeded to start a new amber beard. Also, his moist breath quickly powdered with white his moustache, eyebrows, and lashes. There did not seem to be so many springs on the left fork of the Henderson, and for half an hour the man saw no signs of any. And then it happened. At a place where there were no signs, where the soft, unbroken snow seemed to advertise solidity beneath, the man broke through. It was not deep. He wetted himself half-way to the knees before he floundered out to the firm crust.

He was angry, and cursed his luck aloud. He had hoped to get into camp with the boys at six o'clock, and this would delay him an hour, for he would have to build a fire and dry out his foot-gear. This was imperative at that low temperature—he knew that much; and he turned aside to the bank, which he climbed. On top, tangled in the underbrush about the trunks of several small spruce trees, was a high-water deposit of dry firewood—sticks and twigs principally, but also larger portions of seasoned branches and fine, dry, last-year's grasses. He threw down several large pieces on top of the snow. This served for a foundation and prevented the young flame from drowning itself in the snow it otherwise would melt. The flame he got by touching a match to a small shred of birch-bark that he took from his pocket. This burned even more readily than paper. Placing it on the foundation, he fed the young flame with wisps of dry grass and with the tiniest dry twigs.

He worked slowly and carefully, keenly aware of his danger. Gradually, as the flame grew stronger, he increased the size of the twigs with which he fed it. He squatted in the snow, pulling the twigs out from their entanglement in the brush and feeding directly to the flame. He knew there must be no failure. When it is seventy-five below zero, a man must not fail in his first attempt to build a fire—that is, if his feet are wet. If his feet are dry, and he fails, he can run along the trail for half a mile and restore his circulation. But the circulation of wet and freezing feet cannot be restored by running when it is seventy-five below. No matter how fast he runs, the wet feet will freeze the harder.

All this the man knew. The old-timer on Sulphur Creek had told him about it the previous fall, and now he was appreciating the advice. Already all sensation had gone out of his feet. To build the fire he had been forced to remove his mittens, and the fingers had quickly gone numb. His pace of four miles an hour had kept his heart pumping blood to the surface of his body and to all the extremities. But the instant he stopped, the action of the pump eased down. The cold of space smote the unprotected tip of the planet, and he, being on that unprotected tip, received the full force of the blow. The blood of his body recoiled before it. The blood was alive, like the dog, and like the dog it wanted to hide away and cover itself up from the fearful cold. So long as he walked four miles an hour, he pumped that blood, willy-nilly, to the surface; but now it ebbed away and sank down into the recesses of his body. The extremities were the first to feel its absence. His wet feet froze the faster, and his exposed fingers numbed the faster, though they had not yet begun to freeze. Nose and cheeks were already freezing, while the skin of all his body chilled as it lost its blood.

But he was safe. Toes and nose and cheeks would be only touched by the frost, for the fire was beginning to burn with strength. He was feeding it with twigs the size of his finger. In another minute he would be able to feed it with branches the size of his wrist, and then he could remove his wet foot-gear, and, while it dried, he could keep his naked feet warm by the fire, rubbing them at first, of course, with snow. The fire was a success. He was safe. He remembered the advice of the old-timer on Sulphur Creek, and smiled. The old-timer had been very serious in laying down the law that no man must travel alone in the Klondike after fifty below. Well, here he was; he had had the accident; he was alone; and he had saved himself. Those oldtimers were rather womanish, some of them, he thought. All a man had to do was to keep his head, and he was all right. Any man who was a man could travel alone. But it was surprising, the rapidity with which his cheeks and nose were freezing. And he had not thought his fingers could go lifeless in so short a time. Lifeless they were, for he could scarcely make them move together to grip a twig, and they seemed remote from his body and from him. When he touched a twig, he had to look and see whether or not he had hold of it. The wires were pretty well down between him and his finger-ends.

All of which counted for little. There was the fire, snapping and crackling and promising life with every dancing flame. He started to untie his moccasins. They were coated with ice; the thick German socks were like sheaths of iron half-way to the knees; and the mocassin strings were like rods of steel all twisted and knotted as by some conflagration. For a moment he tugged with his numbed fingers, then, realizing the folly of it, he drew his sheath-knife.

But before he could cut the strings, it happened. It was his own fault or, rather, his mistake. He should not have built the fire under the spruce tree. He should have built it in the open. But it had been easier to pull the twigs from the brush and drop them directly on the fire. Now the tree under which he had done this carried a weight of snow on its boughs. No wind had blown for weeks, and each bough was fully freighted. Each time he had pulled a twig he had communicated a slight agitation to the tree—an imperceptible agitation, so far as he was concerned, but an agitation sufficient to bring about the disaster. High up in the tree one bough capsized its load of snow. This fell on the boughs beneath, capsizing them. This process continued, spreading out and involving the whole tree. It grew like an av-alanche, and it descended without warning upon the man and the fire, and the fire was blotted out! Where it had burned was a mantle of fresh and disordered snow.

The man was shocked. It was as though he had just heard his own sentence of death. For a moment he sat and stared at the spot where the fire had been. Then he grew very calm. Perhaps the old-timer on Sulphur Creek was right. If he had only had a trail-mate he would have been in no danger now. The trail-mate could have built the fire. Well, it was up to him to build the fire over again, and this second time there must be no failure. Even if he succeeded, he would most likely lose some toes. His feet must be badly frozen by now, and there would be some time before the second fire was ready.

Such were his thoughts, but he did not sit and think them. He was busy all the time they were passing through his mind, he made a new foundation for a fire, this time in the open; where no treacherous tree could blot it out. Next, he gathered dry grasses and tiny twigs from the high-water flotsam. He could not bring his fingers together to pull them out, but he was able to gather them by the handful. In this way he got many rotten twigs and bits of green moss that were undesirable, but it was the best he could do. He worked methodically, even collecting an armful of the larger branches to be used later when the fire gathered strength. And all the while the dog sat and watched him, a certain yearning wistfulness in its eyes, for it looked upon him as the fire-provider, and the fire was slow in coming.

When all was ready, the man reached in his pocket for a second piece of birch-bark. He knew the bark was there, and, though he could not feel it with his fingers, he could hear its crisp rustling as he fumbled for it. Try as he would, he could not clutch hold of it. And all the time, in his consciousness, was the knowledge that each instant his feet were freezing. This thought tended to put him in a panic, but he fought against it and kept calm. He pulled on his mittens with his teeth, and threshed his arms back and forth, beating his hands with all his might against his sides. He did this sitting down, and he stood up to do it; and all the while the dog sat in the snow, its wolf-brush of a tail curled around warmly over its forefeet, its sharp wolf-ears pricked forward intently as it watched the man. And the man as he beat and threshed with his arms and hands, felt a great surge of envy as he regarded the creature that was warm and secure in its natural covering.

After a time he was aware of the first far-away signals of sensation in his beaten fingers. The faint tingling grew stronger till it evolved into a stinging ache that was excruciating, but which the man hailed with satisfaction. He stripped the mitten from his right hand and fetched forth the birch-bark. The exposed fingers were quickly going numb again. Next he brought out his bunch of sulphur matches. But the tremendous cold had already driven the life out of his fingers. In his effort to separate one match from the others, the whole bunch fell in the snow. He tried to pick it out of the snow, but failed. The dead fingers could neither touch nor clutch. He was very careful. He drove the thought of his freezing feet; and nose, and cheeks, out of his mind, devoting his whole soul to the matches. He watched, using the sense of vision in place of that of touch, and when he saw his fingers on each side the bunch, he closed them—that is, he willed to close them, for the wires were drawn, and the fingers did not obey. He pulled the mitten on the right hand, and beat it fiercely against his knee. Then, with both mittened hands, he scooped the bunch of matches, along with much snow, into his lap. Yet he was no better off.

After some manipulation he managed to get the bunch between the heels of his mittened hands. In this fashion he carried it to his mouth. The ice crackled and snapped when by a violent effort he opened his mouth. He drew the lower jaw in, curled the upper lip out of the way, and scraped the bunch with his upper teeth in order to separate a match. He succeeded in getting one, which he dropped on his lap. He was no better off. He could not pick it up. Then he devised a way. He picked it up in his teeth and scratched it on his leg. Twenty times he scratched before he succeeded in lighting it. As it flamed he held it with his teeth to the birch-bark. But the burning brimstone went up his nostrils and into his lungs, causing him to cough spasmodically. The match fell into the snow and went out.

The old-timer on Sulphur Creek was right, he thought in the moment of controlled despair that ensued: after fifty below, a man should travel with a partner. He beat his hands, but failed in exciting any sensation. Suddenly he bared both hands, removing the mittens with his teeth. He caught the whole bunch between the heels of his hands. His arm-muscles not being frozen enabled him to press the hand-heels tightly against the matches. Then he scratched the bunch along his leg. It flared into flame, seventy sulphur matches at once! There was no wind to blow them out. He kept his head to one side to escape the strangling fumes, and held the blazing bunch to the birch-bark. As he so held it, he became aware of sensation in his hand. His flesh was burning. He could smell it. Deep down below the surface he could feel it. The sensation developed into pain that grew acute. And still he endured it, holding the flame of the matches clumsily to the bark that would not light readily because his own burning hands were in the way, absorbing most of the flame.

At last, when he could endure no more, he jerked his hands apart. The blazing matches fell sizzling into the snow, but the birch-bark was alight. He began laying dry grasses and the tiniest twigs on the flame. He could not pick and choose, for he had to lift the fuel between the heels of his hands. Small pieces of rotten wood and green moss clung to the twigs, and he bit them off as well as he could with his teeth. He cherished the flame carefully and awkwardly. It meant life, and it must not perish. The withdrawal of blood from the surface of his body now made him begin to shiver, and he grew more awkward. A large piece of green moss fell squarely on the little fire. He tried to poke it out with his fingers, but his shivering frame made him poke too far, and he disrupted the nucleus of the little fire, the burning grasses and tiny twigs separating and scattering. He tried to poke them together again, but in spite of the tenseness of the effort, his shivering got away with him, and the twigs were hopelessly scattered. Each twig gushed a puff of smoke and went out. The fire-provider had failed. As he looked apathetically about him, his eyes chanced on the dog, sitting across the ruins of the fire from him, in the snow, making restless, hunching movements, slightly lifting one forefoot and then the other, shifting its weight back and forth on them with wistful eagerness.

The sight of the dog put a wild idea into his head. He remembered the tale of the man, caught in a blizzard, who killed a steer and crawled inside the carcass, and so was saved. He would kill the dog and bury his hands in the warm body until the numbness went out of them. Then he could build another fire. He spoke to the dog, calling it to him; but in his voice was a strange note of fear that frightened the animal, who had never known the man to speak in such way before. Something was the matter, and its suspicious nature sensed danger,—it knew not what danger but somewhere, somehow, in its brain arose an apprehension of the man. It flattened its ears down at the sound of the man's voice, and its restless, hunching movements and the liftings and shiftings of its forefeet became more pronounced but it would not come to the man. He got on his hands and knees and crawled toward the dog. This unusual posture again excited suspicion, and the animal sidled mincingly away.

The man sat up in the snow for a moment and struggled for calmness. Then he pulled on his mittens, by means of his teeth, and got upon his feet. He glanced down at first in order to assure himself that he was really standing up, for the absence of sensation in his feet left him unrelated to the earth. His erect position in itself started to drive the webs of suspicion from the dog's mind; and when he spoke peremptorily, with the sound of whip-lashes in his voice, the dog rendered its customary allegiance and came to him. As it came within reaching distance, the man lost his control. His arms flashed out to the dog, and he experienced genuine surprise when he discovered that his hands could not clutch, that there was neither bend nor feeling in the lingers. He had forgotten for the moment that they were frozen and that they were freezing more and more. All this happened quickly, and before the animal could get away, he encircled its body with his arms. He sat down in the snow, and in this fashion held the dog, while it snarled and whined and struggled.

But it was all he could do, hold its body encircled in his arms and sit there. He realized that he could not kill the dog. There was no way to do it. With his helpless hands he could neither draw nor hold his sheathknife nor throttle the animal. He released it, and it plunged wildly away, with tail between its legs, and still snarling. It halted forty feet away and surveyed him curiously, with ears sharply pricked forward. The man looked down at his hands in order to locate them, and found them hanging on the ends of his arms. It struck him as curious that one should have to use his eyes in order to find out where his hands were. He began threshing his arms back and forth, beating the mittened hands against his sides. He did this for five minutes, violently, and his heart pumped enough blood up to the surface to put a stop to his shivering. But no sensation was aroused in the hands. He had an impression that they hung like weights on the ends of his arms, but when he tried to run the impression down, he could not find it.

A certain fear of death, dull and oppressive, came to him. This fear quickly became poignant as he realized that it was no longer a mere matter of freezing his fingers and toes, or of losing his hands and feet, but that it was a matter of life and death with the chances against him. This threw him into a panic, and he turned and ran up the creek-bed along the old, dim trail. The dog joined in behind and kept up with him. He ran blindly, without intention, in fear such as he had never known in his life. Slowly, as he ploughed and floundered through the snow, he began to see things again—the banks of the creek, the old timber-jams, the leafless aspens, and the sky. The running made him feel better. He did not shiver. Maybe, if he ran on, his feet would thaw out; and, anyway, if he ran far enough, he would reach camp and the boys. Without doubt he would lose some fingers and toes and some of his face; but the boys would take care of him, and save the rest of him when he got there. And at the same time there was another thought in his mind that said he would never get to the camp and the boys; that it was too many miles away, that the freezing had too great a start on him, and that he would soon be stiff and dead. This thought he kept in the background and refused to consider. Sometimes it pushed itself forward and demanded to be heard, but he thrust it back and strove to think of other things.

It struck him as curious that he could run at all on feet so frozen that he could not feel them when they struck the earth and took the weight of his body. He seemed to himself to skim along above the surface and to have no connection with the earth. Somewhere he had once seen a winged Mercury, and he wondered if Mercury felt as he felt when skimming over the earth.

His theory of running until he reached camp and the boys had one flaw in it: he lacked the endurance. Several times he stumbled, and finally he tottered, crumpled up, and fell. When he tried to rise, he failed. He must sit and rest, he decided, and next time he would merely walk and keep on going. As he sat and regained his breath, he noted that he was feeling quite warm and comfortable. He was not shivering, and it even seemed that a warm glow had come to his chest and trunk. And yet, when he touched his nose or cheeks, there was no sensation. Running would not thaw them out. Nor would it thaw out his hands and feet. Then the thought came to him that the frozen portions of his body must be extending. He tried to keep this thought down, to forget it, to think of something else; he was aware of the panicky feeling that it caused, and he was afraid of the panic. But the thought asserted itself, and persisted, until it produced a vision of his body totally frozen. This was too much, and he made another wild run along the trail. Once he slowed down to a walk, but the thought of the freezing extending itself made him run again.

And all the time the dog ran with him, at his heels. When he fell down a second time, it curled its tail over its forefeet and sat in front of him facing him curiously eager and intent. The warmth and security of the animal angered him, and he cursed it till it flattened down its ears appeasingly. This time the shivering came more quickly upon the man. He was losing in his battle with the frost. It was creeping into his body from all sides. The thought of it drove him on, but he ran no more than a hundred feet, when he staggered and pitched headlong. It was his last panic. When he had recovered his breath and control, he sat up and entertained in his mind the conception of meeting death with dignity. However, the conception did not come to him in such terms. His idea of it was that he had been making a fool of himself, running around like a chicken with its head cut off—such was the simile that occurred to him. Well, he was bound to freeze anyway, and he might as well take it decently. With this new-found peace of mind came the first glimmerings of drowsiness. A good idea, he thought, to sleep off to death. It was like taking an anaesthetic. Freezing was not so bad as people thought. There were lots worse ways to die.

He pictured the boys finding his body next day. Suddenly he found himself with them, coming along the trail and looking for himself. And, still with them, he came around a turn in the trail and found himself lying in the snow. He did not belong with himself any more, for even then he was out of himself, standing with the boys and looking at himself in the snow. It certainly was cold, was his thought. When he got back to the States he could tell the folks what real cold was. He drifted on from this to a vision of the old-timer on Sulphur Creek. He could see him quite clearly, warm and comfortable, and smoking a pipe.

"You were right, old hoss; you were right," the man mumbled to the old-timer of Sulphur Creek.

Then the man drowsed off into what seemed to him the most comfortable and satisfying sleep he had ever known. The dog sat facing him and waiting. The brief day drew to a close in a long, slow twilight. There were no signs of a fire to be made, and, besides, never in the dog's experience had it known a man to sit like that in the snow and make no fire. As the twilight drew on, its eager yearning for the fire mastered it, and with a great lifting and shifting of forefeet, it whined softly, then flattened its ears down in anticipation of being chidden by the man. But the man remained silent. Later, the dog whined loudly. And still later it crept close to the man and caught the scent of death. This made the animal bristle and back away. A little longer it delayed, howling under the stars that leaped and danced and shone brightly in the cold sky. Then it turned and trotted up the trail in the direction of the camp it knew, where were the other food-providers and fire-providers.

3.5.2 Reading and Review Questions

1. Pay close attention to the imagery London uses to describe his Yukon setting. Do human beings belong here?

2. In venturing out into the cold with only a dog, what is the man struggling against?

3. As London's story progresses, he continually invites the reader to contrast the unnamed man with the "proper wolf-dog" that is his companion. What do these comparisons show us about the man, the dog, and their relationships to their environment and each other?

3.6 CHAPTER THREE KEY TERMS

- Charles Darwin
- Émile Zola
- Frank Norris
- Friedrich Nietzsche
- Jack London
- Karl Marx
- Naturalism
- Plot of Decline
- Spanish-American War
- Stephen Crane

4 Turn of the Twentieth Century and the Growth of Modernism (1893 - 1914)

Robert R. Bleil, Jordan Cofer, and Doug Davis

4.1 LEARNING OUTCOMES

After completing this chapter, you should be able to:

- Analyze the ways in which the Industrial Revolution, western expansion, and significant immigration changed the nature of American literature.

- Analyze the ways in which African-American literature develops in this period.

- Explore the ways in which the two decades prior to World War I defined American masculinity for much of the twentieth century.

- Critique the development of Modernist poetry during this period.

4.2 INTRODUCTION

In the twenty-one years between the **World's Columbian Exposition** (also known as the **Chicago World's Fair**) in 1893 and the outbreak of World War I in 1914, the economic, political, and social landscape changed forever. Unprecedented immigration irrevocably changed both the American landscape and American politics, and the colonial powers of nineteenth-century Europe began to lose their grip on their possessions and territories. American literature of the period reflected these changes.

In the United States, the northern and western migration that followed **Reconstruction** (the period between 1865 and 1877 when the Federal government set the conditions by which the states of the former Confederacy would be readmitted to full participation in the national government) caused such rapid growth in Northern cities that the municipal governments were strained to the breaking point as they rushed to deliver services to millions of residents in thousands of languages. In the West, waves of migration were rapidly filling in the plains and prairies; this population boom set up a clash of cultures that continues to have repercussions in contemporary politics. In less than twenty years, the United States marked two population milestones: the population of New York City exceeded five million persons for the first time and, in 1915, the total population of the United States topped one hundred million.

Many immigrants to the United States in this period were fleeing from the collapse of the ancient European monarchies and empires. When Queen Victoria of the United Kingdom died on January 22, 1901, more than half of the persons in the world owed her allegiance; by the outbreak of World War I, a new wave of self-governance had swept through Europe. The political consequences of this destabilization continue to be felt throughout the world today.

These two decades were also remarkable for American literature. F. Scott Fitzgerald, William Faulkner, and Ernest Hemingway were born within three years of each other, and they would collectively reshape the American literary landscape in the twentieth century. Literary contributions were not, however, restricted to white males. Although Mark Twain continued to hold court as the most famous author in the country, Charlotte Perkins Gillman, Kate Chopin, Edith Wharton, and Willa Cather were also making literary and social headlines.

Our readings in this chapter may seem at first to be randomly selected. Not one of the authors mentioned in the previous paragraph appears here; in the case of Fitzgerald, Faulkner, and Hemingway, they had not yet made their mark on literary history. Gillman, Chopin, Wharton, and Cather, although they were writing steadily during this period, had not yet been given appropriate recognition for their literary achievements. Instead, the selections in this chapter speak to two particular aspects of turn-of-the-century American literature: the growth of African-American literary culture and a mythological fascination with the West.

The selections by Booker T. Washington (1901) and W. E. B. Du Bois (1903) both continue the tradition of African-American autobiography begun in the eighteenth and nineteenth centuries by Olaudah Equiano and Frederick Douglass, and forge new ground as political and social manifestoes. In these works both authors advocated passionately, in the wake of the 1896 U.S. Supreme Court decision Plessey v. Ferguson, that the schools and municipal services provided to African-Americans were, in fact, not equal to those provided to the rest of the population. These works are not just autobiography, however: *The Souls of Black Folk* is often considered one of the earliest works in the field of sociology.

The second selection in this chapter, Zane Grey's *Riders of the Purple Sage* (1912), defined a literary genre and an American ideal. Although Owen Wister's *The Virginian* (1902) is often considered the first Western in American fiction, the plot of *The Virginian* is a fairly typical romance that is set in the West. In *Riders of the Purple Sage*, Grey offers readers a new type of character: a rough, independent, introspective cowboy with a pragmatically American, and personal, code of conduct.

The last selection in this chapter, Booker T. Washington's *Up From Slavery* (1895), demonstrates the development of African-American narrative and autobiography. Unlike Frederick Douglass's *Narrative of the Life of Frederick Douglass, an American Slave*, Washington struck a more conciliatory tone aimed at lifting African Americans out of poverty in exchange for lesser political and individual autonomy. In the following decades, the debates between Du Bois and Washington formed the backdrop for the struggle over African-American art and literature during the Harlem Renaissance.

The dawn of the twentieth century witnessed the first significant crisis of American identity since the end of the Civil War, and this time the crisis played out on the world stage. In the decades that followed World War I, the United States would undergo even more dramatic changes, and the most significant literary changes were yet to come.

4.3 BOOKER T. WASHINGTON

(1856 - 1915)

Born a slave in Virginia, Booker T. Washington grew up to become the most influential black author and activist of the late nineteenth and early twentieth centuries. As discussed in his autobiography, *Up from Slavery* (1901), Washington spent his early childhood working as a slave on a plantation. After **Emancipation**, and while still a boy, he first worked with his stepfather in the coalmines and salt foundries of West Virginia and then as a houseboy. At the age of fourteen, Washington left home to attend the Hampton Normal and Agricultural Institute in Virginia, a segregated school for minorities, where he worked as a janitor while learning to be an educator. Washington

Image 4.1 | Booker T. Washington, 1905
Photographer | Harris & Ewing
Source | Wikimedia Commons
License | Public Domain

distinguished himself at the Hampton Institute, ultimately returning after graduation at the invitation of the school's principal to teach there. In 1881, at the age of twenty-five, Washington was hired to build and lead the **Tuskeegee Normal and Industrial Institute** (now Tuskeegee University), a new school in Alabama whose mission was to train African Americans for agricultural and industrial labor. The school was so poorly funded that Washington and his students famously had to make their own bricks and construct their own school buildings. Through Washington's inspiring leadership and tireless fundraising, Tuskeegee grew and prospered. In 1895, Washington gave a five-minute speech at the Atlanta Cotton State and International Exposition that propelled him to the forefront of American politics and culture. American presidents called on him for advice about race relations and white business leaders sought him out to coordinate charitable giving to black institutions, earning Washington the moniker "the Moses of his race" in newspapers of the era.

Washington wrote almost twenty books in his lifetime, including several autobiographies, a biography of Frederick Douglass, and inspirational self-improvement texts such as *Sowing and Reaping* (1900) and *Character Building* (1902). Two chapters from Washington's biography, *Up From Slavery*, are included here. In the first chapter, Washington recounts his childhood up until the time of Emancipation. In the fourteenth chapter, he reprints his Exposition Address and discusses its startlingly positive reception by a largely white audience that up to that point was fearful of America's black population. Unlike contemporaries such as W. E. B. Du Bois, Washington did not criticize the Supreme Court's 1896 ruling in *Plessy v. Ferguson* that the nation's different races should be treated as "separate but equal." Instead, he sought to work within the law's segregationist restrictions. Washington pragmatically wrote his biography to showcase the industry and integrity of all African Americans rather than to demonize his former owners or celebrate his personal accomplishments. As you read Washington's two chapters, consider how Washington uses the form of the slave narrative to give examples not only of the horrors of **slavery** but also of harmonious and honorable race relations.

4.3.1 Selections from *Up From Slavery*

CHAPTER I
A SLAVE AMOUNG SLAVES

I was born a slave on a plantation in Franklin County, Virginia. I am not quite sure of the exact place or exact date of my birth, but at any rate I suspect I must have been born somewhere and at some time. As nearly as I have been able to learn, I was born near a cross-roads post-office called Hale's Ford, and the year was 1858 or 1859. I do not know the month or the day. The earliest impressions I can now recall are of the plantation and the slave quarters—the latter being the part of the plantation where the slaves had their cabins.

My life had its beginning in the midst of the most miserable, desolate, and discouraging surroundings. This was so, however, not because my owners were especially cruel, for they were not, as compared with many others. I was born in a typical log cabin, about fourteen by sixteen feet square. In this cabin I lived with my mother and a brother and sister till after the Civil War, when we were all declared free.

Of my ancestry I know almost nothing. In the slave quarters, and even later, I heard whispered conversations among the coloured people of the tortures which the slaves, including, no doubt, my ancestors on my mother's side, suffered in the middle passage of the slave ship while being conveyed from Africa to America. I have been unsuccessful in securing any information that would throw any accurate light upon the history of my family beyond my mother. She, I remember, had a half-brother and a half-sister. In the days of slavery not very much attention was given to family history and family records—that is, black family records. My mother, I suppose, attracted the attention of a purchaser who was afterward my owner and hers. Her addition to the slave family attracted about as much attention as the purchase of a new horse or cow. Of my father I know even less than of my mother. I do not even know his name. I have heard reports to the effect that he was a white man who lived on one of the near-by plantations. Whoever he was, I never heard of his taking the least interest in me or providing in any way for my rearing. But I do notfind especial fault with him. He was simply another unfortunate victim of the institution which the Nation unhappily had engrafted upon it at that time.

The cabin was not only our living-place, but was also used as the kitchen for the plantation. My mother was the plantation cook. The cabin was without glass windows; it had only openings in the side which let in the light, and also the cold, chilly air of winter. There was a door to the cabin—that is, something that was called a door—but the uncertain hinges by which it was hung, and the large cracks in it, to say nothing of the fact that it was too small, made the room a very uncomfortable one. In addition to these openings there was, in the lower right-hand corner of the room, the "cat-hole,"—a contrivance which almost every mansion or cabin in Virginia possessed during the ante-bellum period. The "cat-hole" was a square opening, about seven by eight inches, provided for the purpose of letting the cat pass in and out of the house at will during the night. In the case of our particular cabin I could never understand the necessity for this convenience, since there were at least a half-dozen other places in the cabin that would have accommodated the cats. There was no wooden floor in our cabin, the naked earth being used as a floor. In the centre of the earthen floor there was a large, deep opening covered with boards, which was used as a place in which to store sweet potatoes during the winter. An impression of this potato-hole is very distinctly engraved upon my memory, because I recall that during the process of putting the potatoes in or taking them out I would often come into possession of one or two, which I roasted and thoroughly enjoyed. There was no cooking-stove on our plantation, and all the cooking for the whites and slaves my mother had to do over an open fireplace, mostly in pots and "skillets." While the poorly built cabin caused us to suffer with cold in the winter, the heat from the open fire-place in summer was equally trying.

The early years of my life, which were spent in the little cabin, were not very different from those of thousands of other slaves. My mother, of course, had little time in which to give attention to the training of her children during the day. She snatched a few moments for our care in the early morning before her work began, and at night after the day's work was done. One of my earliest recollections is that of my mother cooking a chicken late at night, and awakening her children for the purpose of feeding them. How or where she got it I do not know. I presume, however, it was procured from our owner's farm. Some people may call this theft. If such a thing were to happen now, I should condemn it as theft myself. But taking place at the time it did, and for the reason that it did, no one could ever make me believe that my mother was guilty of thieving. She was simply a victim of the system of slavery. I cannot remember having slept in a bed until after our family was declared free by the Emancipation Proclamation. Three children—John, my older brother, Amanda, my sister, and myself—had a pallet on the dirt floor, or, to be more correct, we slept in and on a bundle of filthy rags laid upon the dirt floor.

I was asked not long ago to tell something about the sports and pastimes that I engaged in during my youth. Until that question was asked it had never occurred to me that there was no period of my life that was devoted to play. From the time that I can remember anything, almost every day of my life has been occupied in some kind of labour; though I think I would now be a more useful man if I had had time for sports. During the period that I spent in slavery I was not large enough to be of much service, still I was occupied most of the time in cleaning the yards, carrying water to the men in the fields, or going to the mill, to which I used to take the corn, once a week, to be ground. The mill was about three miles from the plantation. This work I always dreaded. The heavy bag of corn would be thrown across the back of the horse, and the corn divided about evenly on each side; but in some way, almost without exception, on these trips, the corn would so shift as to become unbalanced and would fall off the horse, and often I would fall with it. As I was not strong enough to reload the corn upon the horse, I would have to wait, sometimes for many hours, till a chance passer-by came along who would help me out of my trouble. The hours while waiting for some one were usually spent in crying. The time consumed in this way made me late in reaching the mill, and by the time I got my corn ground and reached home it would be far into the night. The road was a lonely one, and often led through dense forests. I was always frightened. The woods were said to be full of soldiers who had deserted from the army, and I had been told that the first thing a deserter did to a Negro boy when he found him alone was to cut off his ears. Besides, when I was late in getting home I knew I would always get a severe scolding or a flogging.

I had no schooling whatever while I was a slave, though I remember on several occasions I went as far as the schoolhouse door with one of my young mistresses to carry her books. The picture of several dozen boys and girls in a schoolroom engaged in study made a deep impression upon me, and I had the feeling that to get into a schoolhouse and study in this way would be about the same as getting into paradise.

So far as I can now recall, the first knowledge that I got of the fact that we were slaves, and that freedom of the slaves was being discussed, was early one morning before day, when I was awakened by my mother kneeling over her children and fervently praying that Lincoln and his armies might be successful, and that one day she and her children might be free. In this connection I have never been able to understand how the slaves throughout the South, completely ignorant as were the masses so far as books or newspapers were concerned, were able to keep themselves so accurately and completely informed about the great National questions that were agitating the country. From the time that Garrison, Lovejoy, and others began to agitate for freedom, the slaves throughout the South kept in close touch with the progress of the movement. Though I was a mere child during the preparation for the Civil War and during the war itself, I now recall the many late-at-nightwhispered discussions that I heard my mother and the other slaves on the plantation indulge in. These discussions showed that they understood the situation, and that they kept themselves informed of events by what was termed the "grape-vine" telegraph.

During the campaign when Lincoln was first a candidate for the Presidency, the slaves on our far-off plantation, miles from any railroad or large city or daily newspaper, knew what the issues involved were. When war was begun between the North and the South, every slave on our plantation felt and knew that, though other issues were discussed, the primal one was that of slavery. Even the most ignorant members of my race on the remote plantations felt in their hearts, with a certainty that admitted of no doubt, that the freedom of the slaves would be the one great result of the war, if the Northern armies conquered. Every success of the Federal armies and every defeat of the Confederate forces was watched with the keenest and most intense interest. Often the slaves got knowledge of the results of great battles before the white people received it. This news was usually gotten from the coloured man who was sent to the post-office for the mail. In our case the post-office was about three miles from the plantation and the mail came once or twice a week. The man who was sent to the office would linger about the place long enough to get the drift of the conversation from the group of white people who naturally congregated there, after receiving their mail, to discuss the latest news. The mail-carrier on his way back to our master's house would as naturally retail the news that he had secured among the slaves, and in this way they often heard of important events before the white people at the "big house," as the master's house was called.

I cannot remember a single instance during my childhood or early boyhood when our entire family sat down to the table together, and God's blessing was asked, and the family ate a meal in a civilized manner. On the plantation in Virginia, and even later, meals were gotten by the children very much as dumb animals get theirs. It was a piece of bread here and a scrap of meat there. It was a cup of milk at one time and some potatoes at another. Sometimes a portion of our family would eat out of the skillet or pot, while some one else would eat from a tin plate held on the knees, and often using nothing but the hands with which to hold the food. When I had grown to sufficient size, I was required to go to the "big house" at meal-times to fan the flies from the table by means of a large set of paper fans operated by a pully. Naturally much of the conversation of the white people turned upon the subject of freedom and the war, and I absorbed a good deal of it. I remember that at one time I saw two of my young mistresses and some lady visitors eating ginger-cakes, in the yard. At that time those cakes seemed to me to be absolutely the most tempting and desirable things that I had ever seen; and I then and there resolved that, if I ever got free, the height of my ambition would be reached if I could get to the point where I could secure and eat ginger-cakes in the way that I saw those ladies doing.

Of course as the war was prolonged the white people, in many cases, often found it difficult to secure food for themselves. I think the slaves felt the deprivation less than the whites, because the usual diet for the slaves was corn bread and pork, and these could be raised on the plantation; but coffee, tea, sugar, and other articles which the whites had been accustomed to use could not be raised on the plantation, and the conditions brought about by the war frequently made it impossible to secure these things. The whites were often in great straits. Parched corn was used for coffee, and a kind of black molasses was used instead of sugar. Many times nothing was used to sweeten the so-called tea and coffee.

The first pair of shoes that I recall wearing were wooden ones. They had rough leather on the top, but the bottoms, which were about an inch thick, were of wood. When I walked they made a fearful noise, and besides this they were very inconvenient since there was no yielding to the natural pressure of the foot. In wearing them one presented an exceedingly awkward appearance. The most trying ordeal that I was forced to endure as a slave boy, however, was the wearing of a flax shirt. In the portion of Virginia where I lived it was common to use flax as part of the clothing for the slaves. That part of the flax from which our clothing was made was largely the refuse, which of course was the cheapest and roughest part. I can scarcely imagine any torture, except, perhaps, the pulling of a tooth, that is equal to that caused by putting on a new flax shirt for the first time. It is almost equal to the feeling that one would experience if he had a dozen or more chestnut burrs, or a hundred small pin-points, in contact with his flesh. Even to this day I can recall accurately the tortures that I underwent when putting on one of these garments. The fact that my flesh was soft and tender added to the pain. But I had no choice. I had to wear the flax shirt or none; and had it been left to me to choose, I should have chosen to wear no covering. In connection with the flax shirt, my brother John, who is several years older than I am, performed one of the most generous acts that I ever heard of one slave relative doing for another. On several occasions when I was being forced to wear a new flax shirt, he generously agreed to put it on in my stead and wear it for several days, till it was "broken in." Until I had grown to be quite a youth this single garment was all that I wore.

One may get the idea, from what I have said, that there was bitter feeling toward the white people on the part of my race, because of the fact that most of the white population was away fighting in a war which would result in keeping the Negro in slavery if the South was successful. In the case of the slaves on our place this was not true, and it was not true of any large portion of the slave population in the South where the Negro was treated with anything like decency. During the Civil War one of my young masters was killed, and two were severely wounded. I recall the feeling of sorrow which existed among the slaves when they heard of the death of "Mars' Billy." It was no sham sorrow, but real. Some of the slaves had nursed "Mars' Billy"; others had played with him when he was a child. "Mars' Billy" had begged for mercy in the case of others when the overseer or master was thrashing them. The sorrow in the slave quarter was only second to that in the "big house." When the two young masters were brought home wounded the sympathy of the slaves was shown in many ways. They were just as anxious to assist in the nursing as the family relatives of the wounded. Some of the slaves would even beg for the privilege of sitting up at night to nurse their wounded masters. This tenderness and sympathy on the part of those held in bondage was a result of their kindly and generous nature. In order to defend and protect the women and children who were left on the plantations when the white males went to war, the slaves would have laid down their lives. The slave who was selected to sleep in the "big house" during the absence of the males was considered to have the place of honour. Any one attempting to harm "young Mistress" or "old Mistress" during the night would have had to cross the dead body of the slave to do so. I do not know how many have noticed it, but I think that it will be found to be true that there are few instances, either in slavery or freedom, in which a member of my race has been known to betray a specific trust.

As a rule, not only did the members of my race entertain no feelings of bitterness against the whites before and during the war, but there are many instances of Negroes tenderly caring for their former masters and mistresses who for some reason have become poor and dependent since the war. I know of instances where the former masters of slaves have for years been supplied with money by their former slaves to keep them from suffering. I have known of still other cases in which the former slaves have assisted in the education of the descendants of their former owners. I know of a case on a large plantation in the South in which a young white man, the son of the former owner of the estate, has become so reduced in purse and self-control by reason of drink that he is a pitiable creature; and yet, notwithstanding the poverty of the coloured people themselves on this plantation, they have for years supplied this young white man with the necessities of life. One sends him a little coffee or sugar, another a little meat, and so on. Nothing that the coloured people possess is too good for the son of "old Mars' Tom," who will perhaps never be permitted to suffer while any remain on the place who knew directly or indirectly of "old Mars' Tom."

I have said that there are few instances of a member of my race betraying a specific trust. One of the best illustrations of this which I know of is in the case of an ex-slave from Virginia whom I met not long ago in a little town in the state of Ohio. I found that this man had made a contract with his master, two or three years previous to the Emancipation Proclamation, to the effect that the slave was to be permitted to buy himself, by paying so much per year for his body; and while he was paying for himself, he was to be permitted to labour where and for whom he pleased. Finding that he could secure better wages in Ohio, he went there. When freedom came, he was still in debt to his master some three hundred dollars. Notwithstanding that the Emancipation Proclamation freed him from any obligation to his master, this black man walked the greater portion of the distance back to where his old master lived in Virginia, and placed the last dollar, with interest, in his hands. In talking to me about this, the man told me that he knew that he did not have to pay the debt, but that he had given his word to his master, and his word he had never broken. He felt that he could not enjoy his freedom till he had fulfilled his promise.

From some things that I have said one may get the idea that some of the slaves did not want freedom. This is not true. I have never seen one who did not want to be free, or one who would return to slavery.

I pity from the bottom of my heart any nation or body of people that is so unfortunate as to get entangled in the net of slavery. I have long since ceased to cherish any spirit of bitterness against the Southern white people on account of the enslavement of my race. No one section of our country was wholly responsible for its introduction, and, besides, it was recognized and protected for years by the General Government. Having once got its tentacles fastened on to the economic and social life of the Republic, it was no easy matter for the country to relieve itself of the institution. Then, when we rid ourselves of prejudice, or racial feeling, and look facts in the face, we must acknowledge that, notwithstanding the cruelty and moral wrong of slavery, the ten million Negroes inhabiting this country, who themselves or whose ancestors went through the school of American slavery, are in a stronger and more hopeful condition, materially, intellectually, morally, and religiously, than is true of an equal number of black people in any other portion of the globe. This is so to such an extent that Negroes in this country, who themselves or whose forefathers went through the school of slavery, are constantly returning to Africa as missionaries to enlighten those who remained in the fatherland. This I say, not to justify slavery—on the other hand, I condemn it as an institution, as we all know that in America it was established for selfish and financial reasons, and not from a missionary motive—but to call attention to a fact, and to show how Providence so often uses men and institutions to accomplish a purpose. When persons ask me in these days how, in the midst of what sometimes seem hopelessly discouraging conditions, I can have such faith in the future of my race in this country, I remind them of the wilderness through which and out of which, a good Providence has already led us.

Ever since I have been old enough to think for myself, I have entertained the idea that, notwithstanding the cruel wrongs inflicted upon us, the black man got nearly as much out of slavery as the white man did. The hurtful influences of the institution were not by any means confined to the Negro. This was fully illustrated by the life upon our own plantation. The whole machinery of slavery was so constructed as to cause labour, as a rule, to be looked upon as a badge of degradation, of inferiority. Hence labour was something that both races on the slave plantation sought to escape. The slave system on our place, in a large measure, took the spirit of self-reliance and self-help out of the white people. My old master had many boys and girls, but not one, so far as I know, ever mastered a single trade or special line of productive industry. The girls were not taught to cook, sew, or to take care of the house. All of this was left to the slaves. The slaves, of course, had little personal interest in the life of the plantation, and their ignorance prevented them from learning how to do things in the most improved and thorough manner. As a result of the system, fences were out of repair, gates were hanging half off the hinges, doors creaked, window-panes were out, plastering had fallen but was not replaced, weeds grew in the yard. As a rule, there was food for whites and blacks, but inside the house, and on the dining room table, there was wanting that delicacy and refinement of touch and finish which can make a home the most convenient, comfortable, and attractive place in the world. Withal there was a waste of food and other materials which was sad. When freedom came, the slaves were almost as well fitted to begin life anew as the master, except in the matter of book-learning and ownership of property. The slave owner and his sons had mastered no special industry. They unconsciously had imbibed the feeling that manual labour was not the proper thing for them. On the other hand, the slaves, in many cases, had mastered some handicraft, and none were ashamed, and few unwilling, to labour.

Finally the war closed, and the day of freedom came. It was a momentous and eventful day to all upon our plantation. We had been expecting it. Freedom was in the air, and had been for months. Deserting soldiers returning to their homes were to be seen every day. Others who had been discharged, or whose regiments had been paroled, were constantly passing near our place. The "grape-vine telegraph" was kept busy night and day. The news and mutterings of great events were swiftly carried from one plantation to another. In the fear of "Yankee" invasions, the silverware and other valuables were taken from the "big house," buried in the woods, and guarded by trusted slaves. Woe be to any one who would have attempted to disturb the buried treasure. The slaves would give the Yankee soldiers food, drink, clothing—anything but that which had been specifically intrusted to their care and honour. As the great day drew nearer, there was more singing in the slave quarters than usual. It was bolder, had more ring, and lasted later into the night. Most of the verses of the plantation songs had some reference to freedom. True, they had sung those same verses before, but they had been careful to explain that the "freedom" in these songs referred to the next world, and had no connection with life in this world. Now they gradually threw off the mask, and were not afraid to let it be known that the "freedom" in their songs meant freedom of the body in this world. The night before the eventful day, word was sent to the slave quarters to the effect that something unusual was going to take place at the "big house" the next morning. There was little, if any, sleep that night. All was excitement and expectancy. Early the next morning word was sent to all the slaves, old and young, to gather at the house. In company with my mother, brother, and sister, and a large number of other slaves, I went to the master's house. All of our master's family were either standing or seated on the veranda of the house, where they could see what was to take place and hear what was said. There was a feeling of deep interest, or perhaps sadness, on their faces, but not bitterness. As I now recall the impression they made upon me, they did not at the moment seem to be sad because of the loss of property, but rather because of parting with those whom they had reared and who were in many ways very close to them. The most distinct thing that I now recall in connection with the scene was that some man who seemed to be a stranger (a United States officer, I presume) made a little speech and then read a rather long paper—the Emancipation Proclamation, I think. After the reading we were told that we were all free, and could go when and where we pleased. My mother, who was standing by my side, leaned over and kissed her children, while tears of joy ran down her cheeks. She explained to us what it all meant, that this was the day for which she had been so long praying, but fearing that she would never live to see.

For some minutes there was great rejoicing, and thanksgiving, and wild scenes of ecstasy. But there was no feeling of bitterness. In fact, there was pity among the slaves for our former owners. The wild rejoicing on the part of the emancipated coloured people lasted but for a brief period, for I noticed that by the time they returned to their cabins there was a change in their feelings. The great responsibility of being free, of having charge of themselves, of having to think and plan for themselves and their children, seemed to take possession of them. It was very much like suddenly turning a youth of ten or twelve years out into the world to provide for himself. In a few hours the great questions with which the Anglo-Saxon race had been grappling for centuries had been thrown upon these people to be solved. These were the questions of a home, a living, the rearing of children, education, citizenship, and the establishment and support of churches. Was it any wonder that within a few hours the wild rejoicing ceased and a feeling of deep gloom seemed to pervade the slave quarters? To some it seemed that, now that they were in actual possession of it, freedom was a more serious thing than they had expected to find it. Some of the slaves were seventy or eighty years old; their best days were gone. They had no strength with which to earn a living in a strange place and among strange people, even if they had been sure where to find a new place of abode. To this class the problem seemed especially hard. Besides, deep down in their hearts there was a strange and peculiar attachment to "old Marster" and "old Missus," and to their children, which they found it hard to think of breaking off. With these they had spent in some cases nearly a half-century, and it was no light thing to think of parting. Gradually, one by one, stealthily at first, the older slaves began to wander from the slave quarters back to the "big house" to have a whispered conversation with their former owners as to the future.

CHAPTER 14
THE ATLANTA EXPOSITION ADDRESS

The Atlanta Exposition, at which I had been asked to make an address as a representative of the Negro race, as stated in the last chapter, was opened with a short address from Governor Bullock. After other interesting exercises, including an invocation from Bishop Nelson, of Georgia, a dedicatory ode by Albert Howell, Jr., and addresses by the President of the Exposition and Mrs. Joseph Thompson, the President of the Woman's Board, Governor Bullock introduced me with the words, "We have with us to-day a representative of Negro enterprise and Negro civilization."

When I arose to speak, there was considerable cheering, especially from the coloured people. As I remember it now, the thing that was uppermost in my mind was the desire to say something that would cement the friendship of the races and bring about hearty cooperation between them. So far as my outward surroundings were concerned, the onlything that I recall distinctly now is that when I got up, I saw thousands of eyes looking intently into my face. The following is the address which I delivered:—

Mr. President and Gentlemen of the Board of Directors and Citizens.

One-third of the population of the South is of the Negro race. No enterprise seeking the material, civil, or moral welfare of this section can disregard this element of our population and reach the highest success. I but convey to you, Mr. President and Directors, the sentiment of the masses of my race when I say that in no way have the value and manhood of the American Negro been more fittingly and generously recognized than by the managers of this magnificent Exposition at every stage of its progress. It is a recognition that will do more to cement the friendship of the two races than any occurrence since the dawn of our freedom.

Not only this, but the opportunity here afforded will awaken among us a new era of industrial progress. Ignorant and inexperienced, it is not strange that in the first years of our new life we began at the top instead of at the bottom; that a seat in Congress or the state legislature was more sought than real estate or industrial skill; that the political convention of stump speaking had more attraction than starting a dairy farm or truck garden.

A ship lost at sea for many days suddenly sighted a friendly vessel. From the mast of the unfortunate vessel was seen a signal, "Water, water; we die of thirst!" The answer from the friendly vessel at once came back, "Cast down your bucket where you are." A second time the signal, "Water, water; send us water!" ran up from the distressed vessel, and was answered, "Cast down your bucket where you are." And a third and fourth signal for water was answered, "Cast down your bucket where you are." The captain of the distressed vessel, at last heeding the injunction, cast down his bucket, and it came up full of fresh, sparkling water from the mouth of the Amazon River. To those of my race who depend on bettering their condition in a foreign land or who underestimate the importance of cultivating friendly relations with the Southern white man, who is their next-door neighbour, I would say: "Cast down your bucket where you are"—cast it down in making friends in every manly way of the people of all races by whom we are surrounded.

Cast it down in agriculture, mechanics, in commerce, in domestic service, and in the professions. And in this connection it is well to bear in mind that whatever other sins the South may be called to bear, when it comes to business, pure and simple, it is in the South that the Negro is given a man's chance in the commercial world, and in nothing is this Exposition more eloquent than in emphasizing this chance. Our greatest danger is that in the great leap from slavery to freedom we may overlook the fact that the masses of us are to live by the productions of our hands, and fail to keep in mind that we shall prosper in proportion as we learn to dignify and glorify common labour and put brains and skill into the common occupations of life; shall prosper in proportion as we learn to draw the line between the superficial and the substantial, the ornamental gewgaws of life and the useful. No race can prosper till it learns that there is as much dignity in tilling a field as in writing a poem. It is at the bottom of life we must begin, and not at the top. Nor should we permit our grievances to overshadow our opportunities.

To those of the white race who look to the incoming of those of foreign birth and strange tongue and habits for the prosperity of the South, were I permitted I would repeat what I say to my own race, "Cast down your bucket where you are." Cast it down among the eight millions of Negroes whose habits you know, whose fidelity and love you have tested in days when to have proved treacherous meant the ruin of your firesides. Cast down your bucket among these people who have, without strikes and labour wars, tilled your fields, cleared your forests, builded your railroads and cities, and brought forth treasures from the bowels of the earth, and helped make possible this magnificent representation of the progress of the South. Casting down your bucket among my people, helping and encouraging them as you are doing on these grounds, and to education of head, hand, and heart, you will find that they will buy your surplus land, make blossom the waste places in your fields, and run your factories. While doing this, you can be sure in the future, as in the past, that you and your families will be surrounded by the most patient, faithful, law-abiding, and unresentful people that the world has seen. As we have proved our loyalty to you in the past, in nursing your children, watching by the sick-bed of your mothers and fathers, and often following them with tear-dimmed eyes to their graves, so in the future, in our humble way, we shall stand by you with a devotion that no foreigner can approach, ready to lay down our lives, if need be, in defence of yours, interlacing our industrial, commercial, civil, and religious life with yours in a way that shall make the interests of both races one. In all things that are purely social we can be as separate as the fingers, yet one as the hand in all things essential to mutual progress.

There is no defence or security for any of us except in the highest intelligence and development of all. If anywhere there are efforts tending to curtail the fullest growth of the Negro, let these efforts be turned into stimulating, encouraging, and making him the most useful and intelligent citizen. Effort or means so invested will pay a thousand per cent. interest. These efforts will be twice blessed—"blessing him that gives and him that takes."

There is no escape through law of man or God from the inevitable:—

> The laws of changeless justice bind
>   Oppressor with oppressed;
> And close as sin and suffering joined
>   We march to fate abreast.

Nearly sixteen millions of hands will aid you in pulling the load upward, or they will pull against you the load downward. We shall constitute one-third and more of the ignorance and crime of the South, or one-third its intelligence and progress; we shall contribute one-third to the business and industrial prosperity of the South, or we shall prove a veritable body of death, stagnating, depressing, retarding every effort to advance the body politic.

Gentlemen of the Exposition, as we present to you our humble effort at an exhibition of our progress, you must not expect overmuch. Starting thirty years ago with ownership here and there in a few quilts and pumpkins and chickens (gathered from miscellaneous sources), remember the path that has led from these to the inventions and production of agricultural implements, buggies, steam-engines, newspapers, books, statuary, carving, paintings, the management of drug-stores and banks, has not been trodden without contact with thorns and thistles. While we take pride in what we exhibit as a result of our independent efforts, we do not for a moment forget that our part in this exhibition would fall far short of your expectations but for the constant help that has come to our educational life, not only from the Southern states, but especially from Northern philanthropists, who have made their gifts a constant stream of blessing and encouragement.

The wisest among my race understand that the agitation of questions of social equality is the extremest folly, and that progress in the enjoyment of all the privileges that will come to us must be the result of severe and constant struggle rather than of artificial forcing. No race that has anything to contribute to the markets of the world is long in any degree ostracized. It is important and right that all privileges of the law be ours, but it is vastly more important that we be prepared for the exercises of these privileges. The opportunity to earn a dollar in a factory just now is worth infinitely more than the opportunity to spend a dollar in an opera-house.

In conclusion, may I repeat that nothing in thirty years has given us more hope and encouragement, and drawn us so near to you of the white race, as this opportunity offered by the Exposition; and here bending, as it were, over the altar that represents the results of the struggles of your race and mine, both starting practically empty-handed three decades ago, I pledge that in your effort to work out the great and intricate problem which God has laid at the doors of the South, you shall have at all times the patient, sympathetic help of my race; only let this be constantly in mind, that, while from representations in these buildings of the product of field, of forest, of mine, of factory, letters and art, much good will come, yet far above and beyond material benefits will be that higher good, that, let us pray God, will come, in a blotting out of sectional differences and racial animosities and suspicions, in a determination to administer absolute justice, in a willing obedience among all classes to the mandates of law. This, this, coupled with our material prosperity, will bring into our beloved South a new heaven and a new earth.

The first thing that I remember, after I had finished speaking, was that Governor Bullock rushed across the platform and took me by the hand, and that others did the same. I received so many and such hearty congratulations that I found it difficult to get out of the building. I did not appreciate to any degree, however, the impression which my address seemed to have made, until the next morning, when I went into the business part of the city. As soon as I was recognized, I was surprised to find myself pointed out and surrounded by a crowd of men who wished to shake hands with me. This was kept up on every street on to which I went, to an extent which embarrassed me so much that I went back to my boarding-place. The next morning I returned to Tuskegee. At the station in Atlanta, and at almost all of the stations at which the train stopped between that city and Tuskegee, I found a crowd of people anxious to shake hands with me.

The papers in all parts of the United States published the address in full, and for months afterward there were complimentary editorial references to it. Mr. Clark Howell, the editor of the Atlanta *Constitution,* telegraphed to a New York paper, among other words, the following, "I do not exaggerate when I say that Professor Booker T. Washington's address yesterday was one of the most notable speeches, both as to character and as to the warmth of its reception, ever delivered to a Southern audience. The address was a revelation. The whole speech is a platform upon which blacks and whites can stand with full justice to each other."

The Boston *Transcript* said editorially: "The speech of Booker T. Washington at the Atlanta Exposition, this week, seems to have dwarfed all the other proceedings and the Exposition itself. The sensation that it has caused in the press has never been equalled."

I very soon began receiving all kinds of propositions from lecture bureaus, and editors of magazines and papers, to take the lecture platform, and to write articles. One lecture bureau offered me fifty thousand dollars, or two hundred dollars a night and expenses, if I would place my services at its disposal for a given period. To all these communications I replied that my life-work was at Tuskegee; and that whenever I spoke it must be in the interests of the Tuskegee school and my race, and that I would enter into no arrangements that seemed to place a mere commercial value upon my services.

Some days after its delivery I sent a copy of my address to the President of the United States, the Hon. Grover Cleveland. I received from him the following autograph reply:—

GRAY GABLES, BUZZARD'S BAY, MASS.,
OCTOBER 6, 1895.

BOOKER T. WASHINGTON, ESQ.:

MY DEAR SIR: I thank you for sending me a copy of your address delivered at the Atlanta Exposition.

I thank you with much enthusiasm for making the address. I have read it with intense interest, and I think the Exposition would be fully justified if it did not do more than furnish the opportunity for its delivery. Your words cannot fail to delight and encourage all who wish well for your race; and if our coloured fellow-citizens do not from your utterances gather new hope and form new determinations to gain every valuable advantage offered them by their citizenship, it will be strange indeed.

Yours very truly,
GROVER CLEVELAND

Later I met Mr. Cleveland, for the first time, when, as President, he visited the Atlanta Exposition. At the request of myself and others he consented to spend an hour in the Negro Building, for the purpose of inspecting the Negro exhibit and of giving the coloured people in attendance an opportunity to shake hands with him. As soon as I met Mr. Cleveland I became impressed with his simplicity, greatness, and rugged honesty. I have met him many times since then, both at public functions and at his private residence in Princeton, and the more I see of him the more I admire him. When he visited the Negro Building in Atlanta he seemed to give himself up wholly, for that hour, to the coloured people. He seemed to be as careful to shake hands with some old coloured "auntie" clad partially in rags, and to take as much pleasure in doing so, as if he were greeting some millionaire. Many of the coloured people took advantage of the occasion to get him to write his name in a book or on a slip of paper. He was as careful and patient in doing this as if he were putting his signature to some great state document.

Mr. Cleveland has not only shown his friendship for me in many personal ways, but has always consented to do anything I have asked of him for our school. This he has done, whether it was to make a personal donation or to use his influence in securing the donations of others. Judging from my personal acquaintance with Mr. Cleveland, I do not believe that he is conscious of possessing any colour prejudice. He is too great for that. In my contact with people I find that, as a rule, it is only the little, narrow people who live for themselves, who never read good books, who do not travel, who never open up their souls in a way to permit them to come into contact with other souls—with the great outside world. No man whose vision is bounded by colour can come into contact with what is highest and best in the world. In meeting men, in many places, I have found that the happiest people are those who do the most for others; the most miserable are those who do the least. I have also found that few things, if any, are capable of making one so blind and narrow as race prejudice. I often say to our students, in the course of my talks to them on Sunday evenings in the chapel, that the longer I live and the more experience I have of the world, the more I am convinced that, after all, the one thing that is most worth living for—and dying for, if need be—is the opportunity of making some one else more happy and more useful.

The coloured people and the coloured newspapers at first seemed to be greatly pleased with the character of my Atlanta address, as well as with its reception. But after the first burst of enthusiasm began to die away, and the coloured people began reading the speech in cold type, some of them seemed to feel that they had been hypnotized. They seemed to feel that I had been too liberal in my remarks toward the Southern whites, and that I had not spoken out strongly enough for what they termed the "rights" of the race. For a while there was a reaction, so far as a certain element of my own race was concerned, but later these reactionary ones seemed to have been won over to my way of believing and acting.

While speaking of changes in public sentiment, I recall that about ten years after the school at Tuskegee was established, I had an experience that I shall never forget. Dr. Lyman Abbott, then the pastor of Plymouth Church, and also editor of the *Outlook* (then the *Christian Union*), asked me to write a letter for his paper giving my opinion of the exact condition, mental and moral, of the coloured ministers in the South, as based upon my observations. I wrote the letter, giving the exact facts as I conceived them to be. The picture painted was a rather black one—or, since I am black, shall I say "white"? It could not be otherwise with a race but a few years out of slavery, a race which had not had time or opportunity to produce a competent ministry.

What I said soon reached every Negro minister in the country, I think, and the letters of condemnation which I received from them were not few. I think that for a year after the publication of this article every association and every conference or religious body of any kind, of my race, that met, did not fail before adjourning to pass a resolution condemning me, or calling upon me to retract or modify what I had said. Many of these organizations went so far in their resolutions as to advise parents to cease sending their children to Tuskegee. One association even appointed a "missionary" whose duty it was to warn the people against sending their children to Tuskegee. This missionary had a son in the school, and I noticed that, whatever the "missionary" might have said or done with regard to others, he was careful not to take his son away from the institution. Many of the coloured papers, especially those that were the organs of religious bodies, joined in the general chorus of condemnation or demands for retraction.

During the whole time of the excitement, and through all the criticism, I did not utter a word of explanation or retraction. I knew that I was right, and that time and the sober second thought of the people would vindicate me. It was not long before the bishops and other church leaders began to make a careful investigation of the conditions of the ministry, and they found out that I was right. In fact, the oldest and most influential bishop in one branch of the Methodist Church said that my words were far too mild. Very soon public sentiment began making itself felt, in demanding a purifying of the ministry. While this is not yet complete by any means, I think I may say, without egotism, and I have been told by many of our most influential ministers, that my words had much to do with starting a demand for the placing of a higher type of men in the pulpit. I have had the satisfaction of having many who once condemned me thank me heartily for my frank words.

The change of the attitude of the Negro ministry, so far as regards myself, is so complete that at the present time I have no warmer friends among any class than I have among the clergymen. The improvement in the character and life of the Negro ministers is one of the most gratifying evidences of the progress of the race. My experience with them as well as other events in my life, convince me that the thing to do, when one feels sure that he has said or done the right thing, and is condemned, is to stand still and keep quiet. If he is right, time will show it.

In the midst of the discussion which was going on concerning my Atlanta speech, I received the letter which I give below, from Dr. Gilman, the President of Johns Hopkins University, who had been made chairman of the judges of award in connection with the Atlanta Exposition:—

JOHNS HOPKINS UNIVERSITY, BALTIMORE,
PRESIDENT'S OFFICE, SEPTEMBER 30, 1895.

DEAR MR. WASHINGTON: Would it be agreeable to you to be one of the Judges of Award in the Department of Education at Atlanta? If so, I shall be glad to place your name upon the list. A line by telegraph will be welcomed.
Yours very truly,
D. C. GILMAN.

I think I was even more surprised to receive this invitation than I had been to receive the invitation to speak at the opening of the Exposition. It was to be a part of my duty, as one of the jurors, to pass not only upon the exhibits of the coloured schools, but also upon those of the white schools. I accepted the position, and spent a month in Atlanta in performance of the duties which it entailed. The board of jurors was a large one, consisting in all of sixty members. It was about equally divided between Southern white people and Northern white people. Among them were college presidents, leading scientists and men of letters, and specialists in many subjects. When the group of jurors to which I was assigned met for organization, Mr. Thomas Nelson Page, who was one of the number, moved that I be made secretary of that division, and the motion was unanimously adopted. Nearly half of our division were Southern people. In performing my duties in the inspection of the exhibits of white schools I was in every case treated with respect, and at the close of our labours I parted from my associates with regret.

I am often asked to express myself more freely than I do upon the political condition and the political future of my race. These recollections of my experience in Atlanta give me the opportunity to do so briefly. My own belief is, although I have never before said so in so many words, that the time will come when the Negro in the South will be accorded all the political rights which his ability, character, and material possessions entitle him to. I think, though, that the opportunity to freely exercise such political rights will not come in any large degree through outside or artificial forcing, but will be accorded to the Negro by the Southern white people themselves, and that they will protect him in the exercise of those rights. Just as soon as the South gets over the old feeling that it is being forced by "foreigners," or "aliens," to do something which it does not want to do, I believe that the change in the direction that I have indicated is going to begin. In fact, there are indications that it is already beginning in a slight degree.

Let me illustrate my meaning. Suppose that some months before the opening of the Atlanta Exposition there had been a general demand from the press and public platform outside the South that a Negro be given a place on the opening programme, and that a Negro be placed upon the board of jurors of award. Would any such recognition of the race have taken place? I do not think so. The Atlanta officials went as far as they did because they felt it to be a pleasure, as well as a duty, to reward what they considered merit in the Negro race. Say what we will, there is something in human nature which we cannot blot out, which makes one man, in the end, recognize and reward merit in another, regardless of colour or race.

I believe it is the duty of the Negro—as the greater part of the race is already doing—to deport himself modestly in regard to political claims, depending upon the slow but sure influences that proceed from the possession of property, intelligence, and high character for the full recognition of his political rights. I think that the according of the full exercise of political rights is going to be a matter of natural, slow growth, not an over-night, gourd-vine affair. I do not believe that the Negro should cease voting, for a man cannot learn the exercise of self-government by ceasing to vote any more than a boy can learn to swim by keeping out of the water, but I do believe that in his voting he should more and more be influenced by those of intelligence and character who are his next-door neighbours.

I know coloured men who, through the encouragement, help, and advice of Southern white people, have accumulated thousands of dollars' worth of property, but who, at the same time, would never think of going to those same persons for advice concerning the casting of their ballots. This, it seems to me, is unwise and unreasonable, and should cease. In saying this I do not mean that the Negro should buckle, or not vote from principle, for the instant he ceases to vote from principle he loses the confidence and respect of the Southern white man even.

I do not believe that any state should make a law that permits an ignorant and poverty-stricken white man to vote, and prevents a black man in the same condition from voting. Such a law is not only unjust, but it will react, as all unjust laws do, in time; for the effect of such a law is to encourage the Negro to secure education and property, and at the same time it encourages the white man to remain in ignorance and poverty. I believe that in time, through the operation of intelligence and friendly race relations, all cheating at the ballot-box in the South will cease. It will become apparent that the white man who begins by cheating a Negro out of his ballot soon learns to cheat a white man out of his, and that the man who does this ends his career of dishonesty by the theft of property or by some equally serious crime. In my opinion, the time will come when the South will encourage all of its citizens to vote. It will see that it pays better, from every standpoint, to have healthy, vigorous life than to have that political stagnation which always results when one-half of the population has no share and no interest in the Government.

As a rule, I believe in universal, free suffrage, but I believe that in the South we are confronted with peculiar conditions that justify the protection of the ballot in many of the states, for a while at least, either by an educational test, a property test, or by both combined; but whatever tests are required, they should be made to apply with equal and exact justice to both races.

4.3.2 Reading and Review Questions

1. In his opening chapter, what examples does Washington give of harmonious race relations under slavery?

2. Washington tells the story of a former slave who, after Emancipation, travelled back to the South to finish paying his former owner for his freedom. What is the purpose of this story?

3. Washington's Exposition address in chapter fourteen is often called the "**Atlanta Compromise**" speech because in it Washington calls for greater economic and educational opportunities for African Americans while also supporting the policy of racial **segregation**. Other black leaders and intellectuals such as W. E. B. Du Bois, who demanded full equality between the races, criticized Washington's compromise in the years following his famous address for being too politically timid. How does Washington craft his Exposition Address to allay the fears of his white audience while simultaneously making a persuasive case that African Americans merit more educational support and economic opportunity?

4.4 W. E. B. DU BOIS

(1868 - 1963)

William Edward Burghardt Du Bois was born in Massachusetts to an affluent family in Great Barrington, a town with few African-American families. Du Bois describes his youth as pleasant until, while in school, he realized that his skin color, not his academic ability, set him apart from his peers. While growing up in Massachusetts, Du Bois self-identified as "mulatto" before moving to Nashville to attend Fisk University, where he first began to encounter Jim Crow laws. After finishing his bachelor's degree at Fisk University, Du Bois began graduate study at Harvard University. While completing his graduate work, Du Bois

Image 4.2 | W. E. B. Du Bois, 1918
Photographer | Cornelius Marion Battey
Source | Wikimedia Commons
License | Public Domain

was awarded a prestigious one-year fellowship at the University of Berlin, where he was able to work with some of the most prominent social scientists of his day. In 1895, Du Bois completed his Ph.D., becoming the first African American to earn a Ph.D. from Harvard University. While at Harvard, Du Bois was an academic standout; indeed, Harvard University Press later published his dissertation as the first volume in their Harvard Historical Studies series.

After completing his Ph.D., Du Bois went on to hold multiple teaching appointments, first at Wilberforce College, then at the University of Pennsylvania, before moving to Atlanta University where he produced his classic work, *Souls of Black Folk* (1905). In 1910, Du Bois left the academy to move to New York City, where he co-founded the National Association for the Advancement of Colored People (NAACP) and served as the editor of the NAACP's official publication, *The Crisis*. Furthermore, Du Bois was a central orchestrator of the Harlem Renaissance. His essay "**The Talented Tenth**," which was a chapter from his book, *The Negro Problem* (1903), argued that the best African-American artists (the talented "tenth" he dubbed them) were capable of producing art as complex as any white artist. In his writings, Du Bois was openly critical of Washington, whom he saw as an accommodationist (Du Bois disagreed with many of Washington's views and was especially angered by the result of *Plessy v. Ferguson*). By 1920, Du Bois grew frustrated with what he viewed as a lack of positive movement on racial progress. He spent the second half of his career focusing on legislative reform for national race relations, as well turning his attention to the socio-economic conditions of African Americans in the U.S. Late in life, a disillusioned Du Bois renounced his American citizenship, joined the Communist party, and moved to Ghana (1961), where he remained until his death in 1963.

Throughout his life, Du Bois remained one of the most influential academics of his time; however, he is best known for his book, *Souls of Black Folks,* which is a compilation of fourteen essays. In "Of Our Spiritual Strivings," Du Bois introduces the idea of "**double consciousness**," possibly his most famous literary/academic contribution. Du Bois describes double consciousness as the "sense of always looking at one's self through the eyes of others, of measuring one's soul by the tape of a world that looks on in amused contempt and pity. One ever feels his two-ness—an American, a Negro; two souls, two thoughts" (12).

4.4.1 Selections from *The Souls of Black Folk*

THE FORETHOUGHT

Herein lie buried many things which if read with patience may show the strange meaning of being black here at the dawning of the Twentieth Century. This meaning is not without interest to you, Gentle Reader; for the problem of the Twentieth Century is the problem of the color line. I pray you, then, receive my little book in all charity, studying my words with me, forgiving mistake and foible for sake of the faith and passion that is in me, and seeking the grain of truth hidden there.

I have sought here to sketch, in vague, uncertain outline, the spiritual world in which ten thousand thousand Americans live and strive. First, in two chapters I have tried to show what Emancipation meant to them, and what was its aftermath. In a third chapter I have pointed out the slow rise of personal leadership, and criticized candidly the leader who bears the chief burden of his race to-day. Then, in two other chapters I have sketched in swift outline the two worlds within and without the Veil, and thus have come to the central problem of training men for life. Venturing now into deeper detail, I have in two chapters studied the struggles of the massed millions of the black peasantry, and in another have sought to make clear the present relations of the sons of master and man. Leaving, then, the white world, I have stepped within the Veil, raising it that you may view faintly its deeper recesses,—the meaning of its religion, the passion of its human sorrow, and the struggle of its greater souls. All this I have ended with a tale twice told but seldom written, and a chapter of song.

Some of these thoughts of mine have seen the light before in other guise. For kindly consenting to their republication here, in altered and extended form, I must thank the publishers of the Atlantic Monthly, The World's Work, the Dial, The New World, and the Annals of the American Academy of Political and Social Science. Before each chapter, as now printed, stands a bar of the Sorrow Songs,—some echo of haunting melody from the only American music which welled up from black souls in the dark past. And, finally, need I add that I who speak here am bone of the bone and flesh of the flesh of them that live within the Veil?
W.E.B Du B.
ATLANTA, GA., FEB. 1, 1903.

CHAPTER I
OF OUR SPIRITUAL STRIVINGS

O water, voice of my heart, crying in the sand,
All night long crying with a mournful cry,
As I lie and listen, and cannot understand
The voice of my heart in my side or the voice of the sea,
O water, crying for rest, is it I, is it I?
All night long the water is crying to me.

Unresting water, there shall never be rest
Till the last moon droop and the last tide fail,
And the fire of the end begin to burn in the west;
And the heart shall be weary and wonder and cry like the sea,
All life long crying without avail,
As the water all night long is crying to me.

ARTHUR SYMONS.

Between me and the other world there is ever an unasked question: unasked by some through feelings of delicacy; by others through the difficulty of rightly framing it. All, nevertheless, flutter round it. They approach me in a half-hesitant sort of way, eye me curiously or compassionately, and then, instead of saying directly,

How does it feel to be a problem? they say, I know an excellent colored man in my town; or, I fought at Mechanicsville; or, Do not these Southern outrages make your blood boil? At these I smile, or am interested, or reduce the boiling to a simmer, as the occasion may require. To the real question, How does it feel to be a problem? I answer seldom a word.

And yet, being a problem is a strange experience,—peculiar even for one who has never been anything else, save perhaps in babyhood and in Europe. It is in the early days of rollicking boyhood that the revelation first bursts upon one, all in a day, as it were. I remember well when the shadow swept across me. I was a little thing, away up in the hills of New England, where the dark Housatonic winds between Hoosac and Taghkanic to the sea. In a wee wooden schoolhouse, something put it into the boys' and girls' heads to buy gorgeous visiting-cards—ten cents a package—and exchange. The exchange was merry, till one girl, a tall newcomer, refused my card,—refused it peremptorily, with a glance. Then it dawned upon me with a certain suddenness that I was different from the others; or like, mayhap, in heart and life and longing, but shut out from their world by a vast veil. I had thereafter no desire to tear down that veil, to creep through; I held all beyond it in common contempt, and lived above it in a region of blue sky and great wandering shadows. That sky was bluest when I could beat my mates at examination-time, or beat them at a foot-race, or even beat their stringy heads. Alas, with the years all this fine contempt began to fade; for the words I longed for, and all their dazzling opportunities, were theirs, not mine. But they should not keep these prizes, I said; some, all, I would wrest from them. Just how I would do it I could never decide: by reading law, by healing the sick, by telling the wonderful tales that swam in my head,—some way. With other black boys the strife was not so fiercely sunny: their youth shrunk into tasteless sycophancy, or into silent hatred of the pale world about them and mocking distrust of everything white; or wasted itself in a bitter cry, Why did God make me an outcast and a stranger in mine own house? The shades of the prison-house closed round about us all: walls strait and stubborn to the whitest, but relentlessly narrow, tall, and unscalable to sons of night who must plod darkly on in resignation, or beat unavailing palms against the stone, or steadily, half hopelessly, watch the streak of blue above.

After the Egyptian and Indian, the Greek and Roman, the Teuton and Mongolian, the Negro is a sort of seventh son, born with a veil, and gifted with second-sight in this American world,—a world which yields him no true self-consciousness, but only lets him see himself through the revelation of the other world. It is a peculiar sensation, this double-consciousness, this sense of always looking at one's self through the eyes of others, of measuring one's soul by the tape of a world that looks on in amused contempt and pity. One ever feels his twoness,—an American, a Negro; two souls, two thoughts, two unreconciled strivings; two warring ideals in one dark body, whose dogged strength alone keeps it from being torn asunder.

The history of the American Negro is the history of this strife,—this longing to attain self-conscious manhood, to merge his double self into a better and truer self. In this merging he wishes neither of the older selves to be lost. He would not Africanize America, for America has too much to teach the world and Africa. He would not bleach his Negro soul in a flood of white Americanism, for he knows that Negro blood has a message for the world. He simply wishes to make it possible for a man to be both a Negro and an American, without being cursed and spit upon by his fellows, without having the doors of Opportunity closed roughly in his face.

This, then, is the end of his striving: to be a co-worker in the kingdom of culture, to escape both death and isolation, to husband and use his best powers and his latent genius. These powers of body and mind have in the past been strangely wasted, dispersed, or forgotten. The shadow of a mighty Negro past flits through the tale of Ethiopia the Shadowy and of Egypt the Sphinx. Through history, the powers of single black men flash here and there like falling stars, and die sometimes before the world has rightly gauged their brightness. Here in America, in the few days since Emancipation, the black man's turning hither and thither in hesitant and doubtful striving has often made his very strength to lose effectiveness, to seem like absence of power, like weakness. And yet it is not weakness,—it is the contradiction of double aims. The double-aimed struggle of the black artisan—on the one hand to escape white contempt for a nation of mere hewers of wood and drawers of water, and on the other hand to plough and nail and dig for a poverty-stricken horde—could only result in making him a poor craftsman, for he had but half a heart in either cause. By the poverty and ignorance of his people, the Negro minister or doctor was tempted toward quackery and demagogy; and by the criticism of the other world, toward ideals that made him ashamed of his lowly tasks. The would-be black savant was confronted by the paradox that the knowledge his people needed was a twice-told tale to his white neighbors, while the knowledge which would teach the white world was Greek to his own flesh and blood. The innate love of harmony and beauty that set the ruder souls of his people a-dancing and a-singing raised but confusion and doubt in the soul of the black artist; for the beauty revealed to him was the soul-beauty of a race which his larger audience despised, and he could not articulate the message of another people. This waste of double aims, this seeking to satisfy two unreconciled ideals, has wrought sad havoc with the courage and faith and deeds of ten thousand thousand people,— has sent them often wooing false gods and invoking false means of salvation, and at times has even seemed about to make them ashamed of themselves.

Away back in the days of bondage they thought to see in one divine event the end of all doubt and disappointment; few men ever worshipped Freedom with half such unquestioning faith as did the American Negro for two centuries. To him, so far as he thought and dreamed, slavery was indeed the sum of all villainies, the cause of all sorrow, the root of all prejudice; Emancipation was the key to a promised land of sweeter beauty than ever stretched before the eyes of wearied Israelites. In song and exhortation swelled one refrain—Liberty; in his tears and curses the God he implored had Freedom in his right hand. At last it came,—suddenly, fearfully, like a dream. With one wild carnival of blood and passion came the message in his own plaintive cadences:—

> "Shout, O children!
> Shout, you're free!
> For God has bought your liberty!"

Years have passed away since then,—ten, twenty, forty; forty years of national life, forty years of renewal and development, and yet the swarthy spectre sits in its accustomed seat at the Nation's feast. In vain do we cry to this our vastest social problem:—

> "Take any shape but that, and my firm nerves
> Shall never tremble!"

The Nation has not yet found peace from its sins; the freedman has not yet found in freedom his promised land. Whatever of good may have come in these years of change, the shadow of a deep disappointment rests upon the Negro people,—a disappointment all the more bitter because the unattained ideal was unbounded save by the simple ignorance of a lowly people.

The first decade was merely a prolongation of the vain search for freedom, the boon that seemed ever barely to elude their grasp,—like a tantalizing will-o'-the-wisp, maddening and misleading the headless host. The holocaust of war, the terrors of the Ku-Klux Klan, the lies of carpet-baggers, the disorganization of industry, and the contradictory advice of friends and foes, left the bewildered serf with no new watchword beyond the old cry for freedom. As the time flew, however, he began to grasp a new idea. The ideal of liberty demanded for its attainment powerful means, and these the Fifteenth Amendment gave him. The ballot, which before he had looked upon as a visible sign of freedom, he now regarded as the chief means of gaining and perfecting the liberty with which war had partially endowed him. And why not? Had not votes made war and emancipated millions? Had not votes enfranchised the freedmen? Was anything impossible to a power that had done all this? A million black men started with renewed zeal to vote themselves into the kingdom. So the decade flew away, the revolution of 1876 came, and left the half-free serf weary, wondering, but still inspired. Slowly but steadily, in the following years, a new vision began gradually to replace the dream of political power,—a powerful movement, the rise of another ideal to guide the unguided, another pillar of fire by night after a clouded day. It was the ideal of "book-learning"; the curiosity, born of compulsory ignorance, to know and test the power of the cabalistic letters of the white man, the longing to know. Here at last seemed to have been discovered the mountain path to Canaan; longer than the highway of Emancipation and law, steep and rugged, but straight, leading to heights high enough to overlook life.

Up the new path the advance guard toiled, slowly, heavily, doggedly; only those who have watched and guided the faltering feet, the misty minds, the dull under-standings, of the dark pupils of these schools know how faithfully, how piteously this people strove to learn. It was weary work. The cold statistician wrote down the inches of progress here and there, noted also where here and there a foot had slipped or some one had fallen. To the tired climbers, the horizon was ever dark, the mists were often cold, the Canaan was always dim and far away. If, however, the vistas disclosed as yet no goal, no resting-place, little but flattery and criticism, the journey at least gave leisure for reflection and self-examination; it changed the child of Emancipation to the youth with dawning self-consciousness, self-realiza-tion, self-respect. In those sombre forests of his striving his own soul rose before him, and he saw himself,—darkly as through a veil; and yet he saw in himself some faint revelation of his power, of his mission. He began to have a dim feeling that, to attain his place in the world, he must be himself, and not another. For the first time he sought to analyze the burden he bore upon his back, that dead-weight of social degradation partially masked behind a half-named Negro problem. He felt his poverty; without a cent, without a home, without land, tools, or savings, he had entered into competition with rich, landed, skilled neighbors.

To be a poor man is hard, but to be a poor race in a land of dollars is the very bottom of hardships. He felt the weight of his ignorance,—not simply of letters, but of life, of business, of the humanities; the accumulated sloth and shirking and awkwardness of decades and centuries shackled his hands and feet. Nor was his burden all poverty and ignorance. The red stain of bastardy, which two centuries of systematic legal defilement of Negro women had stamped upon his race, meant not only the loss of ancient African chastity, but also the hereditary weight of a mass of corruption from white adulterers, threatening almost the obliteration of the Negro home.

A people thus handicapped ought not to be asked to race with the world, but rather allowed to give all its time and thought to its own social problems. But alas! While sociologists gleefully count his bastards and his prostitutes, the very soul of the toiling, sweating black man is darkened by the shadow of a vast despair. Men call the shadow prejudice, and learnedly explain it as the natural defence of culture against barbarism, learning against ignorance, purity against crime, the "higher" against the "lower" races.

To which the Negro cries Amen! and swears that to so much of this strange prejudice as is founded on just homage to civilization, culture, righteousness, and progress, he humbly bows and meekly does obeisance. But before that nameless prejudice that leaps beyond all this he stands helpless, dismayed, and well-nigh speechless; before that personal disrespect and mockery, the ridicule and system-atic humiliation, the distortion of fact and wanton license of fancy, the cynical ig-noring of the better and the boisterous welcoming of the worse, the all-pervading desire to inculcate disdain for everything black, from Toussaint to the devil,—be-fore this there rises a sickening despair that would disarm and discourage any na-tion save that black host to whom "discouragement" is an unwritten word.

But the facing of so vast a prejudice could not but bring the inevitable self-ques-tioning, self-disparagement, and lowering of ideals which ever accompany repres-sion and breed in an atmosphere of contempt and hate. Whisperings and portents came home upon the four winds: Lo! we are diseased and dying, cried the dark hosts; we cannot write, our voting is vain; what need of education, since we must always cook and serve? And the Nation echoed and enforced this self-criticism, saying: Be content to be servants, and nothing more; what need of higher culture for half-men? Away with the black man's ballot, by force or fraud,—and behold the suicide of a race! Nevertheless, out of the evil came something of good,—the more careful adjustment of education to real life, the clearer perception of the Negroes' social responsibilities, and the sobering realization of the meaning of progress.

So dawned the time of Sturm und Drang: storm and stress to-day rocks our lit-tle boat on the mad waters of the world-sea; there is within and without the sound of conflict, the burning of body and rending of soul; inspiration strives with doubt, and faith with vain questionings. The bright ideals of the past,—physical freedom, political power, the training of brains and the training of hands,—all these in turn have waxed and waned, until even the last grows dim and overcast. Are they all wrong,—all false? No, not that, but each alone was over-simple and incomplete,—the dreams of a credulous race-childhood, or the fond imaginings of the other world which does not know and does not want to know our power. To be really true, all these ideals must be melted and welded into one. The training of the schools we need to-day more than ever,—the training of deft hands, quick eyes and ears, and above all the broader, deeper, higher culture of gifted minds and pure hearts. The power of the ballot we need in sheer self-defence,—else what shall save us from a second slavery? Freedom, too, the long-sought, we still seek,—the freedom of life and limb, the freedom to work and think, the freedom to love and aspire. Work, culture, liberty,—all these we need, not singly but together, not successively but to-gether, each growing and aiding each, and all striving toward that vaster ideal that swims before the Negro people, the ideal of human brotherhood, gained through the unifying ideal of Race; the ideal of fostering and developing the traits and tal-ents of the Negro, not in opposition to or contempt for other races, but rather in large conformity to the greater ideals of the American Republic, in order that some day on American soil two world-races may give each to each those characteristics both so sadly lack. We the darker ones come even now not altogether empty-hand-ed: there are to-day no truer exponents of the pure human spirit of the Declaration of Independence than the American Negroes; there is no true American music but the wild sweet melodies of the Negro slave; the American fairy tales and folklore are Indian and African; and, all in all, we black men seem the sole oasis of simple faith and reverence in a dusty desert of dollars and smartness. Will America be poorer if she replace her brutal dyspeptic blundering with light-hearted but deter-mined Negro humility? or her coarse and cruel wit with loving jovial good-humor? or her vulgar music with the soul of the Sorrow Songs?

Merely a concrete test of the underlying principles of the great republic is the

Negro Problem, and the spiritual striving of the freedmen's sons is the travail of souls whose burden is almost beyond the measure of their strength, but who bear it in the name of an historic race, in the name of this the land of their fathers' fathers, and in the name of human opportunity.

And now what I have briefly sketched in large outline let me on coming pages tell again in many ways, with loving emphasis and deeper detail, that men may listen to the striving in the souls of black folk.

CHAPTER III
OF MR. BOOKER T. WASHINGTON AND OTHERS

From birth till death enslaved; in word, in deed, unmanned!

* * * * * * * * * * * * * * * * *

Hereditary bondsmen! Know ye not
Who would be free themselves must strike the blow?
BYRON.

Easily the most striking thing in the history of the American Negro since 1876 is the ascendancy of Mr. Booker T. Washington. It began at the time when war memories and ideals were rapidly passing; a day of astonishing commercial development was dawning; a sense of doubt and hesitation overtook the freedmen's sons,—then it was that his leading began. Mr. Washington came, with a simple definite programme, at the psychological moment when the nation was a little ashamed of having bestowed so much sentiment on Negroes, and was concentrating its energies on Dollars. His programme of industrial education, conciliation of the South, and submission and silence as to civil and political rights, was not wholly original; the Free Negroes from 1830 up to war-time had striven to build industrial schools, and the American Missionary Association had from the first taught various trades; and Price and others had sought a way of honorable alliance with the best of the Southerners. But Mr. Washington first indissolubly linked these things; he put enthusiasm, unlimited energy, and perfect faith into his programme, and changed it from a by-path into a veritable Way of Life. And the tale of the methods by which he did this is a fascinating study of human life.

It startled the nation to hear a Negro advocating such a programme after many decades of bitter complaint; it startled and won the applause of the South, it interested and won the admiration of the North; and after a confused murmur of protest, it silenced if it did not convert the Negroes themselves.

To gain the sympathy and cooperation of the various elements comprising the white South was Mr. Washington's first task; and this, at the time Tuskegee was founded, seemed, for a black man, well-nigh impossible. And yet ten years later it was done in the word spoken at Atlanta: "In all things purely social we can be as separate as the five fingers, and yet one as the hand in all things essential to mutual progress." This "Atlanta Compromise" is by all odds the most notable thing in Mr. Washington's career. The South interpreted it in different ways: the radicals received it as a complete surrender of the demand for civil and political equality; the conservatives, as a generously conceived working basis for mutual understanding. So both approved it, and to-day its author is certainly the most distinguished Southerner since Jefferson Davis, and the one with the largest personal following.

Next to this achievement comes Mr. Washington's work in gaining place and consideration in the North. Others less shrewd and tactful had formerly essayed to sit on these two stools and had fallen between them; but as Mr. Washington knew the heart of the South from birth and training, so by singular insight he intuitively grasped the spirit of the age which was dominating the North. And so thoroughly did he learn the speech and thought of triumphant commercialism, and the ideals of material prosperity, that the picture of a lone black boy poring over a French grammar amid the weeds and dirt of a neglected home soon seemed to him the acme of absurdities. One wonders what Socrates and St. Francis of Assisi would say to this.

And yet this very singleness of vision and thorough oneness with his age is a mark of the successful man. It is as though Nature must needs make men narrow in order to give them force. So Mr. Washington's cult has gained unquestioning followers, his work has wonderfully prospered, his friends are legion, and his enemies are confounded. Today he stands as the one recognized spokesman of his ten million fellows, and one of the most notable figures in a nation of seventy millions. One hesitates, therefore, to criticise a life which, beginning with so little, has done so much. And yet the time is come when one may speak in all sincerity and utter courtesy of the mistakes and shortcomings of Mr. Washington's career, as well as of his triumphs, without being thought captious or envious, and without forgetting that it is easier to do ill than well in the world.

The criticism that has hitherto met Mr. Washington has not always been of this broad character. In the South especially has he had to walk warily to avoid the harshest judgments,—and naturally so, for he is dealing with the one subject of deepest sensitiveness to that section. Twice—once when at the Chicago celebration of the Spanish-American War he alluded to the color-prejudice that is "eating away the vitals of the South," and once when he dined with President Roosevelt—has the resulting Southern criticism been violent enough to threaten seriously his popularity. In the North the feeling has several times forced itself into words, that Mr. Washington's counsels of submission overlooked certain elements of true manhood, and that his educational programme was unnecessarily narrow. Usually, however, such criticism has not found open expression, although, too, the spiritual sons of the Abolitionists have not been prepared to acknowledge that the schools founded before Tuskegee, by men of broad ideals and self-sacrificing spirit, were wholly failures or worthy of ridicule. While, then, criticism has not failed to follow Mr. Washington, yet the prevailing public opinion of the land has been but too willing to deliver the solution of a wearisome problem into his hands, and say, "If that is all you and your race ask, take it."

Among his own people, however, Mr. Washington has encountered the strongest and most lasting opposition, amounting at times to bitterness, and even today continuing strong and insistent even though largely silenced in outward expression by the public opinion of the nation. Some of this opposition is, of course, mere envy; the disappointment of displaced demagogues and the spite of narrow minds. But aside from this, there is among educated and thoughtful colored men in all parts of the land a feeling of deep regret, sorrow, and apprehension at the wide currency and ascendancy which some of Mr. Washington's theories have gained. These same men admire his sincerity of purpose, and are willing to forgive much to honest endeavor which is doing something worth the doing. They cooperate with Mr. Washington as far as they conscientiously can; and, indeed, it is no ordinary tribute to this man's tact and power that, steering as he must between so many diverse interests and opinions, he so largely retains the respect of all.

But the hushing of the criticism of honest opponents is a dangerous thing. It leads some of the best of the critics to unfortunate silence and paralysis of effort, and others to burst into speech so passionately and intemperately as to lose listeners. Honest and earnest criticism from those whose interests are most nearly touched,—criticism of writers by readers,—this is the soul of democracy and the safeguard of modern society. If the best of the American Negroes receive by outer pressure a leader whom they had not recognized before, manifestly there is here a certain palpable gain. Yet there is also irreparable loss,—a loss of that peculiarly valuable education which a group receives when by search and criticism it finds and commissions its own leaders. The way in which this is done is at once the most elementary and the nicest problem of social growth. History is but the record of such group-leadership; and yet how infinitely changeful is its type and character! And of all types and kinds, what can be more instructive than the leadership of a group within a group?—that curious double movement where real progress may be negative and actual advance be relative retrogression. All this is the social student's inspiration and despair.

Now in the past the American Negro has had instructive experience in the choosing of group leaders, founding thus a peculiar dynasty which in the light of present conditions is worth while studying. When sticks and stones and beasts form the sole environment of a people, their attitude is largely one of determined opposition to and conquest of natural forces. But when to earth and brute is added an environment of men and ideas, then the attitude of the imprisoned group may take three main forms,—a feeling of revolt and revenge; an attempt to adjust all thought and action to the will of the greater group; or, finally, a determined effort at self-realization and self-development despite environing opinion. The influence of all of these attitudes at various times can be traced in the history of the American Negro, and in the evolution of his successive leaders.

Before 1750, while the fire of African freedom still burned in the veins of the slaves, there was in all leadership or attempted leadership but the one motive of revolt and revenge,—typified in the terrible Maroons, the Danish blacks, and Cato of Stono, and veiling all the Americas in fear of insurrection. The liberalizing tendencies of the latter half of the eighteenth century brought, along with kindlier relations between black and white, thoughts of ultimate adjustment and assimilation. Such aspiration was especially voiced in the earnest songs of Phyllis, in the martyrdom of Attucks, the fighting of Salem and Poor, the intellectual accomplishments of Banneker and Derham, and the political demands of the Cuffes.

Stern financial and social stress after the war cooled much of the previous humanitarian ardor. The disappointment and impatience of the Negroes at the persistence of slavery and serfdom voiced itself in two movements. The slaves in the South, aroused undoubtedly by vague rumors of the Haytian revolt, made three fierce attempts at insurrection,—in 1800 under Gabriel in Virginia, in 1822 under Vesey in Carolina, and in 1831 again in Virginia under the terrible Nat Turner. In the Free States, on the other hand, a new and curious attempt at self-development was made. In Philadelphia and New York color-prescription led to a withdrawal of Negro communicants from white churches and the formation of a peculiar socio-religious institution among the Negroes known as the African Church,—an organization still living and controlling in its various branches over a million of men.

Walker's wild appeal against the trend of the times showed how the world was changing after the coming of the cotton-gin. By 1830 slavery seemed hopelessly fastened on the South, and the slaves thoroughly cowed into submission. The free Negroes of the North, inspired by the mulatto immigrants from the West Indies, began to change the basis of their demands; they recognized the slavery of slaves, but insisted that they themselves were freemen, and sought assimilation and amalgamation with the nation on the same terms with other men. Thus, Forten and Purvis of Philadelphia, Shad of Wilmington, Du Bois of New Haven, Barbadoes of Boston, and others, strove singly and together as men, they said, not as slaves; as "people of color," not as "Negroes." The trend of the times, however, refused them recognition save in individual and exceptional cases, considered them as one with all the despised blacks, and they soon found themselves striving to keep even the rights they formerly had of voting and working and moving as freemen. Schemes of migration and colonization arose among them; but these they refused to entertain, and they eventually turned to the Abolition movement as a final refuge.

Here, led by Remond, Nell, Wells-Brown, and Douglass, a new period of self-assertion and self-development dawned. To be sure, ultimate freedom and assimilation was the ideal before the leaders, but the assertion of the manhood rights of the Negro by himself was the main reliance, and John Brown's raid was the extreme of its logic. After the war and emancipation, the great form of Frederick Douglass, the greatest of American Negro leaders, still led the host. Self-assertion, especially in political lines, was the main programme, and behind Douglass came Elliot, Bruce, and Langston, and the Reconstruction politicians, and, less conspicuous but of greater social significance, Alexander Crummell and Bishop Daniel Payne.

Then came the Revolution of 1876, the suppression of the Negro votes, the changing and shifting of ideals, and the seeking of new lights in the great night. Douglass, in his old age, still bravely stood for the ideals of his early manhood,—ultimate assimilation through self-assertion, and on no other terms. For a time Price arose as a new leader, destined, it seemed, not to give up, but to re-state the old ideals in a form less repugnant to the white South. But he passed away in his prime. Then came the new leader. Nearly all the former ones had become leaders by the silent suffrage of their fellows, had sought to lead their own people alone, and were usually, save Douglass, little known outside their race. But Booker T. Washington arose as essentially the leader not of one race but of two,—a compromiser between the South, the North, and the Negro. Naturally the Negroes resented, at first bitterly, signs of compromise which surrendered their civil and political rights, even though this was to be exchanged for larger chances of economic development. The rich and dominating North, however, was not only weary of the race problem, but was investing largely in Southern enterprises, and welcomed any method of peaceful cooperation. Thus, by national opinion, the Negroes began to recognize Mr. Washington's leadership; and the voice of criticism was hushed.

Mr. Washington represents in Negro thought the old attitude of adjustment and submission; but adjustment at such a peculiar time as to make his programme unique. This is an age of unusual economic development, and Mr. Washington's programme naturally takes an economic cast, becoming a gospel of Work and Money to such an extent as apparently almost completely to overshadow the higher aims of life. Moreover, this is an age when the more advanced races are coming in closer contact with the less developed races, and the race-feeling is therefore intensified; and Mr. Washington's programme practically accepts the alleged inferiority of the Negro races. Again, in our own land, the reaction from the sentiment of war time has given impetus to race-prejudice against Negroes, and Mr. Washington withdraws many of the high demands of Negroes as men and American citizens. In other periods of intensified prejudice all the Negro's tendency to self-assertion has been called forth; at this period a policy of submission is advocated. In the history of nearly all other races and peoples the doctrine preached at such crises has been that manly self-respect is worth more than lands and houses, and that a people who voluntarily surrender such respect, or cease striving for it, are not worth civilizing.

In answer to this, it has been claimed that the Negro can survive only through submission. Mr. Washington distinctly asks that black people give up, at least for the present, three things,—

First, political power,

Second, insistence on civil rights,

Third, higher education of Negro youth,—and concentrate all their energies on industrial education, and accumulation of wealth, and the conciliation of the South. This policy has been courageously and insistently advocated for over fifteen years, and has been triumphant for perhaps ten years. As a result of this tender of the palm-branch, what has been the return? In these years there have occurred:

1. The disfranchisement of the Negro.

2. The legal creation of a distinct status of civil inferiority for the Negro.

3. The steady withdrawal of aid from institutions for the higher training of the Negro.

These movements are not, to be sure, direct results of Mr. Washington's teachings; but his propaganda has, without a shadow of doubt, helped their speedier accomplishment. The question then comes: Is it possible, and probable, that nine millions of men can make effective progress in economic lines if they are deprived of political rights, made a servile caste, and allowed only the most meagre chance for developing their exceptional men? If history and reason give any distinct answer to these questions, it is an emphatic NO. And Mr. Washington thus faces the triple paradox of his career:

1. He is striving nobly to make Negro artisans business men and property-owners; but it is utterly impossible, under modern competitive methods, for workingmen and property-owners to defend their rights and exist without the right of suffrage.

2. He insists on thrift and self-respect, but at the same time counsels a silent submission to civic inferiority such as is bound to sap the manhood of any race in the long run.

3. He advocates common-school and industrial training, and depreciates institutions of higher learning; but neither the Negro common-schools, nor Tuskegee itself, could remain open a day were it not for teachers trained in Negro colleges, or trained by their graduates.

This triple paradox in Mr. Washington's position is the object of criticism by two classes of colored Americans. One class is spiritually descended from Toussaint the Savior, through Gabriel, Vesey, and Turner, and they represent the attitude of revolt and revenge; they hate the white South blindly and distrust the white race generally, and so far as they agree on definite action, think that the Negro's only hope lies in emigration beyond the borders of the United States. And yet, by the irony of fate, nothing has more effectually made this programme seem hopeless than the recent course of the United States toward weaker and darker peoples in the West Indies, Hawaii, and the Philippines,—for where in the world may we go and be safe from lying and brute force?

The other class of Negroes who cannot agree with Mr. Washington has hitherto said little aloud. They deprecate the sight of scattered counsels, of internal disagreement; and especially they dislike making their just criticism of a useful and earnest man an excuse for a general discharge of venom from small-minded opponents. Nevertheless, the questions involved are so fundamental and serious that it is difficult to see how men like the Grimkes, Kelly Miller, J. W. E. Bowen, and other representatives of this group, can much longer be silent. Such men feel in conscience bound to ask of this nation three things:

1. The right to vote.

2. Civic equality.

3. The education of youth according to ability. They acknowledge Mr. Washington's invaluable service in counselling patience and courtesy in such demands; they do not ask that ignorant black men vote when ignorant whites are debarred, or that any reasonable restrictions in the suffrage should not be applied; they know that the low social level of the mass of the race is responsible for much discrimination against it, but they also know, and the nation knows, that relentless color-prejudice is more often a cause than a result of the Negro's degradation; they seek the abatement of this relic of barbarism, and not its systematic encouragement and pampering by all agencies of social power from the Associated Press to the Church of Christ. They advocate, with Mr. Washington, a broad system of Negro common schools supplemented by thorough industrial training; but they are surprised that a man of Mr. Washington's insight cannot see that no such educational system ever has rested or can rest on any other basis than that of the well-equipped college and university, and they insist that there is a demand for a few such institutions throughout the South to train the best of the Negro youth as teachers, professional men, and leaders.

This group of men honor Mr. Washington for his attitude of conciliation toward the white South; they accept the "Atlanta Compromise" in its broadest interpretation; they recognize, with him, many signs of promise, many men of high purpose and fair judgment, in this section; they know that no easy task has been laid upon a region already tottering under heavy burdens. But, nevertheless, they insist that the way to truth and right lies in straightforward honesty, not in indiscriminate flattery; in praising those of the South who do well and criticising uncompromisingly those who do ill; in taking advantage of the opportunities at hand and urging their fellows to do the same, but at the same time in remembering that only a firm adherence to their higher ideals and aspirations will ever keep those ideals within the realm of possibility. They do not expect that the free right to vote, to enjoy civic rights, and to be educated, will come in a moment; they do not expect to see the bias and prejudices of years disappear at the blast of a trumpet; but they are absolutely certain that the way for a people to gain their reasonable rights is not by voluntarily throwing them away and insisting that they do not want them; that the way for a people to gain respect is not by continually belittling and ridiculing themselves; that, on the contrary, Negroes must insist continually, in season and out of season, that voting is necessary to modern manhood, that color discrimination is barbarism, and that black boys need education as well as white boys.

In failing thus to state plainly and unequivocally the legitimate demands of their people, even at the cost of opposing an honored leader, the thinking classes of American Negroes would shirk a heavy responsibility,—a responsibility to themselves, a responsibility to the struggling masses, a responsibility to the darker races of men whose future depends so largely on this American experiment, but especially a responsibility to this nation,—this common Fatherland. It is wrong to encourage a man or a people in evil-doing; it is wrong to aid and abet a national crime simply because it is unpopular not to do so. The growing spirit of kindliness and reconciliation between the North and South after the frightful difference of a generation ago ought to be a source of deep congratulation to all, and especially to those whose mistreatment caused the war; but if that reconciliation is to be marked by the industrial slavery and civic death of those same black men, with permanent legislation into a position of inferiority, then those black men, if they are really men, are called upon by every consideration of patriotism and loyalty to oppose such a course by all civilized methods, even though such opposition involves disagreement with Mr. Booker T. Washington. We have no right to sit silently by while the inevitable seeds are sown for a harvest of disaster to our children, black and white.

First, it is the duty of black men to judge the South discriminatingly. The present generation of Southerners are not responsible for the past, and they should not be blindly hated or blamed for it. Furthermore, to no class is the indiscriminate endorsement of the recent course of the South toward Negroes more nauseating than to the best thought of the South. The South is not "solid"; it is a land in the ferment of social change, wherein forces of all kinds are fighting for supremacy; and to praise the ill the South is today perpetrating is just as wrong as to condemn the good. Discriminating and broad-minded criticism is what the South needs,— needs it for the sake of her own white sons and daughters, and for the insurance of robust, healthy mental and moral development.

Today even the attitude of the Southern whites toward the blacks is not, as so many assume, in all cases the same; the ignorant Southerner hates the Negro, the workingmen fear his competition, the money-makers wish to use him as a laborer, some of the educated see a menace in his upward development, while others—usually the sons of the masters—wish to help him to rise. National opinion has enabled this last class to maintain the Negro common schools, and to protect the Negro partially in property, life, and limb. Through the pressure of the money-makers, the Negro is in danger of being reduced to semi-slavery, especially in the country districts; the workingmen, and those of the educated who fear the Negro, have united to disfranchise him, and some have urged his deportation; while the passions of the ignorant are easily aroused to lynch and abuse any black man. To praise this intricate whirl of thought and prejudice is nonsense; to inveigh indiscriminately against "the South" is unjust; but to use the same breath in praising Governor Aycock, exposing Senator Morgan, arguing with Mr. Thomas Nelson Page, and denouncing Senator Ben Tillman, is not only sane, but the imperative duty of thinking black men.

It would be unjust to Mr. Washington not to acknowledge that in several instances he has opposed movements in the South which were unjust to the Negro;

he sent memorials to the Louisiana and Alabama constitutional conventions, he has spoken against lynching, and in other ways has openly or silently set his influence against sinister schemes and unfortunate happenings. Notwithstanding this, it is equally true to assert that on the whole the distinct impression left by Mr. Washington's propaganda is, first, that the South is justified in its present attitude toward the Negro because of the Negro's degradation; secondly, that the prime cause of the Negro's failure to rise more quickly is his wrong education in the past; and, thirdly, that his future rise depends primarily on his own efforts. Each of these propositions is a dangerous half-truth. The supplementary truths must never be lost sight of: first, slavery and race-prejudice are potent if not sufficient causes of the Negro's position; second, industrial and common-school training were necessarily slow in planting because they had to await the black teachers trained by higher institutions,—it being extremely doubtful if any essentially different development was possible, and certainly a Tuskegee was unthinkable before 1880; and, third, while it is a great truth to say that the Negro must strive and strive mightily to help himself, it is equally true that unless his striving be not simply seconded, but rather aroused and encouraged, by the initiative of the richer and wiser environing group, he cannot hope for great success.

In his failure to realize and impress this last point, Mr. Washington is especially to be criticised. His doctrine has tended to make the whites, North and South, shift the burden of the Negro problem to the Negro's shoulders and stand aside as critical and rather pessimistic spectators; when in fact the burden belongs to the nation, and the hands of none of us are clean if we bend not our energies to righting these great wrongs.

The South ought to be led, by candid and honest criticism, to assert her better self and do her full duty to the race she has cruelly wronged and is still wronging. The North—her co-partner in guilt—cannot salve her conscience by plastering it with gold. We cannot settle this problem by diplomacy and suaveness, by "policy" alone. If worse come to worst, can the moral fibre of this country survive the slow throttling and murder of nine millions of men?

The black men of America have a duty to perform, a duty stern and delicate,—a forward movement to oppose a part of the work of their greatest leader. So far as Mr. Washington preaches Thrift, Patience, and Industrial Training for the masses, we must hold up his hands and strive with him, rejoicing in his honors and glorying in the strength of this Joshua called of God and of man to lead the headless host. But so far as Mr. Washington apologizes for injustice, North or South, does not rightly value the privilege and duty of voting, belittles the emasculating effects of caste distinctions, and opposes the higher training and ambition of our brighter minds,—so far as he, the South, or the Nation, does this,—we must unceasingly and firmly oppose them. By every civilized and peaceful method we must strive for the rights which the world accords to men, clinging unwaveringly to those great words which the sons of the Fathers would fain forget: "We hold these truths to be self-evident: That all men are created equal; that they are endowed by their Creator with certain unalienable rights; that among these are life, liberty, and the pursuit of happiness."

4.4.2 Reading and Review Questions

1. Why does Du Bois include the musical bars at the beginning of each chapter?

2. How does Du Bois's essay, "Of Mr. Booker T. Washington and Others" differ from Washington's "Atlanta Exposition"?

4.5 ZANE GREY

(1872 - 1939)

On July 12, 1893, during a meeting of the American Historical Association held in conjunction with the World Columbian Exposition in Chicago, the historian Frederick Jackson Turner (1861-1932) opened his remarks by quoting from the 1890 U.S. Census:

> Up to and including 1880 the country had a frontier of settlement, but at present the unsettled area has been so broken into by isolated bodies of settlement that there can hardly be said to be a frontier line. In the discussion of its extent, its westward movement, etc., it can not, therefore, any longer have a place in the census reports.[1]

Image 4.3 | Zane Grey
Photographer | Unknown
Source | Wikimedia Commons
License | Public Domain

For Turner and his contemporaries, the closing of the American frontier was significant not merely for the manifest destiny that the closing described, but for the institutions which shaped, and were shaped by, these settlements. Jackson continues:

> Behind institutions, behind constitutional forms and modifications, lie the vital forces that call these organs into life and shape them to meet changing conditions. The peculiarity of American institutions is, the fact that they have been compelled to adapt themselves to the changes of an expanding people— to the changes involved in crossing a continent, in winning a wilderness, and in developing at each area of this progress out of the primitive economic and political conditions of the frontier into the complexity of city life.[2]

---

1   Turner, Frederick Jackson, "The Significance of the Frontier in American History," (1893) retrieved from: http://nationalhumanitiescenter.org/pds/gilded/empire/text1/turner.pdf on 12 February 2014.
2   Ibid. paragraph 2.

In the passage above, Jackson draws our attention to the continual adaptation and change that was, for him, part of the American character. Everywhere he looked, the only constant in the American experience was an experience of change, and the constancy of this change shaped and developed the American character, American democracy, and American values. Like his half-contemporary, Charles Saunders Pierce (1839-1914), the founder of modern pragmatism, Turner believed in the practical application of ideas. Read this way, we can see that the frontier thesis, and the closing of the frontier, represented a watershed moment for the American experience. For the first century of the American republic, the West represented an eternally renewing ideal, even an Eden, if you will. If you did not care for your lot in life, strike out for the western territories; if you did not care for the government of your particular state, strike out for the western territories; if you wanted to make your escape, strike out for points unknown, lands undocumented, and resources unclaimed.

Zane Grey (1872-1939) was just twenty-one when Turner first articulated his "frontier thesis," but Grey's novels of western expansion are a testament to the pervasiveness of the western ideal in American literature and American culture. The son of a dentist who was raised in Zanesville, Ohio, on the eastern edge of the colonial frontier, Grey recognized a chance for self-expression and self-determination under the open skies of the western states and territories. While Owen Wister's *The Virginian* (1902) is often credited as the first Western in American literature, *The Virginian* is, at its core, a traditional novel of courtly love, the importance of authority, and the uniting and healing forces of marriage and family. Grey's *Riders of the Purple Sage* (1912) is a different kind of novel set in a different kind of America: rough, opportunistic, pragmatic, and individualistic. Set on the very edge of the frontier in a border town in southern Utah, *Riders of the Purple Sage* challenges readers to celebrate both the outlaw Jim Lassiter and the rugged pioneer woman Jane Withersteen as they struggle to make a new life together as outcasts from the edge of society. While *The Virginian* ends happily in marriage and the security of family, *Riders* offers readers a new kind of family, one that unites faith, culture, and individual identity in a new kind of bond.

While *Riders of the Purple Sage* is often read today as an early critique of conformity and a celebration of American independence, it is also a literary bridge between Realism, Naturalism, and Modernism. Richly and precisely detailed, *Riders of the Purple Sage* presents readers with a hero and heroine who overcome both their circumstances and surroundings, risking almost certain death, to conduct their lives on their own terms. In this way, *Riders of the Purple Sage* can be read as the first true Western, a novel not merely set in the West and espousing orthodox values, but a novel that takes readers to the edge of society and asks essential questions about the creation of a new society.

4.5.1 *RIDERS OF THE PURPLE SAGE*

CHAPTER I

LASSITER

A sharp clip-crop of iron-shod hoofs deadened and died away, and clouds of yellow dust drifted from under the cottonwoods out over the sage.

Jane Withersteen gazed down the wide purple slope with dreamy and troubled eyes. A rider had just left her and it was his message that held her thoughtful and almost sad, awaiting the churchmen who were coming to resent and attack her right to befriend a Gentile.

She wondered if the unrest and strife that had lately come to the little village of Cottonwoods was to involve her. And then she sighed, remembering that her father had founded this remotest border settlement of southern Utah and that he had left it to her. She owned all the ground and many of the cottages. Withersteen House was hers, and the great ranch, with its thousands of cattle, and the swiftest horses of the sage. To her belonged Amber Spring, the water which gave verdure and beauty to the village and made living possible on that wild purple upland waste. She could not escape being involved by whatever befell Cottonwoods.

That year, 1871, had marked a change which had been gradually coming in the lives of the peace-loving Mormons of the border. Glaze—Stone Bridge—Sterling, villages to the north, had risen against the invasion of Gentile settlers and the forays of rustlers. There had been opposition to the one and fighting with the other. And now Cottonwoods had begun to wake and bestir itself and grown hard.

Jane prayed that the tranquillity and sweetness of her life would not be permanently disrupted. She meant to do so much more for her people than she had done. She wanted the sleepy quiet pastoral days to last always. Trouble between the Mormons and the Gentiles of the community would make her unhappy. She was Mormon-born, and she was a friend to poor and unfortunate Gentiles. She wished only to go on doing good and being happy. And she thought of what that great ranch meant to her. She loved it all—the grove of cottonwoods, the old stone house, the amber-tinted water, and the droves of shaggy, dusty horses and mustangs, the sleek, clean-limbed, blooded racers, and the browsing herds of cattle and the lean, sun-browned riders of the sage.

While she waited there she forgot the prospect of untoward change. The bray of a lazy burro broke the afternoon quiet, and it was comfortingly suggestive of the drowsy farmyard, and the open corrals, and the green alfalfa fields. Her clear sight intensified the purple sage-slope as it rolled before her. Low swells of prairie-like ground sloped up to the west. Dark, lonely cedar-trees, few and far between, stood out strikingly, and at long distances ruins of red rocks. Farther on, up the gradual slope, rose a broken wall, a huge monument, looming dark purple and stretching its solitary, mystic way, a wavering line that faded in the north. Here to the westward was the light and color and beauty. Northward the slope descended to a dim line of canyons from which rose an up-Hinging of the earth, not mountainous, but a vast heave of purple uplands, with ribbed and fan-shaped walls, castle-crowned cliffs, and gray escarpments. Over it all crept the lengthening, waning afternoon shadows.

The rapid beat of hoofs recalled Jane Withersteen to the question at hand. A group of riders cantered up the lane, dismounted, and threw their bridles. They were seven in number, and Tull, the leader, a tall, dark man, was an elder of Jane's church.

"Did you get my message?" he asked, curtly. "Yes," replied Jane.

"I sent word I'd give that rider Venters half an hour to come down to the village. He didn't come."

"He knows nothing of it;" said Jane. "I didn't tell him. I've been waiting here for you."

"Where is Venters?"

"I left him in the courtyard."

"Here, Jerry," called Tull, turning to his men, "take the gang and fetch Venters out here if you have to rope him."

The dusty-booted and long-spurred riders clanked noisily into the grove of cottonwoods and disappeared in the shade.

"Elder Tull, what do you mean by this?" demanded Jane. "If you must arrest Venters you might have the courtesy to wait till he leaves my home. And if you do arrest him it will be adding insult to injury. It's absurd to accuse Venters of being mixed up in that shooting fray in the village last night. He was with me at the time. Besides, he let me take charge of his guns. You're only using this as a pretext. What do you mean to do to Venters?"

"I'll tell you presently," replied Tull. "But first tell me why you defend this worthless rider?"

"Worthless!" exclaimed Jane, indignantly. "He's nothing of the kind. He was the best rider I ever had. There's not a reason why I shouldn't champion him and every reason why I should. It's no little shame to me, Elder Tull, that through my friendship he has roused the enmity of my people and become an outcast. Besides I owe him eternal gratitude for saving the life of little Fay."

"I've heard of your love for Fay Larkin and that you intend to adopt her. But— Jane Withersteen, the child is a Gentile!"

"Yes. But, Elder, I don't love the Mormon children any less because I love a Gentile child. I shall adopt Fay if her mother will give her to me."

"I'm not so much against that. You can give the child Mormon teaching," said Tull. "But I'm sick of seeing this fellow Venters hang around you. I'm going to put a stop to it. You've so much love to throw away on these beggars of Gentiles that I've an idea you might love Venters."

Tull spoke with the arrogance of a Mormon whose power could not be brooked and with the passion of a man in whom jealousy had kindled a consuming fire.

"Maybe I do love him," said Jane. She felt both fear and anger stir her heart. "I'd never thought of that. Poor fellow! he certainly needs some one to love him."

"This'll be a bad day for Venters unless you deny that," returned Tull, grimly.

Tull's men appeared under the cottonwoods and led a young man out into the lane. His ragged clothes were those of an outcast. But he stood tall and straight, his wide shoulders flung back, with the muscles of his bound arms rippling and a blue flame of defiance in the gaze he bent on Tull.

For the first time Jane Withersteen felt Venters's real spirit. She wondered if she would love this splendid youth. Then her emotion cooled to the sobering sense of the issue at stake.

"Venters, will you leave Cottonwoods at once and forever?" asked Tull, tensely.

"Why?" rejoined the rider. "Because I order it."

Venters laughed in cool disdain.

The red leaped to Tull's dark cheek.

"If you don't go it means your ruin," he said, sharply.

"Ruin!" exclaimed Venters, passionately. "Haven't you already ruined me? What do you call ruin? A year ago I was a rider. I had horses and cattle of my own. I had a good name in Cottonwoods. And now when I come into the village to see this woman you set your men on me. You hound me. You trail me as if I were a rustler. I've no more to lose—except my life."

"Will you leave Utah?"

"Oh! I know," went on Venters, tauntingly, "it galls you, the idea of beautiful Jane Withersteen being friendly to a poor Gentile. You want her all yourself. You're a wiving Mormon. You have use for her—and Withersteen House and Amber Spring and seven thousand head of cattle!"

Tull's hard jaw protruded, and rioting blood corded the veins of his neck. "Once more. Will you go?"

"NO!"

"Then I'll have you whipped within an inch of your life," replied Tull, harshly. "I'll turn you out in the sage. And if you ever come back you'll get worse."

Venters's agitated face grew coldly set and the bronze changed Jane impulsively stepped forward. "Oh! Elder Tull!" she cried. "You won't do that!" Tull lifted a shaking finger toward her.

"That'll do from you. Understand, you'll not be allowed to hold this boy to a friendship that's offensive to your Bishop. Jane Withersteen, your father left you wealth and power. It has turned your head. You haven't yet come to see the place of Mormon women. We've reasoned with you, borne with you. We've patiently waited. We've let you have your fling, which is more than I ever saw granted to a Mormon woman. But you haven't come to your senses. Now, once for all, you can't have any further friendship with Venters. He's going to be whipped, and he's got to leave Utah!"

"Oh! Don't whip him! It would be dastardly!" implored Jane, with slow certainty of her failing courage. Tull always blunted her spirit, and she grew conscious that she had feigned a boldness which she did not possess. He loomed up now in different guise, not as a jealous suitor, but embodying the mysterious despotism she had known from childhood—the power of her creed.

"Venters, will you take your whipping here or would you rather go out in the sage?" asked Tull. He smiled a flinty smile that was more than inhuman, yet seemed to give out of its dark aloofness a gleam of righteousness.

"I'll take it here—if I must," said Venters. "But by God!—Tull you'd better kill me outright. That'll be a dear whipping for you and your praying Mormons. You'll make me another Lassiter!"

The strange glow, the austere light which radiated from Tull's face, might have been a holy joy at the spiritual conception of exalted duty. But there was something more in him, barely hidden, a something personal and sinister, a deep of himself, an engulfing abyss. As his religious mood was fanatical and inexorable, so would his physical hate be merciless.

"Elder, I—I repent my words," Jane faltered. The religion in her, the long habit of obedience, of humility, as well as agony of fear, spoke in her voice. "Spare the boy!" she whispered.

"You can't save him now," replied Tull stridently.

Her head was bowing to the inevitable. She was grasping the truth, when suddenly there came, in inward constriction, a hardening of gentle forces within her breast. Like a steel bar it was stiffening all that had been soft and weak in her. She felt a birth in her of something new and unintelligible. Once more her strained gaze sought the sage-slopes. Jane Withersteen loved that wild and purple wilderness. In times of sorrow it had been her strength, in happiness its beauty was her continual delight. In her extremity she found herself murmuring, "Whence cometh my help!" It was a prayer, as if forth from those lonely purple reaches and walls of red and clefts of blue might ride a fearless man, neither creed-bound nor creed-mad, who would hold up a restraining hand in the faces of her ruthless people.

The restless movements of Tull's men suddenly quieted down. Then followed a low whisper, a rustle, a sharp exclamation.

"Look!" said one, pointing to the west. "A rider!"

Jane Withersteen wheeled and saw a horseman, silhouetted against the western sky, coming riding out of the sage. He had ridden down from the left, in the golden glare of the sun, and had been unobserved till close at hand. An answer to her prayer!

"Do you know him? Does any one know him?" questioned Tull, hurriedly. His men looked and looked, and one by one shook their heads.

"He's come from far," said one. "Thet's a fine hoss," said another. "A strange rider."

"Huh! he wears black leather," added a fourth.

With a wave of his hand, enjoining silence, Tull stepped forward in such a way that he concealed Venters. The rider reined in his mount, and with a lithe forward-slipping action appeared to reach the ground in one

long step. It was a peculiar movement in its quickness and inasmuch that while performing it the rider did not swerve in the slightest from a square front to the group before him.

"Look!" hoarsely whispered one of Tull's companions. "He packs two black-butted guns—low down—they're

hard to see—black akin them black chaps."

"A gun-man!" whispered another. "Fellers, careful now about movin' your hands."

The stranger's slow approach might have been a mere leisurely manner of gait or the cramped short steps of a rider unused to walking; yet, as well, it could have been the guarded advance of one who took no chances with men.

"Hello, stranger!" called Tull. No welcome was in this greeting only a gruff curiosity.

The rider responded with a curt nod. The wide brim of a black sombrero cast a dark shade over his face. For a moment he closely regarded Tull and his comrades, and then, halting in his slow walk, he seemed to relax.

"Evenin', ma'am," he said to Jane, and removed his sombrero with quaint grace.

Jane, greeting him, looked up into a face that she trusted instinctively and which riveted her attention. It had all the characteristics of the range rider's—the leanness, the red burn of the sun, and the set changelessness that came from years of silence and solitude. But it was not these which held her, rather the intensity of his gaze, a strained weariness, a piercing wistfulness of keen, gray sight, as if the man was forever looking for that which he never found. Jane's subtle woman's intuition, even in that brief instant, felt a sadness, a hungering, a secret.

"Jane Withersteen, ma'am?" he inquired. "Yes," she replied.

"The water here is yours?"

"Yes."

"May I water my horse?"

"Certainly. There's the trough."

"But mebbe if you knew who I was—" He hesitated, with his glance on the listening men. "Mebbe you wouldn't let me water him—though I ain't askin' none for myself."

"Stranger, it doesn't matter who you are. Water your horse. And if you are thirsty and hungry come into my house."

"Thanks, ma'am. I can't accept for myself—but for my tired horse—"

Trampling of hoofs interrupted the rider. More restless movements on the part of Tull's men broke up the little circle, exposing the prisoner Venters.

"Mebbe I've kind of hindered somethin'—for a few moments, perhaps?" inquired the rider. "Yes," replied Jane Withersteen, with a throb in her voice.

She felt the drawing power of his eyes; and then she saw him look at the bound Venters, and at the men who held him, and their leader.

"In this here country all the rustlers an' thieves an' cut-throats an' gun-throwers an' all-round no-good men jest happen to be Gentiles. Ma'am, which of the no-good class does that young feller belong to?"

"He belongs to none of them. He's an honest boy."

"You KNOW that, ma'am?"

"Yes—yes."

"Then what has he done to get tied up that way?"

His clear and distinct question, meant for Tull as well as for Jane Withersteen, stilled the restlessness and brought a momentary silence.

"Ask him," replied Jane, her voice rising high.

The rider stepped away from her, moving out with the same slow, measured stride in which he had approached, and the fact that his action placed her wholly to one side, and him no nearer to Tull and his men, had a penetrating significance.

"Young feller, speak up," he said to Venters.

"Here stranger, this's none of your mix," began Tull. "Don't try any interference. You've been asked to drink and eat. That's more than you'd have got in any other village of the Utah border. Water your horse and be on your way."

"Easy—easy—I ain't interferin' yet," replied the rider. The tone of his voice had undergone a change. A different man had spoken. Where, in addressing Jane, he had been mild and gentle, now, with his first speech to Tull, he was dry, cool, biting. "I've lest stumbled onto a queer deal. Seven Mormons all packin' guns, an' a Gentile tied with a rope, an' a woman who swears by his honesty! Queer, ain't that?"

"Queer or not, it's none of your business," retorted Tull.

"Where I was raised a woman's word was law. I ain't quite outgrowed that yet." Tull fumed between amaze and anger.

"Meddler, we have a law here something different from woman's whim— Mormon law! . . . Take care you don't transgress it."

"To hell with your Mormon law!"

The deliberate speech marked the rider's further change, this time from kindly interest to an awakening menace. It produced a transformation in Tull and his companions. The leader gasped and staggered backward at a blasphemous affront to an institution he held most sacred. The man Jerry, holding the horses, dropped the bridles and froze in his tracks. Like posts the other men stood watchful-eyed, arms hanging rigid, all waiting.

"Speak up now, young man. What have you done to be roped that way?"

"It's a damned outrage!" burst out Venters. "I've done no wrong. I've offended this Mormon Elder by being a friend to that woman."

"Ma'am, is it true—what he says?" asked the rider of Jane, but his quiveringly alert eyes never left the little

knot of quiet men.

"True? Yes, perfectly true," she answered.

"Well, young man, it seems to me that bein' a friend to such a woman would be what you wouldn't want to help an' couldn't help . . . . .What's to be done to you for it?"

"They intend to whip me. You know what that means—in Utah!"

"I reckon," replied the rider, slowly.

With his gray glance cold on the Mormons, with the restive bit-champing of the horses, with Jane failing to repress her mounting agitations, with Venters standing pale and still, the tension of the moment tightened. Tull broke the spell with a laugh, a laugh without mirth, a laugh that was only a sound betraying fear.

"Come on, men!" he called.

Jane Withersteen turned again to the rider. "Stranger, can you do nothing to save Venters?"

"Ma'am, you ask me to save him—from your own people?"

"Ask you? I beg of you!"

"But you don't dream who you're askin'."

"Oh, sir, I pray you—save him!"

These are Mormons, an' I . . . "

"At—at any cost—save him. For I—I care for him!"

Tull snarled. "You love-sick fool! Tell your secrets. There'll be a way to teach you what you've never learned . . . .Come men out of here!"

"Mormon, the young man stays," said the rider. Like a shot his voice halted Tull.

"What!"

"Who'll keep him? He's my prisoner!" cried Tull, hotly. "Stranger, again I tell you—don't mix here. You've meddled enough. Go your way now or—"

"Listen! . . . He stays."

Absolute certainty, beyond any shadow of doubt, breathed in the rider's low voice. "Who are you? We are seven here."

The rider dropped his sombrero and made a rapid movement, singular in that it left him somewhat crouched, arms bent and stiff, with the big black gun-sheaths swung round to the fore. "LASSITER!"

It was Venters's wondering, thrilling cry that bridged the fateful connection between the rider's singular position and the dreaded name.

Tull put out a groping hand. The life of his eyes dulled to the gloom with which men of his fear saw the approach of death. But death, while it hovered over him, did not descend, for the rider waited for the twitching fingers, the downward flash of hand that did not come. Tull, gathering himself together, turned to the horses, attended by his pale comrades.

CHAPTER II
COTTONWOODS

Venters appeared too deeply moved to speak the gratitude his face expressed. And Jane turned upon the rescuer and gripped his hands. Her smiles and tears seemingly dazed him. Presently as something like calmness returned, she went to Lassiter's weary horse.

"I will water him myself," she said, and she led the horse to a trough under a huge old cottonwood. With nimble fingers she loosened the bridle and removed the bit. The horse snorted and bent his head. The trough was of solid stone, hollowed out, moss-covered and green and wet and cool, and the clear brown water that fed it spouted and splashed from a wooden pipe.

"He has brought you far to-day?"

"Yes, ma'am, a matter of over sixty miles, mebbe seventy."

"A long ride—a ride that—Ah, he is blind!"

"Yes, ma'am," replied Lassiter. "What blinded him?"

"Some men once roped an' tied him, an' then held white-iron close to his eyes."

"Oh! Men? You mean devils. . . .Were they your enemies—Mormons?"

"Yes, ma'am."

"To take revenge on a horse! Lassiter, the men of my creed are unnaturally cruel. To my everlasting sorrow I confess it. They have been driven, hated, scourged till their hearts have hardened. But we women hope and pray for the time when our men will soften."

"Beggin' your pardon, ma'am—that time will never come."

"Oh, it will! . . . Lassiter, do you think Mormon women wicked? Has your hand been against them, too?"

"No. I believe Mormon women are the best and noblest, the most long-sufferin', and the blindest, unhappiest women on earth."

"Ah!" She gave him a grave, thoughtful look. "Then you will break bread with me?"

Lassiter had no ready response, and he uneasily shifted his weight from one leg to another, and turned his sombrero round and round in his hands. "Ma'am," he began, presently, "I reckon your kindness of heart makes you overlook things. Perhaps I ain't well known hereabouts, but back up North there's Mormons who'd rest uneasy in their graves at the idea of me sittin' to table with you."

"I dare say. But—will you do it, anyway?" she asked.

"Mebbe you have a brother or relative who might drop in an' be offended, an' I wouldn't want to—"

"I've not a relative in Utah that I know of. There's no one with a right to question my actions." She turned smilingly to Venters. "You will come in, Bern, and Lassiter will come in. We'll eat and be merry while we may."

"I'm only wonderin' if Tull an' his men'll raise a storm down in the village," said Lassiter, in his last weakening stand.

"Yes, he'll raise the storm—after he has prayed," replied Jane. "Come."

She led the way, with the bridle of Lassiter's horse over her arm. They entered a grove and walked down a wide path shaded by great low-branching cottonwoods. The last rays of the setting sun sent golden bars through the leaves. The grass was deep and rich, welcome contrast to sage-tired eyes. Twittering quail darted across the path, and from a tree-top somewhere a robin sang its evening song, and on the still air floated the freshness and murmur of flowing water.

The home of Jane Withersteen stood in a circle of cottonwoods, and was a flat, long, red-stone structure with a covered court in the center through which flowed a lively stream of amber-colored water. In the massive blocks of stone and heavy timbers and solid doors and shutters showed the hand of a man who had builded against pillage and time; and in the flowers and mosses lining the stone-bedded stream, in the bright colors of rugs and blankets on the court floor, and the cozy corner with hammock and books and the clean-linened table, showed the grace of a daughter who lived for happiness and the day at hand.

Jane turned Lassiter's horse loose in the thick grass. "You will want him to be near you," she said, "or I'd have him taken to the alfalfa fields." At her call appeared women who began at once to bustle about, hurrying to and fro, setting the table. Then Jane, excusing herself, went within.

She passed through a huge low ceiled chamber, like the inside of a fort, and into a smaller one where a bright wood-fire blazed in an old open fireplace, and from this into her own room. It had the same comfort as was manifested in the home-like outer court; moreover, it was warm and rich in soft hues.

Seldom did Jane Withersteen enter her room without looking into her mirror. She knew she loved the reflection of that beauty which since early childhood she had never been allowed to forget. Her relatives and friends, and later a horde of Mormon and Gentile suitors, had fanned the flame of natural vanity in her. So that at twenty-eight she scarcely thought at all of her wonderful influence for good in the little community where her father had left her practically its beneficent land-lord, but cared most for the dream and the assurance and the allurement of her beauty. This time, however, she gazed into her glass with more than the usual happy motive, without the usual slight conscious smile. For she was thinking of more than the desire to be fair in her own eyes, in those of her friend; she wondered if she were to seem fair in the eyes of this Lassiter, this man whose name had crossed the long, wild brakes of stone and plains of sage, this gentle-voiced, sad-faced man who was a hater and a killer of Mormons. It was not now her usual half-conscious vain obsession that actuated her as she hurriedly changed her riding-dress to one of white, and then looked long at the stately form with its gracious contours, at the fair face with its strong chin and full firm lips, at the dark-blue, proud, and passionate eyes.

"If by some means I can keep him here a few days, a week—he will never kill another Mormon," she mused. "Lassiter! . . . I shudder when I think of that name, of him. But when I look at the man I forget who he is—I almost like him. I remember only that he saved Bern. He has suffered. I wonder what it was—did he love a Mormon woman once? How splendidly he championed us poor misunderstood souls! Somehow he knows—much."

Jane Withersteen joined her guests and bade them to her board. Dismissing her woman, she waited upon them with her own hands. It was a bountiful supper and a strange company. On her right sat the ragged and half-starved Venters; and though blind eyes could have seen what he counted for in the sum of her happiness, yet he looked the gloomy outcast his allegiance had made him, and about him there was the shadow of the ruin presaged by Tull. On her left sat black-leather-garbed Lassiter looking like a man in a dream. Hunger was not with him, nor composure, nor speech, and when he twisted in frequent unquiet movements the heavy guns that he had not removed knocked against the table-legs. If it had been otherwise possible to forget the presence of Lassiter those telling little jars would have rendered it unlikely. And Jane Withersteen talked and smiled and laughed with all the dazzling play of lips and eyes that a beautiful, daring woman could summon to her purpose.

When the meal ended, and the men pushed back their chairs, she leaned closer to Lassiter and looked square into his eyes.

"Why did you come to Cottonwoods?"

Her question seemed to break a spell. The rider arose as if he had just remembered himself and had tarried longer than his wont.

"Ma'am, I have hunted all over the southern Utah and Nevada for— somethin'. An' through your name I learned where to find it—here in Cottonwoods."

"My name! Oh, I remember. You did know my name when you spoke first. Well, tell me where you heard it and from whom?"

"At the little village—Glaze, I think it's called—some fifty miles or more west of here. An' I heard it from a Gentile, a rider who said you'd know where to tell me to find—"

"What?" she demanded, imperiously, as Lassiter broke off.

"Milly Erne's grave," he answered low, and the words came with a wrench.

Venters wheeled in his chair to regard Lassiter in amazement, and Jane slowly raised herself in white, still wonder.

"Milly Erne's grave?" she echoed, in a whisper. "What do you know of Milly Erne, my best-beloved friend—who died in my arms? What were you to her?"

"Did I claim to be anythin'?" he inquired. "I know people—relatives— who have long wanted to know where she's buried, that's all."

"Relatives? She never spoke of relatives, except a brother who was shot in Texas. Lassiter, Milly Erne's grave is in a secret burying-ground on my property."

"Will you take me there? . . . You'll be offendin' Mormons worse than by breakin' bread with me."

"Indeed yes, but I'll do it. Only we must go unseen. To-morrow, perhaps."

"Thank you, Jane Withersteen," replied the rider, and he bowed to her and stepped backward out of the court. "Will you not stay—sleep under my roof?" she asked.

"No, ma'am, an' thanks again. I never sleep indoors. An' even if I did there's that gatherin' storm in the village below. No, no. I'll go to the sage. I hope you won't suffer none for your kindness to me."

"Lassiter," said Venters, with a half-bitter laugh, "my bed too, is the sage. Perhaps we may meet out there."

"Mebbe so. But the sage is wide an' I won't be near. Good night."

At Lassiter's low whistle the black horse whinnied, and carefully picked his blind way out of the grove. The rider did not bridle him, but walked beside him, leading him by touch of hand and together they passed slowly into the shade of the cottonwoods.

"Jane, I must be off soon," said Venters. "Give me my guns. If I'd had my guns—"

"Either my friend or the Elder of my church would be lying dead," she interposed "Tull would be—surely."

"Oh, you fierce-blooded, savage youth! Can't I teach you forebearance, mercy? Bern, it's divine to forgive your enemies. 'Let not the sun go down upon thy wrath.'"

"Hush! Talk to me no more of mercy or religion—after to-day. To-day this strange coming of Lassiter left me still a man, and now I'll die a man! . . . Give me my guns."

Silently she went into the house, to return with a heavy cartridge-belt and gun-filled sheath and a long rifle;

these she handed to him, and as he buckled on the belt she stood before him in silent eloquence.

"Jane," he said, in gentler voice, "don't look so. I'm not going out to murder your churchman. I'll try to avoid him and all his men. But can't you see I've reached the end of my rope? Jane, you're a wonderful woman. Never was there a woman so unselfish and good. Only you're blind in one way . . . .Listen!"

From behind the grove came the clicking sound of horses in a rapid trot.

"Some of your riders," he continued. "It's getting time for the night shift. Let us go out to the bench in the grove and talk there."

It was still daylight in the open, but under the spreading cottonwoods shadows were obscuring the lanes. Venters drew Jane off from one of these into a shrub-lined trail, just wide enough for the two to walk abreast, and in a roundabout way led her far from the house to a knoll on the edge of the grove. Here in a secluded nook was a bench from which, through an opening in the tree-tops, could be seen the sage-slope and the wall of rock and the dim lines of canyons. Jane had not spoken since Venters had shocked her with his first harsh speech; but all the way she had clung to his arm, and now, as he stopped and laid his rifle against the bench, she still clung to him.

"Jane, I'm afraid I must leave you."

"Bern!" she cried.

"Yes, it looks that way. My position is not a happy one—I can't feel right—I've lost all—"

"I'll give you anything you—"

"Listen, please. When I say loss I don't mean what you think. I mean loss of good-will, good name—that which would have enabled me to stand up in this village without bitterness. Well, it's too late . . . .Now, as to the future, I think you'd do best to give me up. Tull is implacable. You ought to see from his intention to-day

that—But you can't see. Your blindness—your damned religion! . . . Jane, forgive me—I'm sore within and something rankles. Well, I fear that invisible hand will turn its hidden work to your ruin."

"Invisible hand? Bern!"

"I mean your Bishop." Venters said it deliberately and would not release her as she started back. "He's the law. The edict went forth to ruin me. Well, look at me! It'll now go forth to compel you to the will of the Church."

"You wrong Bishop Dyer. Tull is hard, I know. But then he has been in love with me for years."

"Oh, your faith and your excuses! You can't see what I know—and if you did see it you'd not admit it to save your life. That's the Mormon of you. These elders and bishops will do absolutely any deed to go on building up the power and wealth of their church, their empire. Think of what they've done to the Gentiles here, to me—think of Milly Erne's fate!"

"What do you know of her story?"

"I know enough—all, perhaps, except the name of the Mormon who brought her here. But I must stop this kind of talk."

She pressed his hand in response. He helped her to a seat beside him on the bench. And he respected a silence that he divined was full of woman's deep emotion beyond his understanding.

It was the moment when the last ruddy rays of the sunset brightened momentarily before yielding to twilight. And for Venters the outlook before him was in some sense similar to a feeling of his future, and with searching eyes he studied the beautiful purple, barren waste of sage. Here was the unknown and the perilous.

The whole scene impressed Venters as a wild, austere, and mighty manifestation of nature. And as it somehow reminded him of his prospect in life, so it suddenly resembled the woman near him, only in her there were greater beauty and peril, a mystery more unsolvable, and something nameless that numbed his heart and dimmed his eye.

"Look! A rider!" exclaimed Jane, breaking the silence. "Can that be Lassiter?"

Venters moved his glance once more to the west. A horseman showed dark on the sky-line, then merged into the color of the sage.

"It might be. But I think not—that fellow was coming in. One of your riders, more likely. Yes, I see him clearly now. And there's another."

"I see them, too."

"Jane, your riders seem as many as the bunches of sage. I ran into five yesterday 'way down near the trail to

Deception Pass. They were with the white herd."

"You still go to that canyon? Bern, I wish you wouldn't. Oldring and his rustlers live somewhere down there."

"Well, what of that?"

"Tull has already hinted to your frequent trips into Deception Pass."

"I know." Venters uttered a short laugh. "He'll make a rustler of me next. But, Jane, there's no water for fifty miles after I leave here, and the nearest is in the canyon. I must drink and water my horse. There! I see more riders. They are going out."

"The red herd is on the slope, toward the Pass."

Twilight was fast falling. A group of horsemen crossed the dark line of low ground to become more distinct as they climbed the slope. The silence broke to a clear call from an incoming rider, and, almost like the peal of a hunting-horn, floated back the answer. The outgoing riders moved swiftly, came sharply into sight as they topped a ridge to show wild and black above the horizon, and then passed down, dimming into the purple of the sage.

"I hope they don't meet Lassiter," said Jane.

"So do I," replied Venters. "By this time the riders of the night shift know what happened to-day. But Lassiter will likely keep out of their way."

"Bern, who is Lassiter? He's only a name to me—a terrible name."

"Who is he? I don't know, Jane. Nobody I ever met knows him. He talks a little like a Texan, like Milly Erne. Did you note that?"

"Yes. How strange of him to know of her! And she lived here ten years and has been dead two. Bern, what do you know of Lassiter? Tell me what he has done—why you spoke of him to Tull—threatening to become another Lassiter yourself?"

"Jane, I only heard things, rumors, stories, most of which I disbelieved. At Glaze his name was known, but none of the riders or ranchers I knew there ever met him. At Stone Bridge I never heard him mentioned. But at Sterling and villages north of there he was spoken of often. I've never been in a village which he had been known to visit. There were many conflicting stories about him and his doings. Some said he had shot up this and that Mormon village, and others denied it. I'm inclined to believe he has, and you know how Mormons hide the truth. But there was one feature about Lassiter upon which all agree—that he was what riders in this country call a gun-man. He's a man with a marvelous quickness and accuracy in the use of a Colt. And now that I've seen him I know more. Lassiter was born without fear. I watched him with eyes which saw him my friend. I'll never forget the moment I recognized him from what had been told me of his crouch before the draw. It was then I yelled his name. I believe that yell saved Tull's life. At any rate, I know this, between Tull and death then there was not the breadth of the littlest hair. If he or any of his men had moved a finger downward—"

Venters left his meaning unspoken, but at the suggestion Jane shuddered.

The pale afterglow in the west darkened with the merging of twilight into night. The sage now spread out

black and gloomy. One dim star glimmered in the southwest sky. The sound of trotting horses had ceased, and there was silence broken only by a faint, dry pattering of cottonwood leaves in the soft night wind.

Into this peace and calm suddenly broke the high-keyed yelp of a coyote, and from far off in the darkness came the faint answering note of a trailing mate.

"Hello! the sage-dogs are barking," said Venters.

"I don't like to hear them," replied Jane. "At night, sometimes when I lie awake, listening to the long mourn or breaking bark or wild howl, I think of you asleep somewhere in the sage, and my heart aches."

"Jane, you couldn't listen to sweeter music, nor could I have a better bed."

"Just think! Men like Lassiter and you have no home, no comfort, no rest, no place to lay your weary heads. Well! . . . Let us be patient. Tull's anger may cool, and time may help us. You might do some service to the village—who can tell? Suppose you discovered the long-unknown hiding-place of Oldring and his band, and told it to my riders? That would disarm Tull's ugly hints and put you in favor. For years my riders have trailed the tracks of stolen cattle. You know as well as I how dearly we've paid for our ranges in this wild country. Oldring drives our cattle down into the network of deceiving canyons, and somewhere far to the north or east he drives them up and out to Utah markets. If you will spend time in Deception Pass try to find the trails."

"Jane, I've thought of that. I'll try."

"I must go now. And it hurts, for now I'll never be sure of seeing you again. But to-morrow, Bern?"

"To-morrow surely. I'll watch for Lassiter and ride in with him."

"Good night."

Then she left him and moved away, a white, gliding shape that soon vanished in the shadows.

Venters waited until the faint slam of a door assured him she had reached the house, and then, taking up his rifle, he noiselessly slipped through the bushes, down the knoll, and on under the dark trees to the edge of the grove. The sky was now turning from gray to blue; stars had begun to lighten the earlier blackness; and from the wide flat sweep before him blew a cool wind, fragrant with the breath of sage. Keeping close to the edge of the cottonwoods, he went swiftly and silently westward. The grove was long, and he had not reached the end when he heard something that brought him to a halt. Low padded thuds told him horses were coming this way. He sank down in the gloom, waiting, listening. Much before he had expected, judging from sound, to his amazement he descried horsemen near at hand. They were riding along the border of the sage, and instantly he knew the hoofs of the horses were muffled. Then the pale starlight afforded him indistinct sight of the riders. But his eyes were keen and used to the dark, and by peering closely he recognized the huge bulk and black-bearded visage of Oldring and the lithe, supple form of the rustler's lieutenant, a masked rider. They passed on; the darkness swallowed them. Then, farther out on the sage, a dark, compact body of horsemen went by, almost without sound, almost like specters, and they, too, melted into the night.

CHAPTER III
AMBER SPRING

No unusual circumstances was it for Oldring and some of his men to visit Cottonwoods in the broad light of day, but for him to prowl about in the dark with the hoofs of his horses muffled meant that mischief was brewing. Moreover, to Venters the presence of the masked rider with Oldring seemed especially ominous. For about this man there was mystery, he seldom rode through the village, and when he did ride through it was swiftly; riders seldom met by day on the sage, but wherever he rode there always followed deeds as dark and mysterious as the mask he wore. Oldring's band did not confine themselves to the rustling of cattle.

Venters lay low in the shade of the cottonwoods, pondering this chance meeting, and not for many moments did he consider it safe to move on. Then, with sudden impulse, he turned the other way and went back along the grove. When he reached the path leading to Jane's home he decided to go down to the village. So he hurried onward, with quick soft steps. Once beyond the grove he entered the one and only street. It was wide, lined with tall poplars, and under each row of trees, inside the foot-path, were ditches where ran the water from Jane Withersteen's spring.

Between the trees twinkled lights of cottage candles, and far down flared bright windows of the village stores. When Venters got closer to these he saw knots of men standing together in earnest conversation. The usual lounging on the corners and benches and steps was not in evidence. Keeping in the shadow Venters went closer and closer until he could hear voices. But he could not distinguish what was said. He recognized many Mormons, and looked hard for Tull and his men, but looked in vain. Venters concluded that the rustlers had not passed along the village street. No doubt these earnest men were discussing Lassiter's coming. But Venters felt positive that Tull's intention toward himself that day had not been and would not be revealed.

So Venters, seeing there was little for him to learn, began retracing his steps. The church was dark, Bishop Dyer's home next to it was also dark, and likewise Tull's cottage. Upon almost any night at this hour there would be lights here, and Venters marked the unusual omission.

As he was about to pass out of the street to skirt the grove, he once more slunk down at the sound of trotting horses. Presently he descried two mounted men riding toward him. He hugged the shadow of a tree. Again the starlight, brighter now, aided him, and he made out Tull's stalwart figure, and beside him the short, frog-like shape of the rider Jerry. They were silent, and they rode on to disappear.

Venters went his way with busy, gloomy mind, revolving events of the day, trying to reckon those brooding in the night. His thoughts overwhelmed him. Up in that dark grove dwelt a woman who had been his friend. And he skulked about her home, gripping a gun stealthily as an Indian, a man without place or people or purpose. Above her hovered the shadow of grim, hidden, secret power. No queen could have given more royally out of a bounteous store than Jane Withersteen gave her people, and likewise to those unfortunates whom her people hated. She asked only the divine right of all women—freedom; to love and to live as her heart willed. And yet prayer and her hope were vain.

"For years I've seen a storm clouding over her and the village of Cottonwoods," muttered Venters, as he strode on. "Soon it'll burst. I don't like the prospects." That night the villagers whispered in the street—and night-riding rustlers muffled horses—and Tull was at work in secret—and out there in the sage hid a man who meant something terrible—Lassiter!

Venters passed the black cottonwoods, and, entering the sage, climbed the gradual slope. He kept his direction in line with a western star. From time to time he stopped to listen and heard only the usual familiar bark of coyote and sweep of wind and rustle of sage. Presently a low jumble of rocks loomed up darkly somewhat to his right, and, turning that way, he whistled softly. Out of the rocks glided a dog that leaped and whined about him. He climbed over rough, broken rock, picking his way carefully, and then went down. Here it was darker, and sheltered from the wind. A white object guided him. It was another dog, and this one was asleep, curled up between a saddle and a pack. The animal awoke and thumped his tail in greeting. Venters placed the saddle for a pillow, rolled in his blankets, with his face upward to the stars. The white dog snuggled close to him.

The other whined and pattered a few yards to the rise of ground and there crouched on guard. And in that wild covert Venters shut his eyes under the great white stars and intense vaulted blue, bitterly comparing their loneliness to his own, and fell asleep.

When he awoke, day had dawned and all about him was bright steel-gray. The air had a cold tang. Arising, he greeted the fawning dogs and stretched his cramped body, and then, gathering together bunches of dead sage sticks, he lighted a fire. Strips of dried beef held to the blaze for a moment served him and the dogs. He drank from a canteen. There was nothing else in his outfit; he had grown used to a scant fire. Then he sat over the fire, palms outspread, and waited. Waiting had been his chief occupation for months, and he scarcely knew what he waited for unless it was the passing of the hours. But now he sensed action in the immediate present; the day promised another meeting with Lassiter and Lane, perhaps news of the rustlers; on the morrow he meant to take the trail to Deception Pass.

And while he waited he talked to his dogs. He called them Ring and Whitie; they were sheep-dogs, half collie, half deerhound, superb in build, perfectly trained. It seemed that in his fallen fortunes these dogs understood the nature of their value to him, and governed their affection and faithfulness accordingly. Whitie watched him with somber eyes of love, and Ring, crouched on the little rise of ground above, kept tireless guard. When the sun rose, the white dog took the place of the other, and Ring went to sleep at his master's feet.

By and by Venters rolled up his blankets and tied them and his meager pack together, then climbed out to look for his horse. He saw him, presently, a little way off in the sage, and went to fetch him. In that country, where every rider boasted of a fine mount and was eager for a race, where thoroughbreds dotted the wonderful grazing ranges, Venters rode a horse that was sad proof of his misfortunes.

Then, with his back against a stone, Venters faced the east, and, stick in hand and idle blade, he waited. The glorious sunlight filled the valley with purple fire. Before him, to left, to right, waving, rolling, sinking, rising, like low swells of a purple sea, stretched the sage. Out of the grove of cottonwoods, a green patch on the purple, gleamed the dull red of Jane Withersteen's old stone house. And from there extended the wide green of the village gardens and orchards marked by the graceful poplars; and farther down shone the deep, dark richness of the alfalfa fields. Numberless red and black and white dots speckled the sage, and these were cattle and horses.

So, watching and waiting, Venters let the time wear away. At length he saw a horse rise above a ridge, and he knew it to be Lassiter's black. Climbing to the highest rock, so that he would show against the sky-line, he stood and waved his hat. The almost instant turning of Lassiter's horse attested to the quickness of that rider's eye. Then Venters climbed down, saddled his horse, tied on his pack, and, with a word to his dogs, was about to ride out to meet Lassiter, when he concluded to wait for him there, on higher ground, where the outlook was commanding.

It had been long since Venters had experienced friendly greeting from a man. Lassiter's warmed in him something that had grown cold from neglect. And when he had returned it, with a strong grip of the iron hand that held his, and met the gray eyes, he knew that Lassiter and he were to be friends.

"Venters, let's talk awhile before we go down there," said Lassiter, slipping his bridle. "I ain't in no hurry. Them's sure fine dogs you've got." With a rider's eye he took in the points of Venter's horse, but did not speak his thought. "Well, did anythin' come off after I left you last night?"

Venters told him about the rustlers.

"I was snug hid in the sage," replied Lassiter, "an' didn't see or hear no one. Oldrin's got a high hand here, I reckon. It's no news up in Utah how he holes in canyons an' leaves no track." Lassiter was silent a moment. "Me an' Oldrin' wasn't exactly strangers some years back when he drove cattle into Bostil's Ford, at the head of the Rio Virgin. But he got harassed there an' now he drives some place else."

"Lassiter, you knew him? Tell me, is he Mormon or Gentile?"

"I can't say. I've knowed Mormons who pretended to be Gentiles."

"No Mormon ever pretended that unless he was a rustler" declared Venters.

"Mebbe so."

"It's a hard country for any one, but hardest for Gentiles. Did you ever know or hear of a Gentile prospering in a Mormon community?"

"I never did."

"Well, I want to get out of Utah. I've a mother living in Illinois. I want to go home. It's eight years now." The older man's sympathy moved Venters to tell his story. He had left Quincy, run off to seek his fortune in the gold fields had never gotten any farther than Salt Lake City, wandered here and there as helper, teamster, shepherd, and drifted southward over the divide and across the barrens and up the rugged plateau through the passes to the last border settlements. Here he became a rider of the sage, had stock of his own, and for a time prospered, until chance threw him in the employ of Jane Withersteen.

"Lassiter, I needn't tell you the rest."

"Well, it'd be no news to me. I know Mormons. I've seen their women's strange love en' patience en' sacrifice an' silence en' whet I call madness for their idea of

God. An' over against that I've seen the tricks of men. They work hand in hand, all together, an' in the dark. No man can hold out against them, unless he takes to packin' guns. For Mormons are slow to kill. That's the only good I ever seen in their religion. Venters, take this from me, these Mormons ain't just right in their minds. Else could a Mormon marry one woman when he already has a wife, an' call it duty?"

"Lassiter, you think as I think," returned Venters.

"How'd it come then that you never throwed a gun on Tull or some of them?" inquired the rider, curiously. "Jane pleaded with me, begged me to be patient, to overlook. She even took my guns from me. I lost all before I knew it," replied Venters, with the red color in his face. "But, Lassiter, listen. "Out of the wreck I saved a Winchester, two Colts, and plenty of shells. I packed these down into Deception Pass. There, almost every day for six months, I have practiced with my rifle till the barrel burnt my hands. Practised the draw—the firing of a Colt, hour after hour!"

"Now that's interestin' to me," said Lassiter, with a quick uplift of his head and a concentration of his gray gaze on Venters. "Could you throw a gun before you began that practisin'?"

"Yes. And now . . . " Venters made a lightning-swift movement.

Lassiter smiled, and then his bronzed eyelids narrowed till his eyes seemed mere gray slits. "You'll kill Tull!" He did not question; he affirmed.

"I promised Jane Withersteen I'd try to avoid Tull. I'll keep my word. But sooner or later Tull and I will meet. As I feel now, if he even looks at me I'll draw!"

"I reckon so. There'll be hell down there, presently." He paused a moment and flicked a sage-brush with his quirt. "Venters, seein' as you're considerable worked up, tell me Milly Erne's story."

Venters's agitation stilled to the trace of suppressed eagerness in Lassiter's query.

"Milly Erne's story? Well, Lassiter, I'll tell you what I know. Milly Erne had been in Cottonwoods years when I first arrived there, and most of what I tell you happened before my arrival. I got to know her pretty well. She was a slip of a woman, and crazy on religion. I conceived an idea that I never mentioned—I thought she was at heart more Gentile than Mormon. But she passed as a Mormon, and certainly she had the Mormon woman's locked lips. You know, in every Mormon village there are women who seem mysterious to us, but about Milly there was more than the ordinary mystery. When she came to Cottonwoods she had a beautiful little girl whom she loved passionately. Milly was not known openly in Cottonwoods as a Mormon wife. That she really was a Mormon wife I have no doubt. Perhaps the Mormon's other wife or wives would not acknowledge Milly. Such things happen in these villages. Mormon wives wear yokes, but they get jealous. Well, whatever had brought Milly to this country—love or madness of religion—she repented of it. She gave up teaching the village school. She quit the church. And she began to fight Mormon upbringing for her baby girl. Then the Mormons put on the screws—slowly, as is their way. At last the child disappeared. 'Lost' was the report. The child was stolen, I know that. So do you. That wrecked Milly Erne. But she lived on in hope. She became a slave. She worked her heart and soul and life out to get back her child. She never heard of it again. Then she sank . . . .I can see her now, a frail thing, so transparent you could almost look through her—white like ashes—and her eyes! . . . Her eyes have always haunted me. She had one real friend—Jane Withersteen. But Jane couldn't mend a broken heart, and Milly died." For moments Lassiter did not speak, or turn his head.

"The man!" he exclaimed, presently, in husky accents.

"I haven't the slightest idea who the Mormon was," replied Venters; "nor has any Gentile in Cottonwoods."

"Does Jane Withersteen know?"

"Yes. But a red-hot running-iron couldn't burn that name out of her!"

Without further speech Lassiter started off, walking his horse and Venters followed with his dogs. Half a mile down the slope they entered a luxuriant growth of willows, and soon came into an open space carpeted with grass like deep green velvet. The rushing of water and singing of birds filled their ears. Venters led his comrade to a shady bower and showed him Amber Spring. It was a magnificent outburst of clear, amber water pouring from a dark, stone-lined hole. Lassiter knelt and drank, lingered there to drink again. He made no comment, but Venters did not need words. Next to his horse a rider of the sage loved a spring. And this spring was the most beautiful and remarkable known to the upland riders of southern Utah. It was the spring that made old Withersteen a feudal lord and now enabled his daughter to return the toll which her father had exacted from the toilers of the sage.

The spring gushed forth in a swirling torrent, and leaped down joyously to make its swift way along a willow-skirted channel. Moss and ferns and lilies overhung its green banks. Except for the rough-hewn stones that held and directed the water, this willow thicket and glade had been left as nature had made it.

Below were artificial lakes, three in number, one above the other in banks of raised earth, and round about them rose the lofty green-foliaged shafts of poplar trees. Ducks dotted the glassy surface of the lakes; a blue heron stood motionless on a water-gate; kingfishers darted with shrieking flight along the shady banks; a white hawk sailed above; and from the trees and shrubs came the song of robins and cat-birds. It was all in strange contrast to the endless slopes of lonely sage and the wild rock environs beyond. Venters thought of the woman who loved the birds and the green of the leaves and the murmur of the water.

Next on the slope, just below the third and largest lake, were corrals and a wide stone barn and open sheds and coops and pens. Here were clouds of dust, and cracking sounds of hoofs, and romping colts and heehawing burros. Neighing horses trampled to the corral fences. And on the little windows of the barn projected bobbing heads of bays and blacks and sorrels. When the two men entered the immense barnyard, from all around the din increased. This welcome, however, was not seconded by the several men and boys who vanished on sight.

Venters and Lassiter were turning toward the house when Jane appeared in the lane leading a horse. In riding-skirt and blouse she seemed to have lost some of her statuesque proportions, and looked more like a girl rider than the mistress of Withersteen. She was brightly smiling, and her greeting was warmly cordial.

"Good news," she announced. "I've been to the village. All is quiet. I expected—I don't know what. But there's no excitement. And Tull has ridden out on his way to Glaze."

"Tull gone?" inquired Venters, with surprise. He was wondering what could have taken Tull away. Was it to avoid another meeting with Lassiter that he went? Could it have any connection with the probable nearness of Oldring and his gang?

"Gone, yes, thank goodness," replied Jane. "Now I'll have peace for a while. Lassiter, I want you to see my horses. You are a rider, and you must be a judge of horseflesh. Some of mine have Arabian blood. My father got his best strain in Nevada from Indians who claimed their horses were bred down from the original stock left by the Spaniards."

"Well, ma'am, the one you've been ridin' takes my eye," said Lassiter, as he walked round the racy, clean-limbed, and fine-pointed roan.

"Where are the boys?" she asked, looking about. "Jerd, Paul, where are you? Here, bring out the horses."

The sound of dropping bars inside the barn was the signal for the horses to jerk their heads in the windows, to snort and stamp. Then they came pounding out of the door, a file of thoroughbreds, to plunge about the barnyard, heads and tails up, manes flying. They halted afar off, squared away to look, came slowly forward with whinnies for their mistress, and doubtful snorts for the strangers and their horses.

"Come—come—come," called Jane, holding out her hands. "Why, Bells— Wrangle, where are your manners? Come, Black Star—come, Night. Ah, you beauties! My racers of the sage!"

Only two came up to her; those she called Night and Black Star. Venters never looked at them without delight. The first was soft dead black, the other glittering black, and they were perfectly matched in size, both being high and long-bodied, wide through the shoulders, with lithe, powerful legs. That they were a woman's pets showed in the gloss of skin, the fineness of mane. It showed, too, in the light of big eyes and the gentle reach of eagerness.

"I never seen their like," was Lassiter's encomium, "an' in my day I've seen a sight of horses. Now, ma'am, if you was wantin' to make a long an' fast ride across the sage—say to elope—"

Lassiter ended there with dry humor, yet behind that was meaning. Jane blushed and made arch eyes at him. "Take care, Lassiter, I might think that a proposal," she replied, gaily. "It's dangerous to propose elopement to a Mormon woman. Well, I was expecting you. Now will be a good hour to show you Milly Erne's grave. The day-riders have gone, and the night-riders haven't come in. Bern, what do you make of that? Need I worry? You know I have to be made to worry."

"Well, it's not usual for the night shift to ride in so late," replied Venters, slowly, and his glance sought Lassiter's. "Cattle are usually quiet after dark. Still, I've known even a coyote to stampede your white herd."

"I refuse to borrow trouble. Come," said Jane.

They mounted, and, with Jane in the lead, rode down the lane, and, turning off into a cattle trail, proceeded westward. Venters's dogs trotted behind them. On this side of the ranch the outlook was different from that on the other; the immediate foreground was rough and the sage more rugged and less colorful; there were no dark-blue lines of canyons to hold the eye, nor any uprearing rock walls. It was a long roll and slope into gray obscurity. Soon Jane left the trail and rode into the sage, and presently she dismounted and threw her bridle. The men did likewise. Then, on foot, they followed her, coming out at length on the rim of a low escarpment. She passed by several little ridges of earth to halt before a faintly defined mound. It lay in the shade of a sweeping sage-brush close to the edge of the promontory; and a rider could have jumped his horse over it without recognizing a grave.

"Here!"

She looked sad as she spoke, but she offered no explanation for the neglect of an unmarked, uncared-for grave. There was a little bunch of pale, sweet lavender daisies, doubtless planted there by Jane.

"I only come here to remember and to pray," she said. "But I leave no trail!"

A grave in the sage! How lonely this resting-place of Milly Erne! The cottonwoods or the alfalfa fields were not in sight, nor was there any rock or ridge or cedar to lend contrast to the monotony. Gray slopes, tinging the purple, barren and wild, with the wind waving the sage, swept away to the dim horizon.

Lassiter looked at the grave and then out into space. At that moment he seemed a figure of bronze. Jane touched Venters's arm and led him back to the horses.

"Bern!" cried Jane, when they were out of hearing. "Suppose Lassiter were Milly's husband—the father of that little girl lost so long ago!"

"It might be, Jane. Let us ride on. If he wants to see us again he'll come."

So they mounted and rode out to the cattle trail and began to climb. From the height of the ridge, where they had started down, Venters looked back. He did not see Lassiter, but his glance, drawn irresistibly farther out on the gradual slope, caught sight of a moving cloud of dust.

"Hello, a rider!"

"Yes, I see," said Jane.

"That fellow's riding hard. Jane, there's something wrong."

"Oh yes, there must be . . . .How he rides!"

The horse disappeared in the sage, and then puffs of dust marked his course.

"He's short-cut on us—he's making straight for the corrals."

Venters and Jane galloped their steeds and reined in at the turning of the lane. This lane led down to the right of the grove. Suddenly into its lower entrance flashed a bay horse. Then Venters caught the fast rhythmic beat of pounding hoofs. Soon his keen eye recognized the swing of the rider in his saddle.

"It's Judkins, your Gentile rider!" he cried. "Jane, when Judkins rides like that it means hell!"

CHAPTER IV
DECEPTION PASS

The rider thundered up and almost threw his foam-flecked horse in the sudden stop. He was a giant form, and with fearless eyes.

"Judkins, you're all bloody!" cried Jane, in affright. "Oh, you've been shot!"

"Nothin' much Miss Withersteen. I got a nick in the shoulder. I'm some wet an' the hoss's been throwin' lather, so all this ain't blood."

"What's up?" queried Venters, sharply. "Rustlers sloped off with the red herd."

"Where are my riders?" demanded Jane.

"Miss Withersteen, I was alone all night with the herd. At daylight this mornin' the rustlers rode down. They began to shoot at me on sight. They chased me hard an' far, burnin' powder all the time, but I got away."

"Jud, they meant to kill you," declared Venters.

"Now I wonder," returned Judkins. "They wanted me bad. An' it ain't regular for rustlers to waste time chasin' one rider."

"Thank heaven you got away," said Jane. "But my riders—where are they?"

"I don't know. The night-riders weren't there last night when I rode down, en' this mornin' I met no day-riders."

"Judkins! Bern, they've been set upon—killed by Oldring's men!"

"I don't think so," replied Venters, decidedly. "Jane, your riders haven't gone out in the sage."

"Bern, what do you mean?" Jane Withersteen turned deathly pale.

"You remember what I said about the unseen hand?"

"Oh! . . . Impossible!"

"I hope so. But I fear—" Venters finished, with a shake of his head.

"Bern, you're bitter; but that's only natural. We'll wait to see what's happened to my riders. Judkins, come to the house with me. Your wound must be attended to."

"Jane, I'll find out where Oldring drives the herd," vowed Venters.

"No, no! Bern, don't risk it now—when the rustlers are in such shooting mood."

"I'm going. Jud, how many cattle in that red herd?"

"Twenty-five hundred head."

"Whew! What on earth can Oldring do with so many cattle? Why, a hundred head is a big steal. I've got to find out."

"Don't go," implored Jane.

"Bern, you want a hoss thet can run. Miss Withersteen, if it's not too bold of me to advise, make him take a fast hoss or don't let him go."

"Yes, yes, Judkins. He must ride a horse that can't be caught. Which one—Black Star—Night?"

"Jane, I won't take either," said Venters, emphatically. "I wouldn't risk losing one of your favorites."

"Wrangle, then?"

"Thet's the hoss," replied Judkins. "Wrangle can outrun Black Star an' Night. You'd never believe it, Miss Withersteen, but I know. Wrangle's the biggest en' fastest hoss on the sage."

"Oh no, Wrangle can't beat Black Star. But, Bern, take Wrangle if you will go. Ask Jerd for anything you need. Oh, be watchful careful . . . . God speed you."

She clasped his hand, turned quickly away, and went down a lane with the rider.

Venters rode to the barn, and, leaping off, shouted for Jerd. The boy came running. Venters sent him for meat, bread, and dried fruits, to be packed in saddlebags. His own horse he turned loose into the nearest corral. Then he went for Wrangle. The giant sorrel had earned his name for a trait the opposite of amiability. He came readily out of the barn, but once in the yard he broke from Venters, and plunged about with ears laid back. Venters had to rope him, and then he kicked down a section of fence, stood on his hind legs, crashed down and fought the rope. Jerd returned to lend a hand.

"Wrangle don't git enough work," said Jerd, as the big saddle went on. "He's unruly when he's corralled, an' wants to run. Wait till he smells the sage!"

"Jerd, this horse is an iron-jawed devil. I never straddled him but once. Run? Say, he's swift as wind!"

When Venters's boot touched the stirrup the sorrel bolted, giving him the rider's flying mount. The swing of this fiery horse recalled to Venters days that were not really long past, when he rode into the sage as the leader of Jane Withersteen's riders. Wrangle pulled hard on a tight rein. He galloped out of the lane, down the shady border of the grove, and hauled up at the watering-trough, where he pranced and champed his bit. Venters got off and filled his canteen while the horse drank. The dogs, Ring and Whitie, came trotting up for their drink. Then Venters remounted and turned Wrangle toward the sage.

A wide, white trail wound away down the slope. One keen, sweeping glance told Venters that there was neither man nor horse nor steer within the limit of his vision, unless they were lying down in the sage. Ring loped in the lead and Whitie loped in the rear. Wrangle settled gradually into an easy swinging canter, and Venters's thoughts, now that the rush and flurry of the start were past, and the long miles stretched before him, reverted to a calm reckoning of late singular coincidences.

There was the night ride of Tull's, which, viewed in the light of subsequent events, had a look of his covert machinations; Oldring and his Masked Rider and his rustlers riding muffled horses; the report that Tull had ridden out that morning with his man Jerry on the trail to Glaze, the strange disappearance of Jane Withersteen's riders, the unusually determined attempt to kill the one Gentile still in her employ, an intention frustrated, no doubt, only by Judkin's magnificent riding of her racer, and lastly the driving of the red herd. These events, to Venters's color of mind, had a dark relationship. Remembering Jane's accusation of bitterness, he tried hard to put aside his rancor in judging Tull. But it was bitter knowledge that made him see the truth. He had felt the shadow of an unseen hand; he had watched till he saw its dim outline, and then he had traced it to a man's hate, to the rivalry of a Mormon Elder, to the power of a Bishop, to the long, far-reaching arm of a terrible creed. That unseen hand had made its first move against Jane Withersteen. Her riders had been called in, leaving her without help to drive seven thousand head of cattle. But to Venters it seemed extraordinary that the power which had called in these riders had left so many cattle to be driven by rustlers and harried by wolves. For hand in glove with that power was an insatiate greed; they were one and the same.

"What can Oldring do with twenty-five hundred head of cattle?" muttered Venters. "Is he a Mormon? Did he meet Tull last night? It looks like a black plot to me. But Tull and his churchmen wouldn't ruin Jane Withersteen unless the Church was to profit by that ruin. Where does Oldring come in? I'm going to find out about these things."

Wrangle did the twenty-five miles in three hours and walked little of the way. When he had gotten warmed up he had been allowed to choose his own gait. The afternoon had well advanced when Venters struck the trail of the red herd and found where it had grazed the night before. Then Venters rested the horse and used his eyes. Near at hand were a cow and a calf and several yearlings, and farther out in the sage some straggling steers.

He caught a glimpse of coyotes skulking near the cattle. The slow sweeping gaze of the rider failed to find other living things within the field of sight. The sage about him was breast-high to his horse, oversweet with its warm, fragrant breath, gray where it waved to the light, darker where the wind left it still, and beyond the wonderful haze-purple lent by distance. Far across that wide waste began the slow lift of uplands through which Deception Pass cut its tortuous many-canyoned way.

Venters raised the bridle of his horse and followed the broad cattle trail. The crushed sage resembled the path of a monster snake. In a few miles of travel he passed several cows and calves that had escaped the drive. Then he stood on the last high bench of the slope with the floor of the valley beneath. The opening of the canyon showed in a break of the sage, and the cattle trail paralleled it as far as he could see. That trail led to an undiscovered point where Oldring drove cattle into the pass, and many a rider who had followed it had never returned. Venters satisfied himself that the rustlers had not deviated from their usual course, and then he turned at right angles off the cattle trail and made for the head of the pass.

The sun lost its heat and wore down to the western horizon, where it changed from white to gold and rested like a huge ball about to roll on its golden shadows down the slope. Venters watched the lengthening of the rays and bars, and marveled at his own league-long shadow. The sun sank. There was instant shading of brightness about him, and he saw a kind of cold purple bloom creep ahead of him to cross the canyon, to mount the opposite slope and chase and darken and bury the last golden flare of sunlight.

Venters rode into a trail that he always took to get down into the canyon. He dismounted and found no tracks but his own made days previous. Nevertheless he sent the dog Ring ahead and waited. In a little while Ring returned. Whereupon Venters led his horse on to the break in the ground.

The opening into Deception Pass was one of the remarkable natural phenomena in a country remarkable for vast slopes of sage, uplands insulated by gigantic red walls, and deep canyons of mysterious source and outlet. Here the valley floor was level, and here opened a narrow chasm, a ragged vent in yellow walls of stone. The trail down the five hundred feet of sheer depth always tested Venters's nerve. It was bad going for even a burro. But Wrangle, as Venters led him, snorted defiance or disgust rather than fear, and, like a hobbled horse on the jump, lifted his ponderous iron-shod fore hoofs and crashed down over the first rough step. Venters warmed to greater admiration of the sorrel; and, giving him a loose bridle, he stepped down foot by foot.

Oftentimes the stones and shale started by Wrangle buried Venters to his knees; again he was hard put to it to dodge a rolling boulder, there were times when he could not see Wrangle for dust, and once he and the horse rode a sliding shelf of yellow, weathered cliff. It was a trail on which there could be no stops, and, therefore, if perilous, it was at least one that did not take long in the descent.

Venters breathed lighter when that was over, and felt a sudden assurance in the success of his enterprise. For at first it had been a reckless determination to achieve something at any cost, and now it resolved itself into an adventure worthy of all his reason and cunning, and keenness of eye and ear.

Pinyon pines clustered in little clumps along the level floor of the pass. Twilight had gathered under the walls. Venters rode into the trail and up the canyon. Gradually the trees and caves and objects low down turned black, and this blackness moved up the walls till night enfolded the pass, while day still lingered above. The sky darkened; and stars began to show, at first pale and then bright. Sharp notches of the rim-wall, biting like teeth into the blue, were landmarks by which Venters knew where his camping site lay. He had to feel his way through a thicket of slender oaks to a spring where he watered Wrangle and drank himself. Here he unsaddled and turned Wrangle loose, having no fear that the horse would leave the thick, cool grass adjacent to the spring. Next he satisfied his own hunger, fed Ring and Whitie and, with them curled beside him, composed himself to await sleep.

There had been a time when night in the high altitude of these Utah uplands had been satisfying to Venters. But that was before the oppression of enemies had made the change in his mind. As a rider guarding the herd he had never thought of the night's wildness and loneliness; as an outcast, now when the full silence set in, and the deep darkness, and trains of radiant stars shone cold and calm, he lay with an ache in his heart. For a year he had lived as a black fox, driven from his kind. He longed for the sound of a voice, the touch of a hand. In the daytime there was riding from place to place, and the gun practice to which something drove him, and other tasks that at least necessitated action, at night, before he won sleep, there was strife in his soul. He yearned to leave the endless sage slopes, the wilderness of canyons, and it was in the lonely night that this yearning grew unbearable. It was then that he reached forth to feel Ring or Whitie, immeasurably grateful for the love and companionship of two dogs.

On this night the same old loneliness beset Venters, the old habit of sad thought and burning unquiet had its way. But from it evolved a conviction that his useless life had undergone a subtle change. He had sensed it first when Wrangle swung him up to the high saddle, he knew it now when he lay in the gateway of Deception Pass. He had no thrill of adventure, rather a gloomy perception of great hazard, perhaps death. He meant to find Oldring's retreat. The rustlers had fast horses, but none that could catch Wrangle. Venters knew no rustler could creep upon him at night when Ring and Whitie guarded his hiding-place. For the rest, he had eyes and ears, and a long rifle and an unerring aim, which he meant to use. Strangely his foreshadowing of change did not hold a thought of the killing of Tull. It related only to what was to happen to him in Deception Pass; and he could no more lift the veil of that mystery than tell where the trails led to in that unexplored canyon. Moreover, he did not care. And at length, tired out by stress of thought, he fell asleep.

When his eyes unclosed, day had come again, and he saw the rim of the opposite wall tipped with the gold of sunrise. A few moments sufficed for the morning's simple camp duties. Near at hand he found Wrangle, and to his surprise the horse came to him. Wrangle was one of the horses that left his viciousness in the home corral. What he wanted was to be free of mules and burros and steers, to roll in dust-patches, and then to run down the wide, open, windy sage-plains, and at night browse and sleep in the cool wet grass of a springhole. Jerd knew the sorrel when he said of him, "Wait till he smells the sage!"

Venters saddled and led him out of the oak thicket, and, leaping astride, rode up the canyon, with Ring and Whitie trotting behind. An old grass-grown trail followed the course of a shallow wash where flowed a thin stream of water. The canyon was a hundred rods wide, its yellow walls were perpendicular; it had abundant sage and a scant growth of oak and pinon. For five miles it held to a comparatively straight bearing, and then began a heightening of rugged walls and a deepening of the floor. Beyond this point of sudden change in the character of the canyon Venters had never explored, and here was the real door to the intricacies of Deception Pass.

He reined Wrangle to a walk, halted now and then to listen, and then proceeded cautiously with shifting and alert gaze. The canyon assumed proportions that dwarfed those of its first ten miles. Venters rode on and on, not losing in the interest of his wide surroundings any of his caution or keen search for tracks or sight of living thing. If there ever had been a trail here, he could not find it. He rode through sage and clumps of pinon trees and grassy plots where long-petaled purple lilies bloomed. He rode through a dark constriction of the pass no wider than the lane in the grove at Cottonwoods. And he came out into a great amphitheater into which jutted huge towering corners of a confluences of intersecting canyons.

Venters sat his horse, and, with a rider's eye, studied this wild cross-cut of huge stone gullies. Then he went on, guided by the course of running water. If it had not been for the main stream of water flowing north he would never have been able to tell which of those many openings was a continuation of the pass. In crossing this amphitheater he went by the mouths of five canyons, fording little streams that flowed into the larger one. Gaining the outlet which he took to be the pass, he rode on again under over hanging walls. One side was dark in shade, the other light in sun. This narrow passageway turned and twisted and opened into a valley that amazed Venters.

Here again was a sweep of purple sage, richer than upon the higher levels. The valley was miles long, several wide, and inclosed by unscalable walls. But it was the background of this valley that so forcibly struck him. Across the sage-flat rose a strange up-flinging of yellow rocks. He could not tell which were close and which were distant. Scrawled mounds of stone, like mountain waves, seemed to roll up to steep bare slopes and towers.

In this plain of sage Venters flushed birds and rabbits, and when he had pro-ceeded about a mile he caught sight of the bobbing white tails of a herd of running antelope. He rode along the edge of the stream which wound toward the western end of the slowly looming mounds of stone. The high slope retreated out of sight behind the nearer protection. To Venters the valley appeared to have been filled in by a mountain of melted stone that had hardened in strange shapes of rounded outline. He followed the stream till he lost it in a deep cut. Therefore Venters quit the dark slit which baffled further search in that direction, and rode out along the curved edge of stone where it met the sage. It was not long before he came to a low place, and here Wrangle readily climbed up.

All about him was ridgy roll of wind-smoothed, rain-washed rock. Not a tuft of grass or a bunch of sage colored the dull rust-yellow. He saw where, to the right, this uneven flow of stone ended in a blunt wall. Leftward, from the hollow that lay at his feet, mounted a gradual slow-swelling slope to a great height topped by leaning, cracked, and ruined crags. Not for some time did he grasp the wonder of that acclivity. It was no less than a mountain-side, glistening in the sun like pol-ished granite, with cedar-trees springing as if by magic out of the denuded surface. Winds had swept it clear of weathered shale, and rains had washed it free of dust. Far up the curved slope its beautiful lines broke to meet the vertical rim-wall, to lose its grace in a different order and color of rock, a stained yellow cliff of cracks and caves and seamed crags. And straight before Venters was a scene less striking but more significant to his keen survey. For beyond a mile of the bare, hummocky rock began the valley of sage, and the mouths of canyons, one of which surely was another gateway into the pass.

He got off his horse, and, giving the bridle to Ring to hold, he commenced a search for the cleft where the stream ran. He was not successful and concluded the water dropped into an underground passage. Then he returned to where he had left Wrangle, and led him down off the stone to the sage. It was a short ride to the opening canyons. There was no reason for a choice of which one to enter. The one he rode into was a clear, sharp shaft in yellow stone a thousand feet deep, with wonderful wind-worn caves low down and high above buttressed and turreted ramparts. Farther on Venters came into a region where deep indentations marked the line of canyon walls. These were huge, cove-like blind pockets extending back to a sharp corner with a dense growth of underbrush and trees.

Venters penetrated into one of these offshoots, and, as he had hoped, he found abundant grass. He had to bend the oak saplings to get his horse through. Deciding to make this a hiding-place if he could find water, he worked back to the limit of the shelving walls. In a little cluster of silver spruces he found a spring. This inclosed nook seemed an ideal place to leave his horse and to camp at night, and from which to make stealthy trips on foot. The thick grass hid his trail; the dense growth of oaks in the opening would serve as a barrier to keep Wrangle in, if, indeed, the luxuriant browse would not suffice for that. So Venters, leaving Whitie with the horse, called Ring to his side, and, rifle in hand, worked his way out to the open. A careful photographing in mind of the formation of the bold outlines of rimrock assured him he would be able to return to his retreat even in the dark.

Bunches of scattered sage covered the center of the canyon, and among these Venters threaded his way with the step of an Indian. At intervals he put his hand on the dog and stopped to listen. There was a drowsy hum of insects, but no other sound disturbed the warm midday stillness. Venters saw ahead a turn, more abrupt than any yet. Warily he rounded this corner, once again to halt bewildered.

The canyon opened fan-shaped into a great oval of green and gray growths. It was the hub of an oblong wheel, and from it, at regular distances, like spokes, ran the outgoing canyons. Here a dull red color predominated over the fading yellow. The corners of wall bluntly rose, scarred and scrawled, to taper into towers and serrated peaks and pinnacled domes.

Venters pushed on more heedfully than ever. Toward the center of this circle the sage-brush grew smaller and farther apart He was about to sheer off to the right, where thickets and jumbles of fallen rock would afford him cover, when he ran right upon a broad cattle trail. Like a road it was, more than a trail, and the cattle tracks were fresh. What surprised him more, they were wet! He pondered over this feature. It had not rained. The only solution to this puzzle was that the cattle had been driven through water, and water deep enough to wet their legs.

Suddenly Ring growled low. Venters rose cautiously and looked over the sage. A band of straggling horsemen were riding across the oval. He sank down, startled and trembling. "Rustlers!" he muttered. Hurriedly he glanced about for a place to hide. Near at hand there was nothing but sage-brush. He dared not risk crossing the open patches to reach the rocks. Again he peeped over the sage. The rustlers—four—five—seven—eight in all, were approaching, but not directly in line with him. That was relief for a cold deadness which seemed to be creeping inward along his veins. He crouched down with bated breath and held the bristling dog.

He heard the click of iron-shod hoofs on stone, the coarse laughter of men, and then voices gradually dying away. Long moments passed. Then he rose. The rustlers were riding into a canyon. Their horses were tired, and they had several pack animals; evidently they had traveled far. Venters doubted that they were the rustlers who had driven the red herd. Olding's band had split. Venters watched these horsemen disappear under a bold canyon wall.

The rustlers had come from the northwest side of the oval. Venters kept a steady gaze in that direction, hoping, if there were more, to see from what canyon they rode. A quarter of an hour went by. Reward for his vigilance came when he descried three more mounted men, far over to the north. But out of what canyon they had ridden it was too late to tell. He watched the three ride across the oval and round the jutting red corner where the others had gone.

"Up that canyon!" exclaimed Venters. "Oldring's den! I've found it!"

A knotty point for Venters was the fact that the cattle tracks all pointed west. The broad trail came from the direction of the canyon into which the rustlers had ridden, and undoubtedly the cattle had been driven out of it across the oval. There were no tracks pointing the other way. It had been in his mind that Oldring had driven the red herd toward the rendezvous, and not from it. Where did that broad trail come down into the pass, and where did it lead? Venters knew he wasted time in pondering the question, but it held a fascination not easily dispelled. For many years Oldring's mysterious entrance and exit to Deception Pass had been all-absorbing topics to sage-riders.

All at once the dog put an end to Venters's pondering. Ring sniffed the air, turned slowly in his tracks with a whine, and then growled. Venters wheeled. Two horsemen were within a hundred yards, coming straight at him. One, lagging behind the other, was Oldring's Masked Rider.

Venters cunningly sank, slowly trying to merge into sage-brush. But, guarded as his action was, the first horse detected it. He stopped short, snorted, and shot up his ears. The rustler bent forward, as if keenly peering ahead. Then, with a swift sweep, he jerked a gun from its sheath and fired.

The bullet zipped through the sage-brush. Flying bits of wood struck Venters, and the hot, stinging pain seemed to lift him in one leap. Like a flash the blue barrel of his rifle gleamed level and he shot once—twice.

The foremost rustler dropped his weapon and toppled from his saddle, to fall with his foot catching in a stirrup. The horse snorted wildly and plunged away, dragging the rustler through the sage.

The Masked Rider huddled over his pommel slowly swaying to one side, and then, with a faint, strange cry, slipped out of the saddle.

CHAPTER V
THE MASKED RIDER

Venters looked quickly from the fallen rustlers to the canyon where the others had disappeared. He calculated on the time needed for running horses to return to the open, if their riders heard shots. He waited breathlessly. But the estimated time dragged by and no riders appeared. Venters began presently to believe that the rifle reports had not penetrated into the recesses of the canyon, and felt safe for the immediate present.

He hurried to the spot where the first rustler had been dragged by his horse. The man lay in deep grass, dead, jaw fallen, eyes protruding—a sight that sickened Venters. The first man at whom he had ever aimed a weapon he had shot through the heart. With the clammy sweat oozing from every pore Venters dragged the rustler in among some boulders and covered him with slabs of rock. Then he smoothed out the crushed trail in grass and sage. The rustler's horse had stopped a quarter of a mile off and was grazing.

When Venters rapidly strode toward the Masked Rider not even the cold nausea that gripped him could wholly banish curiosity. For he had shot Oldring's infamous lieutenant, whose face had never been seen. Venters experienced a grim pride in the feat. What would Tull say to this achievement of the outcast who rode too often to Deception Pass?

Venters's curious eagerness and expectation had not prepared him for the shock he received when he stood over a slight, dark figure. The rustler wore the black mask that had given him his name, but he had no weapons. Venters glanced at the drooping horse, there were no gun-sheaths on the saddle.

"A rustler who didn't pack guns!" muttered Venters. "He wears no belt. He couldn't pack guns in that rig . . . .Strange!"

A low, gasping intake of breath and a sudden twitching of body told Venters the rider still lived. "He's alive! . . . I've got to stand here and watch him die. And I shot an unarmed man."

Shrinkingly Venters removed the rider's wide sombrero and the black cloth mask. This action disclosed bright chestnut hair, inclined to curl, and a white, youthful face. Along the lower line of cheek and jaw was a clear demarcation, where the brown of tanned skin met the white that had been hidden from the sun.

"Oh, he's only a boy! . . . What! Can he be Oldring's Masked Rider?"

The boy showed signs of returning consciousness. He stirred; his lips moved; a small brown hand clenched in his blouse.

Venters knelt with a gathering horror of his deed. His bullet had entered the rider's right breast, high up to the shoulder. With hands that shook, Venters untied a black scarf and ripped open the blood-wet blouse.

First he saw a gaping hole, dark red against a whiteness of skin, from which welled a slender red stream. Then the graceful, beautiful swell of a woman's breast!

"A woman!" he cried. "A girl! . . . I've killed a girl!"

She suddenly opened eyes that transfixed Venters. They were fathomless blue. Consciousness of death was there, a blended terror and pain, but no consciousness of sight. She did not see Venters. She stared into the unknown.

Then came a spasm of vitality. She writhed in a torture of reviving strength, and in her convulsions she almost tore from Ventner's grasp. Slowly she relaxed and sank partly back. The ungloved hand sought the wound, and pressed so hard that her wrist half buried itself in her bosom. Blood trickled between her spread fingers. And she looked at Venters with eyes that saw him.

He cursed himself and the unerring aim of which he had been so proud. He had seen that look in the eyes of a crippled antelope which he was about to finish with his knife. But in her it had infinitely more—a revelation of mortal spirit. The instinctive bringing to life was there, and the divining helplessness and the terrible accusation of the stricken.

"Forgive me! I didn't know!" burst out Venters.

"You shot me—you've killed me!" she whispered, in panting gasps. Upon her lips appeared a fluttering, bloody froth. By that Venters knew the air in her lungs was mixing with blood. "Oh, I knew—it would—come—some day! . . . Oh, the burn! . . . Hold me—I'm sinking—it's all dark . . . .Ah, God! . . . Mercy—"

Her rigidity loosened in one long quiver and she lay back limp, still, white as snow, with closed eyes. Venters thought then that she died. But the faint pulsation of her breast assured him that life yet lingered.

Death seemed only a matter of moments, for the bullet had gone clear through her. Nevertheless, he tore sageleaves from a bush, and, pressing them tightly over her wounds, he bound the black scarf round her shoulder, tying it securely under her arm. Then he closed the blouse, hiding from his sight that blood-stained, accusing breast.

"What—now?" he questioned, with flying mind. "I must get out of here. She's dying—but I can't leave her." He rapidly surveyed the sage to the north and made out no animate object. Then he picked up the girl's sombrero and the mask. This time the mask gave him as great a shock as when he first removed it from her face. For in the woman he had forgotten the rustler, and this black strip of felt-cloth established the identity of Oldring's Masked Rider. Venters had solved the mystery. He slipped his rifle under her, and, lifting her carefully upon it, he began to retrace his steps. The dog trailed in his shadow. And the horse, that had stood drooping by, followed without a call. Venters chose the deepest tufts of grass and clumps of sage on his return. From time to time he glanced over his shoulder. He did not rest. His concern was to avoid jarring the girl and to hide his trail. Gaining the narrow canyon, he turned and held close to the wall till he reached his hiding-place. When he entered the dense thicket of oaks he was hard put to it to force a way through. But he held his burden almost upright, and by slipping side wise and bending the saplings he got in. Through sage and grass he hurried to the grove of silver spruces.

He laid the girl down, almost fearing to look at her. Though marble pale and cold, she was living. Venters then appreciated the tax that long carry had been to his strength. He sat down to rest. Whitie sniffed at the pale girl and whined and crept to Venters's feet. Ring lapped the water in the runway of the spring.

Presently Venters went out to the opening, caught the horse and, leading him through the thicket, unsaddled him and tied him with a long halter. Wrangle left his browsing long enough to whinny and toss his head. Venters felt that he could not rest easily till he had secured the other rustler's horse; so, taking his rifle and calling for Ring, he set out. Swiftly yet watchfully he made his way through the canyon to the oval and out to the cattle trail. What few tracks might have betrayed him he obliterated, so only an expert tracker could have trailed him. Then, with many a wary backward glance across the sage, he started to round up the rustler's horse. This was unexpectedly easy. He led the horse to lower ground, out of sight from the opposite side of the oval along the shadowy western wall, and so on into his canyon and secluded camp.

The girl's eyes were open; a feverish spot burned in her cheeks she moaned something unintelligible to Venters, but he took the movement of her lips to mean that she wanted water. Lifting her head, he tipped the canteen to her lips. After that she again lapsed into unconsciousness or a weakness which was its counterpart. Venters noted, however, that the burning flush had faded into the former pallor.

The sun set behind the high canyon rim, and a cool shade darkened the walls. Venters fed the dogs and put a halter on the dead rustlers horse. He allowed Wrangle to browse free. This done, he cut spruce boughs and made a lean-to for the girl. Then, gently lifting her upon a blanket, he folded the sides over her. The other blanket he wrapped about his shoulders and found a comfortable seat against a spruce-tree that upheld the little shack. Ring and Whitie lay near at hand, one asleep, the other watchful.

Venters dreaded the night's vigil. At night his mind was active, and this time he had to watch and think and feel beside a dying girl whom he had all but murdered. A thousand excuses he invented for himself, yet not one made any difference in his act or his self-reproach.

It seemed to him that when night fell black he could see her white face so much more plainly. "She'll go, presently," he said, "and be out of agony—thank God!"

Every little while certainty of her death came to him with a shock; and then he would bend over and lay his ear on her breast. Her heart still beat.

The early night blackness cleared to the cold starlight. The horses were not moving, and no sound disturbed the deathly silence of the canyon.

"I'll bury her here," thought Venters, "and let her grave be as much a mystery as her life was." For the girl's few words, the look of her eyes, the prayer, had strangely touched Venters.

"She was only a girl," he soliloquized. "What was she to Oldring? Rustlers don't have wives nor sisters nor daughters. She was bad—that's all. But somehow . . . well, she may not have willingly become the companion of rustlers. That prayer of hers to God for mercy! . . . Life is strange and cruel. I wonder if other members of Oldring's gang are women? Likely enough. But what was his game? Oldring's Mask Rider! A name to make villagers hide and lock their doors. A name credited with a dozen murders, a hundred forays, and a thousand stealings of cattle. What part did the girl have in this? It may have served Oldring to create mystery."

Hours passed. The white stars moved across the narrow strip of dark-blue sky above. The silence awoke to the low hum of insects. Venters watched the immovable white face, and as he watched, hour by hour waiting for death, the infamy of her passed from his mind. He thought only of the sadness, the truth of the moment. Whoever she was—whatever she had done—she was young and she was dying.

The after-part of the night wore on interminably. The starlight failed and the gloom blackened to the darkest hour. "She'll die at the gray of dawn," muttered Venters, remembering some old woman's fancy. The blackness paled to gray, and the gray lightened and day peeped over the eastern rim. Venters listened at the breast of the girl. She still lived. Did he only imagine that her heart beat stronger, ever so slightly, but stronger? He pressed his ear closer to her breast. And he rose with his own pulse quickening.

"If she doesn't die soon—she's got a chance—the barest chance to live," he said.

He wondered if the internal bleeding had ceased. There was no more film of blood upon her lips. But no corpse could have been whiter. Opening her blouse, he untied the scarf, and carefully picked away the sage leaves from the wound in her shoulder. It had closed. Lifting her lightly, he ascertained that the same was true of the hole where the bullet had come out. He reflected on the fact that clean wounds closed quickly in the healing upland air. He recalled instances of riders who had been cut and shot apparently to fatal issues; yet the blood had clotted, the wounds closed, and they had recovered. He had no way to tell if internal hemorrhage still went on, but he believed that it had stopped. Otherwise she would surely not have lived so long. He marked the entrance of the bullet, and concluded that it had just touched the upper lobe of her lung. Perhaps the wound in the lung had also closed. As he began to wash the blood stains from her breast and carefully rebandage the wound, he was vaguely conscious of a strange, grave happiness in the thought that she might live.

Broad daylight and a hint of sunshine high on the cliff-rim to the west brought him to consideration of what he had better do. And while busy with his few camp tasks he revolved the thing in his mind. It would not be wise for him to remain long in his present hiding-place. And if he intended to follow the cattle trail and try to find the rustlers he had better make a move at once. For he knew that rustlers, being riders, would not make much of a day's or night's absence from camp for one or two of their number; but when the missing ones failed to show up in reasonable time there would be a search. And Venters was afraid of that.

"A good tracker could trail me," he muttered. "And I'd be cornered here. Let's see. Rustlers are a lazy set when they're not on the ride. I'll risk it. Then I'll change my hiding-place."

He carefully cleaned and reloaded his guns. When he rose to go he bent a long glance down upon the unconscious girl. Then ordering Whitie and Ring to keep guard, he left the camp

The safest cover lay close under the wall of the canyon, and here through the dense thickets Venters made his slow, listening advance toward the oval. Upon gaining the wide opening he decided to cross it and follow the left wall till he came to the cattle trail. He scanned the oval as keenly as if hunting for antelope. Then, stooping, he stole from one cover to another, taking advantage of rocks and bunches of sage, until he had reached the thickets under the opposite wall. Once there, he exercised extreme caution in his surveys of the ground ahead, but increased his speed when moving. Dodging from bush to bush, he passed the mouths of two canyons, and in the entrance of a third canyon he crossed a wash of swift clear water, to come abruptly upon the cattle trail.

It followed the low bank of the wash, and, keeping it in sight, Venters hugged the line of sage and thicket. Like the curves of a serpent the canyon wound for a mile or more and then opened into a valley. Patches of red showed clear against the purple of sage, and farther out on the level dotted strings of red led away to the wall of rock.

"Ha, the red herd!" exclaimed Venters.

Then dots of white and black told him there were cattle of other colors in this inclosed valley. Oldring, the rustler, was also a rancher. Venters's calculating eye took count of stock that outnumbered the red herd.

"What a range!" went on Venters. "Water and grass enough for fifty thousand head, and no riders needed!" After his first burst of surprise and rapid calculation Venters lost no time there, but slunk again into the sage on his back trail. With the discovery of Oldring's hidden cattle-range had come enlightenment on several problems. Here the rustler kept his stock, here was Jane Withersteen's red herd; here were the few cattle that had disappeared from the Cottonwoods slopes during the last two years. Until Oldring had driven the red herd his thefts of cattle for that time had not been more than enough to supply meat for his men. Of late no drives had been reported from Sterling or the villages north. And Venters knew that the riders had wondered at Oldring's inactivity in that particular field. He and his band had been active enough in their visits to Glaze and Cottonwoods; they always had gold; but of late the amount gambled away and drunk and thrown away in the villages had given rise to much conjecture. Oldring's more frequent visits had resulted in new saloons, and where there had formerly been one raid or shooting fray in the little hamlets there were now many. Perhaps Oldring had another range farther on up the pass, and from there drove the cattle to distant Utah towns where he was little known But Venters came finally to doubt this. And, from what he had learned in the last few days, a belief began to form in Venters's mind that Oldring's intimidations of the villages and the mystery of the Masked Rider, with his alleged evil deeds, and the fierce resistance offered any trailing riders, and the rustling of cattle— these things were only the craft of the rustler-chief to conceal his real life and purpose and work in Deception Pass.

And like a scouting Indian Venters crawled through the sage of the oval valley, crossed trail after trail on the north side, and at last entered the canyon out of which headed the cattle trail, and into which he had watched the rustlers disappear.

If he had used caution before, now he strained every nerve to force himself to creeping stealth and to sensitiveness of ear. He crawled along so hidden that he could not use his eyes except to aid himself in the toilsome progress through the brakes and ruins of cliff-wall. Yet from time to time, as he rested, he saw the massive red walls growing higher and wilder, more looming and broken. He made note of the fact that he was turning and climbing. The sage and thickets of oak and brakes of alder gave place to pinyon pine growing out of rocky soil. Suddenly a low, dull murmur assailed his ears. At first he thought it was thunder, then the slipping of a weathered slope of rock. But it was incessant, and as he progressed it filled out deeper and from a murmur changed into a soft roar.

"Falling water," he said. "There's volume to that. I wonder if it's the stream I lost."

The roar bothered him, for he could hear nothing else. Likewise, however, no rustlers could hear him. Emboldened by this and sure that nothing but a bird could see him, he arose from his hands and knees to hurry on. An opening in the pinyons warned him that he was nearing the height of slope.

He gained it, and dropped low with a burst of astonishment. Before him stretched a short canyon with rounded stone floor bare of grass or sage or tree, and with curved, shelving walls. A broad rippling stream flowed toward him, and at the back of the canyon waterfall burst from a wide rent in the cliff, and, bounding down in two green steps, spread into a long white sheet.

If Venters had not been indubitably certain that he had entered the right canyon his astonishment would not have been so great. There had been no breaks in the walls, no side canyons entering this one where the rustlers' tracks and the cattle trail had guided him, and, therefore, he could not be wrong. But here the canyon ended, and presumably the trails also.

"That cattle trail headed out of here," Venters kept saying to himself. "It headed out. Now what I want to know is how on earth did cattle ever get in here?"

If he could be sure of anything it was of the careful scrutiny he had given that cattle track, every hoofmark of which headed straight west. He was now looking east at an immense round boxed corner of canyon down which tumbled a thin, white veil of water, scarcely twenty yards wide. Somehow, somewhere, his calculations had gone wrong. For the first time in years he found himself doubting his rider's skill in finding tracks, and his memory of what he had actually seen. In his anxiety to keep under cover he must have lost himself in this offshoot of Deception Pass, and thereby in some unaccountable manner, missed the canyon with the trails. There was nothing else for him to think. Rustlers could not fly, nor cattle jump down thousand-foot precipices. He was only proving what the sage-riders had long said of this labyrinthine system of deceitful canyons and valleys—trails led down into Deception Pass, but no rider had ever followed them.

On a sudden he heard above the soft roar of the waterfall an unusual sound that he could not define. He dropped flat behind a stone and listened. From the direction he had come swelled something that resembled a strange muffled pounding and splashing and ringing. Despite his nerve the chill sweat began to dampen his forehead. What might not be possible in this stonewalled maze of mystery? The unnatural sound passed beyond him as he lay gripping his rifle and fighting for coolness. Then from the open came the sound, now distinct and different. Venters recognized a hobble-bell of a horse, and the cracking of iron on submerged stones, and the hollow splash of hoofs in water.

Relief surged over him. His mind caught again at realities, and curiosity prompted him to peep from behind the rock.

In the middle of the stream waded a long string of packed burros driven by three superbly mounted men. Had Venters met these dark-clothed, dark-visaged, heavily armed men anywhere in Utah, let alone in this robbers' retreat, he would have recognized them as rustlers. The discerning eye of a rider saw the signs of a long, arduous trip. These men were packing in supplies from one of the northern villages. They were tired, and their horses were almost played out, and the burros plodded on, after the manner of their kind when exhausted, faithful and patient, but as if every weary, splashing, slipping step would be their last.

All this Venters noted in one glance. After that he watched with a thrilling eagerness. Straight at the waterfall the rustlers drove the burros, and straight through the middle, where the water spread into a fleecy, thin film like dissolving smoke. Following closely, the rustlers rode into this white mist, showing in bold black relief for an instant, and then they vanished.

Venters drew a full breath that rushed out in brief and sudden utterance.

"Good Heaven! Of all the holes for a rustler! . . . There's a cavern under that waterfall, and a passageway leading out to a canyon beyond. Oldring hides in there. He needs only to guard a trail leading down from the sage-flat above. Little danger of this outlet to the pass being discovered. I stumbled on it by luck, after I had given up. And now I know the truth of what puzzled me most—why that cattle trail was wet!"

He wheeled and ran down the slope, and out to the level of the sage-brush. Returning, he had no time to spare, only now and then, between dashes, a moment when he stopped to cast sharp eyes ahead. The abundant grass left no trace of his trail. Short work he made of the distance to the circle of canyons. He doubted that he would ever see it again; he knew he never wanted to; yet he looked at the red corners and towers with the eyes of a rider picturing landmarks never to be forgotten.

Here he spent a panting moment in a slow-circling gaze of the sage-oval and the gaps between the bluffs. Nothing stirred except the gentle wave of the tips of the brush. Then he pressed on past the mouths of several canyons and over ground new to him, now close under the eastern wall. This latter part proved to be easy traveling, well screened from possible observation from the north and west, and he soon covered it and felt safer in the deepening shade of his own canyon. Then the huge, notched bulge of red rim loomed over him, a mark by which he knew again the deep cove where his camp lay hidden. As he penetrated the thicket, safe again for the present, his thoughts reverted to the girl he had left there. The afternoon had far advanced. How would he find her? He ran into camp, frightening the dogs.

The girl lay with wide-open, dark eyes, and they dilated when he knelt beside her. The flush of fever shone in her cheeks. He lifted her and held water to her dry lips, and felt an inexplicable sense of lightness as he saw her swallow in a slow, choking gulp. Gently he laid her back.

"Who—are—you?" she whispered, haltingly. "I'm the man who shot you," he replied. "You'll—not—kill me—now?"

"No, no."

"What—will—you—do—with me?"

"When you get better—strong enough—I'll take you back to the canyon where the rustlers ride through the waterfall."

As with a faint shadow from a flitting wing overhead, the marble whiteness of her face seemed to change. "Don't—take—me—back—there!"

CHAPTER VI
THE MILL-WHEEL OF STEERS

Meantime, at the ranch, when Judkins's news had sent Venters on the trail of the rustlers, Jane Withersteen led the injured man to her house and with skilled fingers dressed the gunshot wound in his arm.

"Judkins, what do you think happened to my riders?"

"I—I d rather not say," he replied.

"Tell me. Whatever you'll tell me I'll keep to myself. I'm beginning to worry about more than the loss of a herd of cattle. Venters hinted of—but tell me, Judkins."

"Well, Miss Withersteen, I think as Venters thinks—your riders have been called in."

"Judkins! . . . By whom?"

"You know who handles the reins of your Mormon riders."

"Do you dare insinuate that my churchmen have ordered in my riders?"

"I ain't insinuatin' nothin', Miss Withersteen," answered Judkins, with spirit. "I know what I'm talking about. I didn't want to tell you."

"Oh, I can't believe that! I'll not believe it! Would Tull leave my herds at the mercy of rustlers and wolves just because—because—? No, no! It's unbelievable."

"Yes, thet particular thing's onheard of around Cottonwoods But, beggin' pardon, Miss Withersteen, there never was any other rich Mormon woman here on the border, let alone one thet's taken the bit between her teeth."

That was a bold thing for the reserved Judkins to say, but it did not anger her. This rider's crude hint of her spirit gave her a glimpse of what others might think. Humility and obedience had been hers always. But had she taken the bit between her teeth? Still she wavered. And then, with quick spurt of warm blood along her veins, she thought of Black Star when he got the bit fast between his iron jaws and ran wild in the sage. If she ever started to run! Jane smothered the glow and burn within her, ashamed of a passion for freedom that opposed her duty.

"Judkins, go to the village," she said, "and when you have learned anything definite about my riders please come to me at once."

When he had gone Jane resolutely applied her mind to a number of tasks that of late had been neglected. Her father had trained her in the management of a hundred employees and the working of gardens and fields; and to keep record of the movements of cattle and riders. And beside the many duties she had added to this work was one of extreme delicacy, such as required all her tact and ingenuity. It was an unobtrusive, almost secret aid which she rendered to the Gentile families of the village. Though Jane Withersteen never admitted so to herself, it amounted to no less than a system of charity. But for her invention of numberless kinds of employment, for which there was no actual need, these families of Gentiles, who had failed in a Mormon community, would have starved.

In aiding these poor people Jane thought she deceived her keen churchmen, but it was a kind of deceit for which she did not pray to be forgiven. Equally as difficult was the task of deceiving the Gentiles, for they were as proud as they were poor. It had been a great grief to her to discover how these people hated her people; and it had been a source of great joy that through her they had come to soften in hatred. At any time this work called for a clearness of mind that precluded anxiety and worry; but under the present circumstances it required all her vigor and obstinate tenacity to pin her attention upon her task.

Sunset came, bringing with the end of her labor a patient calmness and power to wait that had not been hers earlier in the day. She expected Judkins, but he did not appear. Her house was always quiet; to-night, however, it seemed unusually so. At supper her women served her with a silent assiduity; it spoke what their sealed lips could not utter—the sympathy of Mormon women. Jerd came to her with the key of the great door of the stone stable, and to make his daily report about the horses. One of his daily duties was to give Black Star and Night and the other racers a ten-mile run. This day it had been omitted, and the boy grew confused in explanations that she had not asked for. She did inquire if he would return on the morrow, and Jerd, in mingled surprise and relief, assured her he would always work for her. Jane missed the rattle and trot, canter and gallop of the incoming riders on the hard trails. Dusk shaded the grove where she walked; the birds ceased singing; the wind sighed through the leaves of the cottonwoods, and the running water murmured down its stone-bedded channel. The glimmering of the first star was like the peace and beauty of the night. Her faith welled up in her heart and said that all would soon be right in her little world. She pictured Venters about his lonely camp-fire sitting between his faithful dogs. She prayed for his safety, for the success of his undertaking.

Early the next morning one of Jane's women brought in word that Judkins wished to speak to her. She hurried out, and in her surprise to see him armed with rifle and revolver, she forgot her intention to inquire about his wound.

"Judkins! Those guns? You never carried guns."

"It's high time, Miss Withersteen," he replied. "Will you come into the grove? It ain't jest exactly safe for me to be seen here."

She walked with him into the shade of the cottonwoods. "What do you mean?"

"Miss Withersteen, I went to my mother's house last night. While there, some one knocked, an' a man asked for me. I went to the door. He wore a mask. He said I'd better not ride any more for Jane Withersteen. His voice was hoarse an' strange, disguised I reckon, like his face. He said no more, an' ran off in the dark."

"Did you know who he was?" asked Jane, in a low voice. "Yes."

Jane did not ask to know; she did not want to know; she feared to know. All her calmness fled at a single thought "Thet's why I'm packin' guns," went on Judkins. "For I'll never quit ridin' for you, Miss Withersteen, till you let me go."

"Judkins, do you want to leave me?"

"Do I look thet way? Give me a hoss—a fast hoss, an' send me out on the sage."

"Oh, thank you, Judkins! You're more faithful than my own people. I ought not accept your loyalty—you might suffer more through it. But what in the world can I do? My head whirls. The wrong to Venters—the stolen herd—these masks, threats, this coil in the dark! I can't understand! But I feel something dark and terrible closing in around me."

"Miss Withersteen, it's all simple enough," said Judkins, earnestly. "Now please listen—an' beggin' your pardon—jest turn thet deaf Mormon ear aside, an' let me talk clear an' plain in the other. I went around to the saloons an' the stores an' the loafin' places yesterday. All your riders are in. There's talk of a vigilance band organized to hunt down rustlers. They call themselves 'The Riders.' Thet's the report—thet's the reason given for your riders leavin' you. Strange thet only a few riders of other ranchers joined the band! An' Tull's man, Jerry Card— he's the leader. I seen him en' his hoss. He 'ain't been to Glaze. I'm not easy to fool on the looks of a hoss thet's traveled the sage. Tull an' Jerry didn't ride to Glaze! . . . Well, I met Blake en' Dorn, both good friends of mine, usually, as far as their Mormon lights will let 'em go. But these fellers couldn't fool me, an' they didn't try very hard. I asked them, straight out like a man, why they left you like thet. I didn't forget to mention how you nursed Blake's poor old mother when she was sick, an' how good you was to Dorn's kids. They looked ashamed, Miss Withersteen. An' they jest froze up—thet dark set look thet makes them strange an' different to me. But I could tell the difference between thet first natural twinge of conscience an' the later look of some secret thing. An' the difference I caught was thet they couldn't help themselves. They hadn't no say in the matter. They looked as if their bein' unfaithful to you was bein' faithful to a higher duty. An' there's the secret. Why it's as plain as—as sight of my gun here."

"Plain! . . . My herds to wander in the sage—to be stolen! Jane Withersteen a poor woman! Her head to be brought low and her spirit broken! . . . Why, Judkins, it's plain enough."

"Miss Withersteen, let me get what boys I can gather, an' hold the white herd. It's on the slope now, not ten miles out—three thousand head, an' all steers. They're wild, an' likely to stampede at the pop of a jack-rabbit's ears. We'll camp right with them, en' try to hold them."

"Judkins, I'll reward you some day for your service, unless all is taken from me. Get the boys and tell Jerd to give you pick of my horses, except Black Star and Night. But—do not shed blood for my cattle nor heedlessly risk your lives."

Jane Withersteen rushed to the silence and seclusion of her room, and there could not longer hold back the bursting of her wrath. She went stone-blind in the fury of a passion that had never before showed its power. Lying upon her bed, sightless, voiceless, she was a writhing, living flame. And she tossed there while her fury burned and burned, and finally burned itself out.

Then, weak and spent, she lay thinking, not of the oppression that would break her, but of this new revelation of self. Until the last few days there had been little in her life to rouse passions. Her forefathers had been Vikings, savage chieftains who bore no cross and brooked no hindrance to their will. Her father had inherited that temper; and at times, like antelope fleeing before fire on the slope, his people fled from his red rages. Jane Withersteen realized that the spirit of wrath and war had lain dormant in her. She shrank from black depths hitherto unsuspected. The one thing in man or woman that she scorned above all scorn, and which she could not forgive, was hate. Hate headed a flaming pathway straight to hell. All in a flash, beyond her control there had been in her a birth of fiery hate. And the man who had dragged her peaceful and loving spirit to this degradation was a minister of God's word, an Elder of her church, the counselor of her beloved Bishop.

The loss of herds and ranges, even of Amber Spring and the Old Stone House, no longer concerned Jane Withersteen, she faced the foremost thought of her life, what she now considered the mightiest problem—the salvation of her soul.

She knelt by her bedside and prayed; she prayed as she had never prayed in all her life—prayed to be forgiven for her sin to be immune from that dark, hot hate; to love Tull as her minister, though she could not love him as a man; to do her duty by her church and people and those dependent upon her bounty; to hold reverence of God and womanhood inviolate.

When Jane Withersteen rose from that storm of wrath and prayer for help she was serene, calm, sure—a changed woman. She would do her duty as she saw it, live her life as her own truth guided her. She might never be able to marry a man of her choice, but she certainly never would become the wife of Tull. Her churchmen might take her cattle and horses, ranges and fields, her corrals and stables, the house of Withersteen and the water that nourished the village of Cottonwoods; but they could not force her to marry Tull, they could not change her decision or break her spirit. Once resigned to further loss, and sure of herself, Jane Withersteen attained a peace of mind that had not been hers for a year. She forgave Tull, and felt a melancholy regret over what she knew he considered duty, irrespective of his personal feeling for her. First of all, Tull, as he was a man, wanted her for himself; and secondly, he hoped to save her and her riches for his church. She did not believe that Tull had been actuated solely by his minister's zeal to save her soul. She doubted her interpretation of one of his dark sayings—that if she were lost to him she might as well be lost to heaven. Jane Withersteen's common sense took arms against the binding limits of her religion; and she doubted that her Bishop, whom she had been taught had direct communication with God—would damn her soul for refusing to marry a Mormon. As for Tull and his churchmen, when they had harassed her, perhaps made her poor, they would find her unchangeable, and then she would get back most of what she had lost. So she reasoned, true at last to her faith in all men, and in their ultimate goodness.

The clank of iron hoofs upon the stone courtyard drew her hurriedly from her retirement. There, beside his horse, stood Lassiter, his dark apparel and the great black gun-sheaths contrasting singularly with his gentle smile. Jane's active mind took up her interest in him and her half-determined desire to use what charm she had to foil his evident design in visiting Cottonwoods. If she could mitigate his hatred of Mormons, or at least keep him from killing more of them, not only would she be saving her people, but also be leading back this bloodspiller to some semblance of the human.

"Mornin', ma'am," he said, black sombrero in hand.

"Lassiter I'm not an old woman, or even a madam," she replied, with her bright smile. "If you can't say Miss Withersteen—call me Jane."

"I reckon Jane would be easier. First names are always handy for me."

"Well, use mine, then. Lassiter, I'm glad to see you. I'm in trouble."

Then she told him of Judkins's return, of the driving of the red herd, of Venters's departure on Wrangle, and the calling-in of her riders.

"'Pears to me you're some smilin' an' pretty for a woman with so much trouble," he remarked.

"Lassiter! Are you paying me compliments? But, seriously I've made up my mind not to be miserable. I've lost much, and I'll lose more. Nevertheless, I won't be sour, and I hope I'll never be unhappy—again."

Lassiter twisted his hat round and round, as was his way, and took his time in replying.

"Women are strange to me. I got to back-trailin' myself from them long ago. But I'd like a game woman. Might I ask, seein' as how you take this trouble, if you're goin' to fight?"

"Fight! How? Even if I would, I haven't a friend except that boy who doesn't dare stay in the village."

"I make bold to say, ma'am—Jane—that there's another, if you want him."

"Lassiter! . . . Thank you. But how can I accept you as a friend? Think! Why, you'd ride down into the village with those terrible guns and kill my enemies—who are also my churchmen."

"I reckon I might be riled up to jest about that," he replied, dryly. She held out both hands to him.

"Lassiter! I'll accept your friendship—be proud of it—return it—if I may keep you from killing another Mormon."

"I'll tell you one thing," he said, bluntly, as the gray lightning formed in his eyes. "You're too good a woman to be sacrificed as you're goin' to be . . . . No, I reckon you an' me can't be friends on such terms."

In her earnestness she stepped closer to him, repelled yet fascinated by the sudden transition of his moods. That he would fight for her was at once horrible and wonderful.

"You came here to kill a man—the man whom Milly Erne—"

"The man who dragged Milly Erne to hell—put it that way! . . . Jane Withersteen, yes, that's why I came here. I'd tell so much to no other livin' soul . . . .There're things such a woman as you'd never dream of—so don't mention her again. Not till you tell me the name of the man!"

"Tell you! I? Never!"

"I reckon you will. An' I'll never ask you. I'm a man of strange beliefs an' ways of thinkin', an' I seem to see into the future an' feel things hard to explain. The trail I've been followin' for so many years was twisted en' tangled, but it's straightenin' out now. An', Jane Withersteen, you crossed it long ago to ease poor Milly's agony. That, whether you want or not, makes Lassiter your friend. But you cross it now strangely to mean somethin to me—God knows what!—unless by your noble blindness to incite me to greater hatred of Mormon men."

Jane felt swayed by a strength that far exceeded her own. In a clash of wills with this man she would go to the wall. If she were to influence him it must be wholly through womanly allurement. There was that about Lassiter which commanded her respect. She had abhorred his name; face to face with him, she found she feared only his deeds. His mystic suggestion, his foreshadowing of something that she was to mean to him, pierced deep into her mind. She believed fate had thrown in her way the lover or husband of Milly Erne. She believed that through her an evil man might be reclaimed. His allusion to what he called her blindness

terrified her. Such a mistaken idea of his might unleash the bitter, fatal mood she sensed in him. At any cost she must placate this man; she knew the die was cast, and that if Lassiter did not soften to a woman's grace and beauty and wiles, then it would be because she could not make him.

"I reckon you'll hear no more such talk from me," Lassiter went on, presently. "Now, Miss Jane, I rode in to tell you that your herd of white steers is down on the slope behind them big ridges. An' I seen somethin' goin' on that'd be mighty interestin' to you, if you could see it. Have you a field-glass?"

"Yes, I have two glasses. I'll get them and ride out with you. Wait, Lassiter, please," she said, and hurried within. Sending word to Jerd to saddle Black Star and fetch him to the court, she then went to her room and changed to the riding-clothes she always donned when going into the sage. In this male attire her mirror showed her a jaunty, handsome rider. If she expected some little need of admiration from Lassiter, she had no cause for disappointment. The gentle smile that she liked, which made of him another person, slowly overspread his face.

"If I didn't take you for a boy!" he exclaimed. "It's powerful queer what difference clothes make. Now I've been some scared of your dignity, like when the other night you was all in white but in this rig—"

Black Star came pounding into the court, dragging Jerd half off his feet, and he whistled at Lassiter's black. But at sight of Jane all his defiant lines seemed to soften, and with tosses of his beautiful head he whipped his bridle.

"Down, Black Star, down," said Jane.

He dropped his head, and, slowly lengthening, he bent one foreleg, then the other, and sank to his knees. Jane slipped her left foot in the stirrup, swung lightly into the saddle, and Black Star rose with a ringing stamp. It was not easy for Jane to hold him to a canter through the grove. and like the wind he broke when he saw the sage. Jane let him have a couple of miles of free running on the open trail, and then she coaxed him in and waited for her companion. Lassiter was not long in catching up, and presently they were riding side by side. It reminded her how she used to ride with Venters. Where was he now? She gazed far down the slope to the curved purple lines of Deception Pass and involuntarily shut her eyes with a trembling stir of nameless fear.

"We'll turn off here," Lassiter said, "en' take to the sage a mile or so. The white herd is behind them big ridges."

"What are you going to show me?" asked Jane. "I'm prepared—don't be afraid."

He smiled as if he meant that bad news came swiftly enough without being presaged by speech.

When they reached the lee of a rolling ridge Lassiter dismounted, motioning to her to do likewise. They left the horses standing, bridles down. Then Lassiter, carrying the field-glasses began to lead the way up the slow rise of ground. Upon nearing the summit he halted her with a gesture.

"I reckon we'd see more if we didn't show ourselves against the sky," he said. "I was here less than an hour ago. Then the herd was seven or eight miles south, an' if they ain't bolted yet—"

"Lassiter! . . . Bolted?"

"That's what I said. Now let's see."

Jane climbed a few more paces behind him and then peeped over the ridge. Just beyond began a shallow swale that deepened and widened into a valley and then swung to the left. Following the undulating sweep of sage, Jane saw the straggling lines and then the great body of the white herd. She knew enough about steers, even at a distance of four or five miles, to realize that something was in the wind. Bringing her field-glass into use, she moved it slowly from left to right, which action swept the whole herd into range. The stragglers were restless; the more compactly massed steers were browsing. Jane brought the glass back to the big sentinels of the herd, and she saw them trot with quick steps, stop short and toss wide horns, look everywhere, and then trot in another direction.

"Judkins hasn't been able to get his boys together yet," said Jane. "But he'll be there soon. I hope not too late. Lassiter, what's frightening those big leaders?"

"Nothin' jest on the minute," replied Lassiter. "Them steers are quietin' down. They've been scared, but not bad yet. I reckon the whole herd has moved a few miles this way since I was here."

"They didn't browse that distance—not in less than an hour. Cattle aren't sheep."

"No, they jest run it, en' that looks bad."

"Lassiter, what frightened them?" repeated Jane, impatiently.

"Put down your glass. You'll see at first better with a naked eye. Now look along them ridges on the other side of the herd, the ridges where the sun shines bright on the sage . . . .That's right. Now look en' look hard en' wait."

Long-drawn moments of straining sight rewarded Jane with nothing save the low, purple rim of ridge and the shimmering sage.

"It's begun again!" whispered Lassiter, and he gripped her arm. "Watch . . . .There, did you see that?"

"No, no. Tell me what to look for?"

"A white flash—a kind of pin-point of quick light—a gleam as from sun shinin' on somethin' white."

Suddenly Jane's concentrated gaze caught a fleeting glint. Quickly she brought her glass to bear on the spot. Again the purple sage, magnified in color and size and wave, for long moments irritated her with its monotony. Then from out of the sage on the ridge flew up a broad, white object, flashed in the sunlight and vanished. Like magic it was, and bewildered Jane.

"What on earth is that?"

"I reckon there's some one behind that ridge throwin' up a sheet or a white blanket to reflect the sunshine."

"Why?" queried Jane, more bewildered than ever.

"To stampede the herd," replied Lassiter, and his teeth clicked.

"Ah!" She made a fierce, passionate movement, clutched the glass tightly, shook as with the passing of a spasm, and then dropped her head. Presently she raised it to greet Lassiter with something like a smile. "My righteous brethren are at work again," she said, in scorn. She had stifled the leap of her wrath, but for perhaps the first time in her life a bitter derision curled her lips. Lassiter's cool gray eyes seemed to pierce her. "I said I was prepared for anything; but that was hardly true. But why would they—anybody stampede my cattle?"

"That's a Mormon's godly way of bringin' a woman to her knees."

"Lassiter, I'll die before I ever bend my knees. I might be led I won't be driven. Do you expect the herd to bolt?"

"I don't like the looks of them big steers. But you can never tell. Cattle sometimes stampede as easily as buffalo. Any little flash or move will start them. A rider gettin' down an' walkin' toward them sometimes will make them jump an' fly. Then again nothin' seems to scare them. But I reckon that white flare will do the biz. It's a new one on me, an' I've seen some ridin' an' rustlin'. It jest takes one of them God-fearin' Mormons to think of devilish tricks."

"Lassiter, might not this trick be done by Oldring's men?" asked Jane, ever grasping at straws.

"It might be, but it ain't," replied Lassiter. "Oldring's an honest thief. He don't skulk behind ridges to scatter your cattle to the four winds. He rides down on you, an' if you don't like it you can throw a gun."

Jane bit her tongue to refrain from championing men who at the very moment were proving to her that they were little and mean compared even with rustlers.

"Look! . . . Jane, them leadin' steers have bolted. They're drawin' the stragglers, an' that'll pull the whole herd." Jane was not quick enough to catch the details called out by Lassiter, but she saw the line of cattle lengthening. Then, like a stream of white bees pouring from a huge swarm, the steers stretched out from the main body. In a few moments, with astonishing rapidity, the whole herd got into motion. A faint roar of trampling hoofs came to Jane's ears, and gradually swelled; low, rolling clouds of dust began to rise above the sage.

"It's a stampede, an' a hummer," said Lassiter.

"Oh, Lassiter! The herd's running with the valley! It leads into the canyon! There's a straight jump-off!"

"I reckon they'll run into it, too. But that's a good many miles yet. An', Jane, this valley swings round almost north before it goes east. That stampede will pass within a mile of us."

The long, white, bobbing line of steers streaked swiftly through the sage, and a funnel-shaped dust-cloud arose at a low angle. A dull rumbling filled Jane's ears.

"I'm thinkin' of millin' that herd," said Lassiter. His gray glance swept up the slope to the west. "There's some specks an' dust way off toward the village. Mebbe that's Judkins an' his boys. It ain't likely he'll get here in time to help. You'd better hold Black Star here on this high ridge."

He ran to his horse and, throwing off saddle-bags and tightening the cinches, he leaped astride and galloped straight down across the valley.

Jane went for Black Star and, leading him to the summit of the ridge, she mounted and faced the valley with excitement and expectancy. She had heard of milling stampeded cattle, and knew it was a feat accomplished by only the most daring riders.

The white herd was now strung out in a line two miles long. The dull rumble of thousands of hoofs deepened into continuous low thunder, and as the steers swept swiftly closer the thunder became a heavy roll. Lassiter crossed in a few moments the level of the valley to the eastern rise of ground and there waited the coming of the herd. Presently, as the head of the white line reached a point opposite to where Jane stood, Lassiter spurred his black into a run Jane saw him take a position on the off side of the leaders of the stampede, and there he rode. It was like a race. They swept on down the valley, and when the end of the white line neared Lassiter's first stand the head had begun to swing round to the west. It swung slowly and stubbornly, yet surely, and gradually assumed a long, beautiful curve of moving white. To Jane's amaze she saw the leaders swinging, turning till they headed back toward her and up the valley. Out to the right of these wild plunging steers ran Lassiter's black, and Jane's keen eye appreciated the fleet stride and sure-footedness of the blind horse. Then it seemed that the herd moved in a great curve, a huge half-moon with the points of head and tail almost opposite, and a mile apart But Lassiter relentlessly crowded the leaders, sheering them to the left, turning them little by little. And the dust-blinded wild followers plunged on madly in the tracks of their leaders. This ever-moving, ever-changing curve of steers rolled toward Jane and when below her, scarce half a mile, it began to narrow and close into a circle. Lassiter had ridden parallel with her position, turned toward her, then aside, and now he was riding directly away from her, all the time pushing the head of that bobbing line inward.

It was then that Jane, suddenly understanding Lassiter's feat stared and gasped at the riding of this intrepid man. His horse was fleet and tireless, but blind. He had pushed the leaders around and around till they were about to turn in on the inner side of the end of that line of steers. The leaders were already running in a circle; the end of the herd was still running almost straight. But soon they would be wheeling. Then, when Lassiter had the circle formed, how would he escape? With Jane Withersteen prayer was as ready as praise; and she prayed for this man's safety. A circle of dust began to collect. Dimly, as through a yellow veil, Jane saw Lassiter press the leaders inward to close the gap in the sage. She lost sight of him in the dust, again she thought she saw the black, riderless now, rear and drag himself and fall. Lassiter had been thrown—lost! Then he reappeared running out of the dust into the sage. He had escaped, and she breathed again.

Spellbound, Jane Withersteen watched this stupendous millwheel of steers. Here was the milling of the herd. The white running circle closed in upon the open space of sage. And the dust circles closed above into a pall. The ground quaked and the incessant thunder of pounding hoofs rolled on. Jane felt deafened, yet she thrilled to a new sound. As the circle of sage lessened the steers began to bawl, and when it closed entirely there came a great upheaval in the center, and a terrible thumping of heads and clicking of horns. Bawling, climbing, goring, the great mass of steers on the inside wrestled in a crashing din, heaved and groaned under the pressure. Then came a deadlock. The inner strife ceased, and the hideous roar and crash. Movement went on in the outer circle, and that, too, gradually stilled. The white herd had come to a stop, and the pall of yellow dust began to drift away on the wind.

Jane Withersteen waited on the ridge with full and grateful heart. Lassiter appeared, making his weary way toward her through the sage. And up on the slope Judkins rode into sight with his troop of boys. For the present, at least, the white herd would be looked after.

When Lassiter reached her and laid his hand on Black Star's mane, Jane could not find speech. "Killed—my—hoss," he panted.

"Oh! I'm sorry," cried Jane. "Lassiter! I know you can't replace him, but I'll give you any one of my racers—Bells, or Night, even Black Star."

"I'll take a fast hoss, Jane, but not one of your favorites," he replied. "Only—will you let me have Black Star now an' ride him over there an' head off them fellers who stampeded the herd?"

He pointed to several moving specks of black and puffs of dust in the purple sage. "I can head them off with this hoss, an' then—"

"Then, Lassiter?"

"They'll never stampede no more cattle."

"Oh! No! No! . . . Lassiter, I won't let you go!"

But a flush of fire flamed in her cheeks, and her trembling hands shook Black Star's bridle, and her eyes fell before Lassiter's.

CHAPTER VII
THE DAUGHTER OF WITHERSTEEN

"Lassiter, will you be my rider?" Jane had asked him. "I reckon so," he had replied.

Few as the words were, Jane knew how infinitely much they implied. She wanted him to take charge of her cattle and horse and ranges, and save them if that were possible. Yet, though she could not have spoken aloud all she meant, she was perfectly honest with herself. Whatever the price to be paid, she must keep Lassiter close to her; she must shield from him the man who had led Milly Erne to Cottonwoods. In her fear she so controlled her mind that she did not whisper this Mormon's name to her own soul, she did not even think it. Besides, beyond this thing she regarded as a sacred obligation thrust upon her, was the need of a helper, of a friend, of a champion in this critical time. If she could rule this gunman, as Venters had called him, if she could even keep him from shedding blood, what strategy to play his flame and his presence against the game of oppression her churchmen were waging against her? Never would she forget the effect on Tull and his men when Venters shouted Lassiter's name. If she could not wholly control Lassiter, then what she could do might put off the fatal day.

One of her safe racers was a dark bay, and she called him Bells because of the way he struck his iron shoes on the stones. When Jerd led out this slender, beautifully built horse Lassiter suddenly became all eyes. A rider's love of a thoroughbred shone in them. Round and round Bells he walked, plainly weakening all the time in his determination not to take one of Jane's favorite racers.

"Lassiter, you're half horse, and Bells sees it already," said Jane, laughing. "Look at his eyes. He likes you. He'll love you, too. How can you resist him? Oh, Lassiter, but Bells can run! It's nip and tuck between him and Wrangle, and only Black Star can beat him. He's too spirited a horse for a woman. Take him. He's yours."

"I jest am weak where a hoss's concerned," said Lassiter. "I'll take him, an' I'll take your orders, ma'am."

"Well, I'm glad, but never mind the ma'am. Let it still be Jane."

From that hour, it seemed, Lassiter was always in the saddle, riding early and late, and coincident with his part in Jane's affairs the days assumed their old tranquillity. Her intelligence told her this was only the lull before the storm, but her faith would not have it so.

She resumed her visits to the village, and upon one of these she encountered Tull. He greeted her as he had before any trouble came between them, and she, responsive to peace if not quick to forget, met him halfway with manner almost cheerful. He regretted the loss of her cattle; he assured her that the vigilantes which had been organized would soon rout the rustlers; when that had been accomplished her riders would likely return to her.

"You've done a headstrong thing to hire this man Lassiter," Tull went on, severely. "He came to Cottonwoods with evil intent."

"I had to have somebody. And perhaps making him my rider may turn out best in the end for the Mormons of Cottonwoods."

"You mean to stay his hand?"

"I do—if I can."

"A woman like you can do anything with a man. That would be well, and would atone in some measure for the errors you have made."

He bowed and passed on. Jane resumed her walk with conflicting thoughts. She resented Elder Tull's cold, impassive manner that looked down upon her as one who had incurred his just displeasure. Otherwise he would have been the same calm, dark-browed, impenetrable man she had known for ten years. In fact, except when he had revealed his passion in the matter of the seizing of Venters, she had never dreamed he could be other than the grave, reproving preacher. He stood out now a strange, secretive man. She would have thought better of him if he had picked up the threads of their quarrel where they had parted. Was Tull what he appeared to be? The question flung itself in-voluntarily over Jane Withersteen's inhibitive habit of faith without question. And she refused to answer it. Tull could not fight in the open Venters had said, Lassiter had said, that her Elder shirked fight and worked in the dark. Just now in this meeting Tull had ignored the fact that he had sued, exhorted, demanded that she marry him. He made no mention of Venters. His manner was that of the minister who had been outraged, but who overlooked the frailties of a woman. Beyond question he seemed unutterably aloof from all knowledge of pressure being brought to bear upon her, absolutely guiltless of any connection with secret power over riders, with night journeys, with rustlers and stampedes of cattle. And that convinced her again of unjust suspicions. But it was convincement through an obstinate faith. She shuddered as she accepted it, and that shudder was the nucleus of a terrible revolt.

Jane turned into one of the wide lanes leading from the main street and entered a huge, shady yard. Here were sweet-smelling clover, alfalfa, flowers, and vegetables, all growing in happy confusion. And like these fresh green things were the dozens of babies, tots, toddlers, noisy urchins, laughing girls, a whole multitude of children of one family. For Collier Brandt, the father of all this numerous progeny, was a Mormon with four wives.

The big house where they lived was old, solid, picturesque the lower part built of logs, the upper of rough clapboards, with vines growing up the outside stone chimneys. There were many wooden-shuttered windows, and one pretentious window of glass proudly curtained in white. As this house had four mistresses, it likewise had four separate sections, not one of which communicated with another, and all had to be entered from the outside.

In the shade of a wide, low, vine-roofed porch Jane found Brandt's wives entertaining Bishop Dyer. They were motherly women, of comparatively similar ages, and plain-featured, and just at this moment anything but grave. The Bishop was rather tall, of stout build, with iron-gray hair and beard, and eyes of light blue. They were merry now; but Jane had seen them when they were not, and then she feared him as she had feared her father.

The women flocked around her in welcome.

"Daughter of Withersteen," said the Bishop, gaily, as he took her hand, "you have not been prodigal of your gracious self of late. A Sabbath without you at service! I shall reprove Elder Tull."

"Bishop, the guilt is mine. I'll come to you and confess," Jane replied, lightly; but she felt the undercurrent of her words.

"Mormon love-making!" exclaimed the Bishop, rubbing his hands. "Tull keeps you all to himself."

"No. He is not courting me."

"What? The laggard! If he does not make haste I'll go a-courting myself up to Withersteen House."

There was laughter and further bantering by the Bishop, and then mild talk of village affairs, after which he took his leave, and Jane was left with her friend, Mary Brandt.

"Jane, you're not yourself. Are you sad about the rustling of the cattle? But you have so many, you are so rich."

Then Jane confided in her, telling much, yet holding back her doubts of fear. "Oh, why don't you marry Tull and be one of us?"

"But, Mary, I don't love Tull," said Jane, stubbornly.

"I don't blame you for that. But, Jane Withersteen, you've got to choose between the love of man and love of God. Often we Mormon women have to do that. It's not easy. The kind of happiness you want I wanted once. I never got it, nor will you, unless you throw away your soul. We've all watched your affair with Venters in fear and trembling. Some dreadful thing will come of it. You don't want him hanged or shot—or treated worse, as that Gentile boy was treated in Glaze for fooling round a Mormon woman. Marry Tull. It's your duty as a Mormon. You'll feel no rapture as his wife—but think of Heaven! Mormon women don't marry for what they expect on earth. Take up the cross, Jane. Remember your father found Amber Spring, built these old houses, brought Mormons here, and fathered them. You are the daughter of Withersteen!"

Jane left Mary Brandt and went to call upon other friends. They received her with the same glad welcome as had Mary, lavished upon her the pent-up affection of Mormon women, and let her go with her ears ringing of Tull, Venters, Lassiter, of duty to God and glory in Heaven.

"Verily," murmured Jane, "I don't know myself when, through all this, I remain unchanged—nay, more fixed of purpose."

She returned to the main street and bent her thoughtful steps toward the center of the village. A string of wagons drawn by oxen was lumbering along. These "sage-freighters," as they were called, hauled grain and flour and merchandise from Sterling, and Jane laughed suddenly in the midst of her humility at the thought that they were her property, as was one of the three stores for which they freighted goods. The water that flowed along the path at her feet, and turned into each cottage-yard to nourish garden and orchard, also was hers, no less her private property because she chose to give it free. Yet in this village of Cottonwoods, which her father had founded and which she maintained she was not her own mistress; she was not able to abide by her own choice of a husband. She was the daughter of Withersteen. Suppose she proved it, imperiously! But she quelled that proud temptation at its birth.

Nothing could have replaced the affection which the village people had for her; no power could have made her happy as the pleasure her presence gave. As she went on down the street past the stores with their rude platform entrances, and the saloons where tired horses stood with bridles dragging, she was again assured of what was the bread and wine of life to her—that she was loved. Dirty boys playing in the ditch, clerks, teamsters, riders, loungers on the corners, ranchers on dusty horses little girls running errands, and women hurrying to the stores all looked up at her coming with glad eyes.

Jane's various calls and wandering steps at length led her to the Gentile quarter of the village. This was at the extreme southern end, and here some thirty Gentile families lived in huts and shacks and log-cabins and several dilapidated cottages. The fortunes of these inhabitants of Cottonwoods could be read in their abodes. Water they had in abundance, and therefore grass and fruit-trees and patches of alfalfa and vegetable gardens. Some of the men and boys had a few stray cattle, others obtained such intermittent employment as the Mormons reluctantly tendered them. But none of the families was prosperous, many were very poor, and some lived only by Jane Withersteen's beneficence.

As it made Jane happy to go among her own people, so it saddened her to come in contact with these Gentiles. Yet that was not because she was unwelcome; here she was gratefully received by the women, passionately by the children. But poverty and idleness, with their attendant wretchedness and sorrow, always hurt her. That she could alleviate this distress more now than ever before proved the adage that it was an ill wind that blew nobody good. While her Mormon riders were in her employ she had found few Gentiles who would stay with her, and now she was able to find employment for all the men and boys. No little shock was it to have man after man tell her that he dare not accept her kind offer.

"It won't do," said one Carson, an intelligent man who had seen better days. "We've had our warning. Plain and to the point! Now there's Judkins, he packs guns, and he can use them, and so can the daredevil boys he's hired. But they've little responsibility. Can we risk having our homes burned in our absence?"

Jane felt the stretching and chilling of the skin of her face as the blood left it. "Carson, you and the others rent these houses?" she asked.

"You ought to know, Miss Withersteen. Some of them are yours."

"I know? . . . Carson, I never in my life took a day's labor for rent or a yearling calf or a bunch of grass, let alone gold."

"Bivens, your store-keeper, sees to that."

"Look here, Carson," went on Jane, hurriedly, and now her cheeks were burning. "You and Black and Willet pack your goods and move your families up to my cabins in the grove. They're far more comfortable than these. Then go to work for me. And if aught happens to you there I'll give you money—gold enough to leave Utah!"

The man choked and stammered, and then, as tears welled into his eyes, he found the use of his tongue and cursed. No gentle speech could ever have equaled that curse in eloquent expression of what he felt for Jane Withersteen. How strangely his look and tone reminded her of Lassiter!

"No, it won't do," he said, when he had somewhat recovered himself. "Miss Withersteen, there are things that you don't know, and there's not a soul among us who can tell you."

"I seem to be learning many things, Carson. Well, then, will you let me aid you—say till better times?"

"Yes, I will," he replied, with his face lighting up. "I see what it means to you, and you know what it means to me. Thank you! And if better times ever come, I'll be only too happy to work for you."

"Better times will come. I trust God and have faith in man. Good day, Carson."

The lane opened out upon the sage-inclosed alfalfa fields, and the last habitation, at the end of that lane of hovels, was the meanest. Formerly it had been a shed; now it was a home. The broad leaves of a wide-spreading cottonwood sheltered the sunken roof of weathered boards. Like an Indian hut, it had one floor. Round about it were a few scanty rows of vegetables, such as the hand of a weak woman had time and strength to cultivate. This little dwelling-place was just outside the village limits, and the widow who lived there had to carry her water from the nearest irrigation ditch. As Jane Withersteen entered the unfenced yard a child saw her, shrieked with joy, and came tearing toward her with curls flying. This child was a little girl of four called Fay. Her name suited her, for she was an elf, a sprite, a creature so fairy-like and beautiful that she seemed unearthly.

"Muvver sended for oo," cried Fay, as Jane kissed her, "an' oo never tome."

"I didn't know, Fay; but I've come now."

Fay was a child of outdoors, of the garden and ditch and field, and she was dirty and ragged. But rags and dirt did not hide her beauty. The one thin little bedraggled garment she wore half covered her fine, slim body. Red as cherries were her cheeks and lips; her eyes were violet blue, and the crown of her childish loveliness was the curling golden hair. All the children of Cottonwoods were Jane

Withersteen's friends, she loved them all. But Fay was dearest to her. Fay had few playmates, for among the Gentile children there were none near her age, and the Mormon children were forbidden to play with her. So she was a shy, wild, lonely child.

"Muvver's sick," said Fay, leading Jane toward the door of the hut.

Jane went in. There was only one room, rather dark and bare, but it was clean and neat. A woman lay upon a bed.

"Mrs. Larkin, how are you?" asked Jane, anxiously. "I've been pretty bad for a week, but I'm better now."

"You haven't been here all alone—with no one to wait on you?"

"Oh no! My women neighbors are kind. They take turns coming in."

"Did you send for me?"

"Yes, several times."

"But I had no word—no messages ever got to me."

"I sent the boys, and they left word with your women that I was ill and would you please come."

A sudden deadly sickness seized Jane. She fought the weakness, as she fought to be above suspicious thoughts, and it passed, leaving her conscious of her utter impotence. That, too, passed as her spirit rebounded. But she had again caught a glimpse of dark underhand domination, running its secret lines this time into her own household. Like a spider in the blackness of night an unseen hand had begun to run these dark lines, to turn and twist them about her life, to plait and weave a web. Jane Withersteen knew it now, and in the realization further coolness and sureness came to her, and the fighting courage of her ancestors.

"Mrs. Larkin, you're better, and I'm so glad," said Jane. "But may I not do something for you—a turn at nursing, or send you things, or take care of Fay?"

"You're so good. Since my husband's been gone what would have become of Fay and me but for you? It was about Fay that I wanted to speak to you. This time I thought surely I'd die, and I was worried about Fay. Well, I'll be around all right shortly, but my strength's gone and I won't live long. So I may as well speak now. You remember you've been asking me to let you take Fay and bring her up as your daughter?"

"Indeed yes, I remember. I'll be happy to have her. But I hope the day—"

"Never mind that. The day'll come—sooner or later. I refused your offer, and now I'll tell you why."

"I know why," interposed Jane. "It's because you don't want her brought up as a Mormon."

"No, it wasn't altogether that." Mrs. Larkin raised her thin hand and laid it appealingly on Jane's. "I don't like to tell you. But—it's this: I told all my friends what you wanted. They know you, care for you, and they said for me to trust Fay to you. Women will talk, you know. It got to the ears of Mormons—gossip of your love for Fay and your wanting her. And it came straight back to me, in jealousy, perhaps, that you wouldn't take Fay as much for love of her as because of your religious duty to bring up another girl for some Mormon to marry."

"That's a damnable lie!" cried Jane Withersteen.

"It was what made me hesitate," went on Mrs. Larkin, "but I never believed it at heart. And now I guess I'll let you—"

"Wait! Mrs. Larkin, I may have told little white lies in my life, but never a lie that mattered, that hurt any one. Now believe me. I love little Fay. If I had her near me I'd grow to worship her. When I asked for her I thought only of that love . . . .Let me prove this. You and Fay come to live with me. I've such a big house, and I'm so lonely. I'll help nurse you, take care of you. When you're better you can work for me. I'll keep little Fay and bring her up—without Mormon teaching. When she's grown, if she should want to leave me, I'll send her, and not empty-handed, back to Illinois where you came from. I promise you."

"I knew it was a lie," replied the mother, and she sank back upon her pillow with something of peace in her white, worn face. "Jane Withersteen, may Heaven bless you! I've been deeply grateful to you. But because you're a Mormon I never felt close to you till now. I don't know much about religion as religion, but your God and my God are the same."

CHAPTER VIII

SURPRISE VALLEY

Back in that strange canyon, which Venters had found indeed a valley of surprises, the wounded girl's whispered appeal, almost a prayer, not to take her back to the rustlers crowned the events of the last few days with a confounding climax. That she should not want to return to them staggered Venters. Presently, as logical thought returned, her appeal confirmed his first impression—that she was more unfortunate than bad—and he experienced a sensation of gladness. If he had known before that Oldring's Masked Rider was a woman his opinion would have been formed and he would have considered her abandoned. But his first knowledge had come when he lifted a white face quivering in a convulsion of agony; he had heard God's name whispered by blood-stained lips; through her solemn and awful eyes he had caught a glimpse of her soul. And just now had come the entreaty to him, "Don't—take—me—back—there!"

Once for all Venters's quick mind formed a permanent conception of this poor girl. He based it, not upon what the chances of life had made her, but upon the revelation of dark eyes that pierced the infinite, upon a few pitiful, halting words that betrayed failure and wrong and misery, yet breathed the truth of a tragic fate rather than a natural leaning to evil.

"What's your name?" he inquired. "Bess," she answered.

"Bess what?"

"That's enough—just Bess."

The red that deepened in her cheeks was not all the flush of fever. Venters marveled anew, and this time at the tint of shame in her face, at the momentary drooping of long lashes. She might be a rustler's girl, but she was still capable of shame, she might be dying, but she still clung to some little remnant of honor.

"Very well, Bess. It doesn't matter," he said. "But this matters—what shall I do with you?"

"Are—you—a rider?" she whispered.

"Not now. I was once. I drove the Withersteen herds. But I lost my place—lost all I owned—and now I'm—I'm a sort of outcast. My name's Bern Venters."

"You won't—take me—to Cottonwoods—or Glaze? I'd be—hanged."

"No, indeed. But I must do something with you. For it's not safe for me here. I shot that rustler who was with you. Sooner or later he'll be found, and then my tracks. I must find a safer hiding-place where I can't be trailed."

"Leave me—here."

"Alone—to die!"

"Yes."

"I will not." Venters spoke shortly with a kind of ring in his voice.

"What—do you want—to do—with me?" Her whispering grew difficult, so low and faint that Venters had to stoop to hear her.

"Why, let's see," he replied, slowly. "I'd like to take you some place where I could watch by you, nurse you, till you're all right."

"And—then?"

"Well, it'll be time to think of that when you're cured of your wound. It's a bad one. And—Bess, if you don't want to live—if you don't fight for life—you'll never—"

"Oh! I want—to live! I'm afraid—to die. But I'd rather—die—than go back—to—to—"

"To Oldring?" asked Venters, interrupting her in turn.

Her lips moved in an affirmative.

"I promise not to take you back to him or to Cottonwoods or to Glaze."

The mournful earnestness of her gaze suddenly shone with unutterable gratitude and wonder. And as suddenly Venters found her eyes beautiful as he had never seen or felt beauty. They were as dark blue as the sky at night. Then the flashing changed to a long, thoughtful look, in which there was a wistful, unconscious searching of his face, a look that trembled on the verge of hope and trust.

"I'll try—to live," she said. The broken whisper just reached his ears. "Do what—you want—with me."

"Rest then—don't worry—sleep," he replied.

Abruptly he arose, as if words had been decision for him, and with a sharp command to the dogs he strode from the camp. Venters was conscious of an indefinite conflict of change within him. It seemed to be a vague passing of old moods, a dim coalescing of new forces, a moment of inexplicable transition. He was both cast down and uplifted. He wanted to think and think of the meaning, but he resolutely dispelled emotion. His imperative need at present was to find a safe retreat, and this called for action.

So he set out. It still wanted several hours before dark. This trip he turned to the left and wended his skulking way southward a mile or more to the opening of the valley, where lay the strange scrawled rocks. He did not, however, venture boldly out into the open sage, but clung to the right-hand wall and went along that till its perpendicular line broke into the long incline of bare stone.

Before proceeding farther he halted, studying the strange character of this slope and realizing that a moving black object could be seen far against such background. Before him ascended a gradual swell of smooth stone. It was hard, polished, and full of pockets worn by centuries of eddying rain-water. A hundred yards up began a line of grotesque cedar-trees, and they extended along the slope clear to its most southerly end. Beyond that end Venters wanted to get, and he concluded the cedars, few as they were, would afford some cover.

Therefore he climbed swiftly. The trees were farther up than he had estimated, though he had from long habit made allowance for the deceiving nature of distances in that country. When he gained the cover of cedars he paused to rest and look, and it was then he saw how the trees sprang from holes in the bare rock. Ages of rain had run down the slope, circling, eddying in depressions, wearing deep round holes. There had been dry seasons, accumulations of dust, wind-blown seeds, and cedars rose wonderfully out of solid rock. But these were not beautiful cedars. They were gnarled, twisted into weird contortions, as if growth were torture, dead at the tops, shrunken, gray, and old. Theirs had been a bitter fight, and Venters felt a strange sympathy for them. This country was hard on trees—and men.

He slipped from cedar to cedar, keeping them between him and the open valley. As he progressed, the belt of trees widened and he kept to its upper margin. He passed shady pockets half full of water, and, as he marked the location for possible future need, he reflected that there had been no rain since the winter snows. From one of these shady holes a rabbit hopped out and squatted down, laying its ears flat.

Venters wanted fresh meat now more than when he had only himself to think of. But it would not do to fire his rifle there. So he broke off a cedar branch and threw it. He crippled the rabbit, which started to flounder up the slope. Venters did not wish to lose the meat, and he never allowed crippled game to escape, to die lingeringly in some covert. So after a careful glance below, and back toward the canyon, he began to chase the rabbit.

The fact that rabbits generally ran uphill was not new to him. But it presently seemed singular why this rabbit, that might have escaped downward, chose to ascend the slope. Venters knew then that it had a burrow higher up. More than once he jerked over to seize it, only in vain, for the rabbit by renewed effort eluded his grasp. Thus the chase continued on up the bare slope. The farther Venters climbed the more determined he grew to catch his quarry. At last, panting and sweating, he captured the rabbit at the foot of a steeper grade. Laying his rifle on the bulge of rising stone, he killed the animal and slung it from his belt.

Before starting down he waited to catch his breath. He had climbed far up that wonderful smooth slope, and had almost reached the base of yellow cliff that rose skyward, a huge scarred and cracked bulk. It frowned down upon him as if to forbid further ascent. Venters bent over for his rifle, and, as he picked it up from where it leaned against the steeper grade, he saw several little nicks cut in the solid stone.

They were only a few inches deep and about a foot apart. Venters began to count them—one—two—three—four—on up to sixteen. That number carried his glance to the top of his first bulging bench of cliff-base. Above, after a more level offset, was still steeper slope, and the line of nicks kept on, to wind round a projecting corner of wall.

A casual glance would have passed by these little dents; if Venters had not known what they signified he would never have bestowed upon them the second glance. But he knew they had been cut there by hand, and, though age-worn, he recognized them as steps cut in the rock by the cliff-dwellers. With a pulse beginning to beat and hammer away his calmness, he eyed that indistinct line of steps, up to where the buttress of wall hid further sight of them. He knew that behind the corner of stone would be a cave or a crack which could never be suspected from below. Chance, that had sported with him of late, now directed him to a probable hiding-place. Again he laid aside his rifle, and, removing boots and belt, he began to walk up the steps. Like a mountain goat, he was agile, sure-footed, and he mounted the first bench without bending to use his hands. The next ascent took grip of fingers as well as toes, but he climbed steadily, swiftly, to reach the projecting corner, and slipped around it. Here he faced a notch in the cliff. At the apex he turned abruptly into a ragged vent that split the ponderous wall clear to the top, showing a narrow streak of blue sky.

At the base this vent was dark, cool, and smelled of dry, musty dust. It zigzagged so that he could not see ahead more than a few yards at a time. He noticed tracks of wildcats and rabbits in the dusty floor. At every turn he expected to come upon a huge cavern full of little square stone houses, each with a small aperture like a staring dark eye. The passage lightened and widened, and opened at the foot of a narrow, steep, ascending chute.

Venters had a moment's notice of the rock, which was of the same smoothness and hardness as the slope below, before his gaze went irresistibly upward to the precipitous walls of this wide ladder of granite. These were ruined walls of yellow sandstone, and so split and splintered, so overhanging with great sections of balancing rim, so impending with tremendous crumbling crags, that Venters caught his breath sharply, and, appalled, he instinctively recoiled as if a step upward might jar the ponderous cliffs from their foundation. Indeed, it seemed that these ruined cliffs were but awaiting a breath of wind to collapse and come tumbling down. Venters hesitated. It would be a foolhardy man who risked his life under the leaning, waiting avalanches of rock in that gigantic split. Yet how many years had they leaned there without falling! At the bottom of the incline was an immense heap of weathered sandstone all crumbling to dust, but there were no huge rocks as large as houses, such as rested so lightly and frightfully above, waiting patiently and inevitably to crash down. Slowly split from the parent rock by the weathering process, and carved and sculptured by ages of wind and rain, they waited their moment. Venters felt how foolish it was for him to fear these broken walls; to fear that, after they had endured for thousands of years, the moment of his passing should be the one for them to slip. Yet he feared it.

"What a place to hide!" muttered Venters. "I'll climb—I'll see where this thing goes. If only I can find water!" With teeth tight shut he essayed the incline. And as he climbed he bent his eyes downward. This, however, after a little grew impossible; he had to look to obey his eager, curious mind. He raised his glance and saw light between row on row of shafts and pinnacles and crags that stood out from the main wall. Some leaned against the cliff, others against each other; many stood sheer and alone; all were crumbling, cracked, rotten. It was a place of yellow, ragged ruin. The passage narrowed as he went up; it became a slant, hard for him to stick on; it was smooth as marble. Finally he surmounted it, surprised to find the walls still several hundred feet high, and a narrow gorge leading down on the other side. This was a divide between two inclines, about twenty yards wide. At one side stood an enormous rock. Venters gave it a second glance, because it rested on a pedestal. It attracted closer attention. It was like a colossal pear of stone standing on its stem. Around the bottom were thousands of little nicks just distinguishable to the eye. They were marks of stone hatchets. The cliff-dwellers had chipped and chipped away at this boulder fill it rested its tremendous bulk upon a mere pin-point of its surface. Venters pondered. Why had the little stone-men hacked away at that big boulder? It bore no semblance to a statue or an idol or a godhead or a sphinx. Instinctively he put his hands on it and pushed; then his shoulder and heaved. The stone seemed to groan, to stir, to grate, and then to move. It tipped a little downward and hung balancing for a long instant, slowly returned, rocked slightly, groaned, and settled back to its former position.

Venters divined its significance. It had been meant for defense. The cliff-dwellers, driven by dreaded enemies to this last stand, had cunningly cut the rock until it balanced perfectly, ready to be dislodged by strong hands. Just below it leaned a tottering crag that would have toppled, starting an avalanche on an acclivity where no sliding mass could stop. Crags and pinnacles, splintered cliffs, and leaning shafts and monuments, would have thundered down to block forever the outlet to Deception Pass.

"That was a narrow shave for me," said Venters, soberly. "A balancing rock! The cliff-dwellers never had to roll it. They died, vanished, and here the rock stands, probably little changed . . . .But it might serve another lonely dweller of the cliffs. I'll hide up here somewhere, if I can only find water."

He descended the gorge on the other side. The slope was gradual, the space narrow, the course straight for many rods. A gloom hung between the up-sweeping walls. In a turn the passage narrowed to scarce a dozen feet, and here was darkness of night. But light shone ahead; another abrupt turn brought day again, and then wide open space.

Above Venters loomed a wonderful arch of stone bridging the canyon rims, and through the enormous round portal gleamed and glistened a beautiful valley shining under sunset gold reflected by surrounding cliffs. He gave a start of surprise. The valley was a cove a mile long, half that wide, and its enclosing walls were smooth and stained, and curved inward, forming great caves. He decided that its floor was far higher than the level of Deception Pass and the intersecting canyons. No purple sage colored this valley floor. Instead there were the white of aspens, streaks of branch and slender trunk glistening from the green of leaves, and the darker green of oaks, and through the middle of this forest, from wall to wall, ran a winding line of brilliant green which marked the course of cottonwoods and willows.

"There's water here—and this is the place for me," said Venters. "Only birds can peep over those walls, I've gone Oldring one better."

Venters waited no longer, and turned swiftly to retrace his steps. He named the canyon Surprise Valley and the huge boulder that guarded the outlet Balancing Rock. Going down he did not find himself attended by such fears as had beset him in the climb; still, he was not easy in mind and could not occupy himself with plans of moving the girl and his outfit until he had descended to the notch. There he rested a moment and looked about him. The pass was darkening with the approach of night. At the corner of the wall, where the stone steps turned, he saw a spur of rock that would serve to hold the noose of a lasso. He needed no more aid to scale that place. As he intended to make the move under cover of darkness, he wanted most to be able to tell where to climb up. So, taking several small stones with him, he stepped and slid down to the edge of the slope where he had left his rifle and boots. He placed the stones some yards apart. He left the rabbit lying upon the bench where the steps began. Then he addressed a keen-sighted, remembering gaze to the rim-wall above. It was serrated, and between two spears of rock, directly in line with his position, showed a zigzag crack that at night would let through the gleam of sky. This settled, he put on his belt and boots and prepared to descend. Some consideration was necessary to decide whether or not to leave his rifle there. On the return, carrying the girl and a pack, it would be added encumbrance; and after debating the matter he left the rifle leaning against the bench. As he went straight down the slope he halted every few rods to look up at his mark on the rim. It changed, but he fixed each change in his memory. When he reached the first cedar-tree, he tied his scarf upon a dead branch, and then hurried toward camp, having no more concern about finding his trail upon the return trip.

Darkness soon emboldened and lent him greater speed. It occurred to him, as he glided into the grassy glade near camp and head the whinny of a horse, that he had forgotten Wrangle. The big sorrel could not be gotten into Surprise Valley. He would have to be left here.

Venters determined at once to lead the other horses out through the thicket and turn them loose. The farther they wandered from this canyon the better it would suit him. He easily descried Wrangle through the gloom, but the others were not in sight. Venters whistled low for the dogs, and when they came trotting to him he sent them out to search for the horses, and followed. It soon developed that they were not in the glade nor the thicket. Venters grew cold and rigid at the thought of rustlers having entered his retreat. But the thought passed, for the demeanor of Ring and Whitie reassured him. The horses had wandered away.

Under the clump of silver spruces a denser mantle of darkness, yet not so thick that Venter's night-practiced eyes could not catch the white oval of a still face. He bent over it with a slight suspension of breath that was both caution lest he frighten her and chill uncertainty of feeling lest he find her dead. But she slept, and he arose to renewed activity.

He packed his saddle-bags. The dogs were hungry, they whined about him and nosed his busy hands; but he took no time to feed them nor to satisfy his own hunger. He slung the saddlebags over his shoulders and made them secure with his lasso. Then he wrapped the blankets closer about the girl and lifted her in his arms. Wrangle whinnied and thumped the ground as Venters passed him with the dogs. The sorrel knew he was being left behind, and was not sure whether he liked it or not. Venters went on and entered the thicket. Here he had to feel his way in pitch blackness and to wedge his progress between the close saplings. Time meant little to him now that he had started, and he edged along with slow side movement till he got clear of the thicket. Ring and Whitie stood waiting for him. Taking to the open aisles and patches of the sage, he walked guardedly, careful not to stumble or step in dust or strike against spreading sage-branches.

If he were burdened he did not feel it. From time to time, when he passed out of the black lines of shade into the wan starlight, he glanced at the white face of the girl lying in his arms. She had not awakened from her sleep or stupor. He did not rest until he cleared the black gate of the canyon. Then he leaned against a stone breast-high to him and gently released the girl from his hold. His brow and hair and the palms of his hands were wet, and there was a kind of nervous contraction of his muscles. They seemed to ripple and string tense. He had a desire to hurry and no sense of fatigue. A wind blew the scent of sage in his face. The first early blackness of night passed with the brightening of the stars. Somewhere back on his trail a coyote yelped, splitting the dead silence. Venters's faculties seemed singularly acute.

He lifted the girl again and pressed on. The valley better traveling than the canyon. It was lighter, freer of sage, and there were no rocks. Soon, out of the pale gloom shone a still paler thing, and that was the low swell of slope. Venters mounted it and his dogs walked beside him. Once upon the stone he slowed to snail pace, straining his sight to avoid the pockets and holes. Foot by foot he went up. The weird cedars, like great demons and witches chained to the rock and writhing in silent anguish, loomed up with wide and twisting naked arms. Venters crossed this belt of cedars, skirted the upper border, and recognized the tree he had marked, even before he saw his waving scarf.

Here he knelt and deposited the girl gently, feet first and slowly laid her out full length. What he feared was to reopen one of her wounds. If he gave her a violent jar, or slipped and fell! But the supreme confidence so strangely felt that night admitted no such blunders.

The slope before him seemed to swell into obscurity to lose its definite outline in a misty, opaque cloud that shaded into the over-shadowing wall. He scanned the rim where the serrated points speared the sky, and he found the zigzag crack. It was dim, only a shade lighter than the dark ramparts, but he distinguished it, and that served.

Lifting the girl, he stepped upward, closely attending to the nature of the path under his feet. After a few steps he stopped to mark his line with the crack in the rim. The dogs clung closer to him. While chasing the rabbit this slope had appeared interminable to him; now, burdened as he was, he did not think of length or height or toil. He remembered only to avoid a misstep and to keep his direction. He climbed on, with frequent stops to watch the rim, and before he dreamed of gaining the bench he bumped his knees into it, and saw, in the dim gray light, his rifle and the rabbit. He had come straight up without mishap or swerving off his course, and his shut teeth unlocked.

As he laid the girl down in the shallow hollow of the little ridge with her white face upturned, she opened her eyes. Wide, staring black, at once like both the night and the stars, they made her face seem still whiter.

"Is—it—you?" she asked, faintly. "Yes," replied Venters.

"Oh! Where—are we?"

"I'm taking you to a safe place where no one will ever find you. I must climb a little here and call the dogs. Don't be afraid. I'll soon come for you."

She said no more. Her eyes watched him steadily for a moment and then closed. Venters pulled off his boots and then felt for the little steps in the rock. The shade of the cliff above obscured the point he wanted to gain, but he could see dimly a few feet before him. What he had attempted with care he now went at with surpassing lightness. Buoyant, rapid, sure, he attained the corner of wall and slipped around it. Here he could not see a hand before his face, so he groped along, found a little flat space, and there removed the saddle-bags. The lasso he took back with him to the corner and looped the noose over the spur of rock.

"Ring—Whitie—come," he called, softly.

Low whines came up from below.

"Here! Come, Whitie—Ring," he repeated, this time sharply.

Then followed scraping of claws and pattering of feet; and out of the gray gloom below him swiftly climbed the dogs to reach his side and pass beyond.

Venters descended, holding to the lasso. He tested its strength by throwing all his weight upon it. Then he gathered the girl up, and, holding her securely in his left arm, he began to climb, at every few steps jerking his right hand upward along the lasso. It sagged at each forward movement he made, but he balanced himself lightly during the interval when he lacked the support of a taut rope. He climbed as if he had wings, the strength of a giant, and knew not the sense of fear. The sharp corner of cliff seemed to cut out of the darkness. He reached it and the protruding shelf, and then, entering the black shade of the notch, he moved blindly but surely to the place where he had left the saddle-bags. He heard the dogs, though he could not see them. Once more he carefully placed the girl at his feet. Then, on hands and knees, he went over the little flat space, feeling for stones. He removed a number, and, scraping the deep dust into a heap, he unfolded the outer blanket from around the girl and laid her upon this bed. Then he went down the slope again for his boots, rifle, and the rabbit, and, bringing also his lasso with him, he made short work of that trip.

"Are—you—there?" The girl's voice came low from the blackness.

"Yes," he replied, and was conscious that his laboring breast made speech difficult. "Are we—in a cave?"

"Yes."

"Oh, listen! . . . The waterfall! . . . I hear it! You've brought me back!"

Venters heard a murmuring moan that one moment swelled to a pitch almost softly shrill and the next lulled to a low, almost inaudible sigh.

"That's—wind blowing—in the—cliffs," he panted. "You're far from Oldring's—canyon."

The effort it cost him to speak made him conscious of extreme lassitude following upon great exertion. It seemed that when he lay down and drew his blanket over him the action was the last before utter prostration. He stretched inert, wet, hot, his body one great strife of throbbing, stinging nerves and bursting veins. And there he lay for a long while before he felt that he had begun to rest.

Rest came to him that night, but no sleep. Sleep he did not want. The hours of strained effort were now as if they had never been, and he wanted to think. Earlier in the day he had dismissed an inexplicable feeling of change; but now, when there was no longer demand on his cunning and strength and he had time to think, he could not catch the illusive thing that had sadly perplexed as well as elevated his spirit.

Above him, through a V-shaped cleft in the dark rim of the cliff, shone the lustrous stars that had been his lonely accusers for a long, long year. To-night they were different. He studied them. Larger, whiter, more radiant they seemed; but that was not the difference he meant. Gradually it came to him that the distinction was not one he saw, but one he felt. In this he divined as much of the baffling change as he thought would be revealed to him then. And as he lay there, with the singing of the cliff-winds in his ears, the white stars above the dark, bold vent, the difference which he felt was that he was no longer alone.

CHAPTER IX
SILVER SPRUCE AND ASPENS

The rest of that night seemed to Venters only a few moments of starlight, a dark overcasting of sky, an hour or so of gray gloom, and then the lighting of dawn.

When he had bestirred himself, feeding the hungry dogs and breaking his long fast, and had repacked his saddle-bags, it was clear daylight, though the sun had not tipped the yellow wall in the east. He concluded to make the climb and descent into Surprise Valley in one trip. To that end he tied his blanket upon Ring and gave Whitie the extra lasso and the rabbit to carry. Then, with the rifle and saddle-bags slung upon his back, he took up the girl. She did not awaken from heavy slumber.

That climb up under the rugged, menacing brows of the broken cliffs, in the face of a grim, leaning boulder that seemed to be weary of its age-long wavering, was a tax on strength and nerve that Venters felt equally with something sweet and strangely exulting in its accomplishment. He did not pause until he gained the narrow divide and there he rested. Balancing Rock loomed huge, cold in the gray light of dawn, a thing without life, yet it spoke silently to Venters: "I am waiting to plunge down, to shatter and crash, roar and boom, to bury your trail, and close forever the outlet to Deception Pass!"

On the descent of the other side Venters had easy going, but was somewhat concerned because Whitie appeared to have succumbed to temptation, and while carrying the rabbit was also chewing on it. And Ring evidently regarded this as an injury to himself, especially as he had carried the heavier load. Presently he snapped at one end of the rabbit and refused to let go. But his action prevented Whitie from further misdoing, and then the two dogs pattered down, carrying the rabbit between them.

Venters turned out of the gorge, and suddenly paused stock-still, astounded at the scene before him. The curve of the great stone bridge had caught the sunrise, and through the magnificent arch burst a glorious stream of gold that shone with a long slant down into the center of Surprise Valley. Only through the arch did any sunlight pass, so that all the rest of the valley lay still asleep, dark green, mysterious, shadowy, merging its level into walls as misty and soft as morning clouds.

Venters then descended, passing through the arch, looking up at its tremendous height and sweep. It spanned the opening to Surprise Valley, stretching in almost perfect curve from rim to rim. Even in his hurry and concern Venters could not but feel its majesty, and the thought came to him that the cliff-dwellers must have regarded it as an object of worship.

Down, down, down Venters strode, more and more feeling the weight of his burden as he descended, and still the valley lay below him. As all other canyons and coves and valleys had deceived him, so had this deep, nestling oval. At length he passed beyond the slope of weathered stone that spread fan-shape from the arch, and encountered a grassy terrace running to the right and about on a level with the tips of the oaks and cottonwoods below. Scattered here and there upon this shelf were clumps of aspens, and he walked through them into a glade that surpassed in beauty and adaptability for a wild home, any place he had ever seen. Silver spruces bordered the base of a precipitous wall that rose loftily. Caves indented its surface, and there were no detached ledges or weathered sections that might dislodge a stone. The level ground, beyond the spruces, dropped down into a little ravine. This was one dense line of slender aspens from which came the low splashing of water. And the terrace, lying open to the west, afforded unobstructed view of the valley of green treetops.

For his camp Venters chose a shady, grassy plot between the silver spruces and the cliff. Here, in the stone wall, had been wonderfully carved by wind or washed by water several deep caves above the level of the terrace. They were clean, dry, roomy.

He cut spruce boughs and made a bed in the largest cave and laid the girl there. The first intimation that he had of her being aroused from sleep or lethargy was a low call for water.

He hurried down into the ravine with his canteen. It was a shallow, grass-green place with aspens growing up everywhere. To his delight he found a tiny brook of swift-running water. Its faint tinge of amber reminded him of the spring at Cottonwoods, and the thought gave him a little shock. The water was so cold it made his fingers tingle as he dipped the canteen. Having returned to the cave, he was glad to see the girl drink thirstily. This time he noted that she could raise her head slightly without his help.

"You were thirsty," he said. "It's good water. I've found a fine place. Tell me—how do you feel?"

"There's pain—here," she replied, and moved her hand to her left side.

"Why, that's strange! Your wounds are on your right side. I believe you're hungry. Is the pain a kind of dull ache—a gnawing?"

"It's like—that."

"Then it's hunger." Venters laughed, and suddenly caught himself with a quick breath and felt again the little shock. When had he laughed? "It's hunger," he went on. "I've had that gnaw many a time. I've got it now. But you mustn't eat. You can have all the water you want, but no food just yet."

"Won't I—starve?"

"No, people don't starve easily. I've discovered that. You must lie perfectly still and rest and sleep—for days."

"My hands—are dirty; my face feels—so hot and sticky; my boots hurt." It was her longest speech as yet, and it trailed off in a whisper. "Well, I'm a fine nurse!"

It annoyed him that he had never thought of these things. But then, awaiting her death and thinking of her comfort were vastly different matters. He unwrapped the blanket which covered her. What a slender girl she was! No wonder he had been able to carry her miles and pack her up that slippery ladder of stone. Her boots were of soft, fine leather, reaching clear to her knees. He recognized the make as one of a boot-maker in Sterling. Her spurs, that he had stupidly neglected to remove, consisted of silver frames and gold chains, and the rowels, large as silver dollars, were fancifully engraved. The boots slipped off rather hard. She wore heavy woollen rider's stockings, half length, and these were pulled up over the ends of her short trousers. Venters took off the stockings to note her little feet were red and swollen. He bathed them. Then he removed his scarf and bathed her face and hands.

"I must see your wounds now," he said, gently.

She made no reply, but watched him steadily as he opened her blouse and untied the bandage. His strong fingers trembled a little as he removed it. If the wounds had reopened! A chill struck him as he saw the angry red bullet-mark, and a tiny stream of blood winding from it down her white breast. Very carefully he lifted her to see that the wound in her back had closed perfectly. Then he washed the blood from her breast, bathed the wound, and left it unbandaged, open to the air.

Her eyes thanked him.

"Listen," he said, earnestly. "I've had some wounds, and I've seen many. I know a little about them. The hole in your back has closed. If you lie still three days the one in your breast will close and you'll be safe. The danger from hemorrhage will be over."

He had spoken with earnest sincerity, almost eagerness.

"Why—do you—want me—to get well?" she asked, wonderingly.

The simple question seemed unanswerable except on grounds of humanity. But the circumstances under which he had shot this strange girl, the shock and realization, the waiting for death, the hope, had resulted in a condition of mind wherein Venters wanted her to live more than he had ever wanted anything. Yet he could not tell why. He believed the killing of the rustler and the subsequent excitement had disturbed him. For how else could he explain the throbbing of his brain, the heat of his blood, the undefined sense of full hours, charged, vibrant with pulsating mystery where once they had dragged in loneliness?

"I shot you," he said, slowly, "and I want you to get well so I shall not have killed a woman. But—for your own sake, too—"

A terrible bitterness darkened her eyes, and her lips quivered. "Hush," said Venters. "You've talked too much already."

In her unutterable bitterness he saw a darkness of mood that could not have been caused by her present weak and feverish state. She hated the life she had led, that she probably had been compelled to lead. She had suffered some unforgivable wrong at the hands of Oldring. With that conviction Venters felt a shame throughout his body, and it marked the rekindling of fierce anger and ruthlessness. In the past long year he had nursed resentment. He had hated the wilderness—the loneliness of the uplands. He had waited for something to come to pass. It had come. Like an Indian stealing horses he had skulked into the recesses of the canyons. He had found Oldring's retreat; he had killed a rustler; he had shot an unfortunate girl, then had saved her from this unwitting act, and he meant to save her from the consequent wasting of blood, from fever and weakness. Starvation he had to fight for her and for himself. Where he had been sick at the letting of blood, now he remembered it in grim, cold calm. And as he lost that softness of nature, so he lost his fear of men. He would watch for Oldring, biding his time, and he would kill this great black-bearded rustler who had held a girl in bondage, who had used her to his infamous ends.

Venters surmised this much of the change in him—idleness had passed; keen, fierce vigor flooded his mind and body; all that had happened to him at Cotton-woods seemed remote and hard to recall; the difficulties and perils of the present absorbed him, held him in a kind of spell.

First, then, he fitted up the little cave adjoining the girl's room for his own comfort and use. His next work was to build a fireplace of stones and to gather a store of wood. That done, he spilled the contents of his saddle-bags upon the grass and took stock. His outfit consisted of a small-handled axe, a hunting-knife, a large number of cartridges for rifle or revolver, a tin plate, a cup, and a fork and spoon, a quantity of dried beef and dried fruits, and small canvas bags containing tea, sugar, salt, and pepper. For him alone this supply would have been bountiful to begin a sojourn in the wilderness, but he was no longer alone. Starvation in the uplands was not an unheard-of thing; he did not, however, worry at all on that score, and feared only his possible inability to supply the needs of a woman in a weakened and extremely delicate condition.

If there was no game in the valley—a contingency he doubted—it would not be a great task for him to go by night to Oldring's herd and pack out a calf. The exigency of the moment was to ascertain if there were game in Surprise Valley. Whitie still guarded the dilapidated rabbit, and Ring slept near by under a spruce. Venters called Ring and went to the edge of the terrace, and there halted to survey the valley.

He was prepared to find it larger than his unstudied glances had made it appear; for more than a casual idea of dimensions and a hasty conception of oval shape and singular beauty he had not had time. Again the felicity of the name he had given the valley struck him forcibly. Around the red perpendicular walls, except under the great arc of stone, ran a terrace fringed at the cliff-base by silver spruces; below that first terrace sloped another wider one densely overgrown with aspens, and the center of the valley was a level circle of oaks and alders, with the glittering green line of willows and cottonwood dividing it in half. Venters saw a number and variety of birds flitting among the trees. To his left, facing the stone bridge, an enormous cavern opened in the wall; and low down, just above the tree-tops, he made out a long shelf of cliff-dwellings, with little black, staring windows or doors. Like eyes they were, and seemed to watch him. The few cliff-dwellings he had seen—all ruins—had left him with haunting memory of age and solitude and of something past. He had come, in a way, to be a cliff-dweller himself, and those silent eyes would look down upon him, as if in surprise that after thousands of years a man had invaded the valley. Venters felt sure that he was the only white man who had ever walked under the shadow of the wonderful stone bridge, down into that wonderful valley with its circle of caves and its terraced rings of silver spruce and aspens.

The dog growled below and rushed into the forest. Venters ran down the declivity to enter a zone of light shade streaked with sunshine. The oak-trees were slender, none more than half a foot thick, and they grew close together, intermingling their branches. Ring came running back with a rabbit in his mouth. Venters took the rabbit and, holding the dog near him, stole softly on. There were fluttering of wings among the branches and quick bird-notes, and rustling of dead leaves and rapid patterings. Venters crossed well-worn trails marked with fresh tracks; and when he had stolen on a little farther he saw many birds and running quail, and more rabbits than he could count. He had not penetrated the forest of oaks for a hundred yards, had not approached anywhere near the line of willows and cotton-woods which he knew grew along a stream. But he had seen enough to know that Surprise Valley was the home of many wild creatures.

Venters returned to camp. He skinned the rabbits, and gave the dogs the one they had quarreled over, and the skin of this he dressed and hung up to dry, feeling that he would like to keep it. It was a particularly rich, furry pelt with a beautiful white tail. Venters remembered that but for the bobbing of that white tail catching his eye he would not have espied the rabbit, and he would never have discovered Surprise Valley. Little incidents of chance like this had turned him here and there in Deception Pass; and now they had assumed to him the significance and direction of destiny.

His good fortune in the matter of game at hand brought to his mind the necessity of keeping it in the valley. Therefore he took the axe and cut bundles of aspens and willows, and packed them up under the bridge to the narrow outlet of the gorge. Here he began fashioning a fence, by driving aspens into the ground and lacing them fast with willows. Trip after trip he made down for more building material, and the afternoon had passed when he finished the work to his satisfaction. Wildcats might scale the fence, but no coyote could come in to search for prey, and no rabbits or other small game could escape from the valley.

Upon returning to camp he set about getting his supper at ease, around a fine fire, without hurry or fear of discovery. After hard work that had definite purpose, this freedom and comfort gave him peculiar satisfaction. He caught himself often, as he kept busy round the camp-fire, stopping to glance at the quiet form in the cave, and at the dogs stretched cozily near him, and then out across the beautiful valley. The present was not yet real to him.

While he ate, the sun set beyond a dip in the rim of the curved wall. As the morning sun burst wondrously through a grand arch into this valley, in a golden, slanting shaft, so the evening sun, at the moment of setting, shone through a gap of cliffs, sending down a broad red burst to brighten the oval with a blaze of fire. To Venters both sunrise and sunset were unreal.

A cool wind blew across the oval, waving the tips of oaks, and while the light lasted, fluttering the aspen leaves into millions of facets of red, and sweeping the graceful spruces. Then with the wind soon came a shade and a darkening, and suddenly the valley was gray. Night came there quickly after the sinking of the sun. Venters went softly to look at the girl. She slept, and her breathing was quiet and slow. He lifted Ring into the cave, with stern whisper for him to stay there on guard. Then he drew the blanket carefully over her and returned to the camp-fire.

Though exceedingly tired, he was yet loath to yield to lassitude, but this night it was not from listening, watchful vigilance; it was from a desire to realize his position. The details of his wild environment seemed the only substance of a strange dream. He saw the darkening rims, the gray oval turning black, the undulating surface of forest, like a rippling lake, and the spear-pointed spruces. He heard the flutter of aspen leaves and the soft, continuous splash of falling water. The melancholy note of a canyon bird broke clear and lonely from the high cliffs. Venters had no name for this night singer, and he had never seen one, but the few notes, always pealing out just at darkness, were as familiar to him as the canyon silence. Then they ceased, and the rustle of leaves and the murmur of water hushed in a growing sound that Venters fancied was not of earth. Neither had he a name for this, only it was inexpressibly wild and sweet. The thought came that it might be a moan of the girl in her last outcry of life, and he felt a tremor shake him. But no! This sound was not human, though it was like despair. He began to doubt his sensitive perceptions, to believe that he half-dreamed what he thought he heard. Then the sound swelled with the strengthening of the breeze, and he realized it was the singing of the wind in the cliffs.

By and by a drowsiness overcame him, and Venters began to nod, half asleep, with his back against a spruce. Rousing himself and calling Whitie, he went to the cave. The girl lay barely visible in the dimness. Ring crouched beside her, and the patting of his tail on the stone assured Venters that the dog was awake and faithful to his duty. Venters sought his own bed of fragrant boughs; and as he lay back, somehow grateful for the comfort and safety, the night seemed to steal away from him and he sank softly into intangible space and rest and slumber.

Venters awakened to the sound of melody that he imagined was only the haunting echo of dream music. He opened his eyes to another surprise of this valley of beautiful surprises. Out of his cave he saw the exquisitely fine foliage of the silver spruces crossing a round space of blue morning sky; and in this lacy leafage fluttered a number of gray birds with black and white stripes and long tails. They were mocking-birds, and they were singing as if they wanted to burst their throats. Venters listened. One long, silver-tipped branch dropped almost to his cave, and upon it, within a few yards of him, sat one of the graceful birds. Venters saw the swelling and quivering of its throat in song. He arose, and when he slid down out of his cave the birds fluttered and flew farther away.

Venters stepped before the opening of the other cave and looked in. The girl was awake, with wide eyes and listening look, and she had a hand on Ring's neck.

"Mocking-birds!" she said.

"Yes," replied Venters, "and I believe they like our company."

"Where are we?"

"Never mind now. After a little I'll tell you."

"The birds woke me. When I heard them—and saw the shiny trees—and the blue sky—and then a blaze of gold dropping down—I wondered—"

She did not complete her fancy, but Venters imagined he understood her meaning. She appeared to be wandering in mind. Venters felt her face and hands and found them burning with fever. He went for water, and was glad to find it almost as cold as if flowing from ice. That water was the only medicine he had, and he put faith in it. She did not want to drink, but he made her swallow, and then he bathed her face and head and cooled her wrists.

The day began with the heightening of the fever. Venters spent the time reducing her temperature, cooling her hot cheeks and temples. He kept close watch over her, and at the least indication of restlessness, that he knew led to tossing and rolling of the body, he held her tightly, so no violent move could reopen her wounds. Hour after hour she babbled and laughed and cried and moaned in delirium; but whatever her secret was she did not reveal it. Attended by something somber for Venters, the day passed. At night in the cool winds the fever abated and she slept.

The second day was a repetition of the first. On the third he seemed to see her wither and waste away before his eyes. That day he scarcely went from her side for a moment, except to run for fresh, cool water; and he did not eat. The fever broke on the fourth day and left her spent and shrunken, a slip of a girl with life only in her eyes. They hung upon Venters with a mute observance, and he found hope in that.

To rekindle the spark that had nearly flickered out, to nourish the little life and vitality that remained in her, was Venters's problem. But he had little resource other than the meat of the rabbits and quail; and from these he made broths and soups as best he could, and fed her with a spoon. It came to him that the human body, like the human soul, was a strange thing and capable of recovering from terrible shocks. For almost immediately she showed faint signs of gathering strength. There was one more waiting day, in which he doubted, and spent long hours by her side as she slept, and watched the gentle swell of her breast rise and fall in breathing, and the wind stir the tangled chestnut curls. On the next day he knew that she would live.

Upon realizing it he abruptly left the cave and sought his accustomed seat against the trunk of a big spruce, where once more he let his glance stray along the sloping terraces. She would live, and the somber gloom lifted out of the valley, and he felt relief that was pain. Then he roused to the call of action, to the many things he needed to do in the way of making camp fixtures and utensils, to the necessity of hunting food, and the desire to explore the valley.

But he decided to wait a few more days before going far from camp, because he fancied that the girl rested easier when she could see him near at hand. And on the first day her languor appeared to leave her in a renewed grip of life. She awoke stronger from each short slumber; she ate greedily, and she moved about in her bed of boughs; and always, it seemed to Venters, her eyes followed him. He knew now that her recovery would be rapid. She talked about the dogs, about the caves, the valley, about how hungry she was, till Venters silenced her, asking her to put off further talk till another time. She obeyed, but she sat up in her bed, and her eyes roved to and fro, and always back to him.

Upon the second morning she sat up when he awakened her, and would not permit him to bathe her face and feed her, which actions she performed for herself. She spoke little, however, and Venters was quick to catch in her the first intimations of thoughtfulness and curiosity and appreciation of her situation. He left camp and took Whitie out to hunt for rabbits. Upon his return he was amazed and somewhat anxiously concerned to see his invalid sitting with her back to a corner of the cave and her bare feet swinging out. Hurriedly he approached, intending to advise her to lie down again, to tell her that perhaps she might overtax her strength. The sun shone upon her, glinting on the little head with its tangle of bright hair and the small, oval face with its pallor, and dark-blue eyes underlined by dark-blue circles. She looked at him and he looked at her. In that exchange of glances he imagined each saw the other in some different guise. It seemed impossible to Venters that this frail girl could be Oldring's Masked Rider. It flashed over him that he had made a mistake which presently she would explain.

"Help me down," she said.

"But—are you well enough?" he protested. "Wait—a little longer."

"I'm weak—dizzy. But I want to get down."

He lifted her—what a light burden now!—and stood her upright beside him, and supported her as she essayed to walk with halting steps. She was like a stripling of a boy; the bright, small head scarcely reached his shoulder. But now, as she clung to his arm, the rider's costume she wore did not contradict, as it had done at first, his feeling of her femininity. She might be the famous Masked Rider of the uplands, she might resemble a boy; but her outline, her little hands and feet, her hair, her big eyes and tremulous lips, and especially a something that Venters felt as a subtle essence rather than what he saw, proclaimed her sex.

She soon tired. He arranged a comfortable seat for her under the spruce that overspread the camp-fire. "Now tell me—everything," she said.

He recounted all that had happened from the time of his discovery of the rustlers in the canyon up to the present moment.

"You shot me—and now you've saved my life?"

"Yes. After almost killing you I've pulled you through."

"Are you glad?"

"I should say so!"

Her eyes were unusually expressive, and they regarded him steadily; she was unconscious of that mirroring of her emotions and they shone with gratefulness and interest and wonder and sadness.

"Tell me—about yourself?" she asked.

He made this a briefer story, telling of his coming to Utah, his various occupations till he became a rider, and then how the Mormons had practically driven him out of Cottonwoods, an outcast.

Then, no longer able to withstand his own burning curiosity, he questioned her in turn. "Are you Oldring's Masked Rider?"

"Yes," she replied, and dropped her eyes.

"I knew it—I recognized your figure—and mask, for I saw you once. Yet I can't believe it! . . . But you never were really that rustler, as we riders knew him? A thief—a marauder—a kidnapper of women—a murderer of sleeping riders!"

"No! I never stole—or harmed any one—in all my life. I only rode and rode—"

"But why—why?" he burst out. "Why the name? I understand Oldring made you ride. But the black mask—the mystery—the things laid to your hands—the threats in your infamous name—the night-riding credited to you—the evil deeds deliberately blamed on you and acknowledged by rustlers—even Oldring himself! Why? Tell me why?"

"I never knew that," she answered low. Her drooping head straightened, and the large eyes, larger now and darker, met Venters's with a clear, steadfast gaze in which he read truth. It verified his own conviction.

"Never knew? That's strange! Are you a Mormon?"

"No."

"Is Oldring a Mormon?"

"No."

"Do you—care for him?"

"Yes. I hate his men—his life—sometimes I almost hate him!"

Venters paused in his rapid-fire questioning, as if to brace him self to ask for a truth that would be abhorrent for him to confirm, but which he seemed driven to hear.

"What are—what were you to Oldring?"

Like some delicate thing suddenly exposed to blasting heat, the girl wilted; her head dropped, and into her white, wasted cheeks crept the red of shame.

Venters would have given anything to recall that question. It seemed so different—his thought when spoken. Yet her shame established in his mind something akin to the respect he had strangely been hungering to feel for her.

"D—n that question!—forget it!" he cried, in a passion of pain for her and anger at himself. "But once and for all—tell me—I know it, yet I want to hear you say so—you couldn't help yourself?"

"Oh no."

"Well, that makes it all right with me," he went on, honestly. "I—I want you to feel that . . . you see—we've been thrown together—and—and I want to help you—not hurt you. I thought life had been cruel to me, but when I think of yours I feel mean and little for my complaining. Anyway, I was a lonely outcast. And now! . . . I don't see very clearly what it all means. Only we are here—together. We've got to stay here, for long, surely till you are well. But you'll never go back to Oldring. And I'm sure helping you will help me, for I was sick in mind. There's something now for me to do. And if I can win back your strength—then get you away, out of this wild country—help you somehow to a happier life—just think how good that'll be for me!"

CHAPTER X
LOVE

During all these waiting days Venters, with the exception of the afternoon when he had built the gate in the gorge, had scarcely gone out of sight of camp and never out of hearing. His desire to explore Surprise Valley was keen, and on the morning after his long talk with the girl he took his rifle and, calling Ring, made a move to start. The girl lay back in a rude chair of boughs he had put together for her. She had been watching him, and when he picked up the gun and called the dog Venters thought she gave a nervous start.

"I'm only going to look over the valley," he said. "Will you be gone long?"

"No," he replied, and started off. The incident set him thinking of his former impression that, after her recovery from fever, she did not seem at ease unless he was close at hand. It was fear of being alone, due, he concluded, most likely to her weakened condition. He must not leave her much alone.

As he strode down the sloping terrace, rabbits scampered before him, and the beautiful valley quail, as purple in color as the sage on the uplands, ran fleetly along the ground into the forest. It was pleasant under the trees, in the gold-flecked shade, with the whistle of quail and twittering of birds everywhere. Soon he had passed the limit of his former excursions and entered new territory. Here the woods began to show open glades and brooks running down from the slope, and presently he emerged from shade into the sunshine of a meadow.

The shaking of the high grass told him of the running of animals, what species he could not tell, but from Ring's manifest desire to have a chase they were evidently some kind wilder than rabbits. Venters approached the willow and cottonwood belt that he had observed from the height of slope. He penetrated it to find a considerable stream of water and great half-submerged mounds of brush and sticks, and all about him were old and new gnawed circles at the base of the cottonwoods.

"Beaver!" he exclaimed. "By all that's lucky! The meadow's full of beaver! How did they ever get here?" Beaver had not found a way into the valley by the trail of the cliff-dwellers, of that he was certain; and he began to have more than curiosity as to the outlet or inlet of the stream. When he passed some dead water, which he noted was held by a beaver dam, there was a current in the stream, and it flowed west. Following its course, he soon entered the oak forest again, and passed through to find himself before massed and jumbled ruins of cliff wall. There were tangled thickets of wild plum-trees and other thorny growths that made passage extremely laborsome. He found innumerable tracks of wildcats and foxes. Rustlings in the thick undergrowth told him of stealthy movements of these animals. At length his further advance appeared futile, for the reason that the stream disappeared in a split at the base of immense rocks over which he could not climb. To his relief he concluded that though beaver might work their way up the narrow chasm where the water rushed, it would be impossible for men to enter the valley there.

This western curve was the only part of the valley where the walls had been split asunder, and it was a wildly rough and inaccessible corner. Going back a little way, he leaped the stream and headed toward the southern wall. Once out of the oaks he found again the low terrace of aspens, and above that the wide, open terrace fringed by silver spruces. This side of the valley contained the wind or water worn caves. As he pressed on, keeping to the upper terrace, cave after cave opened out of the cliff; now a large one, now a small one. Then yawned, quite suddenly and wonderfully above him, the great cavern of the cliff-dwellers.

It was still a goodly distance, and he tried to imagine, if it appeared so huge from where he stood, what it would be when he got there. He climbed the terrace and then faced a long, gradual ascent of weathered rock and dust, which made climbing too difficult for attention to anything else. At length he entered a zone of

shade, and looked up. He stood just within the hollow of a cavern so immense that he had no conception of its real dimensions. The curved roof, stained by ages of leakage, with buff and black and rust-colored streaks, swept up and loomed higher and seemed to soar to the rim of the cliff. Here again was a magnificent arch, such as formed the grand gateway to the valley, only in this instance it formed the dome of a cave instead of the span of a bridge.

Venters passed onward and upward. The stones he dislodged rolled down with strange, hollow crack and roar. He had climbed a hundred rods inward, and yet he had not reached the base of the shelf where the cliff-dwellings rested, a long half-circle of connected stone house, with little dark holes that he had fancied were eyes. At length he gained the base of the shelf, and here found steps cut in the rock. These facilitated climbing, and as he went up he thought how easily this vanished race of men might once have held that stronghold against an army. There was only one possible place to ascend, and this was narrow and steep.

Venters had visited cliff-dwellings before, and they had been in ruins, and of no great character or size but this place was of proportions that stunned him, and it had not been desecrated by the hand of man, nor had it been crumbled by the hand of time. It was a stupendous tomb. It had been a city. It was just as it had been left by its builders. The little houses were there, the smoke-blackened stains of fires, the pieces of pottery scattered about cold hearths, the stone hatchets; and stone pestles and mealing-stones lay beside round holes polished by years of grinding maize—lay there as if they had been carelessly dropped yesterday. But the cliff-dwellers were gone!

Dust! They were dust on the floor or at the foot of the shelf, and their habitations and utensils endured. Venters felt the sublimity of that marvelous vaulted arch, and it seemed to gleam with a glory of something that was gone. How many years had passed since the cliff-dwellers gazed out across the beautiful valley as he was gazing now? How long had it been since women ground grain in those polished holes? What time had rolled by since men of an unknown race lived, loved, fought, and died there? Had an enemy destroyed them? Had disease destroyed them, or only that greatest destroyer—time? Venters saw a long line of blood-red hands painted low down upon the yellow roof of stone. Here was strange portent, if not an answer to his queries. The place oppressed him. It was light, but full of a transparent gloom. It smelled of dust and musty stone, of age and disuse. It was sad. It was solemn. It had the look of a place where silence had become master and was now irrevocable and terrible and could not be broken. Yet, at the moment, from high up in the carved crevices of the arch, floated down the low, strange wail of wind—a knell indeed for all that had gone.

Venters, sighing, gathered up an armful of pottery, such pieces as he thought strong enough and suitable for his own use, and bent his steps toward camp. He mounted the terrace at an opposite point to which he had left. He saw the girl looking in the direction he had gone. His footsteps made no sound in the deep grass, and he approached close without her being aware of his presence. Whitie lay on the ground near where she sat, and he manifested the usual actions of welcome, but the girl did not notice them. She seemed to be oblivious to everything near at hand. She made a pathetic figure drooping there, with her sunny hair contrasting so markedly with her white, wasted cheeks and her hands listlessly clasped and her little bare feet propped in the framework of the rude seat. Venters could have sworn and laughed in one breath at the idea of the connection between this girl and Oldring's Masked Rider. She was the victim of more than accident of fate—a victim to some deep plot the mystery of which burned him. As he stepped forward with a half-formed thought that she was absorbed in watching for his return, she turned her head and saw him. A swift start, a change rather than rush of blood under her white cheeks, a flashing of big eyes that fixed their glance upon him, transformed her face in that single instant of turning, and he knew she had been watching for him, that his return was the one thing in her mind. She did not smile; she did not flush; she did not look glad. All these would have meant little compared to her indefinite expression. Venters grasped the peculiar, vivid, vital something that leaped from her face. It was as if she had been in a dead, hopeless clamp of inaction and feeling, and had been suddenly shot through and through with quivering animation. Almost it was as if she had returned to life.

And Venters thought with lightning swiftness, "I've saved her—I've unlinked her from that old life—she was watching as if I were all she had left on earth—she belongs to me!" The thought was startlingly new. Like a blow it was in an unprepared moment. The cheery salutation he had ready for her died unborn and he tumbled the pieces of pottery awkwardly on the grass while some unfamiliar, deep-seated emotion, mixed with pity and glad assurance of his power to succor her, held him dumb.

"What a load you had!" she said. "Why, they're pots and crocks! Where did you get them?"

Venters laid down his rifle, and, filling one of the pots from his canteen, he placed it on the smoldering campfire.

"Hope it'll hold water," he said, presently. "Why, there's an enormous cliff-dwelling just across here. I got the pottery there. Don't you think we needed something? That tin cup of mine has served to make tea, broth, soup—everything."

"I noticed we hadn't a great deal to cook in."

She laughed. It was the first time. He liked that laugh, and though he was tempted to look at her, he did not want to show his surprise or his pleasure.

"Will you take me over there, and all around in the valley—pretty soon, when I'm well?" she added. "Indeed I shall. It's a wonderful place. Rabbits so thick you can't step without kicking one out. And quail, beaver, foxes, wildcats. We're in a regular den. But—haven't you ever seen a cliff-dwelling?"

"No. I've heard about them, though. The—the men say the Pass is full of old houses and ruins."

"Why, I should think you'd have run across one in all your riding around," said Venters. He spoke slowly, choosing his words carefully, and he essayed a perfectly casual manner, and pretended to be busy assorting pieces of pottery. She must have no cause again to suffer shame for curiosity of his. Yet never in all his days had he been so eager to hear the details of anyone's life "When I rode—I rode like the wind," she replied, "and never had time to stop for anything."

"I remember that day I—I met you in the Pass—how dusty you were, how tired your horse looked. Were you always riding?"

"Oh, no. Sometimes not for months, when I was shut up in the cabin." Venters tried to subdue a hot tingling.

"You were shut up, then?" he asked, carelessly.

"When Oldring went away on his long trips—he was gone for months sometimes—he shut me up in the cabin."

"What for?"

"Perhaps to keep me from running away. I always threatened that. Mostly, though, because the men got drunk at the villages. But they were always good to me. I wasn't afraid."

"A prisoner! That must have been hard on you?"

"I liked that. As long as I can remember I've been locked up there at times, and those times were the only happy ones I ever had. It's a big cabin, high up on a cliff, and I could look out. Then I had dogs and pets I had tamed, and books. There was a spring inside, and food stored, and the men brought me fresh meat. Once I was there one whole winter."

It now required deliberation on Venters's part to persist in his unconcern and to keep at work. He wanted to look at her, to volley questions at her.

"As long as you can remember—you've lived in Deception Pass?" he went on.

"I've a dim memory of some other place, and women and children; but I can't make anything of it. Sometimes I think till I'm weary."

"Then you can read—you have books?"

"Oh yes, I can read, and write, too, pretty well. Oldring is educated. He taught me, and years ago an old rustler lived with us, and he had been something different once. He was always teaching me."

"So Oldring takes long trips," mused Venters. "Do you know where he goes?"

"No. Every year he drives cattle north of Sterling—then does not return for months. I heard him accused once of living two lives—and he killed the man. That was at Stone Bridge."

Venters dropped his apparent task and looked up with an eagerness he no longer strove to hide.

"Bess," he said, using her name for the first time, "I suspected Oldring was something besides a rustler. Tell me, what's his purpose here in the Pass? I believe much that he has done was to hide his real work here."

"You're right. He's more than a rustler. In fact, as the men say, his rustling cattle is now only a bluff. There's gold in the canyons!"

"Ah!"

"Yes, there's gold, not in great quantities, but gold enough for him and his men. They wash for gold week in and week out. Then they drive a few cattle and go into the villages to drink and shoot and kill—to bluff the riders."

"Drive a few cattle! But, Bess, the Withersteen herd, the red herd—twenty-five hundred head! That's not a few. And I tracked them into a valley near here."

"Oldring never stole the red herd. He made a deal with Mormons. The riders were to be called in, and Oldring was to drive the herd and keep it till a certain time—I won't know when—then drive it back to the range. What his share was I didn't hear."

"Did you hear why that deal was made?" queried Venters.

"No. But it was a trick of Mormons. They're full of tricks. I've heard Oldring's men tell about Mormons. Maybe the Withersteen woman wasn't minding her halter! I saw the man who made the deal. He was a little, queer-shaped man, all humped up. He sat his horse well. I heard one of our men say afterward there was no better rider on the sage than this fellow. What was the name? I forget."

"Jerry Card?" suggested Venters.

"That's it. I remember—it's a name easy to remember—and Jerry Card appeared to be on fair terms with Oldring's men."

"I shouldn't wonder," replied Venters, thoughtfully. Verification of his suspicions in regard to Tull's underhand work—for the deal with Oldring made by Jerry Card assuredly had its inception in the Mormon Elder's brain, and had been accomplished through his orders—revived in Venters a memory of hatred that had been smothered by press of other emotions. Only a few days had elapsed since the hour of his encounter with Tull, yet they had been forgotten and now seemed far off, and the interval one that now appeared large and profound with incalculable change in his feelings. Hatred of Tull still existed in his heart, but it had lost its white heat. His affection for Jane Withersteen had not changed in the least; nevertheless, he seemed to view it from another angle and see it as another thing—what, he could not exactly define. The recalling of these two feelings was to Venters like getting glimpses into a self that was gone; and the wonder of them—perhaps the change which was too illusive for him—was the fact that a strange irritation accompanied the memory and a desire to dismiss it from mind. And straightway he did dismiss it, to return to thoughts of his significant present.

"Bess, tell me one more thing," he said. "Haven't you known any women— any young people?"

"Sometimes there were women with the men; but Oldring never let me know them. And all the young people I ever saw in my life was when I rode fast through the villages."

Perhaps that was the most puzzling and thought-provoking thing she had yet said to Venters. He pondered, more curious the more he learned, but he curbed his inquisitive desires, for he saw her shrinking on the verge of that shame, the causing of which had occasioned him such self-reproach. He would ask no more. Still he had to think, and he found it difficult to think clearly. This sad-eyed girl was so utterly different from what it would have been reason to believe such a remarkable life would have made her. On this day he had found her simple and frank, as natural as any girl he had ever known. About her there was something sweet. Her voice was low and well modulated. He could not look into her face, meet her steady, unabashed, yet wistful eyes, and think of her as the woman she had confessed herself. Oldring's Masked Rider sat before him, a girl dressed as a man. She had been made to ride at the head of infamous forays and drives. She had been imprisoned for many months of her life in an obscure cabin. At times the most vicious of men had been her companions; and the vilest of women, if they had not been permitted to approach her, had, at least, cast their shadows over her. But—but in spite of all this—there thundered at Venters some truth that lifted its voice higher than the clamoring facts of dishonor, some truth that was the very life of her beautiful eyes; and it was innocence.

In the days that followed, Venters balanced perpetually in mind this haunting conception of innocence over against the cold and sickening fact of an unintentional yet actual gift. How could it be possible for the two things to be true? He believed the latter to be true, and he would not relinquish his conviction of the former; and these conflicting thoughts augmented the mystery that appeared to be a part of Bess. In those ensuing days, however, it became clear as clearest light that Bess was rapidly regaining strength; that, unless reminded of her long association with Oldring, she seemed to have forgotten it; that, like an Indian who lives solely from moment to moment, she was utterly absorbed in the present.

Day by day Venters watched the white of her face slowly change to brown, and the wasted cheeks fill out by imperceptible degrees. There came a time when he could just trace the line of demarcation between the part of her face once hidden by a mask and that left exposed to wind and sun. When that line disappeared in clear bronze tan it was as if she had been washed clean of the stigma of Oldring's Masked Rider. The suggestion of the mask always made Venters remember; now that it was gone he seldom thought of her past. Occasionally he tried to piece together the several stages of strange experience and to make a whole. He had shot a masked outlaw the very sight of whom had been ill omen to riders; he had carried off a wounded woman whose bloody lips quivered in prayer; he had nursed what seemed a frail, shrunken boy; and now he watched a girl whose face had become strangely sweet, whose dark-blue eyes were ever upon him without boldness, without shyness, but with a steady, grave, and growing light. Many times Venters found the clear gaze embarrassing to him, yet, like wine, it had an exhilarating effect. What did she think when she looked at him so? Almost he believed she had no thought at all. All about her and the present there in Surprise Valley, and the dim yet subtly impending future, fascinated Venters and made him thoughtful as all his lonely vigils in the sage had not.

Chiefly it was the present that he wished to dwell upon; but it was the call of the future which stirred him to action. No idea had he of what that future had in store for Bess and him. He began to think of improving Surprise Valley as a place to live in, for there was no telling how long they would be compelled to stay there. Venters stubbornly resisted the entering into his mind of an insistent thought that, clearly realized, might have made it plain to him that he did not want to leave Surprise Valley at all. But it was imperative that he consider practical matters; and whether or not he was destined to stay long there, he felt the immediate need of a change of diet. It would be necessary for him to go farther afield for a variety of meat, and also that he soon visit Cottonwoods for a supply of food.

It occurred again to Venters that he could go to the canyon where Oldring kept his cattle, and at little risk he could pack out some beef. He wished to do this, however, without letting Bess know of it till after he had made the trip. Presently he hit upon the plan of going while she was asleep.

That very night he stole out of camp, climbed up under the stone bridge, and entered the outlet to the Pass. The gorge was full of luminous gloom. Balancing Rock loomed dark and leaned over the pale descent. Transformed in the shadowy light, it took shape and dimensions of a spectral god waiting—waiting for the moment to hurl himself down upon the tottering walls and close forever the outlet to Deception Pass. At night more than by day Venters felt something fearful and fateful in that rock, and that it had leaned and waited through a thousand years to have somehow to deal with his destiny.

"Old man, if you must roll, wait till I get back to the girl, and then roll!" he said, aloud, as if the stones were indeed a god.

And those spoken words, in their grim note to his ear, as well as contents to his mind, told Venters that he was all but drifting on a current which he had not power nor wish to stem.

Venters exercised his usual care in the matter of hiding tracks from the outlet, yet it took him scarcely an hour to reach Oldring's cattle. Here sight of many calves changed his original intention, and instead of packing out meat he decided to take a calf out alive. He roped one, securely tied its feet, and swung it over his shoulder. Here was an exceedingly heavy burden, but Venters was powerful—he could take up a sack of grain and with ease pitch it over a pack-saddle—and he made long distance without resting. The hardest work came in the climb up to the outlet and on through to the valley. When he had accomplished it, he became fired with another idea that again changed his intention. He would not kill the calf, but keep it alive. He would go back to Oldring's herd and pack out more calves. Thereupon he secured the calf in the best available spot for the moment and turned to make a second trip.

When Venters got back to the valley with another calf, it was close upon daybreak. He crawled into his cave and slept late. Bess had no inkling that he had been absent from camp nearly all night, and only remarked solicitously that he appeared to be more tired than usual, and more in the need of sleep. In the afternoon Venters built a gate across a small ravine near camp, and here corralled the calves; and he succeeded in completing his task without Bess being any the wiser.

That night he made two more trips to Oldring's range, and again on the following night, and yet another on the next. With eight calves in his corral, he concluded that he had enough; but it dawned upon him then that he did not want to kill one. "I've rustled Oldring's cattle," he said, and laughed. He noted then that all the calves were red. "Red!" he exclaimed. "From the red herd. I've stolen Jane Withersteen's cattle! . . . That's about the strangest thing yet."

One more trip he undertook to Oldring's valley, and this time he roped a yearling steer and killed it and cut out a small quarter of beef. The howling of coyotes told him he need have no apprehension that the work of his knife would be discovered. He packed the beef back to camp and hung it upon a spruce-tree. Then he sought his bed.

On the morrow he was up bright and early, glad that he had a surprise for Bess. He could hardly wait for her to come out. Presently she appeared and walked under the spruce. Then she approached the camp-fire. There was a tinge of healthy red in the bronze of her cheeks, and her slender form had begun to round out in graceful lines.

"Bess, didn't you say you were tired of rabbit?" inquired Venters. "And quail and beaver?"

"Indeed I did."

"What would you like?"

"I'm tired of meat, but if we have to live on it I'd like some beef."

"Well, how does that strike you?" Venters pointed to the quarter hanging from the spruce-tree. "We'll have fresh beef for a few days, then we'll cut the rest into strips and dry it."

"Where did you get that?" asked Bess, slowly. "I stole that from Oldring."

"You went back to the canyon—you risked—" While she hesitated the tinge of bloom faded out of her cheeks. "It wasn't any risk, but it was hard work."

"I'm sorry I said I was tired of rabbit. Why! How—When did you get that beef?"

"Last night."

"While I was asleep?"

"Yes."

"I woke last night sometime—but I didn't know."

Her eyes were widening, darkening with thought, and whenever they did so the steady, watchful, seeing gaze gave place to the wistful light. In the former she saw as the primitive woman without thought; in the latter she looked inward, and her gaze was the reflection of a troubled mind. For long Venters had not seen that dark change, that deepening of blue, which he thought was beautiful and sad. But now he wanted to make her think.

"I've done more than pack in that beef," he said. "For five nights I've been working while you slept. I've got eight calves corralled near a ravine. Eight calves, all alive and doing fine!"

"You went five nights!"

All that Venters could make of the dilation of her eyes, her slow pallor, and her exclamation, was fear—fear for herself or for him.

"Yes. I didn't tell you, because I knew you were afraid to be left alone."

"Alone?" She echoed his word, but the meaning of it was nothing to her. She had not even thought of being left alone. It was not, then, fear for herself, but for him. This girl, always slow of speech and action, now seemed almost stupid. She put forth a hand that might have indicated the groping of her mind. Suddenly she stepped swiftly to him, with a look and touch that drove from him any doubt of her quick intelligence or feeling.

"Oldring has men watch the herds—they would kill you. You must never go again!"

When she had spoken, the strength and the blaze of her died, and she swayed toward Venters. "Bess, I'll not go again," he said, catching her.

She leaned against him, and her body was limp and vibrated to a long, wavering tremble. Her face was upturned to his. Woman's face, woman's eyes, woman's lips—all acutely and blindly and sweetly and terribly truthful in their betrayal! But as her fear was instinctive, so was her clinging to this one and only friend.

Venters gently put her from him and steadied her upon her feet; and all the while his blood raced wild, and a thrilling tingle unsteadied his nerve, and something—that he had seen and felt in her—that he could not understand—seemed very close to him, warm and rich as a fragrant breath, sweet as nothing had ever before been sweet to him.

With all his will Venters strove for calmness and thought and judgment unbiased by pity, and reality unswayed by sentiment. Bess's eyes were still fixed upon him with all her soul bright in that wistful light. Swiftly, resolutely he put out of mind all of her life except what had been spent with him. He scorned himself for the intelligence that made him still doubt. He meant to judge her as she had judged him. He was face to face with the inevitableness of life itself. He saw destiny in the dark, straight path of her wonderful eyes. Here was the simplicity, the sweetness of a girl contending with new and strange and enthralling emotions here the living truth of innocence; here the blind terror of a woman confronted with the thought of death to her savior and protector. All this Venters saw, but, besides, there was in Bess's eyes a slow-dawning consciousness that seemed about to break out in glorious radiance.

"Bess, are you thinking?" he asked. "Yes—oh yes!"

"Do you realize we are here alone—man and woman?"

"Yes."

"Have you thought that we may make our way out to civilization, or we may have to stay here—alone—hidden from the world all our lives?"

"I never thought—till now."

"Well, what's your choice—to go—or to stay here—alone with me?"

"Stay!" New-born thought of self, ringing vibrantly in her voice, gave her answer singular power.

Venters trembled, and then swiftly turned his gaze from her face—from her eyes. He knew what she had only half divined—that she loved him.

CHAPTER XI
FAITH AND UNFAITH

At Jane Withersteen's home the promise made to Mrs. Larkin to care for little Fay had begun to be fulfilled. Like a gleam of sunlight through the cottonwoods was the coming of the child to the gloomy house of Withersteen. The big, silent halls echoed with childish laughter. In the shady court, where Jane spent many of the hot July days, Fay's tiny feet pattered over the stone flags and splashed in the amber stream. She prattled incessantly. What difference, Jane thought, a child made in her home! It had never been a real home, she discovered. Even the tidiness and neatness she had so observed, and upon which she had insisted to her women, became, in the light of Fay's smile, habits that now lost their importance. Fay littered the court with Jane's books and papers, and other toys her fancy improvised, and many a strange craft went floating down the little brook.

And it was owing to Fay's presence that Jane Withersteen came to see more of Lassiter. The rider had for the most part kept to the sage. He rode for her, but he did not seek her except on business; and Jane had to acknowledge in pique that her overtures had been made in vain. Fay, however, captured Lassiter the moment he first laid eyes on her.

Jane was present at the meeting, and there was something about it which dimmed her sight and softened her toward this foe of her people. The rider had clanked into the court, a tired yet wary man, always looking for the attack upon him that was inevitable and might come from any quarter; and he had walked right upon little Fay. The child had been beautiful even in her rags and amid the surroundings of the hovel in the sage, but now, in a pretty white dress, with her shining curls brushed and her face clean and rosy, she was lovely. She left her play and looked up at Lassiter.

If there was not an instinct for all three of them in that meeting, an unreasoning tendency toward a closer intimacy, then Jane Withersteen believed she had been subject to a queer fancy. She imagined any child would have feared Lassiter. And Fay Larkin had been a lonely, a solitary elf of the sage, not at all an ordinary child, and exquisitely shy with strangers. She watched Lassiter with great, round, grave eyes, but showed no fear. The rider gave Jane a favorable report of cattle and horses; and as he took the seat to which she invited him, little Fay edged as much as half an inch nearer. Jane replied to his look of inquiry and told Fay's story. The rider's gray, earnest gaze troubled her. Then he turned to Fay and smiled in a way that made Jane doubt her sense of the true relation of things. How could Lassiter smile so at a child when he had made so many children fatherless? But he did smile, and to the gentleness she had seen a few times he added something that was infinitely sad and sweet. Jane's intuition told her that Lassiter had never been a father, but if life ever so blessed him he would be a good one. Fay, also, must have found that smile singularly winning. For she edged closer and closer, and then, by way of feminine capitulation, went to Jane, from whose side she bent a beautiful glance upon the rider.

Lassiter only smiled at her.

Jane watched them, and realized that now was the moment she should seize, if she was ever to win this man from his hatred. But the step was not easy to take. The more she saw of Lassiter the more she respected him, and the greater her respect the harder it became to lend herself to mere coquetry. Yet as she thought of her great motive, of Tull, and of that other whose name she had schooled herself never to think of in connection with Milly Erne's avenger, she suddenly found she had no choice. And her creed gave her boldness far beyond the limit to which vanity would have led her.

"Lassiter, I see so little of you now," she said, and was conscious of heat in her cheeks. "I've been riding hard," he replied.

"But you can't live in the saddle. You come in sometimes. Won't you come here to see me—oftener?"

"Is that an order?"

"Nonsense! I simply ask you to come to see me when you find time."

"Why?"

The query once heard was not so embarrassing to Jane as she might have imagined. Moreover, it established in her mind a fact that there existed actually other than selfish reasons for her wanting to see him. And as she had been bold, so she determined to be both honest and brave.

"I've reasons—only one of which I need mention," she answered. "If it's possible I want to change you toward my people. And on the moment I can conceive of little I wouldn't do to gain that end."

How much better and freer Jane felt after that confession! She meant to show him that there was one Mormon who could play a game or wage a fight in the open.

"I reckon," said Lassiter, and he laughed.

It was the best in her, if the most irritating, that Lassiter always aroused.

"Will you come?" She looked into his eyes, and for the life of her could not quite subdue an imperiousness that rose with her spirit. "I never asked so much of any man—except Bern Venters."

"'Pears to me that you'd run no risk, or Venters, either. But mebbe that doesn't hold good for me."

"You mean it wouldn't be safe for you to be often here? You look for ambush in the cottonwoods?"

"Not that so much."

At this juncture little Fay sidled over to Lassiter. "Has oo a little dirl?" she inquired.

"No, lassie," replied the rider.

Whatever Fay seemed to be searching for in Lassiter's sun-reddened face and quiet eyes she evidently found. "Oo tan tom to see me," she added, and with that, shyness gave place to friendly curiosity. First his sombrero with its leather band and silver ornaments commanded her attention; next his quirt, and then the clinking, silver spurs. These held her for some time, but presently, true to childish fickleness, she left off playing with them to look for something else. She laughed in glee as she ran her little hands down the slippery, shiny surface of Lassiter's leather chaps. Soon she discovered one of the hanging gun— sheaths, and she dragged it up and began tugging at the huge black handle of the gun. Jane Withersteen repressed an exclamation. What significance there was to her in the little girl's efforts to dislodge that heavy weapon! Jane Withersteen saw Fay's play and her beauty and her love as most powerful allies to her own woman's part in a game that suddenly had acquired a strange zest and a hint of danger. And as for the rider, he appeared to have forgotten Jane in the wonder of this lovely child playing about him. At first he was much the shyer of the two. Gradually her confidence overcame his backwardness, and he had the temerity to stroke her golden curls with a great hand. Fay rewarded his boldness with a smile, and when he had gone to the extreme of closing that great hand over her little brown one, she said, simply, "I like oo!"

Sight of his face then made Jane oblivious for the time to his character as a hater of Mormons. Out of the mother longing that swelled her breast she divined the child hunger in Lassiter.

He returned the next day, and the next; and upon the following he came both at morning and at night. Upon the evening of this fourth day Jane seemed to feel the breaking of a brooding struggle in Lassiter. During all these visits he had scarcely a word to say, though he watched her and played absent-mindedly with Fay. Jane had contented herself with silence. Soon little Fay substituted for the expression of regard, "I like oo," a warmer and more generous one, "I love oo."

Thereafter Lassiter came oftener to see Jane and her little protegee. Daily he grew more gentle and kind, and gradually developed a quaintly merry mood. In the morning he lifted Fay upon his horse and let her ride as he walked beside her to the edge of the sage. In the evening he played with the child at an infinite variety of games she invented, and then, oftener than not, he accepted Jane's invitation to supper. No other visitor came to Withersteen House during those days. So that in spite of watchfulness he never forgot, Lassiter began to show he felt at home there. After the meal they walked into the grove of cottonwoods or up by the lakes, and little Fay held Lassiter's hand as much as she held Jane's. Thus a strange relationship was established, and Jane liked it. At twilight they always returned to the house, where Fay kissed them and went in to her mother. Lassiter and Jane were left alone.

Then, if there were anything that a good woman could do to win a man and still preserve her self-respect, it was something which escaped the natural subtlety of a woman determined to allure. Jane's vanity, that after all was not great, was soon satisfied with Lassiter's silent admiration. And her honest desire to lead him from his dark, blood-stained path would never have blinded her to what she owed herself. But the driving passion of her religion, and its call to save Mormons' lives, one life in particular, bore Jane Withersteen close to an infringement of her womanhood. In the beginning she had reasoned that her appeal to Lassiter must be through the senses. With whatever means she possessed in the way of adornment she enhanced her beauty. And she stooped to artifices that she knew were unworthy of her, but which she deliberately chose to employ. She made of herself a girl in every variable mood wherein a girl might be desirable. In those moods she was not above the methods of an inexperienced though natural flirt. She kept close to him whenever opportunity afforded; and she was forever playfully, yet passionately underneath the surface, fighting him for possession of the great black guns. These he would never yield to her. And so in that manner their hands were often and long in contact. The more of simplicity that she sensed in him the greater the advantage she took.

She had a trick of changing—and it was not altogether voluntary—from this gay, thoughtless, girlish coquettishness to the silence and the brooding, burning mystery of a woman's mood. The strength and passion and fire of her were in her eyes, and she so used them that Lassiter had to see this depth in her, this haunting promise more fitted to her years than to the flaunting guise of a wilful girl.

The July days flew by. Jane reasoned that if it were possible for her to be happy during such a time, then she was happy. Little Fay completely filled a long aching void in her heart. In fettering the hands of this Lassiter she was accomplishing the greatest good of her life, and to do good even in a small way rendered happiness to Jane Withersteen. She had attended the regular Sunday services of her church; otherwise she had not gone to the village for weeks. It was unusual that none of her churchmen or friends had called upon her of late; but it was neglect for which she was glad. Judkins and his boy riders had experienced no difficulty in driving the white herd. So these warm July days were free of worry, and soon Jane hoped she had passed the crisis; and for her to hope was presently to trust, and then to believe. She thought often of Venters, but in a dreamy, abstract way. She spent hours teaching and playing with little Fay. And the activity of her mind centered around Lassiter. The direction she had given her will seemed to blunt any branching off of thought from that straight line. The mood came to obsess her.

In the end, when her awakening came, she learned that she had builded better than she knew. Lassiter, though kinder and gentler than ever, had parted with his quaint humor and his coldness and his tranquillity to become a restless and unhappy man. Whatever the power of his deadly intent toward Mormons, that passion now had a rival, the one equally burning and consuming. Jane Withersteen had one moment of exultation before the dawn of a strange uneasiness. What if she had made of herself a lure, at tremendous cost to him and to her, and all in vain!

That night in the moonlit grove she summoned all her courage and, turning suddenly in the path, she faced

Lassiter and leaned close to him, so that she touched him and her eyes looked up to his. "Lassiter! . . . Will you do anything for me?"

In the moonlight she saw his dark, worn face change, and by that change she seemed to feel him immovable as a wall of stone.

Jane slipped her hands down to the swinging gun-sheaths, and when she had locked her fingers around the huge, cold handles of the guns, she trembled as with a chilling ripple over all her body.

"May I take your guns?"

"Why?" he asked, and for the first time to her his voice carried a harsh note. Jane felt his hard, strong hands close round her wrists. It was not wholly with intent that she leaned toward him, for the look of his eyes and the feel of his hands made her weak.

"It's no trifle—no woman's whim—it's deep—as my heart. Let me take them?"

"Why?"

"I want to keep you from killing more men—Mormons. You must let me save you from more wickedness—more wanton bloodshed—" Then the truth forced itself falteringly from her lips. "You must—let—help me to keep my vow to Milly Erne. I swore to her—as she lay dying—that if ever any one came here to avenge her—I swore I would stay his hand. Perhaps I—I alone can save the—the man who—who—Oh, Lassiter! . . . I feel that I can't change you—then soon you'll be out to kill—and you'll kill by instinct—and among the Mormons you kill will be the one—who . . . Lassiter, if you care a little for me—let me—for my sake—let me take your guns!"

As if her hands had been those of a child, he unclasped their clinging grip from the handles of his guns, and, pushing her away, he turned his gray face to her in one look of terrible realization and then strode off into the shadows of the cottonwoods.

When the first shock of her futile appeal to Lassiter had passed, Jane took his cold, silent condemnation and abrupt departure not so much as a refusal to her entreaty as a hurt and stunned bitterness for her attempt at his betrayal. Upon further thought and slow consideration of Lassiter's past actions, she believed he would return and forgive her. The man could not be hard to a woman, and she doubted that he could stay away from her. But at the point where she had hoped to find him vulnerable she now began to fear he was proof against all persuasion. The iron and stone quality that she had early suspected in him had actually cropped out as an impregnable barrier. Nevertheless, if Lassiter remained in Cottonwoods she would never give up her hope and desire to change him. She would change him if she had to sacrifice everything dear to her except hope of heaven. Passionately devoted as she was to her religion, she had yet refused to marry a Mormon. But a situation had developed wherein self paled in the great white light of religious duty of the highest order. That was the leading motive, the divinely spiritual one; but there were other motives, which, like tentacles, aided in drawing her will to the acceptance of a possible abnegation. And through the watches of that sleepless night Jane Withersteen, in fear and sorrow and doubt, came finally to believe that if she must throw herself into Lassiter's arms to make him abide by "Thou shalt not kill!" she would yet do well.

In the morning she expected Lassiter at the usual hour, but she was not able to go at once to the court, so she sent little Fay. Mrs. Larkin was ill and required attention. It appeared that the mother, from the time of her arrival at Withersteen House, had relaxed and was slowly losing her hold on life. Jane had believed that absence of worry and responsibility coupled with good nursing and comfort would mend Mrs. Larkin's broken health. Such, however, was not the case.

When Jane did get out to the court, Fay was there alone, and at the moment embarking on a dubious voyage down the stone-lined amber stream upon a craft of two brooms and a pillow. Fay was as delightfully wet as she could possibly wish to get.

Clatter of hoofs distracted Fay and interrupted the scolding she was gleefully receiving from Jane. The sound was not the light-spirited trot that Bells made when Lassiter rode him into the outer court. This was slower and heavier, and Jane did not recognize in it any of her other horses. The appearance of Bishop Dyer startled Jane. He dismounted with his rapid, jerky motion flung the bridle, and, as he turned toward the inner court and stalked up on the stone flags, his boots rang. In his authoritative front, and in the red anger unmistakably flaming in his face, he reminded Jane of her father.

"Is that the Larkin pauper?" he asked, bruskly, without any greeting to Jane. "It's Mrs. Larkin's little girl," replied Jane, slowly.

"I hear you intend to raise the child?"

"Yes."

"Of course you mean to give her Mormon bringing-up?"

"No."

His questions had been swift. She was amazed at a feeling that some one else was replying for her. "I've come to say a few things to you." He stopped to measure her with stern, speculative eye.

Jane Withersteen loved this man. From earliest childhood she had been taught to revere and love bishops of her church. And for ten years Bishop Dyer had been the closest friend and counselor of her father, and for the greater part of that period her own friend and Scriptural teacher. Her interpretation of her creed and her religious activity in fidelity to it, her acceptance of mysterious and holy Mormon truths, were all invested in this Bishop. Bishop Dyer as an entity was next to God. He was God's mouthpiece to the little Mormon community at Cottonwoods. God revealed himself in secret to this mortal.

And Jane Withersteen suddenly suffered a paralyzing affront to her consciousness of reverence by some strange, irresistible twist of thought wherein she saw this Bishop as a man. And the train of thought hurdled the rising, crying protests of that other self whose poise she had lost. It was not her Bishop who eyed her in curious measurement. It was a man who tramped into her presence without removing his hat, who had no greeting for her, who had no semblance of courtesy. In looks, as in action, he made her think of a bull stamping cross-grained into a corral. She had heard of Bishop Dyer forgetting the minister in the fury of a common man, and now she was to feel it. The glance by which she measured him in turn momentarily veiled the divine in the ordinary. He looked a rancher; he was booted, spurred, and covered with dust; he carried a gun at his hip, and she remembered that he had been known to use it. But during the long moment while he watched her there was nothing commonplace in the slow-gathering might of his wrath.

"Brother Tull has talked to me," he began. "It was your father's wish that you marry Tull, and my order. You

refused him?"

"Yes."

"You would not give up your friendship with that tramp Venters?"

"No."

"But you'll do as I order!" he thundered. "Why, Jane Withersteen, you are in danger of becoming a heretic! You can thank your Gentile friends for that. You face the damning of your soul to perdition."

In the flux and reflux of the whirling torture of Jane's mind, that new, daring spirit of hers vanished in the old habitual order of her life. She was a Mormon, and the Bishop regained ascendance.

"It's well I got you in time, Jane Withersteen. What would your father have said to these goings-on of yours? He would have put you in a stone cage on bread and water. He would have taught you something about Mormonism. Remember, you're a born Mormon. There have been Mormons who turned heretic—damn their souls!—but no born Mormon ever left us yet. Ah, I see your shame. Your faith is not shaken. You are only a wild girl." The Bishop's tone softened. "Well, it's enough that I got to you in time . . . .Now tell me about this Lassiter. I hear strange things."

"What do you wish to know?" queried Jane. "About this man. You hired him?"

"Yes, he's riding for me. When my riders left me I had to have any one I could get."

"Is it true what I hear—that he's a gun-man, a Mormon-hater, steeped in blood?"

"True—terribly true, I fear."

"But what's he doing here in Cottonwoods? This place isn't notorious enough for such a man. Sterling and the villages north, where there's universal gun-packing and fights every day—where there are more men like him, it seems to me they would attract him most. We're only a wild, lonely border settlement. It's only recently that the rustlers have made killings here. Nor have there been saloons till lately, nor the drifting in of outcasts. Has not this gun-man some special mission here?"

Jane maintained silence.

"Tell me," ordered Bishop Dyer, sharply. "Yes," she replied.

"Do you know what it is?"

"Yes."

"Tell me that."

"Bishop Dyer, I don't want to tell."

He waved his hand in an imperative gesture of command. The red once more leaped to his face, and in his steel-blue eyes glinted a pin-point of curiosity.

"That first day," whispered Jane, "Lassiter said he came here to find— Milly Erne's grave!"

With downcast eyes Jane watched the swift flow of the amber water. She saw it and tried to think of it, of the stones, of the ferns; but, like her body, her mind was in a leaden vise. Only the Bishop's voice could release her. Seemingly there was silence of longer duration than all her former life.

"For what—else?" When Bishop Dyer's voice did cleave the silence it was high, curiously shrill, and on the point of breaking. It released Jane's tongue, but she could not lift her eyes.

"To kill the man who persuaded Milly Erne to abandon her home and her husband—and her God!"

With wonderful distinctness Jane Withersteen heard her own clear voice. She heard the water murmur at her feet and flow on to the sea; she heard the rushing of all the waters in the world. They filled her ears with low, unreal murmurings— these sounds that deadened her brain and yet could not break the long and terrible silence. Then, from somewhere— from an immeasurable distance—came a slow, guarded, clinking, clanking step. Into her it shot electrifying life. It released the weight upon her numbed eyelids. Lifting her eyes she saw—ashen, shaken, stricken— not the Bishop but the man! And beyond him, from round the corner came that soft, silvery step. A long black boot with a gleaming spur swept into sight—and then Lassiter! Bishop Dyer did not see, did not hear: he stared at Jane in the throes of sudden revelation.

"Ah, I understand!" he cried, in hoarse accents. "That's why you made love to this Lassiter—to bind his hands!"

It was Jane's gaze riveted upon the rider that made Bishop Dyer turn. Then clear sight failed her. Dizzily, in a blur, she saw the Bishop's hand jerk to his hip. She saw gleam of blue and spout of red. In her ears burst a thundering report. The court floated in darkening circles around her, and she fell into utter blackness.

The darkness lightened, turned to slow-drifting haze, and lifted. Through a thin film of blue smoke she saw the rough-hewn timbers of the court roof. A cool, damp touch moved across her brow. She smelled powder, and it was that which galvanized her suspended thought. She moved, to see that she lay prone upon the stone flags with her head on Lassiter's knee, and he was bathing her brow with water from the stream. The same swift glance, shifting low, brought into range of her sight a smoking gun and splashes of blood.

"Ah-h!" she moaned, and was drifting, sinking again into darkness, when Lassiter's voice arrested her. "It's all right, Jane. It's all right."

"Did—you—kill—him?" she whispered.

"Who? That fat party who was here? No. I didn't kill him."

"Oh! . . . Lassiter!"

"Say! It was queer for you to faint. I thought you were such a strong woman, not faintish like that. You're all right now—only some pale. I thought you'd never come to. But I'm awkward round women folks. I couldn't think of anythin'."

"Lassiter! . . . the gun there! . . . the blood!"

"So that's troublin' you. I reckon it needn't. You see it was this way. I come round the house an' seen that fat party an' heard him talkin' loud. Then he seen me, an' very impolite goes straight for his gun. He oughtn't have tried to throw a gun on me—whatever his reason was. For that's meetin' me on my own grounds. I've seen runnin' molasses that was quicker 'n him. Now I didn't know who he was, visitor or friend or relation of yours, though I seen he was a Mormon all over, an' I couldn't get serious about shootin'. So I winged him—put a bullet through his arm as he was pullin' at his gun. An' he dropped the gun there, an' a little blood. I told him he'd introduced himself sufficient, an' to please move out of my vicinity. An' he went."

Lassiter spoke with slow, cool, soothing voice, in which there was a hint of levity, and his touch, as he continued to bathe her brow, was gentle and steady. His impassive face, and the kind gray eyes, further stilled her agitation.

"He drew on you first, and you deliberately shot to cripple him—you wouldn't kill him—you—Lassiter?"

"That's about the size of it."

Jane kissed his hand.

All that was calm and cool about Lassiter instantly vanished.

"Don't do that! I won't stand it! An' I don't care a damn who that fat party was."

He helped Jane to her feet and to a chair. Then with the wet scarf he had used to bathe her face he wiped the blood from the stone flags and, picking up the gun, he threw it upon a couch. With that he began to pace the court, and his silver spurs jangled musically, and the great gun-sheaths softly brushed against his leather chaps.

"So—it's true—what I heard him say?" Lassiter asked, presently halting before her. "You made love to me—to bind my hands?"

"Yes," confessed Jane. It took all her woman's courage to meet the gray storm of his glance.

"All these days that you've been so friendly an' like a pardner—all these evenin's that have been so bewilderin' to me—your beauty—an'—an' the way you looked an' came close to me—they were woman's tricks to bind my hands?"

"Yes."

"An' your sweetness that seemed so natural, an' your throwin' little Fay an' me so much together—to make me love the child—all that was for the same reason?"

"Yes."

Lassiter flung his arms—a strange gesture for him.

"Mebbe it wasn't much in your Mormon thinkin', for you to play that game. But to ring the child in—that was hellish!"

Jane's passionate, unheeding zeal began to loom darkly.

"Lassiter, whatever my intention in the beginning, Fay loves you dearly— and I—I've grown to—to like you."

"That's powerful kind of you, now," he said. Sarcasm and scorn made his voice that of a stranger. "An' you sit there an' look me straight in the eyes! You're a wonderful strange woman, Jane Withersteen."

"I'm not ashamed, Lassiter. I told you I'd try to change you."

"Would you mind tellin' me just what you tried?"

"I tried to make you see beauty in me and be softened by it. I wanted you to care for me so that I could influence you. It wasn't easy. At first you were stone-blind. Then I hoped you'd love little Fay, and through that come to feel the horror of making children fatherless."

"Jane Withersteen, either you're a fool or noble beyond my understandin'. Mebbe you're both. I know you're blind. What you meant is one thing—what you did was to make me love you."

"Lassiter!"

"I reckon I'm a human bein', though I never loved any one but my sister, Milly Erne. That was long—"

"Oh, are you Milly's brother?"

"Yes, I was, an' I loved her. There never was any one but her in my life till now. Didn't I tell you that long ago I back-trailed myself from women? I was a Texas ranger till—till Milly left home, an' then I became somethin' else—Lassiter! For years I've been a lonely man set on one thing. I came here an' met you. An' now I'm not the man I was. The change was gradual, an' I took no notice of it. I understand now that never-satisfied longin' to see you, listen to you, watch you, feel you near me. It's plain now why you were never out of my thoughts.

I've had no thoughts but of you. I've lived an' breathed for you. An' now when I know what it means—what you've done—I'm burnin' up with hell's fire!"

"Oh, Lassiter—no—no—you don't love me that way!" Jane cased. "If that's what love is, then I do."

"Forgive me! I didn't mean to make you love me like that. Oh, what a tangle of our lives! You—Milly Erne's brother! And I—heedless, mad to melt your heart toward Mormons. Lassiter, I may be wicked but not wicked enough to hate. If I couldn't hate Tull, could I hate you?"

"After all, Jane, mebbe you're only blind—Mormon blind. That only can explain what's close to selfishness—"

"I'm not selfish. I despise the very word. If I were free—"

"But you're not free. Not free of Mormonism. An' in playin' this game with me you've been unfaithful."

"Un-faithful!" faltered Jane.

"Yes, I said unfaithful. You're faithful to your Bishop an' unfaithful to yourself. You're false to your womanhood an' true to your religion. But for a savin' innocence you'd have made yourself low an' vile— betrayin' yourself, betrayin' me—all to bind my hands an' keep me from snuffin' out Mormon life. It's your damned Mormon blindness."

"Is it vile—is it blind—is it only Mormonism to save human life? No, Lassiter, that's God's law, divine, universal for all Christians."

"The blindness I mean is blindness that keeps you from seein' the truth. I've known many good Mormons. But some are blacker than hell. You won't see that even when you know it. Else, why all this blind passion to save the life of that—that . . . ."

Jane shut out the light, and the hands she held over her eyes trembled and quivered against her face.

"Blind—yes, en' let me make it clear en' simple to you," Lassiter went on, his voice losing its tone of anger. "Take, for instance, that idea of yours last night when you wanted my guns. It was good an' beautiful, an' showed your heart—but—why, Jane, it was crazy. Mind I'm assumin' that life to me is as sweet as to any other man. An' to preserve that life is each man's first an' closest thought. Where would any man be on this border without guns? Where, especially, would Lassiter be? Well, I'd be under the sage with thousands of other men now livin' an' sure better men than me. Gun-packin' in the West since the Civil War has growed into a kind of moral law. An' out here on this border it's the difference between a man an' somethin' not a man. Look what your takin' Venters's guns from him all but made him! Why, your churchmen carry guns. Tull has killed a man an' drawed on others. Your Bishop has shot a half dozen men, an' it wasn't through prayers of his that they recovered. An' to-day he'd have shot me if he'd been quick enough on the draw. Could I walk or ride down into Cottonwoods without my guns? This is a wild time, Jane Withersteen, this year of our Lord eighteen seventy- one."

"No time—for a woman!" exclaimed Jane, brokenly. "Oh, Lassiter, I feel help-less—lost—and don't know where to turn. If I am blind—then—I need some one—a friend—you, Lassiter—more than ever!"

"Well, I didn't say nothin' about goin' back on you, did I?"

CHAPTER XII
THE INVISIBLE HAND

Jane received a letter from Bishop Dyer, not in his own handwriting, which stated that the abrupt termination of their interview had left him in some doubt as to her future conduct. A slight injury had incapacitated him from seeking another meeting at present, the letter went on to say, and ended with a request which was virtually a command, that she call upon him at once.

The reading of the letter acquainted Jane Withersteen with the fact that something within her had all but changed. She sent no reply to Bishop Dyer nor did she go to see him. On Sunday she remained absent from the service—for the second time in years—and though she did not actually suffer there was a dead-lock of feelings deep within her, and the waiting for a balance to fall on either side was almost as bad as suffering. She had a gloomy expectancy of untoward circumstances, and with it a keen-edged curiosity to watch developments. She had a half-formed conviction that her future conduct—as related to her churchmen—was beyond her control and would be governed by their attitude toward her. Something was changing in her, forming, waiting for decision to make it a real and fixed thing. She had told Lassiter that she felt helpless and lost in the fateful tangle of their lives; and now she feared that she was approaching the same chaotic condition of mind in regard to her religion. It appalled her to find that she questioned phases of that religion. Absolute faith had been her serenity. Though leaving her faith unshaken, her serenity had been disturbed, and now it was broken by open war between her and her ministers. That something within her—a whisper—which she had tried in vain to hush had become a ringing voice, and it called to her to wait. She had transgressed no laws of God. Her churchmen, however invested with the power and the glory of a wonderful creed, however they sat in inexorable judgment of her, must now practice toward her the simple, common, Christian virtue they professed to preach, "Do unto others as you would have others do unto you!"

Jane Withersteen, waiting in darkness of mind, remained faithful still. But it was darkness that must soon be pierced by light. If her faith were justified, if her churchmen were trying only to intimidate her, the fact would soon be manifest, as would their failure, and then she would redouble her zeal toward them and toward what had been the best work of her life—work for the welfare and happiness of those among whom she lived, Mormon and Gentile alike. If that secret, intangible power closed its toils round her again, if that great invisible hand moved here and there and everywhere, slowly paralyzing her with its mystery and its inconceivable sway over her affairs, then she would know beyond doubt that it was not chance, nor jealousy, nor intimidation, nor ministerial wrath at her revolt, but a cold and calculating policy thought out long before she was born, a dark, immutable will of whose empire she and all that was hers was but an atom.

Then might come her ruin. Then might come her fall into black storm. Yet she would rise again, and to the light. God would be merciful to a driven woman who had lost her way.

A week passed. Little Fay played and prattled and pulled at Lassiter's big black guns. The rider came to Withersteen House oftener than ever. Jane saw a change in him, though it did not relate to his kindness and gentleness. He was quieter and more thoughtful. While playing with Fay or conversing with Jane he seemed to be possessed of another self that watched with cool, roving eyes, that listened, listened always as if the murmuring amber stream brought messages, and the moving leaves whispered something. Lassiter never rode Bells into the court any more, nor did he come by the lane or the paths. When he appeared it was suddenly and noiselessly out of the dark shadow of the grove.

"I left Bells out in the sage," he said, one day at the end of that week. "I must carry water to him."

"Why not let him drink at the trough or here?" asked Jane, quickly.

"I reckon it'll be safer for me to slip through the grove. I've been watched when

I rode in from the sage."

"Watched? By whom?"

"By a man who thought he was well hid. But my eyes are pretty sharp. An', Jane," he went on, almost in a whisper, "I reckon it'd be a good idea for us to talk low. You're spied on here by your women."

"Lassiter!" she whispered in turn. "That's hard to believe. My women love me."

"What of that?" he asked. "Of course they love you. But they're Mormon women." Jane's old, rebellious loyalty clashed with her doubt.

"I won't believe it," she replied, stubbornly.

"Well then, just act natural an' talk natural, an' pretty soon—give them time to hear us—pretend to go over there to the table, en' then quick-like make a move for the door en' open it."

"I will," said Jane, with heightened color. Lassiter was right; he never made mistakes; he would not have told her unless he positively knew. Yet Jane was so tenacious of faith that she had to see with her own eyes, and so constituted that to employ even such small deceit toward her women made her ashamed, and angry for her shame as well as theirs. Then a singular thought confronted her that made her hold up this simple ruse— which hurt her, though it was well justified—against the deceit she had wittingly and eagerly used toward Lassiter. The difference was staggering in its suggestion of that blindness of which he had accused her. Fairness and justice and mercy, that she had imagined were anchor-cables to hold fast her soul to righteousness had not been hers in the strange, biased duty that had so exalted and confounded her.

Presently Jane began to act her little part, to laugh and play with Fay, to talk of horses and cattle to Lassiter. Then she made deliberate mention of a book in which she kept records of all pertaining to her stock, and she walked slowly toward the table, and when near the door she suddenly whirled and thrust it open. Her sharp action nearly knocked down a woman who had undoubtedly been listening.

"Hester," said Jane, sternly, "you may go home, and you need not come back."

Jane shut the door and returned to Lassiter. Standing unsteadily, she put her hand on his arm. She let him see that doubt had gone, and how this stab of disloyalty pained her.

"Spies! My own women! . . . Oh, miserable!" she cried, with flashing, tearful eyes.

"I hate to tell you," he replied. By that she knew he had long spared her. "It's begun again—that work in the dark."

"Nay, Lassiter—it never stopped!"

So bitter certainty claimed her at last, and trust fled Withersteen House and fled forever. The women who owed much to Jane Withersteen changed not in love for her, nor in devotion to their household work, but they poisoned both by a thousand acts of stealth and cunning and duplicity. Jane broke out once and caught them in strange, stone-faced, unhesitating falsehood. Thereafter she broke out no more. She forgave them because they were driven. Poor, fettered, and sealed Hagars, how she pitied them! What terrible thing bound them and locked their lips, when they showed neither consciousness of guilt toward their benefactress nor distress at the slow wearing apart of long-established and dear ties?

"The blindness again!" cried Jane Withersteen. "In my sisters as in me! . . . O God!"

There came a time when no words passed between Jane and her women. Silently they went about their household duties, and secretly they went about the underhand work to which they had been bidden. The gloom of the house and the gloom of its mistress, which darkened even the bright spirit of little Fay, did not pervade these women. Happiness was not among them, but they were aloof from gloom. They spied and listened; they received and sent secret messengers; and they stole Jane's books and records, and finally the papers that were deeds of her possessions. Through it all they were silent, rapt in a kind of trance. Then one by one, without leave or explanation or farewell, they left Withersteen House, and never returned.

Coincident with this disappearance Jane's gardeners and workers in the alfalfa fields and stable men quit her, not even asking for their wages. Of all her Mormon employees about the great ranch only Jerd remained. He went on with his duty, but talked no more of the change than if it had never occurred.

"Jerd," said Jane, "what stock you can't take care of turn out in the sage. Let your first thought be for Black Star and Night. Keep them in perfect condition. Run them every day and watch them always."

Though Jane Withersteen gave them such liberality, she loved her possessions. She loved the rich, green stretches of alfalfa, and the farms, and the grove, and the old stone house, and the beautiful, ever-faithful amber spring, and every one of a myriad of horses and colts and burros and fowls down to the smallest rabbit that nipped her vegetables; but she loved best her noble Arabian steeds. In common with all riders of the upland sage Jane cherished two material things—the cold, sweet, brown water that made life possible in the wilderness and the horses which were a part of that life. When Lassiter asked her what Lassiter would be without his guns he was assuming that his horse was part of himself. So Jane loved Black Star and Night because it was her nature to love all beautiful creatures—perhaps all living things; and then she loved them because she herself was of the sage and in her had been born and bred the rider's instinct to rely on his four-footed brother. And when Jane gave Jerd the order to keep her favorites trained down to the day it was a half-conscious admission that presaged a time when she would need her fleet horses.

Jane had now, however, no leisure to brood over the coils that were closing round her. Mrs. Larkin grew weaker as the August days began; she required constant care; there was little Fay to look after; and such household work as was imperative. Lassiter put Bells in the stable with the other racers, and directed his efforts to a closer attendance upon Jane. She welcomed the change. He was always at hand to help, and it was her fortune to learn that his boast of being awkward around women had its root in humility and was not true.

His great, brown hands were skilled in a multiplicity of ways which a woman might have envied. He shared Jane's work, and was of especial help to her in nursing Mrs. Larkin. The woman suffered most at night, and this often broke Jane's rest. So it came about that Lassiter would stay by Mrs. Larkin during the day, when she needed care, and Jane would make up the sleep she lost in night-watches. Mrs. Larkin at once took kindly to the gentle Lassiter, and, without ever asking who or what he was, praised him to Jane. "He's a good man and loves children," she said. How sad to hear this truth spoken of a man whom Jane thought lost beyond all redemption! Yet ever and ever Lassiter towered above her, and behind or through his black, sinister figure shone something luminous that strangely affected Jane. Good and evil began to seem incomprehensibly blended in her judgment. It was her belief that evil could not come forth from good; yet here was a murderer who dwarfed in gentleness, patience, and love any man she had ever known.

She had almost lost track of her more outside concerns when early one morning Judkins presented himself before her in the courtyard.

Thin, hard, burnt, bearded, with the dust and sage thick on him, with his leather wrist-bands shining from use, and his boots worn through on the stirrup side, he looked the rider of riders. He wore two guns and carried a Winchester.

Jane greeted him with surprise and warmth, set meat and bread and drink before him; and called Lassiter out to see him. The men exchanged glances, and the meaning of Lassiter's keen inquiry and Judkins's bold reply, both unspoken, was not lost upon Jane.

"Where's your hoss?" asked Lassiter, aloud.

"Left him down the slope," answered Judkins. "I footed it in a ways, an' slept last night in the sage. I went to the place you told me you 'moss always slept, but didn't strike you."

"I moved up some, near the spring, an' now I go there nights."

"Judkins—the white herd?" queried Jane, hurriedly.

"Miss Withersteen, I make proud to say I've not lost a steer. Fer a good while after thet stampede Lassiter milled we hed no trouble. Why, even the sage dogs left us. But it's begun agin—thet flashin' of lights over ridge tips, an' queer puffin' of smoke, en' then at night strange whistles en' noises. But the herd's acted magnificent. An' my boys, say, Miss Withersteen, they're only kids, but I ask no better riders. I got the laugh in the village fer takin' them out. They're a wild lot, an' you know boys hev more nerve than grown men, because they don't know what danger is. "I'm not denyin' there's danger. But they glory in it, an' mebbe I like it myself—anyway, we'll stick. We're goin' to drive the herd on the far side of the first break of Deception Pass. There's a great round valley over there, an' no ridges or piles of rocks to aid these stampeders. The rains are due. We'll hev plenty of water fer a while. An' we can hold thet herd from anybody except Oldrin'. I come in fer supplies. I'll pack a couple of burros an' drive out after dark to-night."

"Judkins, take what you want from the store-room. Lassiter will help you. I—I can't thank you enough . . . but—wait."

Jane went to the room that had once been her father's, and from a secret chamber in the thick stone wall she took a bag of gold, and, carrying it back to the court, she gave it to the rider.

"There, Judkins, and understand that I regard it as little for your loyalty. Give what is fair to your boys, and keep the rest. Hide it. Perhaps that would be wisest."

"Oh . . . Miss Withersteen!" ejaculated the rider. "I couldn't earn so much in—in ten years. It's not right—I oughtn't take it."

"Judkins, you know I'm a rich woman. I tell you I've few faithful friends. I've fallen upon evil days. God only knows what will become of me and mine! So take the gold."

She smiled in understanding of his speechless gratitude, and left him with Lassiter. Presently she heard him speaking low at first, then in louder accents emphasized by the thumping of his rifle on the stones. "As infernal a job as even you, Lassiter, ever heerd of."

"Why, son," was Lassiter's reply, "this breakin' of Miss Withersteen may seem bad to you, but it ain't bad—yet. Some of these wall-eyed fellers who look jest as if they was walkin' in the shadow of Christ himself, right down the sunny road, now they can think of things en' do things that are really hell-bent."

Jane covered her ears and ran to her own room, and there like caged lioness she paced to and fro till the coming of little Fay reversed her dark thoughts.

The following day, a warm and muggy one threatening rain awhile Jane was resting in the court, a horseman clattered through he grove and up to the hitching-rack. He leaped off and approached Jane with the manner of a man determined to execute difficult mission, yet fearful of its reception. In the gaunt, wiry figure and the lean, brown face Jane recognized one of her Mormon riders, Blake. It was he of whom Judkins had long since spoken. Of all the riders ever in her employ Blake owed her the most, and as he stepped before her, removing his hat and making manly efforts to subdue his emotion, he showed that he remembered.

"Miss Withersteen, mother's dead," he said.

"Oh—Blake!" exclaimed Jane, and she could say no more.

"She died free from pain in the end, and she's buried—resting at last, thank God! . . . I've come to ride for you again, if you'll have me. Don't think I mentioned mother to get your sympathy. When she was living and your riders quit, I had to also. I was afraid of what might be done—said to her . . . .Miss Withersteen, we can't talk of—of what's going on now—"

"Blake, do you know?"

"I know a great deal. You understand, my lips are shut. But without explanation or excuse I offer my services. I'm a Mormon—I hope a good one. But—there are some things! . . . It's no use, Miss Withersteen, I can't say any more—what I'd like to. But will you take me back?"

"Blake! . . . You know what it means?"

"I don't care. I'm sick of—of—I'll show you a Mormon who'll be true to you!"

"But, Blake—how terribly you might suffer for that!"

"Maybe. Aren't you suffering now?"

"God knows indeed I am!"

"Miss Withersteen, it's a liberty on my part to speak so, but I know you pretty well—know you'll never give in. I wouldn't if I were you. And I—I must—Something makes me tell you the worst is yet to come. That's all. I absolutely can't say more. Will you take me back—let me ride for you—show everybody what I mean?"

"Blake, it makes me happy to hear you. How my riders hurt me when they quit!" Jane felt the hot tears well to her eyes and splash down upon her hands. "I thought so much of them—tried so hard to be good to them. And not one was true. You've made it easy to forgive. Perhaps many of them really feel as you do, but dare not return to me. Still, Blake, I hesitate to take you back. Yet I want you so much."

"Do it, then. If you're going to make your life a lesson to Mormon women, let me make mine a lesson to the men. Right is right. I believe in you, and here's my life to prove it."

"You hint it may mean your life!" said Jane, breathless and low.

"We won't speak of that. I want to come back. I want to do what every rider aches in his secret heart to do for you . . . .Miss Withersteen, I hoped it'd not be necessary to tell you that my mother on her deathbed told me to have courage. She knew how the thing galled me—she told me to come back . . . .Will you take me?"

"God bless you, Blake! Yes, I'll take you back. And will you—will you accept gold from me?"

"Miss Withersteen!"

"I just gave Judkins a bag of gold. I'll give you one. If you will not take it you must not come back. You might ride for me a few months— weeks—days till the storm breaks. Then you'd have nothing, and be in disgrace with your people. We'll forearm you against poverty, and me against endless regret. I'll give you gold which you can hide—till some future time."

"Well, if it pleases you," replied Blake. "But you know I never thought of pay. Now, Miss Withersteen, one thing more. I want to see this man Lassiter. Is he here?"

"Yes, but, Blake—what—Need you see him? Why?" asked Jane, instantly worried. "I can speak to him—tell him about you."

"That won't do. I want to—I've got to tell him myself. Where is he?"

"Lassiter is with Mrs. Larkin. She is ill. I'll call him," answered Jane, and going to the door she softly called for the rider. A faint, musical jingle preceded his step— then his tall form crossed the threshold.

"Lassiter, here's Blake, an old rider of mine. He has come back to me and he wishes to speak to you." Blake's brown face turned exceedingly pale.

"Yes, I had to speak to you," he said, swiftly. "My name's Blake. I'm a Mormon and a rider. Lately I quit Miss Withersteen. I've come to beg her to take me back. Now I don't know you; but I know—what you are. So I've this to say to your face. It would never occur to this woman to imagine—let alone suspect me to be a spy. She couldn't think it might just be a low plot to come here and shoot you in the back. Jane Withersteen hasn't that kind of a mind . . . .Well, I've not come for that. I want to help her—to pull a bridle along with Judkins and—and you. The thing is—do you believe me?"

"I reckon I do," replied Lassiter. How this slow, cool speech contrasted with Blake's hot, impulsive words! "You might have saved some of your breath. See here, Blake, cinch this in your mind. Lassiter has met some square Mormons! An' mebbe—"

"Blake," interrupted Jane, nervously anxious to terminate a colloquy that she perceived was an ordeal for him. "Go at once and fetch me a report of my horses."

"Miss Withersteen! . . . You mean the big drove—down in the sage-cleared fields?"

"Of course," replied Jane. "My horses are all there, except the blooded stock I keep here."

"Haven't you heard—then?"

"Heard? No! What's happened to them?"

"They're gone, Miss Withersteen, gone these ten days past. Dorn told me, and I rode down to see for myself."

"Lassiter—did you know?" asked Jane, whirling to him.

"I reckon so . . . .But what was the use to tell you?"

It was Lassiter turning away his face and Blake studying the stone flags at his feet that brought Jane to the understanding of what she betrayed. She strove desperately, but she could not rise immediately from such a blow.

"My horses! My horses! What's become of them?"

"Dorn said the riders report another drive by Oldring . . . .And I trailed the horses miles down the slope toward Deception Pass."

"My red herd's gone! My horses gone! The white herd will go next. I can stand that. But if I lost Black Star and Night, it would be like parting with my own flesh and blood. Lassiter—Blake—am I in danger of losing my racers?"

"A rustler—or—or anybody stealin' hosses of yours would most of all want the blacks," said Lassiter. His evasive reply was affirmative enough. The other rider nodded gloomy acquiescence.

"Oh! Oh!" Jane Withersteen choked, with violent utterance.

"Let me take charge of the blacks?" asked Blake. "One more rider won't be any great help to Judkins. But I might hold Black Star and Night, if you put such store on their value."

"Value! Blake, I love my racers. Besides, there's another reason why I mustn't lose them. You go to the stables. Go with Jerd every day when he runs the horses, and don't let them out of your sight. If you would please me—win my gratitude, guard my black racers."

When Blake had mounted and ridden out of the court Lassiter regarded Jane with the smile that was becoming rarer as the days sped by.

"'Pears to me, as Blake says, you do put some store on them hosses. Now I ain't gainsayin' that the Arabians are the handsomest hosses I ever seen. But Bells can beat Night, an' run neck en' neck with Black Star."

"Lassiter, don't tease me now. I'm miserable—sick. Bells is fast, but he can't stay with the blacks, and you know it. Only Wrangle can do that."

"I'll bet that big raw-boned brute can more'n show his heels to your black racers. Jane, out there in the sage, on a long chase, Wrangle could kill your favorites."

"No, no," replied Jane, impatiently. "Lassiter, why do you say that so often? I know you've teased me at times, and I believe it's only kindness. You're always trying to keep my mind off worry. But you mean more by this repeated mention of my racers?"

"I reckon so." Lassiter paused, and for the thousandth time in her presence moved his black sombrero round and round, as if counting the silver pieces on the band. "Well, Jane, I've sort of read a little that's passin' in your mind."

"You think I might fly from my home—from Cottonwoods—from the Utah border?"

"I reckon. An' if you ever do an' get away with the blacks I wouldn't like to see Wrangle left here on the sage. Wrangle could catch you. I know Venters had him. But you can never tell. Mebbe he hasn't got him now . . . .Besides—things are happenin', an' somethin' of the same queer nature might have happened to Venters."

"God knows you're right! . . . Poor Bern, how long he's gone! In my trouble I've been forgetting him. But, Lassiter, I've little fear for him. I've heard my riders say he's as keen as a wolf . . . . "As to your reading my thoughts—well, your suggestion makes an actual thought of what was only one of my dreams. I believe I dreamed of flying from this wild borderland, Lassiter. I've strange dreams. I'm not always practical and thinking of my many duties, as you said once. For instance—if I dared—if I dared I'd ask you to saddle the blacks and ride away with me—and hide me."

"Jane!"

The rider's sunburnt face turned white. A few times Jane had seen Lassiter's cool calm broken—when he had met little Fay, when he had learned how and why he had come to love both child and mistress, when he had stood beside Milly Erne's grave. But one and all they could not be considered in the light of his present agitation. Not only did Lassiter turn white—not only did he grow tense, not only did he lose his coolness, but also he suddenly, violently, hungrily took her into his arms and crushed her to his breast.

"Lassiter!" cried Jane, trembling. It was an action for which she took sole blame. Instantly, as if dazed, weakened, he released her. "Forgive me!" went on Jane. "I'm always forgetting your—your feelings. I thought of you as my faithful friend. I'm always making you out more than human . . . only, let me say—I meant that—about riding away. I'm wretched, sick of this—this—Oh, something bitter and black grows on my heart!"

"Jane, the hell—of it," he replied, with deep intake of breath, "is you can't ride away. Mebbe realizin' it accounts for my grabbin' you—that way, as much as the crazy boy's rapture your words gave me. I don't understand myself . . . . But the hell of this game is—you can't ride away."

"Lassiter! . . . What on earth do you mean? I'm an absolutely free woman."

"You ain't absolutely anythin' of the kind . . . . I reckon I've got to tell you!"

"Tell me all. It's uncertainty that makes me a coward. It's faith and hope—blind love, if you will, that makes me miserable. Every day I awake believing—still believing. The day grows, and with it doubts, fears, and that black bat hate that bites hotter and hotter into my heart. Then comes night—I pray—I pray for all, and for myself—I sleep—and I awake free once more, trustful, faithful, to believe—to hope! Then, O my God! I grow and live a thousand years till night again! . . . But if you want to see me a woman, tell me why I can't ride away—tell me what more I'm to lose—tell me the worst."

"Jane, you're watched. There's no single move of yours, except when you're hid in your house, that ain't seen by sharp eyes. The cottonwood grove's full of creepin', crawlin' men. Like Indians in the grass. When you rode, which wasn't often lately, the sage was full of sneakin' men. At night they crawl under your windows into the court, an' I reckon into the house. Jane Withersteen, you know, never locked a door! This here grove's a hummin' bee-hive of mysterious happenin's. Jane, it ain't so much that these soles keep out of my way as me keepin' out of theirs. They're goin' to try to kill me. That's plain. But mebbe I'm as hard to shoot in the back as in the face. So far I've seen fit to watch only. This all means, Jane, that you're a marked woman. You can't get away— not now. Mebbe later, when you're broken, you might. But that's sure doubtful. Jane, you're to lose the cattle that's left—your home en' ranch—en' amber Spring. You can't even hide a sack of gold! For it couldn't be slipped out of the house, day or night, an' hid or buried, let alone be rid off with. You may lose all. I'm tellin' you, Jane, hopin' to prepare you, if the worst does come. I told you once before about that strange power I've got to feel things."

"Lassiter, what can I do?"

"Nothin', I reckon, except know what's comin' an' wait an' be game. If you'd let me make a call on Tull, an' a long-deferred call on—"

"Hush! . . . Hush!" she whispered.

"Well, even that wouldn't help you any in the end."

"What does it mean? Oh, what does it mean? I am my father's daughter—a Mormon, yet I can't see! I've not failed in religion—in duty. For years I've given with a free and full heart. When my father died I was rich. If I'm still rich it's because I couldn't find enough ways to become poor. What am I, what are my possessions to set in motion such intensity of secret oppression?"

"Jane, the mind behind it all is an empire builder."

"But, Lassiter, I would give freely—all I own to avert this—this wretched thing. If I gave—that would leave me with faith still. Surely my—my churchmen think of my soul? If I lose my trust in them—"

"Child, be still!" said Lassiter, with a dark dignity that had in it something of pity. "You are a woman, fine en' big an' strong, an' your heart matches your size. But in mind you're a child. I'll say a little more—then I'm done. I'll never mention this again. Among many thousands of women you're one who has bucked against your churchmen. They tried you out, an' failed of persuasion, an' finally of threats. You meet now the cold steel of a will as far from Christlike as the universe is wide. You're to be broken. Your body's to be held, given to some man, made, if possible, to bring children into the world. But your soul? . . . What do they care for your soul?"

CHAPTER XIII

SOLITUDE AND STORM

In his hidden valley Venters awakened from sleep, and his ears rang with innumerable melodies from full-throated mockingbirds, and his eyes opened wide upon the glorious golden shaft of sunlight shining through the great stone bridge. The circle of cliffs surrounding Surprise Valley lay shrouded in morning mist, a dim blue low down along the terraces, a creamy, moving cloud along the ramparts. The oak forest in the center was a plumed and tufted oval of gold.

He saw Bess under the spruces. Upon her complete recovery of strength she always rose with the dawn. At the moment she was feeding the quail she had tamed. And she had begun to tame the mocking-birds. They fluttered among the branches overhead and some left off their songs to flit down and shyly hop near the twittering quail. Little gray and white rabbits crouched in the grass, now nibbling, now laying long ears flat and watching the dogs.

Venters's swift glance took in the brightening valley, and Bess and her pets, and Ring and Whitie. It swept over all to return again and rest upon the girl. She had changed. To the dark trousers and blouse she had added moccasins of her own make, but she no longer resembled a boy. No eye could have failed to mark the rounded contours of a woman. The change had been to grace and beauty. A glint of warm gold gleamed from her hair, and a tint of red shone in the clear dark brown of cheeks. The haunting sweetness of her lips and eyes, that earlier had been illusive, a promise, had become a living fact. She fitted harmoniously into that wonderful setting; she was like Surprise Valley—wild and beautiful.

Venters leaped out of his cave to begin the day.

He had postponed his journey to Cottonwoods until after the passing of the summer rains. The rains were due soon. But until their arrival and the necessity for his trip to the village he sequestered in a far corner of mind all thought of peril, of his past life, and almost that of the present. It was enough to live. He did not want to know what lay hidden in the dim and distant future. Surprise Valley had enchanted him. In this home of the cliff-dwellers there were peace and quiet and solitude, and another thing, wondrous as the golden morning shaft of sunlight, that he dared not ponder over long enough to understand.

The solitude he had hated when alone he had now come to love. He was assimilating something from this valley of gleams and shadows. From this strange girl he was assimilating more.

The day at hand resembled many days gone before. As Venters had no tools with which to build, or to till the terraces, he remained idle. Beyond the cooking of the simple fare there were no tasks. And as there were no tasks, there was no system. He and Bess began one thing, to leave it; to begin another, to leave that; and then do nothing but lie under the spruces and watch the great cloud-sails majestically move along the ramparts, and dream and dream. The valley was a golden, sunlit world. It was silent. The sighing wind and the twittering quail and the singing birds, even the rare and seldom-occurring hollow crack of a sliding weathered stone, only thickened and deepened that insulated silence. Venters and Bess had vagrant minds.

"Bess, did I tell you about my horse Wrangle?" inquired Venters. "A hundred times," she replied.

"Oh, have I? I'd forgotten. I want you to see him. He'll carry us both."

"I'd like to ride him. Can he run?"

"Run? He's a demon. Swiftest horse on the sage! I hope he'll stay in that canyon. "He'll stay."

They left camp to wander along the terraces, into the aspen ravines, under the gleaming walls. Ring and Whitie wandered in the fore, often turning, often trotting back, open-mouthed and solemn-eyed and happy. Venters lifted his gaze to the grand archway over the entrance to the valley, and Bess lifted hers to follow his, and both were silent. Sometimes the bridge held their attention for a long time. To-day a soaring eagle attracted them.

"How he sails!" exclaimed Bess. "I wonder where his mate is?"

"She's at the nest. It's on the bridge in a crack near the top. I see her often. She's almost white."

They wandered on down the terrace, into the shady, sun-flecked forest. A brown bird fluttered crying from a bush. Bess peeped into the leaves. "Look! A nest and four little birds. They're not afraid of us. See how they open their mouths. They're hungry."

Rabbits rustled the dead brush and pattered away. The forest was full of a drowsy hum of insects. Little darts of purple, that were running quail, crossed the glades. And a plaintive, sweet peeping came from the coverts. Bess's soft step disturbed a sleeping lizard that scampered away over the leaves. She gave chase and caught it, a slim creature of nameless color but of exquisite beauty.

"Jewel eyes," she said. "It's like a rabbit—afraid. We won't eat you. There—go."

Murmuring water drew their steps down into a shallow shaded ravine where a brown brook brawled softly over mossy stones. Multitudes of strange, gray frogs with white spots and black eyes lined the rocky bank and leaped only at close approach. Then Venters's eye descried a very thin, very long green snake coiled round a sapling. They drew closer and closer till they could have touched it. The snake had no fear and watched them with scintillating eyes.

"It's pretty," said Bess. "How tame! I thought snakes always ran."

"No. Even the rabbits didn't run here till the dogs chased them."

On and on they wandered to the wild jumble of massed and broken fragments of cliff at the west end of the valley. The roar of the disappearing stream dinned in their ears. Into this maze of rocks they threaded a tortuous way, climbing, descending, halting to gather wild plums and great lavender lilies, and going on at the will of fancy. Idle and keen perceptions guided them equally.

"Oh, let us climb there!" cried Bess, pointing upward to a small space of terrace left green and shady between huge abutments of broken cliff. And they climbed to the nook and rested and looked out across the valley to the curling column of blue smoke from their campfire. But the cool shade and the rich grass and the fine view were not what they had climbed for. They could not have told, although whatever had drawn them was well-satisfying. Light, sure-footed as a mountain goat, Bess pattered down at Venters's heels; and they went on, calling the dogs, eyes dreamy and wide, listening to the wind and the bees and the crickets and the birds.

Part of the time Ring and Whitie led the way, then Venters, then Bess; and the direction was not an object. They left the sun-streaked shade of the oaks, brushed the long grass of the meadows, entered the green and fragrant swaying willows, to stop, at length, under the huge old cottonwoods where the beavers were busy.

Here they rested and watched. A dam of brush and logs and mud and stones backed the stream into a little lake. The round, rough beaver houses projected from the water. Like the rabbits, the beavers had become shy. Gradually, however, as Venters and Bess knelt low, holding the dogs, the beavers emerged to swim with logs and gnaw at cottonwoods and pat mud walls with their paddle-like tails, and, glossy and shiny in the sun, to go on with their strange, persistent industry. They were the builders. The lake was a mud-hole, and the immediate environment a scarred and dead region, but it was a wonderful home of wonderful animals.

"Look at that one—he puddles in the mud," said Bess. "And there! See him dive! Hear them gnawing! I'd think they'd break their teeth. How's it they can stay out of the water and under the water?"

And she laughed.

Then Venters and Bess wandered farther, and, perhaps not all unconsciously this time, wended their slow steps to the cave of the cliff-dwellers, where she liked best to go.

The tangled thicket and the long slant of dust and little chips of weathered rock and the steep bench of stone and the worn steps all were arduous work for Bess in the climbing. But she gained the shelf, gasping, hot of cheek, glad of eye, with her hand in Venters's. Here they rested. The beautiful valley glittered below with its millions of wind-turned leaves bright-faced in the sun, and the mighty bridge towered heavenward, crowned with blue sky. Bess, however, never rested for long. Soon she was exploring, and Venters followed; she dragged forth from corners and shelves a multitude of crudely fashioned and painted pieces of pottery, and he carried them. They peeped down into the dark holes of the kivas, and Bess gleefully dropped a stone and waited for the long-coming hollow sound to rise. They peeped into the little globular houses, like mud-wasp nests, and wondered if these had been store-places for grain, or baby cribs, or what; and they crawled into the larger houses and laughed when they bumped their heads on the low roofs, and they dug in the dust of the floors. And they brought from dust and darkness armloads of treasure which they carried to the light. Flints and stones and strange curved sticks and pottery they found; and twisted grass rope that crumbled in their hands, and bits of whitish stone which crushed to powder at a touch and seemed to vanish in the air.

"That white stuff was bone," said Venters, slowly. "Bones of a cliff-dweller."

"No!" exclaimed Bess.

"Here's another piece. Look! . . . Whew! dry, powdery smoke! That's bone."

Then it was that Venters's primitive, childlike mood, like a savage's, seeing, yet unthinking, gave way to the encroachment of civilized thought. The world had not been made for a single day's play or fancy or idle watching. The world was old. Nowhere could be gotten a better idea of its age than in this gigantic silent tomb. The gray ashes in Venters's hand had once been bone of a human being like himself. The pale gloom of the cave had shadowed people long ago. He saw that Bess had received the same shock—could not in moments such as this escape her feeling living, thinking destiny. "Bern, people have lived here," she said, with wide, thoughtful eyes. "Yes," he replied.

"How long ago?"

"A thousand years and more."

"What were they?"

"Cliff-dwellers. Men who had enemies and made their homes high out of reach."

"They had to fight?"

"Yes."

"They fought for—what?"

"For life. For their homes, food, children, parents—for their women!"

"Has the world changed any in a thousand years?"

"I don't know—perhaps a little."

"Have men?"

"I hope so—I think so."

"Things crowd into my mind," she went on, and the wistful light in her eyes told Venters the truth of her thoughts. "I've ridden the border of Utah. I've seen people—know how they live—but they must be few of all who are living. I had my books and I studied them. But all that doesn't help me any more. I want to go out into the big world and see it. Yet I want to stay here more. What's to become of us? Are we cliff-dwellers? We're alone here. I'm happy when I don't think. These—these bones that fly into dust—they make me sick and a little afraid. Did the people who lived here once have the same feelings as we have? What was the good of their living at all? They're gone! What's the meaning of it all—of us?"

"Bess, you ask more than I can tell. It's beyond me. Only there was laughter here once—and now there's silence. There was life—and now there's death. Men cut these little steps, made these arrow-heads and mealing-stones, plaited the ropes we found, and left their bones to crumble in our fingers. As far as time is concerned it might all have been yesterday. We're here to-day. Maybe we're higher in the scale of human beings—in intelligence. But who knows? We can't be any higher in the things for which life is lived at all."

"What are they?"

"Why—I suppose relationship, friendship—love."

"Love!"

"Yes. Love of man for woman—love of woman for man. That's the nature, the meaning, the best of life itself." She said no more. Wistfulness of glance deepened into sadness.

"Come, let us go," said Venters.

Action brightened her. Beside him, holding his hand she slipped down the shelf, ran down the long, steep slant of sliding stones, out of the cloud of dust, and likewise out of the pale gloom.

"We beat the slide," she cried.

The miniature avalanche cracked and roared, and rattled itself into an inert mass at the base of the incline. Yellow dust like the gloom of the cave, but not so changeless, drifted away on the wind; the roar clapped in echo from the cliff, returned, went back, and came again to die in the hollowness. Down on the sunny terrace there was a different atmosphere. Ring and Whitie leaped around Bess. Once more she was smiling, gay, and thoughtless, with the dream-mood in the shadow of her eyes.

"Bess, I haven't seen that since last summer. Look!" said Venters, pointing to the scalloped edge of rolling purple clouds that peeped over the western wall. "We're in for a storm."

"Oh, I hope not. I'm afraid of storms."

"Are you? Why?"

"Have you ever been down in one of these walled-up pockets in a bad storm?"

"No, now I think of it, I haven't."

"Well, it's terrible. Every summer I get scared to death and hide somewhere in the dark. Storms up on the sage are bad, but nothing to what they are down here in the canyons. And in this little valley—why, echoes can rap back and forth so quick they'll split our ears."

"We're perfectly safe here, Bess."

"I know. But that hasn't anything to do with it. The truth is I'm afraid of lightning and thunder, and thunder-claps hurt my head. If we have a bad storm, will you stay close to me?"

"Yes."

When they got back to camp the afternoon was closing, and it was exceedingly sultry. Not a breath of air stirred the aspen leaves, and when these did not quiver the air was indeed still. The dark-purple clouds moved almost imperceptibly out of the west.

"What have we for supper?" asked Bess. "Rabbit."

"Bern, can't you think of another new way to cook rabbit?" went on Bess, with earnestness. "What do you think I am—a magician?" retorted Venters.

"I wouldn't dare tell you. But, Bern, do you want me to turn into a rabbit?"

There was a dark-blue, merry flashing of eyes and a parting of lips; then she laughed. In that moment she was naive and wholesome.

"Rabbit seems to agree with you," replied Venters. "You are well and strong—and growing very pretty." Anything in the nature of compliment he had never before said to her, and just now he responded to a sudden curiosity to see its effect. Bess stared as if she had not heard aright, slowly blushed, and completely lost her poise in happy confusion.

"I'd better go right away," he continued, "and fetch supplies from Cotton-woods."

A startlingly swift change in the nature of her agitation made him reproach himself for his abruptness.

"No, no, don't go!" she said. "I didn't mean—that about the rabbit. I—I was only trying to be—funny. Don't leave me all alone!"

"Bess, I must go sometime."

"Wait then. Wait till after the storms."

The purple cloud-bank darkened the lower edge of the setting sun, crept up and up, obscuring its fiery red heart, and finally passed over the last ruddy crescent of its upper rim.

The intense dead silence awakened to a long, low, rumbling roll of thunder. "Oh!" cried Bess, nervously.

"We've had big black clouds before this without rain," said Venters. "But there's no doubt about that thunder. The storms are coming. I'm glad. Every rider on the sage will hear that thunder with glad ears."

Venters and Bess finished their simple meal and the few tasks around the camp, then faced the open terrace, the valley, and the west, to watch and await the approaching storm.

It required keen vision to see any movement whatever in the purple clouds. By infinitesimal degrees the dark cloud-line merged upward into the golden-red haze of the afterglow of sunset. A shadow lengthened from under the western wall across the valley. As straight and rigid as steel rose the delicate spear-pointed silver spruces; the aspen leaves, by nature pendant and quivering, hung limp and heavy; no slender blade of grass moved. A gentle splashing of water came from the ravine. Then again from out of the west sounded the low, dull, and rumbling roll of thunder.

A wave, a ripple of light, a trembling and turning of the aspen leaves, like the approach of a breeze on the water, crossed the valley from the west; and the lull and the deadly stillness and the sultry air passed away on a cool wind.

The night bird of the canyon, with clear and melancholy notes announced the twilight. And from all along the cliffs rose the faint murmur and moan and mourn of the wind singing in the caves. The bank of clouds now swept hugely out of the western sky. Its front was purple and black, with gray between, a bulging, mushrooming, vast thing instinct with storm. It had a dark, angry, threatening aspect. As if all the power of the winds were pushing and piling behind, it rolled ponderously across the sky. A red flare burned out instantaneously, flashed from the west to east, and died. Then from the deepest black of the purple cloud burst a boom. It was like the bowling of a huge boulder along the crags and ramparts, and seemed to roll on and fall into the valley to bound and bang and boom from cliff to cliff.

"Oh!" cried Bess, with her hands over her ears. "What did I tell you?"

"Why, Bess, be reasonable!" said Venters.

"I'm a coward."

"Not quite that, I hope. It's strange you're afraid. I love a storm."

"I tell you a storm down in these canyons is an awful thing. I know Oldring hated storms. His men were afraid of them. There was one who went deaf in a bad storm, and never could hear again."

"Maybe I've lots to learn, Bess. I'll lose my guess if this storm isn't bad enough. We're going to have heavy wind first, then lightning and thunder, then the rain. Let's stay out as long as we can."

The tips of the cottonwoods and the oaks waved to the east, and the rings of aspens along the terraces twinkled their myriad of bright faces in fleet and glancing gleam. A low roar rose from the leaves of the forest, and the spruces swished in the rising wind. It came in gusts, with light breezes between. As it increased in strength the lulls shortened in length till there was a strong and steady blow all the time, and violent puffs at intervals, and sudden whirling currents. The clouds spread over the valley, rolling swiftly and low, and twilight faded into a sweeping darkness. Then the singing of the wind in the caves drowned the swift roar of rustling leaves; then the song swelled to a mourning, moaning wail; then with the gathering power of the wind the wail changed to a shriek. Steadily the wind strengthened and constantly the strange sound changed.

The last bit of blue sky yielded to the on-sweep of clouds. Like angry surf the pale gleams of gray, amid the purple of that scudding front, swept beyond the eastern rampart of the valley. The purple deepened to black. Broad sheets of lightning flared over the western wall. There were not yet any ropes or zigzag streaks darting down through the gathering darkness. The storm center was still beyond Surprise Valley.

"Listen! . . . Listen!" cried Bess, with her lips close to Venters's ear. "You'll hear Oldring's knell!"

"What's that?"

"Oldring's knell. When the wind blows a gale in the caves it makes what the rustlers call Oldring's knell. They believe it bodes his death. I think he believes so, too. It's not like any sound on earth . . . .It's beginning. Listen!"

The gale swooped down with a hollow unearthly howl. It yelled and pealed and shrilled and shrieked. It was made up of a thousand piercing cries. It was a rising and a moving sound. Beginning at the western break of the valley, it rushed along each gigantic cliff, whistling into the caves and cracks, to mount in power, to bellow a blast through the great stone bridge. Gone, as into an engulfing roar of surging waters, it seemed to shoot back and begin all over again.

It was only wind, thought Venters. Here sped and shrieked the sculptor that carved out the wonderful caves in the cliffs. It was only a gale, but as Venters listened, as his ears became accustomed to the fury and strife, out of it all or through it or above it pealed low and perfectly clear and persistently uniform a strange sound that had no counterpart in all the sounds of the elements. It was not of earth or of life. It was the grief and agony of the gale. A knell of all upon which it blew!

Black night enfolded the valley. Venters could not see his companion, and knew of her presence only through the tightening hold of her hand on his arm. He felt the dogs huddle closer to him. Suddenly the dense, black vault overhead split asunder to a blue-white, dazzling streak of lightning. The whole valley lay vividly clear and luminously bright in his sight. Upreared, vast and magnificent, the stone bridge glimmered like some grand god of storm in the lightning's fire. Then all flashed black again—blacker than pitch—a thick, impenetrable coal-blackness. And there came a ripping, crashing report. Instantly an echo resounded with clapping crash. The initial report was nothing to the echo. It was a terrible, living, reverberating, detonating crash. The wall threw the sound across, and could have made no greater roar if it had slipped in avalanche. From cliff to cliff the echo went in crashing retort and banged in lessening power, and boomed in thinner volume, and clapped weaker and weaker till a final clap could not reach across the waiting cliff.

In the pitchy darkness Venters led Bess, and, groping his way, by feel of hand found the entrance to her cave and lifted her up. On the instant a blinding flash of lightning illumined the cave and all about him. He saw Bess's face white now with dark, frightened eyes. He saw the dogs leap up, and he followed suit. The golden glare vanished; all was black; then came the splitting crack and the infernal din of echoes.

Bess shrank closer to him and closer, found his hands, and pressed them tightly over her ears, and dropped her face upon his shoulder, and hid her eyes.

Then the storm burst with a succession of ropes and streaks and shafts of lightning, playing continuously, filling the valley with a broken radiance; and the cracking shots followed each other swiftly till the echoes blended in one fearful, deafening crash.

Venters looked out upon the beautiful valley—beautiful now as never before—mystic in its transparent, luminous gloom, weird in the quivering, golden haze of lightning. The dark spruces were tipped with glimmering lights; the aspens bent low in the winds, as waves in a tempest at sea; the forest of oaks tossed wildly and shone with gleams of fire. Across the valley the huge cavern of the cliff-dwellers yawned in the glare, every little black window as clear as at noonday; but the night and the storm added to their tragedy. Flung arching to the black clouds, the great stone bridge seemed to bear the brunt of the storm. It caught the full fury of the rushing wind. It lifted its noble crown to meet the lightnings. Venters thought of the eagles and their lofty nest in a niche under the arch. A driving pall of rain, black as the clouds, came sweeping on to obscure the bridge and the gleaming walls and the shining valley. The lightning played incessantly, streaking down through opaque darkness of rain. The roar of the wind, with its strange knell and the re-crashing echoes, mingled with the roar of the flooding rain, and all seemingly were deadened and drowned in a world of sound.

In the dimming pale light Venters looked down upon the girl. She had sunk into his arms, upon his breast, burying her face. She clung to him. He felt the softness of her, and the warmth, and the quick heave of her breast. He saw the dark, slender, graceful outline of her form. A woman lay in his arms! And he held her closer. He who had been alone in the sad, silent watches of the night was not now and never must be again alone. He who had yearned for the touch of a hand felt the long tremble and the heart-beat of a woman. By what strange chance had she come to love him! By what change—by what marvel had she grown into a treasure!

No more did he listen to the rush and roar of the thunder-storm. For with the touch of clinging hands and the throbbing bosom he grew conscious of an inward storm—the tingling of new chords of thought, strange music of unheard, joyous bells sad dreams dawning to wakeful delight, dissolving doubt, resurging hope, force, fire, and freedom, unutterable sweetness of desire. A storm in his breast—a storm of real love.

CHAPTER XIV
WEST WIND

When the storm abated Venters sought his own cave, and late in the night, as his blood cooled and the stir and throb and thrill subsided, he fell asleep.

With the breaking of dawn his eyes unclosed. The valley lay drenched and bathed, a burnished oval of glittering green. The rain-washed walls glistened in the morning light. Waterfalls of many forms poured over the rims. One, a broad, lacy sheet, thin as smoke, slid over the western notch and struck a ledge in its downward fall, to bound into broader leap, to burst far below into white and gold and rosy mist.

Venters prepared for the day, knowing himself a different man. "It's a glorious morning," said Bess, in greeting.

"Yes. After the storm the west wind," he replied.

"Last night was I—very much of a baby?" she asked, watching him. "Pretty much."

"Oh, I couldn't help it!"

"I'm glad you were afraid."

"Why?" she asked, in slow surprise.

"I'll tell you some day," he answered, soberly. Then around the camp-fire and through the morning meal he was silent; afterward he strolled thoughtfully off alone along the terrace. He climbed a great yellow rock raising its crest among the spruces, and there he sat down to face the valley and the west.

"I love her!"

Aloud he spoke—unburdened his heart—confessed his secret. For an instant the golden valley swam before his eyes, and the walls waved, and all about him whirled with tumult within.

"I love her! . . . I understand now."

Reviving memory of Jane Withersteen and thought of the complications of the present amazed him with proof of how far he had drifted from his old life. He discovered that he hated to take up the broken threads, to delve into dark problems and difficulties. In this beautiful valley he had been living a beautiful dream. Tranquillity had come to him, and the joy of solitude, and interest in all the wild creatures and crannies of this incomparable valley—and love. Under the shadow of the great stone bridge God had revealed Himself to Venters.

"The world seems very far away," he muttered, "but it's there—and I'm not yet done with it. Perhaps I never shall be . . . .Only—how glorious it would be to live here always and never think again!"

Whereupon the resurging reality of the present, as if in irony of his wish, steeped him instantly in contending thought. Out of it all he presently evolved these things: he must go to Cottonwoods; he must bring supplies back to Surprise Valley; he must cultivate the soil and raise corn and stock, and, most imperative of all, he must decide the future of the girl who loved him and whom he loved. The first of these things required tremendous effort, the last one, concerning Bess, seemed simply and naturally easy of accomplishment. He would marry her. Suddenly, as from roots of poisonous fire, flamed up the forgotten truth concerning her. It seemed to wither and shrivel up all his joy on its hot, tearing way to his heart. She had been Oldring's Masked Rider. To Venters's question, "What were you to Oldring?" she had answered with scarlet shame and drooping head.

"What do I care who she is or what she was!" he cried, passionately. And he knew it was not his old self speaking. It was this softer, gentler man who had awakened to new thoughts in the quiet valley. Tenderness, masterful in him now, matched the absence of joy and blunted the knife-edge of entering jealousy. Strong and passionate effort of will, surprising to him, held back the poison from piercing his soul.

"Wait! . . . Wait!" he cried, as if calling. His hand pressed his breast, and he might have called to the pang there. "Wait! It's all so strange—so wonderful. Anything can happen. Who am I to judge her? I'll glory in my love for her. But I can't tell it—can't give up to it."

Certainly he could not then decide her future. Marrying her was impossible in Surprise Valley and in any village south of Sterling. Even without the mask she had once worn she would easily have been recognized as Oldring's Rider. No man who had ever seen her would forget her, regardless of his ignorance as to her sex. Then more poignant than all other argument was the fact that he did not want to take her away from Surprise Valley. He resisted all thought of that. He had brought her to the most beautiful and wildest place of the uplands; he had saved her, nursed her back to strength, watched her bloom as one of the valley lilies; he knew her life there to be pure and sweet—she belonged to him, and he loved her. Still these were not all the reasons why he did not want to take her away. Where could they go? He feared the rustlers—he feared the riders—he feared the Mormons. And if he should ever succeed in getting Bess safely away from these immediate perils, he feared the sharp eyes of women and their tongues, the big outside world with its problems of existence. He must wait to decide her future, which, after all, was deciding his own. But between her future and his something hung impending. Like Balancing Rock, which waited darkly over the steep gorge, ready to close forever the outlet to Deception Pass, that nameless thing, as certain yet intangible as fate, must fall and close forever all doubts and fears of the future.

"I've dreamed," muttered Venters, as he rose. "Well, why not? . . . To dream is happiness! But let me just once see this clearly wholly; then I can go on dreaming till the thing falls. I've got to tell Jane Withersteen. I've dangerous trips to take. I've work here to make comfort for this girl. She's mine. I'll fight to keep her safe from that old life. I've already seen her forget it. I love her. And if a beast ever rises in me I'll burn my hand off before I lay it on her with shameful intent. And, by God! sooner or later I'll kill the man who hid her and kept her in Deception Pass!"

As he spoke the west wind softly blew in his face. It seemed to soothe his passion. That west wind was fresh, cool, fragrant, and it carried a sweet, strange burden of far-off things—tidings of life in other climes, of sunshine asleep on other walls—of other places where reigned peace. It carried, too, sad truth of human hearts and mystery—of promise and hope unquenchable. Surprise Valley was only a little niche in the wide world whence blew that burdened wind. Bess was only one of millions at the mercy of unknown motive in nature and life. Content had come to Venters in the valley; happiness had breathed in the slow, warm air; love as bright as light had hovered over the walls and descended to him; and now on the west wind came a whisper of the eternal triumph of faith over doubt.

"How much better I am for what has come to me!" he exclaimed. "I'll let the future take care of itself. Whatever falls, I'll be ready."

Venters retraced his steps along the terrace back to camp, and found Bess in the old familiar seat, waiting and watching for his return.

"I went off by myself to think a little," he explained.

"You never looked that way before. What—what is it? Won't you tell me?"

"Well, Bess, the fact is I've been dreaming a lot. This valley makes a fellow dream. So I forced myself to think. We can't live this way much longer. Soon I'll simply have to go to Cottonwoods. We need a whole pack train of supplies. I can get—"

"Can you go safely?" she interrupted.

"Why, I'm sure of it. I'll ride through the Pass at night. I haven't any fear that Wrangle isn't where I left him. And once on him—Bess, just wait till you see that horse!"

"Oh, I want to see him—to ride him. But—but, Bern, this is what troubles me," she said. "Will—will you come back?"

"Give me four days. If I'm not back in four days you'll know I'm dead. For that only shall keep me."

"Oh!"

"Bess, I'll come back. There's danger—I wouldn't lie to you—but I can take care of myself."

"Bern, I'm sure—oh, I'm sure of it! All my life I've watched hunted men. I can tell what's in them. And I believe you can ride and shoot and see with any rider of the sage. It's not—not that I—fear."

"Well, what is it, then?"

"Why—why—why should you come back at all?"

"I couldn't leave you here alone."

"You might change your mind when you get to the village—among old friends—"

"I won't change my mind. As for old friends—" He uttered a short, expressive laugh.

"Then—there—there must be a—a woman!" Dark red mantled the clear tan of temple and cheek and neck. Her eyes were eyes of shame, upheld a long moment by intense, straining search for the verification of her fear. Suddenly they drooped, her head fell to her knees, her hands flew to her hot cheeks.

"Bess—look here," said Venters, with a sharpness due to the violence with which he checked his quick, surging emotion.

As if compelled against her will—answering to an irresistible voice— Bess raised her head, looked at him with sad, dark eyes, and tried to whisper with tremulous lips.

"There's no woman," went on Venters, deliberately holding her glance with his. "Nothing on earth, barring the chances of life, can keep me away."

Her face flashed and flushed with the glow of a leaping joy; but like the vanishing of a gleam it disappeared to leave her as he had never beheld her.

"I am nothing—I am lost—I am nameless!"

"Do you want me to come back?" he asked, with sudden stern coldness. "Maybe you want to go back to Oldring!"

That brought her erect, trembling and ashy pale, with dark, proud eyes and mute lips refuting his insinuation. "Bess, I beg your pardon. I shouldn't have said that. But you angered me. I intend to work—to make a home for you here—to be a—a brother to you as long as ever you need me. And you must forget what you are— were—I mean, and be happy. When you remember that old life you are bitter, and it hurts me."

"I was happy—I shall be very happy. Oh, you're so good that—that it kills me! If I think, I can't believe it. I grow sick with wondering why. I'm only a let me say it—only a lost, nameless—girl of the rustlers. Oldring's Girl, they called me. That you should save me—be so good and kind—want to make me happy—why, it's beyond belief. No wonder I'm wretched at the thought of your leaving me. But I'll be wretched and bitter no more. I promise you. If only I could repay you even a little—"

"You've repaid me a hundredfold. Will you believe me?"

"Believe you! I couldn't do else."

"Then listen! . . . Saving you, I saved myself. Living here in this valley with you, I've found myself. I've learned to think while I was dreaming. I never troubled myself about God. But God, or some wonderful spirit, has whispered to me here. I absolutely deny the truth of what you say about yourself. I can't explain it. There are things too deep to tell. Whatever the terrible wrongs you've suffered, God holds you blameless. I see that—feel that in you every moment you are near me. I've a mother and a sister 'way back in Illinois. If I could I'd take you to them—to-mor-row."

"If it were true! Oh, I might—I might lift my head!" she cried. "Lift it then—you child. For I swear it's true."

She did lift her head with the singular wild grace always a part of her actions, with that old unconscious intimation of innocence which always tortured Venters, but now with something more—a spirit rising from the depths that linked itself to his brave words.

"I've been thinking—too," she cried, with quivering smile and swelling breast. "I've discovered myself—too. I'm young—I'm alive—I'm so full—oh! I'm a woman!"

"Bess, I believe I can claim credit of that last discovery—before you," Venters said, and laughed. "Oh, there's more—there's something I must tell you."

"Tell it, then."

"When will you go to Cottonwoods?"

"As soon as the storms are past, or the worst of them."

"I'll tell you before you go. I can't now. I don't know how I shall then. But it must be told. I'd never let you leave me without knowing. For in spite of what you say there's a chance you mightn't come back."

Day after day the west wind blew across the valley. Day after day the clouds clustered gray and purple and black. The cliffs sang and the caves rang with Old-ring's knell, and the lightning flashed, the thunder rolled, the echoes crashed and crashed, and the rains flooded the valley. Wild flowers sprang up everywhere, sway-ing with the lengthening grass on the terraces, smiling wanly from shady nooks, peeping wondrously from year-dry crevices of the walls. The valley bloomed into a paradise. Every single moment, from the breaking of the gold bar through the bridge at dawn on to the reddening of rays over the western wall, was one of color-ful change. The valley swam in thick, transparent haze, golden at dawn, warm and white at noon, purple in the twilight. At the end of every storm a rainbow curved down into the leaf-bright forest to shine and fade and leave lingeringly some faint essence of its rosy iris in the air.

Venters walked with Bess, once more in a dream, and watched the lights change on the walls, and faced the wind from out of the west.

Always it brought softly to him strange, sweet tidings of far-off things. It blew from a place that was old and whispered of youth. It blew down the grooves of time. It brought a story of the passing hours. It breathed low of fighting men and praying women. It sang clearly the song of love. That ever was the burden of its tidings—youth in the shady woods, waders through the wet meadows, boy and girl at the hedgerow stile, bathers in the booming surf, sweet, idle hours on grassy, windy hills, long strolls down moonlit lanes—everywhere in far-off lands, fingers locked and bursting hearts and longing lips—from all the world tidings of unquenchable love.

Often, in these hours of dreams he watched the girl, and asked himself of what was she dreaming? For the changing light of the valley reflected its gleam and its color and its meaning in the changing light of her eyes. He saw in them infinitely more than he saw in his dreams. He saw thought and soul and nature—strong vision of life. All tidings the west wind blew from distance and age he found deep in those dark-blue depths, and found them mysteries solved. Under their wistful shadow he softened, and in the softening felt himself grow a sadder, a wiser, and a better man.

While the west wind blew its tidings, filling his heart full, teaching him a man's part, the days passed, the purple clouds changed to white, and the storms were over for that summer.

"I must go now," he said. "When?" she asked.

"At once—to-night."

"I'm glad the time has come. It dragged at me. Go—for you'll come back the sooner."

Late in the afternoon, as the ruddy sun split its last flame in the ragged notch of the western wall, Bess walked with Venters along the eastern terrace, up the long, weathered slope, under the great stone bridge. They entered the narrow gorge to climb around the fence long before built there by Venters. Farther than this she had never been. Twilight had already fallen in the gorge. It brightened to waning shadow in the wider ascent. He showed her Balancing Rock, of which he had often told her, and explained its sinister leaning over the outlet. Shuddering, she looked down the long, pale incline with its closed-in, toppling walls.

"What an awful trail! Did you carry me up here?"

"I did, surely," replied he.

"It frightens me, somehow. Yet I never was afraid of trails. I'd ride anywhere a horse could go, and climb where he couldn't. But there's something fearful here. I feel as—as if the place was watching me."

"Look at this rock. It's balanced here—balanced perfectly. You know I told you the cliff-dwellers cut the rock, and why. But they're gone and the rock waits. Can't you see—feel how it waits here? I moved it once, and I'll never dare again. A strong heave would start it. Then it would fall and bang, and smash that crag, and jar the walls, and close forever the outlet to Deception Pass!"

"Ah! When you come back I'll steal up here and push and push with all my might to roll the rock and close forever the outlet to the Pass!" She said it lightly, but in the undercurrent of her voice was a heavier note, a ring deeper than any ever given mere play of words.

"Bess! . . . You can't dare me! Wait till I come back with supplies— then roll the stone."

"I—was—in—fun." Her voice now throbbed low. "Always you must be free to go when you will. Go now . . . this place presses on me—stifles me."

"I'm going—but you had something to tell me?"

"Yes . . . .Will you—come back?"

"I'll come if I live."

"But—but you mightn't come?"

"That's possible, of course. It'll take a good deal to kill me. A man couldn't have a faster horse or keener dog. And, Bess, I've guns, and I'll use them if I'm pushed. But don't worry."

"I've faith in you. I'll not worry until after four days. Only— because you mightn't come—I must tell you—" She lost her voice. Her pale face, her great, glowing, earnest eyes, seemed to stand alone out of the gloom of the gorge. The dog whined, breaking the silence.

"I must tell you—because you mightn't come back," she whispered. "You must know what—what I think of your goodness—of you. Always I've been tongue-tied. I seemed not to be grateful. It was deep in my heart. Even now—if I were other than I am—I couldn't tell you. But I'm nothing—only a rustler's girl—nameless—infamous. You've saved me— and I'm—I'm yours to do with as you like . . . .With all my heart and soul—I love you!"

CHAPTER XV
SHADOWS ON THE SAGE-SLOPE

In the cloudy, threatening, waning summer days shadows lengthened down the sage-slope, and Jane Withersteen likened them to the shadows gathering and closing in around her life.

Mrs. Larkin died, and little Fay was left an orphan with no known relative. Jane's love redoubled. It was the saving brightness of a darkening hour. Fay turned now to Jane in childish worship. And Jane at last found full expression for the mother-longing in her heart. Upon Lassiter, too, Mrs. Larkin's death had some subtle reaction. Before, he had often, without explanation, advised Jane to send Fay back to any Gentile family that would take her in. Passionately and reproachfully and wonderingly Jane had refused even to entertain such an idea. And now Lassiter never advised it again, grew sadder and quieter in his contemplation of the child, and infinitely more gentle and loving. Sometimes Jane had a cold, inexplicable sensation of dread when she saw Lassiter watching Fay. What did the rider see in the future? Why did he, day by day, grow more silent, calmer, cooler, yet sadder in prophetic assurance of something to be?

No doubt, Jane thought, the rider, in his almost superhuman power of foresight, saw behind the horizon the dark, lengthening shadows that were soon to crowd and gloom over him and her and little Fay. Jane Withersteen awaited the long-deferred breaking of the storm with a courage and embittered calm that had come to her in her extremity. Hope had not died. Doubt and fear, subservient to her will, no longer gave her sleepless nights and tortured days. Love remained. All that she had loved she now loved the more. She seemed to feel that she was defiantly flinging the wealth of her love in the face of misfortune and of hate. No day passed but she prayed for all—and most fervently for her enemies. It troubled her that she had lost, or had never gained, the whole control of her mind. In some measure reason and wisdom and decision were locked in a chamber of her brain, awaiting a key. Power to think of some things was taken from her. Meanwhile, abiding a day of judgment, she fought ceaselessly to deny the bitter drops in her cup, to tear back the slow, the intangibly slow growth of a hot, corrosive lichen eating into her heart.

On the morning of August 10th, Jane, while waiting in the court for Lassiter, heard a clear, ringing report of a rifle. It came from the grove, somewhere toward the corrals. Jane glanced out in alarm. The day was dull, windless, soundless. The leaves of the cottonwoods drooped, as if they had foretold the doom of Withersteen House and were now ready to die and drop and decay. Never had Jane seen such shade. She pondered on the meaning of the report. Revolver shots had of late cracked from different parts of the grove—spies taking snap-shots at Lassiter from a cowardly distance! But a rifle report meant more. Riders seldom used rifles. Judkins and Venters were the exceptions she called to mind. Had the men who hounded her hidden in her grove, taken to the rifle to rid her of Lassiter, her last friend? It was probable—it was likely. And she did not share his cool assumption that his death would never come at the hands of a Mormon. Long had she expected it. His constancy to her, his singular reluctance to use the fatal skill for which he was famed—both now plain to all Mormons—laid him open to inevitable assassination. Yet what charm against ambush and aim and enemy he seemed to bear about him! No, Jane reflected, it was not charm; only a wonderful training of eye and ear, and sense of impending peril. Nevertheless that could not forever avail against secret attack.

That moment a rustling of leaves attracted her attention; then the familiar clinking accompaniment of a slow, soft, measured step, and Lassiter walked into the court.

"Jane, there's a fellow out there with a long gun," he said, and, removing his sombrero, showed his head bound in a bloody scarf.

"I heard the shot; I knew it was meant for you. Let me see—you can't be badly injured?"

"I reckon not. But mebbe it wasn't a close call! . . . I'll sit here in this corner where nobody can see me from the grove." He untied the scarf and removed it to show a long, bleeding furrow above his left temple.

"It's only a cut," said Jane. "But how it bleeds! Hold your scarf over it just a moment till I come back." She ran into the house and returned with bandages; and while she bathed and dressed the wound Lassiter talked.

"That fellow had a good chance to get me. But he must have flinched when he pulled the trigger. As I dodged down I saw him run through the trees. He had a rifle. I've been expectin' that kind of gun play. I reckon now I'll have to keep a little closer hid myself. These fellers all seem to get chilly or shaky when they draw a bead on me, but one of them might jest happen to hit me."

"Won't you go away—leave Cottonwoods as I've begged you to—before some one does happen to hit you?" she appealed to him.

"I reckon I'll stay."

"But, oh, Lassiter—your blood will be on my hands!"

"See here, lady, look at your hands now, right now. Aren't they fine, firm, white hands? Aren't they bloody now? Lassiter's blood! That's a queer thing to stain your beautiful hands. But if you could only see deeper you'd find a redder color of blood. Heart color, Jane!"

"Oh! . . . My friend!"

"No, Jane, I'm not one to quit when the game grows hot, no more than you. This game, though, is new to me, an' I don't know the moves yet, else I wouldn't have stepped in front of that bullet."

"Have you no desire to hunt the man who fired at you—to find him—and— and kill him?"

"Well, I reckon I haven't any great hankerin' for that."

"Oh, the wonder of it! . . . I knew—I prayed—I trusted. Lassiter, I almost gave— all myself to soften you to Mormons. Thank God, and thank you, my friend . . . .But, selfish woman that I am, this is no great test. What's the life of one of those sneaking cowards to such a man as you? I think of your great hate toward him who—I think of your life's implacable purpose. Can it be—"

"Wait! . . . Listen!" he whispered. "I hear a hoss."

He rose noiselessly, with his ear to the breeze. Suddenly he pulled his sombrero down over his bandaged head and, swinging his gun-sheaths round in front, he stepped into the alcove.

"It's a hoss—comin' fast," he added.

Jane's listening ear soon caught a faint, rapid, rhythmic beat of hoofs. It came from the sage. It gave her a thrill that she was at a loss to understand. The sound rose stronger, louder. Then came a clear, sharp difference when the horse passed from the sage trail to the hard-packed ground of the grove. It became a ringing run—swift in its bell-like clatterings, yet singular in longer pause than usual between the hoofbeats of a horse. "It's Wrangle! . . . It's Wrangle!" cried Jane Withersteen. "I'd know him from a million horses!"

Excitement and thrilling expectancy flooded out all Jane Withersteen s calm. A tight band closed round her breast as she saw the giant sorrel flit in reddish-brown flashes across the openings in the green. Then he was pounding down the lane— thundering into the court—crashing his great iron-shod hoofs on the stone flags. Wrangle it was surely, but shaggy and wild-eyed, and sage-streaked, with dust-caked lather staining his flanks. He reared and crashed down and plunged. The rider leaped off, threw the bridle, and held hard on a lasso looped round Wrangle's head and neck. Janet's heart sank as she tried to recognize Venters in the rider. Something familiar struck her in the lofty stature in the sweep of powerful shoulders. But this bearded, longhaired, unkempt man, who wore ragged clothes patched with pieces of skin, and boots that showed bare legs and feet—this dusty, dark, and wild rider could not possibly be Venters.

"Whoa, Wrangle, old boy! Come down. Easy now. So—so—so. You're home, old boy, and presently you can have a drink of water you'll remember."

In the voice Jane knew the rider to be Venters. He tied Wrangle to the hitching-rack and turned to the court. "Oh, Bern! . . . You wild man!" she exclaimed.

"Jane—Jane, it's good to see you! Hello, Lassiter! Yes, it's Venters."

Like rough iron his hard hand crushed Jane's. In it she felt the difference she saw in him. Wild, rugged, unshorn—yet how splendid! He had gone away a boy—he had returned a man. He appeared taller, wider of shoulder, deeper-chested, more powerfully built. But was that only her fancy—he had always been a young giant—was the change one of spirit? He might have been absent for years, proven by fire and steel, grown like Lassiter, strong and cool and sure. His eyes—were they keener, more flashing than before?—met hers with clear, frank, warm regard, in which perplexity was not, nor discontent, nor pain.

"Look at me long as you like," he said, with a laugh. "I'm not much to look at. And, Jane, neither you nor Lassiter, can brag. You're paler than I ever saw you. Lassiter, here, he wears a bloody bandage under his hat. That reminds me. Some one took a flying shot at me down in the sage. It made Wrangle run some . . . . Well, perhaps you've more to tell me than I've got to tell you."

Briefly, in few words, Jane outlined the circumstances of her undoing in the weeks of his absence. Under his beard and bronze she saw his face whiten in terrible wrath.

"Lassiter—what held you back?"

No time in the long period of fiery moments and sudden shocks had Jane Withersteen ever beheld Lassiter as calm and serene and cool as then.

"Jane had gloom enough without my addin' to it by shootin' up the village," he said.

As strange as Lassiter's coolness was Venters's curious, intent scrutiny of them both, and under it Jane felt a flaming tide wave from bosom to temples.

"Well—you're right," he said, with slow pause. "It surprises me a little, that's all."

Jane sensed then a slight alteration in Venters, and what it was, in her own confusion, she could not tell. It had always been her intention to acquaint him with the deceit she had fallen to in her zeal to move Lassiter. She did not mean to spare herself. Yet now, at the moment, before these riders, it was an impossibility to explain. Venters was speaking somewhat haltingly, without his former frankness. "I found Oldring's hiding-place and your red herd. I learned—I know— I'm sure there was a deal between Tull and Oldring." He paused and shifted his position and his gaze. He looked as if he wanted to say something that he found beyond him. Sorrow and pity and shame seemed to contend for mastery over him. Then he raised himself and spoke with effort. "Jane I've cost you too much. You've almost ruined yourself for me. It was wrong, for I'm not worth it. I never deserved such friendship. Well, maybe it's not too late. You must give me up. Mind, I haven't changed. I am just the same as ever. I'll see Tull while I'm here, and tell him to his face."

"Bern, it's too late," said Jane.

"I'll make him believe!" cried Venters, violently. "You ask me to break our friendship?"

"Yes. If you don't, I shall."

"Forever?"

"Forever!"

Jane sighed. Another shadow had lengthened down the sage slope to cast further darkness upon her. A melancholy sweetness pervaded her resignation. The boy who had left her had returned a man, nobler, stronger, one in whom she divined something unbending as steel. There might come a moment later when she would wonder why she had not fought against his will, but just now she yielded to it. She liked him as well—nay, more, she thought, only her emotions were deadened by the long, menacing wait for the bursting storm.

Once before she had held out her hand to him—when she gave it; now she stretched it tremblingly forth in acceptance of the decree circumstance had laid upon them. Venters bowed over it kissed it, pressed it hard, and half stifled a sound very like a sob. Certain it was that when he raised his head tears glistened in his eyes.

"Some—women—have a hard lot," he said, huskily. Then he shook his powerful form, and his rags lashed about him. "I'll say a few things to Tull—when I meet him."

"Bern—you'll not draw on Tull? Oh, that must not be! Promise me—"

"I promise you this," he interrupted, in stern passion that thrilled while it terrorized her. "If you say one more word for that plotter I'll kill him as I would a mad coyote!"

Jane clasped her hands. Was this fire-eyed man the one whom she had once made as wax to her touch? Had Venters become Lassiter and Lassiter Venters? "I'll—say no more," she faltered.

"Jane, Lassiter once called you blind," said Venters. "It must be true. But I won't upbraid you. Only don't rouse the devil in me by praying for Tull! I'll try to keep cool when I meet him. That's all. Now there's one more thing I want to ask of you—the last. I've found a valley down in the Pass. It's a wonderful place. I intend to stay there. It's so hidden I believe no one can find it. There's good water, and browse, and game. I want to raise corn and stock. I need to take in supplies. Will you give them to me?"

"Assuredly. The more you take the better you'll please me—and perhaps the less my—my enemies will get."

"Venters, I reckon you'll have trouble packin' anythin' away," put in Lassiter.

"I'll go at night."

"Mebbe that wouldn't be best. You'd sure be stopped. You'd better go early in the mornin'—say, just after dawn. That's the safest time to move round here."

"Lassiter, I'll be hard to stop," returned Venters, darkly. "I reckon so."

"Bern," said Jane, "go first to the riders' quarters and get yourself a complete outfit. You're a—a sight. Then help yourself to whatever else you need—burros, packs, grain, dried fruits, and meat. You must take coffee and sugar and flour—all kinds of supplies. Don't forget corn and seeds. I remember how you used to starve.

Please—please take all you can pack away from here. I'll make a bundle for you, which you mustn't open till you're in your valley. How I'd like to see it! To judge by you and Wrangle, how wild it must be!"

Jane walked down into the outer court and approached the sorrel. Upstarting, he laid back his ears and eyed her.

"Wrangle—dear old Wrangle," she said, and put a caressing hand on his matted mane. "Oh, he's wild, but he knows me! Bern, can he run as fast as ever?"

"Run? Jane, he's done sixty miles since last night at dark, and I could make him kill Black Star right now in a ten-mile race."

"He never could," protested Jane. "He couldn't even if he was fresh."

"I reckon mebbe the best hoss'll prove himself yet," said Lassiter, "an', Jane, if it ever comes to that race I'd like you to be on Wrangle."

"I'd like that, too," rejoined Venters. "But, Jane, maybe Lassiter's hint is extreme. Bad as your prospects are, you'll surely never come to the running point."

"Who knows!" she replied, with mournful smile.

"No, no, Jane, it can't be so bad as all that. Soon as I see Tull there'll be a change in your fortunes. I'll hurry down to the village . . . .Now don't worry."

Jane retired to the seclusion of her room. Lassiter's subtle forecasting of disaster, Venters's forced optimism, neither remained in mind. Material loss weighed nothing in the balance with other losses she was sustaining. She wondered dully at her sitting there, hands folded listlessly, with a kind of numb deadness to the passing of time and the passing of her riches. She thought of Venters's friendship. She had not lost that, but she had lost him. Lassiter's friendship—that was more than love—it would endure, but soon he, too, would be gone. Little Fay slept dreamlessly upon the bed, her golden curls streaming over the pillow. Jane had the child's worship. Would she lose that, too? And if she did, what then would be left? Conscience thundered at her that there was left her religion. Conscience thundered that she should be grateful on her knees for this baptism of fire; that through misfortune, sacrifice, and suffering her soul might be fused pure gold. But the old, spontaneous, rapturous spirit no more exalted her. She wanted to be a woman—not a martyr. Like the saint of old who mortified his flesh, Jane Withersteen had in her the temper for heroic martyrdom, if by sacrificing herself she could save the souls of others. But here the damnable verdict blistered her that the more she sacrificed herself the blacker grew the souls of her churchmen. There was something terribly wrong with her soul, something terribly wrong with her churchmen and her religion. In the whirling gulf of her thought there was yet one shining light to guide her, to sustain her in her hope; and it was that, despite her errors and her frailties and her blindness, she had one absolute and unfaltering hold on ultimate and supreme justice. That was love. "Love your enemies as yourself!" was a divine word, entirely free from any church or creed.

Jane's meditations were disturbed by Lassiter's soft, tinkling step in the court. Always he wore the clinking spurs. Always he was in readiness to ride. She passed out and called him into the huge, dim hall.

"I think you'll be safer here. The court is too open," she said.

"I reckon," replied Lassiter. "An' it's cooler here. The day's sure muggy. Well, I went down to the village with Venters."

"Already! Where is he?" queried Jane, in quick amaze.

"He's at the corrals. Blake's helpin' him get the burros an' packs ready. That Blake is a good fellow."

"Did—did Bern meet Tull?"

"I guess he did," answered Lassiter, and he laughed dryly.

"Tell me! Oh, you exasperate me! You're so cool, so calm! For Heaven's sake, tell me what happened!"

"First time I've been in the village for weeks," went on Lassiter, mildly. "I reckon there 'ain't been more of a show for a long time. Me an' Venters walkin' down the road! It was funny. I ain't sayin' anybody was particular glad to see us. I'm not much thought of hereabouts, an' Venters he sure looks like what you called him, a wild man. Well, there was some runnin' of folks before we got to the stores. Then everybody vamoosed except some surprised rustlers in front of a saloon. Venters went right in the stores an' saloons, an' of course I went along. I don't know which tickled me the most—the actions of many fellers we met, or Venters's nerve. Jane, I was downright glad to be along. You see that sort of thing is my element, an' I've been away from it for a spell. But we didn't find Tull in one of them places. Some Gentile feller at last told Venters he'd find Tull in that long buildin' next to Parsons's store. It's a kind of meetin'-room; and sure enough, when we peeped in, it was half full of men.

"Venters yelled: 'Don't anybody pull guns! We ain't come for that!' Then he tramped in, an' I was some put to keep alongside him. There was a hard, scrapin' sound of feet, a loud cry, an' then some whisperin', an' after that stillness you could cut with a knife. Tull was there, an' that fat party who once tried to throw a gun on me, an' other important-lookin' men, en' that little frog-legged feller who was with Tull the day I rode in here. I wish you could have seen their faces, 'specially Tull's an' the fat party's. But there ain't no use of me tryin' to tell you how they looked.

"Well, Venters an' I stood there in the middle of the room with that batch of men all in front of us, en' not a blamed one of them winked an eyelash or moved a finger. It was natural, of course, for me to notice many of them packed guns. That's a way of mine, first noticin' them things. Venters spoke up, an' his voice sort of chilled an' cut, en' he told Tull he had a few things to say."

Here Lassiter paused while he turned his sombrero round and round, in his familiar habit, and his eyes had the look of a man seeing over again some thrilling spectacle, and under his red bronze there was strange animation.

"Like a shot, then, Venters told Tull that the friendship between you an' him was all over, an' he was leaving your place. He said you'd both of you broken off in the hope of propitiatin' your people, but you hadn't changed your mind otherwise, an' never would.

"Next he spoke up for you. I ain't goin' to tell you what he said. Only—no other woman who ever lived ever had such tribute! You had a champion, Jane, an' never fear that those thick-skulled men don't know you now. It couldn't be otherwise. He spoke the ringin', lightnin' truth . . . .Then he accused Tull of the underhand, miserable robbery of a helpless woman. He told Tull where the red herd was, of a deal made with Oldrin', that Jerry Card had made the deal. I thought Tull was goin' to drop, an' that little frog-legged cuss, he looked some limp an' white. But Venters's voice would have kept anybody's legs from bucklin'. I was stiff myself. He went on an' called Tull—called him every bad name ever known to a rider, an' then some. He cursed Tull. I never hear a man get such a cursin'. He laughed in scorn at the idea of Tull bein' a minister. He said Tull an' a few more dogs of hell builded their empire out of the hearts of such innocent an' God-fearin' women as Jane Withersteen. He called Tull a binder of women, a callous beast who hid behind a mock mantle of righteousness—an' the last an' lowest coward on the face of the earth. To prey on weak women through their religion—that was the last unspeakable crime!

"Then he finished, an' by this time he'd almost lost his voice. But his whisper was enough. 'Tull,' he said, 'she begged me not to draw on you to-day. She would pray for you if you burned her at the stake . . . .But listen! . . . I swear if you and I ever come face to face again, I'll kill you!'

"We backed out of the door then, an' up the road. But nobody follered us."

Jane found herself weeping passionately. She had not been conscious of it till Lassiter ended his story, and she experienced exquisite pain and relief in shedding tears. Long had her eyes been dry, her grief deep; long had her emotions been dumb. Lassiter's story put her on the rack; the appalling nature of Venters's act and speech had no parallel as an outrage; it was worse than bloodshed. Men like Tull had been shot, but had one ever been so terribly denounced in public? Over-mounting her horror, an uncontrollable, quivering passion shook her very soul. It was sheer human glory in the deed of a fearless man. It was hot, primitive instinct to live—to fight. It was a kind of mad joy in Venters's chivalry. It was close to the wrath that had first shaken her in the beginning of this war waged upon her.

"Well, well, Jane, don't take it that way," said Lassiter, in evident distress. "I had to tell you. There's some things a feller jest can't keep. It's strange you give up on hearin' that, when all this long time you've been the gamest woman I ever seen. But I don't know women. Mebbe there's reason for you to cry. I know this—nothin' ever rang in my soul an' so filled it as what Venters did. I'd like to have done it, but—I'm only good for throwin' a gun, en' it seems you hate that . . . .Well, I'll be goin' now."

"Where?"

"Venters took Wrangle to the stable. The sorrel's shy a shoe, an' I've got to help hold the big devil an' put on another."

"Tell Bern to come for the pack I want to give him—and—and to say good-by," called Jane, as Lassiter went out.

Jane passed the rest of that day in a vain endeavor to decide what and what not to put in the pack for Venters. This task was the last she would ever perform for him, and the gifts were the last she would ever make him.

So she picked and chose and rejected, and chose again, and often paused in sad revery, and began again, till at length she filled the pack.

It was about sunset, and she and Fay had finished supper and were sitting in the court, when Venters's quick steps rang on the stones. She scarcely knew him, for he had changed the tattered garments, and she missed the dark beard and long hair. Still he was not the Venters of old. As he came up the steps she felt herself pointing to the pack, and heard herself speaking words that were meaningless to her. He said good-by; he kissed her, released her, and turned away. His tall figure blurred in her sight, grew dim through dark, streaked vision, and then he vanished.

Twilight fell around Withersteen House, and dusk and night. Little Fay slept; but Jane lay with strained, aching eyes. She heard the wind moaning in the cotton-woods and mice squeaking in the walls. The night was interminably long, yet she prayed to hold back the dawn. What would another day bring forth? The blackness of her room seemed blacker for the sad, entering gray of morning light. She heard the chirp of awakening birds, and fancied she caught a faint clatter of hoofs. Then low, dull distant, throbbed a heavy gunshot. She had expected it, was waiting for it; nevertheless, an electric shock checked her heart, froze the very living fiber of her bones. That vise-like hold on her faculties apparently did not relax for a long time, and it was a voice under her window that released her.

"Jane! . . . Jane!" softly called Lassiter. She answered somehow.

"It's all right. Venters got away. I thought mebbe you'd heard that shot, en' I was worried some."

"What was it—who fired?"

"Well—some fool feller tried to stop Venters out there in the sage—an' he only stopped lead! . . . I think it'll be all right. I haven't seen or heard of any other fellers round. Venters'll go through safe. An', Jane, I've got Bells saddled, an' I'm going to trail Venters. Mind, I won't show myself unless he falls foul of somebody an' needs me. I want to see if this place where he's goin' is safe for him. He says nobody can track him there. I never seen the place yet I couldn't track a man to. Now, Jane, you stay indoors while I'm gone, an' keep close watch on Fay. Will you?"

"Yes! Oh yes!"

"An' another thing, Jane," he continued, then paused for long—"another thing—if you ain't here when I come back—if you're gone—don't fear, I'll trail you—I'll find you out."

"My dear Lassiter, where could I be gone—as you put it?" asked Jane, in curious surprise.

"I reckon you might be somewhere. Mebbe tied in an old barn—or corralled in some gulch—or chained in a cave! Milly Erne was—till she give in! Mebbe that's news to you . . . .Well, if you're gone I'll hunt for you."

"No, Lassiter," she replied, sadly and low. "If I'm gone just forget the unhappy woman whose blinded selfish deceit you repaid with kindness and love."

She heard a deep, muttering curse, under his breath, and then the silvery tinkling of his spurs as he moved away.

Jane entered upon the duties of that day with a settled, gloomy calm. Disaster hung in the dark clouds, in the shade, in the humid west wind. Blake, when he reported, appeared without his usual cheer; and Jerd wore a harassed look of a worn and worried man. And when Judkins put in appearance, riding a lame horse, and dismounted with the cramp of a rider, his dust-covered figure and his darkly grim, almost dazed expression told Jane of dire calamity. She had no need of words.

"Miss Withersteen, I have to report—loss of the—white herd," said Judkins, hoarsely.

"Come, sit down, you look played out," replied Jane, solicitously. She brought him brandy and food, and while he partook of refreshments, of which he appeared badly in need, she asked no questions.

"No one rider—could hev done more—Miss Withersteen," he went on, presently.

"Judkins, don't be distressed. You've done more than any other rider. I've long expected to lose the white herd. It's no surprise. It's in line with other things that are happening. I'm grateful for your service."

"Miss Withersteen, I knew how you'd take it. But if anythin', that makes it harder to tell. You see, a feller wants to do so much fer you, an' I'd got fond of my job. We led the herd a ways off to the north of the break in the valley. There was a big level an' pools of water an' tip-top browse. But the cattle was in a high nervous condition. Wild—as wild as antelope! You see, they'd been so scared they never slept. I ain't a-goin' to tell you of the many tricks that were pulled off out there in the sage. But there wasn't a day for weeks thet the herd didn't get started to run. We allus managed to ride 'em close an' drive 'em back an' keep 'em bunched. Honest, Miss Withersteen, them steers was thin. They was thin when water and grass was everywhere. Thin at this season—thet'll tell you how your steers was pestered. Fer instance, one night a strange runnin' streak of fire run right through the herd. That streak was a coyote—with an oiled an' blazin' tail! Fer I shot it an' found out. We had hell with the herd that night, an' if the sage an' grass hadn't been wet—we, hosses, steers, an' all would hev burned up. But I said I wasn't goin' to tell you any of the tricks . . . Strange now, Miss Withersteen, when the stampede did come it was from natural cause—jest a whirlin' devil of dust. You've seen the like often. An' this wasn't no big whirl, fer the dust was mostly settled. It had dried out in a little swale, an' ordinarily no steer would ever hev run fer it. But the herd was nervous en' wild. An' jest as Lassiter said, when that bunch of white steers got to movin' they was as bad as buffalo. I've seen some buffalo stampedes back in Nebraska, an' this bolt of the steers was the same kind.

"I tried to mill the herd jest as Lassiter did. But I wasn't equal to it, Miss Withersteen. I don't believe the rider lives who could hev turned thet herd. We kept along of the herd fer miles, an' more 'n one of my boys tried to get the steers a-millin'. It wasn't no use. We got off level ground, goin' down, an' then the steers ran somethin' fierce. We left the little gullies an' washes level-full of dead steers. Finally I saw the herd was makin' to pass a kind of low pocket between ridges. There was a hog-back—as we used to call 'em—a pile of rocks stickin' up, and I saw the herd was goin' to split round it, or swing out to the left. An' I wanted 'em to go to the right so mebbe we'd be able to drive 'em into the pocket. So, with all my boys except three, I rode hard to turn the herd a little to the right. We couldn't budge 'em. They went on en' split round the rocks, en' the most of 'em was turned sharp to the left by a deep wash we hedn't seen—hed no chance to see.

"The other three boys—Jimmy Vail, Joe Willis, an' thet little Cairns boy—a nervy kid! they, with Cairns leadin', tried to buck thet herd round to the pocket. It was a wild, fool idee. I couldn't do nothin'. The boys got hemmed in between the steers an' the wash—thet they hedn't no chance to see, either. Vail an' Willis was run down right before our eyes. An' Cairns, who rode a fine hoss, he did some ridin'. I never seen equaled, en' would hev beat the steers if there'd been any room to run in. I was high up an' could see how the steers kept spillin' by twos an' threes over into the wash. Cairns put his hoss to a place thet was too wide fer any hoss, an' broke his neck an' the hoss's too. We found that out after, an' as fer Vail an' Willis— two thousand steers ran over the poor boys. There wasn't much left to pack home fer buryin'! . . . An', Miss Withersteen, thet all happened yesterday, en' I believe, if the white herd didn't run over the wall of the Pass, it's runnin' yet."

On the morning of the second day after Judkins's recital, during which time Jane remained indoors a prey to regret and sorrow for the boy riders, and a new and now strangely insistent fear for her own person, she again heard what she had missed more than she dared honestly confess—the soft, jingling step of Lassiter. Almost overwhelming relief surged through her, a feeling as akin to joy as any she could have been capable of in those gloomy hours of shadow, and one that suddenly stunned her with the significance of what Lassiter had come to mean to her. She had begged him, for his own sake, to leave Cottonwoods. She might yet beg that, if her weakening courage permitted her to dare absolute loneliness and helplessness, but she realized now that if she were left alone her life would become one long, hideous nightmare.

When his soft steps clinked into the hall, in answer to her greeting, and his tall, black-garbed form filled the door, she felt an inexpressible sense of immediate safety. In his presence she lost her fear of the dim passageways of Withersteen House and of every sound. Always it had been that, when he entered the court or the hall, she had experienced a distinctly sickening but gradually lessening shock at sight of the huge black guns swinging at his sides. This time the sickening shock again visited her, it was, however, because a revealing flash of thought told her that it was not alone Lassiter who was thrillingly welcome, but also his fatal weapons. They meant so much. How she had fallen—how broken and spiritless must she be—to have still the same old horror of Lassiter's guns and his name, yet feel some-how a cold, shrinking protection in their law and might and use.

"Did you trail Venters—find his wonderful valley?" she asked, eagerly. "Yes, an' I reckon it's sure a wonderful place."

"Is he safe there?"

"That's been botherin' me some. I tracked him an' part of the trail was the hardest I ever tackled. Mebbe there's a rustler or somebody in this country who's as good at trackin' as I am. If that's so Venters ain't safe."

"Well—tell me all about Bern and his valley."

To Jane's surprise Lassiter showed disinclination for further talk about his trip. He appeared to be extremely fatigued. Jane reflected that one hundred and twenty miles, with probably a great deal of climbing on foot, all in three days, was enough to tire any rider. Moreover, it presently developed that Lassiter had returned in a mood of singular sadness and preoccupation. She put it down to a moodiness over the loss of her white herd and the now precarious condition of her fortune.

Several days passed, and as nothing happened, Jane's spirits began to bright-en. Once in her musings she thought that this tendency of hers to rebound was as sad as it was futile. Meanwhile, she had resumed her walks through the grove with little Fay.

One morning she went as far as the sage. She had not seen the slope since the beginning of the rains, and now it bloomed a rich deep purple. There was a high wind blowing, and the sage tossed and waved and colored beautifully from light to dark. Clouds scudded across the sky and their shadows sailed darkly down the sunny slope.

Upon her return toward the house she went by the lane to the stables, and she had scarcely entered the great open space with its corrals and sheds when she saw Lassiter hurriedly approaching. Fay broke from her and, running to a corral fence, began to pat and pull the long, hanging ears of a drowsy burro.

One look at Lassiter armed her for a blow.

Without a word he led her across the wide yard to the rise of the ground upon which the stable stood. "Jane—look!" he said, and pointed to the ground.

Jane glanced down, and again, and upon steadier vision made out splotches of blood on the stones, and broad, smooth marks in the dust, leading out toward the sage.

"What made these?" she asked.

"I reckon somebody has dragged dead or wounded men out to where there was hosses in the sage."

"Dead—or—wounded—men!"

"I reckon—Jane, are you strong? Can you bear up?"

His hands were gently holding hers, and his eyes—suddenly she could no longer look into them. "Strong?" she echoed, trembling. "I—I will be."

Up on the stone-flag drive, nicked with the marks made by the iron-shod hoofs of her racers, Lassiter led her, his grasp ever growing firmer.

"Where's Blake—and—and Jerb?" she asked, haltingly.

"I don't know where Jerb is. Bolted, most likely," replied Lassiter, as he took her through the stone door. "But Blake—poor Blake! He's gone forever! . . . Be prepared, Jane."

With a cold prickling of her skin, with a queer thrumming in her ears, with fixed and staring eyes, Jane saw a gun lying at her feet with chamber swung and empty, and discharged shells scattered near.

Outstretched upon the stable floor lay Blake, ghastly white—dead—one hand clutching a gun and the other twisted in his bloody blouse.

"Whoever the thieves were, whether your people or rustlers—Blake killed some of them!" said Lassiter. "Thieves?" whispered Jane.

"I reckon. Hoss-thieves! . . . Look!" Lassiter waved his hand toward the stalls.

The first stall—Bells's stall—was empty. All the stalls were empty. No racer whinnied and stamped greeting to her. Night was gone! Black Star was gone!

CHAPTER XVI
GOLD

As Lassiter had reported to Jane, Venters "went through" safely, and after a toilsome journey reached the peaceful shelter of Surprise Valley. When finally he lay wearily down under the silver spruces, resting from the strain of dragging packs and burros up the slope and through the entrance to Surprise Valley, he had leisure to think, and a great deal of the time went in regretting that he had not been frank with his loyal friend, Jane Withersteen.

But, he kept continually recalling, when he had stood once more face to face with her and had been shocked at the change in her and had heard the details of her adversity, he had not had the heart to tell her of the closer interest which had entered his life. He had not lied; yet he had kept silence.

Bess was in transports over the stores of supplies and the outfit he had packed from Cottonwoods. He had certainly brought a hundred times more than he had gone for; enough, surely, for years, perhaps to make permanent home in the valley. He saw no reason why he need ever leave there again.

After a day of rest he recovered his strength and shared Bess's pleasure in rummaging over the endless packs, and began to plan for the future. And in this planning, his trip to Cottonwoods, with its revived hate of Tull and consequent unleashing of fierce passions, soon faded out of mind. By slower degrees his friendship for Jane Withersteen and his contrition drifted from the active preoccupation of his present thought to a place in memory, with more and more infrequent recalls.

And as far as the state of his mind was concerned, upon the second day after his return, the valley, with its golden hues and purple shades, the speaking west wind and the cool, silent night, and Bess's watching eyes with their wonderful light, so wrought upon Venters that he might never have left them at all.

That very afternoon he set to work. Only one thing hindered him upon beginning, though it in no wise checked his delight, and that in the multiplicity of tasks planned to make a paradise out of the valley he could not choose the one with which to begin. He had to grow into the habit of passing from one dreamy pleasure to another, like a bee going from flower to flower in the valley, and he found this wandering habit likely to extend to his labors. Nevertheless, he made a start.

At the outset he discovered Bess to be both a considerable help in some ways and a very great hindrance in others. Her excitement and joy were spurs, inspirations; but she was utterly impracticable in her ideas, and she flitted from one plan to another with bewildering vacillation. Moreover, he fancied that she grew more eager, youthful, and sweet; and he marked that it was far easier to watch her and listen to her than it was to work. Therefore he gave her tasks that necessitated her going often to the cave where he had stored his packs.

Upon the last of these trips, when he was some distance down the terrace and out of sight of camp, he heard a scream, and then the sharp barking of the dogs.

For an instant he straightened up, amazed. Danger for her had been absolutely out of his mind. She had seen a rattlesnake—or a wildcat. Still she would not have been likely to scream at sight of either; and the barking of the dogs was ominous. Dropping his work, he dashed back along the terrace. Upon breaking through a clump of aspens he saw the dark form of a man in the camp. Cold, then hot, Venters burst into frenzied speed to reach his guns. He was cursing himself for a thoughtless fool when the man's tall form became familiar and he recognized Lassiter. Then the reversal of emotions changed his run to a walk; he tried to call out, but his voice refused to carry; when he reached camp there was Lassiter staring at the white-faced girl. By that time Ring and Whitie had recognized him.

"Hello, Venters! I'm makin' you a visit," said Lassiter, slowly. "An' I'm some surprised to see you've a—a young feller for company."

One glance had sufficed for the keen rider to read Bess's real sex, and for once his cool calm had deserted him. He stared till the white of Bess's cheeks flared into crimson. That, if it were needed, was the concluding evidence of her femininity, for it went fittingly with her sun-tinted hair and darkened, dilated eyes, the sweetness of her mouth, and the striking symmetry of her slender shape.

"Heavens! Lassiter!" panted Venters, when he caught his breath. "What relief—it's only you! How—in the name of all that's wonderful—did you ever get here?"

"I trailed you. We—I wanted to know where you was, if you had a safe place. So I trailed you."

"Trailed me," cried Venters, bluntly.

"I reckon. It was some of a job after I got to them smooth rocks. I was all day trackin' you up to them little cut steps in the rock. The rest was easy."

"Where's your hoss? I hope you hid him."

"I tied him in them queer cedars down on the slope. He can't be seen from the valley."

"That's good. Well, well! I'm completely dumfounded. It was my idea that no man could track me in here."

"I reckon. But if there's a tracker in these uplands as good as me he can find you."

"That's bad. That'll worry me. But, Lassiter, now you're here I'm glad to see you. And—and my companion here is not a young fellow! . . . Bess, this is a friend of mine. He saved my life once."

The embarrassment of the moment did not extend to Lassiter. Almost at once his manner, as he shook hands with Bess, relieved Venters and put the girl at ease. After Venters's words and one quick look at Lassiter, her agitation stilled, and, though she was shy, if she were conscious of anything out of the ordinary in the situation, certainly she did not show it.

"I reckon I'll only stay a little while," Lassiter was saying. "An' if you don't mind troublin', I'm hungry. I fetched some biscuits along, but they're gone. Venters, this place is sure the wonderfullest ever seen. Them cut steps on the slope! That outlet into the gorge! An' it's like climbin' up through hell into heaven to climb through that gorge into this valley! There's a queer-lookin' rock at the top of the passage. I didn't have time to stop. I'm wonderin' how you ever found this place. It's sure interestin'."

During the preparation and eating of dinner Lassiter listened mostly, as was his wont, and occasionally he spoke in his quaint and dry way. Venters noted, however, that the rider showed an increasing interest in Bess. He asked her no questions, and only directed his attention to her while she was occupied and had no opportunity to observe his scrutiny. It seemed to Venters that Lassiter grew more and more absorbed in his study of Bess, and that he lost his coolness in some strange, softening sympathy. Then, quite abruptly, he arose and announced the necessity for his early departure. He said good-by to Bess in a voice gentle and somewhat broken, and turned hurriedly away. Venters accompanied him, and they had traversed the terrace, climbed the weathered slope, and passed under the stone bridge before either spoke again.

Then Lassiter put a great hand on Venters's shoulder and wheeled him to meet a smoldering fire of gray eyes. "Lassiter, I couldn't tell Jane! I couldn't," burst out Venters, reading his friend's mind. "I tried. But I couldn't.

She wouldn't understand, and she has troubles enough. And I love the girl!"

"Venters, I reckon this beats me. I've seen some queer things in my time, too. This girl—who is she?"

"I don't know."

"Don't know! What is she, then?"

"I don't know that, either. Oh, it's the strangest story you ever heard. I must tell you. But you'll never believe."

"Venters, women were always puzzles to me. But for all that, if this girl ain't a child, an' as innocent, I'm no fit person to think of virtue an' goodness in anybody.

Are you goin' to be square with her?"

"I am—so help me God!"

"I reckoned so. Mebbe my temper oughtn't led me to make sure. But, man, she's a woman in all but years. She's sweeter 'n the sage."

"Lassiter, I know, I know. And the hell of it is that in spite of her innocence and charm she's—she's not what she seems!"

"I wouldn't want to—of course, I couldn't call you a liar, Venters," said the older man. "What's more, she was Oldring's Masked Rider!"

Venters expected to floor his friend with that statement, but he was not in any way prepared for the shock his words gave. For an instant he was astounded to see Lassiter stunned; then his own passionate eagerness to unbosom himself, to tell the wonderful story, precluded any other thought.

"Son, tell me all about this," presently said Lassiter as he seated himself on a stone and wiped his moist brow. Thereupon Venters began his narrative at the point where he had shot the rustler and Oldring's Masked Rider, and he rushed through it, telling all, not holding back even Bess's unreserved avowal of her love or his deepest emotions.

"That's the story," he said, concluding. "I love her, though I've never told her. If I did tell her I'd be ready to marry her, and that seems impossible in this country. I'd be afraid to risk taking her anywhere. So I intend to do the best I can for her here."

"The longer I live the stranger life is," mused Lassiter, with downcast eyes. "I'm reminded of somethin' you once said to Jane about hands in her game of life. There's that unseen hand of power, an' Tull's black hand, an' my red one, an' your indifferent one, an' the girl's little brown, helpless one. An', Venters there's another one that's all-wise an' all-wonderful. That's the hand guidin' Jane Withersteen's game of life! . . . Your story's one to daze a far clearer head than mine. I can't offer no advice, even if you asked for it. Mebbe I can help you. Anyway, I'll hold Oldrin' up when he comes to the village an' find out about this girl. I knew the rustler years ago. He'll remember me."

"Lassiter, if I ever meet Oldring I'll kill him!" cried Venters, with sudden intensity. "I reckon that'd be perfectly natural," replied the rider.

"Make him think Bess is dead—as she is to him and that old life."

"Sure, sure, son. Cool down now. If you're goin' to begin pullin' guns on Tull an' Oldin' you want to be cool. I reckon, though, you'd better keep hid here. Well, I must be leavin'."

"One thing, Lassiter. You'll not tell Jane about Bess? Please don't!"

"I reckon not. But I wouldn't be afraid to bet that after she'd got over anger at your secrecy—Venters, she'd be furious once in her life!—she'd think more of you. I don't mind sayin' for myself that I think you're a good deal of a man."

In the further ascent Venters halted several times with the intention of saying good-by, yet he changed his mind and kept on climbing till they reached Balancing Rock. Lassiter examined the huge rock, listened to Venters's idea of its position and suggestion, and curiously placed a strong hand upon it.

"Hold on!" cried Venters. "I heaved at it once and have never gotten over my scare."

"Well, you do seem uncommon nervous," replied Lassiter, much amused. "Now, as for me, why I always had the funniest notion to roll stones! When I was a kid I did it, an' the bigger I got the bigger stones I'd roll. Ain't that funny? Honest—even now I often get off my hoss just to tumble a big stone over a precipice, en' watch it drop, en' listen to it bang an' boom. I've started some slides in my time, an' don't you forget it. I never seen a rock I wanted to roll as bad as this one! Wouldn't there jest be roarin', crashin' hell down that trail?"

"You'd close the outlet forever!" exclaimed Venters. "Well, good-by, Lassiter. Keep my secret and don't forget me. And be mighty careful how you get out of the valley below. The rustlers' canyon isn't more than three miles up the Pass. Now you've tracked me here, I'll never feel safe again."

In his descent to the valley, Venters's emotion, roused to stirring pitch by the recital of his love story, quieted gradually, and in its place came a sober, thoughtful mood. All at once he saw that he was serious, because he would never more regain his sense of security while in the valley. What Lassiter could do another skilful tracker might duplicate. Among the many riders with whom Venters had ridden he recalled no one who could have taken his trail at Cottonwoods and have followed it to the edge of the bare slope in the pass, let alone up that glistening smooth stone. Lassiter, however, was not an ordinary rider. Instead of hunting cattle tracks he had likely spent a goodly portion of his life tracking men. It was not improbable that among Oldring's rustlers there was one who shared Lassiter's gift for trailing. And the more Venters dwelt on this possibility the more perturbed he grew.

Lassiter's visit, moreover, had a disquieting effect upon Bess, and Venters fancied that she entertained the same thought as to future seclusion. The breaking of their solitude, though by a well-meaning friend, had not only dispelled all its dream and much of its charm, but had instilled a canker of fear. Both had seen the footprint in the sand.

Venters did no more work that day. Sunset and twilight gave way to night, and the canyon bird whistled its melancholy notes, and the wind sang softly in the cliffs, and the camp-fire blazed and burned down to red embers. To Venters a subtle difference was apparent in all of these, or else the shadowy change had been in him. He hoped that on the morrow this slight depression would have passed away.

In that measure, however, he was doomed to disappointment. Furthermore, Bess reverted to a wistful sadness that he had not observed in her since her recovery. His attempt to cheer her out of it resulted in dismal failure, and consequently in a darkening of his own mood. Hard work relieved him; still, when the day had passed, his unrest returned. Then he set to deliberate thinking, and there came to him the startling conviction that he must leave Surprise Valley and take Bess with him. As a rider he had taken many chances, and as an adventurer in Deception Pass he had unhesitatingly risked his life, but now he would run no preventable hazard of Bess's safety and happiness, and he was too keen not to see that hazard. It gave him a pang to think of leaving the beautiful valley just when he had the means to establish a permanent and delightful home there. One flashing thought tore in hot temptation through his mind—why not climb up into the gorge, roll Balancing Rock down the trail, and close forever the outlet to Deception Pass? "That was the beast in me—showing his teeth!" muttered Venters, scornfully. "I'll just kill him good and quick! I'll be fair to this girl, if it's the last thing I do on earth!"

Another day went by, in which he worked less and pondered more and all the time covertly watched Bess. Her wistfulness had deepened into downright unhappiness, and that made his task to tell her all the harder. He kept the secret another day, hoping by some chance she might grow less moody, and to his exceeding anxiety she fell into far deeper gloom. Out of his own secret and the torment of it he divined that she, too, had a secret and the keeping of it was torturing her. As yet he had no plan thought out in regard to how or when to leave the valley, but he decided to tell her the necessity of it and to persuade her to go. Furthermore, he hoped his speaking out would induce her to unburden her own mind.

"Bess, what's wrong with you?" he asked. "Nothing," she answered, with averted face.

Venters took hold of her gently, though masterfully, forced her to meet his eyes.

"You can't look at me and lie," he said. "Now—what's wrong with you? You're keeping something from me. Well, I've got a secret, too, and I intend to tell it presently."

"Oh—I have a secret. I was crazy to tell you when you came back. That's why I was so silly about everything. I kept holding my secret back—gloating over it. But when Lassiter came I got an idea—that changed my mind. Then I hated to tell you."

"Are you going to now?"

"Yes—yes. I was coming to it. I tried yesterday, but you were so cold. I was afraid. I couldn't keep it much longer."

"Very well, most mysterious lady, tell your wonderful secret."

"You needn't laugh," she retorted, with a first glimpse of reviving spirit. "I can take the laugh out of you in one second."

"It's a go."

She ran through the spruces to the cave, and returned carrying something which was manifestly heavy. Upon nearer view he saw that whatever she held with such evident importance had been bound up in a black scarf he well remembered. That alone was sufficient to make him tingle with curiosity.

"Have you any idea what I did in your absence?" she asked.

"I imagine you lounged about, waiting and watching for me," he replied, smiling. "I've my share of conceit, you know."

"You're wrong. I worked. Look at my hands." She dropped on her knees close to where he sat, and, carefully depositing the black bundle, she held out her hands. The palms and inside of her fingers were white, puckered, and worn.

"Why, Bess, you've been fooling in the water," he said.

"Fooling? Look here!" With deft fingers she spread open the black scarf, and the bright sun shone upon a dull, glittering heap of gold.

"Gold!" he ejaculated.

"Yes, gold! See, pounds of gold! I found it—washed it out of the stream—picked it out grain by grain, nugget by nugget!"

"Gold!" he cried.

"Yes. Now—now laugh at my secret!"

For a long minute Venters gazed. Then he stretched forth a hand to feel if the gold was real. "Gold!" he almost shouted. "Bess, there are hundreds—thousands of dollars' worth here!"

He leaned over to her, and put his hand, strong and clenching now, on hers. "Is there more where this came from?" he whispered.

"Plenty of it, all the way up the stream to the cliff. You know I've often washed for gold. Then I've heard the men talk. I think there's no great quantity of gold here, but enough for—for a fortune for you."

"That—was—your—secret! "

"Yes. I hate gold. For it makes men mad. I've seen them drunk with joy and dance and fling themselves around. I've seen them curse and rave. I've seen them fight like dogs and roll in the dust. I've seen them kill each other for gold."

"Is that why you hated to tell me?"

"Not—not altogether." Bess lowered her head. "It was because I knew you'd never stay here long after you found gold."

"You were afraid I'd leave you?"

"Yes.

"Listen! . . . You great, simple child! Listen . . . You sweet, wonderful, wild, blue-eyed girl! I was tortured by my secret. It was that I knew we—we must leave the valley. We can't stay here much longer. I couldn't think how we'd get away—out of the country—or how we'd live, if we ever got out. I'm a beggar. That's why I kept my secret. I'm poor. It takes money to make way beyond Sterling. We couldn't ride horses or burros or walk forever. So while I knew we must go, I was distracted over how to go and what to do. Now! We've gold! Once beyond Sterling, well be safe from rustlers. We've no others to fear.

"Oh! Listen! Bess!" Venters now heard his voice ringing high and sweet, and he felt Bess's cold hands in his crushing grasp as she leaned toward him pale, breathless. "This is how much I'd leave you! You made me live again! I'll take you away—far away from this wild country. You'll begin a new life. You'll be happy. You shall see cities, ships, people. You shall have anything your heart craves. All the shame and sorrow of your life shall be forgotten—as if they had never been. This is how much I'd leave you here alone—you sad-eyed girl. I love you! Didn't you know it? How could you fail to know it? I love you! I'm free! I'm a man—a man you've made—no more a beggar! . . . Kiss me! This is how much I'd leave you here alone—you beautiful, strange, unhappy girl. But I'll make you happy. What—what do I care for—your past! I love you! I'll take you home to Illinois—to my mother.

Then I'll take you to far places. I'll make up all you've lost. Oh, I know you love me—knew it before you told me. And it changed my life. And you'll go with me, not as my companion as you are here, nor my sister, but, Bess, darling! . . . As my wife!"

CHAPTER XVII
WRANGLE'S RACE RUN

The plan eventually decided upon by the lovers was for Venters to go to the village, secure a horse and some kind of a disguise for Bess, or at least less striking apparel than her present garb, and to return post-haste to the valley. Meanwhile, she would add to their store of gold. Then they would strike the long and perilous trail to ride out of Utah. In the event of his inability to fetch back a horse for her, they intended to make the giant sorrel carry double. The gold, a little food, saddle blankets, and Venters's guns were to compose the light outfit with which they would make the start.

"I love this beautiful place," said Bess. "It's hard to think of leaving it."

"Hard! Well, I should think so," replied Venters. "Maybe—in years—" But he did not complete in words his thought that might be possible to return after many years of absence and change.

Once again Bess bade Venters farewell under the shadow of Balancing Rock, and this time it was with whispered hope and tenderness and passionate trust. Long after he had left her, all down through the outlet to the Pass, the clinging clasp of her arms, the sweetness of her lips, and the sense of a new and exquisite birth of character in her remained hauntingly and thrillingly in his mind. The girl who had sadly called herself nameless and nothing had been marvelously transformed in the moment of his avowal of love. It was something to think over, something to warm his heart, but for the present it had absolutely to be forgotten so that all his mind could be addressed to the trip so fraught with danger.

He carried only his rifle, revolver, and a small quantity of bread and meat, and thus lightly burdened, he made swift progress down the slope and out into the valley. Darkness was coming on, and he welcomed it. Stars were blinking when he reached his old hiding-place in the split of canyon wall, and by their aid he slipped through the dense thickets to the grassy enclosure. Wrangle stood in the center of it with his head up, and he appeared black and of gigantic proportions in the dim light. Venters whistled softly, began a slow approach, and then called. The horse snorted and, plunging away with dull, heavy sound of hoofs, he disappeared in the gloom. "Wilder than ever!" muttered Venters. He followed the sorrel into the narrowing split between the walls, and presently had to desist because he could not see a foot in advance. As he went back toward the open Wrangle jumped out of an ebony shadow of cliff and like a thunderbolt shot huge and black past him down into the starlit glade. Deciding that all attempts to catch Wrangle at night would be useless, Venters repaired to the shelving rock where he had hidden saddle and blanket, and there went to sleep.

The first peep of day found him stirring, and as soon as it was light enough to distinguish objects, he took his lasso off his saddle and went out to rope the sorrel. He espied Wrangle at the lower end of the cove and approached him in a perfectly natural manner. When he got near enough, Wrangle evidently recognized him, but was too wild to stand. He ran up the glade and on into the narrow lane between the walls. This favored Venters's speedy capture of the horse, so, coiling his noose ready to throw, he hurried on. Wrangle let Venters get to within a hundred feet and then he broke. But as he plunged by, rapidly getting into his stride, Venters made a perfect throw with the rope. He had time to brace himself for the shock; nevertheless, Wrangle threw him and dragged him several yards before halting.

"You wild devil," said Venters, as he slowly pulled Wrangle up. "Don't you know me? Come now—old fellow—so—so—"

Wrangle yielded to the lasso and then to Venters's strong hand. He was as straggly and wild-looking as a horse left to roam free in the sage. He dropped his long ears and stood readily to be saddled and bridled. But he was exceedingly sensitive, and quivered at every touch and sound. Venters led him to the thicket, and, bending the close saplings to let him squeeze through, at length reached the open. Sharp survey in each direction assured him of the usual lonely nature of the canyon, then he was in the saddle, riding south.

Wrangle's long, swinging canter was a wonderful ground-gainer. His stride was almost twice that of an ordinary horse; and his endurance was equally remarkable. Venters pulled him in occasionally, and walked him up the stretches of rising ground and along the soft washes. Wrangle had never yet shown any indication of distress while Venters rode him. Nevertheless, there was now reason to save the horse, therefore Venters did not resort to the hurry that had characterized his former trip. He camped at the last water in the Pass. What distance that was to Cottonwoods he did not know; he calculated, however, that it was in the neighborhood of fifty miles.

Early in the morning he proceeded on his way, and about the middle of the forenoon reached the constricted gap that marked the southerly end of the Pass, and through which led the trail up to the sage-level. He spied out Lassiter's tracks in the dust, but no others, and dismounting, he straightened out Wrangle's bridle and began to lead him up the trail. The short climb, more severe on beast than on man, necessitated a rest on the level above, and during this he scanned the wide purple reaches of slope.

Wrangle whistled his pleasure at the smell of the sage. Remounting, Venters headed up the white trail with the fragrant wind in his face. He had proceeded for perhaps a couple of miles when Wrangle stopped with a suddenness that threw Venters heavily against the pommel.

"What's wrong, old boy?" called Venters, looking down for a loose shoe or a snake or a foot lamed by a picked-up stone. Unrewarded, he raised himself from his scrutiny. Wrangle stood stiff head high, with his long ears erect. Thus guided, Venters swiftly gazed ahead to make out a dust-clouded, dark group of horsemen riding down the slope. If they had seen him, it apparently made no difference in their speed or direction.

"Wonder who they are!" exclaimed Venters. He was not disposed to run. His cool mood tightened under grip of excitement as he reflected that, whoever the approaching riders were, they could not be friends. He slipped out of the saddle and led Wrangle behind the tallest sage-brush. It might serve to conceal them until the riders were close enough for him to see who they were; after that he would be indifferent to how soon they discovered him.

After looking to his rifle and ascertaining that it was in working order, he watched, and as he watched, slowly the force of a bitter fierceness, long dormant, gathered ready to flame into life. If those riders were not rustlers he had forgotten how rustlers looked and rode. On they came, a small group, so compact and dark that he could not tell their number. How unusual that their horses did not see Wrangle! But such failure, Venters decided, was owing to the speed with which they were traveling. They moved at a swift canter affected more by rustlers than by riders. Venters grew concerned over the possibility that these horsemen would actually ride down on him before he had a chance to tell what to expect. When they were within three hundred yards he deliberately led Wrangle out into the trail.

Then he heard shouts, and the hard scrape of sliding hoofs, and saw horses rear and plunge back with up-flung heads and flying manes. Several little white puffs of smoke appeared sharply against the black background of riders and horses, and shots rang out. Bullets struck far in front of Venters, and whipped up the dust and then hummed low into the sage. The range was great for revolvers, but whether the shots were meant to kill or merely to check advance, they were enough to fire that waiting ferocity in Venters. Slipping his arm through the bridle, so that Wrangle could not get away, Venters lifted his rifle and pulled the trigger twice.

He saw the first horseman lean sideways and fall. He saw another lurch in his saddle and heard a cry of pain. Then Wrangle, plunging in fright, lifted Venters and nearly threw him. He jerked the horse down with a powerful hand and leaped into the saddle. Wrangle plunged again, dragging his bridle, that Venters had not had time to throw in place. Bending over with a swift movement, he secured it and dropped the loop over the pommel. Then, with grinding teeth, he looked to see what the issue would be.

The band had scattered so as not to afford such a broad mark for bullets. The riders faced Venters, some with red-belching guns. He heard a sharper report, and just as Wrangle plunged again he caught the whim of a leaden missile that would have hit him but for Wrangle's sudden jump. A swift, hot wave, turning cold, passed over Venters. Deliberately he picked out the one rider with a carbine, and killed him. Wrangle snorted shrilly and bolted into the sage. Venters let him run a few rods, then with iron arm checked him.

Five riders, surely rustlers, were left. One leaped out of the saddle to secure his fallen comrade's carbine. A shot from Venters, which missed the man but sent the dust flying over him made him run back to his horse. Then they separated. The crippled rider went one way; the one frustrated in his attempt to get the carbine rode another, Venters thought he made out a third rider, carrying a strange-appearing bundle and disappearing in the sage. But in the rapidity of action and vision he could not discern what it was. Two riders with three horses swung out to the right. Afraid of the long rifle—a burdensome weapon seldom carried by rustlers or riders—they had been put to rout.

Suddenly Venters discovered that one of the two men last noted was riding Jane Withersteen's horse Bells—the beautiful bay racer she had given to Lassiter. Venters uttered a savage outcry. Then the small, wiry, frog-like shape of the second rider, and the ease and grace of his seat in the saddle—things so strikingly incongruous—grew more and more familiar in Venters's sight.

"Jerry Card!" cried Venters.

It was indeed Tull's right-hand man. Such a white hot wrath inflamed Venters that he fought himself to see with clearer gaze.

"It's Jerry Card!" he exclaimed, instantly. "And he's riding Black Star and leading Night!"

The long-kindling, stormy fire in Venters's heart burst into flame. He spurred Wrangle, and as the horse lengthened his stride Venters slipped cartridges into the magazine of his rifle till it was once again full. Card and his companion were now half a mile or more in advance, riding easily down the slope. Venters marked the smooth gait, and understood it when Wrangle galloped out of the sage into the broad cattle trail, down which Venters had once tracked Jane Withersteen's red herd. This hard-packed trail, from years of use, was as clean and smooth as a road. Venters saw Jerry Card look back over his shoulder, the other rider did likewise. Then the three racers lengthened their stride to the point where the swinging canter was ready to break into a gallop.

"Wrangle, the race's on," said Venters, grimly. "We'll canter with them and gallop with them and run with them. We'll let them set the pace."

Venters knew he bestrode the strongest, swiftest, most tireless horse ever ridden by any rider across the Utah uplands. Recalling Jane Withersteen's devoted assurance that Night could run neck and neck with Wrangle, and Black Star could show his heels to him, Venters wished that Jane were there to see the race to recover her blacks and in the unqualified superiority of the giant sorrel. Then Venters found himself thankful that she was absent, for he meant that race to end in Jerry Card's death. The first flush, the raging of Venters's wrath, passed, to leave him in sullen, almost cold possession of his will. It was a deadly mood, utterly foreign to his nature, engendered, fostered, and released by the wild passions of wild men in a wild country. The strength in him then—the thing rife in him that was note hate, but something as remorseless—might have been the fiery fruition of a whole lifetime of vengeful quest. Nothing could have stopped him.

Venters thought out the race shrewdly. The rider on Bells would probably drop behind and take to the sage. What he did was of little moment to Venters. To stop Jerry Card, his evil hidden career as well as his present flight, and then to catch the blacks—that was all that concerned Venters. The cattle trail wound for miles and miles down the slope. Venters saw with a rider's keen vision ten, fifteen, twenty miles of clear purple sage.

There were no on-coming riders or rustlers to aid Card. His only chance to escape lay in abandoning the stolen horses and creeping away in the sage to hide. In ten miles Wrangle could run Black Star and Night off their feet, and in fifteen he could kill them outright. So Venters held the sorrel in, letting Card make the running. It was a long race that would save the blacks.

In a few miles of that swinging canter Wrangle had crept appreciably closer to the three horses. Jerry Card turned again, and when he saw how the sorrel had gained, he put Black Star to a gallop. Night and Bells, on either side of him, swept into his stride.

Venters loosened the rein on Wrangle and let him break into a gallop. The sorrel saw the horses ahead and wanted to run. But Venters restrained him. And in the gallop he gained more than in the canter. Bells was fast in that gait, but Black Star and Night had been trained to run. Slowly Wrangle closed the gap down to a quarter of a mile, and crept closer and closer.

Jerry Card wheeled once more. Venters distinctly saw the red flash of his red face. This time he looked long. Venters laughed. He knew what passed in Card's mind. The rider was trying to make out what horse it happened to be that thus gained on Jane Withersteen's peerless racers. Wrangle had so long been away from the village that not improbably Jerry had forgotten. Besides, whatever Jerry's qualifications for his fame as the greatest rider of the sage, certain it was that his best point was not far-sightedness. He had not recognized Wrangle. After what must have been a searching gaze he got his comrade to face about. This action gave Venters amusement. It spoke so surely of the facts that neither Card nor the rustler actually knew their danger. Yet if they kept to the trail—and the last thing such men would do would be to leave it—they were both doomed.

This comrade of Card's whirled far around in his saddle, and he even shaded his eyes from the sun. He, too, looked long. Then, all at once, he faced ahead again and, bending lower in the saddle, began to fling his right arm up and down. That flinging Venters knew to be the lashing of Bells. Jerry also became active. And the three racers lengthened out into a run.

"Now, Wrangle!" cried Venters. "Run, you big devil! Run!"

Venters laid the reins on Wrangle's neck and dropped the loop over the pommel. The sorrel needed no guiding on that smooth trail. He was surer-footed in a run than at any other fast gait, and his running gave the impression of something devilish. He might now have been actuated by Venters's spirit; undoubtedly his savage running fitted the mood of his rider. Venters bent forward swinging with the horse, and gripped his rifle. His eye measured the distance between him and Jerry Card.

In less than two miles of running Bells began to drop behind the blacks, and Wrangle began to overhaul him. Venters anticipated that the rustler would soon take to the sage. Yet he did not. Not improbably he reasoned that the powerful sorrel could more easily overtake Bells in the heavier going outside of the trail. Soon only a few hundred yards lay between Bells and Wrangle. Turning in his saddle, the rustler began to shoot, and the bullets beat up little whiffs of dust. Venters raised his rifle, ready to take snap shots, and waited for favorable opportunity when Bells was out of line with the forward horses. Venters had it in him to kill these men as if they were skunk-bitten coyotes, but also he had restraint enough to keep from shooting one of Jane's beloved Arabians.

No great distance was covered, however, before Bells swerved to the left, out of line with Black Star and Night. Then Venters, aiming high and waiting for the pause between Wrangle's great strides, began to take snap shots at the rustler. The fleeing rider presented a broad target for a rifle, but he was moving swiftly forward and bobbing up and down. Moreover, shooting from Wrangle's back was shooting from a thunderbolt. And added to that was the danger of a low-placed bullet taking effect on Bells. Yet, despite these considerations, making the shot exceedingly difficult, Venters's confidence, like his implacability, saw a speedy and fatal termination of that rustler's race. On the sixth shot the rustler threw up his arms and took a flying tumble off his horse. He rolled over and over, hunched himself to a half-erect position, fell, and then dragged himself into the sage. As Venters went thundering by he peered keenly into the sage, but caught no sign of the man. Bells ran a few hundred yards, slowed up, and had stopped when Wrangle passed him.

Again Venters began slipping fresh cartridges into the magazine of his rifle, and his hand was so sure and steady that he did not drop a single cartridge. With the eye of a rider and the judgment of a marksman he once more measured the distance between him and Jerry Card. Wrangle had gained, bringing him into rifle range. Venters was hard put to it now not to shoot, but thought it better to withhold his fire. Jerry, who, in anticipation of a running fusillade, had huddled himself into a little twisted ball on Black Star's neck, now surmising that this pursuer would make sure of not wounding one of the blacks, rose to his natural seat in the saddle.

In his mind perhaps, as certainly as in Venters's, this moment was the beginning of the real race.

Venters leaned forward to put his hand on Wrangle's neck, then backward to put it on his flank. Under the shaggy, dusty hair trembled and vibrated and rippled a wonderful muscular activity. But Wrangle's flesh was still cold. What a cold-blooded brute thought Venters, and felt in him a love for the horse he had never given to any other. It would not have been humanly possible for any rider, even though clutched by hate or revenge or a passion to save a loved one or fear of his own life, to be astride the sorrel to swing with his swing, to see his magnificent stride and hear the rapid thunder of his hoofs, to ride him in that race and not glory in the ride.

So, with his passion to kill still keen and unabated, Venters lived out that ride, and drank a rider's sage-sweet cup of wildness to the dregs.

When Wrangle's long mane, lashing in the wind, stung Venters in the cheek, the sting added a beat to his flying pulse. He bent a downward glance to try to see Wrangle's actual stride, and saw only twinkling, darting streaks and the white rush of the trail. He watched the sorrel's savage head, pointed level, his mouth still closed and dry, but his nostrils distended as if he were snorting unseen fire. Wrangle was the horse for a race with death. Upon each side Venters saw the sage merged into a sailing, colorless wall. In front sloped the lay of ground with its purple breadth split by the white trail. The wind, blowing with heavy, steady blast into his face, sickened him with enduring, sweet odor, and filled his ears with a hollow, rushing roar.

Then for the hundredth time he measured the width of space separating him from Jerry Card. Wrangle had ceased to gain. The blacks were proving their fleetness. Venters watched Jerry Card, admiring the little rider's horsemanship. He had the incomparable seat of the upland rider, born in the saddle. It struck Venters that Card had changed his position, or the position of the horses. Presently Venters remembered positively that

Jerry had been leading Night on the right-hand side of the trail. The racer was now on the side to the left.

No—it was Black Star. But, Venters argued in amaze, Jerry had been mounted on Black Star. Another clearer, keener gaze assured Venters that Black Star was really riderless. Night now carried Jerry Card.

"He's changed from one to the other!" ejaculated Venters, realizing the astounding feat with unstinted admiration. "Changed at full speed! Jerry Card, that's what you've done unless I'm drunk on the smell of sage. But I've got to see the trick before I believe it."

Thenceforth, while Wrangle sped on, Venters glued his eyes to the little rider. Jerry Card rode as only he could ride. Of all the daring horsemen of the uplands, Jerry was the one rider fitted to bring out the greatness of the blacks in that long race. He had them on a dead run, but not yet at the last strained and killing pace.

From time to time he glanced backward, as a wise general in retreat calculating his chances and the power and speed of pursuers, and the moment for the last desperate burst. No doubt, Card, with his life at stake, gloried in that race, perhaps more wildly than Venters. For he had been born to the sage and the saddle and the wild. He was more than half horse. Not until the last call—the sudden up-flashing instinct of self-preservation—would he lose his skill and judgment and nerve and the spirit of that race. Venters seemed to read Jerry's mind. That little crime-stained rider was actually thinking of his horses, husbanding their speed, handling them with knowledge of years, glorying in their beautiful, swift, racing stride, and wanting them to win the race when his own life hung suspended in quivering balance. Again Jerry whirled in his saddle and the sun flashed red on his face. Turning, he drew Black Star closer and closer toward Night, till they ran side by side, as one horse. Then Card raised himself in the saddle, slipped out of the stirrups, and, somehow twisting himself, leaped upon Black Star. He did not even lose the swing of the horse. Like a leech he was there in the other saddle, and as the horses separated, his right foot, that had been apparently doubled under him, shot down to catch the stirrup. The grace and dexterity and daring of that rider's act won something more than admiration from Venters.

For the distance of a mile Jerry rode Black Star and then changed back to Night. But all Jerry's skill and the running of the blacks could avail little more against the sorrel.

Venters peered far ahead, studying the lay of the land. Straightaway for five miles the trail stretched, and then it disappeared in hummocky ground. To the right, some few rods, Venters saw a break in the sage, and this was the rim of Deception Pass. Across the dark cleft gleamed the red of the opposite wall. Venters imagined that the trail went down into the Pass somewhere north of those ridges. And he realized that he must and would overtake Jerry Card in this straight course of five miles.

Cruelly he struck his spurs into Wrangle's flanks. A light touch of spur was sufficient to make Wrangle plunge. And now, with a ringing, wild snort, he seemed to double up in muscular convulsions and to shoot forward with an impetus that almost unseated Venters. The sage blurred by, the trail flashed by, and the wind robbed him of breath and hearing. Jerry Card turned once more. And the way he shifted to Black Star showed he had to make his last desperate running. Venters aimed to the side of the trail and sent a bullet puffing the dust beyond Jerry. Venters hoped to frighten the rider and get him to take to the sage. But Jerry returned the shot, and his ball struck dangerously close in the dust at Wrangle's flying feet. Venters held his fire then, while the rider emptied his revolver. For a mile, with Black Star leaving Night behind and doing his utmost, Wrangle did not gain; for another mile he gained little, if at all. In the third he caught up with the now galloping Night and began to gain rapidly on the other black.

Only a hundred yards now stretched between Black Star and Wrangle. The giant sorrel thundered on—and on—and on. In every yard he gained a foot. He was whistling through his nostrils, wringing wet, flying lather, and as hot as fire. Savage as ever, strong as ever, fast as ever, but each tremendous stride jarred Venters out of the saddle! Wrangle's power and spirit and momentum had begun to run him off his legs. Wrangle's great race was nearly won—and run. Venters seemed to see the expanse before him as a vast, sheeted, purple plain sliding under him. Black Star moved in it as a blur. The rider, Jerry Card, appeared a mere dot bobbing dimly. Wrangle thundered on—on—on! Venters felt the increase in quivering, straining shock after every leap. Flecks of foam flew into Venters's eyes, burning him, making him see all the sage as red. But in that red haze he saw, or seemed to see, Black Star suddenly riderless and with broken gait. Wrangle thundered on to change his pace with a violent break. Then Venters pulled him hard. From run to gallop, gallop to canter, canter to trot, trot to walk, and walk to stop, the great sorrel ended his race.

Venters looked back. Black Star stood riderless in the trail. Jerry Card had taken to the sage. Far up the white trail Night came trotting faithfully down. Venters leaped off, still half blind, reeling dizzily. In a moment he had recovered sufficiently to have a care for Wrangle. Rapidly he took off the saddle and bridle. The sorrel was reeking, heaving, whistling, shaking. But he had still the strength to stand, and for him Venters had no fears.

As Venters ran back to Black Star he saw the horse stagger on shaking legs into the sage and go down in a heap. Upon reaching him Venters removed the saddle and bridle. Black Star had been killed on his legs, Venters thought. He had no hope for the stricken horse. Black Star lay flat, covered with bloody froth, mouth wide, tongue hanging, eyes glaring, and all his beautiful body in convulsions.

Unable to stay there to see Jane's favorite racer die, Venters hurried up the trail to meet the other black. On the way he kept a sharp lookout for Jerry Card. Venters imagined the rider would keep well out of range of the rifle, but, as he would be lost on the sage without a horse, not improbably he would linger in the vicinity on the chance of getting back one of the blacks. Night soon came trotting up, hot and wet and run out. Venters led him down near the others, and unsaddling him, let him loose to rest. Night wearily lay down in the dust and rolled, proving himself not yet spent.

Then Venters sat down to rest and think. Whatever the risk, he was compelled to stay where he was, or comparatively near, for the night. The horses must rest and drink. He must find water. He was now seventy miles from Cottonwoods, and, he believed, close to the canyon where the cattle trail must surely turn off and go down into the Pass. After a while he rose to survey the valley.

He was very near to the ragged edge of a deep canyon into which the trail turned. The ground lay in uneven ridges divided by washes, and these sloped into the canyon. Following the canyon line, he saw where its rim was broken by other intersecting canyons, and farther down red walls and yellow cliffs leading toward a deep blue cleft that he made sure was Deception Pass. Walking out a few rods to a promontory, he found where the trail went down. The descent was gradual, along a stone-walled trail, and Venters felt sure that this was the place where Oldring drove cattle into the Pass. There was, however, no indication at all that he ever had driven cattle out at this point. Oldring had many holes to his burrow.

In searching round in the little hollows Venters, much to his relief, found water. He composed himself to rest and eat some bread and meat, while he waited for a sufficient time to elapse so that he could safely give the horses a drink. He judged the hour to be somewhere around noon. Wrangle lay down to rest and Night followed suit. So long as they were down Venters intended to make no move. The longer they rested the better, and the safer it would be to give them water. By and by he forced himself to go over to where Black Star lay, expecting to find him dead. Instead he found the racer partially if not wholly recovered. There was recognition, even fire, in his big black eyes. Venters was overjoyed. He sat by the black for a long time. Black Star presently labored to his feet with a heave and a groan, shook himself, and snorted for water. Venters repaired to the little pool he had found, filled his sombrero, and gave the racer a drink. Black Star gulped it at one draught, as if it were but a drop, and pushed his nose into the hat and snorted for more. Venters now led Night down to drink, and after a further time Black Star also. Then the blacks began to graze.

The sorrel had wandered off down the sage between the trail and the canyon. Once or twice he disappeared in little swales. Finally Venters concluded Wrangle had grazed far enough, and, taking his lasso, he went to fetch him back. In crossing from one ridge to another he saw where the horse had made muddy a pool of water. It occurred to Venters then that Wrangle had drunk his fill, and did not seem the worse for it, and might be anything but easy to catch. And, true enough, he could not come within roping reach of the sorrel. He tried for an hour, and gave up in disgust. Wrangle did not seem so wild as simply perverse. In a quandary Venters returned to the other horses, hoping much, yet doubting more, that when Wrangle had grazed to suit himself he might be caught.

As the afternoon wore away Venters's concern diminished, yet he kept close watch on the blacks and the trail and the sage. There was no telling of what Jerry Card might be capable. Venters sullenly acquiesced to the idea that the rider had been too quick and too shrewd for him. Strangely and doggedly, however, Venters clung to his foreboding of Card's downfall.

The wind died away; the red sun topped the far distant western rise of slope; and the long, creeping purple shadows lengthened. The rims of the canyons gleamed crimson and the deep clefts appeared to belch forth blue smoke. Silence enfolded the scene.

It was broken by a horrid, long-drawn scream of a horse and the thudding of heavy hoofs. Venters sprang erect and wheeled south. Along the canyon rim, near the edge, came Wrangle, once more in thundering flight.

Venters gasped in amazement. Had the wild sorrel gone mad? His head was high and twisted, in a most singular position for a running horse. Suddenly Venters descried a frog-like shape clinging to Wrangle's neck. Jerry Card! Somehow he had straddled Wrangle and now stuck like a huge burr. But it was his strange position and the sorrel's wild scream that shook Venters's nerves. Wrangle was pounding toward the turn where the trail went down. He plunged onward like a blind horse. More than one of his leaps took him to the very edge of the precipice.

Jerry Card was bent forward with his teeth fast in the front of Wrangle's nose! Venters saw it, and there flashed over him a memory of this trick of a few desperate riders. He even thought of one rider who had worn off his teeth in this terrible hold to break or control desperate horses. Wrangle had indeed gone mad. The marvel was what guided him. Was it the half-brute, the more than half-horse instinct of Jerry Card? Whatever the mystery, it was true. And in a few more rods Jerry would have the sorrel turning into the trail leading down into the canyon.

"No—Jerry!" whispered Venters, stepping forward and throwing up the rifle. He tried to catch the little humped, frog-like shape over the sights. It was moving too fast; it was too small. Yet Venters shot once . . . twice . . . the third time . . . four times . . . five! all wasted shots and precious seconds!

With a deep-muttered curse Venters caught Wrangle through the sights and pulled the trigger. Plainly he heard the bullet thud. Wrangle uttered a horrible strangling sound. In swift death action he whirled, and with one last splendid leap he cleared the canyon rim. And he whirled downward with the little frog-like shape clinging to his neck!

There was a pause which seemed never ending, a shock, and an instant silence.

Then up rolled a heavy crash, a long roar of sliding rocks dying away in distant echo, then silence unbroken. Wrangle's race was run.

CHAPTER XVIII
OLDRING'S KNELL

Some forty hours or more later Venters created a commotion in Cottonwoods by riding down the main street on Black Star and leading Bells and Night. He had come upon Bells grazing near the body of a dead rustler, the only incident of his quick ride into the village.

Nothing was farther from Venters's mind than bravado. No thought came to him of the defiance and boldness of riding Jane Withersteen's racers straight into the arch-plotter's stronghold. He wanted men to see the famous Arabians; he wanted men to see them dirty and dusty, bearing all the signs of having been driven to their limit; he wanted men to see and to know that the thieves who had ridden them out into the sage had not ridden them back. Venters had come for that and for more—he wanted to meet Tull face to face; if not Tull, then Dyer; if not Dyer, then anyone in the secret of these master conspirators. Such was Venters's passion. The meeting with the rustlers, the unprovoked attack upon him, the spilling of blood, the recognition of Jerry Card and the horses, the race, and that last plunge of mad Wrangle—all these things, fuel on fuel to the smoldering fire, had kindled and swelled and leaped into living flame. He could have shot Dyer in the midst of his religious services at the altar; he could have killed Tull in front of wives and babes.

He walked the three racers down the broad, green-bordered village road. He heard the murmur of running water from Amber Spring. Bitter waters for Jane Withersteen! Men and women stopped to gaze at him and the horses. All knew him; all knew the blacks and the bay. As well as if it had been spoken, Venters read in the faces of men the intelligence that Jane Withersteen's Arabians had been known to have been stolen. Venters reined in and halted before Dyer's residence. It was a low, long, stone structure resembling Withersteen House. The spacious front yard was green and luxuriant with grass and flowers; gravel walks led to the huge porch; a well-trimmed hedge of purple sage separated the yard from the church grounds; birds sang in the trees; water flowed musically along the walks; and there were glad, careless shouts of children. For Venters the beauty of this home, and the serenity and its apparent happiness, all turned red and black. For Venters a shade overspread the lawn, the flowers, the old vine-clad stone house. In the music of the singing birds, in the murmur of the running water, he heard an ominous sound. Quiet beauty—sweet music—innocent laughter! By what monstrous abortion of fate did these abide in the shadow of Dyer?

Venters rode on and stopped before Tull's cottage. Women stared at him with white faces and then flew from the porch. Tull himself appeared at the door, bent low, craning his neck. His dark face flashed out of sight; the door banged; a heavy bar dropped with a hollow sound.

Then Venters shook Black Star's bridle, and, sharply trotting, led the other horses to the center of the village. Here at the intersecting streets and in front of the stores he halted once more. The usual lounging atmosphere of that prominent corner was not now in evidence. Riders and ranchers and villagers broke up what must have been absorbing conversation. There was a rush of many feet, and then the walk was lined with faces.

Venters's glance swept down the line of silent stone-faced men. He recognized many riders and villagers, but none of those he had hoped to meet. There was no expression in the faces turned toward him. All of them knew him, most were inimical, but there were few who were not burning with curiosity and wonder in regard to the return of Jane Withersteen's racers. Yet all were silent. Here were the familiar characteristics—masked feeling—strange secretiveness—expressionless expression of mystery and hidden power.

"Has anybody here seen Jerry Card?" queried Venters, in a loud voice.

In reply there came not a word, not a nod or shake of head, not so much as dropping eye or twitching lip—nothing but a quiet, stony stare.

"Been under the knife? You've a fine knife-wielder here—one Tull, I believe! . . . Maybe you've all had your tongues cut out?"

This passionate sarcasm of Venters brought no response, and the stony calm was as oil on the fire within him. "I see some of you pack guns, too!" he added, in biting scorn. In the long, tense pause, strung keenly as a tight wire, he sat motionless on Black Star. "All right," he went on. "Then let some of you take this message to Tull. Tell him I've seen Jerry Card! . . . Tell him Jerry Card will never return!"

Thereupon, in the same dead calm, Venters backed Black Star away from the curb, into the street, and out of range. He was ready now to ride up to Withersteen House and turn the racers over to Jane.

"Hello, Venters!" a familiar voice cried, hoarsely, and he saw a man running toward him. It was the rider Judkins who came up and gripped Venters's hand. "Venters, I could hev dropped when I seen them hosses. But thet sight ain't a marker to the looks of you. What's wrong? Hev you gone crazy? You must be crazy to ride in here this way—with them hosses—talkie' thet way about Tull en' Jerry Card."

"Jud, I'm not crazy—only mad clean through," replied Venters.

"Mad, now, Bern, I'm glad to hear some of your old self in your voice. Fer when you come up you looked like the corpse of a dead rider with fire fer eyes. You hed thet crowd too stiff fer throwin' guns. Come, we've got to hev a talk. Let's go up the lane. We ain't much safe here."

Judkins mounted Bells and rode with Venters up to the cottonwood grove. Here they dismounted and went among the trees.

"Let's hear from you first," said Judkins. "You fetched back them hosses. Thet is the trick. An', of course, you got Jerry the same as you got Horne."

"Horne!"

"Sure. He was found dead yesterday all chewed by coyotes, en' he'd been shot plumb center."

"Where was he found?"

"At the split down the trail—you know where Oldring's cattle trail runs off north from the trail to the pass."

"That's where I met Jerry and the rustlers. What was Horne doing with them? I thought Horne was an honest cattle-man."

"Lord—Bern, don't ask me thet! I'm all muddled now tryin' to figure things." Venters told of the fight and the race with Jerry Card and its tragic conclusion.

"I knowed it! I knowed all along that Wrangle was the best hoss!" exclaimed Judkins, with his lean face working and his eyes lighting. "Thet was a race! Lord, I'd like to hev seen Wrangle jump the cliff with Jerry. An' thet was good-by to the grandest hoss an' rider ever on the sage! . . . But, Bern, after you got the hosses why'd you want to bolt right in Tull's face?"

"I want him to know. An' if I can get to him I'll—"

"You can't get near Tull," interrupted Judkins. "Thet vigilante bunch hev taken to bein' bodyguard for Tull an' Dyer, too."

"Hasn't Lassiter made a break yet?" inquired Venters, curiously.

"Naw!" replied Judkins, scornfully. "Jane turned his head. He's mad in love over her—follers her like a dog. He ain't no more Lassiter! He's lost his nerve, he doesn't look like the same feller. It's village talk. Everybody knows it. He hasn't thrown a gun, an' he won't!"

"Jud, I'll bet he does," replied Venters, earnestly. "Remember what I say. This Lassiter is something more than a gun-man. Jud, he's big—he's great! . . . I feel that in him. God help Tull and Dyer when Lassiter does go after them. For horses and riders and stone walls won't save them."

"Wal, hev it your way, Bern. I hope you're right. Nat'rully I've been some sore on Lassiter fer gittin' soft. But I ain't denyin' his nerve, or whatever's great in him thet sort of paralyzes people. No later 'n this mornin' I seen him saunterin' down the lane, quiet an' slow. An' like his guns he comes black—black, thet's Lassiter. Wal, the crowd on the corner never batted an eye, en' I'll gamble my hoss thet there wasn't one who hed a heartbeat till Lassiter got by. He went in Snell's saloon, an' as there wasn't no gun play I had to go in, too. An' there, darn my pictures, if Lassiter wasn't standin' to the bar, drinking en' talkin' with Oldrin'."

"Oldring!" whispered Venters. His voice, as all fire and pulse within him, seemed to freeze.

"Let go my arm!" exclaimed Judkins. "Thet's my bad arm. Sure it was Oldrin'. What the hell's wrong with you, anyway? Venters, I tell you somethin's wrong. You're whiter 'n a sheet. You can't be scared of the rustler. I don't believe you've got a scare in you. Wal, now, jest let me talk. You know I like to talk, an' if I'm slow I allus git there sometime. As I said, Lassiter was talkie' chummy with Oldrin'. There wasn't no hard feelin's.

An' the gang wasn't payin' no pertic'lar attention. But like a cat watchin' a mouse I hed my eyes on them two fellers. It was strange to me, thet confab. I'm gittin' to think a lot, fer a feller who doesn't know much. There's been some queer deals lately an' this seemed to me the queerest. These men stood to the bar alone, an' so close their big gun-hilts butted together. I seen Oldrin' was some surprised at first, an' Lassiter was cool as ice. They talked, an' presently at somethin' Lassiter said the rustler bawled out a curse, an' then he jest fell up against the bar, an' sagged there. The gang in the saloon looked around an' laughed, an' thet's about all. Finally Oldrin' turned, and it was easy to see somethin' hed shook him. Yes, sir, thet big rustler—you know he's as broad as he is long, an' the powerfulest build of a man—yes, sir, the nerve had been taken out of him. Then, after a little, he began to talk an' said a lot to Lassiter, an' by an' by it didn't take much of an eye to see thet Lassiter was gittin' hit hard. I never seen him anyway but cooler 'n ice—till then. He seemed to be hit harder 'n Oldrin', only he didn't roar out thet way. He jest kind of sunk in, an' looked an' looked, an' he didn't see a livin' soul in thet saloon. Then he sort of come to, an' shakin' hands—mind you, shakin' hands with Oldrin'—he went out. I couldn't help thinkin' how easy even a boy could hev dropped the great gun-man then! . . . Wal, the rustler stood at the bar fer a long time, en' he was seein' things far off, too; then he come to an' roared fer whisky, an' gulped a drink thet was big enough to drown me."

"Is Oldring here now?" whispered Venters. He could not speak above a whisper. Judkins's story had been meaningless to him.

"He's at Snell's yet. Bern, I hevn't told you yet thet the rustlers hev been raisin' hell. They shot up Stone Bridge an' Glaze, an' fer three days they've been here drinkin' an' gamblin' an' throwin' of gold. These rustlers hev a pile of gold. If it was gold dust or nugget gold I'd hev reason to think, but it's new coin gold, as if it had jest come from the United States treasury. An' the coin's genuine. Thet's all been proved. The truth is Oldrin's on a rampage. A while back he lost his Masked Rider, an' they say he's wild about thet. I'm wonderin' if Lassiter could hev told the rustler anythin' about thet little masked, hard-ridin' devil. Ride! He was most as good as Jerry Card. An', Bern, I've been wonderin' if you know—"

"Judkins, you're a good fellow," interrupted Venters. "Some day I'll tell you a story. I've no time now. Take the horses to Jane."

Judkins stared, and then, muttering to himself, he mounted Bells, and stared again at Venters, and then, leading the other horses, he rode into the grove and disappeared.

Once, long before, on the night Venters had carried Bess through the canyon and up into Surprise Valley, he had experienced the strangeness of faculties singularly, tinglingly acute. And now the same sensation recurred. But it was different in that he felt cold, frozen, mechanical incapable of free thought, and all about him seemed unreal, aloof, remote. He hid his rifle in the sage, marking its exact location with extreme care. Then he faced down the lane and strode toward the center of the village. Perceptions flashed upon him, the faint, cold touch of the breeze, a cold, silvery tinkle of flowing water, a cold sun shining out of a cold sky, song of birds and laugh of children, coldly distant. Cold and intangible were all things in earth and heaven. Colder and tighter stretched the skin over his face; colder and harder grew the polished butts of his guns; colder and steadier became his hands as he wiped the clammy sweat from his face or reached low to his gun-sheaths. Men meeting him in the walk gave him wide berth. In front of Bevin's store a crowd melted apart for his passage, and their faces and whispers were faces and whispers of a dream. He turned a corner to meet Tull face to face, eye to eye. As once before he had seen this man pale to a ghastly, livid white so again he saw the change. Tull stopped in his tracks, with right hand raised and shaking. Suddenly it dropped, and he seemed to glide aside, to pass out of Venters's sight. Next he saw many horses with bridles down—all clean-limbed, dark bays or blacks—rustlers' horses! Loud voices and boisterous laughter, rattle of dice and scrape of chair and clink of gold, burst in mingled din from an open doorway. He stepped inside.

With the sight of smoke-hazed room and drinking, cursing, gambling, dark-visaged men, reality once more dawned upon Venters.

His entrance had been unnoticed, and he bent his gaze upon the drinkers at the bar. Dark-clothed, dark-faced men they all were, burned by the sun, bow-legged as were most riders of the sage, but neither lean nor gaunt. Then Venters's gaze passed to the tables, and swiftly it swept over the hard-featured gamesters, to alight upon the huge, shaggy, black head of the rustler chief.

"Oldring!" he cried, and to him his voice seemed to split a bell in his ears. It stilled the din.

That silence suddenly broke to the scrape and crash of Oldring's chair as he rose; and then, while he passed, a great gloomy figure, again the thronged room stilled in silence yet deeper.

"Oldring, a word with you!" continued Venters.

"Ho! What's this?" boomed Oldring, in frowning scrutiny.

"Come outside, alone. A word for you—from your Masked Rider!"

Oldring kicked a chair out of his way and lunged forward with a stamp of heavy boot that jarred the floor. He waved down his muttering, rising men.

Venters backed out of the door and waited, hearing, as no sound had ever before struck into his soul, the rapid, heavy steps of the rustler.

Oldring appeared, and Venters had one glimpse of his great breadth and bulk, his gold-buckled belt with hanging guns, his high-top boots with gold spurs. In that moment Venters had a strange, unintelligible curiosity to see Oldring alive. The rustler's broad brow, his large black eyes, his sweeping beard, as dark as the wing of a raven, his enormous width of shoulder and depth of chest, his whole splendid presence so wonderfully charged with vitality and force and strength, seemed to afford Venters an unutterable fiendish joy because for that magnificent manhood and life he meant cold and sudden death.

"Oldring, Bess is alive! But she's dead to you—dead to the life you made her lead—dead as you will be in one second!"

Swift as lightning Venters's glance dropped from Oldring's rolling eyes to his hands. One of them, the right, swept out, then toward his gun—and Venters shot him through the heart.

Slowly Oldring sank to his knees, and the hand, dragging at the gun, fell away. Venters's strangely acute faculties grasped the meaning of that limp arm, of the swaying hulk, of the gasp and heave, of the quivering beard. But was that awful spirit in the black eyes only one of vitality?

"Man—why—didn't—you—wait? Bess—was—" Oldring's whisper died under his beard, and with a heavy lurch he fell forward.

Bounding swiftly away, Venters fled around the corner, across the street, and, leaping a hedge, he ran through yard, orchard, and garden to the sage. Here, under cover of the tall brush, he turned west and ran on to the place where he had hidden his rifle. Securing that, he again set out into a run, and, circling through the sage, came up behind Jane Withersteen's stable and corrals. With laboring, dripping chest, and pain as of a knife thrust in his side, he stopped to regain his breath, and while resting his eyes roved around in search of a horse. Doors and windows of the stable were open wide and had a deserted look. One dejected, lonely burro stood in the near corral. Strange indeed was the silence brooding over the once happy, noisy home of Jane Withersteen's pets.

He went into the corral, exercising care to leave no tracks, and led the burro to the watering-trough. Venters, though not thirsty, drank till he could drink no more. Then, leading the burro over hard ground, he struck into the sage and down the slope.

He strode swiftly, turning from time to time to scan the slope for riders. His head just topped the level of sage-brush, and the burro could not have been seen at all. Slowly the green of Cottonwoods sank behind the slope, and at last a wavering line of purple sage met the blue of sky.

To avoid being seen, to get away, to hide his trail—these were the sole ideas in his mind as he headed for Deception Pass, and he directed all his acuteness of eye and ear, and the keenness of a rider's judgment for distance and ground, to stern accomplishment of the task. He kept to the sage far to the left of the trail leading into the Pass. He walked ten miles and looked back a thousand times. Always the graceful, purple wave of sage remained wide and lonely, a clear, undotted waste. Coming to a stretch of rocky ground, he took advantage of it to cross the trail and then continued down on the right. At length he persuaded himself that he would be able to see riders mounted on horses before they could see him on the little burro, and he rode bareback.

Hour by hour the tireless burro kept to his faithful, steady trot. The sun sank and the long shadows lengthened down the slope. Moving veils of purple twilight crept out of the hollows and, mustering and forming on the levels, soon merged and shaded into night. Venters guided the burro nearer to the trail, so that he could see its white line from the ridges, and rode on through the hours.

Once down in the Pass without leaving a trail, he would hold himself safe for the time being. When late in the night he reached the break in the sage, he sent the burro down ahead of him, and started an avalanche that all but buried the animal at the bottom of the trail. Bruised and battered as he was, he had a moment's elation, for he had hidden his tracks. Once more he mounted the burro and rode on. The hour was the blackest of the night when he made the thicket which inclosed his old camp. Here he turned the burro loose in the grass near the spring, and then lay down on his old bed of leaves.

He felt only vaguely, as outside things, the ache and burn and throb of the muscles of his body. But a dammed-up torrent of emotion at last burst its bounds, and the hour that saw his release from immediate action was one that confounded him in the reaction of his spirit. He suffered without understanding why. He caught glimpses into himself, into unlit darkness of soul. The fire that had blistered him and the cold which had frozen him now united in one torturing possession of his mind and heart, and like a fiery steed with ice-shod feet, ranged his being, ran rioting through his blood, trampling the resurging good, dragging ever at the evil.

Out of the subsiding chaos came a clear question. What had happened? He had left the valley to go to Cottonwoods. Why? It seemed that he had gone to kill a man—Oldring! The name riveted his consciousness upon the one man of all men upon earth whom he had wanted to meet. He had met the rustler. Venters recalled the smoky haze of the saloon, the dark-visaged men, the huge Oldring. He saw him step out of the door, a splendid specimen of manhood, a handsome giant with purple-black and sweeping beard. He remembered inquisitive gaze of falcon eyes. He heard himself repeating: "OLDRING, BESS IS ALIVE! BUT SHE'S DEAD TO YOU," and he felt himself jerk, and his ears throbbed to the thunder of a gun, and he saw the giant sink slowly to his knees. Was that only the vitality of him—that awful light in the eyes—only the hard-dying life of a tremendously powerful brute? A broken whisper, strange as death:

"MAN—WHY—DIDN'T—YOU WAIT! BESS—WAS—" And Oldring plunged face forward, dead.

"I killed him," cried Venters, in remembering shock. "But it wasn't THAT. Ah, the look in his eyes and his whisper!"

Herein lay the secret that had clamored to him through all the tumult and stress of his emotions. What a look in the eyes of a man shot through the heart! It had been neither hate nor ferocity nor fear of men nor fear of death. It had been no passionate glinting spirit of a fearless foe, willing shot for shot, life for life, but lacking physical power. Distinctly recalled now, never to be forgotten, Venters saw in Oldring's magnificent eyes the rolling of great, glad surprise—softness—love! Then came a shadow and the terrible superhuman striving of his spirit to speak. Oldring shot through the heart, had fought and forced back death, not for a moment in which to shoot or curse, but to whisper strange words.

What words for a dying man to whisper! Why had not Venters waited? For what? That was no plea for life. It was regret that there was not a moment of life left in which to speak. Bess was—Herein lay renewed torture for Venters. What had Bess been to Oldring? The old question, like a specter, stalked from its grave to haunt him. He had overlooked, he had forgiven, he had loved and he had forgotten; and now, out of the mystery of a dying man's whisper rose again that perverse, unsatisfied, jealous uncertainty. Bess had loved that splendid, black-crowned giant—by her own confession she had loved him; and in Venters's soul again flamed up the jealous hell. Then into the clamoring hell burst the shot that had killed Oldring, and it rang in a wild fiendish gladness, a hateful, vengeful joy. That passed to the memory of the love and light in Oldring's eyes and the mystery in his whisper. So the changing, swaying emotions fluctuated in Venters's heart.

This was the climax of his year of suffering and the crucial struggle of his life. And when the gray dawn came he rose, a gloomy, almost heartbroken man, but victor over evil passions. He could not change the past; and, even if he had not loved Bess with all his soul, he had grown into a man who would not change the future he had planned for her. Only, and once for all, he must know the truth, know the worst, stifle all these insistent doubts and subtle hopes and jealous fancies, and kill the past by knowing truly what Bess had been to Oldring. For that matter he knew—he had always known, but he must hear it spoken. Then, when they had safely gotten out of that wild country to take up a new and an absorbing life, she would forget, she would be happy, and through that, in the years to come, he could not but find life worth living.

All day he rode slowly and cautiously up the Pass, taking time to peer around corners, to pick out hard ground and grassy patches, and to make sure there was no one in pursuit. In the night sometime he came to the smooth, scrawled rocks dividing the valley, and here set the burro at liberty. He walked beyond, climbed the slope and the dim, starlit gorge. Then, weary to the point of exhaustion, he crept into a shallow cave and fell asleep.

In the morning, when he descended the trail, he found the sun was pouring a golden stream of light through the arch of the great stone bridge. Surprise Valley, like a valley of dreams, lay mystically soft and beautiful, awakening to the golden flood which was rolling away its slumberous bands of mist, brightening its walled faces.

While yet far off he discerned Bess moving under the silver spruces, and soon the barking of the dogs told him that they had seen him. He heard the mocking-birds singing in the trees, and then the twittering of the quail. Ring and Whitie came bounding toward him, and behind them ran Bess, her hands outstretched.

"Bern! You're back! You're back!" she cried, in joy that rang of her loneliness. "Yes, I'm back," he said, as she rushed to meet him.

She had reached out for him when suddenly, as she saw him closely, something checked her, and as quickly all her joy fled, and with it her color, leaving her pale and trembling.

"Oh! What's happened?"

"A good deal has happened, Bess. I don't need to tell you what. And I'm played out. Worn out in mind more than body."

"Dear—you look strange to me!" faltered Bess.

"Never mind that. I'm all right. There's nothing for you to be scared about. Things are going to turn out just as we have planned. As soon as I'm rested we'll make a break to get out of the country. Only now, right now, I must know the truth about you."

"Truth about me?" echoed Bess, shrinkingly. She seemed to be casting back into her mind for a forgotten key. Venters himself, as he saw her, received a pang.

"Yes—the truth. Bess, don't misunderstand. I haven't changed that way. I love you still. I'll love you more afterward. Life will be just as sweet—sweeter to us. We'll be—be married as soon as ever we can. We'll be happy—but there's a devil in me. A perverse, jealous devil! Then I've queer fancies. I forgot for a long time. Now all those fiendish little whispers of doubt and faith and fear and hope come torturing me again. I've got to kill them with the truth."

"I'll tell you anything you want to know," she replied, frankly.

"Then by Heaven! we'll have it over and done with! . . . Bess—did Oldring love you?"

"Certainly he did."

"Did—did you love him?"

"Of course. I told you so."

"How can you tell it so lightly?" cried Venters, passionately. "Haven't you any sense of—of—" He choked back speech. He felt the rush of pain and passion. He seized her in rude, strong hands and drew her close. He looked straight into her dark-blue eyes. They were shadowing with the old wistful light, hut they were as clear as the limpid water of the spring. They were earnest, solemn in unutterable love and faith and abnegation. Venters shivered. He knew he was looking into her soul. He knew she could not lie in that moment; but that she might tell the truth, looking at him with those eyes, almost killed his belief in purity.

"What are—what were you to—to Oldring?" he panted, fiercely. "I am his daughter," she replied, instantly.

Venters slowly let go of her. There was a violent break in the force of his feeling—then creeping blankness. "What—was it—you said?" he asked, in a kind of dull wonder.

"I am his daughter."

"Oldring's daughter?" queried Venters, with life gathering in his voice. "Yes."

With a passionately awakening start he grasped her hands and drew her close. "All the time—you've been Oldring's daughter?"

"Yes, of course all the time—always."

"But Bess, you told me—you let me think—I made out you were—a—so—so ashamed."

"It is my shame," she said, with voice deep and full, and now the scarlet fired her cheek. "I told you—I'm nothing—nameless—just Bess, Oldring's girl!"

"I know—I remember. But I never thought—" he went on, hurriedly, huskily. "That time—when you lay dying—you prayed—you—somehow I got the idea you were bad."

"Bad?" she asked, with a little laugh.

She looked up with a faint smile of bewilderment and the absolute unconsciousness of a child. Venters gasped in the gathering might of the truth. She did not understand his meaning.

"Bess! Bess!" He clasped her in his arms, hiding her eyes against his breast. She must not see his face in that moment. And he held her while he looked out across the valley. In his dim and blinded sight, in the blur of golden light and moving mist, he saw Oldring. She was the rustler's nameless daughter. Oldring had loved her. He had so guarded her, so kept her from women and men and knowledge of life that her mind was as a child's. That was part of the secret—part of the mystery. That was the wonderful truth. Not only was she not bad, but good, pure, innocent above all innocence in the world—the innocence of lonely girlhood.

He saw Oldring's magnificent eyes, inquisitive, searching, softening. He saw them flare in amaze, in gladness, with love, then suddenly strain in terrible effort of will. He heard Oldring whisper and saw him sway like a log and fall. Then a million bellowing, thundering voices—gunshots of conscience, thunderbolts of remorse—dinned horribly in his ears. He had killed Bess's father. Then a rushing wind filled his ears like a moan of wind in the cliffs, a knell indeed—Oldring's knell.

He dropped to his knees and hid his face against Bess, and grasped her with the hands of a drowning man.

"My God! . . . My God! . . . Oh, Bess! . . . Forgive me! Never mind what I've done—what I've thought. But forgive me. I'll give you my life. I'll live for you. I'll love you. Oh, I do love you as no man ever loved a woman. I want you to know—to remember that I fought a fight for you—however blind I was. I thought—I thought—never mind what I thought—but I loved you—I asked you to marry me. Let that—let me have that to hug to my heart. Oh, Bess, I was driven! And I might have known! I could not rest nor sleep till I had this mystery solved.

God! how things work out!"

"Bern, you're weak—trembling—you talk wildly," cried Bess. "You've overdone your strength. There's nothing to forgive. There's no mystery except your love for me. You have come back to me!"

And she clasped his head tenderly in her arms and pressed it closely to her throbbing breast.

CHAPTER XIX
FAY

At the home of Jane Withersteen Little Fay was climbing Lassiter's knee. "Does oo love me?" she asked.

Lassiter, who was as serious with Fay as he was gentle and loving, assured her in earnest and elaborate speech that he was her devoted subject. Fay looked thoughtful and appeared to be debating the duplicity of men or searching for a supreme test to prove this cavalier.

"Does oo love my new mower?" she asked, with bewildering suddenness.

Jane Withersteen laughed, and for the first time in many a day she felt a stir of her pulse and warmth in her cheek.

It was a still drowsy summer of afternoon, and the three were sitting in the shade of the wooded knoll that faced the sage-slope Little Fay's brief spell of unhappy longing for her mother—the childish, mystic gloom—had passed, and now where Fay was there were prattle and laughter and glee. She had emerged Iron sorrow to be the incarnation of joy and loveliness. She had growl supernaturally sweet and beautiful. For Jane Withersteen the child was an answer to prayer, a blessing, a possession infinitely more precious than all she had lost. For Lassiter, Jane divined that little Fay had become a religion.

"Does oo love my new mower?" repeated Fay.

Lassiter's answer to this was a modest and sincere affirmative. "Why don't oo marry my new mower an' be my favver?"

Of the thousands of questions put by little Fay to Lassiter the was the first he had been unable to answer. "Fay—Fay, don't ask questions like that," said Jane.

"Why?"

"Because," replied Jane. And she found it strangely embarrassing to meet the child's gaze. It seemed to her that Fay's violet eyes looked through her with piercing wisdom.

"Oo love him, don't oo?"

"Dear child—run and play," said Jane, "but don't go too far. Don't go from this little hill." Fay pranced off wildly, joyous over freedom that had not been granted her for weeks. "Jane, why are children more sincere than grown-up persons?" asked Lassiter.

"Are they?"

"I reckon so. Little Fay there—she sees things as they appear on the face. An Indian does that. So does a dog. An' an Indian an' a dog are most of the time right in what they see. Mebbe a child is always right."

"Well, what does Fay see?" asked Jane.

"I reckon you know. I wonder what goes on in Fay's mind when she sees part of the truth with the wise eyes of a child, an' wantin' to know more, meets with strange falseness from you? Wait! You are false in a way, though you're the best woman I ever knew. What I want to say is this. Fay has taken you're pretendin' to—to care for me for the thing it looks on the face. An' her little formin' mind asks questions. An' the answers she gets are different from the looks of things. So she'll grow up gradually takin' on that falseness, an' be like the rest of the women, an' men, too. An' the truth of this falseness to life is proved by your appearin' to love me when you don't. Things aren't what they seem."

"Lassiter, you're right. A child should be told the absolute truth. But—is that possible? I haven't been able to do it, and all my life I've loved the truth, and I've prided myself upon being truthful. Maybe that was only egotism. I'm learning much, my friend. Some of those blinding scales have fallen from my eyes. And—and as to caring for you, I think I care a great deal. How much, how little, I couldn't say. My heart is almost broken. Lassiter. So now is not a good time to judge of affection. I can still play and be merry with Fay. I can still dream. But when I attempt serious thought I'm dazed. I don't think. I don't care any more. I don't pray! . . . Think of that, my friend! But in spite of my numb feeling I believe I'll rise out of all this dark agony a better woman, with greater love of man and God. I'm on the rack now; I'm senseless to all but pain, and growing dead to that. Sooner or later I shall rise out of this stupor. I'm waiting the hour."

"It'll soon come, Jane," replied Lassiter, soberly. "Then I'm afraid for you. Years are terrible things, an' for years you've been bound. Habit of years is strong as life itself. Somehow, though, I believe as you—that you'll come out of it all a finer woman. I'm waitin', too. An' I'm wonderin'—I reckon, Jane, that marriage between us is out of all human reason?"

"Lassiter! . . . My dear friend! . . . It's impossible for us to marry!"

"Why—as Fay says?" inquired Lassiter, with gentle persistence.

"Why! I never thought why. But it's not possible. I am Jane, daughter of Withersteen. My father would rise out of his grave. I'm of Mormon birth. I'm being broken. But I'm still a Mormon woman. And you—you are Lassiter!"

"Mebbe I'm not so much Lassiter as I used to be."

"What was it you said? Habit of years is strong as life itself! You can't change the one habit—the purpose of your life. For you still pack those black guns! You still nurse your passion for blood."

A smile, like a shadow, flickered across his face. "No."

"Lassiter, I lied to you. But I beg of you—don't you lie to me. I've great respect for you. I believe you're softened toward most, perhaps all, my people except—But when I speak of your purpose, your hate, your guns, I have only him in mind. I don't believe you've changed."

For answer he unbuckled the heavy cartridge-belt, and laid it with the heavy, swing gun-sheaths in her lap. "Lassiter!" Jane whispered, as she gazed from him to the black, cold guns. Without them he appeared shorn of strength, defenseless, a smaller man. Was she Delilah? Swiftly, conscious of only one motive—refusal to see this man called craven by his enemies—she rose, and with blundering fingers buckled the belt round his waist where it belonged.

"Lassiter, I am a coward."

"Come with me out of Utah—where I can put away my guns an' be a man," he said. "I reckon I'll prove it to you then! Come! You've got Black Star back, an' Night an' Bells. Let's take the racers an' little Fay, en' race out of Utah. The hosses an' the child are all you have left. Come!"

"No, no, Lassiter. I'll never leave Utah. What would I do in the world with my broken fortunes and my broken heart? Ill never leave these purple slopes I love so well."

"I reckon I ought to 've knowed that. Presently you'll be livin' down here in a hovel, en' presently Jane Withersteen will be a memory. I only wanted to have a chance to show you how a man—any man—can be better 'n he was. If we left Utah I could prove—I reckon I could prove this thing you call love. It's strange, an' hell an' heaven at once, Jane Withersteen. 'Pears to me that you've thrown away your big heart on love—love of religion an' duty an' churchmen, an' riders an' poor families an' poor children! Yet you can't see what love is—how it changes a person! . . . Listen, an' in tellin' you Milly Erne's story I'll show you how love changed her.

"Milly an' me was children when our family moved from Missouri to Texas, an' we growed up in Texas ways same as if we'd been born there. We had been poor, an' there we prospered. In time the little village where we went became a town, an' strangers an' new families kept movin' in. Milly was the belle them days. I can see her now, a little girl no bigger 'n a bird, an' as pretty. She had the finest eyes, dark blue-black when she was excited, an' beautiful all the time. You remember Milly's eyes! An' she had light-brown hair with streaks of gold, an' a mouth that every feller wanted to kiss.

"An' about the time Milly was the prettiest an' the sweetest, along came a young minister who began to ride some of a race with the other fellers for Milly. An' he won. Milly had always been strong on religion, an' when she met Frank Erne she went in heart an' soul for the salvation of souls. Fact was, Milly, through study of the Bible an' attendin' church an' revivals, went a little out of her head. It didn't worry the old folks none, an' the only worry to me was Milly's everlastin' prayin' an' workin' to save my soul. She never converted me, but we was the best of comrades, an' I reckon no brother an' sister ever loved each other better. Well, Frank Erne an me hit up a great friendship. He was a strappin' feller, good to look at, an' had the most pleasin' ways. His religion never bothered me, for he could hunt an' fish an' ride an' be a good feller. After buffalo once, he come pretty near to savin' my life. We got to be thick as brothers, an' he was the only man I ever seen who I thought was good enough for Milly. An' the day they were married I got drunk for the only time in my life.

"Soon after that I left home—it seems Milly was the only one who could keep me home—an' I went to the bad, as to prosperin' I saw some pretty hard life in the Pan Handle, an' then I went North. In them days Kansas an' Nebraska was as bad, come to think of it, as these days right here on the border of Utah. I got to be pretty handy with guns. An' there wasn't many riders as could beat me ridin'. An' I can say all modest-like that I never seen the white man who could track a hoss or a steer or a man with me. Afore I knowed it two years slipped by, an' all at once I got homesick, en' purled a bridle south.

"Things at home had changed. I never got over that homecomin'. Mother was dead an' in her grave. Father was a silent, broken man, killed already on his feet. Frank Erne was a ghost of his old self, through with workin', through with preach-in', almost through with livin', an' Milly was gone! . . . It was a long time before I got the story. Father had no mind left, an' Frank Erne was afraid to talk. So I had to pick up whet 'd happened from different people.

"It 'pears that soon after I left home another preacher come to the little town. An' he an' Frank become rivals. This feller was different from Frank. He preached some other kind of religion, and he was quick an' passionate, where Frank was slow an' mild. He went after people, women specially. In looks he couldn't compare to Frank Erne, but he had power over women. He had a voice, an' he talked an' talked an' preached an' preached. Milly fell under his influence.. She became mightily interested in his religion. Frank had patience with her, as was his way, an' let her be as interested as she liked. All religions were devoted to one God, he said, an' it wouldn't hurt Milly none to study a different point of view. So the new preacher often called on Milly, an' sometimes in Frank's absence. Frank was a cattle-man between Sundays.

"Along about this time an incident come off that I couldn't get much light on. A stranger come to town, an' was seen with the preacher. This stranger was a big man with an eye like blue ice, an' a beard of gold. He had money, an' he 'peered a man of mystery, an' the town went to buzzin' when he disappeared about the same time as a young woman known to be mightily interested in the new preacher's religion. Then, presently, along comes a man from somewheres in Illinois, en' he up an' spots this preacher as a famous Mormon proselyter. That riled Frank Erne as nothin' ever before, an' from rivals they come to be bitter enemies. An' it ended in Frank goin' to the meetin'-house where Milly was listenin', en' before her en' everybody else he called that preacher—called him, well, almost as hard as Venters called Tull here sometime back. An' Frank followed up that call with a hosswhippin', en' he drove the proselyter out of town.

"People noticed, so 'twas said, that Milly's sweet disposition changed. Some said it was because she would soon become a mother, en' others said she was pinin' after the new religion. An' there was women who said right out that she was pinin' after the Mormon. Anyway, one mornin' Frank rode in from one of his trips, to find Milly gone. He had no real near neighbors—livin' a little out of town—but those who was nearest said a wagon had gone by in the night, an' they though it stopped at her door. Well, tracks always tell, an' there was the wagon tracks an' hoss tracks an' man tracks. The news spread like wildfire that Milly had run off from her husband. Everybody but Frank believed it an' wasn't slow in tellin' why she run off. Mother had always hated that strange streak of Milly's, takin' up with the new religion as she had, an' she believed Milly ran off with the Mormon. That hastened mother's death, an' she died unforgivin'. Father wasn't the kind to bow down under disgrace or misfortune but he had surpassin' love for Milly, an' the loss of her broke him.

"From the minute I heard of Milly's disappearance I never believed she went off of her own free will. I knew Milly, an' I knew she couldn't have done that. I stayed at home awhile, tryin' to make Frank Erne talk. But if he knowed anythin' then he wouldn't tell it. So I set out to find Milly. An' I tried to get on the trail of that proselyter. I knew if I ever struck a town he'd visited that I'd get a trail. I knew, too, that nothin' short of hell would stop his proselytin'. An' I rode from town to town. I had a blind faith that somethin' was guidin' me. An' as the weeks an' months went by I growed into a strange sort of a man, I guess. Anyway, people were afraid of me. Two years after that, way over in a corner of Texas, I struck a town where my man had been. He'd jest left. People said he came to that town without a woman. I back-trailed my man through Arkansas an' Mississippi, an' the old trail got hot again in Texas. I found the town where he first went after leavin' home. An' here I got track of Milly. I found a cabin where she had given birth to her baby. There was no way to tell whether she'd been kept a prisoner or not. The feller who owned the place was a mean, silent sort of a skunk, an' as I was leavin' I jest took a chance an' left my mark on him. Then I went home again.

"It was to find I hadn't any home, no more. Father had been dead a year. Frank Erne still lived in the house where Milly had left him. I stayed with him awhile, an' I grew old watchin' him. His farm had gone to weed, his cattle had strayed or been rustled, his house weathered till it wouldn't keep out rain nor wind. An' Frank set on the porch and whittled sticks, an' day by day wasted away. There was times when he ranted about like a crazy man, but mostly he was always sittin' an' starin' with eyes that made a man curse. I figured Frank had a secret fear that I needed to know. An' when I told him I'd trailed Milly for near three years an' had got trace of her, an' saw where she'd had her baby, I thought he would drop dead at my feet. An' when he'd come round more natural-like he begged me to give up the trail. But he wouldn't explain. So I let him alone, an' watched him day en' night.

"An' I found there was one thing still precious to him, an' it was a little drawer where he kept his papers. This was in the room where he slept. An' it 'peered he seldom slept. But after bein' patient I got the contents of that drawer an' found two letters from Milly. One was a long letter written a few months after her disappearance. She had been bound an' gagged an' dragged away from her home by three men, an' she named them—Hurd, Metzger, Slack. They was strangers to her. She was taken to the little town where I found trace of her two years after. But she didn't send the letter from that town. There she was penned in. 'Peared that the proselytes, who had, of course, come on the scene, was not runnin' any risks of losin' her. She went on to say that for a time she was out of her head, an' when she got right again all that kept her alive was the baby. It was a beautiful baby, she said, an' all she thought an' dreamed of was somehow to get baby back to its father, an' then she'd thankfully lay down and die. An' the letter ended abrupt, in the middle of a sentence, en' it wasn't signed.

"The second letter was written more than two years after the first. It was from Salt Lake City. It simply said that Milly had heard her brother was on her trail. She asked Frank to tell her brother to give up the search because if he didn't she would suffer in a way too horrible to tell. She didn't beg. She just stated a fact an' made the simple request. An' she ended that letter by sayin' she would soon leave Salt Lake City with the man she had come to love, en' would never be heard of again.

"I recognized Milly's handwritin', an' I recognized her way of puttin' things.

But that second letter told me of some great change in her. Ponderin' over it, I felt at last she'd either come to love that feller an' his religion, or some terrible fear made her lie an' say so. I couldn't be sure which. But, of course, I meant to find out. I'll say here, if I'd known Mormons then as I do now I'd left Milly to her fate. For mebbe she was right about what she'd suffer if I kept on her trail. But I was young an' wild them days. First I went to the town where she'd first been taken, an' I went to the place where she'd been kept. I got that skunk who owned the place, an' took him out in the woods, an' made him tell all he knowed. That wasn't much as to length, but it was pure hell's-fire in substance. This time I left him some incapaci-tated for any more skunk work short of hell. Then I hit the trail for Utah.

"That was fourteen years ago. I saw the incomin' of most of the Mormons. It was a wild country an' a wild time. I rode from town to town, village to village, ranch to ranch, camp to camp. I never stayed long in one place. I never had but one idea. I never rested. Four years went by, an' I knowed every trail in northern Utah. I kept on an' as time went by, an' I'd begun to grow old in my search, I had firmer, blinder faith in whatever was guidin' me. Once I read about a feller who sailed the seven seas an' traveled the world, an' he had a story to tell, an' whenever he seen the man to whom he must tell that story he knowed him on sight. I was like that, only I had a question to ask. An' always I knew the man of whom I must ask. So I never really lost the trail, though for many years it was the dimmest trail ever fol-lowed by any man.

"Then come a change in my luck. Along in Central Utah I rounded up Hurd, an' I whispered somethin' in his ear, an' watched his face, an' then throwed a gun against his bowels. An' he died with his teeth so tight shut I couldn't have pried them open with a knife. Slack an' Metzger that same year both heard me whisper the same question, an' neither would they speak a word when they lay dyin'. Long before I'd learned no man of this breed or class—or God knows what—would give up any secrets! I had to see in a man's fear of death the connections with Milly Erne's fate. An' as the years passed at long intervals I would find such a man.

"So as I drifted on the long trail down into southern Utah my name preceded me, an' I had to meet a people prepared for me, an' ready with guns. They made me a gun-man. An' that suited me. In all this time signs of the proselyter an' the giant with the blue-ice eyes an' the gold beard seemed to fade dimmer out of the trail. Only twice in ten years did I find a trace of that mysterious man who had visited the proselyter at my home village. What he had to do with Milly's fate was beyond all hope for me to learn, unless my guidin' spirit led me to him! As for the other man, I knew, as sure as I breathed en' the stars shone en' the wind blew, that I'd meet him some day.

"Eighteen years I've been on the trail. An' it led me to the last lonely villages of the Utah border. Eighteen years! . . . I feel pretty old now. I was only twenty when I hit that trail. Well, as I told you, back here a ways a Gentile said Jane Withersteen could tell me about Milly Erne an' show me her grave!"

The low voice ceased, and Lassiter slowly turned his sombrero round and round, and appeared to be counting the silver ornaments on the band. Jane, leaning toward him, sat as if petrified, listening intently, waiting to hear more. She could have shrieked, but power of tongue and lips were denied her. She saw only this sad, gray, passion-worn man, and she heard only the faint rustling of the leaves.

"Well, I came to Cottonwoods," went on Lassiter, "an' you showed me Milly's grave. An' though your teeth have been shut tighter 'n them of all the dead men lyin' back along that trail, jest the same you told me the secret I've lived these eighteen years to hear! Jane, I said you'd tell me without ever me askin'. I didn't need to ask my question here. The day, you remember, when that fat party throwed a gun on me in your court, an'—"

"Oh! Hush!" whispered Jane, blindly holding up her hands.

"I seen in your face that Dyer, now a bishop, was the proselyter who ruined Milly Erne."

For an instant Jane Withersteen's brain was a whirling chaos and she recovered to find herself grasping at Lassiter like one drowning. And as if by a lightning stroke she sprang from her dull apathy into exquisite torture.

"It's a lie! Lassiter! No, no!" she moaned. "I swear—you're wrong!"

"Stop! You'd perjure yourself! But I'll spare you that. You poor woman! Still blind! Still faithful! . . . Listen. I know. Let that settle it. An' I give up my purpose!"

"What is it—you say?"

"I give up my purpose. I've come to see an' feel differently. I can't help poor Milly. An' I've outgrowed revenge. I've come to see I can be no judge for men. I can't kill a man jest for hate. Hate ain't the same with me since I loved you and little Fay."

"Lassiter! You mean you won't kill him?" Jane whispered. "No."

"For my sake?"

"I reckon. I can't understand, but I'll respect your feelin's."

"Because you—oh, because you love me? . . . Eighteen years! You were that terrible Lassiter! And now—because you love me?"

"That's it, Jane."

"Oh, you'll make me love you! How can I help but love you? My heart must be stone. But—oh, Lassiter, wait, wait! Give me time. I'm not what I was. Once it was so easy to love. Now it's easy to hate. Wait! My faith in God—some God—still lives. By it I see happier times for you, poor passion-swayed wanderer! For me—a miserable, broken woman. I loved your sister Milly. I will love you. I can't have fallen so low—I can't be so abandoned by God—that I've no love left to give you. Wait! Let us forget Milly's sad life. Ah, I knew it as no one else on earth! There's one thing I shall tell you—if you are at my death-bed, but I can't speak now."

"I reckon I don't want to hear no more," said Lassiter.

Jane leaned against him, as if some pent-up force had rent its way out, she fell into a paroxysm of weeping.

Lassiter held her in silent sympathy. By degrees she regained composure, and she was rising, sensible of being relieved of a weighty burden, when a sudden start on Lassiter's part alarmed her.

"I heard hosses—hosses with muffled hoofs!" he said; and he got up guardedly.

"Where's Fay?" asked Jane, hurriedly glancing round the shady knoll. The bright-haired child, who had appeared to be close all the time, was not in sight.

"Fay!" called Jane.

No answering shout of glee. No patter of flying feet. Jane saw Lassiter stiffen. "Fay—oh—Fay!" Jane almost screamed.

The leaves quivered and rustled; a lonesome cricket chirped in the grass, a bee hummed by. The silence of the waning afternoon breathed hateful portent. It terrified Jane. When had silence been so infernal?

"She's—only—strayed—out—of earshot," faltered Jane, looking at Lassiter.

Pale, rigid as a statue, the rider stood, not in listening, searching posture, but in one of doomed certainty. Suddenly he grasped Jane with an iron hand, and, turning his face from her gaze, he strode with her from the knoll.

"See—Fay played here last—a house of stones an' sticks . . . .An' here's a corral of pebbles with leaves for hosses," said Lassiter, stridently, and pointed to the ground. "Back an' forth she trailed here . . . .See, she's buried somethin'—a dead grasshopper—there's a tombstone . . . here she went, chasin' a lizard—see the tiny streaked trail . . . she pulled bark off this cottonwood . . . look in the dust of the path—the letters you taught her—she's drawn pictures of birds en' hosses an' people . . . .Look, a cross! Oh, Jane, your cross!"

Lassiter dragged Jane on, and as if from a book read the meaning of little Fay's trail. All the way down the knoll, through the shrubbery, round and round a cottonwood, Fay's vagrant fancy left records of her sweet musings and innocent play. Long had she lingered round a bird-nest to leave therein the gaudy wing of a butterfly. Long had she played beside the running stream sending adrift vessels freighted with pebbly cargo. Then she had wandered through the deep grass, her tiny feet scarcely turning a fragile blade, and she had dreamed beside some old faded flowers. Thus her steps led her into the broad lane. The little dimpled imprints of her bare feet showed clean-cut in the dust they went a little way down the lane; and then, at a point where they stopped, the great tracks of a man led out from the shrubbery and returned.

CHAPTER XX

LASSITER'S WAY

Footprints told the story of little Fay's abduction. In anguish Jane Withersteen turned speechlessly to Lassiter, and, confirming her fears, she saw him gray-faced, aged all in a moment, stricken as if by a mortal blow.

Then all her life seemed to fall about her in wreck and ruin.

"It's all over," she heard her voice whisper. "It's ended. I'm going—I'm going—"

"Where?" demanded Lassiter, suddenly looming darkly over her.

"To—to those cruel men—"

"Speak names!" thundered Lassiter.

"To Bishop Dyer—to Tull," went on Jane, shocked into obedience. "Well—what for?"

"I want little Fay. I can't live without her. They've stolen her as they stole Milly Erne's child. I must have little Fay. I want only her. I give up. I'll go and tell Bishop Dyer—I'm broken. I'll tell him I'm ready for the yoke—only give me back Fay— and—and I'll marry Tull!"

"Never!" hissed Lassiter.

His long arm leaped at her. Almost running, he dragged her under the cotton-woods, across the court, into the huge hall of Withersteen House, and he shut the door with a force that jarred the heavy walls. Black Star and Night and Bells, since their return, had been locked in this hall, and now they stamped on the stone floor.

Lassiter released Jane and like a dizzy man swayed from her with a hoarse cry and leaned shaking against a table where he kept his rider's accoutrements. He began to fumble in his saddlebags. His action brought a clinking, metallic sound— the rattling of gun-cartridges. His fingers trembled as he slipped cartridges into an extra belt. But as he buckled it over the one he habitually wore his hands became steady. This second belt contained two guns, smaller than the black ones swinging low, and he slipped them round so that his coat hid them. Then he fell to swift action. Jane Withersteen watched him, fascinated but uncomprehending and she saw him rapidly saddle Black Star and Night. Then he drew her into the light of the huge windows, standing over her, gripping her arm with fingers like cold steel.

"Yes, Jane, it's ended—but you're not goin' to Dyer! . . . I'm goin' instead!"

Looking at him—he was so terrible of aspect—she could not comprehend his words. Who was this man with the face gray as death, with eyes that would have made her shriek had she the strength, with the strange, ruthlessly bitter lips? Where was the gentle Lassiter? What was this presence in the hall, about him, about her—this cold, invisible presence?

"Yes, it's ended, Jane," he was saying, so awfully quiet and cool and implacable, "an' I'm goin' to make a little call. I'll lock you in here, an' when I get back have the saddle-bags full of meat an bread. An' be ready to ride!"

"Lassiter!" cried Jane.

Desperately she tried to meet his gray eyes, in vain, desperately she tried again, fought herself as feeling and thought resurged in torment, and she succeeded, and then she knew.

"No—no—no!" she wailed. "You said you'd foregone your vengeance. You promised not to kill Bishop Dyer."

"If you want to talk to me about him—leave off the Bishop. I don't understand that name, or its use."

"Oh, hadn't you foregone your vengeance on—on Dyer? "Yes."

But—your actions—your words—your guns—your terrible looks! . . . They don't seem foregoing vengeance?"

"Jane, now it's justice."

"You'll—kill him?"

"If God lets me live another hour! If not God—then the devil who drives me!"

"You'll kill him—for yourself—for your vengeful hate?"

"No!"

"For Milly Erne's sake?"

"No."

"For little Fay's?"

"No!"

"Oh—for whose?"

"For yours!"

"His blood on my soul!" whispered Jane, and she fell to her knees. This was the long-pending hour of fruition. And the habit of years—the religious passion of her life—leaped from lethargy, and the long months of gradual drifting to doubt were as if they had never been. "If you spill his blood it'll be on my soul—and on my father's. Listen." And she clasped his knees, and clung there as he tried to raise her. "Listen. Am I nothing to you?"

"Woman—don't trifle at words! I love you! An' I'll soon prove it."

"I'll give myself to you—I'll ride away with you—marry you, if only you'll spare him?" His answer was a cold, ringing, terrible laugh.

"Lassiter—I'll love you. Spare him!"

"No."

She sprang up in despairing, breaking spirit, and encircled his neck with her arms, and held him in an embrace that he strove vainly to loosen. "Lassiter, would you kill me? I'm fighting my last fight for the principles of my youth—love of religion, love of father. You don't know—you can't guess the truth, and I can't speak ill. I'm losing all. I'm changing. All I've gone through is nothing to this hour. Pity me— help me in my weakness. You're strong again—oh, so cruelly, coldly strong! You're killing me. I see you—feel you as some other Lassiter! My master, be merciful—spare him!"

His answer was a ruthless smile.

She clung the closer to him, and leaned her panting breast on him, and lifted her face to his. "Lassiter, I do love you! It's leaped out of my agony. It comes suddenly with a terrible blow of truth. You are a man! I never knew it till now. Some wonderful change came to me when you buckled on these guns and showed that gray, awful face. I loved you then. All my life I've loved, but never as now. No woman can love like a broken woman. If it were not for one thing—just one thing—and yet! I can't speak it—I'd glory in your manhood—the lion in you that means to slay for me. Believe me—and spare Dyer. Be merciful—great as it's in you to be great .
. . .Oh, listen and believe—I have nothing, but I'm a woman—a beautiful woman, Lassiter—a passionate, loving woman—and I love you! Take me—hide me in some wild place—and love me and mend my broken heart. Spare him and take me away."

She lifted her face closer and closer to his, until their lips nearly touched, and she hung upon his neck, and with strength almost spent pressed and still pressed her palpitating body to his.

"Kiss me!" she whispered, blindly.

"No—not at your price!" he answered. His voice had changed or she had lost clearness of hearing. "Kiss me! . . . Are you a man? Kiss me and save me!"

"Jane, you never played fair with me. But now you're blisterin' your lips—blackenin' your soul with lies!"

"By the memory of my mother—by my Bible—no! No, I have no Bible! But by my hope of heaven I swear I love you!"

Lassiter's gray lips formed soundless words that meant even her love could not avail to bend his will. As if the hold of her arms was that of a child's he loosened it and stepped away.

"Wait! Don't go! Oh, hear a last word! . . . May a more just and merciful God than the God I was taught to worship judge me—forgive me—save me! For I can no longer keep silent! . . . Lassiter, in pleading for Dyer I've been pleading more for my father. My father was a Mormon master, close to the leaders of the church. It was my father who sent Dyer out to proselyte. It was my father who had the blue-ice eye and the beard of gold. It was my father you got trace of in the past years. Truly, Dyer ruined Milly Erne—dragged her from her home—to Utah—to Cottonwoods. But it was for my father! If Milly Erne was ever wife of a Mormon that Mormon was my father! I never knew—never will know whether or not she was a wife. Blind I may be, Lassiter—fanatically faithful to a false religion I may have been but I know justice, and my father is beyond human justice. Surely he is meeting just punishment—somewhere. Always it has appalled me—the thought of your killing Dyer for my father's sins. So I have prayed!"

"Jane, the past is dead. In my love for you I forgot the past. This thing I'm about to do ain't for myself or Milly or Fay. It s not because of anythin' that ever happened in the past, but for what is happenin' right now. It's for you! . . . An' listen. Since I was a boy I've never thanked God for anythin'. If there is a God—an' I've come to believe it—I thank Him now for the years that made me Lassiter! . . . I can reach down en' feel these big guns, en' know what I can do with them. An', Jane, only one of the miracles Dyer professes to believe in can save him!"

Again for Jane Withersteen came the spinning of her brain in darkness, and as she whirled in endless chaos she seemed to be falling at the feet of a luminous figure—a man—Lassiter—who had saved her from herself, who could not be changed, who would slay rightfully. Then she slipped into utter blackness.

When she recovered from her faint she became aware that she was lying on a couch near the window in her sitting-room. Her brow felt damp and cold and wet, some one was chafing her hands; she recognized Judkins, and then saw that his lean, hard face wore the hue and look of excessive agitation.

"Judkins!" Her voice broke weakly.

"Aw, Miss Withersteen, you're comin' round fine. Now jest lay still a little. You're all right; everythin's all right."

"Where is—he?"

"Who?"

"Lassiter!"

"You needn't worry none about him."

"Where is he? Tell me—instantly."

"Wal, he's in the other room patchin' up a few triflin' bullet holes."

"Ah! . . . Bishop' Dyer?"

"When I seen him last—a matter of half an hour ago, he was on his knees. He was some busy, but he wasn't prayin'!"

"How strangely you talk! I'll sit up. I'm—well, strong again. Tell me. Dyer on his knees! What was he doing?"

"Wal, beggin' your pardon fer blunt talk, Miss Withersteen, Dyer was on his knees an' not prayin'. You remember his big, broad hands? You've seen 'em raised in blessin' over old gray men an' little curly-headed

children like—like Fay Larkin! Come to think of thet, I disremember ever hearin' of his liftin' his big hands in blessin' over a woman. Wal, when I seen him last—jest a little while ago—he was on his knees, not prayin', as I remarked—an' he was pressin' his big hands over some bigger wounds."

"Man, you drive me mad! Did Lassiter kill Dyer?"

"Yes."

"Did he kill Tull?"

"No. Tull's out of the village with most of his riders. He's expected back before evenin'. Lassiter will hev to git away before Tull en' his riders come in. It's sure death fer him here. An' wuss fer you, too, Miss Withersteen. There'll be some of an uprisin' when Tull gits back."

"I shall ride away with Lassiter. Judkins, tell me all you saw—all you know about this killing." She realized, without wonder or amaze, how Judkins's one word, affirming the death of Dyer—that the catastrophe had fallen—had completed the change whereby she had been molded or beaten or broken into another woman. She felt calm, slightly cold, strong as she had not been strong since the first shadow fell upon her.

"I jest saw about all of it, Miss Withersteen, an' I'll be glad to tell you if you'll only hev patience with me," said Judkins, earnestly. "You see, I've been pecooliarly interested, an' nat'rully I'm some excited. An' I talk a lot thet mebbe ain't necessary, but I can't help thet.

"I was at the meetin'-house where Dyer was holdin' court. You know he allus acts as magistrate an' judge when Tull's away. An' the trial was fer tryin' what's left of my boy riders—thet helped me hold your cattle—fer a lot of hatched-up things the boys never did. We're used to thet, an' the boys wouldn't hev minded bein' locked up fer a while, or hevin' to dig ditches, or whatever the judge laid down. You see, I divided the gold you give me among all my boys, an' they all hid it, en' they all feel rich. Howsomever, court was adjourned before the judge passed sentence. Yes, ma'm, court was adjourned some strange an' quick, much as if lightnin' hed struck the meetin'-house.

"I hed trouble attendin' the trial, but I got in. There was a good many people there, all my boys, an' Judge Dyer with his several clerks. Also he hed with him the five riders who've been guardin' him pretty close of late.

They was Carter, Wright, Jengessen, an' two new riders from Stone Bridge. I didn't hear their names, but I heard they was handy men with guns an' they looked more like rustlers than riders. Anyway, there they was, the five all in a row.

"Judge Dyer was tellin' Willie Kern, one of my best an' steadiest boys—Dyer was tellin' him how there was a ditch opened near Willie's home lettin' water through his lot, where it hadn't ought to go. An' Willie was tryin' to git a word in to prove he wasn't at home all the day it happened—which was true, as I know—but Willie couldn't git a word in, an' then Judge Dyer went on layin' down the law. An' all to onct he happened to look down the long room. An' if ever any man turned to stone he was thet man.

"Nat'rully I looked back to see what hed acted so powerful strange on the judge. An' there, half-way up the room, in the middle of the wide aisle, stood Lassiter! All white an' black he looked, an' I can't think of anythin' he resembled, onless it's death. Venters made thet same room some still an' chilly when he called Tull; but this was different. I give my word, Miss Withersteen, thet I went cold to my very marrow. I don't know why. But Lassiter had a way about him thet's awful. He spoke a word—a name—I couldn't understand it, though he spoke clear as a bell. I was too excited, mebbe. Judge Dyer must hev understood it, an' a lot more thet was mystery to me, for he pitched forrard out of his chair right onto the platform.

"Then them five riders, Dyer's bodyguards, they jumped up, an' two of them thet I found out afterward were the strangers from Stone Bridge, they piled right out of a winder, so quick you couldn't catch your breath. It was plain they wasn't Mormons.

"Jengessen, Carter, an' Wright eyed Lassiter, for what must hev been a second an' seemed like an hour, an' they went white en' strung. But they didn't weaken nor lose their nerve.

"I hed a good look at Lassiter. He stood sort of stiff, bendin' a little, an' both his arms were crooked an' his hands looked like a hawk's claws. But there ain't no tellin' how his eyes looked. I know this, though, an' thet is his eyes could read the mind of any man about to throw a gun. An' in watchin' him, of course, I couldn't see the three men go fer their guns. An' though I was lookin' right at Lassiter—lookin' hard—I couldn't see how he drawed. He was quicker 'n eyesight—thet's all. But I seen the red spurtin' of his guns, en' heard his shots jest the very littlest instant before I heard the shots of the riders. An' when I turned, Wright an' Carter was down, en' Jengessen, who's tough like a steer, was pullin' the trigger of a wabblin' gun. But it was plain he was shot through, plumb center. An' sudden he fell with a crash, an' his gun clattered on the floor.

"Then there was a hell of a silence. Nobody breathed. Sartin I didn't, anyway. I saw Lassiter slip a smokin' gun back in a belt. But he hadn't throwed either of the big black guns, an' I thought thet strange. An' all this was happenin' quick—you can't imagine how quick.

"There come a scrapin' on the floor an' Dyer got up, his face like lead. I wanted to watch Lassiter, but Dyer's face, onct I seen it like thet, glued my eyes. I seen him go fer his gun—why, I could hev done better, quicker—an' then there was a thunderin' shot from Lassiter, an' it hit Dyer's right arm, an' his gun went off as it dropped. He looked at Lassiter like a cornered sage-wolf, an' sort of howled, an' reached down fer his gun. He'd jest picked it off the floor an' was raisin' it when another thunderin' shot almost tore thet arm off—so it seemed to me. The gun dropped again an' he went down on his knees, kind of flounderin' after it. It was some strange an' terrible to see his awful earnestness. Why would such a man cling so to life? Anyway, he got the gun with left hand an' was raisin' it, pullin' trigger in his madness, when the third thunderin' shot hit his left arm, an' he dropped the gun again. But thet left arm wasn't useless yet, fer he grabbed up the gun, an' with a shakin' aim thet would hev been pitiful to me—in any other man—he began to shoot. One wild bullet struck a man twenty feet from Lassiter. An' it killed thet man, as I seen afterward. Then come a bunch of thunderin' shots—nine I calkilated after, fer they come so quick I couldn't count them—an' I knew Lassiter hed turned the black guns loose on Dyer.

"I'm tellin' you straight, Miss Withersteen, fer I want you to know. Afterward you'll git over it. I've seen some soul-rackin' scenes on this Utah border, but this was the awfulest. I remember I closed my eyes, an' fer a minute I thought of the strangest things, out of place there, such as you'd never dream would come to mind. I saw the sage, an' runnin' hosses—an' thet's the beautfulest sight to me—an' I saw dim things in the dark, an' there was a kind of hummin' in my ears. An' I remember distinctly—fer it was what made all these things whirl out of my mind an' opened my eyes—I remember distinctly it was the smell of gunpowder.

"The court had about adjourned fer thet judge. He was on his knees, en' he wasn't prayin'. He was gaspin' an' tryin' to press his big, floppin', crippled hands over his body. Lassiter had sent all those last thunderin' shots through his body. Thet was Lassiter's way.

"An' Lassiter spoke, en' if I ever forgit his words I'll never forgit the sound of his voice.

"'Proselyter, I reckon you'd better call quick on thet God who reveals Hisself to you on earth, because He won't be visitin' the place you're goin' to!'

"An' then I seen Dyer look at his big, hangin' hands thet wasn't big enough fer the last work he set them to. An' he looked up at Lassiter. An' then he stared horrible at somethin' thet wasn't Lassiter, nor anyone there, nor the room, nor the branches of purple sage peepin' into the winder. Whatever he seen, it was with the look of a man who discovers somethin' too late. Thet's a terrible look! . . . An' with a horrible understandin' cry he slid forrard on his face."

Judkins paused in his narrative, breathing heavily while he wiped his perspiring brow.

"Thet's about all," he concluded. "Lassiter left the meetin'-house an' I hurried to catch up with him. He was bleedin' from three gunshots, none of them much to bother him. An' we come right up here. I found you layin' in the hall, an' I hed to work some over you."

Jane Withersteen offered up no prayer for Dyer's soul.

Lassiter's step sounded in the hall—the familiar soft, silver-clinking step—and she heard it with thrilling new emotions in which was a vague joy in her very fear of him. The door opened, and she saw him, the old Lassiter, slow, easy, gentle, cool, yet not exactly the same Lassiter. She rose, and for a moment her eyes blurred and swam in tears.

"Are you—all—all right?" she asked, tremulously. "I reckon."

"Lassiter, I'll ride away with you. Hide me till danger is past—till we are forgotten—then take me where you will. Your people shall be my people, and your God my God!"

He kissed her hand with the quaint grace and courtesy that came to him in rare moments. "Black Star an' Night are ready," he said, simply.

His quiet mention of the black racers spurred Jane to action. Hurrying to her room, she changed to her rider's suit, packed her jewelry, and the gold that was left, and all the woman's apparel for which there was space in the saddle-bags, and then returned to the hall. Black Star stamped his iron-shod hoofs and tossed his beautiful head, and eyed her with knowing eyes.

"Judkins, I give Bells to you," said Jane. "I hope you will always keep him and be good to him." Judkins mumbled thanks that he could not speak fluently, and his eyes flashed.

Lassiter strapped Jane's saddle-bags upon Black Star, and led the racers out into the court.

"Judkins, you ride with Jane out into the sage. If you see any riders comin' shout quick twice. An', Jane, don't look back! I'll catch up soon. We'll get to the break into the Pass before midnight, an' then wait until mornin' to go down."

Black Star bent his graceful neck and bowed his noble head, and his broad shoulders yielded as he knelt for Jane to mount.

She rode out of the court beside Judkins, through the grove, across the wide lane into the sage, and she realized that she was leaving Withersteen House forever, and she did not look back. A strange, dreamy, calm peace pervaded her soul. Her doom had fallen upon her, but, instead of finding life no longer worth living she found it doubly significant, full of sweetness as the western breeze, beautiful and unknown as the sage-slope stretching its purple sunset shadows before her. She became aware of Judkins's hand touching hers; she heard him speak a husky good-by; then into the place of Bells shot the dead-black, keen, racy nose of Night, and she knew Lassiter rode beside her.

"Don't—look—back!" he said, and his voice, too, was not clear.

Facing straight ahead, seeing only the waving, shadowy sage, Jane held out her gauntleted hand, to feel it enclosed in strong clasp. So she rode on without a backward glance at the beautiful grove of Cottonwoods. She did not seem to think of the past of what she left forever, but of the color and mystery and wildness of the sage-slope leading down to Deception Pass, and of the future. She watched the shadows lengthen down the slope; she felt the cool west wind sweeping by from the rear; and she wondered at low, yellow clouds sailing swiftly over her and beyond.

"Don't look—back!" said Lassiter.

Thick-driving belts of smoke traveled by on the wind, and with it came a strong, pungent odor of burning wood.

Lassiter had fired Withersteen House! But Jane did not look back.

A misty veil obscured the clear, searching gaze she had kept steadfastly upon the purple slope and the dim lines of canyons. It passed, as passed the rolling clouds of smoke, and she saw the valley deepening into the shades of twilight. Night came on, swift as the fleet racers, and stars peeped out to brighten and grow, and the huge, windy, eastern heave of sage-level paled under a rising moon and turned to silver. Blanched in moonlight, the sage yet seemed to hold its hue of purple and was infinitely more wild and lonely. So the night hours wore on, and Jane Withersteen never once looked back.

CHAPTER XXI
BLACK STAR AND NIGHT

The time had come for Venters and Bess to leave their retreat. They were at great pains to choose the few things they would be able to carry with them on the journey out of Utah.

"Bern, whatever kind of a pack's this, anyhow?" questioned Bess, rising from her work with reddened face. Venters, absorbed in his own task, did not look up at all, and in reply said he had brought so much from Cottonwoods that he did not recollect the half of it.

"A woman packed this!" Bess exclaimed.

He scarcely caught her meaning, but the peculiar tone of her voice caused him instantly to rise, and he saw Bess on her knees before an open pack which he recognized as the one given him by Jane. "By George!" he ejaculated, guiltily, and then at sight of Bess's face he laughed outright. "A woman packed this," she repeated, fixing woeful, tragic eyes on him.

"Well, is that a crime?'

"There—there is a woman, after all!"

"Now Bess—"

"You've lied to me!"

Then and there Venters found it imperative to postpone work for the present. All her life Bess had been isolated, but she had inherited certain elements of the eternal feminine.

"But there was a woman and you did lie to me," she kept repeating, after he had explained.

"What of that? Bess, I'll get angry at you in a moment. Remember you've been pent up all your life. I venture to say that if you'd been out in the world you d have had a dozen sweethearts and have told many a lie before this."

"I wouldn't anything of the kind," declared Bess, indignantly.

"Well—perhaps not lie. But you'd have had the sweethearts—You couldn't have helped that—being so pretty." This remark appeared to be a very clever and fortunate one; and the work of selecting and then of stowing all the packs in the cave went on without further interruption.

Venters closed up the opening of the cave with a thatch of willows and aspens, so that not even a bird or a rat could get in to the sacks of grain. And this work was in order with the precaution habitually observed by him. He might not be able to get out of Utah, and have to return to the valley. But he owed it to Bess to make the attempt, and in case they were compelled to turn back he wanted to find that fine store of food and grain intact. The outfit of implements and utensils he packed away in another cave.

"Bess, we have enough to live here all our lives," he said once, dreamily.

"Shall I go roll Balancing Rock?" she asked, in light speech, but with deep-blue fire in her eyes. "No—no."

"Ah, you don't forget the gold and the world," she sighed.

"Child, you forget the beautiful dresses and the travel—and everything."

"Oh, I want to go. But I want to stay!"

"I feel the same way."

They let the eight calves out of the corral, and kept only two of the burros Venters had brought from Cottonwoods. These they intended to ride. Bess freed all her pets—the quail and rabbits and foxes.

The last sunset and twilight and night were both the sweetest and saddest they had ever spent in Surprise Valley. Morning brought keen exhilaration and excitement. When Venters had saddled the two burros, strapped on the light packs and the two canteens, the sunlight was dispersing the lazy shadows from the valley. Taking a last look at the caves and the silver spruces, Venters and Bess made a reluctant start, leading the burros. Ring and Whitie looked keen and knowing. Something seemed to drag at Venters's feet and he noticed Bess lagged behind. Never had the climb from terrace to bridge appeared so long.

Not till they reached the opening of the gorge did they stop to rest and take one last look at the valley. The tremendous arch of stone curved clear and sharp in outline against the morning sky. And through it streaked the golden shaft. The valley seemed an enchanted circle of glorious veils of gold and wraiths of white and silver haze and dim, blue, moving shade—beautiful and wild and unreal as a dream.

"We—we can—th—think of it—always—re—remember," sobbed Bess.

"Hush! Don't cry. Our valley has only fitted us for a better life somewhere. Come!"

They entered the gorge and he closed the willow gate. From rosy, golden morning light they passed into cool, dense gloom. The burros pattered up the trail with little hollow-cracking steps. And the gorge widened to narrow outlet and the gloom lightened to gray. At the divide they halted for another rest. Venters's keen, remembering gaze searched Balancing Rock, and the long incline, and the cracked toppling walls, but failed to note the slightest change.

The dogs led the descent; then came Bess leading her burro; then Venters leading his. Bess kept her eyes bent downward. Venters, however, had an irresistible desire to look upward at Balancing Rock. It had always haunted him, and now he wondered if he were really to get through the outlet before the huge stone thundered down. He fancied that would be a miracle. Every few steps he answered to the strange, nervous fear and turned to make sure the rock still stood like a giant statue. And, as he descended, it grew dimmer in his sight. It changed form; it swayed it nodded darkly; and at last, in his heightened fancy, he saw it heave and roll. As in a dream when he felt himself falling yet knew he would never fall, so he saw this long-standing thunderbolt of the little stone-men plunge down to close forever the outlet to Deception Pass.

And while he was giving way to unaccountable dread imaginations the descent was accomplished without mishap.

"I'm glad that's over," he said, breathing more freely. "I hope I'm by that hanging rock for good and all. Since almost the moment I first saw it I've had an idea that it was waiting for me. Now, when it does fall, if I'm thousands of miles away, I'll hear it."

With the first glimpses of the smooth slope leading down to the grotesque cedars and out to the Pass, Venters's cool nerve returned. One long survey to the left, then one to the right, satisfied his caution. Leading the burros down to the spur of rock, he halted at the steep incline.

"Bess, here's the bad place, the place I told you about, with the cut steps. You start down, leading your burro. Take your time and hold on to him if you slip. I've got a rope on him and a half-hitch on this point of rock, so I can let him down safely. Coming up here was a killing job. But it'll be easy going down."

Both burros passed down the difficult stairs cut by the cliff-dwellers, and did it without a misstep. After that the descent down the slope and over the mile of scrawled, ripped, and ridged rock required only careful guidance, and Venters got the burros to level ground in a condition that caused him to congratulate himself.

"Oh, if we only had Wrangle!" exclaimed Venters. "But we're lucky. That's the worst of our trail passed. We've only men to fear now. If we get up in the sage we can hide and slip along like coyotes."

They mounted and rode west through the valley and entered the canyon. From time to time Venters walked, leading his burro. When they got by all the canyons and gullies opening into the Pass they went faster and with fewer halts. Venters did not confide in Bess the alarming fact that he had seen horses and smoke less than a mile up one of the intersecting canyons. He did not talk at all. And long after he had passed this canyon and felt secure once more in the certainty that they had been unobserved he never relaxed his watchfulness. But he did not walk any more, and he kept the burros at a steady trot. Night fell before they reached the last water in the Pass and they made camp by starlight. Venters did not want the burros to stray, so he tied them with long halters in the grass near the spring. Bess, tired out and silent, laid her head in a saddle and went to sleep between the two dogs. Venters did not close his eyes. The canyon silence appeared full of the low, continuous hum of insects. He listened until the hum grew into a roar, and then, breaking the spell, once more he heard it low and clear. He watched the stars and the moving shadows, and always his glance returned to the girl's dimly pale face. And he remembered how white and still it had once looked in the starlight. And again stern thought fought his strange fancies. Would all his labor and his love be for naught? Would he lose her, after all? What did the dark shadow around her portend? Did calamity lurk on that long upland trail through the sage? Why should his heart swell and throb with nameless fear? He listened to the silence and told himself that in the broad light of day he could dispel this leaden-weighted dread.

At the first hint of gray over the eastern rim he awoke Bess, saddled the burros, and began the day's travel. He wanted to get out of the Pass before there was any chance of riders coming down. They gained the break as the first red rays of the rising sun colored the rim.

For once, so eager was he to get up to level ground, he did not send Ring or Whitie in advance. Encouraging Bess to hurry pulling at his patient, plodding burro, he climbed the soft, steep trail.

Brighter and brighter grew the light. He mounted the last broken edge of rim to have the sun-fired, purple sage-slope burst upon him as a glory. Bess panted up to his side, tugging on the halter of her burro.

"We're up!" he cried, joyously. "There's not a dot on the sage We're safe. We'll not be seen! Oh, Bess—" Ring growled and sniffed the keen air and bristled. Venters clutched at his rifle. Whitie sometimes made a mistake, but Ring never. The dull thud of hoofs almost deprived Venters of power to turn and see from where disaster threatened. He felt his eyes dilate as he stared at Lassiter leading Black Star and Night out of the sage, with Jane Withersteen, in rider's costume, close beside them.

For an instant Venters felt himself whirl dizzily in the center of vast circles of sage. He recovered partially, enough to see Lassiter standing with a glad smile and Jane riveted in astonishment.

"Why, Bern!" she exclaimed. "How good it is to see you! We're riding away, you see. The storm burst—and I'm a ruined woman! . . . I thought you were alone."

Venters, unable to speak for consternation, and bewildered out of all sense of what he ought or ought not to do, simply stared at Jane.

"Son, where are you bound for?" asked Lassiter.

"Not safe—where I was. I'm—we're going out of Utah—back East," he found tongue to say.

"I reckon this meetin's the luckiest thing that ever happened to you an' to me— an' to Jane—an' to Bess," said Lassiter, coolly.

"Bess!" cried Jane, with a sudden leap of blood to her pale cheek. It was entirely beyond Venters to see any luck in that meeting.

Jane Withersteen took one flashing, woman's glance at Bess's scarlet face, at her slender, shapely form. "Venters! is this a girl—a woman?" she questioned, in a voice that stung.

"Yes."

"Did you have her in that wonderful valley?"

"Yes, but Jane—"

"All the time you were gone?"

"Yes, but I couldn't tell—"

"Was it for her you asked me to give you supplies? Was it for her that you wanted to make your valley a paradise?"

"Oh—Jane—"

"Answer me."

"Yes."

"Oh, you liar!" And with these passionate words Jane Withersteen succumbed to fury. For the second time in her life she fell into the ungovernable rage that had been her father's weakness. And it was worse than his, for she was a jealous woman—jealous even of her friends.

As best he could, he bore the brunt of her anger. It was not only his deceit to her that she visited upon him, but her betrayal by religion, by life itself.

Her passion, like fire at white heat, consumed itself in little time. Her physical strength failed, and still her spirit attempted to go on in magnificent denunciation of those who had wronged her. Like a tree cut deep into its roots, she began to quiver and shake, and her anger weakened into despair. And her ringing voice sank into a broken, husky whisper. Then, spent and pitiable, upheld by Lassiter's arm, she turned and hid her face in Black Star's mane.

Numb as Venters was when at length Jane Withersteen lifted her head and looked at him, he yet suffered a pang.

"Jane, the girl is innocent!" he cried.

"Can you expect me to believe that?" she asked, with weary, bitter eyes.

"I'm not that kind of a liar. And you know it. If I lied—if I kept silent when honor should have made me speak, it was to spare you. I came to Cottonwoods to tell you. But I couldn't add to your pain. I intended to tell you I had come to love this girl. But, Jane I hadn't forgotten how good you were to me. I haven't changed at all toward you. I prize your friendship as I always have. But, however it may look to you—don't be unjust. The girl is innocent. Ask Lassiter."

"Jane, she's jest as sweet an' innocent as little Fay," said Lassiter. There was a faint smile upon his face and a beautiful light.

Venters saw, and knew that Lassiter saw, how Jane Withersteen's tortured soul wrestled with hate and threw it—with scorn doubt, suspicion, and overcame all.

"Bern, if in my misery I accused you unjustly, I crave forgiveness," she said. "I'm not what I once was. Tell me—who is this girl?"

"Jane, she is Oldring's daughter, and his Masked Rider. Lassiter will tell you how I shot her for a rustler, saved her life—all the story. It's a strange story, Jane, as wild as the sage. But it's true—true as her innocence. That you must believe,"

"Oldring's Masked Rider! Oldring's daughter!" exclaimed Jane "And she's innocent! You ask me to believe much. If this girl is—is what you say, how could she be going away with the man who killed her father?"

"Why did you tell that?" cried Venters, passionately.

Jane's question had roused Bess out of stupefaction. Her eyes suddenly darkened and dilated. She stepped toward Venters and held up both hands as if to ward off a blow.

"Did—did you kill Oldring?"

"I did, Bess, and I hate myself for it. But you know I never dreamed he was your father. I thought he'd wronged you. I killed him when I was madly jealous."

For a moment Bess was shocked into silence.

"But he was my father!" she broke out, at last. "And now I must go back—I can't go with you. It's all over—that beautiful dream. Oh, I knew it couldn't come true. You can't take me now."

"If you forgive me, Bess, it'll all come right in the end!" implored Venters.

"It can't be right. I'll go back. After all, I loved him. He was good to me. I can't forget that."

"If you go back to Oldring's men I'll follow you, and then they'll kill me," said Venters, hoarsely.

"Oh no, Bern, you'll not come. Let me go. It's best for you to forget mot I've brought you only pain and dishonor."

She did not weep. But the sweet bloom and life died out of her face. She looked haggard and sad, all at once stunted; and her hands dropped listlessly; and her head drooped in slow, final acceptance of a hopeless fate.

"Jane. look there!" cried Venters, in despairing grief. "Need you have told her? Where was all your kindness of heart? This girl has had a wretched, lonely life. And I'd found a way to make her happy. You've killed it. You've killed something sweet and pure and hopeful, just as sure as you breathe."

"Oh, Bern! It was a slip. I never thought—I never thought!" replied Jane. "How could I tell she didn't know?" Lassiter suddenly moved forward, and with the beautiful light on his face now strangely luminous, he looked at Jane and Venters and then let his soft, bright gaze rest on Bess.

"Well, I reckon you've all had your say, an' now it's Lassiter's turn. Why, I was jest praying for this meetin'. Bess, jest look here."

Gently he touched her arm and turned her to face the others, and then outspread his great hand to disclose a shiny, battered gold locket.

"Open it," he said, with a singularly rich voice. Bess complied, but listlessly.

"Jane—Venters—come closer," went on Lassiter. "Take a look at the picture. Don't you know the woman?" Jane, after one glance, drew back.

"Milly Erne!" she cried, wonderingly.

Venters, with tingling pulse, with something growing on him, recognized in the faded miniature portrait the eyes of Milly Erne.

"Yes, that's Milly," said Lassiter, softly. "Bess, did you ever see her face—look hard—with all your heart an' soul?"

"The eyes seem to haunt me," whispered Bess. "Oh, I can't remember— they're eyes of my dreams—but—but—" Lassiter's strong arm went round her and he bent his head.

"Child, I thought you'd remember her eyes. They're the same beautiful eyes you'd see if you looked in a mirror or a clear spring. They're your mother's eyes. You are Milly Erne's child. Your name is Elizabeth Erne. You're not Oldring's daughter. You're the daughter of Frank Erne, a man once my best friend. Look! Here's his picture beside Milly's. He was handsome, an' as fine an' gallant a Southern gentleman as I ever seen. Frank came of an old family. You come of the best of blood, lass, and blood tells."

Bess slipped through his arm to her knees and hugged the locket to her bosom, and lifted wonderful, yearning eyes.

"It—can't—be—true!"

"Thank God, lass, it is true," replied Lassiter. "Jane an' Bern here—they both recognize Milly. They see Milly in you. They're so knocked out they can't tell you, that's all."

"Who are you?" whispered Bess.

"I reckon I'm Milly's brother an' your uncle! . . . Uncle Jim! Ain't that fine?"

"Oh, I can't believe—Don't raise me! Bern, let me kneel. I see truth in your face—in Miss Withersteen's. But let me hear it all—all on my knees. Tell me how it's true!"

"Well, Elizabeth, listen," said Lassiter. "Before you was born your father made a mortal enemy of a Mormon named Dyer. They was both ministers an' come to be rivals. Dyer stole your mother away from her home. She gave birth to you in Texas eighteen years ago. Then she was taken to Utah, from place to place, an' finally to the last border settlement—Cottonwoods. You was about three years old when you was taken away from Milly. She never knew what had become of you. But she lived a good while hopin' and prayin' to have you again. Then she gave up an' died. An' I may as well put in here your father died ten years ago. Well, I spent my time tracin' Milly, an' some months back I landed in Cottonwoods. An' jest lately I learned all about you. I had a talk with Oldrin' an' told him you was dead, an' he told me what I had so long been wantin' to know. It was Dyer, of course, who stole you from Milly. Part reason he was sore because Milly refused to give you Mormon teachin', but mostly he still hated Frank Erne so infernally that he made a deal with Oldrin' to take you an' bring you up as an infamous rustler an' rustler's girl. The idea was to break Frank Erne's heart if he ever came to Utah—to show him his daughter with a band of low rustlers. Well—Oldrin' took you, brought you up from childhood, an' then made you his Masked Rider. He made you infamous. He kept that part of the contract, but he learned to love you as a daughter an' never let any but his own men know you was a girl. I heard him say that with my own ears, an' I saw his big eyes grow dim. He told me how he had guarded you always, kept you locked up in his absence, was always at your side or near you on those rides that made you famous on the sage. He said he an' an old rustler whom he trusted had taught you how to read an' write. They selected the books for you. Dyer had wanted you brought up the vilest of the vile! An' Oldrin' brought you up the innocentest of the innocent. He said you didn't know what vileness was. I can hear his big voice tremble now as he said it. He told me how the men—rustlers an' outlaws—who from time to time tried to approach you familiarly—he told me how he shot them dead. I'm tellin' you this 'specially because you've showed such shame—sayin' you was nameless an' all that. Nothin' on earth can be wronger than that idea of yours. An' the truth of it is here. Oldrin' swore to me that if Dyer died, releasin' the contract, he intended to hunt up your father an' give you back to him. It seems Oldrin' wasn't all bad, en' he sure loved you."

Venters leaned forward in passionate remorse.

"Oh, Bess! I know Lassiter speaks the truth. For when I shot Oldring he dropped to his knees and fought with unearthly power to speak. And he said: 'Man—why—didn't—you—wait? Bess was—' Then he fell dead. And I've been haunted by his look and words. Oh, Bess, what a strange, splendid thing for Oldring to do! It all seems impossible. But, dear, you really are not what you thought."

"Elizabeth Erne!" cried Jane Withersteen. "I loved your mother and I see her in you!"

What had been incredible from the lips of men became, in the tone, look, and gesture of a woman, a wonderful truth for Bess. With little tremblings of all her slender body she rocked to and fro on her knees. The yearning wistfulness of her eyes changed to solemn splendor of joy. She believed. She was realizing happiness. And as the process of thought was slow, so were the variations of her expression. Her eyes reflected the transformation of her soul. Dark, brooding, hopeless belief—clouds of gloom—drifted, paled, vanished in glorious light. An exquisite rose flush—a glow—shone from her face as she slowly began to rise from her knees. A spirit uplifted her. All that she had held as base dropped from her.

Venters watched her in joy too deep for words. By it he divined something of what Lassiter's revelation meant to Bess, but he knew he could only faintly understand. That moment when she seemed to be lifted by some spiritual transfiguration was the most beautiful moment of his life. She stood with parted, quivering lips, with hands tightly clasping the locket to her heaving breast. A new conscious pride of worth dignified the old wild, free grace and poise.

"Uncle Jim!" she said, tremulously, with a different smile from any Venters had ever seen on her face. Lassiter took her into his arms.

"I reckon. It's powerful fine to hear that," replied Lassiter, unsteadily.

Venters, feeling his eyes grow hot and wet, turned away, and found himself looking at Jane Withersteen. He had almost forgotten her presence. Tenderness and sympathy were fast hiding traces of her agitation. Venters read her mind—felt the reaction of her noble heart—saw the joy she was beginning to feel at the happiness of others. And suddenly blinded, choked by his emotions, he turned from her also. He knew what she would do presently; she would make some magnificent amend for her anger; she would give some manifestation of her love; probably all in a moment, as she had loved Milly Erne, so would she love Elizabeth Erne.

"'Pears to me, folks, that we'd better talk a little serious now," remarked Lassiter, at length. "Time flies."

"You're right," replied Venters, instantly. "I'd forgotten time—place— danger. Lassiter, you're riding away.

Jane's leaving Withersteen House?"

"Forever," replied Jane.

"I fired Withersteen House," said Lassiter. "Dyer?" questioned Venters, sharply.

"I reckon where Dyer's gone there won't be any kidnappin' of girls."

"Ah! I knew it. I told Judkins—And Tull?" went on Venters, passionately.

"Tull wasn't around when I broke loose. By now he's likely on our trail with his riders."

"Lassiter, you're going into the Pass to hide till all this storm blows over?"

"I reckon that's Jane's idea. I'm thinkin' the storm'll be a powerful long time blowin' over. I was comin' to join you in Surprise Valley. You'll go back now with me?"

"No. I want to take Bess out of Utah. Lassiter, Bess found gold in the valley. We've a saddle-bag full of gold. If we can reach Sterling—"

"Man! how're you ever goin' to do that? Sterlin' is a hundred miles."

"My plan is to ride on, keeping sharp lookout. Somewhere up the trail we'll take to the sage and go round Cottonwoods and then hit the trail again."

"It's a bad plan. You'll kill the burros in two days."

"Then we'll walk."

"That's more bad an' worse. Better go back down the Pass with me."

"Lassiter, this girl has been hidden all her life in that lonely place," went on Venters. "Oldring's men are hunting me. We'd not be safe there any longer. Even if we would be I'd take this chance to get her out. I want to marry her. She shall have some of the pleasures of life—see cities and people. We've gold—we'll be rich. Why, life opens sweet for both of us. And, by Heaven! I'll get her out or lose my life in the attempt!"

"I reckon if you go on with them burros you'll lose your life all right. Tull will have riders all over this sage. You can't get out on them burros. It's a fool idea. That's not doin' best by the girl. Come with me en' take chances on the rustlers."

Lassiter's cool argument made Venters waver, not in determination to go, but in hope of success.

"Bess, I want you to know. Lassiter says the trip's almost useless now. I'm afraid he's right. We've got about one chance in a hundred to go through. Shall we take it? Shall we go on?"

"We'll go on," replied Bess. "That settles it, Lassiter."

Lassiter spread wide his hands, as if to signify he could do no more, and his face clouded.

Venters felt a touch on his elbow. Jane stood beside him with a hand on his arm. She was smiling. Something radiated from her, and like an electric current accelerated the motion of his blood.

"Bern, you'd be right to die rather than not take Elizabeth out of Utah—out of this wild country. You must do it. You'll show her the great world, with all its wonders. Think how little she has seen! Think what delight is in store for her! You have gold, You will be free; you will make her happy. What a glorious prospect! I share it with you. I'll think of you—dream of you—pray for you."

"Thank you, Jane," replied Venters, trying to steady his voice. "It does look bright. Oh, if we were only across that wide, open waste of sage!"

"Bern, the trip's as good as made. It'll be safe—easy. It'll be a glorious ride," she said, softly.

Venters stared. Had Jane's troubles made her insane? Lassiter, too, acted queerly, all at once beginning to turn his sombrero round in hands that actually shook.

"You are a rider. She is a rider. This will be the ride of your lives," added Jane, in that same soft undertone, almost as if she were musing to herself.

"Jane!" he cried.

"I give you Black Star and Night!"

"Black Star and Night!" he echoed.

"It's done. Lassiter, put our saddle-bags on the burros."

Only when Lassiter moved swiftly to execute her bidding did Venters's clogged brain grasp at literal meanings. He leaped to catch Lassiter's busy hands.

"No, no! What are you doing?" he demanded, in a kind of fury. "I won't take her racers. What do you think I

am? It'd be monstrous. Lassiter! stop it, I say! . . . You've got her to save. You've miles and miles to go. Tull is trailing you. There are rustlers in the Pass. Give me back that saddle-bag!"

"Son—cool down," returned Lassiter, in a voice he might have used to a child. But the grip with which he tore away Venters's grasping hands was that of a giant. "Listen—you fool boyl Jane's sized up the situation. The burros'll do for us. Well sneak along an' hide. I'll take your dogs an' your rifle. Why, it's the trick. The blacks are yours, an' sure as I can throw a gun you're goin' to ride safe out of the sage."

"Jane—stop him—please stop him," gasped Venters. "I've lost my strength. I can't do—anything. This is hell for me! Can't you see that? I've ruined you—it was through me you lost all. You've only Black Star and Night left. You love these horses. Oh! I know how you must love them now! And—you're trying to give them to me. To help me out of Utah! To save the girl I love!"

"That will be my glory."

Then in the white, rapt face, in the unfathomable eyes, Venters saw Jane Withersteen in a supreme moment. This moment was one wherein she reached up to the height for which her noble soul had ever yearned. He, after disrupting the calm tenor of her peace, after bringing down on her head the implacable hostility of her churchmen, after teaching her a bitter lesson of life—he was to be her salvation. And he turned away again, this time shaken to the core of his soul. Jane Withersteen was the incarnation of selflessness. He experienced wonder and terror, exquisite pain and rapture. What were all the shocks life had dealt him compared to the thought of such loyal and generous friendship?

And instantly, as if by some divine insight, he knew himself in the remaking—tried, found wanting; but stronger, better, surer—and he wheeled to Jane Withersteen, eager, joyous, passionate, wild, exalted. He bent to her; he left tears and kisses on her hands.

"Jane, I—I can't find words—now," he said. "I'm beyond words. Only—I understand. And I'll take the blacks."

"Don't be losin' no more time," cut in Lassiter. "I ain't certain, but I think I seen a speck up the sage-slope.

Mebbe I was mistaken. But, anyway, we must all be movin'. I've shortened the stirrups on Black Star. Put Bess on him."

Jane Withersteen held out her arms.

"Elizabeth Erne!" she cried, and Bess flew to her.

How inconceivably strange and beautiful it was for Venters to see Bess clasped to Jane Withersteen's breast! Then he leaped astride Night.

"Venters, ride straight on up the slope," Lassiter was saying, "'an if you don't meet any riders keep on till you're a few miles from the village, then cut off in the sage an' go round to the trail. But you'll most likely meet riders with Tull. Jest keep right on till you're jest out of gunshot an' then make your cut-off into the sage. They'll ride after you, but it won't be no use. You can ride, an' Bess can ride. When you're out of reach turn on round to the west, an' hit the trail somewhere. Save the hosses all you can, but don't be afraid. Black Star and Night are good for a hundred miles before sundown, if you have to push them. You can get to Sterlin' by night if you want. But better make it along about to-morrow mornin'. When you get through the notch on the Glaze trail, swing to the right. You'll be able to see both Glaze an' Stone Bridge. Keep away from them villages. You won't run no risk of meetin' any of Oldrin's rustlers from Sterlin' on. You'll find water in them deep hollows north of the Notch. There's an old trail there, not much used, en' it leads to Sterlin'. That's your trail. An' one thing more. If Tull pushes you—or keeps on persistent-like, for a few miles—jest let the blacks out an' lose him an' his riders."

"Lassiter, may we meet again!" said Venters, in a deep voice.

"Son, it ain't likely—it ain't likely. Well, Bess Oldrin'—Masked Rider—Elizabeth Erne—now you climb on Black Star. I've heard you could ride. Well, every rider loves a good horse. An', lass, there never was but one that could beat Black Star."

"Ah, Lassiter, there never was any horse that could beat Black Star," said Jane, with the old pride.

"I often wondered—mebbe Venters rode out that race when he brought back the blacks. Son, was Wrangle the best hoss?"

"No, Lassiter," replied Venters. For this lie he had his reward in Jane's quick smile.

"Well, well, my hoss-sense ain't always right. An' here I'm talkie' a lot, wastin' time. It ain't so easy to find an' lose a pretty niece all in one hour! Elizabeth—good-by!"

"Oh, Uncle Jim! . . . Good-by!"

"Elizabeth Erne, be happy! Good-by," said Jane.

"Good-by—oh—good-by!" In lithe, supple action Bess swung up to Black Star's saddle. "Jane Withersteen! . . . Good-by!" called Venters hoarsely.

"Bern—Bess—riders of the purple sage—good-by!"

CHAPTER XXII
RIDERS OF THE PURPLE SAGE

Black Star and Night, answering to spur, swept swiftly westward along the white, slow-rising, sage-bordered trail. Venters heard a mournful howl from Ring, but Whitie was silent. The blacks settled into their fleet, long-striding gallop. The wind sweetly fanned Venters's hot face. From the summit of the first low-swelling ridge he looked back. Lassiter waved his hand; Jane waved her scarf. Venters replied by standing in his stirrups and holding high his sombrero. Then the dip of the ridge hid them. From the height of the next he turned once more. Lassiter, Jane, and the burros had disappeared. They had gone down into the Pass. Venters felt a sensation of irreparable loss.

"Bern—look!" called Bess, pointing up the long slope.

A small, dark, moving dot split the line where purple sage met blue sky. That dot was a band of riders. "Pull the black, Bess."

They slowed from gallop to canter, then to trot. The fresh and eager horses did not like the check. "Bern, Black Star has great eyesight."

"I wonder if they're Tull's riders. They might be rustlers. But it's all the same to us."

The black dot grew to a dark patch moving under low dust clouds. It grew all the time, though very slowly. There were long periods when it was in plain sight, and intervals when it dropped behind the sage. The blacks trotted for half an hour, for another half-hour, and still the moving patch appeared to stay on the horizon line. Gradually, however, as time passed, it began to enlarge, to creep down the slope, to encroach upon the intervening distance.

"Bess, what do you make them out?" asked Venters. "I don't think they're rustlers."

"They're sage-riders," replied Bess. "I see a white horse and several grays. Rustlers seldom ride any horses but bays and blacks."

"That white horse is Tull's. Pull the black, Bess. I'll get down and cinch up. We're in for some riding. Are you afraid?"

"Not now," answered the girl, smiling.

"You needn't be. Bess, you don't weigh enough to make Black Star know you're on him. I won't be able to stay with you. You'll leave Tull and his riders as if they were standing still."

"How about you?"

"Never fear. If I can't stay with you I can still laugh at Tull."

"Look, Bern! They've stopped on that ridge. They see us."

"Yes. But we're too far yet for them to make out who we are. They'll recognize the blacks first. We've passed most of the ridges and the thickest sage. Now, when I give the word, let Black Star go and ride!"

Venters calculated that a mile or more still intervened between them and the riders. They were approaching at a swift canter. Soon Venters recognized Tull's white horse, and concluded that the riders had likewise recognized Black Star and Night. But it would be impossible for Tull yet to see that the blacks were not ridden by Lassiter and Jane. Venters noted that Tull and the line of horsemen, perhaps ten or twelve in number, stopped several times and evidently looked hard down the slope. It must have been a puzzling circumstance for Tull. Venters laughed grimly at the thought of what Tull's rage would be when he finally discovered the trick. Venters meant to sheer out into the sage before Tull could possibly be sure who rode the blacks.

The gap closed to a distance to half a mile. Tull halted. His riders came up and formed a dark group around him. Venters thought he saw him wave his arms and was certain of it when the riders dashed into the sage, to right and left of the trail. Tull had anticipated just the move held in mind by Venters.

"Now Bess!" shouted Venters. "Strike north. Go round those riders and turn west."

Black Star sailed over the low sage, and in a few leaps got into his stride and was running. Venters spurred Night after him. It was hard going in the sage. The horses could run as well there, but keen eyesight and judgment must constantly be used by the riders in choosing ground. And continuous swerving from aisle to aisle between the brush, and leaping little washes and mounds of the pack-rats, and breaking through sage, made rough riding. When Venters had turned into a long aisle he had time to look up at Tull's riders. They were now strung out into an extended line riding northeast. And, as Venters and Bess were holding due north, this meant, if the horses of Tull and his riders had the speed and the staying power, they would head the blacks and turn them back down the slope. Tull's men were not saving their mounts; they were driving them desperately. Venters feared only an accident to Black Star or Night, and skilful riding would mitigate possibility of that. One glance ahead served to show him that Bess could pick a course through the sage as well as he. She looked neither back nor at the running riders, and bent forward over Black Star's neck and studied the ground ahead.

It struck Venters, presently, after he had glanced up from time to time, that Bess was drawing away from him as he had expected. He had, however, only thought of the light weight Black Star was carrying and of his superior speed; he saw now that the black was being ridden as never before, except when Jerry Card lost the race to Wrangle. How easily, gracefully, naturally, Bess sat her saddle! She could ride! Suddenly Venters remembered she had said she could ride. But he had not dreamed she was capable of such superb horsemanship. Then all at once, flashing over him, thrilling him, came the recollection that Bess was Oldring's Masked Rider.

He forgot Tull—the running riders—the race. He let Night have a free rein and felt him lengthen out to suit himself, knowing he would keep to Black Star's course, knowing that he had been chosen by the best rider now on the upland sage. For Jerry Card was dead. And fame had rivaled him with only one rider, and that was the slender girl who now swung so easily with Black Star's stride. Venters had abhorred her notoriety, but now he took passionate pride in her skill, her daring, her power over a horse. And he delved into his memory, recalling famous rides which he had heard related in the villages and round the camp-fires. Oldring's Masked Rider! Many times this strange rider, at once well known and unknown, had escaped pursuers by matchless riding. He had to run the gantlet of vigilantes down the main street of Stone Bridge, leaving dead horses and dead rustlers behind. He had jumped his horse over the Gerber Wash, a deep, wide ravine separating the fields of Glaze from the wild sage. He had been surrounded north of Sterling; and he had broken through the line. How often had been told the story of day stampedes, of night raids, of pursuit, and then how the Masked Rider, swift as the wind, was gone in the sage! A fleet, dark horse—a slender, dark form—a black mask—a driving run down the slope—a dot on the purple sage—a shadowy, muffled steed disappearing in the night!

And this Masked Rider of the uplands had been Elizabeth Erne!

The sweet sage wind rushed in Venters's face and sang a song in his ears. He heard the dull, rapid beat of Night's hoofs; he saw Black Star drawing away, farther and farther. He realized both horses were swinging to the west. Then gunshots in the rear reminded him of Tull. Venters looked back. Far to the side, dropping behind, trooped the riders. They were shooting. Venters saw no puffs or dust, heard no whistling bullets. He was out of range. When he looked back again Tull's riders had given up pursuit. The best they could do, no doubt, had been to get near enough to recognize who really rode the blacks. Venters saw Tull drooping in his saddle.

Then Venters pulled Night out of his running stride. Those few miles had scarcely warmed the black, but Venters wished to save him. Bess turned, and, though she was far away, Venters caught the white glint of her waving hand. He held Night to a trot and rode on, seeing Bess and Black Star, and the sloping upward stretch of sage, and from time to time the receding black riders behind. Soon they disappeared behind a ridge, and he turned no more. They would go back to Lassiter's trail and follow it, and follow in vain. So Venters rode on, with the wind growing sweeter to taste and smell, and the purple sage richer and the sky bluer in his sight; and the song in his ears ringing. By and by Bess halted to wait for him, and he knew she had come to the trail. When he reached her it was to smile at sight of her standing with arms round Black Star's neck.

"Oh, Bern! I love him!" she cried. "He's beautiful; he knows; and how he can run! I've had fast horses. But Black Star! . . . Wrangle never beat him!"

"I'm wondering if I didn't dream that. Bess, the blacks are grand. What it must have cost Jane—ah!—well, when we get out of this wild country with Star and Night, back to my old home in Illinois, we'll buy a beautiful farm with meadows and springs and cool shade. There we'll turn the horses free—free to roam and browse and drink—never to feel a spur again—never to be ridden!"

"I would like that," said Bess.

They rested. Then, mounting, they rode side by side up the white trail. The sun rose higher behind them. Far to the left a low fine of green marked the site of Cottonwoods. Venters looked once and looked no more. Bess gazed only straight ahead. They put the blacks to the long, swinging rider's canter, and at times pulled them to a trot, and occasionally to a walk. The hours passed, the miles slipped behind, and the wall of rock loomed in the fore. The Notch opened wide. It was a rugged, stony pass, but with level and open trail, and Venters and Bess ran the blacks through it. An old trail led off to the right, taking the line of the wall, and his Venters knew to be the trail mentioned by Lassiter.

The little hamlet, Glaze, a white and green patch in the vast waste of purple, lay miles down a slope much like the Cottonwoods slope, only this descended to the west. And miles farther west a faint green spot marked the location of Stone Bridge. All the rest of that world was seemingly smooth, undulating sage, with no ragged lines of canyons to accentuate its wildness.

"Bess, we're safe—we're free!" said Venters. "We're alone on the sage. We're half way to Sterling."

"Ah! I wonder how it is with Lassiter and Miss Withersteen."

"Never fear, Bess. He'll outwit Tull. He'll get away and hide her safely. He might climb into Surprise Valley, but I don't think he'll go so far."

"Bern, will we ever find any place like our beautiful valley?"

"No. But, dear, listen. Well go back some day, after years—ten years. Then we'll be forgotten. And our valley will be just as we left it."

"What if Balancing Rock falls and closes the outlet to the Pass?"

"I've thought of that. I'll pack in ropes and ropes. And if the outlet's closed we'll climb up the cliffs and over them to the valley and go down on rope ladders. It could be done. I know just where to make the climb, and I'll never forget."

"Oh yes, let us go back!"

"It's something sweet to look forward to. Bess, it's like all the future looks to me."

"Call me—Elizabeth," she said, shyly.

"Elizabeth Erne! It's a beautiful name. But I'll never forget Bess. Do you know—have you thought that very soon—by this time to-morrow—you will be Elizabeth Venters?"

So they rode on down the old trail. And the sun sloped to the west, and a golden sheen lay on the sage. The hours sped now; the afternoon waned. Often they rested the horses. The glisten of a pool of water in a hollow caught Venters's eye, and here he unsaddled the blacks and let them roll and drink and browse. When he and Bess rode up out of the hollow the sun was low, a crimson ball, and the valley seemed veiled in purple fire and smoke. It was that short time when the sun appeared to rest before setting, and silence, like a cloak of invisible life, lay heavy on all that shimmering world of sage.

They watched the sun begin to bury its red curve under the dark horizon.

"We'll ride on till late," he said. "Then you can sleep a little, while I watch and graze the horses. And we'll ride into Sterling early to-morrow. We'll be married! . . . We'll be in time to catch the stage. We'll tie Black Star and Night behind—and then—for a country not wild and terrible like this!"

"Oh, Bern! . . . But look! The sun is setting on the sage—the last time for us till we dare come again to the Utah border. Ten years! Oh, Bern, look, so you will never forget!"

Slumbering, fading purple fire burned over the undulating sage ridges. Long streaks and bars and shafts and spears fringed the far western slope. Drifting, golden veils mingled with low, purple shadows. Colors and shades changed in slow, wondrous transformation.

Suddenly Venters was startled by a low, rumbling roar—so low that it was like the roar in a sea-shell. "Bess, did you hear anything?" he whispered.

"No."

"Listen! . . . Maybe I only imagined—Ah!"

Out of the east or north from remote distance, breathed an infinitely low, continuously long sound—deep, weird, detonating, thundering, deadening—dying.

CHAPTER XXIII
THE FALL OF BALANCING ROCK

Through tear-blurred sight Jane Withersteen watched Venters and Elizabeth Erne and the black racers disappear over the ridge of sage.

"They're gone!" said Lassiter. "An' they're safe now. An' there'll never be a day of their comin' happy lives but what they'll remember Jane Withersteen an'—an' Uncle Jim! . . . I reckon, Jane, we'd better be on our way."

The burros obediently wheeled and started down the break with little cautious steps, but Lassiter had to leash the whining dogs and lead them. Jane felt herself bound in a feeling that was neither listlessness nor indifference, yet which rendered her incapable of interest. She was still strong in body, but emotionally tired. That hour at the entrance to Deception Pass had been the climax of her suffering— the flood of her wrath—the last of her sacrifice—the supremacy of her love—and the attainment of peace. She thought that if she had little Fay she would not ask any more of life.

Like an automaton she followed Lassiter down the steep trail of dust and bits of weathered stone; and when the little slides moved with her or piled around her knees she experienced no alarm. Vague relief came to her in the sense of being enclosed between dark stone walls, deep hidden from the glare of sun, from the glistening sage. Lassiter lengthened the stirrup straps on one of the burros and bade her mount and ride close to him. She was to keep the burro from cracking his little hard hoofs on stones. Then she was riding on between dark, gleaming walls. There were quiet and rest and coolness in this canyon. She noted indifferently that they passed close under shady, bulging shelves of cliff, through patches of grass and sage and thicket and groves of slender trees, and over white, pebbly washes, and around masses of broken rock. The burros trotted tirelessly; the dogs, once more free, pattered tirelessly; and Lassiter led on with never a stop, and at every open place he looked back. The shade under the walls gave place to sunlight. And presently they came to a dense thicket of slender trees, through which they passed to rich, green grass and water. Here Lassiter rested the burros for a little while, but he was restless, uneasy, silent, always listening, peering under the trees. She dully reflected that enemies were behind them—before them; still the thought awakened no dread or concern or interest.

At his bidding she mounted and rode on close to the heels of his burro. The canyon narrowed; the walls lifted their rugged rims higher; and the sun shone down hot from the center of the blue stream of sky above. Lassiter traveled slower, with more exceeding care as to the ground he chose, and he kept speaking low to the dogs. They were now hunting-dogs—keen, alert, suspicious, sniffing the warm breeze. The monotony of the yellow walls broke in change of color and smooth surface, and the rugged outline of rims grew craggy. Splits appeared in deep breaks, and gorges running at right angles, and then the Pass opened wide at a junction of intersecting canyons.

Lassiter dismounted, led his burro, called the dogs close, and proceeded at snail pace through dark masses of rock and dense thickets under the left wall. Long he watched and listened before venturing to cross the mouths of side canyons. At length he halted, fled his burro, lifted a warning hand to Jane, and then slipped away among the boulders, and, followed by the stealthy dogs, disappeared from sight. The time he remained absent was neither short nor long to Jane Withersteen.

When he reached her side again he was pale, and his lips were set in a hard line, and his gray eyes glittered coldly. Bidding her dismount, he led the burros into a covert of stones and cedars, and tied them.

"Jane, I've run into the fellers I've been lookin' for, an' I'm goin' after them," he said. "Why?" she asked.

"I reckon I won't take time to tell you."

"Couldn't we slip by without being seen?"

"Likely enough. But that ain't my game. An' I'd like to know, in case I don't come back, what you'll do."

"What can I do?"

"I reckon you can go back to Tull. Or stay in the Pass an' be taken off by rustlers. Which'll you do?"

"I don't know. I can't think very well. But I believe I'd rather be taken off by rustlers."

Lassiter sat down, put his head in his hands, and remained for a few moments in what appeared to be deep and painful thought. When he lifted his face it was haggard, lined, cold as sculptured marble.

"I'll go. I only mentioned that chance of my not comin' back. I'm pretty sure to come."

"Need you risk so much? Must you fight more? Haven't you shed enough blood?"

"I'd like to tell you why I'm goin'," he continued, in coldness he had seldom used to her. She remarked it, but it was the same to her as if he had spoken with his old gentle warmth. "But I reckon I won't. Only, I'll say that mercy an' goodness, such as is in you, though they're the grand things in human nature, can't be lived up to on this Utah border. Life's hell out here. You think—or you used to think—that your religion made this life heaven. Mebbe them scales on your eyes has dropped now. Jane, I wouldn't have you no different, an' that's why I'm going to try to hide you somewhere in this Pass. I'd like to hide many more women, for I've come to see there are more like you among your people. An' I'd like you to see jest how hard an' cruel this border life is. It's bloody. You'd think churches an' church-men would make it better. They make it worse. You give names to things—bish-ops, elders, ministers, Mormonism, duty, faith, glory. You dream—or you're driven mad. I'm a man, an' I know. I name fanatics, followers, blind women, oppressors, thieves, ranchers, rustlers, riders. An' we have—what you've lived through these last months. It can't be helped. But it can't last always. An' remember his—some day the border'll be better, cleaner, for the ways of ten like Lassiter!"

She saw him shake his tall form erect, look at her strangely and steadfastly, and then, noiselessly, stealthily slip away amid the rocks and trees. Ring and Whitie, not being bidden to follow, remained with Jane. She felt extreme weariness, yet somehow it did not seem to be of her body. And she sat down in the shade and tried to think. She saw a creeping lizard, cactus flowers, the drooping burros, the resting dogs, an eagle high over a yellow crag. Once the meanest flower, a color, the flight of the bee, or any living thing had given her deepest joy. Lassiter had gone off, yielding to his incurable blood lust, probably to his own death; and she was sorry, but there was no feeling in her sorrow.

Suddenly from the mouth of the canyon just beyond her rang out a clear, sharp report of a rifle. Echoes clapped. Then followed a piercingly high yell of anguish, quickly breaking. Again echoes clapped, in grim imitation. Dull revolver shots—hoarse yells—pound of hoofs—shrill neighs of horses—commingling of echoes—and again silence! Lassiter must be busily engaged, thought Jane, and no chill trembled over her, no blanching tightened her skin. Yes, the border was a bloody place. But life had always been bloody. Men were blood-spillers. Phases of the history of the world flashed through her mind—Greek and Roman wars, dark, mediaeval times, the crimes in the name of religion. On sea, on land, everywhere—shooting, stab-bing, cursing, clashing, fighting men! Greed, power, oppression, fanaticism, love, hate, revenge, justice, freedom—for these, men killed one another.

She lay there under the cedars, gazing up through the delicate lacelike foliage at the blue sky, and she thought and wondered and did not care.

More rattling shots disturbed the noonday quiet. She heard a sliding of weathered rock, a hoarse shout of warning, a yell of alarm, again the clear, sharp crack of the rifle, and another cry that was a cry of death. Then rifle reports pierced a dull volley of revolver shots. Bullets whizzed over Jane's hiding-place; one struck a stone and whined away in the air. After that, for a time, succeeded desultory shots; and then they ceased under long, thundering fire from heavier guns.

Sooner or later, then, Jane heard the cracking of horses' hoofs on the stones, and the sound came nearer and nearer. Silence intervened until Lassiter's soft, jingling step assured her of his approach. When he appeared he was covered with blood.

"All right, Jane," he said. "I come back. An' don't worry."

With water from a canteen he washed the blood from his face and hands.

"Jane, hurry now. Tear my scarf in two, en' tie up these places. That hole through my hand is some inconvenient, worse 'n this at over my ear. There—you're doin' fine! Not a bit nervous—no tremblin'. I reckon I ain't done your courage justice. I'm glad you're brave jest now—you'll need to be. Well, I was hid pretty good, enough to keep them from shootin' me deep, but they was slingin' lead close all the time. I used up all the rifle shells, an' en I went after them. Mebbe you heard. It was then I got hit. Had to use up every shell in my own gun, an' they did, too, as I seen. Rustlers an' Mormons, Jane! An' now I'm packin' five bullet holes in my carcass, an' guns without shells. Hurry, now."

He unstrapped the saddle-bags from the burros, slipped the saddles and let them lie, turned the burros loose, and, calling the dogs, led the way through stones and cedars to an open where two horses stood.

"Jane, are you strong?" he asked.

"I think so. I'm not tired," Jane replied.

"I don't mean that way. Can you bear up?"

"I think I can bear anything."

"I reckon you look a little cold an' thick. So I'm preparin' you."

"For what?"

"I didn't tell you why I jest had to go after them fellers. I couldn't tell you. I believe you'd have died. But I can tell you now—if you'll bear up under a shock?"

"Go on, my friend."

"I've got little Fay! Alive—bad hurt—but she'll live!"

Jane Withersteen's dead-locked feeling, rent by Lassiter's deep, quivering voice, leaped into an agony of sensitive life.

"Here," he added, and showed her where little Fay lay on the grass.

Unable to speak, unable to stand, Jane dropped on her knees. By that long, beautiful golden hair Jane recognized the beloved Fay. But Fay's loveliness was gone. Her face was drawn and looked old with grief. But she was not dead—her heart beat—and Jane Withersteen gathered strength and lived again.

"You see I jest had to go after Fay," Lassiter was saying, as he knelt to bathe her little pale face. "But I reckon I don't want no more choices like the one I had to make. There was a crippled feller in that bunch, Jane. Mebbe Venters crippled him. Anyway, that's why they were holding up here. I seen little Fay first thing, en' was hard put to it to figure out a way to get her. An' I wanted hosses, too. I had to take chances. So I crawled close to their camp. One feller jumped a hoss with little Fay, an' when I shot him, of course she dropped. She's stunned an' bruised—she fell right on her head. Jane, she's comin' to! She ain't bad hurt!"

Fay's long lashes fluttered; her eyes opened. At first they seemed glazed over. They looked dazed by pain. Then they quickened, darkened, to shine with intelligence—bewilderment—memory—and sudden wonderful joy.

"Muvver—Jane!" she whispered.

"Oh, little Fay, little Fay!" cried Jane, lifting, clasping the child to her.

"Now, we've got to rustle!" said Lassiter, in grim coolness. "Jane, look down the Pass!"

Across the mounds of rock and sage Jane caught sight of a band of riders filing out of the narrow neck of the Pass; and in the lead was a white horse, which, even at a distance of a mile or more, she knew. "Tull!" she almost screamed.

"I reckon. But, Jane, we've still got the game in our hands. They're ridin' tired hosses. Venters likely give them a chase. He wouldn't forget that. An' we've fresh hosses."

Hurriedly he strapped on the saddle-bags, gave quick glance to girths and cinches and stirrups, then leaped astride.

"Lift little Fay up," he said.

With shaking arms Jane complied.

"Get back your nerve, woman! This's life or death now. Mind that. Climb up! Keep your wits. Stick close to me. Watch where your hoss's goin' en' ride!"

Somehow Jane mounted; somehow found strength to hold the reins, to spur, to cling on, to ride. A horrible quaking, craven fear possessed her soul. Lassiter led the swift flight across the wide space, over washes, through sage, into a narrow canyon where the rapid clatter of hoofs rapped sharply from the walls. The wind roared in her ears; the gleaming cliffs swept by; trail and sage and grass moved under her. Lassiter's bandaged, blood-stained face turned to her; he shouted encouragement; he looked back down the Pass; he spurred his horse. Jane clung on, spurring like-wise. And the horses settled from hard, furious gallop into a long-stridng, driving run. She had never ridden at anything like that pace; desperately she tried to get the swing of the horse, to be of some help to him in that race, to see the best of the ground and guide him into it. But she failed of everything except to keep her seat the saddle, and to spur and spur. At times she closed her eyes unable to bear sight of Fay's golden curls streaming in the wind. She could not pray; she could not rail; she no longer cared for herself. All of life, of good, of use in the world, of hope in heaven entered in Lassiter's ride with little Fay to safety. She would have tried to turn the iron-jawed brute she rode, she would have given herself to that relentless, dark-browed Tull. But she knew Lassiter would turn with her, so she rode on and on.

Whether that run was of moments or hours Jane Withersteen could not tell. Lassiter's horse covered her with froth that blew back in white streams. Both horses ran their limit, were allowed slow down in time to save them, and went on dripping, heaving, staggering.

"Oh, Lassiter, we must run—we must run!"

He looked back, saying nothing. The bandage had blown from his head, and blood trickled down his face. He was bowing under the strain of injuries, of the ride, of his burden. Yet how cool and gay he looked—how intrepid!

The horses walked, trotted, galloped, ran, to fall again to walk. Hours sped or dragged. Time was an instant—an eternity. Jane Withersteen felt hell pursuing her, and dared not look back for fear she would fall from her horse.

"Oh, Lassiter! Is he coming?"

The grim rider looked over his shoulder, but said no word. Fay's golden hair floated on the breeze. The sun shone; the walls gleamed; the sage glistened. And then it seemed the sun vanished, the walls shaded, the sage paled. The horses walked—trotted—galloped—ran—to fall again to walk. Shadows gathered under shelving cliffs. The canyon turned, brightened, opened into a long, wide, wall-enclosed valley. Again the sun, lowering in the west, reddened the sage. Far ahead round, scrawled stone appeared to block the Pass.

"Bear up, Jane, bear up!" called Lassiter. "It's our game, if you don't weaken."

"Lassiter! Go on—alone! Save little Fay!"

"Only with you!"

"Oh!—I'm a coward—a miserable coward! I can't fight or think or hope or pray! I'm lost! Oh, Lassiter, look back! Is he coming? I'll not—hold out—"

"Keep your breath, woman, an' ride not for yourself or for me, but for Fay!" A last breaking run across the sage brought Lassiter's horse to a walk.

"He's done," said the rider. "Oh, no—no!" moaned Jane.

"Look back, Jane, look back. Three—four miles we've come across this valley, en' no Tull yet in sight. Only a few more miles!"

Jane looked back over the long stretch of sage, and found the narrow gap in the wall, out of which came a file of dark horses with a white horse in the lead. Sight of the riders acted upon Jane as a stimulant. The weight of cold, horrible terror lessened. And, gazing forward at the dogs, at Lassiter's limping horse, at the blood on his face, at the rocks growing nearer, last at Fay's golden hair, the ice left her veins, and slowly, strangely, she gained hold of strength that she believed would see her to the safety Lassiter promised. And, as she gazed, Lassiter's horse stumbled and fell.

He swung his leg and slipped from the saddle.

"Jane, take the child," he said, and lifted Fay up. Jane clasped her arms suddenly strong. "They're gainin'," went on Lassiter, as he watched the pursuing riders. "But we'll beat 'em yet."

Turning with Jane's bridle in his hand, he was about to start when he saw the saddle-bag on the fallen horse.

"I've jest about got time," he muttered, and with swift fingers that did not blunder or fumble he loosened the bag and threw it over his shoulder. Then he started to run, leading Jane's horse, and he ran, and trotted, and walked, and ran again. Close ahead now Jane saw a rise of bare rock. Lassiter reached it, searched along the base, and, finding a low place, dragged the weary horse up and over round, smooth stone. Looking backward, Jane saw Tull's white horse not a mile distant, with riders strung out in a long line behind him. Looking forward, she saw more valley to the right, and to the left a towering cliff. Lassiter pulled the horse and kept on.

Little Fay lay in her arms with wide-open eyes—eyes which were still shadowed by pain, but no longer fixed, glazed in terror. The golden curls blew across Jane's lips; the little hands feebly clasped her arm; a ghost of a troubled, trustful smile hovered round the sweet lips. And Jane Withersteen awoke to the spirit of a lioness.

Lassiter was leading the horse up a smooth slope toward cedar trees of twisted and bleached appearance. Among these he halted.

"Jane, give me the girl en' get down," he said. As if it wrenched him he unbuckled the empty black guns with a strange air of finality. He then received Fay in his arms and stood a moment looking backward. Tull's white horse mounted the ridge of round stone, and several bays or blacks followed. "I wonder what he'll think when he sees them empty guns. Jane, bring your saddle-bag and climb after me."

A glistening, wonderful bare slope, with little holes, swelled up and up to lose itself in a frowning yellow cliff. Jane closely watched her steps and climbed behind Lassiter. He moved slowly. Perhaps he was only husbanding his strength. But she saw drops of blood on the stone, and then she knew. They climbed and climbed without looking back. Her breast labored; she began to feel as if little points of fiery steel were penetrating her side into her lungs. She heard the panting of Lassiter and the quicker panting of the dogs.

"Wait—here," he said.

Before her rose a bulge of stone, nicked with little cut steps, and above that a corner of yellow wall, and overhanging that a vast, ponderous cliff.

The dogs pattered up, disappeared round the corner. Lassiter mounted the steps with Fay, and he swayed like a drunken man, and he too disappeared. But instantly he returned alone, and half ran, half slipped down to her.

Then from below pealed up hoarse shouts of angry men. Tull and several of his riders had reached the spot where Lassiter had parted with his guns.

"You'll need that breath—mebbe!" said Lassiter, facing downward, with glittering eyes.

"Now, Jane, the last pull," he went on. "Walk up them little steps. I'll follow an' steady you. Don't think. Jest go. Little Fay's above. Her eyes are open. She jest said to me, 'Where's muvver Jane?'"

Without a fear or a tremor or a slip or a touch of Lassiter's hand Jane Withersteen walked up that ladder of cut steps.

He pushed her round the corner of the wall. Fay lay, with wide staring eyes, in the shade of a gloomy wall. The dogs waited. Lassiter picked up the child and turned into a dark cleft. It zigzagged. It widened. It opened. Jane was amazed at a wonderfully smooth and steep incline leading up between ruined, splintered, toppling walls. A red haze from the setting sun filled this passage. Lassiter climbed with slow, measured steps, and blood dripped from him to make splotches on the white stone. Jane tried not to step in his blood, but was compelled, for she found no other footing. The saddle-bag began to drag her down; she gasped for breath, she thought her heart was bursting. Slower, slower yet the rider climbed, whistling as he breathed. The incline widened. Huge pinnacles and monuments of stone stood alone, leaning fearfully. Red sunset haze shone through cracks where the wall had split. Jane did not look high, but she felt the overshadowing of broken rims above. She felt that it was a fearful, menacing place. And she climbed on in heartrending effort. And she fell beside Lassiter and Fay at the top of the incline in a narrow, smooth divide.

He staggered to his feet—staggered to a huge, leaning rock that rested on a small pedestal. He put his hand on it—the hand that had been shot through—and Jane saw blood drip from the ragged hole. Then he fell.

"Jane—I—can't—do—it!" he whispered. "What?"

"Roll the—stone! . . . All my—life I've loved—to roll stones—en' now I—can't!"

"What of it? You talk strangely. Why roll that stone?"

"I planned to—fetch you here—to roll this stone. See! It'll smash the crags—loosen the walls—close the outlet!"

As Jane Withersteen gazed down that long incline, walled in by crumbling cliffs, awaiting only the slightest jar to make them fall asunder, she saw Tull appear at the bottom and begin to climb. A rider followed him— another—and another.

"See! Tull! The riders!"

"Yes—they'll get us—now."

"Why? Haven't you strength left to roll the stone?"

"Jane—it ain't that—I've lost my nerve!"

"You! . . . Lassiter!"

"I wanted to roll it—meant to—but I—can't. Venters's valley is down behind here. We could—live there. But if I roll the stone—we're shut in for always. I don't dare. I'm thinkin' of you!"

"Lassiter! Roll the stone!" she cried.

He arose, tottering, but with set face, and again he placed the bloody hand on the Balancing Rock. Jane Withersteen gazed from him down the passageway. Tull was climbing. Almost, she thought, she saw his dark, relentless face. Behind him more riders climbed. What did they mean for Fay—for Lassiter—for herself?

"Roll the stone! . . . Lassiter, I love you!"

Under all his deathly pallor, and the blood, and the iron of seared cheek and lined brow, worked a great change. He placed both hands on the rock and then leaned his shoulder there and braced his powerful body.

ROLL THE STONE!

It stirred, it groaned, it grated, it moved, and with a slow grinding, as of wrathful relief, began to lean. It had waited ages to fall, and now was slow in starting. Then, as if suddenly instinct with life, it leaped hurtingly down to alight on the steep incline, to bound more swiftly into the air, to gather momentum, to plunge into the lofty leaning crag below. The crag thundered into atoms. A wave of air—a splitting shock! Dust shrouded the sunset red of shaking rims; dust shrouded Tull as he fell on his knees with uplifted arms. Shafts and monuments and sections of wall fell majestically.

From the depths there rose a long-drawn rumbling roar. The outlet to Deception Pass closed forever.

4.5.2 Reading and Review Questions

1. What roles do men and women play in *Riders of the Purple Sage*? How do those roles, and the reactions of the characters, shape our understanding of the outcome of the action?

2. Zane Grey travelled widely in the American West, and he lived for some time among the Mormons. What does Grey's portrayal of the Mormon elders tell us about his views?

3. How is the relationship between Jane Withersteen and Lassiter shaped by their surroundings?

4. Many readers comment that the landscape is a character in *Riders of the Purple Sage*. In what ways does the landscape take over from the characters?

5. How does Turner's frontier thesis expand our understanding of the tension between continuing westward migration, even as the available land in the western United States began to dwindle?

4.6 CHAPTER FOUR KEY TERMS

- Atlanta Compromise
- Atlanta Exposition
- Booker T. Washington
- Chicago World's Fair
- Emancipation
- Reconstruction
- Segregation
- Slavery
- Tuskegee Normal and Industrial Institute
- W. E. B. Du bois
- World's Columbian Exposition
- Zane Grey

Modernism (1914 - 1945)

Amy Berke, Robert R. Bleil, Jordan Cofer, and Doug Davis

5.1 LEARNING OUTCOMES

After completing this chapter, you should be able to:

- Identify the causes and effects of Modernism
- Differentiate between High Modernism and Low Modernism
- Identify the social, cultural, and political movements occurring during Modernism
- Identify several major Modernist works

5.2 INTRODUCTION

The biggest driver for **Modernism** was World War I, also known as the **Great War**, and the social and political turmoil that ensued. Much of the innovative work of the Modernist period seemed to follow writer Ezra Pound's credo of **"Make It New!"** Whether it was technology, art, architecture, or poetry, **Modernism** sought to reinvent the world. Uninhibited by the past, the Modernist era redefined America's political, religious, economic, and social values. From areas of **women's suffrage** to the invention of the assembly line, from **Harlem** to the Deep South, Modernism was a time of social upheaval, extraordinary growth, and accelerated change for America.

5.2.1 The Great War

World War I, which lasted from 1914-1918, was largely a European conflict with Great Britain, France, Russia, and Italy serving as the pillars of the Allied Forces, and Germany and Austria-Hungary and the Ottoman Empire anchoring the Central powers. Yet it brought turbulent changes to the entire world, America included. Although America did not officially enter the war effort until 1917, many young men already volunteered before then to fight with other detachments, such men including Ernest Hemingway, who was stationed as an ambulance driver on the Italian front. This war was the first global war and, as the world evolved, so did warfare. Additionally, this war was the first fully-industrialized war, featuring shelling, machine guns, mustard gas, and several other kinds of advanced weaponry. Indeed this war was the likes of which no one had ever seen. As such, it was a war of attrition, with over 30 million casualties. Never before in the history of civilization had there been such a large and full-scale military affair. Although in 1918, the **Armistice** signaled the end to World War I, many tensions and hostilities remained, especially among the combatants who felt disillusioned and used by their country. It's no coincidence that in 1919, just one year later, riots broke out across the United States. After the dust settled, one thing was clear: the world had changed permanently; this change would be at the heart of Modernist literature and art.

Of course World War I did not end European conflict; tension began to arise when Adolf Hitler came to power in the 1930s and bristled under Germany's heavy sanctions imposed by the Armistice. Hitler's rise in Germany would lead to World War II, which the United States tried to avoid using isolationist policies. However, Japan's attack on Pearl Harbor (December 7, 1941) served as the catalyst for America's entrance into World War II. This period between the two wars marks an important time in American life and culture. During this time, America grew and matured, largely in reaction to these events that unified the nation against common enemies. This unprecedented American growth included growth from immigration, industrialization, technological developments, and the development of the modern cities.

5.2.2 Une Generation Perdue…(A Lost Generation)

If the mantra of Modernism was Pound's "Make it New," then the defining characteristic for the generation comes from Gertrude Stein's comment to young Ernest Hemingway that you are all "une generation perdue" (you all are a *lost* generation). With the economy at an all-time high—due to the increased industrial manufacturing and development of so many new industries—came an increase in wealth in America; indeed, the Modernist period is characterized by the boom of a growing economy before the bust of the Great Depression. While overall wealth increased, dissatisfaction with America also increased and a growing number of young people, artists and veterans alike lived as expatriates outside the country—largely taking up residence in France and Spain. Most notable among these expatriates were writers T. S. Eliot, F. Scott Fitzgerald, and Ernest Hemingway. This movement is depicted in Hemingway's novel, *The Sun Also Rises.*

5.2.3 A Modern Nation

The industrial revolution and the meteoric rise of factories helped shift the nation's economy from its agricultural roots to an industry based economy. World War I (which began in 1914) along with America's entrance into the war (1917) put pressure on all of the citizens to ration goods and supplies. To meet demand, more factories began to experiment with mass production. This boom led to more jobs and a stronger economy, often referred to as the Boom years. Furthermore, while live music led to the prevalence of nightclubs, Prohibition created an underground industry of bootlegging to supply alcohol for these entertainment and music venues. This instant wealth led to a greater population of the newly rich and encouraged growth throughout the country. Often called "**The Jazz Age,**" this era of wealth was written about by many different Modernists, but made famous by F. Scott Fitzgerald.

However, the Boom years did not last forever. This age of prosperity came to a sudden halt in October 1929, when the sudden stock market collapse led to the **Great Depression**. The economic downturn led to more than 10,000 banks shutting down and more than 15 million workers becoming unemployed. Worse still, a series of droughts in the early 1930s, known as the **"Dust Bowl,"** left 500,000 people homeless, as many of these families moved to California, looking for work. The Great Depression became a major literary theme chronicled, most notably, by John Steinbeck in his novel, *The Grapes of Wrath.*

The election of Franklin Roosevelt (1932) ushered in the age of "The New Deal." During the New Deal era, Roosevelt created the Works Progress Administration (WPA) which used Federal funds to put more people to work, building America's infrastructure. The WPA was responsible for roads, various public buildings, and other projects, most notably the Hoover Dam, using Federal funds. The WPA provided employment for millions, including writers and artists who were sponsored by the **Federal Writers' Project**. James Agee's *Let Us Now Praise Famous*

Men, featuring the photography of Walker Evans, was an eye-opening book that captured the extent of **New Deal** poverty in the American South

At the same time, more and more people started migrating out of small rural agricultural areas into cities. Most notable among this time period is **the Great Migration**, during which African-Americans left the South to escape poverty and **Jim Crow** laws and moved to larger cities like Chicago, Detroit, Cleveland, Philadelphia, and New York. The Great Migration included as many as 1.5 million African-Americans and represents the greatest population shift in American history. These cultural and population shifts, along with the freedom of transportation, caused cultural cross-pollination, as people brought their old customs to new places. These shifts helped spark regional cultural revolutions, such as the **Harlem Renaissance** in Harlem—which brought many important African-American artists to the forefront and is captured in works like Zora Neal Huston's *Their Eyes Were Watching God* or Jean Toomer's *Cane*—as well the **Southern Literary Renaissance**, also referred to by Southern Writers as the **Southern Literary Renascence**—which foregrounded the creativity of the South and brought authors like William Faulkner and Eudora Welty to national prominence.

5.2.3 Technology

New technologies were changing the face of modern life. The Brooklyn Bridge, completed in 1883, was a giant suspension bridge which connected Brooklyn with Manhattan. Although it pre-dates Modernism, it was seen as one of America's greatest technological achievements and was the subject of Hart Crane's famous Modernist poem *The Bridge.* The invention of the automobile by inventors like Henry Ford and the development of the assembly line in the early 1920s not only created an industry, but also spurred investments in America's infrastructure, that is, its roads, highways. Suddenly, all of America was connected and personal travel was more readily available. The mass production of phonographs, projection reels, and telephones made these technologies more accessible to the public and allowed for more recording, making mass culture possible. The same could be said about the publishing industry, which flourished during this time. The paperback book made books more affordable, and the development of Book-of-the-Month clubs and subscription reading programs allowed for mass audiences, giving rise to the modern day "best seller." The affordability of magazines also made them a popular venue for many writers, as F. Scott Fitzgerald regularly published in *The Saturday Evening Post,* while many famous Modernist writers, such as Ezra Pound, held editorial positions for magazines, and literary magazines, such as *The Dial,* became popular venues for Modernist writers to publish.

5.2.4 Modernist Literature

The term Modernism as a literary term is largely used as a catchall for a global movement that was centered in the United States and Europe, for literature written during the two wars, which is said to be the first industrialized modern period. In another sense, Modernism refers to the general theme: much of the literature of the period is written in reaction to these accelerated times. After World War I, many writers felt betrayed by the United States, but even more than that, there was a general feeling of change, of progress, of questioning the ways of the past. Throughout the art of this time period, whether it is painting, sculpture, poetry, fiction, or non-fiction, all question the truths of the past, all question the status quo. Largely, this attitude goes hand-in-hand with the disaffection with politics caused by World War I.

Poetry

There is no single style that would encompass all of Modernist poetry; rather, a lot of Modernist poetry could be separated as **High Modernism** and **Low Modernism**. These terms are not meant to serve as an aesthetic judgment about the quality of the work, but rather help us understand the range of experimentation occurring during this period. High Modernism features poets who are much more formal, such as T. S. Eliot with his "The Love Song of J. Alfred Prufrock," and who look at the modern era as a period of loss, in some ways, looking at how much America has changed and fearing that the change might be for the worse. Essentially, in high modernist works, the authors realize that society has shifted so much, it will never be possible to return to the old ways, so they often represent the world as fragmented, disjointed, or chaotic. High Modernist poetry also maintains a traditional structure and form and often contains explicit allusions to history, myth, or religion, such as the epigraph from Dante's *Inferno* which begins T. S. Eliot's "The Love Song of J. Alfred Prufrock."

Low Modernism is much less formal, experimenting with form. The poetry of William Carlos Williams, the doctor turned poet, is a great example of Low Modernism. His poetry—like "This is Just to Say" and "The Red Wheelbarrow"—often plays with the traditional structure of a poem. These writers tend to be so different that first-time readers often questioned whether these works—Williams's "This is Just to Say"; Pound's "In a Station of the Metro"; Cummings's "In Just"—are poems. Ezra Pound did not even consider himself a poet; rather, in his essay, "A Few Don'ts by an Imagiste," he refers to himself as an imagiste, or one who creates images.

Prose

Experimentation was not limited to Modernist poetry, as **prose** (fiction and non-fiction) writers were also challenging form, style, and content, that is, what you could or could not write about. Authors such as Faulkner experimented with how to tell a story, especially by using a rotating cast of characters often set in the same county of Yoknapatawpha, while Gertrude Stein's *Tender Buttons* experimented with what exactly was a story. Sherwood Anderson's book, *Winesburg, Ohio,* was able to blur the line between short stories and the novel by writing a book of short stories that fit together as a novel. In much the same way, Jean

Toomer's *Cane* combined poetry, prose, and drama in one strange and beautiful book, foregrounding the dangerous racial politics of the time. Modernist prose was much more than just experimentation, though, in that it also introduced new subject matter. Writers no longer felt the need to veil their opinions; instead, many were explicit in their political critiques. The Great Depression gave rise to Communism among many artists, especially in the works of Ellison and Baldwin, while the **Women's Suffrage Movement** highlighted early **feminism**. Furthermore, the widespread distribution of easily affordable magazines and paperbacks meant that these writers were reaching a wider audience with a more radical message.

Drama

The Modernist period was perhaps the birth of the American playwright. Before Modernism, theater consisted of largely vaudeville or productions of European works. However, the success of Eugene O'Neil paved the way for several other successful American playwrights, such as Arthur Miller and Tennessee Williams.

Although theirs was a time of great change, the common thread that ties the Modernist writers together—whether they write poetry, prose, or drama—is the techniques they invented. Writers such as Faulkner, whose novel *The Sound and the Fury* offered an entirely new way to narrate a book, or Langston Hughes, whose poetry blended music and verse, developed entirely new ways of telling a story. Modernist writers radically rejected previous standards in an attempt to "make it new" and, in the process, changed the course of literary history.

5.2.5 Further Reading: Additional Secondary Sources

Modernism: A Very Short Introduction	Christopher Butler
The Concept of Modernism	Astradur Eysteinsson
After the Great Divide: Modernism, Mass Culture, Postmodernism	Andreas Huyssen
The Pound Era	Hugh Kenner
The American Adam	RWB Lewis
The Turning Word	Joseph Riddel

5.3 ROBERT FROST

(1874 - 1963)

When Robert Frost was asked to recite "The Gift Outright" at the inauguration of President John F. Kennedy in 1961, he was not only the first poet to be invited to participate in a presidential inauguration, he was also an American icon whose poetry was as recognizable to the nation as were Norman Rockwell's *Saturday Evening Post* covers. Yet like his contemporary Rockwell, Frost's poems reflect a rapidly changing cultural landscape in which the warm glow of memory was tinted by the cold reality of a highly mechanized, and often cruel, world. Frost was no passive megaphone for a comfortable past; like other Modernists, Frost melded traditional forms to the American vernacular to produce poetry that was strikingly American and contemporary.

Image 5.1 | Robert Frost, circa 1910
Photographer | Unknown
Source | Wikimedia Commons
License | Public Domain

Listeners and readers who are unfamiliar with Frost's poetry often remark on the consistency of his poetic voice. Many of the poems, in fact, appear to originate from the same person, an older New England gentleman who spends much of his time reminiscing about the past, remarking wistfully on the changes taking place around him, and celebrating those rare moments when he has stepped out of the norm. Thus, poems like "The Road Not Taken," are often recited at high school graduation ceremonies as a way to encourage students to take risks and celebrate life. Closer inspection of the poems reveals that this voice is not Frost's at all, but that of an alter ego who exists not to highlight the past glories, but to underline very contemporary frustrations with a decaying world.

"Mending Wall," a poem written around the time of Frost's fortieth birthday in 1914, is a strong introduction to his use of this alter ego. A dramatic monologue in forty-five lines of iambic pentameter, the poem opens with the vague pronouncement, "Something there is that doesn't love a wall," and proceeds to spell out the conditions for this seasonal activity, that of mending the fence that separates two farms. As the speaker and his neighbor proceed to rebuild the wall, each one responsible for the stones that have fallen onto his own side, the first farmer pauses to reflect on how it is that every year the wall requires new attention even though no one, save for a few hunters, has been observed disturbing the stones. This annual cycle of decay and reconstruction is at the heart of this poem, and the need for annual maintenance occurs not only in the world of fences, but in the world of human relationships as well.

This idea of continual decay and maintenance in human relationships provides a useful frame for understanding "Home Burial," a longer narrative poem that describes the apparently divergent responses of a husband and wife to the death of one of their children. A primer in the relationship between appearance and reality as the wife and husband struggle to understand their individual responses to this most recent death, the poem continues the theme of decay and rebuilding that is apparent in "Mending Wall." As the husband and wife appear to move closer together in the poem, they must also rebuild trust in their own relationship. Throughout Frost's poetry this cycle of decay and reconstruction continues unabated.

5.3.1 "Mending Wall"

Something there is that doesn't love a wall,
That sends the frozen-ground-swell under it,
And spills the upper boulders in the sun;
And makes gaps even two can pass abreast.
The work of hunters is another thing:
I have come after them and made repair
Where they have left not one stone on a stone,
But they would have the rabbit out of hiding,
To please the yelping dogs. The gaps I mean,
No one has seen them made or heard them made,
But at spring mending-time we find them there.
I let my neighbour know beyond the hill;
And on a day we meet to walk the line
And set the wall between us once again.
We keep the wall between us as we go.
To each the boulders that have fallen to each.
And some are loaves and some so nearly balls
We have to use a spell to make them balance:
"Stay where you are until our backs are turned!"
We wear our fingers rough with handling them.
Oh, just another kind of out-door game,
One on a side. It comes to little more:
There where it is we do not need the wall:
He is all pine and I am apple orchard.
My apple trees will never get across
And eat the cones under his pines, I tell him.
He only says, "Good fences make good neighbours."
Spring is the mischief in me, and I wonder
If I could put a notion in his head:
"*Why* do they make good neighbours? Isn't it
Where there are cows? But here there are no cows.
Before I built a wall I'd ask to know
What I was walling in or walling out,
And to whom I was like to give offence.

Something there is that doesn't love a wall,
That wants it down." I could say "Elves" to him,
But it's not elves exactly, and I'd rather
He said it for himself. I see him there
Bringing a stone grasped firmly by the top
In each hand, like an old-stone savage armed.
He moves in darkness as it seems to me,
Not of woods only and the shade of trees.
He will not go behind his father's saying,
And he likes having thought of it so well
He says again, "Good fences make good neighbours."

5.3.2 "Home Burial"

He saw her from the bottom of the stairs
Before she saw him. She was starting down,
Looking back over her shoulder at some fear.
She took a doubtful step and then undid it
To raise herself and look again. He spoke
Advancing toward her: "What is it you see
From up there always—for I want to know."
She turned and sank upon her skirts at that,
And her face changed from terrified to dull.
He said to gain time: "What is it you see,"
Mounting until she cowered under him.
"I will find out now—you must tell me, dear."
She, in her place, refused him any help
With the least stiffening of her neck and silence.
She let him look, sure that he wouldn't see,
Blind creature; and awhile he didn't see.
But at last he murmured, "Oh," and again, "Oh."

"What is it—what?" she said.

                    "Just that I see."

"You don't," she challenged. "Tell me what it is."

"The wonder is I didn't see at once.
I never noticed it from here before.
I must be wonted to it—that's the reason.
The little graveyard where my people are!
So small the window frames the whole of it.
Not so much larger than a bedroom, is it?

There are three stones of slate and one of marble,
Broad-shouldered little slabs there in the sunlight
On the sidehill. We haven't to mind *those*.
But I understand: it is not the stones,
But the child's mound—"

        "Don't, don't, don't, don't," she cried.

She withdrew shrinking from beneath his arm
That rested on the banister, and slid downstairs;
And turned on him with such a daunting look,
He said twice over before he knew himself:
"Can't a man speak of his own child he's lost?"

"Not you! Oh, where's my hat? Oh, I don't need it!
I must get out of here. I must get air.
I don't know rightly whether any man can."

"Amy! Don't go to someone else this time.
Listen to me. I won't come down the stairs."
He sat and fixed his chin between his fists.
"There's something I should like to ask you, dear."

"You don't know how to ask it."

        "Help me, then."

Her fingers moved the latch for all reply.

"My words are nearly always an offense.
I don't know how to speak of anything
So as to please you. But I might be taught
I should suppose. I can't say I see how.
A man must partly give up being a man
With women-folk. We could have some arrangement
By which I'd bind myself to keep hands off
Anything special you're a-mind to name.
Though I don't like such things 'twixt those that love.
Two that don't love can't live together without them.
But two that do can't live together with them."
She moved the latch a little. "Don't—don't go.
Don't carry it to someone else this time.
Tell me about it if it's something human.

Let me into your grief. I'm not so much
Unlike other folks as your standing there
Apart would make me out. Give me my chance.
I do think, though, you overdo it a little.
What was it brought you up to think it the thing
To take your mother-loss of a first child
So inconsolably—in the face of love.
You'd think his memory might be satisfied—"

"There you go sneering now!"

                    "I'm not, I'm not!
You make me angry. I'll come down to you.
God, what a woman! And it's come to this,
A man can't speak of his own child that's dead."

"You can't because you don't know how to speak.
If you had any feelings, you that dug
With your own hand—how could you?—his little grave;
I saw you from that very window there,
Making the gravel leap and leap in air,
Leap up, like that, like that, and land so lightly
And roll back down the mound beside the hole.
I thought, Who is that man? I didn't know you.
And I crept down the stairs and up the stairs
To look again, and still your spade kept lifting.
Then you came in. I heard your rumbling voice
Out in the kitchen, and I don't know why,
But I went near to see with my own eyes.
You could sit there with the stains on your shoes
Of the fresh earth from your own baby's grave
And talk about your everyday concerns.
You had stood the spade up against the wall
Outside there in the entry, for I saw it."

"I shall laugh the worst laugh I ever laughed.
I'm cursed. God, if I don't believe I'm cursed."

"I can repeat the very words you were saying:
"Three foggy mornings and one rainy day
Will rot the best birch fence a man can build."
Think of it, talk like that at such a time!
What had how long it takes a birch to rot

To do with what was in the darkened parlor?
You *couldn't* care! The nearest friends can go
With anyone to death, comes so far short
They might as well not try to go at all.
No, from the time when one is sick to death,
One is alone, and he dies more alone.
Friends make pretense of following to the grave,
But before one is in it, their minds are turned
And making the best of their way back to life
And living people, and things they understand.
But the world's evil. I won't have grief so
If I can change it. Oh, I won't, I won't!"

"There, you have said it all and you feel better.
You won't go now. You're crying. Close the door.
The heart's gone out of it: why keep it up.
Amy! There's someone coming down the road!"

"*You*—oh, you think the talk is all. I must go—
Somewhere out of this house. How can I make you—"

"If—you—do!" She was opening the door wider.
"Where do you mean to go? First tell me that.
I'll follow and bring you back by force. I *will!*—"

5.3.3 Reading and Review Questions

1. Compare and contrast the speakers in "Mending Wall" and "Home Burial." How does each of these men understand the world around them?

2. The two figures in "Mending Wall" rebuild the wall in silence. What does their silence tell us about their relationship?

3. At the end of "Home Burial," Amy appears ready to exit the house? Does she depart?

4. Compare Frost's "Home Burial" to Williams's "The Dead Baby."

5.4 WALLACE STEVENS

(1879 - 1955)

Wallace Stevens's reputation as an American poet has undergone something of a transformation over the sixty years since his death in the middle of the twentieth century. Celebrated during his lifetime for his imagery and for his attempts to unite the real world with the imagination, Stevens was also the target of frequent criticism for both the ordinary subjects of his early poetry and for the abstractness of his later work. Those who celebrate Stevens's work often point to this dichotomy, between the world of commerce and the world of the mind, as evidence of Stevens's particularly American upbringing.

Image 5.2 | Wallace Stevens
Photographer | Unknown
Source | Wikipedia
License | Fair Use

Unlike many of his generation, Stevens did not shy from commerce or industry in pursuit of his art; instead, he embraced both halves of himself by working during the day as a lawyer and insurance company executive and by writing poetry in the evenings and on vacation. While many modernist poets considered it a badge of honor to support themselves solely through their writings, Stevens saw no conflict in pursuing both the world of real things and the flights of the imagination. These were the stuff of poetry, not of conflict. From his first collection, *Harmonium*, published in 1923, to *The Collected Poems of Wallace Stevens*, published in 1954, the year before his death, Stevens resolutely mixed the ordinary and the imaginary in poems that are technically sophisticated while accessible to a wider audience.

The two selections from Stevens in this section highlight these two aspects of his poetry. In the first, "The Emperor of Ice-Cream" (1923), the poet uses just sixteen lines to connect the reader to an ordinary funeral, one in which there are no grand flourishes or flagrant displays, but only mourners in everyday clothes, bouquets of flowers wrapped in newspaper, and a widow who covers her face with a dresser cloth. Juxtaposed against a poet like Whitman, who celebrates the body, here in this poem we never even see the deceased in repose; nonetheless we know that he is an ordinary man. By 1923 Stevens warns us that the only emperor, the only one to deserve or receive a grand funeral, is the emperor of ice cream.

The second selection from Stevens is the much-quoted "Of Modern Poetry" (1942), which has become an iconic twentieth-century poem. Here Stevens makes his own argument for poetry that picks up on Marianne Moore's call for more precise language that is found in her own poem, "Poetry" (1921), included earlier in this chapter. Stevens, like Moore, argues that a poem "has to be living" (7), and therefore poetry must embrace the simple language of ordinary things in order for the imagination to create images. Yet, Stevens cautions poets and readers that modern poetry must not seek merely to represent an image; it must also connect to the imagination in order for it to succeed. These two selections are but a small portion of Stevens's rich body of work, but in reflecting both the early and the later parts of his career as a poet, they show a consistency of purpose, and a dedication to the natural language of readers, that few equaled in the twentieth century.

5.4.1 "The Emperor of Ice Cream"

Call the roller of big cigars,
The muscular one, and bid him whip
In kitchen cups concupiscent curds.
Let the wenches dawdle in such dress
As they are used to wear, and let the boys
Bring flowers in last month's newspapers.
Let be be finale of seem.
The only emperor is the emperor of ice-cream.

Take from the dresser of deal,
Lacking the three glass knobs, that sheet
On which she embroidered fantails once
And spread it so as to cover her face.
If her horny feet protrude, they come
To show how cold she is, and dumb.
Let the lamp affix its beam.
The only emperor is the emperor of ice-cream.

5.4.2 "Of Modern Poetry"

Please click the link below to access this selection:
http://www.poetryfoundation.org/poem/172210

5.4.3 Reading and Review Questions

1. How does Stevens's use of everyday language and situations shape the subjects of his poetry?

2. Compare Stevens's "Of Modern Poetry" to Marianne Moore's "Poetry." How do these authors understand the roles and responsibilities of poets?

5.5 WILLIAM CARLOS WILLIAMS

(1883 - 1963)

Affectionately known as "the good doctor," the prolific William Carlos Williams published dozens of works of literature in his lifetime, including novels, plays, essay and poetry collections, an autobiography, and one of the longest modernist poems ever composed, the five-part epic *Paterson*. Born in Rutherford, New Jersey, in 1883, Williams attended medical school at the University of Pennsylvania, where he met fellow poets Hilda Doolittle (H. D.) and Ezra Pound. Soon after graduating, Williams settled back home in Rutherford with his wife and family to run a medical practice, delivering over 2000 babies during his lifelong career as a pediatrician. While establishing himself as a

Image 5.3 | William Carlos Williams, 1921
Photographer | Unknown
Source | Wikimedia Commons
License | Public Domain

successful neighborhood doctor, Williams also established himself as an influential voice in New York City's Modernist art scene, befriending writers such as Wallace Stevens and Marianne Moore and experimental painters such as Marcel Duchamp. In 1913, the International Exhibition of Modern Art at New York City's 69th Regiment Armory introduced Americans to radical new styles of painting such as **Cubism** and **Fauvism**. Inspired by these new forms of visual art, Williams sought to craft a similarly new form of poetry for modern America. Like the modern painters, Williams focuses on the details of urban life through shifting perspectives and juxtaposed images. To both free his poetry from the restrictions of traditional verse forms and save it from the anarchy of free verse, Williams devised a new poetic rhythm called "the variable foot" that he used to structure his poems organically according to the rhythms of everyday American speech.

At a time when many American modernist authors were moving to Europe to find artistic inspiration, Williams found inspiration in his native New Jersey, taking its small cities and working people as the subjects for his poetry. Stylistically, Williams's poetry is rooted in the **Imagism** championed by his friend Ezra Pound, as evidenced by the short imagist poem, "The Red Wheelbarrow" presented here. In his *Autobiography*, Williams writes that the poet is "not to talk in vague categories but to write particularly, as a physician works, upon a patient, upon the thing before him, in the particular to discover the universal." Williams's insistence on writing about the particular led him to differ from poets such as Pound and Eliot, who eventually sought to make modern poetry more universal by making it more international, infusing it with different cultures and languages. Williams chose instead to write most of his poems—to use the title of one of his essay collections—"in the American grain," finding the universal in the everyday experiences of his native land. For example, in "The Dead Baby," Williams draws from his own experience as a doctor to explore a sadly common but usually unsung moment of grief. In "This Is Just To Say," Williams combines the linguistic economy of an Imagist poet with the shifts in perspective of a Cubist painter, presenting multiple perspectives on a small family drama over the course of three brief stanzas.

5.5.1 "The Red Wheelbarrow"

Please click the link below to access this selection:

http://www.poetryfoundation.org/learning/guide/178804#poem

5.5.2 "This Is Just To Say"

Please click the link below to access this selection:

http://www.poetryfoundation.org/poem/245576

5.5.3 "The Dead Baby"

Please click the link below to access this selection:

http://www.poetrynook.com/poem/dead-baby-1

5.5.4 Reading and Review Questions

1. In his poem *Paterson*, Williams famously writes that there are "no ideas but in things." What ideas do you find in "The Red Wheelbarrow"?

2. Discuss the use of repetition in "The Dead Baby." What universal meanings can be derived by Williams's careful observation of the particular repetitive behavior in this poem?

3. Explore the shifting perspectives in "This Is Just to Say." How does the idea of the plums change over the poem's course?

5.6 EZRA POUND

(1885 - 1972)

Image 5.4 | Ezra Pound, 1913
Photographer | Alvin Langdon Coburn
Source | Wikimedia Commons
License | Public Domain

As brilliant as he was controversial, Ezra Pound more than any other single poet or editor shaped modernist poetry into the forms you find in this chapter. Pound grew up in Philadelphia and attended the University of Pennsylvania, where he studied world languages and became friends with fellow poets Hilda Doolittle (H. D.) and William Carlos Williams. After being fired from his first college teaching job at Wabash College for his idiosyncratic behavior, Pound moved to London in 1908, working as a teacher, book reviewer, and secretary to William Butler Yeats. The energetic and prolific Pound soon became a force within London's literary scene, urging his fellow poets to break from poetic tradition and, as he famously wrote, "make it new." Over his lifetime Pound published collections of critical essays such as "Make it New" (1934) and *The ABC of Reading* (1934), translations of Chinese and Japanese poetry, and volumes of his own poetry, most notably his 116 *Cantos*, a decades-long project that he envisioned as the sum total of his life's learnings and observations. After the World War I, Pound became disillusioned with free-market democratic society, blaming it for both the immediate war and the general decline of civilization. He moved to Italy and became enamored with Italy's fascist government, recording hundreds of pro-fascist radio programs for Rome Radio that were broadcast to allied troops. After the war, Pound was arrested for treason, found mentally unfit, and incarcerated in Washington, D.C.'s Saint Elizabeth's Hospital until 1958, when his fellow poets successfully lobbied to have him freed.

Pound influenced modernist literature in two ways: by championing and editing numerous writers such as H. D., Robert Frost, James Joyce, Ernest Hemingway, Wyndham Lewis, and T. S. Eliot (whose *The Waste Land* he substantially revised); and by campaigning for the Imagist and Vorticist poetic movements. "In a Station of the Metro" is a perfect example of an Imagist poem. The poem is based on an experience Pound had of stepping off a train in Paris's underground Metro. As he writes in his essay, "From Vorticism," he "saw suddenly a beautiful face, and then another and another...and I tried all that day to find words for what this had meant to me..." It took Pound an entire year to find those words. His first draft of the poem was thirty lines long. His second draft was fifteen lines long. Still unable to express the emotion he felt that day, Pound continued to cut verbiage from the poem until it came closer in form to a Japanese haiku than a traditional Western lyric. The final two-line poem exemplifies Pound's three criteria for an Imagist poem: that the poet must treat things directly; eliminate unnecessary words; and use rhythm musically, not mechanically.

5.6.1 "In a Station of the Metro"

The apparition of these faces in the crowd:
Petals on a wet, black bough.

5.6.2 Reading and Review Questions

1. Consider the title as part of the poem. How does the title set your expectations for what follows?

2. Explore the word "apparition" in the poem's first line. What meanings and associations does this one word evoke?

3. What emotions does the imagery of petals and water in the poem's second line convey?

4. Scan the poem's meter. How does the poem's rhythm—its music— correspond to its imagery?

5.7 MARIANNE MOORE

(1887 - 1972)

If Robert Frost's poems demonstrate a continuing fascination with decay, it may be said
that Marianne Moore's poetry reveals an equally compelling fascination with development.
Like Dickinson and Whitman in the previous
century, Moore was a compulsive editor and
revisionist who apparently struggled over the
publication of each of her poems. Like Dickinson, she wished to see her poems laid out exactly
as she wished, but as a professional, rather than
an amateur poet, she seized upon each opportunity for publication as a chance for revision.
Thus, like with Whitman's *Leaves of Grass*, it is
difficult to call any of Moore's poems finished.

Image 5.5 | Marianne Moore, 1935
Photographer | George Platt Lynes
Source | Wikimedia Commons
License | Public Domain

Each time they were printed anew, she revised them. In this way, Moore's poetry
works on a number of textual levels. Like Dickinson, Moore expressed hesitation at
the appearance of her published work, but like her Modernist contemporaries, she
embraced the opportunities that twentieth-century publishing, and the existence
of numerous "little magazines," offered.

Moore's first published poems appeared in these "little magazines," the literary
and artistic journals of the early twentieth century, around 1915, and her work was
widely praised by the literary gatekeepers of the day, including Ezra Pound and
T. S. Eliot. But it was her first collection of twenty-four entries, *Poems*, published
without her knowledge in July 1921, that made her name widely known in the literary world. By the time that Moore herself produced a collection of poems, 1924's
Observations, she was beginning to develop a reputation as a "poet's poet" that
was only strengthened by winning the *Dial* prize in 1925. After winning the prize in
1925, Moore became editor of the *Dial*, a post that she held for the next four years.

"Poetry," the selection that follows, is a manifesto for Modernism, a demonstration of Moore's command of both technique and artistry, and an instruction
manual. As a manifesto, "Poetry" is both disdainful of the rigid forms that dominated most poetry—what Moore calls, "this fiddle,"—and celebratory of the experience of reading poetry. The experience of reading poetry, she argues, must yield an
understanding of "imaginary gardens with real toads in them," and not be merely
sites for "high-sounding," but "unintelligible," attempts at communication. Thus
poetry, Moore argues, must be both precise and genuine.

Moore demonstrates both precision and authenticity throughout the poem by
using concrete, rather than traditionally poetic, language and by avoiding many of
our expectations about poetry. Not only does Moore's poetry fail to rhyme, but she
also rejects Dickinson's rigid hymnody, eschews Whitman's free verse, and ignores

Frost's blank verse in favor of poetry that shares more of its syntax with prose and the spoken word than it does with traditional poetic forms. In place of lines and stanzas, Moore forces us to confront her poetry as a single unit where the expression begins with the first capital "I," and concludes with a single period at the end of the last line. Entangled in this extended expression, Moore guides the reader to a new understanding of poetry that reminds readers of Whitman's *Song of Myself* while it advocates not for a song in the traditional sense but for the importance of ordinary human speech. While reading "Poetry," careful readers should take note of the differences between Moore's monologue, in which no response is required from the reader, and the dramatic monologues of Frost whose speaker is always questioning.

5.7.1 "Poetry"

I, too, dislike it: there are things that are important beyond
    all this fiddle.
  Reading it, however, with a perfect contempt for it, one
    discovers in
  it after all, a place for the genuine.
    Hands that can grasp, eyes
    that can dilate, hair that can rise
      if it must, these things are important not because a

high-sounding interpretation can be put upon them but because
    they are
  useful. When they become so derivative as to become
    unintelligible,
  the same thing may be said for all of us, that we
    do not admire what
    we cannot understand: the bat
      holding on upside down or in quest of something to

eat, elephants pushing, a wild horse taking a roll, a tireless
    wolf under
  a tree, the immovable critic twitching his skin like a horse
    that feels a flea, the base-
  ball fan, the statistician—
    nor is it valid
      to discriminate against "business documents and

school-books"; all these phenomena are important. One must make
    a distinction
  however: when dragged into prominence by half poets, the
    result is not poetry,
  nor till the poets among us can be

"literalists of
  the imagination"—above
    insolence and triviality and can present

for inspection, "imaginary gardens with real toads in them,"
    shall we have
  it. In the meantime, if you demand on the one hand,
  the raw material of poetry in
    all its rawness and
    that which is on the other hand
      genuine, you are interested in poetry.

5.7.2 Reading and Review Questions

1. How does the presentation of Moore's poem—the ragged lines, the uneven breaks—shape our understanding of the poem?

2. How does Moore distinguish her work from the work of her predecessors like Dickinson and Whitman?

5.8 T. S. ELIOT

(1888 - 1965)

Image 5.6 | T. S. Elliot, 1934
Photographer | Lady Ottoline Morrell
Source | Wikimedia Commons
License | Public Domain

Thomas Stearns Eliot was born in St. Louis, Missouri. Eliot's father, Henry Eliot, was a successful businessman, while his mother, Charlotte Stearns, wrote poetry and was involved in St. Louis's cultural scene. Eliot lived in St. Louis until 1906, when he enrolled at Harvard University where he studied until 1910. Later that year, Eliot left to study at the Sorbonne in Paris for a year, before returning to Harvard to begin work on a Ph.D. In 1914, Eliot left the United States and accepted a scholarship at Oxford University, where he stayed for a year. Although he did not finish his studies at Oxford, Eliot remained in England, completing his dissertation for Harvard University, since World War I prevented Eliot from returning to the U.S. Instead Eliot stayed in London, later renouncing his American citizenship in favor of British citizenship (1927). Although he was a successful writer, Eliot also worked for a living, first as a teacher, then a banker, before accepting a position at Faber and Faber Publishing House. Eliot would become a tastemaker of the Modernist period, discovering and publishing many Modernist writers and eventually serving as the director of Faber and Faber. Although Eliot never moved back to the United States, he returned quite often to visit as well as to give lectures and readings.

Eliot began writing poetry in college, but it was after he moved to England (1914) that he began to write in earnest. Once he started to publish, Eliot's reputation grew until he became one of the central figures of the modernist movement. His essay, "Tradition and the Individual Talent," offered a highly influential approach for reading and interpreting literature. However, Eliot's poem, *The Waste Land* (1922), was possibly the most famous work of the Modernist era, one that is considered a masterpiece and significantly raised Eliot's profile. Written with editorial guidance from fellow Modernist poet Ezra Pound, *The Waste Land* sought to express the disillusionment of the post WWI Modernist era. It is a poem that many other Modernist writers used in their own writing. Throughout his career, Eliot produced several major works spanning multiple genres, including his poems, "The Love Song of J. Alfred Prufrock," *The Waste Land,* "The Hollow Men," "Ash Wednesday," and *The Four Quartets*, as well as the famous essay, "Tradition and the Individual Talent" and the play, *Murder in the Cathedral* (1935). Common themes in his work include isolation, religious insecurities, and frustration.

Eliot's poem, "The Love Song of J. Alfred Prufrock," which begins with an **epigraph** from Dante's *Inferno*, is innovative in form because it is formatted as a **dramatic monologue** without a clearly identified audience. It quickly becomes evident to the reader that this poem defies the conventions of a traditional love letter; rather, it reads like a confessional, with Prufrock confessing his feelings to the reader. The reader is privy to Prufrock's own insecurities and self-doubt that cannot be assuaged by God/religion, his fear of rejection, and his fear of dying alone.

5.8.1 "The Love Song of J. Alfred Prufrock"

> *S'io credesse che mia risposta fosse*
> *A persona che mai tornasse al mondo,*
> *Questa fiamma staria senza piu scosse.*
> *Ma percioche giammai di questo fondo*
> *Non torno vivo alcun, s'i'odo il vero,*
> *Senza tema d'infamia ti rispondo.*

Let us go then, you and I,
When the evening is spread out against the sky
Like a patient etherized upon a table;
Let us go, through certain half-deserted streets,
The muttering retreats
Of restless nights in one-night cheap hotels
And sawdust restaurants with oyster-shells:
Streets that follow like a tedious argument
Of insidious intent
To lead you to an overwhelming question . . .

Oh, do not ask, "What is it?"
Let us go and make our visit.

In the room the women come and go
Talking of Michelangelo.

The yellow fog that rubs its back upon the window-panes,
The yellow smoke that rubs its muzzle on the window-panes,
Licked its tongue into the corners of the evening,
Lingered upon the pools that stand in drains,
Let fall upon its back the soot that falls from chimneys,
Slipped by the terrace, made a sudden leap,
And seeing that it was a soft October night,
Curled once about the house, and fell asleep.

And indeed there will be time
For the yellow smoke that slides along the street,
Rubbing its back upon the window-panes;
There will be time, there will be time
To prepare a face to meet the faces that you meet;
There will be time to murder and create,
And time for all the works and days of hands
That lift and drop a question on your plate;
Time for you and time for me,
And time yet for a hundred indecisions,
And for a hundred visions and revisions,
Before the taking of a toast and tea.

In the room the women come and go
Talking of Michelangelo.

And indeed there will be time
To wonder, "Do I dare?" and, "Do I dare?"
Time to turn back and descend the stair,
With a bald spot in the middle of my hair—
(They will say: "How his hair is growing thin!")
My morning coat, my collar mounting firmly to the chin,
My necktie rich and modest, but asserted by a simple pin—
(They will say: "But how his arms and legs are thin!")
Do I dare
Disturb the universe?
In a minute there is time
For decisions and revisions which a minute will reverse.

For I have known them all already, known them all:
Have known the evenings, mornings, afternoons,
I have measured out my life with coffee spoons;
I know the voices dying with a dying fall
Beneath the music from a farther room.
            So how should I presume?

And I have known the eyes already, known them all—
The eyes that fix you in a formulated phrase,
And when I am formulated, sprawling on a pin,
When I am pinned and wriggling on the wall,
Then how should I begin
To spit out all the butt-ends of my days and ways?
            And how should I presume?

And I have known the arms already, known them all—
Arms that are braceleted and white and bare
(But in the lamplight, downed with light brown hair!)
Is it perfume from a dress
That makes me so digress?
Arms that lie along a table, or wrap about a shawl.
            And should I then presume?
            And how should I begin?

Shall I say, I have gone at dusk through narrow streets
And watched the smoke that rises from the pipes
Of lonely men in shirt-sleeves, leaning out of windows? . . .

I should have been a pair of ragged claws
Scuttling across the floors of silent seas.

And the afternoon, the evening, sleeps so peacefully!
Smoothed by long fingers,
Asleep . . . tired . . . or it malingers,
Stretched on the floor, here beside you and me.
Should I, after tea and cakes and ices,
Have the strength to force the moment to its crisis?
But though I have wept and fasted, wept and prayed,
Though I have seen my head (grown slightly bald) brought in upon a platter,
I am no prophet—and here's no great matter;
I have seen the moment of my greatness flicker,
And I have seen the eternal Footman hold my coat, and snicker,
And in short, I was afraid.

And would it have been worth it, after all,
After the cups, the marmalade, the tea,
Among the porcelain, among some talk of you and me,
Would it have been worth while,
To have bitten off the matter with a smile,
To have squeezed the universe into a ball
To roll it towards some overwhelming question,
To say: "I am Lazarus, come from the dead,
Come back to tell you all, I shall tell you all"—
If one, settling a pillow by her head
          Should say: "That is not what I meant at all;
          That is not it, at all."

And would it have been worth it, after all,
Would it have been worth while,
After the sunsets and the dooryards and the sprinkled streets,
After the novels, after the teacups, after the skirts that trail along the floor—
And this, and so much more?—
It is impossible to say just what I mean!
But as if a magic lantern threw the nerves in patterns on a screen:
Would it have been worth while
If one, settling a pillow or throwing off a shawl,
And turning toward the window, should say:
          "That is not it at all,
          That is not what I meant, at all."

No! I am not Prince Hamlet, nor was meant to be;
Am an attendant lord, one that will do
To swell a progress, start a scene or two,
Advise the prince; no doubt, an easy tool,
Deferential, glad to be of use,
Politic, cautious, and meticulous;
Full of high sentence, but a bit obtuse;
At times, indeed, almost ridiculous—
Almost, at times, the Fool.

I grow old ... I grow old ...
I shall wear the bottoms of my trousers rolled.

Shall I part my hair behind? Do I dare to eat a peach?
I shall wear white flannel trousers, and walk upon the beach.
I have heard the mermaids singing, each to each.

I do not think that they will sing to me.

I have seen them riding seaward on the waves
Combing the white hair of the waves blown back
When the wind blows the water white and black.
We have lingered in the chambers of the sea
By sea-girls wreathed with seaweed red and brown
Till human voices wake us, and we drown.

5.8.2 Reading and Review Questions

1. The poem is titled "The Love Song of J. Alfred Prufrock." How does this poem differ from what we usually consider the typical themes of a love song? Are there any similarities to a love song?

2. Eliot's famous line, "Do I Dare Disturb the Universe," has been seen as the central line in this poem. What is Prufrock referring to in this line? How could he disturb the universe?

5.9 EDNA ST. VINCENT MILLAY
(1892 - 1950)

Image 5.7 | Edna St. Vincent Millay, 1933
Photographer | Carl Van Vechten
Source | Wikimedia Commons
License | Public Domain

When the first of our selections from Edna St. Vincent Millay, "First Fig," was published in *Poetry* in October 1918, the twenty-six year old author was already a published poet and a rising figure in the Greenwich Village literary scene. Yet "First Fig," and the four other lyrics that appeared alongside it in that issue, are notable because they demonstrate—in a total of just twenty lines—both Millay's mastery of the lyric form and her determined frankness. In this way, Millay represents both a continuation of poetic traditions and a new approach to appropriate subject matter for women's poetry. Like many female poets of the early part of the twentieth century, Millay appears at once to straddle two worlds: on one hand her poetry shows great technical skill, which permits her entry into the ranks of so-called serious poets, while on the other hand, her verses show a lightness, a frankness, and a freshness from which a poet like Dickinson would retreat. For Millay and other female poets, as for their African-American contemporaries like Countee Cullen, it was often necessary to embrace traditional poetic forms even as their subject matter was decidedly modern.

One of three daughters of a divorced mother at the turn of the century, Millay's early successes resulted in the unusual opportunity to attend Vassar College in her early twenties, and these social and educational connections proved highly useful to the young writer. A gifted playwright as well as a poet, Millay was a member of the experimental theatre group, the Provincetown Players, for whom she frequently wrote while also composing several books of poetry. As a sometime expatriate in the 1920s, Millay liberally combined traditional poetic forms and contemporary subjects in her verse, prose, and drama. The winner of the **Pulitzer Prize** for poetry in 1923, for *The Ballad of the Harp-Weaver*, Millay was both a critically and a commercially successful writer.

"First Fig," the opening lyric in a group known as *Figs from Thistles*, is familiar to many readers who encountered it in high school, where it is often included as a tool for teaching about scansion and prosody. Composed of just four lines that alternate between iambic pentameter and iambic tetrameter, and featuring a strong end-rhyme, "First Fig" is often a gateway work in modernist poetry because it mimics forms with which readers are already comfortable. Yet the poem quickly challenges our expectations by celebrating excess: "My candle burns at both ends," for example, and then acknowledging the speaker's foes as readily as the speaker's friends. These elements combined with the exclamatory, "It gives a lovely light!" in the last line transport the imagery from the usual one of decay into a celebration. This celebration of rapid change unites "First Fig" with the other four lyrics with which it was first published into a celebration of the present.

The second selection from Millay, "I Think I Should Have Loved You Presently" (1922), provides additional evidence of the poet's technical skills. A sonnet in the Shakespearean tradition, "I Think I Should Have Loved You Presently," uses the occasion of an absent lover not as a moment for regret but as an occasion to acknowledge the impermanence of romantic love. In the first few lines, the speaker makes clear that it was a choice, and not mere caprice that caused her to act as she did in jesting with a recent lover. Despite the loss of her lover's affections, the speaker would not change her ways, instead choosing to "Cherish no less the certain stakes I gained" (11) than to regret her dalliance. For these and other epigrammatic lines, Millay remains one of the most quoted modernist poets.

5.9.1 "First Fig"

My candle burns at both ends;
    It will not last the night;
But ah, my foes, and oh, my friends—
    It gives a lovely light!

5.9.2 "I Think I Should Have Loved You Presently"

I think I should have loved you presently,
And given in earnest words I flung in jest;

And lifted honest eyes for you to see,
And caught your hand against my cheek and breast;
And all my pretty follies flung aside
That won you to me, and beneath your gaze,
Naked of reticence and shorn of pride,
Spread like a chart my little wicked ways.
I, that had been to you, had you remained,
But one more waking from a recurrent dream,
Cherish no less the certain stakes I gained,
And walk your memory's halls, austere, supreme,
A ghost in marble of a girl you knew
Who would have loved you in a day or two.

5.9.3 Reading and Review Questions

1. How does Millay's choice of the sonnet form distinguish her work from that of other Modernists such as Eliot, Moore, Stevens, and Williams? Also, why do writers like Cullen and Millay experiment with the sonnet form?

2. Millay is one of the first American poets to write candidly about female sexuality. How does Millay's poetry reflect the attitudes of Modernism in relation to female sexuality?

5.10 E. E. CUMMINGS

(1894 - 1962)

Like a number of the modernist poets, e. e. cummings came from a family of teachers and ministers. But while many of his contemporaries were active members of the artistic communities of New York, Boston, and Philadelphia, cummings was a more solitary figure whose poetry and politics tended toward the everyday and the common. This is not to say that cummings was a passive observer of the world around him: while serving overseas during World War I, cummings and a friend were held by the French on charges that their letters home were derisive of authority and of the general war effort. At home in New York, however, cummings seems to have avoided the style of poetry and pronouncements that made his contemporaries like Pound, Williams, Moore, and Stevens into vanguards of Modernist poetry.

Image 5.8 | e. e. cummings, 1953
Photographer | Walter Albertin
Source | Wikimedia Commons
License | Public Domain

Nonetheless, contemporary readers are often startled by the appearance of cummings's poetry on the printed page. Eschewing capitalization, punctuation, and standard verse forms, cummings's works take full advantage of the printed page to present poems that are often better suited to private reading than public performance. Where the lack of punctuation and capitalization may disarm readers more accustomed to being told how to vocalize a poem, cummings's verses are presented without a beginning or an ending so as to allow the reader to move through a collection of cummings's verse in a way that befits the private reading experience. Like Marianne Moore, who also paid careful attention to the presentation of her works in print, cummings embraced the opportunities that modern print culture provided to poets.

The selection from cummings in this unit, "in Just-," published in 1920, demonstrates many of the attributes that are common in cummings's verse. This poem can be said to begin without a beginning, withholding even the suggestion of where these lines fall in the consciousness of the poetic voice. And yet, while cummings does away with many aspects of poetry, the beginning of the poem is still familiar to the reader. Consider the beginning of the poem written out in prose: in Just-spring when the world is mud-luscious the little lame balloonman whistles far and wee. Written out this way, the reader can quickly ascertain the meaning of the first few lines, but it is not the form on the page, verse or prose, that makes this possible, but the fact that these lines follow an elementary syntax that feels natural to the ear, even if the eye is confused by the physical arrangement.

Once the first lines of the poem have been mastered, more traditional patterns begin to emerge for the reader. The three-times repetition of the words, "balloonman whistles far and wee," divides the poem into two sections describing the games and adventures of two groups of children, Eddie and Bill and Betty and Isbel. With these children, celebrating the early days of spring, the Just-spring of the opening lines are full of movement and energy in contrast to the infirmities of the balloonman; nonetheless, all five are part of a vignette whose appearance in the poem suggests further adventures to come. Although unusual in its shape and punctuation, cummings's poetry is linked to the same rhythms of life that have captivated poets from Chaucer to Eliot.

5.10.1 "in Just-"

in Just-
spring　　　when the world is mud-
luscious the little
lame balloonman

whistles　　　far　　　and wee

and eddieandbill come
running from marbles and

piracies and it's
spring

when the world is puddle-wonderful

the queer
old balloonman whistles
far   and   wee
and bettyandisbel come dancing

from hop-scotch and jump-rope and

it's
spring
and

      the

         goat-footed

balloonMan   whistles
far
and
wee

5.10.2 Reading and Review Questions

1. How does cummings's resistance to punctuation shape your understanding of this poem? Can you determine an internal structure in the poem that replaces the need for standard punctuation?

2. How does cummings's poetry compare to other iconic American poets like Whitman or Williams? Is cummings's rejection of punctuation and traditional forms part of the American quality of his poetry?

3. Analyze the ways in which cummings uses hyphenation and line breaks in "in Just-" to create a sense of overlapping time.

5.11 F. SCOTT FITZGERALD

(1896 - 1940)

F. Scott Fitzgerald was born in 1896 to a comfortable, solidly middle-class family in St. Paul, Minnesota. A social and cultural beneficiary of the Gilded Age, Fitzgerald's family did not enjoy the prominence and ease of the Carnegies, the Vanderbilts, or the Rockefellers, but in the fluidity of the 1890s a young man like Fitzgerald could, with the right manners and reading, pass among the wealthy without causing much of a stir. In an era when the ultra-rich and the working poor were separated by an unbridgeable chasm, Fitzgerald's modest means still placed him closer to the rich than the poor. Fitzgerald was nevertheless acutely aware of the shortcomings of his limited means and his Midwestern heritage. In his stories and novels,

Image 5.9 | F. Scott Fitzgerald, 1937
Photographer | Carl Van Vechten
Source | Wikimedia Commons
License | Public Domain

Fitzgerald returned time and again to three areas: money, unattainable love, and individual identity. The three short stories selected here present these themes in abundance.

Fitzgerald's short fiction has been overwhelmed by interest in his novel *The Great Gatsby*, but Fitzgerald survived by writing short stories for popular magazines like the *Saturday Evening Post*, *Metropolitan*, and *Cosmopolitan*. The selections that follow, each from the first decade of Fitzgerald's career, show his development as a writer of social fiction, and they allow us to understand his longer works in a new light. In "The Rich Boy," a story from 1926 and not reprinted in this collection, Fitzgerald clearly describes the project of his short stories:

> Begin with an individual, and before you know it you find that you have created a type; begin with a type, and you find that you have created—nothing. That is because we are all queer fish, queerer behind our faces and voices than we want any one to know or than we know ourselves.[1]

These lines are particularly important to understanding Fitzgerald because they remind us that his characters are not intended to represent anything larger than the essential character. While Gatsby may be great, his story is uniquely his own and unrepresentative of any other industrial baron, brewer, or bootlegger of the 1920s. Thus, Fitzgerald portrays his most famous character through the eyes of a single, flawed narrator. We are not meant to know all of Gatsby's secrets, and, by not knowing his secrets, the story of Gatsby's rise and fall is both individual and universal.

---

1   Fitzgerald, F. Scott. The Fitzgerald Reader. New York: Scribner, 1963. Print., 239

Later in "The Rich Boy," Fitzgerald's narrator offers one of the most memorable and misquoted passages in American literature:

> Let me tell you about the very rich. They are different from you and me. They possess and enjoy early, and it does something to them, makes them soft where we are hard, and cynical where we are trustful, in a way that, unless you were born rich, it is very difficult to understand. They think, deep in their hearts, that they are better than we are because we had to discover the compensations and refuges of life for ourselves. Even when they enter deep into our world or sink below us, they still think that they are better than we are. They are different.[2]

The essential differences of the rich fascinated Fitzgerald and his readers. Throughout the 1920s, the rich and mysterious filled dozens of short stories that enabled Fitzgerald to marry Zelda Sayre, a Southern debutante, and to start a family. But constant exposure to the rich, without being rich, took its toll on both of them. The three stories here: "Bernice Bobs Her Hair," "Winter Dreams," and "The Diamond as Big as the Ritz," are ultimately stories of disillusionment with a strong moral center. Filled with wonder and caution, these three stories blend realism and fable into a uniquely modernist take on wealth, love, and success.

The first of our stories, "Bernice Bobs Her Hair," developed out of an actual letter that Fitzgerald wrote to his younger sister Annabel when she was a teenager. By the second decade of the twentieth century, Fitzgerald already had deep exposure to the wealthy that he would later write about, and in this early letter, he gives his sister advice meant to ease her transition into society. As we can see from the story, that transition into society required a sufficient degree of caution and self-protection. The second and third of our selections, "Winter Dreams" and "The Diamond as Big as the Ritz," explore themes that are more closely related to Fitzgerald: young love between a rich girl and a middle-class boy. In both stories, however, the moral compass is very clear: the Midwesterner who stays true to his values will survive even as his romantic heart is damaged. Although each of these stories is from the early years of Fitzgerald's career, readers will surely recognize these themes and their distinctly American ethic and tone.

5.11.1 "Winter Dreams"

Some of the caddies were poor as sin and lived in one-room houses with a neurasthenic cow in the front yard, but Dexter Green's father owned the second best grocery-store in Black Bear—the best one was "The Hub," patronized by the wealthy people from Sherry Island—and Dexter caddied only for pocket-money.

In the fall when the days became crisp and gray, and the long Minnesota winter shut down like the white lid of a box, Dexter's skis moved over the snow that hid the fairways of the golf course. At these times the country gave him a feeling of

---

2   Ibid.

profound melancholy—it offended him that the links should lie in enforced fallow-ness, haunted by ragged sparrows for the long season. It was dreary, too, that on the tees where the gay colors fluttered in summer there were now only the desolate sand-boxes knee-deep in crusted ice. When he crossed the hills the wind blew cold as misery, and if the sun was out he tramped with his eyes squinted up against the hard dimensionless glare.

In April the winter ceased abruptly. The snow ran down into Black Bear Lake scarcely tarrying for the early golfers to brave the season with red and black balls. Without elation, without an interval of moist glory, the cold was gone.

Dexter knew that there was something dismal about this Northern spring, just as he knew there was something gorgeous about the fall. Fall made him clinch his hands and tremble and repeat idiotic sentences to himself, and make brisk abrupt gestures of command to imaginary audiences and armies. October filled him with hope which November raised to a sort of ecstatic triumph, and in this mood the fleet-ing brilliant impressions of the summer at Sherry Island were ready grist to his mill. He became a golf champion and defeated Mr. T. A. Hedrick in a marvellous match played a hundred times over the fairways of his imagination, a match each detail of which he changed about untiringly—sometimes he won with almost laughable ease, sometimes he came up magnificently from behind. Again, stepping from a Pierce-Ar-row automobile, like Mr. Mortimer Jones, he strolled frigidly into the lounge of the Sherry Island Golf Club—or perhaps, surrounded by an admiring crowd, he gave an exhibition of fancy diving from the spring-board of the club raft. . . . Among those who watched him in open-mouthed wonder was Mr. Mortimer Jones.

And one day it came to pass that Mr. Jones—himself and not his ghost—came up to Dexter with tears in his eyes and said that Dexter was the—best caddy in the club, and wouldn't he decide not to quit if Mr. Jones made it worth his while, because every other caddy in the club lost one ball a hole for him—regularly—

"No, sir," said Dexter decisively, "I don't want to caddy any more." Then, after a pause: "I'm too old."

"You're not more than fourteen. Why the devil did you decide just this morning that you wanted to quit? You promised that next week you'd go over to the State tournament with me."

"I decided I was too old."

Dexter handed in his "A Class" badge, collected what money was due him from the caddy master, and walked home to Black Bear Village.

"The best—caddy I ever saw," shouted Mr. Mortimer Jones over a drink that afternoon. "Never lost a ball! Willing! Intelligent! Quiet! Honest! Grateful!"

The little girl who had done this was eleven—beautifully ugly as little girls are apt to be who are destined after a few years to be inexpressibly lovely and bring no end of misery to a great number of men. The spark, however, was perceptible. There was a general ungodliness in the way her lips twisted ,down at the corners when she smiled, and in the—Heaven help us!—in the almost passionate quality of her eyes. Vitality is born early in such women. It was utterly in evidence now, shining through her thin frame in a sort of glow.

She had come eagerly out on to the course at nine o'clock with a white linen nurse and five small new golf-clubs in a white canvas bag which the nurse was carrying. When Dexter first saw her she was standing by the caddy house, rather ill at ease and trying to conceal the fact by engaging her nurse in an obviously unnatural conversation graced by startling and irrelevant grimaces from herself.

"Well, it's certainly a nice day, Hilda," Dexter heard her say. She drew down the corners of her mouth, smiled, and glanced furtively around, her eyes in transit falling for an instant on Dexter.

Then to the nurse:

"Well, I guess there aren't very many people out here this morning, are there?"

The smile again—radiant, blatantly artificial—convincing.

"I don't know what we're supposed to do now," said the nurse, looking nowhere in particular.

"Oh, that's all right. I'll fix it up.

Dexter stood perfectly still, his mouth slightly ajar. He knew that if he moved forward a step his stare would be in her line of vision—if he moved backward he would lose his full view of her face. For a moment he had not realized how young she was. Now he remembered having seen her several times the year before in bloomers.

Suddenly, involuntarily, he laughed, a short abrupt laugh—then, startled by himself, he turned and began to walk quickly away.

"Boy!"

Dexter stopped.

"Boy—"

Beyond question he was addressed. Not only that, but he was treated to that absurd smile, that preposterous smile—the memory of which at least a dozen men were to carry into middle age.

"Boy, do you know where the golf teacher is?"

"He's giving a lesson."

"Well, do you know where the caddy-master is?"

"He isn't here yet this morning."

"Oh." For a moment this baffled her. She stood alternately on her right and left foot.

"We'd like to get a caddy," said the nurse. "Mrs. Mortimer Jones sent us out to play golf, and we don't know how without we get a caddy."

Here she was stopped by an ominous glance from Miss Jones, followed immediately by the smile.

"There aren't any caddies here except me," said Dexter to the nurse, "and I got to stay here in charge until the caddy-master gets here."

"Oh."

Miss Jones and her retinue now withdrew, and at a proper distance from Dexter became involved in a heated conversation, which was concluded by Miss Jones taking one of the clubs and hitting it on the ground with violence. For further emphasis she raised it again and was about to bring it down smartly upon the nurse's bosom, when the nurse seized the club and twisted it from her hands.

"You damn little mean old thing!" cried Miss Jones wildly.

Another argument ensued. Realizing that the elements of the comedy were implied in the scene, Dexter several times began to laugh, but each time restrained the laugh before it reached audibility. He could not resist the monstrous conviction that the little girl was justified in beating the nurse.

The situation was resolved by the fortuitous appearance of the caddymaster, who was appealed to immediately by the nurse.

"Miss Jones is to have a little caddy, and this one says he can't go."

"Mr. McKenna said I was to wait here till you came," said Dexter quickly.

"Well, he's here now." Miss Jones smiled cheerfully at the caddy-master. Then she dropped her bag and set off at a haughty mince toward the first tee.

"Well?" The caddy-master turned to Dexter. "What you standing there like a dummy for? Go pick up the young lady's clubs."

"I don't think I'll go out to-day," said Dexter.

"You don't—"

"I think I'll quit."

The enormity of his decision frightened him. He was a favorite caddy, and the thirty dollars a month he earned through the summer were not to be made elsewhere around the lake. But he had received a strong emotional shock, and his perturbation required a violent and immediate outlet.

It is not so simple as that, either. As so frequently would be the case in the future, Dexter was unconsciously dictated to by his winter dreams.

II

Now, of course, the quality and the seasonability of these winter dreams varied, but the stuff of them remained. They persuaded Dexter several years later to pass up a business course at the State university—his father, prospering now, would have paid his way—for the precarious advantage of attending an older and more famous university in the East, where he was bothered by his scanty funds. But do not get the impression, because his winter dreams happened to be concerned at first with musings on the rich, that there was anything merely snobbish in the boy. He wanted not association with glittering things and glittering people—he wanted the glittering things themselves. Often he reached out for the best without knowing why he wanted it—and sometimes he ran up against the mysterious denials and prohibitions in which life indulges. It is with one of those denials and not with his career as a whole that this story deals.

He made money. It was rather amazing. After college he went to the city from which Black Bear Lake draws its wealthy patrons. When he was only twenty-three and had been there not quite two years, there were already people who liked to say: "Now there's a boy—" All about him rich men's sons were peddling bonds precariously, or investing patrimonies precariously, or plodding through the two dozen volumes of the "George Washington Commercial Course," but Dexter borrowed a thousand dollars on his college degree and his confident mouth, and bought a partnership in a laundry.

It was a small laundry when he went into it but Dexter made a specialty of learning how the English washed fine woollen golf-stockings without shrinking them, and within a year he was catering to the trade that wore knickerbockers. Men were insisting that their Shetland hose and sweaters go to his laundry just as they had insisted on a caddy who could find golfballs. A little later he was doing their wives' lingerie as well—and running five branches in different parts of the city. Before he was twenty-seven he owned the largest string of laundries in his section of the country. It was then that he sold out and went to New York. But the part of his story that concerns us goes back to the days when he was making his first big success.

When he was twenty-three Mr. Hart—one of the gray-haired men who like to say "Now there's a boy"—gave him a guest card to the Sherry Island Golf Club for a week-end. So he signed his name one day on the register, and that afternoon played golf in a foursome with Mr. Hart and Mr. Sandwood and Mr. T. A. Hedrick. He did not consider it necessary to remark that he had once carried Mr. Hart's bag over this same links, and that he knew every trap and gully with his eyes shut—but he found himself glancing at the four caddies who trailed them, trying to catch a gleam or gesture that would remind him of himself, that would lessen the gap which lay between his present and his past.

It was a curious day, slashed abruptly with fleeting, familiar impressions. One minute he had the sense of being a trespasser—in the next he was impressed by the tremendous superiority he felt toward Mr. T. A. Hedrick, who was a bore and not even a good golfer any more.

Then, because of a ball Mr. Hart lost near the fifteenth green, an enormous thing happened. While they were searching the stiff grasses of the rough there was a clear call of "Fore!" from behind a hill in their rear. And as they all turned abruptly from their search a bright new ball sliced abruptly over the hill and caught Mr. T. A. Hedrick in the abdomen.

"By Gad!" cried Mr. T. A. Hedrick, "they ought to put some of these crazy women off the course. It's getting to be outrageous."

A head and a voice came up together over the hill:

"Do you mind if we go through?"

"You hit me in the stomach!" declared Mr. Hedrick wildly.

"Did I?" The girl approached the group of men. "I'm sorry. I yelled 'Fore!'"

Her glance fell casually on each of the men—then scanned the fairway for her ball.

"Did I bounce into the rough?"

It was impossible to determine whether this question was ingenuous or malicious. In a moment, however, she left no doubt, for as her partner came up over the hill she called cheerfully:

"Here I am! I'd have gone on the green except that I hit something."

As she took her stance for a short mashie shot, Dexter looked at her closely. She wore a blue gingham dress, rimmed at throat and shoulders with a white edging that accentuated her tan. The quality of exaggeration, of thinness, which had made her passionate eyes and down-turning mouth absurd at eleven, was gone now. She was arrestingly beautiful. The color in her cheeks was centered like the color in a picture—it was not a "high" color, but a sort of fluctuating and feverish warmth, so shaded that it seemed at any moment it would recede and disappear. This color and the mobility of her mouth gave a continual impression of flux, of intense life, of passionate vitality—balanced only partially by the sad luxury of her eyes.

She swung her mashie impatiently and without interest, pitching the ball into a sand-pit on the other side of the green. With a quick, insincere smile and a careless "Thank you!" she went on after it.

"That Judy Jones!" remarked Mr. Hedrick on the next tee, as they waited—some moments—for her to play on ahead. "All she needs is to be turned up and spanked for six months and then to be married off to an oldfashioned cavalry captain."

"My God, she's good-looking!" said Mr. Sandwood, who was just over thirty.

"Good-looking!" cried Mr. Hedrick contemptuously, "she always looks as if she wanted to be kissed! Turning those big cow-eyes on every calf in town!"

It was doubtful if Mr. Hedrick intended a reference to the maternal instinct.

"She'd play pretty good golf if she'd try," said Mr. Sandwood.

"She has no form," said Mr. Hedrick solemnly.

"She has a nice figure," said Mr. Sandwood.

"Better thank the Lord she doesn't drive a swifter ball," said Mr. Hart, winking at Dexter.

Later in the afternoon the sun went down with a riotous swirl of gold and varying blues and scarlets, and left the dry, rustling night of Western summer. Dexter watched from the veranda of the Golf Club, watched the even overlap of the waters in the little wind, silver molasses under the harvest-moon. Then the moon held a finger to her lips and the lake became a clear pool, pale and quiet. Dexter put on his bathing-suit and swam out to the farthest raft, where he stretched dripping on the wet canvas of the springboard.

There was a fish jumping and a star shining and the lights around the lake were gleaming. Over on a dark peninsula a piano was playing the songs of last summer and of summers before that—songs from "Chin-Chin" and "The Count of Luxemburg" and "The Chocolate Soldier"—and because the sound of a piano over a stretch of water had always seemed beautiful to Dexter he lay perfectly quiet and listened.

The tune the piano was playing at that moment had been gay and new five years before when Dexter was a sophomore at college. They had played it at a prom once when he could not afford the luxury of proms, and he had stood outside the gymnasium and listened. The sound of the tune precipitated in him a sort of ecstasy and it was with that ecstasy he viewed what happened to him now. It was a mood of intense appreciation, a sense that, for once, he was magnificently attune to life and that everything about him was radiating a brightness and a glamour he might never know again.

A low, pale oblong detached itself suddenly from the darkness of the Island, spitting forth the reverberate sound of a racing motor-boat. Two white streamers of cleft water rolled themselves out behind it and almost immediately the boat was beside him, drowning out the hot tinkle of the piano in the drone of its spray. Dexter raising himself on his arms was aware of a figure standing at the wheel, of two dark eyes regarding him over the lengthening space of water—then the boat had gone by and was sweeping in an immense and purposeless circle of spray round and round in the middle of the lake. With equal eccentricity one of the circles flattened out and headed back toward the raft.

"Who's that?" she called, shutting off her motor. She was so near now that Dexter could see her bathing-suit, which consisted apparently of pink rompers.

The nose of the boat bumped the raft, and as the latter tilted rakishly he was precipitated toward her. With different degrees of interest they recognized each other.

"Aren't you one of those men we played through this afternoon?" she demanded.

He was.

"Well, do you know how to drive a motor-boat? Because if you do I wish you'd drive this one so I can ride on the surf-board behind. My name is Judy Jones"—she favored him with an absurd smirk—rather, what tried to be a smirk, for, twist her mouth as she might, it was not grotesque, it was merely beautiful—"and I live in a house over there on the Island, and in that house there is a man waiting for me. When he drove up at the door I drove out of the dock because he says I'm his ideal."

There was a fish jumping and a star shining and the lights around the lake were gleaming. Dexter sat beside Judy Jones and she explained how her boat was driven. Then she was in the water, swimming to the floating surfboard with a sinuous crawl. Watching her was without effort to the eye, watching a branch waving or a sea-gull flying. Her arms, burned to butternut, moved sinuously among the dull platinum ripples, elbow appearing first, casting the forearm back with a cadence of falling water, then reaching out and down, stabbing a path ahead.

They moved out into the lake; turning, Dexter saw that she was kneeling on the low rear of the now uptilted surf-board.

"Go faster," she called, "fast as it'll go."

Obediently he jammed the lever forward and the white spray mounted at the bow. When he looked around again the girl was standing up on the rushing board, her arms spread wide, her eyes lifted toward the moon.

"It's awful cold," she shouted. "What's your name?"

He told her.

"Well, why don't you come to dinner to-morrow night?"

His heart turned over like the fly-wheel of the boat, and, for the second time, her casual whim gave a new direction to his life.

III

Next evening while he waited for her to come down-stairs, Dexter peopled the soft deep summer room and the sun-porch that opened from it with the men who had already loved Judy Jones. He knew the sort of men they were—the men who when he first went to college had entered from the great prep schools with graceful clothes and the deep tan of healthy summers. He had seen that, in one sense, he was better than these men. He was newer and stronger. Yet in acknowledging to himself that he wished his children to be like them he was admitting that he was but the rough, strong stuff from which they eternally sprang.

When the time had come for him to wear good clothes, he had known who were the best tailors in America, and the best tailors in America had made him the suit he wore this evening. He had acquired that particular reserve peculiar to his university, that set it off from other universities. He recognized the value to him of such a mannerism and he had adopted it; he knew that to be careless in dress and manner required more confidence than to be careful. But carelessness was for his children. His mother's name had been Krimslich. She was a Bohemian of the peasant class and she had talked broken English to the end of her days. Her son must keep to the set patterns.

At a little after seven Judy Jones came down-stairs. She wore a blue silk afternoon dress, and he was disappointed at first that she had not put on something more elaborate. This feeling was accentuated when, after a brief greeting, she went to the door of a butler's pantry and pushing it open called: "You can serve dinner, Martha." He had rather expected that a butler would announce dinner, that there would be a cocktail. Then he put these thoughts behind him as they sat down side by side on a lounge and looked at each other.

"Father and mother won't be here," she said thoughtfully.

He remembered the last time he had seen her father, and he was glad the parents were not to be here to-night—they might wonder who he was. He had been born in Keeble, a Minnesota village fifty miles farther north, and he always gave Keeble as his home instead of Black Bear Village. Country towns were well enough to come from if they weren't inconveniently in sight and used as footstools by fashionable lakes.

They talked of his university, which she had visited frequently during the past two years, and of the near-by city which supplied Sherry Island with its patrons, and whither Dexter would return next day to his prospering laundries.

During dinner she slipped into a moody depression which gave Dexter a feeling of uneasiness. Whatever petulance she uttered in her throaty voice worried him. Whatever she smiled at—at him, at a chicken liver, at nothing—it disturbed him that her smile could have no root in mirth, or even in amusement. When the scarlet corners of her lips curved down, it was less a smile than an invitation to a kiss.

Then, after dinner, she led him out on the dark sun-porch and deliberately changed the atmosphere.

"Do you mind if I weep a little?" she said.

"I'm afraid I'm boring you," he responded quickly.

"You're not. I like you. But I've just had a terrible afternoon. There was a man I cared about, and this afternoon he told me out of a clear sky that he was poor as a church-mouse. He'd never even hinted it before. Does this sound horribly mundane?"

"Perhaps he was afraid to tell you."

"Suppose he was," she answered. "He didn't start right. You see, if I'd thought of him as poor—well, I've been mad about loads of poor men, and fully intended to marry them all. But in this case, I hadn't thought of him that way, and my interest in him wasn't strong enough to survive the shock. As if a girl calmly informed her fianc_ that she was a widow. He might not object to widows, but—

"Let's start right," she interrupted herself suddenly. "Who are you, anyhow?"

For a moment Dexter hesitated. Then:

"I'm nobody," he announced. "My career is largely a matter of futures."

"Are you poor?"

"No," he said frankly, "I'm probably making more money than any man my age in the Northwest. I know that's an obnoxious remark, but you advised me to start right."

There was a pause. Then she smiled and the corners of her mouth drooped and an almost imperceptible sway brought her closer to him, looking up into his eyes. A lump rose in Dexter's throat, and he waited breathless for the experiment, facing the unpredictable compound that would form mysteriously from the elements of their lips. Then he saw—she communicated her excitement to him, lavishly, deeply, with kisses that were not a promise but a fulfillment. They aroused in him not hunger demanding renewal but surfeit that would demand more surfeit . . . kisses that were like charity, creating want by holding back nothing at all.

It did not take him many hours to decide that he had wanted Judy Jones ever since he was a proud, desirous little boy.

IV

It began like that—and continued, with varying shades of intensity, on such a note right up to the dénouement. Dexter surrendered a part of himself to the most direct and unprincipled personality with which he had ever come in contact. Whatever Judy wanted, she went after with the full pressure of her charm. There was no divergence of method, no jockeying for position or premeditation of effects—there was a very little mental side to any of her affairs. She simply made men conscious to the highest degree of her physical loveliness. Dexter had no desire to change her. Her deficiencies were knit up with a passionate energy that transcended and justified them.

When, as Judy's head lay against his shoulder that first night, she whispered, "I don't know what's the matter with me. Last night I thought I was in love with a man and to-night I think I'm in love with you—"—it seemed to him a beautiful and romantic thing to say. It was the exquisite excitability that for the moment he controlled and owned. But a week later he was compelled to view this same quality in a different light. She took him in her roadster to a picnic supper, and after supper she disappeared, likewise in her roadster, with another man. Dexter became enormously upset and was scarcely able to be decently civil to the other people present. When she assured him that she had not kissed the other man, he knew she was lying—yet he was glad that she had taken the trouble to lie to him.

He was, as he found before the summer ended, one of a varying dozen who circulated about her. Each of them had at one time been favored above all others—about half of them still basked in the solace of occasional sentimental revivals. Whenever one showed signs of dropping out through long neglect, she granted him a brief honeyed hour, which encouraged him to tag along for a year or so longer. Judy made these forays upon the helpless and defeated without malice, indeed half unconscious that there was anything mischievous in what she did.

When a new man came to town every one dropped out—dates were automatically cancelled.

The helpless part of trying to do anything about it was that she did it all herself. She was not a girl who could be "won" in the kinetic sense—she was proof against cleverness, she was proof against charm; if any of these assailed her too strongly she would immediately resolve the affair to a physical basis, and under the magic of her physical splendor the strong as well as the brilliant played her game and not their own. She was entertained only by the gratification of her desires and by the direct exercise of her own charm. Perhaps from so much youthful love, so many youthful lovers, she had come, in self-defense, to nourish herself wholly from within.

Succeeding Dexter's first exhilaration came restlessness and dissatisfaction. The helpless ecstasy of losing himself in her was opiate rather than tonic. It was fortunate for his work during the winter that those moments of ecstasy came infrequently. Early in their acquaintance it had seemed for a while that there was a deep and spontaneous mutual attraction that first August, for example—three days of long evenings on her dusky veranda, of strange wan kisses through the late afternoon, in shadowy alcoves or behind the protecting trellises of the garden arbors, of mornings when she was fresh as a dream and almost shy at meeting him in the clarity of the rising day. There was all the ecstasy of an engagement about it, sharpened by his realization that there was no engagement. It was during those three days that, for the first time, he had asked her to marry him. She said "maybe some day," she said "kiss me," she said "I'd like to marry you," she said "I love you"—she said—nothing.

The three days were interrupted by the arrival of a New York man who visited at her house for half September. To Dexter's agony, rumor engaged them. The man was the son of the president of a great trust company. But at the end of a month it was reported that Judy was yawning. At a dance one night she sat all evening in a motor-boat with a local beau, while the New Yorker searched the club for her frantically. She told the local beau that she was bored with her visitor, and two days later he left. She was seen with him at the station, and it was reported that he looked very mournful indeed.

On this note the summer ended. Dexter was twenty-four, and he found himself increasingly in a position to do as he wished. He joined two clubs in the city and lived at one of them. Though he was by no means an integral part of the stag-lines at these clubs, he managed to be on hand at dances where Judy Jones was likely to appear. He could have gone out socially as much as he liked—he was an eligible young man, now, and popular with down-town fathers. His confessed devotion to Judy Jones had rather solidified his position. But he had no social aspirations and rather despised the dancing men who were always on tap for the Thursday or Saturday parties and who filled in at dinners with the younger married set. Already he was playing with the idea of going East to New York. He wanted to take Judy Jones with him. No disillusion as to the world in which she had grown up could cure his illusion as to her desirability.

Remember that—for only in the light of it can what he did for her be understood.

Eighteen months after he first met Judy Jones he became engaged to another girl. Her name was Irene Scheerer, and her father was one of the men who had always believed in Dexter. Irene was light-haired and sweet and honorable, and a little stout, and she had two suitors whom she pleasantly relinquished when Dexter formally asked her to marry him.

Summer, fall, winter, spring, another summer, another fall—so much he had given of his active life to the incorrigible lips of Judy Jones. She had treated him with interest, with encouragement, with malice, with indifference, with contempt. She had inflicted on him the innumerable little slights and indignities possible in such a case—as if in revenge for having ever cared for him at all. She had beckoned him and yawned at him and beckoned him again and he had responded often with bitterness and narrowed eyes. She had brought him ecstatic happiness and intolerable agony of spirit. She had caused him untold inconvenience and not a little trouble. She had insulted him, and she had ridden over him, and she had played his interest in her against his interest in his work—for fun. She had done everything to him except to criticise him—this she had not done—it seemed to him only because it might have sullied the utter indifference she manifested and sincerely felt toward him.

When autumn had come and gone again it occurred to him that he could not have Judy Jones. He had to beat this into his mind but he convinced himself at last. He lay awake at night for a while and argued it over. He told himself the trouble and the pain she had caused him, he enumerated her glaring deficiencies as a wife. Then he said to himself that he loved her, and after a while he fell asleep. For a week, lest he imagined her husky voice over the telephone or her eyes opposite him at lunch, he worked hard and late, and at night he went to his office and plotted out his years.

At the end of a week he went to a dance and cut in on her once. For almost the first time since they had met he did not ask her to sit out with him or tell her that she was lovely. It hurt him that she did not miss these things—that was all. He was not jealous when he saw that there was a new man to-night. He had been hardened against jealousy long before.

He stayed late at the dance. He sat for an hour with Irene Scheerer and talked about books and about music. He knew very little about either. But he was beginning to be master of his own time now, and he had a rather priggish notion that he—the young and already fabulously successful Dexter Green—should know more about such things.

That was in October, when he was twenty-five. In January, Dexter and Irene became engaged. It was to be announced in June, and they were to be married three months later.

The Minnesota winter prolonged itself interminably, and it was almost May when the winds came soft and the snow ran down into Black Bear Lake at last. For the first time in over a year Dexter was enjoying a certain tranquility of spirit. Judy Jones had been in Florida, and afterward in Hot Springs, and somewhere she had been engaged, and somewhere she had broken it off. At first, when Dexter had definitely given her up, it had made him sad that people still linked them together and asked for news of her, but when he began to be placed at dinner next to Irene Scheerer people didn't ask him about her any more—they told him about her. He ceased to be an authority on her.

May at last. Dexter walked the streets at night when the darkness was damp as rain, wondering that so soon, with so little done, so much of ecstasy had gone from him. May one year back had been marked by Judy's poignant, unforgivable, yet forgiven turbulence—it had been one of those rare times when he fancied she had grown to care for him. That old penny's worth of happiness he had spent for this bushel of content. He knew that Irene would be no more than a curtain spread behind him, a hand moving among gleaming tea-cups, a voice calling to children . . . fire and loveliness were gone, the magic of nights and the wonder of the varying hours and seasons . . . slender lips, down-turning, dropping to his lips and bearing him up into a heaven of eyes. . . . The thing was deep in him. He was too strong and alive for it to die lightly.

In the middle of May when the weather balanced for a few days on the thin bridge that led to deep summer he turned in one night at Irene's house. Their engagement was to be announced in a week now—no one would be surprised at it. And to-night they would sit together on the lounge at the University Club and look on for an hour at the dancers. It gave him a sense of solidity to go with her—she was so sturdily popular, so intensely "great."

He mounted the steps of the brownstone house and stepped inside.

"Irene," he called.

Mrs. Scheerer came out of the living-room to meet him.

"Dexter," she said, "Irene's gone up-stairs with a splitting headache. She wanted to go with you but I made her go to bed."

"Nothing serious, I—"

"Oh, no. She's going to play golf with you in the morning. You can spare her for just one night, can't you, Dexter?"

Her smile was kind. She and Dexter liked each other. In the living-room he talked for a moment before he said good-night.

Returning to the University Club, where he had rooms, he stood in the doorway for a moment and watched the dancers. He leaned against the door-post, nodded at a man or two—yawned.

"Hello, darling."

The familiar voice at his elbow startled him. Judy Jones had left a man and crossed the room to him—Judy Jones, a slender enamelled doll in cloth of gold: gold in a band at her head, gold in two slipper points at her dress's hem. The fragile glow of her face seemed to blossom as she smiled at him. A breeze of warmth and light blew through the room. His hands in the pockets of his dinner-jacket tightened spasmodically. He was filled with a sudden excitement.

"When did you get back?" he asked casually.

"Come here and I'll tell you about it."

She turned and he followed her. She had been away—he could have wept at the wonder of her return. She had passed through enchanted streets, doing things that were like provocative music. All mysterious happenings, all fresh and quickening hopes, had gone away with her, come back with her now.

She turned in the doorway.

"Have you a car here? If you haven't, I have."

"I have a coup_."

In then, with a rustle of golden cloth. He slammed the door. Into so many cars she had stepped—like this—like that—her back against the leather, so—her elbow resting on the door—waiting. She would have been soiled long since had there been anything to soil her—except herself—but this was her own self outpouring.

With an effort he forced himself to start the car and back into the street. This was nothing, he must remember. She had done this before, and he had put her behind him, as he would have crossed a bad account from his books.

He drove slowly down-town and, affecting abstraction, traversed the deserted streets of the business section, peopled here and there where a movie was giving out its crowd or where consumptive or pugilistic youth lounged in front of pool halls. The clink of glasses and the slap of hands on the bars issued from saloons, cloisters of glazed glass and dirty yellow light.

She was watching him closely and the silence was embarrassing, yet in this crisis he could find no casual word with which to profane the hour. At a convenient turning he began to zigzag back toward the University Club.

"Have you missed me?" she asked suddenly.

"Everybody missed you."

He wondered if she knew of Irene Scheerer. She had been back only a day—her absence had been almost contemporaneous with his engagement.

"What a remark!" Judy laughed sadly—without sadness. She looked at him searchingly. He became absorbed in the dashboard.

"You're handsomer than you used to be," she said thoughtfully. "Dexter, you have the most rememberable eyes."

He could have laughed at this, but he did not laugh. It was the sort of thing that was said to sophomores. Yet it stabbed at him.

"I'm awfully tired of everything, darling." She called every one darling, endowing the endearment with careless, individual comraderie. "I wish you'd marry me."

The directness of this confused him. He should have told her now that he was going to marry another girl, but he could not tell her. He could as easily have sworn that he had never loved her.

"I think we'd get along," she continued, on the same note, "unless probably you've forgotten me and fallen in love with another girl."

Her confidence was obviously enormous. She had said, in effect, that she found such a thing impossible to believe, that if it were true he had merely committed a childish indiscretion—and probably to show off. She would forgive him, because it was not a matter of any moment but rather something to be brushed aside lightly.

"Of course you could never love anybody but me," she continued. "I like the way you love me. Oh, Dexter, have you forgotten last year?"

"No, I haven't forgotten."

"Neither have I! "

Was she sincerely moved—or was she carried along by the wave of her own acting?

"I wish we could be like that again," she said, and he forced himself to answer:

"I don't think we can."

"I suppose not. . . . I hear you're giving Irene Scheerer a violent rush."

There was not the faintest emphasis on the name, yet Dexter was suddenly ashamed.

"Oh, take me home," cried Judy suddenly; "I don't want to go back to that idiotic dance—with those children."

Then, as he turned up the street that led to the residence district, Judy began to cry quietly to herself. He had never seen her cry before.

The dark street lightened, the dwellings of the rich loomed up around them, he stopped his coup_ in front of the great white bulk of the Mortimer Joneses house, somnolent, gorgeous, drenched with the splendor of the damp moonlight. Its solidity startled him. The strong walls, the steel of the girders, the breadth and beam and pomp of it were there only to bring out the contrast with the young beauty beside him. It was sturdy to accentuate her slightness—as if to show what a breeze could be generated by a butterfly's wing.

He sat perfectly quiet, his nerves in wild clamor, afraid that if he moved he would find her irresistibly in his arms. Two tears had rolled down her wet face and trembled on her upper lip.

"I'm more beautiful than anybody else," she said brokenly, "why can't I be happy?" Her moist eyes tore at his stability—her mouth turned slowly downward with an exquisite sadness: "I'd like to marry you if you'll have me, Dexter. I suppose you think I'm not worth having, but I'll be so beautiful for you, Dexter."

A million phrases of anger, pride, passion, hatred, tenderness fought on his lips. Then a perfect wave of emotion washed over him, carrying off with it a sediment of wisdom, of convention, of doubt, of honor. This was his girl who was speaking, his own, his beautiful, his pride.

"Won't you come in?" He heard her draw in her breath sharply.

Waiting.

"All right," his voice was trembling, "I'll come in.

V

It was strange that neither when it was over nor a long time afterward did he regret that night. Looking at it from the perspective of ten years, the fact that Judy's flare for him endured just one month seemed of little importance. Nor did it matter that by his yielding he subjected himself to a deeper agony in the end and gave serious hurt to Irene Scheerer and to Irene's parents, who had befriended him. There was nothing sufficiently pictorial about Irene's grief to stamp itself on his mind.

Dexter was at bottom hard-minded. The attitude of the city on his action was of no importance to him, not because he was going to leave the city, but because any outside attitude on the situation seemed superficial. He was completely indifferent to popular opinion. Nor, when he had seen that it was no use, that he did not possess in himself the power to move fundamentally or to hold Judy Jones, did he bear any malice toward her. He loved her, and he would love her until the day he was too old for loving—but he could not have her. So he tasted the deep pain that is reserved only for the strong, just as he had tasted for a little while the deep happiness.

Even the ultimate falsity of the grounds upon which Judy terminated the engagement that she did not want to "take him away" from Irene—Judy, who had wanted nothing else—did not revolt him. He was beyond any revulsion or any amusement.

He went East in February with the intention of selling out his laundries and settling in New York—but the war came to America in March and changed his plans. He returned to the West, handed over the management of the business to his partner, and went into the first officers' training-camp in late April. He was one of those young thousands who greeted the war with a certain amount of relief, welcoming the liberation from webs of tangled emotion.

VI

This story is not his biography, remember, although things creep into it which have nothing to do with those dreams he had when he was young. We are almost done with them and with him now. There is only one more incident to be related here, and it happens seven years farther on.

It took place in New York, where he had done well—so well that there were no barriers too high for him. He was thirty-two years old, and, except for one flying trip immediately after the war, he had not been West in seven years. A man named Devlin from Detroit came into his office to see him in a business way, and then and there this incident occurred, and closed out, so to speak, this particular side of his life.

"So you're from the Middle West," said the man Devlin with careless curiosity. "That's funny—I thought men like you were probably born and raised on Wall

Street. You know—wife of one of my best friends in Detroit came from your city. I was an usher at the wedding."

Dexter waited with no apprehension of what was coming.

"Judy Simms," said Devlin with no particular interest; "Judy Jones she was once."

"Yes, I knew her." A dull impatience spread over him. He had heard, of course, that she was married—perhaps deliberately he had heard no more.

"Awfully nice girl," brooded Devlin meaninglessly, "I'm sort of sorry for her."

"Why?" Something in Dexter was alert, receptive, at once.

"Oh, Lud Simms has gone to pieces in a way. I don't mean he ill-uses her, but he drinks and runs around "

"Doesn't she run around?"

"No. Stays at home with her kids."

"Oh."

"She's a little too old for him," said Devlin.

"Too old!" cried Dexter. "Why, man, she's only twenty-seven."

He was possessed with a wild notion of rushing out into the streets and taking a train to Detroit. He rose to his feet spasmodically.

"I guess you're busy," Devlin apologized quickly. "I didn't realize—"

"No, I'm not busy," said Dexter, steadying his voice. "I'm not busy at all. Not busy at all. Did you say she was—twenty-seven? No, I said she was twenty-seven."

"Yes, you did," agreed Devlin dryly.

"Go on, then. Go on."

"What do you mean?"

"About Judy Jones."

Devlin looked at him helplessly.

"Well, that's, I told you all there is to it. He treats her like the devil. Oh, they're not going to get divorced or anything. When he's particularly outrageous she forgives him. In fact, I'm inclined to think she loves him. She was a pretty girl when she first came to Detroit."

A pretty girl! The phrase struck Dexter as ludicrous

"Isn't she—a pretty girl, any more?"

"Oh, she's all right."

"Look here," said Dexter, sitting down suddenly, "I don't understand. You say she was a 'pretty girl' and now you say she's 'all right.' I don't understand what you mean—Judy Jones wasn't a pretty girl, at all. She was a great beauty. Why, I knew her, I knew her. She was—"

Devlin laughed pleasantly.

"I'm not trying to start a row," he said. "I think Judy's a nice girl and I like her. I can't understand how a man like Lud Simms could fall madly in love with her, but he did." Then he added: "Most of the women like her."

Dexter looked closely at Devlin, thinking wildly that there must be a reason for this, some insensitivity in the man or some private malice.

"Lots of women fade just like that," Devlin snapped his fingers. "You must have seen it happen. Perhaps I've forgotten how pretty she was at her wedding. I've seen her so much since then, you see. She has nice eyes."

A sort of dulness settled down upon Dexter. For the first time in his life he felt like getting very drunk. He knew that he was laughing loudly at something Devlin had said, but he did not know what it was or why it was funny. When, in a few minutes, Devlin went he lay down on his lounge and looked out the window at the New York sky-line into which the sun was sinking in dull lovely shades of pink and gold.

He had thought that having nothing else to lose he was invulnerable at last—but he knew that he had just lost something more, as surely as if he had married Judy Jones and seen her fade away before his eyes.

The dream was gone. Something had been taken from him. In a sort of panic he pushed the palms of his hands into his eyes and tried to bring up a picture of the waters lapping on Sherry Island and the moonlit veranda, and gingham on the golf-links and the dry sun and the gold color of her neck's soft down. And her mouth damp to his kisses and her eyes plaintive with melancholy and her freshness like new fine linen in the morning. Why, these things were no longer in the world! They had existed and they existed no longer.

For the first time in years the tears were streaming down his face. But they were for himself now. He did not care about mouth and eyes and moving hands. He wanted to care, and he could not care. For he had gone away and he could never go back any more. The gates were closed, the sun was gone down, and there was no beauty but the gray beauty of steel that withstands all time. Even the grief he could have borne was left behind in the country of illusion, of youth, of the richness of life, where his winter dreams had flourished.

"Long ago," he said, "long ago, there was something in me, but now that thing is gone. Now that thing is gone, that thing is gone. I cannot cry. I cannot care. That thing will come back no more."

5.11.2 "The Diamond as Big as the Ritz"

John T. Unger came from a family that had been well known in Hades—a small town on the Mississippi River—for several generations. John's father had held the amateur golf championship through many a heated contest; Mrs. Unger was known "from hot-box to hot-bed," as the local phrase went, for her political addresses; and young John T. Unger, who had just turned sixteen, had danced all the latest dances from New York before he put on long trousers. And now, for a certain time, he was to be away from home. That respect for a New England education which is the bane of all provincial places, which drains them yearly of their most promising young men, had seized upon his parents. Nothing would suit them but that he should go to St. Midas's School near Boston—Hades was too small to hold their darling and gifted son.

Now in Hades—as you know if you ever have been there—the names of the more fashionable preparatory schools and colleges mean very little. The inhabitants have been so long out of the world that, though they make a show of keeping up-to-date in dress and manners and literature, they depend to a great extent on hearsay, and a function that in Hades would be considered elaborate would doubtless be hailed by a Chicago beef-princess as "perhaps a little tacky."

John T. Unger was on the eve of departure. Mrs. Unger, with maternal fatuity, packed his trunks full of linen suits and electric fans, and Mr. Unger presented his son with an asbestos pocket-book stuffed with money.

"Remember, you are always welcome here," he said. "You can be sure, boy, that we'll keep the home fires burning."

"I know," answered John huskily.

"Don't forget who you are and where you come from," continued his father proudly, "and you can do nothing to harm you. You are an Unger—from Hades."

So the old man and the young shook hands, and John walked away with tears streaming from his eyes. Ten minutes later he had passed outside the city limits and he stopped to glance back for the last time. Over the gates the old-fashioned Victorian motto seemed strangely attractive to him. His father had tried time and time again to have it changed to something with a little more push and verve about it, such as "Hades—Your Opportunity," or else a plain "Welcome" sign set over a hearty handshake pricked out in electric lights. The old motto was a little depressing, Mr. Unger had thought—but now . . .

So John took his look and then set his face resolutely toward his destination. And, as he turned away, the lights of Hades against the sky seemed full of a warm and passionate beauty.

St. Midas's School is half an hour from Boston in a Rolls-Pierce motor-car. The actual distance will never be known, for no one, except John T. Unger, had ever arrived there save in a Rolls-Pierce and probably no one ever will again. St. Midas's is the most expensive and the most exclusive boys' preparatory school in the world.

John's first two years there passed pleasantly. The fathers of all the boys were money-kings, and John spent his summer visiting at fashionable resorts. While he was very fond of all the boys he visited, their fathers struck him as being much of a piece, and in his boyish way he often wondered at their exceeding sameness. When he told them where his home was they would ask jovially, "Pretty hot down there?" and John would muster a faint smile and answer, "It certainly is." His response would have been heartier had they not all made this joke—at best varying it with, "Is it hot enough for you down there?" which he hated just as much.

In the middle of his second year at school, a quiet, handsome boy named Percy Washington had been put in John's form. The new-comer was pleasant in his manner and exceedingly well dressed even for St. Midas's, but for some reason he kept aloof from the other boys. The only person with whom he was intimate was John T. Unger, but even to John he was entirely uncommunicative concerning his home or his family. That he was wealthy went without saying, but beyond a few such deductions John knew little of his friend, so it promised rich confectionery for his curiosity when Percy invited him to spend the summer at his home "in the West." He accepted, without hesitation.

It was only when they were in the train that Percy became, for the first time, rather communicative. One day while they were eating lunch in the dining-car and discussing the imperfect characters of several of the boys at school, Percy suddenly changed his tone and made an abrupt remark.

"My father," he said, "is by far the richest man in the world."

"Oh," said John politely. He could think of no answer to make to this confidence. He considered "That's very nice," but it sounded hollow and was on the point of saying, "Really?" but refrained since it would seem to question Percy's statement. And such an astounding statement could scarcely be questioned.

"By far the richest," repeated Percy.

"I was reading in the World Almanac," began John, "that there was one man in America with an income of over five million a years and four men with incomes of over three million a year, and—"

"Oh, they're nothing." Percy's mouth was a half-moon of scorn. "Catch-penny capitalists, financial small-fry, petty merchants and money-lenders. My father could buy them out and not know he'd done it."

"But how does he—"

"Why haven't they put down his income-tax? Because he doesn't pay any. At least he pays a little one—but he doesn't pay any on his real income."

"He must be very rich," said John simply, "I'm glad. I like very rich people.

"The richer a fella is, the better I like him." There was a look of passionate frankness upon his dark face. "I visited the Schnlitzer-Murphys last Easter. Vivian Schnlitzer-Murphy had rubies as big as hen's eggs, and sapphires that were like globes with lights inside them—"

"I love jewels," agreed Percy enthusiastically. "Of course I wouldn't want any one at school to know about it, but I've got quite a collection myself. I used to collect them instead of stamps."

"And diamonds," continued John eagerly. "The Schnlitzer-Murphys had diamonds as big as walnuts—"

"That's nothing." Percy had leaned forward and dropped his voice to a low whisper. "That's nothing at all. My father has a diamond bigger than the Ritz-Carlton Hotel."

2

The Montana sunset lay between two mountains like a gigantic bruise from which dark arteries spread themselves over a poisoned sky. An immense distance under the sky crouched the village of Fish, minute, dismal, and forgotten. There were twelve men, so it was said, in the village of Fish, twelve sombre and inexplicable souls who sucked a lean milk from the almost literally bare rock upon which a mysterious populatory force had begotten them. They had become a race apart, these twelve men of Fish, like some species developed by an early whim of nature, which on second thought had abandoned them to struggle and extermination.

Out of the blue-black bruise in the distance crept a long line of moving lights upon the desolation of the land, and the twelve men of Fish gathered like ghosts at the shanty depot to watch the passing of the seven o'clock train, the Transcontinental Express from Chicago. Six times or so a year the Transcontinental Express, through some inconceivable jurisdiction, stopped at the village of Fish, and when this occurred a figure or so would disembark, mount into a buggy that always appeared from out of the dusk, and drive off toward the bruised sunset. The observation of this pointless and preposterous phenomenon had become a sort of cult among the men of Fish. To observe, that was all; there remained in them none of the vital quality of illusion which would make them wonder or speculate, else a religion might have grown up around these mysterious visitations. But the men of Fish were beyond all religion—the barest and most savage tenets of even Christianity could gain no foothold on that barren rock—so there was no altar, no priest, no sacrifice; only each night at seven the silent concourse by the shanty depot, a congregation who lifted up a prayer of dim, anaemic wonder.

On this June night, the Great Brakeman, whom, had they deified any one, they might well have chosen as their celestial protagonist, had ordained that the seven o'clock train should leave its human (or inhuman) deposit at Fish. At two minutes after seven Percy Washington and John T. Unger disembarked, hurried past the spellbound, the agape, the fearsome eyes of the twelve men of Fish, mounted into a buggy which had obviously appeared from nowhere, and drove away.

After half an hour, when the twilight had coagulated into dark, the silent negro who was driving the buggy hailed an opaque body somewhere ahead of them in the gloom. In response to his cry, it turned upon them a luminous disc which regarded them like a malignant eye out of the unfathomable night. As they came closer, John saw that it was the tail-light of an immense automobile, larger and more magnificent than any he had ever seen. Its body was of gleaming metal richer than nickel and lighter than silver, and the hubs of the wheels were studded with iridescent geometric figures of green and yellow—John did not dare to guess whether they were glass or jewel.

Two negroes, dressed in glittering livery such as one sees in pictures of royal processions in London, were standing at attention beside the car and, as the two young men dismounted from the buggy, they were greeted in some language which the guest could not understand, but which seemed to be an extreme form of the Southern negro's dialect.

"Get in," said Percy to his friend, as their trunks were tossed to the ebony roof of the limousine. "Sorry we had to bring you this far in that buggy, but of course it wouldn't do for the people on the train or those God-forsaken fellas in Fish to see this automobile."

"Gosh! What a car!" This ejaculation was provoked by its interior. John saw that the upholstery consisted of a thousand minute and exquisite tapestries of silk, woven with jewels and embroideries, and set upon a background of cloth of gold. The two armchair seats in which the boys luxuriated were covered with stuff that resembled duvetyn, but seemed woven in numberless colours of the ends of ostrich feathers.

"What a car!" cried John again, in amazement.

"This thing?" Percy laughed. "Why, it's just an old junk we use for a station wagon."

By this time they were gliding along through the darkness toward the break between the two mountains.

"We'll be there in an hour and a half," said Percy, looking at the clock. "I may as well tell you it's not going to be like anything you ever saw before."

If the car was any indication of what John would see, he was prepared to be astonished indeed. The simple piety prevalent in Hades has the earnest worship of and respect for riches as the first article of its creed—had John felt otherwise than radiantly humble before them, his parents would have turned away in horror at the blasphemy.

They had now reached and were entering the break between the two mountains and almost immediately the way became much rougher.

"If the moon shone down here, you'd see that we're in a big gulch," said Percy, trying to peer out of the window. He spoke a few words into the mouthpiece and immediately the footman turned on a searchlight and swept the hillsides with an immense beam.

"Rocky, you see. An ordinary car would be knocked to pieces in half an hour. In fact, it'd take a tank to navigate it unless you knew the way. You notice we're going uphill now."

They were obviously ascending, and within a few minutes the car was crossing a high rise, where they caught a glimpse of a pale moon newly risen in the distance. The car stopped suddenly and several figures took shape out of the dark beside it—these were negroes also. Again the two young men were saluted in the same dimly recognisable dialect; then the negroes set to work and four immense cables dangling from overhead were attached with hooks to the hubs of the great jewelled wheels. At a resounding "Hey-yah!" John felt the car being lifted slowly from the ground—up and up—clear of the tallest rocks on both sides—then higher, until he could see a wavy, moonlit valley stretched out before him in sharp contrast to the quagmire of rocks that they had just left. Only on one side was there still rock—and then suddenly there was no rock beside them or anywhere around.

It was apparent that they had surmounted some immense knife-blade of stone, projecting perpendicularly into the air. In a moment they were going down again, and finally with a soft bump they were landed upon the smooth earth.

"The worst is over," said Percy, squinting out the window. "It's only five miles from here, and our own road—tapestry brick—all the way. This belongs to us. This is where the United States ends, father says."

"Are we in Canada?"

"We are not. We're in the middle of the Montana Rockies. But you are now on the only five square miles of land in the country that's never been surveyed."

"Why hasn't it? Did they forget it?"

"No," said Percy, grinning, "they tried to do it three times. The first time my grandfather corrupted a whole department of the State survey; the second time he had the official maps of the United States tinkered with—that held them for fifteen years. The last time was harder. My father fixed it so that their compasses were in the strongest magnetic field ever artificially set up. He had a whole set of surveying instruments made with a slight defection that would allow for this territory not to appear, and he substituted them for the ones that were to be used. Then he had a river deflected and he had what looked like a village up on its banks—so that they'd see it, and think it was a town ten miles farther up the valley. There's only one thing my father's afraid of," he concluded, "only one thing in the world that could be used to find us out."

"What's that?"

Percy sank his voice to a whisper.

"Aeroplanes," he breathed. "We've got half a dozen anti-aircraft guns and we've arranged it so far—but there've been a few deaths and a great many prisoners. Not that we mind that, you know, father and I, but it upsets mother and the girls, and there's always the chance that some time we won't be able to arrange it."

Shreds and tatters of chinchilla, courtesy clouds in the green moon's heaven, were passing the green moon like precious Eastern stuffs paraded for the inspection of some Tartar Khan. It seemed to John that it was day, and that he was looking at some lads sailing above him in the air, showering down tracts and patent medicine circulars, with their messages of hope for despairing, rock-bound hamlets. It seemed to him that he could see them look down out of the clouds and stare—and stare at whatever there was to stare at in this place whither he was bound—What then? Were they induced to land by some insidious device to be immured far from patent medicines and from tracts until the judgment day—or, should they fail to fall into the trap, did a quick puff of smoke and the sharp round of a splitting shell bring them drooping to earth—and "upset" Percy's mother and sisters. John shook his head and the wraith of a hollow laugh issued silently from his parted lips. What desperate transaction lay hidden here? What a moral expedient of a bizarre Croesus? What terrible and golden mystery? . . .

The chinchilla clouds had drifted past now and, outside the Montana night was bright as day the tapestry brick of the road was smooth to the tread of the great tyres as they rounded a still, moonlit lake; they passed into darkness for a moment, a pine grove, pungent and cool, then they came out into a broad avenue of lawn, and John's exclamation of pleasure was simultaneous with Percy's taciturn "We're home."

Full in the light of the stars, an exquisite château rose from the borders of the lake, climbed in marble radiance half the height of an adjoining mountain, then melted in grace, in perfect symmetry, in translucent feminine languor, into the massed darkness of a forest of pine. The many towers, the slender tracery of the sloping parapets, the chiselled wonder of a thousand yellow windows with their oblongs and hectagons and triangles of golden light, the shattered softness of the intersecting planes of star-shine and blue shade, all trembled on John's spirit like a chord of music. On one of the towers, the tallest, the blackest at its base, an arrangement of exterior lights at the top made a sort of floating fairyland—and as John gazed up in warm enchantment the faint acciaccare sound of violins drifted down in a rococo harmony that was like nothing he had ever heard before. Then in a moment the car stepped before wide, high marble steps around which the night air was fragrant with a host of flowers. At the top of the steps two great doors swung silently open and amber light flooded out upon the darkness, silhouetting the figure of an exquisite lady with black, high-piled hair, who held out her arms toward them.

"Mother," Percy was saying, "this is my friend, John Unger, from Hades."

Afterward John remembered that first night as a daze of many colours, of quick sensory impressions, of music soft as a voice in love, and of the beauty of things, lights and shadows, and motions and faces. There was a white-haired man who stood drinking a many-hued cordial from a crystal thimble set on a golden stem. There was a girl with a flowery face, dressed like Titania with braided sapphires in her hair. There was a room where the solid, soft gold of the walls yielded to the pressure of his hand, and a room that was like a platonic conception of the ultimate prison—ceiling, floor, and all, it was lined with an unbroken mass of diamonds, diamonds of every size and shape, until, lit with tall violet lamps in the corners, it dazzled the eyes with a whiteness that could be compared only with itself, beyond human wish, or dream.

Through a maze of these rooms the two boys wandered. Sometimes the floor under their feet would flame in brilliant patterns from lighting below, patterns of barbaric clashing colours, of pastel delicacy, of sheer whiteness, or of subtle and in-tricate mosaic, surely from some mosque on the Adriatic Sea. Sometimes beneath layers of thick crystal he would see blue or green water swirling, inhabited by vivid fish and growths of rainbow foliage. Then they would be treading on furs of every texture and colour or along corridors of palest ivory, unbroken as though carved complete from the gigantic tusks of dinosaurs extinct before the age of man . . . .

Then a hazily remembered transition, and they were at dinner—where each plate was of two almost imperceptible layers of solid diamond between which was curi-ously worked a filigree of emerald design, a shaving sliced from green air. Music, plangent and unobtrusive, drifted down through far corridors—his chair, feathered and curved insidiously to his back, seemed to engulf and overpower him as he drank his first glass of port. He tried drowsily to answer a question that had been asked him, but the honeyed luxury that clasped his body added to the illusion of sleep—jewels, fabrics, wines, and metals blurred before his eyes into a sweet mist . . .

"Yes," he replied with a polite effort, "it certainly is hot enough for me down there."

He managed to add a ghostly laugh; then, without movement, without resis-tance, he seemed to float off and away, leaving an iced dessert that was pink as a dream . . . . He fell asleep.

When he awoke he knew that several hours had passed. He was in a great quiet room with ebony walls and a dull illumination that was too faint, too subtle, to be called a light. His young host was standing over him.

"You fell asleep at dinner," Percy was saying. "I nearly did, too—it was such a treat to be comfortable again after this year of school. Servants undressed and bathed you while you were sleeping."

"Is this a bed or a cloud?" sighed John. "Percy, Percy—before you go, I want to apologise."

"For what?"

"For doubting you when you said you had a diamond as big as the Ritz-Carlton Hotel."

Percy smiled.

"I thought you didn't believe me. It's that mountain, you know."

"What mountain?"

"The mountain the chateau rests on. It's not very big, for a mountain. But except about fifty feet of sod and gravel on top it's solid diamond. One diamond, one cubic mile without a flaw. Aren't you listening? Say—"

But John T. Unger had again fallen asleep.

3

Morning. As he awoke he perceived drowsily that the room had at the same moment become dense with sunlight. The ebony panels of one wall had slid aside on a sort of track, leaving his chamber half open to the day. A large negro in a white uniform stood beside his bed.

"Good-evening," muttered John, summoning his brains from the wild places.

"Good-morning, sir. Are you ready for your bath, sir? Oh, don't get up—I'll put you in, if you'll just unbutton your pyjamas—there. Thank you, sir."

John lay quietly as his pyjamas were removed—he was amused and delighted; he expected to be lifted like a child by this black Gargantua who was tending him, but nothing of the sort happened; instead he felt the bed tilt up slowly on its side—he began to roll, startled at first, in the direction of the wall, but when he reached the wall its drapery gave way, and sliding two yards farther down a fleecy incline he plumped gently into water the same temperature as his body.

He looked about him. The runway or rollway on which he had arrived had folded gently back into place. He had been projected into another chamber and was sitting in a sunken bath with his head just above the level of the floor. All about him, lining the walls of the room and the sides and bottom of the bath itself, was a blue aquarium, and gazing through the crystal surface on which he sat, he could see fish swimming among amber lights and even gliding without curiosity past his outstretched toes, which were separated from them only by the thickness of the crystal. From overhead, sunlight came down through sea-green glass.

"I suppose, sir, that you'd like hot rosewater and soapsuds this morning, sir—and perhaps cold salt water to finish."

The negro was standing beside him.

"Yes," agreed John, smiling inanely, "as you please." Any idea of ordering this bath according to his own meagre standards of living would have been priggish and not a little wicked.

The negro pressed a button and a warm rain began to fall, apparently from overhead, but really, so John. discovered after a moment, from a fountain arrangement near by. The water turned to a pale rose colour and jets of liquid soap spurted into it from four miniature walrus heads at the corners of the bath. In a moment a dozen little paddle-wheels, fixed to the sides, had churned the mixture into a radiant rainbow of pink foam which enveloped him softly with its delicious lightness, and burst in shining, rosy bubbles here and there about him.

"Shall I turn on the moving-picture machine, sir?" suggested the negro deferentially. "There's a good one-reel comedy in this machine to-day, or I can put in a serious piece in a moment, if you prefer it.

"No, thanks," answered John, politely but firmly. He was enjoying his bath too much to desire any distraction. But distraction came. In a moment he was listening intently to the sound of flutes from just outside, flutes dripping a melody that was like a waterfall, cool and green as the room itself, accompanying a frothy piccolo, in play more fragile than the lace of suds that covered and charmed him.

After a cold salt-water bracer and a cold fresh finish, he stepped out and into a fleecy robe, and upon a couch covered with the same material he was rubbed with oil, alcohol, and spice. Later he sat in a voluptuous while he was shaved and his hair was trimmed.

"Mr. Percy is waiting in your sitting-room," said the negro, when these operations were finished. "My name is Gygsum, Mr. Unger, sir. I am to see to Mr. Unger every morning."

John walked out into the brisk sunshine of his living-room, where he found breakfast waiting for him and Percy, gorgeous in white kid knickerbockers, smoking in an easy chair.

4

This is a story of the Washington family as Percy sketched it for John during breakfast.

The father of the present Mr. Washington had been a Virginian, a direct descendant of George Washington, and Lord Baltimore. At the close of the Civil War he was a twenty-five-year-old Colonel with a played-out plantation and about a thousand dollars in gold.

Fitz-Norman Culpepper Washington, for that was the young Colonel's name, decided to present the Virginia estate to his younger brother and go West, He selected two dozen of the most faithful blacks, who, of course, worshipped him, and bought twenty-five tickets to the West, where he intended to take out land in their names and start a sheep and cattle ranch.

When he had been in Montana for less than a month and things were going very poorly indeed, he stumbled on his great discovery. He had lost his way when riding in the hills, and after a day without food he began to grow hungry. As he was without his rifle, he was forced to pursue a squirrel, and, in the course of the pursuit, he noticed that it was carrying something shiny in its mouth. Just before it vanished into its hole—for Providence did not intend that this squirrel should alleviate his hunger—it dropped its burden. Sitting down to consider the situation

Fitz-Norman's eye was caught by a gleam in the grass beside him. In ten seconds he had completely lost his appetite and gained one hundred thousand dollars. The squirrel, which had refused with annoying persistence to become food, had made him a present of a large and perfect diamond.

Late that night he found his way to camp and twelve hours later all the males among his darkies were back by the squirrel hole digging furiously at the side of the mountain. He told them he had discovered a rhinestone mine, and, as only one or two of them had ever seen even a small diamond before, they believed him, without question. When the magnitude of his discovery became apparent to him, he found himself in a quandary. The mountain was a diamond—it was literally nothing else but solid diamond. He filled four saddle bags full of glittering samples and started on horseback for St. Paul. There he managed to dispose of half a dozen small stones—when he tried a larger one a storekeeper fainted and Fitz-Norman was arrested as a public disturber. He escaped from jail and caught the train for New York, where he sold a few medium-sized diamonds and received in exchange about two hundred thousand dollars in gold. But he did not dare to produce any exceptional gems—in fact, he left New York just in time. Tremendous excitement had been created in jewellery circles, not so much by the size of his diamonds as by their appearance in the city from mysterious sources. Wild rumours became current that a diamond mine had been discovered in the Catskills, on the Jersey coast, on Long Island, beneath Washington Square. Excursion trains, packed with men carrying picks and shovels, began to leave New York hourly, bound for various neighbouring El Dorados. But by that time young Fitz-Norman was on his way back to Montana.

By the end of a fortnight he had estimated that the diamond in the mountain was approximately equal in quantity to all the rest of the diamonds known to exist in the world. There was no valuing it by any regular computation, however, for it was one solid diamond—and if it were offered for sale not only would the bottom fall out of the market, but also, if the value should vary with its size in the usual arithmetical progression, there would not be enough gold in the world to buy a tenth part of it. And what could any one do with a diamond that size?

It was an amazing predicament. He was, in one sense, the richest man that ever lived—and yet was he worth anything at all? If his secret should transpire there was no telling to what measures the Government might resort in order to prevent a panic, in gold as well as in jewels. They might take over the claim immediately and institute a monopoly.

There was no alternative—he must market his mountain in secret. He sent South for his younger brother and put him in charge of his coloured following, darkies who had never realised that slavery was abolished. To make sure of this, he read them a proclamation that he had composed, which announced that General Forrest had reorganised the shattered Southern armies and defeated the North in one pitched battle. The negroes believed him implicitly. They passed a vote declaring it a good thing and held revival services immediately.

Fitz-Norman himself set out for foreign parts with one hundred thousand dollars and two trunks filled with rough diamonds of all sizes. He sailed for Russia in a Chinese junk, and six months after his departure from Montana he was in St. Petersburg. He took obscure lodgings and called immediately upon the court jeweller, announcing that he had a diamond for the Czar. He remained in St. Petersburg for two weeks, in constant danger of being murdered, living from lodging to lodging, and afraid to visit his trunks more than three or four times during the whole fortnight.

On his promise to return in a year with larger and finer stones, he was allowed to leave for India. Before he left, however, the Court Treasurers had deposited to his credit, in American banks, the sum of fifteen million dollars—under four different aliases.

He returned to America in 1868, having been gone a little over two years. He had visited the capitals of twenty-two countries and talked with five emperors, eleven kings, three princes, a shah, a khan, and a sultan. At that time Fitz-Norman estimated his own wealth at one billion dollars. One fact worked consistently against the disclosure of his secret. No one of his larger diamonds remained in the public eye for a week before being invested with a history of enough fatalities, amours, revolutions, and wars to have occupied it from the days of the first Babylonian Empire.

From 1870 until his death in 1900, the history of Fitz-Norman Washington was a long epic in gold. There were side issues, of course—he evaded the surveys, he married a Virginia lady, by whom he had a single son, and he was compelled, due to a series of unfortunate complications, to murder his brother, whose unfortunate habit of drinking himself into an indiscreet stupor had several times endangered their safety. But very other murders stained these happy years of progress and exspansion.

Just before he died he changed his policy, and with all but a few million dollars of his outside wealth bought up rare minerals in bulk, which he deposited in the safety vaults of banks all over the world, marked as bric-a-brac. His son, Braddock Tarleton Washington, followed this policy on an even more tensive scale. The minerals were converted into the rarest of all elements—radium—so that the equivalent of a billion dollars in gold could be placed in a receptacle no bigger than a cigar box.

When Fitz-Norman had been dead three years his son, Braddock, decided that the business had gone far enough. The amount of wealth that he and his father had taken out of the mountain was beyond all exact computation. He kept a note-book in cipher in which he set down the approximate quantity of radium in each of the thousand banks he patronised, and recorded the alias under which it was held. Then he did a very simple thing—he sealed up the mine.

He sealed up the mine. What had been taken out of it would support all the Washingtons yet to be born in unparalleled luxury for generations. His one care must be the protection of his secret, lest in the possible panic attendant on its discovery he should be reduced with all the property-holders in the world to utter poverty.

This was the family among whom John T. Unger was staying. This was the story he heard in his silver-walled living-room the morning after his arrival.

5

After breakfast, John found his way out the great marble entrance, and looked curiously at the scene before him. The whole valley, from the diamond mountain to the steep granite cliff five miles away, still gave off a breath of golden haze which hovered idly above the fine sweep of lawns and lakes and gardens. Here and there clusters of elms made delicate groves of shade, contrasting strangely with the tough masses of pine forest that held the hills in a grip of dark-blue green. Even as John looked he saw three fawns in single file patter out from one clump about a half-mile away and disappear with awkward gaiety into the black-ribbed half-light of another. John would not have been surprised to see a goat-foot piping his way among the trees or to catch a glimpse of pink nymph-skin and flying yellow hair between the greenest of the green leaves.

In some such cool hope he descended the marble steps, disturbing faintly the sleep of two silky Russian wolfhounds at the bottom, and set off along a walk of white and blue brick that seemed to lead in no particular direction.

He was enjoying himself as much as he was able. It is youth's felicity as well as its insufficiency that it can never live in the present, but must always be measuring up the day against its own radiantly imagined future—flowers and gold, girls and stars, they are only prefigurations and prophecies of that incomparable, unattainable young dream.

John rounded a soft corner where the massed rosebushes filled the air with heavy scent, and struck off across a park toward a patch of moss under some trees. He had never lain upon moss, and he wanted to see whether it was really soft enough to justify the use of its name as an adjective. Then he saw a girl coming toward him over the grass. She was the most beautiful person he had ever seen.

She was dressed in a white little gown that came just below her knees, and a wreath of mignonettes clasped with blue slices of sapphire bound up her hair. Her pink bare feet scattered the dew before them as she came. She was younger than John—not more than sixteen.

"Hallo," she cried softly, "I'm Kismine."

She was much more than that to John already. He advanced toward her, scarcely moving as he drew near lest he should tread on her bare toes.

"You haven't met me," said her soft voice. Her blue eyes added, "Oh, but you've missed a great deal!" . . . "You met my sister, Jasmine, last night. I was sick with lettuce poisoning," went on her soft voice, and her eye continued, "and when I'm sick I'm sweet—and when I'm well."

"You have made an enormous impression on me," said John's eyes, "and I'm not so slow myself"—"How do you do?" said his voice. "I hope you're better this morning."—"You darling," added his eyes tremulously.

John observed that they had been walking along the path. On her suggestion they sat down together upon the moss, the softness of which he failed to determine.

He was critical about women. A single defect—a thick ankle, a hoarse voice, a glass eye—was enough to make him utterly indifferent. And here for the first time in his life he was beside a girl who seemed to him the incarnation of physical perfection.

"Are you from the East?" asked Kismine with charming interest.

"No," answered John simply. "I'm from Hades."

Either she had never heard of Hades, or she could think of no pleasant comment to make upon it, for she did not discuss it further.

"I'm going East to school this fall" she said. "D'you think I'll like it? I'm going to New York to Miss Bulge's. It's very strict, but you see over the weekends I'm going to live at home with the family in our New York house, because father heard that the girls had to go walking two by two."

"Your father wants you to be proud," observed John.

"We are," she answered, her eyes shining with dignity. "None of us has ever been punished. Father said we never should be. Once when my sister Jasmine was a little girl she pushed him downstairs and he just got up and limped away.

"Mother was—well, a little startled," continued Kismine, "when she heard that you were from—from where you are from, you know. She said that when she was a young girl—but then, you see, she's a Spaniard and old-fashioned."

"Do you spend much time out here?" asked John, to conceal the fact that he was somewhat hurt by this remark. It seemed an unkind allusion to his provincialism.

"Percy and Jasmine and I are here every summer, but next summer Jasmine is going to Newport. She's coming out in London a year from this fall. She'll be presented at court."

"Do you know," began John hesitantly, "you're much more sophisticated than I thought you were when I first saw you?"

"Oh, no, I'm not," she exclaimed hurriedly. "Oh, I wouldn't think of being. I think that sophisticated young people are terribly common, don't you? I'm not all, really. If you say I am, I'm going to cry."

She was so distressed that her lip was trembling. John was impelled to protest:

"I didn't mean that; I only said it to tease you."

"Because I wouldn't mind if I were," she persisted, "but I'm not. I'm very innocent and girlish. I never smoke, or drink, or read anything except poetry. I know scarcely any mathematics or chemistry. I dress very simply—in fact, I scarcely dress at all. I think sophisticated is the last thing you can say about me. I believe that girls ought to enjoy their youths in a wholesome way."

"I do, too," said John, heartily,

Kismine was cheerful again. She smiled at him, and a still-born tear dripped from the corner of one blue eye.

"I like you," she whispered intimately. "Are you going to spend all your time with Percy while you're here, or will you be nice to me? Just think—I'm absolutely fresh ground. I've never had a boy in love with me in all my life. I've never been allowed even to see boys alone—except Percy. I came all the way out here into this grove hoping to run into you, where the family wouldn't be around."

Deeply flattered, John bowed from the hips as he had been taught at dancing school in Hades.

"We'd better go now," said Kismine sweetly. "I have to be with mother at eleven. You haven't asked me to kiss you once. I thought boys always did that nowadays"

John drew himself up proudly.

"Some of them do," he answered, "but not me. Girls don't do that sort of thing—in Hades."

Side by side they walked back toward the house.

6

John stood facing Mr. Braddock Washington in the full sunlight. The elder man was about forty, with a proud, vacuous face, intelligent eyes, and a robust figure. In the mornings he smelt of horses—the best horses. He carried a plain walking-stick of gray birch with a single large opal for a grip. He and Percy were showing John around.

"The slaves' quarters are there." His walking-stick indicated a cloister of marble on their left that ran in graceful Gothic along the side of the mountain. "In my youth I was distracted for a while from the business of life by a period of absurd idealism. During that time they lived in luxury. For instance, I equipped every one of their rooms with a tile bath."

"I suppose," ventured John, with an ingratiating laugh, "that they used the bathtubs to keep coal in. Mr. Schnlitzer-Murphy told me that once he—"

"The opinions of Mr. Schnlitzer-Murphy are of little importance, I should imagine," interrupted Braddock Washington coldly. "My slaves did not keep coal in their bathtubs. They had orders to bathe every day, and they did. If they hadn't I might have ordered a sulphuric acid shampoo. I discontinued the baths for quite another reason. Several of them caught cold and died. Water is not good for certain races—except as a beverage."

John laughed, and then decided to nod his head in sober agreement. Braddock Washington made him uncomfortable.

"All these negroes are descendants of the ones my father brought North with him. There are about two hundred and fifty now. You notice that they've lived so long apart from the world that their original dialect has become an almost indistinguishable patois. We bring a few of them up to speak English—my secretary and two or three of the house servants.

"This is the golf course," he continued, as they strolled along the velvet winter grass. "It's all a green, you see—no fairway, no rough, no hazards."

He smiled pleasantly at John.

"Many men in the cage, father?" asked Percy suddenly.

Braddock Washington stumbled, and let forth an involuntary curse.

"One less than there should be," he ejaculated darkly—and then added after a moment, "We've had difficulties."

"Mother was telling me," exclaimed Percy, "that Italian teacher—"

"A ghastly error," said Braddock Washington angrily. "But of course there's a good chance that we may have got him. Perhaps he fell somewhere in the woods or stumbled over a cliff. And then there's always the probability that if he did get away his story wouldn't be believed. Nevertheless, I've had two dozen men looking for him in different towns around here."

"And no luck?"

"Some. Fourteen of them reported to my agent they'd each killed a man answering to that description, but of course it was probably only the reward they were after—"

He broke off. They had come to a large cavity in the earth about the circumference of a merry-go-round, and covered by a strong iron grating. Braddock Washington beckoned to John, and pointed his cane down through the grating. John stepped to the edge and gazed. Immediately his ears were assailed by a wild clamor from below.

"Come on down to Hell!"

"Hallo, kiddo, how's the air up there?"

"Hey! Throw us a rope!"

"Got an old doughnut, Buddy, or a couple of second-hand sandwiches?"

"Say, fella, if you'll push down that guy you're with, we'll show you a quick disappearance scene."

"Paste him one for me, will you?"

It was too dark to see clearly into the pit below, but John could tell from the coarse optimism and rugged vitality of the remarks and voices that they proceeded from middle-class Americans of the more spirited type. Then Mr. Washington put out his cane and touched a button in the grass, and the scene below sprang into light.

"These are some adventurous mariners who had the misfortune to discover El Dorado," he remarked.

Below them there had appeared a large hollow in the earth shaped like the interior of a bowl. The sides were steep and apparently of polished glass, and on its slightly concave surface stood about two dozen men clad in the half costume, half uniform, of aviators. Their upturned faces, lit with wrath, with malice, with despair, with cynical humour, were covered by long growths of beard, but with the exception of a few who had pined perceptibly away, they seemed to be a well-fed, healthy lot.

Braddock Washington drew a garden chair to the edge of the pit and sat down.

"Well, how are you, boys?" he inquired genially.

A chorus of execration, in which all joined except a few too dispirited to cry out, rose up into the sunny air, but Braddock Washington heard it with unruffled composure. When its last echo had died away he spoke again.

"Have you thought up a way out of your difficulty?"

From here and there among them a remark floated up.

"We decided to stay here for love!"

"Bring us up there and we'll find us a way!"

Braddock Washington waited until they were again quiet. Then he said:

"I've told you the situation. I don't want you here, I wish to heaven I'd never seen you. Your own curiosity got you here, and any time that you can think of a way out which protects me and my interests I'll be glad to consider it. But so long as you confine your efforts to digging tunnels—yes, I know about the new one you've started—you won't get very far. This isn't as hard on you as you make it out, with all your howling for the loved ones at home. If you were the type who worried much about the loved ones at home, you'd never have taken up aviation."

A tall man moved apart from the others, and held up his hand to call his captor's attention to what he was about to say.

"Let me ask you a few questions!" he cried. "You pretend to be a fair-minded man."

"How absurd. How could a man of my position be fair-minded toward you? You might as well speak of a Spaniard being fair-minded toward a piece of steak."

At this harsh observation the faces of the two dozen fell, but the tall man continued:

"All right!" he cried. "We've argued this out before. You're not a humanitarian and you're not fair-minded, but you're human—at least you say you are—and you ought to be able to put yourself in our place for long enough to think how—how—how—"

"How what?" demanded Washington, coldly.

"—how unnecessary—"

"Not to me."

"Well—how cruel—"

"We've covered that. Cruelty doesn't exist where self-preservation is involved. You've been soldiers; you know that. Try another."

"Well, then, how stupid."

"There," admitted Washington, "I grant you that. But try to think of an alternative. I've offered to have all or any of you painlessly executed if you wish. I've offered to have your wives, sweethearts, children, and mothers kidnapped and brought out here. I'll enlarge your place down there and feed and clothe you the rest of your lives. If there was some method of producing permanent amnesia I'd have all of you operated on and released immediately, somewhere outside of my preserves. But that's as far as my ideas go."

"How about trusting us not to peach on you?" cried some one.

"You don't proffer that suggestion seriously," said Washington, with an expression of scorn. "I did take out one man to teach my daughter Italian. Last week he got away."

A wild yell of jubilation went up suddenly from two dozen throats and a pandemonium of joy ensued. The prisoners clog-danced and cheered and yodled and wrestled with one another in a sudden uprush of animal spirits. They even ran up the glass sides of the bowl as far as they could, and slid back to the bottom upon the natural cushions of their bodies. The tall man started a song in which they all joined—

"Oh, we'll hang the kaiser

On a sour apple-tree—"

Braddock Washington sat in inscrutable silence until the song was over.

"You see," he remarked, when he could gain a modicum of attention. "I bear you no ill-will. I like to see you enjoying yourselves. That's why I didn't tell you the whole story at once. The man—what was his name? Critchtichiello?—was shot by some of my agents in fourteen different places."

Not guessing that the places referred to were cities, the tumult of rejoicing subsided immediately.

"Nevertheless," cried Washington with a touch of anger, "he tried to run away. Do you expect me to take chances with any of you after an experience like that?"

Again a series of ejaculations went up.

"Sure!"

"Would your daughter like to learn Chinese?"

"Hey, I can speak Italian! My mother was a wop."

"Maybe she'd like t'learna speak N'Yawk!"

"If she's the little one with the big blue eyes I can teach her a lot of things better than Italian."

"I know some Irish songs—and I could hammer brass once't."

Mr. Washington reached forward suddenly with his cane and pushed the button in the grass so that the picture below went out instantly, and there remained only that great dark mouth covered dismally with the black teeth of the grating.

"Hey!" called a single voice from below, "you ain't goin' away without givin' us your blessing?"

But Mr. Washington, followed by the two boys, was already strolling on toward the ninth hole of the golf course, as though the pit and its contents were no more than a hazard over which his facile iron had triumphed with ease.

7

July under the lee of the diamond mountain was a month of blanket nights and of warm, glowing days. John and Kismine were in love. He did not know that the little gold football (inscribed with the legend Pro deo et patria et St. Mida) which he had given her rested on a platinum chain next to her bosom. But it did. And she for her part was not aware that a large sapphire which had dropped one day from her simple coiffure was stowed away tenderly in John's jewel box.

Late one afternoon when the ruby and ermine music room was quiet, they spent an hour there together. He held her hand and she gave him such a look that he whispered her name aloud. She bent toward him—then hesitated.

"Did you say 'Kismine'?" she asked softly, "or—"

She had wanted to be sure. She thought she might have misunderstood.

Neither of them had ever kissed before, but in the course of an hour it seemed to make little difference.

The afternoon drifted away. That night, when a last breath of music drifted down from the highest tower, they each lay awake, happily dreaming over the separate minutes of the day. They had decided to be married as soon as possible.

8

Every day Mr. Washington and the two young men went hunting or fishing in the deep forests or played golf around the somnolent course—games which John diplomatically allowed his host to win—or swam in the mountain coolness of the lake. John found Mr. Washington a somewhat exacting personality—utterly uninterested in any ideas or opinions except his own. Mrs. Washington was aloof and reserved at all times. She was apparently indifferent to her two daughters, and entirely absorbed in her son Percy, with whom she held interminable conversations in rapid Spanish at dinner.

Jasmine, the elder daughter, resembled Kismine in appearance—except that she was somewhat bow-legged, and terminated in large hands and feet—but was utterly unlike her in temperament. Her favourite books had to do with poor girls who kept house for widowed fathers. John learned from Kismine that Jasmine had never recovered from the shock and disappointment caused her by the termination of the World War, just as she was about to start for Europe as a canteen expert. She had even pined away for a time, and Braddock Washington had taken steps to promote a new war in the Balkans—but she had seen a photograph of some wounded Serbian soldiers and lost interest in the whole proceedings. But Percy and Kismine seemed to have inherited the arrogant attitude in all its harsh magnificence from their father. A chaste and consistent selfishness ran like a pattern through their every idea.

John was enchanted by the wonders of the château and the valley. Braddock Washington, so Percy told him, had caused to be kidnapped a landscape gardener, an architect, a designer of state settings, and a French decadent poet left over from the last century. He had put his entire force of negroes at their disposal, guaranteed to supply them with any materials that the world could offer, and left them to work out some ideas of their own. But one by one they had shown their uselessness. The decadent poet had at once begun bewailing his separation, from the boulevards in spring—he made some vague remarks about spices, apes, and ivories, but said nothing that was of any practical value. The stage designer on his part wanted to make the whole valley a series of tricks and sensational effects—a state of things that the Washingtons would soon have grown tired of. And as for the architect and the landscape gardener, they thought only in terms of convention. They must make this like this and that like that.

But they had, at least, solved the problem of what was to be done with them—they all went mad early one morning after spending the night in a single room trying to agree upon the location of a fountain, and were now confined comfortably in an insane asylum at Westport, Connecticut.

"But," inquired John curiously, "who did plan all your wonderful reception rooms and halls, and approaches and bathrooms—?"

"Well," answered Percy, "I blush to tell you, but it was a moving-picture fella. He was the only man we found who was used to playing with an unlimited amount of money, though he did tuck his napkin in his collar and couldn't read or write."

As August drew to a close John began to regret that he must soon go back to school. He and Kismine had decided to elope the following June.

"It would be nicer to be married here," Kismine confessed, "but of course I could never get father's permission to marry you at all. Next to that I'd rather elope. It's terrible for wealthy people to be married in America at present—they always have to send out bulletins to the press saying that they're going to be married in remnants, when what they mean is just a peck of old second-hand pearls and some used lace worn once by the Empress Eugenie."

"I know," agreed John fervently. "When I was visiting the Schnlitzer-Murphys, the eldest daughter, Gwendolyn, married a man whose father owns half of West Virginia. She wrote home saying what a tough struggle she was carrying on on his salary as a bank clerk—and then she ended up by saying that 'Thank God, I have four good maids anyhow, and that helps a little.'"

"It's absurd," commented Kismine—"Think of the millions and millions of people in the world, labourers and all, who get along with only two maids."

One afternoon late in August a chance remark of Kismine's changed the face of the entire situation, and threw John into a state of terror.

They were in their favourite grove, and between kisses John was indulging in some romantic forebodings which he fancied added poignancy to their relations.

"Sometimes I think we'll never marry," he said sadly. "You're too wealthy, too magnificent. No one as rich as you are can be like other girls. I should marry the daughter of some well-to-do wholesale hardware man from Omaha or Sioux City, and be content with her half-million."

"I knew the daughter of a wholesale hardware man once," remarked Kismine. "I don't think you'd have been contented with her. She was a friend of my sister's. She visited here."

"Oh, then you've had other guests?" exclaimed John in surprise.

Kismine seemed to regret her words.

"Oh, yes," she said hurriedly, "we've had a few."

"But aren't you—wasn't your father afraid they'd talk outside?"

"Oh, to some extent, to some extent," she answered, "Let's talk about something pleasanter."

But John's curiosity was aroused.

"Something pleasanter!" he demanded. "What's unpleasant about that? Weren't they nice girls?"

To his great surprise Kismine began to weep.

"Yes—th—that's the—the whole t-trouble. I grew qu-quite attached to some of them. So did Jasmine, but she kept inv-viting them anyway. I couldn't understand it."

A dark suspicion was born in John's heart.

"Do you mean that they told, and your father had them—removed?"

"Worse than that," she muttered brokenly. "Father took no chances—and Jasmine kept writing them to come, and they had such a good time!"

She was overcome by a paroxysm of grief.

Stunned with the horror of this revelation, John sat there open-mouthed, feeling the nerves of his body twitter like so many sparrows perched upon his spinal column.

"Now, I've told you, and I shouldn't have," she said, calming suddenly and drying her dark blue eyes.

"Do you mean to say that your father had them murdered before they left?"

She nodded.

"In August usually—or early in September. It's only natural for us to get all the pleasure out of them that we can first."

"How abominable! How—why, I must be going crazy! Did you really admit that—"

"I did," interrupted Kismine, shrugging her shoulders. "We can't very well imprison them like those aviators, where they'd be a continual reproach to us every day. And it's always been made easier for Jasmine and me, because father had it done sooner than we expected. In that way we avoided any farewell scene-"

"So you murdered them! Uh!" cried John.

"It was done very nicely. They were drugged while they were asleep—and their families were always told that they died of scarlet fever in Butte."

"But—I fail to understand why you kept on inviting them!"

"I didn't," burst out Kismine. "I never invited one. Jasmine did. And they always had a very good time. She'd give them the nicest presents toward the last. I shall probably have visitors too—I'll harden up to it. We can't let such an inevitable thing as death stand in the way of enjoying life while we have it. Think of how lonesome it'd be out here if we never had any one. Why, father and mother have sacrificed some of their best friends just as we have."

"And so," cried John accusingly, "and so you were letting me make love to you and pretending to return it, and talking about marriage, all the time knowing perfectly well that I'd never get out of here alive—"

"No," she protested passionately. "Not any more. I did at first. You were here. I couldn't help that, and I thought your last days might as well be pleasant for both of us. But then I fell in love with you, and—and I'm honestly sorry you're going to—going to be put away—though I'd rather you'd be put away than ever kiss another girl."

"Oh, you would, would you?" cried John ferociously.

"Much rather. Besides, I've always heard that a girl can have more fun with a man whom she knows she can never marry. Oh, why did I tell you? I've probably spoiled your whole good time now, and we were really enjoying things when you didn't know it. I knew it would make things sort of depressing for you."

"Oh, you did, did you?" John's voice trembled with anger. "I've heard about enough of this. If you haven't any more pride and decency than to have an affair with a fellow that you know isn't much better than a corpse, I don't want to have any more to with you!"

"You're not a corpse!" she protested in horror. "You're not a corpse! I won't have you saying that I kissed a corpse!"

"I said nothing of the sort!"

"You did! You said I kissed a corpse!"

"I didn't!"

Their voices had risen, but upon a sudden interruption they both subsided into immediate silence. Footsteps were coming along the path in their direction, and a moment later the rose bushes were parted displaying Braddock Washington, whose intelligent eyes set in his good-looking vacuous face were peering in at them.

"Who kissed a corpse?" he demanded in obvious disapproval.

"Nobody," answered Kismine quickly. "We were just joking."

"What are you two doing here, anyhow?" he demanded gruffly. "Kismine, you ought to be—to be reading or playing golf with your sister. Go read! Go play golf! Don't let me find you here when I come back!"

Then he bowed at John and went up the path.

"See?" said Kismine crossly, when he was out of hearing. "You've spoiled it all. We can never meet any more. He won't let me meet you. He'd have you poisoned if he thought we were in love."

"We're not, any more!" cried John fiercely, "so he can set his mind at rest upon that. Moreover, don't fool yourself that I'm going to stay around here. Inside of six hours I'll be over those mountains, if I have to gnaw a passage through them, and on my way East." They had both got to their feet, and at this remark Kismine came close and put her arm through his.

"I'm going, too."

"You must be crazy—"

"Of course I'm going," she interrupted impatiently.

"You most certainly are not. You—"

"Very well," she said quietly, "we'll catch up with father and talk it over with him."

Defeated, John mustered a sickly smile.

"Very well, dearest," he agreed, with pale and unconvincing affection, "we'll go together."

His love for her returned and settled placidly on his heart. She was his—she would go with him to share his dangers. He put his arms about her and kissed her fervently. After all she loved him; she had saved him, in fact.

Discussing the matter, they walked slowly back toward the château. They decided that since Braddock Washington had seen them together they had best depart the next night. Nevertheless, John's lips were unusually dry at dinner, and he nervously emptied a great spoonful of peacock soup into his left lung. He had to be carried into the turquoise and sable card-room and pounded on the back by one of the under-butlers, which Percy considered a great joke.

9

Long after midnight John's body gave a nervous jerk, he sat suddenly upright, staring into the veils of somnolence that draped the room. Through the squares of blue darkness that were his open windows, he had heard a faint far-away sound that died upon a bed of wind before identifying itself on his memory, clouded with uneasy dreams. But the sharp noise that had succeeded it was nearer, was just outside the room—the click of a turned knob, a footstep, a whisper, he could not tell; a hard lump gathered in the pit of his stomach, and his whole body ached in the moment that he strained agonisingly to hear. Then one of the veils seemed to dissolve, and he saw a vague figure standing by the door, a figure only faintly limned and blocked in upon the darkness, mingled so with the folds of the drapery as to seem distorted, like a reflection seen in a dirty pane of glass.

With a sudden movement of fright or resolution John pressed the button by his bedside, and the next moment he was sitting in the green sunken bath of the adjoining room, waked into alertness by the shock of the cold water which half filled it.

He sprang out, and, his wet pyjamas scattering a heavy trickle of water behind him, ran for the aquamarine door which he knew led out on to the ivory landing of the second floor. The door opened noiselessly. A single crimson lamp burning in a great dome above lit the magnificent sweep of the carved stairways with a poignant beauty. For a moment John hesitated, appalled by the silent splendour massed about him, seeming to envelop in its gigantic folds and contours the solitary drenched little figure shivering upon the ivory landing. Then simultaneously two things happened. The door of his own sitting-room swung open, precipitating three naked negroes into the hall—and, as John swayed in wild terror toward the stairway, another door slid back in the wall on the other side of the corridor, and John saw Braddock Washington standing in the lighted lift, wearing a fur coat and a pair of riding boots which reached to his knees and displayed, above, the glow of his rose-colored pyjamas.

On the instant the three negroes—John had never seen any of them before, and it flashed through his mind that they must be the professional executioners paused in their movement toward John, and turned expectantly to the man in the lift, who burst out with an imperious command:

"Get in here! All three of you! Quick as hell!"

Then, within the instant, the three negroes darted into the cage, the oblong of light was blotted out as the lift door slid shut, and John was again alone in the hall. He slumped weakly down against an ivory stair.

It was apparent that something portentous had occurred, something which, for the moment at least, had postponed his own petty disaster. What was it? Had the negroes risen in revolt? Had the aviators forced aside the iron bars of the grating? Or had the men of Fish stumbled blindly through the hills and gazed with bleak, joyless eyes upon the gaudy valley? John did not know. He heard a faint whir of air as the lift whizzed up again, and then, a moment later, as it descended. It was probable that Percy was hurrying to his father's assistance, and it occurred to John that this was his opportunity to join Kismine and plan an immediate escape. He waited until the lift had been silent for several minutes; shivering a little with the night cool that whipped in through his wet pyjamas, he returned to his room and dressed himself quickly. Then he mounted a long flight of stairs and turned down the corridor carpeted with Russian sable which led to Kismine's suite.

The door of her sitting-room was open and the lamps were lighted. Kismine, in an angora kimono, stood near the window Of the room in a listening attitude, and as John entered noiselessly she turned toward him.

"Oh, it's you!" she whispered, crossing the room to him. "Did you hear them?"
I heard your father's slaves in my—"

"No," she interrupted excitedly. "Aeroplanes!"

"Aeroplanes? Perhaps that was the sound that woke me."

"There're at least a dozen. I saw one a few moments ago dead against the moon. The guard back by the cliff fired his rifle and that's what roused father. We're going to open on them right away."

"Are they here on purpose?"

"Yes—it's that Italian who got away—"

Simultaneously with her last word, a succession of sharp cracks tumbled in through the open window. Kismine uttered a little cry, took a penny with fumbling fingers from a box on her dresser, and ran to one of the electric lights. In an instant the entire chateau was in darkness—she had blown out the fuse.

"Come on!" she cried to him. "We'll go up to the roof garden, and watch it from there!"

Drawing a cape about her, she took his hand, and they found their way out the door. It was only a step to the tower lift, and as she pressed the button that shot them upward he put his arms around her in the darkness and kissed her mouth. Romance had come to John Unger at last. A minute later they had stepped out upon the star-white platform. Above, under the misty moon, sliding in and out of the patches of cloud that eddied below it, floated a dozen dark-winged bodies in a constant circling course. From here and there in the valley flashes of fire leaped toward them, followed by sharp detonations. Kismine clapped her hands with pleasure, which, a moment later, turned to dismay as the aeroplanes, at some prearranged signal, began to release their bombs and the whole of the valley became a panorama of deep reverberate sound and lurid light.

Before long the aim of the attackers became concentrated upon the points where the anti-aircraft guns were situated, and one of them was almost immediately reduced to a giant cinder to lie smouldering in a park of rose bushes.

"Kismine," begged John, "you'll be glad when I tell you that this attack came on the eve of my murder. If I hadn't heard that guard shoot off his gun back by the pass I should now be stone dead—"

"I can't hear you!" cried Kismine, intent on the scene before her. "You'll have to talk louder!"

"I simply said," shouted John, "that we'd better get out before they begin to shell the chateau!"

Suddenly the whole portico of the negro quarters cracked asunder, a geyser of flame shot up from under the colonnades, and great fragments of jagged marble were hurled as far as the borders of the lake.

"There go fifty thousand dollars' worth of slaves," cried Kismine, "at pre-war prices. So few Americans have any respect for property."

John renewed his efforts to compel her to leave. The aim of the aeroplanes was becoming more precise minute by minute, and only two of the anti-aircraft guns were still retaliating. It was obvious that the garrison, encircled with fire, could not hold out much longer.

"Come on!" cried John, pulling Kismine's arm, "we've got to go. Do you realise that those aviators will kill you without question if they find you?"

She consented reluctantly.

"We'll have to wake Jasmine!" she said, as they hurried toward the lift. Then she added in a sort of childish delight: "We'll be poor, won't we? Like people in books. And I'll be an orphan and utterly free. Free and poor! What fun!" She stopped and raised her lips to him in a delighted kiss.

"It's impossible to be both together," said John grimly. "People have found that out. And I should choose to be free as preferable of the two. As an extra caution you'd better dump the contents of your jewel box into your pockets."

Ten minutes later the two girls met John in the dark corridor and they descended to the main floor of the chateau. Passing for the last time through the magnificence of the splendid halls, they stood for a moment out on the terrace, watching the burning negro quarters and the flaming embers of two planes which had fallen on the other side of the lake. A solitary gun was still keeping up a sturdy popping, and the attackers seemed timorous about descending lower, but sent their thunderous fireworks in a circle around it, until any chance shot might annihilate its Ethiopian crew.

John and the two sisters passed down the marble steps, turned sharply to the left, and began to ascend a narrow path that wound like a garter about the diamond mountain. Kismine knew a heavily wooded spot half-way up where they could lie concealed and yet be able to observe the wild night in the valley—finally to make an escape, when it should be necessary, along a secret path laid in a rocky gully.

10

It was three o'clock when they attained their destination. The obliging and phlegmatic Jasmine fell off to sleep immediately, leaning against the trunk of a large tree, while John and Kismine sat, his arm around her, and watched the desperate ebb and flow of the dying battle among the ruins of a vista that had been a garden spot that morning. Shortly after four o'clock the last remaining gun gave out a clanging sound, and went out of action in a swift tongue of red smoke. Though the moon was down, they saw that the flying bodies were circling closer to the earth. When the planes had made certain that the beleaguered possessed no further resources they would land and the dark and glittering reign of the Washingtons would be over.

With the cessation of the firing the valley grew quiet. The embers of the two aeroplanes glowed like the eyes of some monster crouching in the grass. The château stood dark and silent, beautiful without light as it had been beautiful in the sun, while the woody rattles of Nemesis filled the air above with a growing and receding complaint. Then John perceived that Kismine, like her sister, had fallen sound asleep.

It was long after four when he became aware of footsteps along the path they had lately followed, and he waited in breathless silence until the persons to whom they belonged had passed the vantage-point he occupied. There was a faint stir in the air now that was not of human origin, and the dew was cold; be knew that the dawn would break soon. John waited until the steps had gone a safe distance up the mountain and were inaudible. Then he followed. About half-way to the steep summit the trees fell away and a hard saddle of rock spread itself over the diamond beneath. Just before he reached this point he slowed down his pace warned by an animal sense that there was life just ahead of him. Coming to a high boulder, he lifted his head gradually above its edge. His curiosity was rewarded; this is what he saw:

Braddock Washington was standing there motionless, silhouetted against the gray sky without sound or sign of life. As the dawn came up out of the east, lending a gold green colour to the earth, it brought the solitary figure into insignificant contrast with the new day,

While John watched, his host remained for a few moments absorbed in some inscrutable contemplation; then he signalled to the two negroes who crouched at his feet to lift the burden which lay between them. As they struggled upright, the first yellow beam of the sun struck through the innumerable prisms of an immense and exquisitely chiselled diamond—and a white radiance was kindled that glowed upon the air like a fragment of the morning star. The bearers staggered beneath its weight for a moment—then their rippling muscles caught and hardened under the wet shine of the skins and the three figures were again motionless in their defiant impotency before the heavens.

After a while the white man lifted his head and slowly raised his arms in a gesture of attention, as one who would call a great crowd to hear—but there was no crowd, only the vast silence of the mountain and the sky, broken by faint bird voices down among the trees. The figure on the saddle of rock began to speak ponderously and with an inextinguishable pride.

"You—out there—!" he cried in a trembling voice.

"You—there—!" He paused, his arms still uplifted, his head held attentively as though he were expecting an answer. John strained his eyes to see whether there might be men coming down the mountain, but the mountain was bare of human life. There was only sky and a mocking flute of wind along the treetops. Could Washington be praying? For a moment John wondered. Then the illusion passed—there was something in the man's whole attitude antithetical to prayer.

"Oh, you above there!"

The voice was become strong and confident. This was no forlorn supplication.

If anything, there was in it a quality of monstrous condescension.

"You there—" Words, too quickly uttered to be understood, flowing one into the other . . . . John listened breathlessly, catching a phrase here and there, while the voice broke off, resumed, broke off again—now strong and argumentative, now coloured with a slow, puzzled impatience, Then a conviction commenced to dawn on the single listener, and as realisation crept over him a spray of quick blood rushed through his arteries. Braddock Washington was offering a bribe to God!

That was it—there was no doubt. The diamond in the arms of his slaves was some advance sample, a promise of more to follow.

That, John perceived after a time, was the thread running through his sentences. Prometheus Enriched was calling to witness forgotten sacrifices, forgotten rituals, prayers obsolete before the birth of Christ. For a while his discourse took the farm of reminding God of this gift or that which Divinity had deigned to accept from men—great churches if he would rescue cities from the plague, gifts of myrrh and gold, of human lives and beautiful women and captive armies, of children and queens, of beasts of the forest and field, sheep and goats, harvests and cities, whole conquered lands that had been offered up in lust or blood for His appeasal, buying a meed's worth of alleviation from the Divine wrath—and now he, Braddock Washington, Emperor of Diamonds, king and priest of the age of gold, arbiter of splendour and luxury, would offer up a treasure such as princes before him had never dreamed of, offer it up not in suppliance, but in pride.

He would give to God, he continued, getting down to specifications, the greatest diamond in the world. This diamond would be cut with many more thousand facets than there were leaves on a tree, and yet the whole diamond would be shaped with the perfection of a stone no bigger than a fly. Many men would work upon it for many years. It would be set in a great dome of beaten gold, wonderfully carved and equipped with gates of opal and crusted sapphire. In the middle would be hollowed out a chapel presided over by an altar of iridescent, decomposing, ever-changing radium which would burn out the eyes of any worshipper who lifted up his head from prayer—and on this altar there would be slain for the amusement of the Divine Benefactor any victim He should choose, even though it should be the greatest and most powerful man alive.

In return he asked only a simple thing, a thing that for God would be absurdly easy—only that matters should be as they were yesterday at this hour and that they should so remain. So very simple! Let but the heavens open, swallowing these men and their aeroplanes—and then close again. Let him have his slaves once more, restored to life and well.

There was no one else with whom he had ever needed: to treat or bargain.

He doubted only whether he had made his bribe big enough. God had His price, of course. God was made in man's image, so it had been said: He must have His price. And the price would be rare—no cathedral whose building consumed many years, no pyramid constructed by ten thousand workmen, would be like this cathedral, this pyramid.

He paused here. That was his proposition. Everything would be up to specifications, and there was nothing vulgar in his assertion that it would be cheap at the price. He implied that Providence could take it or leave it.

As he approached the end his sentences became broken, became short and uncertain, and his body seemed tense, seemed strained to catch the slightest pressure or whisper of life in the spaces around him. His hair had turned gradually white as he talked, and now he lifted his head high to the heavens like a prophet of old—magnificently mad.

Then, as John stared in giddy fascination, it seemed to him that a curious phenomenon took place somewhere around him. It was as though the sky had darkened for an instant, as though there had been a sudden murmur in a gust of wind, a sound of far-away trumpets, a sighing like the rustle of a great silken robe—for a time the whole of nature round about partook of this darkness; the birds' song ceased; the trees were still, and far over the mountain there was a mutter of dull, menacing thunder.

That was all. The wind died along the tall grasses of the valley. The dawn and the day resumed their place in a time, and the risen sun sent hot waves of yellow mist that made its path bright before it. The leaves laughed in the sun, and their laughter shook until each bough was like a girl's school in fairyland. God had refused to accept the bribe.

For another moment John, watched the triumph of the day. Then, turning, he saw a flutter of brown down by the lake, then another flutter, then another, like the dance of golden angels alighting from the clouds. The aeroplanes had come to earth.

John slid off the boulder and ran down the side of the mountain to the clump of trees, where the two girls were awake and waiting for him. Kismine sprang to her feet, the jewels in her pockets jingling, a question on her parted lips, but instinct told John that there was no time for words. They must get off the mountain without losing a moment. He seized a hand of each, and in silence they threaded the tree-trunks, washed with light now and with the rising mist. Behind them from the valley came no sound at all, except the complaint of the peacocks far away and the pleasant of morning.

When they had gone about half a mile, they avoided the park land and entered a narrow path that led over the next rise of ground. At the highest point of this they paused and turned around. Their eyes rested upon the mountainside they had just left—oppressed by some dark sense of tragic impendency.

Clear against the sky a broken, white-haired man was slowly descending the steep slope, followed by two gigantic and emotionless negroes, who carried a burden between them which still flashed and glittered in the sun. Half-way down two other figures joined them—John could see that they were Mrs. Washington and her son, upon whose arm she leaned. The aviators had clambered from their machines to the sweeping lawn in front of the chateau, and with rifles in hand were starting up the diamond mountain in skirmishing formation.

But the little group of five which had formed farther up and was engrossing all the watchers' attention had stopped upon a ledge of rock. The negroes stooped and pulled up what appeared to be a trap-door in the side of the mountain. Into this they all disappeared, the white-haired man first, then his wife and son, finally the two negroes, the glittering tips of whose jewelled head-dresses caught the sun for a moment before the trap-door descended and engulfed them all.

Kismine clutched John's arm.

"Oh," she cried wildly, "where are they going? What are they going to do?"

"It must be some underground way of escape—"

A little scream from the two girls interrupted his sentence.

"Don't you see?" sobbed Kismine hysterically. "The mountain is wired!"

Even as she spoke John put up his hands to shield his sight. Before their eyes the whole surface of the mountain had changed suddenly to a dazzling burning yellow, which showed up through the jacket of turf as light shows through a human hand. For a moment the intolerable glow continued, and then like an extinguished filament it disappeared, revealing a black waste from which blue smoke arose slowly, carrying off with it what remained of vegetation and of human flesh. Of the aviators there was left neither blood nor bone—they were consumed as completely as the five souls who had gone inside.

Simultaneously, and with an immense concussion, the château literally threw itself into the air, bursting into flaming fragments as it rose, and then tumbling back upon itself in a smoking pile that lay projecting half into the water of the lake. There was no fire—what smoke there was drifted off mingling with the sunshine, and for a few minutes longer a powdery dust of marble drifted from the great featureless pile that had once been the house of jewels. There was no more sound and the three people were alone in the valley.

9

At sunset John and his two companions reached the huge cliff which had marked the boundaries of the Washington's dominion, and looking back found the valley tranquil and lovely in the dusk. They sat down to finish the food which Jasmine had brought with her in a basket,

"There!" she said, as she spread the table-cloth and put the sandwiches in a neat pile upon it. "Don't they look tempting? I always think that food tastes better outdoors."

"With that remark," remarked Kismine, "Jasmine enters the middle class."

"Now," said John eagerly, "turn out your pocket and let's see what jewels you brought along. If you made a good selection we three ought to live comfortably all the rest of our lives."

Obediently Kismine put her hand in her pocket and tossed two handfuls of glittering stones before him. "Not so bad," cried John enthusiastically. "They aren't very big, but-Hallo!" His expression changed as he held one of them up to the declining sun. "Why, these aren't diamonds! There's something the matter!"

"By golly!" exclaimed Kismine, with a startled look. "What an idiot I am!"

"Why, these are rhinestones!" cried John.

"I know." She broke into a laugh. "I opened the wrong drawer. They belonged on the dress of a girl who visited Jasmine. I got her to give them to me in exchange for diamonds. I'd never seen anything but precious stones before."

"And this is what you brought?"

"I'm afraid so." She fingered the brilliants wistfully. "I think I like these better. I'm a little tired of diamonds."

"Very well," said John gloomily. "We'll have to live in Hades. And you will grow old telling incredulous women that you got the wrong drawer. Unfortunately, your father's bank-books were consumed with him."

"Well, what's the matter with Hades?"

"If I come home with a wife at my age my father is just as liable as not to cut me off with a hot coal, as they say down there."

Jasmine spoke up.

"I love washing," she said quietly. "I have always washed my own handkerchiefs. I'll take in laundry and support you both."

"Do they have washwomen in Hades?" asked Kismine innocently.

"Of course," answered John. "It's just like anywhere else."

"I thought—perhaps it was too hot to wear any clothes."

John laughed.

"Just try it!" he suggested. "They'll run you out before you're half started."

"Will father be there?" she asked.

John turned to her in astonishment.

"Your father is dead," he replied sombrely. "Why should he go to Hades? You have it confused with another place that was abolished long ago."

After supper they folded up the table-cloth and spread their blankets for the night.

"What a dream it was," Kismine sighed, gazing up at the stars. "How strange it seems to be here with one dress and a penniless fiancée!

"Under the stars," she repeated. "I never noticed the stars before. I always thought of them as great big diamonds that belonged to some one. Now they frighten me. They make me feel that it was all a dream, all my youth."

"It was a dream," said John quietly. "Everybody's youth is a dream, a form of chemical madness."

"How pleasant then to be insane!"

"So I'm told," said John gloomily. "I don't know any longer. At any rate, let us love for a while, for a year or so, you and me. That's a form of divine drunkenness that we can all try. There are only diamonds in the whole world, diamonds and perhaps the shabby gift of disillusion. Well, I have that last and I will make the usual nothing of it." He shivered. "Turn up your coat collar, little girl, the night's full of chill and you'll get pneumonia. His was a great sin who first invented consciousness. Let us lose it for a few hours."

So wrapping himself in his blanket he fell off to sleep.

5.11.3 "Bernice Bobs Her Hair"

After dark on Saturday night one could stand on the first tee of the golf-course and see the country-club windows as a yellow expanse over a very black and wavy ocean. The waves of this ocean, so to speak, were the heads of many curious caddies, a few of the more ingenious chauffeurs, the golf professional's deaf sister— and there were usually several stray, diffident waves who might have rolled inside had they so desired. This was the gallery.

The balcony was inside. It consisted of the circle of wicker chairs that lined the wall of the combination clubroom and ballroom. At these Saturday-night dances it was largely feminine; a great babel of middle-aged ladies with sharp eyes and icy hearts behind lorgnettes and large bosoms. The main function of the balcony was critical, it occasionally showed grudging admiration, but never approval, for it is well known among ladies over thirty-five that when the younger set dance in the summer-time it is with the very worst intentions in the world, and if they are not bombarded with stony eyes stray couples will dance weird barbaric interludes in the corners, and the more popular, more dangerous, girls will sometimes be kissed in the parked limousines of unsuspecting dowagers.

But, after all, this critical circle is not close enough to the stage to see the actors' faces and catch the subtler byplay. It can only frown and lean, ask questions and make satisfactory deductions from its set of postulates, such as the one which states that every young man with a large income leads the life of a hunted partridge. It never really appreciates the drama of the shifting, semi-cruel world of adolescence. No; boxes, orchestra-circle, principals, and chorus be represented by the medley of faces and voices that sway to the plaintive African rhythm of Dyer's dance orchestra.

From sixteen-year-old Otis Ormonde, who has two more years at Hill School, to G. Reece Stoddard, over whose bureau at home hangs a Harvard law diploma; from little Madeleine Hogue, whose hair still feels strange and uncomfortable on top of her head, to Bessie MacRae, who has been the life of the party a little too long—more than ten years—the medley is not only the centre of the stage but contains the only people capable of getting an unobstructed view of it.

With a flourish and a bang the music stops. The couples exchange artificial, effortless smiles, facetiously repeat "LA-de-DA-DA dum-DUM," and then the clatter of young feminine voices soars over the burst of clapping.

A few disappointed stags caught in midfloor as they bad been about to cut in subsided listlessly back to the walls, because this was not like the riotous Christmas dances—these summer hops were considered just pleasantly warm and exciting, where even the younger marrieds rose and performed ancient waltzes and terrifying fox trots to the tolerant amusement of their younger brothers and sisters.

Warren McIntyre, who casually attended Yale, being one of the unfortunate stags, felt in his dinner-coat pocket for a cigarette and strolled out onto the wide, semidark veranda, where couples were scattered at tables, filling the lantern-hung night with vague words and hazy laughter. He nodded here and there at the less absorbed and as he passed each couple some half-forgotten fragment of a story played in his mind, for it was not a large city and every one was Who's Who to every one else's past. There, for example, were Jim Strain and Ethel Demorest, who had been privately engaged for three years. Every one knew that as soon as Jim managed to hold a job for more than two months she would marry him. Yet how bored they both looked, and how wearily Ethel regarded Jim sometimes, as if she wondered why she had trained the vines of her affection on such a wind-shaken poplar.

Warren was nineteen and rather pitying with those of his friends who hadn't gone East to college. But, like most boys, he bragged tremendously about the girls of his city when he was away from it. There was Genevieve Ormonde, who regularly made the rounds of dances, house-parties, and football games at Princeton, Yale, Williams, and Cornell; there was black-eyed Roberta Dillon, who was quite as famous to her own generation as Hiram Johnson or Ty Cobb; and, of course, there was Marjorie Harvey, who besides having a fairylike face and a dazzling, bewildering tongue was already justly celebrated for having turned five cart-wheels in succession during the last pump-and-slipper dance at New Haven.

Warren, who had grown up across the street from Marjorie, had long been "crazy about her." Sometimes she seemed to reciprocate his feeling with a faint gratitude, but she had tried him by her infallible test and informed him gravely that she did not love him. Her test was that when she was away from him she forgot him and had affairs with other boys. Warren found this discouraging, especially as Marjorie had been making little trips all summer, and for the first two or three days after each arrival home he saw great heaps of mail on the Harveys' hall table addressed to her in various masculine handwritings. To make matters worse, all during the month of August she had been visited by her cousin Bernice from Eau Claire, and it seemed impossible to see her alone. It was always necessary to hunt round and find some one to take care of Bernice. As August waned this was becoming more and more difficult.

Much as Warren worshipped Marjorie he had to admit that Cousin Bernice was sorta dopeless. She was pretty, with dark hair and high color, but she was no fun on a party. Every Saturday night he danced a long arduous duty dance with her to please Marjorie, but he had never been anything but bored in her company.

"Warren"—a soft voice at his elbow broke in upon his thoughts, and he turned to see Marjorie, flushed and radiant as usual. She laid a hand on his shoulder and a glow settled almost imperceptibly over him.

"Warren," she whispered "do something for me—dance with Bernice. She's been stuck with little Otis Ormonde for almost an hour."

Warren's glow faded.

"Why—sure," he answered half-heartedly.

"You don't mind, do you? I'll see that you don't get stuck."

"'Sall right."

Marjorie smiled—that smile that was thanks enough.

"You're an angel, and I'm obliged loads."

With a sigh the angel glanced round the veranda, but Bernice and Otis were not in sight. He wandered back inside, and there in front of the women's dressing-room he found Otis in the centre of a group of young men who were convulsed with laughter. Otis was brandishing a piece of timber he had picked up, and discoursing volubly.

"She's gone in to fix her hair," he announced wildly. "I'm waiting to dance another hour with her."

Their laughter was renewed.

"Why don't some of you cut in?" cried Otis resentfully. "She likes more variety."

"Why, Otis," suggested a friend "you've just barely got used to her."

"Why the two-by-four, Otis?" inquired Warren, smiling.

"The two-by-four? Oh, this? This is a club. When she comes out I'll hit her on the head and knock her in again."

Warren collapsed on a settee and howled with glee.

"Never mind, Otis," he articulated finally. "I'm relieving you this time."

Otis simulated a sudden fainting attack and handed the stick to Warren.

"If you need it, old man," he said hoarsely.

No matter how beautiful or brilliant a girl may be, the reputation of not being frequently cut in on makes her position at a dance unfortunate. Perhaps boys prefer her company to that of the butterflies with whom they dance a dozen times an but, youth in this jazz-nourished generation is temperamentally restless, and the idea of fox-trotting more than one full fox trot with the same girl is distasteful, not to say odious. When it comes to several dances and the intermissions between she can be quite sure that a young man, once relieved, will never tread on her wayward toes again.

Warren danced the next full dance with Bernice, and finally, thankful for the intermission, he led her to a table on the veranda. There was a moment's silence while she did unimpressive things with her fan.

"It's hotter here than in Eau Claire," she said.

Warren stifled a sigh and nodded. It might be for all he knew or cared. He wondered idly whether she was a poor conversationalist because she got no attention or got no attention because she was a poor conversationalist.

"You going to be here much longer?" he asked and then turned rather red. She might suspect his reasons for asking.

"Another week," she answered, and stared at him as if to lunge at his next remark when it left his lips.

Warren fidgeted. Then with a sudden charitable impulse he decided to try part of his line on her. He turned and looked at her eyes.

"You've got an awfully kissable mouth," he began quietly.

This was a remark that he sometimes made to girls at college proms when they were talking in just such half dark as this. Bernice distinctly jumped. She turned an ungraceful red and became clumsy with her fan. No one had ever made such a remark to her before.

"Fresh!"—the word had slipped out before she realized it, and she bit her lip.

Too late she decided to be amused, and offered him a flustered smile.

Warren was annoyed. Though not accustomed to have that remark taken seriously, still it usually provoked a laugh or a paragraph of sentimental banter. And he hated to be called fresh, except in a joking way. His charitable impulse died and he switched the topic.

"Jim Strain and Ethel Demorest sitting out as usual," he commented.

This was more in Bernice's line, but a faint regret mingled with her relief as the subject changed. Men did not talk to her about kissable mouths, but she knew that they talked in some such way to other girls.

"Oh, yes," she said, and laughed. "I hear they've been mooning around for years without a red penny. Isn't it silly?"

Warren's disgust increased. Jim Strain was a close friend of his brother's, and anyway he considered it bad form to sneer at people for not having money. But Bernice had had no intention of sneering. She was merely nervous.

II

When Marjorie and Bernice reached home at half after midnight they said good night at the top of the stairs. Though cousins, they were not intimates. As a matter of fact Marjorie had no female intimates—she considered girls stupid. Bernice on the contrary all through this parent-arranged visit had rather longed to exchange those confidences flavored with giggles and tears that she considered an indispensable factor in all feminine intercourse. But in this respect she found Marjorie rather cold; felt somehow the same difficulty in talking to her that she had in talking to men. Marjorie never giggled, was never frightened, seldom embarrassed, and in fact had very few of the qualities which Bernice considered appropriately and blessedly feminine.

As Bernice busied herself with tooth-brush and paste this night she wondered for the hundredth time why she never had any attention when she was away from home. That her family were the wealthiest in Eau Claire; that her mother entertained tremendously, gave little diners for her daughter before all dances and bought her a car of her own to drive round in, never occurred to her as factors in her home-town social success. Like most girls she had been brought up on the warm milk prepared by Annie Fellows Johnston and on novels in which the female was beloved because of certain mysterious womanly qualities always mentioned but never displayed.

Bernice felt a vague pain that she was not at present engaged in being popular. She did not know that had it not been for Marjorie's campaigning she would have danced the entire evening with one man; but she knew that even in Eau Claire other girls with less position and less pulchritude were given a much bigger rush. She attributed this to something subtly unscrupulous in those girls. It had never worried her, and if it had her mother would have assured her that the other girls cheapened themselves and that men really respected girls like Bernice.

She turned out the light in her bathroom, and on an impulse decided to go in and chat for a moment with her aunt Josephine, whose light was still on. Her soft slippers bore her noiselessly down the carpeted hall, but hearing voices inside she stopped near the partly openers door. Then she caught her own name, and without any definite intention of eavesdropping lingered—and the thread of the conversation going on inside pierced her consciousness sharply as if it had been drawn through with a needle.

"She's absolutely hopeless!" It was Marjorie's voice. "Oh, I know what you're going to say! So many people have told you how pretty and sweet she is, and how she can cook! What of it? She has a bum time. Men don't like her."

"What's a little cheap popularity?"

Mrs. Harvey sounded annoyed.

"It's everything when you're eighteen," said Marjorie emphatically. "I've done my best. I've been polite and I've made men dance with her, but they just won't stand being bored. When I think of that gorgeous coloring wasted on such a ninny, and think what Martha Carey could do with it—oh!"

"There's no courtesy these days."

Mrs. Harvey's voice implied that modern situations were too much for her. When she was a girl all young ladies who belonged to nice families had glorious times.

"Well," said Marjorie, "no girl can permanently bolster up a lame-duck visitor, because these days it's every girl for herself. I've even tried to drop hints about clothes and things, and she's been furious—given me the funniest looks. She's sensitive enough to know she's not getting away with much, but I'll bet she consoles herself by thinking that she's very virtuous and that I'm too gay and fickle and will come to a bad end. All unpopular girls think that way. Sour grapes! Sarah Hopkins refers to Genevieve and Roberta and me as gardenia girls! I'll bet she'd give ten years of her life and her European education to be a gardenia girl and have three or four men in love with her and be cut in on every few feet at dances."

"It seems to me," interrupted Mrs. Harvey rather wearily, "that you ought to be able to do something for Bernice. I know she's not very vivacious."

Marjorie groaned.

"Vivacious! Good grief! I've never heard her say anything to a boy except that it's hot or the floor's crowded or that she's going to school in New York next year. Sometimes she asks them what kind of car they have and tells them the kind she has. Thrilling!"

There was a short silence and then Mrs. Harvey took up her refrain:

"All I know is that other girls not half so sweet and attractive get partners. Martha Carey, for instance, is stout and loud, and her mother is distinctly common. Roberta Dillon is so thin this year that she looks as though Arizona were the place for her. She's dancing herself to death."

"But, mother," objected Marjorie impatiently, "Martha is cheerful and awfully witty and an awfully slick girl, and Roberta's a marvellous dancer. She's been popular for ages!"

Mrs. Harvey yawned.

"I think it's that crazy Indian blood in Bernice," continued Marjorie. "Maybe she's a reversion to type. Indian women all just sat round and never said anything."

"Go to bed, you silly child," laughed Mrs. Harvey. "I wouldn't have told you that if I'd thought you were going to remember it. And I think most of your ideas are perfectly idiotic," she finished sleepily.

There was another silence, while Marjorie considered whether or not convincing her mother was worth the trouble. People over forty can seldom be permanently convinced of anything. At eighteen our convictions are hills from which we look; at forty-five they are caves in which we hide.

Having decided this, Marjorie said good night. When she came out into the hall it was quite empty.

III

While Marjorie was breakfasting late next day Bernice came into the room with a rather formal good morning, sat down opposite, stared intently over and slightly moistened her lips.

"What's on your mind?" inquired Marjorie, rather puzzled.

Bernice paused before she threw her hand-grenade.

"I heard what you said about me to your mother last night."

Marjorie was startled, but she showed only a faintly heightened color and her voice was quite even when she spoke.

"Where were you?"

"In the hall. I didn't mean to listen—at first."

After an involuntary look of contempt Marjorie dropped her eyes and became very interested in balancing a stray corn-flake on her finger."

"I guess I'd better go back to Eau Claire—if I'm such a nuisance." Bernice's lower lip was trembling violently and she continued on a wavering note: "I've tried to be nice, and—and I've been first neglected and then insulted. No one ever visited me and got such treatment."

Marjorie was silent.

"But I'm in the way, I see. I'm a drag on you. Your friends don't like me." She paused, and then remembered another one of her grievances. "Of course I was furious last week when you tried to hint to me that that dress was unbecoming. Don't you think I know how to dress myself?"

"No," murmured less than half-aloud.

"What?"

"I didn't hint anything," said Marjorie succinctly. "I said, as I remember, that it was better to wear a becoming dress three times straight than to alternate it with two frights."

"Do you think that was a very nice thing to say?"

"I wasn't trying to be nice." Then after a pause: "When do you want to go?"

Bernice drew in her breath sharply.

"Oh!" It was a little half-cry.

Marjorie looked up in surprise.

"Didn't you say you were going?"

"Yes, but—"

"Oh, you were only bluffing!"

They stared at each other across the breakfast-table for a moment. Misty waves were passing before Bernice's eyes, while Marjorie's face wore that rather hard expression that she used when slightly intoxicated undergraduate's were making love to her.

"So you were bluffing," she repeated as if it were what she might have expected.

Bernice admitted it by bursting into tears. Marjorie's eyes showed boredom.

"You're my cousin," sobbed Bernice. "I'm v-v-visiting you. I was to stay a month, and if I go home my mother will know and she'll wah-wonder—"

Marjorie waited until the shower of broken words collapsed into little sniffles.

"I'll give you my month's allowance," she said coldly, "and you can spend this last week anywhere you want. There's a very nice hotel—"

Bernice's sobs rose to a flute note, and rising of a sudden she fled from the room.

An hour later, while Marjorie was in the library absorbed in composing one of those non-committal marvelously elusive letters that only a young girl can write, Bernice reappeared, very red-eyed, and consciously calm. She cast no glance at Marjorie but took a book at random from the shelf and sat down as if to read. Marjorie seemed absorbed in her letter and continued writing. When the clock showed noon Bernice closed her book with a snap.

"I suppose I'd better get my railroad ticket."

This was not the beginning of the speech she had rehearsed up-stairs, but as Marjorie was not getting her cues—wasn't urging her to be reasonable; it's an a mistake—it was the best opening she could muster.

"Just wait till I finish this letter," said Marjorie without looking round. "I want to get it off in the next mail."

After another minute, during which her pen scratched busily, she turned round and relaxed with an air of "at your service." Again Bernice had to speak.

"Do you want me to go home?"

"Well," said Marjorie, considering, "I suppose if you're not having a good time you'd better go. No use being miserable."

"Don't you think common kindness—"

"Oh, please don't quote 'Little Women'!" cried Marjorie impatiently. "That's out of style."

"You think so?"

"Heavens, yes! What modern girl could live like those inane females?"

"They were the models for our mothers."

Marjorie laughed.

"Yes, they were—not! Besides, our mothers were all very well in their way, but they know very little about their daughters' problems."

Bernice drew herself up.

"Please don't talk about my mother."

Marjorie laughed.

"I don't think I mentioned her."

Bernice felt that she was being led away from her subject.

"Do you think you've treated me very well?"

"I've done my best. You're rather hard material to work with."

The lids of Bernice's eyes reddened.

"I think you're hard and selfish, and you haven't a feminine quality in you."

"Oh, my Lord!" cried Marjorie in desperation "You little nut! Girls like you are responsible for all the tiresome colorless marriages; all those ghastly inefficiencies that pass as feminine qualities. What a blow it must be when a man with imagination marries the beautiful bundle of clothes that he's been building ideals round, and finds that she's just a weak, whining, cowardly mass of affectations!"

Bernice's mouth had slipped half open.

"The womanly woman!" continued Marjorie. "Her whole early life is occupied in whining criticisms of girls like me who really do have a good time."

Bernice's jaw descended farther as Marjorie's voice rose.

"There's some excuse for an ugly girl whining. If I'd been irretrievably ugly I'd never have forgiven my parents for bringing me into the world. But you're starting life without any handicap—" Marjorie's little fist clinched, "If you expect me to weep with you you'll be disappointed. Go or stay, just as you like." And picking up her letters she left the room.

Bernice claimed a headache and failed to appear at luncheon. They had a matinée date for the afternoon, but the headache persisting, Marjorie made explanation to a not very downcast boy. But when she returned late in the afternoon she found Bernice with a strangely set face waiting for her in her bedroom.

"I've decided," began Bernice without preliminaries, "that maybe you're right about things—possibly not. But if you'll tell me why your friends aren't—aren't interested in me I'll see if I can do what you want me to."

Marjorie was at the mirror shaking down her hair.

"Do you mean it?"

"Yes."

"Without reservations? Will you do exactly what I say?"

"Well, I—"

"Well nothing! Will you do exactly as I say?"

"If they're sensible things."

"They're not! You're no case for sensible things."

"Are you going to make—to recommend—"

"Yes, everything. If I tell you to take boxing-lessons you'll have to do it. Write home and tell your mother you're going' to stay another two weeks.

"If you'll tell me—"

"All right—I'll just give you a few examples now. First you have no ease of manner. Why? Because you're never sure about your personal appearance. When a girl feels that she's perfectly groomed and dressed she can forget that part of her. That's charm. The more parts of yourself you can afford to forget the more charm you have."

"Don't I look all right?"

"No; for instance you never take care of your eyebrows. They're black and lustrous, but by leaving them straggly they're a blemish. They'd be beautiful if you'd take care of them in one-tenth the time you take doing nothing. You're going to brush them so that they'll grow straight."

Bernice raised the brows in question.

"Do you mean to say that men notice eyebrows?"

"Yes—subconsciously. And when you go home you ought to have your teeth straightened a little. It's almost imperceptible, still—"

"But I thought," interrupted Bernice in bewilderment, "that you despised little dainty feminine things like that."

"I hate dainty minds," answered Marjorie. "But a girl has to be dainty in person. If she looks like a million dollars she can talk about Russia, ping-pong, or the League of Nations and get away with it."

"What else?"

"Oh, I'm just beginning! There's your dancing."

"Don't I dance all right?"

"No, you don't—you lean on a man; yes, you do—ever so slightly. I noticed it when we were dancing together yesterday. And you dance standing up straight instead of bending over a little. Probably some old lady on the side-line once told you that you looked so dignified that way. But except with a very small girl it's much harder on the man, and he's the one that counts."

"Go on." Bernice's brain was reeling.

"Well, you've got to learn to be nice to men who are sad birds. You look as if you'd been insulted whenever you're thrown with any except the most popular boys. Why, Bernice, I'm cut in on every few feet—and who does most of it? Why, those very sad birds. No girl can afford to neglect them. They're the big part of any crowd. Young boys too shy to talk are the very best conversational practice. Clumsy boys are the best dancing practice. If you can follow them and yet look graceful you can follow a baby tank across a barb-wire sky-scraper."

Bernice sighed profoundly, but Marjorie was not through.

"If you go to a dance and really amuse, say, three sad birds that dance with you; if you talk so well to them that they forget they're stuck with you, you've done something. They'll come back next time, and gradually so many sad birds will dance with you that the attractive boys will see there's no danger of being stuck—then they'll dance with you."

"Yes," agreed Bernice faintly. "I think I begin to see."

"And finally," concluded Marjorie, "poise and charm will just come. You'll wake up some morning knowing you've attained it and men will know it too."

Bernice rose.

"It's been awfully kind of you—but nobody's ever talked to me like this before, and I feel sort of startled."

Marjorie made no answer but gazed pensively at her own image in the mirror.

"You're a peach to help me," continued Bernice.

Still Marjorie did not answer, and Bernice thought she had seemed too grateful.

"I know you don't like sentiment," she said timidly.

Marjorie turned to her quickly.

"Oh, I wasn't thinking about that. I was considering whether we hadn't better bob your hair."

Bernice collapsed backward upon the bed.

IV

On the following Wednesday evening there was a dinner-dance at the country club. When the guests strolled in Bernice found her place-card with a slight feeling of irritation. Though at her right sat G. Reece Stoddard, a most desirable and distinguished young bachelor, the all-important left held only Charley Paulson. Charley lacked height, beauty, and social shrewdness, and in her new enlightenment Bernice decided that his only qualification to be her partner was that he had never been stuck with her. But this feeling of irritation left with the last of the soup-plates, and Marjorie's specific instruction came to her. Swallowing her pride she turned to Charley Paulson and plunged.

"Do you think I ought to bob my hair, Mr. Charley Paulson?"

Charley looked up in surprise.

"Why?"

"Because I'm considering it. It's such a sure and easy way of attracting attention."

Charley smiled pleasantly. He could not know this had been rehearsed. He replied that he didn't know much about bobbed hair. But Bernice was there to tell him.

"I want to be a society vampire, you see," she announced coolly, and went on to inform him that bobbed hair was the necessary prelude. She added that she wanted to ask his advice, because she had heard he was so critical about girls.

Charley, who knew as much about the psychology of women as he did of the mental states of Buddhist contemplatives, felt vaguely flattered.

"So I've decided," she continued, her voice rising slightly, "that early next week I'm going down to the Sevier Hotel barber-shop, sit in the first chair, and get my hair bobbed." She faltered noticing that the people near her had paused in their conversation and were listening; but after a confused second Marjorie's coaching told, and she finished her paragraph to the vicinity at large. "Of course I'm charging admission, but if you'll all come down and encourage me I'll issue passes for the inside seats."

There was a ripple of appreciative laughter, and under cover of it G. Reece Stoddard leaned over quickly and said close to her ear: "I'll take a box right now."

She met his eyes and smiled as if he had said something surprisingly brilliant.

"Do you believe in bobbed hair?" asked G. Reece in the same undertone.

"I think it's unmoral," affirmed Bernice gravely. "But, of course, you've either got to amuse people or feed 'em or shock 'em." Marjorie had culled this from Oscar Wilde. It was greeted with a ripple of laughter from the men and a series of quick, intent looks from the girls. And then as though she had said nothing of wit or moment Bernice turned again to Charley and spoke confidentially in his ear.

"I want to ask you your opinion of several people. I imagine you're a wonderful judge of character."

Charley thrilled faintly—paid her a subtle compliment by overturning her water.

Two hours later, while Warren McIntyre was standing passively in the stag line abstractedly watching the dancers and wondering whither and with whom Marjorie had disappeared, an unrelated perception began to creep slowly upon him—a perception that Bernice, cousin to Marjorie, had been cut in on several times in the past five minutes. He closed his eyes, opened them and looked again. Several minutes back she had been dancing with a visiting boy, a matter easily accounted for; a visiting boy would know no better. But now she was dancing with some one else, and there was Charley Paulson headed for her with enthusiastic determination in his eye. Funny—Charley seldom danced with more than three girls an evening.

Warren was distinctly surprised when—the exchange having been effected—the man relieved proved to be none ether than G. Reece Stoddard himself. And G. Reece seemed not at all jubilant at being relieved. Next time Bernice danced near, Warren regarded her intently. Yes, she was pretty, distinctly pretty; and to-night her face seemed really vivacious. She had that look that no woman, however histrionically proficient, can successfully counterfeit—she looked as if she were having a good time. He liked the way she had her hair arranged, wondered if it was brilliantine that made it glisten so. And that dress was becoming—a dark red that set off her shadowy eyes and high coloring. He remembered that he had thought her pretty when she first came to town, before he had realized that she was dull. Too bad she was dull—dull girls unbearable—certainly pretty though.

His thoughts zigzagged back to Marjorie. This disappearance would be like other disappearances. When she reappeared he would demand where she had been—would be told emphatically that it was none of his business. What a pity she was so sure of him! She basked in the knowledge that no other girl in town interested him; she defied him to fall in love with Genevieve or Roberta.

Warren sighed. The way to Marjorie's affections was a labyrinth indeed. He looked up. Bernice was again dancing with the visiting boy. Half unconsciously he took a step out from the stag line in her direction, and hesitated. Then he said to himself that it was charity. He walked toward her—collided suddenly with G. Reece Stoddard.

"Pardon me," said Warren.

But G. Reece had not stopped to apologize. He had again cut in on Bernice.

That night at one o'clock Marjorie, with one hand on the electric-light switch in the hall, turned to take a last look at Bernice's sparkling eyes.

"So it worked?"

"Oh, Marjorie, yes!" cried Bernice.

"I saw you were having a gay time."

"I did! The only trouble was that about midnight I ran short of talk. I had to repeat myself—with different men of course. I hope they won't compare notes."

"Men don't," said Marjorie, yawning, "and it wouldn't matter if they did—they'd think you were even trickier."

She snapped out the light, and as they started up the stairs Bernice grasped the banister thankfully. For the first time in her life she had been danced tired.

"You see," said Marjorie it the top of the stairs, "one man sees another man cut in and he thinks there must be something there. Well, we'll fix up some new stuff to-morrow. Good night."

"Good night."

As Bernice took down her hair she passed the evening before her in review. She had followed instructions exactly. Even when Charley Paulson cut in for the eighth time she had simulated delight and had apparently been both interested and flattered. She had not talked about the weather or Eau Claire or automobiles or her school, but had confined her conversation to me, you, and us.

But a few minutes before she fell asleep a rebellious thought was churning drowsily in her brain—after all, it was she who had done it. Marjorie, to be sure, had given her her conversation, but then Marjorie got much of her conversation out of things she read. Bernice had bought the red dress, though she had never valued it highly before Marjorie dug it out of her trunk—and her own voice had said the words, her own lips had smiled, her own feet had danced. Marjorie nice girl—vain, though—nice evening—nice boys—like Warren—Warren—Warren—what's his name—Warren—

She fell asleep.

V

To Bernice the next week was a revelation. With the feeling that people really enjoyed looking at her and listening to her came the foundation of self-confidence. Of course there were numerous mistakes at first. She did not know, for instance, that Draycott Deyo was studying for the ministry; she was unaware that he had cut in on her because he thought she was a quiet, reserved girl. Had she known these things she would not have treated him to the line which began "Hello, Shell Shock!" and continued with the bathtub story—"It takes a frightful lot of energy to fix my hair in the summer—there's so much of it—so I always fix it first and powder my face and put on my hat; then I get into the bathtub, and dress afterward. Don't you think that's the best plan?"

Though Draycott Deyo was in the throes of difficulties concerning baptism by immersion and might possibly have seen a connection, it must be admitted that he did not. He considered feminine bathing an immoral subject, and gave her some of his ideas on the depravity of modern society.

But to offset that unfortunate occurrence Bernice had several signal successes to her credit. Little Otis Ormonde pleaded off from a trip East and elected instead to follow her with a puppylike devotion, to the amusement of his crowd and to the irritation of G. Reece Stoddard, several of whose afternoon calls Otis completely ruined by the disgusting tenderness of the glances he bent on Bernice. He even told her the story of the two-by-four and the dressing-room to show her how frightfully mistaken he and every one else had been in their first judgment of her. Bernice laughed off that incident with a slight sinking sensation.

Of all Bernice's conversation perhaps the best known and most universally approved was the line about the bobbing of her hair.

"Oh, Bernice, when you goin' to get the hair bobbed?"

"Day after to-morrow maybe," she would reply, laughing. "Will you come and see me? Because I'm counting on you, you know."

"Will we? You know! But you better hurry up."

Bernice, whose tonsorial intentions were strictly dishonorable, would laugh again.

"Pretty soon now. You'd be surprised."

But perhaps the most significant symbol of her success was the gray car of the hypercritical Warren McIntyre, parked daily in front of the Harvey house. At first the parlor-maid was distinctly startled when he asked for Bernice instead of Marjorie; after a week of it she told the cook that Miss Bernice had gotta holda Miss Marjorie's best fella.

And Miss Bernice had. Perhaps it began with Warren's desire to rouse jealousy in Marjorie; perhaps it was the familiar though unrecognized strain of Marjorie in Bernice's conversation; perhaps it was both of these and something of sincere attraction besides. But somehow the collective mind of the younger set knew within a week that Marjorie's most reliable beau had made an amazing face-about and was giving an indisputable rush to Marjorie's guest. The question of the moment was how Marjorie would take it. Warren called Bernice on the 'phone twice a day, sent her notes, and they were frequently seen together in his roadster, obviously engrossed in one of those tense, significant conversations as to whether or not he was sincere.

Marjorie on being twitted only laughed. She said she was mighty glad that Warren had at last found some one who appreciated him. So the younger set laughed, too, and guessed that Marjorie didn't care and let it go at that.

One afternoon when there were only three days left of her visit Bernice was waiting in the hall for Warren, with whom she was going to a bridge party. She was in rather a blissful mood, and when Marjorie—also bound for the party—appeared beside her and began casually to adjust her hat in the mirror, Bernice was utterly unprepared for anything in the nature of a clash. Marjorie did her work very coldly and succinctly in three sentences.

"You may as well get Warren out of your head," she said coldly.

"What?" Bernice was utterly astounded.

"You may as well stop making a fool of yourself over Warren McIntyre. He doesn't care a snap of his fingers about you."

For a tense moment they regarded each other—Marjorie scornful, aloof; Bernice astounded, half-angry, half-afraid. Then two cars drove up in front of the house and there was a riotous honking. Both of them gasped faintly, turned, and side by side hurried out.

All through the bridge party Bernice strove in vain to master a rising uneasiness. She had offended Marjorie, the sphinx of sphinxes. With the most wholesome and innocent intentions in the world she had stolen Marjorie's property. She felt suddenly and horribly guilty. After the bridge game, when they sat in an informal circle and the conversation became general, the storm gradually broke. Little Otis Ormonde inadvertently precipitated it.

"When you going back to kindergarten, Otis?" some one had asked.

"Me? Day Bernice gets her hair bobbed."

"Then your education's over," said Marjorie quickly. "That's only a bluff of hers. I should think you'd have realized."

"That a fact?" demanded Otis, giving Bernice a reproachful glance.

Bernice's ears burned as she tried to think up an effectual come-back. In the face of this direct attack her imagination was paralyzed.

"There's a lot of bluffs in the world," continued Marjorie quite pleasantly. "I should think you'd be young enough to know that, Otis."

"Well," said Otis, "maybe so. But gee! With a line like Bernice's—"

"Really?" yawned Marjorie. "What's her latest bon mot?"

No one seemed to know. In fact, Bernice, having trifled with her muse's beau, had said nothing memorable of late.

"Was that really all a line?" asked Roberta curiously.

Bernice hesitated. She felt that wit in some form was demanded of her, but under her cousin's suddenly frigid eyes she was completely incapacitated.

"I don't know," she stalled.

"Splush!" said Marjorie. "Admit it!"

Bernice saw that Warren's eyes had left a ukulele he had been tinkering with and were fixed on her questioningly.

"Oh, I don't know!" she repeated steadily. Her cheeks were glowing.

"Splush!" remarked Marjorie again.

"Come through, Bernice," urged Otis. "Tell her where to get off." Bernice looked round again—she seemed unable to get away from Warren's eyes.

"I like bobbed hair," she said hurriedly, as if he had asked her a question, "and I intend to bob mine."

"When?" demanded Marjorie.

"Any time."

"No time like the present," suggested Roberta.

Otis jumped to his feet.

"Good stuff!" he cried. "We'll have a summer bobbing party. Sevier Hotel barber-shop, I think you said."

In an instant all were on their feet. Bernice's heart throbbed violently.

"What?" she gasped.

Out of the group came Marjorie's voice, very clear and contemptuous.

"Don't worry—she'll back out!"

"Come on, Bernice!" cried Otis, starting toward the door.

Four eyes—Warren's and Marjorie's—stared at her, challenged her, defied her. For another second she wavered wildly.

"All right," she said swiftly "I don't care if I do."

An eternity of minutes later, riding down-town through the late afternoon beside Warren, the others following in Roberta's car close behind, Bernice had all the sensations of Marie Antoinette bound for the guillotine in a tumbrel. Vaguely she wondered why she did not cry out that it was all a mistake. It was all she could do to keep from clutching her hair with both bands to protect it from the suddenly hostile world. Yet she did neither. Even the thought of her mother was no deterrent now. This was the test supreme of her sportsmanship; her right to walk unchallenged in the starry heaven of popular girls.

Warren was moodily silent, and when they came to the hotel he drew up at the curb and nodded to Bernice to precede him out. Roberta's car emptied a laughing crowd into the shop, which presented two bold plate-glass windows to the street.

Bernice stood on the curb and looked at the sign, Sevier Barber-Shop. It was a guillotine indeed, and the hangman was the first barber, who, attired in a white coat and smoking a cigarette, leaned non-chalantly against the first chair. He must have heard of her; he must have been waiting all week, smoking eternal cigarettes beside that portentous, too-often-mentioned first chair. Would they blind-fold her? No, but they would tie a white cloth round her neck lest any of her blood—nonsense—hair—should get on her clothes.

"All right, Bernice," said Warren quickly.

With her chin in the air she crossed the sidewalk, pushed open the swinging screen-door, and giving not a glance to the uproarious, riotous row that occupied the waiting bench, went up to the fat barber.

"I want you to bob my hair."

The first barber's mouth slid somewhat open. His cigarette dropped to the floor.

"Huh?"

"My hair—bob it!"

Refusing further preliminaries, Bernice took her seat on high. A man in the chair next to her turned on his side and gave her a glance, half lather, half amazement. One barber started and spoiled little Willy Schuneman's monthly haircut. Mr. O'Reilly in the last chair grunted and swore musically in ancient Gaelic as a razor bit into his cheek. Two bootblacks became wide-eyed and rushed for her feet. No, Bernice didn't care for a shine.

Outside a passer-by stopped and stared; a couple joined him; half a dozen small boys' nose sprang into life, flattened against the glass; and snatches of conversation borne on the summer breeze drifted in through the screen-door.

"Lookada long hair on a kid!"

"Where'd yuh get 'at stuff? 'At's a bearded lady he just finished shavin'."

But Bernice saw nothing, heard nothing. Her only living sense told her that this man in the white coat had removed one tortoise-shell comb and then another; that his fingers were fumbling clumsily with unfamiliar hairpins; that this hair, this wonderful hair of hers, was going—she would never again feel its long voluptuous pull as it hung in a dark-brown glory down her back. For a second she was near breaking down, and then the picture before her swam mechanically into her vision—Marjorie's mouth curling in a faint ironic smile as if to say:

"Give up and get down! You tried to buck me and I called your bluff. You see you haven't got a prayer."

And some last energy rose up in Bernice, for she clinched her hands under the white cloth, and there was a curious narrowing of her eyes that Marjorie remarked on to some one long afterward.

Twenty minutes later the barber swung her round to face the mirror, and she flinched at the full extent of the damage that had been wrought. Her hair was not curls and now it lay in lank lifeless blocks on both sides of her suddenly pale face. It was ugly as sin—she had known it would be ugly as sin. Her face's chief charm had been a Madonna-like simplicity. Now that was gone and she was—well frightfully mediocre—not stagy; only ridiculous, like a Greenwich Villager who had left her spectacles at home.

As she climbed down from the chair she tried to smile—failed miserably. She saw two of the girls exchange glances; noticed Marjorie's mouth curved in attenuated mockery—and that Warren's eyes were suddenly very cold.

"You see,"—her words fell into an awkward pause—"I've done it."

"Yes, you've—done it," admitted Warren.

"Do you like it?"

There was a half-hearted "Sure" from two or three voices, another awkward pause, and then Marjorie turned swiftly and with serpentlike intensity to Warren.

"Would you mind running me down to the cleaners?" she asked. "I've simply got to get a dress there before supper. Roberta's driving right home and she can take the others."

Warren stared abstractedly at some infinite speck out the window. Then for an instant his eyes rested coldly on Bernice before they turned to Marjorie.

"Be glad to," he said slowly.

VI

Bernice did not fully realize the outrageous trap that had been set for her until she met her aunt's amazed glance just before dinner.

"Why Bernice!"

"I've bobbed it, Aunt Josephine."

"Why, child!"

"Do you like it?"

"Why Bernice!"

"I suppose I've shocked you."

"No, but what'll Mrs. Deyo think tomorrow night? Bernice, you should have wait-ed until after the Deyo's dance—you should have waited if you wanted to do that."

"It was sudden, Aunt Josephine. Anyway, why does it matter to Mrs. Deyo par-ticularly?"

"Why child," cried Mrs. Harvey, "in her paper on 'The Foibles of the Younger Generation' that she read at the last meeting of the Thursday Club she devoted fifteen minutes to bobbed hair. It's her pet abomination. And the dance is for you and Marjorie!"

"I'm sorry."

"Oh, Bernice, what'll your mother say? She'll think I let you do it."

"I'm sorry."

Dinner was an agony. She had made a hasty attempt with a curling-iron, and burned her finger and much hair. She could see that her aunt was both worried and grieved, and her uncle kept saying, "Well, I'll be darned!" over and over in a hurt and faintly hostile torte. And Marjorie sat very quietly, intrenched behind a faint smile, a faintly mocking smile.

Somehow she got through the evening. Three boy's called; Marjorie disap-peared with one of them, and Bernice made a listless unsuccessful attempt to en-tertain the two others—sighed thankfully as she climbed the stairs to her room at half past ten. What a day!

When she had undressed for the night the door opened and Marjorie came in.

"Bernice," she said "I'm awfully sorry about the Deyo dance. I'll give you my word of honor I'd forgotten all about it."

"'Sall right," said Bernice shortly. Standing before the mirror she passed her comb slowly through her short hair.

"I'll take you down-town to-morrow," continued Marjorie, "and the hairdress-er'll fix it so you'll look slick. I didn't imagine you'd go through with it. I'm really mighty sorry."

"Oh, 'sall right!"

"Still it's your last night, so I suppose it won't matter much."

Then Bernice winced as Marjorie tossed her own hair over her shoulders and began to twist it slowly into two long blond braids until in her cream-colored neg-ligée she looked like a delicate painting of some Saxon princess. Fascinated, Ber-nice watched the braids grow. Heavy and luxurious they were moving under the supple fingers like restive snakes—and to Bernice remained this relic and the curl-ing-iron and a to-morrow full of eyes. She could see G. Reece Stoddard, who liked her, assuming his Harvard manner and telling his dinner partner that Bernice shouldn't have been allowed to go to the movies so much; she could see Draycott Deyo exchanging glances with his mother and then being conscientiously charita-ble to her. But then perhaps by to-morrow Mrs. Deyo would have heard the news; would send round an icy little note requesting that she fail to appear—and behind her back they would all laugh and know that Marjorie had made a fool of her; that her chance at beauty had been sacrificed to the jealous whim of a selfish girl. She sat down suddenly before the mirror, biting the inside of her cheek.

"I like it," she said with an effort. "I think it'll be becoming."

Marjorie smiled.

"It looks all right. For heaven's sake, don't let it worry you!"

"I won't."

"Good night Bernice."

But as the door closed something snapped within Bernice. She sprang dynamically to her feet, clinching her hands, then swiftly and noiseless crossed over to her bed and from underneath it dragged out her suitcase. Into it she tossed toilet articles and a change of clothing, Then she turned to her trunk and quickly dumped in two drawerfulls of lingerie and stammer dresses. She moved quietly. but deadly efficiency, and in three-quarters of an hour her trunk was locked and strapped and she was fully dressed in a becoming new travelling suit that Marjorie had helped her pick out.

Sitting down at her desk she wrote a short note to Mrs. Harvey, in which she briefly outlined her reasons for going. She sealed it, addressed it, and laid it on her pillow. She glanced at her watch. The train left at one, and she knew that if she walked down to the Marborough Hotel two blocks away she could easily get a taxicab.

Suddenly she drew in her breath sharply and an expression flashed into her eyes that a practiced character reader might have connected vaguely with the set look she had worn in the barber's chair—somehow a development of it. It was quite a new look for Bernice—and it carried consequences.

She went stealthily to the bureau, picked up an article that lay there, and turning out all the lights stood quietly until her eyes became accustomed to the darkness. Softly she pushed open the door to Marjorie's room. She heard the quiet, even breathing of an untroubled conscience asleep.

She was by the bedside now, very deliberate and calm. She acted swiftly. Bending over she found one of the braids of Marjorie's hair, followed it up with her hand to the point nearest the head, and then holding it a little slack so that the sleeper would feel no pull, she reached down with the shears and severed it. With the pigtail in her hand she held her breath. Marjorie had muttered something in her sleep. Bernice deftly amputated the other braid, paused for an instant, and then flitted swiftly and silently back to her own room.

Down-stairs she opened the big front door, closed it carefully behind her, and feeling oddly happy and exuberant stepped off the porch into the moonlight, swinging her heavy grip like a shopping-bag. After a minute's brisk walk she discovered that her left hand still held the two blond braids. She laughed unexpectedly—had to shut her mouth hard to keep from emitting an absolute peal. She was passing Warren's house now, and on the impulse she set down her baggage, and swinging the braids like piece of rope flung them at the wooden porch, where they landed with a slight thud. She laughed again, no longer restraining herself.

"Huh," she giggled wildly. "Scalp the selfish thing!"

Then picking up her staircase she set off at a half-run down the moonlit street.

5.11.4 Reading and Review Questions

1. Each of these stories presents a certain type of woman, commonly known as a "flapper." What are the common characteristics of Fitzgerald's female characters? What do those characters tell us about gender roles and expectations in Fitzgerald's fiction?

2. What do Fitzgerald's stories tell us about the American dream?

3. What role does money play in Fitzgerald's stories?

4. How does Fitzgerald treat matters of geography? What is Fitzgerald's attitude toward the eastern, midwestern, and western parts of the United States?

5.12 ERNEST HEMINGWAY

(1899 - 1961)

Image 5.10 | Ernest Hemingway, 1923
Photographer | Unknown
Source | Wikimedia Commons
License | Public Domain

Ernest Hemingway was born and raised in Oak Park, Illinois, an affluent suburb of Chicago. His father, who was prone to depression and would later commit suicide, was a physician and his mother was a singer turned music teacher. Because Hemingway's father was an avid outdoorsman, the family spent many of their summers in northern Michigan, which is where Hemingway set many of his short fiction, including the Nick Adams stories.

In 1917, Hemingway, at that time a writer for *The Kansas City Star,* was eager to join the Armed Forces to fight in the Great War (World War I) but was medically disqualified. Undiscouraged, he joined the ambulance corps and served on the Italian front. During shelling, Hemingway received a shrapnel injury but still carried a comrade to safety and was decorated as a hero.

When Hemingway returned to the States, living ultimately in Chicago, he fell under the mentorship of fellow modernist, Sherwood Anderson, who encouraged Hemingway to move to Paris. In 1920, Hemingway married Hadley Richardson; soon afterwards, the couple left for Paris. Surrounded by other writers of the period, such as Gertrude Stein, F. Scott Fitzgerald, Ezra Pound, Hemingway used these connections to help develop his own writing career. With F. Scott Fitzgerald's help, Hemingway published his first novel *The Sun Also Rises* (1926) to great acclaim. The novel established Hemingway's simplistic writing style while expressing the frustration that many felt about World War I. His second novel, *A Farewell to Arms* (1929), another critical success, once again, captured the disillusionment of the modernist period.

While Hemingway had a turbulent personal life, filled with divorces and failed relationships, he continued to write successful works including several collections of short fiction, for which he was well known, as well as novels and non-fiction. Some of his many works are *Death in the Afternoon* (1932), bringing bullfighting to a larger audience; *To Have and Have Not* (1937); and *For Whom the Bell Tolls* (1940), a classic novel on the Spanish Civil War. In 1952, Hemingway wrote what many consider to be his finest work, *Old Man and the Sea*, which was awarded the Pulitzer Prize and led to his Nobel Prize for Literature in 1954. In 1961, after struggling with depression for years, Ernest Hemingway took his own life in Ketchum, Idaho. In 1964, Scribners published his posthumous memoir, *A Moveable Feast*, which details both Hemingway and Hadley's expatriate life in Paris during the modernist period.

Hemingway's writing was well known stylistically for its short declarative sentences and lack of detail. Hemingway often said this style based on his iceberg approach to narrative, where, like an iceberg, ten percent of the story was on the surface and ninety percent was under the water. Hemingway attributes this style to his time spent as a journalist. Due to his distinctive style, Hemingway remained an immensely popular writer and his novels were not only critically acclaimed but also best sellers. In both "The Short Happy Life of Francis Macomber" and "The Snows of Kilimanjaro," Hemingway writes about couples on safari in Africa and both stories feature couples with troubled relationships. These two stories are great examples of Hemingway's technique since it is clear to the reader that the narrator is leaving out many details about the characters' history.

5.12.1 "The Short Happy Life of Francis Macomber"

Please click the link below to access this selection:

http://m.learning.hccs.edu/faculty/selena.anderson/engl2328/readings/the-short-happy-life-of-francis-maccomber-by-ernest-hemingway

5.12.2 "The Snows of Kilimanjaro"

Please click the link below to access this selection:

http://xroads.virginia.edu/~drbr/heming.html

5.12.3 Reading and Review Questions

1. Looking at the two stories, side by side, what similarities do you notice between Macomber and Harry? What message is Hemingway trying to send to readers?

2. Do you notice any similarities between Margaret Macomber and Helen as well?

3. Hemingway is often accused of being a chauvinistic writer, after reading

these two stories—do you think this is a fair critique? Does he have a preference for his male characters? Are his female characters fully formed and believable?

5.13 ARTHUR MILLER

(1915 - 2005)

Known best for his ironic commentaries on the American dream, Arthur Miller's plays capture the disillusionment, the emptiness, and the ambivalence of individual Americans in the twentieth century. His most famous plays, *Death of a Salesman* (1949) and *The Crucible* (1953), are staples in American literature courses from high school through university, and his precise excoriation of the American experience of freedom continues to captivate audiences.

Miller believed that playgoers responded to drama because they experienced examples of acting throughout their daily lives. In his remarks upon receiving the 2001 National Endowment for the Humanities Jefferson Medal, Miller observed:

Image 5.11 | Arthur Miller, 1966
Photographer | Eric Koch
Source | Wikimedia Commons
License | CC BY-SA 3.0

> The fact is that acting is inevitable as soon as we walk out our front doors into society. . . and in fact we are ruled more by the arts of performance, by acting in other words, than anybody wants to think about for very long.
>
> But in our time television has created a quantitative change in all this; one of the oddest things about millions of lives now is that ordinary individuals, as never before in human history, are so surrounded by acting. Twenty-four hours a day everything seen on the tube is either acted or conducted by actors in the shape of news anchor men and women, including their hairdos. It may be that the most impressionable form of experience now, for many if not most people, consists of their emotional transactions with actors which happen far more of the time than with real people.[3]

In this way, Miller may be said to democratize theatre. Building on the work of the Scandinavian playwrights of the nineteenth century, Miller, along with his contemporaries Eugene O'Neill and Tennessee Williams, wrote plays that featured ordinary persons who were tortured to the point of madness by ordinary life. In doing so, Miller, O'Neill, and Williams captured the confusion, despair, and hopelessness of modern life and assured themselves a place in the American national conversation.

---

3   "Arthur Miller Lecture." *NEH.gov*. National Endowment for the Humanities, 26 Mar. 2001. Web. 10 Dec. 2015

In *Death of a Salesman*, Miller presents a tragedy for the common man. Willy Loman, a marginally successful traveling salesman of women's undergarments, is, as many students learned in high school, a low man, the most common of a type of road warrior who today fills the nation's airports instead of its highways. Frustrated by the unbearable sameness of his travels, Willy lives within his own fantasies, and those fantasies ultimately include Willy's dreams for his sons, Biff and Happy, while excluding Willy's devoted wife, Linda. Willy Loman is Everyman for the twentieth century, a character whose work produces nothing and generates little in the way of material comfort. Living from paycheck to paycheck, Willy merely survives. When, ultimately, he can be neither a role model to his family nor their provider, he chooses to die rather than face exile into a state of irrelevance. *Death of a Salesman* is a Greek tragedy for the twentieth century in which a man who does not know who he is chooses death when he realizes his mistakes.

5.13.1 *Death of a Salesman*

Please click the link below to access this selection:

http://www.pelister.org/literature/ArthurMiller/Miller_Salesman.pdf

5.13.2 Reading and Review Questions

1. Why does Willy consistently fail to communicate with Happy and Biff?

2. What impact does Linda have on her husband and sons? Is she a positive influence in their lives?

3. Willy Loman is often referred to as representative of the "common man." What does this term mean for Willy and those like him?

4. How does Miller use natural and man-made elements in the play? What does the juxtaposition of the city and country tell us about Willy's life?

5. What does the play suggest about the responsibilities of fathers?

5.11 SOUTHERN RENAISSANCE – FIRST WAVE
(1920 – 1940)

After the Civil War, Southern literature had been mostly of the Local Color variety, as Thomas Nelson Page became one of the most prolific Southern writers in postbellum America with his plantation myth stories. However, by the end of the nineteenth century, a number of Southern writers, educated, well-traveled, and well-read, began to break from the "moonlight and magnolias" tradition of Page that evinced nostalgia for the Old South. James Lane Allen from Kentucky, Kate Chopin and Grace King from Louisiana, Ellen Glasgow, Amélie Rives, and Mary Johnston from Virginia took on a wide variety of edgy topics in their works, including a critique of traditional social roles for women and an exploration of sexual desire repressed by rigid cultural norms. Ellen Glasgow, in particular, led the way toward a new Southern literature in her call for more "blood and irony" in Southern fiction.[4] She calls for an invigorated literature that rejects the false veneer of Southern culture and probes the reality of life that is limited or repressed by rigid social norms and develops characters who exhibit fortitude and endurance in spite of such limitations. She is the first voice of the Southern Renaissance, which bloomed fully in the 1920s and 30s within the Modernist temperament of the early twentieth century.

Another seminal "call" for a new Southern literature came in 1917 when cultural critic H. L. Mencken published his famous essay, "The Sahara of the Bozart," in the New York *Evening Mail.* Mencken's acerbic wit was biting, as he likened Southern culture to the sterility of the Sahara Desert. After World War I, writers such as William Faulkner, Thomas Wolfe, Eudora Welty, Katherine Anne Porter, John Crowe Ransom, and Robert Penn Warren responded to this call by producing a body of literary work that won national and international acclaim as part of a revival of Southern letters and culture. William Faulkner, in particular, who went on to win the Nobel Prize for Literature in 1949, created a body of work against which future Southern writers would be measured.

The first wave of writers in the Southern Renaissance probed a number of themes, but for the most part the writers had to come to terms with the South's past, particularly slavery. Racial tensions, racial inequality, white guilt associated with slavery, and the haunting specter of slavery became themes and motifs throughout the literature. Writers also attempted to define the South as a distinct and unique place rather than as simply a region of the United States, especially within the context of social and economic changes that were beginning to erase the distinctive features of the South. Narrative techniques in the literature from this time period are often borrowed from oral storytelling or from other oral traditions in Southern culture, traditions such as preaching, conversing, and memorializing. First Wave writers, like their Local Color predecessors, attempted to capture in print the distinctive features of Southern dialects that were beginning to disappear. Religion and religious images infused much of Southern writing during this time. A particular sub-genre of Southern writing emerged: the Southern gothic story or novel. Southern gothic writing borrowed from elements of eighteenth-century British works written in the style of Gothic, or "Dark Romanticism." In these stories the fantastic and the macabre were central. In the Southern gothic, writers focused less on supernatural events and more on ways in which the seemingly pretty, orderly surface veneer of the Southern social order hid deep, dark, disturbing secrets or distorted the dark nature of reality behind the curtain of respectability and gentility. Most Southern gothic works also contain some aspect of the grotesque as well. This sub-genre of Southern literature, often termed the Southern grotesque, features images of physical disfigurement, physical decay, mental disability, incest, deviance, extreme violence, illness, suffering, and death. The grotesque motif features prominently in most Southern gothic stories and comment, usually, on some

---

4   Glasgow, Ellen. *A Certain Measure: An Interpretation of Prose Fiction.* New York: Harcourt Brace and Co., 1938.

aspects of a disintegrating people and culture.

5.14 ELLEN GLASGOW

(1873 - 1945)

Ellen Glasgow was born in 1873 to a wealthy Virginia family. Her father was a successful owner of an ironworks company in Richmond, Virginia. Glasgow's mother, who bore ten children, became an invalid, suffering from a variety of nervous disorders. Glasgow was educated at home, and she exhibited intellectual independence from a young age. She read widely in her father's library, tackling subjects from literature to philosophy and political theory. Glasgow began her own foray into fiction writing and was immediately successful. In novels such as *The Descendant* (1897), *The Deliverance* (1904), *Virginia* (1913), and *Barren Ground* (1925), Glasgow predicted the first wave of the Southern Renaissance as she rigorously chronicled the death of the Old South,

Image 5.12 | Ellen Glasgow, n.d.
Photographer | Unknown
Source | Wikimedia Commons
License | Public Domain

as well as rebelled against the contemporary artifice and restrictions of Victorian gentility. *Barren Ground*, in particular, established her reputation as a writer who moved beyond the styles of the Realist and Naturalist in the 1890s more fully into the temperament of the Modernist and feminist writer. Glasgow continued writing until her death, publishing later works such as *The Sheltered Life* (1932), *Vein of Iron* (1935), and *In This Our Life* (1941), which won the Pulitzer Prize for the novel in 1942. While she had love interests during her life, Glasgow remained single, valuing her independence. During her life, Glasgow suffered from a variety of illnesses and ailments, including heart disease. She died in her sleep at home in 1945.

Ellen Glasgow changed the course of Southern literature in the 1890s in her striking departure from traditional Southern literary fare dominated by Thomas Nelson Page's fictional accounts of the plantation myth. Like literary Naturalists such as Frank Norris and Jack London, Glasgow absorbed ideas from Charles Darwin's works and became one of the first Southern writers of substance to incorporate Darwinian themes in her fiction. She was influenced by Darwin's views on heredity and environment as factors that strongly determined human behavior. As a young writer, she fearlessly confronted uncomfortable truths about human nature, eschewing the ever popular "moonlight and magnolias" fictional representation of life in the South and calling for more "blood and irony" in Southern fiction. She heeded her own call, producing a strong body of work that dealt with a variety of realistic, naturalistic, and even modernist, themes: women confronting their own biological impulses, social classes in conflict, women deconstructing social codes as artificial barriers to self-determination, rural farming families at odds with new industrialization and urbanization, and the transition of the Old South into the New South. Throughout her fiction, illusions about the present are shattered under the intense light of reality, and nostalgia for the past is revealed as a form of "evasive idealism," a way of thinking that Glasgow deplored. In "Dare's Gift," one of many stories that Glasgow wrote about seemingly haunted dwellings, Glasgow explores the residual "haunting" of the present by the past, particularly by a past infected with the actions of a woman whose loyalty to an abstraction or dogmatic creed supersede her loyalty to her fiancé.

5.14.1 "Dare's Gift"

A year has passed, and I am beginning to ask myself if the thing actually happened? The whole episode, seen in clear perspective, is obviously incredible. There are, of course, no haunted houses in this age of science; there are merely hallucinations, neurotic symptoms, and optical illusions. Any one of these practical diagnoses would, no doubt, cover the impossible occurrence, from my first view of that dusky sunset on James River to the erratic behavior of Mildred during the spring we spent in Virginia. There is—I admit it readily!—a perfectly rational explanation of every mystery. Yet, while I assure myself that the supernatural has been banished, in the evil company of devils, black plagues, and witches, from this sanitary century, a vision of Dare's Gift, amid its clustering cedars under the shadowy arch of the sunset, rises before me, and my feeble scepticism surrenders to that invincible spirit of darkness. For once in my life—the ordinary life of a corporation lawyer in Washington—the impossible really happened. It was the year after Mildred's first nervous breakdown, and Drayton, the great specialist in whose care she had been for some months, advised me to take her away from Washington until she recovered her health. As a busy man I couldn't spend the whole week out of town; but if we could find a place near enough—somewhere in Virginia! we both exclaimed, I remember—it would be easy for me to run down once a fortnight. The thought was with me when Harrison asked me to join him for a week's hunting on James River; and it was still in my mind, though less distinctly, on the evening when I stumbled alone, and for the first time, on Dare's Gift.

I had hunted all day—a divine day in October—and at sunset, with a bag full of partridges, I was returning for the night to Chericoke, where Harrison kept his bachelor's house. The sunset had been wonderful; and I had paused for a moment with my back to the bronze sweep of the land, when I had a swift impression that the memories of the old river gathered around me. It was at this instant—I recall even the trivial detail that my foot caught in a brier as I wheeled quickly about— that I looked past the sunken wharf on my right, and saw the garden of Dare's Gift falling gently from its almost obliterated terraces to the scalloped edge of the river. Following the steep road, which ran in curves through a stretch of pines and across an abandoned pasture or two, I came at last to an iron gate and a grassy walk leading, between walls of box, to the open lawn planted in elms. With that first glimpse the Old World charm of the scene held me captive. From the warm red of its brick walls to the pure Colonial lines of its doorway, and its curving wings mantled in roses and ivy, the house stood there, splendid and solitary. The rows of darkened windows sucked in without giving back the last flare of daylight; the heavy cedars crowding thick up the short avenue did not stir as the wind blew from the river; and above the carved pineapple on the roof, a lonely bat was wheeling high against the red disc of the sun. While I had climbed the rough road and passed more slowly between the marvelous walls of the box, I had told myself that the place must be Mildred's and mine at any cost. On the upper terrace, before several crude modern additions to the wings, my enthusiasm gradually ebbed, though I still asked myself incredulously, "Why have I never heard of it? To whom does it belong? Has it a name as well known in Virginia as Shirley or Brandon?" The house was of great age, I knew, and yet from obvious signs I discovered that it was not too old to be lived in. Nowhere could I detect a hint of decay or dilapidation. The sound of cattle bells floated up from a pasture somewhere in the distance. Through the long grass on the lawn little twisted paths, like sheep tracks, wound back and forth under the fine old elms, from which a rain of bronze leaves fell slowly and ceaselessly in the wind. Nearer at hand, on the upper terrace, a few roses were blooming; and when I passed between two marble urns on the right of the house, my feet crushed a garden of "simples" such as our grandmothers used to grow.

As I stepped on the porch I heard a child's voice on the lawn, and a moment afterwards a small boy, driving a cow, appeared under the two cedars at the end of the avenue. At sight of me he flicked the cow with the hickory switch he held and bawled, "Ma! thar's a stranger out here, an' I don't know what he wants."

At his call the front door opened, and a woman in a calico dress, with a sunbonnet pushed back from her forehead, came out on the porch.

"Hush yo' fuss, Eddy!" she remarked authoritatively. "He don't want nothint." Then, turning to me, she added civilly, "Good evenin', suh. You must be the gentleman who is visitin' over at Chericoke?"

"Yes, I am staying with Mr. Harrison. You know him, of course?" "Oh, Lordy, yes. Everybody aroun' here knows Mr. Harrison. His folks have been here goin' on mighty near forever. I don't know what me and my children would come to it if wa'n't for him. He is gettin' me my divorce now. It's been three years and mo' sence Tom deserted me."

"Divorce?" I had not expected to find this innovation on James River.

"Of course it ain't the sort of thing anybody would want to come to. But if a woman in the State ought to have one easy, I reckon it's me. Tom went off with another woman—and she my own sister—from this very house—"

"From this house—and, by the way, what is the name of it?" "Name of what? This place? Why, it's Dare's Gift. Didn't you know it? Yes, suh, it happened right here in this very house, and that, too, when we hadn't been livin' over here mo' than three months. After Mr. Duncan got tired and went away he left us as caretakers, Tom and me, and I asked Tilly to come and stay with us and help me look after the children. It came like a lightning stroke to me, for Tom and Tilly had known each other all their lives, and he'd never taken any particular notice of her till they moved over here and began to tend the cows together. She wa'n't much for beauty, either. I was always the handsome one of the family—though you mightn't think it now, to look at me—and Tom was the sort that never could abide red hair—"

"And you've lived at Dare's Gift ever since?" I was more interested in the house than in the tenant.

"I didn't have nowhere else to go, and the house has got to have a caretaker till it is sold. It ain't likely that anybody will want to rent an out—of—the—way place like this—though now that automobiles have come to stay that don't make so much difference."

"Does it still belong to the Dares?"

"Now, suh; they had to sell it at auction right after the war on account of mort-gages and debts—old Colonel Dare died the very year Lee surrendered, and Miss Lucy she went off somewhere to strange parts. Sence their day it has belonged to so many different folks that you can't keep account of it. Right now it's owned by a Mr. Duncan, who lives out in California. I don't know that he'll ever come back here he couldn't get on with the neighbors—and he is trying to sell it. No wonder, too, a great big place like this, and he ain't even a Virginian—"

"I wonder if he would let it for a season?" It was then, while I stood there in the brooding dusk of the doorway, that the idea of the spring at Dare's Gift first occurred to me.

"If you want it, you can have it for 'most nothing, I reckon. Would you like to step inside and go over the rooms?"

That evening at supper I asked Harrison about Dare's Gift, and gleaned the salient facts of its history.

"Strange to say, the place, charming as it is, has never been well known in Vir-ginia. There's historical luck, you know, as well as other kinds, and the Dares—after that first Sir Roderick, who came over in time to take a stirring part in Bacon's Re-bellion, and, tradition says, to betray his leader—have never distinguished them-selves in the records of the State. The place itself, by the way, is about a fifth of the original plantation of three thousand acres, which was given—though I imagine there was more in that than appears in history—by some Indian chief of forgotten name to this notorious Sir Roderick. The old chap—Sir Roderick, I mean—seems to have been something of a fascinator in his day. Even Governor Berkeley, who hanged half the colony, relented, I believe, in the case of Sir Roderick, and that un-usual clemency gave rise, I sup—pose, to the legend of the betrayal. But, however that may be, Sir Roderick had more miraculous escapes than John Smith himself, and died at last in his bed at the age of eighty from overeating cherry pie." "And now the place has passed away from the family?"

"Oh, long ago—though not so long, after all, when one comes to think of it. When the old Colonel died the year after the war, it was discovered that he had mortgaged the farm up to the last acre. At that time real estate on James River wasn't regarded as a particularly profit–able investment, and under the hammer Dare's Gift went for a song."

"Was the Colonel the last of his name?" "He left a daughter—a belle, too, in her youth, my mother says—but she died—at least I think she did—only a few months after her father."

Coffee was served on the veranda, and while I smoked my cigar and sipped my brandy—Harrison had an excellent wine cellar—I watched the full moon shining like a yellow lantern through the diaphanous mist on the river. Downshore, in the sparkling reach of the water, an immense cloud hung low over the horizon, and between the cloud and the river a band of silver light quivered faintly, as if it would go out in an instant.

"It is over there, isn't it?"—I pointed to the silver light—"Dare's Gift, I mean."

"Yes, it's somewhere over yonder—five miles away by the river, and nearly seven by the road."

"It is the dream of a house, Harrison, and there isn't too much history attached to it—nothing that would make a modern beggar ashamed to live in it."

"By Jove! so you are thinking of buying it?" Harrison was beaming. "It is downright ridiculous, I declare, the attraction that place has for strangers. I never knew a Virginian who wanted it; but you are the third Yankee of my acquaintance—and I don't know many—who has fallen in love with it. I searched the title and drew up the deed for John Duncan exactly six years ago—though I'd better not boast of that transaction, I reckon."

"He still owns it, doesn't he?"

"He still owns it, and it looks as if he would continue to own it unless you can be persuaded to buy it. It is hard to find purchasers for these old places, especially when the roads are uncertain and they happen to be situated on the James River. We live too rapidly in these days to want to depend on a river, even on a placid old fellow like the James."

"Duncan never really lived here, did he?"

"At first he did. He began on quite a royal scale; but, somehow, from the very start things appeared to go wrong with him. At the outset he prejudiced the neighbors against him—I never knew exactly why—by putting on airs, I imagine, and boasting about his money. There is something in the Virginia blood that resents boasting about money. How—ever that may be, he hadn't been here six months before he was at odds with every living thing in the county, white, black, and spotted—for even the dogs snarled at him. Then his secretary—a chap he had picked up starving in London, and had trusted absolutely for years—made off with a lot of cash and securities, and that seemed the last straw in poor Duncan's ill luck. I believe he didn't mind the loss half so much—he refused to prosecute the fellow— as he minded the betrayal of confidence. He told me, I remember, before he went away, that it had spoiled Dare's Gift for him. He said he had a feeling that the place had come too high; it had cost him his belief in human nature."

"Then I imagine he'd be disposed to consider an offer?"

"Oh, there isn't a doubt of it. But, if I were you, I shouldn't be too hasty. Why not rent the place for the spring months? It's beautiful here in the spring, and Duncan has left furniture enough to make the house fairly comfortable."

"Well, I'll ask Mildred. Of course Mildred must have the final word in the matter."

"As if Mildred's final word would be anything but a repetition of yours!" Harrison laughed slyly—for the perfect harmony in which we lived had been for ten years a pleasant jest among our friends. Harrison had once classified wives as belonging to two distinct groups—the group of those who talked and knew nothing about their husbands' affairs, and the group of those who knew everything and kept silent. Mildred, he had added politely, had chosen to belong to the latter division.

The next day I went back to Washington, and Mildred's first words to me in the station were,

"Why, Harold, you look as if you had bagged all the game in Virginia!"

"I look as if I had found just the place for you!"

When I told her about my discovery, her charming face sparkled with interest. Never once, not even during her illness, had she failed to share a single one of my enthusiasms; never once, in all the years of our marriage, had there been so much as a shadow between us. To understand the story of Dare's Gift, it is necessary to realize at the beginning all that Mildred meant and means in my life.

Well, to hasten my slow narrative, the negotiations dragged through most of the winter. At first, Harrison wrote me, Duncan couldn't be found, and a little later that he was found, but that he was opposed, from some inscrutable motive, to the plan of renting Dare's Gift. He wanted to sell it outright, and he'd be hanged if he'd do anything less than get the place clean off his hands. "As sure as I let it"—Harrison sent me his letter—"there is going to be trouble, and somebody will come down on me for damages. The damned place has cost me already twice as much as I paid for it."

In the end, however—Harrison has a persuasive way—the arrangements were concluded. "Of course," Duncan wrote after a long silence, "Dare's Gift may be as healthy as heaven. I may quite as easily have contracted this confounded rheumatism, which makes life a burden, either in Italy or from too many cocktails. I've no reason whatever for my dislike for the place; none, that is, except the incivility of my neighbors—where, by the way, did you Virginians manufacture your reputation for manners?—and my unfortunate episode with Paul Grymes. That, as you remark, might, no doubt, have occurred anywhere else, and if a man is going to steal he could have found all the opportunities he wanted in New York or London. But the fact remains that one can't help harboring associations, pleasant or unpleasant, with the house in which one has lived, and from start to finish my associations with Dare's Gift are frankly unpleasant. If, after all, however, your friend wants the place, and can afford to pay for his whims—let him have it! I hope to Heaven he'll be ready to buy it when his lease has run out. Since he wants it for a hobby, I suppose one place is as good as another; and I can assure him that by the time he has owned it for a few years—especially if he under—takes to improve the motor road up to Richmond—he will regard a taste for Chinese porcelain as an inexpensive diversion." Then, as if impelled by a twist of ironic humor, he added, "He will find the shooting good anyhow."

By early spring Dare's Gift was turned over to us—Mildred was satisfied, if Duncan wasn't—and on a showery day in April, when drifting clouds cast faint gauzy shadows over the river, our boat touched at the old wharf, where carpenters were working, and rested a minute before steaming on the Chericoke Landing five miles away. The spring was early that year—or perhaps the spring is always early on James River. I remember the song of birds in the trees; the veil of bright green over the distant forests; the broad reach of the river scalloped with silver; the dappled sunlight on the steep road which climbed from the wharf to the iron gates; the roving fragrance from lilacs on the lower terrace; and, sur—mounting all, the two giant cedars which rose like black crags against the changeable blue of the sky—I remember these things as distinctly as if I had seen them this morning.

We entered the wall of box through a living door, and strolled up the grassy walk from the lawn to the terraced garden. Within the garden the air was perfumed with a thousand scents—with lilacs, with young box, with flags and violets and lilies, with aromatic odors from the garden of "simples," and with the sharp sweetness of sheep—mint from the mown grass on the lawn.

"This spring is fine, isn't it?" As I turned to Mildred with the question, I saw for the first time that she looked pale and tired—or was it merely the green light from the box wall that fell over her features? "The trip has been too much for you. Next time we'll come by motor."

"Oh, no, I had a sudden feeling of faintness. It will pass in a minute. What an adorable place, Harold!"

She was smiling again with her usual brightness, and as we passed from the box wall to the clear sunshine on the terrace her face quickly resumed its natural color. To this day—for Mildred has been strangely reticent about Dare's Gift—I do not know whether her pallor was due to the shade in which we walked or whether, at the instant when I turned to her, she was visited by some intuitive warning against the house we were approaching. Even after a year the events of Dare's Gift are not things I can talk over with Mildred; and, for my part, the occurrence remains, like the house in its grove of cedars, wrapped in an impenetrable mystery. I don't in the least pretend to know how or why the thing happened. I only know that it did happen—that it happened, word for word as I record it. Mildred's share in it will, I think, never become clear to me. What she felt, what she imagined, what she believed, I have never asked her. Whether the doctor's explanation is history or fiction, I do not attempt to decide. He is an old man, and old men, since Biblical times, have seen visions. There were places in his story where it seemed to me that he got historical data a little mixed—or it may be that his memory failed him. Yet, in spite of his liking for romance and his French education, he is without constructive imagination—at least he says that he is without it—and the secret of Dare's

Gift, if it is not fact, could have sprung only from the ultimate chaos of imagination.

But I think of these things a year afterwards, and on that April morning the house stood there in the sunlight, presiding over its grassy terraces with an air of gracious and intimate hospitality. From the symbolic pineapple on its sloping roof to the twittering sparrows that flew in and out of its ivied wings, it reaffirmed that first flawless impression. Flaws, of course, there were in the fact, yet the recollection of it to—day—the garnered impression of age, of formal beauty, of clustering memories—is one of exquisite harmony. We found later, as Mildred pointed out, architectural absurdities—wanton excrescences in the mod—ern additions, which had been designed apparently with the purpose of providing space at the least possible cost of material and labor. The rooms, when we passed through the fine old doorway, appeared cramped and poorly lighted; broken pieces of the queer mullioned window, where the tracery was of wood, not stone, had been badly repaired, and much of the original detail work of the mantels and cornices had been blurred by recent disfigurements. But these discoveries came afterwards. The first view of the place worked like a magic spell—like an intoxicating perfume—on our senses.

"It is just as if we had stepped into another world," said Mildred, looking up at the row of windows, from which the ivy had been carefully clipped. "I feel as if I had ceased to be myself since I left Washington." Then she turned to meet Harrison, who had ridden over to welcome us. We spent a charming fortnight together at Dare's Gift—Mildred happy as a child in her garden, and I satisfied to lie in the shadow of the box wall and watch her bloom back to health. At the end of the fortnight I was summoned to an urgent conference in Washington. Some philanthropic busybody, employed to nose out corruption, had scented legal game in the affairs of the Atlantic & Eastern Railroad, and I had been retained as special counsel by that corporation. The fight would be long, I knew—I had already thought of it as one of my great cases—and the evidence was giving me no little anxiety. "It is my last big battle," I told Mildred, as I kissed her good—bye on the steps. "If I win, Dare's Gift shall be your share of the spoils; if I lose—well, I'll be like any other general who has met a better man in the field."

"Don't hurry back, and don't worry about me. I am quite happy here."

"I shan't worry, but all the same I don't like leaving you. Remember, if you need advice or help about anything, Harrison is always at hand."

"Yes, I'll remember."

With this assurance I left her standing in the sunshine, with the windows of the house staring vacantly down on her.

When I try now to recall the next month, I can bring back merely a turmoil of legal wrangles. I contrived in the midst of it all to spend two Sundays with Mildred, but I remember nothing of them except the blessed wave of rest that swept over me as I lay on the grass under the elms. On my second visit I saw that she was looking badly, though when I commented on her pallor and the darkened circles under her eyes, she laughed and put my anxious questions aside.

"Oh, I've lost sleep, that's all," she answered, vaguely, with a swift glance at the house. "Did you ever think how many sounds there are in the country that keep one awake?"

As the day went on I noticed, too, that she had grown restless, and once or twice while I was going over my case with her—I always talked over my cases with Mildred because it helped to clarify my opinions—she returned with irritation to some obscure legal point I had passed over. The flutter of her movements—so unlike my calm Mildred—disturbed me more than I confessed to her, and I made up my mind before night that I would consult Drayton when I went back to Washington. Though she had always been sensitive and impressionable, I had never seen her until that second Sunday in a condition of feverish excitability.

In the morning she was so much better that by the time I reached Washington I forgot my determination to call on her physician. My work was heavy that week—the case was developing into a direct attack upon the management of the road and in seeking evidence to rebut the charges of illegal rebates to the American Steel Company, I stumbled by accident upon a mass of damaging records. It was a clear case of some—body having blundered—or the records would not have been left for me to discover—and with disturbed thoughts I went down for my third visit to Dare's Gift. It was in my mind to draw out of the case, if an honorable way could be found, and I could barely wait until dinner was over before I unburdened my conscience to Mildred.

"The question has come to one of personal honesty." I remember that I was emphatic. "I've nosed out something real enough this time. There is material for a dozen investigations in Dowling's transactions alone."

The exposure of the Atlantic & Eastern Railroad is public property by this time, and I needn't resurrect the dry bones of that deplorable scandal. I lost the case, as everyone knows; but all that concerns me in it today is the talk I had with Mildred on the darkening terrace at Dare's Gift. It was a reckless talk, when one comes to think of it. I said, I know, a great deal that I ought to have kept to myself; but, after all, she is my wife; I had learned in ten years that I could trust her discretion, and there was more than a river between us and the Atlantic & Eastern Railroad.

Well, the sum of it is that I talked foolishly, and went to bed feeling justified in my folly. Afterwards I recalled that Mildred had been very quiet, though whenever I paused she questioned me closely, with a flash of irritation as if she were impatient of my slowness or my lack of lucidity. At the end she flared out for a moment into the excitement I had noticed the week before; but at the time I was so engrossed in my own affairs that this scarcely struck me as unnatural. Not until the blow fell did I recall the hectic flush in her face and the quivering sound of her voice, as if she were trying not to break down and weep.

It was long before either of us got to sleep that night, and Mildred moaned a little under her breath as she sank into unconsciousness. She was not well, I knew, and I resolved again that I would see Drayton as soon as I reached Washington. Then, just before falling asleep, I became acutely aware of all the noises of the country which Mildred said had kept her awake—of the chirping of the crickets in the fireplace, of the fluttering of swallows in the chimney, of the sawing of innumerable insects in the night outside, of the croaking of frogs in the marshes, of the distant solitary hooting of an owl, of the whispering sound of wind in the leaves, of the stealthy movement of a myriad creeping lives in the ivy. Through the open window the moonlight fell in a milk—white flood, and in the darkness the old house seemed to speak with a thousand voices. As I dropped off I had a confused sensation—less a perception than an apprehension—that all these voices were urging me to something—somewhere—

The next day I was busy with a mass of evidence—dull stuff, I remember. Harrison rode over for luncheon, and not until late afternoon, when I strolled out, with my hands full of papers, for a cup of tea on the terrace, did I have a chance to see Mildred alone. Then I noticed that she was breathing quickly, as if from a hurried walk. "Did you go to meet the boat, Mildred?"

"No, I've been nowhere—nowhere. I've been on the lawn all day," she answered sharply—so sharply that I looked at her in surprise.

In the ten years that I had lived with her I had never before seen her irritated without cause—Mildred's disposition, I had once said, was as flawless as her profile—and I had for the first time in my life that baffled sensation which comes to men whose perfectly normal wives reveal flashes of abnormal psychology. Mildred wasn't Mildred, that was the upshot of my conclusions; and, hang it all! I didn't know any more than Adam what was the matter with her. There were lines around her eyes, and her sweet mouth had taken an edge of bitterness.

"Aren't you well, dear?" I asked.

"Oh, I'm perfectly well," she replied, in a shaking voice, "only I wish you would leave me alone!" And then she burst into tears.

While I was trying to comfort her the servant came with the tea things, and she kept him about some trivial orders until the big touring car of one of our neighbors rushed up the drive and halted under the terrace.

In the morning Harrison motored up to Richmond with me, and on the way he spoke gravely of Mildred.

"Your wife isn't looking well, Beckwith. I shouldn't wonder if she were a bit seedy—and if I were you I'd get a doctor to look at her. There is a good man down at Chericoke Landing—old Palham Lakeby. I don't care if he did get his training in France half a century ago; he knows more than your half—baked modern scientists."

"I'll speak to Drayton this very day," I answered, ignoring his suggestion of the physician. "You have seen more of Mildred this last month than I have. How long have you noticed that she isn't herself?"

"A couple of weeks. She is usually so jolly, you know." Harrison had played with Mildred in his childhood. "Yes, I shouldn't lose any time over the doctor. Though, of course, it may be only the spring," he added, reassuringly.

"I'll drop by Drayton's office on my way uptown," I replied, more alarmed by Harrison's manner than I had been by Mildred's condition.

But Drayton was not in his office, and his assistant told me that the great specialist would not return to town until the end of the week. It was impossible for me to discuss Mildred with the earnest young man who discoursed so eloquently of the experiments in the Neurological Institute, and I left without mentioning her, after making an appointment for Saturday morning. Even if the consultation delayed my return to Dare's Gift until the afternoon, I was determined to see Drayton, and, if possible, take him back with me. Mildred's last nervous breakdown had been too serious for me to neglect this warning.

I was still worrying over that case—wondering if I could find a way to draw out of it—when the catastrophe overtook me. It was on Saturday morning, I remember, and after a reassuring talk with Drayton, who had promised to run down to Dare's Gift for the coming weekend, I was hurrying to catch the noon train for Richmond. As I passed through the station, one of the Observer's sensational "war extras" caught my eye, and I stopped for an instant to buy the paper before I hastened through the gate to the train. Not until we had started, and I had gone back to the dining car, did I unfold the pink sheets and spread them out on the table before me. Then, while the waiter hung over me for the order, I felt the headlines on the front page slowly burn themselves into my brain—for, instead of the news of the great French drive I was expecting, there flashed back at me, in large type, the name of the opposing counsel in the case against the Atlantic & Eastern. The Observer's "extra" battened not on the war this time, but on the gross scandal of the railroad; and the front page of the paper was devoted to a personal interview with Herbert Tremaine, the great Tremaine, that philanthropic busybody who had first scented corruption. It was all there, every ugly detail—every secret proof of the illegal transactions on which I had stumbled. It was all there, phrase for phrase, as I alone could have told it—as I alone, in my folly, had told it to Mildred. The Atlantic & Eastern had been betrayed, not privately, not secretly, but in large type in the public print of a sensational newspaper. And not only the road! I also had been betrayed – betrayed so wantonly, so irrationally, that it was like an incident out of melodrama.

It was conceivable that the simple facts might have leaked out through other channels, but the phrases, the very words of Tremaine's interview, were mine.

The train had started; I couldn't have turned back even if I had wanted to do so. I was bound to go on, and some intuition told me that the mystery lay at the end of my journey. Mildred had talked indiscreetly to someone, but to whom? Not to Harrison, surely! Harrison, I knew, I could count on, and yet whom had she seen except Harrison? After my first shock the absurdity of the thing made me laugh aloud. It was all as ridiculous, I realized, as it was disastrous! It might so easily not have happened. If only I hadn't stumbled on those accursed records! If only I had kept my mouth shut about them! If only Mildred had not talked unwisely to someone! But I wonder if there was ever a tragedy so inevitable that the victim, in looking back, could not see a hundred ways, great or small, of avoiding or preventing it?—a hundred trivial incidents which, falling differently, might have transformed the event into pure comedy?

The journey was unmitigated torment. In Richmond the car did not meet me, and I wasted half an hour in looking for a motor to take me to Dare's Gift. When at last I got off, the road was rougher than ever, plowed into heavy furrows after the recent rains, and filled with mud—holes from which it seemed we should never emerge. By the time we puffed exhaustedly up the rocky road from the river's edge, and ran into the avenue, I had worked myself into a state of nervous apprehension bordering on panic. I don't know what I expected, but I think I shouldn't have been surprised if Dare's Gift had lain in ruins before me. Had I found the house leveled to ashes by a divine visitation, I believe I should have accepted the occurrence as within the bounds of natural phenomena.

But everything—even the young peacocks on the lawn—was just as I had left it. The sun, setting in a golden ball over the pineapple on the roof, appeared as unchangeable, while it hung there in the glittering sky, as if it were made of metal. From the somber dusk of the wings, where the ivy lay like a black shadow, the clear front of the house, with its formal doorway and its mullioned windows, shone with an intense brightness, the last beams of sunshine lingering there before they faded into the profound gloom of the cedars. The same scents of roses and sage and mown grass and sheep—mint hung about me; the same sounds—the croaking of frogs and the sawing of katydids—floated up from the low grounds; the very books I had been reading lay on one of the tables on the terrace, and the front door still stood ajar as if it had not closed since I passed through it.

I dashed up the steps, and in the hall Mildred's maid met me. "Mrs. Beckwith was so bad that we sent for the doctor—the one Mr. Harrison recommended. I don't know what it is, sir, but she doesn't seem like herself. She talks as if she were quite out of her head."

"What does the doctor say?"

"He didn't tell me. Mr. Harrison saw him. He—the doctor, I mean—has sent a nurse, and he is coming again in the morning. But she isn't herself, Mr. Beckwith. She says she doesn't want you to come to her—"

"Mildred!" I had already sprung past the woman, calling the beloved name aloud as I ran up the stairs.

In her chamber, standing very straight, with hard eyes, Mildred met me. "I had to do it, Harold," she said coldly—so coldly that my outstretched arms fell to my sides. "I had to tell all I knew."

"You mean you told Tremaine—you wrote to him—you, Mildred?"

"I wrote to him—I had to write. I couldn't keep it back any longer. No, don't touch me. You must not touch me. I had to do it. I would do it again."

Then it was, while she stood there, straight and hard, and rejoiced because she had betrayed me—then it was that I knew that Mildred's mind was unhinged.

"I had to do it. I would do it again," she repeated, pushing me from her.

II

All night I sat by Mildred's bedside, and in the morning, without having slept, I went downstairs to meet Harrison and the doctor.

"You must get her away, Beckwith," began Harrison with a curious, suppressed excitement. "Dr. Lakeby says she will be all right again as soon as she gets back to Washington."

"But I brought her away from Washington because Drayton said it was not good for her."

"I know, I know." His tone was sharp, "But it's different now Dr. Lakeby wants you to take her back as soon as you can."

The old doctor was silent while Harrison spoke, and it was only after I had agreed to take Mildred away tomorrow that he murmured something about "bromide and chloral," and vanished up the staircase. He impressed me then as a very old man—old not so much in years as in experience, as if, living there in that flat and remote country, he had exhausted all human desires. A leg was missing, I saw, and Harrison explained that the doctor had been dangerously wounded in the battle of Seven Pines, and had been obliged after that to leave the army and take up again the practice of medicine.

"You had better get some rest," Harrison said, as he parted from me. "It is all right about Mildred, and nothing else matters. The doctor will see you in the afternoon, when you have had some sleep, and have a talk with you. He can explain things better than I can."

Some hours later, after a profound slumber, which lasted well into the afternoon, I waited for the doctor by the tea table, which had been laid out on the upper terrace. It was a perfect afternoon—a serene and cloudless afternoon in early summer. All the brightness of the day gathered on the white porch and the red walls, while the clustering shadows slipped slowly over the box garden to the lawn and the river.

I was sitting there, with a book I had not even attempted to read, when the doctor joined me; and while I rose to shake hands with him I received again the impression of weariness, of pathos and disappointment, which his face had given me in the morning. He was like sun—dried fruit, I thought, fruit that has ripened and dried under the open sky, not withered in tissue paper.

Declining my offer of tea, he sat down in one of the wicker chairs, selecting, I noticed, the least comfortable among them, and filled his pipe from a worn leather pouch.

"She will sleep all night," he said; "I am giving her bromide every three hours, and tomorrow you will be able to take her away. In a week she will be herself again. These nervous natures yield quickest to the influence, but they recover quickest also. In a little while this illness, as you choose to call it, will have left no mark upon her. She may even have forgotten it. I have known this to happen."

"You have known this to happen?" I edged my chair nearer.

"They all succumb to it—the neurotic temperament soonest, the phlegmatic one later—but they all succumb to it in the end. The spirit of the place is too strong for them. The surrender to the thought of the house—to the psychic force of its memories—"

"There are memories, then? Things have happened here?"

"All old houses have memories, I suppose. Did you ever stop to wonder about the thoughts that must have gathered within walls like these?—to wonder about the impressions that must have lodged in the bricks, in the crevices, in the timber and the masonry? Have you ever stopped to think that these multiplied impressions might create a current of thought—a mental atmosphere—an inscrutable power of suggestion?"

"Even when one is ignorant? When one does not know the story?"

"She may have heard scraps of it from the servants—who knows? One can never tell how traditions are kept alive. Many things have been whispered about Dare's Gift; some of these whispers may have reached her. Even without her knowledge she may have absorbed the suggestion; and some day, with that suggestion in her mind, she may have gazed too long at the sunshine on these marble urns before she turned back into the haunted rooms where she lived. After all, we know so little, so pitifully little about these things. We have only touched, we physicians, the outer edges of psychology. The rest lies in darkness—"

I jerked him up sharply. "The house, then, is haunted?"

For a moment he hesitated. "The house is saturated with a thought. It is haunted by treachery."

"You mean something happened here?"

"I mean—" He bent forward, groping for the right word, while his gaze sought the river, where a golden web of mist hung midway between sky and water. "I am an old man, and I have lived long enough to see every act merely as the husk of an idea. The act dies; it decays like the body, but the idea is immortal. The thing that happened at Dare's Gift was over fifty years ago, but the thought of it still lives — still utters its profound and terrible message. The house is a shell, and if one listens long enough one can hear in its heart the low murmur of the past — of that past which is but a single wave of the great sea of human experience —"

"But the story?" I was becoming impatient with his theories. After all, if Mildred was the victim of some phantasmal hypnosis, I was anxious to meet the ghost who had hypnotized her. Even Drayton, I reflected, keen as he was about the fact of mental suggestion, would never have regarded seriously the suggestion of a phantom. And the house looked so peaceful — so hospitable in the afternoon light.

"The story? Oh, I am coming to that — but of late the story has meant so little to me beside the idea. I like to stop by the way. I am getting old, and an amble suits me better than too brisk a trot — particularly in this weather —"

Yes, he was getting old. I lit a fresh cigarette and waited impatiently. After all, this ghost that he rambled about was real enough to destroy me, and my nerves were quivering like harp strings.

"Well, I came into the story — I was in the very thick of it, by accident, if there is such a thing as accident in this world of incomprehensible laws. The Incomprehensible! That has always seemed to me the supreme fact of life, the one truth overshadowing all others—the truth that we know nothing. We nibble at the edges of the mystery, and the great Reality—the Incomprehensible—is still untouched, undiscovered. It unfolds hour by hour, day by day, creating, enslaving, killing us, while we painfully gnaw off—what? A crumb or two, a grain from that vastness which envelops us, which remains impenetrable—"

Again he broke off, and again I jerked him back from his reverie.

"As I have said, I was placed, by an act of Providence, or of chance, in the very heart of the tragedy. I was with Lucy Dare on the day, the unforgettable day, when she made her choice—her heroic or devilish choice, according to the way one has been educated. In Europe a thousand years ago such an act committed for the sake of religion would have made her a saint; in New England, a few centuries past, it would have entitled her to a respectable position in history—the little history of New England. But Lucy Dare was a Virginian, and in Virginia—except in the brief, exalted Virginia of the Confederacy—the personal loyalties have always been esteemed beyond the impersonal. I cannot imagine us as a people canonizing a woman who sacrificed the human ties for the superhuman—even for the divine. I cannot imagine it, I repeat; and so Lucy Dare—though she rose to greatness in that one instant of sacrifice—has not even a name among us today. I doubt if you can find a child in the State who has ever heard of her—or a grown man, outside of this neighborhood, who could give you a single fact of her history. She is as completely forgotten as Sir Roderick, who betrayed Bacon—she is forgotten because the thing she did, though it might have made a Greek tragedy, was alien to the temperament of the people among whom she lived. Her tremendous sacrifice failed to arrest the imagination of her time. After all, the sublime cannot touch us unless it is akin to our ideal; and though Lucy Dare was sublime, according to the moral code of the Romans, she was a stranger to the racial soul of the South. Her memory died because it was the bloom of an hour—because there was nothing in the soil of her age for it to thrive on. She missed her time; she is one of the mute inglorious heroines of history; and yet, born in another century, she might have stood side by side with Antigone—" For an instant he paused. "But she has always seemed to me diabolical," he added.

"What she did, then, was so terrible that it has haunted the house ever since?" I asked again, for, wrapped in memories, he had lost the thread of his story.

"What she did was so terrible that the house has never forgotten. The thought in Lucy Dare's mind during those hours while she made her choice has left an ineffaceable impression on the things that surrounded her. She created in the horror of that hour an unseen environment more real, because more spiritual, than the material fact of the house. You won't believe this, of course—if people believed in the unseen as in the seen, would life be what it is?"

The afternoon light slept on the river; the birds were mute in the elm trees; from the garden of herbs at the end of the terrace an aromatic fragrance rose like invisible incense.

"To understand it all, you must remember that the South was dominated, was possessed by an idea—the idea of the Confederacy. It was an exalted idea supremely vivid, supremely romantic—but, after all, it was only an idea. It existed nowhere within the bounds of the actual unless the souls of its devoted people may be re-garded as actual. But it is the dream, not the actuality, that commands the noblest devotion, the completest self—sacrifice. It is the dream, the ideal, that has ruled mankind from the beginning.

"I saw a great deal of the Dares that year. It was a lonely life I led after I lost my leg at Seven Pines and dropped out of the army, and, as you may imagine, a country doctor's practice in wartimes was far from lucrative. Our one comfort was that we were all poor, that we were all starving together; and the Dares—there were only two of them, father and daughter—were as poor as the rest of us. They had given their last coin to the government had poured their last bushel of meal into the sacks of the army. I can imagine the superb gesture with which Lucy Dare flung her dearest heirloom—her one remaining brooch or pin—into the bare coffers of the Confed-eracy. She was a small woman, pretty rather than beautiful—not the least heroic in build—yet I wager that she was heroic enough on that occasion. She was a strange soul, though I never so much as suspected her strangeness while I knew her—while she moved among us with her small oval face, her gentle blue eyes, her smoothly banded hair, which shone like satin in the sunlight. Beauty she must have had in a way, though I confess a natural preference for queenly women; I dare say I should have preferred Octavia to Cleopatra, who, they tell me, was small and slight. But Lucy Dare wasn't the sort to blind your eyes when you first looked at her. Her charm was like a fragrance rather than a color—a subtle fragrance that steals into the senses and is the last thing a man ever forgets. I knew half a dozen men who would have died for her—and yet she gave them nothing, nothing, barely a smile. She appeared cold—she who was destined to flame to life in an act. I can see her distinctly as she looked then, in that last year—grave, still, with the curious, unearthly loveliness that comes to pretty women who are underfed—who are slowly starving for bread and meat, for bodily nourishment. She had the look of one dedicated—as ethereal as a saint, and yet I never saw it at the time; I only remember it now, after fifty years, when I think of her. Starvation, when it is slow, not quick—when it means, not acute hunger, but merely lack of the right food, of the blood—making, nerve—building el-ements—starvation like this often plays strange pranks with one. The visions of the saints, the glories of martyrdom, come to the underfed, the anemic. Can you recall one of the saints—the genuine sort—whose regular diet was roast beef and ale?

"Well, I have said that Lucy Dare was a strange soul, and she was, though to this day I don't know how much of her strangeness was the result of improper nourishment, of too little blood to the brain. Be that as it may, she seems to me when I look back on her to have been one of those women whose characters are shaped entirely by external events—who are the playthings of circumstance. There are many such women. They move among us in obscurity—reserved, passive, com-monplace—and we never suspect the spark of fire in their natures until it flares up at the touch of the unexpected. In ordinary circumstances Lucy Dare would have been ordinary, submissive, feminine, domestic; she adored children. That she possessed a stronger will than the average Southern girl, brought up in the conventional manner, none of us—least of all I, myself—ever imagined. She was, of course, intoxicated, obsessed, with the idea of the Confederacy; but, then, so were all of us. There wasn't anything unusual or abnormal in that exalted illusion. It was the common property of our generation. . . .

"Like most noncombatants, the Dares were extremists, and I, who had got rid of a little of my bad blood when I lost my leg, used to regret sometimes that the Colonel—I never knew where he got his title—was too old to do a share of the actual fighting. There is nothing that takes the fever out of one so quickly as a fight; and in the army I had never met a hint of this concentrated, vitriolic bitterness towards the enemy. Why, I've seen the Colonel, sitting here on this terrace, and crippled to the knees with gout, grow purple in the face if I spoke so much as a good word for the climate of the North. For him, and for the girl, too, the Lord had drawn a divine circle round the Confederacy. Everything inside of that circle was perfection; everything outside of it was evil. Well, that was fifty years ago, and his hate is all dust now; yet I can sit here, where he used to brood on this terrace, sipping his blackberry wine—I can sit here and remember it all as if it were yesterday. The place has changed so little, except for Duncan's grotesque additions to the wings, that one can scarcely believe all these years have passed over it. Many an afternoon just like this I've sat here, while the Colonel nodded and Lucy knitted for the soldiers, and watched these same shadows creep down the terrace and that mist of light—it looks just as it used to—hang there over the James. Even the smell from those herbs hasn't changed. Lucy used to keep her little garden at the end of the terrace, for she was fond of making essences and beauty lotions. I used to give her all the prescriptions I could find in old books I read—and I've heard people say that she owed her wonderful white skin to the concoctions she brewed from shrubs and herbs. I couldn't convince them that lack of meat, not lotions, was responsible for the pallor – pallor was all the fashion then—that they admired and envied."

He stopped a minute, just long enough to refill his pipe, while I glanced with fresh interest at the garden of herbs.

"It was a March day when it happened," he went on presently; "cloudless, mild, with the taste and smell of spring in the air. I had been at Dare's Gift almost every day for a year. We had suffered together, hoped, feared, and wept together, hungered and sacrificed together. We had felt together the divine, invincible sway of an idea.

"Stop for a minute and picture to yourself what it is to be of a war and yet not in it; to live in imagination until the mind becomes inflamed with the vision; to have no outlet for the passion that consumes one except the outlet of thought. Add to this the fact that we really knew nothing. We were as far away from the truth, stranded here on our river, as if we had been anchored in a canal on Mars. Two men—one crippled, one too old to fight—and a girl—and the three living for a country which in a few weeks would be nothing—would be nowhere—not on any map of the world. . . .

"When I look back now it seems to me incredible that at that time any persons in the Confederacy should have been ignorant of its want of resources. Yet remember we lived apart, remote, unvisited, out of touch with realities, thinking the one thought. We believed in the ultimate triumph of the South with that indomitable belief which is rooted not in reason, but in emotion. To believe had become an act of religion; to doubt was rank infidelity. So we sat there in our little world, the world of unrealities, bounded by the river and the garden, and talked from noon till sunset about our illusion—not daring to look a single naked fact in the face—talking of plenty when there were no crops in the ground and no flour in the store-room, prophesying victory while the Confederacy was in her death struggle. Folly! All folly, and yet I am sure even now that we were sincere, that we believed the nonsense we were uttering. We believed, I have said, because to doubt would have been far too horrible. Hemmed in by the river and the garden, there wasn't anything left for us to do since we couldn't fight—but believe. Someone has said, or ought to have said, that faith is the last refuge of the inefficient. The twin devils of famine and despair were at work in the country, and we sat there—we three, on this damned terrace—and prophesied about the second president of the Confederacy. We agreed, I remember, that Lee would be the next president. And all the time, a few miles away, the demoralization of defeat was abroad, was around us, was in the air . . .

"It was a March afternoon when Lucy sent for me, and while I walked up the drive—there was not a horse left among us, and I made all my rounds on foot—I noticed that patches of spring flowers were blooming in the long grass on the lawn. The air was as soft as May, and in the woods at the back of the house buds of maple trees ran like a flame. There were, I remember, leaves—dead leaves, last year's leaves—everywhere, as if, in the demoralization of panic, the place had been forgotten, had been untouched since autumn. I remember rotting leaves that gave like moss underfoot; dried leaves that stirred and murmured as one walked over them; black leaves, brown leaves, wine—colored leaves, and the still glossy leaves of the evergreens. But they were everywhere—in the road, over the grass on the lawn, beside the steps, piled in wind drifts against the walls of the house.

"On the terrace, wrapped in shawls, the old Colonel was sitting; and he called out excitedly, 'Are you bringing news of a victory?' Victory! when the whole country had been scraped with a fine—tooth comb for provisions.

"'No, I bring no news except that Mrs. Morson has just heard of the death of her youngest son in Petersburg. Gangrene, they say. The truth is the men are so ill—nourished that the smallest scratch turns to gangrene—'

"'Well, it won't be for long—not for long. Let Lee and Johnston get together and things will go our way with a rush. A victory or two, and the enemy will be asking for terms of peace before the summer is over.'

"A lock of his silver—white hair had fallen over his forehead, and pushing it back with his clawlike hand, he peered up at me with his little nearsighted eyes, which were of a peculiar burning blackness, like the eyes of some small enraged animal. I can see him now as vividly as if I had left him only an hour ago, and yet it is fifty years since then—fifty years filled with memories and with forgetfulness. Behind him the warm red of the bricks glowed as the sunshine fell, sprinkled with shadows, through the elm boughs. Even the soft wind was too much for him, for he shivered occasionally in his blanket shawls, and coughed the dry, hacking cough which had troubled him for a year. He was a shell of a man—a shell vitalized and animated by an immense, an indestructible illusion. While he sat there, sipping his blackberry wine, with his little fiery dark eyes searching the river in hope of something that would end his interminable expectancy, there was about him a fitful somber gleam of romance. For him the external world, the actual truth of things, had vanished all of it, that is, except the shawl that wrapped him and the glass of blackberry wine he sipped. He had died already to the material fact, but he lived intensely, vividly, profoundly, in the idea. It was the idea that nourished him, that gave him his one hold on reality.

"'It was Lucy who sent for you,' said the old man presently. 'She has been on the upper veranda all day overlooking something—the sunning of winter clothes, I think. She wants to see you about one of the servants—a sick child, Nancy's child, in the quarters.'

"'Then I'll find her,' I answered readily, for I had, I confess, a mild curiosity to find out why Lucy had sent for me.

"She was alone on the upper veranda, and I noticed that she closed her Bible and laid it aside as I stepped through the long window that opened from the end of the hall. Her face, usually so pale, glowed now with a wan illumination, like ivory before the flame of a lamp. In this illumination her eyes, beneath delicately penciled eyebrows, looked unnaturally large and brilliant, and so deeply, so angel-ically blue that they made me think of the Biblical heaven of my childhood. Her beauty, which had never struck me sharply before, pierced through me. But it was her fate—her misfortune perhaps—to appear commonplace, to pass unrecognized, until the fire shot from her soul.

"'No, I want to see you about myself, not about one of the servants.' "At my first question she had risen and held out her hand—a white, thin hand, small and frail as a child's.

"'You are not well, then?' I had known from the first that her starved look meant something.

"'It isn't that; I am quite well.' She paused a moment, and then looked at me with a clear shining gaze. 'I have had a letter,' she said.

"'A letter?' I have realized since how dull I must have seemed to her in that moment of excitement, of exaltation.

"'You didn't know. I forgot that you didn't know that I was once engaged long ago—before the beginning of the war. I cared a great deal—we both cared a great deal, but he was not one of us; he was on the other side—and when the war came, of course there was no question. We broke if off; we had to break it off. How could it have been possible to do otherwise?'

"'How, indeed!' I murmured; and I had a vision of the old man downstairs on the terrace, of the intrepid and absurd old man.

"'My first duty is to my country,' she went on after a minute, and the words might have been spoken by her father. 'There has been no thought of anything else in my mind since the beginning of the war. Even if peace comes I can never feel the same again I can never forget that he has been a part of all we have suffered—of the thing that has made us suffer. I could never forget—I can never forgive.'

"Her words sound strange now, you think, after fifty years; but on that day, in this house surrounded by dead leaves, inhabited by an inextinguishable ideal—in this country, where the spirit had fed on the body until the impoverished brain reacted to transcendent visions—in this place, at that time, they were natural enough. Scarcely a woman of the South but would have uttered them from her soul. In every age one ideal enthralls the imagination of mankind; it is in the air; it subjugates the will; it enchants the emotions. Well, in the South fifty years ago this ideal was patriotism; and the passion of patriotism, which bloomed like some red flower, the flower of carnage, over the land, had grown in Lucy Dare's soul into an exotic blossom.

"Yet even today, after fifty years, I cannot get over the impression she made upon me of a woman who was, in the essence of her nature, thin and colorless. I may have been wrong. Perhaps I never knew her. It is not easy to judge people, especially women, who wear a mask by instinct. What I thought lack of character, of personality, may have been merely reticence; but again and again there comes back to me the thought that she never said or did a thing—except the one terrible thing—that one could remember. There was nothing remarkable that one could point to about her. I cannot recall either her smile or her voice, though both were sweet, no doubt, as the smile and the voice of a Southern woman would be. Until that morning on the upper veranda I had not noticed that her eyes were wonderful. She was like a shadow, a phantom, that attains in one supreme instant, by one immortal gesture, union with reality. Even I remember her only by that one lurid flash.

"'And you say you have had a letter?'

"'It was brought by one of the old servants—Jacob, the one who used to wait on him when he stayed here. He was a prisoner. A few days ago he escaped. He asked me to see him—and I told him to come. He wishes to see me once again before he goes North—forever—' She spoke in gasps in a dry voice. Never once did she mention his name. Long afterwards I remembered that I had never heard his name spoken. Even today I do not know it. He also was a shadow, a phantom—a part of the encompassing unreality.

"'And he will come here?'

"For a moment she hesitated; then she spoke quite simply, knowing that she could trust me.

"'He is here. He is in the chamber beyond.' She pointed to one of the long windows that gave on the veranda. 'The blue chamber at the front.'

"I remember that I made a step towards the window when her voice arrested me. 'Don't go in. He is resting. He is very tired and hungry.'

"'You didn't send for me, then, to see him?'

"'I sent for you to be with father. I knew you would help me—that you would keep him from suspecting. He must not know, of course. He must be kept quiet.'

"'I will stay with him,' I answered, and then, 'Is that all you wish to say to me?'

"'That is all. It is only for a day or two. He will go on in a little while, and I can never see him again. I do not wish to see him again.'

"I turned away, across the veranda, entered the hall, walked the length of it, and descended the staircase. The sun was going down in a ball—just as it will begin to go down in a few minutes—and as I descended the stairs I saw it through the mullioned window over the door—huge and red and round above the black cloud of the cedars.

"The old man was still on the terrace. I wondered vaguely why the servants had not brought him indoors; and then, as I stepped over the threshold, I saw that a company of soldiers—Confederates—had crossed the lawn and were already gathering about the house. The commanding officer—I was shaking hands with him presently—was a Dare, a distant cousin of the Colonel's, one of those excitable, nervous, and slightly theatrical natures who become utterly demoralized under the spell of any violent emotion. He had been wounded at least a dozen times, and his lean, sallow, still handsome features had the greenish look which I had learned to associate with chronic malaria.

"When I look back now I can see it all as a part of the general disorganization—of the fever, the malnutrition, the complete demoralization of panic. I know now that each man of us was facing in his soul defeat and despair; and that we—each one of us—had gone mad with the thought of it. In a little while, after the certainty of failure had come to us, we met it quietly—we braced our souls for the issue; but in those last weeks defeat had all the horror, all the insane terror of a nightmare, and all the vividness. The thought was like a delusion from which we fled, and which no flight could put farther away from us.

"Have you ever lived, I wonder, from day to day in that ever—present and unchanging sense of unreality, as if the moment before you were but an imaginary experience which must dissolve and evaporate before the touch of an actual event? Well, that was the sensation I had felt for days, weeks, months, and it swept over me again while I stood there, shaking hands with the Colonel's cousin, on the terrace. The soldiers, in their ragged uniforms, appeared as visionary as the world in which we had been living. I think now that they were as ignorant as we were of the things that had happened—that were happening day by day to the army. The truth is that it was impossible for a single one of us to believe that our heroic army could be beaten even by unseen powers—even by hunger and death.

"'And you say he was a prisoner?' It was the old man's quavering voice, and it sounded avid for news, for certainty.

'Caught in disguise. Then he slipped through our fingers.' The cousin's tone was querulous, as if he were irritated by loss of sleep or of food. 'Nobody knows how it happened. Nobody ever knows. But he has found out things that will ruin us. He has plans. He has learned things that mean the fall of Richmond if he escapes.'

"Since then I have wondered how much they sincerely believed—how much was simply the hallucination of fever, of desperation? Were they trying to bully themselves by violence into hoping? Or had they honestly convinced themselves that victory was still possible? If one only repeats a phrase often and emphatically enough one comes in time to believe it; and they had talked so long of that coming triumph, of the established Confederacy, that it had ceased to be, for them at least, merely a phrase. It wasn't the first occasion in life when I had seen words bullied—yes, literally bullied into beliefs.

"Well, looking back now after fifty years, you see, of course, the weakness of it all, the futility. At that instant, when all was lost, how could any plans, any plotting have ruined us? It seems irrational enough now—a dream, a shadow, that belief—and yet not one of us but would have given our lives for it. In order to understand you must remember that we were, one and all, victims of an idea—of a divine frenzy.

"'And we are lost—the Confederacy is lost, you say, if he escapes?'

"It was Lucy's voice; and turning quickly, I saw that she was standing in the doorway. She must have followed me closely. It was possible that she had over-heard every word of the conversation.

"'If Lucy knows anything, she will tell you. There is no need to search the house,' quavered the old man, 'she is my daughter.'

"'Of course we wouldn't search the house—not Dare's Gift,' said the cousin. He was excited, famished, malarial, but he was a gentleman, every inch of him.

"He talked on rapidly, giving details of the capture, the escape, the pursuit. It was all rather confused. I think he must have frightfully exaggerated the incident. Nothing could have been more unreal than it sounded. And he was just out of a hospital—was suffering still, I could see, from malaria. While he drank his black-berry wine—the best the house had to offer—I remember wishing that I had a good dose of quinine and whiskey to give him.

"The narrative lasted a long time; I think he was glad of a rest and of the black-berry wine and biscuits. Lucy had gone to fetch food for the soldiers; but after she had brought it she sat down in her accustomed chair by the old man's side and bent her head over her knitting. She was a wonderful knitter. During all the years of the war I seldom saw her without her ball of yarn and her needles—the long wooden kind that the women used at the time. Even after the dusk fell in the evenings the click of her needles sounded in the darkness.

"'And if he escapes it will mean the capture of Richmond?' she asked once again when the story was finished. There was no hint of excitement in her manner. Her voice was perfectly toneless. To this day I have no idea what she felt—what she was thinking.

"'If he gets away it is the ruin of us—but he won't get away. We'll find him be-fore morning.'

"Rising from his chair, he turned to shake hands with the old man before de-scending the steps. 'We've got to go on now. I shouldn't have stopped if we hadn't been half starved. You've done us a world of good, Cousin Lucy. I reckon you'd give your last crust to the soldiers?'

"'She'd give more than that,' quavered the old man. 'You'd give more than that, wouldn't you, Lucy?'

"'Yes, I'd give more than that,' repeated the girl quietly, so quietly that it came as a shock to me—like a throb of actual pain in the midst of a nightmare—when she rose to her feet and added, without a movement, without a gesture, 'You must not go, Cousin George. He is upstairs in the blue chamber at the front of the house.'

"For an instant surprise held me speechless, transfixed, incredulous; and in that instant I saw a face—a white face of horror and disbelief—look down on us from one of the side windows of the blue chamber. Then, in a rush it seemed to me the soldiers were everywhere, swarming over the terrace, into the hall, surrounding the house. I had never imagined that a small body of men in uniforms, even ragged uniforms, could so possess and obscure one's surroundings. The three of us waited there—Lucy had sat down again and taken up her knitting—for what seemed hours, or an eternity. We were still waiting—though, for once, I noticed, the needles did not click in her fingers—when a single shot, followed by a volley, rang out from the rear of the house, from the veranda that looked down on the grove of oaks and the kitchen.

"Rising, I left them—the old man and the girl—and passed from the terrace down the little walk which led to the back. As I reached the lower veranda one of the soldiers ran into me.

"'I was coming after you,' he said, and I observed that his excitement had left him. 'We brought him down while he was trying to jump from the veranda. He is there now on the grass.'

"The man on the grass was quite dead, shot through the heart; and while I bent over to wipe the blood from his lips, I saw him for the first time distinctly. A young face, hardly more than a boy—twenty—five at the most. Handsome, too, in a poetic and dreamy way; just the face, I thought, that a woman might have fallen in love with. He had dark hair, I remember, though his features have long ago faded from my memory. What will never fade, what I shall never forget, is the look he wore— the look he was still wearing when we laid him in the old graveyard next day—a look of mingled surprise, disbelief, terror, and indignation.

"I had done all that I could, which was nothing, and rising to my feet, I saw for the first time that Lucy had joined me. She was standing perfectly motionless. Her knitting was still in her hands, but the light had gone from her face, and she looked old—old and gray—beside the glowing youth of her lover. For a moment her eyes held me while she spoke as quietly as she had spoken to the soldiers on the terrace.

"'I had to do it,' she said. 'I would do it again.'"

Suddenly, like the cessation of running water, or of wind in the treetops, the doctor's voice ceased. For a long pause we stared in silence at the sunset; then, without looking at me, he added slowly:

"Three weeks later Lee surrendered and the Confederacy was over."

III

The sun had slipped, as if by magic, behind the tops of the cedars, and dusk fell quickly, like a heavy shadow, over the terrace. In the dimness a piercing sweetness floated up from the garden of herbs, and it seemed to me that in a minute the twilight was saturated with fragrance. Then I heard the cry of a solitary whippoorwill in the graveyard, and it sounded so near that I started.

"So she died of the futility, and her unhappy ghost haunts the house?"

"No, she is not dead. It is not her ghost; it is the memory of her act that has haunted the house. Lucy Dare is still living. I saw her a few months ago."

"You saw her? You spoke to her after all these years?"

He had refilled his pipe, and the smell of it gave me a comfortable assurance that I was living here, now, in the present. A moment ago I had shivered as if the hand of the past, reaching from the open door at my back, had touched my shoulder.

"I was in Richmond. My friend Beverly, an old classmate, had asked me up for a weekend, and on Saturday afternoon, before motoring into the country for supper, we started out to make a few calls which had been left over from the morning. For a doctor, a busy doctor, he had always seemed to me to possess unlimited leisure, so I was not surprised when a single visit sometimes stretched over twenty—five minutes. We had stopped several times, and I confess that I was getting a little impatient when he remarked abruptly while he turned his car into a shady street,

"'There is only one more. If you don't mind, I'd like you to see her. She is a friend of yours, I believe.'

"Before us, as the car stopped, I saw a red—brick house, very large, with green shutters, and over the wide door, which stood open, a sign reading 'St. Luke's Church Home.' Several old ladies sat, half asleep, on the long veranda; a clergyman, with a prayer book in his hand, was just leaving; a few pots of red geraniums stood on little green wicker stands; and from the hall, through which floated the smell of freshly baked bread, there came the music of a Victrola—sacred music, I remember. Not one of these details escaped me. It was as if every trivial impression was stamped indelibly in my memory by the shock of the next instant.

"In the center of the large, smoothly shaven lawn an old woman was sitting on a wooden bench under an ailanthus tree which was in blossom. As we approached her, I saw that her figure was shapeless, and that her eyes, of a faded blue, had the vacant and listless expression of the old who have ceased to think, who have ceased even to wonder or regret. So unlike was she to anything I had ever imagined Lucy Dare could become, that not until my friend called her name and she glanced up from the muffler she was knitting—the omnipresent dun—colored muffler for the war relief associations—not until then did I recognize her.

"'I have brought an old friend to see you, Miss Lucy.'

"She looked up, smiled slightly, and after greeting me pleasantly, relapsed into silence. I remembered that the Lucy Dare I had known was never much of a talker.

"Dropping on the bench at her side, my friend began asking her about her sciatica, and, to my surprise, she became almost animated. Yes, the pain in her hip was better – far better than it had been for weeks. The new medicine had done her a great deal of good; but her fingers were getting rheumatic. She found trouble holding her needles. She couldn't knit as fast as she used to.

"Unfolding the end of the muffler, she held it out to us. 'I have managed to do twenty of these since Christmas. I've promised fifty to the War Relief Association by autumn, and if my finger don't get stiff I can easily do them.'

"The sunshine falling through the ailanthus tree powdered with dusty gold her shapeless, relaxed figure and the dun—colored wool of the muffler. While she talked her fingers flew with the click of the needles – older fingers than they had been at Dare's Gift, heavier, stiffer, and little knotted in the joints. As I watched her the old familiar sense of strangeness, of encompassing and hostile mystery, stole over me.

"When we rose to go she looked up, and, without pausing for an instant in her knitting, said, gravely, 'It gives me something to do, this work for the Allies. It helps to pass the time, and in an Old Ladies' Home one has so much time on one's hands.'

"Then, as we parted from her, she dropped her eyes again to her needles. Looking back at the gate, I saw that she still sat there in the faint sunshine—knitting—knitting—"

"And you think she has forgotten?"

He hesitated, as if gathering his thoughts. "I was with her when she came back from the shock – from the illness that followed – and she had forgotten. Yes, she has forgotten, but the house has remembered."

Pushing back from his chair, he rose unsteadily on his crutch, and stood staring across that twilight which was spangled with fireflies. While I waited I heard again the loud cry of the whippoorwill.

"Well, what could one expect?" he asked, presently. "She had drained the whole experience in an instant, and there was left to her only the empty and withered husks of the hours. She had felt too much ever to fell again. After all," he added slowly, "it is the high moments that make a life, and the flat ones that fill the years."

5.14.2 Reading and Review Questions

1. What does the title "Dare's Gift" mean?

2. How is Mildred affected by past events in the house, according to Dr. Lakeby? How does Dr. Lakeby present the events in the house as scientific rather than supernatural? Does he believe his own explanations?

3. Examine the theme of betrayal in the story.

4. How are Mildred's and Lucy's decisions and actions similar or different?

5. Why does Lucy have no memory of her decision to turn in her fiancé?

6. What role does the past play in the story, especially the past as represented by the Old South?

5.15 WILLIAM FAULKNER

(1897 - 1962)

William Faulkner is the most important writer of the Southern Renaissance. Flannery O'Connor once compared the overpowering force of his influence to a thundering train, remarking that "nobody wants his mule and wagon stalled on the same track the **Dixie Limited** is roaring down." Faulkner was born in Mississippi and raised on tales of his legendary great-great grandfather—the "Old Colonel," who led a group of raiders in the civil war, built his own railroad, served in the state legislature, and was murdered by a political rival—and prominent great-grandfather, the "Young Colonel," who was an assistant United States attorney and banker. Dropping out of high school, Faulkner left Mississippi to pursue his interests in drawing and poetry. During World War I, Faulkner pretended to be English and enlisted in the Royal Air Force, although he never saw combat. He picked up his poetic career after the war, ultimately publishing his first book in 1924, a collection of poetry called *The Marble Faun*. Turning his attention to fiction writing, Faulkner then wrote two timely novels. His first novel, *Soldier's Pay* (1926), explores the states of mind of those who did and did not fight in World War I. His second novel, *Mosquitos* (1927), exposes the triviality of the New Orleans art community of which Faulkner was briefly a part. However, it is with his third novel, *Sartoris* (1929), that Faulkner made what he called his "great discovery": the fictional possibilities contained within his home state of Mississippi. Returning to Oxford, MI, with his new wife, Faulkner moved into an antebellum mansion and began turning the tales he heard growing up about his hometown and surrounding area into one of the greatest inventions in American literary history: Yoknapatawpha County.

Faulkner eventually wrote thirteen novels set in Yoknapatawpha County. Beginning with his fourth novel, *The Sound and the Fury* (1929), Faulkner began to incorporate modernist literary techniques such as stream-of-consciousness narration and non-linear plotting into his already lofty style. *The Sound and the Fury* describes the fall of the Compson family through four distinct psychological points of view, one of which is that of a young man who commits suicide, and another belonging to an illiterate who is severely mentally handicapped. *As I Lay Dying* (1930) describes the death and burial of a matriarch from the perspective of fifteen different characters in fifty-seven sections of often stream-of-consciousness prose. In *Absalom, Absalom!* (1936), four narrators relate the same story yet also change it to arrive at four very different meanings. Modernist techniques such as these enabled Faulkner to show how the particulars of everyday life in the rural American South dramatize what he saw as the universal truths of humanity as a whole. While stylistically modernist, Faulkner's collective epic of Yoknapatawpha County ultimately explores not so much the future of narrative as the human condition itself as lensed through generation-spanning histories of great and low families. Two of Faulkner's Yoknapatawpha stories are included here: "Barn Burning," an early story of the Snopes family about whom Faulkner would eventually write a trilogy of novels; and "A Rose for Emily," one of his many tales about the decline of formerly-great Southern families. These short stories are good representatives of both the range of Faulkner's style and his ambition as a storyteller. In deeply regional tales that are at once grotesque, tragic, brilliant, profound, loving, and hilarious, Faulkner leads us to the source, as he once put it, from which drama flows: "the problems of the human heart in conflict with itself."

5.15.1 "A Rose For Emily"

Please click the link below to access this selection:

http://xroads.virginia.edu/~drbr/wf_rose.html

5.15.2 "Barn Burning"

Please click the link below to access this selection:

http://www.griffinhighschool.org/wp-content/uploads/2015/12/Barn-Burning-by-William-Faulkner-1.pdf

5.15.3 Reading and Review Questions

1. At the end of "Barn Burning," what is young Sarty running from? Why does he not look back?

2. Why does Abner Snopes burn barns?

3. Why is the discovery of the single grey hair at the end of "A Rose for Emily" significant?

4. Faulkner received the Nobel Prize for Literature in 1950. In his award speech, he lamented that many of America's young authors had forgotten "the problems of the human heart in conflict with itself which alone can make good writing." Discuss how "Barn Burning" and "A Rose for Emily" show the human heart in conflict with itself.

5. How does Faulkner represent the relationship between parents and children in "Barn Burning"?

5.16 EUDORA ALICE WELTY

(1909 - 2001)

Eudora Alice Welty was born in Jackson, Mississippi, the daughter of an insurance agent father and a retired teacher mother. Her family had moved to Mississippi from the Ohio Valley region, and Welty enjoyed an idyllic childhood spent in Mississippi with summers visiting relatives in the

Image 5.14 | Eudora Alice Welty, 1988
Photographer | Mildred Nungester Wolfe
Source | National Portrait Gallery
License | Fair Use

Midwest. While in high school, Welty published works in a national magazine before attending Mississippi State College for Women for an Associate degree, then transferring to the University of Wisconsin in order to finish her Bachelor's degree in English. After earning that degree (1929), Welty enrolled at Columbia University but could not find full time work in New York City during the depression; due to finances, she returned home to Jackson (1931) where she would reside for the rest of her life.

Once home, Welty held a series of jobs to help support her mother, including working as a publicity agent for the Works Progress Administration (WPA). In 1936, Welty published her first short story, "Death of a Traveling Salesman," in *Manuscript* magazine. After this success, she continued to publish in many prominent journals and magazines, including *Harper's Bazaar* and *Atlantic Monthly*. Her first collection of short stories, *A Curtain of Green and Other Stories* (1941), was largely well-received. Her follow-up novella, *The Robber Bridegroom* (1942), brought her national attention. Soon, Welty was receiving encouragement from fellow Mississippi native William Faulkner.

In both 1943 and 1944, Welty won the O. Henry Award, a prestigious award given for outstanding short fiction. Soon after, Welty would go on to write her classic, *The Golden Apples* (1949). After publishing *The Bride of the Innisfallen* (1955), Welty took a fifteen-year hiatus from writing fiction before returning with her novel, *The Optimist Daughter* (1972), which was awarded the Pulitzer Prize. In 1980, Welty was awarded the Presidential Medal of Freedom before publishing her best-selling autobiography, *One Writer's Beginnings*. Welty died in Jackson, Mississippi in 2001.

Although she won a Pulitzer Prize for her novel, *The Optimist's Daughter,* Welty is largely known as a master of short fiction. Her work engages Southern themes, often dealing with the problems of post-Reconstruction South. "A Worn Path," originally published in *Atlantic Monthly,* is one of Welty's most famous and most anthologized short stories. It transposes the hero's journey (tales in which a hero sets off on an adventure and is changed at the end) on to a seemingly simple tale of an elderly African-American grandmother, Phoenix Jackson, retrieving medication for her sick grandson.

5.16.1 "A Worn Path"

Please click the link below to access this selection:
   http://xroads.virginia.edu/~drbr/ew_path.html

5.16.2 Reading and Review Questions

1. Do you think Phoenix Jackson's grandson is still alive? Why, or why not?

2. What is the significance of her name, Phoenix? Why is this important in the context of the story?

3. How does Welty take the details of the mundane and transform them into the mystical?

5.17 THE HARLEM RENAISSANCE

The early years of the twentieth century transformed the United States from a nation of agrarian settlers into a nation of industrial immigrants. With the collapse of the plantation economy and the closing of the western frontier, the United States suddenly became a nation of city-dwellers. The urban economies of the north thrived during this period, and internal migration brought about significant changes in cultural production. While these migratory patterns often reinforced regional identities, they also provided the conditions for the creation of new identities. For African-Americans of the early twentieth century, the Harlem Renaissance was the most significant period of cultural formation since the end of the Civil War.

The Harlem Renaissance is commonly defined as a period of cultural activity by African-American artists that began in Harlem, a New York City neighborhood in northern Manhattan, in the 1920s and ended in the years leading up to World War II. Yet that short span of approximately fifteen years neither accurately describes the period, nor indicates the lasting influence that the Harlem Renaissance continues to have on American literature. In order to locate the roots of the Harlem Renaissance, we need to go back at least as far as 1910 and the founding of *The Crisis*, the journal of the National Association for the Advancement of Colored People (NAACP). Many members of the Harlem Renaissance, including early luminaries such as Countee Cullen and Jessie Redmon Fauset, were closely associated with *The Crisis* and with the high ideals of its editorial page "[to] stand for the right of men, irrespective of color or race, for the highest ideals of American democracy" (Du Bois, November 1910). This dedication to the idealized principles of Ameri-can democracy and a celebration of the achievements of African-Americans had a direct influence on the early members of the Harlem Renaissance. Many, like Cullen and Fauset, were highly and traditionally educated, and their poetry and fiction descend directly from the English literary traditions of the eighteenth and nineteenth centuries. While other African-American writers of the time embraced folklore traditions, Cullen and many others celebrated their association with the highest forms of English literature.

From the very beginnings of the Harlem Renaissance, the movement lacked unity. Although some members embraced the high language of Du Bois and those closest to him, others argued for a literature that responded to the writers' Afri-can heritage instead of their European connection. Alain Locke's *The New Negro* (1925) is often regarded as the manifesto of this pan-Africanism. Writers like Rich-ard Wright, Langston Hughes, and Zora Neale Hurston, are often considered to be part of this second branch of the Harlem Renaissance.

By the 1930s, the Harlem Renaissance no longer signified a unified artistic ideal, and its many voices and members were scattered around the globe by evolving racial tensions in the United States. Beyond Harlem, African-American communities were thriving in cities like Chicago, Memphis, Detroit, Baltimore, Washington, and Pittsburgh; furthermore, the wars in Europe were redrawing political boundaries worldwide. Almost as quickly as it began, the Harlem Renaissance faded, but it left behind a legacy of independence in literature, music, and heart that can be traced directly to jazz, the blues, Motown, rock, rap, and hip-hop.

5.17 JESSIE REDMON FAUSET

(1882 - 1961)

Jessie Redmon Fauset, like her younger con-temporary Countee Cullen, belongs to the first generation of Harlem Renaissance writers who used traditional literary forms to explore issues important to the African-American community. In this way, the growth of these writers can be likened to the path traced by nineteenth-century British women writers and outlined in Elaine Showalter's book *A Literature of Their Own* (1977). In her study of women writers, Showal-ter traced three stages of literary development. In the first stage, underrepresented authors use traditional forms and adopt traditional view-points in order to gain wider acceptance. In the

Image 5.15 | Jessie Redmon Fauset, n.d.
Photographer | Unknown
Source | Wikimedia Commons
License | Fair Use

second stage, authors begin to use traditional forms to advance new viewpoints while, in the third stage, authors adopt new forms to advance progressive view-points. In many ways, these same three stages that Showalter assigned to British women writers of the nineteenth century can be applied to the writers of the Har-lem Renaissance. Both Fauset and Cullen can be classified as second stage writers: those who used traditional forms to celebrate new ideas.

For much of the early twentieth century, Fauset was the literary editor of *The Crisis*, and her selections, as well as her own writing, adhered to W. E. B. Du Bois's mission statement for the magazine:

> The object of this publication is to set forth those facts and arguments which show the danger of race prejudice, particularly as manifested today toward colored people. . . . The policy of *The Crisis* will be simple and well defined: It will first and foremost be a newspaper, . . . Secondly it will be a review of opinion and literature, . . . Thirdly it will publish a few short articles, . . . Fi-nally, its editorial page will stand for the right of men, irrespective of color or race, for the highest ideals of American democracy, and for reasonable but earnest and persistent attempt to gain these rights and realize these ideals. The Magazine will be the organ of no clique or party and will avoid personal rancor of all sorts. In the absence of proof to the contrary it will assume hon-esty of purpose on the part of all men, North and South, white and black.[5]

5   "The Crisis." Editorial. *The Crisis.* ed. Nov. 1910. Web. 10 Dec. 2015.

As the first African-American elected to the Phi Beta Kappa honor society at Cornell University (1905) and as a master's graduate of the University of Pennsylvania, Fauset was well positioned to advance Du Bois's goals. Like Cullen and other early members of the Harlem Renaissance, Fauset was an articulate voice for a certain segment of the African-American community.

While Fauset's relatively privileged position granted her access to mainstream literary circles of her time, this same privilege ultimately alienated her from other members of the Harlem Renaissance. Many of Fauset's works concern the struggles of light-skinned, middle-class African-Americans to assimilate and succeed over the limitations of their racial identities, and this largely positive portrayal of assimilation and passing angered other members of the movement like Langston Hughes who argued for a full embrace of African-American racial identity.

The selection from Fauset, "The Sleeper Wakes" (1920), challenges both our preconceptions about Fauset and the attacks on her by Hughes. Although the story directly concerns the life of a light-skinned African-American who is married to a white husband, Fauset's heroine, Amy, is ultimately unsettled by her success at passing. Stirred to action by her husband's mistreatment of an African-American servant, Amy recognizes her racial identity and awakens as the title suggests. Awakened to her racial identity, Amy leaves her husband and his money behind in order to live a more direct representation of her identity. Although Fauset and Cullen both embrace traditional literary forms, their presentation of race demonstrates their active engagement with issues of identity, politics, and the promises of the American experiment that are more progressive than their forms suggest.

5.17.1 "The Sleeper Wakes"

Amy recognized the incident as the beginning of one of her phases. Always from a child she had been able to tell when "something was going to happen." She had been standing in Marshall's store, her young, eager gaze intent on the lovely little sample dress which was not from Paris, but quite as dainty as anything that Paris could produce. It was not the lines or even the texture that fascinated Amy so much, it was the grouping of colors—of shades. She knew the combination was just right for her.

"Let me slip it on, Miss," said the saleswoman suddenly. She had nothing to do just then, and the girl was so evidently charmed and so pretty—it was a pleasure to wait on her.

"Oh no," Amy had stammered. "I haven't time." She had already wasted two hours at the movies, and she knew at home they were waiting for her.

The saleswoman slipped the dress over the girl's pink blouse, and tucked the linen collar under so as to bring the edge of the dress next to her pretty neck. The dress was apricot-color shading into a shell pink and the shell pink shaded off again into the pearl and pink whiteness of Amy's skin. The saleswoman beamed as Amy, entranced, surveyed herself naively in the tall looking-glass.

Then it was that the incident befell. Two men walking idly through the dress-salon stopped and looked—she made an unbelievably pretty picture. One of them with a short, soft brown beard,—"fuzzy" Amy thought to herself as she caught his glance in the mirror—spoke to his companion.

"Jove, how I'd like to paint her!" But it was the look on the other man's face that caught her and thrilled her. "My God! Can't a girl be beautiful!" he said half to himself. The pair passed on.

Amy stepped out of the dress and thanked the saleswoman half absently. She wanted to get home and think, think to herself about that look. She had seen it before in men's eyes, it had been in the eyes of the men in the moving-picture which she had seen that afternoon. But she had not thought *she* could cause it. Shut up in her little room, she pondered over it. Her beauty,—she was really good-looking then—she could stir people—men! A girl of seventeen has no psychology, she does not go beneath the surface, she accepts. But she knew she was entering on one of her phases.

She was always living in some sort of story. She had started it when as a child of five she had driven with the tall, proud, white woman to Mrs. Boldin's home. Mrs. Boldin was a bride of one year's standing then. She was slender and very, very comely, with her rich brown skin and her hair that crinkled thick and soft above a low forehead. The house was still redolent of new furnoiture; Mr. Boldin was spick and span—he, unlike the furniture, remained so for that matter. The white woman had told Amy that this henceforth was to be her home.

Amy was curious, fond of adventure; she did not cry. She did not, of course, realize that she was to stay here indefinitely, but if she had, even at that age she would hardly have shed tears, she was always too eager, too curious to know, to taste what was going to happen next. Still since she had had almost no dealings with colored people and knew absolutely none of the class to which Mrs. Boldin belonged, she did venture one question.

"Am I going to be colored now?"

The tall white woman had flushed and paled. "You—" she began, but the words choked her. "Yes, you are going to be colored now," she ended finally. She was a proud woman, in a moment she had recovered her usual poise. Amy carried with her for many years the memory of that proud head. She never saw her again.

When she was sixteen she asked Mrs. Boldin the question which in the light of that memory had puzzled her always. "Mrs. Boldin, tell me—am I white or colored?"

And Mrs. Boldin had told her and told her truly that she did not know.

"A—a—mee!" Mrs. Bolding's voice mounted on the last syllable in a shrill crescendo. Amy rose and went downstairs.

Down in the comfortable, but rather shabby dining-room which the Boldins used after meals to sit in, Mr. Boldin, a tall black man, with aristocratic features, sat reading; little Cornelius Boldin sat practicing on a cornet, and Mrs. Boldin sat rocking. In all of their eyes was the manifestation of the light that Amy loved, but how truly she loved it, she was not to guess till years later.

"Amy," Mr. Boldin paused in her rocking, "did you get the braid?" Of couse she had not, though that was the thing she had gone to Marshall's for. Amy always went willingly, it was for the pure joy of going. Who knew what angels might meet one unawares? Not that Amy though in biblical or in literary phrases. She was in the High School, it is true, but she was simply passing through, "getting by" she would have said carelessly. The only reading that had ever made any impression on her had been fairy tales read to her in those long remote days when she had lived with the tall, proud woman; and descriptions in novels or histories of beautiful stately palaces tenanted by beautiful, stately women. She could pore over such pages for hours, her face flushed, her eyes eager.

At present she cast about for an excuse. She had so meant to get the braid. "There was a dress—" she began lamely, she was never deliberately dishonest.

Mr. Boldin cleared his throat and nervously fingered his paper. Cornelius ceased his awful playing and blinked at her shortsightedly through his thick glasses. Both of these, the man and the little boy, loved the beautiful, inconsequential creature with her airy, irresponsible ways. But Mrs. Boldin loved her too, and because she loved her she could not scold.

"Of course you forgot," she began chidingly. Then she smiled. "There was a dress that you looked at *perhaps*. But confess, didn't you go to the movies first?"

Yes, Amy confessed she had done just that. "And oh, Mrd. Boldin, it was the most wonderful picture—a girl—such a pretty one—and she was poor, awfully. And somehow se met the most wonderful people and they were so kind to her. And she married a man who was just tremendously rich and he gave her everything. I did so want Cornelius to see it."

"Huh!" said Cornelius who had been listening not because he was interested, but because he wanted to call Amy's attention to his playing as soon as possible. "Huh! I don't want to look at no pretty girl. Did they have anybody looping the loop in an airship?"

"You'd better stop seeing pretty girl pictures, Amy," said Mr. Boldin kindly. "They're not always true to life. Besides, I know where you can see all the pretty girls you want without bothering to pay twenty-five cents for it."

Amy smiled at the implied compliment and went on happily studying her lessons. They were all happy in their own way. Amy because she was sure of their love and admiration, Mr. and Mrs. Boldin because of her beauty and innocence and Cornelius because he knew he had in his foster-sister a listener whom his terrible practicing could never bore. He played brokenly a piece he had found in an old music-book. *"There's an aching void in every heart, brother."*

"Where *do* you pick up those old things, Neely?" said his mother fretfully. But Amy could not have her favorite's feelings injured.

"I think it's lovely," she announced defensively. "Cornelius, I'll ask Sadie Murray to lend me her brother's book. He's learning the cornet, too, and you can get some new pieces. Of, isn't it awful to have to go to bed? Good-night, everybody." She smiled her charming, ever ready smile, the mere reflex of youth and beauty and content.

"You do spoil her, Mattie," said Mr. Boldin after she had left the room. "She's only seventeen—here, Cornelius, you go to bed—but it seems to me she ought to be more dependable about errands. Though she is splendid about some things," he defended her. "Look how willingly she goes off to bed. She'll be asleep before she knows it when most girls of her age would want to be in the street."

But upstairs Amy was far from sleep. She lit on gas-jet and pulled down the shades. Then she stuffed tissue paper in the keyhole and under the doors, and lit the remaining gas-jets. The light thus thrown on the mirror of the ugly oak dresser was perfect. She slipped off the pink blouse and found two scarfs, a soft yellow and soft pink,—se had had them in a scarf-dance for a school entertainment. She wound them and draped them about her pretty shoulders and loosened her hair. In the mirror she apostrophized the beautiful, glowing vision of herself.

"There," she said, "I'm like the girl in the picture. She had nothing but her beautiful face—and she did so want to be happy." She sat down on the side of the rather lumpy bed and stretched out her arms. "I want to be happy, too." She intoned it earnestly, almost like an incantation. "I want wonderful clothes, and people around me, men adoring me, and the world before me. I want—everything! It will come, it will all come because I want it so." She sat frowning intently as she was apt to do when very much engrossed. "And we'd all be so happy. I'd give Mr. and Mrs. Boldin money! And Cornelius—he'd go to college and learn all about his old airships. Oh, if I only knew how to begin!"

Smiling, she turned off the lights and crept to bed.

II

Quite suddenly she knew she was going to run away. That was in October. By December she had accomplished her purpose. Not that she was to least bit unhappy but because she must get out in the world,—she felt caged, imprisoned. "Trenton is stifling me," she would have told you, in her unconsciously adopted "movie" diction. New York she knew was the place for her. She had her plans all made. She had sewed steadily after school for two months—as she frequently did when she wanted to buy her season's wardrobe, so besides her carfare she had $25. She went immediately to a white Y. W. C. A., stayed there two nights, found and answered an advertisement for clerk and waitress in a small confectionery and bakery-shop, was accepted and there she was launched.

Perhaps it was because of her early experience when as a tiny child she was taken from that so different home and left at Mrs. Boldin's, perhaps it was some fault in her own disposition, concentrated and egotistic as she was, but certainly she felt no pangs of separation, no fear of her future. She was cold too,—unfired though so to speak rather than icy,—and fastidious. This last quality kept her safe where morality or religion, of neither of which had she any conscious endowment, would have availed her nothing. Unbelievably then she lived two years in New York, unspoiled, untouched going to her work on the edge of Greenwich Village early and coming back late, knowing almost no one and yet altogether happy in the expectation of something wonderful, which she knew some day must happen.

It was at the end of the second year that she met Zora Harrisson. Zora used to come into lunch with a group of habitués of the place—all of them artists and writers Amy gathered. Mrs. Harrisson (for she was married as Amy later learned) appealed to the girl because she knew so well how to afford the contrast to her blonde, golden beauty. Purple, dark and regal, developed in velvets and heavy silks, and strange marine blues she wore, and thus made Amy absolutely happy. Singularly enough, the girl intent as she was on her own life and experiences, had felt up to this time no yearning to know these strange, happy beings who surrounded her. She did miss Cornelius, but otherwise she was never lonely, or if she was she hardly knew it, for she had always lived an inner life to herself. But Mrs. Harrisson magnetized her—she could not keep her eyes from her face, from her wonderful clothes. She made conjectures about her.

The wonderful lady came in late one afternoon—an unusual thing for her. She smiled at Amy invitingly, asked some banal questions and their first conversation began. The acquaintance once struck up progressed rapidly—after a few weeks Mrs. Harrisson invited the girl to come to see her. Amy accepted quietly, unaware that anything extraordinary was happening. Zora noticed this and liked it. She had an apartment in 12th Street in a house inhabited only by artists—she was no mean one herself. Amy was fascinated by the new world into which she found herself ushered; Zora's surroundings were very beautiful and Zora herself was a study. She opened to the girl's amazed vision fields of thought and conjecture, phases of whose existence Amy, who was a builder of phases, had never dreamed. Zora had been a poor girl of good family. She had wanted to study art, she had deliberately married a rich man and as deliberately obtained in the course of four years a divorce, and she was now living in New York studying by means of her alimony and enjoying to its fullest the life she loved. She took Amy on a footing with herself—the girl's refinement, her beauty, her interest in colors (though this in Amy at the time was purely sporadic, never consciously encouraged), all this gave Zora a figure about which to plan and build a romance. Amy had told her to truth, but not all about her coming to New York. She had grown tired of Trenton—her people were all dead—the folks with whom she lived were kind and good but not "inspiring" (she had borrowed the term from Zora and it was true, the Boldins, when one came to think of it, were not "inspiring"), so she had run away.

Zora had gone into raptures. "What an adventure! My dear, the world is yours. Why, with your looks and your birth, for I suppose you really belong to the Kildares who used to live in Philadelphia, I think there was a son who ran off and married an actress or someone—they disowned him I remember,—you can reach any height. You must marry a wealthy man—perhaps someone who is interested in art and who will let you pursue your studies." She insisted always that Amy had run away in order to study art. "But luck like that comes to few," she sighed, remembering her own plight, for Mr. Harrisson had been decidedly unwilling to let her pursue her studies, at least to the extent she wished. "Anyway you must marry wealth,—

one can always get a divorce," she ended sagely.

Amy—she came to Zora's every night now—used to listen dazedly at first. She had accepted willingly enough Zora's conjecture about her birth, came to believe it in fact—but she drew back somewhat at such wholesale exploitation of people to suit one's own convenience, still she did not probe too far into this thought—nor did she grasp at all the infamy of exploitation of self. She ventured one or two objections, however, but Zora brushed everything aside.

"Everybody is looking out for himself," she said airily. "I am interested in you, for instance, not for philanthropy's sake, but because I am lonely, and you are charming and pretty and don't get tired of hearing me talk. You'd better come and live with me awhile, my dear, six months or a year. It doesn't cost any more for two than for one, and you can always leave when we get tired of each other. A girl like you can always get a job. If you are worried about being dependent you can pose for me and design my frocks, and oversee Julienne"—her maid-of-all-work—"I'm sure she's a stupendous robber."

Amy came, not at all overwhelmed by the good luck of it—good luck was around the corner more or less for everyone, she supposed. Moreover, she was beginning to absorb some of Zora's doctrine—she, too, must look out for herself. Zora *was* lonely, she *did* need companionship; Julienne *was* careless about change and odd blouses and left-over dainties. Amy had her own sense of honor. She carried out faithfully her share of the bargain, cut down waste, renovated Zora's clothes, posed for her, listened to her endlessly and bore with her fitfulness. Zora was truly grateful for this last. She was temperamental but Amy had good nerves and her strong natural inclination to let people do as they wanted stood her in good stead. She was a little stolid, a little unfeeling under her lovely exterior. Her looks at this time belied her—her perfect ivory-pink face, her deep luminous eyes,—very brown they were with purple depths that made one think of pansies—her charming, rather wide mouth, her whole face set in a frame of very soft, very live, brown hair which grew in wisps and tendrils and curls and waves back from her smooth, young forehead. All this made one look for softness and ingenuousness. The ingenuousness was there, but not the softness—except of her fresh, vibrant loveliness.

On the whole then she progressed famously with Zora. Sometimes the latter's callousness shocked her, as when they would go strolling through the streets south of Washing Square. The children, the people all foreign, all dirty, often very artistic, always immensely human, disgusted Zora except for "local color"—she really could reproduce them wonderfully. But she almost hated them for being what they were.

"Br-r-r, dirty little brats!" she would say to Amy. "Don't let them touch me." She was frequently amazed at her protégée's utter indifference to their appearance, for Amy herself was the pink of daintiness. They were turning from MacDougall into Bleecker Street one day and Amy had patted a child—dirty, but lovely—on the head.

"They are all people just like anybody else, just like you and me, Zora," she said in answer to her friend's protest.

"You *are* the true democrat," Zora returned with a shrug. But Amy did not understand her.

Not the least of Amy's services was to come between and the too pressing attention of the men who thronged about her.

"Oh, go and talk to Amy," Zora would say, standing slim and gorgeous in some wonderful evening gown. She was extraordinarily attractive creature, very white and pink, with great ropes of dazzling gold hair, and that look of no-age which only American women possess. As a matter of fact she was thirty-nine, immensely sophisticated and selfish, even Amy thought, a little cruel. Her present mode of living just suited her; she could not stand any condition that bound her, anything at all *exigeant*. It was useless for anyone to try to influence her. If she did not want to talk, she would not.

The men used to obey her orders and seek Amy sulkily at first, but afterwards with considerably more interest. She was so lovely to look at. But they really, as Zora knew, preferred to talk to the older woman, for while with Zora indifference was a role, second nature by now but still a role—with Amy it was natural and she was also trifle shallow. She had the admiration she craved, she was comfortable, she asked no more. Moreover she thought the men, with the exception of Stuart James Wynne, rather uninteresting—they were faddists for the most part, crazy not about art or music, but merely about some phase such s cubism or syncopation.

Wynne, who was much older than the other half-dozen men who weekly paid Zora homage—impressed her by his suggestion of power. He was a retired broker, immensely wealthy (Zora, who had known him since childhood, informed her), very set and purposeful and very polished. He was perhaps fifty-five, widely traveled, of medium height, very white skin and clear frosty blue eyes, with sharp, proud features. He liked Amy from the beginning, her childishness touched him. In particular he admired her pliability—not knowing it was really indifference. He had been married twice; one wife had divorced him, the other had died. Both marriages were unsuccessful owing to his dominant, rather unsympathetic nature. But he had softened considerably with years, though he still had decided views, was glad to see that Amy, in spite of Zora's influence, neither smoked nor drank. He liked her shallowness—she fascinated him.

III

From the very beginning *he* was different form what she had supposed. To start with he was far, far wealthier, and he had, too, a tradition, a family-pride which to Amy was inexplicable. Still more inexplicably he had a race-pride. To his wife this was not only strange but foolish. She was as Zora had once suggested, the true democrat. Not that she preferred the company of her maids, though the reason for this did not lie *per se* in the fact that they were maids. There was simply no common ground. But she was uniformly kind, a trait which had she been older would have irritated her husband. As it was, he saw in it only an additional indication of her freshness, her lack of worldliness which seemed to him the attributes of an inherent refinement and goodness untouched by experience.

He, himself, was intolerant of all people of inferior birth or standing and looked with contempt on foreigners, except the French and English. All the rest were variously "guinerys," "niggers," and "wops," and all of them he genuinely despised and hated, and talked of them with the huge intolerant carelessness characteristic of occidental civilization. Amy was never able to understand it. People were always first and last, just people to her. Growing up as the average colored American girl does grow up, surrounded by types of every hue, color and facial configuration she had had no absolute ideal. She was not even aware that there was one. Wynne, who in his grim way had a keen sense of humor, used to be vastly amused at the artlessness with which she let him know that she did not consider him good-looking. She never wanted him to wear anything but dark blue, or somber mixtures always.

"They take away from that awful whiteness of your skin," she used to tell him, "and deepen the blue of your eyes."

In the main she made no attempt to understand him, as indeed she made no attempt to understand anything. The result, of course, was that such ideas as seeped into her mind stayed there, took growth and later bore fruit. But just at this period she was like a well-cared for, sleek, house-pet, delicately nurtured, velvety, content to let her days pass by. She thought almost nothing of her art just now, except as her sensibilities were jarred by an occasional disharmony. Likewise, even to herself, she never criticized Wynne, except when some act or attitude of his stung. She could never understand why he, so fastidious, so versed in elegance of word and speech, so careful in his surroundings, even down to the last detail of glass and napery, should take such evident pleasure in literature of a certain prurient type. He would get her to read to him, partly because he liked to be read to, mostly because he enjoyed the realism and in a slighter degree because he enjoyed seeing her shocked. Her point of view amused him.

"What funny people," she would say naively, "to do such things." She could not understand the liaisons and intrigues of women in the society novels, such infamy was stupid and silly. If one starved, it was conceivable that one might steal; if one were intentionally injured, one might hit back, even murder; but deliberate nastiness she could not envisage. The stories, after she had read them to him, passed out of her mind as completely as though they had never existed.

Picture the two of them spending three years together with practically no friction. To his dominance and intolerance she opposed a soft and unobtrusive indifference. What she wanted she had, ease, wealth , adoration, love, too, passionate and imperious, but she had never known any other kind. She was growing cleverer also, her knowledge of French was increasing, she was acquiring a knowledge of politics, of commerce and of the big social questions, for Wynne's interests were exhaustive and she did most of his reading for him. Another woman might have yearned for a more youthful companion, but her native coldness kept her content. She did not love him, she had never really loved anybody, but little Cornelius Boldin—he had been such a n enchanting, such a darling baby, she remembered,—her heart contracted painfully when she thought as she did very of ten of his warm softness.

"He must be a big boy now," she would think almost maternally, wondering—once she had been so sure!—if she would ever see him again. But she was very fond of Wynne, and he was crazy over he r just as Zora had predicted. He loaded her with gifts, dresses, flowers, jewels—she amused him because none but colored stones appealed to her.

"Diamonds are so hard, so cold, and pearls are dead," she told him.

Nothing ever came between them, but his ugliness, his hatefulness to dependents. It hurt her so, for she was naturally kind in her careless, uncomprehending way. True, she had left Mrs. Boldin without a word, but she did not guess how completely Mrs. Boldin loved her. She wo uld have been aghast had she realized how stricken her flight had left them. At twenty-two, Amy was still as good, as unspoiled, as pure as a child. Of course with all this she was too unquestioning, too selfish, too vain, but they were all faults of her lovely, lovely flesh. Wynne's intolerance finally got on her nerves. She used to blush for his unkindness. All the servants were colored, but she had long since ceased to think that perhaps she, too, was colored , except when he, by insult toward an employee, overt always at least implied, made her realize his contemptuous dislike and disregard for a dark skin or Negro blood .

"Stuart, how can you say such things?" she would expostulate. "You can't expect a man to stand such language as that." And Wynne would sneer, "A man—you don't consider a nigger a man, do you? Oh, Amy, don't be such a fool. You've got to keep them in their places."

Some innate sense of the fitness of things kept her from condoling outspokenly with the servants, but they knew she was ashamed of her husband's ways. Of course, they left—it seemed to Amy that Peter, the butler, was always getting new "help",—but most of the upper servants stayed, for Wynne paid handsomely and although his orders were meticulous and insistent, the retinue of employees was so large that the individual's work was light.

Most of the servants who did stay on in spite of Wynne's occasional insults had a purpose in view. Callie, the cook, Amy found out, had two children at Howard University—of course she n ever came in contact wit h Wynne—the chauffeur had a crippled sister. Rose, Amy's maid and purveyor of much outside information, was the chief support of her family. About Peter, Amy knew nothing; he was a striking, taciturn man, very competent, who had left the Wynnes' service years before and had returned in Amy's third year. Wynne treated him with comparative respect. But Stephen, the new valet, met with entirely different treatment. Amy's heart yearned toward him, he was like Cornelius, with short sighted, patient eyes, always willing, a little over-eager. Amy recognized him for what he was ; a boy of respectable, ambitious parentage, striving for the means for an education; naturally far above his present calling, yet willing to pass through all this as a means to an end. She questioned Rosa about him.

"Oh , Stephen," Rosa told her, "yes'm, he's workin' for fair. He's got a brother at the Howard's and a sister at Smith's. Yes'm, it do seem a little hard on him, but Stephen, he say, they're both goin' to turn roun' and help him when they get through. That blue silk has a rip in it, Miss Amy, if you was thinkin' of wearin' that. Yes'm, somehow I don't think Steve's very strong, kinda worries like. I guess he's sorta nervous."

Amy told Wynne. "He's such a nice boy, Stuart," she pleaded, "it hurts me to have you so cross with him. Anyway don't call him names." She was both surprised and fightened at the feeling in her that prompted her to interfere. She had held so aloof from other people's interests all these years.

"I *am* colored," she told herself that night. "I feel it inside of me. I must be or I couldn't care so about Stephen. Poor boy, I suppose Cornelius is just like him. I wish Stuart would let him alone. I wonder if all white people are like that. Zora was hard, too, on unfortunate people." She pondered over it a bit. "I wonder what Stuart would say if he knew I was colored?" She lay perfectly still, her smooth brow knitted, thinking hard. "But he loves me," she said to herself still silently. "He'll always love my looks," and she fell to thinking that all the wonderful happenings in her sheltered, pampered life had come to her through her beauty. She reached out an exquisite arm, switched on a light, and picking up a hand-mirror from a dressing-table, fell to studying her face. She was right. It was her chiefest asset. She forgot Stephen and fell asleep.

But in the morning her husband's voice issuing from his dressing-room across the hall, awakened her. She listened drowsily. Stephen, leaving the house the day before, had been met by a boy with a telegram. He had taken it, slipped it in to his pocket, (he was just going to the mail-box) and had forgotten to deliver it until now, nearly twenty-four hours later. She could hear Stuart's storm of abuse—it was terrible, made up as it was of oaths and insults to the boy's ancestry. There was a moment's lull. Then she heard him again.

"If your brains are a fair sample of that black wench of a sister of yours—"

She sprang up then thrusting her arms as she ran into her pink dressing-gown. She got there just in time. Stephen, his face quivering, was standing looking straight in to Wynne's smoldering eyes. In spite of herself, Amy was glad to see the boy's bearing. But he did not notice her.

"You devil!" he was saying. "You white faced devil! I'll make you pay for that!" He raised his arm. Wynne did not blench.

With a scream she was between them. "Go, Stephen, go,—get out of the house. Where do you think you are? Don't you know you'll be hanged, lynched, tortured?" Her voice shrilled at him.

Wynne tried to thrust aside her arms that clung and twisted. But she held fast till the door slammed behind the fleeing boy.

"God, let me by, Amy!" As suddenly as she had clasped him she let him go, ran to the door, fastened it and threw the key out the window.

He took her by the arm and shook her. "Are you mad? Didn't you hear him threaten me, me,—a nigger threaten me?" His voice broke with anger, "And you're letting him get away! Why, I'll get him. I'll set bloodhounds on him, I'll have every white man in this town after him! He'll be hanging so high by midnight—" he made for the other door, cursing, half-insane.

How, *how* could she keep him back! She hated her weak arms with their futile beauty! She sprang toward him. "Stuart, wait," she was breathless and sobbing. She said the first thing that came into her head. "Wait, Stuart, you cannot do this thing." She thought of Cornelius—suppose it had been he—"Stephen,—that boy,—he is my brother."

He turned on her. "What!" he said fiercely, then laughed a short laugh of disdain. "You are crazy," he said roughly, "My God, Amy! How can you even in jest associate yourself with these people? Don't you suppose I know a white girl when I see one? There's no use in telling a lie like that."

Well, there was no help for it. There was only one way. He had turned back for a moment, but she must keep him many moments—an hour. Stephen must get out of town.

She caught his arm again. "Yes," she told him, "I did lie. Stephen is not my brother, I never saw him before." The light of relief that crept into his eyes did not escape her, it only nerved her. "But I *am* colored," she ended.

Before he could stop her she had told him all about the tall white woman. "She took me to Mrs. Boldin's and gave me to her to keep. She would never have taken me to her if I had been white. If you lynch this boy, I'll let the world, your world, know that your wife is a colored woman."

He sate down like a man suddenly stricken old, his face ashen. "Tell me about it again," he commanded. And she obeyed, going mercilessly into every damning detail.

IV

Amazingly her beauty availed her nothing. If she had been an older woman, if she had had Zora's age and experience, she would have been able to gauge exactly her influence over Wynne. Through even then in similar circumstances she would have taken the risk and acted in just the same manner. But she was a little bewildered at her utter miscalculation. She had though he might not wasn't his friends—his world by which he set such store—to know that she was colored, but she had not dreamed it could make any real difference to him. He had chosen her, poor and ignorant, out of a host of women, and had told her countless times of his love. To herself Amy Wynne was in comparison with Zora for instance, stupid and uninteresting. But his constant, unsolicited iterations had made her accept his idea.

She was just the same woman she told herself, she had not changed, she was still beautiful, still charming, still "different." Perhaps that very difference had its being in the fact of her mixed blood. She had been his wife—there were memories—she could not see how he could give her up. The suddenness of the divorce carried her off her feet. Dazedly she left him—thought almost without a pang for she had only like him. She had bee perfectly honest about this, and he, although consume by the fierceness of his emotion toward her, had gradually forced himself to be content, for at least she had never made him jealous. She was to live in a small house of his in New York, up town in the 80's. Peter was in charge and there were a new maid and a cook. the servants, of course, knew od the separation, but nobody guess why/ She was living on a much smaller basis than the one to which she had become so accustomed in the last three years. But she was very comfortable. She felt, at any rate she manifested, no qualms at receiving alimony from Wynne. That was the way things happened, she supposed when she thought of it at all. Moreover, it seemed to her perfectly in keeping with Wynne's former attitude toward her; she did not see how he could do less. She expected people to be consistent. That was why she was so amazed that he in spite of his oft iterated love, could let her go. If she had felt half the love for him which he had professed for her, she would not have sent him away if she had been a leper.

"Why I'd stay with him," she told herself, "If he were one, even as I feel now."

She was lonely in New York. Perhaps it was the first time in her life that she had felt so. Zora had gone to Paris the first of the year of her marriage and had not come back.

The days dragged on emptily. One thing helped her. She had gone one day to the modiste from whom she had bought her trousseau. The woman remembered her perfectly—"The lady with the exquisite taste for colors—ah, madame, but you have the rare gift." Amy was grateful to be taken out of her thoughts. She bought one of two daring but altogether lovely creations and let fall a few suggestions:

"That brown frock, Madame,—you say it has been on your hands a long time? Yes? But no wonder. See, instead of that dead white you should have a shade of ivory, that white cheapens it." Deftly she caught up a bit of ivory satin and worked out her idea. Madame was ravished.

"But yes, Madame Wen is correct,—as always. Oh, what a pity that the Madame is so wealthy. If she were only a poor girl—Mlle. Antoine with the best eye for color in the place has just left, gone back to France to nurse her brother—this World War is of such horror! If someone like Madame, now, could be found, to take the little Antoine's place!"

Some obscure impulse drove Amy to accept the half proposal: "Oh! I don't know, I have nothing to do just now. My husband is abroad." Wynne had left her with that impression. "I could contribute the money to the Red Cross or to charity."

The work was the best thing in the world for her. It kept her from becoming too introspective, though even then she did more serious, connected thinking than she had done in all the years of her varied life.

She missed Wynne definitely, chiefly as a guiding influence for she had rarely planned even her own amusements. Her dependence on him had been absolute. She used to picture him to herself as he was before the trouble—and his changing expressions as he looked at her, of amusement, interest, pride, a certain little teasing quality that used to come into his eyes, which always made her adopt her "spoiled child air," as he used to call it. It was the way he liked her best. Then last, there was that look he had given her the morning she had told him she was colored—it had depicted so many emotions, various and yet distinct. There were dismay, disbelief, coldness, a final aloofness.

There was another expression, too, that she thought of sometimes—the look on the face of Mr. Packard, Wynne's lawyer. She, herself, had attempted no defense.

"For God's sake why did you tell him, Mrs. Wynne?" Packard asked her. His curiosity got the better of him. "You couldn't have been in love with that yellow rascal," he blurted out. "She's too cold really, to love anybody," he told himself. "If you didn't care about the boy why should you have told?"

She defended herself feebly. "He looked so like little Cornelius Boldin," she replied vaguely, "and he couldn't help being colored." A clerk came in then and Packard said no mare. But into his eyes had crept a certain reluctant respect. She remembered the look, but could not define it.

She was so sorry about the trouble now, she wished it had never happened. Still if she had it to repeat she would act in the same way again. "There was nothing else for me to do," she used to tell herself.

But she missed Wynne unbelievably.

If it had not been for Peter, he life would have been almost that of a nun. But Peter, who read the papers and kept abreast of the times, constantly called her attention with all due respect, to the meetings, the plays, the sights which she ought to attend or see. She was truly grateful to him. She was very kind to all three of the servants. They had the easiest "places" in New York, the maids used to tell their friends. As she never entertained, and frequently dined out, they had a great deal of time off.

She had been separated from Wynne for ten months before she began to make any definite plans for her future. Of course, she could not go on like this always. It came to her suddenly that probably she would go to Paris and live there—why or how she did not know. Only Zora was there and lately she had begun to think that her life was to be like Zora's. They had been amazingly parallel up to this time. Of course she would have to wait until after the war.

She sat musing about it one day in the big sitting-room which she had had fitted over into a luxurious studio. There was a sewing-room off to the side from which Peter used to wheel into the room waxen figures of all colorings and contours so hat she could drape the various fabrics about them to be sure of the bext results. But today she was working out a scheme for one of Madame's customers, who was of her own color and size and she was her own lay-figure. She sat in front of the huge pier glass, a wonderful soft yellow silk draped about her radiant loveliness.

"I could do some serious work in Paris," she said half aloud to herself. "I suppose if I really wanted to, I could be very successful along this line."

Somewhere downstairs and electric bell buzzed, at first softly then after a slight pause, louder, and more insistently.

"If Madame send me that lace today," she was thinking, idly, "I could finish this and start on the pink. I wonder why Peter doesn't answer the bell."

She remembered then that Peter had gone to New Rochelle on business and she had sent Ellen to Altman's to find a certain rare velvet and had allowed Mary to go with her. She would dine out, she told them, so they need not hurry. Evidently she was alone in the house.

Well she could answer the bell. She had done it often enough in the old days at

Mrs. Boldin's. Of course it was the lace. She smiled a bit as she went down stairs thinking how surprised the delivery-boy would be to see her arrayed thus early in the afternoon. She hoped he wouldn't go. She could see him through the long, thick panels of glass in the vestibule and front door. He was just turning about as she opened the door.

This was no delivery-boy, this man whose gaze fell on her hungry and avid. This was Wynne. She stood for a second leaning against the door-lamb, a strange figure surely in the sharp November weather/ Some leaves—brown, skeleton shapes—rose and swirled unnoticed about her head. A passing letter-carrier looked at them curiously.

"What are you doing answering the door?" Wynne asked her roughly. "Where is Peter? Go in, you'll catch cold."

She was glad to see him. She took him into the drawing room—a wonderful study in browns—and looked at him and looked at him.

"Well," he asked her, his voice eager in spite of the commonplace words, "are you glad to see me? Tell me what do you do with yourself."

She could not talk fast enough, her eyes clinging to his face. Once it struck her that he had changed in some indefinable way. Was it a slight coarsening of that refined aristocratic aspect? Even in her sub-consciousness she denied it.

He had come back to her.

"So I design for Madame when I feel like it, and send the money to the Red Cross and wonder when you are coming back to me." For the first time in their acquaintanceship she was conscious deliberately of trying to attract, to hold him. She put on her spoiled child air which had once been so successful.

"It took you long enough to get here," she pouted. She was certain of him now. His mere presence assured her.

They sat silent a moment, the later November sun bathing her head in an austere glow of chilly gold. As she sat there in the big brown chair she was, in her yellow dress, like some mysterious emanation, some wraith-like aura developed from the tone of her surroundings.

He rose and came toward her, still silent. She grew nervous, and talked incessantly with sudden unusual gestures. "Oh, Stuart, let me give you tea. It's right there in the pantry off the dining-room. I can wheel the table in." She rose, a lovely creature in her yellow robe. He watched her intently.

"Wait," he bade her.

She paused almost on tiptoe, a dainty golden butterfly.

"You are coming back to live with me?" he asked her hoarsely.

For the first time in her life she loved him.

"Of course I am coming back," she told him softly. "Aren't you glad? Haven't you missed me? I didn't see how you could stay away. Oh! Stuart, what a wonderful ring!"

For he had slipped on her finger a heavy dull gold band, with an immense sapphire in an oval setting—a beautiful thing of Italian workmanship.

"It is so like you to remember," she told him gratefully. "I love colored stones."

She admired it, turning it around and around on her slender finger.

How silent he was, standing there watching her with his somber yet eager gaze. It made her troubled, uneasy. She cast about for something to say.

"You can't think how I've improved since I saw you, Stuart. I've read all sorts of books—Oh! I'm learned," she smiled at him. "And Stuart," she went a little closer to him, twisting the button on his perfect coat, "I'm so sorry about it all,—about Stephen, that boy you know. I just couldn't help interfering. But when we're married again, if you'll just remember how it hurts me to have you so cross—"

He interrupted her. "I wasn't aware that I spoke of our marrying again," he told her, his voice steady, his blue eyes cold.

She thought he was teasing. "Why you just asked me to. You said 'aren't you coming back to live with me—'"

"Yes," he acquiesced, "I said just that—'to live with me'."

Still she didn't comprehend. "But what do you mean?" she asked bewildered.

"What do you suppose a man means," he returned deliberately, "when he asks a woman to live with him, but not to marry him?"

She sat down heavily in the brown chair, all glowing ivory and yellow against its somber depths.

"Like the women in those awful novels?" she whispered. "Not like those women!—Oh Stuart! you don't mean it!" Her heart was numb.

"But you must care a little—" she was amazed at her own depth of feeling. "Why I care—there are all those me memories back of us—you must want me really—"

"I do want you," he told her tensely. "I want you damnably. But—well—I might as well out with it—A white man like me simply doesn't marry a colored woman. After all what difference need it make to you? We'll live abroad—you'll travel, have all the things you love. Many a white woman would envy you." He stretched out an eager hand.

She evaded it, holding herself aloof as though his touch were contaminating. Her movement angered him.

Like a rending veil suddenly the veneer of his high polish cracked and the man stood revealed.

"Oh, hell!" he snarled at her roughly. "Why don't you stop posing? What do you think you are anyway? Do you suppose I'd take you for my wife—what do you think can happen to you? What man of your own race could give you what you want? You don't suppose I am going to support you this way forever, do you? The court imposed no alimony. You've got to come to it sooner or later—you're bound to fall to some white man. What's the matter—I'm not rich enough?"

Her face flamed at that—"As though it were *that* that mattered!"

He gave her a deadly look. "Well, isn't it? Ah, my girl, you forget you told me you didn't love me when you married me. You sold yourself to me then. Haven't I reason to suppose you are waiting for a higher bidder?"

At these words something in her died forever, her youth, her happy, happy blindness. She saw life leering mercilessly in her face. It seemed to her that she would give all her future to stamp out, to kill the contempt in his frosty insolent eyes. In a sudden rush of savagery she struck him, struck him across his hateful sneering mouth with the hand which wore his ring.

As *she* fell, reeling under the fearful impact of his brutal but involuntary blow, her mind caught at, registered two things. A little thin stream of blood was trickling across his chin. She had cut him with the ring, she realized with a certain savage satisfaction. And there was something else which she must remember, which she *would* remember if only she could fight her way out of this dreadful clinging blackness, which was bearing down upon her—closing her in.

When she came to she sat up holding her bruised, aching head in her palms, trying to recall what it was that had impressed her so.

Oh, yes, her very mind ached with the realization. She lay back again on the floor, prone, anything to relieve that intolerable pain. But her memory, her thoughts went on.

"Nigger," he had called her as she fell, "nigger, nigger," and again, "nigger."

"He despised me absolutely," she said to herself wonderingly, "Because I was colored. And yet he wanted me."

V

Somehow she reached her room. Long after the servants had come in, she lay face downward across her bed, thinking. How she hated Wynne, how she hated herself! And for ten months she had been living off his money although in no way had she a claim on him. Her whole body burned with the shame of it.

In the morning she rang for Peter. She faced him, white and haggard, but if the man noticed her condition, he made no sign. He was, if possible, more imperturbable than ever.

"Peter," she told him, her eyes and voice very steady, "I am leaving this house today and shall never come back."

"Yes, Miss."

"I shall want you to see to the packing and storing of the goods and to send the keys and the receipts for the jewelry and valuables to Mr. Packard in Baltimore."

"Yes, Miss."

"And, Peter, I am very poor now and shall have no money besides what I can make for myself."

"Yes, Miss."

Would nothing surprise him, she wondered dully. She went on "I don't know whether you knew it or not, Peter, but I am colored, and hereafter I mean to live among my own people. Do you think you could find me a little house or a little cottage not too far from New York?"

He had a little place in New Rochelle, he told her, his manner altering not one whit, or better yet his sister had a four room house in Orange, with a garden, if he remembered correctly. Yes, he was sure there was a garden. It would be just the thing for Mrs. Wynne.

She had four hundred dollars of her very own which she had earned by designing f or Madame. She paid the maids a month in advance—they were to stay as long as Peter needed them. She, herself, went to a small hotel in Twenty-eighth Street, and here Peter came for her at the end of ten days, with the acknowledgement of the keys and receipts from Mr. Packard. Then he accompanied her to Orange and installed her in her new home.

"I wish I could afford to keep you, Peter," she said a little wistfully, "but I am very poor. I am heavily in debt and I must get that off my shoulders at once."

Mrs. Wynne was very kind, he was sure; he could think of no one with whom he would prefer to work. Furthermore, he of ten ran down from New Rochelle to see his sister; he would come in from time to time, and in the spring would plant the garden if she wished.

She hated to see him go, but she did not dwell long on that. Her only thought was to work and work and work and save until she could pay Wynne back. She had not lived very extravagantly during those ten months and Peter was a perfect manager—in spite of her remonstrances he had given her every month an account of his expenses. She had made arrangements with Madame to be her regular designer. The French woman guessing that more than whim was behind this move drove a very shrewd bargain, but even then the pay was excellent. With care, she told herself, she could be free within two years, three at most.

She lived a dull enough existence now, going to work steadily every morning and getting home late at night. Almost it was like those early days when she had first left Mrs. Boldin, except that now she had no high sense of adventure, no expectation of great things to come, which might buoy her up. She no longer thought of phases and the proper setting for her beauty. Once indeed catching sight of her face late one night in the mirror in her tiny work-room in Orange, she stopped and scanned herself, loathing what she saw there.

"You *thing!*" she said to the image in the glass, "if you hadn't been so vain, so shallow!" And she had struck herself violently again and again across the face until her head ached.

But such fits of passion were rare. She had a curious sense of freedom in these days, a feeling that at last her brain, her senses were liberated from some hateful clinging thralldom. Her thoughts were always busy. She used to go over that last scene with Wynne again and again trying to probe the inscrutable mystery which she felt was at the bottom of the affair. She groped her way toward a solution, but always something stopped her. Her impulse to strike, she realized, and his brutal rejoinder had been actuated by something more than mere sex antagonism, there was *race* antagonism there—two elements clashing. That much she could fathom. But that he despising her, hating her for not being white should yet desire her! It seemed to her that his attitude toward her—hate and yet desire, was the attitude in microcosm of the whole white world toward her own, toward that world to which those few possible strains of black blood so tenuously and yet so tenaeciously linked her.

Once she got hold of a big thought. Perhaps there *was* some root, some racial distinction woven in with the stuff of which she was formed which made her persistently kind and unexacting. And perhaps in the same way this difference, help-lessly, inevitably operated in making Wynne and his kind, cruel or at best indiffer-ent. Her reading for Wynne reacted to her thought—she remembered the grating insolence of white exploiters in foreign lands, the wrecking of African villages, the destruction of homes in Tasmania. She couldn't imagine where Tasmania was, but wherever it was, it had been the realest thing in the world to its crude inhabitants.

Gradually she reached a decision. There were two divisions of people in the world—on the one hand insatiable desire for power; keenness, mentality; a vast and cruel pride. On the other there was ambition, it is true, but modified, a certain humble sweetness, too much inclination to trust, an unthinking, unswerving loy-alty. All the advantages in the world accrued to the first division. But without bit-terness she chose the second. She wanted to be colored, she hoped she was colored. She wished even that she did not have to take advantage of her appearance to earn her living. But that was to meet an end. After all she had contracted her debt with a white man, she would pay him with a white man's money.

The years slipped by—four of them. One day a letter came from Mr. Packard. Mrs. Wynne had sent him the last penny of the sum received from Mr. Wynne from February to November, 1914. Mr. Wynne had refused to touch the money, it was and would be indefinitely at Mrs. Wynne's disposal.

She never even answered the letter. Instead she dismissed the whole inci-dent,—Wynne and all,—from her mind and began to plan for her future. She was free, free! She had paid back her sorry debt with labor, money and anguish. From now on she could do as she pleased. Almost she caught herself saying "something is going to happen." But she checked herself, she hated her old attitude.

But something *was* happening. Insensibly from the moment she knew of her deliverance, her thoughts turned back to a stifled hidden longing, which had lain, it seemed to her, an eternity in her heart. Those days with Mrs. Boldin! At night,—on her way to New York,—in the workrooms,—her mind was busy with little intimate pictures of that happy, wholesome, unpretentious life. She could see Mrs. Boldin, clean and portly, in a lilac chambray dress, upbraiding her for some trifling, yet exasperating fault. And Mr. Boldin, immaculate and slender, with his noticeably polished air—how kind he had always been, she remembered. And lastly, Corne-lius; Cornelius in a thousand attitudes and engaged in a thousand occupations, brown and near-sighted and sweet—devoted to his pretty sister, as he used to call her; Cornelius, who used to come to her as a baby as willingly as to his mother; Cornelius spelling out colored letters on his blocks, pointing to them stickily with a brown, perfect finger; Cornelius singing like an angel in his breathy, sexless voice and later murdering everything possible on his terrible cornet. How had she ever been able to leave them all and the dear shabbiness of that home! Nothing, she re-alized, in all these years had touched her inmost being, had penetrated to the core of her cold heart like the memories of those early, misty scenes.

One day she wrote a letter to Mrs. Boldin. She, the writer, Madame A. Wynne, had come across a young woman, Amy Kildare, who said that as a girl she had run away from home and now she would like to come back. But she was ashamed to write. Madame Wynne had questioned the girl closely and she was quite sure that this Miss Kildare had in no way incurred shame or dis grace. It had been some time since Madame Wynne had seen the girl but if Mrs. Boldin wished, she would try to find her again—perhaps Mrs. Boldin would like to get in touch with her. The letter ended on a tentative note.

The answer came at once. My dear Madame Wynne:

My mother told me to write you this letter. She says even if Amy Kildare had done something terrible, she would want her to come home again. My father says so too. My mother says, please find her as soon as you can and tell her to come back. She still misses her. We all miss her. I was a little boy when she left, but though I am in the High School now and play in the school orchestra, I would rather see her than do anything I know. If you see her, be sure to tell her to come right away. My mother says thank you.

Yours respectfully,
CORNELIUS BOLDIN.

The letter came to the modiste's establishment in New York. Amy read it and went with it to Madame. "I have had wonderful news," she told her, "I must go away immediately, I can't come back—you may have these last two weeks f or nothing." Madame, who had surmised long since the separation, looked curiously at the girl's flushed cheeks, and decided that "Monsieur Ween" had returned. She gave her fatalistic shrug. All Americans were crazy.

"But, yes, Madame,—if you must go—absolument."

When she reached the ferry, Amy looked about her searchingly. "I hope I'm seeing you for the last time—I'm going home, home!" Oh, the unbelievable kindness! She had left them without a word and they still wanted her back!

Eventually she got to Orange and to the little house. She sent a message to Peter's sister and set about her packing. But first she sat down in the little house and looked about her. She would go home, home—how she loved the word, she would stay there a while, but always there was life, still beckoning. It would beckon forever she realized to her adventurousness. Afterwards she would set up an establishment of her own,—she reviewed possibilities—in a rich suburb, where white women would pay and pay for her expertness, caring nothing f or realities, only for externals.

"As I myself used to care," she sighed. Her thoughts flashed on. "Then some day I'll work and help with colored people—the only ones who have really cared for and wanted me." Her eyes blurred.

She would never make any attempt to find out who or what she was. If she were white, there would always be people urging her to keep up the silliness of racial prestige. How she hated it all!

"Citizen of the world, that's what I'll be. And now I'll go home."

Peter's sister's little girl came over to be with the pretty lady whom she adored.

"You sit here, Angel, and watch me pack," Amy said, placing her in a little arm-chair. And the baby sat there in silent observation, one tiny leg crossed over the other, surely the quaintest, gravest bit of bronze, Amy thought, that ever lived.

"Miss Amy cried," the child told her mother afterwards.

Perhaps Amy did cry, but if so she was unaware. Certainly she laughed more happily, more spontaneously than she had done for years. Once she got down on her knees in front of the little arm-chair and buried her face in the baby's tiny bosom.

"Oh Angel, Angel," she whispered, "do you suppose Cornelius still plays on that cornet?"

5.17.2 Reading and Review Questions

1. The story opens with Amy in a dressmaker's shop trying on a new and expensive gown. What does the story's fascination with costume suggest about Amy's racial identity?

2. How does Fauset's treatment of Amy's "awakening" compare to the presentation of race in the work of Nella Larsen and Zora Neale Hurston?

3. Compare and contrast Amy's relationships with other women in the story.

5.18 ZORA NEALE HURSTON

(1891 - 1960)

Zora Neale Hurston was born in 1891 in Alabama, moving with her family when she was a young child to Eatonville, Florida, one of the nation's first all-black towns. Hurston enjoyed a happy childhood in Eatonville. In 1904, however, Hurston's idyllic young life came to an end when her mother died. Hurston's father soon remarried, and family life for Hurston became complicated. She moved frequently, living with relatives and working to support herself. Even-

Image 5.16 | Zora Neale Hurston, circa 1935
Photographer | Unknown
Source | Wikimedia Commons
License | Public Domain

tually, she attended Howard University where she nurtured her writing talent. She later attended Barnard College where she studied anthropology, earning her bachelor's degree in 1928. In the 1920s, Hurston became one of the most important figures of the Harlem Renaissance, producing a number of literary pieces and working with Langston Hughes to launch a literary magazine that promoted the talents of young African-American writers. In the 1930s, Hurston enjoyed one of her most productive decades. She conducted anthropological fieldwork across the South, studying African-American folklore, and she traveled in Haiti and Jamaica, where she conducted research on spiritual practices including hoodoo and voodoo. Her book *Mules and Men*, published in 1935, remains an important work on African-American folklore. In 1937, she published her most well-known novel, *Their Eyes Were Watching God*, an early African-American feminist work that inspired later writers such as Alice Walker. During the next twenty years, Hurston continued to work as a journalist and a freelance writer. She married twice, but each marriage ended. By the time of her death, she was living in Florida in relative obscurity and poverty, dying of a stroke in 1960.

Unlike her contemporaries, Richard Wright and Ralph Ellison, Hurston in her fiction did not take on overtly political or racial themes. Like many artists in the Harlem Renaissance in the 1920s, Hurston's art was essentially apolitical. Hurston's work celebrated racial pride and African-American culture without any filtering, and characters' power came from their own self-discoveries and their own inner resources. In her most critically acclaimed novel, *Their Eyes Were Watching God*, the main character Janie Crawford comes of age, moving from a young girl taught by her grandmother that she must be cared for by a man to a young woman trapped in an abusive marriage to a self-actualized woman who loves herself and lives life on her own terms, including freely expressing her sexuality. In "Sweat," Hurston explores a similar theme of self-liberation. Delia Jones, trapped in an abusive marriage to Sykes, a brutal man who beats her and uses her for material gain, finds within herself the power to stand up to him and order him from the home and business she has built through her own sweat. When he plans retribution by exposing Delia to a rattlesnake in her home, she beats him at his own game. Sykes, at the end of the story, sweats for a change.

5.18.1 "Sweat"

Please click the link below to access this selection:
http://wwwi.mcpherson.edu/~claryb/en255/handouts/sweat.pdf

5.18.2 Reading and Review Questions

1. Analyze the title of the story "Sweat." How does the title comment upon the theme of the story?

2. Why does Delia continue to stay with a husband who abuses her?

3. How do the community members react to Sykes's treatment of Delia?

4. How does Delia's discovery of Sykes's bullwhip foreshadow what is to come later in the story?

5. When Delia finally stands up to Sykes and tells him to leave her house, how does he react? Why doesn't he carry through with his threats to hurt her?

6. Why does Delia not attempt to save Sykes? Do you think she will later have regrets?

5.19 NELLA LARSEN

(1891 - 1964)

Image 5.17 | Nella Larsen, 1928
Photographer | James Allen
Source | Wikimedia Commons
License | Public Domain

Nella Larsen is a groundbreaking figure in American history. Trained professionally as both a nurse and a librarian, Larsen is the first African-American to receive a degree from a school of library science in the United States and the first African-American woman to receive a prestigious **Guggenheim Fellowship**. She is also the first African-American author to publish a short story—"Sanctuary," included here—in the esteemed literary magazine, *The Forum*. In the two novels and single short story she published over the course of her brief writing career, Larsen drew upon her personal history of living as a woman on both sides of the color line to explore nothing less than the experience of race, class, gender, and sexuality in the early twentieth century. Larsen was born in Chicago to a Danish immigrant mother and a Caribbean father. After her father abandoned the family, her mother remarried a fellow Dane, leaving Larsen as the only black member of a white household, attending separate schools than her white half-sister, and also living for years in Denmark with her white relatives. Leaving Chicago during her teens, Larsen enrolled in the racially segregated high school associated with Fisk University and then worked as head nurse of the Tuskeegee Institute's School of Nursing. However, she chafed at what she saw as the limited mission and puritanical culture of these black institutions, even criticizing them in her loosely autobiographical novel, *Quicksand* (1928).

Moving to Harlem with her husband in 1920 and taking a job at the New York Public Library on 135th Street, Larsen found a more satisfactory model for black American culture in the historic neighborhood's music and literary scene. In her first novel, *Quicksand*, Larsen uses her experiences growing up in a mixed-race home, working in fabled black institutions, and living in Denmark and Harlem to represent the often cruel vagaries of racial identification and class division. In her second novel, *Passing* (1929), Larsen writes about two light-skinned Afriimmigrant mother and a Caribbean father. After her father abandoned the family, her mother remarried a fellow Dane, leaving Larsen as the only black member of a white household, attending separate schools than her white half-sister, and also living for years in Denmark with her white relatives. Leaving Chicago during her teens, Larsen enrolled in the racially segregated high school associated with Fisk University and then worked as head nurse of the Tuskeegee Institute's School of Nursing. However, she chafed at what she saw as the limited mission and puritanical culture of these black institutions, even criticizing them in her loosely autobiographical novel, *Quicksand* (1928).

Moving to Harlem with her husband in 1920 and taking a job at the New York Public Library on 135th Street, Larsen found a more satisfactory model for black American culture in the historic neighborhood's music and literary scene. In her first novel, *Quicksand*, Larsen uses her experiences growing up in a mixed-race home, working in fabled black institutions, and living in Denmark and Harlem to represent the often cruel vagaries of racial identification and class division. In her second novel, *Passing* (1929), Larsen writes about two light-skinned African-American childhood friends, one of whom grows up to hide her race, pass as a white woman, and marry into a wealthy white family. The other embraces her black community yet secretly indulges in passing as well. Through the tale of these two women's lives passing through different races and social classes, Larsen not only illuminates the workings of race and class in America but also the bonds of female friendship and sexuality.

After publishing two successful novels and winning a Guggenheim, the publication of "Sanctuary" in *The Forum* should have been another step upwards in Larsen's career. Instead, it embroiled Larsen in controversy and was the last thing she ever published. Readers of Larsen's tale pointed out great similarities between it and a story published eight years earlier by Sheila Kaye-Smith, "Mrs. Adis." Both stories have the same plot, similar dialogue, and the same ironic ending. However, Kaye-Smith's story takes place in Sussex, England, and features two white working-class characters. Larsen's similarly-plotted tale takes place in the American South and features two black working-class characters. While both Larsen and the editors of *The Forum* defended the story, Larsen could not find a publisher for the novel she wrote during her Guggenheim fellowship. She divorced her husband for infidelity in 1933 and returned to her first career of nursing for the remainder of her life.

5.19.1 "Sanctuary"

Please click the link below to access this selection:

http://eiffel.ilt.columbia.edu/teachers/cluster_teachers/Dick_Parsons/Cluster_2/ Amy's%20web%20Quest/larsen_sanctuary.htm

5.19.2 Reading and Review Questions

1. Discuss why, after criticizing Jim Hammer for being "no 'count trash," Annie Poole still protects him.

5.20 LANGSTON HUGHES

(1902 - 1967)

"We younger Negro artists who create now intend to express our individual dark-skinned selves without fear or shame," Langston Hughes writes in his 1926 manifesto for the younger generation of Harlem Renaissance artists, "The Negro Artist and the Racial Mountain." He continues, "If white people are pleased we are glad. If they are not, it doesn't matter. We know we are beautiful." Celebrated as "the poet laureate of Harlem," Langston Hughes was born in Joplin, Missouri, and traveled extensively before settling in the neighborhood he came to call home. When growing up, Hughes lived variously with his grandmother in Lawrence, Kansas, his father in Mexico, and his mother in Washington, D.C. After just one year at Columbia University, Hughes left college to explore the world, working as a cabin boy on ships bound for Africa and as

Image 5.18 | Langston Hughes, 1936
Photographer | Carl Van Vechten
Source | Wikimedia Commons
License | Public Domain

a cook in a Paris kitchen. Throughout these early years, Hughes published poems in the African-American magazines *The Crisis* and *Opportunity*; these poems soon earned him recognition as a rising star of the Harlem Renaissance who excelled at the lyrical use of the music, speech, and experiences of urban, working-class African-Americans. Hughes published his first book of poetry, *The Weary Blues*, at the age of twenty-four while still a student at Lincoln University in Pennsylvania. Over the course of his long and influential literary career, Hughes worked extensively in all areas of African-American literature, writing novels, short stories, plays, essays, and works of history; translating work by black authors; and editing numerous anthologies of African-American history and culture, such as *The First Book of Jazz* (1955) and *The Best Short Stories by Negro Writers* (1969).

Hughes's poems embody one of the major projects of the Harlem Renaissance: to create distinctively African-American art. By the turn of the twentieth century, African-Americans had awakened to the realization that two hundred years of slavery had simultaneously erased their connections to their African heritage and created, in its wake, new, vital forms of distinctively African-American culture. Accordingly, politicians, authors, and artists associated with the Harlem Renaissance reconstructed that lost history and championed art rooted in the black American experience. Hughes's poems from the 1920s are particularly notable for celebrating black culture while also honestly representing the deprivations of working-class African-American life. In "The Negro Speaks of Rivers," Hughes connects African-American culture to the birth of civilization in Africa and the Middle East. In "Mother to Son," Hughes draws upon the music of the blues and black dialect to celebrate the indomitable heart of working black America. Hughes grew increasingly radicalized in the 1930s following such high-profile examples of American racism as the 1931 Scottsboro trial in Alabama. He travelled to the Soviet Union in 1932 to work on an unfinished film about race in the American South and published in leftist publications associated with the **American Communist Party**, the only political party at the time to oppose segregation. "Christ in Alabama" is a good example of Hughes's more pointed political style, in which the poet criticizes the immorality of racism by equating the suffering of African-Americans in Alabama with the suffering of Christ. Poems such as "I, too," and "Theme for English B," in turn, combine Hughes's provocative politics with his cultural lyricism to articulate a theme that runs throughout his life's work: that the American experience is as black as it is white.

5.20.1 "Christ in Alabama"

Please click the link below to access this selection:

http://xroads.virginia.edu/~ma05/dulis/poetry/Hughes/hughes2.html

5.20.2 "The Negro Speaks of Rivers"

I've known rivers
I've known rivers ancient as the world and older than the flow of human blood in
    human veins.

My soul has grown deep like the rivers.

I bathed in the Euphrates when dawns were young.
I built my hut near the Congo and it lulled me to sleep.
I looked upon the Nile and raised the pyramids above it.
I heard the singing of the Mississippi when Abe Lincoln went down to New
    Orleans, and I've seen its muddy bosom turn all golden in the sunset.

I've known rivers:
Ancient, dusky rivers.

My soul has grown deep like the rivers.

5.20.3 "Theme for English B"

Please click the link below to access this selection:

http://www.eecs.harvard.edu/~keith/poems/English_B.html

5.20.4 Reading and Review Questions

1. What is significant about the rivers—the Euphrates, the Congo, the Nile, and the Mississippi—that Hughes names in "The Negro Speaks of Rivers"?

2. Jesus Christ is often represented as being white in Western art. What does Hughes's identification of Christ as "a nigger" say about the Christians of the segregated American South of the early twentieth century?

3. The semi-autobiographical poem "Theme for English B" was first published in 1946, decades after Hughes attended his one year of college at Columbia "on the hill above Harlem." However, Hughes writes the poem not in the past tense but in the present tense. How does Hughes's use of the present tense affect the meaning of the poem?

5.21 COUNTEE CULLEN

(1903 - 1946)

Image 5.19 | Countee Cullen, 1941
Photographer | Carl Van Vechten
Source | Wikimedia Commons
License | Public Domain

Countee Cullen, one of the most successful writers of the early Harlem Renaissance, was himself a poetic creation. Born sometime around the turn of the twentieth century and raised until his middle teens by a woman who may have been his paternal grandmother, Cullen's academic skills gained him early recognition and entry into New York University, where he graduated with Phi Beta Kappa honors in 1925. Nurtured in the university environment, Cullen published poetry throughout his time at NYU and during his graduate studies at Harvard. While other members of the Harlem Renaissance, like Alain Locke, author of *The New Negro* (1925), advocated for artistic production that embraced distinctly African themes and styles, Cullen was a traditionalist who believed that African-American writers were entitled to the forms of English literature. In the forward to his 1927 collection *Caroling Dusk*, Cullen made his case succinctly: "Negro poets, dependent as they are on the English language, may have more to gain from the rich background of English and American poetry than from any nebulous atavistic yearnings toward an African influence."[6] While Cullen's contemporaries like Langston Hughes argued for a more clearly and uniquely defined African-American literature, Cullen focused on traditional forms in his poetry and drew inspiration from the works of John Keats and A. E. Houseman.

---

6   "Excerpts from Countee Cullen's Forward to Caroling Dusk." *Modern American Poetry Site*. Ed. Cary Nelson and Bartholomew Brinkman. Department of English, University of Illinois at Urbana-Champaign, n.d. Web. 10 July 2015.

Our two selections from Cullen's poetry, "Yet Do I Marvel" and "Heritage," demonstrate both Cullen's command of the historical traditions of English and American poetry and a deep sense of irony regarding his own role as an African-American poet. Both poems were published in 1925 and showcase Cullen's technical skill and his ambivalence. "Yet Do I Marvel," an Italian sonnet in iambic pentameter, uses Cullen's technical skills to remind his audience of the audacity of being a young, well-educated, African-American poet in the early twentieth century. Throughout the poem Cullen creates a sense of irony through the skill with which he interweaves classical references with nods to both John Milton and Percy Bysshe and Mary Shelley only to close with a sense of curiosity that this black poet has been made to sing in classical tones.

"Heritage," also from 1925, uses a longer form to ask essential questions about the relationship between African-American poets and African cultural heritage. From the earliest lines of the poem, Cullen expresses distance from the African heritage embraced by other authors of the Harlem Renaissance. Building on the question, "What is Africa to me?" (10), the poem becomes a meditation on the divided self of the young African-American poet. In "Heritage," Cullen reflects on the tensions inherent in the Harlem Renaissance: that the very education that allows a poet like Cullen to achieve widespread notoriety also exposes cultural barriers among the members of the Harlem Renaissance.

5.21.1 "Heritage"

Please click the link below to access this selection:

http://www.sas.upenn.edu/~jenglish/Courses/Spring02/104/Cullen_Heritage.html

5.21.2 "Yet Do I Marvel"

Please click the link below to access this selection:

http://allpoetry.com/Yet-Do-I-Marvel

5.21.3 Reading and Review Questions

1. Compare and contrast Cullen's views on poetry to those of Langston Hughes.

2. How does Cullen use traditional literary forms to critique the position of African-American poets?

3. Analyze Cullen's portrayal of African, American, and European cultures as those cultures collided during the Harlem Renaissance. How does Cullen's poetry explore these cultural intersections?

5.22 JEAN TOOMER

(1894 - 1967)

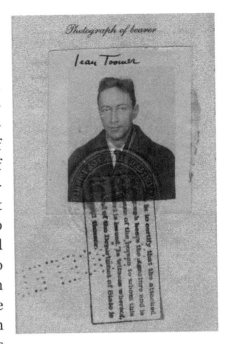

Image 5.20 | Jean Toomer, 1926
Photographer | U.S. State Dept.
Source | Wikimedia Commons
License | Public Domain

Nathan Eugene Toomer, known as Jean, was born in Washington D.C. to a bi-racial father, Nathan Toomer from Georgia, and a bi-racial mother, Nina Pinchback, the daughter of P. B. S. Pinchback, who was the first person of African descent to serve as Governor of Louisiana. Toomer never knew his father, who left the family shortly after Toomer's birth due to conflicts with his father-in-law, and was raised by the Pinchbacks, a well-respected family who had moved from New Orleans to Washington D.C. in order to escape Jim Crow laws. Since Toomer could "pass" as white and lived in an affluent neighborhood, his racial identity was of little consequence for most of his young life. It was not until he was fourteen, when Toomer moved in with his Uncle Bismark in a working-class African-American neighborhood, that Toomer began to experience racial tension of the period. After graduating high school, Toomer left for the University of Wisconsin to study agriculture, where, according to his own unpublished autobiography, he fully realized the stark racial conflicts between blacks and whites. Toomer dropped out of the University of Wisconsin, briefly studied biology at the University of Chicago, and later attended New York University. During this time, Toomer struggled with his own self-identity since he had always been able to pass as white, yet he began to self-identify as African-American.

Toomer held odd jobs in Chicago and New York, while becoming active politically in the Socialist movement and gaining a growing reputation as a writer. However, it was Toomer's year as the principle of an industrial and agricultural school for African-Americans in Sparta, Georgia that became the inspiration for many of the stories in his groundbreaking work, *Cane* (1923). As Toomer developed a growing reputation, publishing in notable places and working with W. E. B. Du Bois as part of the "**talented tenth**" in the Harlem Renaissance, *Cane* became a critical success. However, just as *Cane* began to raise his profile, Toomer began to feel hesitant about identifying as African-American and started withdrawing from public life, abandoning fiction and eventually writing philosophical treatises. *Cane* fell out of favor and was almost nearly a lost work, until it was re-discovered in the 1960s and has been highly acclaimed ever since.

Originally published with Boni & Liveright, an avante-garde press of the time, *Cane* is today considered a modernist classic, but it is the only work associated with Toomer. It is hailed not only for its historical significance within the Harlem Renaissance, but also for its experimental form. *Cane* combines poetry, prose, short fiction, and even a play in the three-part book. In the short story "Blood Burning Moon" Toomer combines both poetry and prose. Hence, the book resists genre classification as a novel, a short story collection, or a book of poetry.

Toomer's own racial background became a major theme of his work, especially the conflict between races appearing in short stories such as "Blood Burning Moon." Other themes include the great migration of African-Americans from the rural South to urbanized areas, as well as the juxtaposition of the beautiful imagery of rural America ("Portrait in Georgia") and the containment of the city (or slavery) which appear in works such as "Box Seat" and "Kabnis."

5.22.1 Selections from *Cane*

"Blood Burning Moon"
Please click the link below to access this selection:
   http://english204-dcc.blogspot.com/2011/04/blood-burning-moon-toomer.html

"Portrait in Georgia"
Please click the link below to access this selection:
   https://www.poets.org/poetsorg/poem/portrait-georgia

5.22.2 Reading and Review Questions

1. Why does Toomer include the verses in between sections of "Blood Burning Moon"? What effect does this have on readers? Does it change the meaning of the story?

2. In the short poem "Portrait in Georgia," how does Toomer's conciseness affect readers? What type of images is he using in this poem? Why?

5.23 CHAPTER FIVE KEY TERMS

- American Communist Party
- Armistice
- Arthur Miller
- Countee Cullen
- Cubism
- Dixie Limited
- Dramatic Monologue
- Dust Bowl
- e. e. cummings
- Edna St. Vincent Millay
- Ellen Glasgow
- Epigraph
- Ernest Hemingway
- Eudora Welty

- Jean Toomer
- Jessie Redmon Fauset
- Langston Hughes
- Low Modernism
- "Make It New!"
- Marianne Moore
- Modernism
- Modernist
- Nella Larsen
- Nobel Prize
- Prose
- Pulitzer Prize
- Racial Inequality
- Robert Frost

American Literature Since 1945 (1945 - Present)

Amy Berke, Robert R. Bleil, Jordan Cofer, and Doug Davis

6.1 LEARNING OUTCOMES

After completing this chapter, you should be able to:

- Identify Second Wave writers of the Southern Literary Renaissance
- Explain how the Second Wave of the Southern Literary Renaissance differed from the First Wave
- Describe the impact that World War II had on the Southern Literary Renaissance
- Identify selected writers and works of American literature since 1945
- Interpret, compare and contrast selected works of American literature since 1945
- Describe how selected works represent American culture of the 1940s, 1950s, 1960s, 1970s and beyond
- Explain how literary postmodernism relates to literary modernism
- Describe the postmodern style and sensibility of selected works of American literature since 1945

6.2 INTRODUCTION

Since the end of the Second World War to the present day, the people of the United States of America have witnessed the incredible economic and technological growth of their nation into a global cultural and military superpower. These years of growth also have often been times of radical cultural transformation, during which the nation reassessed its traditions. Americans in this period lived through times of war and times of peace, decades of cultural conformity and decades of social revolt. For the first two decades of this period, Americans lived in a racially segregated nation; they now live in a multicultural nation that has twice elected a black president. For much of this period, Americans lived in a world of ideologically warring superpowers poised on the brink of nuclear annihilation; they now live in a world intimately connected by massive computer networks and a complex global economy, yet one still riven by dangerous religious and economic disputes. In popular culture, Americans' tastes in music have moved from jazz and rock and roll to hip-hop and electronic music. In the visual arts, Americans have seen the explosive canvases of abstract expressionists such as Jackson Pollock become the Campbell's Soup cans of pop artists such as Andy Warhol and then the video screens of cable television's MTV and multimedia artists on YouTube. Their art and entertainment have come to them increasingly through technologies, starting with film and radio, then television, and now the Internet. In the literature of this amazingly transformative era, we find a record of how the nation has known, questioned, and even redefined itself.

When the United States ended the Second World War by dropping atomic bombs on the Japanese cities of Hiroshima and Nagasaki, the nation was well positioned to assume a role of global leadership. While the cities and factories of both its enemies Germany and Japan and its allies Britain and the Soviet Union were destroyed in the war, the continental U.S. was never attacked. The American industries that won the war quickly retooled to win the peace, selling cars, radios, and washing machines within an increasingly global economy and ushering in an era of unparalleled American prosperity. The United States government spent tens of billions of dollars in foreign aid to rebuild its former enemies Germany and Japan, ensuring that they would be both economic and military allies in the future. The **GI Bill** paid for an unprecedented number of young American men to attend colleges and buy homes, creating a huge professional middle class eager to work for the nation's mighty high-tech corporations and live in its swiftly growing new suburbs. The decade and a half following the Second World War is often called the age of conformity, as the nation's large, college-educated middle class embraced the values of the nuclear family and sought happiness, after years of desperate war, in their society's newfound abundance of consumer goods.

Yet the peace was short lived, and there was dissent at home. In the midst of this postwar era of prosperity, Allen Ginsberg composed his great poem "Howl," in which he lambasted the nation's conformist culture for destroying its best and brightest citizens. Authors of the Beat movement of the 1950s such as Ginsberg celebrated America's countercultures and sought to free literature from traditional formalism and align it more closely with the improvisatory musical solos of jazz, the spontaneous drips and splashes of abstract expressionist action painting, and the everyday utterances of the American street. Storytellers of the second wave of the Southern Renaissance resisted America's culture of conformity and embraced their distinctive regionality, with Georgia author Flannery O'Connor lamenting in her essay, "The Fiction Writer and His Country," that the traditional American South was "getting more and more like" the rest of the materialistic, money-hungry nation. Poets during this period, such as Theodore Roethke and Sylvia Plath, began sharing intimate, sometimes disturbing details from their lives in a newly confessional mode of poetry that showed how the nuclear family could be a source of stress as well as stability, ultimately showing the nation how the personal situation of the writer could represent the politics of the nation as a whole.

On the world stage, the Soviet Union organized the Eastern European nations it had conquered during the Second World War into a political bloc dedicated to Russian-led state socialism under which the state owns all businesses and administers all social services as opposed to American-led free-market capitalism, under which private individuals own all businesses. The former allies found themselves competing for the hearts and minds of the world over the value of their respective social systems. When the Soviet Union tested its own atomic bomb in 1949, the U.S. and the Soviet Union entered into a conflict called the **Cold War**. The two enemies proceeded to build tens of thousands of nuclear weapons over the following decades to deter each from attacking the other, accumulating enough atomic bombs to destroy human civilization many times over. The U.S. committed itself to a policy of Soviet containment, checking the influence of the so-called red menace abroad through foreign aid and limited military action, and prosecuting American artists and activists with leftist sympathies at home through such venues as the House Un-American Activities Committee. Some of the authors in this chapter had their careers curtailed during this fearful period because of their political beliefs, as when poet William Carlos Williams was stripped of his consultancy to the Library of Congress in 1952 for once having written a poem titled "Russia."

In addition to grappling with the threats of nuclear war and the red menace, Americans at this time were also grappling with the homegrown injustice of racial segregation. Up until 1965, Americans in many states lived under **Jim Crow** laws that disenfranchised African-Americans, keeping black American citizens socially separate from and legally inferior to white citizens. The civil rights and black power movements of the 1950s and 60s, led by Dr. Martin Luther King and Malcolm X, increasingly showed the nation that the experience of its prosperous, college-educated white middle class was not the experience of all Americans. The often-violent struggle to desegregate America was televised across the nation, unifying the country within a new television culture in the very act of displaying its deep ideological divisions. The works in this chapter by Toni Morrison, James Baldwin, and Ralph Ellison present a good record of what life was like in segregated America and during the civil rights movement.

In 1963, American President John F. Kennedy was assassinated. In 1974, another American president, Richard M. Nixon, resigned from office in disgrace. The tumultuous decade in between these two events is known as the Sixties. During this decade, America was fighting a seemingly endless war of containment in Vietnam. Students on college campuses protested the war and the policies of their own government. Urban populations rioted against racism and economic disparity. Artists and intellectuals radically reassessed America's prosperous postwar era as a culture of one-dimensional organization men trapped in skyscrapers and servile women trapped by what feminist critic Betty Friedan called the feminine mystique. Led by author-activists such as Betty Friedan and Gloria Steinem, women in the 1960s and '70s launched a second wave of feminist political activity, demanding full social and economic equality with men. Poets such as Adrienne Rich embodied the radical politics of their era, composing feminist poems, such as the one by her included in this chapter.

America returned to a Cold War culture of conformity in the decade preceding the collapse of the Soviet Union in 1991. Yet the changes the Sixties had wrought in the nation's culture were permanent. From the time of the civil rights movement to the present day, American writers have increasingly come to see the U.S. as being home to several different kinds of Americans—African-Americans, Native Americans, Asian Americans, Straight Americans, Queer Americans—each with their own unique experience of life in America. The civil rights and feminist movements of the 1960s and 1970s were followed by the gay rights and multicultural movements of the 1980s, 1990s, and early twenty-first century. Western culture itself became more welcoming of difference after the fall of the Soviet Union and the end of the Cold War as the nations of Europe cast aside millennia of enmities and joined in a European Union, sharing a common currency, the Euro, and a common economic fate. While the terrorist attacks of September 11, 2001 illustrated how economically and technologically connected the world had become, they also drove home how socially and ideologically divided it remains in the early twenty-first century.

America's growing multicultural sensibility and tolerance of diversity has been both empowering and challenging, reflecting new kinds of political identity that often conflict with Americans' senses of who they are. Beholding the diversity within America, authors of the 1960s once worried about the "death of the novel." It no longer felt possible for a single story to represent the American experience as a whole. Back in 1949, Arthur Miller's salesman Willy Loman in his play, *Death of a Salesman*, could stand on stage as an American Everyman dreaming the American dream. Yet Willy's life is far from representative of every life in America, starting with the lives of every American woman and extending to every member of an American minority. American authors of the following decades began to represent America multiculturally as a nation of indigenous peoples and immigrants from other lands. The short stories by Alice Walker and Leslie Marmon Silko are good examples of multicultural literature. Silko draws specifically on her Native American heritage while Alice Walker shows us the tensions that arise as her characters negotiate an identity that is grounded in both Africa and America.

The changes that the nation has undergone since 1945 have often been disorienting, a disorientation that is reflected in Donald Barthleme's story, also found in this chapter, "The School," in which the reader struggles to make sense of all the odd and terrible things that happen in Barthleme's average American school. The United States has remained an economic and cultural global superpower since 1945, but the politics of both the nation and the world during this time have been radically in flux, seeing the rise and fall of global empires, the emergence of new social justice movements, and the creation of new senses of national identity. Science and technology, so important to winning the Second World War, have penetrated more and more parts of American society. The computer has been the most influential invention of the era, changing the way Americans both work and play. The media of the book, radio, and film have been joined by the new media of the television and computer screen, giving Americans since 1945 an overwhelming variety of often contradictory ways to know themselves, their fellow citizens, and their world.

With so many media in which to see, know, and communicate with one another, Americans in the final decades of the twentieth century developed a growing sense of the "textuality" of experience, the recognition that their lives are increasingly lived through signs and images seen on life's many screens, that videos and computer simulations have become an indispensable part of, and perhaps have even taken the place of, their reality. This sensibility is reflected in the transition from literary modernism to Postmodernism during this period. You will read more about this transition later in this chapter. Postmodernist authors such as Barthleme playfully use all the experimental literary techniques developed by the modernists in the first half of the century to represent the many lives Americans live in the century's second half and beyond. The characters in Don DeLillo's 1985 postmodernist novel *White Noise* anticipate the twenty-first century's obsession with social media as they realize that the many photographs of "the most photographed barn in America" are more real than the actual barn being photographed. David Foster Wallace's "maximalist" essay "Consider the Lobster" likewise represents the information overload Americans experience in the twenty-first century, his many footnotes creating a hyperlinked, postmodern style of prose that reflects the superabundance of information available on the Internet.

American literature since 1945 has seen the rise of countercultural Beats and the confessional poets. It contains the voices of radical feminists, conservative regionalists, and proud multiculturalists. It presides over the reinvention of America as its modernist storytellers of one American experience now stand beside the postmodernist storytellers of many American experiences. In all these ways and more, the American writers who lived through the extraordinary era since 1945 present us with an insightful record of what their nation and its people once were, of what they are, and of what they may become.

6.3 SOUTHERN LITERARY RENAISSANCE - SECOND WAVE (1945-1965)

While the first wave of Southern writers were writing with an agenda, in reaction to H.L. Menken's claims that the South could not produce great art, the Post-1945 Southern writers came of age under the spell of the a group of writers studying at Vanderbilt University who named themselves the Agrarians (John Crow Ransom, Allen Tate, Robert Penn Warren, Andrew Lytle, etc) as well as several commercially successful Southern writers such as William Faulkner. In turn, they internalized a story telling tradition that was already on-going. These Second Wave writers had concerns of their own, as the South, along with the rest of the World, entered the **Cold War,** in the post **World War II** period. Yet, while the South tried to keep pace with a changing world, Southern literature continued to produce some of the most innovative, critically acclaimed work of the time period. Eudora Welty's debut novel, *The Robber Bridegroom* (1942), gained national attention for her as a short story writer who had already won back-to-back O. Henry awards, including one for her well anthologized short story, "A Worn Path." Carson McCullers was the literary "wunderkind" who exploded onto the national spotlight at the age of twenty-three with her debut novel, *The Heart is a Lonely Hunter* (1940). Flannery O'Connor emerged as the super star of the Iowa Writer's Workshop, winning multiple accolades, including two O. Henry Awards, as her short story "A Good Man Is Hard to Find" (1955) became widely anthologized. Doctor turned lawyer, Walker Percy's debut novel, *The Movie Goer* (1961), won the National Book Award for mixing theology, philosophy, and the Mardi Gras into one beautifully written novel. From Percy to Porter to Peter Taylor, the Southern Literary Renaissance remained strong well after 1945.

6.3.1 The Cold War and the Southern Literary Renaissance

America's war efforts bolstered the national economy, especially in the South, which is home to several military training bases. While the South still suffered from Jim Crow laws and antiquated racial politics, it did offer more progressive roles for women who found themselves taking professional jobs, filling positions vacated by men who had left for war. This shift became a major theme in Katherine Ann Porter's "Miranda" stories. Flannery O'Connor saw such role changes firsthand when she studied at Georgia College for Women where the WAVES (Women Accepted for Voluntary Emergency Services), a female naval reserve unit, were training. As the country continued to change drastically after World War II, the South tried to keep pace.

6.3.2 Economic Prosperity

The post World War II South was positioned for economic prosperity, as soldiers returned home to find more infrastructure and a trained workforce. The rise of the middle class also helped develop major Southern cities, such as Atlanta and Birmingham, into national prominence. The South had finally begun to embrace the shift from agricultural to industrial economy. With a growing middle and professional class, the South began to shake off the image of rural poverty with which it was associated in works such as Erskine Caldwell's *Tobacco Road* and *God's Little Acre* or the influence of Margaret Mitchell's **Gone with the Wind**.

6.3.3 The Civil Rights Movement in the South

Unfortunately, the South's prosperity during this time was marred by its bigotry and antiquated racial politics as many of the South's preeminent African-American authors, such as Richard Wright, James Baldwin, and Ralph Ellison, left the South to escape the antagonism and racism they encountered. As the segregationists dug in their heels, the Civil Rights movement became a major theme of the Southern Literary Renaissance. Although the South was growing, the legacy of racism—as the Civil Rights Movement gained national attention in the 1950s and 1960s—gave the region a national black eye, but also gave birth to the Civil Rights movement, the Black Power movement and the Black Arts movement. A strong literary tradition developed around these movements, giving rise to powerful writers such as Nikki Giovanni and Maya Angelou.

6.3.4 New Criticism and the Rise of the MFA program

One unexpected result of the Southern Literary Renaissance was the creation of the first Southern literary celebrities. This rise to prominence of Southern literary authors coincided with the return of thousands of soldiers entering college for the first time, courtesy of the GI Bill. Suddenly these soldiers were enrolling in creative writing classes, wanting to tell their own stories.

Around this time, the University of Iowa and Stanford University piloted the nation's very first graduate creative writing programs, offering a Masters of Fine Arts (MFA) degree. These creative writing programs, especially the Iowa Writers Workshop, were heavily influenced by the Southern literary celebrities. While Columbia University's writing program featured Thomas Wolfe, the early faculty at the Iowa Writers Workshop included Allen Tate and John Crowe Ransom, while Robert Penn Warren, a professor at Louisiana State University, was a featured speaker on numerous occasions. The instruction at the Iowa Writers Workshop was based upon the textbooks *Understanding Poetry* and *Understanding Fiction,* which were co-written by Warren and Cleanth Brooks, a professor at LSU and co-founder of *The Southern Review.* Through their celebrity, Southern writers exerted national influence over these creative writing programs as well as the early classes of writers who enrolled in these creative writing programs, such as Flannery O'Connor who was a student at the Iowa Writers Workshop from 1945-1948. Additionally, many of the early creative writing textbooks and anthologies featured these Southern writers; for example, Caroline Gordon's *The House of Fiction* was extremely popular in creative writing programs. In fact, the second editions of both *Understanding Fiction* and *The House of Fiction* would feature work from Iowa alum, Flannery O'Connor. Thus, the Southern Literary Renaissance writers continued to exert influence on creative writing, with everyone from Caroline Gordon, Katherine Ann Porter, and even Peter Taylor becoming associated with these programs.

6.3.5 Innovation

Like their predecessors, from whom they learned, the Second Wave of the Southern Literary Renaissance featured writers continuing the legacy of reinvention. Flannery O'Connor's fiction was particularly noteworthy for its marriage of violence, humor, and religious themes, a mixture that amused and baffled readers. On the opposite end of the spectrum, Walker Percy's experiment with blending philosophy and fiction captivated a national audience, while Tennessee Williams revolutionized theater with his hits *A Streetcar Named Desire* (1947) and *Cat on a Hot Tin Roof* (1955), both of which highlighted the complex sexual politics of the South while also capturing its dialect and storytelling tradition.

The Southern Literary Renaissance, much like the South itself, was a diverse movement with wide regional variations. Although it started as reactionary, with the work of the Fugitives, it grew in ways that the original authors of *I'll Take My Stand* could have never predicted, producing some of America's most famous writers and forever changing the way writing was viewed in the United States. After World War II, a new generation of Southern writers took up the cause. While not always responding to Menken, these writers continued the artistry, experimentation, and innovation of the previous generation.

6.4 TENNESSEE WILLIAMS

(1911 - 1983)

Born Thomas Lanier Williams III in Mississippi, Williams later adopted the pen name "Tennessee" after he began his writing career. Williams's early life was fraught with family dysfunction. Williams's father was a shoe salesman who struggled with alcoholism and at times exhibited violent tendencies. Williams's mother, Edwina, covered for her husband's often embarrassing behavior, attempting to maintain a veneer of Southern gentility. Williams and his two siblings, Dakin and Rose, weathered the family

Image 6.1 | Tennessee Williams, 1965
Photographer | Orlando Fernandez
Source | Wikimedia Commons
License | Public Domain

dynamics for a time, until Rose was diagnosed with schizophrenia. After years of treatment proved inadequate, Williams's mother eventually approved a lobotomy for Rose, and after the procedure, the young woman was never the same, spending the rest of her life in an institution. Williams, who was very close to Rose, was tormented about his sister, and many of his plays dealt in some way with the trauma Rose endured. Williams attended college for a time as he developed his writing skills, attempting to garner attention for his work. It was not until the 1940s that Williams enjoyed his first success with *The Glass Menagerie*, which opened in Chicago and eventually made its way to New York and enjoyed a long run on Broadway. Williams followed that success in 1947 with *A Streetcar Named Desire*, one of his most enduring plays. Throughout the 1940s and 1950s, Williams enjoyed a string of successes and saw a number of his plays adapted for film. By 1959, he had won multiple Pulitzer prizes for his work. In the 1930s, Williams had accepted his sexual orientation as a gay man but maintained a private life. In later years, Williams struggled with alcoholism and prescription drug addiction. After the painful loss of his partner of fourteen years, Frank Merlo, Williams faced serious depression, and over the last twenty years of his life, Williams struggled to reignite his writing career while his health and mental state deteriorated. In February 1983, Williams was found dead in a hotel room in New York after apparently choking on a bottle cap.

Tennessee Williams's style is often referred to as poetic realism or poetic expressionism. Expressionism is a part of the modernist movement in art and literature, where the expression of emotion or emotional experience takes precedence over the materialistic depiction of physical reality. Williams's plays typically contain stage directions that call not for a physical setting but for a creation of mood. Physical setting is often altered, augmented, or distorted in order to create a mood or to suggest an emotion. Music, lighting, and screen legends are used symbolically to create this kind of effect. In terms of characterization, Williams's plays often center on misfits or outcasts—outsiders who are often very sensitive and completely out of tune with contemporary times. Characters may be at odds with restrictive Southern mores, and they may struggle with sexual repression. In *A Streetcar Named Desire,* Blanche DuBois is a complicated character who at times performs the role of Southern Belle, slightly down on her luck but steeped in Southern gentility with fine manners. At other times, the mask slips, and we see Blanche the sexually hungry woman, who gives a predatory stare at the young newspaper boy. At still other times, we see Blanche in all of her raw vulnerability, terrified of being "played out," of having lost her youth and looks, of being utterly alone.

6.4.1 *A Street Car Named Desire*

Please click the link below to access this selection:
   http://www.metropolitancollege.com/Streetcar.pdf

6.4.2 Reading and Review Questions

1. How is "desire" defined in the play?

2. Compare and contrast Blanche and Stella. What is the symbolic significance of their names?

3. Compare and contrast Blanche and Stanley; are they attracted to one another or repelled by one another? Why?

4. Select and analyze any of the following for symbolic significance in the play: the poker game, the streetcars and their names, Blanche's trunk, images of water, images of light, the flower seller, the newspaper boy, or Belle Reve.

5. Contrast Blanche with her "performance" of Blanche: what are the distinguishing features between the woman and the mask she sometimes creates for others? Does she create different personas for different people in the play? Who is the "real" Blanche?

6. What is the connection between sex and death in the play?

6.5 JAMES DICKEY

(1923 - 1997)

Image 6.1 | James Dickey, n.d.
Photographer | Unknown
Source | Wikipedia
License | Fair Use

James Dickey, whose Byronic demeanor and athletic prowess earned him the nickname the "bare-chested bard," was born in Atlanta, Georgia and grew up in Buckhead. Excelling at both football and track in high school, Dickey enrolled in Clemson A&M in 1942 to play football. He left Clemson after only one semester to enlist in the Army Air Corps, joining the 418th Night Fighter Squadron and flying over 100 missions in the Pacific Theater. Dickey discovered poetry during the war, spending his time between deadly night missions reading all the literature he could find in the base libraries where he was stationed. After the war, he attended Vanderbilt University as an English major, distinguishing himself in both academics and track. MA in hand, Dickey taught English at Rice Institute and the University of Florida, returning to the military during the **Korean War** to teach aviation for the Air Force. In the mid-1950s, Dickey suddenly quit teaching and moved to New York to work as a copywriter for an advertising agency, writing poetry only in the evenings. Growing to feel that "I was selling my soul to the devil during the day and trying to get it back at night," as he told *Life* magazine in 1966, Dickey quit his lucrative advertising job after six years. While unemployed and on welfare, he won a $5000 Guggenheim Fellowship that allowed him to travel and focus his creative energies entirely on poetry. Dickey then returned to academia and dedicated himself for the rest of his life to writing and teaching, while continuing to play the sports he loved.

Dickey published nineteen volumes of poetry, three essay collections, two children's books, and three novels, including the best-selling novel *Deliverance*

(1972), a thrilling tale set in north Georgia about four suburban Atlanta river rafters who find themselves in a fight for their lives against homicidal mountain men. Over the forty years of his writing career, Dickey continually sought new ways to give voice to intense, violent, and powerful experiences such as combat, hunting, and sports. He continually experimented with new poetic forms of his own invention, such as "open verse," "split lines," and "associational imagery," as well as new typographical arrangements of the printed page. Although Dickey's poetry is informed by both his wartime experience and love of the physical life, he does not usually reflect upon his own adventures in his work. Instead—and unlike his era's confessional poets, who reflect deeply upon personal experience—Dickey frequently writes in a narrative mode as an explorer of someone else's extreme situation. In this way, the narrators of his poems reflect the act of reading itself, imaginatively inhabiting the characters they observe and vicariously experiencing the life-and-death situations they describe. For example, in the poem "Drinking from a Helmet," one soldier experiences the thoughts of a recently deceased soldier by wearing his helmet. Likewise, in "Falling," a poem based on a real event, a third-person narrator enters the consciousness of a stewardess during her fatal plunge to earth after being thrown from the open door of an airplane. Not all of Dickey's poems are this dramatic, as evidenced by the early narrative poem included here, "Cherrylog Road." Yet even this poem about an illicit tryst is set in "the parking lot of the dead," its narrator musing more upon the past lives and adventures contained in the wrecked cars around him than about the girl he is soon to meet.

6.5.1 "Cherrylog Road"

Please click the link below to access this selection:
http://www.poetryfoundation.org/poem/171426

6.5.2 Reading and Review Questions

1. The poem's narrator devotes much of the poem to describing the cars around him, noting their physical condition and wondering about their previous owners. However, he never describes what Doris Holbrook looks like or tells us anything about her past. Why is this?

2. What do the histories that the narrator imagines are contained within the wrecked cars tell us about the narrator himself?

3. In stanzas 15 and 16, the narrator compares himself and Doris to a blacksnake and then to beetles, respectively. Closely read these stanzas and discuss the significance of the poem's comparisons of people to animals and bugs.

6.6 FLANNERY O'CONNOR

(1925 - 1964)

Mary Flannery O'Connor was born in Savannah, Georgia and lived there until 1938. An Orthodox Catholic family, the O'Connor family lived in Lafayette Square, a largely Catholic neighborhood of Savannah, mainly through the generosity of her second cousin, Kate Semmes (whom O'Connor would call "Cousin Katie"). In 1936, O'Connor's father, Edwin, was diagnosed with lupus and was hospitalized in Atlanta; his diagnosis would later force the family to leave Savannah. While Edwin sought treatment, both Regina and Flannery would often stay with family in Milledgeville.

Image 6.3 | Flannery O'Connor, 1947
Photographer | C. Cameron Macauley
Source | Wikimedia Commons
License | CC BY-SA 3.0

In 1941, Edwin's death would imprint itself on O'Connor, who was close with her father. Both Flannery and her mother, Regina, subsequently moved to live at Andalusia, the maternal family farm in Milledgeville. After high school, O'Connor enrolled in Georgia College for Women (now Georgia College) in Milledgeville, where she completed a degree in English and Sociology. In college, O'Connor was active with both the literary magazine, *The Corinthian,* and the yearbook, *The Spectrum.* After college, O'Connor enrolled in journalism school at the University of Iowa but, once there, enrolled in the Iowa Writer's Workshop, where she was able to work with many of the most influential writers of her time.

At the Writer's Workshop, O'Connor established herself as one of their most promising writers, winning a book contract, as well as a prestigious Yaddo fellowship at the Yaddo Writers Colony in New York. However, after being diagnosed with lupus in 1951, Flannery O'Connor returned to Andalusia, where she remained. At the age of twenty-five, she published her first novel, *Wise Blood* (1952) and followed it up with her first collection of short stories, *A Good Man is Hard to Find and Other Stories* (1955). Her second published novel, *The Violent Bear It Away* (1960), was nominated for a **National Book Award**. Up until her death from lupus, at the young age of thirty-nine, she was working on her second collection of stories, *Everything That Rises Must Converge* (1965). In 1971, O'Connor's friend and literary executor, Sally Fitzgerald, helped publish *The Complete Stories of Flannery O'Connor* which won the National Book Award and was later awarded the Reader's Choice Best of the National Book Award (2010).

O'Connor's fiction is famous for its **Southern gothic** settings and her use of dark humor. Other themes in her fiction include the following: her relationship with her mother, life at Andalusia, and her Orthodox Catholicism. "A Good Man is Hard to Find" is O'Connor's most anthologized story and one of her most violent.

The story follows a family of six that, while on vacation to Florida, encounter the Misfit, a pensive, yet troubled serial killer, and one of O'Connor's most famous characters. The Misfit states that his troubles center on Christ's claims of resurrecting the dead. In "Good Country People," Joy-Hulga, a philosophy Ph.D. with a wooden leg, tries to seduce Manly Pointer, a naïve traveling bible salesman.

6.6.1 "A Good Man is Hard to Find"

Please click the link below to access this selection:

http://xroads.virginia.edu/~drbr/goodman.html

6.6.2 "Good Country People"

Please click the link below to access this selection:

http://faculty.weber.edu/Jyoung/English%206710/Good%20Country%20People.pdf

6.6.3 Reading and Review Questions

1. What do these two stories, "A Good Man is Hard to Find" and "Good Country People," have in common?

2. What does the Misfit mean with his final line, "She would have been a good woman. . . if it had been somebody there to shoot her every minute of her life"?

6.7 POSTMODERNISM

Postmodernism is difficult to define. Don DeLillo is recognized as one of America's premier postmodernist novelists, yet he rejects the term entirely. "If I had to classify myself," he explains in a 2010 interview in the *Saint Louis Beacon*, "it would be in the long line of modernists, from James Joyce through William Faulkner and so on. That has always been my model." Literally, the term postmodernism refers to culture that comes after Modernism, referring specifically to works of art created in the decades following the 1950s. The term's most precise definition comes from architecture, where it refers to a contemporary style of building that rejects the austerity and minimalism of modernist architecture's glass boxes and towers; postmodernist architects retain the functionalist core of the modernist building but then decorate their boxes and towers with playful colors, forms, and ornaments that reference disparate historical eras. Indeed, play—with media and materials, and with forms, styles, and content—is one of the chief characteristics of postmodernist art.

While postmodernist architects play with the material of their buildings, postmodernist writers play with the material that their poems and stories are made of, namely language and the book. Postmodernist writers freely use all the challenging experimental literary techniques developed by the modernists earlier in the twentieth century as well as new, even more experimental techniques of their own invention. In fiction, many postmodernist authors adopt the self-referential style of "**metafiction**," a story that is just as much about the process of telling a story as it is about describing characters and events. Donald Barthelme's postmodernist short story, "The School," contains metafictional elements that comment on the process of storytelling and meaning-making, as when the narrator describes how the "lesson plan called for tropical fish input" even though all the students in the schoolroom knew the fish would soon die. Who is telling this story? Bartheleme? The unnamed narrator? The lesson plan? The stories that make up history itself are often a playground for postmodernist authors, as they take material found in history books and weave it into new tales that reveal secret histories and dimly perceived conspiracies. David Foster Wallace's essay, "Consider the Lobster," is a good example of the narrative excess found in postmodern literature. In this essay written for *Gourmet* magazine, Wallace uses his visit to the Maine Lobster Festival to tell a history of the lobster since the Jurassic period that eventually turns against the organizers of the festival themselves, who may or may not be covering up the truth about how much lobsters suffer in their cooking pots. The form of the essay cannot even contain Wallace's ideas, which spill over into twenty excessively long footnotes, many of which are little essays in themselves. In addition to playing with the form of literature and the notion of authorship, postmodernist writers also often play with popular sub-genres such as the detective story, horror, and science fiction. For example, in her poem "Diving into the Wreck," Adrienne Rich evokes both the detective story and science fiction as she imagines a futuristic diver visiting a deep sea wreck in order to solve the mystery of why literature and history have been mostly about men and not women.

Not all works of postmodernist literature are stylistically experimental or playful. Rather, their authors explore the meaning and value of postmodernity as a cultural condition. Several philosophers and literary critics—many of whose names have become synonymous with postmodernism itself—have helped us understand what the postmodern condition may be. "Poststructuralist" philosophers such as Jacques Derrida and Jean Baudrillard have argued that words and texts do not reflect the world but instead exist as their own self-referential systems, containing and even creating the world they describe. When we perceive the world, Derrida's philosophy of "deconstruction" claims, we see not things but "signs" that can be understood only through their relation to other signs. "There is no outside the text," Derrida famously claimed in his book *Of Grammatology* (1967). In this way, words and books and texts are powerful things, for in them our world itself is created—an insight that many postmodernist creative writers share. Baudrillard, in turn, argues in his book, *Simulacra and Simulation* (1981), that the real world has been filled up with and even replaced by simulations that we now treat as reality: simulacra. These postmodern sensibilities are reflected in both Allen Ginsberg's poem, "A Supermarket in California," and our selection from DeLillo's *White Noise*. In Ginsberg's poem, food has become "brilliant stacks of cans" knowable only by their similarity to each other. The "neon fruit supermarket" is not even a simulation of a real farm but instead is a simulacra full of families who have probably never even seen a farm. In DeLillo's novel, we find the insight that the collected photographs of "the most photographed barn in America" are more real than the physical barn being photographed. Nobody knows why this particular barn is the most photographed barn in America. The barn is famous simply because it is a much-copied text, valued more as a sign in relation to other signs (all those photos of the same thing) than as a thing in itself with a specific history and a particular use. In his book *Postmodernism* (1991), the leftist critic Frederic Jameson chastises postmodernism for being the "cultural logic of late capitalism," which for him is a culture that erases the real meanings and relations of things such as the most photographed barn in America, replacing true history with nostalgic simulacra.

The culture of postmodernism in general exhibits a skepticism towards the grand truth claims and unifying narratives that have organized culture since the time of the Enlightenment. In postmodern culture, history becomes a field of competing histories and the self becomes a hybrid being with multiple, partial identities. In his provocative study, *The Postmodern Condition* (1979), the philosopher Jean Francois Lyotard argues that what defines the present postmodern historical era is the collapse of "grand narratives" that explain all experience, faiths, and truths, such as those found in science, politics, and religion; in place of all-explaining master narratives, he argues, we now know the world through smaller micro-narratives that don't all fit together into a greater coherent whole. These insights are thoroughly explored in the confessional, feminist, and multicultural American literature of this era, whose authors write from their subjective points of view rather than presuming to represent the sum total of all American experiences, and whose works show us that American history has been far from the same experience for all Americans. For example, both Sylvia Plath and Theodore Roethke have poems about their fathers, but their appreciation of their respective fathers is shaped by both their genders and their own personal histories. Roethke feels a kinship with his father. Plath, however, sees her father as an enemy. The Native American author Leslie Marmon Silko tells her story specifically from the point of view of a member of the Laguna Pueblo tribe, whose members use old stories about the Yellow Woman and the ka'tsina spirit to understand their tribe's relationship to the rest of America. In the works of African-American literature in this section, we find similar explorations of cultural identity. James Baldwin uses the African-American music of the blues and jazz to describe the relationship between the two brothers in his story, "Sonny's Blues." Ralph Ellison, in the first chapter from his novel *Invisible Man* (1952), writes about the experience of attending a segregated school that keeps black Americans separate from white Americans. Toni Morrison and Alice Walker, in their stories, explore the hybrid nature of African-American identity itself, showing us the tensions that arise when one's identity is both American and black.

The varied, playful, experimental literature of postmodernism, the critic Brian McHale helpfully observes in his book *Constructing Postmodernism* (1993), presents readers not with many ways to know our one world but instead with many knowable worlds created within many disparate works in many different ways. Modernist authors all strove to devise new techniques with which to accurately represent the world, McHale observes. Postmodernist authors, however, are no longer concerned with representing one knowable world but instead with creating many literary worlds that represent a diversity of experiences. Thus, much as the American literature of the contemporary era presents us with a record of how the nation has known, questioned, and even redefined itself, so too does the literature of postmodernism present us with a record of how writers have known, questioned, and even redefined what literature is.

6.8 THEODORE ROETHKE

(1908 - 1963)

Image 6.4 | Theodore Roethke, 1959
Photographer | Imogen Cunningham
Source | Wikipedia
License | Fair Use

Theodore Roethke is one of the most influential poets of the postmodern era. A student of the Modernists, who ultimately outgrew their poetry, Roethke's world is filled with contrasting images of nature and industry that create a sense of hope that distinguishes him from the Modernists, and a sense of insecurity that seems aptly suited to the middle years of the twentieth century. The winner of the Pulitzer Prize for Poetry and two National Book Awards, Roethke is frequently remembered as a teacher, and the work of his own students often obscured the work of the master. The centenary of Roethke's birth in 2008, however, brought renewed attention to his poetic career.

Roethke's earliest works of poetry are restrained and spare, as the last lines of "Cuttings" (1948) demonstrate:

> One nub of growth
> Nudges a sand-crumb loose,
> Pokes through a musty sheath
> Its pale tendrilous horn. (5-8)

Even in these short lines, however, Roethke's gift for the lyric is clearly visible with the repeated opening sounds of "nub" and "nudges" pushing the reader to the end of the poem. At the same time, the sounds and rhythms of Roethke's poems, with their short lines and broken rhythms, evoke images of constraint and hesitation.

The selection from Roethke included here, "My Papa's Waltz," also from 1948, takes us from the world of hothouses into the hot and enclosed houses of American life. Much like the young plants struggling to grow in "Cuttings," the young boy in "My Papa's Waltz" struggles to grow in his home environment. Arranged in broken three-quarter time, "My Papa's Waltz" evokes contrasting images of playful roughhousing and domestic abuse. These contrasting images often lead to heated discussions among readers who are divided by their interpretations of this poem as one of joyous abandon and one of repeated brutality. Just what is the nature of this waltz that the boy and his father engage in, and how can it be wondrous if the mother's gaze is so disapproving? That Roethke's poetry invites such disparate responses is both a testament to his craftsmanship and a reaction to his deliberate ambiguity. Like the other postmodern poets in this section, Roethke's poems reveal the many shadows of modern life.

6.8.1 "My Papa's Waltz"

Please click the link below to access this selection:
   http://www.poetryfoundation.org/poem/172103

6.8.2 Reading and Review Questions

1. Describe the scene in the kitchen. Is this a happy occasion or is there a darker meaning here?

2. Describe the speaker's attitude toward the mother and the father.

3. What does the poem suggest about a father's responsibilities?

6.9 RALPH ELLISON

(1914 - 1994)

Ralph Waldo Ellison was born in Oklahoma City, Oklahoma. Ellison's father, Lewis, a manual laborer who delivered ice and coal, was an avid reader who named his son after Ralph Waldo Emerson and who hoped that his son would grow up to be a poet. Unfortunately he died of a work-related accident when Ellison was three, which left the two brothers, Robert and Herbert, to be raised by their single mother, Ida. The absence of his father would remain a recurring theme in Ellison's work.

Image 6.5 | Ralph Ellison, 1961
Photographer | Houghton Mifflin
Source | Wikimedia Commons
License | Public Domain

As a young man, Ellison was interested in arts and culture, specifically, music. In 1933, he enrolled at the Tuskegee Institute, a historically black college which offered one of the nation's top programs in music. During his time at Tuskegee,

Ellison gained a reputation for spending long hours in the library, reading heavily from several Modernist writers. Ellison cites T. S. Eliot's *The Waste Land* as a major influence in his life, inspiring him to be a writer. After college, Ellison moved to New York, where he met influential artist Romare Bearden as well as writer Richard Wright, both of whom were important influences on Ellison's life. During this time in New York, Ellison began to publish short stories, essays, and book reviews.

In 1952, Ellison published his debut novel, *The Invisible Man,* a critical best seller which won the National Book Award. The novel vaulted him into the international spotlight as a writer, a position that he did not always embrace. *The Invisible Man* describes how the protagonist (who is never named and is, hence, "invisible") experiences various incidents of racism throughout his life after moving from the South to New York. The novel, Ellison's only one published during his lifetime, has remained one of the most famous and most influential novels in American literature. He spent the remainder of his life working on a follow-up novel. In 1967, he claimed to be near completion of this novel when a house fire consumed his drafts. After his death, his posthumous follow-up was published under the title *Juneteenth* (1999); later a longer version of this novel was published under the title *Three Days Before the Shooting* (2010).

Although he never published a second novel in his lifetime, he did publish several essays, including essays about his lifelong love of music. His essay collection *Shadow and Act* (1964) was named one of the top 100 best non-fiction books of the twentieth century. One of the common themes of Ellison's work, both in fiction and non-fiction, was the idea of cultural ancestry—the idea that our cultural ancestors could be as influential as our biological ancestors. "Battle Royale," the opening chapter of *The Invisible Man,* describes the protagonist's humiliating experience accepting a scholarship from a local civic organization. Although it is the introductory chapter, it has been highly anthologized as a short story.

6.9.1 Selection from *Invisible Man*

Chapter 1
Please click the link below to access this selection:

http://bpi.edu/ourpages/auto/2010/5/11/36901472/Ralph%20Ellison%20-%20Invisible%20Man%20v3_0.pdf

6.9.2 Reading and Review Questions

1. What is the significance of the protagonist's dream? What does his grandfather's appearance symbolize?

2. Why do you think the protagonist still gives his speech even after he's been humiliated?

6.10 JAMES BALDWIN

(1924 - 1987)

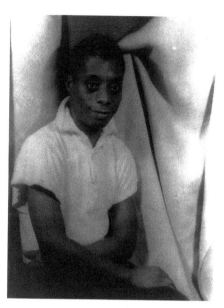

Image 6.6 | James Baldwin, 1955
Photographer | Carl Van Vechten
Source | Wikimedia Commons
License | Public Domain

James Baldwin was born in Harlem, the oldest of nine children. Although he did not know his biological father, Baldwin's rocky relationship with his stepfather, a lay preacher who shared his name of James Baldwin, was a major influence in both Baldwin's writings and life. At the age of fourteen, a young Baldwin tried to follow in his stepfather's footsteps as a preacher, but his interest was short lived. In high school, Baldwin joined the school's literary magazine and began making trips to Greenwich Village. These trips only further sparked his interests in the arts and befriended many professional artists, including Beauford Delaney, an African-American painter who found fame during the Harlem Renaissance. As he recounts in his essay, "Notes on a Native Son," Baldwin's stepfather died in 1943 and was buried on Baldwin's nineteenth birthday, which was, subsequently, both the day his youngest brother was born as well as the day of the Harlem Riot.

In 1944, after the death of his stepfather, Baldwin moved to Greenwich Village, to focus on becoming a writer. It was here that Baldwin found an artistic community, forming friendships with artists such as Marlon Brando and his literary hero, Richard Wright. With Wright's help, Baldwin was awarded the Eugene Saxton fellowship (1945). Baldwin began to publish essays in influential magazines, such as *The Nation* and *Partisan Review*; however, in 1948, due to his disillusionment as a black, gay man in America, Baldwin followed in the path of other expatriates, including Wright, by moving to Paris. Although he would live in both Switzerland and Turkey, Baldwin eventually settled in Saint-Paul de Vence, South of France.

Baldwin's first novel, *Go Tell It on the Mountain* (1953), was a major critical and commercial success. Despite being fiction, the biographical similarities in the novel about a young man, John Grimes—who questions the hypocrisy of the church, his own religious upbringing, his own sexuality, and his frustrations with being an African-American—were quite transparent. In 1955, he released his first collection of essays, the influential *Notes on a Native Son,* but it was his follow up novel, *Giovanni's Room* (1956), which was the subject of international controversy for its homoerotic content. The novel follows David who, after his girlfriend leaves him, has an affair with an Italian bartender, Giovanni.

The debut of Baldwin's book of essays *The Fire Next Time* (1963) only further cemented his reputation as one of the most famous and influential American writers of the twentieth century. Baldwin, despite living in France, was an extremely influential figure during the American Civil Rights movement, aligning himself with the Student

Nonviolent Coordinating Committee (SNCC), making several trips to the American South, working with figures such as Martin Luther King Jr. In 1963, he was featured on the cover of *Time* magazine for his work on the Civil Rights movement.

In his famous short story, "Sonny's Blues," Baldwin deals with the conflict between two brothers, one a math teacher and the other, Sonny, a musician recently released from jail. Throughout the story, it becomes clear that the two brothers do not know each other very well and that, although Sonny's troubles are **explicit,** the narrator's troubles are more **implicit.**

6.10.1 "Sonny's Blues"

Please click the link below to access this selection:

http://swcta.net/moore/files/2012/02/sonnysblues.pdf

6.10.2 Reading and Review Questions

1. The story describes a Cain and Abel-type relationship between the narrator and his brother. Can you find any other biblical allusions in the story?

2. To what does the title, "Sonny's Blues," refer? How is Sonny misrepresented by his brother? Why does his brother show up at the concert at the end of the story?

3. What do you see as the central theme of this story—addiction? Reconciliation? Individuality?

6.11 ALLEN GINSBERG

(1926 - 1997)

Ever since he read his groundbreaking poem "Howl" in 1954 to a shocked and enthralled audience at the Six Gallery in San Francisco, Allen Ginsberg has been the poetic voice of America's counterculture. Ginsberg grew up in Patterson, New Jersey and attended Columbia University in New York City, where he met fellow authors Jack Kerouac (author of *On the Road* published

Image 6.7 | Allen Ginsberg, 1979
Photographer | Michiel Hendryckx
Source | Wikimedia Commons
License | CC BY-SA 3.0

in 1957) and William S. Burroughs (author of *Naked Lunch* published in 1959). Although a distinguished student, Ginsberg was temporarily expelled from Columbia for profanity and later spent eight months in a mental institution after pleading insanity when caught storing stolen goods for a drug addict friend. Upon his release, he was befriended by the poet William Carlos Williams, who recognized in Ginsberg a singular talent. After graduating from Columbia and supporting himself with a series of menial jobs in Harlem, Ginsberg moved to San Francisco in 1953 and began a successful, if brief, career as a market researcher. Yet his true calling remained poetry; he was soon fired from his job and, while on unemployment, wrote the poem that would make his reputation as a major American poet: the explosive, furious "Howl," whose opening lines famously read, "I have seen the best minds of my generation destroyed by madness, starving hysterical naked, / dragging themselves through the negro streets at dawn looking for an angry fix, / angelheaded hipsters burning for the ancient heavenly connection to the starry dynamo in the machine of night..." In San Francisco, Ginsberg found a welcoming community of poets centered around Lawrence Ferlinghetti's City Lights Bookshop. In 1956, **City Lights Books** published Ginsberg's first collection, *Howl and Other Poems* (which includes the poem selected here, "A Supermarket in California") only to have the book seized and prosecuted by U.S. Customs for its allegedly indecent depiction of sexuality. From that point on, in numerous volumes of poetry as well as direct political actions from sit-ins to Congressional testimonies, Ginsberg became a singularly oppositional voice in American culture, howling against conformity and war, championing environmentalism and gay rights, and finding beauty in all that American society has beaten down.

Ginsberg's *Howl and Other Poems* and his friend Jack Kerouac's novel *On the Road* (a *roman à clef* in which the leftist Ginsberg is the character "Carlo Marx") are the two definitive works of **Beat literature**, depicting the countercultural lives of their artists in an improvisatory, spontaneous style akin to jazz music. In 1948, while still living in Harlem, Ginsberg experienced a days-long **cosmic vision** in which he beheld the beauty of all divine creation and heard the godly voice of British romantic poet William Blake in the sky reciting his *Songs of Innocence and Experience* (1798). Inspired by this vision and writing under the mentorship of William Carlos Williams, Ginsberg began crafting the poetic style for which he is now known: long, free Whitmanesque lines that find their rhythms in everyday American speech and contain the shockingly personal confessions of the poet himself on topics ranging from his mother's mental illness to his own open homosexuality. For Ginsberg, the American experience is often one of oppression and loss; Ginsberg's poetic mission, accordingly, is to recover the beauty of those people and things America herself has cast aside. In the poem "A Supermarket in California" included here, Ginsberg imagines walking with his poetic ancestor Walt Whitman through a modern-day supermarket, showing the great American romantic what his beautiful nation has become.

6.10.2 "Supermarket in California"

Please click the link below to access this selection:

http://www.english.illinois.edu/maps/poets/g_l/ginsberg/onlinepoems.htm

6.10.3 Reading and Review Questions

1. Making reference to the imagery in Ginsberg's poem, describe the America Walt Whitman finds in a mid-twentieth-century American supermarket.

2. Why does Ginsberg "feel absurd" when dreaming of his "odyssey in the

supermarket" with Whitman?

3. Whitman asks three questions while in the supermarket: "Who killed the pork chops? What price bananas? Are you my Angel?" Imagine going into Publix, Kroger, or Ingles and asking these same three questions. How would the staff in the produce section or behind the meat counter respond? Could they even answer all three questions? And what do their responses tell us about the kinds of thought that are encouraged in modern consumer America—and the kinds of thought that are not?

6.11 ADRIENNE RICH

(1929 - 2012)

Adrienne Rich is one of the most important poets and feminists of the middle to late
twentieth century. Taken together, the twenty-five collections of poetry and numerous essays she published in her lifetime are a powerful literary expression of this period's radical
politics. Born in Baltimore, Maryland, Rich
was encouraged to write poetry at an early
age by her father, a pathologist at Johns Hopkins Medical School with a passion for English
verse. She distinguished herself as a poet early
in life, publishing her first book of poems, *A
Change of World*, in 1951 while still a senior
at Radcliffe College. The renowned poet W.
H. Auden selected Rich's work for publication
in the prestigious Yale Younger Poets Series
based on what he perceived as the delicacy
and restraint of her style. In 1952, Rich won
her first of two coveted Guggenheim Fellow-

Image 6.8 | Adrienne Rich, 1980
Photographer | K. Kendall
Source | Wikimedia Commons
License | CC BY 2.0

ships, which funded a year-long trip to England and Italy. In 1953, she married
an economics professor from Harvard, giving birth to three children before the
end of the decade. In this formative decade, Rich faced a dilemma still familiar
to women today: how to maintain her career while shouldering full responsibility
for her children and home. In the volumes of poetry she published in the early
1960s, Rich turns an increasingly critical eye on an American society that subordinates women to the will of men and that asks only women to choose between
family and career. Rich's delicate and restrained poetry became radicalized over
the course of the 1960s as she realized that her personal situation was also political, an expression of social forces and institutions that the poet herself could
change. From then on, as she writes in her 1968 poem "Implosions," "I wanted to

choose words that even you/ would have to be changed by."

From the 1960s until she published her final collection in 2010, Rich used poetry to criticize war, sexism, and environmental destruction and to imagine a world free of gender divisions and male domination. Beginning in the 1970s, Rich became an outspoken advocate for lesbian rights in her poetry as well. As she describes in her book Of Woman Born: Motherhood as Experience and Institution (1976), over the course of the 1960s Rich came to realize that she had been living as a "suppressed lesbian" her entire life. She separated from her husband in 1970 and entered into a relationship with the novelist Michelle Cliff in 1974, with whom she remained partners until her death 2012. Rich's National Book Award winning collection of 1973, Diving into the Wreck, exemplifies her poetry of political conviction. Published during the second wave feminist movement, the poems in this volume describe women as a vast global sisterhood that has been written out of history. Rich optimistically imagines that this oppressive situation can change as society itself changes, in part through the force of the poet's voice. The history of Western civilization, as Rich writes in in the closing lines of the titular poem presented here, "Diving into the Wreck," is "a book of myths / in which / our names do not appear." The wreck in this poem is the wreck of western civilization itself, containing the ruins of both patriarchy and poetry. The poem's narrator is a person unimaginable in traditional Western society: someone who identifies with both genders at once and who transforms the decline of one civilization into the art of its successor. This hybrid narrator takes the reader on a dramatic journey into this dangerous wreck so that the reader, too, can imagine the end of a divisive civilization in which men dominate women.

6.11.1 "Diving into the Wreck"

Please click the link below to access this selection:
https://www.poets.org/poetsorg/poem/diving-wreck

6.11.2 Reading and Review Questions

1. The book of myths is a metaphor for all the writings of Western civilization. Why does the poem's narrator "first [have] to read the books of myths" before making this metaphoric dive into the wreck of Western civilization?

2. In the final stanza, Rich contradictorily writes that the narrator finds her way "by cowardice or courage...back to this scene." If cowardice, then what fear is she succumbing to? If courage, then what fear is she facing?

3. Rich's narrator worries in stanza five that "it is easy to forget / what I came for." What does the narrator come to the wreck for? Why is it so easy to forget this goal?

6.12 TONI MORRISON

(1931 -)

Image 6.9 | Toni Morrison, 2008
Photographer | Angela Radulescu
Source | Wikimedia Commons
License | CC BY-SA 2.0

The first African-American to win a Nobel Prize for Literature, Toni Morrison is one of the most important American authors of the past century. In the eleven exquisitely crafted novels she has published to date, Morrison combines folk and postmodernist storytelling techniques to explore what it means to be both black and a woman in America. Morrison was born in Loraine, Ohio, and earned a Bachelor's degree in English from Howard University and a Master's Degree from Cornell University. Although she began writing creative fiction at Howard, Morrison worked primarily as a college professor in the decade following her graduation from Cornell, teaching at Texas Southern University and then at Howard. In 1964, Morrison divorced the husband she met at Howard, moved to New York, and worked as a senior editor for Random House publishers, where she championed the writing of several notable African-American authors including Angela Davis and Toni Cade Bambara. Morrison continued to write and teach at colleges while working at Random House, publishing her first novel, *The Bluest Eye*, in 1970. Since then she has taught at numerous institutions, including schools in the New York state university system, Yale, Bard, and finally Princeton, where she is currently an emerita professor. In addition to working as an editor, novelist, and professor, Morrison is also a prolific essayist and public intellectual, publishing editorials in venues such as *The New York Times* and appearing on popular TV programs such as *The Late Show with Stephen Colbert*. She has also written three children's books with her son, Slade Morrison, and the libretto for an opera based on the life of the American slave Margaret Garner, who is also the inspiration for her Pulitzer Prize winning novel, *Beloved* (1987).

Morrison describes the postmodernist literary technique she has developed in her novels as that of "enchantment," a blending of historical realism with the myths and supernatural tales she learned as a child. "That's the way the world was for me and for the black people I knew," she tells Christina Davis in a 1986 interview in *Conversations with Toni Morrison*. "There was this other knowledge or perception, always discredited but nevertheless there, which informed their sensibilities and clarified their activities...they had some sweet, intimate connection with things that were not empirically verifiable." Examples of enchantment abound in Morrison's work. In her novel *Song of Solomon* (1977), a story of a man coming to terms with his African-American identity, one character gives birth to herself—and thus does not have a navel—while another learns to fly as legendary African tribesmen once did. In *Tar Baby* (1981), a novel about people who trap themselves in self-deceptions, Morrison structures her tale around the African-American fable of the trickster rabbit who gets caught by a deceptive figure made out of tar. In *Beloved*, a powerful novel about the legacy of slavery, the ghost of a slain baby haunts the home of an escaped slave. The short story "Recitatif" included here, originally published in Amiri and Amina Baraka's anthology *Confirmation* (1983), is the only short story that Morrison ever published. While it does not directly reference the supernatural, "Recitatif" features other postmodernist techniques common to Morrison's work, from its estranging opening lines to the historical revisionism that the two central characters, Twyla and Roberta, engage in over the story's course.

6.12.1 "Recitatif"

Please click the link below to access this selection:

http://www.mychandlerschools.org/cms/lib6/AZ01001175/Centricity/ Domain/1073/Morrison_recitatifessay.doc.pdf

6.12.2 Reading and Review Questions

1. Look up the meaning of the word "Recitatif." Discuss why Morrison chose this term for her story's title.

2. Twyla and Roberta are inseparable friends at St. Bonny's. Why don't Twyla and Roberta stay friends over the course of their lives?

3. Discuss why Twyla and Roberta have different memories of—and tell different stories about—Maggie.

6.13 Donald Barthelme

(1931 - 1989)

Donald Barthelme was born in Philadelphia, but grew up in Houston, Texas, where his father was a professor of architecture at the University of Houston. From an early age, Barthelme showed an interest in writing, and in high school he won a Scholastic Writing Award, given to young writers. Yet, Barthelme had a strained relationship with his father, who disagreed with his choice of literature and whom Barthelme believed was too demanding and controlling. Despite this rocky relationship, Barthelme attended the University of Houston, where his father worked, and studied journalism. As a student, Barthelme began writing for the *Houston Post*. In 1953, he was drafted into

Image 6.10 | Donald Barthelme, n.d.
Publisher | University of Houston
Source | Wikimedia Commons
License | Public Domain

service for the U.S. Army, but arrived in Korea at the very end of the Korean War; thus, he was never in combat. When Barthelme returned to the states, he continued writing for the *Houston Post* and returned to the University of Houston, this time studying philosophy, although he never earned a degree.

Barthelme's literary output is most known for his short stories, with his Postmodern fiction being entirely unique. Indeed, he is considered a pioneer of **flash fiction.** Barthelme's experimental short stories avoid many of the common traits of a story, with their elements of plot or a linear narrative by instead experimenting with just about every constitutive element. Furthermore, his fiction was highly influenced by his own interest in philosophy, which gave his work an element of **gravitas.**

In 1961, Barthelme became the director of the Contemporary Arts Museum in Houston; in the same year, he published his first short story in *The New Yorker*. Soon after, he moved to New York to edit a journal, *Locomotion,* and would go on to publish several short stories in *The New Yorker* magazine. In 1964, he published his first collection of short stories, *Come Back, Dr. Caligiri,* but it was his 1968 book of short stories, *Unspeakable Practices, Unnatural Acts,* featuring his famous work, "The Balloon," which brought Barthelme acclaim as a master of the short story. From there, his reputation as a Postmodern writer, primarily of short stories, continued to grow, although he did publish three novels in his lifetime and one posthumous novel. Barthelme helped start a creative writing program at the University of Houston, where he mentored young writers. He also taught creative writing at Boston University and the University of Buffalo. He was married four times and had two daughters. In 1989, Donald Barthelme died of throat cancer.

Barthelme's short story, "The School," is an excellent example of his style as a writer. Barthelme is able to take the general concerns of our human condition—concerns over the purpose of life or the reasons we die—and put them in the mouths of school children. Also, he blends both humor and seriousness in one story.

6.13.1 "The School"

Please click the link below to access this selection:

http://www.npr.org/programs/death/readings/stories/bart.html

6.13.2 Reading and Review Questions

1. How does Barthelme use humor as a rhetorical technique in this story? What about death as a rhetorical technique?

2. At what point does the story feel unrealistic to you as a reader?

3. What do you think will happen to the gerbil at the end of the story?

4. What, if anything, do you think that Barthelme's story has to say about schools?

5. How is this story similar to and different from other postmodern stories that you've read?

6.14 SYLVIA PLATH

(1932 - 1963)

Image 6.11 | Sylvia Plath, n.d.
Photographer | Unknown
Source | Wikipedia
License | Fair Use

Sylvia Plath was born in Boston, Massachusetts. Plath's father, a professor of biology at Boston University and an authoritarian figure within the family, died when Plath was eight years old, and Plath struggled for the rest of her life to come to terms with her complicated feelings for him. Plath's mother went to work to provide for Plath and her brother. From a young age, Plath was a high achiever, showing an early talent as a writer and poet. She received a scholarship to Smith College and, after graduating, was awarded a Fulbright Scholarship to Cambridge University. In spite of a history of depression and one suicide attempt, Plath excelled at academics and worked diligently on her writing, periodically publishing her work. At Cambridge, Plath met the young, upcoming British poet Ted Hughes; the two shared an intense and immediate attraction, marrying only a few months later. Plath and Hughes enjoyed their first years together as writing partners, encouraging each other as poets. The two lived for a time in America, travelled broadly, and eventually returned to England to live. Plath gave birth to two children and engaged in domestic routines while still working on poems which would eventually be included in her posthumous collection, *Ariel* (1965). She continued to struggle with depression, and after discovering Ted Hughes's affair with a mutual friend, Assia Wevill, Plath's depression worsened. She eventually separated from Hughes and moved to London with her children in an attempt to start over on her own. Most of the poems that comprise *Ariel* were written while she lived in London. During a particularly difficult winter where she saw her novel *The Bell Jar* published to less than enthusiastic reviews in January 1963, Plath's mental state deteriorated. She committed suicide in February 1963, leaving her children behind, as well as the new collection of poems that would eventually make her famous after her death.

Plath's most critically acclaimed poems are those that appeared in her posthumous collection, *Ariel.* In these last poems composed before her suicide, Plath appears to have reached a new level of creative complexity in imagery and theme. Her poems exhibit a raw power and anger, as she battles with despair and attempts to find the fortitude to endure her psychic pain. Within the postmodern milieu and contributing to its innovations, Plath does not create a distinct persona through which she filters these intense, private emotions. Poetic form and tradition become less significant with postmodern poets, and the poet's voice achieves primacy, especially in the school of poetry termed "Confessional." Poets such as Allen Ginsberg, Anne Sexton, and Plath in the 1950s were willing to probe their psyches in very private, personal ways, "confessing" their deepest, most private, even disturbing feelings. In the time period, this kind of psychological probing of the self was new and provocative. From a feminist perspective, Plath in the *Ariel* poems openly explores her feelings of rage against the men in her life and against patriarchal authority in general. Plath also explores her feelings of ambivalence about being a mother, the cultural pressures she experienced of becoming a wife and mother, the pain she endured as a result of her husband's infidelity, and her battle with depression that culminated in suicide attempts. In "Daddy," the prevalent Nazi imagery is not autobiographical but is used to depict the extreme emotions at work in the narrative voice's desperate, raging attempt to cut the cord of paternalistic domination. The narrative voice urgently and angrily wants to break from daddy's control, domination, and influence in order to forge her own identity as a woman and as a person. In "Fever 103°," the narrative voice offers hallucinogenic images of a fevered self, burned pure of fleshly needs and desires into an acetylene virgin, a bodiless entity that is almost invisible but nevertheless combustible. In her virginal state, untouched by the "lecherous" patriarchy, she is most volatile—and powerful.

6.14.1 "Daddy"

Please click the link below to access this selection:

http://www.poetryfoundation.org/poem/178960

6.14.2 "Fever 103"

Please click the link below to access this selection:

http://www.poetryfoundation.org/learning/guide/179981#poem

6.14.3 Reading and Review Questions

1. In Plath's "Daddy," analyze the imagery of Nazism associated with the "father" in the poem. What is the meaning of the imagery? Why is it so extreme?

2. In "Daddy," who or what is the narrator trying to break away from? Explain the nature of this break or escape the narrator is trying to make.

3. How would you describe the narrator of "Daddy": a victim? a survivor? a heroine?

4. In "Fever 103°" examine ways in which the flesh and the spirit (or soul) are distinguished through imagery.

5. Examine the nature of "fever" in "Fever 103°." What is the symbolic significance of "fever" in the poem?

6. Analyze the terms "purity" and "sin" in the poem in light the narrator's apparent transformation.

6.15 DON DELILLO

(1936 -)

In the sixteen darkly satiric novels he has published to date, Don DeLillo shows us how disorienting, mysterious and absurd life in postmodern America can be. DeLillo was born in Brooklyn, New York, and graduated from Fordham University in the Bronx. While DeLillo is known for his careful research and erudition, he admits that "I never liked school" in a rare 2000 interview in the *South Atlantic Quarterly*. Instead, he explains that he received his education primarily from New York City itself, in particular from the city's intense

Image 6.12 | Don DeLillo, 2011
Photographer | User "Thousand Robots"
Source | Wikimedia Commons
License | CC BY-SA 2.0

avant-garde artistic culture on display in its modern art museums, jazz clubs, and art cinemas. After college, DeLillo stayed in the city to work for an advertising agency, quitting in 1964 after five years to pursue a career as a writer. Since then he has published in venues ranging from *The Kenyon Review* and *The New Yorker* to *Rolling Stone* and *Sports Illustrated* and has won dozens of awards, including a Guggenheim Fellowship, the National Book Award for Fiction, and the **PEN/ Faulkner Award**. DeLillo's capacious work centers around a wide cast of familiar American characters, from football players, rock stars, writers, and child prodigies to college professors, spies, stock brokers, and the real-world assassin, Lee Harvey Oswald—all of whom live in an America that is saturated with media, obsessed with violent entertainment, prone to conspiracy, overloaded with sensation, overcrowded with the detritus of militarism and capitalism, and poised on the brink of apocalypse. To represent the superabundance of contemporary American culture—from the lives we live to those we mythologize to those we know only through movies and TV—DeLillo has worked in numerous narrative forms, including the sports novel (*End Zone* 1972 and *Amazons* 1980), the rock and role **satire** (*Great Jones Street* 1972), science fiction (*Ratner's Star* 1976), the thriller (*Players* 1977, *Running Dog* 1978, and *The Names* 1982), the weighty modernist odyssey (*Cosmopolis* 2003), the dense postmodernist historical novel (*Underworld* 1997, *Libra* 1988, and *Mao II* 1991), and even closely observed American realism (*Falling Man* 2007).

DeLillo's academic satire *White Noise*, a selection of which is included here, received the National Book Award for Fiction in 1985. *White Noise* represents what everyday American life is like for "men and women who live," as DeLillo describes in a 1993 *Paris Review* interview, "in the particular skin of the late twentieth century." *White Noise* holds an estranging mirror to 1980s Cold War American culture, foregrounding the absurdity behind much everyday American behavior. The novel is narrated by Jake Gladney—a professor of an invented academic field called "Hitler Studies"—who is so disconnected from the real Adolph Hitler that he doesn't even know German and does not study the Holocaust. A four-time divorcee, Jake lives in a house full of the children from his past marriages and his present wife, a woman addicted to a drug that cures her fear of death. DeLillo uses the misadventures of Professor Gladney to explore themes ranging from consumerism, non-traditional families, addiction, and medicalization to conspiracies, mass destruction, the relation of media to reality, and the mystery of life itself. In the brief section included here, Jake has accompanied his colleague Murray Jay Siskind (a professor who wants to create a new academic field modeled on Hitler Studies called "Elvis Presley Studies") to "The Most Photographed Barn in America." The visit to this piece of Americana then becomes an occasion for DeLillo's characters to converse about what it means to live in America today.

6.15.1 "The Most Photographed Barn in America" (excerpt from *White Noise*)

Please click the link below to access this selection:

http://text-relations.blogspot.com/2011/03/most-photographed-barn-in-america.html

6.15.2 Reading and Review Questions

1. "No one sees the barn," Murray observes. Why does no one see the barn?

2. In his influential essay, "The Work of Art in the Age of Mechanical Reproduction," the cultural theorist Walter Benjamin argues that photographs and films strip their original objects of the "aura" of authenticity by removing them from the traditions and situations of which they are organically a part. One cannot photograph the entire material history of a work of art, after all. Murray argues that "every photograph" taken of the barn actually "reinforces the aura" it possesses. If photographs strip things of their aura of authenticity then how can this be? Describe the aura these pictures reinforce. What is unique or artistic about this barn, if anything? What do we see when we look within the barn's much-photographed aura?

6.16 ALICE WALKER

(1944 -)

Born in Eatonton, Georgia, Alice Walker grew up in rural middle Georgia. Her father was a sharecropper, and her mother was a maid. Although they lived under Jim Crow laws in Georgia, in which African-Americans were discouraged from education, Walker's parents turned her away from working in the fields, espousing instead the importance of education and enrolling her in school at an early age. Walker describes writing at the age of eight years old, largely as a result of growing up in what was a strong oral culture.

In 1952, Walker injured her eye after her brother accidently shot her with a BB gun. Since the family did not have a car, it was a week before Walker received medical attention.

Image 6.13 | Alice Walker, n.d.
Photographer | User "Applegirl77"
Source | Wikimedia Commons
License | CC BY-SA 4.0

By this time, she was blind in that eye, with scar tissue forming. As a result, Walker became shy and withdrawn, yet, years later, after the scar tissue healed, she became more confident and gregarious, graduating high school as the valedictorian, Walker writes about this in her essay, "Beauty: When the Other Dancer is the Self." Walker left Eatonton for Atlanta, attending Spelman College, a prestigious Historically Black College for women, and later receiving a scholarship to Sarah Lawrence College in New York. Walker considers her time in New York as critical for her development. While there, Walker became involved in the Black Arts movement before her work in the Civil Rights movement brought her back to the South. In 1969, Walker took a teaching position as Writer-in-Residence at Jackson State College in Jackson, Mississippi before accepting the same position at Tougaloo College in Tougaloo, Mississippi. While there, she published her debut novel, *The Third Life of Grange Copeland* (1970). However, Walker soon returned to New York to join the editorial staff of *Ms.* magazine. Her second novel, *Meridian* (1976), received positive reviews, but her third novel, *The Color Purple* (1982), perhaps best showcases her writing talents. This novel draws on some of Walker's personal experiences as well as demonstrates Walker's own creativity. For it, she won the National Book Award and the Pulitzer Prize. This novel was later adapted as a popular film.

In addition to her engagement as an activist in many key issues, Walker has continued to write, publishing the famous book of essays, *In Search of Our Mother's Gardens* (1983), as well as several other novels, such as *Possessing the Secret of Joy* (1992). One theme that emerges in Walker's work is acknowledging the contributions of, often under-appreciated, African-American writers, such writers as Zora Neale Hurston. Furthermore, Walker's writing calls attention to the discrepancies in America's treatment of African-Americans, while also acknowledging the importance of all Americans' shared past. In "Everyday Use," we see many of these themes coalesce in the conflict between sisters Dee and Magee. Although they are sisters, these two have very different lives, which leads to the central tension of the story—their argument over the quilt.

6.16.1 "Everyday Use"

Please click the link below to access this selection:

http://xroads.virginia.edu/~ug97/quilt/walker.html

6.16.2 Reading and Review Questions

1. Why does Dee take Polaroids? Why does she change her name? What does this signify?

2. What does the quilt represent?

3. Dee and Magee are both interested in the quilt for different reasons. Why is each sister interested in the quilt? Who does Mama side with in this conflict? Why?

6.17 LESLIE MARMON SILKO

(1948 -)

Leslie Marmon Silko was born in Albuquerque, New Mexico, but raised in the outskirts of Old Laguna, a Pueblo village. Silko describes a lively childhood spent outdoors, one which included riding horses and hunting deer. Although Silko enjoys one-fourth Pueblo ancestry, she also shares Mexican ancestry; Silko did not live on the Laguna Pueblo reservation, and Silko was not allowed to participate in many Pueblo rituals. Through the fourth grade, she

Image 6.14 | Leslie Marmon Silko, 2011
Photographer | Uche Ohbuji
Source | Wikimedia Commons
License | CC BY-SA 2.0

attended a Bureau of Indian Affairs (BIA) school, only to later commute to Manzano Day School, a Catholic private school in Albuquerque. After high school, Silko enrolled at the University of New Mexico, where she earned a bachelor's degree in English. After college, Silko taught creative writing courses at the University of New Mexico before enrolling in their American Indian law program. As her literary career blossomed, Silko dropped out to focus on her writing. Silko would later spend several years as a professor of English and Creative Writing at the University of Arizona in Tucson, where she currently resides.

Silko's first published short story, "The Man to Send Rain Clouds" (1969), was originally written for a class in college and was based around a similar autobiographic event. The story earned Silko an National Endowment for the Humanities (NEH) grant and, as Silko continued to publish, her literary reputation grew. In 1974, her first book, *Laguna Woman,* featured a selection of Silko's poems and short fiction; however, it was the emergence of her debut novel, *Ceremony* (1977), which brought her national recognition and established her as a prominent Native American writer. Since then, Silko has remained one of the most respected contemporary American writers: her short story collection, *Storyteller* (1981), was well received and, in the same year, Silko was awarded the famed MacArthur Genius Grant. Her other novels include *Almanac of the Dead* (1991) and *Gardens in the Dunes* (1999). In 1996, Silko published *Yellow Woman and a Beauty of the Spirit,* a collection of essays on Native American life; these essays discuss many contemporary issues relevant to Native Americans as well as her own reflections on her storytelling background and writing process.

Silko's Native American heritage, especially her Pueblo upbringing, is a major thematic element which emerges within her writing regardless of its genre, albeit poetry, fiction, or nonfiction. In "Yellow Woman," a part of her *Storyteller* collection, Silko is able to merge traditional Pueblo legends with a contemporary tale. Part action/adventure story and part mythology, "Yellow Woman" seamlessly tells the tale of a narrator who may or may not be caught up in Laguna ancestral lore.

6.17.1 "The Yellow Woman"

Please click the link below to access this selection:

https://moodle2.unifr.ch/pluginfile.php/268379/mod_resource/content/1/Silko%20Yellow%20Woman.pdf

6.17.2 Reading and Review Questions

1. What elements seem out of time? What effect on readers do these anachronistic elements have?

2. Is this a story of alienation or community? How does the narrator use the Kachina yellow woman story to connect with her community?

3. Is this a story about humanity or the mystical?

6.18 DAVID FOSTER WALLACE

(1962 - 2008)

David Foster Wallace was born in Ithaca, New York, but was raised in Urbana, Illinois. The son of two academics, his father, James Donald Wallace, was a philosophy professor at the University of Illinois, while his mother, Mary Jean Foster, was an English professor at Parkland College. During his youth, Wallace was a regionally ranked junior tennis player (an interest that would emerge as a subject in many

Image 6.15 | David Foster Wallace, 2006
Photographer | Steve Rhodes
Source | Wikimedia Commons
License | CC SA 2.0

of his writings). Wallace attended Amherst College, where he majored in both English and Philosophy. His first novel, *The Broom of the System* (1987), was based on his undergraduate thesis. After his undergraduate studies, Wallace enrolled at the University of Arizona, where he earned his M.F.A. in fiction; he then enrolled in a philosophy graduate program at Harvard University before dropping out during his first semester and admitting himself into a mental institution. From this time onward, Wallace began to take a greater interest in fiction, especially postmodern fiction, reading writers such as John Barth and Donald Barthleme, who were influential on his writing.

Wallace's debut novel, *The Broom of the System,* led to several influential publications, yet, it was his novel, *Infinite Jest* (1996), which earned him universal accolades, including landing him on the cover of *Time Magazine*. It also earned him the MacArthur Genius Grant (1997). Considered one of the greatest novels in the last fifty years, *Infinite Jest* deals with popular themes found in Wallace's work, such as addiction and media's growing influence in our culture.

Wallace was a rare writer, who wrote about a variety of topics, ranging from tennis, to writing the first critical study of rap, to a book on the concept of infinity. In 2004, he married painter Karen Green and, in 2008, after years of dealing with clinical depression, Wallace committed suicide. Posthumously, his estate published the novel *The Pale King* (2011) which was a finalist for the Pulitzer Prize. Since his suicide, Wallace has captivated the public and been the subject of countless essays and features. In 2009, Jon Krasinski adapted a film version of Wallace's book *Brief Interviews with Hideous Men*. In 2015, a film based on David Lipski's book length interview with Wallace, *Although in the End You End Up Becoming Yourself* (2010), was released under the title, *At the End of the Tour*.

"Consider the Lobster," originally published in *Gourmet* magazine, is a great example of Wallace's mass appeal, his ability to write about a seemingly simple event, a Lobster Festival, with humor and nuance, while uncovering the complex issues that arise from the festival. In many ways, Wallace's commencement speech to Kenyon College, "This is Water" (2005), later published as a stand-alone book, *This is Water* (2009), perfects that approach of writing for a mass audience. "This is Water" is said to be the culmination of his common themes as a writer, the most important of which is sincerity. In the speech, Wallace reminds audiences that although we all tend towards narcissism, it is important to try to be altruistic. Other themes found in Wallace's work include a growing concern with our changing culture, the increasing presence of media, as well as the effects of addiction.

6.18.1 "This is Water"

Please click the link below to access this selection:

http://www.metastatic.org/text/This%20is%20Water.pdf

6.18.2 "Consider the Lobster"

Please click the link below to access this selection:

http://www.columbia.edu/~col8/lobsterarticle.pdf

6.18.3 Reading and Review Questions

1. What does the title "This is Water" mean? How does this title emerge as a main theme of his speech?

2. What does Wallace mean by "default mode"? For example, how, according to Wallace, can our default mode be dangerous? Why does Wallace feel this is such an important lesson for graduates?

3. Examine the structure of "Consider the Lobster." How does Wallace develop his argument about the ethos of eating lobster? What is his argument?

4. How do you think the original readers of *Gourmet,* where "Consider the Lobster" was first published, reacted to this essay? Why do you think they printed it?

6.19 CHAPTER SIX KEY TERMS

- Adrienne Rich
- Alice Walker
- Allen Ginsberg
- Beat Literature
- City Lights Books
- Cold War
- Cosmic Vision
- David Foster Wallace
- Dialect
- Deconstruction
- Don DeLillo
- Donald Barthleme
- Explicit
- Flannery Othlemer
- Flash Fiction
- GI Bill
- Gravitas
- Implicit
- James Baldwin
- James Dickey

- Jim Crow Laws
- Korean War
- Leslie Marmon Silko
- Metanarrative
- National Book Award
- PEN/Faulkner Award
- Postmodernism
- Poststructuralist
- Pulitzer Prize
- Ralph Ellison
- Satire

- Signs
- Southern Gothic
- Southern Renaissance
- Student Nonviolent Coordinating Committee (SNCC)
- Sylvia Plath
- Tennessee Williams
- Theodore Roethke
- Toni Morrison
- World War II

GLOSSARY

Acadian: In Kate Chopin's work, the Acadians (or 'Cadians) were of French or French-Canadian descent. They may be depicted as having a mixed racial and ethnic heritage, and they do not have the wealth and status that the Creoles have.

Adrienne Rich: A twentieth century American poet associated with the feminist, environmentalist, anti-war and lesbian rights movements. She is the author of numerous collections of poetry including A Change of World (1951) and Diving into the Wreck (1973).

Alice Walker: Born in Eatonton, Georgia, Alice Walker is a contemporary American novelist and essayist whose work often focuses on America's treatment of African-Americans. She is the author of several novels such as The Third Life of Grange Copeland (1970) and The Color Purple (1982).

Allen Ginsberg: A twentieth century American poet associated with the Beat Literature movement. In collections such as Howl and Other Poems (1956), Ginsberg criticizes America's materialist culture and celebrates the nation's outcasts.

Ambrose Bierce: (1842 – 1914?) A short story writer and journalist known in particular for his realistic stories about the Civil War.

American Communist Party: The American Wing of the Communist Party, extremely influential in American politics in the early twentieth century.

Armistice: An agreement to stop fighting. The Armistice to end World War 1 (The Great War) signed on November 11, 1918.

Arthur Miller (1915-2005): An American playwright known for his critique of American society and the American dream. Among his best known plays are *Death of a Salesman* (1949) and *The Crucible* (1953)

Atlanta Compromise: A controversial agreement in 1895 between Booker T. Washington and Southern political leaders that exchanged basic protections for African-Americans for a continuation of white political rule.

Atlanta Exposition: Also called the Cotton States and International Exposition took place from 18 September to 31 December 1895 in Atlanta, Georgia to promote the technological and agricultural abilities of the Southern states and to encourage trade with Latin America.

Beat Literature: Represented in this book by Allen Ginsberg, Beat Literature is the product of a group of mid-twentieth century authors known as the Beat Generation, whose members also include the well-known novelists Jack Kerouac and William S. Burroughs. Authors of the Beat Generation represented America's countercultures while critiquing its materialism during the era of cultural conformity and national prosperity that followed World War II.

Booker T. Washington (1856-1915): An African-American educator, orator, and statesman who founded the Tuskegee Normal and Industrial Institute in 1881 to educate and train African-Americans living in the former Confederacy. As Washington argued in the Atlanta Compromise he believed that educational and business ownership were essential to the success and stability of the African-American community.

Cadence: The natural rhythm or modulation of a line of poetry.

Charles Chesnutt: (1858-1932) An African-American short story writer, novelist, essayist, and activist known for his stories about complex issues of race in the South after the Civil War.

Charles Darwin: Charles Darwin was a British naturalist and author best known for his contributions to evolutionary theory in his description of the process of natural selection. His important work, Origin of the Species (1859), influenced a number of artists and intellectuals of the time.

Charlotte Perkins Gilman: (1860 – 1935) An early feminist and activist known for her poems, short stories, essays, and novels that dealt with women's social and political issues.

Chicago World's Fair: See World's Columbian Exhibition

City Lights Books: Publisher of Allen Ginsberg's *Howl and Other Poems* (1956), City Lights Books is an independent San Francisco bookstore and publisher associated with the Beat Literature movement.

Civil War: The American Civil War was fought between northern states (known as Union forces) and Southern states (known as the Confederacy) from 1861 to 1865. The Civil War pitted the eleven states of the Confederate States of America against the twenty states of the Union (also known as the United States or the Federal Army) over the question of slavery. The war began in Charleston, South Carolina on 12 April 1861 and ended officially at Appomattox Courthouse, Virginia on 9 April 1865.

Cold War: The Cold War is the decades-long military and cultural conflict that developed soon after World War II between the United States and the Soviet Union. During the Cold War, the United States sought to contain the threat of Soviet Communism through military policies such as nuclear deterrence and domestic policies such as the formation of the House Un-American Activities Committee. The Cold War ended with the dissolution of the Soviet Union in 1991.

Cosmic Vision: A phrase associated with the American Beat poet Allen Ginsberg, cosmic vision refers to the days-long state of heightened spiritual awareness the poet reported to have experienced while living in Harlem in 1948.

Countee Cullen (1903-1946): A preeminent poet of the early Harlmen Renaissance who used traditional literary forms borrowed from nineteenth century English poetry to examine and critique the experiences of African-American artists.

Creole: In Kate Chopin's work, the French Creoles are of Spanish or French descent. They are typically white and are considered members of the upper class.

Cubism: A popular style of painting made famous by Pablo Picasso. Instead of realistic representation, objects are depicted in an abstract style, often fractional and cube-like.

David Foster Wallace: David Foster Wallace is a late twentieth century American novelist and essayist associated with the "maximalist" writing style, whose authors deliberately overload their work with excessive information.

Deconstruction: A postmodern philosophy associated with the French philosopher Jacques Derrida that emphasizes the contingency and contextuality of language. Contrary to the traditional definition of a word as the name of a thing, Deconstructionists treat words not as definitions of external, non-linguistic things but as so-called signs that can only continually refer to other signs. The meaning of things thus exists not absolutely in an objective world at large but instead within processions of signs that connect, ultimately, only to each other, and in which meaning is always relative to linguistic and historical context.

Dialect: The term dialect refers to the unique forms of a common language that are associated with different regions and groups. For instance, regional authors often write their dialog in "New England dialect" or "Southern dialect."

Don DeLillo: A contemporary American novelist whose work is often associated with postmodernism. In the wide ranging novels he has published to date, including Underworld (1997) and White Noise (1985), DeLillo represents the national myths, popular media, absurd situations, and everyday people who comprise the twentieth century American experience.

Donald Barthelme: A twentieth century postmodernist short story writer and novelist whose fiction is known for its playful sense of experimentation.

Dramatic Monologue: A lengthy speech by a single person, often seen in plays. Robert Browning's "My Last Duchess," is a famous example.

Dust Bowl: Severe storms and drought that affected American agriculture in the 1930s at the height of the Great Depression. The 'Dust Bowl' usually referred to the Great Plains and Midwest, which was most affected.

e. e. cummings (1894-1962): A twentieth century American modernist poet who wrote around three thousand poems in his lifetime, Cummings's poetry plays with language and bends traditional poetic forms into new shapes.

Edna St. Vincent Millay (1892-1950): A twentieth century American modernist poet known for her portrayal of female sexuality who combined technical skill as a poet with a lightness that contrasted sharply with the work of some of her male contemporaries.

Ellen Glasgow(1873-1945): (1873 - 1945) A Southern writer whose works heralded the Southern Renascence with their modernist and feminist themes concerning the changing South.

Emancipation: The process by which an individual or community is set free from slavery or some other form of legal confinement.

Émile Zola: A French writer known as a leader in the literary movement termed Naturalism. Zola articulated a theory of Naturalism in his important work, Le Roman Expérimental (1880). Zola argued for a kind of intense Realism, one that did not look away from any aspects of life, including the base, dirty, or ugly. His theory of Naturalism was heavily influenced by the works of Charles Darwin. Zola argued that a novel written about the human animal could be set up as a kind of scientific experiment, where, once the ingredients were added, the story would unfold with scientific accuracy. He was particularly interested in how hereditary traits under the influence of a particular social environment might determine a human to behave.

Emily Dickinson (1830-1886): An American poet of the mid-nineteenth century who experimented with verse and poetic forms to free language from the confines of traditional poetry. Even as she experimented with poetic forms, however, Dickinson's poetry explored traditional themes of identity, mortality, and the natural world.

Epigraph: A brief quotation preceding a literary work. For example, T.S. Eliot's 'The Love Song of J. Alfred Prufrock' begins with a brief epigraph from Dante's Inferno.

Ernest Hemingway (1899-1961): A modernist American novelist known for his distinct minimalist style of terse sentences. He is known for his novels The Sun Also Rises, A Farewell to Arms and The Old Man and The Sea.

Eudora Welty (1909-2001): A modernist American writer, Welty is considered a master of short fiction, publishing many famous short stories as well as winning a Pulitzer Prize for her novel, The Optimist's Daughter.

Explicit: The opposite of implicit, the term explicit refers to things that are clearly and directly stated.

Ezra Pound (1885-1972): A modernist poet and editor, known for his imagist poetry, such as "In a Station of the Metro."

F. Scott Fitzgerald (1896-1940): An American author known for his fictional depictions of the rich and famous in the 1920s. Fitzgerald's most famous works, including The Great Gatsby (1925) are sophisticated social satires.

Fauvism: A French style of art, specifically painting, made popular during Modernism, emphasizing color over representation.

Federal Writers' Project: A federal project to support writers during the Great Depression.

Feminism: The advocacy of equality between the sexes. In the United States, feminism can be defined as a series of social, cultural, economic, and political movements that emphasized and called for equality for women.

Flannery O'Connor: Georgia native Flannery O'Connor is a mid-twentieth century short story writer and novelist associated with Southern Gothic literature. In the two novels and two collections of short fiction she published before her early death, O'Connor explores the lives of Southerners caught between Old and New Souths.

Flash Fiction: Associated with the work of Donald Barthelme, the term flash fiction refers to extremely brief works of fiction ranging from 50 to 1000 words.

Frank Norris: (1870 – 1902) A journalist, novelist, and literary theorist, Norris was one of the first writers to embrace French Naturalism and to introduce the style of writing to an American audience.

Free Verse: A poetic form, commonly associated with Walt Whitman and more modern poets, that does not conform to a regular rhythm or set line length. Free verse is often said to suggest the form of ordinary speech.

Friedrich Nietzsche: Friedrich Nietzsche a nineteenth century German philosopher whose rejection of traditional religious views and his writings on nihilism influenced a number of artists and intellectuals of the time.

G.I. Bill: Known formally as The Serviceman's Readjustment Act of 1944, the so-called G.I. Bill provided benefits to servicemen returning from World War II such as funds for college tuition and affordable home and business loans.

Gravitas: Gravitas refers to a quality of seriousness and dignity, as well as a sense of substance and importance, that someone or something may possess.

Great Migration: A major population shift as many Southerners, including a large population of African-Americans, moved from rural Southern states to urban Northeastern, Midwestern and even Western metropolitan areas.

Great War: Another name for World War 1, which lasted from 1914-1918.

Guggenheim Fellowship: Guggenheim Fellowships are prestigious, multi-thousand-dollar grants awarded since 1925 from the John Simon Guggenheim Memorial Foundation to scholars and artists of exceptional ability.

H. L. Mencken: An early twentieth century journalist and social critic who published widely during his lifetime. He is perhaps best known for his news reporting of the Scopes "monkey trial," where a high school teacher in Tennessee was put on trial for violating the state's Butler Act which made the teaching of evolution in state-funded schools illegal.

Harlem Renaissance: A cultural and artistic movement, originating in Harlem in the 1920s, which exposed many African-American artists and musicians to a larger audience.

Harlem: A neighborhood in New York City, influenced culturally by it's African-American population

Henry James: An advocate of Realism, James was a well-known novelist and literary theorist known for his international themes. He spent most of his working life in Britain.

High Modernism: Modernist works that, while more formal, look at the modern era as a period of loss. High modernists realize that the world has changed so much, it is impossible to return to the old ways.

Iconoclast: An iconoclast is a highly independent non-conformist who may rebel against or criticize the status quo.

Imagery: A type of figurative language that invokes a visual image or memory.

Imagism: A movement amongst Modernist poets to focus in on precise images. Ezra Pound's "In a Station of the metro" is a famous example of imagism.

Immigration: America saw a steep rise in immigration in the nineteenth century, as people from other countries moved to America for a variety of personal and political reasons but primarily to find work in America's growing industries, including the building of the transcontinental railroad.

Implicit. The opposite of explicit, the term implicit refers to things that are implied but not directly expressed.

Industrial Age: In America, the rise of industry in the mid to late nineteenth century and beyond caused a shift in America from a primarily agrarian economy to an industrial economy.

Industrialization: In America, industrialization can be seen as the process by which advances in technology in the nineteenth century led to the shift from farm production to manufacturing production.

Jack London: (1876 – 1916) A journalist, fiction writer, and social activist, London is known for elements of Naturalism in his work set in the Klondike region and the South Pacific. **James Baldwin**: A mid-twentieth century American essayist, novelist, playwright and civil rights activist whose work explores the complex interrelationship of race, class, and gender.

James Dickey: The Atlanta-born James Dickey is a mid-twentieth century American poet and novelist whose poetry, like his best-selling novel *Deliverance*, often explores the experiences of people in intense and violent situations.

Jazz Age: Another name for the 1920s in which Jazz became a popular form of music. Also known as "The Roaring 20s," the Jazz Age is said to have died when the Great Depression occured.

Jean Toomer (1894-1967): A Harlem Renaissance writer known primarily for his modernist work Cane.

Jessie Redmon Fauset (1882-1961): An African-American author of the Harlem Renaissance, Fauset was the longtime literary editor of The Crisis, the official magazine of the NAACP. Fauset's works frequently deal with the conflicts faced by light-skinned African-American women.

Jim Crow Laws: Named after a popular racist caricature of the nineteenth century, Jim Crow refers to the racist laws enacted in the states of the American South after Reconstruction that enforced the racial segregation of society under the specious rationale that black and white Americans could be "separate but equal." Jim Crow laws were nullified by the Civil Rights Act of 1964 and the Voting Rights Act of 1965.

Karl Marx: Karl Marx, who was born in Prussia and later lived in London, was a nineteenth century philosopher whose political and economic theories (collectively known as Marxism) formed the basis of the modern practice of Communism. Marx's views on class struggle and power were highly influential during the nineteenth century and beyond.

Kate Chopin: (1850 – 1904) A short story writer and novelist who wrote frankly about women's lives in Louisiana Bayou region and is known as one of the early feminist writers in America.

Korean War: Fought from June of 1950 to July of 1953, The Korean War was a war between North and South Korea, the two parts of Korea that were formed after World War II. The Soviet Union supported the Communist government of North Korea while the United States supported, and sent troops to fight for, its ally South Korea. The Korean War is often seen as an escalation of the Cold War between the Soviet Union and the United States. There was no victor in the Korean War and the country of Korea remains divided between North and South to this day.

Langston Hughes (1902-1967): A Jazz Age poet known for his lyric approach to poetry. Hughes is one of the most influential American poets of the twentieth century.

Leslie Marmon Silko: A late twentieth century Postmodern American novelist and essayist whose work often represents the lives and culture of Native Americans.

Local Color: Local color is a type of writing that became popular after the American Civil War. It is a sub-movement of writing that generally preceded and influenced the rise of Realism in American writing while it still retained some features of the Romanticism, the movement which preceded it. Local color writing focuses on the distinctive features of particular locale, including the customs, language, mannerisms, habits, and peculiarities of people and place, thereby predicting some aspects of the Realists' writing style, which focused on accuracy and detail. However, in Local Color stories, the characters are often predictable character types rather than the complex characters offered by Realist writers. Additionally, Local Color stories often retain Romantic features of emotion (including sentimentality and nostalgia) and idealism (with endings that are neatly resolved). Examples include Mark Twain's Life on the Mississippi.

Low Modernism: Modernist work that is less formal and experiments with form.

Lyric: A short poem that often expresses a single theme such as the speaker's mood or feeling.

Make It New!: A phrase from poet Ezra Pound which becomes the mantra of the modernists.

Marianne Moore (1887-1972): A preeminent modernist poet, Moore favored concrete images and plain language over traditional literary forms.

Mark Twain: (1835 – 1910): A pen name for Samuel Longhorn Clemens, an American author and humorist, who is known for his travel writings, his storytelling on the lecture circuit, and his novels and short stories, particularly Adventures of Huckleberry Finn (1885) which is often touted as the "Great American Novel."

Mary E. Wilkins Freeman: (1852 – 1930) A short story writer and novelist known for her realistic depiction of women's lives in the New England region. She also is known for her collection of ghost stories.

Metafiction: Metafiction is a literary technique in which a story's narrator draws attention to her own act of storytelling, explicitly foregrounding within her narrative the usually implicit processes with which stories are told.

Meter: The regular pattern of stressed and unstressed syllables found in a line of poetry. Free verse is notable for the absence of meter.

Modernism: a global movement centered in the United States and Europe, for literature written during the two wars, which is said to be the first industrialized modern period.

Modernist: An artist associated with the Modernism time period.

The National Association for the Advancement of Colored People (NAACP): founded in 1909 by a group of prominent African-Americans, including W.E.B. Du Bois who responded to the wave of punitive laws and restrictive ordinances enacted against African-Americans after the end of Reconstruction. The founders of the NAACP opposed Booker T. Washington's Atlanta Compromise on the grounds that it did not do enough to protect African-Americans from discriminatory laws and practices.

National Book Award: Starting in 1936, the ever-changing National Book Awards have been awarded annually by various organizations within the publishing industry and, since 1988, by the non-profit National Book Foundation to honor books written exclusively by American authors that have sold well or otherwise merit critical acclaim.

Naturalism: Naturalism was a style of writing that achieved prominence after Realism. Reacting against the Realists, Naturalists rejected Realism as focusing too much on the mundane, day-to-day concerns of average people while avoiding controversial subjects. Willing to tackle stories about prostitution, murder, domestic violence, alcoholism, and madness, Naturalists explored the grittier side of life. Influenced by the literary theories of Emile Zola and by Charles Darwin's writings about evolution, Naturalists typically saw the human being at the mercy of hereditary traits and environmental forces beyond his or her awareness, understanding, or control.

Nella Larsen (1891-1964): A Harlem Renaissance writer, known for her short story "Sanctuary," as well as her novels, Quicksand and Passing.

Nobel Prize: An international award granted for major artistic, cultural and scientific advances. Arguably the most prestigious literary award on Earth, the Nobel Prize in Literature is part of a set of annual awards named after the Swedish inventor Alfred Nobel, whose will created the prize. The prize in literature is awarded by the Swedish Academy to an individual author whose lifetime of work has made an outstanding contribution to the arts of letters. To date, thirteen Americans have received the Nobel Prize in literature, Sinclair Lewis being the first in 1930 and Toni Morrison being the latest in 1993.

Passing: "Passing" is a historical term that describes the process by which light-skinned African-Americans could pass as whites.

PEN/Faulkner Award: In 1980, the PEN/Faulkner Foundation was created after the publishing industry changed the voting rules for the National Book Award to encourage awarding only bestselling books. Since then the Foundation has recognized the best work of the year written by a living American citizen with the PEN/Faulkner Award. The acronym PEN stands for Poets, Essayists, and Novelists.

Plot of decline: The plot of decline is a significant feature in most Naturalistic novels. At some point in the novel, even after enjoying a temporary rise in material circumstances, characters—under the pressures of hereditary traits and environmental forces beyond their awareness, understanding, or control—often start a downward spiral into degeneration and even death.

Post-structuralism: refers to philosophies and critical theories that follow the insights of "structuralism," a twentieth century critical movement that emphasized the role that language plays in the apprehension of meaning and reality. Philosophers such as Jacques Derrida and Jean Baudrillard are poststructuralists.

Postmodernism: The term postmodernism refers both to works of culture that were created since the 1950s following the innovations of Modernism, and to the high-tech, global, cold-warring, consumerist mass-media society that arose in the decades following World War II. In literature, Postmodernism refers to a style of writing such as one finds in the work of Donald Barthleme and David Foster Wallace that employs the experimental techniques of the Modernists in a decidedly playful manner, foregrounding the role that language, text, and technique play in the creation of fiction, poetry, and drama. The term also refers to works such as Don DeLillo's that represents how absurd, overwhelming, and disorienting postmodern society can be.

Prose: A term used for writing which does not fit the poetic structure (does not use metric verse or free verse).

Pulitzer Prize: A very prestigious award for journalism, literature or music granted each year from Columbia University. Established in 1918 in the will of the publisher Joseph Pulitzer and managed by Columbia University, the Pulitzer Prize is awarded annually to writers, journalists, and composers of exemplary works of literature, journalism, and music respectively.

Racial Inequality: The inferior treatment of another person due to their racial heritage.

Ralph Ellison: Ralph Ellison is a mid-twentieth century Modernist American essayist and novelist whose work explores the African-American experience.

Realism: Realism is a type of writing that achieved prominence after the American Civil War. Reacting against the Romantic era of writing that preceded them, Realists rejected Romantic features of emotionalism and idealism. Realists also rejected the creation of larger-than-life characters who were unrealistically all good or all bad. Influenced by Local Color and Regional writers, Realists paid attention to details and accuracy in describing people and places, and they developed characters who used ordinary speech in dialogue, commensurate to the character's social class. However, the Realists moved beyond Local Color and Regional writers in their more complex development of realistic characterization. Characters in Realist stories resembled ordinary people (neither all good nor all bad), often of the middle class, living in ordinary circumstances, who experienced plausible real-life struggles and who often, as in life, were unable to find resolution to their conflicts. In Realistic stories, the plot was formed from the exploration of a character working through or reacting to a particular issue or struggle. In other words, character often drove the plot of the story. Characters in Realistic fiction were three-dimensional, and their inner lives were often revealed through an objective, omniscient narrator. In a Realist story, there are rarely any indications of Romantic features such as nostalgia, sentimentality, or neatly resolved endings.

Reconstruction: The period of American history from the end of the Civil War in 1865 until the formal removal of the U.S. Army from the territory of the former Confederate States of America on 31 March 1877.

Regionalism: Regionalism is a type of writing that was practiced after the American Civil War. It is a sub-movement of writing that generally preceded and influenced the rise of Realism in American writing. Regionalism, like Local Color, employs a focus on the details associated with a particular place, but Regionalist stories often feature a more complex narrative structure, including the creation of a main protagonist who provides the perspective or point of view through which the plot of the story is told. Such a shift in the technique of narration aligns Regionalist writers more closely with Realist writers, who are known for their complex characters who exhibit psychological dimensionality. However, Regionalist stories, like Local Color stories, often retain Romantic features of emotion (including sentimentality and nostalgia) and idealism (with endings that are neatly resolved).

Rest cure: The "rest cure" was a medical treatment for women developed by a nineteenth century physician, Dr. S. Weir Mitchell. Used to treat "hysterical" (or nervous) tendencies in women, the "cure" involved complete bed rest and isolation, with no mental or physical stimulation.

Rhyme: Repetition of sounds within poetry and often at the end of a line.

Robert Frost (1872-1963): American modernist poet best known for his poems like "The Road Not Taken" and "Mending Wall" that feature the voice of an older New England farmer reflecting on themes of nature and mutability.

Romanticism: A literary movement that begin in the late eighteenth century and often focused on unique feelings of the speaker and the importance of nature in relation to individuals.

Sarah Orne Jewett: (1849 – 1909) A short story writer, poet, and novelist known for her realistic depiction of women's lives in the New England region, particularly near the coast of Maine.

Satire: Satire is the use of humor, exaggeration, or ridicule to expose human ignorance, vice, or foolishness—as well as other human weaknesses.

Segregation: The enforced separation of groups of persons based on race.

Signs: In poststructuralist philosophies such as Jacques Derrida's Deconstructionism, language is composed not of words that exactly define specific, concrete things but instead of signs that refer always to other signs in a so-called "chain of signification." The meanings of words-as-signs are thus linguistically and historically relative, indefinite, and prone to change because they refer not to actual things but to long, historically produced assemblages of signs/words.

Slavery: A legal and economic system in which certain individuals are treated as an legally considered the property of others. This form of slavery is also called chattel slavery.

Southern gothic: Southern gothic is a genre of writing that is prevalent in the literary tradition of the American South. Borrowing features from gothic literature of the Romantic period, works may focus on dark themes associated with the supernatural, or they may focus on exaggerated characters that are eccentric, freakish, disfigured, or flawed in some disturbing way. Often, works incorporate elements of the grotesque. Southern writers sometimes used these conventions to critique the underlying Southern social order, illuminating disturbing foundations on which the social order was constructed.

Southern Renaissance: Also known as the Southern Renascence; refers to Modernist literature written in the American South during the 1920s and 30s by such authors as William Faulkner, Katherine Anne Porter, and Eudora Welty. The literature of the Southern Renascence eschewed nostalgic representations of the Old South, featuring instead more realist, violent, experimental and even gothic representations of the region's history and social norms.

Spanish-American War: The Spanish-American War was a war between Spain and the United States in 1898, resulting in Cuban independence.

Stephen Crane

Student Nonviolent Coordinating Committee (SNCC): The Student Nonviolent Coordinating Committee was an influential organization of students during the Civil Rights Movement of the 1960s, organizing public protests such as sit-ins and marches on Washington, D.C. as well as freedom rides and voter registration drives.

Sylvia Plath: Sylvia Plath is a mid-twentieth Century American poet whose work is associated with the confessional style of poetry.

T. S. Eliot (1888-1965): A modernist poet and writer who published The Wasteland, which is perhaps the most famous work of the modernist period. Eliot was one of the most important figures of the modernist period, editing The Dial, where he helped many modernist writers gain a wider audience.

Talented Tenth: A term from W.E.B. DuBois' essay, 'The Talented Tenth,' referring to the top 10% of African-Americans as cultural and political leaders. It was used widely during the Harlem Renaissance.

Tennessee Williams: Tennessee Williams is a Modernist mid-twentieth Century American playwright whose work, often featuring misfits or outcasts, foregrounds the emotional experiences of its characters.

The Great Depression: A period of national economic depression beginning with the Stock Market Crash of 1929 and lasting throughout the 1930s.

The New Deal: A series of federally funded programs started by President Franklin Delano Roosevelt during the Great Depression to build infrastructure and create jobs for the nation.

Theodore Roethke (1908-1963): A preeminent postmodern poet, Roethke's poetry combines natural and industrial elements in a combination of hope and insecurity.

Toni Morrison: A late twentieth century novelist who combines folk and postmodernist storytelling techniques to represent the African-American experience.

Transcontinental Railroad: The Transcontinental Railroad was a network of railroads completed in the nineteenth century that stretched across the country and united America by rail.

Tuskegee Normal and Industrial Institute: A school for the education of African-Americans living in the former confederacy founded by Booker T. Washington at Tuskegee, Alabama in 1881. The school exists today as Tuskegee University.

W. E. B. Du Bois (1868-1963): An African-American historian and sociologist, Du Bois earned the first doctorate at Harvard University and championed the cause of equal rights for African-Americans. Du Bois was a founder of the NAACP and an active supporter of the Harlem Renaissance. He actively opposed the Atlanta Compromise supported by Booker T. Washington.

Wallace Stevens (1874-1955): American modernist poet whose works often feature the common, the contemporary, and the familiar. Unlike the Romantic poets who looked to the natural world for signs of cosmic significance, Stevens's poetry celebrates the ordinary.

Walt Whitman (1819-1892): A leading figure in nineteenth century American poetry, Whitman celebrated the common language of the common man throughout his works.

William Carlos Williams (1883-1963): A modernist poet, who was trained as a medical doctor. Williams is known for experimenting with style in his poetry. William Carlos Williams is known for his poems, "This is Just to Say" and "The Red Wheelbarrow."

William Dean Howells: (1837 - 1920) A founder of the Realism movement, Howells was a well-known and influential writer, literary theorist, and literary critic. He was editor of the Atlantic Monthly from 1871 – 1881.

William Faulkner (1897-1962): One of America's most famous novelists winning both a Nobel and Pulitzer Prize for Fiction. Faulkner was active during the Southern Literary Renaissance and was famous for his stream of consciousness writing, as well as for using the same fictional setting Yoknapatawpha County (and many of the same characters) in his works. He is known for his modernist novels The Sound and the Fury, Absalom, Absalom! and As I Lay Dying.

Woman Suffrage Movement: a movement that began in the mid-nineteenth century, with a focus on achieving for women the legal right to vote. Led to the adoption of the nineteenth amendment of the U.S. Constitution.

World War I: The first global war, (1914-1918). World War I included 9 million combatants and changed the face of modern warfare. It had a major economic, political and artistic impact on the entire world, especially Europe.

World War II: World War II, also known as The Second World War, was a global "total war" involving all the major nations of the world. The United States, The Soviet Union, and Britain were allies during the war, and this coalition of "Allied" powers were victorious over the "Axis" powers of Germany, Japan, Italy and their allies. The war was fought between 1939 and 1945, resulting in up to eighty million deaths.

World's Columbian Exposition: The World's Columbian Exposition, held from 1 May 1893 to 30 October 1893, took place in Chicago's Jackson Park and commemorated 400th anniversary of the arrival of Christopher Columbus in the Caribbean in 1492. The exposition featured exhibits by forty-six nations and represented both growing industrial importance of United States and the significance of the city of Chicago, Illinois as a transportation hub.

Zane Grey (1872-1839): A leading figure in the development of the western in American literature, Zane Grey was a dentist turned prolific author whose novels and short stories about the American West made him one of the most popular and commercially successful writers of the first two decades of the twentieth century.

Zora Neale Hurston (1891-1960): An anthropologist and Harlem Renaissance author known for her highly celebrated novel Their Eyes Were Watching God.

CALIFORNIA

REAL ESTATE PRACTICE

William H. Pivar,
Lowell Anderson,
Daniel S. Otto
with Kartik Subramaniam, Contributing Editor

This publication is designed to provide accurate and authoritative information in regard to the subject matter covered. It is sold with the understanding that the publisher is not engaged in rendering legal, accounting, or other professional advice. If legal advice or other expert assistance is required, the services of a competent professional should be sought.

President: Dr. Andrew Temte
Chief Learning Officer: Dr. Tim Smaby
Executive Director, Real Estate Education: Melissa Kleeman-Moy
Development Editor: Jody Manderfeld

CALIFORNIA REAL ESTATE PRACTICE, NINTH EDITION
©2016 Kaplan, Inc.
Published by DF Institute, Inc., d/b/a Dearborn Real Estate Education
332 Front St. S., Suite 501
La Crosse, WI 54601

Printed in the United States of America
Second revision, April 2017
ISBN: 978-1-4754-3575-7

CONTENTS

INTRODUCTION

California Real Estate Practice is the practical application of real estate knowledge to meet the needs of buyers, sellers, lessors, and lessees. It is a course in what to do for success in meeting these needs.

California Real Estate Practice is not a repetition of *California Real Estate Principles*; however, it does cover the practical application of much of what you learned in Principles, as well as the "how" of being a real estate professional.

Note: Every applicant for a real estate salesperson's examination must complete college-level courses in real estate principles and real estate practice, as well as an approved third course, before sitting for the real estate salesperson's examination.

ACKNOWLEDGMENTS

The authors wish to acknowledge the invaluable assistance given to us in this and previous editions from the following professionals and educators:

Thurza B. Andrew, GRI, Mortgage Broker, Chico Valley Mortgage; Associate Professor, Butte Community College; Leonel "Leo" Bello, MBA, City College of San Francisco; Joyce Emory, Real Estate Advisory Council; Ignacio Gonzalez, Mendocino Community College, Ukiah, California; Professor Donna Grogan, El Camino College; Ted Highland, Kaplan Professional Schools; Margaret McCarthy Johnson, CPA; Don Kalal, GRI, California Brokers Institute; Keith H. Kerr, City College of San Francisco; Charles E. Krackeler, CRS, GRI, College of San Mateo; Fred L. Martinez, City College of San Francisco; Judith Meadows; Joe M. Newton, Bakersfield College; Pamela Pedago-Lowe, RE/MAX South County; Ronald Dean Schultz, Diablo Valley College; Nancy E. Weagley, Saddleback College; Evelyn W. Winkel, Esq., Rancho Santiago College; Janet Wright, Place Title Company; and Bud Zeller, GRI, CRS, RIM, ERA Sierra Properties.

It is with fond memories that we acknowledge the contribution of two exceptional real estate educators, Lowell Anderson and Daniel S. Otto, the original authors of this text. They set the direction to produce a working tool for real estate professionals. Their emphasis was to meet the needs of others.

1

GETTING STARTED IN REAL ESTATE

LEARNING OBJECTIVES

When you have completed this unit, you will be able to

- explain the effect the real estate industry has, both directly and indirectly, on the economy;

- describe the unique nature of the real estate marketplace and changes that are taking place within the real estate profession;

- explain how brokers are compensated and changes taking place as to compensation;

- list specialties available within or related to the real estate profession;

- describe the relationship between brokers and salespeople and factors to consider in choosing a broker; and

- explain the necessity of planning, goal setting, time management, attitude, continued education and training to a real estate career.

KEY TERMS

buyer's market	inventory	personal assistant
California Association of REALTORS®	mentor program	Realtist
	multiple listing service	seller's market
caravans	must-buy buyer	stratified marketplace
completed staff work	must-sell seller	team concepts
daily planning	National Association of REALTORS®	will-buy buyer
e-PRO certification		will-sell seller
employee	office procedures manual	workers' compensation insurance
goal setting	100% commission office	
independent contractor		

WHAT IT MEANS TO BE A REAL ESTATE PROFESSIONAL

It has been said that without the first real estate salesperson, human beings would still be living in caves. This may be an overstatement, but it is true that the real estate profession has played a significant role in improving the living conditions and lifestyles of our citizens.

Although we deal with a product—real estate (namely, the land and that which transfers with it)—the human factor of identifying and fulfilling the needs of others is the dominant emphasis of the real estate profession. We reach success in the real estate profession by first successfully meeting the needs of others. Real estate is, therefore, more a *people* than a *property* profession. Your understanding of people and their motivations will determine your future as a real estate professional. You might consider taking an interest aptitude test to see if you have the *people interests* that fit a career in real estate.

This is a profession that you can be properly proud of, because in its practice you guide buyers in making the largest purchase of their lives, one that will become a significant part of their lives—their homes. You also guide sellers in selling what has likely become more than just real estate but a place of memories. For the buyer as well as the seller, home purchases are important in both emotion and dollars.

REAL ESTATE AND THE ECONOMY

The real estate industry, which includes the production as well as the distribution of real estate, has historically been an engine driving both the California and the U.S. economies.

More jobs have been created in the real estate and related supply, construction, and service industries than from any other source. In addition, the many industries that benefit from a strong real estate market—in new as well as existing proper ties—include those listed below.

Advertising	Escrow
Air-conditioning	Excavating
Aluminum	Fencing
Appliance	Floor coverings
Appraisal	Flooring
Architecture and design	Furniture
Awning	Glass
Banking	Hardware
Bed and bath accessories	Heating
Brick and stone	Home inspection
Cabinetry	Insulation
Carpet cleaning	Insurance
Ceramic	Internet services
Cleaning services	Iron work
Concrete	Landscaping
Construction equipment manufacture and sales	Lawn care
	Lawn equipment and supplies
Construction workers and support	Legal
personnel	Logging
Contracting	Lumber
Crane service	Maintenance
Drywall	Millwork
Electrical equipment and supplies	Mold abatement
	Moving and storage
	Mortgage origination and service
Equipment maintenance	Municipal services

Nursery

Paint

Pest control

Plaster Plastic

Plumbing fixtures

Pools and spas (construction, maintenance and repair)

Portable toilets

Printing

Property inspection

Property management

Remodeling

Road construction

Roofing

Sales (supplies, equipment, and services)

Seal coating

Security (equipment and services)

Septic systems

Service providers

Steel

Stucco

Survey

Textile (fabrics for home furnishings)

Termite

Tile

Title insurance

Tools

Transportation

Vehicle (sales and service)

Wall coverings

Warehousing

Waste removal

Window coverings

Website design

Well (drilling and maintenance)

Real estate salespeople work at the end of the production and marketing pipeline keeping our products moving. If we were unable to effectively market products, the entire process would slow, resulting in increased unemployment that would have been a recessionary effect on our entire economy. The real estate recession of the mid-2000s began with a decrease in lending standards, and the market has been recovering as the remaining toxic inventory moves through the system.

THE REAL ESTATE MARKETPLACE

The real estate marketplace, where you will be aiding buyers and sellers, is generally regarded as an imperfect marketplace. Prices asked for similar properties vary, and the selling price is often less than the asking price. Values generally are set by supply and demand, not by sellers. It is the price a buyer will pay and not the price a seller desires that ultimately determines value. The only constant in the real estate marketplace is change. Inventory and value are not static. The real estate marketplace differs from other commodities. Some of the reasons why the real estate marketplace is unique include the following:

<table>
<tr><td>Real estate is not homogeneous</td></tr>
</table>

- **Product differentiation**—Every property is different. No two locations are the same. There are usually differences in square feet, interior design, architectural style, landscaping, decorating, age, maintenance, and other amenities. Because of these differences, it is impossible to determine value scientifically. An appraiser tries to evaluate these differences but only estimates what the sale price should be.

- **Emotion**—Emotion plays a significant part in a purchase decision. Often a buyer wants just one particular property after having turned down similar offerings without knowing why. This emotional desire can play a significant role in determining what a buyer will pay. Emotion plays a far lesser role for sellers, who are more likely to make their decisions based on logic.

- **Buyer and seller knowledge**—While internet homesites have resulted in better informed buyers and sellers, the listing prices alone can be misleading. List prices are not sale prices and many listings expire unsold. Location also plays a significant role in determining value. Similar houses on different blocks or different streets can have significantly dissimilar values. In a thin market with few sales for a type of property, the internet data can be especially misleading. Some buyers and sellers in the marketplace have imperfect or erroneous knowledge of prices paid for similar properties. Because of this imperfect knowledge, sellers have sold at what we may consider below-market prices, and sellers have priced their properties so high that buyers show no interest in them. Similarly, imperfect knowledge can result in a buyer paying more than what might be regarded as a reasonable price. The growth of buyer brokerage, where a sole agent represents a buyer, has reduced the likelihood of a buyer overpaying.

- **Will-sell versus must-sell owners,** and **will-buy versus must-buy buyers**—Buyer and seller motivation play a significant role in what is asked for a property by an owner, what is offered by a buyer, and what an owner will accept. Unmotivated sellers—that is, **will-sell sellers** (those who don't need to sell but who will sell if the price is right)—frequently place property on the market at above-market prices. Sellers who are motivated to sell will be more realistic in their pricing. When a seller is highly motivated or desperate, a **must-sell seller,** the price asked could be less than the sale prices of similarly desirable properties. The degree of seller motivation also will affect the likelihood of a below-list-price offer being accepted. Included in must-sell sellers are those in foreclosure sales to avoid foreclosure as well as short sales and lender dispositions of lender-owned real estate. Lender-owned real estate is usually called REOs (Real Estate Owned). When many such properties are on the market, they have a negative effect on all similar properties in the marketplace. **Will-buy buyers** are buyers who don't really have to buy. Investors and speculators are included in this group. Will-buy buyers generally look for motivated must-sell sellers; in other words, they're often bargain hunters. Investors are usually will-buy buyers. **Must-buy buyers** generally look for properties that meet their specific needs. While even must-buy buyers like bargains, they are more likely to pay a reasonable price. Successful real estate professionals concentrate their time on probabilities rather than possibilities, which means giving priority to must-sell owners and motivated buyers.

■ **Terms**—Because of the dollar value of the purchase, real estate sales tend to be very sensitive to interest rates. Higher interest rates can depress the marketplace because fewer buyers will qualify for loans. Lower rates tend to stimulate the market as more potential buyers qualify for loans. Investors are less likely to borrow money to invest in real property when interest rates are high, because the rate of return on the investment could be disappointing compared with the interest payments the investor would be required to make. By the same token, an investor would be more likely to borrow funds to invest in real property when interest rates are low. If a seller is willing to finance a buyer at a below-market rate of interest, the seller may be able to obtain a premium price for the property. Lower interest rates alone will not stimulate the economy if lenders are reluctant to loan.

Sale prices in a seller's market may actually be greater than the list price.

The economic forces of **supply and demand** place pressure on prices to rise or fall. In a **seller's market,** buyers must compete among themselves for properties. In a seller's market, there may be multiple offers for a property. Prices will increase in a seller's market. The reverse is true of a **buyer's market**. In a buyer's market, there are many sellers and few buyers, so sellers must compete for the available buyers, which usually means the lowering of prices.

Over the long term, real estate values have tended to increase significantly due to increased demand, which is affected by population movement and growth. However, it is not a truth that real estate values always increase. Economic factors, as well as a perceived desirability, can result in a stable or even declining market. Because price is a function of supply and demand, the areas and properties maintaining the greatest desirability will have the least downward pressure on prices.

A number of factors led to the 2008 meltdown in real estate values. Some of these included the following:

- A rapid rise in real estate values. Where values have increased rapidly, they are likely to show a rapid decline with a change in demand.

- Speculators entering the housing marketplace led to a false sense of actual housing demand. Many developers encouraged multiple sales to speculators, which helped to raise prices. When the market activity slowed, speculators sought to unload their inventory at prices that in many cases were less than what developers were selling the units for. Many speculators defaulted on their loans, resulting in foreclosure sales, which drove prices down further.

- Refinancing of homes became a prime engine of our economy. People were using their homes like credit cards to obtain money for consumer goods. When home values declined, many homeowners realized they were upside down on their loans, meaning that they owed more on their homes than the homes were worth. The result was that many owners walked away, leaving their homes to the lenders.

- Exotic loan types such as option-arms allowed borrowers to qualify for loans with a low monthly payment. When the honeymoon period of low payments ended, the loans required an amortized payment. Payment shock coupled with a declining market encouraged loan defaults.

- No down payment loans or very low down payment loans made from about 2003 until 2007 resulted in many buyers realizing they had no equity in their homes and, in many cases, owed tens or even hundreds of thousands more than similar homes were selling for. This led to a great many loan defaults.

■ Lenders who were not keeping the loans but intended to sell them to others became caught up in a "make hay while the sun shines" attitude. Appraisers who did not rubber stamp purchase prices were replaced by those who were more accommodating.

■ Ready credit led to developers building more and bigger projects. There was a belief that prosperity for them would never end.

■ Rating services gave collateralized mortgage securities investment grade ratings that in retrospect were not justified. The ability to sell these securities fueled the demand for more of them.

■ The economies of the world are interrelated and a world downturn led to lower exports, a lack of consumer confidence, lower imports and loss of jobs in both production and services. With two incomes necessary for many families, the loss of an income or even a reduction in hours led to many owners being unable to make mortgage payments.

In the mid- to late- 2000s we had a depressed real estate market, but the market moves in cycles. There was a brisk market in foreclosed properties, fueled both by families seeking homes and by investors. In 2012, several large investment groups entered the marketplace seeking to buy thousands of lender-owned homes. The increased demand resulted in higher prices being paid for distressed properties and was also reflected in higher prices for the resale market. Because few new homes had been built while the market was depressed, the demand for housing, coupled with low interest rates, caused rents to increase and home construction to come back strong. By 2015, home prices in many areas of California had exceeded the highs of 2007. The marketplace corrected itself.

| The real estate market is stratified based on price. |

The real estate marketplace is also a **stratified marketplace**—stratified based on price range. As an example, there might be a seller's market in homes priced under $250,000, with many more buyers than sellers. At the same time, there might be a glut of homes priced between $800,000 and $1,000,000, with few buyers.

The real estate professional helps to bring a measure of order to what could otherwise be a chaotic marketplace. A broker's knowledge, as well as inventory, gives both buyers and sellers comparables and enables the agent to educate them in the realities of the current marketplace. Membership in a **multiple listing service** (MLS) expands the inventory of comparables to provide information on a much broader scale. This information includes more than offering prices, which can be found on the internet; it also includes actual sale prices, special sale conditions, time to sell, as well as property that failed to sell during the listing period.

By serving as a marketing center or clearinghouse for both knowledge and proper ties, real estate brokers can analyze buyer needs and resources to match buyers with properties and guide them to the culminations of sales.

TRENDS IN REAL ESTATE BROKERAGE

The real estate profession has been undergoing significant change in the past few years. This change has included the following:

- Greater emphasis on determining client needs

- Greater interest in single agency buyer representation

- Better-trained and technology-oriented salespeople who regard real estate as a profession

- Buyers and sellers showing greater interest in professional designations, education, and experience of agents

- Expansion of large franchise offices through the absorption of former independent offices (though there will still be a place for small offices specializing in a geographic area or a type of property)

- Growth of the team concept where real estate salespeople form partnerships within a firm

- Greater use of the internet by homebuyers, as well as for marketing

- Decreasing reliance on traditional print advertising

- Increased number of marketing websites

- Growth of personal and office websites

- Increased website sophistication, with virtual tours, movement, and sound

- Use of informative blogs

- Use of social networking sites

- IDX (Internet Data Exchange) cooperation between brokers allows MLS members to display listings of other offices on their websites

- Electronic signatures—by using electronically stored signatures, DocuSign users can annotate and sign electronic documents, allowing for instantaneous transmission of signed documents

- Use of internet-generated forms

- Greater use of email and other cloud-based services to transmit information and contracts

- Mergers of MLSs, providing greater coverage for listings

- Use of smartphones by salespeople, not only to communicate with clients but also to access information

- Increased use of licensed and unlicensed professional assistants

- A change in the role of real estate brokers. With the internet, more buyers are doing their homework and know values and what is available. Agents are being sought to make showings of buyer-selected properties and help finalize a purchase. This has had an impact on fee schedules with the growth of online brokerage firms.

- Growth in one-stop shopping, where real estate firms are able to offer affiliated services

- Growth in number of firms offering lower rates of commissions with lower levels of services

- Increasing number of brokers and salespeople forming limited liability companies (LLC) to protect personal assets. Members have no personal liability for debts of the LLC.

- Increase in marketing efforts for foreign buyers

- Greater importance on marketing to both seniors and singles

- Increased awareness of the diversity of the people being served, which is not limited to race, nationality, culture, or religion. It includes people with handicaps, people in recovery, veterans, victims of domestic violence, et cetera. Understanding their needs and concerns is essential to serving these diverse groups.

- More negotiation in languages other than English. When the agent does not speak the language, a qualified interpreter should be used (not a minor child).

- Several states have recently eliminated the real estate salesperson's license and are requiring that all licensees be brokers. The purpose stated by legislators is to enhance consumer protection and increase the professional competence of all licensees. Other states have shown interest in this development, and it could become the norm across the nation. For California to adapt the one-license concept, all licensees would have to meet broker licensing requirements rather than the current lesser educational requirements for salespeople.

- Changes in broker compensation

The real estate marketplace is constantly undergoing change. Energy and water problems will affect the industry. Political change could include changes in capital gain rates, as well as loss of all or part of homeowner deductions for interest and taxes. Licensees will have to adapt to conditions beyond their control. Licensees realize that the marketplace is dynamic and not static.

BROKER COMPENSATION

Although there are a number of flat-fee brokerage firms, a broker's fee or commission is generally a percentage of the sales price. The fee is negotiable between the broker and the client, although most brokers will stick to the same percentage fee for similar properties. It is an antitrust violation for brokers to agree among themselves as to minimum fees to be charged; however, most major brokerage firms charge similar fees.

There have always been cut-rate or discount brokers that have used their lower fees to market their services. In order to obtain the cooperation of other brokers for sales purposes, many of these discount brokers will have a commission split whereby the sales broker receives a more normal commission and the listing broker takes less. Assume most brokers charge 6% for a residential sale and the normal commission split is 50% to the listing broker and 50% to the selling broker. If a broker took a listing for 5% commission, the broker might agree to give the selling broker the normal

3% and take 2% for his own efforts. A problem with working for a lesser commission is that the listing broker might rely more on other brokers and reduce marketing efforts and expenses.

In a seller's market, with few sellers and many buyers, discount brokerage firms tend to be more successful. In a buyer's market with fewer buyers and many sellers, discount brokers have greater difficulty competing because of the need to increase sales effort while offering to perform for a lesser fee.

Prosperity in the real estate profession (fueled by low interest rates and escalating prices) had resulted in many new entrants into the real estate profession, as well as different approaches to service and pricing. Some brokerage offices charge flat fees rather than a percentage of the sales price. While some discount brokers offer full brokerage services, there has been a growth in limited-services offerings for discount fees. For example, several brokers agree to make a charitable donation to the buyer's or the seller's charity of choice using an agreed portion of fees received. It makes for "feel good" clients without discounting fees.

Some brokers offer MLS access plans, where for a fixed fee they will place the owner's property on an MLS site. The owner will agree to pay a selling broker a fee but will be saving the listing broker's fee. Some brokers offer a choice of plans with various services.

Some limited-service brokers help the owner to sell without an agent. They prepare ads, provide website placement, provide open house material and For Sale signs, and will write up the sales contract should a buyer be procured by the seller.

Some offices have come up with à la carte fee pricing for their services. The owners decides what they want, including MLS placement, placement on additional websites, internet virtual tours, open houses, brochures, and the writing of sales contracts. The owner pays for services selected even if a sale is not completed.

Some buyer agents charge the buyers for their time much as other professionals do. They might provide the first home tour, of up to three hours, at no charge but have an hourly charge thereafter. If the broker shares in a listing agent's commission, then the hourly fee would be reduced or eliminated.

Some buyer agents offer to rebate a portion of the commission received from the sellers to the buyers. They hope that the rebate will increase the number of buyers, which will more than offset the rebate.

Redfin is a lower-rate online brokerage firm that pays its agents a salary rather than a commission. The firm currently charges a listing commission of 1.5% with a minimum of $5,000. The seller pays the selling agent. Typically the seller would pay 1½% to Redfin and 3% to the selling agent, making a total commission of 4½%. Redfin also acts as a buyer's agent, rebating a portion of the commission received to the buyer based on a sliding scale. There are countless variations on the above fee arrangements. When the real estate market declines, the average commission increases. According to *Real Trends*, an industry publication, the average commission jumped from a low of 5.02% in 2005, a time of great sales activity, to 5.4% in 2010. The statistics indicate that brokers are more likely to work for a lower commission when sales are relatively easy than when sales are expected to take greater effort.

Some analysts have predicted that real estate will follow the path of stock broker age with lower and lower fees and clients who make decisions based solely on costs. These fears are unlikely to be realized. While higher property prices, a strong market, and greater competition can be expected to place pressure on fees, real estate buyers require the services that only working face to face with an agent can provide. It takes people skills to understand peoples' needs, and selling is simply satisfying those needs. A property sale cannot be reduced to moving a cursor and pressing an enter key.

The product, or property, is not homogeneous. There are differences, benefits, and possible problems with every property. The real estate market is local in nature and requires in-depth local knowledge. Each buyer is different as to needs, wants, and purchasing ability. The agent must gain the trust of buyers to lead them through what is likely to be the most important purchase of their lives.

AN OVERVIEW OF GENERAL BROKERAGE

Most real estate licensees are engaged in representing buyers or sellers or both buyers and sellers in the sale of residential property. The reason is obvious: most properties that are sold are improved residential properties, and most of these are single-family dwelling units.

Real estate salespeople find owners willing to sell their properties or buyers desiring to buy property and secure agency agreements (listings). They then seek buyers for their property listings or properties for their buyer-agency listings. Real estate brokers and salespeople are able to expand their activities beyond their own listings because of a unique system of cooperation that exists among brokers.

Brokers who are members of an MLS make their sale listings available for other agents to sell. Therefore, any member of an MLS can show and sell a listing of any other member. Even agents who are not members of an MLS service will generally cooperate on their listings. By having access to this huge market inventory, an agent can locate a property that best meets the needs and is within the resources of a prospective buyer. Cooperation is the cornerstone of modern real estate brokerage. Cooperation includes sharing of commission. Members of an MLS system have agreed on sharing arrangements, but agents who are not members should have commission-sharing agreements in writing to avoid misunderstanding.

AREAS OF SPECIALIZATION

There are other areas of activity besides the listing and selling of traditional single-family homes. These areas of real estate activity include the following:

- **Manufactured home sales**—While the industry prefers the term *manufactured home*, most people still refer to these homes, which are transported to a site on their own chassis, as *mobile homes*. Mobile homes differ from other types of housing in that they are normally located on leased sites (mobile home parks). Real estate licensees can list and sell mobile homes that are 8 feet by 40 feet or larger in rental spaces, as well as with the land. Real estate licensees cannot sell new mobile homes without land. These new mobile homes can be sold only through dealers licensed by the Department of Housing and Community Development. Mobile homes fill a significant need for lower-cost housing, as well as a lifestyle need in retirement housing. Many salespeople specialize in mobile home sales.

■ **Tract sales**—Many salespeople like to sell new homes in subdivisions because they like selling a product at a fixed price. Buyers generally arrive at tract sales because of developer promotion.

■ **Residential income property (multifamily residential units)**—Brokers, as well as salespersons, often choose this specialty, although agents who handle primarily single-family home sales can also be involved with this type of income property.

■ **Speculator (flipper) sales**—Distressed or problem properties are sold to investors who intend to resell at a profit rather than hold for income.

■ **Commercial property**—Brokers and salespeople may choose this as a specialty; furthermore, many agents may specialize by type of property. For example, some agents handle only minimalls, while others may specialize in office buildings, retail stores, or warehouses.

■ **Industrial property**—Factory and warehouse specialists make relatively few sales, but the dollar volume in these sales tends to be high. Within this field, there are subspecialties, such as research and development facilities.

■ **Business opportunities**—Businesses are listed and sold with or without real estate. It is a specialized field, and very few residential sales agents ever get involved in a business opportunity sale. Some specialists handle only particular types of businesses, such as taverns, restaurants, or motels.

■ **Land and farm brokerage**—Generally, these specialists cover large geographic areas. Knowledge of farming is an important attribute for these agents. In California, many agents specialize in selling acreage parcels to investors and/or developers.

■ **Lot sales**—Many agents specialize in listing and selling lots for investment purposes, as well as to provide builders with a supply of real estate. General real estate brokerage offices also handle the sale of lots, as well as sales of land parcels of all sizes.

- **Auction sales**—Auctions are now being used to sell all types of real property. In England and Australia, auctions play a greater role in real estate brokerage activity than in the United States. The importance of auction sales in the United States has been increasing. Many firms hold online auctions. There are a number of firms that deal only in auction sales.

- **Time-shares**—Besides the sale of new time-shares (which is selling a vacation lifestyle), there is also a growing market in time-share resales.

- **Counseling**—Some experienced professionals provide expert advice to buyers, sellers, developers, and builders on a fee basis.

- **Subdividing**—Many real estate professionals have gone into subdividing to provide a stock of parcels for development.

- **Loan brokerage**—Loan brokers generally find investors for trust deeds and property owners who desire to borrow on their properties. They bring these lenders and borrowers together for a fee.

- **Mortgage loan activities**—Real estate licensees may act as lenders or agents in making and arranging loans. These activities differ greatly from normal brokerage activities because greater administrative skills are needed. However, both sales and mortgage activities require a strong desire to meet the needs of others. (Mortgage loan activities that require a real estate license are discussed in Unit 12.)

- **Personal assistants**—Many licensed agents have chosen to work for other agents as salaried assistants. They like the security of a regular paycheck, as well as the chance to use organizational skills. Assistants allow agents to better utilize their time by handling tasks that the agents can delegate. Some agents use virtual assistants for the internet. They update internet information, send additional data to responses, answer email requests, and provide names and information to their employing agent. The National Association of REALTORS® developed a virtual assistants training program for military spouses.

- **Property management**—As in other specialties, there are subspecialties based on the type of property. (Property management is covered in detail in Unit 15.)

- **Leasing agent**—Leasing agents are not necessarily property managers. They generally charge a fee based on the gross receipts of the lease entered into. There are subspecialties such as residential leasing, industrial leasing, and commercial leasing.

- **Appraisal**—Although a separate license is required, a great many appraisers started out in real estate sales.

BROKER/SALESPERSON RELATIONSHIPS

The real estate broker is almost always an **independent contractor**. According to the *Real Estate Reference Book*, "an independent contractor is one who, in rendering services, exercises an independent employment or occupation and is responsible to the employer only as to the results of his or her work." Very simply, this means that an independent contractor is not under the direction and control of the employer regarding the manner in which work is carried out. The independent contractor is responsible to the employer only for the results. For example, real estate brokers are responsible for results to their principal (employer), who could be a buyer, a seller, a lessor, or a lessee.

Real estate brokers are required to have a written contract with their individual salespeople. Most contracts identify the working relationship of the salesperson as that of an independent contractor (Figure 1.1). California Business and Professions Code Section 10032 allows brokers to hire classified salespersons as employees or independent contractors. Most contracts specify an independent contractor choice because it relieves the broker of unemployment compensation, as well as withholding requirements. The statute provides that obligations to the public (liability) apply to the broker regardless of classification of employee or independent contractor. Section 10177(h) of the Business and Professions Code requires that brokers supervise their salespeople, and exercise of supervision in the performance of work precludes an independent contractor relationship as to liability. Formerly, the broker was required to review contracts prepared by salespersons within five days. This has been replaced by a policy of "reasonable supervision."

FIGURE 1.1: **Independent Contractor Agreement**

INDEPENDENT CONTRACTOR EMPLOYMENT AGREEMENT
For Sales Agents and Associated Brokers

NOTE: This form is used by an employing broker when entering into an agreement employing a sales agent or a broker on terms calling for the employee to be treated for tax purposes as an independent contractor, to establish the duties of the broker and agent, earned fees and how the fees due the employee will be allocated and shared.

DATE:_____, 20_____, at _____, California.

Items left blank or unchecked are not applicable

FACTS:

1. Broker hereby employs Agent as a real estate sales agent or broker-associate, until terminated by either party, on the following terms.

   1.1   Agent to be treated as an independent contractor for tax purposes.

2. AGENT agrees:

   2.1   To maintain a real estate license in the State of California.

   2.2   To provide brokerage services only on behalf of Broker.

   2.3   To follow the Broker's policy manual and any directions orally given by Broker.

   2.4   To use only those real estate forms authorized by Broker.

   2.5   To make complete and immediate disclosure to Broker of any correspondence or document made or received.

   2.6   To immediately deliver and account to Broker for funds received by Agent in the course of this employment.

   2.7   To participate in educational programs and meetings specified by Broker.

   2.8   To visually inspect the physical conditions of any property to be sold or bought for clients.

   2.9   To obligate Broker to no agreement without Broker's prior consent.

   2.10 To expose Broker to no liability to any third party without Broker's prior consent.

   2.11 To furnish their own transportation and carry a liability and property damage insurance policy in an amount satisfactory to Broker with a policy rider naming Broker as a co-insured.

   2.12 To faithfully adhere to the Real Estate Law of the State of California.

   2.13 To file and pay quarterly estimated taxes and self-employment taxes.

   2.14 To contribute to the defense and settlement of litigation arising out of transactions in which Agent was to or shared fees, in an amount equal to Agent's percentage share of the fees.

   2.15 To join and pay fees for membership to professional organizations in which broker is a member.

   2.16 Other _____

3. BROKER agrees:

   3.1   To maintain a real estate Broker's license in the State of California.

   3.2   To maintain office(s) with proper facilities to operate a general real estate brokerage business.

   3.3   To maintain membership in the following professional organization(s):

      ☐ Multiple Listing Service

      ☐ Local branch of the California Association of Realtors and National Association of Realtors

      ☐ _____

   3.4   To maintain listings.

   3.5   To provide advertising approved by Broker.

   3.6   To provide worker's compensation insurance for Agent.

   3.7   To file informational tax returns on Agent's fee or other compensation, under State and Federal Tax regulations.

   3.8   To pay Agent as specified in the Broker's fee schedule at section 5.

   3.9   To maintain the following insurance coverage's for Agent:

      ☐ Errors and Omissions   ☐ Life   ☐ Health   ☐ Dental

   3.10 ☐ _____

4. General Provisions:

   4.1   Agent has the right to purchase any properties listed by Broker on full disclosure to the Seller of the Agent's activity as a principal, and without diminution of fees to the Broker.

   4.2   Agent is authorized to enter into any documents required to perform any of the services referenced in this agreement.

   4.3   Broker has the right to reject any listing or retainer agreement obtained by Agent.

   4.4   Broker to determine whether any litigation or dispute involving the Broker, or their business and third parties, arising from Agent's activities, will be prosecuted, defended or settled.

   4.5   Arbitration: Any dispute between the Agent and the Broker or with any other Agent employed by Broker that cannot be settled by the Broker, or resolved by the State Labor Commission or by non-binding mediation, will be arbitrated under the rules of the American Arbitration Association.

   4.6   ☐ **See addendum for additional provisions. [See RPI** Form 250]

— — — — — — — — — — — — — *PAGE ONE OF TWO — FORM 506* — — — — — — — — — — — — — — —

FIGURE 1.1 (continued): **Independent Contractor Agreement**

— — — — — — — — — — — — — PAGE TWO OF TWO — FORM 506 — — — — — — — — — — — — — — —

5. Broker's Fee Schedule and Charges:

5.1 Broker is to pay Agent a fee for participating in a sales transaction evidenced by a purchase agreement which confirms the Agent is acting as an agent for Broker and Broker receives a brokerage fee on the transaction.

5.2 The amount of fee due Agent is _____% of the funds remaining from the brokerage fee received by Broker under sections 5.1 or 5.10b after first deducting the following amounts:

   a. Payment to other brokerage offices of sums due them for their participation in the transaction;

   b. Payment to Broker's franchisor of the fee due the franchisor from the transaction;

   c. Payment to Broker of one-half of the then remaining funds if another Agent of Broker is entitled to a fee for negotiating the other end of the transaction;

   d. Other deductions _____.

5.3 From each fee due Agent and before disbursement, Broker will deduct the following amounts and any amounts otherwise due Broker from the Agent:

   a. An advertising or promo charge of $_____.

   b. An errors and omissions insurance coverage charge of $_____.

   c. A charge of $_____ for _____.

   d. Disbursement to another Agent of Broker, transaction coordinator or finder with whom Agent agreed to share the fee due under section 5.2.

5.4 The percentage participation by Agent in the funds remaining under section 5.2 is adjusted to _____% on the following event _____, and will apply until _____.

5.5 Agent is to pay Broker, on the first of each month of employment, a desk fee of $_____.

5.6 Any expenses incurred by Broker in a transaction negotiated by Agent, such as travel expenses, meals, attorney fees, printing, listing service fees, etc., will be deducted from the fee due Agent.

5.7 If all or part of the fee is received in property other than cash, Agent is to obtain Broker's prior approval. In this event, Broker will make one of the following determinations for disposition of the property:

   a. Divide the property between Broker and Agent in kind, based on the fee schedule; or

   b. Pay Agent their dollar share of the fee in cash; or

   c. Retain the property in the names of Broker and Agent, or their trustee, and thereafter dispose of it when on terms Broker and Agent agree to on its acquisition. Any ownership income and expenses will be shared between Broker and Agent in proportion to their share of ownership.

5.8 On termination, Agent to be paid as follows:

   a. Closed Transactions: Agent will receive their share of fees on all transactions which are closed before termination.

   b. Pending Transactions: Agent will receive their share of fees on all pending transactions which close after termination, subject to fee limitations under section 5.9.

   c. Unexpired Listings and Retainers: Agent will receive their share of fees if the client enters into a transaction during the written listing or retainer period. Agent will not earn a fee under any extension of the listing or retainer obtained after termination, subject to fee limitations under section 5.9.

5.9 Fee Limitation: If on termination Agent has pending transactions under section 5.1 or unexpired listings or retainers procured by Agent which require further services normally rendered by Agent, Broker will direct another employed Agent or himself to perform these services. For these services after termination, a reasonable share of the fee will be deducted from the fee due Agent.

5.10 Compensation From Prior Employment: Monies received by Broker from Agent's prior employing brokers representing fees earned by Agent while employed by that broker are to be disbursed by Broker as follows:

   a. ☐ Agent to receive 100% of the monies received by Broker.

   b. ☐ The monies are to be shared with Agent at the percentage set in section 5.2.

   c. ☐ Broker and Agent, respectively, to share the monies _____ : _____.

I agree to render services on the terms stated above.	I agree to employ Agent on the terms stated above.
Date: _____, 20_____	Date: _____, 20_____
Agent's Name: _____	Broker's Name: _____
Agent's Signature: _____	Broker's Signature: _____
Address: _____	Address: _____
Phone: _____	Phone: _____
Cell: _____	Cell: _____
Email: _____	Email: _____

FORM 506   08-15   ©2015 **RPI – Realty Publications, Inc.** P.O.Box 5707, RIVERSIDE, CA 92517

Brokers and salespeople contract as independent contractors as required by the Internal Revenue Service. The IRS will treat the real estate salesperson as an independent contractor if the following three criteria are met:

1. The salesperson is licensed as a real estate agent.

2. Reimbursement to the salesperson is based solely on sales, not on hours worked.

3. There is a written contract stating that the salesperson will be treated as an independent contractor for tax purposes.

The economic reason a broker wants salespersons to be independent contractors is that if they are independent contractors, the broker is relieved of withholding taxes and Social Security, as well as not contributing to Social Security for the salesperson.

While real estate salespeople are treated as independent contractors for purposes of state and federal income tax reporting and certain other purposes, such as workers' compensation insurance coverage, they are treated as employees in connection with dealing with the public.

Despite the IRS treatment of a real estate salesperson as an independent contractor in California, brokers are responsible for wrongful acts (*torts*) of their salespeople within the course and scope of employment. Because of this potential liability, many brokers require that their salespeople carry high limits of automobile liability insurance and that brokers be named as insured under the policies. If a salesperson has access to the funds of others (such as a property manager who collects rents and deposits), brokers might obtain fidelity bonds to protect themselves from a salesperson's embezzlement. Offices also carry errors and omissions insurance policies that offer liability protection for acts of brokers and agents. Errors and omissions insurance typically does not cover pollution on the property, physical harm to others, or damage to property caused by the insured. Policies typically have deductibles, and the cost of the policy is related to business volume.

FIGURE 1.2:   **Employee or Independent Contractor? IRS Considerations**

Factors Indicating Control	Employee	Independent Contractor
Is the worker required to comply with employer instructions about when, where, and how work is to be performed?	Yes	No
Is the worker required to undergo training?	Yes	No
Does the worker hire, supervise, and pay others to perform work for which she is responsible?	No	Yes
Must the worker's job be performed during certain set hours?	Yes	No
Must the worker devote full time to the job?	Yes	No
Must the work be performed on the employer's property?	Yes	No
Must tasks be performed in a certain order set by the employer?	Yes	No
Is the individual required to submit regular written or oral reports to the employer?	Yes	No
Is payment by the hour, week, or month?	Yes	No
Is payment in a lump sum?	No	Yes
Are the worker's business and travel expenses paid by the employer?	Yes	No
Does the employer furnish the tools and materials required for the job?	Yes	No
Does the worker rent his own office or working space?	No	Yes
Will the worker realize a profit or loss as a result of her services?	No	Yes
Does the individual work for more than one firm at a time?	No	Yes
Does the worker make his services available to the general public?	No	Yes
Does the employer have the right to fire the worker?	Yes	No
Does the worker have the right to quit the job at any time, whether or not a particular task is complete?	Yes	No

Note: These factors are only possible indicators of a worker's status. Each case must be determined on its own facts, based on all the information.

Brokers must carry **workers' compensation insurance** for salespeople who are considered for this purpose to be employees. Brokers need not carry unemployment insurance coverage because commission salespeople are not eligible for unemployment insurance benefits. Also, because salespeople are paid solely by commission, minimum wage laws do not protect them.

Brokers are required to report the annual earnings of a salesperson to both the licensee and the IRS using IRS Form 1099.

SALESPERSON/SALESPERSON CONTRACTS

Real estate salespeople often team up with one or more other salespeople to form a partnership or selling team. These teams sometimes seem to operate as separate brokerage offices within a brokerage office. The teams are usually organized under written agreements, sometimes for a specified period that provides for renewal by agreement. Team agreements cover adding or termination of team membership. They call for a division of the combined earnings of the group. Commission splits are negotiated within the team. Some teams have a broker who selects the team, supervises all activity, and takes a percentage of total earnings. Other teams have a split based on the role of each agent in a transaction, and they might have a set amount or percentage that goes to the team. Some teams divide duties, such as listing specialist, selling specialist, marketing and office management. Further specialization could be type of property, such as commercial, as well as buyer or seller agents. Advantages of team arrangements are as follows:

- The needs of buyers and sellers are better served because of the greater availability of a team member; someone is always available to help in an area where help is needed.

- Members are motivated because they share in one another's successes.

- Members receive more steady income flow because there is a greater likelihood of income being earned every month.

- Such partnerships better utilize the time, talent, and skills of members and paid assistants.

Teams are likely to have their own websites. The website shown in Figure 4.3 of Unit 4 is the home webpage of a team.

The team must take caution to ensure that members are complying with the Real Estate Commissioner's rules. Because the team is ultimately still operating under the employing broker's license, questions might arise as to the ownership of this team name. From the broker's perspective, they might hold the position that the brokerage owns the team name because it is tied to the broker's personal or corporate broker's license.

The team will naturally dispute the broker's claim of ownership because the salespeople are likely spending their own marketing dollars to promote this team name in print and online. If a salesperson were to move to a different brokerage, that salesperson would want the ability to take the team name with her to the new firm. Additionally, any website domains that the team registers are likely to be done by the team itself and not the broker. Therefore, internet control of the team name would be hard for the broker to enforce. Assembly Bill 2018 (Bocanegra) allows a salesperson to "maintain ownership of a fictitious business name" but still requires that this name be used "subject to the control of a responsible broker."

Despite the fact that the "team name" might be owned by the salesperson according to this bill, it is imperative that brokers supervise and manage exactly how these team names are used.

As an example, section (d) of this bill also requires that

> marketing and solicitation materials, including business cards, print or electronic media and "for sale" signage, using a fictitious business name obtained in accordance with subdivision (a) shall include the responsible broker's identity in a manner equally as prominent as the fictitious business name.

Therefore, it is important that brokers have their teams agree that in any of their marketing, the size and prominence of the team name should not be larger than the broker's to avoid giving the appearance that the team is operating without an employing broker. This is despite the fact that the ownership of the team name could be held by the salesperson and not the broker necessarily.

Fictitious Business Names and Teams

Specifically, AB 2018 defines a "team name" as a professional identity or brand name used by a salesperson, and one or more other real estate licensees, for the provision of real estate licensed services. AB 2018 specifies that

> the use of a team name, as defined above, does not constitute a fictitious business name and would not require a separate license if (1) the name is used by two or more real estate licensees who work together to provide licensed real estate services, or who represent themselves to the public as being a part of a team, group, or association to provide

those services, (2) the name includes the surname (last name) of at least one of the licensee members of the team, group, or association in conjunction with the term "associates," "group," or "team," and (3) the name does not include any term or terms, such as "real estate broker," "real estate brokerage," "broker," or "brokerage" or any other term that would lead a member of the public to believe that the team is offering real estate brokerage services, or imply or suggest the existence of a real estate entity independent of a responsible broker.

Ownership of Team Names

When a team name is tied to a given broker at the California Bureau of Real Estate, a question may arise as to the ownership of the team name. The broker may hold the position that he owns the team name because it is tied to his personal or corporate license at the bureau.

Salespeople will naturally be opposed to this because they are likely spending their own marketing dollars to promote this team name in print and online. If the salespeople were to move to a different brokerage, they would want the ability to take this team name with them to the new firm. Additionally, any website domains that the team registers are likely to be done by the team itself and not the broker. Therefore, internet control of the team name would be hard for the broker to enforce.

AB 2018 (Bocanegra) allows a salesperson to "maintain ownership of a fictitious business name" but still requires that this name be used "subject to the control of a responsible broker."

Despite the fact that the "team name" might be owned by the salesperson, according to 2018, it is imperative that brokers supervise and manage exactly how these team names are used.

If a team or any other sales group operates under a name that does not include the surname of every principal, it must comply with the fictitious name statute, which requires filing the name with the county clerk and complying with advertising requirements.

A partnership or team choice should not be taken lightly. You should choose not only a person or persons you like but those who are similarly dedicated. You want partners you can rely on.

CHOOSING A BROKER

Many people enter the real estate profession thinking it is a certain path to riches. While some real estate sales agents earn over $250,000 per year (about 2%), according to the U.S. Bureau of Labor Statistics (2014) the mean income of a real estate salesperson (average income) was $55,300 per year. The median income was $40,900 (median means half the agents made more than that figure and half made less). You should realize that agents' income tends to increase after the first years, so new agents will likely have lower incomes. The broker you choose to go with can have a significant effect on your income.

At one time, most real estate offices seemed to be running a numbers game. They would take in every real estate licensee willing to come to work for them. Most firms have come to realize that such a practice can be counter-productive in that it can waste both time and money. Today, most offices are interested in agents they believe will fit with their office and either have experience or the drive to learn what is necessary for success. Brokers realize that whom they hire can affect their bottom line—their profit. Direct and indirect costs in hiring an agent who fails to produce can be in the thousands of dollars. Brokers often use the term "desk cost." This is the total office operational overhead divided by the number of salespeople. If a salesperson fails to contribute at least that amount to the **company dollar** (broker's share of commission received), then the agent is a negative factor on earnings.

Expect to be asked direct questions about your past work history, what you expect from being a real estate agent, and what you are willing to give to the job as far as effort and dedication. Your job interview is really a two-way interview, with the broker trying to do what is best for the brokerage firm and with you seeking the firm that will best meet your personal goals.

Because your choice of broker could have a significant effect on your success or failure as a real estate professional, don't jump at the first "come to work for me" offer. You could end up wasting a great deal of what otherwise could be productive time. More important, an initial experience of feeling like a square peg in a round hole could lead you to abandon what would otherwise be a rewarding career.

Before you even think about talking to brokers, you should understand why fewer than 50% of new real estate licensees are still actively engaged in real estate one year after starting work. Your careful initial choice of a broker will reduce your likelihood of becoming a "failure statistic."

A contributing reason for such a high rate of failure is lack of training in what to do to be successful. It's true that some successful agents come into an office absolutely green, observe what successful agents are doing, and then do it themselves, but these agents are the exceptions. In some offices, a new licensee is assigned a desk, provided rudimentary information about using the computer, and will maybe receive a 30-minute briefing. The new agent might be given the task to knock on doors for listings. This can be a frightening task for many new licensees who are not used to rejection. New licensees are often left to learn by osmosis, an approach that is far more likely to result in failure than success.

While many experienced agents generate most of their leads, floor time is important for new licensees. The amount of floor time offered by the broker should be an important consideration in choosing a broker.

Many offices have weekly sales meetings with skill improvement sessions. Some offices use a **mentor program** in which the new hire assists a successful salesperson for several months. This approach can be very good if the mentor is knowledgeable. While some successful agents are not interested in being mentors or are not skilled at training others, many successful agents enjoy working with a *protégé*. They will bring new licensees along on some calls and show them what they are doing and why, as well as answer questions and make suggestions. While some mentors will help you at no cost, they are more likely to expect you to do some work for them. Others might expect a percentage of your deals. There are also professional mentors who have programs with set fees. Before you develop any mentor relationship, check the success of the mentor and others who have been mentored.

Most large offices have a formal training program. Some are excellent, providing motivation and the skills necessary for success. Some offices have training directors who not only conduct training sessions but also work closely with agents to improve their performance. Some offices have extensive CD, video, and audio training libraries, as well as excellent books to augment their training programs and to help develop the skills of success.

Your first few months in real estate are critical because if you can't see success in the near future, you are likely to drop by the wayside and become a failure statistic. You need a broker who will provide you with the training you need for success. When you talk to brokers, find out details about their training programs, what the office does about continuing skill improvement, and what the office has in the way of a library and training aids. Ask to talk to a recent licensee who works in the office. Ask pointed questions about the training and broker assistance. You should be actively interviewing the prospective broker rather than being a passive listener.

Find out about the broker's present employees. How long have they been with the office? If everyone seems to be a relative newcomer, it could indicate a serious problem. Find out about the earnings of the full-time salespersons. This is very important because working around successful people can serve as a great personal motivator. If you are working in the midst of a group of marginal producers, their attitudes, perhaps negative, could make it difficult for you to maintain the positive approach required for your success.

You will likely give your greatest consideration to a broker involved in residential sales because most sales are residential. Commercial or industrial sales might offer huge commissions, but the deals that come together are few and often far apart. As a new licensee, you are unlikely to develop the skills needed to succeed in commercial/industrial selling before financial pressures drive you toward a salaried position. In addition, the background and legal knowledge required for commercial, industrial, and business sales are far different than they are for residential sales and generally require intensive education and training. Keep in mind that the sales skills learned in residential sales can be transferred to other areas of real estate. After you have developed these skills, a number of alternatives will be open to you.

Many real estate boards and associations offer training opportunities. The largest broker organization is the **National Association of REALTORS®** (NAR). The **California Association of REALTORS®** (CAR) is the state organization of NAR. Membership in a local board of REALTORS® automatically includes membership in both CAR and NAR. Among the many advantages of becoming a REALTOR® or REALTOR-Associate® are the training opportunities, legal updates, industry news, access to lockboxes, multiple listing services, legal forms (including computer forms), legal services, and interaction with other professionals guided by the same code of ethics. In addition to the National Association of REALTORs®, there are other organizations of real estate professionals that provide educational services and help their members advance in their profession. They include the National Association of Real Estate Brokers (NAREB), whose members use the Realtist designation; the National Association of Hispanic Real Estate Professionals; and the Asian Real Estate Association of America.

Some of these organizations offer regularly scheduled training sessions; others sponsor special training programs. Many board and association offices have libraries that contain excellent training material, and some have bookstores where training materials and supplies can be purchased. The training publications, along with ideas you gain from your local real estate board or association, can materially affect your future.

If you have already achieved success in real estate, the initial training offered by a broker would not be a major consideration in working for that broker, but other support services and commission arrangements could be very important to you. Some offices offer a sliding commission scale under which the individual salespeople keep a greater portion of the commission dollars as their commissions increase. The purpose of this type of arrangement is to motivate salespeople to achieve greater success, as well as to retain top producers. Health insurance coverage with a broker-paid portion (often related to performance) has been an excellent salesperson retention tool for some brokers.

The salesperson pays the broker in a 100% commission office.

There are a number of **100% commission offices**. In these offices, the salesperson pays a flat desk fee or a desk fee plus a transaction fee to the broker and then keeps all the commissions earned. Desk fees vary based on area, broker's facilities, and support services provided by the broker, such as internet and administrative services and insurance coverage. The desk fee is calculated to cover all office overhead plus provide broker compensation. The broker retains responsibility for the salesperson. Generally, the brokers in 100% offices provide little help to the salespeople, and the salespeople pay for many of their own support services. This type of arrangement is not a good choice for a new licensee, although it can offer benefits for experienced real estate professionals who generate much of their own business. If you are just beginning a real estate career, don't worry about commission splits; 100% of nothing is nothing. Generally, the higher the split, the fewer services provided by the broker to the agent. As a new hire, you want all the help you can get. Figure 1.3 is a worksheet for selecting a broker's office that allows the agent to compare three different brokers.

FIGURE 1.3:   **Checklist for Selecting a Broker's Office**

Brokers' Names

1. _____

2. _____

3. _____

Benefits provided by the broker	Broker 1	Broker 2	Broker 3
1. New-agent training program			
2. Ongoing training program			
3. Use of a mentor system			
4. Computer training			
5. Quality phone systems (voice mail, call forwarding, etc.)			
6. Fax machine availability			
7. Email address			
8. Office website (grade on a 1 to 10 scale)			
9. Additional websites used			
10. Multiple listing service (MLS)			
11. Success of current sales staff			
12. Computer forms			
13. Open-house signs and flags			
14. Desk fees and MLS board fees			
15. Advertising support			
16. Distribution of leads generated by company websites and relocation websites.			
17. Organized farm for new agents			
18. Weekly meeting and caravans			
19. Broker's interest in you			
20. Can you work with management?			
21. Estimated start-up costs			

How to Choose Where to Work

A new licensee is wise to go to work for an office

- that offers a training program as good as or better than those offered by other area brokers;

- that offers assistance when you need it (for example, an office with a designated person in charge of your training);

- with a good library of books, audiotapes, CDs, and DVDs available for your use;

- that is primarily devoted to the sale of and/or lease in the real estate specialty area you desire to work in;

- where salespeople have good morale, reflected in their length of employment;

- that has a significant proportion of successful agents; and

- that is comfortable for you. You must feel comfortable with the broker, your co-workers, and the operation of the office. If you are uncomfortable, your chances of success are going to be materially diminished.

Because the Bureau of Real Estate will sell lists of real estate applicants, you may be contacted by several local brokers. Friends in the business may also make suggestions. Take your time in your choice because it can have long-lasting implications.

Many enter the real estate profession with the intention of working part time until they learn the business and develop an income. Part-time agents are far less likely to be successful than full-time agents because of the difficulty in being able to serve the needs of buyers and sellers in a timely manner. In addition, few successful brokerage firms will take on a part-time salesperson. Exceptions are time-share sales at special seminars and tract sales.

Brokers compute desk cost as the total office overhead divided by the number of salespersons. Each salesperson's production is expected to cover desk cost, as well as make a contribution to broker profits. A salesperson who, after a training period, consistently fails to produce office revenue sufficient to cover desk cost is unlikely to continue with the brokerage firm.

SUCCESS AND YOUR ATTITUDE

We know that simply moving an agent's desk can change an agent's production. Having successful co-workers around you can serve to generate ideas and motivation to achieve your own success. Unfortunately, the opposite is also true. Having people around you who are unsuccessful or who have a negative attitude can adversely affect your attitude. If they are failures, your chances of failure will be increased. If you associate with successful people, you will likely be associating with people who have a positive attitude. A positive attitude can be infectious, just as the negative attitude of friends and associates can lead you to failure. A negative attitude will lead to a "they aren't really buyers" prejudgment that can make the difference between marginal results and great success.

No one will stand over you in real estate to watch your every move and prod you on. And even though others may reinforce your resolve to succeed, the real motivation for success comes from you. You must be a self-starter who wants to succeed so much that you will continue to strive despite setbacks or the negative attitudes of others. By completing the Success Questionnaire in Figure 1.4, you will gain an understanding of where you are now as well as areas where improvement is needed.

Certainly, motivational seminars, tapes, videos and books help, but these are short-term motivational aids. Long-term success is based on internal motivation to expend the extra effort to learn, to plan, and to practice for your success. Working hard isn't enough. You have to learn to work smart. Think out what needs to be done and why. Plan your work.

You must be interested in people and truly want to help them in meeting their needs. The desire to help and your belief that your product, real estate, offers a solution to their needs will keep you motivated. Use the success of others as a guide to show yourself what can be done. In the same vein, don't become complacent because you are doing better than others. In real estate, don't feel that you are in competition with any other agent. Your only competitor should be yourself. Of course, when you start to realize success, success itself becomes a motivator.

FIGURE 1.4:   Success Questionnaire

1. Are you enthusiastic about your work?
    Study the unusually successful people you know and you will find them imbued with an enthusiasm for their work that is contagious. Not only are they excited about what they are doing, but they also get you excited. Remember the maxim: "Enthusiasm is like a contagious disease. It must be caught and not taught."

2. How do you overcome objections?
    Numerous spoken questions and written questions are being fired at you every day. Do you answer them without hesitation, drawing on your reservoir of knowledge? Do you do so to the satisfaction of the client or prospect? Or is there sometimes a hesitation followed by a garbled description that leaves the clients as much in the dark as they were before?

3. Are you self-confident?
    Knowledge gives confidence. A thorough knowledge of both the property in question and the exact advantages that the customer will receive develops this quality of confidence in you, which shows itself in your personality. If the client or customer has confidence in you and your company, a sale may result naturally. The main factor that determines whether customers will have confidence in your product or service is whether they have confidence in you. Your knowledge gives you assurance, a prime factor in assuring others.

4. Do you have the courage of your convictions?
    Many times, we cease to be courageous in the face of opposition. It is a sad commentary, but we live in an era when rapid change breeds fear. Conquer fear! Banish worry, because, as someone once said, worry is the interest you pay on trouble before you get it. Keep your fears to yourself, and share your courage with others. Remember, fear is only in the mind.

5. Are your actions and speech positive?
    A number of years ago there was a popular song with the words "accentuate the positive, eliminate the negative." You need to think and act positively.
    Those who think negatively say, "Business is poor; unemployment rates are more than 9%. That means 9% of the people cannot be considered potential prospects."
    Those who think positively say, "Business is great, with only 9% unemployment. That means 91% of the people are potential prospects." However, being positive does not imply that it gives us the right to be dishonest. But we can state facts positively without being dishonest.

6. Are you persistent?
    Customers admire a salesperson who has developed persistence. No one has respect for a quitter, a person who readily takes no for an answer. If only 1 in 20 presentations results in a sale, your attitude should be: "Thanks for the no. I'm now closer to the yes." (You should of course be considering it a goal to reduce 1 in 20 to 1 in 19.)

7. Are you a problem solver?
    Be a problem solver, not a problem. Problem solvers are people helpers. The basic principles of problem solving are the following:

    ■ Despite any problem, you can persevere, think, and reach a solution.

    ■ Use relentless pressure, persistence, and determination.

    ■ Act as if the problem can be solved. Use the power of positive thinking.

    ■ Remember, you do not sell properties; you sell solutions to people's problems.

    ■ Understand completed staff work. The idea of completed staff work is that you should never present your broker with a problem unless you also present your broker with the possible courses of action to take—your recommendations as to a specific action and why.

8. Are you willing to fail?
    Perhaps this should be phrased as "willing to try, regardless of the chance of failure." Success cannot be achieved without failure. An old story is a good example of this concept: Robert Bruce, King of Scotland, had just been defeated for the 11th time by his enemies, the English. He was dejectedly resting by a tree, ready to give up, when he saw a spider persistently trying to spin a web from one limb to another. After the spider failed to reach its goal 11 times, it finally succeeded on the 12th try. Inspired by this incident, Bruce went forth against his enemy for the 12th time. This time he was victorious, defeating the English at Bannockburn, winning independence for Scotland. To be a successful salesperson, you must be willing to try and perhaps to fail in order to succeed in the end.

We are seeing a change in the way that many successful salespersons do business. Many have significantly reduced the number of hours they spend in the broker's office. With smartphones, email, and fax machines, most of their office time has become home based or car based. With reduced direct contact with brokers and co-workers, self-motivation becomes essential for success.

PROFESSIONAL DESIGNATIONS

The National Association of REALTORS® and numerous other real estate organizations offer myriad professional designations. Some designations relate to general brokerage, while others are for specialized areas of activity. Earning these designations requires a course of study and, in some cases, an examination. Achieving these designations opens up many opportunities because they are regarded highly by others. The Seniors Real Estate Specialist® designation (SRES) will provide the expertise to meet real estate needs of seniors and help you reach this market.

The Association of Energy and Environment Real Estate Professionals offers the Eco Broker designation for agents dedicated to reducing our carbon footprints and protecting the environment. Dealing with an Eco Broker is becoming an important consideration to many buyers. A designation frequently sought is the Graduate, REALTOR® Institute (GRI). Achieving designations such as the GRI will increase your confidence, as well as your sense of self-worth.

CONTINUING TRAINING

Training is not a one-time program. As a real estate professional, you should constantly be improving your skills and increasing your knowledge. The most successful agents continually strive for improvement throughout their careers.

Seek out available training sessions and group-sponsored seminars applicable to your work. *California Real Estate Magazine*, the magazine of the California Association of REALTORS®; *Real Estate Today*, the magazine published by the National Association of REALTORS®; and *REALTOR®*

News, the biweekly newspaper of the National Association of REAL-TORS®, are examples of excellent publications with articles that will help you succeed. Many offices have back issues of these publications in their libraries. In addition, some local associations of REALTORS® have newsletters or publications that discuss local issues. A great many relevant articles and blogs are available on the internet.

When a new idea or approach is proposed during office training sessions, take notes and try to use that idea or approach as soon as possible. Keep in mind that listening may give you ideas, but a demonstration is even better because it shows how to apply the ideas. Using the ideas yourself makes them yours, and they become part of your personal "sales software" to be retained in your memory bank and taken out when a situation warrants their use.

Besides office training sessions, you may have a training supervisor who will critique your efforts. Pay attention. Take criticism as an opportunity for improvement. Criticism is feedback for improvement, not an indication of failure.

Ask questions of the more successful salespeople in your office. Generally, they will share ideas gladly. Consider building a special relationship with a successful agent in your office. In doing so, you will be developing your own mentor. Someone who is supportive of you who possesses both knowledge and experience can be a great help during your first few months in real estate. This is especially important in offices where the broker or office manager has limited time to work with you.

You will find that there are more good ideas for prospecting, listing, and selling than one person could possibly use. By trying various ideas, you will find approaches you feel comfortable with, and you will work these with greater enthusiasm and heighten the likelihood of your success.

Check the course offerings of your local colleges and business schools. Besides specific real estate courses, consider more general business courses in salesmanship, marketing, advertising, and so forth. The knowledge gained in many general courses will have direct application to real estate activities. A number of courses also are offered by correspondence. While some correspondence and online courses are quite good, they lack the insights of an instructor and the give and take of a classroom environment. There is a great deal more to learning than just what is "in the book."

Real estate licensees are required to take continuing education courses for license renewal. Many of these courses will provide you with knowledge directly applicable to your work. Even if you are not required to take a course, you should evaluate what the course can do for you.

WEB LINK

The internet can be a great learning tool. Two of the many websites you should consider visiting are www.relibrary.com and www.realtimes.com.

Many excellent commercial seminars are available to licensees. Besides providing new ideas and approaches, these seminars are motivational in nature. In making decisions about which courses and seminars to attend, ask your broker and/or successful salespeople you know who have attended the courses for their evaluations of the programs.

Self-Training

In your training, you should realize that the quicker you acquire the basic skills needed for success, the greater the likelihood you will remain in the real estate profession. The simple economics of trying to survive a lengthy training period forces many agents to leave real estate when they might otherwise have realized great success. Stated simply, the quicker you learn your survival skills, the more likely you are to survive and succeed.

Therefore, it is important to use every bit of available time toward this goal of self-improvement. As a new licensee, you cannot afford the luxury of relaxing in front of the television after an eight-hour day.

Check your office library, as well as city libraries, for real estate training books and videos. Study them, take notes, and then verbalize (role-play) the approaches presented. Chances are a number of people in your office have trainer material from various seminar presenters. Borrow it; some of the private presenter material is excellent.

Learn the inventory in your market area. Only with product knowledge will you be able to successfully match prospective buyers to properties meeting their needs.

Learn about the facilities within your market area. You want to be able to answer the questions that prospective buyers are likely to ask about schools, parks, transportation, recreational facilities, and so on.

As a word of caution, keep in mind that some of the poorest producers may have excellent resource material available, but if unused it becomes worthless.

Role-Playing

Role-playing is acting as the person you wish to be.

To communicate effectively with buyers and sellers, you must be able to take your ideas and verbalize them in an effective manner. By using role-playing, you can train yourself to handle telephone inquiries; make listing, showing, and selling presentations; learn to effectively qualify buyers; and learn to overcome both buyer and seller objections. Role-playing can help you overcome the fear that grips many agents when it comes time to ask an owner or a buyer to sign a contract. Role-playing can give you the self-confidence to close (obtain signatures on the contract) in a natural and effective manner.

Role-playing is a mind game. It is also basic acting. In role-playing, you imagine yourself in a situation where you are confronted by unexpected objections of all sorts and then decide on the best way to handle them. (The training material we discussed will provide you with many ideas.) Verbalize your responses before a mirror. Watch your expressions.

Always remember that you are playing the part of a knowledgeable professional. You should constantly strive for improvement. The beauty of role-playing is that you can do it mentally, even when others are present. You can use otherwise nonproductive driving time for role-playing exercises. By role-playing, you will gain confidence and become at ease in dealing with people. An excellent training approach is to role-play with another person with whom you can exchange characters. This really is a team-teaching exercise. Having a third-party observer will increase the effectiveness of this technique and will help keep you focused.

By recording your role-playing presentations, you will hear how you sound. You might feel you need better enunciation or need to speak with greater confidence. Annoying verbal habits become evident, such as verbalizing your pauses with "ahhh" or repeating a phrase such as "you know." If you realize you have problems, you can work to overcome them. Making presentations before a video camera can reveal problems with facial expressions and body language.

After you make any type of presentation, ask yourself, "Could I have handled the situation better?" By thinking about what you should have said, you are actually preparing yourself for future encounters with similar situations. You can thus benefit by failures as well as successes.

Role-playing will improve your communication skills, and as your skills improve, so will your confidence. You will thus overcome fear, a significant factor in the failure of many salespeople. If you fear failure, you are likely to betray your fear by appearing nervous. A prospective buyer or seller is not likely to become convinced to buy or list property by an agent who appears to lack confidence. As you progress, you will become the person you were portraying in your role-playing: a confident, knowledgeable, and caring person interested in fulfilling the needs of others.

Planning

Planning is the process of plotting your course of action to reach specified goals and objectives. It is a blueprint of what you intend to accomplish. Add a timetable, and you also have a tool to evaluate your performance. Planning is never a waste of time. The less time you have to spare, the more important it is to plan your day carefully. Do not forget the oft-repeated statement that 20% of your effort will produce 80% of your results.

Adopt your own system of planning, but be sure to plan. Any system that does away with time-wasters and puts the focus on planning will increase productivity. Self-discipline is the key. If you have it, you will have great success with time management and the other aspects of your life.

Sometimes it may seem that no matter how hard you apply yourself and how efficiently you allocate your time, you have more work to do and more people to see than you can handle satisfactorily. Time management is part of the solution. A good time-management system rounds out your plan and helps you improve efficiency and income. As you refine your techniques of self-management, you may expect a release from the pressures of time as your first dividend.

Time Management

The paradox of time is that "there is never enough, but we have all there is." A time-management authority who conducted a poll of managers found that 90% said they needed more time to get their jobs done right.

Unsuccessful real estate licensees often waste 40% to 50% of every workday. Just think of your first hour on the job. Are you guilty of the behavior that one time-management expert witnessed? Do you do nothing more than participate in "opening exercises": have a cup of coffee, socialize, read the paper? Little gets done, and that sets a pattern for the day. There's an old proverb that reads as follows: "As the first hour goes, so goes the day."

Time management can make the whole day more productive, allowing you to produce more, get better results, and probably get more rewards as well. Remember, time is capital; know what it is worth.

$$\frac{\text{desired annual earnings}}{1{,}952 \text{ working hours a year}}$$

The figure of 1,952 is based on 244 working days times 8 hours per day.

EXAMPLE Salesperson Graham makes $100,000 per year; his hourly wage is approximately $51 per hour ($100,000 ÷ 1,952 hours = $51, the dollar value of one hour).

Allowing for other activities and unavoidable delays, you will be fortunate to have one-fourth that time (488 hours a year) to actually spend with clients or customers. Thus, the dollar value of your time is even greater than the equation above indicates. To start thinking about how to get the maximum return on your time, ask yourself, "How can I raise the

- number of contacts received and made per week?"
- number of interviews per contact?"
- number of presentations given per interview?"
- number of closes per presentation?"
- number of new prospects per week?"
- number of repeat sales?"
- dollar value of selling time?"

Goal Setting

Can you imagine yourself in a race without a finish line? That is what it is like to work without goals. You can travel a great distance but get nowhere.

Goal setting is a tool for making intelligent decisions. Use the following seven principles to help you set your goals effectively:

1. Goals in real estate selling should be specific rather than abstract. For example:

   ■ Abstract—I will do my best to improve my sales techniques during this week.

   ■ Specific—I will obtain at least one listing and make at least three sales presentations during this week.

   Goals must be measurable. "Doing better" cannot be measured, but giving out 50 calling cards is a measurable goal. If a goal is not measurable, it is not likely to be met.

2. Goals should be in a time frame. Set short-term, intermediate-term, and long-term goals. (The short-term, intermediate-term, and long-term goals listed below are representative only. Goals will vary based on your area of specialization and your geographic area, as well as your individual needs.) For example:
   Short-term (less than one year)

   ■ I will obtain a minimum of three listings this month.

   ■ This week I will enroll in a college-level course in property management.

   Intermediate-term (one to five years)

   ■ I will complete the required eight broker courses within two years.

   ■ I will obtain the GRI designation within four years.

   Long-term (more than five years)

   ■ I will open my own real estate office within eight years.

   (Your short-term and intermediate-term goals should flow toward meeting your long-term goals.)

3. Goals should be put into writing:

   ■ It is easier to determine your priorities when your goals are written.

   ■ Written goals are easier to examine and revise.

   Translating goals onto paper makes them appear more manageable and helps licensees overcome selling fears.

4. Tell someone, such as your spouse or trusted friend, your goals. Telling another person will serve as motivation to continue striving for your goals. You are now accountable to someone besides yourself.

5. Goals should be reasonably attainable. If your goals are not realistic, you are likely to become discouraged and disappointed.

6. Goals should be adopted only after careful and considerable thought.

   Think about what you really want and why. Reaching goals can take hard work, so you probably will devote time and energy only to those you are really committed to.

7. Goals should not be cast in stone. If interests change, the economy changes, or your needs and desires change, your long-term and intermediate-term goals should change accordingly. If you are no longer motivated to reach a goal, your likelihood of accomplishing that goal will be significantly lessened.

You need action steps to meet goals. In other words, a plan so the goal will be met. As an example, the goal to obtain three listings this month might have the following action plan:

■   I will make personal owner contact each week with all for-sale-by-owner ads that include addresses.

■   I will check local bulletin boards each week for for-sale-by-owner ads.

■   I will mail solicitation material each week to all expired listings.

■   I will check the local legal paper for legal notices that could indicate listing opportunities and follow up with personal contacts.

By evaluating yourself, you will discover that wishes can become reality if you have a plan that leads toward their fruition.

Your **daily planning** is the foundation of your goal setting. Your planning for each day should include steps leading to your short-term, intermediate-term, and long-term goals.

Before you start daily planning, precisely log your time for several days. How productive was that 20-minute discussion on the Dodgers? Besides identifying the time-wasters, ask yourself, "Were my efforts devoted more to probabilities rather than mere possibilities?"

Some agents like to divide their activities into A, B, C, and D categories:

Simply increasing "A" Time will increase productivity.

"A" Time—Time spent making listing presentations and showing properties for sale. This is time spent that can lead directly to a commission.

"B" Time—Time spent in prospecting for buyers and sellers and in preparing for showings

"C" Time—Caravanning, studying inventory, and doing necessary tasks and paperwork in support of "A" Time and "B" Time activities

"D" Time—Time spent for personal and non-work-related activities

This simple rating of time presents a basic truth. If you can double your A" Time, you will double your income, even without any improvement in your skills. When coupled with skill improvement, you can readily see how incomes can soar. Some successful agents hire assistants to take care of a great deal of their "B" Time and "C" Time activities. You can see why a productive salesperson would want to do this.

You are now ready for your daily plan. There are quite a few real estate daily planners available. Consider one for your smartphone and/or computer. Figure 1.5 shows a basic daily planning sheet. By having your planner with you on your smartphone, you can set appointments several days in advance when necessary. A smartphone not only provides planning ability, it also provides much of the information needed to fulfill the tasks in your daily plan.

Just having a planner isn't enough—you must use it. Keep in mind that every activity on your daily plan will not be accomplished. Your schedule will change because of unplanned opportunities. Grab an "A" Time opportunity whenever it comes your way.

At the end of each day, evaluate what you have accomplished. If a task was not accomplished but is still relevant, set it forward to the next day; if not, delete it. If a task is unpleasant but must be done, set it for the beginning of a day. After it is accomplished, you will have a sense of relief rather than worrying about it all day.

If you have a goal to earn $100,000 in one year, you would want to know how many sale and listing transactions would have to be closed to meet that goal. Assume that in your office, the average salesperson's commission per transaction is $5,850. In order to earn $100,000, you would have to close 17.1 transactions per year or 1.42 per month ($100,000 ÷ $5,850). Now you must determine the A, B, C, and D time allocations needed to meet this income goal.

Assistants

Some new licensees will work as salaried **personal assistants** to successful sales agents to gain the experience and confidence necessary for success in sales. While assistants do not make much economic sense for new agents (who must learn before they can train others to help them), they can handle a great deal of a successful agent's B, C, and D time activities, thus allowing for greater "A" Time work. Hundreds of agents in California hire paid full-time or part-time assistants, and one agent we know has a personal staff of four full-time aides. (See Figure 1.6.)

FIGURE 1.5:   Daily Planning Sheet

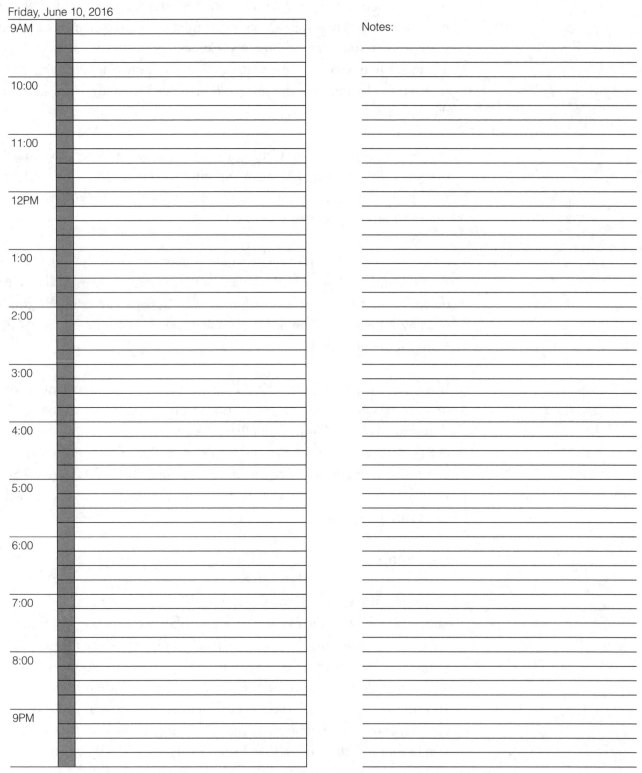

Friday, June 10, 2016

9AM	Notes:
10:00	
11:00	
12PM	
1:00	
2:00	
3:00	
4:00	
5:00	
6:00	
7:00	
8:00	
9PM	

Source: Jim Loonday, *List for Success: How Real Estate Professionals Make Big Money* (Chicago: Real Estate Education Company®, 1986), 10.

FIGURE 1.6:   **Personal Assistant Contract**

CALIFORNIA
ASSOCIATION
OF REALTORS®

PERSONAL ASSISTANT CONTRACT
(Between Associate-Licensee and Licensed or Unlicensed Assistant)
(C.A.R. Form PAC, Revised 06/12)

This Agreement, dated _____, is between _____,
("Associate-Licensee") and _____ ("Assistant").
Assistant desires to work for Associate-Licensee, and Associate-Licensee desires to use the services of Assistant. In consideration for the covenants and representations contained in this Agreement, Associate-Licensee and Assistant agree as follows:

1. **ASSOCIATE-LICENSEE** is a California real estate licensee with a ☐ salesperson's, or ☐ broker's license. Associate-Licensee is licensed under _____, ("Broker") or ☐ (if checked) works for him/herself.

2. **ASSISTANT REAL ESTATE LICENSE:** Assistant ☐ does, ☐ does not, hold a California real estate license. If Assistant does hold a real estate license, the license must be furnished to Broker immediately upon execution of this Agreement.

3. **EMPLOYER-EMPLOYEE RELATIONSHIP:** Assistant shall be an at-will employee of Associate-Licensee. This means either party may terminate this Agreement at any time with or without cause. As Assistant's employer, Associate-Licensee shall be responsible for compliance with all applicable local, state and federal laws including not limited to minimum wage and overtime pay, timekeeping requirements, income and employment tax withholdings, worker's compensation coverage and compliance with employment discrimination including harassment law. If Associate-Licensee and Assistant desire to enter into a different type of working relationship, such as independent contractor, a separate written agreement must be used. The classification of any person who performs services for an Associate-Licensee as an independent contractor has significant legal consequences for both the Associate-Licensee and the person who performs the services and can result in severe penalties and other adverse consequences if a person is misclassified as an independent contractor. Associate-Licensee and Assistant are advised to seek legal and accounting advice before considering classifying Assistant as an independent contractor.

4. **DUTIES:** Assistant shall assist Associate-Licensee in fulfilling Associate-Licensee's obligations under the Independent Contractor agreement (C.A.R. Form ICA, attached) between Associate-Licensee and Broker. Assistant shall comply with all obligations of Associate-Licensee imposed under the terms of that agreement and any office policy established by Broker. Associate-Licensee shall monitor the work and results of Assistant. If Assistant does not have a real estate license, Assistant shall not engage in any activity for which a real estate license is required. (Assistant may become more familiar with these limitations by reading the "DRE Guidelines for Unlicensed Assistants") In addition, and more specifically, Assistant shall perform the following activities: _____
_____
_____
_____

5. **COMPENSATION AND BENEFITS:**
   A. **Base Compensation:** Assistant's base compensation is $_____ per **hour** payable in equal bi-weekly installments every other_____(insert day of the week).
   OR ☐ (If checked) Assistant's base compensation is $_____ per **hour** payable in equal semi-monthly installments on the 15th (or_____) and last (or_____) day of the month.
   OR ☐ (If checked) Assistant's base compensation is shown in Exhibit _____ attached hereto an incorporated as a part of this Agreement by reference.
   B. **Expenses:** Assistant shall be reimbursed for reasonable business expenses incurred by Assistant in performing Assistant's duties under this Agreement.
   C. **Advances:** Assistant shall not be entitled to any advance payment from Associate-Licensee upon future compensation, unless specified in a separate written agreement for each such advance. If Associate-Licensee elects to advance funds to Assistant pursuant to a separate written agreement, Associate-Licensee may deduct the amount advanced from any future paycheck due Assistant as specified in the separate written agreement.
   D. Deductions authorized by Assistant or required by law (including but not limited to FICA, Medicare and Federal and State income tax) will be with held from Assistant's pay.
   E. **Compensation Review:** Associate-Licensee shall review Assistant's base compensation annually. Associate understands and agrees that any such review is not an express or implied commitment to increase such compensation nor is there any express or implied commitment to maintain Assistant's compensation at any particular level in the future.
   F. **Timekeeping:** Associate-Licensee shall record Assistant's time on a daily basis including starting time, ending time and the beginning and ending time for all meal periods.
   G. **Vacation Policy:** Assistant shall be eligible to accrue vacation at the rate of _____ hours per pay period. The maximum unused vacation benefits Assistant may have at any one time shall equal two year's worth of vacation (or a total of _____ hours) OR ☐ as specified in Exhibit _____, attached. If Assistant's earned but unused vacation reaches the maximum accrual amount, Assistant will cease to accrue additional vacation time until Assistant uses enough vacation to fall below the maximum accrual amount. All accrued and unused vacation will be paid to Assistant upon termination of this Agreement as required by law.

Associate Licensee's Initials (_____)(_____)

Assistant's Initials (_____)(_____)

Reviewed by _____ Date _____

EQUAL HOUSING
OPPORTUNITY

PAC REVISED 06/12 (PAGE 1 OF 3) Print Date

PERSONAL ASSISTANT CONTRACT (PAC PAGE 1 OF 3)

FIGURE 1.6 (continued):   Personal Assistant Contract

6. **PROPRIETARY INFORMATION AND FILES:**
   A. Assistant acknowledge that as a result of Assistant's employment created by this Agreement, Assistant may given access to, make use of, create, acquire and/or add to non-public proprietary, confidential information of a secret, special and/or unique nature and value to Broker, including without limitation Broker's internal systems, procedures, manuals, confidential reports, client lists and client information, methods, strategies and/or techniques used by Broker, the equipment and methods used and preferred by Broker's clients, the fees paid by clients and any and all other confidential information of Broker (hereafter collectively and individually "Confidential Information"). Assistant further recognizes and acknowledges that all of Broker's Confidential Information which is now or may hereafter be in their possession is the property of Broker and that protection of this Confidential Information against unauthorized disclosure or use is of critical importance to Broker in order to protect Broker from unfair competition. As a material inducement to Associate-Licensee to enter into this Agreement, Assistant covenants and agrees Assistant will not at any time, either while this Agreement is in force or after it is terminated without the prior written consent of Broker make any independent use of such Confidential Information, or disclose the same, directly or indirectly, to any other person, firm, corporation or other entity, for any reason or purpose whatsoever, except as may be required by law provided that Assistant shall cooperate with Broker in taking all necessary and appropriate steps to assure the protection of such Confidential Information from unauthorized use or disclosure outside of any action, proceeding, inquiry or investigation, or except to the extent that any such Confidential Information shall be in the public domain other than by reason of Assistant's breach of this paragraph 6.
   B. All Confidential Information including without limitation files and documents pertaining to listings, leads, transactions and the operation of Broker's real estate brokerage are property of Broker. Assistant shall, on the termination of this Agreement for any reason, immediately surrender to Broker all such Confidential Information including without limitation all documents and files whether in paper or electronic format.
7. **INSURANCE:**
   A. AUTOMOBILE: Assistant shall maintain automobile insurance coverage for liability and property damage in the following amounts $_____ /$_____, respectively. Associate-Licensee and Broker shall be named as additional insured parties on Assistant's policies. A copy of the endorsement showing the additional insured parties shall be provided to Associate-Licensee.
   B. WORKER'S COMPENSATION: Associate-Licensee's Worker's Compensation carrier is _____.
   The contact information for this carrier is as follows: Address:_____
   _____, Telephone:_____
   C. ERRORS AND OMISSIONS INSURANCE: Associate-Licensee represents that (check one):
      (i) ☐ Assistant is covered by errors and omissions insurance obtained by Broker.
      (ii) ☐ Assistant is covered by errors and omissions insurance obtained by Associate-Licensee.
      (iii) ☐ Assistant is not covered by errors and omissions insurance.
8. **COMPLIANCE WITH APPLICABLE LAWS, RULES, REGULATIONS AND POLICIES:** Assistant agrees to comply with all local, state and federal laws and regulations, and any office policy and procedures to which Associate-Licensee is subject as a result of engaging in real estate activity.
9. **NOTICE OF CLAIMS:** Assistant shall immediately notify Associate-Licensee or Broker in writing if Assistant is served with or becomes aware of any lawsuit, claim or proceeding relating to Associate-Licensee or Broker's brokerage business or the performance of this Agreement.
10. **DISPUTE RESOLUTION:** Associate-Licensee and Assistant agree to mediate all disputes and claims between them arising from or connected in any way with this Agreement before resorting to court action. If any dispute or claim is not resolved through mediation, or otherwise, Associate-Licensee and Assistant may agree to submit the dispute to arbitration at, and pursuant to the rules and bylaws of, the Association of REALTORS®.
11. **OTHER TERMS AND CONDITIONS AND ATTACHED SUPPLEMENTS:**
    ☐ Broker and Associate-Licensee Independent Contractor Agreement (C.A.R. Form ICA)
    ☐ Broker/Associate-Licensee/Assistant Three Party Agreement (C.A.R. Form TPA)
    ☐ Broker Office Policy Manual (or, if checked, ☐ available in Broker's office)
    ☐ DRE Guidelines for Unlicensed Assistants
    ☐ California Association of REALTORS® Real Estate Licensing Chart
    _____
    _____
    _____
    _____
    _____
12. **ATTORNEY FEES:** In any action, proceeding, or arbitration between Associate-Licensee and Assistant arising from or related to this Agreement, the prevailing Associate-Licensee or Assistant shall be entitled to reasonable attorney fees and costs.
13. **ENTIRE AGREEMENT:** This Agreement constitutes the entire Agreement between the parties. Its terms are intended by the parties as a final, complete, exclusive, and integrated expression of their agreement with respect to its subject matter, and may not be contradicted by evidence of any prior agreement or contemporaneous oral agreement. This Agreement may not be amended, modified, altered, or changed except in writing signed by Associate-Licensee and Assistant. If any provision of this Agreement is held invalid and legally unenforceable, the parties agree that such provision shall be deemed amended to the extent necessary to render it and/or the remainder of this Agreement valid and enforceable. Even after termination, this Agreement shall govern all disputes and claims between Associate-Licensee and Assistant connected with their respective obligations under this Agreement, including obligations and liabilities arising from existing and completed listings, transactions and services.

Associate Licensee's Initials (_____)(_____)   Assistant's Initials (_____)(_____)

PAC REVISED 06/12 (PAGE 2 OF 3) Print Date

Reviewed by _____ Date _____

EQUAL HOUSING OPPORTUNITY

PERSONAL ASSISTANT CONTRACT (PAC PAGE 2 OF 3)

FIGURE 1.6 (continued):   Personal Assistant Contract

Associate-Licensee _____ Date _____
                        Signature

Associate-Licensee _____
                        Print Name

Address _____ City _____ State _____ Zip _____

Telephone _____ Fax _____ E-mail _____

Associate-Licensee _____ Date _____
                        Signature

Associate-Licensee _____
                        Print Name

Address _____ City _____ State _____ Zip _____

Telephone _____ Fax _____ E-mail _____

PAC REVISED 06/12 (PAGE 3 OF 3)

Reviewed by _____ Date _____

EQUAL HOUSING OPPORTUNITY

PERSONAL ASSISTANT CONTRACT (PAC PAGE 3 OF 3)

According to the National Association of REALTORS®, 16% of REALTORS® have at least one assistant. While some agents share an assistant, 79% of assistants work for a single agent. Fifty-four percent of personal assistants work part time. Although 48% of assistants are unlicensed, unlicensed assistants are limited in their activities. Some of the activities that might be delegated to assistants include the following:

■ Installing signs and lockboxes

■ Returning calls and handling correspondence and emails

■ Preparing disclosures

■ Conducting or assisting in open houses with the consent of the principal

■ Financial qualifying of prospective buyers

■ Tracking escrows

■ Preparing internet listings and updates

■ Answering emails within minutes and setting up appointments with prospect

■ Preparing property flyers

■ Locating property to show

■ Contacting owners as to showings

■ Managing agent's daily planner

■ Handling agent's social media

Unlicensed assistants are prohibited from the following activities:

■ Attempting to induce a person to use broker services (prohibits communication with the public in a manner structured for solicitation purposes)

■ Showing property, including open houses (simply handing out material is alright)

■ Discussing features of a property, unless taken from a data sheet prepared by a licensee

- Discussing terms and conditions regarding a listing or sale

- Discussing property needs with a client

- Discussing contracts or significance of documents with a client

- Participating in any negotiations

The Bureau of Real Estate published guidelines for unlicensed assistants, setting forth what an unlicensed assistant could and could not do; the *Guidelines for Unlicensed Assistants* was published in *Real Estate Bulletin*, Winter 2003, and can be accessed online at www.dre.ca.gov/files/pdf/guide_unlic_asst.pdf.

WEB LINK

ADDITIONAL PREPARATION

Additional preparation will be required to prepare for your career.

When you go to work for an office, you will want to learn about the office **inventory** as soon as possible. This means you must visit office listings. Call ahead if a listing is inhabited. Don't take too much time with each owner, or you will have a long-term job just visiting inventory. In the case of large offices with hundreds of listings, personal visits to each listing would not be possible. As a suggestion, use your office website to review listings and then visit those listings that are in the area, price range, and of the type you feel you would like to concentrate on. You may wish to take digital photographs of features of the property, if they are not covered by your office website or property flyers. Take notes so you don't confuse property features. Until you know the inventory, you will be unable to field inquiries or properly prepare for a showing.

Another benefit of visiting office inventory is that it will give you a sense of area value based on listing prices. You should be able to judge within a relatively short period of time if a listing is priced competitively. Check out homes listed by other offices within the geographic area or specialization area if you have decided to specialize in a particular market segment. In smaller communities, you might be able to see everything that is available, but in larger markets, you will have to be selective and choose homes for which you feel you might have interested buyers.

Of course, you should go on office and board **caravans** of new listings. Avoid visiting properties where you feel the likelihood of your having a buyer is slight. Try to avoid wasting time. Abraham Lincoln said, "A lawyer's time is his stock in trade." It holds true for real estate agents as well as lawyers.

Office Procedure

If your office or company has a **policy manual** (procedures manual), study it. As soon as possible, learn what is expected of you. Know your office meeting and training schedules, and enter them in your daily planner for the month ahead. Find out what the procedure is for depositing customer trust money. You must know what to do when you take a listing or an offer to purchase. Every office is run a little differently from every other office, so be certain you understand what is expected of you.

Be familiar with the forms used by your office so that you will be able to complete them and explain them to others without hesitation. As a personal training exercise, complete a listing for a property you know of, and then complete an offer to purchase for that property. Have both reviewed by another agent.

Find out how to use your office communications systems. What are the procedures for long distance calls and overnight express services? Understand what systems your office provides and how to use them.

Computer Literacy

A 2014 survey by the National Association of REALTORS® (NAR) revealed that

- the internet was used by 92% of buyers and only 30% used newspapers;

- 91% of REALTORS® used social media to some extent; and

- the top three places where REALTORS® placed their listings, besides their own website, were www.Realtor.com, Zillow, and Trulia.

A 2012 NAR survey revealed that

- 90% of buyers used the internet as their first stop in house hunting and

- 80% of buyers contacted a broker from what they saw on the internet.

In today's sales environment, it is readily apparent that you must have computer knowledge. At a minimum, you should be able to use a computer for the following:

- Sending and accessing email

- Searching for available properties from MLS data based on specific criteria (for example: four-bedroom houses in a particular area priced under $400,000)

- Obtaining a printout of houses sold within an area showing features and sale price

- Knowing your office and MLS website and links

- Accessing additional websites covering your market area

- Preparing a listing for website use

- Using word-processing software to produce personalized sales letters and other correspondence

- Producing an attractive property brief (one-page description) for a listing

- Obtaining comparables (listing and sale prices of similar properties) and preparing a comparative market analysis

- Handling loan-qualifying and loan applications online

You should consider **e-PRO certification**. This is the NAR training program to certify real estate professionals as internet professionals. The educational requirements for certification will prepare you for more effective online communications.

Tax Knowledge

You must understand real property taxation and special benefits available for seniors, low-income individuals, and so on. You should also have knowledge of the income tax benefits of home ownership, as well as the tax treatment for investment and income property, including exchanging. (See Unit 14.) Tax knowledge is also important for tracking your own expenses for income tax preparation. What you can deduct will significantly affect your net income.

Sales Equipment

You must be equipped to be a successful real estate salesperson. You should consider the following:

iPad or other tablet device.   Many real estate agents are relying on iPads or other tablet devices, such as those that run on the Android operating system, to conduct their real estate sales business. Most MLS interfaces are optimized to display on tablet devices. Other agents are using their tablets to generate and sign contracts through applications designed for this purpose.

Wireless printers.   Wireless printers are available starting at about $100. The printers can be mounted in your vehicle and used in conjunction with your netbook or laptop to print out information on properties as well as contracts. With a wireless printer, you can turn your vehicle into a mobile office.

Smartphone.   Over 80% of real estate agents now use smartphones. They do so to increase agent efficiency. Consider a smartphone such as an Apple iPhone with the following features and real estate apps:

- All phone services, including caller ID, call waiting, and recording
- Wireless email
- Daily planning
- Storing of addresses and telephone numbers
- Managing contacts for return calls, action, et cetera.
- Making to-do lists
- Taking notes
- Writing memos
- Amortization schedule
- Doing financial calculations (closing costs, payments, etc.)
- Retrieving and sending emails
- Downloading MLS information and other data from the internet

- Available For Sale by Owner properties

- Zillow value estimates

- Transferring data to and from desktop computers

- Setting an alarm for appointment reminders

- Entering business-related expenses for tax purposes

- Using universal connectors for add-ons, such as portable keyboard, modems, and more

- Accessing a global positioning system (GPS) for driving instructions to addresses from your location; Waze is a community-based traffic navigation system that saves both time and gas.

- Open House Pro is an open house management system that helps follow up leads on walk-ins

- Dropbox is a free service that allows you to bring photos, documents, and videos anywhere. Any file you place in Dropbox is accessible.

- AroundMe identifies where you are and all businesses in the category that you type in

- Camera

- Customizing for specific needs

- Security. Red Alert is a security app that can contact 911 if you are in danger; it also features a built-in alarm.

A 2008 CAR survey revealed that 27% of respondents felt that a hands-free cell phone was their most important business upgrade in the past 12 months. A survey today would reveal that cell phone to be a smartphone with a real estate app. The real estate app gives the agent information on local listing and area information. The NAR has apps that will show sold homes on map zones, price-reduced properties, and foreclosed properties, as well as customized searches. In California, you cannot use a hand-held cell phone while driving.

Using a search engine, you will find App stores that offer a variety of apps, with many designed for real estate agents.

Business cards.   Your license number must be printed on your business card. You should also include your email address and your cell phone number. If you are fluent in another language or languages and are targeting persons who speak that language, then your business card should indicate your language fluency. Your name must appear as it is on your real estate license. A nickname may be highlighted to indicate it is not the salesperson's legal name. The name of your employing broker must be in at least eight-point type. Your photo on your card will help contacts identify you. A fold-out card might be required to provide all pertinent data.

Some brokers do not want photos used on business cards because of agent safety. Brokers feel that "glamour photos" might cause contacts with the agent other than real property–related business. Other brokers fear the photos could encourage racial or ethnic discrimination. You should be aware of these concerns. However, the author believes tasteful business card photos are proper, as well as being a positive business practice.

Electronic business cards have seen increased use by real estate professionals. While they may look like ordinary cards, when they are inserted into a computer, they can provide videos, resumes, and links to social networking, as well as your office site.

A QR code (quick response code) is a bar code readable by smartphones. One phone scans the other for data transfer. Use of a QR code can mean a paperless electronic card.

Your car.   Your car should be kept clean at all times. Avoid smoking in your car because many people are offended by the smell of tobacco. You might want to use an air freshener. If you are going to purchase a car, consider a full-size four-door model or SUV for ease in entering and exiting. This is of particular value when dealing with older prospective buyers. To test for comfort, sit in the rear seat of the vehicle before you decide to purchase.

Carry the following items in the trunk, glove box, or under the seat:

1. A plastic bag with extra forms and pens

2. A flashlight

3. A For Sale sign and stake. Large For Sale signs erected on heavy posts are generally installed by a crew hired by the broker. Many offices install small signs until the large sign can be erected. In addition, many communities limit the size of For Sale signs, so smaller signs must be used.

4. Basic tools (hammer, screwdriver, pliers, assorted nails, screws, nuts, and bolts) for setting or repairing firm signs

5. A 50-foot tape measure (and/or an electronic measuring device)

6. A small tape recorder to record your thoughts or ideas if your smartphone does not have this capability

7. A supply of business cards

8. Maps showing school districts, public transportation, recreational areas, et cetera. (Use colored marking pens.)

9. A digital camera with a minimum of 14 megapixels for clarity

If your office does not have an 800 number and your buyers come primarily from outside your local calling area, you might consider your own 800 number. An 800 number is available at a very reasonable cost. Many independent providers offer these services.

Computer.   As you gain experience and knowledge, you will find that you will be spending more time away from your office. Your office will become more of a place to meet clients than a workstation. Your own computer to access your office computers and MLS services is a necessity. A computer offers the benefit of a larger monitor than a smartphone's screen. Your home office should also include a printer, scanner, fax, and copier (now available as 4-in-1 machines). You will need them. Having a home office will reduce wasted time and allow you to utilize spare time at home. You can track contact information and activities with contact management software. You can even set alarms as to contacts.

Note: You should be aware that a home office may qualify as an IRS tax deduction if the space is used exclusively and regularly as your principal place of business. You should check with your accountant to determine if your home office expenses qualify as tax deductions.

Specialty items.   There are a number of sources for real estate signs, flags, cards, newsletters and give-away advertising items. Many boards of REALTORS® have stores. In addition there are a number of providers on the internet such as www.sanzospecialties.com.

You.   You want to dress as a professional within your area would dress. Your clothes reflect the image you want to convey, that of a person who feels competent in her role. Avoid trendy fashions; conservative is best. Avoid overly flashy or expensive jewelry; you don't want to divert attention from what you are saying. Use cologne or aftershave lotion sparingly. If people can smell you coming, chances are you overdid it.

Learn to smile. Smile while you are on the telephone and when you talk to people. An upbeat person can make others feel good and can set an upbeat mood for a sale.

Take care of yourself. Your body is the only one you have. Watch your diet, get adequate sleep, and exercise on a regular basis. A healthy body will be reflected in your energy and productivity.

Recordkeeping.   Keep records of all written communications and notes of any problems. Do not make verbal promises. Follow up communications with an email. Contemporaneous dated notes are important. Records can be kept electronically. Many of the problems you will encounter are based on understanding later what was communicated. Good records can avoid legal disputes and serve to reinforce your position if disputes do occur.

SUMMARY

Real estate professionals deal in the fulfillment of needs. The product that fulfills these needs is real estate.

Real estate activity can be an important engine for economic growth because more people are employed in real estate and construction-related jobs than in any other industry.

Competition has changed the way many brokers charge for their services.

Real estate professionals work in an imperfect and changing marketplace. The reasons for this imperfection include product differentiation, emotions, imperfect buyer and seller knowledge, buyer and seller motivation, and the differing terms of the sale. The real estate professional brings a degree of order to this marketplace.

Real estate is changing with new technology, as well as with better-educated and trained professionals. Changes are also taking place because of competition.

Most real estate agents are engaged in listing and selling single-family residences. Other areas of activity or specialization include the following:

- Mobile home sales

- Residential income property

- Commercial property

- Industrial property

- Business opportunities

- Land and farm brokerage

- Lot sales

- Auction sales

- Loan brokerage

- Land development

- Property management

- Leasing

The real estate salesperson is considered by real estate law to be an employee of the broker but for tax purposes usually is contractually designated as an independent contractor.

If the salesperson meets the IRS criteria as an independent contractor, withholding tax is not deducted from the salesperson's commission checks. Also, the employer need not contribute to the salesperson's Social Security.

Choosing a broker is an extremely important decision. A new licensee should be particularly interested in the aid and training provided by the broker. Brokers want to hire salespersons who will succeed, and salespersons want a broker who can meet their needs.

Your attitude can be a significant factor in your success. A negative attitude will be reflected in your production.

Working for a REALTOR® or a Realtist will give you the advantage of a broad educational program, as well as access to publications. Keep in mind that training is a career-long activity and is an integral part of your career as a real estate professional. You must equip yourself with the basic tools of the real estate profession and know how to use them. Besides office training and boards of REALTORS® sessions, engage in self-training. This includes reading books and periodicals, using available videos, and, most important, role-playing to prepare yourself to handle any conceivable situation.

Establish goals for yourself. These should include short-term, intermediate-term, and long-term goals. You need a plan to meet these goals. Your planning will reduce wasted time and lead to realization of your goals. The basic building block of your planning is a daily plan.

One of your first steps toward success in a new office is learning your inventory. You must learn office procedures, acquire basic computer literacy, and have basic knowledge of property and income taxes as they relate to real estate sales activities. You must also acquire some basic tools so you can perform as a real estate professional. Keep records of what was communicated and when. Good records can avoid problems.

Of course, you want to personally convey the image of a professional in your dress and manner. Take care of yourself because your health is related to your productivity.

CLASS DISCUSSION TOPICS

1. Describe your local market area and evaluate it. Is your local market stratified? How? If you were to choose an area of specialization, what would it be? (Consider both geographic area and activity.) Justify your choice.

2. Describe the training programs provided by local offices.

3. What are your long-term goals? What short-term and intermediate-term goals would help in meeting these long-term goals?

4. What training material is available for your use in your office?

5. What training material and course offerings are available through your board or association of REALTORS®?

6. Prepare a daily plan in advance. How was your time actually spent on that day? Discuss deviations from the plan and the reasons for the deviations. Were they justified?

7. Evaluate your average day. What percentage of your time is spent in "A" Time activities? "B" Time activities? "C" Time activities? "D" Time activities?

8. What could you do now to increase the percentage of your time spent on "A" Time activities?

9. Do you know of any real estate firms in your area that have merged? If so, what benefits do you feel resulted from the merger?

10. Are there brokers in your area offering lower fees than their competition?

11. Are they providing similar services to those offered by their higher priced competitors?

12. Discuss what you consider to be a successful team. How are team members compensated? What are the benefits of team members?

13. For class discussion, bring to class one current-events article dealing with some aspect of real estate practice.

UNIT 1 QUIZ

1. The real estate marketplace could *BEST* be described as being
   a. homogeneous.
   b. stratified.
   c. perfect.
   d. uninfluenced by emotion.

2. *MOST* real estate agents are primarily engaged in which area of activity?
   a. Residential property
   b. Raw land and lots
   c. Commercial property
   d. Development

3. The IRS will treat real estate salespeople as independent contractors if three criteria are met. Which is *NOT* one of the criteria?
   a. The salesperson's reimbursement is solely based on sales, not hours worked.
   b. The salesperson represents himself as an independent contractor when dealing with third parties.
   c. There is a written contract stating that the salesperson will be treated as an independent contractor for tax purposes.
   d. The salesperson is licensed as a real estate agent.

4. A broker ordinarily would be liable to salespeople for
   a. unemployment compensation.
   b. workers' compensation.
   c. Social Security contributions.
   d. none of these.

5. In choosing a broker, a new licensee should be *LEAST* interested in an office that
   a. has a high percentage of successful salespeople.
   b. has a good library of books, tapes, and videos for training.
   c. offers 100% commission.
   d. is a member of a local multiple listing service.

6.   The *BEST* way to learn is to
   a.   listen to what others say.
   b.   read instructional material.
   c.   watch what others are doing.
   d.   use the ideas you observe or read about.

7.   Which of the following statements regarding role-playing is *TRUE*?
   a.   Role-playing situations are limited only by our own imagination.
   b.   Role-playing can be verbalized or nonverbalized.
   c.   Role-playing exercises can involve more than one person.
   d.   All of these.

8.   Which statement is an example of a specific goal?
   a.   I will work harder next week.
   b.   I will improve my listing presentation.
   c.   I will make 10 calls tomorrow on for-sale-by-owner ads and schedule three property showings by Sunday.
   d.   I will learn by observing successful agents.

9.   All of the following will aid you in goal achievement *EXCEPT*
   a.   that goals should be attainable.
   b.   that goals should be based on what you really want.
   c.   that goals should be kept to yourself because they are personal.
   d.   that goals should be exact so that you can measure their attainment.

10.   Proper daily planning means that you should endeavor to
   a.   reduce "D" Time activities.
   b.   increase "A" Time activities.
   c.   place more emphasis on probabilities than on possibilities.
   d.   accomplish all of these.

UNIT TWO

ETHICS, FAIR HOUSING, TRUST FUNDS, AND OTHER LEGAL ISSUES

LEARNING OBJECTIVES

When you have completed this unit, you will be able to

- define ethics and explain how to evaluate an act as ethical or unethical,

- understand federal and state fair housing laws and regulations and how they relate to real estate practice,

- explain the antitrust provision of the Sherman Antitrust Act and the applicability of the act to real estate practice, and

- understand real estate professionals' responsibility regarding sexual harassment and the handling of trust funds.

KEY TERMS

Americans with Disabilities Act	diversity training	REALTORS® Code of Ethics
blockbusting	*Dred Scott* decision	redlining
Civil Rights Act of 1866	ethics	Rumford Act
Civil Rights Act of 1870	Fair Employment and Housing Act	sexual harassment
Civil Rights Act of 1964	familial status	Sherman Antitrust Act
Civil Rights Act of 1968	Golden Rule	steering
commingling	group boycotting laws	tie-in agreements
conversion	market allocation	trust funds
	place of public accommodation	Unruh Act
	price-fixing	
	readily achievable	

WHAT IS ETHICS?

The word **ethics** comes from the Greek *ethikos*, meaning *moral*, and *ethos*, meaning *character*. Ethics is a moral standard for life, and the test for that standard is quite simple. It is the **Golden Rule**: "Do unto others as you would have them do unto you." To evaluate conduct to determine whether it is ethical, simply ask yourself, "If the roles were reversed, would I consider the conduct I am contemplating to be proper?"

While no person is perfect, real estate professionals should strive for fair and honest dealings with all parties. If they do so, they will be acting in an ethical manner.

Ethics and the Law

The best test of ethics is the Golden Rule.

You should do right not because of a fear of punishment or exposure but because the reward is the conduct itself. George Bernard Shaw stated, "You cannot believe in honor until you have achieved it." Similarly, you cannot truly understand why you should be a moral person until you become such a person.

The fact that everyone is doing an unethical act does not make it right. Nor does the fact that if you didn't do it someone else would.

Ethics has nothing to do with legality or illegality. **Laws** set minimum standards for what a society regards as acceptable behavior. Violation of the law is an illegal act for which the state has set penalties. Laws can change: what is illegal today could be legal tomorrow, and what is legal today could be illegal tomorrow. Similarly, a legal act could be unethical, and an illegal act could be ethical. As an example, adultery may be legal because it may not violate the law, but being unfaithful to a spouse would be considered unethical behavior because it does not pass the test of the Golden Rule. Similarly, failing to have a current dog license would violate the law, but it would not be unethical behavior based on the Golden Rule.

Ethics deals in what is right, not in minimum standards. While laws change to accommodate current attitudes, ethics remains constant. If conduct is wrong, based on the application of the Golden Rule, it remains wrong, even though others may engage in such conduct.

Ethics goes beyond the law.

Ethics tends to precede the law. For instance, in the early 1980s, there was a rash of home purchases with loans being assumed and sellers carrying the balance of the purchase price using a second trust deed. These no-down-payment purchasers would rent the homes, pocket the rent receipts, and then not make payments on either the first or second trust deed, a practice called *rent skimming*. Some purchasers were able to delay foreclosure for more than a year.

Though this practice was not at the time a violation of the law, if you apply the Golden Rule to this conduct, it is reprehensible and, of course, unethical. Statutes were later enacted that made rent skimming illegal.

Gray Ethical Areas

Ethics is not an exact science. What is ethical or unethical is not always clear. Our sense of right and wrong is based on our experiences. If in your heart you believe an action is proper, then it is ethical to you. However, if you have to ask someone if an action is legal, then you clearly feel there is something questionable in the action.

If you would not want others to know what you have done, then it is also clear that you feel the action is tainted. Or if you feel you have to justify an action with a defense such as "If I didn't do it, someone else would," it is clear that you know the action is wrong. Shakespeare said it best over 400 years ago: "To thine own self be true, and it must follow, as the night the day, thou canst not then be false to any man."

Ethics and Motive

Your motive for an action could determine whether the action is ethical or unethical. For example, while on a caravan visiting new listings, you notice several building code violations in one of the properties and you notify the county authorities of the violations. If you did so because you felt the violations presented a real danger to present occupants and any future buyers, then your action would have to be viewed as ethical. But if safety was not a concern, and you reported the violations solely because of animosity toward the listing agent, then your action would clearly be viewed as unethical because you were intentionally trying to hurt another without any redeeming reason.

Ethics and Your Career

Ethics is not incompatible with good business practices. Successfully meeting the needs of buyers and sellers will reinforce your self-esteem and serve as a motivator for further success. Over the long haul, an ethical professional will be rewarded with a loyal clientele and a steady stream of referrals. Most successful real estate salespeople obtain the greater portion of their business from referrals from people with whom they have worked in the past. If you want long-term success, you must earn the trust of others. From a pragmatic viewpoint, good ethics is good business.

Do not fall into the trap of measuring your success by dollars earned rather than by how you have successfully helped others. If you measure success solely in dollars, it becomes easy to take a pragmatic approach to real estate. You can lead yourself to believe that because the end—dollars—is important, the means to reach it are of less importance. You could find yourself acting in a self-serving manner, placing your own interests above the best interests of those you are serving. In short, it can be easy to become an unethical real estate salesperson or broker. Unfortunately, some real estate agents take a pragmatic approach based on "What will it do for me *now?*" A great many real estate license revocations have been the result of this "me" attitude.

CODES OF ETHICS

REALTORS®

A number of professional organizations have codes of ethics. The **REALTORS® Code of Ethics** is based on the Golden Rule and is an excellent guide to ethical behavior. The word *REALTOR®* denotes a member of the National Association of REALTORS® (NAR). But even if you are not a member of the NAR, you should read this code and use it as a guide in your relations with others.

Realtists

At one time, African Americans were excluded from just about every professional business group. In 1947, a group of African American brokers founded the National Association of Real Estate Brokers (NAREB) and adopted the word *Realtist* to designate their members. The NAREB, like the NAR, is constantly striving to increase the professionalism of the real estate industry.

California Code of Ethics

In 1979, former Real Estate Commissioner David Fox expressed a need for a California Code of Ethics. This code was known as the *Commissioner's Code of Ethics*. Because it was a repetition of conduct made illegal by other sections of the law, it was repealed in 1996. While illegal conduct is generally unethical, this code failed to carry ethics beyond the law. Legality or illegality of an act does not make it ethical or unethical. The real estate commissioner has, however, adopted the National Association of REALTORS® Code of Ethics.

The real estate commissioner has issued suggestions for professional conduct in sale, lease, and exchange transactions and suggestions for professional conduct when negotiating or arranging loans secured by real property or the sale of a promissory note secured by real property. These comprise Figure 2.1.

FAIR HOUSING AND ANTIDISCRIMINATION LEGISLATION

Fair housing legislation and practices involve almost every activity in real estate. The federal and state governments have passed legislation in the areas of fair housing and antidiscriminatory practices. Material regarding housing discrimination also appears in the real estate commissioner's Rules and Regulations and in the Business and Professions Code.

Federal Laws

Real estate brokers and salespeople should heed these laws in every stage of the real estate process. An understanding of the history of antidiscrimination laws will help you understand the need for this legislation.

FIGURE 2.1:   Suggestions for Professional Conduct

The Real Estate Commissioner has issued "Suggestions for Professional Conduct in Sale, Lease, and Exchange Transactions" and "Suggestions for Professional Conduct When Negotiating or Arranging Loans Secured by Real Property or Sale of a Promissory Note Secured by Real Property."

The purpose of the Suggestions is to encourage real estate licensees to maintain a high level of ethics and professionalism in their business practices when performing acts for which a real estate license is required.

The Suggestions are not intended as statements of duties imposed by law nor as grounds for disciplinary action by the Bureau of Real Estate but as suggestions for elevating the professionalism of real estate licensees.

As part of the effort to promote ethical business practices of real estate licensees, the real estate commissioner has issued the following Suggestions for Professional Conduct:

(a) Suggestions for Professional Conduct in Sale, Lease, and Exchange Transactions. In order to maintain a high level of ethics and professionalism in their business practices, real estate licensees are encouraged to adhere to the following suggestions in conducting their business activities:

(1) Aspire to give a high level of competent, ethical, and quality service to buyers and sellers in real estate transactions.

(2) Stay in close communication with clients or customers to ensure that questions are promptly answered and all significant events or problems in a transaction are conveyed in a timely manner.

(3) Cooperate with the California Bureau of Real Estate's enforcement of, and report to that Bureau evident violations of, the Real Estate Law.

(4) Use care in the preparation of any advertisement to present an accurate picture or message to the reader, viewer, or listener.

(5) Submit all written offers in a prompt and timely manner.

(6) Keep oneself informed and current on factors affecting the real estate market in which the licensee operates as an agent.

(7) Make a full, open, and sincere effort to cooperate with other licensees, unless the principal has instructed the licensee to the contrary.

(8) Attempt to settle disputes with other licensees through mediation or arbitration.

(9) Advertise or claim to be an expert in an area of specialization in real estate brokerage activity (e.g., appraisal, property management, industrial siting, mortgage loan, etc.), only if the licensee has had special training, preparation, or experience in such areas.

(10) Strive to provide equal opportunity for quality housing and a high level of service to all persons regardless of race, color, sex, religion, ancestry, physical handicap, marital status, or national origin.

(11) Base opinions of value, whether for the purpose of advertising or promoting real estate brokerage business, upon documented objective data.

(12) Make every attempt to comply with these Suggestions for Professional Conduct and the Code of Ethics of any organized real estate industry group of which the licensee is a member.

FIGURE 2.1 (continued):   Suggestions for Professional Conduct

(b) Suggestions for Professional Conduct When Negotiating or Arranging Loans Secured by Real Property or Sale of a Promissory Note Secured by Real Property. In order to maintain a high level of ethics and professionalism in their business practices when performing acts within the meaning of subdivision (d) and (e) of Section 10131 and Sections 10131.1 and 10131.2 of the Business and Professions Code, real estate licensees are encouraged to adhere to the following suggestions, in addition to any applicable provisions of subdivision (a), in conducting their business activities:

   (1)   Aspire to give a high level of competent, ethical, and quality service to borrowers and lenders in loan transactions secured by real estate.

   (2)   Stay in close communication with borrowers and lenders to ensure that reasonable questions are promptly answered and all significant events or problems in a loan transaction are conveyed in a timely manner.

   (3)   Keep oneself informed and current on factors affecting the real estate loan market in which the licensee acts as an agent.

   (4)   Advertise or claim to be an expert in an area of specialization in real estate mortgage loan transactions only if the licensee has had special training, preparation, or experience in such area.

Suggestions for Professional Conduct

   (5)   Strive to provide equal opportunity for quality mortgage loan services and a high level of service to all borrowers or lenders regardless of race, color, sex, religion, ancestry, physical handicap, marital status, or national origin.

   (6)   Base opinions of value in a loan transaction, whether for the purpose of advertising or promoting real estate mortgage loan brokerage business, on documented objective data.

   (7)   Respond to reasonable inquiries of a principal as to the status or extent of efforts to negotiate the sale of an existing loan.

   (8)   Respond to reasonable inquiries of a borrower regarding the net proceeds available from a loan arranged by the licensee.

   (9)   Make every attempt to comply with the standards of professional conduct and the code of ethics of any organized mortgage loan industry group of which the licensee is a member.

The conduct suggestions set forth in subsections (a) and (b) are not intended as statements of duties imposed by law nor as grounds for disciplinary action by the Bureau of Real Estate, but as guidelines for elevating the professionalism of real estate licensees.

Although the Declaration of Independence originally contained language condemning slavery, that language was removed shortly before the document was signed to ensure the consensus of all the states. However, the Declaration of Independence did retain the following statement: "We hold these truths to be self-evident, that all men are created equal, that they are endowed by their Creator with certain Inalienable Rights, that among these are Life, Liberty, and the pursuit of Happiness." There was also an attempt to outlaw slavery when the U.S. Constitution was written. Because of strong opposition, wording that would outlaw slavery was not included based on "practical" considerations.

While there was strong antislavery sentiment in the northern states, by the mid-1800s, the South's economy had become dependent on slave labor. The invention of the cotton gin and the Industrial Revolution had made cotton growing very lucrative. In 1820, the Missouri Compromise allowed Missouri to enter the Union without restrictions as to slavery, while Maine would enter as a free state. The western territories were to be free.

In 1857, the U.S. Supreme Court issued the **Dred Scott decision** that basically ordered the federal government to keep out of the slavery issue because it was a matter for the states to decide. The court held that only a state could exclude slavery and that Congress had exceeded its authority by prohibiting slavery in the territories. The Missouri Compromise was thus held unconstitutional.

> **The Declaration of Independence Is Not Law**
>
> While inspiring, the Declaration of Independence is not law. Had it been law, there likely would not have been the necessity for most of the federal and state antidiscrimination laws. An attempt to include antislavery language in the Constitution failed. In fact, the Constitution provided that a slave should be considered as being only three-fifths of a person in determining the congressional representation of a state.

The court also made clear that "Negroes" were not entitled to rights as U.S. citizens and had "no rights which any white man was bound to respect." The court pointed out that slaves were property and that the U.S. Constitution guaranteed property rights.

The *Dred Scott* decision was received with anger in the North. It led to sectionalism that divided the nation and was a prime cause of the Civil War.

Thirteenth Amendment. The Thirteenth Amendment to the Constitution abolished slavery, but it did not specifically address the rights of former slaves.

Civil Rights Act of 1866. The **Civil Rights Act of 1866** was intended to provide equal treatment for former slaves. It states that "all citizens of the United States shall have the same rights in every state or territory as is enjoyed by white citizens thereof to inherit, purchase, lease, sell, hold, and convey real and personal property."

The Civil Rights Act of 1866 had no exceptions.

While this act was broad in its protection, it applied only to race. There were exceptions to the act, which could be enforced by any individual who was discriminated against. Remedies included injunction and compensatory and punitive damages.

Fourteenth Amendment.   The Fourteenth Amendment to the Constitution was passed after the Civil Rights Act of 1866. Supporters of the amendment pointed out that it would protect the rights granted in the 1866 act by providing protection in the U.S. Constitution. This would prevent a later Congress or court from taking away these rights.

The Fourteenth Amendment states the following:

> All persons born or naturalized in the United States, and subject to the jurisdiction thereof, are citizens of the United States and of the State wherein they reside. No State shall make or enforce any law which shall abridge the privileges or immunities of citizens of the United States; nor shall any State deprive any person of life, liberty, or property, without due process of law; nor deny any person within its jurisdiction the equal protection of the laws.

Obviously, the Fourteenth Amendment did not limit itself to race. A reasonable interpretation of the above quote would be that the Fourteenth Amendment offered comprehensive civil rights protection.

Civil Rights Act of 1870.   Some attorneys were of the opinion that because the Fourteenth Amendment was passed after the Civil Rights Act of 1866, that act had been effectively replaced and was no longer law. So to protect against later courts taking away the remedies granted by the 1866 act, the following statement was tacked onto a voting rights act in 1870 (**Civil Rights Act of 1870**):

> (A)nd be it further enacted that the act to protect all persons in the United States in their civil rights and furnish the means of their vindication, passed April nine, eighteen hundred and sixty-six, is hereby re-enacted.

Thus, the Civil Rights Act of 1866 was passed twice to make certain it would withstand possible future challenges in the courts. However, the act was effectively gutted by state court decisions and failure of the federal courts to enforce the act. The act, as well as the Fourteenth Amendment, was ineffective in providing equal rights for approximately 100 years.

Executive Order 11063.   On November 21, 1962, President John F. Kennedy issued an order that prohibited discrimination in housing wherever federal funds were involved. The order affected property sales involving FHA and VA loans, as well as other government-subsidized programs. It stated that

> the executive branch of the government, in faithfully executing the laws of the United States which authorize federal financial assistance, directly or indirectly for the provision, rehabilitation, and operation of housing and related facilities, is charged with an obligation and duty to assume that the laws are fairly administered and that benefits there under are made available to all Americans without regard to their race, color, creed, or national origin.

Civil Rights Act of 1964.   The **Civil Rights Act of 1964** made the 1962 executive order law and is considered among the first of the modern civil rights acts. While it prohibited discrimination in all federally assisted programs, prior and later acts are far more comprehensive.

Jones v. Mayer.   In the same year that the Civil Rights Act of 1968 was passed (below), the Supreme Court decided the case of *Jones v. Mayer*, which involved a seller who refused to sell a home to an African American. Both the district court and the court of appeals ruled that the Civil Rights Act of 1866 prohibited discrimination by the state but not by individuals. The Supreme Court reversed, ruling that the Civil Rights Act of 1866 applied to private property and could be enforced by the party discriminated against. The court based its decision on the 13th Amendment because the act was passed before passage of the 14th Amendment..

Jones v. Mayer upheld the Civil Rights Act of 1866.

Civil Rights Act of 1968.   The **Civil Rights Act of 1968** prohibited discrimination in housing based on national origin, race, religion, and color. (Sexual discrimination was added in 1974.) The act prohibits the following:

- Discrimination by brokers toward clients and customers

- Refusal to show, rent, or sell through the false representation that a property is not available

- Discrimination as to access to multiple listing services

- Discriminatory sales or loan terms

Steering is directing based on a group.

Blockbusting is inducing panic selling.

Redlining is refusal to loan in designated areas.

- **Steering,** the act of directing people of different races, religions, et cetera, away from or toward particular areas

- **Blockbusting,** the process of inducing panic selling by representing that prices will drop or crime will increase because of the possible entrance of minority group members to the area

- **Redlining,** the refusal to loan within an area

- Retaliatory acts against persons making fair-housing complaints and intimidation to discourage complaints

- Discriminatory advertising, which is prohibited even when related to activities exempt from the act

There has been a great deal of concern as to what advertising might be considered discriminatory. Advertising that a property is close to a particular house of worship or a place that has a racial connotation (such as "Martin Luther King Hospital") has been held to be discriminatory, as have ads that indicate a preference for a particular race or marital status or ads that indicate a member of a protected category is not welcome.

Advertising Terms Acceptable by HUD

HUD has indicated that use of the following terms and phrases are not discriminatory: master bedroom, rare find, desirable neighborhood, kosher meals available, apartment complex with chapel, Santa Claus, Easter Bunny, St. Valentine's Day, Merry Christmas, Happy Easter, mother-in-law suite, bachelor apartment, great view, fourth-floor walkup, walk-in closets, jogging trails, walk to bus stop, nonsmoking, sober, two-bedroom, family room, no bicycles allowed, and quiet streets.

There is still a great deal of confusion as to what HUD will consider discriminatory advertising. Several groups have published lists of terms that are acceptable, that are to be used with caution, or that are to be regarded as discriminatory. However, clearance through one of these lists does not mean that HUD will not regard the language as discriminatory. One problem is that words have different connotations within different groups, as well as regions in the country. HUD has indicated it will not approve any of the published lists. (See Unit 8 for more details.)

There are some exemptions to the Civil Rights Act of 1968. The following exemptions apply to the Civil Rights Act of 1968 but are not exemptions under the Civil Rights Act of 1866 or under California fair housing laws:

- Religious groups, which can discriminate in providing nonprofit housing, provided that the religion is open to all, regardless of race, sex, color, or national origin

- Private clubs, which can discriminate or give preference to members when selling or leasing housing for noncommercial purposes

- Owners of single-family homes, who can discriminate when selling or renting without an agent, provided that they do not own more than three such homes and are not in the business of renting

- Owners of one-to-four-residential-unit buildings who occupy a unit and who can discriminate if an agent is not used in renting

The 1988 Fair Housing Amendments Act extended protection in regard to familial status and the handicapped.

1988 Fair Housing Amendments Act. This important law extended federal protection against housing discrimination to include **familial status** and handicapped persons. It also strengthened the enforcement mechanisms and gave HUD greater enforcement power. Familial status protection refers to persons under age 18 living with a parent or guardian, persons in the process of obtaining legal custody, and pregnant persons.

The real estate agent should also be aware that adult-only designations are no longer possible, although there are exceptions to this rule. Operators of projects can either set up a community in which all residents must be at least age 62 or in which 80% of the units are occupied by at least one person age 55 years or older.

Even if an apartment complex has a family section, designation of an all-adult area still is prohibited. Steering prospective tenants toward a particular area in an apartment complex and away from another area also violates the act.

Apartments can have rules for children's use of facilities when there is a nondiscriminatory reason for the difference in rules. The Civil Rights Act of 1968 does not prohibit owners from setting maximum occupancy of units as long as the rule is enforced without discrimination. (It is likely that unreasonably limited occupancy rules would be unenforceable because they would discriminate against families with children.)

Discrimination against the handicapped is prohibited. The term *handicapped* refers to both mentally and physically handicapped persons. AIDS is considered a handicap under the act, so landlords and sellers cannot discriminate against a person with AIDS or HIV infection. The law specifically prohibits discrimination against guide dogs and support animals. Landlords cannot require additional security deposits because of these animals.

Property managers should be aware that the handicapped must be allowed to alter their units and common areas if such alterations are necessary for reasonable use and enjoyment of the premises. The property manager cannot increase the security deposit because of these alterations. However, the landlord *can* require that the tenant agree to put the premises back as they originally were if an able-bodied person would not wish the alterations to remain.

Brokers should prominently display the Equal Housing Opportunity poster (Figure 2.2) in all rental offices. Failure of the broker to post this poster in the place of business can shift the burden of proof to the broker to prove that an act was nondiscriminatory under federal law, should a complaint be made.

Advertising residential financing must contain an Equal Housing Opportunity logo, slogan, or statement advising the homeseeker that financing is available to all persons regardless of race, color, religion, sex, handicap, familial status, or national origin.

Americans with Disabilities Act.   The **Americans with Disabilities Act (ADA)** prohibits discrimination that would deny the equal enjoyment of goods, services, facilities, and accommodations in any existing place of public accommodation, based on an individual's physical or mental disabilities. A "**place of public accommodation**" applies to stores, offices, and other nonresidential commercial facilities open to the public.

Owners and operators of such establishments (including property management firms) must make the facilities accessible to the extent *readily achievable*. (See Figure 2.3.) "**Readily achievable**" is defined as "easily accomplished without a great deal of expense." This would be based on the cost of compliance related to property values and on the financial abilities of the person(s) involved. New construction must be readily accessible unless it is structurally impractical.

The ADA also applies to employment discrimination. Employers having 15 or more employees must alter their workplaces to provide reasonable accommodations for handicapped employees unless it creates an undue hardship on the business. Compliance for a real estate office might consist of designating parking spaces for the handicapped, ramping curbs, adding railings on steps, lowering counters, creating wider aisles between desks, et cetera.

The act provides for civil penalties of $75,000 for the first discriminatory act and $150,000 for each subsequent violation, including compensatory damages and attorneys' fees. Because of the substantial penalties, owners and property managers should be aware that a cottage industry has evolved of handicapped persons and attorneys who seek out properties with handicapped-access deficiencies to sue for damages. Several handicapped individuals have brought legal action against more than 100 businesses. Businesses usually agree to a settlement rather than a costly trial and possible penalties.

Equal Credit Opportunity Act. This federal act prohibits credit discrimination because of sex, marital status, age, race, religion, national origin, or because the income of a credit applicant is from public assistance.

FIGURE 2.2:   **Equal Housing Opportunity Poster**

U. S. Department of Housing and Urban Development

**EQUAL HOUSING
OPPORTUNITY**

We Do Business in Accordance With the Federal Fair Housing Law

(The Fair Housing Amendments Act of 1988)

It is illegal to Discriminate Against Any Person Because of Race, Color, Religion, Sex, Handicap, Familial Status, or National Origin

---

■ In the sale or rental of housing or residential lots

■ In advertising the sale or rental of housing

■ In the financing of housing

■ In the provision of real estate brokerage services

■ In the appraisal of housing

■ Blockbusting is also illegal

Anyone who feels he or she has been discriminated against may file a complaint of housing discrimination:
     1-800-669-9777 (Toll Free)
     1-800-927-9275 (TTY)
     www.hud.gov/fairhousing

U.S. Department of Housing and
Urban Development
Assistant Secretary for Fair Housing and
Equal Opportunity
Washington, D.C. 20410

Previous editions are obsolete   form HUD-928.1 (6/2011)

California fair housing laws. California has several fair housing laws, as well as administrative regulations dealing with discrimination. A single act could be a violation of more than one state or federal law or regulation, or both.

Unruh Act. The **Unruh Act** prohibits discrimination in all business establishments. The Unruh Act applies to real estate brokers, salespeople, and anyone managing an apartment building or other business establishment. Business discrimination includes housing discrimination based on sex, race, color, religion, ancestry, national origin, disability, medical condition, marital status, familial status, and sexual orientation. ADA provisions have been incorporated into the act.

FIGURE 2.3: Reasonable Modifications to Public Facilities or Services

Provide doors with automatic opening mechanisms

Provide menus (and real estate listings) in a large-print or braille format

Install an intercom so customers can contact a second-floor business in a building without an elevator

Lower public telephones

Add grab bars to public restroom stalls

Permit guide dogs to accompany customers

Provide a shopper's assistant to help disabled customers

Provide ramps in addition to entry stairs

A violation of the Unruh Act, can result in a court award of a maximum of three times actual damages but not less than $4,000. In addition, the violation could result in a civil penalty up to $25,000.

The Unruh Act applies to business discrimination.

The act has been expanded to apply to age discrimination in rental apartments and condominium properties. Housing developed and designed for the special needs of senior citizens is exempt from this act.

Rumford Fair Housing Act.   The **Fair Employment and Housing Act**, also known as the **Rumford Act** (Government Code Sections 12900 et seq.), prohibits discrimination in supplying housing accommodations on the basis of sex, color, race, religion, marital status, family status, sexual orientation, disability, source of income, ancestry, or national origin. Anyone selling, renting, leasing, or financing housing must comply with the Rumford Act.

While the Unruh Act applies to discrimination by businesses, the Rumford Act applies to all housing discrimination by individuals and businesses. Unlike the Unruh Act, it applies only to housing.

At Home With Diversity

In today's market, the average real estate agent no longer reflects the typical buyer. In recognition of our rapidly changing national demographics, the National Association of REALTORS® and the U.S. Department of Housing and Urban Development created the At Home with Diversity program to expand home ownership opportunities for more Americans by training real estate professionals to actively and aggressively seek out potential homebuyers from all racial and cultural backgrounds. Licensees who take this **diversity training** program, sponsored by the NAR, will learn how attending diverse cultural and community events can expand their client base, find out how simple multicultural etiquette can lead to success with new clients and customers, and develop sound diversity strategies to incorporate into their overall business plan.

An individual violating any part of this act may be reported to the Department of Fair Employment and Housing within one year of the occurrence. The Rumford Act predated the Civil Rights Act of 1968. Rumford Act violations are also violations of the federal act.

Business and Professions Code

The California Business and Professions Code governs real estate licensees' behavior, in addition to federal and state fair housing laws. The code provides detailed antidiscrimination material, including a definition of the term *discrimination* as used in the code, and sections detailing behavioral guidelines for licensees and grounds for disciplinary action in cases of noncompliance.

Section 125.6: Disciplinary Provisions for Discriminatory Acts

Under Section 125.6, persons who hold a license under the provisions of the code are subject to disciplinary action if they refuse to perform a licensed activity or make any discrimination or restriction in the performance of the licensed activity because of an applicant's race, color, sex, religion, ancestry, physical handicap, or national origin.

Section 10177(l): Further Grounds for Disciplinary Action

Discrimination occurs

> if a licensee solicited or induced the sale, lease, or listing for sale or lease, of residential property on the ground, wholly or in part, of loss of value, increase in crime, or decline of the quality of the schools, due to the presence or prospective entry into the neighborhood of a person or persons of another race, color, religion, ancestry, or national origin.

Regulations of the Real Estate Commissioner
Section 2780: Discriminatory Conduct as the Basis for Disciplinary Action

Prohibited discriminatory conduct by real estate licensees based on race, color, sex, religion, physical handicap, or national origin includes:

a. refusing to negotiate for the sale, rental, or financing;

b. refusing or failing to show, rent, sell, or finance;

c. discriminating against any person in the sale or purchase, collection of payments, or performance of services;

d. discriminating in the conditions or privileges of sale rental or financing;

e. discriminating in processing applications, referrals, or assigning licenses;

f. representing real property as not available for inspection;

g. processing an application more slowly;

h. making any effort to encourage discrimination;

i. refusing to assist another licensee;

j. making an effort to obstruct, retard, or discourage a purchase;

k. expressing or implying a limitation, preference, or discrimination;

l. coercing, intimidating, threatening, or interfering;

m. soliciting restrictively;

n. maintaining restrictive waiting lists;

o. seeking to discourage or prevent transactions;

p. representing alleged community opposition;

q. representing desirability of particular properties;

r. refusing to accept listings;

s. agreeing not to show property;

t. advertising in a manner that indicates discrimination;

u. using wording that indicates preferential treatment;

v. advertising selectively;

w. maintaining selective pricing, rent, cleaning, or security deposits;

x. financing in a discriminatory manner;

y. discriminating in pricing;

z. discriminating in services;

aa. discriminating against owners, occupants, or guests;

ab. bb. making an effort to encourage discrimination;

cc. implementing discriminatory rule in multiple listings and other services; and

dd. assisting one who intends to discriminate.

Section 2781: Panic Selling

Section 2781 prohibits discriminatory conduct that creates fear or alarm to induce sale or lease because of the entry into an area of people of another race, color, sex, religion, ancestry, or national origin.

Section 2782: Duty to Supervise

Brokers must take reasonable steps to be familiar with, and to familiarize their salespeople with, the federal and state laws pertaining to prohibition of discriminatory process.

Holden Act (Housing Financial Discrimination Act of 1977). The Holden Act prohibits financial institutions from engaging in discriminatory loan activities or practices. Activities covered under this act include awarding building, improvement, purchase, or refinancing loans using the criteria of race, color, national origin, ancestry, sex, religion, or marital status. Discrimination based on the ethnic composition of the area surrounding a property (redlining) is also illegal.

California Omnibus Housing Nondiscrimination Act. This act makes all California's nondiscrimination acts consistent with the California Fair Employment and Housing Act as to coverage. All the acts apply to discrimination on the basis of national origin, ancestry, race, color, gender, religion, marital status, familial status, disability, source of income, and sexual orientation.

COMMISSIONER'S RULES AND REGULATIONS

Article 10 of the Real Estate Commissioner's Rules and Regulations concerns the discriminatory activities of real estate licensees. Regulations 2780, 2781, and 2782, contained within Article 10 (summarized above), list unacceptable discriminatory practices by licensees. Regulation 2780 indicates that discriminatory conduct by real estate licensees is a basis for disciplinary action by the Commissioner.

Licensees must be color-blind in their relations with owners and prospective buyers and tenants. Anything less is a violation of the law, as well as just "bad business."

SEXUAL HARASSMENT

In today's workplace, you must be cognizant of what could be regarded by others as **sexual harassment**. Charges of sexual harassment could result in legal expenses and significant damage awards or settlement costs, as well as being time consuming to resolve. Sexual harassment can be defined by how your actions are viewed by others, not necessarily by your intent.

Besides the costs involved, a claim of sexual harassment can adversely affect your working relationship with others. This would include co-workers, agents in other offices, and buyers and sellers.

Always conduct yourself in a businesslike manner. The only needs of others that you try to fulfill must be those relating to real estate.

> Jokes, remarks, and touching might be regarded by others as sexual harassment.

In general, observe the following:

- Avoid sexually oriented jokes and anecdotes. Don't use "cute," double-meaning terms. Never discuss your love life or that of others in the workplace.

- Avoid patting, hugging, and touching others. What you might regard as a sign of "friendship" might be regarded differently by others.

- Allow others space. While in some cultures it is acceptable to talk to others with your face just inches from the other person, many people regard this closeness as intimidating and/or sexual harassment.

- Avoid romantic overtures or entanglements in the workplace.

- Avoid asking a co-worker for a date. If repeated on numerous occasions, it could be regarded as harassment. If a romantic relationship gets started in the workplace, a difficult working relationship will normally be the result should the romantic relationship end.

- Whenever possible, avoid one-on-one encounters in other than an open area. Some problem tenants have made multiple claims of sexual harassment by owners and property managers.

If a buyer or a seller seems to be inviting sexual advances, ignore the signals. You could be wrong, and if you are, you could find yourself facing a charge of sexual harassment.

SHERMAN ANTITRUST ACT

The **Sherman Antitrust Act** is a federal act to protect consumers from businesses that conspired to control prices and/or competition. Penalties for violation can include imprisonment. The act prohibits the following:

- **Price-fixing** (brokers cannot agree on minimum fees to be charged) Prudent brokers will add a statement in bold to the listing advising the seller of the negotiability of real estate commissions. This is an important aspect of strengthening the industry's compliance with this rule.

- **Market allocation** (it's illegal to divide a marketplace geographically or by type of service because it reduces competition)

- **Group boycotting** (firms may not agree to refuse to do business with a firm or individual)

- **Tie-in agreements** (agreements that require a client to buy additional goods or services as a condition of doing business or cooperating)

In September 2005, the Department of Justice filed a lawsuit alleging that a REALTOR® policy allowing brokers to block their listings from being displayed on other broker websites is a restraint on competition. An antitrust settlement between the National Association of REALTORS® and the

Justice Department in May 2008 prohibits REALTOR® rules that block listings of homes from being displayed on other brokers' websites.

A violation of the Sherman Act is likely to also violate California antitrust laws allowing for damages for injuries suffered.

OTHER LAWS AND REGULATIONS

Besides civil rights and antitrust legislation, there are numerous other federal and state statutes that apply to real estate transactions.

The Real Estate Settlement Procedures Act (RESPA) prohibits kickbacks from service providers to brokers. It makes illegal what was a common but unethical practice of "taking care" of agents who steered business to service providers. By accepting kickbacks of any sort, the agent feels an obligation to the service provider to steer business to that service provider when the agent's obligations should be to best serve the interests of the principal. Kickbacks prohibited by RESPA include cash, free business equipment, nonbusiness meals, tickets to events, and recreation fees.

California regulations include Sections 1000 through 10581 of the Business and Professions Code, which regulates real estate licensing, and Sections 11000 through 11030 of the Code, which regulates real estate licensees.

TRUST FUNDS

Trust funds refer to money or anything of value received by an agent, but not belonging to the agent, and held for the benefit of another. When a broker receives funds for a transaction, the broker must, within three days of receipt of the funds, do one of the following:

- Give the funds to the principal.

- Deposit the funds directly into escrow.

- Place the funds in the broker's trust account. (A broker who does not receive funds in trust does not need to have a trust account.)

Commingling is the mixing of property of another (trust funds) with property of the broker. Commingling is a violation of the Commissioner's Regulations and subject a broker to severe disciplinary action. Holding the funds without authorization is **commingling**. (The broker can hold a check uncashed at the direction of the buyer before acceptance of an offer and at the direction of the seller after acceptance.)

Should a broker misappropriate trust funds for personal or any other use than what was designated, the act would be considered **conversion**, which is a criminal offense.

It is important that **trust funds** be handled properly. Improprieties regarding trust funds are the number one reason for disciplinary action against real estate licensees. Some general rules for trust funds include the following:

- Trust accounts must be in the name of the broker as trustee.

- Unless otherwise agreed, in cooperative sales, listing brokers deposit the funds in their trust account.

- In the absence of written permission from the client, a broker may not receive a commission or consideration of any kind for placement of the trust monies.

- A separate record must be kept of all trust funds received that are not deposited in a trust account (example: checks returned to offeror when offer is rejected). Accounts must be balanced daily and reconciled with bank records monthly.

- Accounts must be demand deposits (non-interest-bearing that can be withdrawn without notice) with the exception that accounts may be kept in a separate interest-bearing account with a federally insured lender at the direction of the owner of the funds. The broker may not benefit from any interest earned. Drawing interest on trust funds for the benefit of the principal can cause an accounting challenge. Interest earned must be prorated if one trust account contains funds for multiple beneficiaries.

- A broker may keep no more than $200 of broker funds in the trust account. This is to cover bank charges. Any greater amount of non-trust money in the account would subject the broker to disciplinary action.

- Earned commissions must be withdrawn from the account within 30 days.

- Columnar records must be kept (double entry) with separate records for each beneficiary and transaction.

- The account must be open for inspection by the Bureau of Real Estate.

- Should a BRE audit reveal a violation of the law, the broker will be assessed the cost of the audit, as well as be subject to disciplinary action, which could result in revocation of the broker's license.

- The broker can designate another person to withdraw trust funds from the trust account, but if that person is not licensed, a bond is required. However, the broker bears liability for any improper action.

- Records must be kept for three years.

- Computer programs are available for trust fund accounting. See Figure 2.4 for a sample Trust Bank Account Record for Trust Funds Deposited and Withdrawn.

There are additional regulations and reporting requirements for trust monies received by mortgage loan brokers.

Penalties for trust fund violations include the following:

- A financial penalty

- Suspension or revocation of license

- Imprisonment

FIGURE 2.4: Trust Bank Account Record for All Trust Funds Deposited and Withdrawn

Reprinted with permission, California Association of REALTORS®. Endorsement not implied.

CASE EXAMPLES

The following case examples are included to help you understand how ethics applies to you and to help you recognize your responsibilities regarding fair housing.

Case Example 1

Broker McIntosh realized that Henry Higgins was extremely naive about financial matters. While McIntosh usually charged a 6% commission for similar residential properties, when she filled out the listing for Higgins's home, she wrote "11%" in the commission block. She did, however, explain to Higgins that her fee was 11% and provided Higgins an estimate of what he would receive based on a sale at the list price, which was realistically set. Analyze McIntosh's actions from an ethical perspective.

Analysis 1

Legally, McIntosh did nothing wrong. Commissions are negotiable, and she simply negotiated to her advantage. Ethically, there are some problems. McIntosh charged almost twice her customary fee for the service, not because of problems the property presented but because she thought she could. This action certainly would not pass the test of the Golden Rule. How do you suppose McIntosh would feel if she found that a mechanic charged her an exorbitant fee for a simple adjustment to her vehicle because she was naive about mechanical matters?

A more interesting ethical question arises regarding other owners who have listed similar properties with McIntosh for a 6% commission. McIntosh is likely to give priority to selling the 11% listing over other listings, which would work to the detriment of other owners who expected the best efforts from McIntosh. Similarly, if McIntosh customarily split commissions with selling agents, other agents would likely give similar preferences. Therefore, applying the Golden Rule from the perspective of other owners also indicates that the 11% commission is unethical.

There could be circumstances, however, in which a higher-than-normal commission is justified. These could include property that requires greater sales effort or situations in which a quick sale is essential to protect the owner's interests (for example, a pending foreclosure).

Case Example 2

Tom Huang wanted to buy a lot in Sunrise Estates. While there were several dozen vacant lots in the subdivision, none currently had For Sale signs. Huang contacted Omni Realty and met with salesperson Upton. Upton told Huang that if a lot could be purchased in Sunrise Estates, she would find it.

Using tax records, Upton contacted owners of the vacant lots and asked them if they wanted to sell their lots. Owner Pike was receptive to the idea of a sale and indicated he would sell if he could net $100,000. Upton knew the lots were worth between $150,000 and $175,000, so she purchased it for $100,000. She then contacted Huang and told him about the lot and that she was now the owner. Huang was delighted and agreed to buy the lot for $160,000. Upton never revealed the transaction to her broker. What ethical problems are raised by this case?

Analysis 2

Tom Huang could reasonably assume that Upton was working on his behalf when she agreed to locate a lot for him. Instead, Upton acted on her own behalf and purchased a lot for herself, which she offered to Huang at a higher price as a principal.

While Huang may have been comfortable with Upton's purchase and may not have objected to the price, what started as a clear buyer's agency relationship was unilaterally changed by Upton to her own benefit. Huang paid more for the lot than he should have, had Upton been properly serving him. Upton had no duty to disclose to Pike that she felt the price was too low or that she had a buyer whom she believed would pay more money. Upton was not Pike's agent.

Although Huang had contacted Upton through Omni Realty, Upton turned what was originally contemplated as a brokerage situation into her own purchase and sale for profit. She in fact deprived her broker of a commission by her self-serving actions. Application of the Golden Rule would indicate unethical conduct on the part of Upton.

Case Example 3

Broker Zwerik was a member of a listing service. While Zwerik usually submitted his listings to the service, whenever he took a high-value listing that was also highly salable, he would recommend to the owner that for the owner's protection it would be best that Zwerik Realty be the only firm allowed to show the property. He would then cross out the listing authorization to cooperate with other agents and to give the listing to a listing service. He had the owner initial these modifications.

When other agents called Zwerik about his signs or ads on the property, Zwerik told them that the owner had specified in writing that only his firm would be allowed to show the property and that the listing information should not be given to any other agent. Was Zwerik's conduct proper?

Analysis 3

Broker Zwerik wants to be able to sell other office listings and wants other offices to help in the sale of most of his listings. But when he takes a listing that offers a substantial commission and is exceptionally desirable, the spirit of cooperation ends. The reason he persuades owners that he alone be allowed to show the property is based solely on the value and salability of the listing, not on the owner's best interests. Apply the Golden Rule: Would Zwerik want other brokers to withhold their better listings from him and give him only properties less likely to be sold? The answer is obvious. Broker Zwerik is guilty of unethical conduct.

In addition, keeping a listing off a listing service reduces the likelihood of a sale. Even for a highly salable listing, it is unethical because it is not in the best interest of Zwerik's client. Zwerik clearly misrepresented the reason to exclude other agents. The owner could have a cause of action against Zwerik.

Case Example 4

Mr. and Mrs. Jones and their two small children call your office inquiring about a three-bedroom condominium that you have advertised for sale. The unit is in a six-unit complex and is four years old. While you had intended to show the prospective buyers other units as well, it's love at first sight and they want to buy the unit advertised. You know that Tom Sinn lives in the unit next to the unit that is for sale. Sinn's well-publicized child molestation conviction was recently set aside by a higher court that ruled the photos taken from Sinn's home were illegally obtained and should not have been allowed admissible as evidence. What should you do?

Analysis 4

Because the conviction was set aside, Sinn is not a convicted sex offender, so even if the buyers checked the Megan's Law website, they would not learn of the allegations made against Sinn.

You have a duty to disclose any detrimental information you know of concerning a property. There is no question that a buyer who has small children would consider this information detrimental.

To fail to inform Mr. and Mrs. Jones about their next-door neighbor could subject their children to danger. Application of the Golden Rule would require disclosure, even though disclosure may not be required by law. Even if the prospective buyers had no children, it's possible that visitors might.

There is another problem as to the agent's duty to the owners. The owners must be told if you will be disclosing information as to the neighbor and why. Because disclosure might materially affect the chances of a sale or the sales price, you should consider offering the owners the opportunity to cancel the listing.

Case Example 5

Salesperson Garcia was contacted by a representative of an organization for the developmentally disabled. The representative was looking for a group home with at least five bedrooms on a large lot. Checking the multiple listings, Garcia discovered that three homes were available that met the location, price, and size criteria of the organization. One of these homes was on the same block as the home of Garcia's broker, Douglas LaRue. Garcia contacted LaRue, who told her to show the other two homes to her prospect but not the home on his block because he thought he had a buyer for it. What ethical issues are raised by this case?

Analysis 5

Garcia should have treated the prospective buyer as any other buyer. By contacting her broker before she showed the properties, Garcia was, in effect, saying, "What do I do if they want to live near you?" She was assuming that these citizens should be treated differently from other buyers, for example, a large family looking for a large house. Garcia's conduct does not pass the test of the Golden Rule.

If broker LaRue did not want the house shown because he felt that it could take away a sale he was going to make, then LaRue is not treating Garcia fairly. The Golden Rule would seem to dictate that until sold, everyone should have an equal opportunity to sell it. There is also an ethical problem as to the owner in that LaRue is withholding a potential buyer from the property. It is in the owner's best interests that the property be available to all prospective buyers.

If Broker LaRue directed that the home on his block not be shown because he believed that the presence of developmentally disabled citizens would be a detriment to the neighborhood, it would clearly be unethical because he is willing to locate them close to someone else and to profit on the sale. This certainly would not pass the test of the Golden Rule.

LaRue and Garcia were likely in violation of the 1988 Amendment to the Civil Rights Act of 1968 in discriminating against the disabled by refusing to tell the organization about an available home they knew could meet the buyer's needs. This action also would be considered steering.

Case Example 6

Henrietta Jackson, a single African American woman, inquired about an apartment with a For Rent sign. The manager showed her a vacant three-bedroom, two-and-a-half-bath unit. The manager told her the rent was $1,850 per month. She was told to think it over, and if she decided that she wanted the apartment, she should contact the manager, who would give her a rental application.

Gomer Clyde, a single white male, inquired about apartments one hour after Henrietta Jackson left. He was shown the three-bedroom apartment, which he was told was the only current vacancy. He was informed that in four days a studio apartment would be available at $700 per month and a one-bedroom apartment would be available in about 40 days for $1,100 per month. The manager took Clyde back to her office, where she showed him diagrams of the floor plans of the two additional apartments.

She asked Clyde which of the three apartments best met his needs. When Clyde indicated that he liked the studio apartment best, the manager handed him an application and said, "Fill out this application now and give me a deposit check for $100. I will call you tomorrow to let you know if your application has been approved." Is there a problem with the actions of the manager?

Analysis 6

It appears that the apartment manager violated the Unruh Act (discrimination by a business), the Rumford Act, probably the Civil Rights Act of 1866, certainly the Civil Rights Act of 1968, and the Commissioner's Regulations.

The two prospective renters were treated differently. Whether the discrimination was because she was a single woman or because she was African American, Jackson was discriminated against. It was illegal as well as unethical. While Jackson was not denied a rental, she was also not told about upcoming vacancies that would better meet her needs. This information was volunteered to Clyde, a single white male.

Jackson was told to think about the unit and contact the manager about a rental application if she was interested. The manager not only did not try to sell her on the units, but the manager's conduct was likely to discourage a rental application. On the other hand, the manager used good sales techniques to get Clyde to submit an application and pay his deposit on the first visit.

The discrimination in this case is certainly subtler than that encountered by African Americans and single women in the past, disparate treatment is still discrimination.

Case Example 7

A country home had been the scene of horrible crimes that had drawn national attention. The home had been boarded up for a number of years, but the present owner had just finished decorating the home and had placed it on the market through your firm. Your broker tells all the agents, "The law does not require disclosure of a death from any cause after three years," implying that the crime need not be mentioned to prospective buyers.

You show the house to a family that is moving to the area due to a job transfer. They have three small children, and they love the huge yard and bright and cheery rooms. Because of the very reasonable list price, they want to put in an offer right away. What do you do?

Analysis 7

This is an example of "when in doubt—disclose." While California law does not mandate a disclosure after three years, place yourself in the shoes of the buyers. Consider how it would affect your peace of mind as well as that of your children (if any) when you learned the history of the house. The application of the Golden Rule clearly indicates that while nondisclosure is legal, in this case it may be unethical.

If you were acting as a buyer's agent or dual agent, you would likely have a duty to disclose what would be regarded by most buyers as material information. This breach of fiduciary duty could result in agent liability for damages.

The owner should have been informed at the time of listing that your office would disclose the crime to any prospective buyers before an offer was taken. The broker's action seemed to encourage nondisclosure by relying on the letter of the law. In this case, such action appears unethical.

Case Example 8

Henry Shibata of Shibata Realty managed a small commercial building in a stable neighborhood of middle-class homes. The building had been vacant for more than six months, and the owner was concerned about the loss of income.

Shibata received a deposit and a lease from Ms. Corcoran, who wished to lease the building for 10 years. The rent specified was higher than the rent being asked for the property. Shibata knew that Corcoran was one of the largest owner/operators of adult bookstores in the region. The lease provision regarding use read "any legal purpose." An adult bookstore was not in violation of the current zoning codes, although there were no such stores within a 3-mile radius of the property. What should Shibata do?

Analysis 8

Shibata must inform the owner about the lease and about the proposed tenant. He can point out that the presence of an adult bookstore might create a great deal of animosity toward the owner, as well as have a possible negative effect on area property values.

If Shibata believes the lease would be detrimental to the community and the owner wants to accept it, an ethical approach would be to ask to be relieved from the management contract. However, if he believes that even though the presence of the business would hurt the area, First Amendment rights of free speech should be paramount and Corcoran should not be stifled, then handling the lease would be ethical conduct.

Case Example 9

The best friend of broker Kritski was Timothy Plunk, a home inspector. Plunk was well qualified as an inspector and had an excellent reputation. Kritski customarily recommended Plunk to buyers, telling them only that he regarded Plunk as being extremely competent. Kritski's buyers were pleased with Plunk.

Every Christmas, Kritski and Plunk exchanged gifts. Plunk would give Kritski a case of his favorite single-malt Scotch whisky, and Kritski would give Plunk a tie. Is there any ethical problem with their relationship?

Analysis 9

There is nothing unethical about recommending a friend for services; however, the close personal relationship should have been revealed. A buyer might feel that the friendship could influence what the inspection disclosed.

The apparent disparity in the value of the gifts exchanged creates, at the very least, an appearance of a kickback for recommending Plunk. The broker should have realized this and either refused the gift or increased the value of his gift to negate the disparity in value. As presented, it appears to be both unethical and illegal conduct.

Case Example 10

Broker Esposito has his office in the small town where he lives. The local high school recently was destroyed by fire. Because the structure was supposed to be "fireproof," the school board had no insurance on the structure. The students are now being bused to five other community high schools. The bus rides for the students range from 40 minutes to almost two hours each way.

A special bond election is coming up for a citizens' vote to provide funds for a new high school. The additional tax burden on the largely low-income and middle-income residents will be significant. Esposito has talked to several retirees who have indicated that they will have to sell their homes and move elsewhere if the bond passes.

The local real estate association has asked for a vote to assess members a special fee to fight against the bond issue because it feels the issue will depress local property values, cause people to move to nearby lower-taxed communities, and increase residential and commercial vacancies. Esposito voted to assess members and to fight the bond issue. Were his actions ethical?

Analysis 10

This case is unusual because a vote either way could be ethical or unethical, based on the reasons for the vote. If Esposito's vote were based on the fact that a bond issue would personally hurt his business, although he believed it was necessary for the long-term growth of the community, then his vote would be ethically wrong. If he voted for the assessment because he felt that the damage to retirees and the community as a whole outweighed having a community high school and the long bus rides, then such a vote would be ethically correct.

Similarly, if Esposito had opposed the assessment, the ethics of his opposition would be based on his reasons. As an example, if Esposito believed the bond issue would be bad for the community and create hardships far beyond the benefits but favored a bond because he had nine children in school, then his decision would be self-serving, and voting against the assessment could be unethical. Esposito could also have ethically voted against an assessment or bond position based on the belief that the real estate association should not be involved in local political decisions.

Case Example 11

LaMont, a mortgage broker, has 14 licensees working at his firm. Most of the loans arranged by LaMont are with a particular institutional lender. The lender currently requires that the borrower pay one point to obtain the quoted rate. LaMont is allowed to keep any overage that he is able to obtain. LaMont splits the overage equally with his salespeople. To determine how he could maximize income, LaMont analyzed loans arranged over the past six months. He discovered that points charged for loans averaged out as follows:

- Loans over $500,000 = 1.1 points

- Loans for $250,000 to $500,000 = 1.35 points

- Loans under $250,000 = 1.64 points

He also discovered that points paid by borrowers varied by race. LaMont's results indicated the following:

- Caucasians = 1.17 points

- Mexican Americans = 1.62 points

- African Americans = 1.73 points

Do these results indicate any ethical problems?

Analysis 11

From the facts, it appears that LaMont's staff is targeting minorities and less-affluent borrowers for disparate treatment. They appear to be taking advantage of these borrowers by quoting and insisting on more points than others are paying. Apparently, LaMont's employees are taking the position that "we will get what the market will bear."

A person applying for a loan would ordinarily believe that the terms quoted are the same for everyone and are not based on race or other factors. The fact that this is not a level playing field does not pass the test of the Golden Rule. Obtaining a loan should not be like buying a used car. Buyers of used cars know that everything is negotiable. Most borrowers wrongfully believe that they are required to pay what is quoted. Borrowers could assume that the loan officer is acting for them in an agency capacity. The borrower could have a cause of action against the loan broker as to a breach of an implied agency. While the agents' intent may not have been to discriminate, that is the result.

Case Example 12

Broker Thall owns Thall Mortgage Company. About 20% of his loans failed to close because of appraisals that were significantly below the purchase prices. The broker for Big Realty Company, which gave Thall Mortgage Company about one-half of its business by referrals, told Thall that the appraiser would have to do better or he would find a more cooperative mortgage company.

Thall told his appraiser, Adam Fine, that appraisals had to more realistically reflect the marketplace. There were too many appraisals below the purchase prices. Fine told Thall that what a single buyer was willing to pay did not change the fair market value. He indicated that he had data to strongly support all of his valuations and had followed the *Uniform Standards of Professional Appraisal Practice (USPAP)*.

Thall stopped using Fine and now uses Willard Fast for the appraisals. For 132 appraisals over the past two-year period, not one came in under the contract purchase price. What, if any, are the problems in this case?

Analysis 12

The broker for Big Realty acted unethically in trying to induce Thall to act in an unethical and illegal manner. Thall and the broker for Big Realty violated Section 2785 of the Real Estate Commissioner's Regulations that prohibit a real estate licensee from improperly influencing or attempting to influence a real estate appraiser. Big Realty also disregarded the interests of its buyers. (If there were a buyer agency or dual agency, they would have breached that agency to the buyer.)

In trying to influence Fine, Thall was encouraging appraisals related to contract prices, not necessarily fair market value. This could be a fraud on both the borrower and the lender, who would be led to believe that the appraisal fairly reflected fair market value. If the lender were federally insured, it would be a federal crime. Foreclosures could result in lender losses because of inflated appraisals and loans.

Willard Fast apparently understood the game that was being played and had agreed to do what was expected of him instead of following the *USPAP*.

SUMMARY

Ethics is fair and honest dealing.

Ethics differs from the law because the law sets minimum standards of acceptable conduct, whereas ethics deals in what is right. The test for determining whether an action is ethical is the Golden Rule.

The National Association of REALTORS® and the National Association of Real Estate Brokers have developed ethical codes to promote professionalism in the real estate industry.

Federal fair housing legislation began with the Civil Rights Act of 1866, which applied to racial discrimination. The Civil Rights Act of 1870 reiterated the 1866 act. The Civil Rights Act of 1964 elevated a 1962 executive order into law. The act prohibited housing discrimination when there was any government assistance or involvement. The Civil Rights Act of 1968 expanded discriminatory protection to include national origin, color, and religion, as well as race. By amendment, the act was extended to sex, physical handicaps, and familial status. The act specifically prohibits steering (that is, directing persons to housing based on race), blockbusting (obtaining listings or sales based on the fear of loss in value because minority group members are entering the area), and redlining (refusing to loan within a certain area).

The Americans with Disabilities Act requires that owners and operators of places of public accommodations make the premises accessible to the extent readily achievable.

Diversity training programs aid licensees in understanding the customs and culture of other peoples, as well as the motivations in their decision-making processes. The National Association of REALTORS® has developed a diversity training program.

The Unruh Act is a California act that prohibits discrimination by a business establishment. The Rumford Act is considered California's fair housing act.

The Holden Act prohibits financial institutions from engaging in discriminatory practices, and the California Business and Professions Code and the Real Estate Commissioner's Rules and Regulations provide details regarding discriminatory practices of California real estate licensees. The Omnibus Housing Nondiscrimination Act makes all California nondiscrimination acts consistent in coverage with the California Fair Employment and Housing Act.

You must be cognizant of the fact that what you regard as innocent conduct could be regarded by others as sexual harassment. You should always conduct yourself in a businesslike manner. An allegation of sexual harassment could be expensive in dollars and time.

The Sherman Antitrust Act prohibits brokers from price-fixing, using a group boycott, and engaging in tie-in sales.

Trust funds must be protected and kept separate from broker funds. Records must be kept for each beneficiary and transaction.

CLASS DISCUSSION TOPICS

1. Without giving names, discuss any ethical problems you have observed in the real estate industry.

2. You have just brought in a cash deposit for which your broker gives you a receipt. Later, you find a duplicate cash deposit slip on the floor for that exact amount for deposit into a personal account of your broker. What should you do?

3. Salesman Rutkowski was showing a couple homes in a beautiful subdivision. Rutkowski took a route to the property that added 3 miles to the trip in order to avoid driving through a racially mixed housing area that contained many structures in need of repair. Discuss the ethics of Rutkowski's actions.

4. Broker Shimato was handling the grand opening of Big Town Estates. To emphasize the desirability of the property, Shimato sent out a press release indicating that 71 of the 400 homes to be built were sold before the grand opening. At the grand opening, the model of the subdivision showed sold flags on a large number of sites. Actually, Shimato had only three advance sales. Analyze Shimato's actions from an ethical standpoint.

5. Salesperson Sven Petersen took a listing for $389,500, although his comparative market analysis indicated a sales price between $295,000 and $310,000. Peterson's broker, Olaf Petersen, told Peterson to "start working on the owner to reduce the price." He told Peterson, "It isn't a good listing now, but it will be one in a few months. Anyway, any listing is better than no listing." Discuss ethical problems raised by this case, if any.

6. In Britain, the National Association of Estate Agents (a real estate professional organization) considers it an unethical practice to contact bereaved relatives of a deceased person in order to obtain a listing. Do you agree? Why?

7. Billie Bob Smith built a model home for his new subdivision. His newspaper ads showed an artist's rendering that made the home appear much larger than it was. In small letters the ad stated "Not to Scale." The price printed next to the drawing was $289,500. The small asterisk at the bottom of the page said "Plus Lot." The

model itself, which had a sign that said "From $289,500," included upgraded carpets, tile, cabinetry, landscaping, patio, et cetera. If a prospect wanted a home just like the model, the price would be $370,450 plus a lot starting at $140,000. Discuss the ethical problems, if any, of Smith's advertising and model home.

8. You are presenting an offer to owners represented by another agent. The offer requires that the owner carry back a second trust deed for $209,000. The other agent tells the owner that the buyer has "ace-high credit, and he has an excellent employment history." You are the selling agent, and you know from prequalifying the buyer that he has had prior credit problems owing to a lengthy period of unemployment; however, he has been working steadily for the past two years and is now up to date on all payments. What should you do?

9. While on caravan viewing new listings, you see another agent from your office, who is a close friend, slip a small Dresden figurine into her purse. What should you do?

10. Figure 2.5 is a list of the most common real estate licensee violations. Which of these reasons are clearly unethical and which could be ethical?

11. Give an example of a broker violation. Using Figure 2.5, what code section was violated?

12. Bring to class one current-events article dealing with some aspect of real estate practice for class discussion.

FIGURE 2.5:   Top Enforcement Violations

The following is a list of the top violations of the real estate law that are filed by the Bureau of Real Estate against real estate licensees. All references refer to sections of the California Business and Professions Code and the Regulations of the Real Estate Commissioner.

(1)   Trust Fund Record Keeping

Section 10145 – General statute governing the handling of trust funds. Regulation 2831 – Maintaining columnar records for trust funds received. Regulation 2831-a – Maintaining separate records for each beneficiary. Regulation 2831.2 – Performing monthly reconciliation of trust fund accounts.

Regulation 2834 – Allowing unlicensed and unbonded signatories on a trust account.

(2)   Trust Fund Shortages

Section 10145 – General statute governing the handling of trust funds. Regulation 2832 – Trust fund handling.

Regulation 2832.1 – Trust fund shortages.

(3)   Failure to Supervise

Section 10177 (h) – Failure to reasonably supervise activities of salesperson.

(4)   Unlicensed Activity Violations

Section 10130 – Act as a real estate licensee without first obtaining a license.

Section 10137 – Unlawful employment or payment to unlicensed individual or salesperson not employed by broker.

(5)   Misrepresentation Violations

Section 10276-a – Substantial misrepresentation in a real estate transaction in which a license is required.

UNIT 2 QUIZ

1.   Three brokers agreed that they would not let a third broker show any of their listings. This action would be regarded as
     a.   a group boycott.
     b.   price-fixing.
     c.   market allocations.
     d.   a tie-in agreement.

2.   Ethics' relationship to law is that
     a.   if an act is illegal it is also unethical.
     b.   ethics tends to precede the law.
     c.   ethics and the law both set minimum standards for behavior.
     d.   what is ethical is legal.

3.   Which of the following phrases would be considered nondiscriminatory in an advertisement for a rental?
     a.   Christian family
     b.   Prefer working married couple
     c.   Just two blocks to St. Michael's
     d.   None of these

4.   A broker with a disabled employee widened the doorway to the restroom to accommodate a wheelchair. This work was performed to comply with the
     a.   Civil Rights Act of 1866.
     b.   Americans with Disabilities Act.
     c.   Rumford Act.
     d.   Fair Housing Amendment Act of 1988.

5.   The Civil Rights Act of 1866 specifically covers what type of discrimination?
     a.   Sex
     b.   Marital status
     c.   Age
     d.   Race

6. A broker showed African American prospective buyers homes in African American and racially mixed neighborhoods. He would show African American prospects homes in predominantly Caucasian areas only if the prospects specifically requested to see homes in those areas. The broker's action would described as

   a. illegal.

   b. unethical.

   c. steering.

   d. all of these.

7. A broker refused to show a young Hispanic family of five a condominium about which they had inquired. The broker's action would be proper if

   a. the broker considered the unit too small for the family.

   b. there were no other children in the development.

   c. the development has an age exemption because all occupants are 55 years of age or older.

   d. 70% of the units are occupied by elderly.

8. A landlord can properly refuse to accept an applicant because the applicant

   a. has a guide dog and the apartment is on the fourth floor.

   b. is a single but obviously pregnant woman.

   c. appears to be gay and the landlord is afraid of catching AIDS.

   d. None of these

9. The state act that specifically prohibits discrimination in business establishments is the

   a. Unruh Act.

   b. Rumford Act.

   c. Holden Act.

   d. Civil Rights Act of 1968.

10. Which of the following actions dealing in trust funds would be a violation of the law?

   a. Giving trust funds received to a principal

   b. Placing depository trust funds directly into escrow

   c. Placing trust funds in a trust account

   d. Placing trust funds in the personal care of a bonded employee

UNIT THREE

3

MANDATORY DISCLOSURES

LEARNING OBJECTIVES

When you have completed this unit, you will be able to

- explain fiduciary- and agency-related disclosures, real estate transfer disclosure, agent's inspection disclosure, disclosure of death or AIDS, and natural and environmental hazards disclosures;

- describe subdivision and common interest development disclosures; and

- explain financing-related and other mandatory disclosures.

KEY TERMS

adjustable-rate loan
   disclosure
advisability of title
   insurance
agency
agency disclosure
Agent's Inspection
   Disclosure
AIDS disclosure
associate licensee
blanket encumbrance
   disclosure
brownfields
buyer's agent
California Land
   Project
carbon monoxide
   detector notice
common interest
   subdivision
Consumer Caution
   and Home
   Ownership
   Counseling Notice
controlled business
   arrangement
designated agent
dual agency
Easton v. Strassburger
elder abuse law
Environmental
   Hazards Disclosure
farming area disclosure

fiduciary responsibility
fire hazard areas
flood hazard areas
Gas or Hazardous
   Liquid Transmission
   Lines Disclosure
hazardous waste
   disclosure
Home Energy Rating
   System (HERS)
home inspection
   notice
*Homeowner's Guide to
   Earthquake Safety*
industrial/airport
   disclosure
Integrated Closing
   Disclosure
interstate land sales
landslide inventory
   report
Loan Estimate
material facts
Megan's Law
Mello-Roos bonds
methamphetamine
   contamination order
military ordnance
   location
Mining Operations
   Notice
nonresidential energy
   use disclosure

public report
Real Estate Transfer
   Disclosure
   Statement (TDS)
red flag
rescission rights
renter notice of
   foreclosure
Residential
   Earthquake Hazards
   Report
seller's agent
seller financing
   addendum and
   disclosure
septic system
   disclosure
sick building syndrome
single agency
smoke detector
   disclosure
stigmatized property
structural pest control
   inspection
Subdivided Lands Law
toxic mold
Truth-in-Lending
   Disclosure
water-conserving
   fixtures
water heater bracing
window security bars

UNDERSTANDING DISCLOSURES

Real estate agents used to say that the three main factors in real estate were "location, location, location." Today, they are "disclosure, disclosure, disclosure." Although the concept of *caveat emptor,* or "let the buyer beware," has been around for centuries, in the past several decades, California legislators, courts, and the Bureau of Real Estate (BRE) have been pushing enactment of disclosure laws. Although many agents think these laws are new, in reality, real estate law has always stressed full disclosure. However, in the past, some agents did not understand what full disclosure meant or when it was necessary to disclose certain circumstances. As a result, buyers and sellers began to take agents to court for nondisclosure. Such court cases became so numerous in certain areas that California legislators and the BRE worked to enact laws and regulations to force agents to disclose certain items. These laws and regulations have led to increased paperwork for real estate transactions, so agents must be familiar with all aspects of disclosure to complete transactions properly.

The disclosure laws discussed in this unit primarily involve 1-4-unit residential real property. Often, commercial buyers are deemed to be more sophisticated than buyers of residential real estate. Therefore, many of the disclosures that a homebuyer would get are absent from a commercial transaction. Also, the information given here is general in nature. In situations involving specific facts, consult your attorney concerning your specific case. To help avoid future disputes and litigation, always disclose the issue in question.

> A material fact is any fact that, if disclosed, could affect the decision of an entity in completing the transaction.

Full disclosure means disclosing, or giving notice of, all **material facts** in a transaction. A *material fact* is any fact that, if disclosed, could affect the decision of an entity (person or persons) in completing (to buy, to sell, etc.) a transaction. Many facets of a property might need to be disclosed to a prospective seller, buyer, or borrower to complete a transaction legally and to secure the financing necessary to purchase the property. The disclosure laws impose obligations not only on real estate licensees but also on the principals to the transaction. This is why the agent must consider all the material facts.

Full disclosure will

- protect the principals (buyers and sellers),

- establish and build trust and confidence between the licensee and principals, and

- satisfy the law.

The agent must not only disclose the information but also make certain that the principal understands the information and the importance of the information disclosed. Disclosures should be in writing to protect all parties involved.

Certain disclosures are mandated. A *mandated disclosure* is an item of information required by law to be conveyed from one entity involved in a real estate transaction to another entity in the same transaction. *Information* means some type of material data, facts, news, or figures. The phrase *required by law* means some obligation imposed by a legal authority, such as the BRE, the state legislature, or a court. *Convey* means to present from one entity (person or persons) to another entity. Thus, a mandated disclosure is simply a material fact obligated by law to be disclosed.

While the latest California Association of REALTORS® forms, as well as the forms from other California forms publishers, provide for most mandatory disclosures, outdated forms (as well as forms produced for national use) can result in a failure to properly disclose. You are not excused from disclosure because a form you used did not include or reference the disclosure.

Disclosure obligations in residential real estate sales of 1–4-unit properties are many and varied. Some are mandatory for real estate agents, some for sellers, some for both licensees and principals. At times, every agent will be in doubt about exactly what to disclose. The general rule is, "When in doubt on a particular issue, always disclose."

FIDUCIARY RESPONSIBILITY AND DISCLOSURES

An agent is one who represents another. When a principal appoints an agent, the principal assumes **vicarious liability** for the act of the agent within the scope of the agency. Of course agents would also be liable for their wrongful or negligent acts. The agency relationship demands that the agent use best efforts to protect the interests of the principal and to carry out the agency responsibilities.

When a real estate broker acts as an agent of only the seller or only the buyer, this is called a **single agency**. The **dual agency** may be used only if the buyer and the seller are both aware of the situation and approve of the arrangements. In many states, dual agency is not allowed because of the problems inherent in conflicting interests. Although this type of agency is in common use, many attorneys look on this arrangement as a conflict of interest ripe for lawsuits. Real estate agents often carry errors and omissions insurance to help protect against this problem. An agent who represents both the buyer and the seller without the approval of both is guilty of an undisclosed *divided* or dual agency and is in violation of the real estate law (Business and Professions Code 10176(d)).

An agent's **fiduciary responsibility** to the principal is one of *trust*. The duties include the following:

■ Loyalty

■ Obedience

■ Confidentiality

■ Disclosure

■ Accounting

The agent must be *loyal* to the principal, placing the principal's interests above those of the agent. An agent's actions, therefore, cannot be inconsistent with the principal's interests. The agent cannot act in a self-serving manner to the detriment of the principal. As an example, assume a buyer's agent, in seeking a property for a buyer, discovered a property meeting the buyer's needs that was bargain priced. If the broker purchased the property to resell at a profit, the broker would be competing with the principal. This would be a breach of fiduciary duty.

Fiduciary duty is one of good faith and trust.

The listing agent has a duty to conduct a diligent visual property inspection.

In dual agency situations, caution must be exercised so that aiding one principal is not detrimental to the other principal.

One duty of the agent to the principal is *obedience*. The agent must obey the principal's *lawful directions*. A principal direction to discriminate or fail to disclose a material fact could not be followed, and the principal should be so advised. These are not lawful directions. Agents also have a duty of *skill* and *diligence* and must diligently exercise their skills in the performance of agency duties.

Their duty of trust prohibits agents from revealing confidential information about the principal to others without the consent of the principal. For example, if a seller's agent revealed to a prospective buyer, without the principal's permission, that the principal was in serious financial straits, the agent's action would be a violation of the duty of trust. This information could seriously reduce the principal's bargaining ability. It could also encourage an offer at a lower price than was originally intended. Similarly, a buyer's agent could not inform a seller that the buyer had a particular need for the seller's property or that the buyer considered the seller's asking price to be extremely low.

The fiduciary duty of the agent includes full disclosure of material facts discovered by the agent that the principal would reasonably want to know in making decisions. Full disclosure would likely include the duty to warn a principal of any known dangers, such as possible problems relating to an offer, a lease, or an option. It also includes a duty to fully and honestly convey information concerning value and market conditions. Again, if there is any doubt as to the material nature of information, disclose.

An agent of a seller would not have a duty to tell a buyer that the agent would receive a greater commission or a bonus if the agent were able to sell a particular property, but if the agent were a buyer's agent, then such a disclosure would be required because failure to do so could create the appearance of a conflict of interest. It is a material fact that the buyer, as principal, would want to know.

The agent must account for all monies received and disbursed. Reasonable records must be kept.

Duty to Other Party (Nonagency)

When dealing with third parties, you are not held to the degree of fiduciary duties to a principal; nevertheless, you have duties of fairness, honesty, and disclosure. You must disclose to the buyer any detrimental information you know concerning a property that might affect its value or desirability to the buyer.

If you realize a buyer is mistaken about a property, you have a duty to let the buyer know the facts. Suppose, for example, that a buyer indicates he wants a site for an automobile repair facility. If you know that the current zoning precludes this use, you have a duty to inform the buyer about the zoning restriction.

If you have knowledge of a problem concerning the property before an offer, your disclosure must be made before the purchase offer. Your duty of disclosure, however, extends beyond the offer and acceptance of the offer. As an example, if you discover a serious structural problem after acceptance of an offer, you have a duty to inform the buyer, as well as the owner, of the problem.

For 1–4-unit residential properties, you have an actual duty to conduct a reasonably diligent visual inspection of the property. (See *Agent's Inspection Disclosure* later in this unit.) While the law does not require a visual inspection for other than 1–4-unit residential properties, you still have a duty to disclose known detrimental information to the buyer.

Facilitators and Designated Agents

When dealing with a broker in another state, California agents should understand that there could be differences in types of agency relationships and duties. Though not allowed in California, real estate brokers in some states are allowed to work as facilitators or intermediaries. These are third parties who are not agents of either the buyer or the seller; instead, they assist the buyer and the seller in the transference of real property ownership. They do, however, have a duty to treat all parties fairly and must disclose known defects in a property.

A number of states allow a broker to designate one salesperson as a principal's sole agent. When the listing broker is also the selling broker, the selling salesperson would then be the buyer's sole agent. An advantage of the **designated agent** concept lies in the fact that it is used to avoid problems often associated with conflicting duties of dual agency. Both buyer and seller have separate agency representation. However, both agencies are under the supervision of a single broker, so an appearance of a conflict of interest is still present. This type of agency relationship has not been adopted in California.

AGENCY DISCLOSURE

Civil Code Sections 2373–2382, which deal with agency relationships in real estate transactions involving 1–4-unit residential properties, became law on January 1, 1988. Any licensee in a transaction involving residential real property of 1–4 units must disclose agency. In 2015, mandatory written agency disclosure was extended to commercial transactions. Agents must disclose their exact agency role in all transactions.

To understand **agency disclosure**, brokers and salespersons must understand the term *agency*. An agent is one who represents another, called the **principal**, in dealings with a third person or persons. Such a representation is called agency. The agency disclosure form defines agency as

> a person acting under provisions of this title in a real property transaction, [including] a person who is licensed as a real estate broker under Unit 3 (commencing with Section 10130) of Part 1 of Division 4 of the Business & Professions Code, and under whose license a listing is executed or an offer to purchase is obtained.

The word *agent* is synonymous with *employing broker*. Though it is common in the real estate industry for salespeople to call themselves *real estate agents*, it is important to understand that there is only one agent in a company, the real estate broker, and all agency comes under that person. The law now uses the term **associate licensee**, defined as "a person who is licensed as a real estate salesperson or broker who is either licensed under a broker or has entered into a written contract with a broker to act as the broker's agent and to function under the broker's supervision." There is but one broker of record or responsible broker per company, and all associate licensees (salespeople) are **subagents** of that broker.

Brokers and salespeople should understand the various ways the word *agent* can be used in a real estate transaction. The licensee who lists the seller's home is called the *listing agent* or seller's agent. The licensee who brings the buyer into the transaction is called the buyer's agent or selling agent. An agent who represents the seller is called the **seller's agent**, and the agent who represents the buyer is called the **buyer's agent**. At one time, selling agents were considered subagents of the listing broker, so they represented the seller and the buyer had no representation. This has changed dramatically.

As previously stated, when an agent represents only a buyer *or* a seller, it is considered a single agency, and when an agent represents both buyer *and* seller, it is known as a dual agency.

Some brokerage offices have elected single agency. *Single agency* means that they will represent the buyer or the seller but not both. Their reason is that they feel duties to both principals in a transaction can create the appearance of a conflict of interest. This can result in lawsuits because of the perception of the parties. Single agency, representing one party to the transaction, reduces the likelihood of misunderstandings.

While the listing agent for a property could be either a seller's sole agent or a dual agent, the selling agent could be a buyer's agent (representing the buyer alone), a seller's agent (representing the seller alone), or a dual agent (representing both buyer and seller) with the knowledge and consent of both.

Even in a large company with multiple offices, there still is only one broker. For example, Bigtime Real Estate Company has an office in Los Angeles and another in San Francisco. If the agent from the Los Angeles office lists a property for sale and the agent from the San Francisco office brings in a buyer, whom does each agent represent or owe a fiduciary responsibility to? Does the listing agent exclusively represent the seller, and the selling agent exclusively represent the buyer? The agents are under the same employing broker (agency), so either both agents represent the seller or both agents represent both the seller *and* the buyer (dual agency).

Note: An agent (broker), however, is supposed to get the best and most honest deal for his principal. In a dual agency situation, the agent is compelled to obtain the highest price and best terms for the seller and also the lowest price and best terms for the buyer. In court, it is often hard to convince the jury that a dual agent has accomplished that. This is why full disclosure is extremely important.

FIGURE 3.1:   **Disclosure Regarding Real Estate Agency Relationships**

AGENCY LAW DISCLOSURE

Disclosure Regarding Real Estate Agency Relationships

Prepared by: Agent _____   Phone _____
            Broker _____   Email _____

NOTE: This form is used by agents as an attachment when preparing a seller's listing agreement, a purchase agreement or a counteroffer on the sale, exchange or lease for more than one year of residential property, nonresidential property or mobilehomes to comply with agency disclosure law controlling the conduct of real estate licensees when in agency relationships. [Calif. Civil Code §§2079 et seq.]

DATE: _____, 20____, at _____, California.

TO THE SELLER AND THE BUYER: _____

1. **FACTS:** When you enter into a discussion with a real estate agent regarding a real estate transaction, you should, from the outset, understand what type of agency relationship or representation you wish to have with the agent in the transaction.

2. **SELLER'S AGENT:** A Seller's Agent under a listing agreement with the Seller acts as the Agent for the Seller only. A Seller's Agent or a subagent of that Agent has the following affirmative obligations:
    2.1   To the Seller:
          a. A fiduciary duty of utmost care, integrity, honesty and loyalty in dealings with the Seller.
    2.2   To the Seller and the Buyer:
          a. Diligent exercise of reasonable skill and care in performance of the Agent's duties.
          b. A duty of honest and fair dealing and good faith.
          c. A duty to disclose all facts known to the Agent materially affecting the value or desirability of the property that are not known to, or within the diligent attention and observation of the parties.
    2.3   An Agent is not obligated to reveal to either party any confidential information obtained from the other party which does not involve the affirmative duties set forth above.

3. **BUYER'S AGENT:** A Selling Agent can, with a Buyer's consent, agree to act as the Agent for the Buyer only. In these situations, the Agent is not the Seller's Agent, even if by agreement the Agent may receive compensation for services rendered, either in full or in part, from the Seller. An Agent acting only for a Buyer has the following affirmative obligations:
    3.1   To the Buyer:
          a. A fiduciary duty of utmost care, integrity, honesty and loyalty in dealings with the Buyer.
    3.2   To the Seller and the Buyer:
          a. Diligent exercise of reasonable skill and care in performance of the Agent's duties.
          b. A duty of honest and fair dealing and good faith.
          c. A duty to disclose all facts known to the Agent materially affecting the value or desirability of the property that are not known to or within the diligent attention and observation of the parties. An Agent is not obligated to reveal to either party any confidential information obtained from the other party which does not involve the affirmative duties set forth above.

4. **AGENT REPRESENTING BOTH THE SELLER AND THE BUYER:** A Real Estate Agent, either acting directly or through one or more associate licensees, can legally be the Agent of both the Seller and the Buyer in a transaction, but only with the knowledge and consent of both the Seller and the Buyer.
    4.1   In a dual agency situation, the Agent has the following affirmative obligations to both the Seller and the Buyer:
          a. A fiduciary duty of utmost care, integrity, honesty and loyalty in the dealings with either the Seller or the Buyer.
          b. Other duties to the Seller and the Buyer as stated above in their respective sections.
    4.2   In representing both the Seller and the Buyer, the Agent may not, without the express permission of the respective party, disclose to the other party that the Seller will accept a price less than the listing price or that the Buyer will pay a price greater than the price offered.

5. The above duties of the Agent in a real estate transaction do not relieve a Seller or a Buyer from the responsibility to protect their own interests. You should carefully read all agreements to assure that they adequately express your understanding of the transaction. A Real Estate Agent is a person qualified to advise about real estate. If legal or tax advice is desired, consult a competent professional.

6. Throughout your real property transaction, you may receive more than one disclosure form depending upon the number of Agents assisting in the transaction. The law requires each Agent with whom you have more than a casual relationship to present you with this disclosure form. You should read its contents each time it is presented to you, considering the relationship between you and the Real Estate Agent in your specific transaction.

7. This disclosure form includes the provisions of §2079.13 to §2079.24, inclusive, of the Calif. Civil Code set forth on the reverse hereof. Read it carefully.

(Buyer's Broker)	Date	(Buyer's Signature)	Date
(Associate Licensee Signature)	Date	(Buyer's Signature)	Date
(Seller's Broker)	Date	(Seller's Signature)	Date
(Associate Licensee Signature)	Date	(Seller's Signature)	Date

-------------------------------- PAGE 1 OF 2 — FORM 305 --------------------------------

©2015 RPI — Realty Publications, Inc.

FIGURE 3.1 (continued):   Disclosure Regarding Real Estate Agency Relationships

-- PAGE 2 OF 2 — FORM 305 ---

2079.13. As used in Sections 2079.14 to 2079.24, inclusive, the following terms have the following meanings:

a. "Agent" means a person acting under provisions of Title 9 (commencing with Section 2295) in a real property transaction, and includes a person who is licensed as a real estate broker under Chapter 3 (commencing with Section 10130) of Part 1 of Division 4 of the Business and Professions Code, and under whose license a listing is executed or an offer to purchase is obtained.

b. "Associate licensee" means a person who is licensed as a real estate broker or salesperson under Chapter 3 (commencing with Section 10130) of Part 1 of Division 4 of the Business and Professions Code and who is either licensed under a broker or has entered into a written contract with a broker to act as the broker's agent in connection with acts requiring a real estate license and to function under the broker's supervision in the capacity of an associate licensee.

The agent in the real property transaction bears responsibility for his or her associate licensees who perform as agents of the agent. When an associate licensee owes a duty to any principal, or to any buyer or seller who is not a principal, in a real property transaction, that duty is equivalent to the duty owed to that party by the broker for whom the associate licensee functions.

c. "Buyer" means a transferee in a real property transaction, and includes a person who executes an offer to purchase real property from a seller through an agent, or who seeks the services of an agent in more than a casual, transitory, or preliminary manner, with the object of entering into a real property transaction. "Buyer" includes vendee or lessee.

d. "Commercial real property" means all real property in the state, except single-family residential real property, dwelling units made subject to Chapter 2 (commencing with Section 1940) of Title 5, mobilehomes, as defined in Section 798.3, or recreational vehicles, as defined in Section 799.29.

e. "Dual agent" means an agent acting, either directly or through an associate licensee, as agent for both the seller and the buyer in a real property transaction.

f. "Listing agreement" means a contract between an owner of real property and an agent, by which the agent has been authorized to sell the real property or to find or obtain a buyer.

g. "Listing agent" means a person who has obtained a listing of real property to act as an agent for compensation.

h. "Listing price" is the amount expressed in dollars specified in the listing for which the seller is willing to sell the real property through the listing agent.

i. "Offering price" is the amount expressed in dollars specified in an offer to purchase for which the buyer is willing to buy the real property.

j. "Offer to purchase" means a written contract executed by a buyer acting through a selling agent that becomes the contract for the sale of the real property upon acceptance by the seller.

k. "Real property" means any estate specified by subdivision (1) or (2) of Section 761 in property that constitutes or is improved with one to four dwelling units, any commercial real property, any leasehold in these types of property exceeding one year's duration, and mobilehomes, when offered for sale or sold through an agent pursuant to the authority contained in Section 10131.6 of the Business and Professions Code.

l. "Real property transaction" means a transaction for the sale of real property in which an agent is employed by one or more of the principals to act in that transaction, and includes a listing or an offer to purchase.

m. "Sell," "sale," or "sold" refers to a transaction for the transfer of real property from the seller to the buyer, and includes exchanges of real property between the seller and buyer, transactions for the creation of a real property sales contract within the meaning of Section 2985, and transactions for the creation of a leasehold exceeding one year's duration.

n. "Seller" means the transferor in a real property transaction, and includes an owner who lists real property with an agent, whether or not a transfer results, or who receives an offer to purchase real property of which he or she is the owner from an agent on behalf of another. "Seller" includes both a vendor and a lessor.

o. "Selling agent" means a listing agent who acts alone, or an agent who acts in cooperation with a listing agent, and who sells or finds and obtains a buyer for the real property, or an agent who locates property for a buyer or who finds a buyer for a property for which no listing exists and presents an offer to purchase to the seller.

p. "Subagent" means a person to whom an agent delegates agency powers as provided in Article 5 (commencing with Section 2349) of Chapter 1 of Title 9. However, "subagent" does not include an associate licensee who is acting under the supervision of an agent in a real property transaction.

§2079.14. Listing agents and selling agents shall provide the seller and buyer in a real property transaction with a copy of the disclosure form specified in Section 2079.16, and, except as provided in subdivision (c), shall obtain a signed acknowledgment of receipt from that seller or buyer, except as provided in this section or Section 2079.15, as follows:

a. The listing agent, if any, shall provide the disclosure form to the seller prior to entering into the listing agreement.

b. The selling agent shall provide the disclosure form to the seller as soon as practicable prior to presenting the seller with an offer to purchase, unless the selling agent previously provided the seller with a copy of the disclosure form pursuant to subdivision (a).

c. Where the selling agent does not deal on a face-to-face basis with the seller, the disclosure form prepared by the selling agent may be furnished to the seller (and acknowledgment of receipt obtained for the selling agent from the seller) by the listing agent, or the selling agent may deliver the disclosure form by certified mail addressed to the seller at his or her last known address, in which case no signed acknowledgment of receipt is required.

d. The selling agent shall provide the disclosure form to the buyer as soon as practicable prior to execution of the buyer's offer to purchase, except that if the offer to purchase is not prepared by the selling agent, the selling agent shall present the disclosure form to the buyer not later than the next business day after the selling agent receives the offer to purchase from the buyer.

§2079.15. In any circumstance in which the seller or buyer refuses to sign an acknowledgment of receipt pursuant to Section 2079.14, the agent, or an associate licensee acting for an agent, shall set forth, sign, and date a written declaration of the facts of the refusal.

§2079.17. (a) As soon as practicable, the selling agent shall disclose to the buyer and seller whether the selling agent is acting in the real property transaction exclusively as the buyer's agent, exclusively as the seller's agent, or as a dual agent representing both the buyer and the seller. This relationship shall be confirmed in the contract to purchase and sell real property or in a separate writing executed or acknowledged by the seller, the buyer, and the selling agent prior to or coincident with execution of that contract by the buyer and the seller, respectively.

b. As soon as practicable, the listing agent shall disclose to the seller whether the listing agent is acting in the real property transaction exclusively as the seller's agent, or as a dual agent representing both the buyer and seller. This relationship shall be confirmed in the contract to purchase and sell real property or in a separate writing executed or acknowledged by the seller and the listing agent prior to or coincident with the execution of that contract by the seller.

c. The confirmation required by subdivisions (a) and (b) shall be in the following form:

<u>　　　　[Do not fill out]　　　　</u> is the agent of (check one):
　　　　　(Name of the Seller's Agent)
☐ the seller exclusively; or
☐ both the buyer and seller.

<u>　　　　[Do not fill out]　　　　</u> is the agent of (check one):
　(Name of the Buyer's Agent if not the same as the Seller's Agent)
☐ the buyer exclusively;
☐ the seller exclusively; or
☐ both the buyer and seller.

d. The disclosures and confirmation required by this section shall be in addition to the disclosure required by Section 2079.14.

§2079.18. No selling agent in a real property transaction may act as an agent for the buyer only, when the selling agent is also acting as the listing agent in the transaction.

§2079.19. The payment of compensation or the obligation to pay compensation to an agent by the seller or buyer is not necessarily determinative of a particular agency relationship between an agent and the seller or buyer. A listing agent and a selling agent may agree to share any compensation or commission paid, or any right to any compensation or commission for which an obligation arises as the result of a real estate transaction, and the terms of any such agreement shall not necessarily be determinative of a particular relationship.

§2079.20. Nothing in this article prevents an agent from selecting, as a condition of the agent's employment, a specific form of agency relationship not specifically prohibited by this article if the requirements of Section 2079.14 and Section 2079.17 are complied with.

§2079.21. A dual agent shall not disclose to the buyer that the seller is willing to sell the property at a price less than the listing price, without the express written consent of the seller. A dual agent shall not disclose to the seller that the buyer is willing to pay a price greater than the offering price, without the expressed written consent of the buyer.

This section does not alter in any way the duty or responsibility of a dual agent to any principal with respect to confidential information other than price.

§2079.22. Nothing in this article precludes a listing agent from also being a selling agent, and the combination of these functions in one agent does not, of itself, make that agent a dual agent.

§2079.23. A contract between the principal and agent may be modified or altered to change the agency relationship at any time before the performance of the act which is the object of the agency with the written consent of the parties to the agency relationship.

§2079.24. Nothing in this article shall be construed to either diminish the duty of disclosure owed buyers and sellers by agents and their associate licensees, subagents, and employees or to relieve agents and their associate licensees, subagents, and employees from liability for their conduct in connection with acts governed by this article or for any breach of a fiduciary duty or a duty of disclosure.

Franchise offices are usually independently owned, with a different broker for each independently owned office. Thus, different agents from different offices may not be under the same agency (the same broker). Because the listing associate licensee is from a different office (different agency), the licensee can exclusively represent the seller, and the selling licensee can create an exclusive agency with the buyer. However, under the law of disclosing agency, all types of agency must be disclosed.

Any associate licensee who acts on behalf of others in selling, buying, exchanging, or leasing real estate creates agency for her broker (the agent).

An agent can receive a commission from a seller but still be the buyer's agent. Agency has nothing to do with who pays the commission (California Civil Code 2079.19). Buyer's agents customarily receive their compensation from the sellers.

Agency relationships can be either *implied* or *express*. Formalities are not necessarily required to create an agency relationship; the licensee can create an implied agency with a buyer or a seller simply through the words used when talking to prospective clients. For example, a court might determine that an implied agency is created when a licensee says to a buyer on the phone, "I have time today to look for property for your specific needs, to help you solve your housing problems." Agency can also be created by an express contract, such as a listing agreement. (See Unit 6.) Remember, once this agency relationship is created, the licensee has a fiduciary relationship with the principal. A fiduciary incurs the highest obligations under the law.

The Disclosure Process

The three-step process of disclosing agency can be remembered by using the acronym *DEC*.

Step 1: Disclose. This step will be in writing. Using a prescribed disclosure form (Figure 3.1), the licensee must educate the principal about the three different types of agents—seller's agent, buyer's agent, and dual agent—and how they operate. After this full disclosure, it is necessary to obtain the principal's signature. In dealing with consumers (buyers), the broker should educate the buyer about agency relationships as soon as possible, provide the potential buyer with the disclosure regarding agency relationships, and obtain the buyer's signature.

Step 2: Elect.   In this step, the agent and the principal decide which type of agency will be used. Because circumstances can change with each transaction, it is imperative that the principal and the agent thoroughly understand the implications of the agency roles they agree on and elect. Nothing has to be signed in this step, but care must be taken that both principal and agent enjoy full understanding (disclosure) of the agency elected.

> The three steps of the disclosure process are Disclose, Elect, and Confirm.

Step 3: Confirm.   The confirmation of the type of agency elected in step 2 must be in writing. The agent and the principal(s) must sign the confirmation statement. Usually this confirmation is included as part of the purchase contract (also known as a *deposit receipt*), but it is also available as a separate document. If dual agency is elected, the agent must disclose that fact to both the buyer and the seller because a dual agent needs the consent of both. Because the broker is the agent, it is the broker's responsibility to make certain that proper disclosures have been made.

The selling agent should confirm the agency with the buyer, even if the buyer is not to be represented by an agent.

Timing of Disclosure

When should an agent disclose agency? The Bureau of Real Estate mandates disclosure "as soon as possible" when more than a casual relationship exists, and most offices have a policy manual that addresses the requirement of prompt disclosure. The three steps in the process may be taken at different times. Below are some general ideas on when to disclose, when to elect, and when to confirm.

Listing agents not selling their own listings.   In these cases, agents should provide the disclosure to the seller before entering into the listing agreement, elect as soon as is practical, and confirm the agency before or coincident with the seller's acceptance of the purchase contract.

Listing agents selling their own listings (in-house). In this case, the agent should disclose (that she is either the seller's exclusive agent or a dual agent of both seller and buyer), elect, and confirm to the seller and the buyer as in the preceding transaction.

Selling agents working with a buyer. Selling agents who are not listing agents always should disclose as soon as is practical and before a buyer's making an offer. As above, they should also elect as soon as is practical and confirm before or coincident with a buyer's and a seller's execution of the purchase contract.

Selling agents working with a seller. Selling agents who are not listing agents should remember to disclose to sellers as soon as is practical. They should elect as soon as is practical and confirm before or coincident with a buyer's and a seller's execution of the deposit receipt.

The chart in Figure 3.2 sums up the important information on agency disclosure that will be found in many offices' policy manuals.

REAL ESTATE TRANSFER DISCLOSURE

Under current law (California Civil Code Sections 1.102–1.102.14), the purchaser of residential real property (including residential stock cooperative housing) of four units or less is entitled to a **Real Estate Transfer Disclosure Statement (TDS)** from the seller. The term *transfer* refers to sale, exchange, real property sales contract (installment land sales contract), option, lease option, and so forth. Since January 1, 1987, any seller, whether represented by an agent or not, has been required to give the buyer a written disclosure statement of the condition of the property. The disclosure statement must identify

- items in the home and whether these items are operational (part A);

- significant defects of the home, if any (part B); and

- all information regarding improvements and alterations, concerns with neighbors and the neighborhood, zoning, a homeowners association, and other possible problem areas (part C).

FIGURE 3.2:   Agency Law Summary Chart

Listing Agent (Representing Seller Only)

What?	Who?	When?	How?	Law
Disclose	Provide disclosure form to seller.	Prior to entering into the listing agreement.	Obtain signed copy of disclosure form (C.A.R. Form AD).	Cal. Civ. Code §§ 2079.14, 2079.16
Confirm	Confirm in writing with the seller and buyer that you are seller's agent exclusively.	Prior to or same time as Seller's Execution of Purchase Agreement (last party to sign purchase contract).	In Purchase Agreement (C.A.R. Form RPA-CA) or another writing signed by buyer, seller, and listing agent (C.A.R. Form AC-6).	Cal. Civ. Code § 2079.17

Dual Agent (Office Represents Seller and Buyer)
For an office selling their own listing, in ADDITION to the above, the office MUST do the following:

What?	Who?	When?	How?	Law
Disclose	Provide disclosure form to buyer.	ASAP before buyer executes offer.	Obtain signed copy of Disclosure Form (C.A.R. Form AD)	Cal. Civ. Code §§ 2079,14, 2079.16
Confirm	Confirm in writing with seller and buyer that your office is the dual agent. (Note: Office is dual agent even if one salesperson in office represents the seller and another salesperson in the same office represents the buyer.)	Prior to or same time as Seller's Execution of Purchase Agreement (last party to sign purchase contract).	In the Purchase Contract (C.A.R. Form RPA-CA) or another writing signed by buyer, seller, and listing agent (C.A.R. Form AC-6).	Cal. Civ. Code § 2079.17

Selling Agent (Representing Buyer Only)

What?	Who?	When?	How?	Law
Disclose	Provide disclosure form to buyer.	ASAP before buyer executes offer (i.e., after more than a casual, transitory, or preliminary inquiry).	Obtain signed copy of disclosure form (C.A.R. Form AD).	Cal. Civ. Code §§ 2079,14, 2079.16
Disclose	Provide disclosure form to seller.	ASAP before presenting seller with offer.	(1) Obtain signed copy directly from seller or through listing agent or (2) provide by certified mail to seller (C.A.R. Form AD – may use new AD form or same form already signed by buyer).	Cal. Civ. Code §§ 2079,14, 2079.16
Confirm	Confirm in writing with buyer and seller whether you are buyer's agent exclusively.	Prior to or same time as seller's execution of purchase contract (last party to accept contract)	In the purchase contract (C.A.R. Form RPA-CA) or another writing signed by buyer, seller, and selling agent (C.A.R. Form AC-6).	Cal. Civ. Code § 2079.17

A copy of the form must be delivered to the buyer. If only one agent is involved, that agent must deliver it to the buyer. If two agents are involved, it is the responsibility of the selling agent (the agent who obtained the offer) to deliver it to the buyer. If the seller has not filled out the disclosure statement, the buyer should be notified in writing of the buyer's right to receive such a statement.

Seller Disclosure Exemptions

Exempted from disclosure are transfers

- requiring public report,
- pursuant to court order,
- by foreclosure,
- by a fiduciary,
- from one co-owner to one or more co-owners,
- between spouses or to a direct blood relative,
- between spouses in connection with a dissolution,
  - by the state controller,
- as a result of failure to pay property taxes,
- to or from any government entity (including exchanges), and
  - from probate.

Right of Termination

The disclosure statement should be delivered as soon as practical and before the execution of the offer to purchase. If the statement is not delivered before the execution, or is later amended, the buyer has the right to cancel the offer within three days after delivery (five days if mailed). To cancel the offer, the buyer must write a notice of termination and deliver it to the seller or the seller's agent. Failure to provide a transfer disclosure statement will not invalidate a closed transaction, but failure to comply could result in liability for damages. The transfer disclosure form is shown in Figure 3.3.

FIGURE 3.3:   Real Estate Transfer Disclosure Statement

THIS FORM FOR USE
IN CALIFORNIA ONLY

Real Estate Forms
Since 1966

REAL ESTATE TRANSFER DISCLOSURE STATEMENT
(Statutory Form)

THIS DISCLOSURE STATEMENT CONCERNS THE REAL PROPERTY SITUATED IN THE CITY OF _____,
COUNTY OF _____, STATE OF CALIFORNIA, DESCRIBED AS _____
_____

THIS STATEMENT IS A DISCLOSURE OF THE CONDITION OF THE ABOVE DESCRIBED PROPERTY IN COMPLIANCE WITH SECTION 1102 OF THE CIVIL CODE AS OF (DATE) _____.   IT IS NOT A WARRANTY OF ANY KIND BY THE SELLER(S) OR ANY AGENT(S) REPRESENTING ANY PRINCIPAL(S) IN THIS TRANSACTION, AND IS NOT A SUBSTITUTE FOR ANY INSPECTIONS OR WARRANTIES THE PRINCIPAL(S) MAY WISH TO OBTAIN.

I. COORDINATION WITH OTHER DISCLOSURE FORMS

This Real Estate Transfer Disclosure Statement is made pursuant to Section 1102 of the Civil Code. Other statutes require disclosures, depending upon the details of the particular real estate transaction (for example: special study zone and purchase-money liens on residential property).

Substituted Disclosures: The following disclosures and other disclosures required by law, including the Natural Hazard Disclosure Report/Statement that may include airport annoyances, earthquake, fire, flood, or special assessment information, have or will be made in connection with this real estate transfer, and are intended to satisfy the disclosure obligations on this form, where the subject matter is the same:

☐ Inspection reports completed pursuant to the contract of sale or receipt for deposit.
☐ Additional inspection reports or disclosures: _____

II. Seller's information

The Seller discloses the following information with the knowledge that even though this is not a warranty, prospective Buyers may rely on this information in deciding whether and on what terms to purchase the subject property. Seller hereby authorizes any agent(s) representing any principal(s) in this transaction to provide a copy of this statement to any person or entity in connection with any actual or anticipated sale of the property.

THE FOLLOWING ARE REPRESENTATIONS MADE BY THE SELLER(S) AND ARE NOT THE REPRESENTATIONS OF THE AGENT(S), IF ANY. THIS INFORMATION IS A DISCLOSURE AND IS NOT INTENDED TO BE PART OF ANY CONTRACT BETWEEN THE BUYER AND SELLER.

Seller ☐ is, ☐ is not occupying the property.

A. The subject property has the items checked below (read across): *

☐ Range   ☐ Oven   ☐ Microwave
☐ Dishwasher   ☐ Trash Compactor   ☐ Garbage Disposal
☐ Washer/Dryer Hookups   ☐ Rain Gutters
☐ Burglar Alarms   ☐ Carbon Monoxide Device(s)   ☐ Fire Alarm
☐ T.V. Antenna   ☐ Satellite Dish   ☐ Intercom
☐ Central Heating   ☐ Central Air Conditioning   ☐ Evaporator Cooler(s)
☐ Wall/Window Air Conditioning   ☐ Sprinklers   ☐ Public Sewer System
☐ Septic Tank   ☐ Sump Pump   ☐ Water Softener
☐ Patio/Decking   ☐ Built-in Barbecue   ☐ Gazebo
☐ Sauna
☐ Hot Tub ☐ Locking Safety Cover   ☐ Pool ☐ Child Resistant Barrier   ☐ Spa ☐ Locking Safety Cover
☐ Security Gate(s)   ☐ Automatic Garage   ☐ Number Remote
                                           Door Opener(s)   Controls _____
☐ Garage: ☐ Attached   ☐ Not Attached   ☐ Carport
☐ Pool/Spa Heater: ☐ Gas   ☐ Solar   ☐ Electric
☐ Water Heater: ☐ Gas
☐ Water Supply: ☐ City   ☐ Well   ☐ Private Utility, or
☐ Gas Supply: ☐ Utility   ☐ Bottled   Other _____
☐ Window Screens   ☐ Window Security Bars,   ☐ Water-Conserving Plumbing Fixtures
                                          ☐ Quick Release Mechanism
                                            on Bedroom Windows

Exhaust Fan(s) in _____ 220 Volt Wiring in _____ Fireplace(s) in _____
Gas Starter _____ Roof(s): Type: _____ Age: _____ (approx.)
Other: _____
Are there, to the best of your (Seller's) knowledge, any of the above that are not in operating condition? ☐ Yes ☐ No. If yes, then describe. (Attach additional sheets if necessary.): _____
_____

* Installation of a listed appliance, device, or amenity is not a precondition of sale or transfer of the dwelling. The carbon monoxide device, garage door opener, or child-resistant pool barrier may not be in compliance with the safety standards relating to, respectively, carbon monoxide device standards of Chapter 8 (commencing with Section 13260) of Part 2 of Division 12 of, automatic reversing device standards of Chapter 12.5 (commencing with Section 19890) of Part 3 of Division 13 of, or the pool safety standards of Article 2.5 (commencing with Section 115920) of Chapter 5 of Part 10 of Division 104 of, the Health and Safety Code. Window security bars may not have quick-release mechanisms in compliance with the 1995 edition of the California Building Standards Code. Section 1101.4 of the Civil Code requires all single-family residences built on or before January 1, 1994, to be equipped with water-conserving plumbing fixtures after January 1, 2017. Additionally, on and after January 1, 2014, a single-family residence built on or before January 1, 1994, that is altered or improved is required to be equipped with water-conserving plumbing fixtures as a condition of final approval. Fixtures in this dwelling may not comply with Section 1101.4 of the Civil Code.

Buyer acknowledges receipt of a copy of this page. [_____] [_____] Date _____

FORM 110.21 CAL (01-2012) COPYRIGHT BY PROFESSIONAL PUBLISHING CORP., NOVATO, CA

**PROFESSIONAL
PUBLISHING**

Form generated by: **TrueForms**™   www.TrueForms.com   800-499-9612

FIGURE 3.3 (continued):   **Real Estate Transfer Disclosure Statement**

Property Address _____

B. **Are you (Seller) aware of any significant defects/malfunctions in any of the following?** ☐ Yes ☐ No. **If yes, check appropriate box(es) below.**

☐ Interior Walls ☐ Ceilings ☐ Floors ☐ Exterior Walls ☐ Insulation ☐ Roof(s) ☐ Windows ☐ Doors ☐ Foundation ☐ Slab(s) ☐ Driveways ☐ Sidewalks ☐ Walls/Fences ☐ Electrical Systems ☐ Plumbing/Sewers/Septics ☐ Other Structural Components (Describe: _____).

If any of the above is checked, explain. (Attach additional sheets if necessary):

_____
_____
_____
_____
_____
_____
_____
_____

C. **Are you (Seller) aware of any of the following:**

1. Substances, materials, or products which may be an environmental hazard such as, but not limited to, asbestos, formaldehyde, radon gas, lead-based paint, mold, fuel or chemical storage tanks, and contaminated soil or water on the subject property . . . . ☐ Yes ☐ No
2. Features of the property shared in common with adjoining landowners, such as walls, fences, and driveways, whose use or responsibility for maintenance may have an effect on the subject property . . . . ☐ Yes ☐ No
3. Any encroachments, easements or similar matters that may affect your interest in the subject property . . . . ☐ Yes ☐ No
4. Room additions, structural modifications, or other alterations or repairs made without necessary permits . . . . . . ☐ Yes ☐ No
5. Room additions, structural modifications, or other alterations or repairs not in compliance with building codes . . . . ☐ Yes ☐ No
6. Fill (compacted or otherwise) on the property or any portion thereof . . . . ☐ Yes ☐ No
7. Any settling from any cause, or slippage, sliding, or other soil problems . . . . ☐ Yes ☐ No
8. Flooding, drainage or grading problems . . . . ☐ Yes ☐ No
9. Major damage to the property or any of the structures from fire, earthquake, floods, or landslides . . . . ☐ Yes ☐ No
10. Any zoning violations, nonconforming uses, violations of "setback" requirements . . . . ☐ Yes ☐ No
11. Neighborhood noise problems or other nuisances . . . . ☐ Yes ☐ No
12. CC&R's or other deed restrictions or obligations . . . . ☐ Yes ☐ No
13. Homeowners' Association which has any authority over the subject property . . . . ☐ Yes ☐ No
14. Any "common area" (facilities such as pools, tennis courts, walkways, or other areas co-owned in undivided interest with others) . . . . ☐ Yes ☐ No
15. Any notices of abatement or citations against the property . . . . ☐ Yes ☐ No
16. Any lawsuits by or against the Seller threatening to or affecting this real property, including any lawsuits alleging a defect or deficiency in this real property or "common areas" (facilities such as pools, tennis courts, walkways, or other areas co-owned in undivided interest with others) . . . . ☐ Yes ☐ No
17. Any Mello-Roos special tax levy lien or fixed lien assessment pursuant to Improvement Bond Act of 1915 on subject property. (If yes, disclosure notice should be obtained from levying agency.) . . . . ☐ Yes ☐ No
18. Any former federal or state ordnance locations (as defined in C.C. 1102.15) within one mile of the subject property ☐ Yes ☐ No
19. Whether subject property is affected by or zoned to allow certain manufacturing or commercial or airport use as set forth in CCP 731a . . . . ☐ Yes ☐ No
20. An order from a local health officer prohibiting the use or occupancy of portions of the property contaminated by methamphetamine. (If so, a copy of the order must be delivered to any prospective purchaser.) . . . . ☐ Yes ☐ No

If the answer to any of these is yes, explain. (Attach additional sheets if necessary.): _____
_____
_____

D. 1. The Seller certifies that the property, as of the close of escrow, will be in compliance with Section 13113.8 of the Health and Safety Code by having operable smoke detectors(s) which are approved, listed, and installed in accordance with the State Fire Marshal's regulations and applicable local standards.

2. The Seller certifies that the property, as of the close of escrow, will be in compliance with Section 19211 of the Health and Safety Code by having the water heater tank(s) braced, anchored, or strapped in place in accordance with applicable law.

Seller certifies that the information herein is true and correct to the best of the Seller's knowledge as of the date signed by the Seller.

Seller _____ Date _____   Seller _____ Date _____

Buyer acknowledges receipt of a copy of this page. [_____] [_____] **Date** _____

Page 2 of 3
FORM 110.22 CAL (01-2012) COPYRIGHT BY PROFESSIONAL PUBLISHING CORP., NOVATO, CA

PROFESSIONAL PUBLISHING

Form generated by: TrueForms™   www.TrueForms.com   800-499-9612

FIGURE 3.3 (continued):   Real Estate Transfer Disclosure Statement

Property Address _____

III. AGENT'S INSPECTION DISCLOSURE (Listing Agent)
(To be completed only if the Seller is represented by an agent in this transaction.)
THE UNDERSIGNED, BASED ON THE ABOVE INQUIRY OF THE SELLER(S) AS TO THE CONDITION OF THE PROPERTY AND BASED ON A REASONABLY COMPETENT AND DILIGENT VISUAL INSPECTION OF THE ACCESSIBLE AREAS OF THE PROPERTY IN CONJUNCTION WITH THAT INQUIRY, STATES THE FOLLOWING:
☐ Agent notes no items for disclosure.
☐ Agent notes the following items:

_____
_____
_____
_____
_____
_____

Agent (Broker
Representing Seller) _____ By _____ Date _____
                     (Please Print)   (Associate Licensee or Broker Signature)

IV. AGENT'S INSPECTION DISCLOSURE (Selling Agent)
(To be completed only if the agent who has obtained the offer is other than the agent above.)
THE UNDERSIGNED, BASED ON A REASONABLY COMPETENT AND DILIGENT VISUAL INSPECTION OF THE ACCESSIBLE AREAS OF THE PROPERTY, STATES THE FOLLOWING:
☐ Agent notes no items for disclosure.
☐ Agent notes the following items:

_____
_____
_____
_____
_____
_____

Agent (Broker
Obtaining the Offer) _____ By _____ Date _____
                     (Please Print)   (Associate Licensee or Broker Signature)

V. BUYER(S) AND SELLER(S) MAY WISH TO OBTAIN PROFESSIONAL ADVICE AND/OR INSPECTIONS OF THE PROPERTY AND TO PRO-VIDE FOR APPROPRIATE PROVISIONS IN A CONTRACT BETWEEN BUYER(S) AND SELLER(S) WITH RESPECT TO ANY ADVICE /IN-SPECTIONS/DEFECTS.

I/WE ACKNOWLEDGE RECEIPT OF A COPY OF THIS STATEMENT.

Seller _____ Date _____ Buyer _____ Date _____

Seller _____ Date _____ Buyer _____ Date _____

Agent (Broker
Representing Seller) _____ By _____ Date _____
                     (Please Print)   (Associate Licensee or Broker Signature)
Agent (Broker
Obtaining the Offer) _____ By _____ Date _____
                     (Please Print)   (Associate Licensee or Broker Signature)

SECTION 1102.3 OF THE CIVIL CODE PROVIDES A BUYER WITH THE RIGHT TO RESCIND A PURCHASE CONTRACT FOR AT LEAST THREE DAYS AFTER THE DELIVERY OF THIS DISCLOSURE IF DELIVERY OCCURS AFTER THE SIGNING OF AN OFFER TO PURCHASE. IF YOU WISH TO RESCIND THE CONTRACT, YOU MUST ACT WITHIN THE PRESCRIBED PERIOD.

A REAL ESTATE BROKER IS QUALIFIED TO ADVISE ON REAL ESTATE. IF YOU DESIRE LEGAL ADVICE, CONSULT YOUR ATTORNEY.

Page 3 of 3
FORM 110.23 CAL (01-2012) COPYRIGHT BY PROFESSIONAL PUBLISHING CORP., NOVATO, CA

Form generated by: **TrueForms™**   **www.TrueForms.com**   800-499-9612

PROFESSIONAL PUBLISHING

Reprinted with permission, Professional Publications. Endorsement not implied.

AGENT'S INSPECTION DISCLOSURE

Whenever agents take listings on 1–4-unit residential properties, they should fill out a Real Estate Transfer Disclosure Statement. Even if the seller is exempt from the transfer disclosure statement requirements—for example, if the property is being sold to a co-owner—the agent is responsible for conducting an investigation and inspection independent of the seller and for filling out a transfer disclosure statement. The agent uses the same disclosure statement as that in Figure 3.3. Section III of that disclosure statement, the **Agent's Inspection Disclosure**, is to be completed if the seller is represented by a listing agent.

On May 31, 1984, the California State Supreme Court refused to hear the **Easton v. Strassburger** ([1984] 152 Ca.3d 90) case, making the decision of the appellate court case law in California final. Under *Easton*, a real estate agent was deemed responsible not only for what was known or accessible only to the agent or the principal but also for what the agent "should have known," following a reasonably competent and diligent inspection. This court case has been codified in the Civil Code, beginning with Section 2079, and became effective January 1, 1986. It requires that all real estate agents conduct a competent and diligent visual inspection of all accessible property areas in a real estate sale involving 1–4-unit residential properties and disclose to the prospective buyer all material facts affecting the value or desirability of the property. There are no exceptions to or exemptions from this law. If an agent does not comply with this code section, the statute of limitations for bringing suit is two years.

A difficulty with this section of code is that it does not tell agents what to inspect or how. The following suggestions may help agents find physical problems and fundamental defects in the home. The major factors contributing to defects in homes are structural failure, material deterioration, water damage, mold, and insect infestation. When one of these factors is found in a home, some or all of the other factors often are present.

Structural Failure

Structural failure can be caused by environmental extremes, poor design, material deterioration, water, or insects. When inspecting for structural failure, agents should look for the following:

- Cracks in structural walls, beams, and columns (outside and inside), particularly foundations, or in corners of walls and around doors and windows (large V-shaped cracks may indicate settlement, upheaval, or lateral movement of soil; minor cracking is normal)

- Severe bulging in floors or structural walls

- Floors that slope

- Excessive deflection of girders and joists evidenced by a caved-in and creaky floor

- Doors that fail to close or that have been trimmed to close

- A roof ridgeline that is not straight

- Instability in any structural member

Material Deterioration

Material deterioration can be produced by substandard material or construction procedures. A moist environment can produce damp rot (a decaying fungus), one of the most severe types of material damage. Principal items to look for when inspecting for material deterioration include the following:

- Decay or warping of wood members (porches are a prime candidate)

- Rotting, cracking, or warping—check around doors and windows especially

- Erosion of concrete, masonry units, or mortar

Water Problems

Water problems can be caused by faulty plumbing, a rising ground water level, seepage, improper drainage, or condensation from inadequate ventilation. Water is a common enemy of a house. Principal items to look for when inspecting for water problems include the following:

- Water stains on ceilings that may be coming from leaky plumbing or a leaky roof

- Mold, mildew, and rust—be particularly alert for black mold

- Loose or warped wood members

- Rotted wood

- Cracked, chipped, or curled tile

- Premature interior paint deterioration—check for peeling and flaking

- Roof defects

Toxic Mold

Sellers of 1–4-unit residential property must disclose in the Real Estate Transfer Disclosure Statement if the owner is aware of mold on the premises.

The presence of **toxic mold** can have serious health effects. It is caused by damp conditions. Solving mold conditions can require walls being torn open. In some cases, buildings have been razed because the cost to cure the problem was too great. If a house has a dampness problem or has a musty odor, you should recommend to a buyer that the home inspector test for mold. Mold detection kits are available at hardware and building supply stores as well as through the internet. Some kits are priced less than $10.

Carpenter ants and subterranean termites are the most damaging of all insects. Both attack wooden structures internally and might leave few visible signs of infestation on the surface, making their presence virtually impossible to detect.

Insect Infestation

Undetected and therefore untreated insect infestation could make the home structurally unsound over time. The following are some insect signs to look for:

- Carpenter ants: wood shavings near wood members

- Termites: earth and wood droppings, which look like sawdust and mud tubes leading from ground to wood or marks where mud tubes were removed

With regard to termite infestation, companies are licensed by the Structural Pest Control Board in California. Copies of termite reports conducted within the last two years are available for a fee to anyone who requests them.

There are two sections to termite reports:

- Section 1 is for what is commonly called active infestation. The industry standard is that the seller would pay for this termite damage.

- Section 2 is for what is generally a condition that could lead to a future problem. Examples of conditions noted in section 2 would be plumbing leaks or excessive moisture conditions. Generally, the buyer would pay to correct section 2 problems.

There are too many possible defects to mention here, but agents have developed inspection techniques to detect some of the more common problems. For example, defective wood framing can be detected after a few years by uneven floors and window sills. If an uncarpeted floor looks uneven, a simple test is to place a marble at several places on the floor; rolling marbles may indicate a problem. Resawn doors or doorjambs reworked because they were no longer perpendicular to the floor signify a structural defect. Sticking doors and windows can indicate green lumber, sloppy workmanship, foundation settling, or imperfect framing. Ceiling stains generally indicate a past or current roof problem. A **red flag** is anything that indicates a possible problem. Any red-flag information should be conveyed to the purchaser with a warning that it could indicate a problem. Remember, agents' legal responsibility extends only to a visual inspection of reasonably accessible areas.

A *red flag* is a visual sign or indication of a defect.

Many agents today use the following three techniques to help protect them in the area of inspection disclosure:

1. Have the buyer pay for a home inspection, whereby a professional inspector examines the property, verifies defects on the transfer disclosure statement, and points out any defects that are not on the statement

2. Obtain a home warranty. The purchase contract may call for the seller to pay the cost, typically between $250 and $400 for one-year coverage. Coverages vary but generally include appliances and electrical, plumbing, heating, and cooling systems. Some brokers offer home warranty protection on all their sales. Buyers often purchase the coverage if not otherwise provided.

3. Have the seller supply the buyer with a pest control inspection report

> Real estate agents are required only to visually inspect one-to-four residential units.

Even if any one or all of these techniques are used, the agent is still responsible for inspecting the home and retains liability for any undisclosed defects that the agent knew about or should have discovered with a reasonably diligent visual inspection.

In addition to physical problems of the property itself, the agent must disclose anything else that might affect the buyer's decision to buy the property. These factors range from the property's being in a flood zone or on or near an earthquake fault to the presence of a nearby nuclear power plant. The agent needs to learn as much as possible about the house and the area around it.

SELLER'S PROPERTY QUESTIONNAIRE

This form is required and is not a substitute for the Real Estate Transfer Disclosure Statement. The seller completes the form to provide additional information about a property.

DISCLOSURE OF DEATH OR AIDS

While the Civil Code does not specifically require disclosure of a death upon the property, Section 1710.2 provides that the agent is not liable for failure to disclose to the buyer any deaths that occurred on the property more than three years before offers to purchase or lease the property. There is, therefore, an understanding that known deaths that occurred within the past three years should be disclosed. **AIDS disclosure** is unnecessary. An agent does not have to disclose that a former owner or resident ever had AIDS or died of AIDS. However, if a buyer asks a direct question concerning cause of deaths, the statute does not protect an agent from misrepresentation.

Stigmatized Property

Stigmatized property is property that may be perceived as undesirable for other than physical or environmental reasons. Besides murder or suicide, a house could be stigmatized by the fact that molestations occurred in the home, that the property has a reputation of being haunted, that satanic rituals had taken place there, or that the property has the reputation of being unlucky because of calamities that befell previous residents.

Because we don't know what a court will say should have been disclosed, as well as because disclosure is the right thing to do, if a fact or reputation could conceivably affect a buyer's decision, disclose it.

Licensed Care Facilities

Opinion 95-907 of the California Attorney General's Office makes it clear that a real estate agent need not disclose the location of a licensed care facility that serves six or fewer people. (A larger facility close to a property being sold would likely require disclosure.)

NATURAL HAZARDS DISCLOSURE

Earthquake Safety

As of January 1, 1993, the state law requires that when selling 1–4-unit residential properties built before January 1, 1960, you must disclose whether the dwelling has earthquake weaknesses. The California Seismic Safety Commission has published *The Homeowner's Guide to Earthquake Safety*, a booklet intended to help buyers, sellers, and real estate agents recognize some of the weaknesses in houses that affect earthquake safety. The buyers should sign that they have received the guide (Figure 3.4).

For all houses sold in California, an earthquake safety disclosure statement must be filled out and signed by the buyer and the seller. This disclosure statement is called the **Residential Earthquake Hazards Report** (Figure 3.5). The agent should prepare to answer the following seven questions, which are answered in the booklet on the pages noted:

1. What is a braced water heater? (page 6)

A braced water heater is one that has metal strips to attach it to the wall.

2. Is the house bolted to the foundation? (page 7)

If the house has a crawl space, you should be able to see the tops of the anchor bolts every 4 to 6 feet along the sill plate.

3. What is a cripple wall? (pages 8 and 9)

A cripple wall is a short wood wall on top of the foundation that creates a crawl space.

4. Is the foundation made of unreinforced masonry? (page 10)

Most brick and stone foundations are unreinforced. For concrete block, check the blocks on the top of the foundation. If they are hollow, the foundation probably is not reinforced. (Generally, steel rods are embedded in grout in the cells if the foundation is reinforced.)

FIGURE 3.4:   Earthquake Safety Client Card

To Whom It May Concern:	
I have received a copy of "The Homeowner's Guide to Earthquake Safety."	
Date:	(Signature)
Time:	(Printed Name)
Date:	(Signature)
Time:	(Printed Name)

FIGURE 3.5:   Residential Earthquake Hazards Report

RESIDENTIAL EARTHQUAKE HAZARDS REPORT

Prepared by: Agent _____   Phone _____
Broker _____   Email _____

NOTE: This form is used by a seller's agent on the sale of a one-to-four unit residential property built prior to 1960 to disclose to a buyer, together with a copy of the "Homeowner's Guide to Earthquake Safety," any potential earthquake weaknesses the property may have. [See ft Form 316-1; Calif. Government Code §§8897 et seq.]

Name _____   Assessor's Parcel No. _____
Street Address _____   Year Built _____
City _____, County _____, Zip Code _____

Answer these questions to the best of your knowledge. If you do not have actual knowledge as to whether the weakness exists, answer "Don't Know." If your house does not have the feature, answer "Doesn't Apply." The page numbers in the right-hand column indicate where in the "Homeowner's Guide to Earthquake Safety" you can find information on each of these features.

	Yes	No	Doesn't Apply	Don't Know	See Page
1. Is the water heater braced, strapped, or anchored to resist falling during an earthquake.	☐	☐	☐	☐	12
2. Is the house anchored or bolted to the foundation?	☐	☐	☐	☐	14
3. If the house has cripple walls:					
3.1 Are the exterior cripple walls braced?	☐	☐	☐	☐	16
3.2 If the exterior foundation consists of unconnected concrete piers and posts, have they been strengthened?	☐	☐	☐	☐	18
4. If the exterior foundation, or part of it, is made of unreinforced masonry, has it been strengthened?	☐	☐	☐	☐	20
5. If the house is built on a hillside:					
5.1 Are the exterior tall foundation walls braced?	☐	☐	☐	☐	22
5.2 Were the tall posts or columns either built to resist earthquakes or have they been strengthened?	☐	☐	☐	☐	22
6. If the exterior walls of the house, or part of them, are made of unreinforced masonry, have they been strengthened?	☐	☐	☐	☐	24
7. If the house has a living area over the garage, was the wall around the garage door opening either built to resist earthquakes or has it been strengthened?	☐	☐	☐	☐	26
8. Is the house outside an Alquist-Priolo Earthquake Fault Zone (zones immediately surrounding known earthquake faults)?	*Lines 8 and 9 to be reported on the Natural Hazards Disclosure Report*				36
9. Is the house outside a Seismic Hazard Zone (zone identified as susceptible to liquefaction or land sliding)?					36

If any of the questions are answered "No," the house is likely to have an earthquake weakness. Questions answered "Don't Know" may indicate a need for further evaluation. If you corrected one or more of these weaknesses, describe the work on a separate page. [See ft Form 250]

As Seller of the property described herein, I have answered the questions above to the best of my knowledge in an effort to disclose fully any potential earthquake weaknesses it may have.

EXECUTED BY:

_____   _____   _____, 20_____
(Seller)   (Seller)   (Date)

I acknowledge receipt of this form, completed and signed by Seller. I understand that if Seller has answered "No" to one or more questions, or if Seller has indicated a lack of knowledge, there may be one or more earthquake weaknesses in this house.

_____   _____   _____, 20_____
(Buyer)   (Buyer)   (Date)

This earthquake disclosure is made in addition to the standard real estate transfer disclosure statement also required by law. [See ft Forms 314 and 304]

©2015 RPI — Realty Publications, Inc.

5. If the house is on a hillside, two questions need to be answered: (1) Are the exterior tall foundation walls braced? (2) Were the tall posts or columns either built to resist earthquakes or have they been strengthened? (page 11)

If wall studs are without plywood sheathing, diagonal wood bracing, or steel bracing, the wall is not braced. Consult an engineer to determine if posts or unbraced walls need strengthening.

6. Are the exterior walls strengthened? (page 12)

If the house was built before 1940, walls are most likely not reinforced. You can check the house plans, which are probably on file with the building department. Otherwise, it could be difficult to determine if walls are reinforced. There are professional testing services that can determine the presence of steel in the walls.

7. If the house has a living area over the garage, was the wall around the garage door strengthened or built to resist earthquakes? (page 13) Check if there are braces or plywood panels around the garage-door opening. If the garage-door opening is in line with the rest of the house, additional bracing is probably not needed.

If these questions cannot readily be answered by a cursory inspection, the services of a professional inspector or engineer may be required.

Commercial Property Earthquake Hazards

Sellers or sellers' agents must give buyers a copy of the *Commercial Property Owner's Guide to Earthquake Safety* for sales or exchanges of any real property built of precast concrete or reinforced masonry walls with wood frame floors or roofs built before January 1, 1975, unless such property falls within an exemption category.

Natural Hazard Disclosure Statement

The Natural Hazards Disclosure Statement sets forth the following additional natural hazard disclosures that must be made on a statutory form when the property lies within one or more state mapped hazard zones. If the property is within a seismic hazard zone as shown by the state geologist, the fact must also be disclosed. Although sellers can take it upon themselves to make such disclosures, many transactions involve a third-party provider such as Property I.D. (www.propertyid.com) or Disclosure Source (www.disclosuresource.com) that interprets the maps for the sellers and makes the statutorily required disclosures to the buyer. These reports cost between $80 and $120, on average. (See Figure 3.6.)

- **Special flood hazard areas**—**Flood hazard areas** are indicated on maps published by the Federal Emergency Management Agency (FEMA). (Maps may be purchased from FEMA by calling 1-800-358-9616.) The seller's agent must disclose this to the buyer if the agent has knowledge that the property is in such a zone or if a list of areas has been posted in the county recorder's office, county assessor's office, and county planning agency.

FIGURE 3.6:   **Natural Hazard Disclosure Statement**

NATURAL HAZARD DISCLOSURE STATEMENT

Prepared by: Agent _____ **Phone** _____
Broker _____ **Email** _____

NOTE: The seller's listing broker (and the seller) must prepare a Natural Hazard Disclosure (NHD) and deliver it to prospective buyers of any property prior to making a purchase agreement offer and indicate compliance in the purchase agreement or a counteroffer. If not so disclosed, the buyer has the right to cancel the purchase agreement within three days of delivery of the disclosure in person. [Calif. Civil Code §1103.3]

DATE:_____, 20_____, at_____, California.

This disclosure statement is prepared for the following:

☐ Seller's listing agreement

☐ Purchase agreement

☐ Counteroffer

☐ _____

dated _____, 20_____, at _____, California,

entered into by _____, as the _____,

regarding real estate referred to as _____

_____.

Natural Hazard Disclosure Statement:

Seller and Seller's Agent(s) or a third-party consultant disclose the following information with the knowledge that even though this is not a warranty, prospective buyers may rely on this information in deciding whether and on what terms to purchase the subject property.

Seller hereby authorizes any agent(s) representing any principal(s) in this action to provide a copy of this statement to any person or entity in connection with any actual or anticipated sale of the property.

THE FOLLOWING ARE REPRESENTATIONS MADE BY SELLER AND SELLER'S AGENT(S) BASED ON THEIR KNOWLEDGE AND MAPS DRAWN BY THE STATE AND FEDERAL GOVERNMENT. THIS INFORMATION IS A DISCLOSURE AND IS NOT INTENDED TO BE PART OF ANY CONTRACT BETWEEN BUYER AND SELLER.

THIS REAL PROPERTY LIES WITHIN THE FOLLOWING HAZARDOUS AREA(S): (Check appropriate response)

1. A SPECIAL FLOOD HAZARD AREA (Any type Zone "A" or "V") designated by the Federal Emergency Management Agency.

    Yes____ No____ Do not know/information not available from local jurisdiction____

2. AN AREA OF POTENTIAL FLOODING shown on an inundation map pursuant to Section 8589.5 of the Government Code.

    Yes____ No____ Do not know/information not available from local jurisdiction____

3. A VERY HIGH FIRE HAZARD SEVERITY ZONE pursuant to Section 51178 or 51179 of the Government Code. The owner of this property is subject to the maintenance requirements of Section 51182 of the Government Code.

    Yes____ No____

4. A WILDLAND AREA THAT MAY CONTAIN SUBSTANTIAL FOREST FIRE RISKS AND HAZARDS pursuant to Section 4125 of the Public Resources Code. The owner of this property is subject to the maintenance requirements of Section 4291 of the Public Resources Code. Additionally, it is not the state's responsibility to provide fire protection services to any building or structure located within the wildlands unless the Department of Forestry and Fire Protection has entered into a cooperative agreement with the local agency for those purposes pursuant to Section 4142 of the Public Resources Code.

    Yes____ No____

5. AN EARTHQUAKE FAULT ZONE pursuant to Section 2622 of the Public Resources Code.

    Yes____ No____

— — — — — — — — — — — — — — — — *PAGE ONE OF TWO — FORM 314* — — — — — — — — — — — — — — — — — —

FIGURE 3.6 (continued):   Natural Hazard Disclosure Statement

— — — — — — — — — — — — — — — — — — *PAGE TWO OF TWO — FORM 314* — — — — — — — — — — — — — — — — — — —

6. A SEISMIC HAZARD ZONE pursuant to Section 2696 of the Public Resources Code.

Yes (Landslide Zone)_____   Yes (Liquefaction Zone)_____

No_____   Map not yet released by state_____

THESE HAZARDS MAY LIMIT YOUR ABILITY TO DEVELOP THE REAL PROPERTY, TO OBTAIN INSURANCE OR TO RECEIVE ASSISTANCE AFTER A DISASTER.

THE MAPS ON WHICH THESE DISCLOSURES ARE BASED ESTIMATE WHERE NATURAL HAZARDS EXIST. THEY ARE NOT DEFINITIVE INDICATORS OF WHETHER OR NOT A PROPERTY WILL BE AFFECTED BY A NATURAL DISASTER. BUYER(S) AND SELLER(S) MAY WISH TO OBTAIN PROFESSIONAL ADVICE REGARDING THOSE HAZARDS AND OTHER HAZARDS THAT MAY AFFECT THE PROPERTY.

Check only one of the following:

☐ Seller and their agent represent that the information herein is true and correct to the best of their knowledge as of the date signed by Seller and Seller's Agent.

☐ Seller and their agent acknowledge that they have exercised good faith in the selection of a third-party report provider as required in Civil Code Section 1103.7, and that the representations made in this Natural Hazard Disclosure Statement are based upon information provided by the independent third-party disclosure provider as a substituted disclosure pursuant to Civil Code Section 1103.4. Neither Seller nor their agent has independently verified the information contained in this statement and report or is personally aware of any errors or inaccuracies in the information contained on the statement. This statement was prepared by

Third-Party Disclosure Provider_____ Date _____

Date:_____, 20_____   Date:_____, 20_____

Seller: _____   Seller's Broker: _____BRE #_____

Seller: _____   Agent: _____BRE #_____

Buyer represents that he has read and understands this document. Pursuant to Civil Code Section 1103.8, the representations made in this Natural Hazard Disclosure Statement do not constitute all of Seller's or Seller's Agent's disclosure obligations in this transaction.

Buyer:_____ Date: _____

Buyer:_____ Date: _____

FORM 314   11-13   ©2013 **first tuesday**, P.O. BOX 5707, RIVERSIDE, CA 92517 (800) 794-0494

©2015 RPI — Realty Publications, Inc.

■ **Areas of potential flooding**—These areas are subject to possible flooding, as shown on a dam failure map. Disclosure must be made if the seller or the seller's agent has knowledge of the designation or a list of properties, including seller's property, has been posted at the county recorder's office, county assessor's office, and county planning agency. (**Note:** If an owner has received federal flood disaster assistance, then the seller must notify the purchaser of the requirement to obtain and maintain flood insurance.)

- **Very high fire hazard zones**—The state has imposed in these **fire hazard areas** fire protection requirements that subject owners to property maintenance requirements.

- **State fire responsibility areas**—These are areas where the state not only sets protection requirements but also has primary firefighting responsibility. This disclosure must be made if the seller or the seller's agent has actual knowledge of this designation or the local agency has a map that includes the seller's property that has been posted at county recorder's office, assessor's office, and planning agency.

- **Wildland area that may contain substantial fire risks and hazards**—Unless the Department of Forestry enters into a cooperative contract, the state is not responsible for fire protection services within wildland areas. The seller must make this disclosure if the seller or the seller's agent has knowledge that the property is in a designated area or if maps showing the property to be in such an area is posted at the office of the country recorder, county assessor, and county planning agency.

WEB LINK

- **Earthquake fault zone as indicated on maps**—Maps can be obtained online through www.consrv.ca.gov/CGS.

- **Seismic hazard zone**—An earthquake in such a zone could result in strong shaking, soil liquefaction, or landslides. The seller or the seller's agent must disclose to the buyer that the property is in such a zone if the seller or the seller's agent has actual knowledge that the property is in such a zone or that maps showing the property is in such a zone have been posted at the offices of the county recorder, county assessor, and county planning agency. **Note:** If upon looking at a map, a reasonable person cannot tell with certainty if a property is within a designated area, then the Natural Hazards Disclosure Statement should be marked "Yes."

Landslide Inventory Report

WEB LINK

A California Geological Survey developed highway corridor landslide hazard maps. The maps provide an inventory of hillside activity along selected corridors. Maps may be downloaded from www.conservation.ca.gov/cgs/rghm/landslides. While there is not a specific requirement for this report, because the potential for landslides or mudflows is a material fact, these potential dangers should be revealed to prospective buyers.

ENVIRONMENTAL HAZARDS DISCLOSURE

California legislation mandates **environmental hazards disclosure** (Civil Code 25417) to inform homeowners and prospective homeowners about environmental hazards located on and affecting residential property. The seller seldom knows if there are any environmental hazards. Thus, a statement that the seller is unaware of environmental hazards is not a guarantee that the property is free of such hazards. It is in the seller's and the future buyer's interest to know what hazards are common, where they might be found, and how they might be alleviated.

California's Environmental Hazards Booklet

The Real Estate Transfer Disclosure Statement specifies environmental hazards. By providing the booklet *Environmental Hazards: A Guide for Homeowners, Buyers, Landlords, and Tenants*, neither the seller nor the seller's agent need furnish the buyer any more information concerning hazards unless the seller or the agent have actual knowledge of environmental hazards concerning the property.

Hazardous Substances Released

Health and Safety Code Section 25359.7(a) requires **hazardous waste disclosure**. Owners of nonresidential property must give prior notice to buyers or lessees if they know of the release of hazardous substances on the property or if they have reasonable cause to believe hazardous substances exist on or beneath the property. *Brownfields* is a term used to describe contaminated soil.

Tenants are required to notify landlords (both residential and nonresidential) of hazardous substances that they know have been released or believe to exist on or beneath the property. Failure to disclose constitutes a default under the lease.

Lead-Based Paint

The seller or the lessor of residential property built before 1978 must deliver to prospective buyers or tenants the booklet ***Protect Your Family from Lead in Your Home***, which was prepared by the federal Environmental Protection Agency.

Providing the California booklet *Environmental Hazards: A Guide for Homeowners, Buyers, Landlords, and Tenants* meets the federal requirement.

Owners must disclose to their agents, as well as prospective buyers and tenants, the presence of known lead-based-paint hazards. Any available records or reports as to lead-based paint must be provided.

Landlords who receive any federal subsidies or have federally related loans, when confronted with deteriorating paint in a pre-1978 housing unit, must alert tenants to the possible health dangers and use government-certified workers and special containment practices to minimize risk of public exposure. As it relates to lead-based paint, the EPA started enforcement of a new rule on October 1, 2010. This new rule requires that contractors and maintenance professionals working in pre-1978 housing be certified, that their employees be trained, and that they follow protective work practice standards.

This applies to renovation, repair, or painting activities affecting more than 6 square feet of lead-based paint in a room or more than 20 square feet of lead-based paint on the exterior.

WEB LINK

Visit www.epa.gov/lead for more information.

Environmental Hazards Booklet

The Bureau of Real Estate and the Department of Health Services have prepared a booklet for homeowners and buyers called *Residential Environmental Hazards*. This booklet is distributed by the California Association of REALTORS®, as well as other form providers, for use by real estate agents to fully disclose environmental hazard issues to prospective buyers. The booklet contains approximately38 pages to be read by buyers, who should sign a form signifying that they have received the booklet. Inside the back cover is a tear-out sheet (Figure 3.7) to be signed by the buyer(s) and retained in the broker's files.

Under the mandated disclosure of environmental hazards, it is important for brokers to have copies of these tear-outs in their files. Sales agents should make their own photocopies to keep in their personal escrow files. The booklet is divided into six sections and two appendixes. The sections are as follows:

- Asbestos
- Formaldehyde
- Lead
- Radon
- Hazardous Waste
- Household Hazardous Wastes

The appendixes contain the following:

- A list of federal and state agencies
- A glossary of terms

All agents should obtain copies of this booklet and familiarize themselves with the six basic topics. You will be asked questions by your buyers and sellers, and every buyer must be given a copy of the booklet.

(**Note:** The above could place a significant financial burden on an owner, and this burden is not limited to 1–4-unit residential properties.)

FIGURE 3.7:   Environmental Hazards Client Card

To Whom It May Concern:

I have received a copy of "Environmental Hazards: A Guide for Homeowners, Buyers, Landlords, and Tenants" from the Broker(s) in this transaction.

Date: _____   _____
                                   (Signature)

Time: _____   _____
                                   (Printed Name)

Date: _____   _____
                                   (Signature)

Time: _____   _____
                                   (Printed Name)

Water Contamination

Well water has been seriously contaminated in many areas of California by industrial, agricultural, farming, and military operations. Many wells have been capped. Besides arsenic from mining, there are countless insecticides and chemicals of all types that were not known to be harmful when discharged.

Perchlorate, the primary ingredient of solid rocket fuel, is believed to be particularly dangerous to health. It alters hormonal balances (thyroid) and impedes metabolism and brain development. The EPA has urged the Pentagon to conduct widespread testing, but the Defense Department has resisted.

If an agent knows of problems in a water supply or a house has its own well in an area where water contamination has been found, then the broker has a duty to provide the information to a prospective buyer.

Sick Building Syndrome

Many modern commercial buildings have sealed windows and receive fresh air through their ventilation systems. Some of these buildings have developed what is known as **sick building syndrome (SBS)**. Common tenant complaints include headaches; eye, nose, and throat irritations; dry cough; dry or itchy skin; dizziness; nausea; difficulty concentrating; fatigue; and sensitivity to odors. The problems relate to time spent in the building, and most sufferers report relief soon after leaving the building.

SBS problems may be located in the entire building or just in one area. A problem with SBS is that a specific cause is not known, although it appears to be related to inadequate ventilation. Corrective action has been to increase ventilation and to clean the ventilation system.

If an agent knows that a property has a reputation as a sick building, the agent should reveal this fact. Failure to do so could expose the agent to significant liability. However, specific SBS disclosure is not mandated by law.

SUBDIVISION DISCLOSURE

There are a number of disclosures that relate to subdivisions.

Public Report

The purpose of the California Subdivided Lands Law is to protect purchasers in new subdivisions from fraud. A disclosure known as a **public report** must be provided to purchasers, who must sign that they have received and accepted the report before they are bound to complete the purchase. The California Real Estate Commissioner must approve the public report, which simply discloses information on the project such as location, size of the offering, identity of the subdivider, the interest to be conveyed, and provisions for handling deposits, purchase money, taxes, and assessments. Also included are use restrictions, unusual costs that a buyer will have to bear at time of purchase, hazards, adverse environmental findings, special permits required, utility availability, and so forth. A public report is good up to five years from date of issuance.

The Real Estate Commissioner may issue a preliminary public report that is good for one year or until the public report is issued, whichever occurs first. A subdivider can accept a deposit with a reservation if there is a preliminary public report, but the purchaser is not obligated until signing that he accepts the public report.

A conditional public report that allows the subdivider to enter into a binding contract can be issued, but the escrow cannot be closed until issuance of the public report. The conditional public report period cannot exceed six months and may be renewed for one six-month period. If the public report is not issued within this period or if the purchaser is not satisfied with the final public report because of material changes, the purchaser is entitled to the full refund of any deposit.

COMMON INTEREST SUBDIVISION

A **common interest subdivision** is a subdivision in which owners own or lease a separate lot or unit together with an undivided interest in the common areas of the project. These common areas usually are governed by a **homeowners association (HOA)**.

In the sale of a common interest subdivision, along with the public report, the purchaser must be given a brochure published by the Bureau of Real Estate titled *Common Interest Development General Information*. In addition, and before transfer of title, owners of condominiums, community apartment projects, cooperatives, and planned unit developments must provide purchasers with a copy of the covenants, conditions, and restrictions; bylaws; and articles of incorporation, plus an owners association financial statement, including the current assessments, late charges, plans on change in assessments, and any delinquent assessments and costs. (A homeowners association must furnish the owner a copy of the latest version of documents within 10 days of request by the owner. Only a reasonable fee beyond actual costs may be charged for this.)

Upon request, HOAs must provide an estimate of the fee for providing prospective buyers with governance documents and required disclosures. The fee must be based on actual costs to the HOA, which cannot bundle nonmandatory documents with the required documents to increase the fee. There cannot be an additional fee for electronic delivery of documents. In addition to required disclosures, 12 months of minutes of the HOA meetings must be supplied upon request.

> For common interest subdivisions, buyers must be provided information about restrictions and the homeowners association (HOA).

If there is an age restriction, a statement must be included that it is only enforceable to the extent permitted by law (citing applicable law).

If there is a drought state of emergency declared by the governor or local government, a homeowners association may not fine a homeowner for reduced watering or ceasing to water plants. If recycled water is used, the association can still fine the owner for not keeping up landscaping. HOA prohibitions on replacing turf with low-water-use plants are void and unenforceable.

Homeowners associations cannot prohibit an owner from keeping one pet (subject to reasonable restrictions), nor can they prohibit solar panels or enforce any prohibition on water-efficient plantings.

Homeowners associations, as well as landlords, cannot prohibit tenants from personal agriculture in portable containers but can specify container requirements.

Civil Code Section 1360.2 requires sellers of common interest developments to disclose whether rental restrictions exist. The code also prohibits an HOA from placing rental restrictions that limit existing owners. Restrictions added to the CC&Rs can apply only to subsequent buyers.

If the association plans to sue or has commenced an action against the developer for damages, the construction defects must be listed. If a settlement has been reached regarding construction defects, the defects to be corrected must be described, and an estimate of when the work will be completed, as well as status of other defects, must be provided to the buyer.

Homeowners associations can record a lien against a member's property for unpaid assessments if the amount exceeds $1,800. There is a 90-day redemption period after lien foreclosure.

Condominium Conversion Notice

When a developer intends to convert an apartment to individual ownership, the developer must notify current and prospective tenants of the intent, the public hearings, and the right to purchase their unit.

Interstate Land Sales Full Disclosure Act

This federal act requires disclosures for interstate sale of remote unimproved lots for subdivisions of 25 or more parcels. The act, which was enacted to prevent fraud, requires disclosures as to title, location, facilities, utilities availability and charges, and soil conditions. After receiving a copy of the property report, the prospective purchaser has a seven-calendar-day *cooling-off period* in which to cancel the transaction.

California Land Project

Similar to the Interstate Act, the California Act applies to 50 or more unimproved parcels in low population density areas. The purchaser must be informed of the 14-day right to cancel the purchase (seven days for federal).

FINANCING DISCLOSURE

There are a number of broker, as well as lender, disclosures relating to financing.

Seller Financing Disclosure

Financial disclosure involving seller carryback financing of 1–4-unit residential properties was one of the first mandated disclosures. In the 1970s, the term *creative financing* became very popular, and in most cases, it meant the seller was to *carry back* (accept a note for part of the purchase price secured by a wraparound or junior mortgage, deed of trust, or contract for deed) a second or third trust deed on the property just sold. Although much of this creative financing was an honest attempt to sell the seller's property and provide a win-win situation for both the buyer and the seller, some agents were not prudent in their judgment. If the seller had to foreclose on the buyer, the payments on the home often were so high that the seller could not handle the foreclosure and would lose the equity in the note she was carrying.

Unethical or unsophisticated agents and buyers developed *walk-away financing* in the late 1970s and early 1980s. An unethical purchaser would convince the seller and his agent to let the purchaser buy the property with a low down payment and then borrow on the property and let the buyer pull cash out. The buyer would make no payments on the property and would let the seller and the lenders reclaim the overencumbered property. Of course, the seller would be on the "short end of the stick."

This kind of financing and the complaints stemming from the victims helped enact Civil Code Sections 2956–2967, which became law on July 1, 1983. These statutes require disclosure of seller carryback financing on 1–4 unit residential property in the **Seller Financing Addendum and Disclosure Statement**. The disclosure must be made to both the buyer and the seller, and the units do not have to be owner-occupied for the statute to govern.

Many items and facts must be disclosed, including these major items:

- The terms of the note, such as original loan amount, interest rate, and term (number of payments)

■ All other liens on the property: the original loan amount, current balance, interest rate and any provisions for variations in the interest rate, term, balloon payments, maturity date, and whether any payments are currently in default

■ That the note, if not fully amortized, will have to be refinanced at maturity and that this might be difficult or impossible to accomplish in the conventional marketplace (If balloon payments are called for, the seller [holder of the note] must notify [send or deliver to] the buyer not less than 60 days or more than 150 days before the due date of the note. The notice must specify to whom payment is due, the due date, and the exact amount due [or a good-faith estimate], including the unpaid balance, interest, and other allowable charges.)

■ That loans have or will have negative amortization, or that deferred interest ARMs (adjustable-rate mortgages) could have negative amortization, must be clearly disclosed and its potential effects explained (negative amortization means that the monthly payments are less than the monthly interest on the loan, with the result that the borrower ends up owing more than the original loan amount)

■ Who is liable for the payoff of the underlying loan in an all-inclusive trust deed (AITD) if the lender accelerates the loan

■ The buyer's creditworthiness (credit report, job verification, etc.)

■ A request for notice of default filed and recorded for the seller to help protect the seller in case any senior loans are foreclosed

■ That a title insurance policy will be obtained and furnished to both buyer and seller

■ That a tax service has been arranged to notify the seller whether property taxes have been paid on the property and who will be responsible for the continued service and compensation of the tax service, and that arrangements have been made to notify the seller if the casualty insurance payments are being paid

■ That the deed of trust securing the note will be recorded, thus avoiding the problems of not recording the trust deed

■ The amount, source of funds, and purpose of the funds when the buyer is to receive cash from the proceeds of the transaction

Remember that the items above represent only a condensed version of the financing disclosure law. How disclosure must be made on the forms is shown in California Civil Code Sections 2956-2967.

Adjustable-Rate Loan Disclosure

Lenders offering an adjustable-rate residential mortgage must provide prospective borrowers the most recent copy of the Federal Reserve publication *Consumer Handbook on Adjustable-Rate Mortgages*.

Blanket Encumbrance Disclosure

If there is an underlying blanket encumbrance that affects more than one parcel, the buyer's funds should be protected unless the unit can be released from the blanket encumbrance. The borrower must be made aware of and sign a notice that her interests could be lost if the holder of the blanket encumbrance forecloses, even though the borrower is current on his or her obligations.

Mortgage Loan Disclosure Statement

When a real estate broker solicits or negotiates loans that are not federally related on behalf of lenders or borrowers, the broker must deliver a mortgage loan disclosure statement (MLDS) to the borrower within three business days of receiving the borrower's written loan application. For federally related loans, the Real Estate Settlement Procedures Act (RESPA) disclosures apply.

Lender/Purchaser Disclosure

This disclosure applies to private-party lenders and pension plans that make or purchase loans through a broker. The broker must provide a disclosure statement as to loan terms and loan status, as well as information about the property securing the loan and other encumbrances.

Borrower's Right to Copy of Appraisal

If the borrower paid for the appraisal, a lender must notify the borrower that the borrower can request and receive a copy of the appraisal report.

TILA-RESPA Rule

The Real Estate Settlement Procedures Act applies to federally related loans for 1–4-unit residential properties. The lender must furnish the buyer with a **Loan Estimate** form showing estimated closing and loan costs within three days of receiving the application and not less than seven days prior to consummation, as well as a booklet called *Your Home Loan Toolkit* within three days of application. Federally related loans include loans made by federally regulated lenders, lenders having federally insured deposits, loans that will be federally insured or guaranteed, and loans that are to be resold to Fannie Mae or Freddie Mac. There must be a justifiable service for every charge made. An administrative fee cannot be charged because it is not for a service performed.

RESPA allows a **controlled business arrangement** where a broker has a financial interest in a service provider. However, the relationship of the broker and the service provider must be fully disclosed, and the buyer must be free to use providers of other service, such as escrow services and loan brokerage services.

Integrated Disclosures

A number of disclosures have been combined as a result of requirements of the Dodd-Frank Wall Street Reform and Consumer Protection Act of 2010 to simplify RESPA and truth-in-lending disclosures. The disclosures have been combined into the following two forms, which are covered in Unit 12:

1. Loan estimate

2. Closing Disclosure

Lender Compensation Disclosure

A broker must reveal to all parties to a transaction if the broker is to receive any compensation from a lender before the transaction closes escrow. **Note:** California law prohibits a broker from receiving referral fees from service providers.

Notice of Transfer of Loan Servicing

For loans secured by 1–4-unit residential properties, the borrower must be notified when the loan servicing function (collection) is transferred.

Consumer Caution and Home Ownership Counseling Notice

This notice must be given to applicants for a covered loan no later than three days before signing loan documents. It warns borrowers they are placing a lien on their home and could lose their home and all their equity. A covered loan is a consumer loan for a 1-4 residential unit building that is the principal residence of the consumer and where the original principal balance does not exceed the current conforming loan (loans that can be purchased by Freddie Mac or Fannie Mae)

Truth in Lending Act (Regulation Z)

This federal consumer protection act requires advertising disclosure of finance charges. Interest expressed as an annual percentage rate (APR) and terms of credit, if trigger terms, are used in the advertisement (see Unit 8). Before a borrower is obligated to complete designated loans, there must be full credit disclosure.

Notice of Adverse Action (Equal Credit Opportunity Act)

When a creditor denies a loan applicant, the creditor must provide a statement of reason for the denial or the applicant's right to obtain such a statement. Generally, this must be provided within 30 days of loan application.

Holden Act Disclosure

At the time of the loan application, borrowers must be notified of the prohibition against lender discriminatory practices and their rights under the law. The act prohibits refusing to lend in designated areas (redlining).

OTHER DISCLOSURES

Methamphetamine Contamination Order

Sellers or landlords must provide buyers and tenants with a copy of the cleanup order for contaminated structures. (**Note:** the cleanup order, not the fact of the contamination, must be disclosed.)

Megan's Law

Megan's Law provides for registration of sex offenders and public availability of knowledge regarding the location of these offenders. Now, every sales contract or lease of 1–4-unit residential properties must include a notice informing buyers or lessees of the public availability of this information on the database website, www.meganslaw.ca.gov.

WEB LINK

Elder Abuse Disclosure

California's Elder Abuse Law requires that escrow holders, realty agents, and others report elder financial abuse, fraud, or undue influence. The county public guardian is authorized to take control of the elder's assets to prevent abuse. If an agent feels that an elderly person is being financially abused, reporting the abuse is mandatory.

Mello-Roos Bond Disclosure

Mello-Roos bonds are municipal-type bonds issued to fund streets, sewers, and so forth for a new development. The bonds shift the expenses from the developer to each homebuyer, who must pay an assessment to retire the bond. The net effect is higher taxes for the homebuyer.

A broker must disclose to a buyer that a project is subject to a Mello-Roos levy for a sale or lease for more than five years. Failure to give notice before signing the sales contract (or lease) gives the buyer or the tenant a three-day right of rescission after receipt of the notice.

Structural Pest Control Inspection and Certification Reports

While the law does not require a **structural pest control inspection**, if required by contract or lender, a copy must be delivered to the buyer, and a copy must be filed with the state Structural Pest Control Board. Section 1 of the report covers visible evidence of active termite infestation, while section 2 covers conditions likely to lead to infestation. (When lender requires clearance, it refers to section 1.)

Septic System Disclosure

The disclosure is required when property is not presently connected to a sewer. The purchaser is alerted to the fact that an inspection may not discover latent defects. The buyer is also made aware of the fact that should a sewer connection be required in the future, the owner will have additional expenses.

Energy Conservation Retrofit and Thermal Insulation Disclosures

Some communities require energy retrofitting as a condition of sale. The seller or the agent should disclose the requirements of local statutes. New-home sellers must disclose in their sales contracts the type, thickness, and R-value of the insulation.

Foreign Investment Real Property Tax Act

The buyer must be informed about the IRS withholding requirement of 10% of the gross sales price when the seller is a foreign person. (See Unit 14 for exemptions.)

The buyer must be informed about the California requirement to withhold 31/3% of the total sale price paid as state income tax. (See Unit 14 for details about this requirement and its exemptions.)

Notice Regarding Advisability of Title Insurance

If no title insurance is to be issued through an escrow, the buyer must receive a separate notice about the advisability of obtaining title insurance. (See Civil Code Section 1057.6.)

Importance of Home Inspection Notice

For the sale of 1–4-unit residential properties (including mobile homes) involving FHA financing or HUD-owned property, the borrower must sign a **home inspection notice** titled The Importance of a Home Inspection.

Smoke Detector Notice

A buyer of a single-family home must receive a **smoke detector disclosure** written statement indicating that the property is in compliance with current California law regarding the presence of smoke detectors. The issuance of a building permit triggers a requirement to update smoke detectors (10 year nonremovable battery).

Carbon Monoxide Detector Notice

Every residential unit that has fossil-fuel heating must have a carbon monoxide detector, and a seller disclosure of the presence or absence of a detector is required.

Window Security Bars

A seller must disclose, on the Real Estate Transfer Disclosure Statement, the presence of **window security bars** and any safety release mechanism on the bars.

Water Heater Bracing

Sellers of real property must certify to prospective purchasers that the **water heater bracing** has been properly installed.

Water Conservancy Plumbing Fixtures

By 2017, single-family residences built before 1994 must be equipped with water conservancy fixtures. By 2019, all multifamily units must have water conservancy fixtures. For property altered or improved after 2014, water conservancy fixtures must be a condition of final permit approval (low-flow toilets, showerheads, and faucets).

Starting in 2017, sellers of single-family residences must disclose to buyers the requirements of plumbing fixtures and whether or not the unit includes noncompliant plumbing. For multifamily units, the disclosure requirement begins in 2019.

Home Energy Rating System (HERS)

The homeseller or the broker must inform the buyer of the existence of the California Whole-House Home Energy Rating Program. Providing the Home Energy Rating System booklet meets the disclosure requirements.

Nonresidential Energy Use Disclosure

To encourage energy efficiency use, owners must disclose the energy consumption to prospective buyers, lessers, and lenders.

Supplemental Tax Bill Disclosure

Residential sellers must disclose to buyers in writing to expect supplemental tax reassessment bills.

Industrial/Airport Disclosure

Sellers of 1–4-unit residential properties must disclose any actual knowledge of airport or industrial use or zoning that could affect the property. Airport noise disclosure has been added to the California Transfer Disclosure Statement.

Farming Area Disclosure

Developers and residential sellers must disclose if property is within 1 mile of a farming operation.

Notice of Mining Operation

If property is within 1 mile of a mining operation, notice must be given.

Gas or Hazardous Liquid Transmission Lines

The sale of 1-4 residential units requires the disclosure of gas or hazardous liquid transmission lines in the vicinity.

Military Ordnance Location

If a transferor has knowledge that a property is within 1 mile of a former **military ordnance location** (military training ground) that may contain explosives, the transferor must disclose in writing that these former federal or state locations may contain potentially explosive ammunition. (the buyer has a statutory right of rescission.)

Commissions

A notice must be given to the party paying any real estate commission that commissions are negotiable. This notice must be in a font not less than 10 points and in bold typeface.

Renter Notice of Foreclosure

Civil Code Section 2924.85 requires that rental applicants be given notice that the owner has received a notice of default and that there is a pending foreclosure.

RIGHT OF RESCISSION

> For detailed California disclosure requirements, check the Bureau of Real Estate website: www.bre.ca.gov.

There are statutory **rescission rights** for a number of transactions. Buyers (or borrowers) must be informed of their rights. Failure to disclose rights of rescission extends this right.

Truth in Lending Act—When a loan for consumer credit is secured by a borrower's residence, a rescission right exists until midnight of the third business day following the completion of the loan.

Interstate Land Sales Full Disclosure Act—This federal act calls for a disclosure statement, known as a *property report*, for subdivisions of 25 or more unimproved residential properties of less than 5 acres each that are sold in interstate commerce. Besides the required disclosures to the purchasers, the purchasers have a seven-day right of rescission.

California land projects—Have a 14-day right of rescission.

Time-share—Because of abusive sales tactics of many time-share developers, purchasers of time-shares now have a rescission right of three days after signing the contract.

Undivided interest subdivision—An undivided interest subdivision is one where the owners are tenants in common with the other owners but don't have an exclusive possessory interest in a particular unit or space. An example is a campground where owners have a right to use a space if available. Purchasers in undivided interest subdivisions have a three-day right of rescission following the day the agreement is signed.

Home equity sales—Because of fraud and unfair dealings by home equity purchasers, a homeowner has a rescission right when selling her equity interest in a residence in foreclosure. There is a right to cancel any contract with an equity purchaser until midnight of the fifth business day following the sales agreement or until 8 am on the day of the sale, whichever occurs first.

Mello-Roos disclosure—Failure to disclose the fact that a property is in a Mello-Roos district would allow the transferee a three- to five-day right of rescission.

BRE DISCLOSURE BOOKLET AND CALIFORNIA ASSOCIATION OF REALTORS® DISCLOSURE CHART

To aid members in understanding the numerous disclosure obligations that real estate professionals should be aware of, the California Association of REALTORS® has prepared a California Real Estate Law Disclosure Chart. This chart is included as Figure 3.8.

California Bureau of Real Estate Disclosure Booklet—The Bureau of Real Estate publishes a booklet titled *Disclosures in Real Property Transactions*. It may be purchased from the BRE or viewed and downloaded free at www.dre.ca.gov/files/pdf/re6.pdf. In Unit 10, you will find that the purchase contract includes many of the required disclosures.

WEB LINK

FIGURE 3.8:   **List of Disclosures**

(The following form is copyrighted by the California Association of REAL-TORS®, © 2014, and is reprinted under a limited license with permission. Photocopying or any other reproduction, whether electronic or otherwise, is strictly prohibited.)

 CALIFORNIA
ASSOCIATION
OF REALTORS®

Summary Disclosure Chart

Member Legal Services
Tel (213) 739-8282
Fax (213) 480-7724
December 19, 2014 (revised)

The Summary Disclosure Chart is designed to provide REALTORS® and their clients with an easy-to-use reference guide for determining the applicability of the state and federal laws to real estate transactions most commonly handled by real estate licensees.

The Summary Disclosure Chart provides a disclosure "trigger" as well as a brief summary of the disclosure requirement, but does not cover all disclosures required by law. More detailed information regarding disclosure and other legal topics is available to C.A.R. members on car.org.

For a quick answer to required disclosures based on the type of property (residential one-to-four units, residential five or more units, commercial property or vacant land, and manufactured or mobile homes, see the **Sales Disclosure Chart**. For information on lease and rental transactions, please refer to the legal chart, **Lease/Rental Disclosure Chart**. For the disclosure requirements involving homes in a new subdivision, please refer to legal chart, **New Home Disclosure Chart**. For the disclosure requirements for foreclosure sales or sales of REO property, see the legal chart, **REO Disclosure Chart**.

For additional disclosure requirements when selling a property in a common interest development, please refer to legal article, **Condominium or Other Common Interest Development Disclosures**.

SUBJECT	DISCLOSURE TRIGGER	DISCLOSURE REQUIREMENT (Brief Summary) FORM	C.A.R. INFORMATION SOURCE LAW CITATION
Advisability of Title Insurance	An escrow transaction for the purchase or simultaneous exchange of real property where a policy of title insurance will <u>not</u> be issued to the buyer.	The buyer must receive the statutory notice. The law does not specify who is responsible for providing this notice. Typically handled by escrow agent.	Cal. Civ. Code § 1057.6.

FIGURE 3.8 (continued): **List of Disclosures**

SUBJECT	DISCLOSURE TRIGGER	DISCLOSURE REQUIREMENT (Brief Summary) FORM	C.A.R. INFORMATION SOURCE LAW CITATION
Agency Disclosure (Education Form) and Agency Confirmation (Who Represents Each Party)	Sale[2] of residential real property of 1-4 units and mobile homes, commercial, vacant land and industrial property, but not residential income of 5 units or more; lease for a term of over one year on the above referenced property.	The buyer must receive the agency disclosure form (AD) from the buyer's agent prior to signing the offer. The seller must receive the agency disclosure form (AD) from the seller's agent prior to signing the listing contract and must receive another agency disclosure form (AD) from the buyer's agent prior to accepting the buyer's offer. The agency confirmation form must be given to the buyer and seller "as soon as practicable." This can be accomplished either by having the language in the purchase agreement or by using a separate form (AC-6). C.A.R. forms AD (disclosure) and AC-6 (confirmation).	Legal Q&As, **Agency Disclosure and Confirmation**, and **Agency Laws Summary Chart** Cal. Civ. Code §§ 2079.13 *et seq.*
Airport in Vicinity	NHD report is completed by third-party disclosure company	The NHD expert must determine if the property is located within an "airport influence area" as defined in Business & Professions Code § 1010(b). If so, the report must contain a statutory statement, *Notice of Airport in Vicinity.*	Cal. Civ. Code § 1103.4(c)(1).
Area of Potential Flooding (in the event of dam or reservoir failure)	Sale of all real property if the seller or the seller's agent has actual knowledge or a list has been compiled by parcel and the notice posted at a local county recorder, assessor and planning agency. Also applies to manufactured homes and personal property mobile homes.	The seller's agent or the seller without an agent must disclose to the buyer if the property is in this Area of Potential Flooding as designated on an inundation map, if a parcel list has been prepared by the county and a notice identifying the location of the list is available at the county assessor, county recorder or county planning	Legal Q&A, **Natural Hazard Disclosure Statement** Cal. Gov't Code §§ 8589.4, 8589.5; Cal. Civ. Code § 1103.

FIGURE 3.8 (continued):   List of Disclosures

SUBJECT	DISCLOSURE TRIGGER	DISCLOSURE REQUIREMENT (Brief Summary) FORM	C.A.R. INFORMATION SOURCE LAW CITATION
		commission office, or if the seller or seller's agent has actual knowledge that the property is in an area. If a TDS is required in the transaction, either C.A.R. Form NHD, *Natural Hazard Disclosure Statement* or an updated Local Option disclosure form must be used to make this disclosure.	
Broker's Statutory Duty to Inspect Property	Sale [3] of all residential real property of 1-4 units (No exemptions except for never-occupied properties where a public report is required or properties exempt from a public report pursuant to Business & Professions Code § 11010.4) Also applies to manufactured and personal property mobile homes.	A real estate licensee must conduct a reasonably competent and diligent visual inspection of the property; this inspection duty does not include areas which are reasonably and normally inaccessible, off the site, or public records or permits concerning the title or use of the property; this inspection duty includes only the unit for sale and not the common areas of a condo or other common interest development. There is no requirement that the inspection report be in writing; however, it is recommended that all licensees put it in writing. C.A.R. Form TDS (or for mobile homes and manufactured housing, C.A.R. Form MHTDS) may be used. If the seller is exempt from the TDS, then C.A.R. Form AVID may be used by the agent.	Legal Q&A, **Real Estate Licensee's Duty to Inspect Residential Property** Cal. Civ. Code §§ 2079 *et seq.*
Carbon Monoxide Detector Disclosure & Compliance	The Carbon Monoxide Poisoning Prevention Act of 2010 requires a carbon monoxide detector device (battery or hard-wired) to be	The C.A.R. Forms TDS and MHTDS add a disclosure regarding these devices. No separate disclosure form is required.	Cal. Civ. Code §§ 1102.6, 1102.6d. Note: Installation is not a precondition

3

FIGURE 3.8 (continued):   List of Disclosures

SUBJECT	DISCLOSURE TRIGGER	DISCLOSURE REQUIREMENT (Brief Summary) FORM	C.A.R. INFORMATION SOURCE LAW CITATION
	installed in all dwelling units. Existing single-family units must have the device installed on or before July 1, 2011 and all other existing dwelling units must have the device installed by Jan. 1, 2013. See manufacturer instructions for the number of devices and location of installation.		of sale or transfer of the dwelling.
Commercial Property Owner's Guide to Earthquake Safety	Mandatory delivery: Sale, transfer, or exchange of any real property or manufactured home or mobile home if built of precast concrete or reinforced/unreinforced masonry with wood frame floors or roofs and built before Jan. 1, 1975, located within a county or city, if not exempt. Almost same exemptions as from Transfer Disclosure Statement.[11] Additional exemption if the buyer agrees, in writing, to demolish the property within one year from date of transfer. Voluntary delivery: Transfer of [4] any real property.	Mandatory delivery: The transferor/transferor's agent must give the transferee a copy of *The Commercial Property Owner's Guide to Earthquake Safety.* [5] Voluntary delivery: If the *Guide* is delivered to the transferee, then the transferor or broker is not required to provide additional information concerning general earthquake hazards. Known earthquake hazards must be disclosed whether delivery is mandatory or voluntary.	Cal. Bus. & Prof. Code § 10147; Cal. Gov't Code §§ 8875.6, 8875.9, 8893.2, 8893.3; Cal. Civ. Code § 2079.9.
Death (in last 3 years)	Sale , lease, or rental of all real property.	The transferor/agent has no liability for not disclosing the fact of any death which occurred more than 3 years prior to the date the transferee offers to buy, lease, or rent the property. Any death which has occurred within a 3-year period should be disclosed if deemed to be "material." Affliction with AIDS or death from AIDS, no matter when it occurred, need not be voluntarily disclosed. However, neither a seller nor	Legal Q&A, **Disclosure of Death and AIDS and the Prohibition Against Discrimination on the Basis of AIDS** Cal. Civ. Code § 1710.2.

4

FIGURE 3.8 (continued):   List of Disclosures

SUBJECT	DISCLOSURE TRIGGER	DISCLOSURE REQUIREMENT (Brief Summary) FORM	C.A.R. INFORMATION SOURCE LAW CITATION
		seller's agent may make an intentional misrepresentation in response to a direct question concerning AIDS/death from AIDS on the property. An agent may simply respond that discussing such information is an invasion of privacy.	
Earthquake Fault Zone[7]	Sale of <u>all</u> real property which does contain or will eventually contain a structure for human occupancy and which is located in an earthquake fault zone (special studies zone) as indicated on maps created by the California Geological Survey.[8] Also applies to manufactured and personal property mobile homes.	The seller's <u>agent</u> or the seller without an agent must disclose to the buyer the fact that the property is in an earthquake fault zone (special studies zone), if maps are available at the county assessor, county recorder, or county planning commission office, or if the seller or seller's agent has actual knowledge that the property is in the zone. If the map is not of sufficient accuracy or scale to determine whether the property is in the zone, then either the agent indicates "yes" that the property is in the zone or the agent may write "no" that the property is <u>not</u> in this zone, but then a report prepared by an expert verifying that fact must be attached to C.A.R. Form NHD. If a TDS is required in the transaction, either C.A.R. Form NHD, *Natural Hazard Disclosure Statement*, or an updated local option disclosure form must be used to make this disclosure.	Legal Q&A, **Natural Hazard Disclosure Statement** Cal. Pub. Res. Code §§ 2621 *et seq.;* Cal. Civ. Code § 1103.
Energy Use Report	Sale of commercial building, lease of entire commercial building or loan application to finance entire commercial	The owner shall disclose energy use report no later than 24 hours prior to execution of sales or lease contract, or submittal of the	Public Resources Code 25402.10. 20 CCR §§ 1680-

FIGURE 3.8 (continued): **List of Disclosures**

SUBJECT	DISCLOSURE TRIGGER	DISCLOSURE REQUIREMENT (Brief Summary) FORM	C.A.R. INFORMATION SOURCE LAW CITATION
	building. The effective date of the law depends on the size of the building. For buildings with sq. ft. 50,000 or more, it is January 1, 2014. For buildings with sq. ft. 10,000 to 50,000, it is January 1, 2014. For buildings with sq. ft. 5,000 to 10,000 it is July 1, 2014.	loan application. An account with the EPA's Energy Star program must be opened or updated 30 days before disclosure is made.	1684.
Farm or Ranch Proximity	NHD report is completed by third-party disclosure company	The NHD expert must determine if the property is located within one mile of real property designated as farm or ranch land on a GIS map. If so, the report must contain a statutory statement, *Notice of Right to Farm*.	Cal. Civ. Code § 1103.4(c)(3).
FHA/HUD Inspection Notice	Sale of HUD-owned residential real property of 1-4 units, including mobile homes on a permanent foundation, or properties which involve FHA loans.	For all existing properties except those "under construction," the borrower must receive from the lender the notice: "For Your Protection: Get a Home Inspection." C.A.R. Form HID.	HUD Mortgagee Letter 06-24

6

FIGURE 3.8 (continued): **List of Disclosures**

SUBJECT	DISCLOSURE TRIGGER	DISCLOSURE REQUIREMENT (Brief Summary) FORM	C.A.R. INFORMATION SOURCE LAW CITATION
Federal Withholding (FIRPTA) and California Withholding Tax	Federal withholding: All sales, including installment sales, exchanges, foreclosures, deeds in lieu of foreclosure and other transactions by a "foreign person." CA withholding: Any "disposition of a California real property interest" (includes sales, exchanges, foreclosures, installment sales, and other types of transfers). See the Legal Q&As for the exemptions.	Federal: Buyers must withhold 10% of the gross sales price and send it to the IRS. If the seller is not a "foreign person," he or she may complete the affidavit of non-foreign status. CA: Buyers must withhold 3 1/3 percent of the gross sales price on any sale of California real property interests, unless an exemption applies, and send it to the FTB. C.A.R. form AS may be used, if applicable, to avoid withholding at time of transfer.	Legal Q&As, **Federal Withholding: The Foreign Investment in Real Property Tax Act (FIRPTA), and** **California Withholding on the Sale of Real Property** 42 U.S.C. § 5154a. Cal. Rev. & Tax Code §§ 18662(e)(f).
Flood Disaster Insurance Requirements (Applicable for any flood disaster[10] declared after Sep. 23, 1994)	Any transfer [6] of personal (e.g., mobile homes), residential, or commercial property where the owner received federal flood disaster assistance conditioned on the owner subsequently obtaining and maintaining flood insurance.	The transferor must notify the transferee in writing on a document "evidencing the transfer of ownership of the property" about the requirement to obtain and maintain flood insurance in accordance with applicable Federal law. Failure to notify the transferee means that in the event the transferee fails to maintain the required flood insurance and the property is damaged by a flood disaster requiring Federal disaster relief, the transferor will be required to reimburse the Federal government. The law is unclear as to what document(s) should contain this notice. C.A.R. Forms RPA-CA and NHD may be acceptable, but technically are not documents that "evidence the transfer of	Legal Q&A, **Federal Flood Insurance Disclosure** 42 U.S.C. § 5154a.

7

FIGURE 3.8 (continued):   List of Disclosures

SUBJECT	DISCLOSURE TRIGGER	DISCLOSURE REQUIREMENT (Brief Summary) FORM	C.A.R. INFORMATION SOURCE LAW CITATION
		ownership." Clearly, a grant deed is such a document.	
Gas and Hazardous Liquid Transmission Pipeline Notice	Every Contract for sale of residential real property.	The Notice informs the buyer that information about the general location of these pipelines is available to the public on line via the National Pipeline Mapping System (NPMS) and provides the web address. The following C.A.R. forms contain this statutory notice: RPA-CA, RIPA, NCPA, NODPA, MHPA.	Cal. Civ. Code § 2079.10.5
Home Energy Ratings System (HERS) Booklet (Optional Disclosure) (Booklet Now Available)	Transfer [9] or exchange of <u>all</u> real property. Also applies to manufactured and personal property mobile homes.	If an energy ratings booklet is delivered to the transferee, then a seller or broker is not required to provide additional information concerning the existence of a statewide energy rating program. *Home Energy Rating System (HERS) Booklet* (part of *Combined Hazards* booklet)	Cal. Civ. Code § 2079.10; Cal. Pub. Res. Code §§ 25402.9, 25942.
Homeowner's Guide to Earthquake Safety Booklet and Residential Earthquake Hazards Report (form in booklet)	<u>Mandatory delivery</u>: Transfer of residential real property of 1-4 units, manufactured homes, and mobile homes, of conventional light frame construction, and built prior to Jan. 1, 1960, if not exempt (almost same exemptions as for the Transfer Disclosure Statement[11]). Additional exemption if the buyer agrees, in writing, to demolish the property within one year from date of transfer. <u>Voluntary delivery</u>: Transfe [6] of <u>any</u> real property.	<u>Mandatory delivery</u>: The licensee must give the transferor the booklet *The Homeowner's Guide to Earthquake Safety*[12] and the transferor must give this booklet to the transferee. Known structural deficiencies must be disclosed by the transferor to the transferee and the form in the booklet entitled *Residential Earthquake Hazards Report* may be used to make this disclosure. <u>Voluntary delivery</u>: If the *Guide* is delivered to	Cal. Bus. & Prof. Code § 10149; Cal. Gov't Code §§ 8897.1, 8897.2, 8897.5; Cal. Civ. Code § 2079.8.

FIGURE 3.8 (continued):   List of Disclosures

SUBJECT	DISCLOSURE TRIGGER	DISCLOSURE REQUIREMENT (Brief Summary) FORM	C.A.R. INFORMATION SOURCE LAW CITATION
		the transferee, then the transferor or broker is not required to provide additional information concerning general earthquake hazards. Known earthquake hazards must be disclosed whether delivery is mandatory or voluntary.	
Industrial Use Zone Location	Transfer[6] or exchange of residential real property of 1-4 units.	The seller of real property subject to the TDS law must disclose "actual knowledge" that the property is affected by or zoned to allow an industrial use of property (manufacturing, commercial, or airport use) as soon as possible before transfer of title. C.A.R. Form SSD or SPQ may be used.	Cal. Civ. Code § 1102.17; Cal. Code Civ. Proc. § 731a.
Lead-Based Paint Pamphlet and Form	Sale or lease of <u>all</u> residential property, built before Jan. 1, 1978, except as indicated below. Also applies to manufactured homes and personal property mobile homes. <u>Exemptions:</u> • foreclosure or trustee's sale transfer (REO properties and deed-in-lieu of foreclosure are NOT exempt!) • zero-bedroom dwelling (loft, efficiency unit, dorm, or studio) • short-term rental (100 or fewer days)	The seller/lessor must provide the buyer/lessee with a lead hazard information pamphlet, disclose the presence of any known lead-based paint and provide a statement signed by the buyer that the buyer has read the warning statement, has received the pamphlet, and has a 10-day opportunity to inspect before becoming obligated under the contract. The purchaser (not lessee) is permitted a 10-day period to conduct an inspection unless the parties mutually agree upon a different time period. The agent, on behalf of the seller/lessor, must ensure compliance with the	Legal Q&As, **Federal Lead-Based Paint Hazard Disclosures**, and **Federal Lead-Based Paint Renovation Rule** Residential Lead-Based Paint Hazard Reduction Act of 1992, 42 U.S.C. § 4852d.

FIGURE 3.8 (continued):   **List of Disclosures**

SUBJECT	DISCLOSURE TRIGGER	DISCLOSURE REQUIREMENT (Brief Summary) FORM	C.A.R. INFORMATION SOURCE LAW CITATION
	• housing for elderly or handicapped (unless children live there) • rental housing certified free of lead paint	requirements of this law. C.A.R. pamphlet, *Protect Your Family From Lead in Your Home*, and C.A.R. form FLD satisfy these requirements (except for sales of HUD properties— then HUD forms required). The C.A.R. Combined Hazards booklet may be used in lieu of the pamphlet mentioned above.	
Material Facts	Any transfer of real property or manufactured homes or mobile homes. No exemptions.	A seller (transferor) or real estate agent involved in the transaction must disclose any <u>known material facts</u> that affect the value or desirability of the property. Whether or not something is deemed material is determined by case law. C.A.R. Form SSD or SPQ may be used.	Case law: *Nussbaum v. Weeks* (1990) 214 Cal. App. 3d 1589 (seller's duty); *Easton v. Strassburger* (1984) 152 Cal. App. 3d 90 (agent's duty); Cal. Civ. Code § 2079 *et seq.*
Megan's Law Disclosure (Registered Sex Offender Database)	Sale[13] or lease/rental of all residential real property of 1-4 units (No exemptions except for never-occupied properties where a public report is required or properties exempted from a public report pursuant to Bus. & Prof. Code § 11010.4)	Every lease or rental agreement and every sales contract is required to include a statutorily-defined notice regarding the existence of public access to database information regarding sex offenders. The following C.A.R. forms contain this statutory notice: RPA-CA, RIPA, PPA, NCPA, NODPA, MHPA, LR, IOA, RLAS	Legal Q&A, **Megan's Law: Disclosure of Registered Sex Offenders** Cal. Civ. Code § 2079.10a.

FIGURE 3.8 (continued):   **List of Disclosures**

SUBJECT	DISCLOSURE TRIGGER	DISCLOSURE REQUIREMENT (Brief Summary) FORM	C.A.R. INFORMATION SOURCE LAW CITATION
Mello-Roos, 1915 Bond Act Assessments, and voluntary contractual assessment.	Transfer[6] or exchange of residential real property of 1-4 units subject to a continuing lien securing the levy of special taxes pursuant to the Mello-Roos Community Facilities Act or the 1915 Bond Act. Same exemptions as for the Transfer Disclosure Statement except that new subdivisions are not exempt.	The transferor must make a good faith effort to obtain a disclosure notice concerning the special tax or assessment from each local agency that levies a special tax or assessment and deliver the notice(s) to the prospective transferee. Transferors may comply with this law by using a third-party disclosure company. The transferee has a 3 or 5-day right of rescission. There is no affirmative duty by an agent to discover a special tax or district or assessment not actually known to the agent.	Legal Q&A, **Mello-Roos District Disclosure Requirements** Cal. Civ. Code § 1102.6b; Cal. Gov't Code § 53340.2 (Mello-Roos Form), § 53341.5 (new subdivisions), § 53754 (bond), Cal. Str. & H. Code § 5898.24.
Meth Lab Clean-Up Order **(Release of Illegal Controlled Substance Remediation Order)**	Transfer by "purchase, exchange, gift, lease, inheritance, or legal action" of any "parcel of land, structure, or part of a structure" where the manufacture of methamphetamine or storage of methamphetamine or a prohibited hazardous chemical occurred.	In the event that toxic contamination by an illegal controlled substance has occurred on a property and upon receipt of a clean-up order from the Dept. of Toxic Substances Control (DTSC) or a Local Health Officer, the transferor must provide a copy of this order to the transferee. In the case of rental property, the landlord must give a prospective tenant a copy of this order which must be attached to the rental agreement. Non-compliance with this law permits the tenant to void the rental agreement. C.A.R. Form SSD, SPQ or MCN may be used.	Cal. Health & Safety Code § 25400.28 (disclosure), § 25400.36 (definitions).

11

FIGURE 3.8 (continued):   List of Disclosures

SUBJECT	DISCLOSURE TRIGGER	DISCLOSURE REQUIREMENT (Brief Summary) FORM	C.A.R. INFORMATION SOURCE LAW CITATION
Military Ordnance Location (former military munitions site)	Transfer [6] or exchange of residential real property of 1-4 units and lease of any residential dwelling unit. Same exemptions as for the Transfer Disclosure Statement.	Disclosure is required when the transferor/lessor has actual knowledge that a former military ordnance location (military training grounds which may contain explosives) is within one mile of the property. The transferor/lessor must disclose in writing to the transferee/lessee, that these former federal or state military ordnance locations may contain potentially explosive munitions. The transferee has a 3 or 5-day right of rescission. C.A.R. Form SSD or SPQ may be used.	Cal. Civ. Code §§ 1102.15, 1940.7.
Mining Operation	NHD report is completed by third-party disclosure company	The NHD expert must determine if the property is located within one mile of a mine operation as reported by the Office of Mine Reclamation map. If so, the report must contain a statutory statement, Notice of Mining Operation.	Cal. Civ. Code § 1103.4 (c)(3).
Mold (Disclosure of Excessive Mold or Health Threat)	Sale, lease, rental, or other transfer of any commercial, industrial or residential property	There are no current disclosure requirements until after the Dept. of Health Services (DHS) develops permissible exposure limits for mold and a consumer booklet. The TDS has been modified to include the word "mold" in paragraph II.C.1. As always, any transferor must disclose actual knowledge of toxic mold on	Legal Q&A, **Mold and Its Impact on Real Estate Transactions** Cal. Health & Safety Code §§ 26100 et seq., §§ 26140, 26141, 26147, 26148.

12

FIGURE 3.8 (continued): **List of Disclosures**

SUBJECT	DISCLOSURE TRIGGER	DISCLOSURE REQUIREMENT (Brief Summary) FORM	C.A.R. INFORMATION SOURCE LAW CITATION
		the property. C.A.R. Form RGM may be used (optional).	
Natural Hazard Disclosure Statement (Form)	Transfer[14] of residential real property of 1-4 units if the property is located in one or more of the following hazard zones: Special Flood Hazard Area, Area of Potential Flooding, Very High Fire Severity Zone, Earthquake Fault Zone, Seismic Hazard Zone, or State Responsibility Area Also applies to manufactured homes and personal property mobile homes. See the Legal Q&A for the list of exemptions.	The seller and the listing agent must sign the statutory form or a substantially equivalent form (provided by a disclosure company or other) to be provided to the buyer. C.A.R. Form NHD (statutory form).	Legal Q&A, **Natural Hazard Disclosure Statement** Cal. Civ. Code §§ 1103 *et seq.*
Pest Control Inspection Report and Certification (wood destroying pests or organisms)	Transfer of title of any real property or the execution of a real property sales contract, as defined in Civil Code Section 2985, <u>only if</u> required by contract or the transferee's lender.	The transferor, fee owner, or his/her agent, must deliver to the transferee a copy of a structural pest control inspection report and certification if any remediation work is required, as soon as practical, before close of escrow or execution of a real property sales contract (land sale contract). Delivery to a transferee means delivery in person or by mail to the transferee him/herself or any person authorized to act for him/her in the transaction or to such additional transferees who have requested such delivery from the transferor or his/her agent in writing. Delivery to either husband or wife will be deemed delivery to a	Cal. Civ. Code § 1099.

13

FIGURE 3.8 (continued): **List of Disclosures**

SUBJECT	DISCLOSURE TRIGGER	DISCLOSURE REQUIREMENT (Brief Summary) FORM	C.A.R. INFORMATION SOURCE LAW CITATION
		transferee, unless the contract affecting the transfer states otherwise.	
Private Transfer Fee	Transfer[6] or exchange of residential real property of 1-4 units. Same exemptions as for the Transfer Disclosure Statement.	If the property being transferred is subject to a transfer fee, as defined in Section 1098, the transferor must provide, at the same time as the TDS, a transfer tax disclosure statement. C.A.R. Form NTF may be used.	Cal. Civ. Code §§ 1102.6e, 1098, 1098.5.
Residential Environmental Hazards Booklet (Optional Disclosure)	Transfer[15] or exchange of all real property. Also applies to manufactured homes and personal property mobile homes.	If a consumer information booklet[16] is delivered to the transferee, then a seller or broker is not required to provide additional information concerning common environmental hazards. Although highly recommended, delivery is voluntary. However, known hazards on the property must be disclosed to the transferee. C.A.R. *Combined Hazards* booklet may be used.	Cal. Civ. Code § 2079.7.
Seismic Hazard Zones	Sale of all real property which does contain or will eventually contain a structure for human habitation and which is located in a seismic hazard zone as indicated on maps created by the California Division of Mines and Geology. Also applies to manufactured homes and personal property mobile homes.	The seller's agent or the seller without an agent must disclose to the buyer the fact that the property is in a seismic hazard zone if maps are available at the county assessor, county recorder, or county planning commission office, or if the seller or seller's agent has actual knowledge that the property is in the zone. If the map is not of sufficient accuracy or scale to determine whether the property is in the zone,	Legal Q&A, **Natural Hazard Disclosure Statement** Cal. Pub. Res. Code § 2690 *et seq.*, § 2694; Cal. Civ. Code § 1103.

14

FIGURE 3.8 (continued):   **List of Disclosures**

SUBJECT	DISCLOSURE TRIGGER	DISCLOSURE REQUIREMENT (Brief Summary) FORM	C.A.R. INFORMATION SOURCE LAW CITATION
		then either the agent indicates "yes" that the property is in the zone or the agent may write "no" that the property is <u>not</u> in this zone, but then a report prepared by an expert verifying that fact must be attached to C.A.R. Form NHD. If a TDS is required in the transaction, either C.A.R. Form NHD, "Natural Hazard Disclosure Statement" or an updated local option disclosure form must be used to make this disclosure.	
Smoke Alarms Must Be In Compliance	All existing real property dwelling units must have a smoke alarm centrally located outside each sleeping area (bedroom or group of bedrooms). All used manufactured homes, used mobile homes, and used multi-family manufactured housing must have a smoke alarm in each room designed for sleeping. However, as point of sale requirement for single family properties and duplexes, the exemptions are the same under the TDS law. Except that, transfers to or from governmental entities, and transfers of property acquired by a beneficiary after a foreclosure or trustee's sale, or after a deed in lieu, which are exempt under the TDS law, are not exempt from compliance as a point of sale requirement. In addition, new real property construction with a permit after Aug. 14, 1992 must have a hard-wired smoke alarm in each bedroom. Any additions, modifications, or repairs to real property (after Aug. 14, 1992) exceeding $1,000 for which a permit is required or the addition of any bedroom will also trigger the requirement of a smoke alarm in each bedroom. (These may be battery operated.)	**LOCAL LAW MAY BE MORE RESTRICTIVE! Check with the local City or County Department of Building and Safety.** See next section for Disclosure requirement.	Legal Q&A, **Smoke Alarm Requirements** Cal. Health & Safety Code §§ 13113.7, 13113.8, 18029.6.

FIGURE 3.8 (continued):   List of Disclosures

SUBJECT	DISCLOSURE TRIGGER	DISCLOSURE REQUIREMENT (Brief Summary) FORM	C.A.R. INFORMATION SOURCE LAW CITATION
Smoke Alarm Written Statement of Compliance	The seller of a single family or two-unit dwellings, factory-built housing, a used manufactured home, used mobile home or used multi-unit manufactured housing must provide the buyer with a written statement indicating that the property is in compliance with current California law. Same exemptions for real property as from the TDS law. However, transfers to or from any governmental entity, and transfers by a beneficiary or mortgagee after foreclosure sale or trustee's sale, which are exempt under the TDS law, are <u>not</u> exempt from this law.	C.A.R. Forms TDS and MHTDS now include a statement of compliance. C.A.R. Form WHSD may be used when no TDS is used in the transaction. HCD Declaration must be used for used mobile homes, used manufactured homes, and used multi-unit manufactured housing, and be given to the buyer within 45 days prior to the transfer of title.	Legal Q&A, **Smoke Alarm Requirements** Cal. Health & Safety Code §§ 13113.8, 18029.6; 25 Cal. Code Regs. § 5545.
Special Flood Hazard Area	Sale of real property located in Zone "A" or " V" as designated by FEMA and if the seller or the seller's agent has actual knowledge <u>or</u> a list has been compiled <u>by parcel</u> and the notice posted at a local county recorder, assessor and planning agency. Also applies to manufactured homes and personal property mobile homes.	The seller's <u>agent</u> or the seller without an agent must disclose to the buyer if the property is in this Special Flood Hazard Area, if a parcel list has been prepared by the county and a notice identifying the location of the list is available at the county assessor, county recorder or county planning commission office, or if the seller or seller's agent has actual knowledge that the property is in an area. If a TDS is required in the transaction, either C.A.R. Form NHD, "Natural Hazard Disclosure Statement" or an updated Local Option disclosure form must be used to make this disclosure.	Legal Q&A, **Natural Hazard Disclosure Statement** Cal. Civ. Code § 1103; Cal. Gov't Code § 8589.3.

16

FIGURE 3.8 (continued):   List of Disclosures

SUBJECT	DISCLOSURE TRIGGER	DISCLOSURE REQUIREMENT (Brief Summary) FORM	C.A.R. INFORMATION SOURCE LAW CITATION
State Responsibility Area (Fire Hazard Area)	Sale of <u>any</u> real property located in a designated state responsibility area (generally a "wildland area") where the state not local or federal govt. has the primary financial responsibility for fire prevention. The California Department of Forestry provides maps to the county assessor of each affected county.[17] Also applies to manufactured homes and personal property mobile homes.	The seller must disclose to the buyer the fact that the property is located in this zone, the risk of fire, state-imposed additional duties such as maintaining fire breaks, and the fact that the state may not provide fire protection services. The disclosure must be made if maps are available at the county assessor, county recorder or county planning commission office, or if the seller has actual knowledge that the property is in the zone. If the map is not of sufficient accuracy or scale to determine whether the property is in this Area, then either the agent indicates "yes" that the property is in this Area or the agent may write "no" that the property is <u>not</u> in this Area, but then a report prepared by an expert verifying that fact must be attached to C.A.R. Form NHD. If a TDS is required in the transaction, either C.A.R. Form NHD, "Natural Hazard Disclosure Statement" or an updated local option disclosure form must be used to make this disclosure.	Legal Q&A, **Natural Hazard Disclosure Statement** Cal. Pub. Res. Code §§ 4125, 4136; Cal. Civ. Code § 1103.
Supplemental Property Tax Notice	Transfer[6] of residential real property of 1-4 units. Same exemptions as for the Transfer Disclosure Statement.	The seller or seller's agent must deliver to the buyer the statutory notice. C.A.R. Form SPT may be used.	Cal. Civ. Code § 1102.6c.

17

FIGURE 3.8 (continued): **List of Disclosures**

SUBJECT	DISCLOSURE TRIGGER	DISCLOSURE REQUIREMENT (Brief Summary) FORM	C.A.R. INFORMATION SOURCE LAW CITATION
Subdivided Lands Law	Sale, leasing, or financing of new developments (condos, PUDs) or conversions consisting of 5 or more lots, parcels, or interests. However, a transfer of a single property to 5 or more unrelated people (unless exempt) may also trigger this law. There are exemptions too numerous to discuss in this chart.	The owner, subdivider, or agent, prior to the execution of the purchase contract or lease, must give the buyer/lessee a copy of the final public report (FPR), preliminary public report (PPR), or the conditional public report (CPR) issued by the DRE. No offers may be solicited until the DRE has issued one of these three reports. If the DRE has issued a CPR or PPR, then offers may be solicited, but close of escrow is contingent upon issuance of the FPR. Contracts entered into pursuant to a PPR may be rescinded by either party; contracts entered into pursuant to a CPR are contingent upon satisfaction of certain specified conditions.	Legal Q&As, **Subdivided Lands Law**, and **Subdivision Applicability Chart** Cal. Bus. & Prof. Code §§ 11018.1, 11018.12; 10 Cal. Code Regs. § 2795. See generally, Cal. Bus. & Prof. Code §§ 11000 *et seq.*; 10 Cal. Code Regs. §§ 2790 *et seq.*
Subdivision Map Act	Any division of real property into 2 or more lots or parcels for the purpose of sale, lease, or financing. There are exemptions too numerous to discuss in this chart.	The owner/subdivider must record either a tentative and final map, or a parcel map (depending on the type of subdivision). Escrow on the transfer cannot close until the appropriate map has been recorded.	Legal Q&A, **Subdivision Applicability Chart** Cal. Gov't Code §§ 66426, 66428. *See generally,* Cal. Gov't Code §§ 66410 *et seq.*
Transfer Disclosure Statement	Transfer[6] of residential real property of 1-4 units. Also applies to manufactured homes and personal property mobile homes.	Sellers and real estate agents must complete a statutory disclosure form. C.A.R. Form TDS (statutory form for real property); C.A.R. Form MHTDS (statutory form for personal property mobile homes)	Legal Q&As, **Transfer Disclosure Statement Law,** and **Transfer Disclosure Statement**

FIGURE 3.8 (continued):   List of Disclosures

SUBJECT	DISCLOSURE TRIGGER	DISCLOSURE REQUIREMENT (Brief Summary) FORM	C.A.R. INFORMATION SOURCE LAW CITATION
			Exemptions Cal. Civ. Code §§ 1102 *et seq.*
Very High Fire Hazard Severity Zone	Sale of any real property. Also applies to manufactured homes and personal property mobile homes.	The seller must disclose the fact that the property is located within this zone and whether it is subject to the requirements of Gov't Code Section 51182 (e.g., clear brush, maintain fire breaks). The disclosure must be made if maps are available at the county assessor, county recorder or county planning commission office, or if the seller has actual knowledge that the property is in the zone. If the map is not of sufficient accuracy or scale to determine whether the property is in this zone, then either the agent indicates "yes" that the property is in this zone or the agent may write "no" that the property is <u>not</u> in this zone, but then a report prepared by an expert verifying that fact must be attached to C.A.R. Form NHD. If a TDS is required in the transaction, either C.A.R. Form NHD, "Natural Hazard Disclosure Statement" or an updated local option disclosure form must be used to make this disclosure.	Legal Q&A, **Natural Hazard Disclosure Statement** Cal. Gov't Code §§ 51178, 51183.5; Cal. Civ. Code § 1103.
Water Conserving Fixtures Compliance	Applies only to real property built on or before Jan. 1, 1994 containing water fixtures. Effective date of law for single-family residential real property is Jan. 1, 2017. Effective date for two or more	Noncompliant plumbing fixtures (defined in Section 1101.3(c)) must be replaced by water conserving plumbing fixtures.	Legal Q&A, Water-Conserving Plumbing Fixtures Cal. Civ. Code § 1101.1 *et seq.*

FIGURE 3.8 (continued):   List of Disclosures

SUBJECT	DISCLOSURE TRIGGER	DISCLOSURE REQUIREMENT (Brief Summary) FORM	C.A.R. INFORMATION SOURCE LAW CITATION
	unit resid. real prop. and commercial real prop is Jan. 1, 2019. Effective date where some types of permitted types of permitted improvements are made is Jan. 1, 2014. Exemptions: • Registered historical sites. • Certified not technically feasible by licensed plumber. • Water service disconnected.		
Water Conserving Fixtures Disclosure	Applies only to real property built on or before Jan. 1, 1994 containing water fixtures. Effective date of law for single-family residential real property is Jan. 1, 2017. Effective date for two or more unit residential real prop. and commercial real prop. is Jan. 1, 2019. Exemptions: • Registered historical sites. • Certified not technically feasible by licensed plumber. • Water service disconnected.	The seller or transferor must disclose in writing to the prospective transferee that the law requires that noncompliant plumbing fixtures must be replaced with water-conserving plumbing fixtures and the required date, and also whether the real property includes any noncompliant plumbing fixtures (Cal. Civ. Code § 1101.4(c) single family and Cal. Civ. Code § 1101.5(a) multi-family and commercial).	Cal. Civ. Code § 1101.1 et seq.
Water Heater Bracing Statement of	All real property with any standard water heater with a	All owners of new or replacement water heaters	Legal Q&A, Water Heater Bracing and

20

FIGURE 3.8 (continued):   **List of Disclosures**

SUBJECT	DISCLOSURE TRIGGER	DISCLOSURE REQUIREMENT (Brief Summary) FORM	C.A.R. INFORMATION SOURCE LAW CITATION
Compliance	capacity of not more than 120 gallons for which a pre-engineered strapping kit is readily available. Legislative intent suggests this law applies only to residential properties, but the language of the statute does not limit the requirement to residential properties. All used mobile homes, used manufactured homes, and used multi-family manufactured housing with a fuel gas-burning water heater.	and all owners of existing residential water heaters must brace, anchor or strap water heaters to resist falling or horizontal displacement due to earthquake motion. Water heaters located in closets are also subject to this law. The seller of real property must certify in writing to a prospective purchaser that he has complied with this section and applicable local code requirements. C.A.R. Forms TDS and MHTDS now include a statement of compliance. C.A.R. Form WHSD may be used when no TDS is used in the transaction. HCD Declaration must be used for used mobile homes, used manufactured homes, and used multi-unit manufactured housing, and be given to the buyer within 45 days prior to the transfer of title.	Disclosure Requirements Cal. Health & Safety Code §§ 19211, 18031.7; 25 Cal. Code Regs. § 4102.

ENDNOTES

1. It is imperative to check local disclosure requirements. Local law may be more stringent than state law in certain areas or there may be additional disclosures required.

2. "Sale" includes exchanges of real property and installment land sale contracts (also called real property sales contracts) (Cal. Civ. Code 2079.13(l)).

3. This provision also applies to leases with an option to purchase, ground leases of land improved with 1-4 residential units, and real property installment sales contracts (Cal. Civ. Code § 2079.1).

4. Transfers which can be made without a public report pursuant to Section 11010.4 of the Business and Professions Code are exempt from a TDS but not from the Homeowner's Guide.

5. This Guide is available from C.A.R. and/or local Boards/Associations.

6. "Transfer" for the purposes of this law means transfer by sale, exchange, lease with option to purchase, purchase option, ground lease coupled with improvements, installment land sale contract, or transfer of a residential stock cooperative (Cal. Civ. Code § 1102).

21

FIGURE 3.8 (continued):   **List of Disclosures**

7. These zones were formerly called, "Special Studies Zones." Some maps may still refer to the old name.

8. The maps may be purchased from BPS Reprographics by calling (415) 512-6550 with the names of the required maps. Special Publication 42 indicates the names of the maps of the Earthquake Fault Zones. This publication is available from the California Geological Survey (formerly the California Division of Mines and Geology) by calling (916) 445-5716.

9. Transfers which can be made without a public report pursuant to Section 11010.4 of the Business and Professions Code are exempt from a TDS but not from the Homeowner's Guide.

10. "Flood disaster area" means an area so designated by the U.S. Secretary of Agriculture or an area the President has declared to be a disaster or emergency as a result of flood conditions.

11. Transfers which can be made without a public report pursuant to Section 11010.4 of the Business and Professions Code are exempt from a TDS but not from the Homeowner's Guide.
12. This Guide is available from C.A.R. and/or local Boards/Associations.

13. This provision also applies to leases with an option to purchase, ground leases of land improved with 1-4 residential units, and real property installment sales contracts (Cal. Civ. Code § 2079.1).

14. "Transfer" for the purposes of this law means transfer by sale, exchange, lease with option to purchase, purchase option, ground lease coupled with improvements, installment land sale contract, or transfer of a residential stock cooperative (Cal. Civ. Code § 1103).

15. Transfers which can be made without a public report pursuant to Section 11010.4 of the Business and Professions Code are exempt from a TDS but not from the Homeowner's Guide.

16. The consumer information booklet entitled *Environmental Hazards, A Guide for Homeowners and Buyers* is available from C.A.R. and/or local Boards/Associations.

17. The Department of Forestry's telephone number is (916) 653-5121.

California law sometimes requires that a specific form (or exact language) be used. Examples are the AD, FLD, TDS, MHTDS, and the NHD. Others times, the law requires a disclosure but doesn't mandate that particular language be used. However, C.A.R. provides forms for that purpose--indicated in this chart by the words "may be used." The law doesn't require the use of these forms. Examples are the AVID, MCN, NTF, SBSA, SSD, SPQ, AS, AB, WHSD, REO, and REOL.

This chart is just one of the many legal publications and services offered by C.A.R. to its members. For a complete listing of C.A.R.'s legal products and services, please visit car.org.

Readers who require specific advice should consult an attorney. C.A.R. members requiring legal assistance may contact C.A.R.'s Member Legal Hotline at (213) 739-8282, Monday through Friday, 9 a.m. to 6 p.m. and Saturday, 10 a.m. to 2 p.m. C.A.R. members who are broker-owners, office managers, or Designated REALTORS® may contact the Member Legal Hotline at (213) 739-8350 to receive expedited service. Members may also submit online requests to speak with an attorney on the Member Legal Hotline by going to http://www.car.org/legal/legal-hotline-access/. Written correspondence should be addressed to:

CALIFORNIA ASSOCIATION OF REALTORS®
Member Legal Services
525 South Virgil Ave.
Los Angeles, CA 90020

22

FIGURE 3.8 (continued):   List of Disclosures

The information contained herein is believed accurate as of December 19, 2014. It is intended to provide general answers to general questions and is not intended as a substitute for individual legal advice. Advice in specific situations may differ depending upon a wide variety of factors. Therefore, readers with specific legal questions should seek the advice of an attorney.

SUMMARY

The purpose of the disclosure requirements in real estate practice is fairness. Parties deserve to have the facts before they make decisions. These facts include detrimental facts known by the agent that the buyer or the seller would likely consider in decision making. The duty of disclosure is inherent in an agency. The fiduciary duty of the agent requires full disclosure. There is also a duty to nonagency third parties to disclose known *detrimental information.*

To avoid misunderstandings, agents must explain the various agency options to both buyer and seller. The agent makes a selection, and the parties confirm the selection.

The seller has disclosure duties to the buyer. For 1–4-unit residential properties, the seller must complete a Real Estate Transfer Disclosure Statement. The agent must also provide the results of his visual inspection to the owner.

An agent need not disclose a death on the premises after three years. An agent also need not disclose that a former resident was afflicted with or died of AIDS. Stigmatized property should be disclosed if a buyer would reasonably want to know about it.

When there is seller financing, a seller financing addendum and disclosure is required. Buyers must be warned of any dangers.

For 1–4-unit residential properties built before January 1, 1960, the agent must disclose whether the dwelling has earthquake weaknesses. This is accomplished with a Residential Earthquake Hazards Report. For commercial property of specified construction, the seller or the seller's agent must give the buyer a copy of the *Commercial Property Owner's Guide to Earthquake Safety.*

Other required natural hazard disclosures are for the following: special flood hazard area, area of potential flooding, very high fire hazard severity zone, wildlife area that may contain substantial forest fire risks and hazards, earthquake fault zone, seismic hazard zone, and landslide inventory report.

These disclosures are made in a statutory form, the Natural Hazard Disclosure Statement.

Homeowners must be informed about environmental hazards on or affecting their property. The broker must provide a booklet to buyers on environmental hazards. Buyers and lessees also must be informed about hazardous substances released on or believed to be present on a property. Tenants must inform landlords if they release hazardous substances on the property.

For 1–4-unit residential properties built before 1978, purchasers must be given a *Protect Your Family from Lead in Your Home* booklet. Giving the buyers the California booklet, *Environmental Hazards: A Guide for Homeowners, Buyers, and Tenants*, also satisfies the federal requirement.

Prospective purchasers must be notified if a property is within 1 mile of a former military ordnance site where explosives might be located. Known water contamination must also be disclosed.

Subdivision disclosures include the public report and common interest information. Notices must also be provided to tenants of their rights when apartments are converted to common interest developments.

The Interstate Land Sales Act is a disclosure act governing sales of unimproved lots in interstate commerce. Its purpose is to prevent fraud. California has similar state disclosure requirements.

For common interest subdivisions, purchasers must be provided an information booklet on common interest subdivisions, as well as a copy of the CC&Rs, articles of incorporation, bylaws, rules and regulations, financial statement including changes, and plans for changes in assessments.

When there is seller financing, a seller financing addendum and disclosure is required. Buyers must be warned of any dangers.

Both federal and state laws require disclosures that must be made where applicable.

There are statutory rights of rescission for a number of disclosures.

CLASS DISCUSSION TOPICS

1. A property you have for sale is about two blocks from a park frequented by homeless people and prostitutes. So as not to offend prospective buyers, you avoid this area by a roundabout drive. Have you acted in a proper manner?

2. A buyer offers to trade 50 emeralds for a home you have listed. What, if any, are your obligations?

3. What environmental hazards would likely be present in your community?

4. Are there agents in your area who operate solely as buyer's agents? What are the advantages to a buyer in dealing with such an agent?

5. You receive what appears to be a fair offer from a prospective buyer; however, you know the buyer has sued sellers after purchasing several other properties. What do you tell your seller?

6. Evaluate your own home for possible environmental hazards.

7. Complete a Real Estate Transfer Disclosure Statement as if you were the seller of the property where you presently live.

8. Bring to class one current-events article dealing with some aspect of real estate practice for class discussion.

UNIT 3 QUIZ

1. Which of the following statements regarding an agent's duty in a real estate transaction is *TRUE?*
    a. An agent has a fiduciary duty to the principal.
    b. An agent must disclose any known detrimental information to a buyer, even when the agent represents the seller.
    c. Any material facts the agent becomes aware of must be disclosed to the principal.
    d. All of these are true.

2. Which of the following statements regarding agency disclosure is *TRUE?*
    a. An agent need not provide a seller of a commercial building with an agency disclosure.
    b. The listing agent cannot elect to be only a buyer's agent.
    c. Both of these are true.
    d. Neither of these is true.

3. Which of the following statements regarding agency disclosure is *TRUE?*
    a. The confirmation of agency must be in writing.
    b. The three steps of the disclosure process are disclose, elect, confirm.
    c. The selling agent must confirm the agency before the buyer makes an offer.
    d. All of these are true.

4. Which seller(s) must provide a Real Estate Transfer Disclosure Statement?
    a. The seller of a lot
    b. The seller of a 4-unit apartment building
    c. The seller of a 16-unit apartment building
    d. All of these

5. Under *Easton*, an agent's duty of inspection and disclosure covers
    a. all types of property.
    b. accessible and inaccessible areas.
    c. a visual inspection and known or should have known defects.
    d. none of these.

6. Which statement regarding earthquake safety disclosure is *TRUE?*
    a. It applies to 1–4-unit residential properties.
    b. It applies only to homes built before 1930.
    c. The buyer can waive her right to a hazards report.
    d. Delivery of a copy of *The Homeowner's Guide to Earthquake Safety* is evidenced by an affidavit from the agent.

7. The buyers sign that they have received a booklet relating to
    a. environmental hazards.
    b. floods, tornados, and earthquakes.
    c. foreclosure rights.
    d. rescission rights.

8. *Brownfields* is a term related to
    a. insect infestation.
    b. soil contamination.
    c. undeveloped acreage.
    d. seller financing.

9. The purpose of the Subdivided Lands Law is to
    a. prohibit premature subdivisions.
    b. set minimum physical standards.
    c. protect purchasers from fraud.
    d. allow for a uniform growth pattern.

10. A right of rescission is provided by law for purchase agreements involving all *EXCEPT*
    a. 1–4-unit residential properties.
    b. time-shares.
    c. undivided interest subdivisions.
    d. both b and c.

PROSPECTING AND BUSINESS DEVELOPMENT

LEARNING OBJECTIVES

When you have completed this unit, you will be able to

■ define prospecting and explain the importance of attitude in prospecting,

■ describe methods of prospecting and sources of leads,

■ understand regulations affecting prospecting, and

■ explain the importance of the internet, farming, and a prospecting plan.

KEY TERMS

bird dogs	door-to-door	niche marketing
CAN-SPAM Act	canvassing	nongeographic farm
centers of influence	endless chain	prospecting
contact management	farming	real estate owned
system	geographic farm	(REO)
do-not-call registry	megafarming	telephone canvassing
	networking	

WHAT IS PROSPECTING?

Prospecting is the process of locating owners who are interested in selling property and prospective buyers who are interested in purchasing property.

> Prospecting is locating potential buyers and sellers.

Without prospecting, you would have much less inventory and fewer buyers. Real estate professionals know that even when buyers and sellers seek them out, it is often the result of prior prospecting or successfully helping someone they know.

Successful real estate agents understand that prospecting is an important element in their success. It is a continuing process of being aware of what is happening around them, organizing their efforts, being persistent, and developing problem-solving and time-management skills. Not only must licensees constantly prospect, they must have the proper attitude toward prospecting. A professional attitude includes considering prospecting a challenge and being positive and enthusiastic in speech and action. The author recommends the SSS system: *see* the people, *serve* the people, *sell* the people.

Develop the Proper Attitude

Prospecting is any method of exposure to people who can buy or sell real estate; hence, it is a major challenge to every licensee. The following questions will help you evaluate your own attitude toward prospecting:

- **Do you consider prospecting a major challenge?** Successful real estate selling entails countless hours and considerable expenditure of energy to keep up with a highly competitive market. Your attitude is the key to your success.

- **Do you recognize the urgency to maintain a constant supply of new prospects?** It is absolutely necessary to provide yourself with a constant supply of customers. Prospects may be found most anywhere; they are all around you.

- **Do you have a well-organized system to use in prospecting?** Because of the many prospect sources available and the necessity of assigning priorities to these sources, advance planning is essential. To get the best results from your prospecting, an effective and well-organized prospecting system is essential.

- **Are you afraid of rejection?** Prospecting is searching for the one among many who needs your services. Therefore, you will encounter rejection more often than success. Fear of being rejected is one of the contributing factors to failure of new licensees. You must take rejection professionally and not personally.

Many successful agents use licensed assistants to aid them in prospecting. When an assistant locates prospective buyers or sellers, the agent then takes over. This frees the agent for "A" Time activities (Unit 1).

METHODS OF PROSPECTING

The successful salesperson is always prospecting. A good prospector knows and accepts that different groups of people have not only varying interests and motivations but also substantially different political, social, philosophical, and economic views. Prospecting is less a matter of getting listings and sales than it is a matter of developing sources for listings and sales. A licensee's ability to do this is limited only by imagination and commitment.

The prospecting method that will produce the best results varies according to the agent and the situation. The broker or the salesperson should choose a method or methods based on the following:

- Type of property involved

- Period of time planned for

- Types of prospects

- Neighborhood and property characteristics, including the properties themselves (number of bedrooms and baths, etc.), income characteristics of the neighborhood (income, family, and social interests), changes taking place (such as a changeover from single-family to multiple-family dwellings), special advantages of the location (schools, shopping centers, recreation areas, and so forth), and special interests and groups to which the agent belongs

After taking these factors into consideration, licensees also should review their own sales skills and personality and choose methods that emphasize their strengths and minimizes their weaknesses. The following material covers just a few of the methods for prospecting. Real estate salespersons should consult with their brokers as to the selection and implementation of prospecting methods.

Door-to-Door Canvassing

While shunned by some real estate agents, **door-to-door canvassing** can be an excellent way to cover a geographic area. Successful canvassers know the number of people they must contact to obtain one good lead. They set goals of a particular number of contacts to achieve the number of leads they desire. They treat a rejection as one contact closer to another lead.

The best times to canvass are obviously when residents are home. With the large percentage of two-income families, early evenings or Saturday mornings are effective times. In retirement areas, daytime canvassing between 9 am and 11 am and between 2 pm and 4 pm could be effective. Do not canvass door to door after dark.

Canvassing an area having many retirees can be particularly beneficial, because many people welcome someone to talk to and can offer valuable information as to needs of neighbors.

When you canvass door to door, step back from the door after you ring the bell so you won't appear menacing. Don't carry a briefcase because this also can be menacing. A notepad or a clipboard is far less intimidating. Smile when you talk, and keep in mind that you must get the homeowner's attention within the first 20 seconds. In some areas, more doors will be opened to women than to men. Women are generally considered less intimidating.

Published reverse directories giving occupants' names from the address are now available in only a few areas. However, internet sites such as www. whitepages.com/ reverse can provide occupants' names from an address. This is particularly valuable when approaching a for sale by owner.

A sample approach for door-to-door canvassing would be as follows:

- Introduce yourself and give your broker affiliation.

- Explain why you are at their front door. An excellent reason is to ask if they can help find a home for a particular family. People often like to help specific persons but have little interest in people in general. Never use a fictitious family. Simply describe one of the people you are working with to find a home. Never give out names or personal information about prospective buyers without their permission. Let the property owner know why you are interested in the specific area, such as a particular school, park, transportation, employment, et cetera.

- Ask if they know of anyone in the area who is planning to move or has had a change in family circumstances that might cause the person to contemplate a move. Also ask owners about their own specific plans. Ask owners if they or any of their neighbors might have any real estate purchase or sale plans for a home, second home, or investment property.

- Ask whether they would like to receive free (monthly) emails or newsletters showing the number of properties in the area that are on the market, the average listing price per square foot, and similar sale information.

- Thank the owner, leave your card, and jot down responses for future reference.

After a home has been sold by you or your office, a door-to-door canvass of the neighborhood can be especially effective. Consider the following approach, replacing the words in brackets with words that fit your situation:

Good morning [Mrs. Smith]. I am [Jane Thomas] from [Uptown Realty]. We have just sold the [Kowalski] home at [211 Elm down the block; the house with the large pine tree in the front yard]. The new owners are [Mr. and Mrs. Collins. He is an engineer, and she teaches first grade at Sunnyside School. They have one daughter, Mary Ann, who is nine years old]. I hope you will welcome them to your neighborhood.

As you undoubtedly realize, you live in a desirable area. In advertising the [Kowalski] home, we were contacted by a number of families whose needs we were unable to meet. Right now, I am looking for a home for a very fine family. [He is an accountant who is being transferred to our area from Ohio. They have two sons, ages three and six.] I need help in finding them a home. Do you know anyone who is planning to move? Has anyone in the area recently had a change in family size because of marriage, divorce, birth, or death, or has anyone recently retired? (Again, never give out personal information without approval. You want to present the prospective buyer as someone who would be welcome as a neighbor.)

Note: You first showed your competence by a sale, gave them information about a new neighbor, and then asked them for help for a particular family.

Consider visiting the clubhouse or pool of common-interest developments. You will often find people who are not only willing but eager to talk to you. This is especially true in retirement communities. By asking questions, you may get referrals of possible sellers or buyers. When you contact these referrals, it is not really a cold call because they were recommended to you by a friend.

Besides canvassing for listings, you can canvass for buyers. By working an area around a new listing, you can approach owners with information about the listing and ask their help in choosing their new neighbors. Most people like their neighborhood and will tell you if they have any friends or acquaintances who might be considering relocating.

When canvassing around a listing, you should tell the party about the home that is available and ask whether they have a friend, family member, or coworker who might like to move to the area. You are giving them an opportunity to help pick their new neighbors.

Canvassing rentals around a new listing can be an effective method of securing buyers.

> (Good Morning) I am _____ from (Realty). We have just listed a (3BR, 2 bath Cape Cod home) on (Sycamore Street) just (2 blocks) from here. I can show you how ownership can be a reality not just a dream. Would you rather remain here as a renter or own your own (single) family home?

With currently rising rents and relatively low interests, home payments are likely to be in line with or lower than rent. If you can get renters to listen to how they can be owners, you will have prospects to work with.

In some areas, agents like to canvass in teams, with each agent taking every other house. Team canvassing can help keep agents motivated to complete the goal you jointly set. A team approach also gives a canvasser a feeling of greater security.

Note: In some communities, door-to-door canvassing is not allowed or might require a permit.

Telephone Canvassing

The Federal Communications Commission has established the National Do Not Call Registry to protect consumers from unwanted commercial solicitations. Landline, as well as all telephone numbers, may be registered. The fine for calling someone whose name appears in the **do-not-call registry** is up to $16,000 per call.

WEB LINK

@

If you make calls seeking buyers, sellers, lessees, or lessors of property or to solicit any services, you should do so only after checking the registry. For detailed information about accessing the registry and exemptions, it is suggested that you check www.donotcall.gov.

There is a relatively simple solution that avoids paging through huge lists. It is the use of a software program that scrubs the number of people who are on the do-not-call registry. There are now dozens of such programs available, such as www.scrubdnc.net/faq.aspx and www.safecaller.com.

WEB LINK

Brokers who do not use a scrubber program can request an account number, which can be given to agents. Agents can then access the registry by area code on the internet at https://www.telemarketing.donotcall.gov. A broker can obtain access to five area codes at no charge, but there is a charge for additional area codes.

WEB LINK

Telephone solicitors often use automatic dialers in conjunction with scrubbers. Automatic dialers are prohibited as to cellphone numbers.

The following are some exceptions to the do-not-call rules:

Do-not-call lists are available from the Federal Trade Commission by area code, and up to five area codes will be provided free of charge. Each additional area code requires a $25 fee. It is necessary to check the updates on the registry at least every 90 days. For greater details, visit the website, *https://www.donotcall.gov*.

- You may call a listed party if you have an existing business relationship (within 18 months of a purchase, sale, or lease).

- You may call a party within three months of an inquiry the party made.

- You may call people who have given you written permission to call.

- You may call commercial numbers (the registry only applies to residential phones).

- You may call the numbers on for-sale-by-owner ads or signs as a buyer representative, but not for the purpose of obtaining seller representation.

- You may call for survey purposes, but no solicitation for representation can be included in the call.

Because of the restrictive do-not-call rules, you should obtain written permission to make further calls when working with buyers, sellers, and even visitors to open houses.

Direct Mail Canvassing

Direct mail is an expensive way to canvass but with do-not-call restrictions, besides direct contact, it is the only way to reach many parties. Because of cost, agents should carefully plan their mailings and keep track of response rates from different mailings. To be effective, a mailing must get attention and result in action. (See Figures 4.1 and 4.2.)

FIGURE 4.1:   **Sample Mailing**

Note: While positive-appearing personal information can be an inducement to help a family, never include personal information without specific permission from the family.

Some general rules for direct mail canvassing include the following:

- Use a #10 plain envelope; don't use a window envelope.

- Don't use a mailing label; type or, preferably, hand-address the envelope.

- Consider first-class stamps (preferably commemorative stamps). If your letter looks like junk mail, it will likely be treated in that manner.

- Don't try to indicate that your letter is something it is not, such as by trying to give it the appearance of a government letter.

- If you get the reader's attention in the first few lines, the letter will be read in its entirety.

- If you indicate you will be contacting the recipient, you force them to consider your message. When you come to the owners' door, they will know why you are there.

- Never send out a mass mailing without test marketing the mailing piece.

- By keeping track of responses to different mailing pieces, you can eliminate ineffective mailings.

- Offering a premium such as a Dodger baseball cap for filling out a questionnaire can be effective in gaining information.

FIGURE 4.2: **Sample Mailing**

UR
HOME REALTY

_____

_____ ◄———— *Date and address*
_____
_____

Dear _____:

I Apologize

If you want to buy a home in [Claridge Estates], I don't really have much to show you. There has been a terrific demand, and the few owners who have taken advantage of the market quickly sold their homes. However, if you really want to buy, call me and I will put your name on my list of buyers, and I will call or e-mail you as soon as properties come on the market.

Now if you are interested in selling, that's a different story! I can prepare a report for you of recent comparable sales indicating the price range we can anticipate from a sale in the current market. This service is at no cost or obligation to you.

Want to take advantage of our offer? Call or e-mail me today.

Yours truly,

_____

P.S. If you would like to be on our e-mail list to receive new listing and sales information in your neighborhood, please sign up on our site, [www.ur-home.net].

If you have already listed your home for sale with another broker, please disregard this letter.

Enclosure: ◄———— *Card*

Email Solicitation

CAN-SPAM is an acronym for Controlling the Assault of Non-Solicited Pornography and Marketing.

To protect consumers from being assaulted by misleading unsolicited email messages, unsolicited emails must include the following:

- Opt-out mechanism where the recipient can indicate no more emails are to be sent

- Functioning return email address

- Valid subject line indicating a message is an advertisement

- Legitimate physical address of the mailer

It is a misdemeanor to send spam with falsified header information. Each violation is subject to a fine of up to $16,000.

Email solicitations are effective for both seller and buyer. A subject header such as "New Listing Edgemont Estates" or "No Down Payment— 4 Bedrooms" will likely get the email opened if it addresses a need or interest of the recipient. For potential sellers, receiving an email heading such as "Real Estate Sales Activity -Edgemont Estates" can be effective. A monthly email showing the number of listings and sales, average price, price per square foot, as well as high and low prices for both listings and sales is of interest to many owners. Many of the same firms that provide mailing lists for areas also provide email addresses by zip code. Because of low costs and a greater consumer reliance on the internet, internet solicitations are playing a significant role in prospecting.

While email solicitations are low cost, you should realize that an estimated 70 to 80% of email real estate solicitations never get opened. Consider using an email distribution program to manage lists and generate reports as related to your email campaigns.

Building an Email Database

An often overlooked aspect of marketing for real estate agents is the amount of people they meet each and every day that could be added to an email database. New agents should make a conscious effort to put every person who comes into an open house, or every prospect they meet, into an email database to receive marketing material from them. Because the sales cycle for real estate can be quite long, staying at the top of a potential client's mind is crucial to getting the deal at the right time.

In terms of for sale by owners and expired listings, we might want to let readers know where they can purchase these leads. If not where, we should probably let them know that they can buy these leads if they want to. The most popular and commonly used are sites such as www.theredx.com and www.landvoice.com.

WEB LINK

Fax Solicitations

The federal Telephone Consumer Protection Act and FCC regulations prohibit sending unsolicited advertisements and solicitations to a fax machine. Permission to send a fax message can be granted only by a signed statement that includes the fax number to which the fax may be sent. This requirement rules out fax messages for initial contacts for real estate solicitation purposes. A penalty of $1,500 may be assessed for each unsolicited fax.

Newsletters

Many brokers have successfully used newsletters as a prospecting tool. Newsletters are more likely to be read if they include local information about events and people, local athletic team event dates and results, recipes, and important local telephone numbers, as well as real estate information such as mortgage rates and market sales data. A number of vendors supply newsletters, some of which can be readily customized. Members of the California Association of REALTORS® have access to a free newsletter that can be personalized by accessing www.car.org and checking on the newsletter sign-up balloon and then selecting Homeowner's Guide. Newsletters can be mailed, emailed, and left in clubhouses and other public places.

WEB LINK

EXPIRED LISTINGS

Never contact owners before their listing has expired. Attempting to solicit a listing away from another REALTOR® is a violation of the NAR Code of Ethics. When contacting the owners, you want to find out immediately if they have relisted the property with their agent or another agent. If they have, wish them well and end the discussion.

When a listing contract expires, it means the listing office was unsuccessful in procuring a buyer for a property during the contract period. Owners will likely sign a new listing contract with their agent if they are satisfied with the efforts of that agent. If not, the owners may try to sell their property without an agent. But, in most cases, they will list their property with another office. Your approach should be low key. You should realize that the owners are likely frustrated and even distrustful of agents. They may have heard a very positive presentation and assurances of success that did not materialize. If you can convince owners that you know why their property didn't sell and show them a plan likely to lead to success, you have a good chance at the listings.

> If you can show why a property failed to sell and how you can succeed, you have an opportunity to list the property.

The reason a property failed to sell could be related to an agent who failed to market it properly. More likely, however, it relates to the price asked and/or the appearance of the property (exposure). Very simply, a home must be competitive in its marketplace to sell. When there are many sellers and few buyers, being competitive is not enough. A home must appear and be priced in such a manner that it stands out above the competition as a "best buy."

If owners are negative or antagonistic during a front-door approach, consider asking for a glass of water. Chances are you won't be refused because the simple act of helping you puts the owners in a better mood. Frustrated sellers need and want to be heard. Let the sellers go on about the failure of their last agent to secure a buyer and be empathetic toward them.

Then ask three questions:

1. Why do you think your home failed to sell?

2. What could have been done better?

3. Would you like to hear my analysis of why there isn't a Sold sign on your home right now?

An advantage of working expired listings is that owners generally now have more realistic expectations than they had when their property was originally listed for sale.

NEWSPAPER LEADS

Newspapers can provide a number of sources of buyers and sellers. When checking newspapers for leads, don't forget that there are other papers besides the large daily papers. There are "shoppers," or throwaway papers, usually devoted entirely to ads; there are papers for groups, such as for mobile home owners; and there is a wide variety of ethnic and foreign language papers. All of these papers contain leads.

For Sale by Owner (FSBO)

A major reason owners try to sell without an agent is that they feel they are saving a commission. Another reason could be related to a prior unpleasant experience with an agent. The owners must be shown that working with an agent is in their best interests, and that the agent will in fact be earning the compensation.

A simple way to get to talk to a for sale by owner (FSBO) is to visit the home and tell the owner about one of the buyers you are working with and then ask, "If I had an offer from this buyer, would you want to see it?"

Because few people would not want to see an offer, the answer likely will be in the affirmative. Of course, this gives you the opportunity to view the home. You could then ask for a one-party short-term listing if you feel you have a prospective buyer who would be interested in the property.

Another approach after introducing yourself might be to ask, "Would you be offended if I asked to see your home?" Most owners will answer in the negative, because, again, to say otherwise would be implying that they are offended.

When viewing a for-sale-by-owner property, you want to come across to the owners as a person they could like. Compliment them on noteworthy things, ask questions, and show you are interested. Make suggestions that will help them sell. Ask how they are advertising the property, what the response has been, their reason for selling, what they will do when they sell, et cetera. Answers can be listing ammunition.

An excellent approach to owners who are advertising their own homes is a front-door offer of a for-sale-by-owner kit:

> [Mr. Chan], I am [Gary Frank from Canyon Realty]. I can help you sell your home without any agent fees. Our office has put together a for-sale-by-owner kit that contains a For Sale sign, contracts, loan contacts, required disclosures, instructions for open houses, and a lot more information. We provide these kits absolutely free as a goodwill gesture. Of course, we hope that if you decide later you want professional assistance, you will consider [Canyon Realty]. I can give you one of these free kits now and show you how to use the forms, although it will take close to an hour to cover the forms and disclosures. Will you [and your wife] be home at seven tonight, or would eight be more convenient?

Your kit should be everything you discussed and more. Put warning labels on sheets that talk about subordination clauses, contingencies, owner points, and so on.

When you meet with the owners, give them the For Sale signs and ask to sit down to go over the forms. Suggest the kitchen table, because it is a non-threatening environment and allows for a physical closeness. Go over the forms, explaining the clauses, the importance of disclosures, and anything else your experience tells you is important for this seller to know. By the time you finish your presentation, the owners will probably be wondering if a sale without an agent is really as simple as they had imagined.

Ask the owner how he or she arrived at the price.

Next, ask, "May I inquire what you're asking for your home? How did you arrive at that price?"

The owners' price likely is based on a single sale or what they would like to get for the property. Continue with, "It would be presumptuous of me to tell you if the price is high or low, but our firm can prepare a comparative market analysis from our computer data. I would like to do a comparative market analysis on your home. This is, of course, provided at no charge."

Chances are the owners will accept your offer. They have already received valuable material, and you have likely sold yourself as a professional. Your appointment to present the market analysis should be on the next day.

After you present the market data analysis, ask the owners if you could just take a few minutes to express why you feel they should consider having an agent. After giving them all this valuable material, the owners will feel obligated to answer in the affirmative. You can then go into a listing presentation. (See Units 5 and 6.)

A variation of the this approach is to offer the owners the use of Open House signs and banners. Use the presence of signs and banners as a reason to follow up with the seller. "How's our sign holding up, Mr. Johnson?" "Is there anything else I can help you with?" These questions provide the agent a reason to continue to follow up with the for sale by owner. Generally, most for sale by owners either end up listing with an agent or taking the property off the market. Consistent follow-up will put you in the front running when the seller does decide to list.

Rental Ads

When a single-family or a mobile home is advertised for rent, it may be a case of an owner who really wants to sell but who needs income for payments. If the owners indicate they will give a tenant an option to purchase, you know they want to sell. Telephone numbers outside the area are more likely than local numbers to signify owners highly motivated to sell. Owner contact can be made face to face or by letter.

Whenever you receive a rental inquiry at your office or through canvassing, don't dismiss the prospect because you don't have any rentals. Prospective renters can frequently be turned into buyers with just a few questions: "Have you considered buying?" "Would you be interested in buying if you could buy with no or very little down payment and have monthly payments similar to what you would pay in rent?"

If you can show prospective renters how they can be buyers, you gain a lead for your existing listings and increase the likelihood of closing a sale. If a prospective renter was formerly an owner, chances are she is not going to be happy as a renter.

Trades

People advertising willingness to trade usually want to sell. By explaining delayed exchanges (see Unit 14), you can show owners how they can sell and still have their trade. Keep in mind that some people advertising trades may be dealers.

Marriage and Engagement Announcements

These announcements can be a source of leads. Perhaps the couple getting married have one or more previous residences each that they want to sell. The couple may also be looking to purchase a new residence. It is also possible that parents of the couple may be wishing to downsize or relocate. These are all prospects worth talking to.

Birth Announcements

Birth announcements could be leads to listings of condominiums or mobile homes and even to sales of single-family homes.

Legal Notices

Notices of legal action can be an excellent source of leads for motivated buyers and sellers. Rather than checking through county records, consider subscribing to a legal notice newspaper in your county.

Foreclosure.   When a notice of default is recorded, it indicates an owner is in trouble. Often the only help is a speedy sale. Keep in mind that just because a property is in foreclosure does not mean it is a good listing opportunity. Before listing, obtain a property profile from a title company. (A *property profile* is a computer printout showing the owner of the property and the liens against the property. It is a free service that title companies provide to the real estate profession.) Keep in mind that even if the liens against the property could exceed the property value, a short sale might be possible.

> Legal notices indicate problems and problems = opportunities.

Probate.   Heirs who inherit property often prefer cash. In other cases, the property must be sold to pay debts of the estate or to carry out the wishes of the deceased. Contact the executor or administrator of the estate for a listing.

Divorce.   The largest asset of most families is their home. Because California is a community property state, divorce often means that a home must be sold so the assets can be divided.

Bankruptcy.   In California, owners in bankruptcy may be able to keep their homes because of their homestead exemption. However, many people in bankruptcy seek a new start and often wish to relocate. A sale listing may therefore be possible. Keep in mind that based on when the listing is taken, the bankruptcy court may need to approve the listing contract and subsequent payment of commissions.

Death notices.   Although death of a spouse frequently means a sale, it can be difficult to solicit a listing after a death. We recommend that no approach be made for at least one month after a death, and then the approach could be to ask the homeowner's help in locating a home in the area for a particular family. An owner who is at all interested in relocating will bring it up.

Evictions.   An eviction means an owner with a problem. When owners of income property don't have problems, they are not likely to be highly motivated to sell. When owners have problems, motivation to sell increases in relation to the seriousness of the problems. Eviction notices are a good source of motivated sellers.

Building permits.   An individual who takes out a building permit could still own another home. Because of the length of the building period, that individual might intend to place the other home on the market later. When the building permit is taken out in the name of the builder, it could mean that a home is being built for speculation. In either case, building permit calls might produce excellent listings.

Code violations.   Notices of code violations and/or fines indicate an owner with a problem property. Owners who don't want to deal with these problems can be motivated sellers.

Tax delinquencies.   Owners delinquent in taxes might have financial problems. The solution to their problem could be a sale. These notices can be an excellent listing source.

When owners have legal problems or personal or family problems, the best approach is to ask the owner's help in meeting the needs of another. Any indication that you are contacting them because they are in serious difficulty would likely result in a defensive and negative reaction.

OTHER PROSPECTING METHODS

Advertising

Besides using it as a selling tool, advertising can be used to obtain listings.

Roy Brooks was a legendary estate agent in England. He gained celebrity status because of his unusual and very effective ads. He found that an advertisement for property to sell that was like everyone else's ads made his ad just one among many. He realized that ads for listings had to stand out from the others. To do this, he advertised for particular prospective buyers. One of the ads Roy Brooks used was the following:

> WE HAVE A RATHER REPULSIVE OLD MAN who, with his child-wife, is looking for an elegant town res. pref. Belgravia, Chelsea, or S. Ken. Price not important but must be realistic as he has, at least, his head screwed on the right way. Usual scale of commission required. ROY BROOKS.

Make your ad stand out.

Note: Before you use an ad such as this, get permission from the "repulsive old man and his child-wife."

Look for Problems

As you drive around, look for problem properties: properties in need of repair, overgrown landscaping, properties obviously vacant, and properties that have had rental signs up for a long time. Also watch for For Sale by Owner signs.

Visible problems usually mean the need for a change in ownership, a problem you, as a real estate professional, are prepared to solve. You can locate the owners of these properties by checking with the county tax assessor's office or a title company.

Internet Site

California Association of REALTORS® surveys illustrate the growing use of the internet by homebuyers. Only 28% of buyers utilized the internet in 2000. In 2005, 62% of homebuyers indicated that the internet was an integral part of their homebuying process, up from 56% in 2004, and by 2007, the number increased to 72%. A 2009 REALTOR® study in Massachusetts revealed that 90% of homebuyers utilized the internet in the buying process, and in 2014 it had risen to 92%.

Studies indicate that internet buyers devoted more time to research before working with an agent and spent just two weeks looking with an agent and viewed just 6.2 homes. Buyers who did not use the internet spent an average of seven weeks working with an agent and viewed 14.5 homes before making a purchase.

The growing importance of the internet reinforces the need for brokers to use internet sites to achieve maximum benefits. An office website or personal website should be referenced on all of your cards, ads, and letters. Such a site could show your success in an area, as well as any value changes in the area. One way to show success is a "success list" of properties sold. The site also could show advantages of low interest rates, indicating that the time to sell or buy couldn't be better.

The design of an internet site is not the place for economy. While there are self-help books and computer programs for designing your own site, and designers who advertise that they will prepare your site for $200 or less, site preparation is not the place for bare-bones economy. Many sites use motion and sound to keep the prospect watching. View a variety of sites, including those of other brokers, and strive for a site designer who will better your competition. The prevalence of IDX searches allows MLS data to be displayed on the agent's website directly. This can be a cost-effective solution and gives the agent the ability to tell a buyer or a seller to search the MLS directly from the agent's website.

We have included a sample home page (Figure 4.3) to give you ideas for what can be done. While there is motion on this site, it doesn't appear in print. The main picture changes with views of Sun City as well as offerings.

Some brokers have home pages on their sites where a viewer can click "find a home" or "What does (Jones Realty) have to offer?" The latter sells your firm's competence and integrity.

The "find a home" portion of your site can result in calls from "half-sold" buyers you didn't know existed but who had visited your firm on a website.

FIGURE 4.3: **Bob & Michael Horne WEBSITE**

Used with the permission of Bob and Michael Horne.

A single property can be presented on numerous separate websites. As an example, a home located in the Coachella Valley could be presented on www.Realtor.com and other national sites. It could also be on an area site. In addition, if the broker belongs to a relocation service or a franchise, or both, property could be presented on additional sites. General websites such as www.craigslist.com attract millions of viewers. Many brokers realize that these sites can be especially productive. It is not unusual for a brokerage firm to have their offerings on from 6 to 10 websites, including their own firm's site.

By checking competitors' internet presentations of their listings, you will see a significant variance. Some properties indicate "picture not available," while others not only have an attractive exterior photo but also allow the viewer to click on additional photos, a detailed property description, and possibly even a virtual tour.

A visitor to your website might not be interested in your offerings and go elsewhere. You want to know who that visitor was and what his interests are. You can get this information with a nonthreatening offer of help. Offering to provide emails of new listings before they are even advertised is a great hook, because most buyers are interested in a first chance, especially in an active market. The visitor would then fill in price parameters, must-have and would-like features, and finally their name and email address.

You can also prospect for both buyers and sellers by using mailings or ads offering to supply owners with details of sales (by email), so that they can understand area values. They would register on your site, giving details of a home that they want comparables for. The emails they would receive would include photos and details, as well as sale prices of similar home sales. Because you are providing an owner with information of interest, a personal contact should result in a positive response.

Just as classified ads (discussed in Unit 8) are in competition with other classified ads, your internet property presentations are in competition with many others. (It is important that you incorporate what you will learn in Unit 8 into your website.)

WEB LINK

@

Websites of others can also be a source for leads. By checking www.forsale-byowner.com, you might find homes in your area that you might not have known were on the market. There are a number of other sites that include for-sale-by-owner listings, such as www.craigslist.org, forsalebyowner.com, www.homepointe.com, www.owners.com, FSBO.com and HomesByOwner.com.

In Unit 8, you will learn many ways to use the internet, including social media sites and blogs.

Check Interested Parties

Property neighbors. When you have a listing of land or income property, contact adjoining property owners, as well as owners of similar property in the area. Neighbors are a source of both buyers and sellers. For residential property, the approach to neighbors could be "Would you like to help choose your new neighbor?" When neighbors have an interest in an outcome, they can be an effective source of prospects.

For income property, as well as farms and raw land, adjoining property owners are good buyer candidates. All many people want is "What's mine and what's next to mine."

Investors and speculators. When an investment property is sold, find out who the buyer is. The same holds true for lots and fixer-uppers. Contact these buyers to find out if they have further interests in purchasing property and, if so, what their interests are. It isn't hard to find the active players in a market. Many of these buyers will welcome an additional pair of eyes, ears, and legs working for them. Keep in mind that these people can be prospects for both listing and selling.

Lenders. Check with local lenders about their **real estate owned (REO)** properties. Find out how to get a key to show the property, as well as what commission will be paid, if any.

Some brokers offer full service for lenders. They offer cleanup service and full maintenance services to protect the property until it can be sold. These services give them an advantage over other brokers as to exclusive listings besides creating another profit center.

Besides local lenders, contact the Department of Housing and Urban Development (HUD) and the Federal Deposit Insurance Corporation (FDIC), as well as the Federal Housing Administration (FHA) and the Department of Veterans Affairs (VA) for foreclosure lists. Many agents specialize in selling lender-owned property.

Chambers of commerce. Check with your local chamber of commerce. Ask to be notified of inquiries made by people or companies planning to relocate to your area. If you can reach them first by letter or email, you may be in a preferred position as a possible selling agent.

Membership in a chamber of commerce will help you obtain inquiry information in a timely fashion. Membership can also provide networking opportunities that can bring business. Many networking groups are limited to one representative from each industry. You don't want to end up in a group dominated by other real estate agents.

Open houses. Open houses can be a good source of both buyer and seller leads. Many people who stop at an open house can't be buyers until they sell their present homes. Some agents will hold open houses on homes listed by other agents within their firm if the property has an attractive exterior (curb appeal) and is on a high-traffic street. Each open house can build a pool of potential buyers with some similarity of interests. If you intend to specialize in an area, price range or type of property, conducting open houses that fall into the category you are interested in can help build a huge pool of new listings to contact. (Open houses are covered in detail in Unit 7.)

> The endless chain method is the process of using prospects to recommend other prospects ad infinitum.

Endless chain. The basis of the **endless chain**, or referral, method of prospecting is to ask every prospect to recommend other prospects. The use of an endless chain can result in an amazing number of referral prospects. For example, if you secure the names of two prospects from every person you interview, you would get two names from your first prospect; these two should yield four; these four should provide eight; and so on. This can continue, eventually resulting in thousands who are at least potential clients, people whose needs have not yet been determined.

Your friends. One of the first things you should do on entering the real estate business is to make a list of all the acquaintances and friends you have made over the years. Your list should contain a minimum of 50 names. A good place to start is your holiday card list. Send these people an announcement that you are in the real estate business and indicate how proud you are that your work may give you an opportunity to help them in the future. Be sure to send announcements to the professional people who serve you and who over the years have had your faith and confidence—your doctor, dentist, attorney, and any other professional people you deal with. Because you do business with them, it is likely they will be willing to do business with you.

Another community resource that should not be overlooked is the people with whom you do non–real estate business. You have to buy food, clothing, gas, personal services, and so on. Tell the people who sell things or services to you that you are in the real estate business. These people come in contact with other people every day, and from time to time they hear of someone who is thinking of listing and selling a home or buying a new home. Such communication is commonly called **networking**.

Your sellers.   A sale normally is part of a chain reaction. Sellers of property generally become buyers of other properties, and those sellers, in turn, buy again. Even before a property is sold, find out the intention of the owners. If they will be buyers within the area, you want to be the agent who will sell to them. If they are leaving the area, consider that a referral fee could be possible from an agent in their new community.

Your buyers.   Most people are glad they purchased their homes. If you sold houses to some of these satisfied buyers, you can turn this positive feeling buyers have about their purchases to your benefit. Stopping by with a small housewarming gift several weeks after they take occupancy will give you an opportunity to talk about their relatives and friends who have real estate needs. Whenever you get a listing in the area, contact former buyers by phone or email to see if they have friends who might be interested.

You can also use the approach of asking them to help another:

> I could use your help. I'm trying to find a home for [a retired couple] who wish to live in your area because [they want to be close to their grandchildren]. Do you know anyone in the area who might consider selling or anyone who has had a change in family size because of marriage, divorce, birth, or graduation?

Note: Always use a real prospect, but never give out personal information without

Your neighbors.   Another broker's sign on a neighbor's home shows that you have failed to make your neighbors realize that you are a real estate professional who is available to meet their needs. When you enter the real estate profession, consider a mailing to your neighbors. Figure 4.4 is a broker letter to neighbors of a new sales associate.

Take a walk around your neighborhood with your child or your dog to give you an opportunity to talk to neighbors. Let them know you are in real estate and where you live. Hand out business cards. By asking questions you can find leads. In most neighborhoods, there are a few people who seem to know everything that is happening. These people should be developed as your extra pairs of eyes and ears.

In condominium complexes and mobile home parks, spend time around the recreational facilities. You will seldom have any trouble finding someone to talk to. By knowing what to ask, you can quickly discover what is happening in the area.

Centers of Influence

Another successful prospecting method is to cultivate the friendship of influential persons in the community or territory. These **centers of influence** can help you obtain prospects by referring people who can use your services. These influential people can tell others about you and tell you about people they know who might require professional real estate services. Centers of influence serve to bring you together with potential sellers and buyers.

The objective of cultivating relationships with centers of influence is to establish genuine friendships, whenever possible. It is important that they know their help will be appreciated in your search for contacts. Let your centers of influence know the results of their efforts. This will come naturally if the friendship is genuine, and it will encourage the person to keep helping you.

Some agents refer to these helpers as **bird dogs**. This term is not derogatory. It merely indicates that they point the way. Keep in mind that help won't come to you unless you ask for it.

> **Centers of influence** are people who are influential in your community.

You must explain what you are looking for, such as a friend or acquaintance who has had a change in family size. Having several dozen extra pairs of eyes and ears working for you can provide a great many leads. The best bird dogs are people who help you because they like you and want to see you succeed. However, for continued effort on your behalf, these helpers must feel they are appreciated. Your appreciation can be verbal; better yet, take them to dinner or give a small personal gift to show your appreciation. While it is a violation of the real estate law to reimburse an unlicensed party for acts requiring a real estate license, compensation may be provided to an individual whose involvement is limited to putting two parties together. Prohibited acts would be paying fees to persons soliciting buyers or sellers, showing property, giving property information, or engaging in any form of negotiation.

FIGURE 4.4:   New Associate Announcement Letter

UR

H O M E   R E A L T Y

_____   ← *Date and address*

_____
_____
_____

Dear _____ :

[Judith Reilly], [your neighbor] who lives [at 111 Midvale Lane in Sunshine Estates], has recently joined our firm as [1. a sales associate 2. an associate broker]. [Judith] has been your neighbor for [four] years. [She] and [her husband] have [two children, Lisa, age nine, and Jeffrey, age seven, both of whom attend Midvale School]. [Judith is a graduate of Ohio State and previously worked in marketing.] [She] has just completed our training program and will be specializing in [residential sales] in [Orchard Ridge]. If you or any of your friends have any real estate needs, we hope you will contact [Judith]. I have enclosed one of [her] new cards.

Sincerely,

_____

Enclosure: ← *Card*

Note: Don't give out personal information about anyone, even your own salespeople, without permission. Many people don't want information about their children given out.

Good Centers of Influence

- Prominent club members
- Friends
- Relatives
- Attorneys
- Doctors
- Accountants
- Physical therapists
- Dog groomers
- Hair dressers
- Prominent members of civic and charitable organizations
- Golf and tennis professionals
- Ministers, priests, and rabbis
- Bankers
- Public officials
- Teachers
- Health club employees
- Business executives
- People with whom you share a mutual interest, such as a hobby or recreational activity

Community Service

Closely akin to the centers-of-influence method is prospecting through local community service groups. Making contacts by participating in community activities can not only bring in more business but also provide personal satisfaction from working for the benefit of others.

Community service organizations recommended for involvement include the following:

- Churches and other houses of worship

- PTAs

- Educational groups

- College associations

- Chambers of commerce

- Civic organizations

- Service groups

- Boys and girls clubs

- Boy Scouts and Girl Scouts

- Recreational clubs (ski, travel, biking, boating, etc.)

- YMCAs and YWCAs

- Political organizations

- Senior centers

Community activities can also provide these benefits:

- Opportunities to counsel fellow members in such areas as investments, property management, and commercial realty

- Constant exposure to referral sources

- Constant exposure to other property owners

- Personal development, by learning and growing through participation

- Development of a more professional image as a real estate licensee

Your peers will have greater respect for a colleague who participates in community activities. The key is to get involved with people and help fulfill their needs. In seeking contacts through community service groups, however, beware of overcommitment. It is important to develop the ability to say no gracefully. Overcommitting yourself can upset your timetable and also may jeopardize your health. Follow these guidelines:

■ Work in only one or two organizations at one time; strive for quality, not quantity

■ Anticipate time-consuming assignments before becoming involved

■ Do not play personalities for an advantage

■ Do not play politics

To stay aware of what is going on, participate where possible in carefully selected committees. Membership on the following committees has proved to be most helpful to licensees:

■ Greeting committee (new members)

■ Membership committee

■ Social or party committee

■ "Sunshine" (visit the sick, etc.) committee

Be cautious in using membership as a prospecting technique, because it is easy to turn off fellow members by being overly aggressive. Obtain help from others, but do not abuse them. When you first join a club or association, keep a low profile. It is advisable to do something for the organization and strengthen your relationships before you ask members for referrals.

Fundraising for a worthwhile charity is an excellent way to meet people. While there may be a negative reaction to having to open their wallets, you will have shown that you are a person with a positive community interest.

> ### Build a Referral List
>
> Agents must bring some sort of order to their prospect lists to avoid getting stuck with a briefcase full of names and little else. To build a list and successfully use referrals, the licensee should follow these guidelines:
>
> **Develop a systematic plan.** This includes studying prospects as you talk to them. Ask for leads as soon after contact as feasible, and ask the prospects how you can improve your services.
>
> **Keep track of the results of your methods.**
>
> **Utilize all sources of information.** This includes friends, neighbors, professionals, people in businesses of all kinds, and social contacts.
>
> **Make them all aware that you are in the real estate business and would appreciate all referrals.**
>
> **Follow up referrals by reporting back to the referrer.** Also important is to use a computer contact management system to record referrals for future calls. A person giving a negative response now may still be in the market in the future.

There are a number of software programs for contact management. Sage Software has *Act! Premium Software,* a specific program for real estate professionals.

FARMING

Farming is working or prospecting an area or area of interest for sellers as well as buyers. The area chosen for farming can be geographic or non-geographic (a special interest area). Your farm should be chosen based on your personal goals, interests, and your specific market area. The longer you work a farm, the more productive it becomes. Farming requires constant attention and regular contacts.

Geographic Farms

A **geographic farm** is a specific area with definite boundaries that is worked by an agent. Within the specific area, the agent seeks a dominant share of the marketplace.

The best geographic farms tend to be homogeneous areas having similarly priced homes, or they share other characteristics such as age, attitude toward recreational activity, family type, and so forth. Areas of common identity, such as a particular subdivision, or mobile home park generally make good farming areas. By farming an area they already live in, agents will have existing contacts and exposure within the farm area.

Farming yields a crop of listings.

In choosing a farm area, consider how you relate to the people in the area or group. If you are comfortable with and have a special interest in the area or group, you are likely to put forth the effort required for success.

If someone already is actively farming an area with great success, you might consider an area with less active competition. Although you should not mind competition, there might be equally desirable areas with little or no competition, which would mean less resistance to overcome. Just one day of knocking on doors could reveal whether an area is being actively farmed by another professional.

Some experts claim that a farm area should not exceed about 500 homes. We believe the size should be based on the size of the area, considering reasonable, identifiable boundaries as well as the agent's available time and techniques used to devote to farming activities. The fact that there are no hard and fast rules governing farm size can be shown by **megafarming**. Some agents farm areas of several thousand homes. Some of these agents use salaried assistants to help them. The internet is an easy and almost cost-free method of farming and allows for larger farms. Still other agents are able to handle larger than normal farms by specializing in listing activities rather than sales.

A farm takes time to produce a crop of sellers and buyers. Like an agricultural farm, it must be constantly worked to be productive. Generally, agents working geographic farms strive for a minimum of one contact per month with every owner within their farm area. The contact might be direct mail, the internet, a phone conversation that does not violate do-not-call rules, or a face-to-face meeting. Besides letters and personal contacts, email newsletters are very effective at minimal cost. Many agents blog on neighborhood group websites and/or have their own blog website. Getting to know owners and, more important, letting them get to know you places you in an excellent position to work with owners as buyers or sellers when a sale or purchase is needed or desired.

Nongeographic Farms/ Social Farm

A **nongeographic farm** is a particular segment of the marketplace defined according to property differentiation or buyer/seller differentiation. For example, an agent could choose to work a particular ethnic group. If an agent works a particular ethnic or nationality segment of the population, it would be a significant plus if the agent were a member of the group and had the necessary language skills of the group.

An agent might work only a type of property for small investors, such as duplexes. There are a number of agents who specialize in horse properties (properties zoned for horses).

A number of agents farm expired listings, providing owners with updates on listings and sales, as well as seeking personal contact. If your broker has an internet address (URL) tied to your farm area, it will show broker commitment to your area. The site could be both a personal site and one that is connected to properties and blogs. It can also be a marketing tool. Brokers who specialize in auction sales often vigorously farm expired listings for their auction sales.

In a nongeographic farm, door-to-door canvassing will seldom be effective. Acquiring membership lists of organizations and even religious groups, as well as buying specialized mailing lists, will allow you to work this type of farm by direct mail.

The internet can be a valuable source for leads when working a nongeographic farm. Using one of the search engines, you should be able to zero in on your area of specialty within your marketing area. You will find organizations, companies, or groups that can provide leads as to buyers, sellers, lessors, or lessees. You will also find organizations, companies, or groups outside your marketing area that have access to information within your marketing area.

Whatever type or area of farm you choose, keep in mind that farming must be continuous. If you slow down your efforts, you will begin to lose market share from your farm at a fairly rapid pace. Although every successful agent does not farm, either by geographic areas or by special interest, every successful agent does prospect for buyers and sellers.

Niche Marketing

Specializing in a narrow segment of the market is known as **niche marketing**. As you gain exposure to the many possibilities of niche marketing, you may decide to choose a niche that you feel best meets your personality, experience, and needs.

In choosing a niche that serves a particular group of buyers or sellers, you must be cognizant of both your moral and your legal responsibilities concerning discrimination. (See Unit 2.)

> Niche marketing is specialization in a narrow segment of the marketplace.

An excellent way to find a niche category of buyers is to go through your old files to see if you have been serving a certain group more than other groups. When you have identified a customer segment, draw a profile of its demographic and psychological characteristics. Prospecting and after-sale surveys are two avenues for accumulating this kind of information. When you analyze past customers, try to determine why they came to you, how effectively you helped them, and the areas in which you feel you may have been weak. This will help you put together a plan to draw more people like them to your customer segment. You also will gain more from your advertising and marketing strategies if these strategies are coordinated around those surveys. Customer segment specialization helps you build a known area of expertise that will enhance your reputation, result in referrals, and keep your customers coming to you, instead of going somewhere else.

Customer segmentation could be flippers who buy, fix and sell, investment property owners, no-down-payment buyers, et cetera. Your niche could be the property type, such as foreclosures, mobile homes, homes with acreage, et cetera.

DEVELOP A PROSPECTING PLAN

Without a definite prospecting plan, prospecting becomes more of a "when you think about it" activity. The results will be far less than optimum. Figure 4.5 shows a sample prospecting plan.

You can evaluate the effectiveness of your prospecting plan by keeping track of the sources of new prospects as well as the results of working with the prospects. Quality of leads is really more important than quantity of leads.

By considering the time spent on your prospecting activities, you may discover that your interests would be better served by a reallocation of time, a change in your plan, or both. Your initial prospecting plan should not be cast in stone. It is a guide that may change, based on your interests and effectiveness in working with different types of situations.

FIGURE 4.5:   Sample Prospecting Plan

1. Each Monday morning call on the weekend FSBO ads as well as FSBO signs you have observed so you can view for your buyer clients.
2. Contact owners within a one-block radius of every new listing taken within three days of listing.
3. Send letters or make personal contact each Friday morning on foreclosures and evictions listed in a legal newspaper.
4. Contact at least one former buyer each week to ask about friends and/or relatives interested in your area or neighbors who might be relocating.
5. Have lunch at least once each week with a person who has provided or can provide referrals.
6. Make a minimum of 30 contacts each week to locate a home for prospective buyers with whom you are working.
7. For new investment property listings, contact owners of similar property within the neighborhood of the listing. (You need not be limited to your office listings.)
8. Conduct at least one open house each week.
9. Ask at least three people each week for referrals and buyer-seller leads.
10. Contact people whom you have previously asked for help at least once each month.
11. Send weekly e-mails about new listings to previous buyers and sellers, as well as any new contacts you are working with.
12. Give out at least five business cards each day.

SUMMARY

Prospecting is a process used to locate prospective buyers and sellers of real property. There are many methods of prospecting, including door-to-door canvassing, direct mail canvassing, emails, expired listings, newspaper leads (For Sale by Owner ads; rental ads; trades; engagement, marriage, and birth announcements; and death notices), legal notices (foreclosures, probate, evictions, building permits, code violations, bankruptcy, tax delinquency), advertising, looking for problems, the internet, property neighbors, investors and speculators, lenders, chambers of commerce, open houses, endless chain referrals, your sellers, your buyers, your neighbors, centers of influence, and community services.

Telephone solicitation has been significantly limited by the do-not-call regulations. Emails must comply with CAN-SPAM regulations, and fax solicitations are limited to recipients who have given written permission for the fax.

The use of the internet has grown in significance, allowing buyers to visualize properties before the first contact.

Farming is working a particular segment of the market intensively. It can be a geographic area or a nongeographic area, which could consist of a certain type of property or an ethnic group.

A prospecting plan forces agents to evaluate how they will prospect and to evaluate results. It is important to have a contact management system so that contacts don't slip away.

CLASS DISCUSSION TOPICS

1. Be prepared to role-play a door-to-door canvassing situation with another student.

2. Identify what you feel would be logical geographic farms in your area, as well as nongeographic farming opportunities.

3. Prepare a prospecting plan for yourself. Include goals and time to be spent executing the plan.

4. List what you expect will be your five best sources of listings in order of effectiveness.

5. Identify three centers of influence that should be useful to you in prospecting.

6. Bring to class one current-events article dealing with some aspect of real estate practice for class discussion.

UNIT 4 QUIZ

1. The CAN-SPAM Act puts controls on unsolicited
    a. fax messages.
    b. misleading emails.
    c. residential phone calls.
    d. real estate assistants.

2. You may legally pay a referral fee to an unlicensed person who
    a. shows listings to prospective buyers.
    b. assists in sale negotiations.
    c. introduces a prospective buyer to the broker.
    d. tells buyers about the beneficial property features.

3. Direct mail solicitation for listings is more effective if you
    a. use window envelopes.
    b. use a mailing machine and bulk rate.
    c. use mailing labels.
    d. indicate you will be contacting them.

4. Under do-not-call regulations, which call would be improper?
    a. Calling for survey purposes
    b. A call to a business phone
    c. A call within three months of an inquiry
    d. A call on a For Sale by Owner ad to solicit a sale listing

5. Which classified ad category is likely to provide listing leads?
    a. Homes for rent
    b. Leases/options to purchase
    c. Mobile homes for rent
    d. All of these

6. Legal notices provide good leads for listings. Which is *NOT* a legal notice?
    a. Eviction
    b. Foreclosure
    c. Probate
    d. Vacancy

7. Which would be an indication that an owner might be interested in selling an income property?
   a. A high vacancy rate
   b. Tenant evictions
   c. Code violations
   d. All of these

8. Endless chain refers to
   a. the long-term effects of advertising.
   b. obtaining additional prospects from every lead.
   c. the fact that your buyer will eventually become a seller.
   d. the fact that most buyers are sellers and sellers are buyers.

9. The term *farming* as used in real estate refers to
   a. determining what your market area will be.
   b. operation by season, such as a listing season, open house season, selling season, and so forth.
   c. specialization in a particular field of real estate activity.
   d. working or prospecting a geographic area or special interest area for buyers and sellers.

10. An example of a nongeographic farm would be specialization in
    a. mobile homes.
    b. income property.
    c. lots.
    d. any of these.

LISTING PRESENTATION PACKAGE

LEARNING OBJECTIVES

When you have completed this unit, you will be able to

- describe a comparative market analysis,

- explain how to estimate seller process,

- list what should be included in a listing presentation, and

- describe the information to be included in buyer listing material.

KEY TERMS

adjusted selling price
comparable properties

comparative market
   analysis
estimated seller's
   proceeds

for sale by owner
listing presentation
   manual

PREPARATION

Getting to the point of an effective face-to-face presentation takes a great deal of effort. An attempt to "wing it" and come in unprepared is more likely to result in failure than success. You should have the material to justify the offering price of the property, to be able to convince the owners that agency representation is in their best interests, and to promote yourself as a professional who understands their needs and is able to meet them.

If your appointment was based on an offer of a **comparative market analysis** (CMA), then we recommend you start at this point. However, if the owners have indicated an interest in listing their property, you might want to start with the listing presentation material.

COMPARATIVE MARKET ANALYSIS

The CMA is really a comparison analysis used by real estate agents to aid in determining a proper list price for a property. Often owners believe their home is worth far more than the CMA would indicate as a fair market value. Your comparables must be presented in an honest, logical, and convincing manner so that the owner realizes that if the property is to sell, it must be priced based on the market. The CMA provides information on **comparable properties** that have been placed in the marketplace, so that they can be compared with the property to be evaluated to determine an offering price. (Comparables are often called *comps*.) Similar property currently on the market is the competition the property owners must go against.

The CMA is not an appraisal. Only certified or licensed appraisers can appraise property. The CMA should be used for single-family residences and for multifamily residential properties of up to four units. In some cases, the CMA can be used for lots. However, it is not an effective tool for larger residential income properties or for commercial or industrial properties.

When relevant property data are selected, the CMA reflects the realities of the marketplace. It should include the following three separate areas:

1. On market now

2. Reported sold prior six months

3. Reported expired prior six months

It is important to have information about all sales in the immediate area over approximately the past six months. If there have been relatively few sales, you might have to go back to expand the analysis to include similarly desirable areas. Similarly, if there were a great many similar sales, the time period could be shortened or the sales area compressed, or both.

An agent could conceivably be liable for damages if a CMA negligently omitted recent similar sales or used unrealistic comparables that resulted in the owner selling a property for less than fair market value. If a court determines that a CMA was prepared to intentionally mislead an owner as to value, then a court might award the owner punitive damages in addition to compensatory damages. For lender-owned properties, you should label them as lender owned and indicate they are offered "as is." Short sales and foreclosure sales should also be indicated as such.

The *on-market-now list* (current listings) merely indicates to an owner the prices that competitors (other owners) are asking for their products (homes). Other owners are competitors because they are seeking to attract the same buyers. The on-market-now list shows an owner what a prospective buyer will see and how the owner's pricing will compare with that of the competition. It does not indicate what an owner can expect to receive from a sale.

> By using comparable properties, the comparative market analysis reflects the reality of the marketplace.

The *reported-sold-prior-six-months list* is more valuable than the list of current properties on the market because it shows actual sales prices. In a market undergoing change, the older the data, the less reliable they are. Prices paid six months ago could be significantly higher than a seller might expect to receive today if the market is falling. On the other hand, prices paid six months ago could be lower than might be anticipated today if the market is rising. Therefore, strive to obtain data covering a period of about the past three months. Use older data only when more current data are not available; even then, older data should be adjusted for market changes.

Adjustments
+ Add for inferior
– Subtract for superior

No two properties are identical. Properties differ by size, age, condition, design, area, view, orientation, and amenities. Adjustments to comparable properties should be made based on the property that is the subject of the CMA. For example, if the comparable property had a better view than the subject property, then the sale price of the comparable would be reduced. If the comparable had two baths and the subject property had 2½ baths, the adjustment would be a higher price for the comparable. The adjusted price is known as the **adjusted selling price**.

Subject Property	Comparable Property	Adjustment to Comparable
2-car garage	3-car garage	–
2½ baths	2 baths	+
9,000 sq. ft. lot	12,000 sq. ft. lot	–
Excellent condition	Needs work	+

There may be sales prices that seem unusual. These too-high or too-low prices are often the result of market imperfections, as covered in Unit 1. Short sales, auctions, and lender "as is" sales could require adjustments. It is also possible that the price paid reflects particular problems or benefits of a property that are not evident from the listing data provided. While prices of sold comparables can be expected to vary within a 10% range of what you consider the value to be (mean point), a variation of 20%, not reflected by the property itself, might be an aberration and not reflect a true market picture. Before you use figures, pull out the old listings and make certain you are not comparing apples and oranges. Information about a property that is significantly different in terms of utility and desirability will give an owner a false sense of value.

The *expired listings* (reported-expired-prior-six-months) *group* is the list of losers. These properties are losers because they failed to sell. Like properties that sold, the more current the expiration of a listing, the more valuable it is for comparison purposes. Often, a property fails to sell because it is overpriced in relation to its competition. From your data, you will likely find that the average list price of homes that failed to sell will be higher than the average list price of homes that sold. Listing prices might be significantly higher than the actual selling prices of the homes that sold. This information can inform owners in a powerful manner that you will not be doing them a favor if you overprice their property. In fact, you could be doing the owners a disservice because the likelihood of selling the property will be decreased. Even when an owner merely hopes for a higher price but will take less, overpricing will keep buyers away. The reported-expired-prior-six-months group also should reinforce your own knowledge that an overpriced listing is not an asset. Instead, it is a liability because it will steal the time and money you spend promoting it with little likelihood of success.

Obtaining Comparables

Comparables are easy to come by. After becoming a member of the local association of REALTORS®, you can log on to the multiple listing service and pull comps from the computer, input the area desired, the square footage, and other amenities to give you a list of comparable homes that have sold recently in the area. You can also perform a radius search. The advantage is speed—the computer produces comps within seconds. You can use the computer to check the current listings as well as the expired listings in the area. There are also services that will prepare comparables for you.

Personalized CMA

If you treat the CMA you have prepared as a valuable document, it will increase the owners' feeling of value. When you give owners a CMA, you want them to feel that you did some hard work on their behalf. A feeling of indebtedness or obligation goes a long way toward the signing of a listing agreement.

Some offices bind a CMA with a plastic ring binder and prepare a nice cover, using their computer printer. The cover indicates that the CMA was prepared for the named owners by the agent and also indicates the basis of the information enclosed. Rather than use a paper presentation, many offices use a laptop computer for their visual presentation. For comparables, they can show virtual tours. The computer presentation allows a more realistic comparison.

The personalized CMA starts with a sheet on the owners' property. It shows owners that you appreciate their home. Be certain that the narrative includes features that owners particularly pointed out to you when they showed you their home. Owners must feel that you have carefully evaluated the property.

Include a view of their home, as well as of the comparables. You should be able to download them from MLS information on the internet. If you don't have a good photo but the comparable has good eye appeal, take the time to get a photograph. A photograph of a house that looks as nice as or better than the home you are attempting to list for sale, coupled with a list price or sale price less than owners have indicated they desire, can go a long way toward putting owners in a realistic frame of mind. It's trite but true: "A picture is worth a thousand words."

If a comparable has features that the home you want to list lacks, Make certain it is covered in your visuals. It emphasizes the strength of the competition.

Your CMA data always should be as accurate and as current as possible. It should lead to your estimate of the price range in which the owners' home could be sold. This estimate should consider the owners' property, comparable sales, and market changes. A range is more realistic than a single price because it allows for minor variations in the marketplace. Be scrupulous in preparing your CMA. Again, using only the comparables that support your own position can be considered fraudulent.

Although an owner might want to list at a price toward the top edge of the range, by using the range, you have prepared the owner to consider any offer within the range as being a reasonable reflection of value. In a sellers' market, with many buyers and few sellers, the range is likely to be far narrower than it would be in a buyers' market, with many more prospective properties available than there are buyers. So, although you show the range, you might want to recommend a listing at the midpoint or even near the low limit of the range, depending on market conditions and the owners' need for a quick sale.. The reasoning for your recommendation should be made clear by the attachments to the CMA.

CMA Software Programs

There are a number of software programs that will make CMA preparation relatively easy and provide a professional-appearing document. These programs use photographs and property details to help you arrive at a recommended list price. We have included CMA material from ToolkitCMA™, a web-based software program of Realty Tools, Inc. (www.realtytools.com) as Figure 5.1A through Figure 5.1H.

WEB LINK

Computer people use the term *GIGO*, which stands for *garbage in, garbage out*. If your comps were not realistic, you would have a hard time developing a trend. A sale far outside your anticipated range is an aberration, but it should be considered in determining averages. (See Figures 5.1A and Figures 5.3 through 5.6I.)

This material can be a help not only in listing at the price indicated by your CMA but also in listing below the price your CMA recommends as a list price when the seller is strongly motivated to sell. Often a sale at a below-market price is in an owner's best interest, when compared with the alternative of not procuring a buyer during the listing period or even facing foreclosure. By using your laptop computer to present your CMA, you can use listing photos, including virtual tours, which will give owners a realistic understanding of the marketplace.

Let Owners See the Competition

Often owners want a price that cannot be justified by market conditions as revealed by your CMA. They need a harsh dose of reality. Some agents will conduct a short excursion with the owners to several comparable properties on the market. The agent asks the owners to compare the features of their home and the homes viewed. The owners are then requested to guess the price asked of the various properties. When the agent tells the owners what the list price is, it can serve as an aid to helping owners understand the reality of the current market.

For comparables, use vacant properties. You do not want to intrude on owners when the benefit is other than a sale of that property.

It is an unethical and unfair practice to take an overpriced listing with the secret intent of then trying to influence the owner to reduce the price or to take the listing to sell other properties. Some agents will show an overpriced property to make another property appear to be bargain priced.

Owners who insist on a price above what you consider to be a fair market value range should realize the following:

1. The higher the price, the longer it will take to sell the property.

2. The higher the price, the lower the chance of sales success .

3. Even if the sale is successful, it is likely to fall in the fair-market range or less.

FIGURES 5.1A – 5.1H: CMA Material from ToolkitCMA™

Determining the Value of Your Home

A Comparative Market Analysis (CMA) is essential to determine the value of residential property. Location and characteristics of the property are the key elements in determining value. Therefore, the basis for valuation is similar properties in your area. The market analysis takes into account the amount received from recent sales of comparable properties and the quantity and quality of comparable properties currently on the market. The desired end result is to find a price that will attract a willing and able buyer in a reasonable time.

Once the value of your home has been determined, you can decide on an offering price that will achieve your goals. Generally, the price should not exceed the value by more than 5% or potential buyers may not even make offers. Naturally, if you want to sell quickly your asking price should be very near the value.

The following are a few things to keep in mind about pricing:

- Realistic pricing will achieve maximum price in a reasonable time.
- Your cost or profit desire is irrelevant; the market determines the price.
- The cost of improvements are almost always more than the added value.
- Houses that remain on the market for a long time do not get shown.
- A house that is priced right from the beginning achieves the highest proceeds.

Angela McKendrick, CRS, GRI
Office: 410-555-1234
Home Office: 410-432-7890
Fax: 410-555-5607
Web Site: www.demorealty.com/angela
Email: angela.mckendrick@demorealty.com

Green Leaf Realty
www.greenleafrealty.com

A.

The Importance of Intelligent Pricing

Determining the best asking price for a home can be one of the most challenging aspects of selling a home. It is also one of the most important. If your home is listed at a price that is above market value, you will miss out on prospective buyers who would otherwise be prime candidates to purchase your home. If you list at a price that is below market value, you will ultimately sell for a price that is not the optimum value for your home. As *Figure 1* illustrates, more buyers purchase their properties at market value than above market value. The percentage increases as the price falls even further below market value. Therefore, by pricing your property at market value, you expose it to a much greater percentage of prospective buyers. This increases your chances for a sale while ensuring a final sale price that properly reflects the market value of your home.

Figure 1 - Percentage of Buyers by Asking Price

Another critical factor to keep in mind when pricing your home is timing. A property attracts the most attention, excitement and interest from the real estate community and potential buyers when it is first listed on the market *(see Figure 2)*. Improper pricing at the initial listing misses out on this peak interest period and may result in your property languishing on the market. This may lead to a below market value sale price *(see Figure 3)*, or, even worse, no sale at all. Therefore, your home has the highest chances for a fruitful sale when it is new on the market and the price is reasonably established.

Figure 2 - Activity versus Timing

We can give you up-to-date information on what is happening in the marketplace and the price, financing, terms, and condition of competing properties. These are key factors in getting your property sold at the best price, quickly and with minimum hassle.

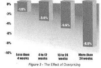
Figure 3 - The Effect of Overpricing

Angela McKendrick, CRS, GRI
Office: 410-555-1234
Home Office: 410-432-7890
Fax: 410-555-5607
Web Site: www.demorealty.com/angela
Email: angela.mckendrick@demorealty.com

Green Leaf Realty
www.greenleafrealty.com

B.

Why use a REALTOR®?

When selling your home, your REALTOR® can give you up-to-date information on what is happening in the marketplace including price, financing and terms of competing properties. These are key factors in a successful sale of your property at the best price in the least amount of time.

Only real estate licensees who are members of the NATIONAL ASSOCIATION OF REALTORS® are properly called REALTORS®. REALTORS® subscribe to a strict code of ethics and are expected to maintain a higher level of knowledge of the process of buying and selling real estate. They are committed to treat all parties to a transaction honestly. REALTOR® business practices are monitored at local board levels. Arbitration and disciplinary systems are in place to address complaints from the public or other board members.

Your REALTOR® can help you objectively evaluate every buyer's proposal and then help write an appropriate legally binding sale agreement. Between the initial sales agreement and settlement, questions may arise. For example, unexpected repairs may be required to obtain financing or a problem with the title is discovered. Your REALTOR® is the best person to help you resolve those issues and move the transaction to settlement.

Angela McKendrick, CRS, GRI
Office: 410-555-1234
Home Office: 410-432-7890
Fax: 410-555-5607
Web Site: www.demorealty.com/angela
Email: angela.mckendrick@demorealty.com

Green Leaf Realty
www.greenleafrealty.com

C.

Important Factors In Choosing A Real Estate Agent

A variety of factors influence a seller's decision to list with a particular real estate agent.

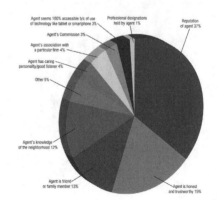

Source: National Association of Realtors®
Profile of Home Buyers and Sellers.

Angela McKendrick, CRS, GRI
Office: 410-555-1234
Home Office: 410-432-7890
Fax: 410-555-5607
Web Site: www.demorealty.com/angela
Email: angela.mckendrick@demorealty.com

Green Leaf Realty
www.greenleafrealty.com

D.

FIGURES 5.1A – 5.1H (continued): CMA Material from ToolkitCMA™

Comparative Market Analysis Summary

Currently On The Market

Address	Neighborhood	Style	Yr Blt	Beds	Bath	Sold Price	List Price
2 Symphony Cir	Laurelford	Modern	2008	4	3/1		$789,000
12218 Cleghorn Road	Laurelford	Modern	1986	4	2/2		$814,900
13213 Beaver Dam Rd	Ivy Hill	Classic	1984	4	3/2		$849,900
84 Warren Rd	Hillsyde	Colonial	1994	5	4/1		$885,000
20 Laurelford Ct	Laurelford	Colonial	1992	4	3/1		$892,000
9 Jules Brentony	Shawan	Colonial	1995	4	3/1		$898,900
510 West Padonia Rd	Springhill Farm	Modern	1991	5	4/1		$899,500

Average of 7 Properties: $861,314   Min: $789,000   Max: $899,500   Median: $885,000

Under Contract

Address	Neighborhood	Style	Yr Blt	Beds	Bath	Sold Price	List Price
13707 Cuba Rd	Hillsyde	Cape Cod	1992	2	2/1		$839,000
9 Ivy Reach Court	Ivy Reach	Colonial	2008	4	2/1		$842,925
3 Indian Spring Court	Sherwood	Colonial	1995	6	4/1		$850,000
15 David Luther Ct	Laurelford/Ivy	Colonial	1990	5	3/1		$899,000
11 Foxtrot Ct	Laurelford/Ivy	Colonial	1993	2	2/1		$899,000

Average of 5 Properties: $865,985   Min: $839,000   Max: $899,000   Median: $850,000

Recently Sold

Address	Neighborhood	Style	Yr Blt	Beds	Bath	Sold Price	List Price
19 Chris Eliot Ct	Ivy Hill	Colonial	1969	3	3/1	$725,000	$849,000
12 Old Padonia Rd	Laurelford	Modern	2008	4	3/1	$755,000	$759,000
4 Chamarat Ct	Ivy Hill	Colonial	1991	4	3/1	$775,000	$799,000
12002 Boxer Hill Rd	Sherwood	Colonial	1995	6	4/1	$790,000	$850,000
12993 Jerome Jay Dr	Laurelford/Ivy	Colonial	1990	5	3/1	$830,000	$899,000
24 Springhill Farm Ct	Springhill Farm	Cottage	2003	4	3/1	$850,000	$899,900
506 Shawan Rd	Hillsyde	Classic	2003	5	4/2	$855,500	$885,000
205 Warren Rd	Laurelford/Ivy	Colonial	1993	2	2/1	$885,000	$899,000

Average of 8 Properties: $808,200   Min: $725,000   Max: $885,000   Median: $810,000

Off The Market

Address	Neighborhood	Style	Yr Blt	Beds	Bath	Sold Price	List Price
10 Loveton Cir	Hillsyde	Classic	1994	5	4/1		$885,000
64 Boxwood Lane	Laurelford	Colonial	1992	4	3/1		$892,000
9 Westcroft Ct	Shawan	Colonial	1995	4	3/1		$898,900
23 Chilcoat Rd	Springhill Farm	Cottage	2003	4	3/1		$899,900

E.

Comparative Market Analysis Graphed by Status

Currently On The Market

Price Range of 7 Properties

Under Contract

Price Range of 5 Properties

Recently Sold

Price Range of 8 Properties

Off The Market

Price Range of 5 Properties

F.

Comparative Market Analysis Statistics

Graphic Analysis of Currently On The Market Properties

Summary Statistics of 7 Properties:

Average Price:	$861,314
High Price:	$899,500
Low Price:	$789,000
Median Price:	$885,000
Average Year Built:	1992

G.

Pricing Your Property to Sell

Pricing your property correctly is crucial. You want to sell your property in a timely manner at the highest price possible. Current market conditions determine the value.

Pricing too high or too low can cost you time and money. Realistic pricing will achieve a maximum sale price in a reasonable amount of time.

Analysis of the comparable properties suggests a list price range of:

$783,954 to $832,446

H.

Used with permission of Realty Tools, Inc.

ESTIMATED SELLER'S PROCEEDS

The **estimated seller's proceeds** (also called the net sheet), what an owner actually receives in cash and/or paper from a sale, are of vital importance to owners. Owners who receive less than what they anticipated are going to be disappointed. They are going to be unhappy with you and your firm. When owners are unhappy, the chances that problems will arise during escrow tend to escalate. From the standpoints of good business, agency duty, and basic fairness, you want the owners to understand what they will net from a sale if sold at list price. The owners should know what costs they will incur.

> The estimated seller's proceeds should show what the seller would net, based on a particular sale price.

While there are computer programs that will give you printouts of seller costs based on data you supply to the computer, the completeness of the form increases the likelihood that actual figures will vary only slightly from the estimate. Make sure that you will know the amounts the seller will likely incur. For example, all counties in California charge a documentary transfer tax, but some cities charge an additional tax. The seller should be made aware of these small but important charges. Many agents like to estimate seller costs just a little on the high side, so any surprises are more likely to be pleasant ones. You would prepare a new Estimated Seller's Proceeds form if the price were adjusted or if an offer were received at a price other than the one set forth in the listing.

THE LISTING PRESENTATION MANUAL

The listing presentation manual is a valuable visual tool for obtaining listings. It can be a paper presentation using a three-ring binder with plastic protector sheets for each page, but agents are more likely to use a laptop display. You want a visual tool that works hand in hand with your dialogue to make a structured and effective presentation. The listing presentation material sells the owner on benefits—the benefit of using an exclusive agent and the benefit of your firm as that agent. It should not be used in place of the verbal presentation. Basically, as the agent turns the pages or changes the images, the visual message reinforces the agent's verbal message. Separate listing presentation visuals should be prepared for sale listings and buyer listings, although some of the pages will be identical.

Using the laptop presentation forces the owners to sit close to you to view the monitor. While prospects are likely to get defensive if you invade their space, with a laptop presentation, they are the ones getting close to you. The advantage of physical proximity is that it is easier to gain trust and acceptance than it is from across a room.

Listing presentation manuals should be divided into two areas:

1. *Why* list?

2. *Why* us? (Your firm and you)

FIGURE 5.2:   Good Faith Estimate of Seller's Net Sales Proceeds

GOOD FAITH ESTIMATE OF SELLER'S NET SALES PROCEEDS
On Sale of Property

Prepared by: Agent _____   **Phone** _____
Broker _____   **Email** _____

> **NOTE:** This net sheet is prepared to assist the Seller by providing an estimate of the amount of net sales proceeds the Seller is likely to receive on closing, based on the price set in the agreement, the estimated amount for expenses likely to be incurred to market the property and close a sale, and any adjustments and pro rates necessitated by the sale.
>
> The figures estimated in the net sheet may vary at the time each is incurred due to periodic changes in charges for professional services, administration fees and work enforcement made necessary by later inspections, and thus constitute an opinion, not a guarantee by the preparer.
>
> If the property disposed of is IRC §1031 property and the seller plans to acquire replacement property, use a §1031 Profit and Basis Recap Sheet to compute the tax consequences of the Seller's §1031 Reinvestment Plan. [See **ft** Form 354]

DATE: _____, 20_____, at _____, California.

1. This is an estimate of the fix-up, marketing and transaction expenses Seller is likely to incur on a sale, and the likely amount of net sales proceeds Seller may anticipate receiving on the close of a sale under the following agreement:

☐ Seller's listing agreement ☐ Purchase agreement ☐ Counteroffer
☐ Escrow instructions ☐ Exchange agreement ☐ Option to buy

1.1 dated _____, 20_____, at _____, California,

1.2 entered into by _____, as the Seller, and

1.3 _____, as the Buyer,

1.4 regarding real estate referred to as _____.

1.5 The day of the month anticipated for closing is _____.

2. **SALES PRICE:**

2.1 Price Received. . . . . (+)$_____

3. **ENCUMBRANCES:**

3.1 First Trust Deed Note. . . . . $_____

3.2 Second Trust Deed Note . . . . $_____

3.3 Other Liens/Bonds/UCC-1 . . . . $_____

3.4 TOTAL ENCUMBRANCES: [Lines 3.1 to 3.3] . . . . (–)$0.00_____

4. **SALES EXPENSES AND CHARGES:**

4.1 Fix-up Cost . . . . $_____

4.2 Structural Pest Control Report . . . . $_____

4.3 Structural Pest Control Clearance . . . . $_____

4.4 Property/Home Inspection Report. . . . . $_____

4.5 Elimination of Property Defects . . . . $_____

4.6 Local Ordinance Compliance Report. . . . . $_____

4.7 Compliance with Local Ordinances. . . . . $_____

4.8 Natural Hazard Disclosure Report . . . . $_____

4.9 Smoke Detector/Water Heater Safety Compliance . . . . . . $_____

4.10 Homeowners' (HOA) Association Document Charge . . . . . $_____

4.11 Mello-Roos Assessment Statement Charge . . . . $_____

4.12 Well Water Reports . . . . $_____

4.13 Septic/Sewer Reports . . . . $_____

4.14 Lead-Based Paint Report . . . . $_____

4.15 Marketing Budget. . . . . $_____

4.16 Home Warranty Insurance. . . . . $_____

4.17 Buyer's Escrow Closing Costs . . . . $_____

4.18 Loan Appraisal Fee . . . . $_____

4.19 Buyer's Loan Charges. $_____

4.20 Escrow Fee. . . . . $_____

4.21 Document Preparation Fee . . . . $_____

FIGURE 5.2 (continued):   Good Faith Estimate of Seller's Net Sales Proceeds

— — — — — — — — — — — — — — — *PAGE TWO OF TWO — FORM 310* — — — — — — — — — — — — — — — —

4.22   Notary Fees . . . . $_____

4.23   Recording Fees/Documentary Transfer Tax . . . . $_____

4.24   Title Insurance Premium. . . . . $_____

4.25   Beneficiary Statement/Demand . . . . $_____

4.26   Prepayment Penalty (first). . . . . $_____

4.27   Prepayment Penalty (second). . . . . $_____

4.28   Reconveyance Fees . . . . $_____

4.29   Brokerage Fees . . . . $_____

4.30   Transaction Coordinator Fee . . . . $_____

4.31   Attorney/Accountant Fees . . . . $_____

4.32   Other _____ . . . . $_____

4.33   Other _____ . . . . $_____

4.34   TOTAL EXPENSES AND CHARGES [Lines 4.1 to 4.33] . . . . (–)$0.00_____

5.   **ESTIMATED NET EQUITY:** . . . . (=)$0.00_____

6.   **PRO RATES DUE BUYER:**

6.1   Unpaid Taxes/Assessments . . . . $_____

6.2   Interest Accrued and Unpaid . . . . $_____

6.3   Unearned Rental Income . . . . $_____

6.4   Tenant Security Deposits . . . . $_____

6.5   TOTAL PRO RATES DUE BUYER [Lines 6.1 to 6.4] . . . . (–)$0.00_____

7.   **PRO RATES DUE SELLER:**

7.1   Prepaid Taxes/Assessments . . . . $_____

7.2   Impound Account Balances . . . . $_____

7.3   Prepaid Association Assessment . . . . $_____

7.4   Prepaid Ground Lease . . . . $_____

7.5   Unpaid Rent Assigned to Buyer . . . . $_____

7.6   Other _____ . . . . $_____

7.7   TOTAL PRO RATES DUE SELLER [Lines 7.1 to 7.6]. . . . . (+)$0.00_____

8.   **ESTIMATED PROCEEDS OF SALE:**. . . . . (=)$0.00_____

8.1   The estimated net proceeds at line 8 from the sale or exchange analyzed in this net sheet will be received in the form of:

a. Cash . . . . $_____

b. Note secured by a Trust Deed. . . . . $_____

c. Equity in Replacement Real Estate. . . . . $_____

d. Other _____ . . . . $_____

I have prepared this estimate based on my knowledge and readily available data.

Date: _____, 20_____

Broker: _____

DRE #: _____

Agent: _____

Signature: _____

I have read and received a copy of this estimate.

Date: _____, 20_____

Seller's Name: _____

Signature: _____

Signature: _____

FORM 310   08-11   2011 **first tuesday**, P.O. BOX 20069, RIVERSIDE, CA 92516 (800) 794-0494

You must convince the owner or the buyer about the concept of a listing as your first step and then show that you should have the listing.

SALE LISTINGS

Owners feel that a listing will cost them money. They are likely to initially view the idea of a listing as negative rather than look at the benefits you can offer. Therefore, you must overcome the negative thoughts and help owners realize the benefits offered.

Why List?

When you deal with a **for sale by owner** (FSBO), realize that a significant reason the owners want to sell the home themselves is to save the commission. They feel if they can sell their property without an agent, the agent's fee will be additional money for them. Therefore, begin your presentation with a discussion of who actually saves when an agent is not involved.

Even when you are not dealing with an FSBO, you could be in competition with the owners, as well as with other agents, for a listing. While not stated or even denied, the owners could be considering selling without an agent as one of their options. Therefore, we believe that all listing presentation material should begin with a discussion of the false savings of FSBO offerings.

Consider starting your presentation with the following visual question and answer:

Question:

Who saves when an owner sells without an agent?

Answer:

The buyer

> The primary reason owners want to sell without an agent is to avoid paying a commission.

Note: This question-and-answer technique is very effective and easy to prepare. Put only one question and answer on a page or screen. For a book, pages should be read on the right side of your book. We show suggested verbal presentations following each question and answer. You can use appropriate ideas to tailor your own presentation materials to your needs.

> I understand why you would want to sell [might consider selling] your home without an agent. You would like to save the agent's fee. Owners who do succeed in selling without an agent—and there aren't that many of them—find that they're not the ones who save. If there are any savings to be had, the buyer enjoys them.

Buyers who approach owners who advertise their homes for sale or put signs in their front yards will want to reduce any offer they might make by at least the amount of the agent's fee, even though the price might have been set to reflect all or part of this savings.

Buyers will not even settle for half because they realize it is buyers, not sellers, who really pay the commission. The price the buyer pays includes a commission, and although the seller may pay it, it is paid for with dollars that come from the buyer's savings and not the seller's pockets. When an owner sells direct, losing the commission is just for starters. Buyers often view for-sale-by-owner situations as opportunities to make a profit for themselves. They believe that for sale by owner indicates a distress sale, and that belief explains some of the ridiculous offers that owners receive.

Question:

Why are most For Sale by Owner signs replaced by agent signs?

Answer:

> Because owners are seldom successful in selling their homes, most owners who try to sell without an agent end up listing their property with a licensed agent. They wasted time and money on their futile effort.

Few buyers seek out For Sale by Owner ads and signs, and when they do give an offer it is usually at a price the owner will not consider. Many times, buyers who are considering making an offer on a for-sale-by-owner property will make an opening offer of at least 5% less than they would otherwise offer because they figure that the seller is not paying a commission. Many buyers use this as a negotiating tool.

Question:

Whom does this sign attract?

Answer:

Bargain hunters

"Lookie Lous"

Unqualified buyers

With a For Sale by Owner sign on your front lawn, you will attract bargain hunters of all types.

Your home will be on the Sunday entertainment tour of "Lookie Lous," who might be interested only in how you have decorated your home or are simply using you as a way to fill an otherwise vacant day.

Your For Sale by Owner ads and signs will attract people who might truly love your home but don't have a prayer of getting necessary financing. These people can waste a great deal of your time. Even if they give you an offer, the sale will never be closed.

A For Sale sign says "come on in" to the whole world. When you show people your home and belongings, you are really allowing strangers in. You let them see into closets and places that your best friend will never see, and you have no idea why they are there. While talking to one prospective buyer, another could be going through your jewelry box or medicine cabinet. I wish it weren't a problem, but safety is a problem today. People put in expensive alarm systems and then invite strangers into their homes, allowing them to see who lives there and what is there. Is this wise?

Question:

What does this sign mean?

Answer:

Wasted time

Wasted effort

Likelihood of legal problems

Failure/discouragement

Owners who try to sell without an agent are prisoners in their own homes, waiting for a phone call on the ad or a passerby to ring their doorbell.

When they accept an offer, they might find that the other party views the agreement differently from what the owners thought was agreed to. The likelihood of a lawsuit is increased many times when an agent is not part of the transaction.

Actually, a lawsuit is seldom a problem, because most owners who try to sell without an agent never even get an offer.

Question:

Why do most serious buyers employ real estate agents?

Answer:

Because agents have the inventory, understand the market, know how to qualify buyers, and can negotiate a sale with all the paperwork.

[Mr. and Mrs.], when you were looking for a home to purchase, I bet you visited real estate agents, am I right? The reason you went to at least one agent is because agents knew what was on the market and were able to quickly locate properties that met your needs. Without agents, buyers would have to contact dozens of individual property owners to check out properties, even though inspection might reveal that a property did not come close to meeting their needs. Buyers today are no different than you were when you purchased this home. Buyers who are serious about buying contact agents. Buyers dealing with agents understand they will have to pay a price dictated by the market and that they are not going to get anything for nothing.

We suggest you take a positive approach regarding the benefits of agency representation. Owners who understand the benefits of professional representation are less likely to resist paying a reasonable fee for these services.

Note: The word *fee* denotes a professional charge for benefits, whereas *commission* has a negative connotation to some people.

> The word *commission* has a negative connotation, but *fee* is positive in that it is a charge for benefits received.

Question:

What do you get for your fee?

Answer:

These important benefits:

Help and advice on making your home more salable

Promotion and advertising (paid by the agent)

Exposure on seven websites

Multiple-listing benefits

Qualifying of all prospects

Freedom to enjoy your time

Advice on offers and counteroffers

Problem solving during escrow

We work with you to make your house salable at the highest possible price. We promote your home with advertising and open houses. We prepare advertising flyers on your home for other agents, for responses to inquiries, and for those visiting your home. We also feature your home on our own website, as well as seven other websites. Of course, we bear all of these costs.

Information on your home is made available through our multiple listing service to [137] offices and more than [1,814] agents and through the website that has [more than 3,000] hits per day. This is the kind of exposure that is possible for your home.

An effective visual tool is to have a computer print-out listing every agent who is a member of your MLS service. The size of the printout helps impress upon the owners the number of people who will be able to work to sell their home.

We properly qualify anyone we bring to your home. We know who they are, where they live and work, and who can afford to buy your home before they cross your threshold.

You receive our advice on all offers received. We will work with you and the buyer in turning an unacceptable offer into an advantageous sale.

We work with buyers in obtaining financing to ensure that the purchase will close.

We monitor escrow to make certain there are no hang-ups. If a problem arises, we inform you and work to overcome it so the sale can progress.

This question-and-answer approach is just one of many approaches that can be used for your listing presentation material. Whatever material you use should flow toward the desired goal of overcoming any resistance by the owners to signing an agency agreement. You must be comfortable with the approach you use. If you are not comfortable with the material, chances are your effort will reflect your attitude, which will translate into few successful listings.

WEB LINK

Figures 5.3 and 5.4 were provided by Realty Tools, Inc. (www.realtytools. com) and show the benefits of listing and having agency representation.

FIGURE 5.3:   Why Use a REALTOR®?

Why use a REALTOR®?

When selling your home, your REALTOR® can give you up-to-date information on what is happening in the marketplace including price, financing and terms of competing properties. These are key factors in a successful sale of your property at the best price in the least amount of time.

Only real estate licensees who are members of the NATIONAL ASSOCIATION OF REALTORS® are properly called REALTORS®. REALTORS® subscribe to a strict code of ethics and are expected to maintain a higher level of knowledge of the process of buying and selling real estate. They are committed to treat all parties to a transaction honestly. REALTOR® business practices are monitored at local board levels. Arbitration and disciplinary systems are in place to address complaints from the public or other board members.

Your REALTOR® can help you objectively evaluate every buyer's proposal and then help write an appropriate legally binding sale agreement. Between the initial sales agreement and settlement, questions may arise. For example, unexpected repairs may be required to obtain financing or a problem with the title is discovered. Your REALTOR® is the best person to help you resolve those issues and move the transaction to settlement.

Angela McKendrick, CRS, GRI
Office: 410-555-1234
Home Office: 410-432-7890
Fax: 410-555-5607
Web Site: www.demorealty.com/angela
Email: angela.mckendrick@demorealty.com

www.greenleafrealty.com

Used with permission of Realty Tools, Inc.

FIGURE 5.4: **Services You Will Receive**

Services You Will Receive

- We will help you determine the best selling price for your home.

- We will suggest what you can do to get your home in top selling condition.

- We will develop a strategy to show your home.

- We will enter your home in the Multiple Listing System.

- We will implement the enclosed marketing plan.

- We will talk with you to review progress periodically.

- We will advise you of changes in the market climate.

- We will present all offers to you promptly and assist in evaluating them.

- We will monitor progress toward closing when a contract is accepted.

- We will monitor the appraisal and buyers loan approval.

- We will immediately advise you of events that may threaten closing.

- We will coordinate and monitor the settlement process.

Angela McKendrick, CRS, GRI
Office: 410-555-1234
Home Office: 410-432-7890
Fax: 410-555-5607
Web Site: www.demorealty.com/angela
Email: angela.mckendrick@demorealty.com

Green Leaf Realty
www.greenleafrealty.com

Used with permission of Realty Tools, Inc.

Why Us?

To obtain a listing, you have to convince owners that you and your firm deserve their trust. This is particularly important when owners are hesitant about listing their property because of a previous unsatisfactory experience with another agent.

You must build rapport with property owners. The owners must not only want to list their property, they also must want to list with you because they feel you are a capable, truthful person representing a reputable firm.

Sell yourself to the owners as a caring person who understands their problems and wants to help produce solutions. If you are unsuccessful, you could end up doing all the groundwork for an easy listing by another agent who has been able to develop greater empathy with the owners.

Listen to what the owners say during and after your presentation. Address them by their last names (Mr. Owner, Mrs. Seller). Answer questions slowly and fully. Ask questions to determine if you are communicating fully with the owners.

Don't *tell* the owners, *ask* them. Don't talk down to them or dismiss questions with flippant remarks. Don't use technical terms or acronyms. They may not understand what this "girl" Fannie Mae has to do with their property. In the initial phase of the presentation, keep in mind that the product you are selling is really yourself.

> You must sell yourself as worthy of an owner's trust.

The *Why Us?* portion of your listing material should cover you personally, as well as your firm. You might want to start with a one-page résumé titled "Want to Know About [Lester Jones]?"

Keep your résumé simple. You should have printed copies of this résumé so you can give the owners a copy. You are asking them to entrust you with the sale of their home, so they deserve to know something about you. When you give the owners your résumé, take no more than one minute to tell them about yourself. You should emphasize knowledge of the community, success in sales, special training, professional designations, and so forth.

A photo of your office or, if more than one office, a collage of photos can be effective. If your office has been in business a long time, a caption such as "Servicing [Midvale] since [1953]" is appropriate. If you are with a large firm or franchise, the caption could read "[8] offices and [146] professionals ready to serve you." If you have a large office, a group photo of your sales force with the name of your firm is effective.

Your narrative could simply be the following:

> We offer the advantage of 8 offices and 146 salespeople. Isn't this the kind of sales force you want for success?

For a franchise, consider this presentation:

> [Franchise Name] [Logo]
> [1,823] Offices
> [36,000] Salespeople
> Our Name Means: Instant Recognition
> National Referrals

Your possible narrative could be this:

> The name [VIP Realty] means instant recognition even to those who are new to our community. Because we are a [VIP] office, you can benefit from our national referral system.

You must sell the benefits that your firm has to offer.

If your firm is small, use a photo of your office and turn your small size into a positive with a narrative such as the following:

> Because we specialize in a small number of select properties, our owners receive maximum service. Your home will not be competing with 400 other office listings. We can provide the individual attention your home deserves in order to have a successful sale.

As an alternative, you might use a caption to illustrate your small firm as part of a large organization:

> [Loring Realty] is part of a multiple listing service offering you [237] offices and more than [2,000] salespeople, all working for your success.

Your narrative might be as follows:

> With [Loring Realty] representing you, you can take advantage of this huge sales force working together for your success.

Perhaps you want a separate sheet providing information on your multiple listing service. Your possible narrative might be this:

> By appointing [Loring Realty] as your agent, [in less than one hour] the information on your home will be available to these [237] offices and more than [2,000] salespeople. This sales force can be working for you.

An alternative narrative for a multiple listing service would be the following:

> Assume every agent in our multiple listing service is working with just two buyers for a home in your home's general price range. Now that may seem to be a very low figure, but consider that tomorrow morning your home can be exposed to those two buyers by [2,000] agents. That's [4,000] potential buyers for your home.

If you are a REALTOR®, consider a sheet with just the REALTOR® trademark. Your narrative could be this one:

> Every broker is not a REALTOR®. Only REALTORS® can use this symbol. [Loring Realty] is a member of the California Association of REALTORS® and the National Association of REALTORS®. As REALTORS® we are pledged to a Code of Professional Conduct.

If your firm is a member of the National Association of Real Estate Brokers, a similar approach could be used.

A collage of press releases can be effective as follows:

> The fact that [Loring Realty] has played a dominant role in [community activities] and [development] brings us instant name recognition as a professional leader.

Tell owners how your firm advertises to attract potential buyers. For a larger firm, you could have a sheet stating this:

2013

[$2 Million] + Advertising Budget

Your narrative could be this one:

Our advertising budget of [$] means [$] per week spent to bring in buyers. This budget has given us name recognition and dominance in the marketplace. Our dominance is reflected in our sales record.

FIGURES 5.5A – 5.5E: **Presentation Samples**

A.

Determining the Value of Your Home

A Comparative Market Analysis (CMA) is essential to determine the value of residential property. Location and characteristics of the property are the key elements in determining value. Therefore, the basis for valuation is similar properties in your area. The market analysis takes into account the amount received from recent sales of comparable properties and the quantity and quality of comparable properties currently on the market. The desired end result is to find a price that will attract a willing and able buyer in a reasonable time.

Once the value of your home has been determined, you can decide on an offering price that will achieve your goals. Generally, the price should not exceed the value by more than 5% or potential buyers may not even make offers. Naturally, if you want to sell quickly your asking price should be very near the value.

The following are a few things to keep in mind about pricing:

- Realistic pricing will achieve maximum price in a reasonable time.
- Your cost or profit desire is irrelevant; the market determines the price.
- The cost of improvements are almost always more than the added value.
- Houses that remain on the market for a long time do not get shown.
- A house that is priced right from the beginning achieves the highest proceeds.

 Angela McKendrick, CRS, GRI
Office: 410-555-1234
Home Office: 410-432-7890
Fax: 410-555-5607
Web Site: www.demorealty.com/angela
Email: angela.mckendrick@demorealty.com

 Green Leaf Realty
www.greenleafrealty.com

B.

In Conclusion

When you choose Angela McKendrick you will receive:

- Excellent service and support.
- A market analysis of your home.
- A winning marketing plan.
- Every effort to sell your home promptly.
- The resources of Green Leaf Realty.

List Your Home Now with Angela McKendrick!

 Angela McKendrick, CRS, GRI
Office: 410-555-1234
Home Office: 410-432-7890
Fax: 410-555-5607
Web Site: www.demorealty.com/angela
Email: angela.mckendrick@demorealty.com

 Green Leaf Realty
www.greenleafrealty.com

C.

Customer References

Sellers...

Fred & Susan Fredericks	23 Elm Street	822-4554
Joe & Lisa Johnson	1400 N. Timonium Road	922-2222
Ron & Dawn Larkin	2311 E. Roundtop Circle	444-3948
Debra Jones	433 Forest Drive	231-6932
Don & Julia Smith	32 E. Running Road	211-4599
Len & Hanna Leonard	443 Forest Drive	343-6798

Buyers...

Mark & Joan Dawson	2300 S. Timonium Road	666-3033
Suzanne Swift	22 Forrest Avenue	667-9888
Ron & Joan Burns	55 W. Running Road	333-9843
Joe & Ann Reese	321 Pine Forest Lane	222-4563
Robert Johnson	324 82nd Terrace	342-6879
Jay & Sarah Volkers	75 Winding Way	234-1098

 Angela McKendrick, CRS, GRI
Office: 410-555-1234
Home Office: 410-432-7890
Fax: 410-555-5607
Web Site: www.demorealty.com/angela
Email: angela.mckendrick@demorealty.com

 Green Leaf Realty
www.greenleafrealty.com

D.

Resume

Angela McKendrick

Experience:
1998-Present: Real Estate Agent specializing in single family, multi-family, condominiums, and land sales.
1994-2002: Marketing Director for McCormick Company.

Affiliations:
Greater Baltimore Board of Realtors.
Maryland Association of Realtors.
National Association of Realtors.
Residential Sales Council.

Education:
Columbia University
North Carroll High School
Professional Courses sponsored by the National Association of Realtors.

Community:
Former American Cancer Society "Person of the Year."
Hunt Valley Community Association.
Greater Baltimore Association.
Scoutmaster Troop 211.

Personal:
Married to Jason McKendrick.
Children: David (31) and Anna (26).
Hobbies: Golf and Tennis.

Green Leaf Realty
www.greenleafrealty.com

FIGURES 5.5A – 5.5E (continued):   Presentation Samples

E.

Used with permission of Realty Tools, Inc.

For a small firm, consider a collage of your ads, web listings, or both. You could say: You can see we publicize our listings.

If your office advertises in a foreign paper places listings on foreign websites or has relationships with brokerage offices in other countries, this should be emphasized. Many owners feel that foreign buyers pay top price, so that access to them is important.

The Only Office in [Sacramento] Advertising in

Nihon Keizai Shimbun
Japan's Largest Business Daily Newspaper

We market our properties to the largest possible market. We go to the buyers. Besides our area advertising, our international advertising has built up a referral network of agents who work with us to locate buyers.

FIGURES 5.6A –5.6I: Presentation Samples

A.

Real Estate Services Proposal

Prepared Especially for:
Tom & Mary White
7 Deep Run Court
Hunt Valley, MD 21030

For marketing the property located at:
7 Deep Run Court

Prepared by:
Angela McKendrick, CRS, GRI
Agent
Green Leaf Realty
123 Main Street
Hunt Valley, MD 21030

Office: 410-555-1234
Home Office: 410-432-7890
Fax: 410-555-5607
Web Site: www.demorealty.com/angela
Email: angela.mckendrick@demorealty.com

Date: August 20, 2015

This analysis is not an appraisal. It is intended only for the purpose of assisting buyers or sellers or prospective buyers or sellers in deciding the listing, offering, or sale price of the real property.

Green Leaf Realty
www.greenleafrealty.com

B.

Real Estate Services Proposal

Prepared Especially for:
Tom & Mary White
7 Deep Run Court
Hunt Valley, MD 21030

For marketing the property located at:
7 Deep Run Court

Prepared by:
Angela McKendrick, CRS, GRI
Agent
Green Leaf Realty
123 Main Street
Hunt Valley, MD 21030

Office: 410-555-1234
Home Office: 410-432-7890
Fax: 410-555-5607
Web Site: www.demorealty.com/angela
Email: angela.mckendrick@demorealty.com

Date: August 20, 2015

This analysis is not an appraisal. It is intended only for the purpose of assisting buyers or sellers or prospective buyers or sellers in deciding the listing, offering, or sale price of the real property.

Green Leaf Realty
www.greenleafrealty.com

C.

Subject Property Profile for

7 Deep Run Court

The following features have been identified to aid in the search for properties that are comparable to yours. This will help in determining proper pricing for your home.

City: Hunt Valley	Neighborhood: Orchard Valley	Year Built: 1988
Fin SqFt: 2160	Lot Desc: Backs To Trees	Lot Size: 1.04
Style: Colonial	Levels: 3	Bedrooms: 3
Bathrooms: 2/1	Const: Cedar Siding	Roofing: Cedar/Shake
Basement: Fully Finished	Basement: Walkout Level	Heat: Heat Pump
Fuel: Electric	Cool: Central A/C	Parking: Garage
Garage Spaces: 2	Exter Feat: Deck	Water: Well
Sewer: Septic	# Fireplaces: 2	Amenities: Auto Gar Dr Opn
Amenities: Built-In Bookcases	Amenities: Mba/Sep Shwr	Other Rms: Den/Stdy/Lib
Other Rms: Family Room		

Angela McKendrick, CRS, GRI
Office: 410-555-1234
Home Office: 410-432-7890
Fax: 410-555-5607
Web Site: www.demorealty.com/angela
Email: angela.mckendrick@demorealty.com

Green Leaf Realty
www.greenleafrealty.com

D.

Marketing Plan of Action

First Week on the Market

- Enter listing into MLS system.
- Put up "For Sale" sign.
- Install lock box.
- Take property photos.
- Prepare property flyer/brochure.
- Submit property listing with photos to select real estate websites.

Second Week on the Market

- Schedule Virtual Tour.
- Invite local Realtors to tour home.
- Prepare and place advertisements with select print and online media outlets.

Third Week on the Market

- Submit Open House announcement to MLS & Office Sales meeting.
- Prepare and distribute special Open House flyer.
- Hold Sunday Open House.

On-going

- Handle incoming calls and schedule showing appointments.
- Update owner on showings.
- Pre-qualify buyers.
- Present all offers and recommend counter-offer strategies.
- Review price based on agent input & market conditions.

ASAP

- Obtain an acceptable contract on your property!

Angela McKendrick, CRS, GRI
Office: 410-555-1234
Home Office: 410-432-7890
Fax: 410-555-5607
Web Site: www.demorealty.com/angela
Email: angela.mckendrick@demorealty.com

Green Leaf Realty
www.greenleafrealty.com

FIGURES 5.6A –5.6I (continued):   Presentation Samples

Subject Property Profile for

7 Deep Run Court

The following features have been identified to aid in the search for properties that are comparable to yours. This will help in determining proper pricing for your home.

City:	Hunt Valley	Neighborhood:	Orchard Valley	Year Built:	1988
Fin SqFt:	2160	Lot Desc:	Backs To Trees	Lot Size:	1.04
Style:	Colonial	Levels:	3	Bedrooms:	3
Bathrooms:	2/1	Const:	Cedar Siding	Roofing:	Cedar/Shake
Basement:	Fully Finished	Basement:	Walkout Level	Heat:	Heat Pump
Fuel:	Electric	Cool:	Central A/C	Parking:	Garage
Garage Spaces:	2	Exter Feat:	Deck	Water:	Well
Sewer:	Septic	# Fireplaces:	2	Amenities:	Auto Gar Dr Opn
Amenities:	Built-In Bookcases	Amenities:	Mba/Sep Shwr	Other Rms:	Den/Stdy/Lib
Other Rms:	Family Room				

 Angela McKendrick, CRS, GRI
Office: 410-555-1234
Home Office: 410-432-7890
Fax: 410-555-5607
Web Site: www.demorealty.com/angela
Email: angela.mckendrick@demorealty.com

www.greenleafrealty.com

E.

Services You Will Receive

- We will help you determine the best selling price for your home.
- We will suggest what you can do to get your home in top selling condition.
- We will develop a strategy to show your home.
- We will enter your home in the Multiple Listing System.
- We will implement the enclosed marketing plan.
- We will talk with you to review progress periodically.
- We will advise you of changes in the market climate.
- We will present all offers to you promptly and assist in evaluating them.

- We will monitor progress toward closing when a contract is accepted.
- We will monitor the appraisal and buyers loan approval.
- We will immediately advise you of events that may threaten closing.
- We will coordinate and monitor the settlement process.

 Angela McKendrick, CRS, GRI
Office: 410-555-1234
Home Office: 410-432-7890
Fax: 410-555-5607
Web Site: www.demorealty.com/angela
Email: angela.mckendrick@demorealty.com

www.greenleafrealty.com

F.

Resume

Angela McKendrick

Experience:
1998-Present: Real Estate Agent specializing in single family, multi-family, condominiums, and land sales.
1994-2002: Marketing Director for McCormick Company.

Affiliations:
Greater Baltimore Board of Realtors.
Maryland Association of Realtors.
National Association of Realtors.
Residential Sales Council.

Education:
Columbia University
North Carroll High School
Professional Courses sponsored by the National Association of Realtors.

Community:
Former American Cancer Society "Person of the Year."
Hunt Valley Community Association.
Greater Baltimore Association.
Scoutmaster Troop 211.

Personal:
Married to Jason McKendrick.
Children: David (31) and Anna (26).
Hobbies: Golf and Tennis.

www.greenleafrealty.com

G.

Customer References

Sellers...

Fred & Susan Fredericks	23 Elm Street	822-4554
Joe & Lisa Johnson	1400 N. Timonium Road	922-2222
Ron & Dawn Larkin	2311 E. Roundtop Circle	444-3948
Debra Jones	433 Forest Drive	231-6932
Don & Julia Smith	32 E. Running Road	211-4599
Len & Hanna Leonard	443 Forest Drive	343-6798

Buyers...

Mark & Joan Dawson	2300 S. Timonium Road	666-3033
Suzanne Swift	22 Forrest Avenue	667-9888
Ron & Joan Burns	55 W. Running Road	333-9843
Joe & Ann Reese	321 Pine Forest Lane	222-4563
Robert Johnson	324 82nd Terrace	342-6879
Jay & Sarah Volkers	75 Winding Way	234-1098

 Angela McKendrick, CRS, GRI
Office: 410-555-1234
Home Office: 410-432-7890
Fax: 410-555-5607
Web Site: www.demorealty.com/angela
Email: angela.mckendrick@demorealty.com

www.greenleafrealty.com

H.

FIGURES 5.6A –5.6I (continued):   Presentation Samples

I.

Used with permission of Realty Tools, Inc.

If your office has a home protection plan, consider this:

[Loring Realty] Offers Buyers
Home Protection Plan
That Makes Your Home More Desirable to Buyers

Our home protection plan protects buyers against structural problems and system breakdowns for [one] year after purchase. This protection has given us a word-of-mouth reputation to the extent that many buyers would not consider using another agent to purchase a home.

If your office belongs to a national referral network but is not a franchise office, consider a sheet or computer screen that reads as follows:

Member
[Home Relocators]
A National Relocation Referral Service
[1,838] Cooperating Member Firms in 50 States

Your possible narrative might be as follows:

> Would you like to take advantage of referrals from every corner of the nation? We constantly receive calls about people relocating to our area because of our [Home Relocators] membership. We want our owners to have every sales advantage possible. I'm sure that's the kind of representation you want.

Emphasize your internet site:

> I'm sure you realize that the internet is of prime importance in selling real estate. These are a few pictures of our internet site.

Show a home presentation from the site, as well as your office home site. If your site features virtual tours, explain what they are and the benefits they offer (with a high-speed wireless connection, you can access the sites on your laptop for a very effective presentation):

> [Loring Realty] takes second place to no one in using technology to market our homes.

Emphasize your internet presence:

> "We will be placing your home (photos, video, virtual tour) on nine websites visited by [over 85,000] viewers each day."

If you purchase enhanced coverage on websites, you should point out how their property will stand out from other listings. If your firm specializes in the area where you are seeking a listing, a sheet should show this specialization:

> *[Palm Desert Greens]*
> *Housing Specialists*

Your narrative could be something like this:

> We specialize in [Palm Desert Greens]. We have built up a reputation of being the [Palm Desert Greens] broker. Prospective buyers come to us because we have the inventory and make the sales. When other agents get a buyer who is interested in [Palm Desert Greens], they frequently

call us. Our cooperation with others and our knowledge of the market have resulted in a record of success in [Palm Desert Greens] that is second to none.

By using computer information from your local multiple listing service, you should be able to find statistics that show your firm is outstanding in several areas. Sheets should be prepared to showcase these distinctions. But be careful when you use statistics. If you emphasize that 50% of your listings are sold, it also points out a 50% failure rate. Approaches that are more positive would be these:

[Loring Realty]
[42%] Better Record of Success

According to the records of the [Tri-County Multiple Listing Service], listings with [Loring Realty] had a [42%] greater chance of success than the board average for [20XX].

[Loring Realty]
We Get More for Your Home

According to the records of the [Tri-County Multiple Listing Service], the average home in [20XX] sold at [84%] of its listed price. In [20XX], [Loring Realty] home sales averaged [94%] of list price. That's [10%] more money in the pockets of our sellers than our competition. Is getting the most money from your home important to you?

Another approach could be this:

For all practical purposes, you get our services free. Let me tell you why. The average sale as reported by the [Tri-County Multiple Listing Service] for [20XX] was at [84%] of list price. In [20XX], [Loring Realty] sales averaged [94%] of list price. Therefore, we were able to get our owners an increase over the average sale in excess of our fees received.

The percentage of your own listings that are sold by your office can be a positive statement about your firm:

[20XX] Multiple Listing Figures
Sales Made by Listing Office
Average [26%]
[Loring Realty] [51%]

At [Loring Realty] we don't just list and hope one of the cooperating offices finds a buyer. From these figures, you can see that we feel obligated to work hard for our owners. When we represent you, you come first.

Would you like to know how we will sell your home?

You should have a visual marketing plan (see Figure 5.5E, page 200). Your plan should indicate the following as applicable:

Signs, talking signs

Property flyers

MLS distribution

Office website

Other websites used (domestic and foreign)

Enhanced websites

Electronic lockboxes

Virtual tours

Agent caravan

Open houses

Papers, magazines, and other media

Owner suggestions

Staging

Owner communications

Communications with other agents

Constant evaluation of efforts, property, and results

The last page or screen of your presentation should really be a trial closing:

[Mr. and Mrs. Garczynski], don't you want [Loring Realty] to represent you?

Your narrative would simply be the question asked.

Additional Listing Tools

Another tool to bring to a listing presentation is a completed property flyer of the owner's home with a good color photograph of the home and known information (other information left blank, as well as price). This should be left with the owner even if the listing is not obtained.

Some agents also prepare a website presentation that can be viewed on a laptop computer. An attractive visual such as this can help convince the owners they should have you as their agent.

If you use talking signs, a rider strip showing the radio frequency, the base unit, and a radio to listen to a prepared voice message could put you a step above much of the competition.

Bring an electronic lockbox the owners can handle. People like to feel things. It is in our human nature. Let owners hold the lockbox while you explain the security aspects and the information it provides.

BUYER LISTINGS

To obtain listings from buyers, you should explain the normal agency where the agent represents the seller or has dual agency duties. An understanding of seller agency will make the need for buyer agency representation very apparent.

Owners must also understand what you will do for them and how you will be paid your fee. You can use a variation of the question-and-answer technique with just questions where the answers are obvious:

Whom does the property listing agent represent?

Will the property listing agent try to find the home that is best for you, or will the agent try to sell his clients' property?

Some lenders selling foreclosed properties pay brokers a selling fee less than is usually charged. Will a seller's agent want to show you these homes when they have listings that offer them higher fees?

Will the property listing agent try to sell you the property at the lowest possible price?

Does the property listing agent get greater compensation when the price is greater?

The sellers have an agent looking out for their best interests. Should you be similarly protected?

You should explain that your services will generally be paid for by the seller because you will accept the multiple listing service commission split as compensation, which is paid by the seller.

For your presentation, consider the similar material developed by Realty Tools, Inc., or by other software suppliers. In addition, some of the same material you developed for sales listings would be applicable to buyer listings.

Note: Buyer presentation material can also be used as an enclosure when responding to an inquiry, as well as presented to prospective buyers where a buyer listing is not being sought.

COMMERCIAL AND INVESTMENT PROPERTY

WEB LINK

While you can modify residential listing presentations for commercial and investment property, a better approach would be to use software designed for the purpose. Some examples of providers of such software are www.realdata.com, www.costart.com, and www.realhound.com.

SUMMARY

The comparative market analysis is an excellent tool for arriving at a recommended list price, as well as for convincing owners that it is in their best interests to initially list their home at a realistic price. The attachments you provide clearly illustrate the effect of pricing on the time to sell, as well as on the likelihood of success.

The Estimated Seller's Proceeds form is really a disclosure form to fully inform the owners of what they will net from a sale at list price. By receiving this information at the time of listing, the owners are prepared for what they will actually receive. Unpleasant surprises can mean sales that fail to close.

The listing presentation manual is a paper or computer visual tool to be used along with the agent's narrative to provide a structured, effective listing presentation.

The presentation manual is broken down into two sections. One is *Why List?* and the other is *Why Us?* The *Why List?* presentation shows owners why it is in their best interests to employ an exclusive selling agent. The *Why Us?* presentation tells the owners about you and your firm. It shows the owners the advantages your firm offers. It is a positive approach because it sells benefits and leads to a trial closing.

A separate listing presentation manual should be prepared for buyer listings.

CLASS DISCUSSION TOPICS

1. Comparative market analysis

Prepare a comparative market analysis on a property (use real or fictitious comparables). Present the analysis to an owner (use another student) and explain how you arrived at your recommendations.

2. Estimated Seller's Proceeds form

Prepare an Estimated Seller's Proceeds form, based on costs in your area, for a home that has a $181,000 first trust deed. The seller will be paying 6% commission on the $300,000 sale. (Do not prorate taxes, insurance, or consider impound accounts.)

3. Listing presentation manual

Prepare either the *Why List?* or *Why Us?* portion of the listing presentation manual. Be prepared to make a presentation in class on your portion of the listing presentation manual to another student as though you were addressing an owner.

4. A prospective seller will be interviewing other agents.

Prepare, in writing, the reasons the prospective seller should choose you or your firm rather than your competitors.

5. Bring to class one current-events article dealing with some aspect of real estate practice for class discussion.

UNIT 5 QUIZ

1. A CMA is *BEST* described as
   a. a formal appraisal.
   b. the cooperative marketing approach of multiple listings.
   c. a reflection of the reality of the marketplace.
   d. the comparative mortgage analysis performed by agents in advising buyers as to lender and loan type.

2. In making your recommendation of list price for a single-family home, the *MOST* important portion of the analysis deals with
   a. list prices of homes on the market now.
   b. list prices of homes where the listings expired.
   c. prices of comparable properties that sold.
   d. possible rental income.

3. You should realize that for data used on a CMA,
   a. the older the data, the less reliable they are.
   b. sales prices that seem unusually high or low are often the result of market imperfections.
   c. both of these are true.
   d. both of these are false.

4. Owners must be made to realize that
   a. the higher they price their home over fair market value, the longer it will take to sell.
   b. the higher they price their home over fair market value, the lower the likelihood of a sale during the listing period.
   c. both of these are true.
   d. both of these are false.

5. A recommended list price below what the CMA indicates as the likely sale range is in an owner's best interest when
   a. a sellers' market exists.
   b. the seller must get the highest net.
   c. the seller must sell quickly.
   d. the seller is not strongly motivated to sell.

6. What a seller receives in hand from a sale is the
   a. gross sale price.
   b. net sale price.
   c. net profit.
   d. seller's net proceeds.

7. The principal reason owners try to sell their homes without an agent is
   a. to have a quick sale.
   b. to save the commission.
   c. to be able to pick the buyer.
   d. none of these.

8. Your listing presentation material should
   a. be organized to follow your listing presentation.
   b. not be used in lieu of a verbal presentation.
   c. be helpful in selling an owner on the concept of listing in general and listing with your firm in particular.
   d. be all of these.

9. Which statement is the *BEST* approach to take when selling the benefits of listing with a small office?
   a. "We try harder because of the competition."
   b. "All we need to find is one buyer, and even we can do that."
   c. "We need the business more than the large firms do."
   d. "We specialize in a small number of select properties."

10. Which would be the MOST effective statement to make during a listing presentation?
   a. Last year we sold 26% of the listings we took during the listing period.
   b. Our office has six full-time and nine part-time salespeople.
   c. Last year our average sale was at 86% of the list price.
   d. Our average time to sell was 32 days last year compared with a MLS average time to sell of 54 days.

UNIT SIX

LISTING PRESENTATIONS AND LISTING CONTRACTS

LEARNING OBJECTIVES

When you have completed this unit, you will be able to

- define listing agreement and explain its elements,

- analyze the exclusive-authorization-and-right-to-sell listing and the exclusive-right-to-represent agreement (buyer's listing), and

- describe the listing transaction.

KEY TERMS

bilateral agreement	exclusive-right-to-represent agreement	safety clause
clincher		short sale
exclusive-agency listing	net listing	trial closing
	open listing	Uniform Electronic Transaction Act
exclusive-authorization-and-right-to-sell listing	option combined with a listing	unilateral contract
	procuring cause	

THE LISTING AGREEMENT

Of all the documents used in the real estate business, none is more important than the listing agreement. This is the instrument that defines a broker's rights and duties. It is the broker's employment contract and gives the broker the right to compensation.

Definition

A *listing agreement*, when executed (signed) by the parties, becomes a legally binding *contract* that authorizes a broker to serve as agent for a principal in a real estate activity. Listing contracts may be entered into for the purpose of securing qualified persons to buy, sell, lease, or rent property or to locate property for lease or purchase. Agents are authorized to find a purchaser or a lessee for a particular property at a specified price and terms, within a certain time limit, or to locate a property for a prospective buyer or a lessee, commonly known as a *buyer agency listing*. The agreement spells out the rights to and obligations of the broker and the seller or the broker and the buyer.

The agreement creates an agency relationship. Brokers who fulfills their part of such contracts are entitled, both legally and morally, to be paid for these efforts. Just a few years ago, buyer agency listings were practically unknown. Now they are quite common because they make sense to buyers who want an agent who represents their interests.

Elements

Because the listing is a contract, it must include all the essential elements of a contract, including competency of parties, lawful object, proper offer and acceptance (mutual consent), and consideration.

California has adopted a modified version of the Uniform Electronic Transaction Act. Parties can agree to conduct a transaction by electronic means. This could apply to listing agreements.

To be enforceable, listing contracts must be in writing [Civil Code 1624(5)]. Oral listings provide the broker with no legal protection whatsoever, because without a written contract, the broker cannot enforce payment of compensation if the principal refuses to pay it. "My word is my bond" is no bond at all in a court of law.

The *consideration* in a listing contract is the broker's promise to "use diligence in locating a ready, willing, and able buyer" in exchange for the seller's promise to pay a commission or the agent's promise to locate a property for a buyer with compensation paid by the buyer or the seller. The promise (seller or buyer to pay commission) given for a promise (broker to use diligence in finding a buyer/property) is a **bilateral agreement**, which is a promise made in exchange for another promise.

The consideration that passes between parties in a real estate contract can be anything of value.

FIGURE 6.1: **Who May Sell a Property and Receive a Commission under Three Types of Listing Agreements**

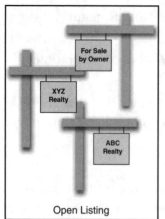
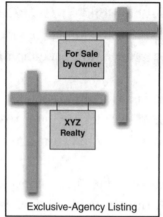

| Open Listing | Exclusive-Agency Listing | Exclusive-Right-to-Sell Listing |

Types of Listing Agreements

There are many variations of the basic listing agreement from various publishers, as well as computer program forms and special forms used by real estate franchises. Some are for general residential property; others are for special types of property, such as industrial, income, farm, or unimproved property. Despite the variations, there are three basic kinds of listings: open listings, exclusive-authorization-and-right-to-sell listings, and exclusive-agency listings. Net listings and option listings are additions to the three aforementioned listing contracts. A buyer's listing can also be an open listing. The purpose of a listing agreement generally is to define the relationship between the seller (or buyer, in the case of a buyer's listing) and the broker. You may find it useful to group listings into two kinds of agreements, exclusive and nonexclusive. Figure 6.1 classifies listings according to the relationship between seller and broker.

Open listing. An **open listing** is a nonexclusive written memorandum that when signed by the seller or buyer, authorizes the broker to serve as an agent for the sale or purchase of property. Under an open listing, the owner agrees to pay a commission if the broker procures a buyer or property that is purchased. Because the broker is not obligated to use diligence to locate a buyer or property, an open listing is considered to be a **unilateral contract**. It is a promise that is accepted by the agent's action in procuring a buyer or a property.

The seller or buyer may give this type of listing to as many brokers as he or she sees fit. If the owner has given agents permission to erect signs, there could be multiple For Sale signs on a property. The first agent who finds, according to the listing terms, a ready, willing, and able buyer acceptable to the seller or an acceptable property for the buyer gets the commission. This cancels all other open listings and negates the payment of any other commission. An open listing allows the owner to sell the property herself or the buyer to buy the property himself without being liable to the broker(s) for any compensation.

From the seller's or the buyer's point of view, open listings may appear to provide a wider market than exclusive agreements. However, more sophisticated sellers and buyers often conclude that brokers receiving this type of listing are unlikely to give them preferred attention. Sellers and buyers soon discover that "what is everybody's business is nobody's business" and that carefully selecting a single competent broker is almost always to their advantage.

Most real estate offices will not take an open sale listing because they know that the likelihood of a sale is slight and that allowing the owner to feel the office is using diligence could be a disservice to the owner. With an open listing, there can be owner/agent competition for the same buyer. Owners will often try to make the sale themselves to avoid paying a commission. In order to be protected as the **"procuring cause"** of a sale, the broker must register a buyer with the owner. The agent who is the procuring cause must have initiated an uninterrupted series of events that led to the sale. Experienced agents will hold out for an exclusive-right-to-sell listing and, if they are unable to obtain one, will walk away. The fact that others might agree to an open listing can actually help them. After the owner and the open listing agents have tried unsuccessfully to market the property for several months, the owner should be more receptive to a prepared marketing plan under an exclusive-right-to-sell listing.

Exclusive-authorization-and-right-to-sell listing. An **exclusive-authorization-and-right-to-sell listing** gives a broker the sole right to procure a purchaser for a property. With this type of listing, the broker is the sole agent and has the right to a commission if a buyer is found for the property by anyone—even the owner—during the term of the listing. The listing broker has earned a commission when a bona fide offer from a ready, willing, and able buyer at a specified or accepted price and terms is produced, whether or not escrow closes. (The listing is to produce a buyer.)

> An exclusive-authorization-and-right-to-sell listing entitles the listing agent to the compensation, no matter who sells the property.

All exclusive listings, by law, must have a definite termination date. Listings should be dated when they are taken, and the effective term should be set forth so clearly and definitely that there can be no mistake. An exclusive listing may not contain such wording as "effective until date of sale" or "until canceled in writing." California Real Estate Law Section 10176(f) states that a licensee is subject to disciplinary action for

> claiming, demanding, or receiving a fee, compensation, or commission under any *exclusive* agreement authorizing or employing a licensee to sell, buy, or exchange real estate for compensation or commission where such agreement does not contain a *definite, specified date* of final and complete termination. [emphasis added]

The agent must give the owner a copy of any exclusive listing at the time it is signed. Because open listings are frequently just letters from an owner and need not be signed by the agent, an agent is not required to give the owner copies of these open listings, although it is strongly recommended that the owner receive copies of all listings. Figure 6.2 is a residential listing agreement, an exclusive-authorization-and-right-to-sell listing form.

FIGURE 6.2:   **Residential Listing Agreement (Exclusive Authorization and Right to Sell)**

(The following form is copyrighted by the California Association of REAL-TORS®, © 2014, and is reprinted under a limited license with permission. Photocopying or any other reproduction, whether electronic or otherwise, is strictly prohibited.)

CALIFORNIA
ASSOCIATION
OF REALTORS®

RESIDENTIAL LISTING AGREEMENT
(Exclusive Authorization and Right to Sell)
(C.A.R. Form RLA, Revised 11/13)

1. **EXCLUSIVE RIGHT TO SELL:** _____ ("Seller")
hereby employs and grants _____ ("Broker")
beginning (date) _____ and ending at 11:59 P.M. on (date) _____ ("Listing Period")
the exclusive and irrevocable right to sell or exchange the real property in the City of _____,
County of_____, Assessor's Parcel No. _____,
California, described as:_____ ("Property").

2. **ITEMS EXCLUDED AND INCLUDED:** Unless otherwise specified in a real estate purchase agreement, all fixtures and fittings that are attached to the Property are included, and personal property items are excluded, from the purchase price.
ADDITIONAL ITEMS EXCLUDED: _____.
ADDITIONAL ITEMS INCLUDED: _____.
Seller intends that the above items be excluded or included in offering the Property for sale, but understands that: (i) the purchase agreement supersedes any intention expressed above and will ultimately determine which items are excluded and included in the sale; and (ii) Broker is not responsible for and does not guarantee that the above exclusions and/or inclusions will be in the purchase agreement.

3. **LISTING PRICE AND TERMS:**
   A. The listing price shall be:_____
   _____ Dollars ($ _____).
   B. Additional Terms: _____
   _____.

4. **COMPENSATION TO BROKER:**
   Notice: The amount or rate of real estate commissions is not fixed by law. They are set by each Broker individually and may be negotiable between Seller and Broker (real estate commissions include all compensation and fees to Broker).
   A. Seller agrees to pay to Broker as compensation for services irrespective of agency relationship(s), either ☐ _____ percent of the listing price (or if a purchase agreement is entered into, of the purchase price), or ☐ $ _____, AND _____, as follows:
      (1) If during the Listing Period, or any extension, Broker, cooperating broker, Seller or any other person procures a ready, willing, and able buyer(s) whose offer to purchase the Property on any price and terms is accepted by Seller, provided the Buyer completes the transaction or is prevented from doing so by Seller. (Broker is entitled to compensation whether any escrow resulting from such offer closes during or after the expiration of the Listing Period, or any extension.)
   OR (2) If within _____ calendar days (a) after the end of the Listing Period or any extension; or (b) after any cancellation of this Agreement, unless otherwise agreed, Seller enters into a contract to sell, convey, lease or otherwise transfer the Property to anyone ("Prospective Buyer") or that person's related entity: (i) who physically entered and was shown the Property during the Listing Period or any extension by Broker or a cooperating broker; or (ii) for whom Broker or any cooperating broker submitted to Seller a signed, written offer to acquire, lease, exchange or obtain an option on the Property. Seller, however, shall have no obligation to Broker under paragraph 4A(2) unless, not later than 3 calendar days after the end of the Listing Period or any extension or cancellation, Broker has given Seller a written notice of the names of such Prospective Buyers.
   OR (3) If, without Broker's prior written consent, the Property is withdrawn from sale, conveyed, leased, rented, otherwise transferred, or made unmarketable by a voluntary act of Seller during the Listing Period, or any extension.
   B. If completion of the sale is prevented by a party to the transaction other than Seller, then compensation due under paragraph 4A shall be payable only if and when Seller collects damages by suit, arbitration, settlement or otherwise, and then in an amount equal to the lesser of one-half of the damages recovered or the above compensation, after first deducting title and escrow expenses and the expenses of collection, if any.
   C. In addition, Seller agrees to pay Broker: _____.
   D. Seller has been advised of Broker's policy regarding cooperation with, and the amount of compensation offered to, other brokers.
      (1) Broker is authorized to cooperate with and compensate brokers participating through the multiple listing service(s) ("MLS") by offering to MLS brokers out of Broker's compensation specified in 4A, either ☐ _____ percent of the purchase price, or ☐ $_____.
      (2) Broker is authorized to cooperate with and compensate brokers operating outside the MLS as per Broker's policy.
   E. Seller hereby irrevocably assigns to Broker the above compensation from Seller's funds and proceeds in escrow. Broker may submit this Agreement, as instructions to compensate Broker pursuant to paragraph 4A, to any escrow regarding the Property involving Seller and a buyer, Prospective Buyer or other transferee.
   F. **(1)** Seller represents that Seller has not previously entered into a listing agreement with another broker regarding the Property, unless specified as follows: _____.
      (2) Seller warrants that Seller has no obligation to pay compensation to any other broker regarding the Property unless the Property is transferred to any of the following individuals or entities: _____.
      (3) If the Property is sold to anyone listed above during the time Seller is obligated to compensate another broker: (i) Broker is

© 2013, California Association of REALTORS®, Inc.

Seller's Initials (_____)(_____)

RLA REVISED 11/13 (PAGE 1 OF 5) Print Date

EQUAL HOUSING
OPPORTUNITY

RESIDENTIAL LISTING AGREEMENT - EXCLUSIVE (RLA PAGE 1 OF 5)

FIGURE 6.2 (continued): **Residential Listing Agreement (Exclusive Authorization and Right to Sell)**

Property Address:_____ Date:_____

not entitled to compensation under this Agreement; and (ii) Broker is not obligated to represent Seller in such transaction.

5. MULTIPLE LISTING SERVICE:

A. Broker is a participant/subscriber to _____ Multiple Listing Service (MLS) and possibly others. Unless otherwise instructed in writing the Property will be listed with the MLS(s) specified above. That MLS is (or if checked ☐ is not) the primary MLS for the geographic area of the Property. All terms of the transaction, including sales price and financing, if applicable, (i) will be provided to the MLS in which the property is listed for publication, dissemination and use by persons and entities on terms approved by the MLS and (ii) may be provided to the MLS even if the Property is not listed with the MLS.

BENEFITS OF USING THE MLS; IMPACT OF OPTING OUT OF THE MLS; PRESENTING ALL OFFERS

WHAT IS AN MLS? The MLS is a database of properties for sale that is available and disseminated to and accessible by all other real estate agents who are participants or subscribers to the MLS. Property information submitted to the MLS describes the price, terms and conditions under which the Seller's property is offered for sale (including but not limited to the listing broker's offer of compensation to other brokers). It is likely that a significant number of real estate practitioners in any given area are participants or subscribers to the MLS. The MLS may also be part of a reciprocal agreement to which other multiple listing services belong. Real estate agents belonging to other multiple listing services that have reciprocal agreements with the MLS also have access to the information submitted to the MLS. The MLS may further transmit the MLS database to Internet sites that post property listings online.

EXPOSURE TO BUYERS THROUGH MLS: Listing property with an MLS exposes a seller's property to all real estate agents and brokers (and their potential buyer clients) who are participants or subscribers to the MLS or a reciprocating MLS.

CLOSED/PRIVATE LISTING CLUBS OR GROUPS: Closed or private listing clubs or groups are not the same as the MLS. The MLS referred to above is accessible to all eligible real estate licensees and provides broad exposure for a listed property. Private or closed listing clubs or groups of licensees may have been formed outside the MLS. Private or closed listing clubs or groups are accessible to a more limited number of licensees and generally offer less exposure for listed property. Whether listing property through a closed, private network - and excluding it from the MLS - is advantageous or disadvantageous to a seller, and why, should be discussed with the agent taking the Seller's listing.

NOT LISTING PROPERTY IN A LOCAL MLS: If the Property is listed in an MLS which does not cover the geographic area where the Property is located then real estate agents and brokers working that territory, and Buyers they represent looking for property in the neighborhood, may not be aware the Property is for sale.

OPTING OUT OF MLS: If Seller elects to exclude the Property from the MLS, Seller understands and acknowledges that: (a) real estate agents and brokers from other real estate offices, and their buyer clients, who have access to that MLS may not be aware that Seller's Property is offered for sale; (b) Information about Seller's Property will not be transmitted to various real estate Internet sites that are used by the public to search for property listings; (c) real estate agents, brokers and members of the public may be unaware of the terms and conditions under which Seller is marketing the Property.

REDUCTION IN EXPOSURE: Any reduction in exposure of the Property may lower the number of offers and negatively impact the sales price.

PRESENTING ALL OFFERS: Seller understands that Broker must present all offers received for Seller's Property unless Seller gives Broker written instructions to the contrary.

Seller's Initials (_____) (_____)	Broker's Initials (_____) (_____)

B. MLS rules generally provide that residential real property and vacant lot listings be submitted to the MLS within 2 days or some other period of time after all necessary signatures have been obtained on the listing agreement. Broker will not have to submit this listing to the MLS if, within that time, Broker submits to the MLS a form signed by Seller (C.A.R. Form SELM or the local equivalent form).

C. MLS rules allow MLS data to be made available by the MLS to additional Internet sites unless Broker gives the MLS instructions to the contrary. Seller acknowledges that for any of the below opt-out instructions to be effective, Seller must make them on a separate instruction to Broker signed by Seller (C.A.R. Form SELI or the local equivalent form). Specific information that can be excluded from the Internet as permitted by (or in accordance with) the MLS is as follows:

(1) Property Availability: Seller can instruct Broker to have the MLS not display the Property on the Internet.

(2) Property Address: Seller can instruct Broker to have the MLS not display the Property address on the Internet. Seller understands that the above opt-outs would mean consumers searching for listings on the Internet may not see the Property or Property's address in response to their search.

(3) Feature Opt-Outs: Seller can instruct Broker to advise the MLS that Seller does not want visitors to MLS Participant or Subscriber Websites or Electronic Displays that display the Property listing to have the features below. Seller understands (i) that these opt-outs apply only to Websites or Electronic Displays of MLS Participants and Subscribers who are real estate broker and agent members of the MLS; (ii) that other Internet sites may or may not have the features set forth herein; and (iii) that neither Broker nor the MLS may have the ability to control or block such features on other Internet sites.

(a) Comments And Reviews: The ability to write comments or reviews about the Property on those sites; or the ability to link to another site containing such comments or reviews if the link is in immediate conjunction with the Property.

Seller's Initials (_____)(_____)

RLA REVISED 11/13 (PAGE 2 OF 5)

RESIDENTIAL LISTING AGREEMENT - EXCLUSIVE (RLA PAGE 2 OF 5)

FIGURE 6.2 (continued):   **Residential Listing Agreement (Exclusive Authorization and Right to Sell)**

Property Address:_____ Date:_____

(b) Automated Estimate Of Value: The ability to create an automated estimate of value or to link to another site containing such an estimate of value if the link is in immediate conjunction with the Property.

6. **SELLER REPRESENTATIONS:** Seller represents that, unless otherwise specified in writing, Seller is unaware of: (i) any Notice of Default recorded against the Property; (ii) any delinquent amounts due under any loan secured by, or other obligation affecting, the Property; (iii) any bankruptcy, insolvency or similar proceeding affecting the Property; (iv) any litigation, arbitration, administrative action, government investigation or other pending or threatened action that affects or may affect the Property or Seller's ability to transfer it; and (v) any current, pending or proposed special assessments affecting the Property. Seller shall promptly notify Broker in writing if Seller becomes aware of any of these items during the Listing Period or any extension thereof.

7. **BROKER'S AND SELLER'S DUTIES:** (a) Broker agrees to exercise reasonable effort and due diligence to achieve the purposes of this Agreement. Unless Seller gives Broker written instructions to the contrary, Broker is authorized to (i) order reports and disclosures as necessary, (ii) advertise and market the Property by any method and in any medium selected by Broker, including MLS and the Internet, and, to the extent permitted by these media, control the dissemination of the information submitted to any medium; and (iii) disclose to any real estate licensee making an inquiry the receipt of any offers on the Property and the offering price of such offers. (b) Seller agrees to consider offers presented by Broker, and to act in good faith to accomplish the sale of the Property by, among other things, making the Property available for showing at reasonable times and, subject to paragraph 4F, referring to Broker all inquiries of any party interested in the Property. Seller is responsible for determining at what price to list and sell the Property. Seller further agrees to indemnify, defend and hold Broker harmless from all claims, disputes, litigation, judgments attorney fees and costs arising from any incorrect information supplied by Seller, or from any material facts that Seller knows but fails to disclose.

8. **DEPOSIT:** Broker is authorized to accept and hold on Seller's behalf any deposits to be applied toward the purchase price.

9. **AGENCY RELATIONSHIPS:**
    A. Disclosure: If the Property includes residential property with one-to-four dwelling units, Seller shall receive a "Disclosure Regarding Agency Relationships" (C.A.R. Form AD) prior to entering into this Agreement.
    B. Seller Representation: Broker shall represent Seller in any resulting transaction, except as specified in paragraph 4F.
    C. Possible Dual Agency With Buyer: Depending upon the circumstances, it may be necessary or appropriate for Broker to act as an agent for both Seller and buyer, exchange party, or one or more additional parties ("Buyer"). Broker shall, as soon as practicable, disclose to Seller any election to act as a dual agent representing both Seller and Buyer. If a Buyer is procured directly by Broker or an associate-licensee in Broker's firm, Seller hereby consents to Broker acting as a dual agent for Seller and Buyer. In the event of an exchange, Seller hereby consents to Broker collecting compensation from additional parties for services rendered, provided there is disclosure to all parties of such agency and compensation. Seller understands and agrees that: (i) Broker, without the prior written consent of Seller, will not disclose to Buyer that Seller is willing to sell the Property at a price less than the listing price; (ii) Broker, without the prior written consent of Buyer, will not disclose to Seller that Buyer is willing to pay a price greater than the offered price; and (iii) except for (i) and (ii) above, a dual agent is obligated to disclose known facts materially affecting the value or desirability of the Property to both parties.
    D. Other Sellers: Seller understands that Broker may have or obtain listings on other properties, and that potential buyers may consider, make offers on, or purchase through Broker, property the same as or similar to Seller's Property. Seller consents to Broker's representation of sellers and buyers of other properties before, during and after the end of this Agreement.
    E. Confirmation: If the Property includes residential property with one-to-four dwelling units, Broker shall confirm the agency relationship described above, or as modified, in writing, prior to or concurrent with Seller's execution of a purchase agreement.

10. **SECURITY AND INSURANCE:** Broker is not responsible for loss of or damage to personal or real property, or person, whether attributable to use of a keysafe/lockbox, a showing of the Property, or otherwise. Third parties, including, but not limited to, appraisers, inspectors, brokers and prospective buyers, may have access to, and take videos and photographs of, the interior of the Property. Seller agrees to: (i) take reasonable precautions to safeguard and protect valuables that might be accessible during showings of the Property; and (ii) to obtain insurance to protect against these risks. Broker does not maintain insurance to protect Seller.

11. **PHOTOGRAPHS AND INTERNET ADVERTISING:**
    A. In order to effectively market the Property for sale it is often necessary to provide photographs, virtual tours and other media to buyers. Seller agrees (or ☐ if checked, does not agree) that Broker may photograph or otherwise electronically capture images of the exterior and interior of the Property ("Images") for static and/or virtual tours of the Property by buyers and others on Broker's website, the MLS, and other marketing sites. Seller acknowledges that once Images are placed on the Internet neither Broker nor Seller has control over who can view such Images and what use viewers may make of the Images, or how long such Images may remain available on the Internet. Seller further agrees that such Images are the property of Broker and that Broker may use such Images for advertisement of Broker's business in the future.
    B. Seller acknowledges that prospective buyers and/or other persons coming onto the property may take photographs, videos or other images of the property. Seller understands that Broker does not have the ability to control or block the taking and use of Images by any such persons. (If checked) ☐ Seller instructs Broker to publish in the MLS that taking of Images is limited to those persons preparing Appraisal or Inspection reports. Seller acknowledges that unauthorized persons may take images who do not have access to or have not read any limiting instruction in the MLS or who take images regardless of any limiting instruction in the MLS. Once Images are taken and/or put into electronic display on the Internet or otherwise, neither Broker nor Seller has control over who views such Images nor what use viewers may make of the Images.

12. **KEYSAFE/LOCKBOX:** A keysafe/lockbox is designed to hold a key to the Property to permit access to the Property by Broker, cooperating brokers, MLS participants, their authorized licensees and representatives, authorized inspectors, and accompanied prospective buyers. Broker, cooperating brokers, MLS and Associations/Boards of REALTORS® are not insurers against injury, theft, loss, vandalism or damage attributed to the use of a keysafe/lockbox. Seller does (or if checked ☐ does not) authorize Broker to install a keysafe/lockbox. If Seller does not occupy the Property, Seller shall be responsible for obtaining occupant(s)' written permission for use of a keysafe/lockbox (C.A.R. Form KLA).

RLA REVISED 11/13 (PAGE 3 OF 5)   Seller's Initials (_____)(_____)

RESIDENTIAL LISTING AGREEMENT - EXCLUSIVE (RLA PAGE 3 OF 5)

FIGURE 6.2 (continued):   **Residential Listing Agreement (Exclusive Authorization and Right to Sell)**

Property Address: _____ Date: _____

13. **SIGN:** Seller does (or if checked ☐ does not) authorize Broker to install a FOR SALE/SOLD sign on the Property.

14. **EQUAL HOUSING OPPORTUNITY:** The Property is offered in compliance with federal, state and local anti-discrimination laws.

15. **ATTORNEY FEES:** In any action, proceeding or arbitration between Seller and Broker regarding the obligation to pay compensation under this Agreement, the prevailing Seller or Broker shall be entitled to reasonable attorney fees and costs from the non-prevailing Seller or Broker, except as provided in paragraph 19A.

16. **ADDITIONAL TERMS:** ☐ REO Advisory Listing (C.A.R. Form REOL) ☐ Short Sale Information and Advisory (C.A.R. Form SSIA)

_____

_____

_____

_____

_____

_____

17. **MANAGEMENT APPROVAL:** If an associate-licensee in Broker's office (salesperson or broker-associate) enters into this Agreement on Broker's behalf, and Broker or Manager does not approve of its terms, Broker or Manager has the right to cancel this Agreement, in writing, within **5 Days** After its execution.

18. **SUCCESSORS AND ASSIGNS:** This Agreement shall be binding upon Seller and Seller's successors and assigns.

19. **DISPUTE RESOLUTION:**

    A. **MEDIATION:** Seller and Broker agree to mediate any dispute or claim arising between them regarding the obligation to pay compensation under this Agreement, before resorting to arbitration or court action. Mediation fees, if any, shall be divided equally among the parties involved. If, for any dispute or claim to which this paragraph applies, any party (i) commences an action without first attempting to resolve the matter through mediation, or (ii) before commencement of an action, refuses to mediate after a request has been made, then that party shall not be entitled to recover attorney fees, even if they would otherwise be available to that party in any such action. THIS MEDIATION PROVISION APPLIES WHETHER OR NOT THE ARBITRATION PROVISION IS INITIALED. **Exclusions from this mediation agreement are specified in paragraph 19C.**

    B. **ARBITRATION OF DISPUTES:**
    Seller and Broker agree that any dispute or claim in Law or equity arising between them regarding the obligation to pay compensation under this Agreement, which is not settled through mediation, shall be decided by neutral, binding arbitration. The arbitrator shall be a retired judge or justice, or an attorney with at least 5 years of residential real estate Law experience, unless the parties mutually agree to a different arbitrator. The parties shall have the right to discovery in accordance with Code of Civil Procedure §1283.05. In all other respects, the arbitration shall be conducted in accordance with Title 9 of Part 3 of the Code of Civil Procedure. Judgment upon the award of the arbitrator(s) may be entered into any court having jurisdiction. Enforcement of this agreement to arbitrate shall be governed by the Federal Arbitration Act. Exclusions from this arbitration agreement are specified in paragraph 19C.
    "NOTICE: BY INITIALING IN THE SPACE BELOW YOU ARE AGREEING TO HAVE ANY DISPUTE ARISING OUT OF THE MATTERS INCLUDED IN THE 'ARBITRATION OF DISPUTES' PROVISION DECIDED BY NEUTRAL ARBITRATION AS PROVIDED BY CALIFORNIA LAW AND YOU ARE GIVING UP ANY RIGHTS YOU MIGHT POSSESS TO HAVE THE DISPUTE LITIGATED IN A COURT OR JURY TRIAL. BY INITIALING IN THE SPACE BELOW YOU ARE GIVING UP YOUR JUDICIAL RIGHTS TO DISCOVERY AND APPEAL, UNLESS THOSE RIGHTS ARE SPECIFICALLY INCLUDED IN THE 'ARBITRATION OF DISPUTES' PROVISION. IF YOU REFUSE TO SUBMIT TO ARBITRATION AFTER AGREEING TO THIS PROVISION, YOU MAY BE COMPELLED TO ARBITRATE UNDER THE AUTHORITY OF THE CALIFORNIA CODE OF CIVIL PROCEDURE. YOUR AGREEMENT TO THIS ARBITRATION PROVISION IS VOLUNTARY."
    "WE HAVE READ AND UNDERSTAND THE FOREGOING AND AGREE TO SUBMIT DISPUTES ARISING OUT OF THE MATTERS INCLUDED IN THE 'ARBITRATION OF DISPUTES' PROVISION TO NEUTRAL ARBITRATION."

    | Seller's Initials ____ / ____ | Broker's Initials ____ / ____ |

    C. **ADDITIONAL MEDIATION AND ARBITRATION TERMS:** The following matters shall be excluded from mediation and arbitration: (i) a judicial or non-judicial foreclosure or other action or proceeding to enforce a deed of trust, mortgage or installment land sale contract as defined in Civil Code §2985; (ii) an unlawful detainer action; (iii) the filing or enforcement of a mechanic's lien; and (iv) any matter that is within the jurisdiction of a probate, small claims or bankruptcy court. The filing of a court action to enable the recording of a notice of pending action, for order of attachment, receivership, injunction, or other provisional remedies, shall not constitute a waiver or violation of the mediation and arbitration provisions.

RLA REVISED 11/13 (PAGE 4 OF 5)

Seller's Initials (_____)(_____)

RESIDENTIAL LISTING AGREEMENT - EXCLUSIVE (RLA PAGE 4 OF 5)

FIGURE 6.2 (continued):   **Residential Listing Agreement (Exclusive Authorization and Right to Sell)**

Property Address:_____ Date:_____

20. **ENTIRE AGREEMENT:** All prior discussions, negotiations and agreements between the parties concerning the subject matter of this Agreement are superseded by this Agreement, which constitutes the entire contract and a complete and exclusive expression of their agreement, and may not be contradicted by evidence of any prior agreement or contemporaneous oral agreement. If any provision of this Agreement is held to be ineffective or invalid, the remaining provisions will nevertheless be given full force and effect. This Agreement and any supplement, addendum or modification, including any photocopy or facsimile, may be executed in counterparts.

21. **OWNERSHIP, TITLE AND AUTHORITY:** Seller warrants that: (i) Seller is the owner of the Property; (ii) no other persons or entities have title to the Property; and (iii) Seller has the authority to both execute this Agreement and sell the Property. Exceptions to ownership, title and authority are as follows: _____
_____.

☐ REPRESENTATIVE CAPACITY: This addendum is being signed for Seller by an individual acting in a Representative Capacity as specified in the attached Representative Capacity Signature Disclosure (C.A.R. Form RCSD). Wherever the signature or initials of the representative identified in the RCSD appear on this Agreement or any related documents, it shall be deemed to be in a representative capacity for the entity described and not in an individual capacity, unless otherwise indicated. Seller (i) represents that the entity for which the individual is signing already exists and (ii) shall Deliver to Broker, within 3 Days After Execution of this Agreement, evidence of authority to act (such as but not limited to: applicable trust document, or portion thereof, letters testamentary, court order, power of attorney, resolution, or formation documents of the business entity).

By signing below, Seller acknowledges that Seller has read, understands, received a copy of and agrees to the terms of this Agreement.

Seller_____ Date _____
Address _____City _____State _____ Zip _____
Telephone _____ Fax _____ Email _____

Seller _____ Date _____
Address _____City _____State _____ Zip _____
Telephone _____ Fax _____ Email _____

Real Estate Broker (Firm) _____ Cal BRE Lic.# _____
By (Agent) _____ Cal BRE Lic.# _____Date _____
Address _____City _____State _____Zip _____
Telephone _____ Fax _____ Email _____

Published and Distributed by:
REAL ESTATE BUSINESS SERVICES, INC.
a subsidiary of the California Association of REALTORS®
525 South Virgil Avenue, Los Angeles, California 90020

Reviewed by _____ Date _____

RLA REVISED 11/13 (PAGE 5 OF 5)

RESIDENTIAL LISTING AGREEMENT - EXCLUSIVE (RLA PAGE 5 OF 5)

> With an exclusive-agency listing, the broker is not entitled to a commission if the owner sells without an agent's assistance.

Exclusive-agency listing. An **exclusive-agency listing** differs from the exclusive-authorization-and-right-to-sell listing in one major respect: the seller will pay a commission to the listing broker regardless of which agency makes the sale, but it does not prevent owners from selling their own property and paying no commission.

Owners will often want an exclusive-agency listing because they have one or more parties who have expressed interest in the property and don't want to have to pay a fee for the agent selling to "their" prospect. In order to avoid competition with the owner, the agent should suggest an exclusive authorization-and-right-to-sell listing with exceptions for named parties for a period of time, such as seven days. If the buyer's prospects are seriously interested, they will have to decide quickly or they will realize that the owner will be paying a fee, which reduces any advantage they may feel they have in buying direct from the owner. Such an agreement helps the owner because it could mean a quick sale or saving wasted time with a party who is not a serious buyer. After the stated time, which in this case was seven days, the broker has an exclusive-authorization-and-right-to-sell listing without exceptions. The broker might also gain prospects for the purchase of other properties.

It is important to keep in mind that whenever there is an excluded party from an exclusive-right-to-sell listing, the listing agent should disclose the exclusion to other agents. Failure to do so could make the listing agent responsible for paying a commission to another agent, even though the listing agent did not receive compensation for the transaction.

Net listing. A **net listing** is not truly a type of listing. Net listings could be open, exclusive-right-to-sell, or exclusive-agency listings. Net refers to commission. A clause in the agreement states that the owner is asking a certain sum of money from the sale of property. All expenses, including the broker's commission, are to be covered by any sum the broker is able to obtain in excess of the selling price (net) specified by the seller.

> Net listings provide that the commission shall be the excess over a net price set by the seller.

Net listings are seldom used. They make agents vulnerable to charges of fraud, misrepresentation, and other abuses against which the real estate law offers sellers protection. For example, a broker might fail to tell an owner that the price the owner wants is too low or be tempted to persuade the seller to ask for the lowest possible amount so that the broker can sell the property at a much higher price to collect a large commission. These types of actions go against the broker's duties as an agent. In fact, net listings are illegal in a number of states because of the inherent conflicts of interest. Even though they are legal in California, they are generally avoided.

Nevertheless, if a broker takes a net listing, California law requires that the broker disclose, in writing, the selling price and the broker's compensation before acceptance of any offer.

Note: An agent's failure to disclose the selling price under a net listing is cause for license revocation or suspension.

Option combined with a listing.   An option is an irrevocable right to buy a property at an agreed price. An **option combined with a listing** entitles the broker to compensation under the listing if the property is sold to a third person, as well as the agent's right to buy the property herself. Law forbids a listing broker who has an option combined with a listing to profit at the expense of the owner. If the broker finds a buyer willing to pay more than the option price, and if the broker then exercises an option to buy to make a greater profit from resale of the property, the broker must make a full disclosure to the owner. California law covering this is stated as follows:

> *If a broker employed to sell property is also given an option to purchase the property himself, he occupies the dual status of agent and purchaser and is not entitled to exercise his option except by divesting himself of his obligation as agent by making a full disclosure of any information in his possession as to the prospect of making a sale to another.*

Even though an option listing may be legal if the proper disclosures are made, an agent who makes an extraordinary profit might nevertheless become involved in a lawsuit. This action could negatively reflect on his or her reputation. It is strongly recommended that both net listings and option listings be avoided.

Buyer broker agreement—exclusive right to represent. Buyers want to be shown the property that best meets the the their needs, regardless of the fact it is listed for sale or for sale by owner or lender. They also want to purchase at the lowest possible price. To accomplish these goals, buyers want their own agents. New contract forms were developed for buyer representation. See Figure 6.3. Although this form is for an exclusive representation, buyer listings (like seller listings) could be exclusive agency, under which a buyer could buy without an agent and not be obligated to pay a fee, or could even be an open listing.

The form is similar in many respects to the exclusive-authorization-and-right-to-sell listing. It gives authority to the broker to act as the agent of the buyer rather than the seller. The buyer's broker looks at the entire transaction from the buyer's standpoint, without a shared loyalty. The new contract form allows the buyer to tailor the broker's services to meet the buyer's needs and adjust the compensation accordingly.

The buyer's broker is held to the same standard of performance in serving the buyer as the listing broker owes to the seller. The commission is negotiable, and the contract must contain a definite termination date.

FIGURE 6.3:   **Buyer's Listing Agreement**

BUYER'S LISTING AGREEMENT
Exclusive Right to Buy, Exchange or Option

Prepared by: Agent _____	**Phone** _____
Broker _____	**Email** _____

NOTE: This form is by a buyer's agent when employed by a buyer as their sole agent to locate and acquire property for a fixed period of time.

DATE: _____, 20_____, at _____, California.
Items left blank or unchecked are not applicable.

1. RETAINER PERIOD:
  1.1   Buyer hereby retains and grants to Broker the exclusive right to locate real property of the type described below and to negotiate the terms and conditions for its purchase, lease or option, acceptable to Buyer, for the period beginning on _____, 20_____ and terminating on _____, 20_____.

2. BROKER'S OBLIGATIONS:
  2.1   Broker to use diligence in the performance of this employment.

3. GENERAL PROVISIONS:
  3.1   Buyer acknowledges receipt of the Agency Law Disclosure. [See **ft** Form 305]
  3.2   Buyer authorizes Broker to cooperate with other brokers and divide with them any compensation due.
  3.3   Before any party to this agreement files an action on a dispute arising out of this agreement which remains unresolved after 30 days of informal negotiations, the parties agree to enter into non-binding mediation administered by a neutral dispute resolution organization and undertake a good faith effort during mediation to settle the dispute.
  3.4   The prevailing party in any action on a dispute will be entitled to attorney fees and costs, unless they file an action without first offering to enter into mediation to resolve the dispute.
  3.5   This agreement will be governed by California law.

4. BROKERAGE FEE:
NOTICE: The amount or rate of real estate fees is not fixed by law. They are set by each Broker individually and may be negotiable between Client and Broker.
  4.1   Buyer agrees to pay Broker ☐ _____% of the purchase price, or ☐ _____, IF:
    a.   Buyer, or any person acting on Buyer's behalf, purchases, leases, exchanges for or obtains a purchase option on real property sought under this agreement during the retainer period.
    b.   Buyer terminates this employment of Broker during the listing period.
    c.   Within one year after termination of this agreement, Buyer enters into negotiations which result in Buyer's acquisition of an interest in any property Broker has solicited information on or negotiated with its owner, directly or indirectly, on behalf of Buyer prior to this agreement's termination. Broker to identify prospective properties by written notice to Buyer within 21 days after termination. [See **ft** Form 123]
  4.2   Buyer's obligation to pay Broker a brokerage fee is extinguished on Broker's acceptance of a fee from Seller or Seller's Broker of property acquired by Buyer.
  4.3   In the event this agreement terminates without Broker receiving a fee under §4.1 or §4.2, Buyer to pay Broker the sum of $_____ per hour of time accounted for by Broker, not to exceed $_____.

TYPE OF PROPERTY SOUGHT:
GENERAL DESCRIPTION _____
LOCATION _____ SIZE _____
RENTAL AMOUNT/TERM _____

I agree to render services on the terms stated above.	**I agree to employ Broker on the terms stated above.**
Date: _____, 20_____	☐ See attached Signature Page Addendum. [**ft** Form 251]
Buyer's Broker: _____	Date: _____, 20_____
Broker's CalBRE #: _____	Buyer's Name: _____
Buyer's Agent: _____	
Agent's CalBRE #: _____	Signature: _____
	Buyer's Name: _____
Signature:_____	Signature: _____
Address: _____	Address: _____
Phone: _____ Cell: _____	Phone: _____ Cell: _____
Email: _____	Email: _____

FORM 103	12-14	©2014 **first tuesday**, P.O. BOX 5707, RIVERSIDE, CA 92517 (951) 781-7300

The buyer's broker, who is entitled to be compensated by the buyer, is motivated to show the buyer all known applicable properties, including:

- For-sale-by-owner properties

- Foreclosure and probate sales

- Unlisted properties

- Open listings

- Any other available properties

Figure 6.3 is a written contract between the broker and a buyer. Therefore, it must be filled out correctly and signed by the necessary parties. (**Note:** Specific clauses and organization will vary in forms prepared by different publishers.)

ANALYSIS OF RESIDENTIAL LISTING AGREEMENT EXCLUSIVE AUTHORIZATION-AND-RIGHT-TO-SELL LISTING FORM

Because the listing agreement is a written contract between the broker and the seller, it must be filled out correctly and signed by the necessary parties. The exact wording on each listing form will vary, depending on the details of the transaction. However, certain basic provisions are part of each listing contract. Figure 6.2 is a form for an exclusive-authorization-and-right-to-sell listing. The following paragraphs analyze this sample form.

Paragraph 1: Exclusive-Right-to-Sell

Enter here the name of the owner and the real estate office or broker receiving the listing. If a salesperson rather than a broker takes the listing, the salesperson should write his or her employing broker's name. The salesperson completing the form signs his or her name at the bottom of the form. Note that the words *exclusive and irrevocable* make this listing an exclusive authorization and right to sell.

After the broker's name, enter the time period, including the beginning and the termination dates. Three-month to six-month periods are common; however, if the broker thinks the property will take longer to sell, he or she may ask for more time.

Next, enter the location of the property by city and county as well as by an unmistakable address within the city. Occasionally, in addition to the street address, the location by lot, block, and tract or a metes-and-bounds legal description may be given. It may be necessary to add a legal description as a signed attachment to the listing.

Paragraph 2: Items Included and Excluded

Items of personal property that may be included in the purchase are listed, as are items of real or personal property excluded from the sale. Misunderstandings can arise as to what property the seller intends to include, and listing the items will help alleviate such a problem. Examples of personal property often sold with a residence are major appliances and drapes.

Paragraph 3: Listing Price and Terms

The terms of sale include the price at which the property is being offered. Additional space is provided for stipulating the exact terms the owner requires to sell the property. This includes financial arrangements, such as cash, second trust deeds, or loan assumptions. Unless terms are specified, the owner is not obligated to pay a commission when he or she refuses a full-price offer unless the offer is for cash.

Paragraph 4: Compensation to Broker

Bold face type points out that commission is negotiable and not set by law. This statement is required for listings of 1–4-unit residential properties.

Subparagraph A indicates the rate or amount of commission that will be paid if the property is sold.

Subparagraph A-1 stipulates that commission is due regardless of who actually produces a potential buyer. All that is required is that the purchase offer either meets the price and terms of the agreement (as stated in Paragraph 2) or includes a different price and terms that are acceptable to the seller. The offer also must be made during the listing period stated in Paragraph 1.

The safety clause protects you from attempts to evade paying your fee even after the listing expires.

Subparagraph A-2 is the **safety clause**. It provides that the listing agent shall be entitled to a commission if the property is sold within a specified number of days after expiration of the listing to a prospective buyer whose name was furnished by the agent to the owner within three calendar days of expiration of the listing or was sold to a buyer who was shown and physically entered the property during the listing period.

Subparagraph A-3 states that the seller agrees to pay a commission if the seller sells, leases, or rents the property; withdraws it from the market without the consent of the broker; or otherwise renders the property unavailable for sale before the expiration date.

Subparagraph B provides that if completion of the sale is prevented by a party other than the seller and the seller collects damages, then the total commission is to be the lesser of the commission due under Paragraph 4A or one-half of the damages recovered after deducting expenses.

Subparagraph C provides for any additional seller compensation, such as MLS fees or other broker expenses.

Note: Several brokerage firms have been charging sellers a transaction fee or document preparation fee in the $200 range in addition to the commission. If any additional charges are to be made to the seller, they should be clearly set forth in the listing contract. If the fee is in conjunction with a federally related loan, then the fee may violate the Real Estate Settlement Procedures Act, which requires an actual service provided for every fee. Agents may not charge duplicate fees.

Subparagraph D provides that the broker may cooperate with other brokers and divide the commission in any manner acceptable to them or an agreed percentage.

Subparagraph E states that the seller irrevocably assigns to the broker the broker's compensation from the seller's proceeds. In the past, some sellers have notified an escrow not to pay the broker but to turn the funds over to the sellers. Because the escrow is not the agent of the broker, the escrows complied. An assignment agreement protects the broker's fee.

Subparagraph F is the owner's warranty that the owner is not obligated to pay a commission to any other broker if the property is sold during the listing period, with the exception of listed prospective buyers. If such a listed buyer purchases the property during the listing, the broker is not obligated to pay the listing broker and the listing broker is not obligated to represent the owner in the sale.

Paragraph 5: Multiple Listing Service

The parties agree that listing information is to be provided to an MLS. Without authorization from the owner, the agent would not have the right to cooperate with subagents or give the listing or sale information to an MLS or to third parties.

The seller has the right to exclude property information from websites, as well as website features such as viewer comments.

Paragraph 6: Seller Representations

Seller represents that he or she is unaware of a notice of default recorded against the property; delinquencies due under loans; bankruptcy, insolvency, or other proceedings affecting the property as well as any litigation pending or threatened that could affect the seller's ability to sell and any current or proposed special assessments. If the seller becomes aware of any of the above during the listing, the seller agrees to promptly notify the agent.

Paragraph 7: Broker's and Seller's Duties

The broker agrees to use diligence in achieving the purpose of the listing agreement. The seller agrees to consider offers received in good faith and to hold the broker harmless for claims resulting from incorrect information supplied or the failure to disclose information to the broker.

Paragraph 8: Deposit

This section authorizes the listing agent to accept the deposit. Without this authorization, an agent taking a deposit could be doing so as the agent of the buyer.

Paragraph 9: Agency Relationships

This paragraph explains that the broker represents the seller and will not be the agent of the buyer; however, if a buyer is procured by the listing agent, it may be necessary for the broker to act in a dual agency capacity. The seller is informed that the broker also represents other sellers. The agency is to be confirmed prior to or concurrent with the execution of a purchase agreement.

Paragraph 10: Security and Insurance

This section explains that the broker is not responsible for loss or damage to personal property, regardless of the presence of a lockbox, and that the owner must take precautions to protect valuables and obtain insurance for risks involved.

Paragraph 11: Photographs and internet Advertising

Owner can agree or refuse to allow photographs to be used for MLS listings and advertising. The owner acknowledges that visitors may take photos but owner has the option of having MLS listing indicate photos are not to be taken.

Paragraph 12: Key Safe/Lockbox

This provides authorization to install a lockbox. The lockbox makes the property more available for showing by other agents in the MLS. The agent is not liable to the owner for loss or damage resulting from access via the lockbox. If the seller wants the property shown by appointment only, then the listing agent may not want to use a lockbox, and the seller can elect whether or not to use it.

Owners should realize that by refusing to allow a lockbox, the number of showings by other offices will likely be reduced. Showings by other offices would likely require the listing agent to accompany selling agents to view the property.

Paragraph 13: Sign

Putting a For Sale sign on the property makes the property more recognizable. However, the agent must obtain authorization from the seller to do so.

Paragraph 14: Equal Housing Opportunity

The property is offered in compliance with antidiscrimination laws. Members of a protected class cannot be denied the right to purchase property due to their protected class

Paragraph 15: Attorney's Fees

If there is any disagreement between the seller and broker and they go either to court or to arbitration, the loser in either incident must pay the costs. This paragraph tends to reduce frivolous lawsuits.

Paragraph 16: Additional Terms

Space is provided for any other owner-broker agreements or terms.

Paragraph 17: Management Approval

If an associate licensee enters into this agreement, the broker or manager has the right to cancel this agreement within five days.

Paragraph 18: Successors and Assigns

This agreement shall be binding upon the seller and seller's successors and assigns.

Paragraph 19: Dispute Resolution

Subparagraph A provides that the broker and seller agree to mediate any disputes arising from this agreement prior to any other action that is available. They are not, however, required to resolve the dispute through mediation.

Subparagraph B provides that by initialing, the parties agree to neutral binding arbitration of any dispute, thus giving up rights to have the dispute litigated in the courts.

Subparagraph C also provides that matters excluded from mediation and arbitration include foreclosure proceedings, unlawful detainer action, mechanics' liens, matters within court jurisdiction, and tort injuries from latent or patent defects to the property.

Paragraph 20: Entire Contract

It is agreed that this agreement is the entire agreement and may not be contradicted by prior agreements or verbal statements.

Paragraph 21: Ownership Title and Authority

This paragraph warrants that the sellers are the only persons who have title to the property unless indicated otherwise, and that the seller has the authority to execute this agreement and sell the property

Signatures

The seller acknowledges that he or she has read, understands, and accepts the agreement and has received a copy of it.

ANALYSIS OF THE BUYER LISTING AGREEMENT—EXCLUSIVE RIGHT TO REPRESENT BUYER

Compare this buyer's listing with the seller listing (exclusive-authorization-and-right-to-sell agreement) in Figure 6.2. You will notice similarities and differences.

The **exclusive-right-to-represent buyer agreement** sets forth the type of property that the buyer wishes to purchase, its size location, and the price. The specific obligations of the broker are set forth.

The general provisions include acknowledgment of agency disclosure, an authorization to cooperate with other brokers, dispute resolution and an attorney fee provision.

The buyer agrees to pay broker agreed compensation if a purchase is made or owner terminates agreement. A safety provision includes entitlement to compensation for one year after termination if a purchase is made of a property the broker introduced the buyer to and identified said property to the buyer within 21 days of termination of the agreement.

The buyer's obligation to pay a brokerage fee is extinguished if broker accepts a fee from seller or seller's agent.

THE LISTING PROCESS

Real estate brokers must pay careful attention to listing details to ensure a smooth transaction.

Preparing for the Listing

An old adage about the listing process is that it is "80% preparation and 20% selling." The time spent on research before the first appointment with a prospective seller is critical in obtaining the listing.

Step 1: Obtain information about the property.   Ownership records, as well as public information about a property, is available online from public as well as private websites. Sites such as *www.propertyshark.com* can provide ownership records, information or recent building permits, taxes, assessor data, etc.

Generally, real estate firms use their title company to obtain property information. A property profile can generally be obtained instantaneously using public records searches available within any local MLS. Besides title and liens, you should ask for a search of federal tax liens. In addition to the public data available through the MLS, your title company also can give you comparable sales by neighborhood, or even by street, and provide copies of deeds if desired.

Step 2: Prepare your comparative market analysis (CMA).   (See Unit 5.)

Step 3: Drive by the current and expired listings and by the property that has sold.   Drive by the prospective property and then by the comparables to get a feeling for the amenities of the property you are going to list as well as to compare it visually with other existing and expired listings in the marketplace. Take photos, if none are available, so the owners can see the types of property their home will be competing with for buyers.

Keep an open mind as to value until you have analyzed the available data. Just like owners, agents will sometimes have preconceived notions about value, based on a single sale or misinformation.

Check comparable properties before you go for your listing presentation. Often what appears as a comparable on your printout is not even close to being a comparable property when utility and desirability are considered. If an owner knows the property you are using as a comparable and knows of problems it has that should have excluded it as a comparable, you will have lost credibility as an expert. Your chances of obtaining a listing could be significantly reduced.

The Sales Listing Interview

With your preparation and research taken care of, you are ready to call on your listing prospect.

On the first visit, you should ascertain the owners' motivation for selling and view the property to prepare your comparative market analysis and your listing presentation. Normally, you will make your listing presentation on your second visit to the property; however, if the owners appear receptive and you have a good feel for the value, you should go into your listing presentation during your first visit to the property.

After arriving for your second visit, ask the owners if it is all right if you go through their home once again. This relieves tension and shows your interest. If you haven't yet determined the owners' reason for selling, ask them. They will generally give you an honest response. Ask what the owners have done to the home. Owners will be more receptive to agents who they feel appreciate their home.

An excellent place to present your material to owners is the kitchen table. It presents a nonthreatening informal setting, and you are able to sit close to the owners.

(It is easier to be argumentative from a distance.) You also want them to be able to easily view your visual material.

The comparative market analysis (CMA).   In presenting your comparative market analysis, don't rush. You must show you appreciate their house, but present the comparables fairly to lead up to your recommendations. Watch owners for reactions. If they show little reaction, ask questions such as "Are there any recent area sales that I missed?"

Sometimes owners have an inflated idea of what their property is worth. It may be based on a sale under different conditions or on what they heard someone say a house sold for. Often owners have a value in mind based simply on what they want. Consider the following:

> *[Mrs. Jones], buyers, not sellers or brokers, determine market value. I have shown you what homes similar to yours are for sale at as well as what similar homes have sold for. Is there any information you know of that I have not considered?*

If the owners say that another agent told them they could get more for their house, ask to see the comparative market analysis that the price was based on. Chances are there won't be one. Then consider the following rebuttal:

> *I don't know how that agent was able to arrive at a value so quickly and without a detailed analysis. A value off the top of one's head is a hunch at best. If it is too high, a listing at that price simply means a lot of time wasted and no sale. I showed you the effect of overpricing a home on the likelihood of a sale. If a hunch is too low, someone will get a bargain at your expense. I won't price your home on a hunch, and I'm sure you wouldn't want me to do that.*

There are many approaches, but all have the same goal: to convince the owners that your value has validity and that offering the property at a competitive price would be in the owners' best interests.

You want to get the owners to agree on an offering price at this time. If you can't obtain an agreement, your further efforts will be futile. However, if the owners agree on an offering price, you are more than halfway along to a listing:

> *Do you agree with my recommendation that your home should be placed on the market for ($___)?*

Accepting a listing at an unreasonably high price could be a violation of your fiduciary duty to your client.

If an owner is adamant about to what you consider an unrealistically high price, a short drive to some neighboring properties for sale might bring the buyers back to earth. Choose unoccupied homes with lockboxes to show without disturbing owners.

If the owners have been very receptive to your presentation with the comparative market analysis or if the owners contacted you to list the property, it should not be necessary for you to go through the listing presentation. You can cut right to the listing. Start by obtaining the owners' signatures on the Estimated Seller's Proceeds form. (See Unit 5.) Never delay when parties are receptive because delay can lead to indecision.

The listing presentation.   After you have finished presenting your comparative market analysis, ask the owners if they can spare a few minutes for you to present some information they will want to hear. Because you have gone to a great deal of effort on behalf of the owners, you can expect a positive response.

Go through the listing presentation book or computer presentation, using narratives such as those developed in Unit 5. Of course, use your narratives with your visuals as you turn the pages of your book. When you have finished, you should be ready for a closing.

PowerPoint, a Microsoft developed program, is an excellent program to use for preparation of a computer presentation. It can combine text with graphics, slides, movies, and audio for a professional and effective presentation. Additionally, if you are making your presentation using an iPad or other tablet device, consider preparing your presentation in Keynote or another third-party application.

> ### Be Positive
> Use positive terms in your presentation. An agency representation indicates you will be doing something for an owner, whereas listing may have a negative connotation. In the same manner, a fee is something that they can understand is due a professional, but commission is a word that can have a negative connotation.

Make certain the owners understand what they will actually net from an offer. Be up front with them. When you use the Estimated Seller's Proceeds form, be realistic in your figures. As previously stated, it is better to be on the low side than to estimate a net significantly higher than the owner will actually receive. Disappointed owners lead to loss of goodwill toward your firm and could result in a failure to close the sale. After the sellers sign the statement, give them a copy.

You should explain agency relationships and have the owners sign that they have received a copy of the agency disclosure (Unit 3). While the signing of the Seller's Estimated Proceeds form and the Disclosure Regarding Real Estate Agency Relationships form do not obligate the owners, it should now be a natural act to sign the listing when it is presented. A **trial closing** tries for an agreement to sign the listing. The choice should not be to list or not to list. As an example, the question "Would you want me to serve as your marketing agent for 90 days or should we make it 120 days?" gives owners a choice between two positives, not between a positive and a negative.

If the owners respond positively to your trial closing, give each of the owners a copy of the listing. It could be prepared in advance so you need to insert only minor items. Go through the listing slowly. Answer any owner questions. When you get to items calling for initials, give each owner a pen and ask each to initial where recommended. Make certain they understand that the option is theirs.

Every presentation you give will not necessarily run smoothly. There will be objections that must be overcome in a straightforward, logical manner. You might consider starting with the following:

I'm glad you mentioned that because. . .

That's an excellent point. You're absolutely right but. . .

Owners who hesitate to sign the agreement are signaling that they have a problem. You must find out what the problem is if you are to overcome it. Most of the objections should be readily overcome by material covered in Unit 5 and included in your listing presentation.

A common objection is, "I want to sell, in fact I need to sell. That's why I can't be tied up with a listing." Your response could be:

That's exactly why I suggest an exclusive-right-to-sell agency agreement at the price I have indicated. We know from experience that it takes longer for an owner not represented by an agent to sell a home than it takes with an agent. In addition, in working on your own, you more than double your chance of running into time-consuming and costly problems when you do find a buyer. You are not tying up your property with an exclusive-right-to-sell agency agreement; instead, you are taking the first step toward a sale.

Many objections center on paying compensation. As previously stated, you should always refer to it as a *fee*. Consider the following approaches:

Who pays your fee?

The fee is paid out of money the buyer puts up. The buyer's price includes the fee so they feel they are the ones paying it. When buyers know that an agent isn't involved, they typically reduce any offer that they're willing to make by an amount to cover the fee involved with an agent even if the price was reduced to reflect this. Buyers may not be willing to split it because they may feel that it comes out of their money.

If an owner asks you to reduce your fee, one approach to use would be:

A reduced fee would not be fair to you. Studies have shown that a reduced fee increases the length of time it takes for a sale as well as reduces the likelihood of a sale.

If there are varying commission rates in your area, check the records of your listing service before making the listing presentation. You may discover that listings taken by firms offering a significantly lower fee have a lower sales record than listings taken by your firm at a more normal fee. If so, you could present this information visually with a bar graph and use a narrative such as:

Based on the computer records of [Cedar Creek Brokers Association], listings taken by [Champion Realty] at a [6%] fee have a [46%] greater likelihood of being sold during the listing period than listings taken by other firms at a [4%] fee. This points out that you get what you pay for. A lower fee simply reduces the likelihood of a sale. A lower fee may mean no fee at all and an unsold house. Is that a bargain?

Another objection concerns *listing price*. Some owners want to add your fee to what they want for the home to determine an offering price. Owners may be unrealistic for many reasons, but it isn't enough just to get a listing; you want a listing that is likely to sell. While you have a duty to an owner to get the maximum possible from a property, you also have a duty to advise the owner as to what would be in the owner's best interests.

Several approaches you can use include:

> *Let's assume that we offer the property at the price you suggest [$]. Assume further that we find a buyer at that price. The sale would be unlikely to be made because lenders make loans based on appraisals of market value, not what a buyer is willing to pay. From my comparables, I have shown you data on market value. Appraisers have access to this same data. What do you suppose will happen when the buyer is notified that the loan is not approved because the property is worth less than the buyer has offered?*

> *Assume you are a buyer and you are looking at homes and you see these comparable properties I have shown you at lower prices than your home is listed at. What do you suppose a buyer's reaction will be? Pricing that is not reflective of the market would not be fair to you, because you would be eliminating many potential buyers.*

Too high a list price does not help the owner.

An overpriced listing is unlikely to sell. Your failure will help another agent in obtaining a listing at a realistic price. By taking an overpriced listing, you will get a reputation both of failure and of having an inventory of overpriced properties.

If the owners indicate that they want to list at their price to see what happens and perhaps reduce the price later, an approach to use would be:

> *When a property is realistically listed, agents are enthusiastic and will spend their best efforts on selling that property. If they regard a listing as a "hard sell," they will show the property only if more attractively priced properties are not available.*

> *When you finally reduce your price, that price adjustment is not greeted with the enthusiasm of a new listing. In addition, when buyers know a price was reduced and the property has been on the market for a long time, they will sense desperation. Any offer will then likely be significantly less than the reduced price. If you really want to sell your home at the best possible price, I suggest we list it at [$]. Doesn't this make sense?*

Sometimes it takes a **clincher**. Final persuasion for an owner who has been trying to sell without an agent could be:

[Mr. and Mrs. Jones], do you realize that this house is holding you captive? With your sign and your ads, you likely feel that you have to be here every weekend waiting for the telephone or doorbell to ring. Even people who say they will be here seldom show up. I'm offering to relieve you of these obligations.

Whenever you make a closing that implies a signature, offer the owner a pen. The owner who puts it down still has questions that must be eliminated. Don't be afraid to try again and again for a closing. A closing is not a one-time win-or-lose proposition.

Prepare yourself so answers to objections and closings come naturally. If you can't close a listing, you won't be able to close a sale. If you can't close a sale, you become an order taker who shows merchandise and waits for a buyer to decide, not a problem solver—and certainly not a professional salesperson.

Follow through.   After you obtain the listing, thank the owners. Be certain you leave the following items:

- A copy of the signed listing with your card attached

- A copy of your comparative market analysis

- The Estimated Seller's Proceeds form

- A copy of the signed agency disclosure form if not covered in the listing

Let the owners know what will be happening (your marketing plan) when the for sale sign will be installed and when you will be contacting them again.

The Buyer Agency Presentation

It is difficult to get buyers to agree that you should be their exclusive agent to find them property to buy unless they feel that you fully understand their needs, that you are competent and able to locate a property for them, and that it would be in their best interests to have you as their exclusive agent. Similarly, you don't want to take an agency responsibility and expend your best efforts for prospective buyers until you realize they are motivated to buy, have the resources and/or credit to consummate a purchase, and have needs you can reasonably fulfill.

A good time to make a presentation for exclusive-agency representation to buyers would be after you have interviewed them about their needs, shown them several properties, and questioned them further about property impressions. By then, you will have understood fairly well the buyers and sold yourself as a professional.

A good approach would be to tell your prospective buyer(s) that you would like to have them obtain preapproval for a loan so that they'll have the financing when they find a property. By handling an internet loan application and printing out a loan preapproval letter, you will show your professionalism and make the prospects feel they are a step closer to a new home. A loan preapproval will also enhance the likelihood of an offer being accepted by an owner.

A number of internet sites are available where your client can get preapproved for a loan in as little as 15 minutes. You should explain to your clients that being preapproved, subject to verification, does not obligate the buyers to deal with that specific lender. The preapproval letter can be attached to any offers made.

You could now conduct a presentation using buyer-listing presentation material, or you could use a narrative such as the following:

> *I would like to help you in finding the best home for you. I imagine we will spend a good deal of time together in accomplishing this goal. Do you feel comfortable working with me?*

You can, of course, expect a positive response and people are unlikely to say they are uncomfortable working with you.

> *Most agents are really agents of the owners and have a duty to get the highest price possible for a property. However, I would like to represent you alone rather than an owner. As your agent, my duty would be to fulfill your needs with the best property for you at the lowest price. Is that what you want?*

Prospective buyers can be expected to give a positive response, as they of course want the best property at the lowest price.

> *I'll be using my best efforts to work for you and to meet your needs. However, my services will likely be paid, not by you, but by sellers who have listed properties with other agents. While I'll share in the fee paid by a seller, my sole obligation will be to you. Does that type of arrangement sound reasonable to you?*

Note: You are asking if it sounds reasonable and the response will likely be positive. It is implied that they are agreeing to an agency relationship.

> *I want you to be partners with me in meeting your needs. If you see a house that is for sale, a house you're interested in, or an internet listing that perks your interest, contact me and I'll get more information for you. If it seems promising, I'll arrange for you to see the property.*

> *I would like to go over the agency representation that I think would best meet your needs.*

You can then give your prospective buyer(s) copies of the exclusive-right-to-represent agreement and go through the agreement with them explaining the meaning of each paragraph. You should explain to the prospective buyers that by signing the agreement, they are not obligated to make any purchase and that in cases where the property is listed for sale with a broker, the seller would be the one paying your fee. By having them initial each page as you complete the agreement, signing it will be a natural act.

Listing a Short Sale

There may be listing situations that at first glance appear hopeless because the owner owes more than can be netted from a sale.

A saleable listing is still possible if you can convince a lender that it is in their best interest to agree to a **short sale** where the lender agrees to accept sale proceeds as settlement of the loan obligation. See Unit 7 for how to handle short-sale situations.

Before a lender will agree to this the lender has to be convinced that the borrower will otherwise default on the loan and that the listing price you are proposing is as good as they can expect in the market. If a lender gives approval for a short sale of 1-4 residential units, a deficiency judgement is not possible.

SUMMARY

A listing contract is an agency contract to sell or locate property.

A valid listing must be in writing and must meet the four requirements of any contract:

1. Competent parties

2. Lawful object

3. Proper offer and acceptance (mutual consent)

4. Consideration

There are six basic types of listings:

1. Open listing (nonexclusive)

2. Exclusive-authorization-and-right-to-sell listing

3. Exclusive-agency listing

4. Net listing

5. Option listing

6. Exclusive-right-to-represent listing

The real estate agent must understand every paragraph used in both the sale and buyer-listing forms to answer owners' and buyers' questions and properly meet owners' and buyers' needs.

The agent must prepare for the listing transaction. The first step is to obtain information about the property; the second step is to prepare the comparative market analysis; the third step is to drive by comparables to make certain that your comparables are truly comparable and that you have a good sense of value.

The listing presentation normally starts with going through the comparative market analysis. The seller should understand the validity of your information before you proceed further.

If the owners are not ready to list their property, go through your listing presentation material, using a narrative with your visuals. This material should answer two owners' questions, why list? and why you? This should lead you to a trial closing that is intended to gain an agreement to sign the listing. After a listing is signed, be certain to leave a copy along with copies of the Estimated Seller's Proceeds form and your comparative market analysis and agency disclosure information if not included in the listing form. Be certain the owners know when you will contact them again.

To obtain a buyer's agency agreement you must prove your competency to locate property and the buyers must feel you fully understand their needs and are willing to work for them.

If a home is encumbered with a trust deed greater than the fair market value of the property, a listing is still possible if the lender will agree to a short sale. In a short sale the lender accepts the net sale proceeds as full settlement for their lien.

CLASS DISCUSSION TOPICS

1. Prepare a list of ten possible objections that an owner might raise to signing a listing.

2. Be prepared to enact a classroom role-playing situation in which objections are raised by the owner. (You might be called on to take the part of either the agent or the owner.)

3. Prepare a five-minute (maximum) presentation to a prospective buyer, showing why he or she should be represented under a signed buyer-listing agreement.

4. Role-play closing a listing with your instructor as the owner. Be prepared with more than one closing.

5. Special assignments (if indicated by instructor):

   a. Using a form supplied by your instructor or one used in your area, complete an exclusive-authorization-and-right-to-sell agreement for the following:

Property:	Single-family residence, 217 W. Clark Lane, Fillmore, California, Ventura County
Owners:	Sam and Loretta Smyth
Broker:	(Name Yourself)
Listing Period:	Four months commencing this date
Price:	$548,000
Personal Property:	Refrigerator, pool equipment, and fireplace accessories go with property
Special Conditions:	No lockbox or sign. Two-hour notice of all showings limited to 3–5 pm daily and 8 am until noon on weekends and holidays.
Broker's Compensation:	Six percent of sale price. 90-day safety period for commissions to parties whom agent(s) negotiated with prior to expiration of listing and whose names were furnished to owner.

b. Using a form supplied by your instructor, complete an exclusive-right-to-represent agreement for the following:

Buyer:	Henry and Sally Corleone
Broker:	(Name Yourself)
Period of Authorization:	Three months from this date
Property:	Single-story 3–4 BR home with 2½ baths, 3-car garage, fireplace, and golf course views in gated community
Price:	$650,000 to $800,000
General Location:	Palm Desert, Rancho Mirage, or Indian Wells, California
Other:	Spanish architecture preferred
Compensation:	3½% of acquiring price. If compensation is paid by another party, any excess shall be paid to broker. If within 60 days of termination buyer buys a property that broker introduced buyer to during life of this agreement, then buyer shall pay broker the compensation.
Agency:	This shall be a single agency only.

6. Explain either a sales listing or buyer agency form, paragraph by paragraph, as if you were explaining it to a prospective seller or buyer.

7. Bring to class one current-events article dealing with some aspect of real estate practice for class discussion.

UNIT 6 QUIZ

1. A valid exclusive listing requires
   a. a lawful purpose.
   b. mutual consent.
   c. consideration.
   d. all of the above.

2. An agent sold a property where the owner had verbally agreed to pay a commission. The agent would be legally entitled to a commission from the owner for the sale if the agent had
   a. relied on the verbal promise.
   b. made a written memorandum of the agreement signed by the agent.
   c. obtained a valid buyer listing agreement.
   d. none of the above.

3. Which listing would you be *LEAST* likely to advertise?
   a. Nonresidential property
   b. An open listing
   c. An exclusive-agency listing
   d. An exclusive-right-to-sell listing

4. A listing under which the owner can sell the listed property without payment of a commission but the agent is nevertheless an exclusive agent is a(n)
   a. open listing.
   b. exclusive-right-to-sell listing.
   c. exclusive-agency listing.
   d. net listing.

5. An agent who did not obtain a purchase offer but who initiated an uninterrupted chain of events that led to a sale would be considered the
   a. agent of record.
   b. procuring cause
   c. exclusive agent.
   d. cooperating broker.

6. An exclusive-right-to-sell listing likely includes
   a. an agency relationship disclosure.
   b. an attorney fee provision.
   c. an arbitration agreement.
   d. all of the above.

7. All of the following statements regarding an exclusive-right-to-sell listing are true *EXCEPT*
   a. escrow does have to close for an agent to be entitled to a commission.
   b. it must have a termination date for the agent to be able to collect a commission.
   c. the agent must give the owner a copy of the listing when the owner signs.
   d. the agent is precluded from working with

8. The type of listing that has the greatest likelihood of resulting in a sale would be a(n)
   a. open listing.
   b. exclusive-agency listing.
   c. exclusive-right-to-sell listing.
   d. reduced-fee listing.

9. An owner tells you that Agent Jones told her she could get far more for her home than your CMA indicates. What is your *BEST* response?
   a. "Many unethical agents will promise the moon to get listings and then fail to perform."
   b. "I am willing to take the listing at that price, but if we don't attract buyers we will reevaluate the price."
   c. "I don't believe it. No agent who knows the market would set a price that high."
   d. "I think my comparative market analysis covers all recent comparables and clearly shows the market value. May I please look at the comparative market analysis that Agent Jones prepared for you?"

10. By taking a listing at a low fee that will result in a less than normal fee for any cooperating brokers, you are benefiting
    a. your office.
    b. a selling office.
    c. the owner.
    d. none of the above.

SERVICING THE LISTING

LEARNING OBJECTIVES

When you have completed this unit, you will be able to

- explain owner/agent communication,

- describe how to prepare a property for a sale,

- describe seller disclosures and explain how to modify or extend a listing,

- list the components of a marketing plan, and

- explain how to handle a short sale listing.

KEY TERMS

agent property evaluation	homeowner instructions	pocket listing
broker open house	information boxes	property brief
caravan	neighborhood	staging
communication	information request	talking sign
Equator Platform	open house	virtual tour
		weekly activity report

OWNER-AGENT COMMUNICATION

The reason most often cited by owners who have been unhappy with the agent who took the listing on their property is not the failure of the agent to secure a buyer; it is the failure of the agent to communicate with them after the listing is signed.

It's easy for owners to feel abandoned by their agents. There is a For Sale sign on the lawn and a listing on the internet. Occasionally, someone calls for an appointment, and people rush through the home in silence.

Owners want to know what is happening. Some agents even become hard to reach when owners want to know what is happening. The agent paved the way so smoothly in the presentation to get the listing, but now there seems to be a communication breakdown.

> Owner discontent is usually based on the agent's failure to communicate with the client.

The problem in these cases may be that the agent failed to explain what would be happening in advance and doesn't want to tell an owner that very little is happening now. Sometimes, unprofessional agents make unrealistic promises to get listings and want to avoid the unpleasant task of telling the owners that they have not located buyers for their properties. When a listing expires, some agents don't even want to face the owners again to try for an extension.

What Will Be Happening

Owner-agent **communication** should start with the listing. Agents should inform owners what will be happening in the few days immediately following. Agents should make definite appointments to meet soon after a listing to discuss their marketing approaches.

Broker Introduction

Chances are the owners have never met your broker. Your broker should send a letter to the owners thanking them for entrusting the sale of their home to his or her firm. The letter should state that the listing agent is the owners' contact person with the firm but that if any problems arise, they should feel free to contact the broker.

Postlisting Meeting

You should consider a post-listing meeting with the owners soon after the listing was obtained. At the post-listing meeting, go through the house again and make recommendations to the owners of things they should do to help with marketing, called "staging," their home. Impress on the owners that marketing is really a team effort.

> The owner's cooperation can increase the likelihood of a sale.

Homeowner instructions. Give the owners **homeowner instructions** to follow. (See Figure 7.1.) When you recognize that work needs to be done, advise the owners to do it or have it done. Show that it is in the owners' interest and not yours that the house appears at its best.

FIGURE 7.1:   **Instructions for Sellers**

Homeowner Hints for a Successful Sale

I. Exterior
   A. Grass and shrubs: Keep trimmed. Consider a fast-greening fertilizer such as ammonium sulfate (inexpensive) for a deep green lawn.
   B. Pets: If you have a dog, clean up any dog dirt on a daily basis. If you have a cat, change your litter box daily. Secure pets when the house is being shown.
   C. Fences: Make any needed repairs. A neat, well-painted fence gives a positive impression.
   D. Flowers: Plant seasonal blooming flowers, especially near the front door and in any patio area. A profusion of color can have your home half-sold before the door is even opened.
   E. Bird feeders: Hummingbird feeders and birdhouses create a pleasant mood, especially when they are close to any patio area.
   F. Paint:
      1. Front door should be refinished or painted if it shows excessive wear.
      2. Check exterior paint. Often only the trim or, depending on sun exposure, only one or two sides of the house need painting. Keep in mind the fact that paint is cheap compared to the extra dollars a home with a clean fresh appearance will bring.
   G. Lawn furniture: Place lawn furniture in an attractive, leisurely manner. A badminton net; croquet set-up or barbeque gives a positive image as well.
   H. Roof: If the roof needs to be repaired or replaced, it's best to have the work done. Otherwise, buyers will want to deduct the cost even if your price already reflects the required work. Delaying repairs can actually cost you twice as much.
II. Interior
   A. Housekeeping: You are competing against model homes, so your home must look as much like a model as possible. Floors, bath fixtures, and appliances must be sparkling. Make beds early in the day. Unmade beds and late sleepers create a very negative image.
   B. Odors and aromas: Avoid using vinegar or frying or cooking strong-smelling foods such as cabbage just before showing. The odors last and work against the image you are trying to create. On the other hand, some smells have a positive effect on people: Baked bread, apple pie, chocolate chip cookies, and cinnamon rolls are examples of foods that can help sell your home. Consider keeping packaged cookie or bread dough in the refrigerator. Just before a scheduled showing, the smell of these baking foods can be a great help to us. Garbage containers should be emptied regularly and cleaned. For exterior garbage cans, seal daily garbage in plastic bags to avoid odor.
   C. Paint: If you have leftover paint, you can accomplish a great deal by touching up paint where needed. If the paint is dark, repaint with light colors such as off-white, oyster, light beige, or pale yellow. Light colors make rooms appear fresh as well as larger.

FIGURE 7.1 (continued): **Instructions for Sellers**

D. Plumbing: Repair any leaky faucets. Make certain you don't have a gurgling toilet or cracked toilet seat.
E. Shades and blinds: Replace any torn shades or broken blinds.
F. Drapes: If drapes need cleaning, have it done. If they are old and worn, stained or dark, consider replacing them with light colors. (Large department stores or catalog houses will have products that can solve the problem.) Vertical blinds might be considered as an alternative to drapes. They are less expensive than all but the cheapest drapes and have a clean, appearance.
G. Carpets: Dirty carpets should be either professionally steam cleaned (preferred), or you should rent a heavy-duty cleaner to do it yourself.
H. Lighting: If any room appears dark, increase the wattage of your light bulbs. Before a showing, open the blinds and drapes and turn on the lights, even during the day. You want the house as light as possible. Make certain your light fixtures and windows are clean.
I. Closets: If closets appear crowded, remove items not needed and put them in boxes. The boxes can then be stacked neatly in a corner of the basement, attic, or garage.
J. Too much furniture: Many houses appear crowded, with too many pieces of large furniture as well as bric-a-brac. Consider putting excess furniture in a rental storage unit.
K. Family photos and mementos: Put very personal items in drawers. While they are important to you, visitors must be able to visualize it as their house, not your house. Many prospects feel intrusive when they are among personal items of others.
L. Garage and basement: Spruce up your work area. Consider a garage sale to get rid of the excess items too good to throw away but of no use to you. Put excess items in boxes and stack them neatly in a corner. Consider using a commercial garage floor cleaner to remove excess oil and grease marks on the garage floor and driveway. You might consider a commercial steam cleaner (not carpet cleaner).
    A. Temperature: On cold days, a natural fire in the fireplace will help us sell your home. Start the fire before the showing is scheduled. On hot days, consider turning the air conditioner several degrees cooler than normal. The contrast will seem phenomenal, giving a very positive reaction. In moderate weather, open windows for fresh air.
III. You
    When your home is shown, it's best that you disappear for a while. Buyers feel restrained with an owner present. If buyers will not voice their concerns, then their questions cannot be answered and their problems cannot be solved. Many buyers will feel they are intruding if you are present. Buyers then tend to spend less time in the property, which can reduce salability.
    If you must remain in the house, try to stay in one area. Excellent places to be are working in the garden, on the lawn, or in the workshop. These activities create a positive image. While soft music is fine, do not have a TV on. Never, never follow the agent around the house during the showing, volunteer any information, or answer questions the buyers may have. You have engaged professional real estate salespersons. We will ask you questions if necessary.
    [Clyde Realty]   [555-8200]   [www.CRE.com]

Besides cleaning and performing needed repairs, there could be a situation in which an improvement might increase property value in excess of the cost of the improvement. Should this be the case, inform the owners of this possibility. In the event they improve the property after it is listed, an adjustment in the list price should be considered.

It is not enough that owners understand what is expected of them, they should understand why. Owners must understand that their house is in competition with other homes for the same buyers. Therefore, they must do everything feasible to make their home a winner.

Some owners may want to meet prospective buyers and follow you around and volunteer information; after all, it is their home. While they have the right to do so, they should understand that being there could inhibit prospective buyers from freely voicing concerns. If a concern of a prospective buyer is not known to you, you can't overcome it. You must explain that like most people, buyers may not want to criticize because it could be taken personally by the owners. On the other hand, voicing a problem to you is really a sign of interest with a "but" attached. Getting rid of the "but" can turn that interest into a sale.

Explain to the owners that at times prospective buyers may come to their door. Owners should ask for the name of the prospect and call your office at once, so an agent can come to show them the home.

Figure 7.2, "Preparing Your Home for Showing and Sale," and Figure 7.3, "When an Appointment Is Made to See Your Home," are taken from the Toolkit for Presentations and are reproduced with the permission of Realty Tools, Inc.

Security.   You should advise owners to secure small expensive items when the home will be available to unsupervised visits by other agents. If the property has a security system, do not make the code readily available to all other agents. Listing agents often arrange to meet buyer agents and disarm the system. Many security systems allow remote monitoring where you can turn off and reset the system when an agent calls your office.

Do not turn off security systems without the owner's permission. While it makes showings easier, it creates great risks. In La Habra, California, an unoccupied furnished home listed on the market was trashed and looted by hundreds of teenagers led to the property by internet party invitations. The security system had been turned off.

Staging.   As the sales market tightens, the need to have properties outshine competing properties is apparent. Owners are competing against other homeowners and even lenders and flippers. The advantage your owner can have is the ability to make their house look move-in ready.

FIGURE 7.2: **Preparing Your Home for Showing and Sale**

Preparing Your Home

Your home has just one chance to make a great impression with each potential buyer. And it can! The following "tricks of the trade" will help you keep track of what needs to be done. The whole idea is to present a clean, spacious clutter-free home--the kind of place you'd like to buy. Accomplish a little everyday, and before long your home will be ready to make the impression that can make the sale.

Your Home's Curb Appeal
- ❑ Mow lawn
- ❑ Trim shrubs
- ❑ Edge gardens and walkways
- ❑ Weed and mulch
- ❑ Sweep walkways and driveway, remove branches, litter or toys
- ❑ Add color and fill in bare spots with plantings
- ❑ Remove mildew or moss from walls or walks with bleach and water or other cleaner
- ❑ Take stains off your driveway with cleanser or kitty litter
- ❑ Stack woodpile neatly
- ❑ Clean and repair patio and deck area
- ❑ Remove any outdoor furniture which is not in good repair
- ❑ Make sure pool or spa sparkles
- ❑ Replace old storm doors
- ❑ Check for flat-fitting roof shingles
- ❑ Repair broken windows and shutters, replace torn screens, make sure frames and seams have solid caulking
- ❑ Hose off exterior wood and trim, replace damaged bricks or wood
- ❑ Touch up exterior paint, repair gutters and eaves
- ❑ Clean and remove rust from any window air conditioning units
- ❑ Paint the front door and mailbox
- ❑ Add a new front door mat and consider a seasonal door decoration
- ❑ Shine brass hardware on front door, outside lighting fixtures, etc.
- ❑ Make sure doorbell is in good working order

General Interior Tips
- ❑ Add a fresh coat of interior paint in light, neutral colors
- ❑ Shampoo carpeting, replace if necessary
- ❑ Clean and wax hardwood floors, refinish if necessary
- ❑ Clean and wash kitchen and bathroom floors
- ❑ Wash all windows, vacuum blinds, wash window sills
- ❑ Clean the fireplace
- ❑ Clean out and organize closets, add extra space by packing clothes and items you won't need again until after you've moved

- ❑ Remove extra furniture, worn rugs, and items you don't use; keep papers, toys, etc. picked up--especially on stairways
- ❑ Repair problems such as loose door knobs, cracked molding, leaking taps and toilets, squeaky doors, closets or screen doors which are off their tracks
- ❑ Add dishes of potpourri, or drop of vanilla or bath oil on light bulbs for scent
- ❑ Secure jewelry, cash and other valuables

The Living Room
- ❑ Make it cozy and inviting, discard chipped or worn furniture and frayed or worn rugs

The Dining Room
- ❑ Polish any visible silver and crystal
- ❑ Set the table for a formal dinner to help viewers imagine entertaining here

The Kitchen
- ❑ Make sure appliances are spotless inside and out (try baking soda for cleaning Formica stains)
- ❑ Make sure all appliances are in perfect working order
- ❑ Clean often forgotten spots on top of refrigerator and under sink
- ❑ Wax or sponge floor to brilliant shine, clean baseboards
- ❑ Unclutter all counter space, remove countertop appliances
- ❑ Organize items inside cabinets, pre-pack anything you won't be using before you move

The Bathrooms
- ❑ Remove all rust and mildew
- ❑ Make sure tile, fixtures, shower doors, etc. are immaculate and shining
- ❑ Make sure all fixtures are in good repair
- ❑ Replace loose caulking or grout
- ❑ Make sure lighting is bright, but soft

The Master Bedroom
- ❑ Organize furnishings to create a spacious look with well-defined sitting, sleeping, and dressing areas

The Garage
- ❑ Sell, give away, or throw out unnecessary items
- ❑ Clean oily cement floor
- ❑ Provide strong overhead light
- ❑ Tidy storage or work areas

The Basement
- ❑ Sell, give away, or throw out unnecessary items
- ❑ Organize and create more floor space by hanging tools and placing items on shelves
- ❑ Clean water heater and drain sediment
- ❑ Change furnace filter
- ❑ Make inspection access easy
- ❑ Clean and paint concrete floor and walls
- ❑ Provide strong overhead light

The Attic
- ❑ Tidy up by discarding or pre-packing
- ❑ Make sure energy-saving insulation is apparent
- ❑ Make sure air vent is in working order
- ❑ Provide strong overhead lighting

When It's Time To Show
- ❑ Make sure your property profile folder, utility bills, MLS profile, house location survey, etc. are available
- ❑ Open all draperies and shades, turn on all lights
- ❑ Pick up toys and other clutter, check to make sure beds are made and clothes are put away
- ❑ Give the carpets a quick vacuuming
- ❑ Add some strategically placed fresh flowers
- ❑ Open bathroom windows for fresh air
- ❑ Pop a spicy dessert or just a pan of cinnamon in the oven for aroma
- ❑ Turn off the television and turn on the radio music at a low volume
- ❑ Make a fire in the fireplace if appropriate
- ❑ Put pets in the backyard or arrange for a friend to keep them
- ❑ Make sure pet areas are clean and odor-free
- ❑ Make sure all trash is disposed of in neatly covered bins

Angela McKendrick, CRS, GRI
Office: 410-555-1234
Home Office: 410-432-7890
Fax: 410-555-5607
Web Site: www.demorealty.com/angela
Email: angela.mckendrick@demorealty.com

Green Leaf Realty
www.greenleafrealty.com

Used with permission of Realty Tools, Inc.

Some agents give advice to owners as to repainting, landscape work, rearranging furniture, storing excess belongings, etc., however many agents lack the training and experience to be really effective.

There are professional stagers who will make a property look as if Martha Stewart lived there. Some will instruct the owner what to do for a few hundred dollars while others will do the entire job. They may just add accessories, remove clutter and use much of what the owner has. In some case they will repaint, refinish floors, change cabinets, paint, re-landscape and completely furnish and accessorize the home with new rental furniture. The property, the market, as well as the owner's willingness to cooperate will determine the extent of the staging. Flippers have found that professionally staged homes sell more quickly than vacant homes and can mean greater profit because of both shorter holding times and higher sale prices. Coldwell Banker tracked 2772 home sales and found that based on list prices, staged homes sold for almost 5% higher price than unstaged homes and took half as long to sell. California does not require licensure to act as a stager.

WEB LINK

@

There are several organizations of home stagers: International Association of Home Staging Professionals at www.iahsp.com and Real Estate Staging Association at www.realestatestagingassociation.com.

Professional Property Inspection

You should inform your owners that your property inspection only covered defects that a reasonable visual inspection would reveal and that most sale contracts provide for the buyer being able to have access for a professional inspection.

Many sales agreements fall apart when defects are found. If corrections are necessary, usually it is the seller who agrees to the cost.

Explain that a better approach would be for the owner to have a professional inspection now so that there will be no surprises and any problems could be solved now. In addition, the professional inspection report could be a sales tool to help convince a buyer.

You could give the owner the names of several inspectors you have had good relations with and consider competent.

FIGURE 7.3:   **When an Appointment Is Made to See Your Home**

When An Appointment Is Made

Agents from many real estate firms will want to show your home. Please allow any agent who calls to show your home at the suggested time. If you are not frequently available, it is suggested that you allow a lockbox to be installed on your door. You will increase your odds for a sale by allowing more qualified buyers to see your home. You do not want to miss an out-of-town transferee because your home was not able to be shown.

During a showing:

- Open all draperies and window shades during daylight hours.

- The kitchen & bathroom should sparkle.

- Open windows one half hour before showing to circulate fresh air.

- Open all the doors between rooms to give an inviting feeling.

- Place fresh flowers on kitchen table and/or in the living room.

- If possible, bake cookies or bread to add an inviting aroma.

- Turn on all lights and replace bulbs with high wattage bulbs where needed.

- Pets should be confined or restricted from view. Eliminate pet odors. Not everyone may share your love of animals. Some people may be allergic to them.

- All jewelry and small valuables should be stored in a safety deposit box or in a locked closet.

- Replace any items not included in the sale, or tag them appropriately with "to be replaced with…" or "not included" signs.

- Beds should be made & clothes picked up. Bathrooms should be clean, with towels folded and toilet lid down.

- When you leave the house, please leave it as if you know it is going to be shown. You never know when the right person is going to look at it!

Angela McKendrick, CRS, GRI
Office: 410-555-1234
Home Office: 410-432-7890
Fax: 410-555-5607
Web Site: www.demorealty.com/angela
Email: angela.mckendrick@demorealty.com

www.greenleafrealty.com

Used with permission of Realty Tools, Inc.

Weekly activity report.   Tell the owners what you have already done, what you are doing, and what you will be doing. Owners should understand that you will be sending them a **weekly activity report**, and that if they have any questions at any time they should call you. (See Figure 7.4.)

While some agents would rather make monthly reports simply because they show more activity, owners don't want to wait that long. Prepare reports on all of your listings every week so they become a part of your routine. Weekly reports also will force you to review your own sales activity and to consider what can or should be done to bring about a sale.

FIGURE 7.4:   Weekly Activity Report Form

[Jones Realty]
Weekly Progress Report   Week Ending _____

Property: _____

Owners: _____

Number of Inquiries: _____

Number of Showings: _____

Advertising: _____

Open House Date(s): _____

Number of Visitors: _____

Comments of Agents and Prospective Buyers: _____

_____

_____

_____

As an attachment to weekly activity reports, you can include any ads for the property, a printout of the property, copies of property postings on internet sites, and even emails sent promoting the property (don't include the addressees or you might find that the seller will contact the prospective buyers directly, posing a problem for the listing agent).

Showings.   Owners must understand that although agents try to give them notice well in advance of a showing, this may not always be practical. Explain that in showing another property, an agent might realize that the owners' property better fits the needs of a certain buyer than properties that originally were selected for viewing. At times, prospective buyers may ask agents about certain houses while looking at other properties. If a property fits a buyer's needs, the prospective buyer could well turn into an actual buyer. The fact that they, not the agent, found the property can influence a sale.

Also explain that the reverse can happen: owners might be prepared for a visit by an agent who fails to show. While you generally will notify owners of canceled appointments, there will be times when such notification is difficult.

During hot weather, suggest that the owner leave soft drinks in the refrigerator for agents from your office and their prospective buyers. Explain that offering prospects cold bottled water or a soda and getting them to sit down can help them view the home from a more relaxed point of view. If the owners agree to do this, and they generally will, make certain the agents within your office know about it. Some agents display their company label on bottled water. Besides stocking owners' refrigerators, they use the bottled water at their office and at open houses as a refreshing advertisement. Incidentally, a good place to sit is close to a pool or garden, if available. Otherwise, pick the room that has the best ambiance.

Your office advertising policy.   You should explain that internet advertising has become the media of choice for most buyers. Classified ads for homes have all but vanished in most newspapers. While you may still spend a significant portion of your advertising dollar in print media, what you do on the internet is of prime importance. Help your owners fully understand your print advertising policy and the media used. Explain that every home is not advertised every day because this isn't necessary to successfully market a property. Explain that buyers often buy a different house from the one in the advertisement that attracted their attention. Explain that many people who answer ads are hoping for a bargain and tend to inquire about homes priced at less than they expect to spend.

A property doesn't need to be advertised every day.

In the same vein, other homes priced in the same or even a higher or a lower price range create inquiries. When qualifying these prospective buyers, the agent may discover that the owners' house is likely to meet the buyers' needs. Thus, advertising for other houses creates prospects for their home. Explain that by endeavoring to cover a range of both price and special features, you can in effect advertise every home in your inventory each day with just a handful of ads.

The owner can be a source of valuable information.

Neighborhood information request. Another way in which you can make the owners feel they are part of your marketing effort is to ask them to complete a **neighborhood information request**. (See Figure 7.5.) This information can be extremely valuable, and filled-out copies should be readily available to all salespersons in your office. Agents who know what buyers want will have special ammunition to sell particular houses. Although other homes might have area activities or neighbors that would make them equally desirable, the agent who does not have the information cannot use it to make the sale. As an example:

Johnny, do you like baseball? Well, you're in luck, there is a Little League here, and they play just two blocks away at McKinley Park.

Knowing the architect.   For distinctive homes, you should ask the owner if they know the name of the architect, being sure to verify this information before using it. Mentioning the architect's name to prospects can add a panache to the property. If the architect is well known, it can reflect in both the sales price and the time required to sell. You can Google the name of the architect and find important buildings/homes that the architect designed. This can be additional sales information. If the owner does not know the architect, you can check with city planning. The building permit records and/or plans on file should reveal the name of the architect.

FIGURE 7.5: **Neighborhood Information Request**

Neighborhood Information Request

Owner: _____   Address: _____

Having an in-depth knowledge of your neighborhood and neighbors can give us a competitive advantage over less informed sales agents who represent other properties.

We would therefore appreciate your completion of this form to the best of your ability.

1. Neighborhood features you feel a buyer would likely be most pleased with: _____
   _____
   _____

2. School districts are:
   _____

3. School bus stops at:
   _____

4. Youth activities in the area (Little League, junior hockey, soccer league, etc.):
   _____

5. Public recreational facilities in area (parks, pools, playgrounds, tennis courts, golf courses, etc.): _____
   _____

6. Hike and/or bike paths:
   _____

7. Nearest public transportation route:
   _____

8. Nearest medical facilities:
   _____

9. Nearest community center (for children, seniors, etc.):
   _____

10. Nearest churches and synagogues (and denominations):
    _____

11. Nearest shopping area:
    _____

12. Any pet-friendly facilities (dog park):
    _____

Please send your completed form to my attention in the enclosed postage paid envelope.

Your help in providing this data is greatly appreciated.

Appreciatively yours,

_____

Change in Agents

If an agent who took a listing leaves the office, the broker should assign another salesperson to serve as listing agent and liaison with the owners. This agent should meet with the owners and go over their work to that point in time as well as to discuss ways the property can be made more readily salable (if applicable).

Preparing the owners for an offer.   Give owners a blank copy of a purchase contract and explain to them that the form is the one that will be used by a buyer. By explaining the clauses and leaving a copy with the owners, you will reduce the chance that they will get upset about any clause when they receive an offer.

Also prepare owners for quick offers. Explain that the first few weeks after a listing is taken can be very productive because other agents as well as prospective buyers tend to get excited over new listings. You can point out that when some owners get a quick offer, they feel that it indicates they set their price too low when it actually means they priced their property right. They reject good offers, and they later regret the rejection. In pointing out this fact, you reduce the likelihood of a negative reaction to a quick offer.

NECESSARY INFORMATION AND DISCLOSURES

You want the sellers to complete the Real Estate Transfer Disclosure Statement (see Unit 3) as soon as possible so it can be given to a prospective buyer. If the owners reveal problems that you feel should be corrected before a sale, you should advise them to take corrective action.

Have the owners complete a FIRPTA/California Withholding form (Unit 14). If the property is leased, obtain copies of lease(s). You should also obtain estoppel certificates from tenant(s) that they have no defenses or offsets against the landlord.

If the property is a common interest development, you should obtain copies of the bylaws, CC&Rs, current financial statement, minutes of meetings, and any information about changes in assessments or pending legal actions. The CAR purchase contract is going to require that this information be provided to the buyers during their contingency periods. It's important to ensure that this information is current and available to buyers.

You should have the sellers sign the Water Heater Statement of Compliance that the water heater will be properly braced as of close of escrow, as well as the Smoke Detector Statement of Compliance that operable smoke detectors shall be in place at close of escrow as required by law.

The Lead-based Paint and Lead-based Hazards Disclosure Acknowledgment and Addendum should also be signed by owners indicating knowledge of any lead-based paint.

You will want a property profile from a title company or through the public records module of the MLS. This could reveal problems that might make a sale difficult or even impossible if not corrected, such as judgments, silent owners, liens, and so forth.

You will also want to know the lot size that may be available from plat maps. You should also obtain the Natural Hazards Disclosure report as soon as practical.

LISTING MODIFICATION (ADJUSTMENT)

If it becomes apparent that you made an error in your assessment of the property value, let the owners know at once. If you suggest a different price, be able to defend your position. When you suggest lowering the price, you are, in effect, asking the owners to give up something they think they have. *Modification* or *adjustment* does not have the immediate negative connotation of *lowering*.

Changes in the market can turn a proper original listing price into a price that is either too high or too low. After taking the listing, for example, several comparable properties are put on the market at significantly lower prices that will affect the ability to attract interest in your property. Taking the owners to visit one or more recently listed, competitively priced, comparable properties, as covered in Unit 5, will help the owners realize that a price adjustment on their property is needed to be competitive.

If owners refuse to adjust their price when you feel such an action is necessary to find a buyer, consider the ultimate in persuasion: offer to return the listing. Ask the owners to sign a release relieving you of all agency obligations under the listing. Ask to be let out of your agreement to exercise diligence on their behalf. Although owners might not really be sold on your representing them, no one likes to be the one rejected. A release offer often convinces owners to adjust their price to the level recommended.

The worst-case scenario is that you will give up an overpriced listing that had less than a good chance of attracting buyers. From a rational point of view, of course, giving up a poor listing makes sense, but you may feel that if you don't succeed, you are a loser. You actually will be a winner, because you will be able to devote your time to probabilities rather than remote possibilities. You do not have to take or retain overpriced listings.

Don't look at this approach as a bluff, because you shouldn't be bluffing. To be sure, it's an either/or approach, but it's unfair to the owners to continue to offer their home at a price that will fail to attract prospective buyers.

Don't change the original listing when making a listing adjustment. Use a modification form or separate signed and dated letter that will enable you to later determine what was done should a problem arise.

A significant downward price adjustment on a listing should be communicated to local area cooperating brokers and salespersons by email. It will get more attention than an MLS computer update by itself. You should update all internet presentations.

LISTING EXTENSION

Several weeks before your listing expires, schedule a meeting with the owners to go over the listing and what you have been doing on their behalf. If the owners feel that you have been diligent in working for them and have kept them informed, you have an excellent chance of obtaining a listing extension. However, if you fail to keep the owners informed and they have to call you to find out what is happening, your chances of obtaining an extension to the listing are materially diminished.

If you obtain an extension, a thank-you letter from your broker is appropriate. Also, don't forget to immediately communicate the extension to your MLS.

If the owners do not wish to extend the listing, supply the names of people who viewed the property. This must be in writing to protect your firm from the owner making a sale to one of these prospects during the safety period.

YOUR MARKETING PLAN

You should have a marketing plan. By following the suggestions in this section, you will see a marketing plan develop. A copy should be provided to the owners as soon as it is prepared. See Figure 5.5E for a sample plan.

Signs

When you obtain the listing, put up a For Sale sign immediately after leaving the house. If you do not, you should tell the owner when one will be installed. If your office uses huge wooden holders for metal signs, you should have smaller lawn signs that can be used in the interim. Tell the owners when your large sign will be installed.

Besides the broker's name and telephone number, some brokers include their website addresses so that prospective buyers can obtain more information right away on their own.

FIGURE 7.6:   Rider Strip Example

Rider strips.   A rider strip can emphasize a desirable feature not evident from the exterior, such as "Pool and Spa," "5 Bedrooms," "Home Theater," etc. See Figure 7.6.

QR codes.   Real estate agents can order signs or create fliers with quick response (QR) codes on them. These codes allow users to scan them quickly using an application on their smartphones or other devices to obtain immediate information on the property in question. These can be just as effective as other advertising media and allow for a call to action to visit a website or call the listing agent from the property itself. The ability to rapidly transmit information through QR codes has made this a popular choice for real estate agents.

Information Boxes

All of the real estate supply houses as well as some REALTOR® board or association office stores carry **information boxes** or tubes that can be attached to your yard signs. These boxes are a low-cost, effective way to interest buyers. Inside the box, insert a supply of property information sheets (briefs) that describe the listed property in a manner that is likely to interest the prospective buyer and encourage them to contact your office. Information boxes can also include information on similar properties and the broker's internet address where more information is available, as well as an email address.

Photos

Photographs of the home should be taken as soon as possible after the listing is taken. You want interior photos emphasizing desirable aspects of the home as well as exterior photos. You want the photos for property magazines, property briefs, ads, mailings, and displays as well as for internet sites. Photos also have to be taken for virtual tours if your internet site includes them.

Lockbox

If possible, install a *lockbox*, or *keybox*, used by your MLS right after taking the listing. If there is going to be a delay, inform the owners when a lockbox will be installed. Lockboxes are simply large boxes that have a separately locked compartment to hold the house keys. They may be locked to door handles, electric meters, metal railings, etc.

The latest lockbox models are electronic marvels. Besides containing the key, they tell you by a simple phone call who has used the lockbox, including date and time. Lockboxes are now available where the agent can access the data online. This information is valuable for security reasons. Electronic lockboxes can even monitor the status of the lockbox battery and restrict access to preselected agents or grant access to agents from other real estate organizations. It also lets you tell the owner in your weekly activity report who entered the property by using the lockbox. You can also call agents who viewed the property for their comments. This is the type of information an owner should be made aware of. Like the talking sign, these electronic lockboxes are a superb marketing tool that can be effectively used in your listing presentation.

There is a REALTOR®-approved lockbox from SentriLock, LLC. You insert a credit-card-sized card in the slot. The card has a microprocessor chip. You then punch in your number on the box's keypad. A green light tells you to remove your card and the box opens. The system logs the last 70 people who entered the property. The lockboxes are sold through REAL-TOR® Associations and MLS services. The California Association of REALTORS® requires the use of approved lockboxes for security reasons, as well as to have uniform access to properties.

Owners should understand that allowing other people access to their homes when they or you are not present does create a security risk. You should suggest that they make certain that their insurance will adequately cover theft or mysterious disappearances of furnishings. You might also suggest that expensive objects be locked up or removed from the premises.

The Multiple Listing Service

To provide greater market coverage for their listings, a group of brokers often conducts a cooperative listing service, or MLS. The group often consists of members of a local real estate board or association; however, membership in the board or association is not a prerequisite to membership in the service. The MLS is used most often with an exclusive-authorization-and-right-to-sell listing, but it may be used with other listings as well. A member of the group who takes any listing turns it in to a central bureau that distributes it to all participants in the service, usually on the internet. All members have the right to sell the property; however, they must have the listing broker's permission to advertise or promote it. When a sale is made on an MLS listing, the listing broker and the broker who found the buyer share the commission.

Suppose, for example, an MLS commission split was 50/50. The listing broker would get 50% of the commission, and the broker who found the buyer would get the other 50%. Within each agency the broker would, according to the contractual agreement between the broker and the salesperson, also split his or her share of the commission with the salesperson who had actual contact with the seller or buyer. (Only brokers can receive commissions, but they may share them with the salespeople who work with them.) Figure 7.7 illustrates a possible split of the 6% commission on a property that sold for $440,000.

Commission splits will vary among offices, often based upon broker services as well as the market. As an example, when there are many buyers and few sellers the listing commission could be greater than the sales commission.

FIGURE 7.7:   Splitting a Commission on an MLS Listing

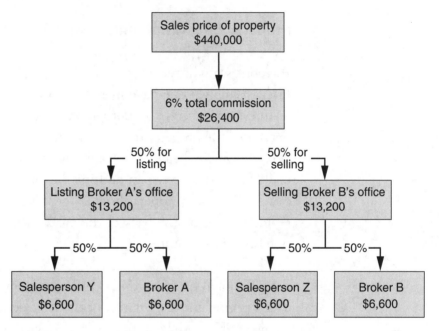

It is important that owners fully understand the role of an MLS service and the agency implications.

If, for any reason, a broker does not submit a listing to the MLS service and precludes other agents from showing the property, it would be considered a *pocket listing*. Refusing cooperation would generally not be in the best interests of the principal and could be a breach of the agent's fiduciary duty as well as MLS rules.

A new listing should be placed on your office website, as well as the other Internet sites that you use, as soon as possible. A printout of the material included on the site should be provided to the owner(s). (For information about what your website should include, see Unit 8.)

Your Website

While other websites might have restrictions, you are not under constraint as to your own office website. You can offer your own format and more data with multiple photos, virtual tours and even videos. A drone's birds-eye view can be an effective means to show the house in its environment as well as focus on area amenities. Drones can produce exceptional videos. Cost for these professionally produced videos has decreased so that they are not limited to the upper end of the price spectrum. Be aware that the use of drones for commercial purposes requires FAA approval.

Property Brief (Information Sheet)

As soon as you have your photographs, prepare a property brief. A **property brief** is simply a one-page flyer about the property pointing out attractive features. It must have a photograph or drawing of the home. If the owners purchased the property from a developer, there is a good chance they have kept the original sales material; check it over if they do have it. There could be an attractive pen-and-ink drawing of the house that would reproduce well for your property brief. If there is a floor plan, it may be possible to reproduce this on the back of the property brief along with some information on special features.

A professional-quality property brief can be prepared in a few minutes with a laser printer and any number of available desktop publishing software programs. Owners will be impressed with a quality flyer featuring their home so soon after you have taken the listing. (See Figure 7.8.)

The backside of this particular property brief provides additional photos.

A property brief is an advertising flyer about a particular property.

The property briefs should include an internet address where the prospect can obtain further information including additional photos on the property as well as other properties.

For your listings, you want the property brief to indicate your name, license, identification number, cellphone number, email address, fax number, personal website, etc. You want to be contacted.

Copies of the property brief should be left at the home to be given to prospects as well as agents who will view the property. Therefore, deliver the property briefs to the home before any visits take place. They should be placed close to the front door, preferably on a table, so that a visitor will not miss them. A small "Take One" sign can be used. If the For Sale sign has an information box, a good supply should be placed inside it. Give a supply of property briefs to every agent in your office. You might also give them to agents from other offices who are particularly active in the area or in the type of property you are offering. Be sure to check the information box on your For Sale sign whenever you visit the property to see whether the property briefs need to be replenished.

Property briefs also are given out at open houses. It is a good idea to have a supply of property briefs on similar homes as well as briefs on the home that is open. Briefs may also be sent in response to mail, phone or internet inquiries.

Other Internet Sites

WEB LINK

The National Association of REALTORS® has a website, www.realtor.com, where a prospective buyer or tenant can find properties in all areas of the country. The site allows a broker to post a picture of the property as well as a great deal of information to interest prospective buyers. The viewer can obtain further information and a blowup picture of the property on request. In addition, a number of boards of REALTORS® and groups of boards have area websites. The appendix includes a list of some of the many internet sites that are available.

You will be limited to what you place on sites that you don't control. You want a good exterior photo as you will likely be allowed to place only one on the website. The information you provide will likely have to be in a specific format. While you should carefully choose descriptive wording on your own website, multiple-broker sites generally limit your descriptions.

If you prepare a video of a listing, it could be used on YouTube and other sites featuring videos.

FIGURE 7.8: **Example of a Property Brief**

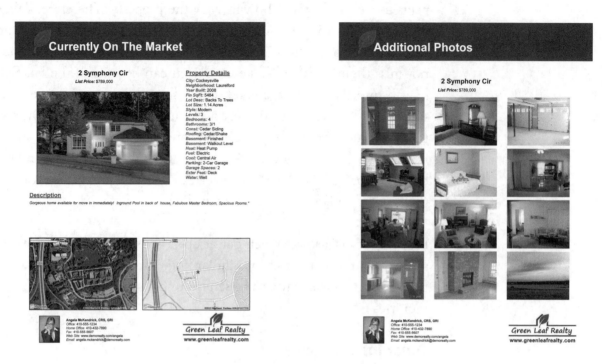

Used with permission of Realty Tools, Inc.

For an additional fee you can get special enhanced coverage for your property on many of the property websites. Realtor.com offers Showcase treatment that can include an agent's photograph and contact information, a yellow banner of search results page, ability to add up to 25 jumbo photos, full motion video and virtual tours, open house alerts, custom headings and descriptions and exposure for up to three additional listings. Your use of showcase treatment will be well received by the owners. It can also be an excellent listing tool.

Virtual Home Tours

Technology has evolved so that it is possible to offer virtual home tours while seated before a personal computer. Providing virtual home tours on the internet impresses owners of listed properties and saves buyers' and agents' time. A viewer can move from side to side, backward and forward, and from room to room when viewing the site. A specially trained photographer usually takes 360-degree photographs of the interior, exterior, and even the neighborhood. Today, software programs are available that allow an agent to prepare a virtual tour using a plain digital camera; such

WEB LINK

a software program costs around $300. If you are interested in creating your own virtual home tour, two of the sources you might wish to consider are www.paradym.com and Photo Vista Virtual Tour available through www.z-law.com. This program can produce film or digital photographs. Homes & Land will prepare a virtual tour for you from six or more photos; however, you must advertise in its home magazine. Its website is www.homesandland.com.

While at present, it is estimated that less than 30% of listings can be seen as a virtual tour, having virtual tours on your website is an excellent marketing tool for both selling properties and obtaining listings.

Before you prepare a virtual tour for the internet, obtain the owner's permission in writing to do so. There is a danger that the virtual tour will provide access information to persons interested in what is in the house and not the house itself. A virtual tour could be a home shopping site for a burglar. Visitors to the home are usually prequalified or register. This is not true of a person who can view the contents on a computer. Owners should be advised to review their insurance coverage, especially if the home contains valuable art objects and/or antiques.

Brokers find that with virtual tours, they can show a home when it is not available for a physical showing. It is believed by many brokers that virtual tours will replace the flat photographs currently used on most websites. Most house hunter sites now offer virtual tours. While virtual tours consist of a number of shots taken from the same point to provide an unbroken panorama, a video tour is a movie using a video camera that provides images as though touring the property. The terms are often used interchangeably.

YouTube sites are now being used for video home tours by many agents. A number of programs are available to make professional quality real estate video tours designed to excite buyers to want more information. If prospective buyers are offered a choice between still photographs and a video of a property, they will usually choose the video. Video tours may also be used on your firm's website. Other real estate websites generally have restrictions.

Advertising

After you have given the listing to your MLS, prepared a property brief, and posted the property information and photograph on the internet, prepare at least three classified advertisements on the property, as well as one open-house ad. Take your time because you want your presentation to have maximum effectiveness. If you are preparing print ads, a number of excellent books can help you produce superior ads. Using different approaches, your ad can be tailored to appeal to various groups of readers, based on features advertised and the form of your appeal. By preparing at least three ads, you are less likely to repeat an ad, which generally results in reduced response. You won't be caught with an ad deadline and six other tasks that need immediate attention, which usually means a mediocre ad at best.

If your firm uses one of the home magazines, prepare an ad for it as well, even though a decision may not yet have been made to advertise the listing there. By having the ad ready, the likelihood of its being used has measurably increased.

Be sure to send owners copies of the ads on their property when it is advertised. Keep in mind that advertising does not sell property—salespersons sell. What advertising does is to create responses that professional agents can convert into sales.

Office Caravans

The owners should be told in advance about the office caravan and the MLS caravan. Many offices **caravan** their office listings. The name *caravan* comes from the long lines of cars that agents drive from home to home to view properties. Have all the salespeople fill out an agent questionnaire after they walk through the property. (See Figure 7.9.) The information from this **agent property evaluation** questionnaire should be supplied to the owners with your suggestions. If the agent property evaluation indicates a serious problem, meet with the owners as soon as possible to decide how to resolve it.

MLS Caravan

Large real estate MLSs have many more listings than the agents could possibly visit in one morning or even in one day. However, the listings are broken down into areas. Most agents want to see only the homes at the price and in the area where they feel they are most likely to have prospective buyers. Again, the effective agent concentrates more on probabilities than on possibilities.

Give the owners as much advance notice as you can about the caravan. The owners should have the property "standing tall (in show condition) for inspection." The following are some general rules for caravans:

- Owners should not be at home. Agents tend to spend more time in a home when owners are not present.

- Offer agents hot coffee or lemonade, depending on the weather. Fill the cups or glasses about two-thirds full, so the agents can carry them while they view the home. This will tend to slow the viewing process.

- Give each agent a property brief. The agents see so many homes that most will not remember which features went with which house.

- Consider mood setting. Have the stereo playing soft music. If the weather is cold, have the fireplace going; if it is hot, set the air-conditioning between 68° and 70° so it feels like a cold blast when agents enter the house.

- Ask the owner to bake some chocolate chip cookies, cinnamon rolls, or fresh bread. The aroma will be pleasant, and agents will like something to eat.

- Be at the house or have an assistant present during the caravan.

Concentrate your viewing time on properties you're most likely to sell.

FIGURE 7.9:   Agent Property Evaluation

Agent Property Evaluation

Property Address _____

1. Features of this house that will be most appealing to buyers: _____
   _____
   _____

2. Features or lack of features that buyers are likely to view as a negative:
   _____

3. I feel that the price is:
   ☐ Too high   ☐ Too low   ☐ Realistic
   By how much? $ _____
   Why? _____
   _____

4. To increase salability, the owner should consider:
   _____
   _____
   _____

During slow markets, some agents put out a buffet lunch for caravan members. In a large MLS, instead of having only 15% of the agents visit the property, you may increase it to 60% or more of the agents on caravan by providing them food. An agent open house is different in that it is designed to attract agents who did not view the property on the MLS caravan. Providing refreshments during the caravan increases caravan viewing, and agents remain in the property for a longer time. An expenditure such as this makes sense for a property that shows well, is priced right and needs a quick sale.

Some agents use the internet to view properties rather than go on caravans. It is likely that at some time in the future, caravans will no longer be necessary.

Area Canvass Letter

Within one week of taking a new listing, you should send a letter to residents living within at least one block of the listed property. This letter informs the neighbors of the listing and asks their help in locating a buyer. (See Figure 7.10.)

Check the Files

As soon as you get a new listing in an office, all salespersons in the office should go through their prospect files to try to match their current prospects with the new listing. This activity has two major advantages:

1. Prospective buyers tend to get excited over brand-new listings. They might treat property on the market for a long period of time as shopworn merchandise, but a new listing elicits interest and can also have a sense of urgency. They are seeing this property before it is being visited by perhaps hundreds of agents, all of whom have prospective buyers. Right now the property can be theirs if they wish. This is one of the reasons that the most productive period for sales tends to be the first 20 days after the listing is taken.

FIGURE 7.10: Canvass Letter

[Date]

_____

_____

_____

Dear [   ]:

Our office has recently listed the home of a neighbor at [322 Maple Lane] for sale. You have probably noticed our For Sale sign.

I am writing to ask for your help in locating a buyer for this fine home.

I have enclosed a descriptive sheet on the property. We think it is a lot of house for the money, and the neighborhood is great so you would be helping anyone you suggest. If you can come up with any suggestions about your friends who might also want to be your neighbors, I would appreciate hearing from you.

Sincerely,

_____

_____

[Note: Be certain to include a property flier and follow through.]

2. The second advantage of immediately calling prospects is that it creates traffic within a few days of taking the listing. The owners' impression of you as a professional and of your firm is likely to be set within the first few weeks of the agency. After that period, it will be difficult to change the owners' perception.

Some brokers make the consideration of new listings part of their weekly meetings. The broker asks agents to think about their prospects and who likely would be interested in the property. By directing thoughts toward solving a problem, agents frequently generate ideas they would not have had otherwise.

Broker Open House

If you have an unusual property, a property that must be sold or several identical properties close to each other, consider a **broker open house**. In large associations, agents can't physically visit every new listing. They have to pick and choose. Therefore, a great many agents could miss your home on a caravan because they only visited, say, 12 of 35 new listings. Even listings that were visited were only viewed for a few minutes, and if you asked an agent a week later which home had which feature, most agents would give you a wrong answer.

Because of the longer period of time spent at a property, an agent open house impresses on agents the details of that property. The offer to stop by for food and drink can bring in many agents. It also serves a dual purpose because owners like these events; it shows extraordinary marketing.

Broker open houses provide maximum exposure of new listings to agents, whereas the MLS caravan only allows quick viewing of a small portion.

Although you may have balloons, flags, and other accoutrements outside, you don't have to host an elaborate party to attract agents. Cheese, crackers, and nuts will do. Wine or champagne should be served in plastic glasses. One way to encourage agents to linger awhile is a drawing using agents' business cards. The prize could be anything from a book of 10 free car washes to a weekend vacation package.

If you have the cards of the agents who were there, you can get them to complete a questionnaire giving their views on the property location and price, as well as letting you know whether they are working with any potential buyers.

While taking an overpriced listing might be a violation of the agent's fiduciary duty, many agents continue to do so.

Open House

Having an open house on an overpriced property will generally be a waste of both time and money. In addition, it will leave viewers with a negative feeling toward you and your firm. Therefore, you want open houses that are priced competitively. Best results can be expected from fresh property (recently listed).

Owners must be encouraged to have the house as presentable as possible for a standard **open house**. Treat the buyer open house as you treated homes for caravans and broker open houses. You want the home to appear light, bright, and as fresh as possible. There is one exception to having the house as close to perfect as is possible. That is an open house for a property advertised as a fixer-upper. If this is the case, the home will need more than minor repairs or touch-ups, although it should be clean.

If you are able to, greet the parties at the door and introduce yourself as you extend your hand. The normal reaction will be to give you their name. Use the prospects' names when answering or asking questions. Use the sales skills of Unit 10; don't be passive.

By asking each visitor to fill out a registration card or guest book, you can find out why they came and if they are buyers or sellers. Instead of registration cards, some agents give visitors clipboards with attached pencils, asking them to rate the house as to how it fits their needs. Figure 7.11 is an example of such a form. Of course, the comments from visitors should be relayed to your owners in their weekly activity report.

Many real estate agents today are relying on iPad or other tablet sign-in sheets for their open houses instead of traditional paper sign in sheets. Some visitors might be hesitant to sign in on a physical sign in sheet but today's consumer is quite accustomed to entering electronic information.

Various apps designed to manage open house leads are available. Many agents are reporting that the consumers are not pushing back at all on these electronic sign-in sheets.

Also, having the consumer information already in a database allows the agent to easily follow up on these leads with emails and phone calls without having to manually move the data into another system.

By offering the viewer notification of new listings, you can obtain email addresses, as well as permission to make phone calls even if they are on the do-not-call registry.

Draw Attention to the Property

Besides ads, you should have signs and arrows directing traffic from major streets. Always ask other property owners if you can put a directional sign on their lawns. They will generally allow you to do so, but if you do not ask, the sign likely will be removed.

Some agents tie a group of balloons to a mailbox or tree to attract attention. This is f ine, as are flags, banners, helium balloons, and so forth. Feather flags are particularly effective in gaining attention. A feather flag is a relatively narrow cloth flag on a vertical pole. Sizes range from 8 inches to around 15 feet in height and from 2 to 4 feet wide. This vertical flag is read from top to bottom. Keep it simple with just Open House in large print. The thin material vibrates with just the slightest breeze and is readily readable. A number of flag companies keep Open House feather flags in stock. One Los Angeles–area broker uses a machine to spew out thousands of large soap bubbles. Another agent flies a 20-foot helium-filled blimp lettered "Open House." Some developments prohibit open house signs and limit For Sale signs as to size and color. By parking an "Open House mobile" or car parked in the driveway with Open House magnetic signs on the sides, you can generally get around these restrictions. Anything to make the house stand out can be used. You don't want to keep an open house a secret. Invite neighbors, as well as prospective buyers you are working with who have not seen the house. You want to generate traffic.

Give every open-house visitor a copy of your property brief and your business card. Property briefs of other homes you have in the same and lower-price brackets also should be available. By questioning visitors, you can find their interests and needs, and you may excite their interest in a property better suited to them. For this reason, it is absolutely critical to be fully aware of any properties that might better suit a prospective buyer's needs.

Open houses are a time to make contacts and gather information, so ask questions. You can use general qualifying questions and determine specific interests. If visitors seem enthusiastic, use a trial closing. Don't think the sole function of an open house is only to show; it is to sell as well. Open houses tend to please owners because they show positive action on your part. They are often a source of listings because many visitors must sell before they can buy. They are a source of prospective buyers for other properties as well as the property shown. Therefore, you should look at the whole picture. With every visitor, ask yourself, "How can I fulfill this person's real estate needs?"

> Open houses provide a variety of benefits.

When you have or your office has several open houses in the same general area and price range, each open house should have a property brief of the other open house(s) and maps showing how to get to each property.

Some brokers advertise an open-house "Lotto," where a visitor to one house gets a card and a sticker. Another sticker is given at each additional home visited. If all the homes are visited, the visitor is awarded a gift, such as a baseball cap (with the firm's name).

It is possible for a single agent to conduct several open houses in a single day. For optimum effect, the homes should be in close proximity and should likely appeal to the same house hunters. The open houses should have staggered times such as 12 to 2 pm and 2:15 to 4 pm.

A variation of the above is an open house caravan where visiting time is relatively short, such as 15 minutes, and the caravan proceeds to the next home. Viewers should also be given clear directions to each home. Again, the homes should all appeal to the same potential buyers.

When a property has been extensively remodeled, neighbors will want to see what has been accomplished. An open house where neighbors have been specially invited can be beneficial not for a sale to the neighbors but for friends of the neighbors who might be interested in a home in the area.

FIGURE 7.11:   Visitor Rating Form

Visitor Rating

Property _____

Your name _____   Phone _____

Address _____   E-mail _____

Date _____

I am visiting this open house because of   ☐ Advertising   ☐ Signs

☐ Other (specify): _____
_____

Features I particularly like: _____
_____
_____

Features I do not like: _____
_____
_____

I believe the price quoted is: ☐ Low   ☐ About right   ☐ High

My reason for visiting is: _____
_____

Do you presently own your home? _____ Is it currently for sale? _____

General comments: _____
_____
_____

☐   I would like to receive e-mails, with pictures, or new listings and other open houses.

☐   You may call me about future new listings.

_____ (Signature)

Facebook Marketing

In this unit, we talk about the marketing plan associated with taking a new listing. Once a listing is taken most real estate agents will do the standard marketing plan consisting of placing a sign on the property, putting it in the MLS and doing some light direct mail. However, the real estate licensee should also have a Facebook strategy in place.

The unique aspect of Facebook advertising is that Facebook has a database of unique information on users. We self-populate what our interests are, where we are at any given time, and who our friends are. This allows marketing to be extremely targeted.

For example, imagine that you have a listing in a given city on a home that has a wine cellar. You could take a picture of the wine cellar and create a Facebook ad around this image. Facebook allows you to target your audience based on interests, gender, age, and other demographic criteria. An agent could target users who live within 15 miles of the listing, are 35 and older, and have indicated interests in "wine," "chardonnay," or other relevant search terms relating to wine.

The thought behind this isn't so much that you are going to find a buyer immediately but that the picture of the wine cellar and your listing will get "liked" and "shared" across the internet and may end up ultimately catching the eye of an interested buyer.

Servicing Buyer Agency Agreements

While keeping in touch with buyers is usually not a problem, prospective buyers you were unsuccessful in helping should not be forgotten, even if you don't have an agency agreement with them. It is a good idea to send emails or letters at least once a week on new listings. Provide website information for viewing or send property briefs. At least every two weeks you should contact the prospects by phone and ask for their comments about properties presented. If positive, set up a showing. It is not uncommon for some buyers to spend months looking for a home. While this is often the fault of the salespersons, some people are just procrastinators when it comes to a final decision. When you have determined that the buyers are ready, willing, and able to buy, keep working and help them decide.

SHORT SALE LISTINGS

A great many homes in America are underwater in that their loan indebtedness exceeds market value. In such cases, sellers would actually have to come up with cash to sell their homes. Most of the time, they are unable to do so. A solution is a short sale in which the lender agrees to accept the net receipts of the sale as a discharge of borrowers' obligations. The advantage to lenders is that they save the time and money a foreclosure would require, do not have to secure the property, and would not be subject to holding costs or the expense of repair and sales expenses. In most cases, a short sale would be an advantage to the lender over foreclosure.

In some instances where there is private mortgage insurance, the lender may want to foreclose and go against the insurer for their loss. Most major lenders use Equator Platform as a standardized short sale system. Agents log in at www.equator.com/ home and click on "Initiate Short Sale." They indicate the lender or the loan servicer and provide the loan number. The agent then completes the short sale application by following the lender's instructions.

Where the Equator Platform is not used, your first step in a short sale should be to contact the lender's loan mitigation officer. Different lenders have different titles. It may take a number of calls to contact the right party. You should tell the officer what you plan to do and indicate you will be sending a package explaining that a short sale is planned. Your package will include the following:

- Comparative market analysis showing all recent comparable sales in the area for three months

- A hardship letter from the owners (letter should show why a sale is needed and why the loan terms cannot be honored [e.g., physical problems and expenses, loss of job, reduced income, job relocation, etc.]) If the homeowner is not in default and there is not a genuine hardship, short sale approval is unlikely.

- Financial statement showing assets and liabilities of the owners

- Copies of bank statements (checking and savings) for past three months

- Credit card statements for past three months

- Estimated lender's net based on list price

- Copy of sale listing

You should ask the loan mitigation officer if there is anything else you should send.

The same package should be sent to the lender when an offer is received, along with the purchase offer and the borrower's prequalification for a loan. While some lenders claim a *fast track* on short sale approvals, a wait of two to four months, and sometimes much longer, is not unusual.

A shorter approval is more likely if the offer is void of contingencies and the earnest money is substantial. If subject to inspection, the period for inspection should be very short.

Some buyer's agents recommend a statement in bold print in their offer that says, "Buyer will pay all closing costs and fees." They believe such a statement will increase the likelihood of a fast approval.

Buyers will sometimes offer several thousand dollars above the broker's advertised price to protect against another agent's submitting a full price offer on the property.

Normally, when a debt is forgiven, the debtor's forgiven obligation is taxed as income. The Mortgage Forgiveness Debt Relief Act removes federal tax liability on such debts. The act was extended through 2015 and further extension is likely. California has a similar act that expired but may be extended.

THE OFFER AND BEYOND

Servicing the listing actually includes your communication and efforts from the time you obtain an offer to purchase until close of escrow. This aspect of servicing the listing is included in Unit 11, "From Offer to Closing."

SUMMARY

In this unit, you learned that honest and complete agent-owner communication, even when the communication is not good news, is better than a breakdown in communication. Owners want and deserve to know what is happening.

Owner-agent communications start with the listing. Owners should know when they will be seeing you again and why. The purpose of your next visit probably will be a postlisting meeting, when you will inform owners what you will be doing, including your marketing plan, and what you expect of them.

The owners should understand the instructions given them and the reasons for those instructions. Owners who do not understand why an instruction is given and that it is given for their best interests are not likely to follow the instruction.

The owners should understand that they will be receiving weekly activity reports about what is happening. Let owners know that if they have any questions or suggestions, they can contact you.

Owners who understand the showing procedure will realize the need to be prepared for showings at short notice.

Owners should realize that when print ads are used to advertise other houses as well, agents are bringing in calls about a wide range of properties. After buyers are qualified, it often is the case that another house better meets their needs than the one they inquired about.

Obtaining neighborhood information from the owners furnishes your office with the special ammunition necessary to give prospective buyers that last little nudge that results in a sale. Knowledge about the neighbors, similar interests, ages of children, and even employment can make a home more desirable to buyers.

Should an agent leave an office, the broker should immediately notify the owners of the departed agent's listings and establish a new contact person to meet with the owners as soon as possible.

The owner should complete the Transfer Disclosure Statement as soon as possible. All owner certificates and disclosures should be signed.

If a listing needs to be modified for any reason, let the owners know and meet with them. If you made a mistake in pricing, admit it and show the owners what it should be. If conditions have changed since the owners gave their listing, show them the changes along with your recommendations.

If you feel a modification is necessary in order to find buyers, and the owners will not accept the modification, ask to be relieved of the listing. This powerful approach will often serve to convince owners to accept your recommendations. If you do give back the listing, chances are you got rid of a liability, not an asset.

Go to owners for an extension before a listing expires. Review what you have done for them. If you have used diligent effort on behalf of the owners and have communicated with them, you will have a good chance of obtaining an extension.

The owners should understand your marketing plan, a plan that likely begins with a For Sale sign. A rider strip showing your evening phone number can give you additional calls. A rider strip for a particularly desirable feature, such as four bedrooms, will increase the sign's effectiveness.

Talking signs are radio transmitters. The sign outside directs people to tune to an AM or FM station number. The signs, usually the property of the listing agent, are an excellent listing tool.

A number of information boxes are available that can be attached to For Sale signs. They are used to hold brochures or property briefs on the property being sold. They are an effective tool to interest prospective buyers.

The lockbox, if appropriate, should be attached as soon as possible after the listing is taken. New electronic lockboxes can provide you with information about all persons who used the lockbox.

Take photographs of the property listed as soon as the proper light is available. They will be needed for the MLS, property briefs, office display boards, window displays, and internet presentations.

Post the property on your internet site, as well as on other sites, as soon as possible. If you prepare a virtual tour, take proper pictures of the property.

Get the listing information to your MLS as soon as possible. Prepare a property brief within a day or two of taking a listing. Also prepare advertisements for placement.

Prepare owners for the office caravan, showing the property to agents from your office. Ask agents to complete an agent property evaluation so you can provide the owners with the reactions of other professionals. The owners should also be prepared for an MLS caravan of agents from other offices. If possible, the listing agent should be at the property during the caravan period.

Immediate interest in the listing can be obtained by direct mail or direct contact with neighbors, asking them for help in finding a buyer, and by all agents going through their files for likely buyers.

An agent open house is another way to bring agents into the property. If you offer food and drinks at the end of the day, many agents will come to these open houses.

Regular open houses must be prepared for in the same manner as a caravan showing. The open house can serve as a source of listings and a source of buyers for other properties, as well as for the open-house property.

If the mortgage amount exceeds fair market value, notify the loan mitigation officer as to a short sale.

Servicing the listing extends all the way until close of escrow. It is a process whereby you make a plan, work your plan, and communicate.

CLASS DISCUSSION TOPICS

1. Prepare a marketing plan with dates from the listing for a single-family home. (Use the following assumptions: The owner is highly motivated to sell, and the property is listed at a price below those of most comparable properties; however, there have been few recent sales in the area.)

2. Prepare a property brief for a specific property.

3. Visit one open house held by another office. Discuss how it was held and what suggestions you would make for the agent (if any).

4. Discuss any property you know of that you feel is not being properly marketed. Be prepared to justify your recommendations.

5. Bring to class one current-events article dealing with some aspect of real estate practice for class discussion.

UNIT 7 QUIZ

1. The reason that an expired listing was not extended with the original listing office MOST likely is dissatisfaction with
    a. the commission percentage.
    b. communications.
    c. price.
    d. the length of listing.

2. Agent advice to owners on showing their home would NOT include
    a. instructions to be present so they can volunteer information.
    b. cleaning instructions.
    c. landscaping instructions.
    d. repair instructions.

3. When there has been little, if any, interest in a property, the listing salesperson should
    a. convey this information.
    b. tell the owner the property is priced 10% too high.
    c. wait until there is something good to report.
    d. tell the owner that you are expecting an offer.

4. The Equator Platform is a system for
    a. locating property.
    b. loan approval..
    c. short-sale approval
    d. a title search.

5. You want owners to give you neighborhood information
    a. to keep the owners busy.
    b. to give your listings a competitive advantage.
    c. to use it to get more listings.
    d. for none of these.

6. An owner should understand that reducing a list price to the CMA value
    a. increases the likelihood of a sale.
    b. does not mean that an owner is giving up anything.
    c. results in both of these.
    d. results in neither of these.

7. If possible, you should place a rider strip on your listing signs that shows
    a. your fax number.
    b. all your professional designations.
    c. a desirable feature.
    d. all of these.

8. A property brief should NOT be used as a
    a. handout at open houses.
    b. substitute for internet advertising.
    c. handout at caravans.
    d. mailing piece to answer inquiries.

9. A broker open house is of greatest value when the property
    a. is in a large market with hundreds of listings.
    b. is overpriced.
    c. has a very limited use.
    d. has been reduced in price.

10. Advantages of open houses include
    a. pleasing owners because they indicate activity.
    b. locating buyers for other property.
    c. obtaining leads for listings.
    d. all of these.

ADVERTISING

LEARNING OBJECTIVES

When you have completed this unit, you will be able to

- explain the objective of advertising and describe the AIDA approach to advertising;

- describe basic advertising guidelines, including media choices;

- evaluate advertising effectiveness;

- explain the legal implications of advertising; and

- describe an advertising budget.

KEY TERMS

AIDA approach
annual percentage rate
bait-and-switch
   advertising
blind ads
business card
car sign
classified advertising

company dollar
direct mail advertising
display advertising
institutional
   advertising
media choice
name tag
newsletters

operational advertising
outdoor advertising
press releases
specialty gifts
specific advertising
Truth in Lending Act

ADVERTISING OBJECTIVES

Advertising is the process of calling people's attention to something to arouse a desire to buy or to obtain more information about the product or service being promoted. The real estate industry could not exist without advertising. In addition to advertising products for lease or sale, the real estate industry also advertises for sellers and for salespeople. You will see that real estate advertising takes many forms.

Real estate advertising may be divided into two major types: institutional advertising and specific advertising. These two categories describe the two goals of real estate advertising.

Institutional advertising attempts to create a favorable image of the real estate company, the broker, and the salesperson. It keeps the company's name in the public eye and aims to inspire trust, confidence, and goodwill. Institutional advertising, often done by organized groups having similar interests, manifests pride in and respect for the real estate business. Individual brokers may be required to share some of the costs incurred in this type of advertising.

Specific advertising, also called **operational advertising**, is concerned with immediate results. It describes a particular piece of property and stimulates activity in a specific property or an entire tract of homes. In specific advertising, a broker's advertisements are in direct competition with the advertisements of other brokers.

THE AIDA APPROACH TO ADVERTISING

The most common, and probably most important, reason for advertising is to find ready, willing, and able buyers for sale listings. All the listings in the world will do you no good unless someone finds a ready, willing, and able buyer and makes that elusive sale.

Why do people buy? Prospective purchasers buy a particular piece of property for the benefits it offers. The most fundamental benefit is shelter, but the property also might provide other things that are important—security, good schools, convenience, recreation, prestige, and a lot more. The purpose of advertising is to communicate these benefits through the property's features—its price, size, location, and so on. People do not buy for the physical features of a property, but rather for the benefits those features offer, such as a relaxing life style, a feeling of security or love of family. Some people buy based upon how others will react.

If an ad is to be read and thus attract buyers, it usually must be designed to grab the reader's Attention, stimulate his or her Interest, generate a Desire, and lead the reader to Action. This is commonly referred to as the **AIDA approach**, from an acronym made up of the first letter of each step involved.

- **Attention**—The first step in any type of advertising is to gain attention. *Attention getters* include headlines that use words and word combinations, as well as typefaces and layouts that attract prospective buyers and encourage them to read further. You might gain attention with color, movement, message, sound, or even something odd or out of place, such as a misspelled word or an outrageous statement. It could even be humor. Whatever is used, you cannot get a message across until you have gained the attention of the intended recipient of the message.

- **Interest**—The ad should arouse interest in the specific product or service offered. Probably one of the best ways to arouse interest is through curiosity. Curiosity can be stimulated by ensuring that the ad allows the reader to imagine using and enjoying the benefits of the product or service.

- **Desire**—Once the person's attention is attracted and her interest is aroused, the ad can create desire by appealing to the senses and emotions. At this stage, language must be clear and concise and inspire the reader's confidence. Wherever possible, the advertising should try to build mental images and picture the reader as the final recipient of the product or service.

- **Action**—Finally, the ad should move potential buyers to take action. The advertisement should be directed toward helping them make a decision, to convince them that they want to know more. The action desired by a real estate advertisement is either a phone call, email, or fax to you or your office; an actual visit to your office, an open house, or a project; or a visit to your website for pictures and more information. If an ad fails to evoke action from a recipient of

The **AIDA** approach: Attention, Interest, Desire, Action

the message, then, to that person, the ad is really institutional in nature. It helps in name identification and general goodwill but has failed to bring in a prospective buyer.

ADVERTISING GUIDELINES

There are five basic tenets of advertising:

1. Advertise the right property

2. Know when to advertise

3. Choose the right market

4. Use the proper media

5. Use effective advertising techniques

By use of the internet, it is now possible for a real estate office to advertise all listings at the same time. This is not possible with print advertising. If you are trying to generate a great number of prospects, consider placing the listings that have the greatest general appeal in a predominant position on your website. We know that buyers responding to a real estate advertisement are likely to buy a property other than the property advertised. For this reason, we strive to advertise properties in areas and/or price ranges where we also have other available properties. This tactic increases the likelihood that prospects who respond to advertisements will become buyers.

Knowing when and where to advertise, whom you want to reach, and the features to emphasize is extremely important. You probably would not feature a swimming pool in an advertisement for a home in northern California at the beginning of a cold winter; a fireplace would be a more appropriate feature. Likewise, you would probably avoid advertising an elegant, expensive home in a local shoppers guide that is distributed primarily to low-income families.

ADVERTISING MEDIA

> ### Choosing Advertising Media
>
> In determining media choice, the advertiser must begin with three basic considerations:
>
> 1. The target audience to be reached
> 2. The message to be conveyed
> 3. The money available for media purchases
>
> This means that in addition to determining what to say, the broker must evaluate which medium or combination of media will deliver the maximum number of potential customers for the expenditure the broker can afford.

Because the message cannot contribute to sales until prospective buyers are exposed to it, the message must be delivered within sight or earshot of such prospects. The various advertising media perform the delivery function.

Media choices available include the following:

- Personal advertising
- Internet property sites
- Office and personal internet sites
- Social media
- General circulation daily
- General circulation weekly
- Weekly throwaway
- Foreign language and ethnic papers
- Special-interest papers (such as mobile home news)
- Special-interest publications
- Homebuyer magazines
- Radio
- Television
- Outdoor advertising

- Signs

- Direct mail

- Newsletters

- Telephone directories

- Press releases

- Specialty gifts

When choosing the medium, keep in mind that the objective is not necessarily to reach the largest number of people but to reach the greatest number of potential prospects at the least possible cost.

In determining the media to be used, ask yourself the following two questions:

1. What are my marketing goals?

   — To get more sale listings?

   — To get more buyer listings?

   — To attract more potential buyers?

   — To increase market share?

   — To enhance recognition of name?

   — To enhance recognition of professionalism?

   — To sell listed properties?

2. Which specific media will reach my target audience?

Personal Advertising

Personal advertising should start with a **name tag** identifying you as a real estate professional. The tag should be readable from at least 6 feet away. Preferably, it should use the same color as your office signs and business cards. If you are a REALTOR®, "REALTOR®" should be on your name tag. If you have achieved a significant professional designation, such as GRI, this also should be on your name tag.

Personal advertising concentrates on you, rather than on your firm.

Your personal advertising should include your **business card**. You want people to be able to identify your card among a group of cards. The easiest way to accomplish this is with your photograph on the card. As stated in Unit 1, your card should include your email address, fax number, and cell phone number. If you have foreign language skills and feel they are important in your work, your card should indicate those skills. Your real estate license number must be on your business card. It is required on cards because they are a first point of contact.

Some agents are now using personal logos on their business cards, personal websites, mailings, property briefs and advertising. While firm information is also provided, the logo helps to distinguish the agent from other agents and sells the individual.

Because of the amount of information that you may require, you might consider a foldout card.

Smartphones can read QR (quick response) codes. A smartphone can scan and capture a business card with a QR code. The code can contain business card data, as well as access to websites, resumes, et cetera. Data can be transferred from one smartphone to another by a simple scanning process.

A magnetic **car sign** is a good low-cost advertising tool. Include your name, the name of your firm, REALTOR® (if applicable), and firm logo (a firm-identifying design). The logo should appear on all advertisements, signs, cards, and so forth. Magnetic signs that proclaim "Open House," as well as your name, can turn your vehicle parked in a driveway into an invitation to visit.

It is a good idea to print out copies of your résumé with your photograph. You can give them to prospective buyers and sellers, as well as use them as an enclosure with mailings (both snail mail and email).

Your own column.   In smaller-circulation local papers, it may be possible to write a weekly real estate column. Being an author of a column will increase your name recognition, as well as show your knowledge and professionalism.

Personal business sites. Many agents now have their own websites that include personal information, as well as information on properties they are offering, frequently with links to other sites. Because salespeople in 100% commission offices act much like independent brokers, it makes sense for such agents to have their own websites.

The salesperson's own website can include many of the links from the office site, but it must include the broker's name and the salesperson's license number.

Blogs. A blog is a website maintained by an individual with emphasis on a particular subject with regularly updated news and comments. Many blogs allow viewers to leave comments. It should be separate from your personal business website. A blog could be centered on an activity or a particular geographical area such as "Sun City Happenings." It might include community events, information on residents, as well as real estate data on listings, sales, rentals and valuation trends. By including valuable information, you promote yourself in a positive manner. There are many sports blogs about particular local teams. There are even blogs as to social activities, such as line dancing or bridge.

A blog should not look like a commercial home page. It should be loaded with information for the targeted audience.

A problem with blogs is that they can take much of your time. Some agents use personal assistants to keep the blogs current after they have been established.

Social networking sites. Social networking is not just for teenagers with agile thumbs. A vast array of social networking sites is now available to help companies and/or an individuals in their business endeavors. Social networking allows a dialog with followers. New ways of using these sites are being discovered almost daily. A growing number of companies on the internet offer tutorials about the business use of social networking and offer to handle your page on a site.

Avoid religion and politics on your websites unless you want to eliminate a great number of potential clients. Don't use social media to make yourself seem important. Use it to show yourself as caring, helpful and community-minded individual. Don't overload your websites with garbage information. Keep in mind that real estate is local, so what is happening in your community will be of greatest interest.

A number of books and videos are available on how to use social networking sites. In addition, a number of firms and organizations offer seminars on social media marketing.

- Twitter is a service that enables users to send and read text messages up to 140 characters. An estimated 500 million tweets are sent daily. While unregistered individuals can read tweets, registered members can post them. Business tweets often talk about non-business items to gain the interest of readers. They can target interest groups.

  Tweets can be inspirational to agents and informative as to offers, price reduction, et cetera. They can be sent to prospective buyers, sellers, and clients. Tweets can be used to invite specific individuals or people in general to an open house or to promote a new listing. They can announce a sale or be used for a welcome to a new neighbor. Tweets are also used to promote blog postings and websites. There is a great deal of free help, as well as a subscription service, about using Twitter for business. The website www.chrisbrogan.com offers free ideas to real estate professionals for using Twitter.

  A hashtag # can be used on Twitter, as well as on other social media. The hashtag is used for key words so the tweet can be found on a tweet search. As an example, #Brentwood Foreclosure or #Yucaipa Horse Ranch.

- Facebook connects people. The largest social networking system available requires participants to register before creating a personal profile. Many firms are now including Facebook link information on their press releases. Some Facebook pages are community oriented with news to garner followers. A Facebook page can include simple sign-ups for emails and newsletters with software such as Mail Chimp (www.mailchimp.com).

- Instagram, owned by Facebook, is a photo and video sharing website. Forty million photos are posted each day. A filter system allows photos to be manipulated in ways similar to Adobe Photoshop. Instagram is available for smartphones and iPads. Hashtags can be used to get attention and listings. Videos are limited to 15 seconds. You can adapt other videos with your voice to describe a property as though you were showing it. One technique is a neighborhood map showing locations of listings giving the user the ability to view each listing with photos or video.

■ LinkedIn is a business networking website that can reach developers, investors, and others who can help your business. You can tell your story on your company page.

■ The above noted sites are just a few of the many available.

YouTube.   Youtube.com is a video-sharing website. Content is uploaded by registered individual users. Unregulated users can view the videos. Many real estate agents post virtual tours of their properties on YouTube. Some agents host their own shows to highlight their knowledge and inform buyers and sellers. YouTube allows for a video blog.

Photo sharing.   Photo sharing is the publishing or transfer of digital images online. Photo blogs allow you to classify photos and add captions and comments.

The internet offers amazing opportunities and is the future of real estate communication.

Newspaper Advertising

Newspapers are the oldest advertising medium in the nation and in the past have been the keystone of the real estate business. Although the first advertisement appeared in the *Boston Newsletter* in 1704, newspapers were rather scarce until 1790. After many decades of phenomenal growth, newspaper sales and readership are now in sharp decline. The high cost of advertising and growth of the internet has resulted in less reliance on real estate classified advertising. The classified ad sections of large circulation newspapers have declined from several pages to a few columns. However, there is still a place for print advertising.

Newspapers have a degree of audience selectivity. Because of their wide circulation, they may be considered to have extensive coverage. They also have time-and-place flexibility and are especially important for local advertising. Because of their tremendous circulation, newspapers reach all classes of consumers. A drawback of newspaper advertising is that its effective life span is short.

Since the 1990s, a third of household growth and about 12% of first-time buyers have been immigrants. Foreign language papers should be considered if an office wishes to tap into this market. Real estate agents must avoid advertising exclusively in minority publications because it might be construed as steering, a violation of the real estate law.

Weekly newspapers in smaller communities are still an effective media for real estate ads because the percentage of readers remains high due to their local news content. The cost of advertising in local weeklies is manageable. Generally, newspaper readers are graying. The average age of readers is increasing. The product advertised can be targeted to the older reader.

Newspaper advertising is divided into classified and display advertisements. Any newspaper ad should provide a broker name, phone number, and internet address. Advertisements that do not identify the advertiser as a broker are called **blind ads** and are illegal in California. A blind ad is deceptive because readers are induced to contact the advertiser in the belief that they are dealing directly with an owner rather than an agent.

Classified advertisements.   All forms of newspaper advertising are important, but the most common form used in the real estate business is still **classified advertising**.

While not as productive as internet sites, print advertising still produces sales. People interested in buying or leasing real estate still check the classifieds where available, although they will likely spend more time on the internet. People older than 60 are more likely than those younger than 50 to seek out classified ads before they use the internet.

Keep in mind that your classified advertisements have a very short lifespan and will be in direct competition with many other ads, including those on the internet. A mediocre ad generally means a mediocre response. Strive for ads that achieve maximum effectiveness by analyzing likely buyers for a property and appealing to those buyers' needs.

Your classified ad should indicate an internet address that offers more information and additional properties: Examples are "More information and properties, www.seeahome.com" or "Property Tour, www.seeahome.com." People who find attractive properties on the internet feel that they played an active role in a home search rather than passively letting a salesperson decide which homes they were going to see. When a prospective buyer "discovers" a property, the chances of an actual offer are enhanced.

Classified ads are read by willing readers looking for properties. Therefore, the best heading would be the most desirable feature of the property: "4 Bedrooms," "Beverly Hills," or even price, "$397,500." However, you would not waste an ad heading such as "Beverly Hills" if the newspaper classification was for "Beverly Hills Property." Avoid redundancy. Figure 8.1 includes examples of ads with headings that cover one or more of a home's prime attractions.

When you don't have a super feature to advertise or there are many competing ads, consider an attention-grabbing heading to make your ad stand out from the others. Figure 8.2 includes examples of such ads.

Advertisements normally tell us how good a product is. If an ad listed the faults of a product, no one would normally be expected to buy it. Real estate, however, is different. Ads for fixer-upper properties often result in an exceptional response. A likely reason is that a property with problems spells opportunity to a great many buyers. The worse you make a property appear, the greater the response. Figure 8.3 includes sample fixer-upper ads. Before you use ads of this type, obtain the owners' permission in writing. Many owners will become upset if you degrade or make fun of their home, even if it brings in a buyer.

FIGURE 8.1:   **Sample Feature Ads**

Westlake

You can own a like-new, 3BR, 2½ bath Tennessee Colonial with all the fine detailing and craftsmanship you thought had been forgotten. A 2½-car garage, central air, a family room and a prestigious

WESTLAKE

address are yours for just $487,500

UR

H O M E   R E A L T Y

Call Amber at 760-555-8200
View at www.ur-home.net

You can call attention to location by using a split heading, which is effective for a highly desirable area.

Spanish Omelet

Arches, tile and huge beams combine to make this 3-bedroom, 2-bath, West Side masterpiece a very tasty dish at

$579,500

Special features include family room, 3-car garage, central air, delightful fenced yard and giant Norway pine. One look and we will put up the "sold" sign. For a virtual tour, check #82 at www.ur-home.net.

UR

H O M E   R E A L T Y

Call Amber at 760-555-8200
Tour at www.ur-homenet

The split heading features architectural style and price. The reader is invited to view the property on the Internet.

Adjectives add desirability to ads.

Adjectives.   The use of adjectives to paint word pictures of features can spark readers' interest. It generally is false economy to write bare-bones ads in a competitive market. Often an ad that is 20% longer because of the use of adjectives earns a response rate that far outweighs the 20% higher ad cost. A response increase exceeding 100% is not uncommon.

As an example of how descriptive words can paint an image, consider how you might describe a bathroom to paint a picture for the reader:

> Sumptuous master bath, sensuous master bath, sinfully sensuous master bath, deliciously sumptuous bath, Roman bath, opulent Phoenician bath, Grecian bath, garden tub, antique claw-footed tub, sky-lit bath, enchanting garden bath

FIGURE 8.2: Sample Attention-Grabbing Ads

Maxine and Marvin Slept Here

for 10 years, but Marvin was transferred to Phoenix, so they must regretfully take their bed and leave this 3BR, 2-bath, red brick Georgian Colonial in the nicest area in all of Woodland Glen. The home features a tantalizing Jacuzzi tub in the master bath, which is why the shower is practically new; walk-in closets; music room for little Ralph, who is learning to play the drums; and a kitchen any chef would fry for. Priced to get Maxine and Marvin on their way at $437,500.

UR

HOME REALTY

760-555-8200
View at www.ur-home.net

Who Used the Tub?

We suspect Mr. Buckley of our office has been bathing in the Italian marble tub in the sumptuous master bath of this 3BR, 2½-bath Italian Renaissance estate in Westhaven. Every afternoon he visits the house and takes along a towel. When he returns, he's singing Italian arias. When you see the tantalizing Roman baths, you'll understand why. The estate has an aura of elegance that makes you want to pamper yourself. With more than 3,500 sq. ft. of sheer luxury and almost a half-acre of grounds, this is your chance to be good to yourself for $849,500. After all, who deserves it more?

UR

HOME REALTY

760-555-8200
View at www.ur-home.net

The above heading is a real attention getter.

Lady Saxophone Player

must sell her 3BR, cedarshake, Westfield Cape Cod in order to seek fame and fortune. There is a garage, several magnificent hickory trees, a family of squirrels, a somewhat neglected garden and a kitchen big enough to seat an 8-piece band. The price hits a pleasant note at $529,500.

UR

HOME REALTY

760-555-8200
www.ur-home.net

Before you feature an owner in your ad, obtain the owner's permission to run the ad.

FIGURE 8.3: Sample Fixer-Upper Ads

A Monument to Bad Taste

If you have more money than taste, you'll love this gaudy French Provincial with Italianate influence, finished to excess in a sort of baroque style. There are 11 huge rooms, all equally ugly. It does command a premier West Hills location, offering every conceivable amenity; but while you might like to visit, you wouldn't want to live here. Mr. Clements of our office, a former Edsel owner, thinks it's beautiful—just the way he imagines a movie star's home to be. It's priced far below reproduction costs at $689,000, but then who would want to reproduce it?

UR
HOME REALTY
760-555-8200
www.ur-home.net

As strange as it may seem, this ad will bring in calls from qualified buyers.

Decorator's Nightmare

Leprous yellow walls, jarring purple accents, and blood-red tile are just a few of the features in this 3-bedroom Dutch Colonial that prove money and good taste aren't synonymous. This appears structurally sound, and it does offer an excellent West Side location as well as an attractive exterior and landscaping. The price reflects the poor taste of the decorator—$369,500.

UR
HOME REALTY
760-555-8200
www.ur-home.net

This ad is a variation on the fixer-upper ad. Be certain you have the owner's permission before you comment negatively on the decorating.

It Could Be Worse

The roof doesn't appear to leak, but just about everything else in this 3BR, 2-bath, brick English Tudor in Westwood is in need of mending. While it has expansive lawns, hedges and flower beds, you'll have to imagine how it will look trimmed without the weeds and bare spots and with flowers blooming. If you love to tinker, you have enough work for a lifetime. The only redeeming feature is the price, $339,500.

UR
HOME REALTY
760-555-8200
www.ur-home.net

Yuk! This Place Is Unbelievable

This 3-bedroom, West Side American Traditional appears to have been neglected from the day it was built. It will take a semi to haul away the junk in the backyard. Perhaps under all that dirt you may find shining spendor, but don't count on it. But then for $189,500, what do you expect?

UR
HOME REALTY
760-555-8200
www.ur-home.net

This was adapted from an ad by Ian Price, Surfer's Paradise, Australia.

You can see that adjectives can bring a desired image to the reader, so use them. The use of adjectives is also important for your internet ads. While you are not limited on your office websites, many websites limit the space allowed for property descriptions.

Large circulation papers.   The greater a paper's circulation, the higher the cost of advertising. It doesn't take many large classified ads in the *Los Angeles Times* to use up the advertising budget of many firms. You can use a relatively short ad to perk a reader's interest to check further on the internet. Here are examples:

Many single-office real estate brokers avoid large newspapers, such as the *Los Angeles Times*, because so much of the circulation is beyond the brokers' market area. They attempt to target their areas by advertising in smaller-circulation papers that are local in scope.

Display advertisements.   **Display advertising** may be either institutional or operational in nature. It may combine the two, so that it is used primarily to build goodwill and prestige and keep the name before the public, while at the same time advertising specific properties. Be sure to include an internet address that can offer additional information.

Because of costs, display ads are primarily used for selling developments rather than single homes. An exception would be newspapers in smaller communities offering lower advertising costs. Consider obtaining professional help for display advertisements.

General Rules for Display Advertising

- Most people read from the upper left corner to the lower right corner.
- Therefore, the ad should be composed with the heading on top, illustration and copy in the center, and firm name, phone number, and Web address in the lower right quarter. One large picture is generally more effective than several small pictures.
- If reproduced well, photographs may be more effective than drawings, but most photographs require professional retouching to increase contrast, remove distracting features, and blur backgrounds.
- Include white space. White space emphasizes the message.
- Don't use more than two typefaces in an ad.
- Ads in the outside columns will generate more interest than ads in the inside columns.
- Typefaces with serifs (the fine lines at the end of letter strokes) are generally more readable than sans-serif typefaces (without the lines).
- Lowercase letters are easier to read than capital letters.
- Short sentences are more readable than long sentences.
- Short words are more readable than long words.
- If you pull readers through the first three lines, they are likely to read the entire ad.
- Use words that are readily understood.
- Don't be too subtle or sophisticated.
- Always tell the reader what to do (call, come in, or check the internet).
- Always use the same logo in your ads.

Magazine Advertising

The cost of advertising in a magazine having mass appeal generally is prohibitive. However, magazines appealing to special-interest groups could be productive for the right property. As an example, if you had 40 acres zoned for a salvage yard with railroad siding access, you might consider advertising it in a trade magazine for salvage yard operators.

Special city or area magazines are usually slick paper magazines with very limited circulation. They are likely to be most effective for very impressive homes.

Area homebuyer magazines are found in most areas of California. These magazines are particularly effective for newcomers to the area. There are variations of these magazines that cover just new home developments and rentals. It is believed that the prevalence of websites will diminish the effectiveness of these magazines.

Similar to homebuyer magazines, e-brochures are for the internet. They can be sent as emails or included on a CD business card. Software to prepare e-brochures can also be used to prepare printed brochures. You might want to check www.imprev.com for more information.

Radio and TV Advertising

Compared with print media, radio broadcasting is a relatively new advertising medium. The first paid advertisement on radio appeared in 1922. Today radio can reach, at one time or another, nearly 99% of the households in the United States. Customers can be reached traveling to and from work, to and from the market, at the beach, or in their own homes. Radio is effective because the audience can listen while doing something else.

In using radio advertising, match the property with the demographics of those who listen to the station. Unless you hope to sell a multimillion-dollar estate to a rock star, don't advertise it on a hard-rock station. Foreign language stations are being used effectively for brokers who are trying to tap into immigrant groups.

Television delivers advertising messages to both the eye and the ear. What's more, it permits the use of motion and color and usually delivers the message in the home. Television advertising, however, is expensive, and it is used sparingly for general real estate advertising. It is used most often by large real estate firms, franchisers, and developers.

Home showcase programs are becoming popular on television, particularly in smaller markets. They allow photos, as well as a verbal descriptions of property benefits. There are cable stations that have 24-hour bulletin boards of things for sale. Some brokers have reported excellent responses to these bulletin-board stations for low-cost and low-down-payment homes as well as rentals.

Outdoor Advertising

Outdoor advertising is used less frequently than other media, depending largely on the size of the town and the availability of advertising billboards. Usually, billboards are used by larger brokerage offices or chain operations.

However, signs may be painted on buildings, fences, bus-stop benches, or other display places by individual real estate offices as well.

Because of their cost, which can be several thousand dollars per month depending on features and location, the real estate use of billboards has been primarily for large new developments.

For Sale Signs

While relatively inexpensive, For Sale signs are effective and they work seven days a week, 24 hours per day. The design of a licensee's For Sale signs should be unique, original, quickly informative, and as attractive as possible. The attention-getting value of the signs will be enhanced through the use of color, unique design, an identifiable logo, and design and size of print. Rather than plain paint for your For Sale signs, consider reflective paint that stands out when light hits the sign. A new twist is a glow-in-the-dark paint that remains bright for several hours after dusk. (Your sign firm should be able to offer this product.) Solar-powered light fixtures are also available that allow signs to stand out at night.

> Your sign should be distinguishable from that of your competition.

Colors used should provide a high degree of contrast for readability (the best color contrast is yellow and black). To distinguish their signs from those of competitors, some brokers have changed the shape of their signs. A simple change is a vertical rectangle rather than a horizontal one. Others have gone to oversized signs or odd-shaped signs. Whatever their makeup, signs should be coordinated with any printed material being created for the office. Riders for special features or for listing a salesperson's name and phone number and even an Web address should be considered. (Talking signs and sign information boxes were covered in Unit 7.)

Direct Mail

Although **direct mail advertising** is rather expensive per contact, it can be an effective way to reach a selected audience. It may be institutional in nature or be designed to promote a new subdivision, an area, or even a specific piece of property. Various vehicles are used in this method of advertising, including pamphlets, brochures, letters, postcards, booklets, pictures, and maps. You can spread the word about new listings with regularly scheduled targeted mail using readily available merge software.

This medium may encourage the reader to seek more information by returning a response device that may result in additional material and inclusion in mailing lists and other sales promotions. An excellent approach is to offer prospective customers free email updates of new listings, including photos, by simply sending you an email. Of course, every direct mail piece should reference your firm's website. Direct mail approaches were more fully discussed in Unit 4.

Direct Email

We have shown you one way to obtain email addresses of prospects with the visitor rating form in Unit 7. We will be showing you more ways to have prospects willingly provide their email addresses. The beauty of a direct approach with email is that, except for preparation time, it is a no-cost approach. Direct approach emails can include colored pictures, movement (motion), and even sound. You can email a zip code by utilizing mailing list firms that also have email addresses. Like any other advertising, you want your direct mail and email ads to stand out from the commonplace. An unsolicited email must clearly indicate that it is an advertisement piece and comply with the CAN-SPAM regulations.

Newsletters

Many offices, as well as individual agents, successfully use **newsletters**. They include information that would be of interest to the recipient, as well as information about the firm or agent. They are particularly valuable in niche marketing. As an example, one agent who has established her niche in marketing mobile homes in a particular park has a monthly newsletter that includes personal information about residents and information on new residents and club schedules and special events. Computer programs and numerous services are available that will allow you to quickly publish a quality newsletter. You can also subscribe to services that print and distribute newsletters with your photo and contact information. Paper newsletters have been diminishing in importance because of the growth of email newsletters and agent blog websites.

Telephone Directories

Although real estate firms have yellow-page listings, often in bold type, display ads in telephone directories are not likely to be as cost-effective as those in other advertising media. The effectiveness of your yellow-page ad can be increased significantly by use of your internet address; for example, "View Available Homes at www.seeahome.com."

Press Releases

Press releases are really free advertisements. If you look in the real estate section or supplement of any newspaper, you will find that most of the articles are taken from press releases. Your local newspaper will publish press releases that are well written and have a newsworthy message. Some examples of such messages are the grand opening of an office, the ground-breaking for a development, the listing of a historic building, any sale where the buyers or sellers are newsworthy, special awards or designations received by agents, and office promotions.

Press releases are free advertisements.

Whenever possible, include a high-quality digital photo. Include a caption, and if people are shown, be sure to identify them in the caption.

Specialty Gifts

Most offices include **specialty gifts**, or promotional giveaway items, in their advertising budget. These may include notepads, maps, magnetic holders, calendars, pencils, directories, and pens with a salesperson's and the firm's identification. Such items promote you or your company continually and can be dispensed through the office, at business and social gatherings, at open houses, and during door-to-door canvassing. They are excellent door openers and can be used effectively to get acquainted in a neighborhood.

The Internet

The internet has become the predominant marketing tool. Just a few years ago, it was rare to have a transaction where the buyer or the seller contact resulted from information contained on a website. Today, many offices are reporting that most of their contacts result from internet postings. Surveys of property buyers reveal that in many areas over 90% of buyers indicated that they used the internet for their property search. Some 63% of buyers say they viewed homes they first found on the internet. While there are a great many sites where you can post your listings, it is extremely important that you have your own office website if you are going to be competitive.

Websites have been getting more elaborate, frequently with multiple pictures of each property and with sound and motion. Virtual tours allow a viewer to "walk through" the property; this virtual "walk-through" can either half-sell the property or eliminate it for a prospective buyer. By paying an extra fee, many home search websites offer enhanced property coverage, which increases the effectiveness of your property presentation.

One advantage of the internet is its relatively low cost once your website has been established. Be sure to include your web address in all your advertising in other media.

A decreasing portion of the advertising pie goes to print advertising. The internet is now considered more productive. Corzen, Inc., a New York–based provider of advertising data, claims that the internet is over twice as effective as print for real estate firms. Because the internet is the best bargain in town, print ads are dwindling in most papers and magazines. The internet allows a small firm to have a large presence within a market area. Some companies are now going 100% internet in their marketing efforts. Other firms claim to be using newspapers sparingly and then primarily to placate owners.

Before you prepare a website, we recommend you view the websites of a number of large brokerage offices in major metropolitan areas across the country. Note the differences in quality of the sites and in site features. Make a note of the features you want in your site, as well as why you feel some sites are outstanding. Now you are ready for your webpage preparation.

Features that you want to include on your website are as follows:

- **About us**—This feature allows a viewer to obtain information about your firm and its personnel; includes résumé and testimonial letters.

- **Inventory**—Here you provide photos and descriptions of your listings. If there are a great many listings, the viewer should be able to enter parameters such as price, size, and location to narrow the search for properties. If a property is advertised by number, the viewer should be able to go directly to that property. The inventory should also include the ability to increase size of photos, as well as view additional photos. Virtual tours should be considered for all listings.

■ **Area map**—This can show the locations of properties, as well as the broker's office.

■ **Email offer**—Each page of your site should offer the viewer an opportunity to receive emails of new listings before they are advertised.

■ **Motion and/or sound**—These features hold the viewer's attention and will distinguish your site from others.

■ **Loan qualifying opportunity**—This viewer option will provide information on the prospect and allow further direct contact.

■ **800 number**—By providing this number, you encourage calls from outside your immediate area.

■ **Back to home page**—This feature should be on every page of your website.

■ **Contact us**—This will allow the viewer to send an email to you. Agents can also include a link that says, "Search MLS here," an, through the use of a system known as IDX, pull MLS data to display on the agent's website.

While agents can prepare their own webpages using one of the inexpensive webpage programs, these are often boilerplate sites and fail to provide maximum viewer impact. As previously stated, we strongly suggest that a professional `webpage designer create your site. Before you hire a designer, be certain to view other sites created by the designer. A correctly designed website can ensure long-term use and will attract prospective buyers, sellers, lessors, and lessees, as well as enhance the image of your firm.

Besides your personal and office websites, it is important that your property information be distributed to MLS and other area and national websites.

Many agents have reported success with internet classified sites such as www.craigslist.org/about/sites and www.wantedwants.com.

Pay-per-click ads.   Many firms have reported success with pay-per-click ads on websites other than real estate sites. Sites that sell the benefit of a community are logical sites for pay-per-click ads. Every time a website viewer clicks on your ad, you pay a small fee. A click on the ad could lead to your website's homepage, which could then lead to information about you and the available inventory.

Other Forms of Advertising

There are many other ways to advertise: movie screens, videotapes, window displays, transit ads, bus shelter and bench ads, electric message boards, marquee ads, supermarket carts, and so on. You will find that your advertising is limited only by the limits of your imagination and the thickness of your pocketbook.

ADVERTISING EFFECTIVENESS

Is your advertising program producing the results you want? There is an old saying in advertising: "Half of my advertising is worth the money. The problem is that I don't know *which* half!" If you don't set up an evaluation system, you will never know. Identifying the part of your advertising dollar that is producing your sales can be critical to success. You must be able to determine which types of advertising are most effective for you and which produce the most income. You can do that by tracking ads and determining their cost compared with the amount of business they generate. You can even pinpoint which approach and/or medium is most effective for a particular type of property.

The key to a good measurement system is simplicity. One method to use when you run a newspaper ad or send out a letter or direct mail piece is to put a code on the bottom of the piece. A simple technique is to use a designated telephone number. Thus, respondents who contact you by a call to that number indicate that they are responding to a particular ad. If possible, try to identify separately for each ad the number of prospects and sales that result, so you will know the quality as well as the quantity of leads you obtain. Then determine the cost of each advertisement. Many offices require that the receptionist who handles incoming calls keep telephone logs. The receptionist can ascertain the type of ad seen by the caller and the ad medium and can enter this information into the log.

> You should evaluate ads for effectiveness.

Just because one medium is not as effective as another in terms of number of responses does not mean the medium is ineffective.

EXAMPLE   Jane Freyman placed two ads in different newspapers for the same period. The ads were identical. She knew that this was important because she wanted to test which publication worked best. If she used different-quality ads, one would naturally pull better because it was a better ad, not because the publication was better. She ran the ads at the same time for the same reason. The only difference was that the ad in paper A directed people to ask for department X, whereas the ad in paper B told people to ask for department Y.

There was a difference in the cost of running the ads. A had a circulation of 20,000 and charged $200 for the ad. B had a circulation of 100,000 and charged $1,000. The following are the results that Freyman tabulated:

Paper A	Paper B
15 prospects	27 prospects
5 eventual sales	9 eventual sales

Which paper is a more attractive advertising medium? Does Freyman simply want greater numbers of sales, or does she want to get more sales more cost-effectively?

Assuming that the amounts of the individual sales were comparable, B probably would be more attractive to Freyman if she wanted more sales. The ad in B generated more eventual sales. However, if Freyman was more interested in cost-effectiveness, she probably would prefer A. The sales numbers were smaller, but so were the costs—not only the cost of the ad but also the cost per sale:

$$\$200 \div 5 \text{ sales} = \$40 \text{ per sale}$$

$$\$1,000 \div 9 \text{ sales} = \$110 \text{ per sale}$$

LEGAL IMPLICATIONS OF ADVERTISING

Advertising of real property is regulated by California real estate law, the regulations of the real estate commissioner, and the federal Consumer Credit Protection Act (Truth in Lending Act). The following sections from the California Business and Professions Code and the Regulations of the Real Estate Commissioner are merely condensations of the actual statues and regulations.

California Real Estate Law

Section 10139—"Penalties for Unlicensed Person."   This law stipulates that any unlicensed person acting as a licensee who advertises using words indicating that she is a broker is subject to a fine not to exceed $20,000 and/or imprisonment in the county jail for a term not to exceed six months. If the violator is a corporation, it is subject to a fine of $60,000.

Section 10140—"False Advertising."   This section states that every officer or employee who knowingly advertises a false statement concerning any land or subdivision is subject to a fine of $1,000 and/or one year's imprisonment. In addition, the licensee may have his license suspended or revoked.

Section 10140.5—"Disclosure of Name."   Each advertisement published by a licensee that offers to assist in filing applications for the purchase or lease of government land must indicate the name of the broker and the state in which she is licensed.

Section 10140.6—"False Advertising."   Licensees may not publish in any newspaper or periodical or by mail an ad for any activity for which a real estate license is required that does not contain a designation disclosure that they are performing acts for which a license is required.

While the law requires licensees to include their license number in contact material, newspaper and periodical advertising are exempt, as are For Sale signs and television ads.

Section 10235—"Misleading Advertisement."   A licensee may not advertise, print, display, publish, distribute, televise, or broadcast false or misleading statements regarding rates and terms or conditions for making, purchasing, or negotiating loans or real property sales contracts, nor may a licensee permit others to do so.

Section 10236.1—"Inducements."   A licensee may not advertise to offer a prospective purchaser, borrower, or lender any gift as an inducement for making a loan or purchasing a promissory note secured directly by a lien on real property or a real property sales contract.

Section 10131.7—"Mobile Home Advertising."   A licensee is prohibited from engaging in the following activities:

- Advertising a mobile home that is not in an established mobile home park or is being sold with the land

- Failing to withdraw an advertisement of a mobile home within 48 hours of removal from the market

- Advertising or representing a used mobile home as a new one

- Making a false statement that a mobile home is capable of traveling on California highways

- Falsely advertising that no down payment is required on the sale of a mobile home when in fact one is required

Regulations of the Real Estate Commissioner

The real estate commissioner can adopt regulations that have the same force and intent as law. Two of these regulations follow.

Article 9, Section 2770.1—"Advertising License Designation."   Use of the terms *broker, agent, REALTOR®, loan correspondent,* or the abbreviations *bro., agt.,* or other terms or abbreviations, is deemed sufficient identification to fulfill the designation requirements of Section 10140.6 of the Business and Professions Code.

Article 9, Section 22773—"Disclosure of License Identification Number on Solicitation Materials."   All first point-of-contact solicitation material must disclose the licensee's eight-digit real estate license number. This includes business cards, stationary, websites, flyers, et cetera.

Code of Ethics of the National Association of REALTORS®

Even though the Code of Ethics of the National Association of REALTORS® is a moral code and as such is not enforceable by law, its guidelines are observed by most real estate licensees in California. Professional courtesy and ethics should not end with those acts that have been sanctioned by law. The individual who tries only to stay on the border of the law may at some time step across that border.

Regarding advertising, Article 12 of the 2015 Code of Ethics states that

> REALTORS® shall be honest and truthful in their real estate communications and shall present a true picture in their advertising, marketing, and other representations. REALTORS® shall ensure that their status as real estate professionals is readily apparent in their advertising, marketing, and other representations, and that the recipients of all real estate communications are, or have been, notified that those communications are from a real estate professional.

12-4   REALTORS® shall not offer for sale/lease or advertise property without authority.

12-5   REALTORS® shall not advertise nor permit any person employed by or affiliated with them to advertise real estate services or listed property in any medium (e.g., electronically, print, radio, television, etc.) without disclosing the name of that REALTOR®'s firm in a reasonable and readily apparent manner.

12-6   REALTORS®, when advertising unlisted real property for sale/lease in which they have an ownership interest, shall disclose their status as both owners/landlords and REALTORS® or real estate licensees.

Truth in Lending Act

The **Truth in Lending Act**, or Regulation Z, a part of the federal Consumer Credit Protection Act of 1968, requires disclosure of credit costs as a percentage, as well as total finance charges. It is enforced by the Federal Trade Commission.

Truth-in-lending applies to credit extended with a finance charge or credit payable in more than four installments. If the amount or percentage of down payment, the number of payments or period of repayment, or the amount of payment or amount of finance charges (trigger terms) is included in any advertisement, then the ad must include three elements:

1. Amount or percentage of down payment

2. Terms of repayment

3. **Annual percentage rate** (APR) (the true interest rate considering points and other loan costs; the nominal rate is the rate stated on the note)

Advertising the APR alone will not trigger the these disclosures.

If creditors extend credit secured by a dwelling more than five times per year, they must furnish the purchaser a truth-in-lending disclosure showing all loan facts. However, the total amount of finance charges for the term of the loan need not be shown for first mortgages or loans used to purchase real property. (Because escrow impounds for taxes and insurance are not considered loan costs, they need not be listed.)

Truth-in-lending makes **bait-and-switch advertising** (advertising property that agents don't intend to sell or that is not available in order to attract buyers for other property) a federal offense.

Rescission right.   If the loan is for consumer credit secured by the borrower's residence, the borrower has the right to reconsider and cancel. This right is valid until midnight on the third business day following loan completion. (Rescission right does not apply to home purchase loans but does apply to home equity loans and home refinancing.)

Exemptions.   Loans exempt from all truth-in-lending disclosure requirements are business loans, agricultural loans, construction loans, personal property loans over $25,000, and interest-free loans with four or fewer installments. Non-owner-occupied housing is considered a business and thus exempt from disclosure. Carryback financing for most sellers (not more than five times per year) also is exempt.

CIVIL RIGHTS ACT OF 1968

The Civil Rights Act of 1968 prohibits discriminatory advertising (see Unit 2). Discriminatory advertising includes advertising that indicates any preference, limitation, or discrimination because of race, color, religion, sex, handicap, familial status, or national origin.

There are some discriminatory words and phrases that are not readily recognized by many as being discriminatory. In addition, some words carry different connotations among different social, ethnic, and economic groups. Words also have different meanings based upon geographic location.

A number of groups have tried to clarify what was and was not acceptable wording for advertising by publishing lists. These lists varied greatly. Some lists went so far as to indicate that advertising the "view" was discriminatory to the blind. Prudent agents will follow the BRE guidelines for advertising (see Figure 8.4).

While the Department of Housing and Urban Development (HUD) enforces the Fair Housing Act, the federal agency was reluctant to provide guidance. There was a partial clarification on January 9, 1995, when HUD sent a memo to its staff as to guidelines for investigation of discrimination allegations. The memo addressed the following five points:

1. **Race, color, national origin.** Complaints should not be filed for use of "master bedroom," "rare find," or "desirable neighborhood." Some groups felt that "master" indicated slavery, and "rare find" and "desirable neighborhood" indicated areas without minorities.

2. **Religion.** Phrases such as "apartment complex with chapel" or "kosher meals available" do not, on their face, state a preference for persons who might use such facilities. Prior to HUD's memo, groups were advising that any reference in an ad to religion would violate the federal Fair Housing Act.

3. **Sex.** Use of the terms "master bedroom," "mother-in-law suite," and "bachelor apartment" does not violate the act because they are commonly used physical descriptions.

4. **Handicap.** Descriptions of properties such as "great view," "fourth-floor walk-up," and "walk-in closets" do not violate the act. Services or facilities such as "jogging trails" or references to neighborhoods such as "walk to bus stop" do not violate the act. Because many handicapped individuals cannot perform these activities, it was formerly thought that references to walking, biking, jogging, and so on would violate the law. It also is acceptable to describe the conduct required of residents, such as "nonsmoking" or "sober." You can't, however, say "nonsmokers" or "no alcoholics" because these describe persons, not barred activities. You can advertise accessibility features such as "wheelchair ramp."

5. **Familial status.** While advertisements may not contain a limitation on the number or ages of children or state a preference for adults, couples, or singles, you are not "facially discriminatory" by advertising properties as "2-BR, cozy, family room," services and facilities with "no bicycles allowed," or neighborhoods with "quiet streets."

The HUD memo still leaves a great deal unanswered; however, HUD seems to indicate that the rule is one of reasonableness. If an ordinary person would feel an ad favored or disfavored a protected group, it would be discriminatory. Organizations have come up with updated lists that tend to reflect this thinking.

FIGURE 8.4:   Advertising Guidelines

STATE OF CALIFORNIA
BUREAU OF REAL ESTATE

LICENSE DISCLOSURE REQUIREMENTS FOR MORTGAGE ADVERTISING

RE 858 (REV. 3/16)

The following chart shows the required disclosures of licensure based on the purpose of the mortgage loan advertisement. In addition to the information in the chart, the requirements of Business and Professions Code (B&P) Section 10140.6(b) apply to all first point-of-contact materials designed to solicit the creation of a professional relationship between the licensee and consumer.
Please note: All disclosure requirements of licensure can be located in B&P Sections 10140.6, 10235.5, 10236.4, and Title 10, beginning with Section 2770, of the Regulations of the Real Estate Commissioner. (See below.)

Advertising Media

The disclosures are required in all advertising including, but not limited to, flyers, mailers, TV, radio, newspapers, magazines, yellow pages, and the Internet.

Questions?

If you have questions, please call the Mortgage Loan Activities section at (916) 263-8941 or write to: Bureau of Real Estate, Attn: Mortgage Loan Activities, P.O. Box 137000, Sacramento, CA 95813-7000.

Required Disclosures	Advertising Purposes		First Point of Contact Only (Business cards, email, etc.)
	Soliciting for Borrowers	Soliciting for Investors/Lenders and/or Note Purchasers	
Phrasing	CA Bur of Real Estate – Real Estate Broker; or Real Estate Broker – CA Bur of Real Estate **- AND -** Broker, agent, Realtor, loan correspondent or abbreviations bro., agt., or other similar terms or abbreviations	Broker, agent, Realtor, loan correspondent or abbreviations bro., agt., or other similar terms or abbreviations	Broker, agent, Realtor, loan correspondent or abbreviations bro., agt., or other similar terms or abbreviations
CalBRE License Number	8-digit license number of each licensee in the advertisement **- AND -** 8-digit license number of the broker	8-digit license number of each licensee in the advertisement **- AND -** 8-digit license number of the broker	8-digit license number of each licensee in the advertisement
NMLS Unique Identifier*	Unique identifier of each licensee in the advertisement* **- AND -** Unique identifier of the broker*	N/A	Unique identifier of each licensee disseminating the materials* (Unique identifier of the employing broker or corporation *not* required)
Font Size Requirement	No less than the smallest font used in the advertisement	No less than the smallest font used in the advertisement	No less than the smallest font used in the advertisement

*Only applies to residential mortgage loan originators, as defined in Section 10166.01 of the Business and Professions Code.

PERTINENT CODES & REGULATIONS

Business and Professions Code

Disclosure of Licensed Status in Advertising
10140.6. (a) A real estate licensee shall not publish, circulate, distribute, or cause to be published, circulated, or distributed in any newspaper or periodical, or by mail, any matter pertaining to any activity for which a real estate license is required that does not contain a designation disclosing that he or she is performing acts for which a real estate license is required.

(b) (1) A real estate licensee shall disclose his or her license identification number and, if that licensee is a mortgage loan originator, the unique identifier assigned to that licensee by the Nationwide Mortgage Licensing System and Registry, on all solicitation materials intended to be the first point of contact with consumers and on real property purchase agreements when acting as an agent in those transactions.

The commissioner may adopt regulations identifying the materials in which a licensee must disclose a license identification number and, if that licensee is a mortgage loan originator, the unique identifier assigned to that licensee by the Nationwide Mortgage Licensing System and Registry.

(2) For purposes of this section, "solicitation materials intended to be the first point of contact with consumers" includes business cards, stationery, advertising fliers, and other materials designed to solicit the creation of a professional relationship between the licensee and a consumer, and excludes an advertisement in print or electronic media and "for sale" signs.

(3) Nothing in this section shall be construed to limit or change the requirement described in Section 10236.4 as applicable to real estate brokers.

FIGURE 8.4 (continued):   Advertising Guidelines

RE 858 – Reverse

(c) The provisions of this section shall not apply to classified rental advertisements reciting the telephone number at the premises of the property offered for rent or the address of the property offered for rent.

(d) "Mortgage loan originator," "unique identifier," and "Nationwide Mortgage Licensing System and Registry" have the meanings set forth in Section 10166.01.

Advertising of Loan – License Disclosure
10235.5. (a) No real estate licensee or mortgage loan originator shall place an advertisement disseminated primarily in this state for a loan unless there is disclosed within the printed text of that advertisement, or the oral text in the case of a radio or television advertisement, the Bureau of Real Estate license number and the unique identifier assigned to that licensee by the Nationwide Mortgage Licensing System and Registry under which the loan would be made or arranged.

(b) "Mortgage loan originator," "unique identifier," and "Nationwide Mortgage Licensing System and Registry" have the meanings set forth in Section 10166.01.

Disclosure of License Number in Advertisement; License Number and CalBRE License Information Telephone Number in Disclosure Statements
10236.4. (a) In compliance with Section 10235.5, every licensed real estate broker shall also display his or her license number on all advertisements where there is a solicitation for borrowers or potential investors. Every mortgage loan originator, as defined in Section 10166.01, shall also display the unique identifier assigned to that individual by the Nationwide Mortgage Licensing System and Registry on all advertisements where there is a solicitation for borrowers.

(b) The disclosures required by Sections 10232.4 and 10240 shall include the licensee's license number, the mortgage loan originator's unique identifier, if applicable, and the department's license information telephone number. *

(c) "Mortgage loan originator," "unique identifier," and "Nationwide Mortgage Licensing System and Registry" have the meanings set forth in Section 10166.01.

[*The CalBRE's licensing information telephone number is not required on advertisements for loan activities. The number is required to be on the Lender/Purchaser Disclosure Statement and the Mortgage Loan Disclosure Statement.]

Commissioner's Regulations

2770.1. Advertising - License Designation.
Use of the terms broker, agent, Realtor, loan correspondent or the abbreviations bro., agt., or other similar terms or abbreviations, is deemed sufficient identification to fulfill the designation requirements of Section 10140.6(a) and (c) of the Business and Professions Code.

Use of the terms and abbreviations set forth above does not satisfy the requirements of Sections 10235.5 and 17539.4 of the Code.

2773. Disclosure of License Identification Number on Solicitation Materials – First Point of Contact with Consumers.

(a) A real estate broker or salesperson, when engaging in acts for which a license is required, shall disclose its, his or her eight (8) digit real estate license identification number on all solicitation materials intended to be the first point of contact with consumers. If the name of more than one licensee appears in the solicitation, the license identification number of each licensee shall be disclosed. The license numbers of employing brokers or corporate brokers whose names or logos or trademarks appear on solicitation materials along with the names and license numbers of licensed employees or broker associates do not need to appear on those materials.

Solicitation materials intended to be the first point of contact with consumers, and in which a licensee must disclose a license identification number, include the following:

(1) Business cards;

(2) Stationery;

(3) Websites owned, controlled, and/or maintained by the soliciting real estate licensee; and

(4) Promotional and advertising fliers, brochures, email and regular mail, leaflets, and any marketing or promotional materials designed to solicit the creation of a professional relationship between the licensee and a consumer, or which is intended to incentivize, induce or entice a consumer to contact the licensee about any service for which a license is required.

The type size of the license identification number shall be no smaller than the smallest size type used in the solicitation material.

(b) For the purposes of Business and Professions Code Section 10140.6, solicitation materials do not include the following:

(1) Advertisements in electronic media (including, without limitation, radio, cinema and television ads, and the opening section of streaming video and audio);

(2) Print advertising in any newspaper or periodical; and

(3) "For Sale" signs placed on or around a property intended to alert the public the property is available for lease, purchase or trade.

2847.3. Disclosure of License and Issuing Department.
(a) Use of either of the following statements shall satisfy the requirements of Sections 10235.5 and 17539.4 of the Code.

(1) Real estate broker, California Bureau of Real Estate.

(2) California Bureau of Real Estate, real estate broker. The words "California" and "Bureau" may be abbreviated only as "CA" or "CAL" or "Calif" and "Bur". A dash (-) may be used in lieu of the comma appearing in the statements set forth above in paragraphs (1) and (2).

(b) The type size of the statement as set forth in subdivision (a) will also satisfy the designation requirements of Section 10140.6 of the Code.

(c) Use of either statement as set forth in subdivision (a) will also satisfy the designation requirements of Section 10140.6(a) and (c) of the Code.

Supervising social media advertising

Real estate licensees should take care to ensure that the names on Instagram, Facebook, and other social media accounts don't give the impression that the salesperson is acting without being under the supervision of a licensed broker.

For example salesperson Betty Thomas at XYZ Brokerage, Inc., should not have an Instagram account that gives the impression that she is operating on her own. One could argue that www.instagram.com/bettythomasrealestatebroker or www.instagram.com/bettythomasrealty could be deemed deceptive and against the rules of the real estate commissioner if obtained by a salesperson.

Ideas of what to post on social media.   As you start your career in real estate, it is important to make a decision as to how your accounts on social media are going to be set up.

- Are your social media accounts going to be separated into personal and business, or are you going to use one account for both?

- If they are going to be split, how often are you going to post to your business account? If you are going to use the same accounts for both, what percentage do you see being devoted to each aspect of your life?

Most social media experts agree that your business posts don't always have to consist of hard-selling content. You can mix lighter material with the fact that you are in business and want more customers.

Here's one idea for posting:

- Photos of houses or properties that you have just sold or listed. As a new real estate licensee, you might not have properties that you have sold or listed yet. In that case, consider posting pictures of properties that your company has listed or sold recently and the caption could be, "Our team just listed 123 Any Street! Message me for details!"

This lets your follower base know that you are active and in the real estate business.

It is a common marketing strategy among real estate agents to send just listed/sold postcards to a given database upon obtaining signatures on a contract. In the world of digital marketing, it should also be standard that a real estate agent post on all social media of their recent success completing a transaction. This means an Instagram, Facebook, and Twitter message announcing your recent transaction.

ADVERTISING BUDGET

Every successful real estate office has developed a system for budgeting its expenses. One of the expenses that must be accounted for is advertising. Advertising is one of the most important steps in the marketing of real property, but it does cost money. Soon after starting in the business, a broker learns that a certain amount of the firm's income dollar must be allocated to this item to maximize returns.

WEB LINK

@

An advertising budget involves more than just the number of dollars to be spent in advertising; it should determine how the dollars should be allocated. According to HomeGain (www.homegain.com), in September 2005 the typical real estate advertising budget was allocated in the following manner:

- Newspapers   39%
- Other print   20%
- Direct mail   17%
- Online   11%
- Yard signs   8%
- Yellow Pages   4%
- Telemarketing   1%

HomeGain believed that a more appropriate budget should be as follows:

- Newspapers   10%
- Other print   5%
- Direct mail   10%

- Online   52%

- Yard signs   20%

- Yellow Pages   3%

- Telemarketing   0%

HomeGains' projections of how a real estate advertising budget should be allocated have been largely realized. According to Borrell Associates, by 2015, real estate agents and brokers had spent nearly 75% of their advertising budget online.

The advertising dollar budget of an office is influenced by the advertising costs within a community, as well as by market conditions. As a rule, the time to increase advertising is when market sales are increasing. It is rare for expansion of advertising in a declining market to make economic sense, although reallocation of expenses should be an ongoing consideration.

Many offices plan their advertising budget as a percentage of their anticipated income dollar. As an example, a firm might plan to use 20% of the office share of commissions (the **company dollar**) for advertising. Because economic changes can be rapid, a budget should be adjusted to reflect market change. In a down market, while total advertising dollars will decrease, the percentage of the company dollar spent on advertising will increase. Similarly, in an active market where total ad dollars will likely increase, the percentage of advertising costs to the company dollar will decrease.

A number of agents who charge reduced fees make up for some of their fee reduction by charging owners advanced advertising expenses. Expenditures are then made with the owner's funds.

SUMMARY

Advertising is the process of calling people's attention to a product or service. The real estate industry could not exist without the ability to disseminate information.

Advertising falls into two broad categories: institutional, which is basically advertising to promote the goodwill of the firm, and specific or operational advertising, which is to sell or lease a particular property.

The AIDA approach to advertising is basically that an effective ad should gain **A**ttention, **I**nterest the party intended, create **D**esire, and result in **A**ction. The five basic tenets or guidelines for advertising are as follows:

1. Advertise the right property

2. Know when to advertise

3. Choose the right market

4. Use the proper media

5. Use effective advertising techniques

Advertising really begins with the salesperson's personal advertising that includes a name tag, business cards, and magnetic car signs.

While a broad array of media choices are available, most of a firm's advertising budget was formerly devoted to classified advertising. To be effective, a classified ad must have a highly desirable feature in the heading or else have an attention-getting heading. While negative ads are generally not successful, in real estate they may be very effective. Fixer-upper ads that emphasize what is wrong with a property often receive an exceptional rate of response. Internet advertising is considered more effective than print ads at a fraction of the cost and has replaced print ads in budget emphasis.

Display advertising, because of cost, is more appropriate for expensive properties or large developments. Specialty magazine ads can also be effective.

The For Sale sign is effective at relatively low cost. Direct mail can be effective, but there is a high cost per contact.

Other advertising includes telephone directories, press releases, newsletters, and specialty gifts.

The internet is the most effective media today including personal and company websites, property websites, classified ad websites, blogs, and social networking sites.

It is essential that a firm understand the effectiveness of its advertising. By keeping track of responses, we can learn which medium or approach is most effective for which type of property. This knowledge will allow advertising planning based on past results, not just by intuition.

As a licensee, you are responsible for knowing the legal implications of real estate advertising. Licensees are prohibited from false, misleading, and discriminatory advertising. Of particular interest is the Truth in Lending Act. Besides prohibiting bait-and-switch advertising, advertising the amount or percentage of down payment, the number of payments or period of repayment, or the amount of payment or finance charge all will trigger the full-disclosure provision of this law. Certain words may have discriminatory connotations, so care must be taken in describing properties.

Today, the largest portion of the advertising budget is related to the internet. The advertising budget of an office will vary based on advertising costs within the market area. Many offices plan advertising based on a percentage of anticipated office income.

CLASS DISCUSSION TOPICS

1. In addition to a photograph, what other ways can agents make their business card stand out?

2. Prepare two classified ads, one with a feature heading and the other with an attention-getting heading, to sell the home in which you live.

3. Discuss all the ways a typical real estate office in your area advertises (include both institutional advertising and specific advertising).

4. Check the websites of local brokers. Evaluate the sites as to quality, giving your reasons for your evaluation.

5. From the cautionary words shown on the Miami Valley word and phrase list, pick out a word that could be used in both a discriminatory and a nondiscriminatory manner and be prepared to give examples.

6. Bring to class one current-events article dealing with some aspect of real estate practice for class discussion.

UNIT 8 QUIZ

1. The AIDA approach does NOT include
   a. attention.
   b. demand.
   c. interest.
   d. action.

2. Personal advertising includes
   a. name tags.
   b. blog websites.
   c. car signs.
   d. all of these.

3. What does the term *logo* refer to?
   a. Your firm name
   b. An identifying design or symbol
   c. Length of gross opportunity, which refers to the time span of attention generated by an ad
   d. None of these

4. Blind ads are ads that fail to include
   a. a price.
   b. the address of property.
   c. broker identification.
   d. property specifics.

5. The MOST cost-effective advertising medium for selling a home likely would be
   a. television.
   b. the internet.
   c. classified newspaper ads.
   d. billboards.

6. Classified ads are different from most other forms of real estate advertising because they are
    a. actually sought out by the reader.
    b. ineffective for expensive homes.
    c. less reader-selective than other printed ads.
    d. unemotional.

7. Real estate professionals know that ads that tell about the problems of a property are
    a. a waste of advertising dollars.
    b. likely to give a firm a bad name.
    c. unlikely to attract any calls.
    d. none of these.

8. An advertiser with an extremely low advertising budget would most likely avoid
    a. press releases.
    b. For Sale signs.
    c. billboards.
    d. the internet.

9. Which statement is *FALSE* about display ads?
    a. Readers' eyes tend to move from upper left to lower right.
    b. One large picture is generally more effective than several smaller ones.
    c. Short words are easier to read than long words.
    d. Capital letters are easier to read than lowercase letters.

10. In preparing display ads, a good advertiser should
    a. eliminate as much white space in the ad as possible for maximum effect.
    b. use different logos in different ads to avoid repetition.
    c. use no more than two typefaces in an ad.
    d. avoid using a serif typeface in the text.

THE BUYER AND THE PROPERTY SHOWING

LEARNING OBJECTIVES

When you have completed this unit, you will be able to

- explain why a call from a prospective buyer resulting from a sign differs from an inquiry resulting from an ad or website;

- describe how to turn inquiries into firm appointments;

- explain how to prepare for your first meeting with prospective buyers and how to qualify these prospective buyers regarding needs, motivation, and financial ability;

- describe how to reduce security risks; and

- describe how to use qualifying information in selecting homes to view and understand that qualifying is an ongoing process.

KEY TERMS

back-end ratio	front-end ratio	open-end questions
closed-end questions	LTV	prequalify
floor time	negative motivation	

THE APPOINTMENT

Your initial buyer contact from advertising generally takes the form of a telephone call. Prospective buyers generally call about ads, For Sale signs, or your website picture and description, rather than coming to your office for general information. Your goal regarding the call is not to sell the property—no one *buys* property over the telephone. Your goal is to turn that call into an appointment so you can be in a position in which a sale is possible.

A call is a valuable commodity. A telephone inquiry from which you fail to obtain an appointment or, at the very least, the caller's name and telephone number is a total loss of overhead dollars. If you were to compute all office overhead, including advertising, and divide that monthly figure by the number of telephone inquiries your office receives in the month, you would understand how much it really costs to bring in each inquiry. Wasting a telephone inquiry might well be equivalent to throwing $100 or $200 into the wind. Good telephone technique reduces the percentage of wasted calls.

Many offices have designated periods of **floor time**, or *opportunity time*, where agents are given inquiries in rotation. If you have floor time, be prepared to turn telephone inquiries into appointments.

Telephone inquiries are not limited to office hours and floor time. Calls can be at all hours and on home phones and personal cell phones. In addition, you will receive inquiries by email and fax messages.

Prepare to Receive Telephone Calls

You should be prepared to field inquiries at all times. Have copies of both your own current ads and your office ads from the prior weekend, as well as all office listings, so that they are readily accessible. Make notations on ads so you know what property each ad refers to. Review the listings so the information is fresh in your mind. Also, consider likely **switch property** priced up to 20% more or less than advertised properties. In the event you reveal some feature that "turns off" the person inquiring, you need something at hand to switch to.

Have a map of your community readily available with numbered adhesive markers referencing all your office listings. If you have wall space near your desk, this is an excellent place for this map, but you also want one to carry with you. This map is essential because callers on For Sale signs often have the wrong street but usually the right general area. Consider switch property for sign inquiries. As a general rule, you know that callers on For Sale signs

- like or would be satisfied with the area, and

- like or would be satisfied with the appearance of a home with a similar exterior.

Handling the Inquiry

> Switch properties are other properties that a caller about a particular property is likely to be interested in.

People calling about ads usually buy property other than the property they initially inquired about. The same is true for calls prompted by For Sale signs. This is why it is important to know your inventory. You will be able to readily switch your discussion to appropriate properties as necessary. For this reason, as you begin your real estate career, it would be wise to spend time each day physically visiting properties for sale and studying the available inventory.

People who call in reference to a sign might not tell you that a price you have quoted is beyond their means. In fact, they might even ask for more information. However, you won't know this unless you mention a switch property priced significantly less than the property called about. If the callers show interest in the switch property, the original property that they called about may be too expensive. As to switch properties, keep in mind that while callers on For Sale signs are often looking beyond their means, callers on priced ads are often hoping to buy a property that is less than they can afford to pay.

If a caller has viewed the property on the internet, you know that the caller likes the appearance of the property and the description seems to "fit" her needs. You also know that the property is priced within the range the caller expects to pay and that the property's location and address are satisfactory. Prospects who call about an internet posting are more likely to buy the property they are interested in than are prospects calling from other advertising. An internet inquiry is, therefore, a valuable inquiry because the callers have half-sold themselves on the property.

The following are some general rules about dealing with telephone inquiries from prospective buyers:

- Obtain the caller's name and telephone number

- Ask questions about family size and needs

- Find out what interested them about the ad

- Find out what the prospective buyer is interested in and why

- Find out if the caller has been prequalified or approved for a loan and for how much

- Hold the details—give a little more information than was in the ad. The less information given, the greater the chance of ending the telephone call with an appointment.

- Answer home elimination questions with a question. For example, if a caller asks, "Does that house have three bedrooms plus a den?" your answer should be "[Mrs. Jones], do you need three bedrooms plus a den?" If the caller asks the price, you should ask, "What price range were you interested in?" If the questioning reveals complete unsuitability of the property, you should be able to switch to a similar property that has the required features.

- Close on an appointment. The choice given should be what time, not whether the caller wants to see the property.

- Set the place for the meeting. There are only two places for an initial meeting with a potential buyer:

  1. At your office (preferred)

  2. At the buyer's home

(You may meet a prospective buyer at a property that the buyer wishes to purchase after having successfully preapproved them with a lender.)

■ Include mention of other property that may interest the prospects. This will help reduce the likelihood of a no-show.

■ Keep the call short and end the call after the appointment is set.

For an internet inquiry, because the caller generally wants to see the property, there should be no difficulty setting up the appointment.

Lovely 3BR, 2-bath ranch home
in Willow Springs.
Reduced to $389,500.
Owner financing available.

Oasis Realty   760-976-4132

www.oasispropertytour.com

A suggested approach to calls on the ad shown is as follows:

My name is Howard Young. What is your name, please?

Note: If the ad indicated a web address, you want to know if the caller viewed the property on the internet. If the caller has, treat the call like gold because the caller is already half-sold on the property.

Yes, that is a lovely three-bedroom home, Mrs. Jones. How large is your family, [Mr./Mrs.] Jones?

That home is in one of the nicer areas of Willow Springs. Is that the area you are interested in?

Are there any other areas that you are considering?

That home is priced at $389,500. Is that the general price range you are interested in?

I can arrange to show this lovely home as well as another home that I think will interest you 5:00 pm today, or would 6:00 pm be more convenient for you?

Notice that the choice is the time, not whether they want to see the property. If your prospective caller indicates neither time is convenient, ask when it would be convenient to show the property.

If the caller indicates he is not free at all that day, say:

Let's set it up for tomorrow at 5:00 pm. I'll meet you and your spouse at my office. Our office is on the corner of Third Street and Lake Boulevard. You can't miss our orange sign.

Have you been prequalified for a loan? (If yes, "For how much?")

(If not), If you could come 15 minutes early, I can get you prequalified so in the event you wish to buy a home, the seller will be more likely to accept any offer you make. Can you come a little early?

If the caller doesn't object, you have a definite appointment. Whenever you have an appointment for the next day, call the prospects in the morning of that day to remind them of the appointment. When you call, be enthusiastic and tell them you have another property you feel they also will be interested in. This will reduce the no-shows. Never indicate you have another property if you don't have one.

> Get more information from the caller than you give.

As you see, asking questions gives you control of the conversation. You get an appointment without giving out too much information and without undue delay and you have set the mood for buying not just looking.

By mentioning another house to Mr. or Mrs. Jones, you probably aroused some interest and set the stage for alternative properties, if necessary. Now say:

I will see you and [Mr./Mrs.] Jones at my office at 6:00 pm. Do you have a pencil and paper handy? Our office is at [1911 Elm Street across from the Security Bank]. Are you familiar with the area? [If not, give specific directions.] Again, my name is Howard Young. I look forward to seeing you.

Your question is about the caller's knowledge of your office location, not where you will meet the caller. You are telling, not asking for, the place of the meeting.

You can see from this sample script that the agent didn't really give information beyond what was in the ad. Instead, the agent asked for information. The call was kept very short and was ended as soon as an appointment had been set.

As we have stated, there are only two places to meet a prospective buyer for the first time. These are at the buyer's home or in the agent's office. Some agents like to visit the buyer's home to get a better insight into the buyer's lifestyle and needs, but the agent's office allows for an uninterrupted qualifying process controlled by the agent. If you are to meet the prospects at their residence, you should let someone in your office know where you are going and whom you are to meet. For safety reasons, you can also check if that person is a resident at that address. You can go to www.msn. intelius.com and click on "Reverse Lookup." Enter the address to get the occupants' names. If you must meet prospective buyers at their homes, you should complete the buyer financial qualifying process before you discuss properties. With wireless access to your MLS, you can go directly from the prospect's home to properties.

Getting a Caller's Name

In some offices, telephone calls are answered by a receptionist, who usually will get a caller's name for you. At times callers will, for one reason or another, resist giving their names. You will also encounter calls where caller ID is blocked. If there is resistance to giving a name, don't make an issue of it because there are a number of simple techniques you can use to get callers' names.

> Let me put you on hold while I get some information that should interest you. In case we get disconnected, what is your telephone number so I can call you back?

If you get the telephone number, there should be no caller hesitancy in proving a name.

If the call results in an appointment, try the following:

> In the unlikely event I get tied up for some reason, what is your home number so I can call you to reset the appointment?

Even though you may have the caller's name and number with your caller ID, you want the caller to give you the number. Callers who give you their number will probably also give their name if asked.

Another effective way to get callers' names owes its effectiveness to the fact that it is nonthreatening:

> I have a flyer with a photo of that property, as well as information on several other properties, one in particular that I feel you will be interested in. Would it be all right if I prepared a packet of information and put it in the mail or emailed it to you?

If you offer sincere, knowledgeable assistance, this nonthreatening approach of mailing the information will result in a positive response in 90% of cases in which prospects initially hesitate to give a name. Callers must now give you a name and an address or email address. Also ask if they would like to receive email alerts as to new listings as soon as they come on the market. Once you have prospects' names, they will provide the other information you need.

If you have not been able to obtain an appointment, the following approach can be very effective in keeping communications open:

> I email pictures and details of new listings to prospective buyers who request them. These are sent out before the property is advertised. Are you interested in being alerted to new listings and having first chance?

Not every contact is a good contact. Reluctance to give a name is often a signal that the caller is not a serious buyer, but it could also mean that the caller is afraid of being harassed by overzealous salespeople. The call could be for information not related to buying, such as a call from a curious neighbor. Your greatest efforts should be directed toward callers who are open as to identity and needs rather than those who are secretive. Your maximum efforts should be directed toward probabilities rather than remote possibilities.

"I Just Want the Address"

You will have callers who haven't used the internet and want the address of the property so they can drive by for a quick look. Generally, the caller wants an exterior look to either eliminate the property from consideration or make a decision to view it. Unfortunately, a drive-by might eliminate you as well as the property from the caller's consideration. As a response to such a request, consider:

> Let me send you some interior photos of the house and back garden. The street view alone doesn't do it justice. What is your email address?

If you are unable to get an appointment with callers and they still want the property address, it is good policy to get the callers' name and telephone number before giving out the address. This is very important because should prospective buyers not be particularly interested in the property from a drive-by look, they would be lost to you for future contact. However, if you have a name and telephone number, you can encourage prospects to drive by the property and also note any other properties nearby with For Sale signs that appear interesting. Let the callers know you will call them back for their impressions of the property and to obtain information for them on other properties that appeared desirable.

Technology and Caller Data

Technology has gone beyond caller ID where you only have the name and number of a caller. It is now possible to know where the caller lives, family size, and even financial data. This information is now available, not just for the calls you answer but also for calls that were unanswered because your line was busy or prospects called and failed to leave a message. If you desire information on such services, one service provider is *www.callsource.com*.

Locking In the Caller

When callers are motivated buyers, there is a good likelihood that they will continue looking through ads, as well as websites, and will contact other agents. You can't do anything about calls made before prospective buyers called you, but it is relatively easy for you to keep them off the phone.

> [Mrs. Smith], if you have the time, I would appreciate it if you could check our website at www.palmspringshomes.com and the classified ads and note any other properties that interest you. Bring the website information and the paper with you when we meet at [4 pm today], and I'll be able to give you information on other properties. Perhaps you might want to see one or more of them. By having you check what interests you, I can also learn a great deal about what you desire and will be able to find the home you will want to own.

This keeps the possible buyer off the phone. It might possibly give you other property to show and provide information on the buyer's desires.

After the appointment—keep the prospect off the phone.

Email Contacts

If you receive an email contact about a property on the web, you will likely also get a name, which allows you to call rather than email your response. It is easier to set up an appointment when in direct phone contact than it is by email. Contacts about a particular property shown on your website should be treated like gold. Be prepared to close on an appointment to show the property.

Can't Get an Appointment

If you can't turn a call into an appointment, use it to set the stage for further contact.

> Would it be all right if I called you should a property be listed that [has five bedrooms and is priced under $300,000]?

This approach will generally result in a positive response and a name and telephone number if you have otherwise been unable to obtain this information.

Similarly, you could ask:

> Would it be all right if I emailed you some information on other properties that I think might interest you?

This nonthreatening approach is likely to receive a positive response.

You should also ask the caller if it would be all right to add them to an email alert system through the MLS that will send them automated information of any new listings that you feel might interest the caller. It's a nonthreatening approach, and you now have a reason to call to discuss any email property you presented. Of course, you should again try to set up an appointment.

Internet Leads

When the buyers' inquiry is from an ad they saw online, they may or may not be serious about purchasing the given property. Previously many real estate brokers and agents would believe that internet leads were worthless, because they didn't take the time to pick up the phone and make an actual call. However, perspective has now shifted as most buyers start their home search online and it is quite common practice for an interested party to make initial contact electronically rather than with a phone call. Therefore, these leads should be taken seriously as well.

The same rules apply with regard to internet leads as they apply to other leads. Here are some best practices with regard to handling internet inquiries:

1. Responsiveness is mandatory. In the age of instantaneous information, your prospects are used to getting fast responses to their inquiries. The buyer is probably surfing around many different websites, and often the most responsive agent is the one that will win.

2. Continuous follow-up is critical with web inquiries. Your prospects are not only on your website. They are visiting the sites of all your competitors too. Couple this with the fact that web inquiries are often long sales cycles, follow-up is mandatory.

3. These buyers should be set up through an automatic drip system in the MLS. Most MLS systems are going to have a mechanism wherein the agent can input the criteria of the buyers and the system will automatically email them listings that match their search. This allows the agent to leverage the technology in the MLS without actually having to pull manual searches each day.

THE MEETING

Your Safety

Unfortunately, personal safety has become an issue in recent years. Agents have been attacked by people posing as "buyers." To reduce jeopardizing your personal safety, meet prospective buyers at your office whenever possible. People who have anything on their minds other than a purchase will generally not want to show themselves to other people. After they come to your office and undergo a qualifying process, the likelihood of a safety problem will be significantly reduced.

Some agents ask to see photo identification to make certain the person is who he claims to be.

Some agents like to introduce prospects to other agents or their broker, as potential troublemakers won't risk being exposed. Other safety precautions include notifying your office or voice mail of a change in a showing schedule, always leaving the front door of a dwelling unlocked during the showing, and having the prospect walk ahead of you. If you must meet a prospect for the first time at a property, you want to make certain an owner, tenant, or another agent from your office will be present.

Always let someone know where you are going. Some offices have a code. As an example, an agent could call an office and say, "Could you check the red file on 1250 North Main Street? I'm there now." The words "red file" could be an alert for agents who feel they are in trouble.

Consider making yourself less attractive as a victim. Avoid ostentatious jewelry; a Gucci bag and/or Rolex watch may be signs of success, but they could also make you a target of opportunity. Stiletto heels or cowboy boots may be fashionable, but they inhibit your ability to move quickly when required.

Many agents now carry pepper spray or electronic devices that emit a loud piercing noise. A loud whistle can also be used.

Avoid parking in the driveway of the property you are showing. Besides showing disrespect for the property, you place yourself in a position where your car can be blocked in case of an emergency.

Never drive to a property in a client's vehicle. If the client insists on driving, take two vehicles.

Some agents take photos of clients and vehicles showing license plate numbers and email the photos to their office.

You lessen your personal danger by telling the prospect that someone else from your office will be arriving shortly.

Safety Issues

Many times, the excitement of getting new clients and meeting them overshadows thoughts of individual safety.

Best practices surrounding safety.   Salespeople should be encouraged to do the following:

1. Require 100% of all potential buyers to be preapproved by a lender before scheduling a tour. Remind your buyer that in the vast majority of cases, the preapproval process is done at no cost or obligation.

2. Always keep your customer in sight while on tour.

3. Let your office manager, receptionist, or another agent know where you are going to be and who you are going to show property to.

4. Have a plan of exit if you feel unsafe in any way.

Brokers should be able to add to the above based on local custom to tailor their own safety program for their sales staff.

Prepare to Meet the Prospective Buyer

Before you meet your prospective buyers for the first time, think through the qualifying process. You also might want to make some tentative appointments to show specific properties.

Schedule your first meeting with a prospective buyer at your office.

Because the qualifying process often reveals that properties inquired about do not really meet the needs, resources, or both of the prospective buyers, you want the owners to understand that the appointments are only tentative at this time and may need to be canceled or postponed.

Make certain you have a "qualifying room," free and clean, with fresh coffee or soft drinks available. We suggest you qualify prospective buyers in a separate office or closing room. This reduces distractions and provides a chance to learn about the prospects without interruption.

First Impressions

When you meet with prospective buyers, make a mental point of remembering their names. By repeating their last name several times to yourself and thinking of people you know with the same first names, you won't have to ask the buyers their names when writing an offer to purchase.

Make certain you are pronouncing names correctly. If you are uncertain, ask. Because people like to be addressed by their names, use them frequently during the discussions. Explain that you will be able to save the prospective buyers a great deal of time by spending just a few minutes to decide what they really need in a home. Serve bottles of water or large cups of hot or iced coffee (or tea). Seat the clients close to you during your qualifying session because it gives you more control.

Needs and Interests

Keep in mind that the primary purpose of this meeting is for you to gain information. When you are talking, it should usually involve asking a question. People like people who are interested in them, and chances are they're not really interested in you. Their interest is in what you can do for them. To communicate effectively, you must ask **open-end questions** that require explanations and reasons rather than **closed-end questions** that can be answered with a simple "yes" or "no" but fail to inform you as to why. Ask about hobbies, special interests and pets. You could be wasting time in showing a house with a small backyard if the prospects own two Great Danes. Keep in mind that the only dumb question is the one you failed to ask.

Some agents use the FORD acronym as a guide to learning about their prospects:

- Family

- Occupation

- Recreation

- Dreams

Many agents use a qualification form so they won't forget the information prospective buyers give them. The use of a form also reduces the chances of forgetting to obtain some needed information. Figure 9.1 is an example of a form you might consider using. You can also put the information directly into your contact management system.

FIGURE 9.1:   **Prospective Buyer Confidential Information Sheet**

Prospective Buyer Confidential Information Sheet

Name(s) _____ Phone no. _____

Fax no. _____ E-mail _____

Address _____

Size of family _____

Names and ages of children or other dependents living with you: _____
_____
_____

Pets _____

Initial contact with the firm was because of (advertisement, Web sites, sign, referral, etc.)
_____

Present address _____

How long at above address? _____

Do you presently own your own home? _____

If yes, must you sell before you buy? _____

If yes, is your present home currently listed for sale? _____

With _____

How long has it been on the market? _____

Your reason for seeking to buy a new home _____

What features do you like about your present home? _____

What features don't you like about your present home? _____

Why? _____

What feature(s) do you consider to be most important for your new home? _____
_____

Why? _____
_____
_____

What are your hobbies or special interests? _____
_____
_____
_____

Have you qualified for or been turned down for a home loan within the past year? _____
_____

If you qualified for a loan, what was the name of the firm and loan amount? _____
_____

How soon would you like to be in your new home? _____

> ### Buyer Qualifying Process
> The qualifying process is really a three-part process involving the following:
> 1. Needs and interests of the buyers
> 2. Buyers' motivation
> 3. Preapproval by an institutional lender

The form tells you the needs of buyers, as well as why they are buyers. Keep in mind that qualifying buyers is a continuing process leading right up to receiving an offer. By asking for reactions to homes shown, you gain insight into what prospective buyers really want. The reality could be far different from what a buyer claims to want. Your contact management systems should not only include the information you obtain about prospect needs and interests but also indicate the properties they have seen and their reactions to the showings.

A simple buyers-needs evaluation can be made by just having the buyers list the 10 most important features they want in their new home. Then have them rate the features in order of importance. This rating will help you in choosing homes to show, as well as in obtaining a purchase offer.

Financial qualifying.   You should know FHA and VA loan limits and down payment requirements if your prospective buyers are likely to be eligible for these types of financing. You also should know down payment requirements for various types of loans.

> You should have an in-depth understanding of current qualifying ratios being used by lenders in your area. You should also understand how the FHA and VA qualify purchasers.

Lenders use the terms *front-end* and *back-end ratios*. **Front-end ratio** customarily refers to the ratio of a buyer's housing costs to income. Generally, gross income is used for front-end qualifying. For many institutional lenders, the front-end ratio is 28%, which means the *buyers' total monthly housing costs (principal, interest, taxes, and insurance [PITI]) cannot exceed 28% of their gross income*.

total monthly payment ÷ gross monthly income = 28% or less

A person's total housing expense plus long-term debt obligations cannot exceed 36% of gross income (**back-end ratio**).

PITI + total monthly credit obligations ÷ gross monthly income
= 36% or less

Qualifying ratios will be covered in more detail in Unit 12.

Down payment requirements vary by the lender and type of loan. Lenders express the loan-to-value ratio by the acronym **LTV**. If the borrower pays for private mortgage insurance, the down payments requirement may be reduced.

Self-employed individuals frequently have difficulty qualifying for loans. Lenders often require that self-employed buyers furnish two years of tax returns with their loan applications. Although buyers may indicate to you or the lender that they make X dollars a year, the tax returns may reveal a very different financial profile. Self-employed buyers may have to consider homes for which seller financing is available, make a larger down payment, or be willing to pay a higher interest rate from a subprime lender.

The maximum loan for which they can qualify plus their down payment sets the maximum limit on housing that prospective buyers can purchase. Further details on financial qualification of buyers are included in Unit 12. Keep in mind that qualification ratios are not rigid. Lenders will make loans to individuals failing to meet qualification tactics when the type of loan, down payment, or interest rate is considered more favorable to the lender.

We recommend that you **prequalify** buyers or obtain lender preapproval whenever possible before you show properties. Failure to prequalify prospective buyers could result in showing the prospects homes they cannot afford. Besides resulting in wasted effort, it becomes difficult to sell the prospects less costly housing later.

By completing a prequalification online, you can get approval for a loan amount based on verification of given information.

You should be sending prequalification lending information to a lender you recommend before you leave your office to show a property. If you don't get an immediate answer, this is a reason for the prospective buyers to come back to your office after the showing. Also, by prequalifying a buyer, you have changed the buyers' attitude from looking to buying. Prequalifying buyers also reduces the likelihood that they will seek out other agents. Prequalifying buyers can make them your customers.

Start the lender financial qualification process before you leave to show homes to customers.

Should prospective buyers be reluctant to give financial information to you, have the prospects complete the computer loan qualification process themselves. They will be less reticent when providing the information directly to the lender.

Actual lender approval is based on more than income and expenses. Their credit score (FICO score) will determine if they will be given a loan, as well as the interest rate and down payment requirements.

Because of the mortgage crisis and its great many defaults, lenders are reluctant to lend to persons with any blemishes on their credit. You might have to consider lower-price homes so that the down payment available will be a larger percentage of the purchase price. Another possibility would be a lease option in which the buyers are lessees until they have enough equity to obtain financing.

If you handle the qualifying process in a professional manner, you will be setting the stage for the buyers to regard you as a professional and a person they can relate to. (Another advantage of financial qualifying is that you tend to eliminate "Lookie Lous.")

After the buyers' financial qualifying, it might become apparent that what the buyers indicate they need may not be possible based upon financial restrictions. Keep in mind what a buyer expresses as a need may be only a "want." The agent must not mislead buyers into believing they can fulfil a wish list when it is clearly not possible because of financial restrictions. Referring to property as a "starter home" allows buyers to keep their perfect dream home alive but postpone it for the future.

As an alternative, you can point out that you will show property with the potential of fulfilling the buyers' wishes through repair, renovation, or future expansion. Explain that their aspirations are within reach if they are able to visualize what a property can become.

Preparing the Buyer

During the financial qualification process, you discussed the down payment. Before you show property, you should discuss earnest money. Earnest money deposits are made with offers. Prospective buyers should understand that their check will be held uncashed until their offer is accepted. Ask a question that makes the prospective buyers visualize writing a check, such as the following:

> If we are fortunate and find the perfect home for you today, would you be able to make a deposit of [$] with your offer? Should we find the home that meets your needs, is there anything that would stop you from making a decision today?"

It is better to know about possible problems as soon as possible so that you can prepare to deal with them. It also lets the prospects anticipate buying rather than just looking.

Give prospective buyers a copy of the purchase contract your office uses before you leave the office. Ask them to look the form over at their convenience and explain that when you succeed in finding them a home they wish to purchase, this will be the form used. Buyers who receive the form up front are less likely to object to the form later, and signing it will be an easier task.

What Happens to the Buyers' Offer?

Buyers should understand that three things can happen when they make an offer:

1. Acceptance means that they have purchased a home.

2. A counteroffer from the owners gives the buyers the opportunity to accept it (and have the house), make their own counter to the counteroffer, or reject it.

3. Rejection of the offer means the entire earnest money deposit is returned to the offerors.

If you approach the qualifying process in an organized fashion, you should be able to start looking at homes less than an hour from the time prospective buyers arrive at your office.

Be certain to explain agencies and have your prospective buyers sign the agency form. (See Unit 3.) You should explain your disclosure obligations, as well as disclosures of the owner when buyers find a home that meets their needs.

You may decide that you can best serve your prospective buyer as a buyer's agent. If this is the case, you should discuss the benefits of exclusive buyer representation with your prospective buyers and obtain a buyer listing.

Planning Your Efforts

From your qualifying questions, you will have determined why the prospective buyers want to buy and if they can buy now. If they must sell a home first to become buyers, discuss an offer contingent on the sale of their own home should they find a house that meets their needs. If your prospects want to sell before they place an offer, you should still spend some time with them to whet their appetites for a new home. An advisable approach would be one showing session plus frequent phone calls about the progress of their own home sale and emails on new listings that you feel would be of interest.

If you know about a person's special interests, you can use this information in selecting homes for showing. As an example, if a prospective buyer has indicates a strong interest in physical fitness, showing a house with a room that is used or could be used as a workout room would be a wise choice.

When the author first began in real estate sales, he showed a listing sight unseen. The prospective buyers, a well-dressed couple with a young daughter, stopped at the office after seeing an ad that indicated the home was located on a large wooded lot, and that it had seven rooms and a large garage-workshop. Because it was located in an excellent area, the potential buyers wanted to know if the listed price of the property, which was low, was a mistake. This untrained agent did everything wrong. He failed to get any qualifying information from the prospective buyers and was off to show a property he knew nothing about other than by reading a few lines on the office listing. Before he showed the property, one of the other agents told him, "It's a dog. You'll never sell it!"

However, he discovered that the home was an old farmhouse with imitation brick, roll-asphalt siding, and the garage was a large machine shed/barn with a dirt floor. The pine floors in the house were covered with linoleum. There were no closets in the bedrooms, and because the house had been vacant for a long time, there was a very unpleasant odor throughout the place.

He asked the prospective buyers what they thought of the home. The response was, "It definitely has possibilities." Fifteen minutes later they signed an offer and within a month had moved into their new home. Because the father was a disabled veteran, this was the only home they could afford in this desirable school district. It was the answer to their dreams, but to other agents it was a dog. If this agent had previously viewed the property and understood the needs and abilities of the buyers, he would have realized the perfect match. There was nothing wrong with the property; it simply needed to be matched with the right buyers. You should not substitute what *you* want for what *others* might want.

In selling, the ability to be a good listener is even more important than the ability to be a good talker. Unfortunately, many people have poor listening skills and pretend to listen, but do not hear. To add to the problem, the human mind can take in and process around 500 words a minute, yet we speak at a rate of only about 100 to 150 words a minute. The difference makes it easy to be distracted and allow your mind to wander. Practice active listening so you will be sure to hear words that are relevant to the customer's needs, problems, and solutions.

A good listener listens actively by reinforcing the speaker with words of understanding, repeating what was said (especially when objections arise), and nodding or making some show of approval.

Silence also is an excellent tool; when in doubt, the best solution is to keep silent. Discreet silence at the right time often shows an excellent command of the language. Also, active listeners do not interrupt or formulate a response when the speaker is talking.

Remember to Listen

Remember, you will not make sales by winning arguments. Speakers need the opportunity to make known their points and voice their feelings of doubt or displeasure. Listen with your eyes, as well as with your ears. Keep a relaxed tone while speaking, and mean what you say. When you are finished, stop.

In selecting property for showing, first consider properties from the internet that the prospective buyers have shown interest in. These properties can be half sold. If the buyers feel they discovered a property, the likelihood of a purchase is enhanced.

Agents must be careful to listen to buyers and choose properties for showing according to wishes and interests shown and not to substitute what the agent likes for what buyers express interest in.

Showing property priced significantly higher than the limits set by buyers when you don't fully realize their financial situation could be a disaster. You could sell buyers on a property or features they cannot obtain.

California is a more mobile society, so neighborhood is less important than in many Eastern communities where family and friends have been located within a small area for generations. When buyers insist on a designated area and their "want" list cannot be met based on their financial ability, consider first showing property within the area and then what a move outside the designated perimeter can achieve as to what they want in a home.

Chinese Buyers

There has been a significant influx of buyers from China. These buyers have been purchasing upscale homes, usually for cash, in prestigious locations.

There are an estimated 2.5 million Chinese millionaires. Many are now seeking a safe place for their wealth, as well as a place for family safety and educational opportunities. A U.S. visa program (EB-5) allows wealthy aliens to obtain permanent residency in the United States if they invest $500,000 to $1 million in a U.S. investment that will create at least 10 jobs. The visa covers the investor's spouse as well as children under age 21. Some 80% of the EB-5 visas have been going to mainland China. China has topped Canada in home purchase dollars. According to the National Association of Realtors®, Chinese buyers purchased $28.6 billion in U.S. real estate in the 12 months preceding March 2015. It is believed that approximately half of this investment has been in California, primarily in the greater Los Angeles area, San Francisco, and San Diego. Buyers have been seeking areas with substantial Chinese populations. Irvine, California, in Orange County has become a mecca for many Chinese buyers. Some subdivisions have reported over 50% of sales to Chinese nationals.

Real estate agents should strive to understand the culture of diverse groups. Chinese buyers often rely heavily on opinions of friends and family members and may wish to consult with them before making a decision. A great many Chinese pay attention to feng shui in home purchase decisions. What you may consider the perfect home for a Chinese family could be rejected because of bad feng shui.

Feng Shui

Feng shui (pronounced fung shway) translates as "wind-water" in English. It is an ancient Chinese practice to orient the energy of a dwelling. It positions objects and structure design for the favorable flow of chi, which is life force for good fortune.

Where a sale to a Chinese national is likely, some agents bring in a feng shui practitioner for an evaluation and hopeful approval. Fees for this service range from under $200 to around $400 depending on area and home size.

Feng shui consultants will offer solutions to correct problems with energy flow. Sometimes a solution can be simple for a property, but at times, the problem can be so severe that many Chinese buyers would not consider the property.

Some problem areas include the following:

- A backyard sloping down, which will take energy away from the house. It can be alleviated with a retaining wall to stop the downward energy flow.

- A T-junction house is considered bad feng shui because the chi coming directly down the road to the house is too aggressive and negatively affects the house.

- A south-facing unit is most preferred and east-facing is considered a bad omen although east-facing windows can create good energy.

- A clean line of sight from the front door to the back door allows good luck to come in and go right out. Minor alterations might solve the problem.

- A front door leading directly to a stairway will allow good energy to flow up or down the stairs to the detriment of the main floor.

- The front door must open inward, not outward which would push away positive energy.

- Trees and shrubs should not block the view of the front door because they would also block energy.

- Sharp corners emit negative energy.

- The bathroom door should not be close to the front door.

- Rooms should be clutter free because clutter resists the flow of positive energy (model homes).

- Work areas (home offices) should be separate from living areas.

- Plants, flowers, and water features are positive energy.

Colors are important to many Chinese buyers. Green is positive because it denotes nature. Yellow equals power, and red and purple are considered lucky.

Numbers are very important to many Chinese. Number 8 is the luckiest of Chinese numbers, while 4 and 14, 5 and 6 are to be avoided. The number 4 is unlucky because it is pronounced similarly to the Chinese word for death (sîwáng).

To avoid the number 4, some agents will set a price, such as $388,888, and a separate price for furnishings, such as $88,888.

Street addresses are also important. Favorable addresses should be emphasized in advertising and in showings.

A basic understanding of feng shui will enable an agent to select homes for showing to Chinese buyers, as well as to consider how to counter possible problem areas.

Prospecting the China Market

China has a number of important home shows that feature foreign property. Beijing luxury property shows brought more than 5,200 wealthy Chinese to view international properties. A number of U.S. brokers have set up elaborate booths at the show. Foreign sellers indicate that setting up a booth at one of many property shows costs from $30,000 to $150,000. Brokers usually represent a new home development or a large condo development with many vacancies. Some brokers travel to China to sell business opportunities to allow Chinese families to obtain a visa. Others enter arrangements with Chinese real estate firms to locate buyers for business opportunities or luxury homes.

There are a number of Chinese real estate websites, some for foreign property. Juwai.com is a global property portal with 2.4 million properties listed in 58 countries.

PROPERTY TOUR PRESENTATION PACKAGE

WEB LINK

@

Just as presentation material can increase the effectiveness of a listing presentation, presentation material can make showings more effective. Material prepared for a buyer makes it easy for the buyer to evaluate and compare offerings and can lead to a natural closing. When you understand the buyer's needs and have prequalified the buyer, a property presentation package should be considered. Figures 9.2A–9.2J from Realty Tools, Inc. (www.realtytools.com) show a sample buyer tour presentation package. You will note that each property presented includes property details, photographs, a map, and space for viewer's comments. The property comparison sheet shows what the buyers have indicated they are seeking.

THE SHOWING

Preparing to Show

To show property to prospective buyers intelligently, you must make adequate preparation:

- Know all available properties in the area

- Be able to identify school boundaries

- Be cognizant of shopping and recreational facilities in the area

- Be aware of public transportation routes

- Be aware of any other information about the area that might help prospects make a favorable decision

FIGURES 9.2A – 9.2J: **Property Tour Presentation Package**

A.

Property Tour

Prepared Especially for:
Tom & Mary White
7 Deep Run Court
Hunt Valley, MD 21030

Prepared by:
Angela McKendrick, CRS, GRI
Agent
Green Leaf Realty
123 Main Street
Hunt Valley, MD 21030

Office: 410-555-1234
Home Office: 410-432-7890
Fax: 410-555-5607
Web Site: www.demorealty.com/angela
Email: angela.mckendrick@demorealty.com

Date: August 20, 2015

Green Leaf Realty
www.greenleafrealty.com

B.

Home Finders' Profile for

Tom & Mary White

You have identified the following criteria to aid us in the search for your new home. Please review this information and notify Angela McKendrick immediately if there are any changes.

City:	Hunt Valley	*Neighborhood:*	Laurelford
Year Built:	1988	*Fin SqFt:*	5384
Lot Desc:	Backs To Trees	*Lot Size:*	1.04
Style:	Colonial	*Levels:*	3
Bedrooms:	4	*Bathrooms:*	3/1
Const:	Cedar Siding	*Roofing:*	Cedar/Shake
Basement:	Fully Finished	*Basement:*	Walkout Level
Heat:	Heat Pump	*Fuel:*	Electric
Cool:	Central A/C	*Parking:*	Garage
Garage Spaces:	2	*Exter Feat:*	Deck
Water:	Well	*Sewer:*	Septic
# Fireplaces:	2	*Amenities:*	Auto Gar Dr Opn
Amenities:	Built-In Bookcases	*Amenities:*	Mba/Sep Shwr
Other Rms:	Den/Stdy/Lib	*Other Rms:*	Family Room

Angela McKendrick, CRS, GRI
Office: 410-555-1234
Home Office: 410-432-7890
Fax: 410-555-5607
Web Site: www.demorealty.com/angela
Email: angela.mckendrick@demorealty.com

Green Leaf Realty
www.greenleafrealty.com

C.

Presenting

Features Include:

City: Hunt Valley
Neighborhood: Shawan
Year Built: 1995
Fin SqFt: 5684
Lot Desc: Cul-De-Sac
Lot Size: 3.05 Acres
Style: Colonial
Levels: 2
Bedrooms: 4
Bathrooms: 3/1
Const: Brick
Roofing: Shingle-Asphalt
Basement: Full
Basement: Unfinished
Heat: Forced Air
Fuel: Gas Heated
Cool: Zoned
Parking: Garage
Garage Spaces: 2
Exter Feat: Deck
Water: Well

9 Jules Brentony
$898,900

Gorgeous Brick Home with Plenty of Amenities. Great Neighborhood. Short Drive to City.

Comments: _____
_____
_____
_____
_____
_____
_____

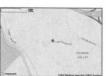

Angela McKendrick, CRS, GRI
Office: 410-555-1234
Home Office: 410-432-7890
Fax: 410-555-5607
Web Site: www.demorealty.com/angela
Email: angela.mckendrick@demorealty.com

Green Leaf Realty
www.greenleafrealty.com

D.

Presenting

Features Include:

City: Cockeysville
Neighborhood: Laurelford
Year Built: 2008
Fin SqFt: 5484
Lot Desc: Backs To Trees
Lot Size: 1.14 Acres
Style: Modern
Levels: 3
Bedrooms: 4
Bathrooms: 3/1
Const: Cedar Siding
Roofing: Cedar/Shake
Basement: Finished
Basement: Walkout Level
Heat: Heat Pump
Fuel: Electric
Cool: Central Air
Parking: 2-Car Garage
Garage Spaces: 2
Exter Feat: Deck
Water: Well

2 Symphony Cir
$789,000

Gorgeous home available for move in immediately! Inground Pool in back of house. Fabulous Master Bedroom, Spacious Rooms."

Comments: _____
_____
_____
_____
_____
_____
_____

Angela McKendrick, CRS, GRI
Office: 410-555-1234
Home Office: 410-432-7890
Fax: 410-555-5607
Web Site: www.demorealty.com/angela
Email: angela.mckendrick@demorealty.com

Green Leaf Realty
www.greenleafrealty.com

FIGURES 9.2A – 9.2J (continued):   Property Tour Presentation Package

Presenting

Features Include:

20 Laurelford Ct
$892,000

City: Cockeysville
Neighborhood: Laurelford
Year Built: 1992
Fin SqFt: 5800
Lot Desc: Backs To Trees
Lot Size: 9 Acres
Style: Colonial
Levels: 3
Bedrooms: 4
Bathrooms: 2/1
Const: Vinyl
Roofing: Shingle
Basement: Full
Basement: Finished
Heat: Forced Air
Fuel: Electric
Cool: Central A/C
Parking: Garage
Garage Spaces: 2
Exter Feat: Balcony
Water: Well

FULLY FINISHED WALK-OUT BASEMENT WITH REC ROOM (30X23), GUEST BEDROOM (18X17), FULL BATH & WINDOWS. THIS IS A FULL BASEMENT. 9 ACRES OF BEAUTIFUL GROUNDS, PARK-SETTING. UPPER 2ND LEVEL HAS 2 ROOMS (20X11 & 20X24) FULLY FINISHED. APPROX. 6,000 FINISHED SQUARE FEET. UNIQUE AND DISTINCTIVE."

Comments: _____

Angela McKendrick, CRS, GRI
Office: 410-555-1234
Home Office: 410-432-7890
Fax: 410-555-5607
Web Site: www.demorealty.com/angela
Email: angela.mckendrick@demorealty.com

Green Leaf Realty
www.greenleafrealty.com

E.

Presenting

Features Include:

13213 Beaver Dam Rd
$849,900

City: Cockeysville
Neighborhood: Ivy Hill
Year Built: 1984
Fin SqFt: 4090
Lot Desc: Back To Woods
Lot Size: 1.89 Acres
Style: Classic
Levels: 3
Bedrooms: 4
Bathrooms: 3/2
Const: Cedar Siding
Roofing: Shingle/F-Glass
Basement: Unfinished
Basement: Walkout Level
Heat: Forced Air
Fuel: Bottled Propane
Cool: Ceiling Fan
Parking: Driveway
Garage Spaces: 3
Exter Feat: Patio
Water: Well

HANDCRAFTED OAK FOYER AND STAIRCASE. THE ATTENTION TO ARCHITECTURAL DETAIL IS OUTSTANDING. AMENITIES SUCH AS HARDWOODS, MARBLE, CERAMIC AND BRASS ADD THE FINISHING TOUCHES!"

Comments: _____

Angela McKendrick, CRS, GRI
Office: 410-555-1234
Home Office: 410-432-7890
Fax: 410-555-5607
Web Site: www.demorealty.com/angela
Email: angela.mckendrick@demorealty.com

Green Leaf Realty
www.greenleafrealty.com

F.

Presenting

Features Include:

12218 Cleghorn Road
$814,900

City: Cockeysville
Neighborhood: Laurelford
Year Built: 1986
Fin SqFt: 3862
Lot Desc: Backs To Trees
Lot Size: 1 Acre
Style: Modern
Levels: 3
Bedrooms: 4
Bathrooms: 2/2
Const: Brick
Roofing: Shingle/Asphalt
Basement: Full
Basement: Unfinished
Heat: Heat Pump
Fuel: Electric
Cool: Central A/C
Parking: Driveway
Garage Spaces: 3
Exter Feat: Balcony
Water: Conditioner

PARK-LIKE GROUNDS. MASTER BEDROOM SUITE WITH BALCONY. STAINED GLASS WINDOWS & LARGE FAMILY ROOM, WET BAR AND ATRIUM DOOR TO SIDE PORCH. LIVING ROOM WITH ATRIUM DOOR TO PATIO. LOTS OF WINDOWS. FLOORS HAVE BEEN REFINISHED. VERY CHARMING HOME WITH ELITE AMENITIES."

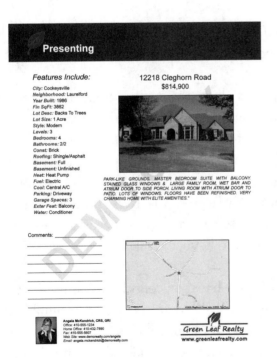

Comments: _____

Angela McKendrick, CRS, GRI
Office: 410-555-1234
Home Office: 410-432-7890
Fax: 410-555-5607
Web Site: www.demorealty.com/angela
Email: angela.mckendrick@demorealty.com

Green Leaf Realty
www.greenleafrealty.com

G.

Buyer Tour Map

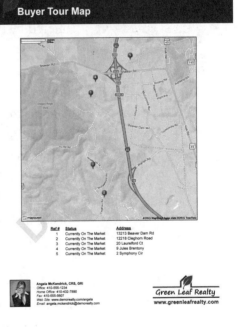

Ref #	Status	Address
1	Currently On The Market	13213 Beaver Dam Rd
2	Currently On The Market	12218 Cleghorn Road
3	Currently On The Market	20 Laurelford Ct
4	Currently On The Market	9 Jules Brentony
5	Currently On The Market	2 Symphony Cir

Angela McKendrick, CRS, GRI
Office: 410-555-1234
Home Office: 410-432-7890
Fax: 410-555-5607
Web Site: www.demorealty.com/angela
Email: angela.mckendrick@demorealty.com

Green Leaf Realty
www.greenleafrealty.com

H.

FIGURES 9.2A – 9.2J (continued): Property Tour Presentation Package

Used with permission of Realty Tools, Inc.

Select previously visited houses for viewing and consider the benefits offered by particular properties to particular buyers.

Don't show a property just to please the owners. Some agents try to show property to impress owners with their work on the owners' behalf rather than to make a sale. This tactic often backfires because prospective buyers will realize that you really aren't listening to them. Instead, you are wasting their time. This tactic materially lessens the likelihood of having a second chance to show properties to these prospects. Don't give preference to your own office listings. What matters is the buyers' needs. By placing buyers' needs first, you are more likely to be successful.

Some agents try to hold back what they consider to be the best property for their prospects. Instead, they show overpriced or unsuitable property first. They believe the property they hope to sell will then appear in a more favorable light. This practice could be considered unethical because the result could be to give prospective buyers a false impression of property values. It is probably best to arrange showings by location to avoid wasting time backtracking.

If the qualifying process indicates that the homes you initially selected for viewing are unsuitable, cancel the appointments and make new ones before leaving your office. Try to show vacant homes on lockboxes first, so that you give owners time to prepare for a showing.

Some agents like to show no more than three or four properties. How many you show should be dictated by the situation. As an example, if buyers have flown into your area to buy a home because of a job transfer, then you want to continue to show them property until a selection can be made. You can keep confusion to a minimum when you show a large number of properties by giving them information sheets with photos of each house. You can break showings into groups of three or four. Take a coffee break after showing each group and discuss the comparative values of the homes. Find out which one of the group buyers liked best. If a clear winner does not appear, consider a second showing of the best home in each group.

Some agents like the idea of showing what they consider the best as their last scheduled showing. They feel that the first homes give the buyers a basis of comparison that allows the benefits of the final home to be fully appreciated. Other agents like to show what they regard as the best first so that other properties, as they are shown, can be compared to the first property.

Successful salespeople will generally show fewer properties per sale than less successful salespeople. Successful salespeople have a better understanding of their buyers and tend to be more selective in properties they show.

Showing Techniques

Sell the neighborhood.   Plan your route to sell the neighborhood. Choose the most scenic route, one that includes schools, public parks, golf courses, and shopping areas. If possible, adapt your route to the interests of the prospective buyers, but do not plan a route to avoid what *you* regard as a negative factor in the area. If you feel there is a negative element that might influence prospective buyers, this must be revealed to them. *However, the presence of a different racial or ethnic group in the area is not considered a negative factor and should not be revealed as if it were.* In fact, if you were to reveal this type of information, it might be regarded as racial steering, that is, directing people based on race. This is a violation of the Civil Rights Act of 1968.

Because people buy a neighborhood as much as they do a specific property, selling the neighborhood cannot be emphasized enough. While driving to the property, endeavor to educate the buyers by discussing only relevant items. If necessary, prepare leading questions. Try to keep the buyers' attention focused on houses of similar price and on the quality of the neighborhood itself. Point out recent sales of comparably priced homes. This should increase the buyers' trust in you and establish a price range in their minds.

A **negative motivation** technique that entails warning buyers about any problem feature often works well. Buyers build these features up in their minds and are relieved when they find a simple solution to a problem or don't perceive the feature as a problem. Also, avoid overenthusiasm on specific points; it may backfire. Instead, permit the buyers' discoveries to be new and exciting experiences.

When you arrive at the property, don't park in the owner's driveway. Park across the street from it if it has good curb appeal. If you pause for a moment when you get out of the car, your buyers will do the same. Ask for their opinion of the house and the area.

Another reason not to park in an owner's driveway is so you don't get blocked in by another vehicle. It also shows respect for the owner's property.

Create a favorable ambiance. It is interesting to note that although some buyers are interested in construction and utility, most are attracted by color, glamour, texture, and style. Don't bore prospects with details unless you are asked. Show a property for the emotional responses. Buyers usually purchase what they want and what they feel good about. Cater to these feelings by creating a favorable ambiance—proper mood and atmosphere. Have the owner provide fresh flowers in vases. Depending on the weather, either prepare the fireplace or have the air-conditioning operating. Encourage the buyer to relax and feel at home.

You want prospective buyers to think like owners. Use language such as "[Jeffrey's school/Longview Middle School] is only three blocks away. Would you like to look at the school after we leave?" You should have ascertained in advance that Jeffrey would indeed be admitted to the school. In some areas, schools have had to limit new students.

If you are unable to answer a prospect's question and you promise to get the information, treat that promise as a priority. It shows you have regard for their concerns and gives you a reason for another contact.

Involve the whole family.   Ask questions of all family members. If you are receiving positive vibrations from prospective buyers, consider "[Jennifer], which bedroom would be yours?" Remember that just because one member of the family is the most vocal does not mean that person is necessarily the decision maker.

Ask, don't tell, if you want to sell.   The following story illustrates what to do and what not to do when you show property:

Mr. and Mrs. Doe are potential real estate buyers. They have decided to go for the traditional afternoon time killer, the Sunday drive. As they tour their town, complaining about the traffic, Mrs. Doe's face lights up when she sees a lovely home with lots of little flags flying. It is crisp, modern, and obviously open for inspection, so she decides that they should stop and look it over. They walk into the house and are greeted by a real estate salesperson, who puts down a comic book and slowly gets up. The salesperson then proceeds to give the demonstration—the cook's tour.

Ask questions and listen to the answers.

"This is the living room," the salesperson proclaims with a sweep of the hand. "This is the dining room; notice the roominess. . . . This is the kitchen. These are the kitchen cabinets. This is the oven; it's big and modern." The salesperson continues, "Notice how wide the hall is. Why don't you both look at this bedroom with me? Isn't your husband interested in bedrooms? This is a closet."

By this time, the couple has had enough. They remember how much they wanted a chocolate malt, and off they go. The salesperson returns to the comic book.

Now imagine the same scene with a different character—a professional salesperson who knows how to communicate:

This salesperson rises but waits to let the customers look around the living room for a moment. Then she turns to Mrs. Doe and says, "Where in this living room would you place your sofa?" (Do not sell the space, sell the benefits of the space.)

In the kitchen, the salesperson opens a cabinet and says, "What would you put in here, dry groceries or your kitchen china?" Opening the oven, the salesperson says, "How big a turkey do you think this oven would take?"

True professionals never say, "This is the second bedroom." They always ask, "Whose bedroom will this be?" A professional does not state obvious facts. A professional *sells* by asking who, what, where, or how for every room and every feature:

> There's plenty of room in the bedroom for a king-size bed plus an office area. Would you put the desk in the window alcove?

> Mr. Thomas, how would you use this workroom?

> Would you use this room as a study or as a spare bedroom?

> How do you think your dog will like having her own trees in the fenced yard? Would you use the covered patio for summer entertaining?

The first minutes of entering a home can set the emotional stage for buying or forgetting the property. You want to get prospective buyers involved:

> What do you like about this [house], [room]? What if anything would you change? Why?

Sell benefits, not features.   A pool is merely a hole in the ground with chlorinated water in it. The wise real estate salesperson remembers that the pool is, in fact, much more than this.

> Imagine on a hot summer day, Mr. and Mrs. Jones, not having to trek the kids all the way down to the local recreation center to go swimming. You will be able to save gas and time by having the kids play right here in the backyard.

A gourmet kitchen is a place to indulge in one's culinary hobby, not to mention a pleasant atmosphere in which to work out tensions. A fireplace contributes to family togetherness and the kindling of romance. A dishwasher is not a luxury; it is a necessity, given the hectic demands on most people's time. A spa and sun deck promote an image of relaxed enjoyment, as well as being status symbols. Listen carefully to uncover features and benefits that are important to the buyer, as well as probing when appropriate, and then sell those features and benefits.

Ask questions, don't state opinions.

Because the qualifying process is a continual one, after each house shown you must *ask questions, not state opinions*. By asking questions about what prospective buyers liked and what they didn't like and probing for the reasons behind these feelings, you may find that your showing schedule needs modification.

Use tie-downs.   A good communicator uses **tie-downs**, a question that calls for a positive response. They can be used to check out whether a benefit is important or to build a sense of ownership. No professional salesperson ever makes a positive statement without tying it down:

- "This is a spacious room, *isn't it?*"

- "You really need four bedrooms, *don't you?*"

- "Your children should be close to school, *shouldn't they?*"

- "This is the sound investment you've been looking for, *isn't it?*"

These words—*isn't it, can it, won't it, don't you, can't you,* and so on—are powerful selling tools. Little yeses easily lead to the big yes. Sell on minor points.

A series of yes responses can lead to the big YES!

Invite comparisons.   The comparison technique gets buyers involved. Ask such questions as "Did you like the vanity off the bedroom, as it was in the house you just saw, or do you prefer this style?" "Will this dining room set off your antique hutch, or can you see it better in the other house?" These questions get the buyers involved in defining what is important to them. Buyers start selling themselves and get prepared to make the big decision by making a lot of little ones.

By use of comparisons you can discover preferences.

Additional showing tips.   If you know that a property has a feature that the buyers will enjoy, don't point it out to them. Let them discover that pool or large oak tree on their own. Here are other items that may enhance your presentation:

- Occasionally allow the buyers privacy. They may want to feel that they're alone when they discuss personal things.

- Do not assume that just because you like a feature of the property, the buyers will like it as well.

- Do not resent the presence of a friend of the family. Use the friend as an ally.

- Always overcome any objections on the scene. If space is an issue, use a tape measure (let the customer measure). Try to settle any questions on the spot.

- Begin and end the tour of the home in the most beautiful and unique part of the house.

- The buyers will follow your lead. Whenever you enter a room, they will follow.

- Involve children. Wherever possible, direct questions to the children.

- Speak plainly, and avoid technical terms. When people do not understand, your point is lost.

- Call attention to outstanding features, but do not go overboard or you will close the door on the sale of another property.

- Show the rooms in the most productive order. In a home, this is usually front hall, living room, dining room, kitchen, bedrooms, yard or garden, and last of all the most attractive rooms on the first floor. This procedure may be varied to suit special cases.

- If the rooms are small, do not stand in the middle of a room; stand along the side.

When showing furnished property be aware that you have a duty of reasonable care as to the possessions of the occupant. Do not allow prospects to wander about out of your sight. Small expensive items can be a temptation for some people. While the listing agent should have advised owners to secure such objects, they don't always do so and some owners fail to heed warnings.

Establishing a list. A valuable technique to use when showing property is to ask prospective buyers if they would want to include the property on their list for consideration. The list approach prepares the buyer for a purchase choice between several properties they have shown a degree of interest in. The choice you're seeking is which property they will buy, not a to-buy-or-not-to-buy decision.

The list can also be used as a closing technique: "This property meets nine out of 10 of the items on your list; you can't get much better than that."

An alternative showing technique. For vacant property, consider opening the door and telling the prospects to take their time and look around and that you will join them shortly.

When you join them, ask questions as to what they thought about particular features or what they like most about the property. By letting them view the property, they will be relaxed making their own decisions and able to privately discuss their feelings. This "on your own" showing technique is particularly effective when you feel that this is the property your prospective buyers will want. Because of security considerations as to the owners' property, don't use this technique when the property has owner furnishings without specific permission by the owner to do so.

Multiple-prospect home tours.   Home tours by bus or caravan are an effective tool to attract prospective buyers and can present competition that can stimulate buying decisions. Buyers do not feel threatened in situations when they are part of a group viewing property. They are more likely to go on a tour of homes than to contact a broker to view particular homes that may interest them.

Most brokers conducting tours require prospects to sign up in advance because space is limited. They also offer to prequalify or even preapprove buyers for loans at no cost or obligation. A call the day before the tour and a little "teaser" information about one property will reduce the number of "no shows." You want a full tour because it can create a feeling of excitement and competition.

Some brokers will offer multiple tours featuring properties based on property type and/or price range. Some tours are limited to new home developments. Others may be limited to properties in foreclosure or short sales. Tours of foreclosed properties, as well as tours of fixer-uppers for flippers, have been very productive. Some brokers advertise the homes they show and the period of time they will be at each property, which allows prospects to go to just one or several of the homes to be viewed.

Providing clipboards with photos and data of each home and places for the prospects to make notes is effective in helping the buyers make their own decisions. With large groups, let the prospects view on their own.

During bus tours, a salesperson will then ask questions of the viewers as to each house after they have seen it. Often a problem raised by one person will be minimized by a solution offered by another viewer.

At the end of the tour, participants are asked to answer a brief question-naire about the benefits of the tour and their feelings about the properties. Participants are asked if they would like to discuss any particular property or if they would like more information.

While offers are received on the day of the tour, especially when more than one prospect shows interest in the same property, other offers may take a few days. Many participants will sign up for additional tours.

Tours should be followed up with a telephone call.

Rules of Professional Conduct

The following rules help you maintain goodwill and a professional manner as you plan for and conduct showings:

- If you arrive at a property and notice that someone else is showing it, wait inconspicuously until the other salesperson and clients have left.

- When showing a home, leave it as you found it. If drapes were closed, see that they're closed when you leave. If inner doors were closed, close them when you leave. Double-check all outside doors to see that they're locked. Be sure to replace the key in the lockbox where you found it. If dogs, cats, or other animals are confined to a given room, yard, garage, and so forth, see that they do not gain access to other rooms or to the street.

- Notify the listing office immediately if something seems to be amiss at a property you have shown. Treat all listings as you would want to have your own listing treated.

- If a listing specifies "call first," never take a customer to the door and ask to show the home. If, while showing a property, you decide to show another and cannot reach the owner by phone, leave the client in the car while you go to the door and ask the owner for belated permission to show the property. Then abide by the owner's wishes.

- If a listing indicates that the property is to be shown only during certain hours or gives other information regarding particular conditions of showing, do not violate these requests. There must be a reason for them.

- Leave your business card at each property. It is a courtesy to the owner (whether at home or not). It also helps to advertise your own office. It is a good idea to write the date and the time on the back of the card.

- Interoffice courtesy requires that when calling another agency for information, you immediately identify yourself and your company.

- Do not enter a house with a lighted cigarette, pipe, or cigar, and do not light one while in a house. Be certain that prospective buyers also abide by these restrictions.

- Avoid making uncomplimentary remarks about a house, its condition, or its furnishings while in the house. The owner may be in the next room and be embarrassed or hurt by your comments.

KEEP THEM YOURS

After you have completed your first session of showing homes to prospective buyers, it is a good idea to ask them to return to the office to discuss the properties they have seen. If a closing is not going to be possible, consider a way to tie down the prospects so they regard you as their agent. Consider the following approach:

I prefer to work with just a few buyers. I dedicate my efforts to finding them a property that best meets their needs. Usually, I'm able to meet the needs of my buyers in just a few weeks. I am willing to work for you and concentrate my efforts on your behalf if you are serious buyers. At times, buyers don't really have the down payment they say they have, or for some other reason are not in a position to buy. If I were able to show you a property that has everything you want, would you make an offer?

> You want prospective buyers to feel an obligation to work with you.

Your buyers can be expected to assure you that they are serious and willing to make an offer. Continue:

If you are willing to let me take over the exclusive responsibility of finding the home you want, I will use all my efforts to locate the property that meets all your needs. If you see an ad or internet listing that interests you, if you drive by a home you like, or even if you see an open-house sign, call me about it. If other brokers contact you, tell them to call me and I will cooperate with them. If you are willing to work with me, I am willing to go all out for you. Does this seem fair?

The answer will usually be positive, and many people will live up to the agreement, but it would be better to bring out a buyer-agency agreement at this time. When you find the house that meets their needs, committed buyers will often feel obligated to make an offer when they might otherwise have procrastinated. If you want to act as a buyer's agent rather than a dual agent or seller's agent, now is a good time to obtain a buyer agent listing.

Video Streaming

You can show property to prospective renters or buyers without their being physically present. Using a smartphone, you can provide live-time viewing with apps such as Skype, Facetime, and Periscope. By coordinating viewing time, clients can see a live video feed as the agent uses a camera function to scan rooms and exterior features while talking to the client. The client can ask for close-ups or to return to a particular feature of the property. While some agents have reported receiving purchase offers online from the live feed, it has been particularly valuable as to relocation rentals. Clients are willing to obligate to a one-year lease more readily than a half a million dollar purchase when they have not physically visited the property.

SUMMARY

Contacts generally begin with a phone call. Be prepared for phone inquiries by having current listings, ads, switch property, and location of office listings readily available.

Prospects calling from a For Sale sign usually like the area and exterior; however, the price may not be suitable. Callers from ads are more likely suitable for switch property at a higher price. Callers from the internet like the appearance and price and are more likely to be purchasers of the property inquired about than callers from other sources.

Find out the names and addresses of callers, as well as their needs. Give minimum property information but extract the maximum information on callers' needs and motivations. By giving callers just enough information to keep their interest level high, you can obtain an appointment using a choice of time, not a choice between meeting and not meeting. By asking motivated prospective buyers to mark other ads that interest them, you can lock the prospects in and keep them from calling other agents.

In preparing to meet prospective buyers, you should have some tentative property-showing appointments and a qualifying plan. Before you show any property, you must ascertain prospects' needs, their motivation to buy, and their financial qualifications: the down payment they can afford and the maximum loan they can carry.

Personal security risks will be reduced by meeting prospects at your office and introducing them to your broker and other employees.

The motivation of prospects will affect the level of priority and energy that should be planned for prospective buyers. Based on prospects' needs and financial abilities, your selection of property for showing might need modification. Do not show prospective buyers properties they cannot afford.

Feng shui is the flow of energy and is of importance when dealing with Chinese buyers.

A property tour presentation package can help the buyer keep track of properties and evaluate them. It can lead naturally to a sale.

Plan your showings and ask questions. Don't give opinions during the showing process. Keep in mind that when you conduct a showing, you are selling benefits. Involve the entire family with your questions. The qualifying process should continue right to the point of sale.

Group tours can be effective in showing similar properties. Competitive situations can spark interest and encourage action.

By having buyers select properties for a list for consideration, they can further narrow their choices by property to buy or not buy.

CLASS DISCUSSION TOPICS

1. Role-play an inquiry about your own home with another student. Your goal will be to obtain a name, address, basic needs, and a firm appointment.

2. Role-play a need and motivation buyer-qualification process with another student.

3. Role-play a showing of your classroom with another student cast as a prospective buyer of a classroom.

4. Bring to class one current-events article dealing with some aspect of real estate practice for class discussion.

UNIT 9 QUIZ

1. Callers from a For Sale sign are likely to be
   a. satisfied with the area.
   b. looking for a more expensive home.
   c. satisfied with the general exterior appearance.
   d. both a and c.

2. If we compare callers from classified ads with those from For Sale signs, in general,
   a. callers from signs are more likely to end up buying homes that cost less than the home they called about.
   b. callers from ads are more likely to end up buying homes that cost more than the home they called about.
   c. both of these are true.
   d. both of these are false.

3. Real estate professionals should
   a. limit showing to their own listings.
   b. show overpriced property first to make the one house seem a bargain.
   c. avoid driving through nearby minority areas.
   d. do none of these.

4. In showing property, you should
   a. never show a prospect more than three homes in one day.
   b. show prospects a really nice home they can't afford in order to keep up their interest.
   c. never change your showing plans once you start.
   d. do none of these.

5. The qualifying process includes discovering
   a. the buyers' motivation.
   b. the buyers' needs and interests.
   c. a down payment they can make and the amount they can finance.
   d. all of these.

6.   The front-end loan-qualifying ratio is the ratio of
   a.   gross housing cost to gross income.
   b.   gross income to net income.
   c.   net housing cost to net income.
   d.   none of these.

7.   The back-end qualifying ratio refers to the ratio of
   a.   gross housing cost to gross income.
   b.   total housing expense plus long-term debt to gross income.
   c.   gross income to net income plus housing cost.
   d.   none of these.

8.   A good policy for a professional real estate salesperson would be to
   a.   meet new prospects at the nicest property you think will interest them.
   b.   avoid discussing financial matters until an offer is received.
   c.   ask open-ended questions of prospective buyers.
   d.   limit appointments to the showing of no more than two properties.

9.   For personal safety concerns, you should
   a.   meet prospects at your office.
   b.   avoid ostentatious jewelry or accessories.
   c.   leave front doors unlocked at showing.
   d.   do all of these.

10.   If another agent is showing a home when you arrive for a showing, what should you do?
   a.   Bring your prospects in and let them know they are competing with other buyers for the house
   b.   Cross the house off your showing list until you are sure it has not been sold
   c.   Wait inconspicuously until the other agent completes his or her showing and leaves
   d.   Tell your clients that you are certain that the other prospects are buyers so they had better act fast

10

OBTAINING THE OFFER AND CREATING THE SALES AGREEMENT

LEARNING OBJECTIVES

When you have completed this unit, you will be able to

- explain what selling is and how it is accomplished;

- describe how to obtain an offer to purchase, recognize buying signals, and deal with objections;

- list various closing techniques;

- explain and complete the California Residential Purchase Agreement and Joint Escrow Instructions; and

- estimate buyer costs.

KEY TERMS

assumptive close	estimated buyer's costs	persuasion
buying motives	inducement	positive choice
buying signals	mirroring	trial close
California Residential Purchase Agreement and Joint Escrow Instructions	negative motivation	

WHAT IS SELLING?

If all you accomplished in real estate was to escort people through houses, you would be a tour guide, not a salesperson. Selling is a noble profession because it helps others fulfill their needs and desires. As a salesperson, you influence the outcome of a showing. You influence prospective buyers to become owners by executing a real property purchase contract. Webster defines selling as "to induce others." While in real estate we induce others to buy benefits, selling begins with uncovering client or customer needs and then working for those needs to be satisfied. In other words, salesmanship involves imparting knowledge, amplifying desire and showing how those desires can be fulfilled.

Selling Is Persuading

Persuasion is the central theme in many descriptions of the selling process:

- The personal or impersonal process of persuading prospective customers to buy a commodity or service

- The art of persuading people to accept or to follow certain ideas that lead them to a desired action

- Persuading people to want what you have in terms of products, services, or ideas

Unfortunately, the word *persuasion* reminds many people of someone who convinces them to buy unnecessary products. You can avoid this problem by understanding that people buy benefits that will satisfy their wants and needs, both conscious and unconscious. Your job is to address the needs and show your customers that satisfying *their* needs is most important to *you*.

The good feelings that result will lead to long-term customer satisfaction and future business.

Selling Is Effective Communication

Without effective communication, there is no understanding. Know what you want to say; use listeners' language. Do not use fancy or technical words when simple ones will do. Use the "KISS" method—**K**eep **I**t **S**imple and **S**incere.

A clear idea, sufficient facts, and proper media are of no avail if the communicator uses language that confuses the listener. Words should be chosen with the utmost care, organized, and delivered meaningfully. When you are dealing with parties who have limited English language skills, slow your speech and ask questions so you are certain you are being understood. Avoid using real estate terminology, such as Fannie Mae, or acronyms, such as MLS and FSBO.

Idea.   The most common cause of poor communication is the communicator's own failure to understand the idea he wants to express. You must have something to communicate. As a rule, if you are unsure about what you really mean or are lacking essential facts, it is best not to try to communicate your thoughts to others.

> For effective communication, Keep It Simple and Sincere!

Facts.   To make the sales message understood, you must provide sufficient facts. Without facts, the person receiving the message cannot form valid conclusions or take effective action. This is illustrated by the story of a temporary post office employee who was told to take a truck and deliver the New York mail. Six hours later, the department received a telephone call: "I'm out of gas on the New Jersey Turnpike, 11 miles out of New York. Can you wire me some money so I can deliver the mail?" What the boss had forgotten to tell the new employee was, "When we say deliver the New York mail, we mean to drive it two blocks to Union Station and leave it on the train platform."

Receiver.   Words or symbols have different meanings for different people. Assess your listener before attempting to communicate. Recognition of experience, mood, and temperament, as well as knowledge of the product or service, will make or break the communication chain.

Your Voice Personality

Does your selling voice communicate well? If not, the following four guidelines will help you relate to your customer more effectively:

1. Articulate clearly

2. Sound positive and friendly

3. Match your customer's speech in volume, speed, and tone (this is sometimes called mirroring). Remember that just because someone speaks slowly, it doesn't mean that person thinks slowly.

4. Use your customer's descriptive words

Selling Is Discovering

Help your client or customer to discover. For example, ask, "Would it be all right if I ask you a few questions?" Evaluate your inquiry style by asking the following questions:

- Do my questions tell my prospect that I understand the client or customer?

- Do I ask property-oriented (fact-finding) questions?

- Do I follow this with people-oriented (feeling-finding) questions?

- Do I ask open-ended questions to get the other party to "open up"?

Open-ended questions ask for reasons and feelings. Example: "Why do you want a three-car garage?"

In qualifying prospective buyers, use open-end questions to gain information rather than closed-end questions. Open-end questions ask for reasons and feelings and aid in the communication process, whereas closed-end questions can be answered with a simple "yes" or "no" that does not provide any background about reasoning and motivation. A child's "Why?" is an example of an open-ended question. By asking questions like "Tell me…," you invite the buyer's participation. The buyer will feel more in control.

If you start with fact-finding questions, which appeal to reason, you accomplish the following three things:

1. You relax the prospect.

2. You indicate to the prospect that you have done your homework.

3. You obtain valuable information that helps guide your sales effort.

Then revert to feeling-finding questions, which appeal to emotions. Remember that people are more likely to buy the product or service if they feel that you understand them. By acknowledging the buyer's needs, you can establish a bond of empathy. You must show that you understand both the needs and the concerns of the buyer.

> Give buyers a rational reason to fulfill an emotional need.

Customers' reasons for buying traditionally have been divided into two major categories: rational and emotional. *Rational motives* are usually defined as including any considerations that have to do with long-term costs, financing, and benefits from proposed expenditures. In other words, rational motives measure all the costs against all the probable gains. There are probably as many *emotional motives* for buying as there are customers. However, a few that are most frequently seen in real estate are love, fear, convenience, prestige or social approval, and self-improvement. Selling often involves giving a prospective buyer a rational reason for fulfilling an emotional need.

Selling Is Knowing Your Customer

Customers are the heart and soul of your business. Your customers do not have to love you but should like and trust you. It is a good idea for you to love your customers. Always keep in mind how you can best serve them.

Customer types.   There have been numerous attempts to pigeonhole prospects and customers. This can be done if you keep in mind the temperamental fluctuations that might occur. Remember, no customer is a single type; each one is a composite of several types. Most experienced licensees have seen an individual display more than one temperament during an interview. Some customers put the salesperson on the defensive; some buyers waver; some are irritable, cynical, or good-humored. Alert salespeople adjust their approaches to the attitudes, temperaments, and buying needs of each customer. Figure 10.1 shows strategies for dealing with various types of prospects.

Selling Is Knowing Your Product

If you are going to satisfy customer needs and wants, you must know what properties are available and their features. Taking a listing, preparing for a showing, going through the multiple listing service listings, and networking with others are all good opportunities for gathering this information. Knowledge and expertise are becoming even more important as consumers become more sophisticated. Several areas of knowledge about your product are discussed in the following paragraphs.

Features of properties include those of the community, as well as those of specific houses. For example, clients may want to know the following:

- Are there good schools nearby? (Private versus public and specialty schools)

- Where is the nearest racquetball court?

- What are the neighborhood amenities?

Because it is difficult to know everything about every community, many salespeople begin by specializing in a specific geographic area. Often, this market area includes the neighborhoods in which you will do the most business. It will serve you well to get involved in these communities, get to know the neighborhood, and keep up with changes.

The brokerage firm, you, and the services you provide also are part of the product. Unanswered questions and objections raised in these areas can kill a sale. Early in your relationship with your clients or prospects, present information that will establish your credibility and show them that you have the resources to work hard for them. Some agents hand out fact sheets or a résumé. An anecdote about a way in which you and the firm have benefited others may help you establish rapport and provide reassurance if the situation seems appropriate:

"There are advantages and disadvantages to this property," said the honest and well-informed real estate agent. "To the north is the gas works, to the east the glue factory, to the south a fish and chips shop, and to the west a sewage farm. These are the disadvantages."

"What are the advantages?" the customer asked.

"You can always tell which way the wind is blowing," was the agent's reply. As this anecdote humorously illustrates, you often can present disadvantages as advantages.

Because it is unlikely that a piece of property will have every feature a client wants, it makes sense to play up the significant features and downplay the ones that are lacking. However, be meticulous about disclosure issues. Do not neglect or change the presentation of negative information just because it is (or may be perceived as) a disadvantage. Both legally and morally, you owe each client a high standard of care—a quality of service that a "reasonably prudent person" would provide. Since the *Easton v. Strassburger* case, awareness of responsibilities has become a prime concern in the real estate profession.

FIGURE 10.1:   Types of Prospects

General Strategies to Use		
Silent Prospect—the "Clam"—Does not indicate whether she is agreeing or disagreeing	=	Ask leading questions; be more personal than usual/
Procrastinator—the "Putter-Offer"—Does not know his own mind; has difficulty making up mind	=	Summarize benefits that prospect will lose if he or she does not act; be positive, self-assured, and dramatic/
Glad-Hander—Talkative or overenthusiastic	=	Lead these prospects back into the sale after letting them talk themselves out!
Argumentative Type—Usually is insincere and tries the salesperson's patience	=	Sincerity and respect on the salesperson's part will create respect. Consider, "You're absolutely right. That's why you'll appreciate . . ."
Slow or Methodical Type—Appears to weigh every word of the salesperson	=	Slow down and simplify details. Adjust your tempo to your prospect's. This approach is often called mirroring and can lead a sales prospect comfortably to a positive decision.
Skeptical or Suspicious Type—Convinced that every salesperson is trying to "pull the wool over her eyes"	=	Stay with the facts, and be conservative in statements. Allay the prospect's fears.
Overcautious or Timid Type—Acts as if he does not trust the salesperson	=	Take it slow and easy. Reassure on every point. Use logic and make it simple.
Impulsive Type—Apt to interrupt presentation before salesperson states all points		Speed up presentation, concentrating only on important points. Omit details when possible.
Opinionated—Ego Type—Is overconfident, with strong opinions		Give these prospects "rope" by appealing to their egos. Listen attentively and guide them, using their opinions.

Selling Is You

You should present a calm rational persona. You must show a desire to understand needs and to help in their fulfillment. If you appear to be trying too hard, buyers are likely to become nervous or defensive, or both. You want to be a person whom the buyers like and trust. You can be that person and it will lead to success.

There will be times when you are not the person who can best serve a particular client. Perhaps the client is looking for a home that lies outside your market area. Or, someone may want a piece of investment property that will involve intricate tax and financing complications. The worst mistake you can make is thinking that you can serve everyone. It is far better to refer people to brokers or other individuals who have the required expertise. Even if you do refer a prospect to another agent, it would be ethical and legal to earn a referral fee from the other agent after the transaction has reached a successful close.

OBTAINING THE OFFER

Closing is simply asking for a decision.

To narrow the number of homes shown for a purchase decision, some brokers create a list. When you show a number of properties to clients, the list approach should be considered. It is a logical approach to selling. After each showing, ask the clients what they liked about the property and what they considered negatives. Then ask if the property should be added to their list for consideration. After you have three or more properties on the list, go over the pluses and minuses of the properties and let the clients tell you which properties they feel they like best. Do not be assertive and try to influence this final decision. Your personal likes and dislikes could turn a decision into no decision at all. Once they have made their choice, ask whether they would like to put an offer on the property. Selling becomes a matter of showing the prospects how and why it should be their home.

In striving to obtain an offer to purchase, you will find that each transaction is unique and has its own approach and required motivation. However, there are some general principles to apply. Understanding why customers buy and the basic steps of transactions help you prepare for a presentation that will lead to an offer. Four basic steps are illustrated in Figure 10.2. They are discussed in the following paragraphs.

Appeal to Buying Motives

Merriam-Webster's Collegiate Dictionary defines *motive* as "something (as a need or desire) that causes a person to act." Understanding a buyer's needs and wants is absolutely essential for optimum results. Remember, you are going to be selling the benefits that match those needs and wants. After all, why should an individual buy a home and be responsible for its maintenance, taxes, and so on, rather than rent for life? Why should a family skimp and save for a down payment and make monthly payments when that family could live in a public housing unit or with relatives?

Ownership of real property satisfies several basic needs or **buying motives**.

Survival.   The most basic human need is survival. If a home has no amenities other than providing shelter, it satisfies the basic human need to survive.

Security.   The desire for security is a fundamental need that has many applications in the selling process. Every licensee should appeal to it. The home often becomes the principal financial asset of many Americans. In times of financial stress, the home might be something to fall back on. People feel secure in their own homes. They do not have to worry about landlords asking them to leave because the landlords want their own children to live there.

FIGURE 10.2:   Steps in Obtaining the Offer

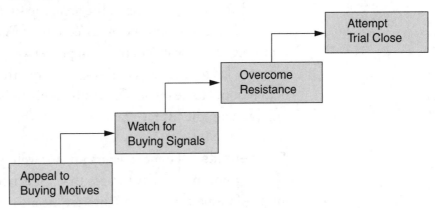

Pride of ownership/social need.   Once buyers obtain basic shelter, pride impels many to pay considerably more for additional benefits. What they feel their friends and/or family will think of the home influences many buyers. By a statement such as "Wouldn't you like to entertain your friends on this delightful patio?" you can create an image of pride in showing the home to others. Many salespeople use pride of ownership immediately by referring to the property being shown as if the prospective buyers were already the owners. Pride of ownership appeal is not limited to luxury estates. It can be used for all types of properties because most buyers are looking at properties with better amenities than they currently enjoy.

Love of family. Desirable school areas, recreational facilities, shopping conveniences, or other factors that may appeal to one or all members of the family often induce the purchase of a certain property. Many times one of the foremost factors in the buyer's mind will be how the home can help the family. Don't forget that in many families, pets are regarded as important family members.

Health. Motivation arising from health interests is closely allied to the survival instinct and can be a determining factor in a decision to buy. The quality of the environment—of the air and water, lower noise levels, the avoidance of urban congestion—often motivates a decision to buy.

Desire for profit or gain (investment). More people have started on the road to financial independence through home ownership than in any other way. Buying a home can be an investment for the future because well-located properties in the long run increase in value, a process called *appreciation*. The amount of appreciation depends on numerous factors, such as the demand for housing in the area, the supply of homes, the availability of good financing, and the area's economy. While we have seen periods of sharp declines in value in the past, property values in California historically have tended to increase an average of more than 3% a year beyond the rate of inflation. Home ownership is still likely to be the best investment or savings program the average family will ever have.

Tax benefits. Home ownership, as well as second-home ownership, offers significant tax advantages that influence many buyers. The deductibility of property taxes and interest means that true costs are significantly less than they appear. The special tax exemptions available for gains on the sale of primary residences is the frosting on the cake, because it makes home ownership extremely attractive for anyone concerned about income taxes. (See Unit 14.)

Comfort and convenience. The human drive for comfort and convenience has less influence than some of the other, previously mentioned factors. When basic needs have been fulfilled, however, these may be considered an added dimension.

Reason versus emotion. *Logic* makes people think, or reason. *Emotion* makes them act. Potential buyers may decide logically that a property is suited for them, but they may not act because the property does not trigger an emotional response. *In most situations, buyers do not buy simply from need, they buy what they want.* While sellers tend to sell based on logic, buyers generally buy based on emotion. The successful salesperson probes to find the buyers' desires that, when satisfied, will trigger their motivation to buy. This is why communication is so important. What a buyer says he or she wants is likely to be based on reason; what the buyer really wants may be based more on emotion than on reason. If you pay attention while showing a house, you can determine the emotional needs of the buyer and select properties to show that meet those needs. You can gain an understanding of which of several properties a buyer actually wants by questions such as "If these properties were priced identically, which property would you prefer?" Follow this up with, "Why?" By listening, you can offer knowledgeable assistance based on experience of other buyers your buyers can relate to. It is much easier to sell buyers a property that appeals to their emotions than one that appears sensible for them.

The author once showed a prospective buyer a luxury home. He could easily afford it but hesitated spending the money because he didn't need that fine a home. Giving the buyer a rational reason to buy resulted in a sale: "It's more than a home, it's an investment, and you don't have to wait to sell it to realize the appreciation. A great many homeowners have sent their children through college by refinancing their homes or using a home equity line of credit." Buyers are usually often receptive to even weak rational reasons to buy property that appeals to their emotions.

Sensory appeal. People learn about the surrounding world through their senses, which include sound, sight, smell, taste, and touch. You can enhance your presentation by employing all the senses and by emphasizing the benefits that can be appreciated by various senses.

In appealing to the sense of *sight*, point out the restful and interesting views from the windows, the lush lawns, the lines of the house, the ample wall space. Be careful not to go overboard about certain colors; they may be your choice but not the buyer's.

The appeal of *sound* may be either its absence or its presence—perhaps it will be music, man-made or natural, to a buyer's ears. Where possible, call attention to the sound made by the ocean, a lake, a babbling brook, or birds. Also, make buyers aware that machinery in the house, such as air conditioners, water closets, and power switches, operate quietly.

To appeal to buyers' sense of *smell*, call attention to the fresh air, flower scents, or, if possible, the smell of cedar from closets or chests.

The sense of *taste* might be appealed to by testing the flavor of well water, vegetables from the garden, or fruit from the trees. If you know there is ripe fruit in the yard, an excellent technique is to bring a pen knife with you and offer a slice of fruit to the prospective buyers.

Appeal to the sense of *touch* by touching the carpeting, knocking on the solid wood paneling, or breaking up a lump of garden soil in your hand. Your prospects will likely do the same. By touching, they come a little closer to ownership.

Negative motivation.   **Negative motivation** applies to knowing what someone does *not* want. There are many things we do not want: pain, hunger, fatigue, worry, strife, just to mention a few. Negative motivation can be more immediate and real to a person than positive motivation. People seem to know what they do not want better than what they do want.

To avoid a fruitless, time-wasting search, the salesperson should endeavor to learn buyers' negative motivations as well as the positive ones. Some disadvantages of home ownership are described in Figure 10.3: large initial investment, risk, increased expenses, restricted mobility, a low level of liquidity, and greater responsibility. If a buyer does not want something, the absence or mitigation of this perceived negative becomes a strong positive factor for a sale.

Watch for Buying Signals

In many situations and at various psychological moments during your presentation, prospects may signal that they are ready to buy. These **buying signals**—some action, word or phrase, or facial expression of buyers—are tip-offs to the salesperson. A buying signal says, "I'm ready to talk terms if you are." These signals are green lights. After prospects have exhibited a buying signal, follow up the opportunity with a closing statement.

Actions.   You are making a presentation, and the prospects stay mum. They do not even grunt. You start to wonder if you are talking their language. Suddenly, one of them picks up the deposit receipt and reads a clause or two. Stop your presentation and swing into your close—they are interested. Prospects also are signaling when they return to an upstairs room for a second look or to measure a room. They are envisioning their placement of furniture. If prospects seem reluctant to leave the room or the property or inspect minute details, it shows positive interest. These actions will often mean "I'm ready to buy."

Words.   Obvious buying signals would be statements such as "This is great!" "Kevin would love this back bedroom," or "I especially like the low maintenance." Even an objection or an expression of resistance can spell a buying signal: "Don't you think the price is a little too high?" The alert salesperson hears it as a signal, because it shows that the buyer actually is thinking about the purchase. Other possible signals occur if a buyer

- asks the salesperson to go over the financing details again,

- inquires about possession time,

- requests information about closing costs,

- starts to whisper with a spouse, or

- makes a statement as to a positive aspect of the property.

FIGURE 10.3: Disadvantages of Home Ownership

■ Large initial investment: Normally, buying a home requires a down payment of 5% to 20% of the purchase price, with the exception of VA loans, some FHA loans, and loans involving secondary financing or high rates of interest. This means the purchase price of a $400,000 home may require a down payment of $20,000 to $80,000. In addition, the closing costs could well be from $4,000 to $10,000.

■ Risk: Whenever customers invest money, they risk losing some or all of it. Changes in market conditions can affect value. However, well-located properties kept in good condition offer less risk over the long term than most other investment choices.

■ Increase in expenses: Although mortgage payments remain constant in the case of fixed-rate loans, other costs may increase. Property taxes and utility costs creep upward. Maintenance costs increase as the home ages. Adjustable-rate loans could have an increase in interest and payments. Buyers have to weigh some of these increased costs against the advantages of ownership, but they should remember that rents also increase.

■ Restricted mobility: To a degree, people are less mobile once they have bought a home. However, houses can be sold or rented out by the owner.

■ Lack of liquidity: Some say they dislike home ownership because their investment is not liquid. While an investment in a home is not as liquid as having money in the bank, homeowners can use their property as a source of cash. For example, homeowners might consider borrowing on the property by taking out a home equity loan. Or they could refinance the first mortgage once sufficient equity has been developed.

■ Greater responsibility: An investment in real property has responsibilities. Buyers must maintain the property properly. For example, they may have to climb a ladder to paint or call a painter and pay the bill. The lawn needs to be watered and cut to protect the investment.

Negative statements can be a signal to buy. A complaint about price could instead mean an offer at a lesser price is imminent. Complaining about problems that can be readily solved, coupled with a reluctance to leave the property, could be a buying tactic to justify a lower offer.

Body language. A salesperson who is not watching customers carefully may easily miss facial-expression signals. Prospects smiling as you make your presentation or nodding at each other are positive signals. A prospect sitting back in the chair and then leaning forward as you make your sales presentation is a sign of interest. Meeting your eye contact, as well as showing signs of relaxing, are also positive indicators.

Overcome Resistance

To obtain the offer, be prepared to answer any objections raised by the buyer. Buyer resistance will vary with each transaction. Typical objections might include some of the following statements:

■ "The price is too high."

■ "The water pressure is too low."

■ "The rooms are too small."

■ "The taxes are too high."

- "I can't buy until I sell."

- "I can't get occupancy soon enough."

- "I'll never get my kids into that school."

Human nature being what it is, some salespeople feel they must conquer objections by crushing them decisively. It is an unfortunate truth that many salespeople feel they must treat objections as barriers raised to block them from their goal— the sale or the offer. They see an objection as being in direct conflict with their best interests, and therefore they fear it and wish to combat it quickly.

In contrast to this, you should treat an objection as a prelude to a sale, a natural part of any sales routine. Objections may occur while showing the house or in your office before signing the offer. Before proceeding to your counterattack, determine two things in your own mind:

1. Is it really an objection or just a comment?

2. Is it an objection you can and should do something about?

There are ways to handle real objections. Five basic steps to be used in meeting objections are shown in Figure 10.4. Carefully following these steps leads to obtaining the offer and closing the sale.

When buyers are hesitant, ask a simple question or two:

What if anything would keep you from buying this house?

How could you overcome this?

If a buyer responds with a solution, you should have an offer.

Welcome objections.   An objection means that you have an interested buyer who has a concern. When you fail to get objections, it could mean that your prospect is not a serious buyer. Do not fear objections; welcome them. Encourage prospects to tell you what is on their minds. Objections help focus your talk on what matters to the prospect. They may be the prospect's way of asking for more information. They may throw some light on the prospect's thinking.

FIGURE 10.4:   Meeting a Buyer's Objections

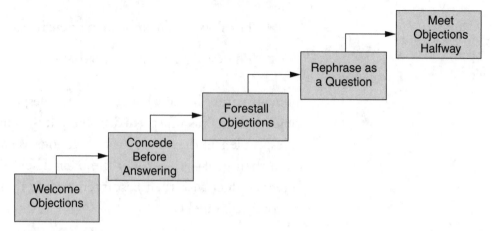

You can't overcome objections if you don't know what they are.

Concede before answering.   To avoid putting the buyers on the defensive, recognize legitimate concerns. Never tell buyers who have a legitimate objection that their position is somehow not valid or less than true. This immediately creates confrontation. You might make a comment such as one of these: "Other clients have felt the same way in the past, but what they have found is that . . .," "I can appreciate your concerns," or "I understand how you feel."

Rephrase an objection as a question.   The buyer might say, "I don't like tract houses," to which you could reply, "As I understand it then, Mr. and Mrs. Buyer, your question is this: 'Am I better off buying a smaller custom home in a less desirable neighborhood for the same money or would I gain greater enjoyment by owning this larger home with more amenities in a great neighborhood?'" Try to restate objections as questions. Doing so shows the buyers that you are working together and that you are most concerned with helping them.

Similarly:

I don't like the color of this room

If this were your house, what color would you paint it?

Do you think [one] gallon of paint would cover it?

If the buyers can solve their own objections, you are on the path to a sale.

What you have done is minimize the objection and the prospective buyers have solved their own objection.

If a prospective buyer objects to a price, your first question should be, "What do you feel would be a fair price for this property?" If the buyer replies with a price, your response could be, "How did you arrive at that price?" Listen attentively. You could correct misconceptions and justify what you feel is a fair price, or you could state, "While I think your price is a little low, let's try it. If the owners accept, I think you'll have made a really advantageous purchase."

Meet objections halfway. A well-known technique for answering objections is the "Yes, but . . ." technique. This technique meets objections halfway. The objection may be, "This is the smallest bedroom I've ever seen." The licensee could answer, "Yes, Ms. Buyer, you're right, that is a small bedroom, and I imagine it was intended for a young person. If this were your house, whose bedroom would this be?" You could then continue, "How would you furnish this room for your [son/daughter]?" If buyers can solve their own objections, you have gone a long way toward making a sale.

Forestall objections. Your experience tells you to expect certain objections from your prospect. Bring up these potential objections before the prospect does. This is known as *forestalling* or *anticipating the objection*. Its effect is to reduce the objection's importance and to show the prospect that you do not fear it. "It could use a new coat of paint. Do you think 10 gallons would do the job?"

When you don't know. If you don't know the answer to a question, never guess. It is better to say you don't know than to fabricate an answer you are unsure of. Consider this example:

"That's a good question, I'll get the answer for you by___."

Answering a question with a question. You must handle questions as well as objections. One way to answer a question from a buyer is to use a "hook." This is the technique of answering a question with a question. It prolongs the sales interview and keeps the buyer in the act. Three examples are these:

1. **Question:** Will the sellers agree to an April 1 closing?

   Wrong answer: I'm pretty sure they will.

   Using a hook: Do you want an April 1 closing?

2. **Question:** Will the sellers consider a lower offer?

   Wrong answer: Yes, they've indicated they might listen to an offer.

   Using a hook: How much are you prepared to offer? (If you feel the figure is unreasonable, you should use it as a starting point and attempt to write a more reasonable offer. If you are a buyer's agent, then you should be recommending an offer price and be prepared to justify it.)

3. **Question:** Is the stove (refrigerator, drapery, carpeting) included?

   Wrong answer: I'll ask the seller.

   Using a hook: Do you want the stove (refrigerator, drapery, carpeting) included?

While these using-a-hook answers imply that the prospect will buy, many agents prefer a nail-down approach: "If _____, would you buy this property?" They have asked for something and the agent is asking, "If you got it, would you buy?"

Listen and minimize. When the property meets most of the buyer's expressed needs, you can summarize benefits and attempt to minimize or overcome the objections. As an example:

This property is nearly perfect for your family.

- It is located in the Newport school district that you indicated you desired.

- It has the formal dining room you said was essential.

- It has the sunlit patio off the kitchen that you liked in the first house I showed you.

- Its size meets all your requirements: 3 bedrooms, 2½ baths, and a 3-car garage.

- The price falls within the guidelines you indicated.

- The condition, I am sure you will agree, is pristine.

- Is my analysis correct except that you don't like the tile in the kitchen and bath and that the light fixture in the dining room is way too small?

If the owner agrees with your analysis, you have emphasized the positive features and exposed the negative features in a way that tends to make them manageable. You might want to continue with, "What do you think it would cost to . . .?" You could then say, "I think an offer for this property would make sense, don't you agree?"

Attempt a Trial Close

If a salesperson successfully builds each part of the sale throughout the presentation, the close will come easily. In many cases, the buyer's reaction says, "I'm ready to make an offer." There is a psychological moment for a **trial close**, but it varies with each transaction.

Attempting a trial close often is called "test and heat." To close any sale and get the buyers' signatures on the deposit receipt, do what your great-grandmother did with the old-fashioned flatiron—test and heat. If the customer is not ready to buy, add a little "heat." This means that you present new evidence or reiterate key sales points and try again.

> With a trial close, you get the buyers to agree to something that indicates they are willing to buy.

Beginning with the first interview, the salesperson must build for this moment during every phase of the sale, because the buyer may make a decision at any time. Although all situations and all buyers are different, the following six basic closing principles can be set forth:

- Throughout the sale, use "you" and "yours" or the customers' name

- Obtain agreement on a variety of things throughout the interview

- Tell a complete story in terms of a customer's buying motives; turn the features into personal benefits and hold some talking points in reserve

- Watch for buying signals

- Say, "Let's go back to the office and see what it looks like on paper"

- Ask for their signatures if they do not volunteer to sign

Closing Techniques

Six basic closing techniques often are employed: the assumptive close, the positive choice, inducement, fear of loss, narrative, and asking for the deposit. Of course, there are hundreds of variations on these closing techniques.

Assumptive close (physical action close). In an **assumptive close**, you assume the buyer is going to buy and you complete the deposit receipt form. This close is a natural follow-through when a buyer flashes a buying-signal question such as "Can I get possession by July 1?" You should respond, "Would you like possession by July 1? We can certainly ask for it . . ."

Other assumptive closings to consider when you are getting a positive feedback include the following:

Does 30 days for closing meet your needs? (If the answer is affirmative or another date is given, you should be writing this offer.)

The property is listed at [$], but you as the buyer decide what you wish to offer. Would you want to offer [$] and be sure you have this home, or would you want to offer a different amount? (If you are a buyer's agent, you should suggest an offer price and be prepared to justify the price with comparables.)

I think we have found your new home; let's put it on paper.

Another approach to the assumptive close would be to talk about the next steps as if the offer were signed.

When we receive confirmation of your offer, we will immediately begin finalizing the loan as well as arrange for a property inspection.

A positive choice is a choice of two factors, either of which indicate a purchase.

Positive choice. Give the buyer a **positive choice**—that is, a choice between two things rather than between something and nothing. The skillful salesperson never asks the buyer a question that can be answered with a flat "no." Here are two examples of positive-choice questions:

Would you prefer government-backed financing with a lower down payment and higher monthly payments or conventional financing with a higher down payment and lower monthly payments?

If the seller will retile the kitchen floor, what size tile do you prefer, 18- or 20-inch?

You have seen [three] houses you really like. Which one do you feel you would be happiest in? Why? Let's see if we can make this your home.

Inducement.   If used properly, an **inducement** can be a powerful stimulant to a close. For example, consider these:

> If you buy now, I believe we can lock in the current (3.6%) interest rate. You would like a 3.6% rate, wouldn't you?

> I'm sure we could arrange the closing of escrow so you will not make double payments. You would like to save that money, wouldn't you?

Be careful when you use this technique. If the outcome of the sale hinges on a lower interest rate, a change of tile, or an added refrigerator and you cannot deliver, you may lose the sale. Try to hedge on your commitment by saying that you will do your best to obtain the inducement.

Fear of loss.   The *fear-of-loss method*, often called the *standing-room-only technique*, is effective only if it is based on fact. Buyers have built up an immunity to such statements as this: "This is the last house in this plot, and the builder doesn't plan any further development." This technique works only if it is based on facts concerning a personal, immediate, and real situation.

Here is an example of a believable fear-of-loss close that is true and is based on researched facts:

> This is the last home by this builder available in this tract. All the others are sold. When the new tract is open, the price will be $20,000 higher for the same home. Wouldn't you rather buy now and save that amount?

When a prospective buyer has made an offer or offers on other properties but lost out to other bidders, fear of loss is a strong motivation to act now. Again, it must be based on fact. "Another agent will be showing this property to an interested couple at 3:30 pm today. If you are interested in this property, I suggest an offer right now that can be accepted before the couple sees this home."

Narrative.   A *narrative close*, or storybook close, involves the use of a third party as an ally. If you are able to produce third-party verification of the fact you are trying to establish, the buyer is likely to accept what you say. For example, you could show a newspaper article stating that interest rates are expected to rise. In this situation, someone else is conveying the information. For example, the buyer may express a concern about some aspect of the property. Use the time-tested "feel, felt, found" technique. The agent might say, "I can appreciate how you FEEL; many of our clients have FELT the same way, but after examining it further, they have FOUND that . . ." Or you could say, "Mr. Jones just down the street had a question similar to yours. We were able to find a solution for him. If you wish, we can call him to verify my story."

If you live in the area, let the buyers know and explain the reasons you chose the location. This will add positive reinforcement for a choice.

Always use real experiences. From interfacing with other agents, you will find out about their experiences and how issues were resolved to the satisfaction of clients.

Ask for the deposit. Many salespeople do an excellent job of making a presentation and even covering all objections, but they are hesitant to ask for the sale. The reason is fear; they get a battlefield fear sensation. They fear a rejection, a "no" answer. Consequently, they overlook asking or are reluctant to ask for the deposit.

> If you want a positive response, you have to ask first.

Buyers will buy if they are asked to buy, but some salespeople rarely ask. Practice and experiment with asking for the deposit. For example, say, "These units do offer an excellent appreciation potential if you're willing to do some fixing up. Why don't you get started on your investment program now? Will you give me your deposit check and let me get your purchase under way?" It's all right to ask again. A coffee salesman we know once asked a close friend, the owner of a large restaurant, why he had never purchased coffee from him. The reply was, "You never asked!"

If one closing doesn't work, continue to emphasize benefits. Suggest another look at the property and try another closing. If the property fits the buyers' needs, they like the property, and they can afford it, then treat a failure as a "maybe." A little more time might be all it takes.

"Let's jot down the issues you want to address in your offer."

Killing a Sale

A positive sales approach is to ask leading questions, gain agreement throughout the sale, then ask for the offer. A salesperson who does not use a positive approach may be the loser. The sale also can be killed by the following:

- Not listening
- Talking too much and too fast
- Being overeager to sell
- Having incomplete knowledge
- Using high-pressure tactics
- Exhibiting fear
- Criticizing competitors
- Straying from the subject
- Displaying a negative selling attitude
- Being argumentative

A Clean Offer

When a buyer is interested but "wants to sleep on it," you should set up a definite appointment, hopefully the next day, for the buyer to make an offer, or continue the home search.

Whenever possible, contingencies should be removed, as should nickel-and-dime items such as "seller to leave the workbench in the garage." Don't deviate from what the seller wants unless absolutely essential. Asking for quicker occupancy could ruin the buyer's chances. To make the offer more desirable, loan qualification information can be attached to the offer. While price is important, a clean sale is also important and a seller is likely to accept a lower offer if the sale appears more certain. Requests for changes can be made after an offer is accepted. While not required to agree to any changes after acceptance, the seller oftentimes will go along with reasonable buyer requests. If the seller counteroffers rather than accepts the offer, then other desired items can be negotiated.

When There Are Other Offers

In the event you have a prospective buyer for a property where another offer has already been made, you could suggest the following tactic to your prospective buyer: An offer for a sum over highest bona fide offer received, such as $5,000, but in no event more than a stated price, which would be the highest price your buyer is willing to pay. If your prospect's offer is accepted, your buyer's offer should allow for verification of the competing offer. This approach assures purchase unless the buyer's maximum has been exceeded.

Buyer Agent Closing

When you are representing the buyer under a buyer-agency agreement, you have a duty to best serve the interests of your principal. Those interests would include finding a house that best meets the needs of your principal at the best price and to protect the buyer against any foreseeable problems. As a buyer's agent, you should have built a trust relationship so you can ask a simple question, "Do you like this house?" and/or "Does this house meet your needs better than anything I have found for you?" Don't ask these questions unless you know the reply will be positive. You could then continue with, "I think we should offer [$] because . . ., and any offer should be contingent upon a professional inspection. Does that make sense to you?" If the response is positive, and it should be, you can begin writing up the offer. Of course, you should justify the offering price based on comparables, changes in market conditions, as well as known facts about the property, and the seller.

ESTIMATED BUYER'S COSTS

When formulating the purchase offer, provide the buyer with the good faith estimate of buyer's acquisition costs—an estimate of the total cash requirements, as well as estimated monthly payments based on the offer (Professional Publishing LLC Form 125 EBECC can be used). Although costs will vary between lenders and escrow companies, you must nevertheless strive to be realistic. Be honest and full in your disclosures. It is best for any error to be on the high side. (Keep in mind that because the dollar amount of real estate transactions is so high, surprises can make people very unhappy.)

Fine-Tuning the Offer

If buyers suggest an offer at an unrealistic price or terms, or both, consider writing up the offer. Before you give it to your prospective buyers to sign, ask the following:

Do you like this house?

You say you like the house, but you want to give an offer that doesn't indicate this. If you were the sellers, what would you think about this offer?

In this market, if you really want this property, I would advise giving your best offer. Raise this offer by just [ ]% and you'll have a chance to be an owner. Let's write it up at [$]. At that price, it is still an exceptional opportunity, and your offer at least will have a fighting chance of being accepted.

Complete this offer and hand it to the prospective buyers, along with a pen.

FIGURE 10.5:   Good Faith Estimate of Buyer's Acquisition Costs

---

GOOD FAITH ESTIMATE OF BUYER'S ACQUISITION COSTS
On Acquisition of Property

Prepared by: Agent _____ Phone _____

Broker _____ Email _____

NOTE: This cost sheet is prepared to assist the buyer to estimate the total cost of acquisition for a property to anticipate the amount of funds likely needed to close, and the source of these funds.

The figures estimated in this cost sheet may vary at the time of closing due to periodic changes in lender demands, escrow fees, other charges and prorates, and thus constitute an opinion, not a guarantee of the preparer.

If acquiring IRC §1031 replacement property, also use a §1031 Profit and Basis Recap Sheet to compute the income tax consequences of the transaction. [See **ft** Form 354]

DATE: _____, 20_____, at _____, California.

1.   This is an estimate of acquisition costs and the funds required to close the following transaction:

☐ Purchase Agreement   ☐ Exchange agreement   ☐ Counteroffer   ☐ Escrow Instructions   ☐ Option

1.1   entered into by _____,

1.2   dated _____, 20_____, at _____, California,

1.3   regarding real estate referred to as _____
_____.

2.   **EXISTING FINANCING ASSUMED:**

2.1   First Trust Deed of Record . . . . $_____

2.2   Second Trust Deed of Record . . . . $_____

2.3   Other Encumbrances/Liens/Bonds . . . . $_____

2.4   TOTAL Encumbrances Assumed [lines 2.1 to 2.4] . . . . (+)$0.00_____

    a.   If loan balance adjustments are to be made in cash, the total funds
required to close escrow at §10 and §12 will vary.

3.   **INSTALLMENT SALE FINANCING:**

3.1   Seller Carryback Financing . . . . (+)$_____

4.   **NEW FINANCING ORIGINATED:**

4.1   New Loan Amount . . . . (+)$_____

4.2   Points/Discount . . . . $_____

4.3   Appraisal Fee . . . . $_____

4.4   Credit Report Fee . . . . $_____

4.5   Miscellaneous Origination Fees . . . . $_____

4.6   Prepaid Interest . . . . $_____

4.7   Mortgage Insurance Premium . . . . $_____

4.8   Lender's Title Policy Premium . . . . $_____

4.9   Tax Service Fee . . . . $_____

4.10   Loan Brokerage Fee . . . . $_____

4.11   Other _____ . . . . $_____

4.12   TOTAL New Financing Costs [lines 4.2 to 4.11] . . . . (+)$0.00_____

5.   **PURCHASE COSTS AND CHARGES:**

5.1   Assumption Fees (First) . . . . $_____

5.2   Assumption Fees (Second) . . . . $_____

5.3   Escrow Fee . . . . $_____

5.4   Notary Fee . . . . $_____

5.5   Document Preparation Fee . . . . $_____

5.6   Recording Fee/Transfer Taxes . . . . $_____

5.7   Title Insurance Premium . . . . $_____

— — — — — — — — — — — — — — — — — *PAGE ONE OF TWO — FORM 311* — — — — — — — — — — — — — — — — —

FIGURE 10.5 (continued):   **Good Faith Estimate of Buyer's Acquisition Costs**

— — — — — — — — — — — — — — — — — — — *PAGE TWO OF TWO — FORM 311* — — — — — — — — — — — — — — — —

5.8   Property Condition Reports . . . . $_____

5.9   Cost of Compliance Repairs . . . . $_____

5.10 Other _____ . . . . $_____

5.11 Other _____ . . . . $_____

5.12 TOTAL Closing Costs [lines 5.1 to 5.11] . . . . (+)$ 0.00 _____

5.13 Down Payment on Price . . . . (+)$_____

6. **TOTAL ESTIMATED ACQUISITION COST** [lines 2.4, 3.1, 4.1, 4.12, 5.12 and 5.13] . . . . . (=)$ 0.00 _____

   6.1 No post-closing repairs or renovation cost are included here.

7. **FUNDS REQUIRED TO CLOSE ESCROW:**

   7.1 Down Payment On Price (From line 5.13) . . . . (+)$_____

   7.2 Closing Costs (From line 5.12) . . . . (+)$ 0.00 _____

   7.3 New Loan Proceeds (From line 4.1) . . . . (+)$_____

   7.4 New Financing Costs (From line 4.12) . . . . (+)$ 0.00 _____

   7.5 Impounds for New Financing . . . . (+)$_____

   7.6 Hazard Insurance Premium . . . . (+)$_____

8. **PRORATES DUE BUYER AT CLOSE:**

   8.1 Unpaid Taxes/Assessments . . . . $_____

   8.2 Interest Accrued and Unpaid . . . . $_____

   8.3 Unearned Rental Income . . . . $_____

   8.4 Tenant Security Deposits . . . . $_____

   8.5 TOTAL Prorates Due Buyer [lines 8.1 to 8.4] . . . . (-)$ 0.00 _____

9. **PRORATES DUE SELLER AT CLOSE:**

   9.1 Prepaid Taxes/Assessments . . . . $_____

   9.2 Impound Account Balance . . . . $_____

   9.3 Prepaid Homeowners' Assessment . . . . $_____

   9.4 Prepaid Ground Lease Rent . . . . $_____

   9.5 Unpaid Rents assigned to Buyer . . . . $_____

   9.6 Other _____ . . . . $_____

   9.7 TOTAL Prorates Due Seller [lines 9.1 to 9.6] . . . . (+)$ 0.00 _____

10. **TOTAL FUNDS REQUIRED TO CLOSE ESCROW:** [lines 6, 7.1 to 7.6, less 8.5 plus 9.7]. (=)$ 0.00 _____

   10.1   See §2.4.a. adjustments.

11. **SOURCE OF FUNDS REQUIRED TO CLOSE ESCROW:**

   11.1 New First Loan Amount (From line 4.1) . . . . $_____

   11.2 New Second Loan Amount (Net loan proceeds) . . . . $_____

   11.3 Third-Party Deposits . . . . $_____

   11.4 Buyer's Cash . . . . $_____

12. **TOTAL FUNDS REQUIRED TO CLOSE ESCROW:** (Same as line 10) . . . . (=)$ 0.00 _____

I have prepared this estimate based on my knowledge and readily available data.

Date: _____, 20_____

Broker: _____

Agent: _____

DRE #: _____

Signature: _____

I have read and received a copy of this estimate.

Date: _____, 20_____

Buyer's Name: _____

Signature: _____

Signature: _____

THE CALIFORNIA RESIDENTIAL PURCHASE AGREEMENT AND JOINT ESCROW INSTRUCTIONS

"An oral contract is not worth the paper it is written on," said Samuel Goldwyn. The California Statute of Frauds stipulates that all real estate sales contracts must be in writing to be enforceable.

When a sale has been consummated and the offer obtained, put everything in writing to avoid costly misunderstanding, bad will, and even litigation in the future. It is essential that the purchase contract include the entire agreement of the parties. There should be no "understood" provisions that are not reduced to writing. Poor draftsmanship of the purchase contract is a significant factor in lawsuits between buyer, seller, and broker, or any combination of the three. Not only must the agreement be complete, but also the parties should fully understand the agreement before signing. Many deposit receipt forms were used in California, and the buyer's offer could be submitted on any of these. However, the number of forms caused a great deal of concern in legal circles and with the California Association of REALTORS® because brokers are seldom attorneys and may be confused by the language employed. As a result, in 1985, the California Association of REALTORS®, in cooperation with the state bar and with the approval of the Bureau of Real Estate, developed a model form, the Residential Purchase Agreement [and Receipt for Deposit], which is now the **California Residential Purchase Agreement and Joint Escrow Instructions.** This form is now widely used in California. (See Figure 10.6.) It is possible to complete your purchase contract online and then print out the contract for signatures. (Other form providers also offer excellent purchasing agreements.)

Content of the Form

Essentially, the form acts as a checklist to ensure that a contract is complete in all respects. The responsible parties must comply with the requirements stipulated to help both parties avoid entangling legal complications. Any changes should be dated and initialed by the principals to the transaction.

FIGURE 10.6: **California Residential Purchase Agreement and Joint Escrow Instructions**

(The following form is copyrighted by the California Association of REALTORS®, © 2014, and is reprinted under a limited license with permission. Photocopying or any other reproduction, whether electronic or otherwise, is strictly prohibited.)

CALIFORNIA ASSOCIATION OF REALTORS®

CALIFORNIA RESIDENTIAL PURCHASE AGREEMENT AND JOINT ESCROW INSTRUCTIONS
(C.A.R. Form RPA-CA, Revised 11/14)

Date Prepared: _____

1. **OFFER:**
   A. **THIS IS AN OFFER FROM** _____ ("Buyer").
   B. **THE REAL PROPERTY** to be acquired is _____, situated in
      _____ (City), _____ (County), California, _____ (Zip Code), Assessor's Parcel No. _____ ("Property").
   C. **THE PURCHASE PRICE** offered is _____
      _____ Dollars $ _____.
   D. **CLOSE OF ESCROW** shall occur on _____ (date)(or _____ **Days** After Acceptance).
   E. Buyer and Seller are referred to herein as the "Parties." Brokers are not Parties to this Agreement.

2. **AGENCY:**
   A. **DISCLOSURE:** The Parties each acknowledge receipt of a ☑"Disclosure Regarding Real Estate Agency Relationships" (C.A.R. Form AD).
   B. **CONFIRMATION:** The following agency relationships are hereby confirmed for this transaction:
      Listing Agent _____ (Print Firm Name) is the agent of (check one):
      ☐ the Seller exclusively; or ☐ both the Buyer and Seller.
      Selling Agent _____ (Print Firm Name) (if not the same as the
      Listing Agent) is the agent of (check one): ☐ the Buyer exclusively; or ☐ the Seller exclusively; or ☐ both the Buyer and Seller.
   C. **POTENTIALLY COMPETING BUYERS AND SELLERS:** The Parties each acknowledge receipt of a ☑"Possible Representation of More than One Buyer or Seller - Disclosure and Consent" (C.A.R. Form PRBS).

3. **FINANCE TERMS:** Buyer represents that funds will be good when deposited with Escrow Holder.
   A. **INITIAL DEPOSIT:** Deposit shall be in the amount of ....$ _____
      (1) Buyer Direct Deposit: Buyer shall deliver deposit directly to Escrow Holder by electronic funds
      transfer, ☐ cashier's check, ☐ personal check, ☐ other _____ within 3 business days
      after Acceptance (or _____);
      OR (2) ☐ **Buyer Deposit with Agent:** Buyer has given the deposit by personal check (or _____)
      to the agent submitting the offer (or to _____), made payable to
      _____. The deposit shall be held uncashed until Acceptance and then deposited
      with Escrow Holder within **3** business days after Acceptance (or _____).
      Deposit checks given to agent shall be an original signed check and not a copy.
      (Note: Initial and increased deposits checks received by agent shall be recorded in Broker's trust fund log.)
   B. **INCREASED DEPOSIT:** Buyer shall deposit with Escrow Holder an increased deposit in the amount of ....$ _____
      within _____ **Days** After Acceptance (or _____).
      If the Parties agree to liquidated damages in this Agreement, they also agree to incorporate the increased
      deposit into the liquidated damages amount in a separate liquidated damages clause (C.A.R. Form RID)
      at the time the increased deposit is delivered to Escrow Holder.
   C. ☐ **ALL CASH OFFER:** No loan is needed to purchase the Property. This offer is NOT contingent on Buyer
      obtaining a loan. Written verification of sufficient funds to close this transaction IS ATTACHED to this offer
      or ☐ Buyer shall, within **3 (or _____) Days** After Acceptance, Deliver to Seller such verification.
   D. **LOAN(S):**
      (1) FIRST LOAN: in the amount of ....$ _____
      This loan will be conventional financing or ☐ FHA, ☐ VA, ☐ Seller financing (C.A.R. Form SFA),
      ☐ assumed financing (C.A.R. Form AFA), ☐ Other _____. This loan shall be at a fixed
      rate not to exceed _____% or, ☐ an adjustable rate loan with initial rate not to exceed _____%.
      Regardless of the type of loan, Buyer shall pay points not to exceed _____% of the loan amount.
      (2) ☐ **SECOND LOAN** in the amount of ....$ _____
      This loan will be conventional financing or ☐ Seller financing (C.A.R. Form SFA), ☐ assumed
      financing (C.A.R. Form AFA), ☐ Other _____. This loan shall be at a fixed rate not to
      exceed _____% or, ☐ an adjustable rate loan with initial rate not to exceed _____%. Regardless of
      the type of loan, Buyer shall pay points not to exceed _____% of the loan amount.
      (3) FHA/VA: For any FHA or VA loan specified in 3D(1), Buyer has **17 (or ___) Days** After Acceptance
      to Deliver to Seller written notice (C.A.R. Form FVA) of any lender-required repairs or costs that
      Buyer requests Seller to pay for or otherwise correct. Seller has no obligation to pay or satisfy lender
      requirements unless agreed in writing. A FHA/VA amendatory clause (C.A.R. Form FVAC) shall be a
      part of this transaction.
   E. **ADDITIONAL FINANCING TERMS:** _____
      _____
   F. **BALANCE OF DOWN PAYMENT OR PURCHASE PRICE** in the amount of ....$ _____
      to be deposited with Escrow Holder pursuant to Escrow Holder instructions.
   G. **PURCHASE PRICE (TOTAL):** ....$ _____

Buyer's Initials (_____)(_____)   Seller's Initials (_____)(_____)

© 1991-2014, California Association of REALTORS®, Inc.
RPA-CA REVISED 11/14 (PAGE 1 OF 10) Print Date

EQUAL HOUSING OPPORTUNITY

CALIFORNIA RESIDENTIAL PURCHASE AGREEMENT (RPA-CA PAGE 1 OF 10)

FIGURE 10.6 (continued):   California Residential Purchase Agreement and Joint Escrow Instructions

Property Address: _____   Date: _____

H. **VERIFICATION OF DOWN PAYMENT AND CLOSING COSTS:** Buyer (or Buyer's lender or loan broker pursuant to paragraph 3J(1)) shall, within **3 (or ____) Days** After Acceptance, Deliver to Seller written verification of Buyer's down payment and closing costs. (☐ Verification attached.)

I. **APPRAISAL CONTINGENCY AND REMOVAL:** This Agreement is (**or** ☐ is NOT) contingent upon a written appraisal of the Property by a licensed or certified appraiser at no less than the purchase price. Buyer shall, as specified in paragraph 14B(3), in writing, remove the appraisal contingency or cancel this Agreement within **17 (or ____) Days** After Acceptance.

J. **LOAN TERMS:**

(1) LOAN APPLICATIONS: Within **3 (or ____) Days** After Acceptance, Buyer shall Deliver to Seller a letter from Buyer's lender or loan broker stating that, based on a review of Buyer's written application and credit report, Buyer is prequalified or preapproved for any NEW loan specified in paragraph 3D. If any loan specified in paragraph 3D is an adjustable rate loan, the prequalification or preapproval letter shall be based on the qualifying rate, not the initial loan rate. (☐ Letter attached.)

(2) LOAN CONTINGENCY: Buyer shall act diligently and in good faith to obtain the designated loan(s). Buyer's qualification for the loan(s) specified above **is a contingency** of this Agreement unless otherwise agreed in writing. If there is no appraisal contingency or the appraisal contingency has been waived or removed, then failure of the Property to appraise at the purchase price does not entitle Buyer to exercise the cancellation right pursuant to the loan contingency if Buyer is otherwise qualified for the specified loan. Buyer's contractual obligations regarding deposit, balance of down payment and closing costs **are not contingencies** of this Agreement.

(3) LOAN CONTINGENCY REMOVAL:
Within **21 (or ____) Days** After Acceptance, Buyer shall, as specified in paragraph 14, in writing, remove the loan contingency or cancel this Agreement. If there is an appraisal contingency, removal of the loan contingency shall not be deemed removal of the appraisal contingency.

(4) ☐ NO LOAN CONTINGENCY: Obtaining any loan specified above is NOT a contingency of this Agreement. If Buyer does not obtain the loan and as a result does not purchase the Property, Seller may be entitled to Buyer's deposit or other legal remedies.

(5) LENDER LIMITS ON BUYER CREDITS: Any credit to Buyer, from any source, for closing or other costs that is agreed to by the Parties ("Contractual Credit") shall be disclosed to Buyer's lender. If the total credit allowed by Buyer's lender ("Lender Allowable Credit") is less than the Contractual Credit, then (i) the Contractual Credit shall be reduced to the Lender Allowable Credit, and (ii) in the absence of a separate written agreement between the Parties, there shall be no automatic adjustment to the purchase price to make up for the difference between the Contractual Credit and the Lender Allowable Credit.

K. **BUYER STATED FINANCING:** Seller is relying on Buyer's representation of the type of financing specified (including but not limited to, as applicable, all cash, amount of down payment, or contingent or non-contingent loan). Seller has agreed to a specific closing date, purchase price and to sell to Buyer in reliance on Buyer's covenant concerning financing. Buyer shall pursue the financing specified in this Agreement. Seller has no obligation to cooperate with Buyer's efforts to obtain any financing other than that specified in the Agreement and the availability of any such alternate financing does not excuse Buyer from the obligation to purchase the Property and close escrow as specified in this Agreement.

4. **SALE OF BUYER'S PROPERTY:**

A. This Agreement and Buyer's ability to obtain financing are NOT contingent upon the sale of any property owned by Buyer.

OR B. ☐ This Agreement and Buyer's ability to obtain financing are contingent upon the sale of property owned by Buyer as specified in the attached addendum (C.A.R. Form COP).

5. **ADDENDA AND ADVISORIES:**

A. **ADDENDA:**

☐ Back Up Offer Addendum (C.A.R. Form BUO)   ☐ Addendum #_____ (C.A.R. Form ADM)
☐ Septic, Well and Property Monument Addendum (C.A.R. Form SWPI)   ☐ Court Confirmation Addendum (C.A.R. Form CCA)
☐ Short Sale Addendum (C.A.R. Form SSA)   ☐ Other_____

B. **BUYER AND SELLER ADVISORIES:**   ☑ Buyer's Inspection Advisory (C.A.R. Form BIA)
☐ Probate Advisory (C.A.R. Form PAK)   ☐ Statewide Buyer and Seller Advisory (C.A.R. Form SBSA)
☐ Trust Advisory (C.A.R. Form TA)   ☐ REO Advisory (C.A.R. Form REO)
☐ Short Sale Information and Advisory (C.A.R. Form SSIA)   ☐ Other_____

6. **OTHER TERMS:**_____
_____
_____
_____

7. **ALLOCATION OF COSTS**

A. INSPECTIONS, REPORTS AND CERTIFICATES: Unless otherwise agreed in writing, this paragraph only determines who is to pay for the inspection, test, certificate or service ("Report") mentioned; it **does not determine who is to pay for any work recommended or identified in the Report.**

(1) ☐ Buyer ☐ Seller shall pay for a natural hazard zone disclosure report, including tax ☐ environmental ☐ Other: _____
_____ prepared by _____.

(2) ☐ Buyer ☐ Seller shall pay for the following Report _____
prepared by_____.

(3) ☐ Buyer ☐ Seller shall pay for the following Report _____
prepared by _____.

Buyer's Initials (_____)(_____)   Seller's Initials (_____)(_____)

RPA-CA REVISED 11/14 (PAGE 2 OF 10) Print Date

CALIFORNIA RESIDENTIAL PURCHASE AGREEMENT (RPA-CA PAGE 2 OF 10)

FIGURE 10.6 (continued):   California Residential Purchase Agreement and Joint Escrow Instructions

Property Address: _____   Date: _____

B. GOVERNMENT REQUIREMENTS AND RETROFIT:
  (1) ☐ Buyer ☐ Seller shall pay for smoke alarm and carbon monoxide device installation and water heater bracing, if required by Law. Prior to Close Of Escrow ("COE"), Seller shall provide Buyer written statement(s) of compliance in accordance with state and local Law, unless Seller is exempt.
  (2) (i) ☐ Buyer ☐ Seller shall pay the cost of compliance with any other minimum mandatory government inspections and reports if required as a condition of closing escrow under any Law.
  (ii) ☐ Buyer ☐ Seller shall pay the cost of compliance with any other minimum mandatory government retrofit standards required as a condition of closing escrow under any Law, whether the work is required to be completed before or after COE.
  (iii) Buyer shall be provided, within the time specified in paragraph 14A, a copy of any required government conducted or point-of-sale inspection report prepared pursuant to this Agreement or in anticipation of this sale of the Property.
C. ESCROW AND TITLE:
  (1) (a) ☐ Buyer ☐ Seller shall pay escrow fee _____.
  (b) Escrow Holder shall be _____.
  (c) The Parties shall, within **5 (or ___) Days** After receipt, sign and return Escrow Holder's general provisions.
  (2) (a) ☐ Buyer ☐ Seller shall pay for **owner's** title insurance policy specified in paragraph 13E _____.
  (b) Owner's title policy to be issued by _____.
  (Buyer shall pay for any title insurance policy insuring Buyer's **lender**, unless otherwise agreed in writing.)
D. OTHER COSTS:
  (1) ☐ Buyer ☐ Seller shall pay County transfer tax or fee _____.
  (2) ☐ Buyer ☐ Seller shall pay City transfer tax or fee _____.
  (3) ☐ Buyer ☐ Seller shall pay Homeowners' Association ("HOA") transfer fee _____.
  (4) Seller shall pay HOA fees for preparing documents required to be delivered by Civil Code §4525.
  (5) ☐ Buyer ☐ Seller shall pay HOA fees for preparing all documents other than those required by Civil Code §4525.
  (6) Buyer to pay for any HOA certification fee.
  (7) ☐ Buyer ☐ Seller shall pay for any private transfer fee _____.
  (8) ☐ Buyer ☐ Seller shall pay for _____.
  (9) ☐ Buyer ☐ Seller shall pay for _____.
  (10) ☐ Buyer ☐ Seller shall pay for the cost, not to exceed $ _____, of a standard (or ☐ upgraded) one-year home warranty plan, issued by _____, with the following optional coverages: ☐ Air Conditioner ☐ Pool/Spa ☐ Other: _____
  Buyer is informed that home warranty plans have many optional coverages in addition to those listed above. Buyer is advised to investigate these coverages to determine those that may be suitable for Buyer.
  OR ☐ **Buyer waives the purchase of a home warranty plan. Nothing in this paragraph precludes Buyer's purchasing a home warranty plan during the term of this Agreement.**
8. ITEMS INCLUDED IN AND EXCLUDED FROM SALE:
  A. NOTE TO BUYER AND SELLER: Items listed as included or excluded in the MLS, flyers or marketing materials are **not** included in the purchase price or excluded from the sale unless specified in paragraph 8 B or C.
  B. ITEMS INCLUDED IN SALE: Except as otherwise specified or disclosed,
  (1) All EXISTING fixtures and fittings that are attached to the Property;
  (2) EXISTING electrical, mechanical, lighting, plumbing and heating fixtures, ceiling fans, fireplace inserts, gas logs and grates, solar power systems, built-in appliances, window and door screens, awnings, shutters, window coverings, attached floor coverings, television antennas, satellite dishes, air coolers/conditioners, pool/spa equipment, garage door openers/remote controls, mailbox, in-ground landscaping, trees/shrubs, water features and fountains, water softeners, water purifiers, security systems/alarms and the following if checked: ☐ all stove(s), except _____; ☐ all refrigerator(s) except _____; ☐ all washer(s) and dryer(s), except _____;
  (3) The following additional items: _____
  (4) Existing integrated phone and home automation systems, including necessary components such as intranet and Internet-connected hardware or devices, control units (other than non-dedicated mobile devices, electronics and computers) and applicable software, permissions, passwords, codes and access information, are (☐ are NOT) included in the sale.
  (5) LEASED OR LIENED ITEMS AND SYSTEMS: Seller shall, within the time specified in paragraph 14A, (i) disclose to Buyer if any item or system specified in paragraph 8B or otherwise included in the sale is leased, or not owned by Seller, or specifically subject to a lien or other encumbrance, and (ii) Deliver to Buyer all written materials (such as lease, warranty, etc.) concerning any such item. Buyer's ability to assume any such lease, or willingness to accept the Property subject to any such lien or encumbrance, is a contingency in favor of Buyer and Seller as specified in paragraph 14B and C.
  (6) Seller represents that all items included in the purchase price, unless otherwise specified, (i) are owned by Seller and shall be transferred free and clear of liens and encumbrances, except the items and systems identified pursuant to 8B(4) and _____, and (ii) are transferred without Seller warranty regardless of value.
  C. ITEMS EXCLUDED FROM SALE: Unless otherwise specified, the following items are excluded from sale: (i) audio and video components (such as flat screen TVs, speakers and other items) if any such item is not itself attached to the Property, even if a bracket or other mechanism attached to the component or item is attached to the Property; (ii) furniture and other items secured to the Property for earthquake purposes; and (iii) _____
  _____. **Brackets attached to walls, floors or ceilings for any such component, furniture or item shall remain with the Property (or ☐ will be removed and holes or other damage shall be repaired, but not painted).**

Buyer's Initials (_____)(_____)   Seller's Initials (_____)(_____)

RPA-CA REVISED 11/14 (PAGE 3 OF 10) Print Date

CALIFORNIA RESIDENTIAL PURCHASE AGREEMENT (RPA-CA PAGE 3 OF 10)

FIGURE 10.6 (continued): **California Residential Purchase Agreement and Joint Escrow Instructions**

Property Address: _____   Date: _____

9. **CLOSING AND POSSESSION:**
   A. Buyer intends (or ☐ does not intend) to occupy the Property as Buyer's primary residence.
   B. **Seller-occupied or vacant property:** Possession shall be delivered to Buyer: (i) at 6 PM or (_____ ☐ AM/☐ PM) on the date of Close Of Escrow; (ii) ☐ no later than ___ calendar days after Close Of Escrow; or (iii) ☐ at ____ ☐ AM/☐ PM on _____.
   C. **Seller remaining in possession After Close Of Escrow:** If Seller has the right to remain in possession after Close Of Escrow, (i) the Parties are advised to sign a separate occupancy agreement such as ☐ C.A.R. Form SIP, for Seller continued occupancy of less than 30 days, ☐ C.A.R. Form RLAS for Seller continued occupancy of 30 days or more; and (ii) the Parties are advised to consult with their insurance and legal advisors for information about liability and damage or injury to persons and personal and real property; and (iii) Buyer is advised to consult with Buyer's lender about the impact of Seller's occupancy on Buyer's loan.
   D. **Tenant-occupied property: Property shall be vacant** at least **5 (or ___) Days** Prior to Close Of Escrow, unless otherwise agreed in writing. **Note to Seller: If you are unable to deliver Property vacant in accordance with rent control and other applicable Law, you may be in breach of this Agreement.**
      OR ☐ **Tenant to remain in possession** (C.A.R. Form TIP).
   E. At Close Of Escrow: Seller assigns to Buyer any assignable warranty rights for items included in the sale; and Seller shall Deliver to Buyer available Copies of any such warranties. Brokers cannot and will not determine the assignability of any warranties.
   F. At Close Of Escrow, unless otherwise agreed in writing, Seller shall provide keys, passwords, codes and/or means to operate all locks, mailboxes, security systems, alarms, home automation systems and intranet and Internet-connected devices included in the purchase price, and garage door openers. If the Property is a condominium or located in a common interest subdivision, Buyer may be required to pay a deposit to the Homeowners' Association ("HOA") to obtain keys to accessible HOA facilities.

10. **STATUTORY AND OTHER DISCLOSURES (INCLUDING LEAD-BASED PAINT HAZARD DISCLOSURES) AND CANCELLATION RIGHTS:**
    A. **(1)** Seller shall, within the time specified in paragraph 14A, Deliver to Buyer: (i) if required by Law, a fully completed: Federal Lead-Based Paint Disclosures (C.A.R. Form FLD) and pamphlet ("Lead Disclosures"); and **(ii)** unless exempt, fully completed disclosures or notices required by sections 1102 et. seq. and 1103 et. seq. of the Civil Code ("Statutory Disclosures"). Statutory Disclosures include, but are not limited to, a Real Estate Transfer Disclosure Statement ("TDS"), Natural Hazard Disclosure Statement ("NHD"), notice or actual knowledge of release of illegal controlled substance, notice of special tax and/or assessments (or, if allowed, substantially equivalent notice regarding the Mello-Roos Community Facilities Act of 1982 and Improvement Bond Act of 1915) and, if Seller has actual knowledge, of industrial use and military ordnance location (C.A.R. Form SPQ or SSD).
       (2) Any Statutory Disclosure required by this paragraph is considered fully completed if Seller has answered all questions and completed and signed the Seller section(s) and the Listing Agent, if any, has completed and signed the Listing Broker section(s), or, if applicable, an Agent Visual Inspection Disclosure (C.A.R. Form AVID). Nothing stated herein relieves a Buyer's Broker, if any, from the obligation to (i) conduct a reasonably competent and diligent visual inspection of the accessible areas of the Property and disclose, on Section IV of the TDS, or an AVID, material facts affecting the value or desirability of the Property that were or should have been revealed by such an inspection or (ii) complete any sections on all disclosures required to be completed by Buyer's Broker.
       (3) Note to Buyer and Seller: Waiver of Statutory and Lead Disclosures is prohibited by Law.
       (4) Within the time specified in paragraph 14A, (i) Seller, unless exempt from the obligation to provide a TDS, shall, complete and provide Buyer with a Seller Property Questionnaire (C.A.R. Form SPQ); (ii) if Seller is not required to provide a TDS, Seller shall complete and provide Buyer with a Supplemental Contractual and Statutory Disclosure (C.A.R. Form SSD).
       (5) Buyer shall, within the time specified in paragraph 14B(1), return Signed Copies of the Statutory, Lead and other disclosures to Seller.
       (6) In the event Seller or Listing Broker, prior to Close Of Escrow, becomes aware of adverse conditions materially affecting the Property, or any material inaccuracy in disclosures, information or representations previously provided to Buyer, Seller shall promptly provide a subsequent or amended disclosure or notice, in writing, covering those items. **However, a subsequent or amended disclosure shall not be required for conditions and material inaccuracies** of which Buyer is otherwise aware, or which are **disclosed in reports provided to or obtained by Buyer or ordered and paid for by Buyer.**
       (7) If any disclosure or notice specified in paragraph 10A(1), or subsequent or amended disclosure or notice is Delivered to Buyer after the offer is Signed, Buyer shall have the right to cancel this Agreement within **3 Days** After Delivery in person, or **5 Days** After Delivery by deposit in the mail, by giving written notice of cancellation to Seller or Seller's agent.
    B. **NATURAL AND ENVIRONMENTAL HAZARD DISCLOSURES AND OTHER BOOKLETS:** Within the time specified in paragraph 14A, Seller shall, if required by Law: (i) Deliver to Buyer earthquake guide(s) (and questionnaire), environmental hazards booklet, and home energy rating pamphlet; (ii) disclose if the Property is located in a Special Flood Hazard Area; Potential Flooding (Inundation) Area; Very High Fire Hazard Zone; State Fire Responsibility Area; Earthquake Fault Zone; and Seismic Hazard Zone; and (iii) disclose any other zone as required by Law and provide any other information required for those zones.
    C. **WITHHOLDING TAXES:** Within the time specified in paragraph 14A, to avoid required withholding, Seller shall Deliver to Buyer or qualified substitute, an affidavit sufficient to comply with federal (FIRPTA) and California withholding Law (C.A.R. Form AS or QS).
    D. **MEGAN'S LAW DATABASE DISCLOSURE:** Notice: Pursuant to Section 290.46 of the Penal Code, information about specified registered sex offenders is made available to the public via an Internet Web site maintained by the Department of Justice at **www.meganslaw.ca.gov.** Depending on an offender's criminal history, this information will include either the address at which the offender resides or the community of residence and ZIP Code in which he or she resides. (Neither Seller nor Brokers are required to check this website. If Buyer wants further information, Broker recommends that Buyer obtain information from this website during Buyer's inspection contingency period. Brokers do not have expertise in this area.)
    E. **NOTICE REGARDING GAS AND HAZARDOUS LIQUID TRANSMISSION PIPELINES:** This notice is being provided simply to inform you that information about the general location of gas and hazardous liquid transmission pipelines is available to the public via the National Pipeline Mapping System (NPMS) Internet Web site maintained by the United States Department of Transportation at **http://www.npms.phmsa.dot.gov/.** To seek further information about possible transmission pipelines near the Property, you may contact your local gas utility or other pipeline operators in the area. Contact information for pipeline operators is searchable by ZIP Code and county on the NPMS Internet Web site.

Buyer's Initials (_____)(_____)   Seller's Initials (_____)(_____)

FIGURE 10.6 (continued):   **California Residential Purchase Agreement and Joint Escrow Instructions**

Property Address: _____   Date: _____

F. CONDOMINIUM/PLANNED DEVELOPMENT DISCLOSURES:
  (1) SELLER HAS: 7 (or ___) Days After Acceptance to disclose to Buyer if the Property is a condominium, or is located in a planned development or other common interest subdivision (C.A.R. Form SPQ or SSD).
  (2) If the Property is a condominium or is located in a planned development or other common interest subdivision, Seller has **3 (or ___) Days** After Acceptance to request from the HOA (C.A.R. Form HOA1): **(i)** Copies of any documents required by Law; **(ii)** disclosure of any pending or anticipated claim or litigation by or against the HOA; **(iii)** a statement containing the location and number of designated parking and storage spaces; **(iv)** Copies of the most recent 12 months of HOA minutes for regular and special meetings; and **(v)** the names and contact information of all HOAs governing the Property (collectively, "CI Disclosures"). Seller shall itemize and Deliver to Buyer all CI Disclosures received from the HOA and any CI Disclosures in Seller's possession. Buyer's approval of CI Disclosures is a contingency of this Agreement as specified in paragraph 14B(3). The Party specified in paragraph 7, as directed by escrow, shall deposit funds into escrow or direct to HOA or management company to pay for any of the above.

11. CONDITION OF PROPERTY: Unless otherwise agreed in writing: **(i)** the Property is sold (a) "AS-IS" in its PRESENT physical condition as of the date of Acceptance and (b) subject to Buyer's Investigation rights; **(ii)** the Property, including pool, spa, landscaping and grounds, is to be maintained in substantially the same condition as on the date of Acceptance; and **(iii)** all debris and personal property not included in the sale shall be removed by Close Of Escrow.
  A. Seller shall, within the time specified in paragraph 14A, DISCLOSE KNOWN MATERIAL FACTS AND DEFECTS affecting the Property, including known insurance claims within the past five years, and make any and all other disclosures required by law.
  B. Buyer has the right to conduct Buyer Investigations of the Property and, as specified in paragraph 14B, based upon information discovered in those investigations: (i) cancel this Agreement; or (ii) request that Seller make Repairs or take other action.
  C. **Buyer is strongly advised to conduct investigations of the entire Property in order to determine its present condition. Seller may not be aware of all defects affecting the Property or other factors that Buyer considers important. Property improvements may not be built according to code, in compliance with current Law, or have had permits issued.**

12. BUYER'S INVESTIGATION OF PROPERTY AND MATTERS AFFECTING PROPERTY:
  A. Buyer's acceptance of the condition of, and any other matter affecting the Property, is a contingency of this Agreement as specified in this paragraph and paragraph 14B. Within the time specified in paragraph 14B(1), Buyer shall have the right, at Buyer's expense unless otherwise agreed, to conduct inspections, investigations, tests, surveys and other studies ("Buyer Investigations"), including, but not limited to, the right to: **(i)** inspect for lead-based paint and other lead-based paint hazards; **(ii)** inspect for wood destroying pests and organisms. Any inspection for wood destroying pests and organisms shall be prepared by a registered Structural Pest Control company; shall cover the main building and attached structures; may cover detached structures; shall NOT include water tests of shower pans on upper level units unless the owners of property below the shower consent; shall NOT include roof coverings; and, if the Property is a unit in a condominium or other common interest subdivision, the inspection shall include only the separate interest and any exclusive-use areas being transferred, and shall NOT include common areas; and shall include a report ("Pest Control Report") showing the findings of the company which shall be separated into sections for evident infestation or infections (Section 1) and for conditions likely to lead to infestation or infection (Section 2); **(iii)** review the registered sex offender database; **(iv)** confirm the insurability of Buyer and the Property including the availability and cost of flood and fire insurance; **(v)** review and seek approval of leases that may need to be assumed by Buyer; and **(vi)** satisfy Buyer as to any matter specified in the attached Buyer's Inspection Advisory (C.A.R. Form BIA). Without Seller's prior written consent, Buyer shall neither make nor cause to be made: **(i)** invasive or destructive Buyer Investigations except for minimally invasive testing required to prepare a Pest Control Report; or **(ii)** inspections by any governmental building or zoning inspector or government employee, unless required by Law.
  B. Seller shall make the Property available for all Buyer Investigations. Buyer shall **(i)** as specified in paragraph 14B, complete Buyer Investigations and either remove the contingency or cancel this Agreement, and **(ii)** give Seller, at no cost, complete Copies of all such Investigation reports obtained by Buyer, which obligation shall survive the termination of this Agreement.
  C. Seller shall have water, gas, electricity and all operable pilot lights on for Buyer's Investigations and through the date possession is made available to Buyer.
  D. **Buyer indemnity and seller protection for entry upon property:** Buyer shall: **(i)** keep the Property free and clear of liens; **(ii)** repair all damage arising from Buyer Investigations; and **(iii)** indemnify and hold Seller harmless from all resulting liability, claims, demands, damages and costs. Buyer shall carry, or Buyer shall require anyone acting on Buyer's behalf to carry, policies of liability, workers' compensation and other applicable insurance, defending and protecting Seller from liability for any injuries to persons or property occurring during any Buyer Investigations or work done on the Property at Buyer's direction prior to Close Of Escrow. Seller is advised that certain protections may be afforded Seller by recording a "Notice of Non-Responsibility" (C.A.R. Form NNR) for Buyer Investigations and work done on the Property at Buyer's direction. Buyer's obligations under this paragraph shall survive the termination of this Agreement.

13. TITLE AND VESTING:
  A. Within the time specified in paragraph 14, Buyer shall be provided a current preliminary title report ("Preliminary Report"). The Preliminary Report is only an offer by the title insurer to issue a policy of title insurance and may not contain every item affecting title. Buyer's review of the Preliminary Report and any other matters which may affect title are a contingency of this Agreement as specified in paragraph 14B. The company providing the Preliminary Report shall, prior to issuing a Preliminary Report, conduct a search of the General Index for all Sellers except banks or other institutional lenders selling properties they acquired through foreclosure (REOs), corporations, and government entities. Seller shall within 7 Days After Acceptance, give Escrow Holder a completed Statement of Information.
  B. Title is taken in its present condition subject to all encumbrances, easements, covenants, conditions, restrictions, rights and other matters, whether of record or not, as of the date of Acceptance except for: **(i)** monetary liens of record (which Seller is obligated to pay off) unless Buyer is assuming those obligations or taking the Property subject to those obligations; and **(ii)** those matters which Seller has agreed to remove in writing.
  C. Within the time specified in paragraph 14A, Seller has a duty to disclose to Buyer all matters known to Seller affecting title, whether of record or not.
  D. At Close Of Escrow, Buyer shall receive a grant deed conveying title (or, for stock cooperative or long-term lease, an assignment of stock certificate or of Seller's leasehold interest), including oil, mineral and water rights if currently owned by Seller. Title shall vest as designated in Buyer's supplemental escrow instructions. THE MANNER OF TAKING TITLE MAY HAVE SIGNIFICANT LEGAL AND TAX CONSEQUENCES. CONSULT AN APPROPRIATE PROFESSIONAL.

Buyer's Initials (_____)(_____)   Seller's Initials (_____)(_____)

RPA-CA REVISED 11/14 (PAGE 5 OF 10) Print Date
CALIFORNIA RESIDENTIAL PURCHASE AGREEMENT (RPA-CA PAGE 5 OF 10)

FIGURE 10.6 (continued):   California Residential Purchase Agreement and Joint Escrow Instructions

Property Address: _____   Date: _____

    E. Buyer shall receive a CLTA/ALTA "Homeowner's Policy of Title Insurance", if applicable to the type of property and buyer. If not, Escrow Holder shall notify Buyer. A title company can provide information about the availability, coverage, and cost of other title policies and endorsements. If the Homeowner's Policy is not available, Buyer shall choose another policy, instruct Escrow Holder in writing and shall pay any increase in cost.

14. TIME PERIODS; REMOVAL OF CONTINGENCIES; CANCELLATION RIGHTS: The following time periods may only be extended, altered, modified or changed by mutual written agreement. Any removal of contingencies or cancellation under this paragraph by either Buyer or Seller must be exercised in good faith and in writing (C.A.R. Form CR or CC).

    A. SELLER HAS: 7 (or ___) Days After Acceptance to Deliver to Buyer all Reports, disclosures and information for which Seller is responsible under paragraphs 5, 6, 7, 8B(4), 10A, B, C, and F, 11A and 13A. If, by the time specified, Seller has not Delivered any such item, Buyer after first Delivering to Seller a Notice to Seller to Perform (C.A.R. Form NSP) may cancel this Agreement.

    B. (1) BUYER HAS: 17 (or ___) Days After Acceptance, unless otherwise agreed in writing, to:
        (i) complete all Buyer Investigations; review all disclosures, reports, lease documents to be assumed by Buyer pursuant to paragraph 8B(4), and other applicable information, which Buyer receives from Seller; and approve all matters affecting the Property; and **(ii)** Deliver to Seller Signed Copies of Statutory and Lead Disclosures and other disclosures Delivered by Seller in accordance with paragraph 10A.
        (2) Within the time specified in paragraph 14B(1), Buyer may request that Seller make repairs or take any other action regarding the Property (C.A.R. Form RR). Seller has no obligation to agree to or respond to (C.A.R. Form RRRR) Buyer's requests.
        (3) By the end of the time specified in paragraph 14B(1) (or as otherwise specified in this Agreement), Buyer shall Deliver to Seller a removal of the applicable contingency or cancellation (C.A.R. Form CR or CC) of this Agreement. However, if any report, disclosure or information for which Seller is responsible is not Delivered within the time specified in paragraph 14A, then Buyer has **5 (or ___) Days** After Delivery of any such items, or the time specified in paragraph 14B(1), whichever is later, to Deliver to Seller a removal of the applicable contingency or cancellation of this Agreement.
        (4) Continuation of Contingency: Even after the end of the time specified in paragraph 14B(1) and before Seller cancels, if at all, pursuant to paragraph 14C, Buyer retains the right, in writing, to either (i) remove remaining contingencies, or (ii) cancel this Agreement based on a remaining contingency. Once Buyer's written removal of all contingencies is Delivered to Seller, Seller may not cancel this Agreement pursuant to paragraph 14C(1).

    C. SELLER RIGHT TO CANCEL:
        (1) Seller right to Cancel; Buyer Contingencies: If, by the time specified in this Agreement, Buyer does not Deliver to Seller a removal of the applicable contingency or cancellation of this Agreement, then Seller, after first Delivering to Buyer a Notice to Buyer to Perform (C.A.R. Form NBP), may cancel this Agreement. In such event, Seller shall authorize the return of Buyer's deposit, except for fees incurred by Buyer.
        (2) Seller right to Cancel; Buyer Contract Obligations: Seller, after first delivering to Buyer a NBP, may cancel this Agreement if, by the time specified in this Agreement, Buyer does not take the following action(s): **(i)** Deposit funds as required by paragraph 3A, or 3B or if the funds deposited pursuant to paragraph 3A or 3B are not good when deposited; **(ii)** Deliver a notice of FHA or VA costs or terms as required by paragraph 3D(3) (C.A.R. Form FVA); **(iii)** Deliver a letter as required by paragraph 3J(1); **(iv)** Deliver verification, or a satisfactory verification if Seller reasonably disapproves of the verification already provided, as required by paragraph 3C or 3H; **(v)** In writing assume or accept leases or liens specified in 8B5; **(vi)** Return Statutory and Lead Disclosures as required by paragraph 10A(5); or **(vii)** Sign or initial a separate liquidated damages form for an increased deposit as required by paragraphs 3B and 21B; or **(viii)** Provide evidence of authority to sign in a representative capacity as specified in paragraph 19. In such event, Seller shall authorize the return of Buyer's deposit, except for fees incurred by Buyer.

    D. NOTICE TO BUYER OR SELLER TO PERFORM: The NBP or NSP shall: **(i)** be in writing; **(ii)** be signed by the applicable Buyer or Seller; and **(iii)** give the other Party at least **2 (or ___) Days** After Delivery (or until the time specified in the applicable paragraph, whichever occurs last) to take the applicable action. A NBP or NSP may not be Delivered any earlier than **2 Days** Prior to the expiration of the applicable time for the other Party to remove a contingency or cancel this Agreement or meet an obligation specified in paragraph 14.

    E. EFFECT OF BUYER'S REMOVAL OF CONTINGENCIES: If Buyer removes, in writing, any contingency or cancellation rights, unless otherwise specified in writing, Buyer shall conclusively be deemed to have: **(i)** completed all Buyer Investigations, and review of reports and other applicable information and disclosures pertaining to that contingency or cancellation right; **(ii)** elected to proceed with the transaction; and **(iii)** assumed all liability, responsibility and expense for Repairs or corrections pertaining to that contingency or cancellation right, or for the inability to obtain financing.

    F. CLOSE OF ESCROW: Before Buyer or Seller may cancel this Agreement for failure of the other Party to close escrow pursuant to this Agreement, Buyer or Seller must first Deliver to the other Party a demand to close escrow (C.A.R. Form DCE). The DCE shall: **(i)** be signed by the applicable Buyer or Seller; and **(ii)** give the other Party at least **3 (or _____) Days** After Delivery to close escrow. A DCE may not be Delivered any earlier than **3 Days** Prior to the scheduled close of escrow.

    G. EFFECT OF CANCELLATION ON DEPOSITS: If Buyer or Seller gives written notice of cancellation pursuant to rights duly exercised under the terms of this Agreement, the Parties agree to Sign mutual instructions to cancel the sale and escrow and release deposits, if any, to the party entitled to the funds, less fees and costs incurred by that party. Fees and costs may be payable to service providers and vendors for services and products provided during escrow. Except as specified below, **release of funds will require mutual Signed release instructions from the Parties, judicial decision or arbitration award.** If either Party fails to execute mutual instructions to cancel escrow, one Party may make a written demand to Escrow Holder for the deposit (C.A.R. Form BDRD or SDRD). Escrow Holder, upon receipt, shall promptly deliver notice of the demand to the other Party. If, within 10 Days After Escrow Holder's notice, the other Party does not object to the demand, Escrow Holder shall disburse the deposit to the Party making the demand. If Escrow Holder complies with the preceding process, each Party shall be deemed to have released Escrow Holder from any and all claims or liability related to the disbursal of the deposit. Escrow Holder, at its discretion, may nonetheless require mutual cancellation instructions. **A Party may be subject to a civil penalty of up to $1,000 for refusal to sign cancellation instructions if no good faith dispute exists as to who is entitled to the deposited funds (Civil Code §1057.3).**

15. FINAL VERIFICATION OF CONDITION: Buyer shall have the right to make a final verification of the Property within **5 (or ☐ ___) Days** Prior to Close Of Escrow, NOT AS A CONTINGENCY OF THE SALE, but solely to confirm: **(i)** the Property is maintained

Buyer's Initials (_____)(_____)   Seller's Initials (_____)(_____)

RPA-CA REVISED 11/14 (PAGE 6 OF 10) Print Date
      CALIFORNIA RESIDENTIAL PURCHASE AGREEMENT (RPA-CA PAGE 6 OF 10)

FIGURE 10.6 (continued):   California Residential Purchase Agreement and Joint Escrow Instructions

Property Address: _____   Date: _____

pursuant to paragraph 11; **(ii)** Repairs have been completed as agreed; and **(iii)** Seller has complied with Seller's other obligations under this Agreement (C.A.R. Form VP).

16. **REPAIRS:** Repairs shall be completed prior to final verification of condition unless otherwise agreed in writing. Repairs to be performed at Seller's expense may be performed by Seller or through others, provided that the work complies with applicable Law, including governmental permit, inspection and approval requirements. Repairs shall be performed in a good, skillful manner with materials of quality and appearance comparable to existing materials. It is understood that exact restoration of appearance or cosmetic items following all Repairs may not be possible. Seller shall: **(i)** obtain invoices and paid receipts for Repairs performed by others; **(ii)** prepare a written statement indicating the Repairs performed by Seller and the date of such Repairs; and **(iii)** provide Copies of invoices and paid receipts and statements to Buyer prior to final verification of condition.

17. **PRORATIONS OF PROPERTY TAXES AND OTHER ITEMS:** Unless otherwise agreed in writing, the following items shall be PAID CURRENT and prorated between Buyer and Seller as of Close Of Escrow: real property taxes and assessments, interest, rents, HOA regular, special, and emergency dues and assessments imposed prior to Close Of Escrow, premiums on insurance assumed by Buyer, payments on bonds and assessments assumed by Buyer, and payments on Mello-Roos and other Special Assessment District bonds and assessments that are now a lien. The following items shall be assumed by Buyer WITHOUT CREDIT toward the purchase price: prorated payments on Mello-Roos and other Special Assessment District bonds and assessments and HOA special assessments that are now a lien but not yet due. Property will be reassessed upon change of ownership. Any supplemental tax bills shall be paid as follows: **(i)** for periods after Close Of Escrow, by Buyer; and **(ii)** for periods prior to Close Of Escrow, by Seller (see C.A.R. Form SPT or SBSA for further information). TAX BILLS ISSUED AFTER CLOSE OF ESCROW SHALL BE HANDLED DIRECTLY BETWEEN BUYER AND SELLER. Prorations shall be made based on a 30-day month.

18. **BROKERS:**
   A. **COMPENSATION:** Seller or Buyer, or both, as applicable, agree to pay compensation to Broker as specified in a separate written agreement between Broker and that Seller or Buyer. Compensation is payable upon Close Of Escrow, or if escrow does not close, as otherwise specified in the agreement between Broker and that Seller or Buyer.
   B. **SCOPE OF DUTY:** Buyer and Seller acknowledge and agree that Broker: **(i)** Does not decide what price Buyer should pay or Seller should accept; **(ii)** Does not guarantee the condition of the Property; **(iii)** Does not guarantee the performance, adequacy or completeness of inspections, services, products or repairs provided or made by Seller or others; **(iv)** Does not have an obligation to conduct an inspection of common areas or areas off the site of the Property; **(v)** Shall not be responsible for identifying defects on the Property, in common areas, or offsite unless such defects are visually observable by an inspection of reasonably accessible areas of the Property or are known to Broker; **(vi)** Shall not be responsible for inspecting public records or permits concerning the title or use of Property; **(vii)** Shall not be responsible for identifying the location of boundary lines or other items affecting title; **(viii)** Shall not be responsible for verifying square footage, representations of others or information contained in Investigation reports, Multiple Listing Service, advertisements, flyers or other promotional material; **(ix)** Shall not be responsible for determining the fair market value of the Property or any personal property included in the sale; **(x)** Shall not be responsible for providing legal or tax advice regarding any aspect of a transaction entered into by Buyer or Seller; and **(xi)** Shall not be responsible for providing other advice or information that exceeds the knowledge, education and experience required to perform real estate licensed activity. Buyer and Seller agree to seek legal, tax, insurance, title and other desired assistance from appropriate professionals.

19. **REPRESENTATIVE CAPACITY:** If one or more Parties is signing this Agreement in a representative capacity and not for him/herself as an individual then that Party shall so indicate in paragraph 31 or 32 and attach a Representative Capacity Signature Disclosure (C.A.R. Form RCSD). Wherever the signature or initials of the representative identified in the RCSD appear on this Agreement or any related documents, it shall be deemed to be in a representative capacity for the entity described and not in an individual capacity, unless otherwise indicated. The Party acting in a representative capacity (i) represents that the entity for which that party is acting already exists and (ii) shall Deliver to the other Party and Escrow Holder, within 3 Days After Acceptance, evidence of authority to act in that capacity (such as but not limited to: applicable portion of the trust or Certification Of Trust (Probate Code §18100.5), letters testamentary, court order, power of attorney, corporate resolution, or formation documents of the business entity).

20. **JOINT ESCROW INSTRUCTIONS TO ESCROW HOLDER:**
   A. **The following paragraphs, or applicable portions thereof, of this Agreement constitute the joint escrow instructions of Buyer and Seller to Escrow Holder,** which Escrow Holder is to use along with any related counter offers and addenda, and any additional mutual instructions to close the escrow: paragraphs 1, 3, 4B, 5A, 6, 7, 10C, 13, 14G, 17, 18A, 19, 20, 26, 29, 30, 31, 32 and paragraph D of the section titled Real Estate Brokers on page 10. If a Copy of the separate compensation agreement(s) provided for in paragraph 18A, or paragraph D of the section titled Real Estate Brokers on page 10 is deposited with Escrow Holder by Broker, Escrow Holder shall accept such agreement(s) and pay out from Buyer's or Seller's funds, or both, as applicable, the Broker's compensation provided for in such agreement(s). The terms and conditions of this Agreement not set forth in the specified paragraphs are additional matters for the information of Escrow Holder, but about which Escrow Holder need not be concerned. Buyer and Seller will receive Escrow Holder's general provisions, if any, directly from Escrow Holder and will execute such provisions within the time specified in paragraph 7C(1)(c). To the extent the general provisions are inconsistent or conflict with this Agreement, the general provisions will control as to the duties and obligations of Escrow Holder only. Buyer and Seller will execute additional instructions, documents and forms provided by Escrow Holder that are reasonably necessary to close the escrow and, as directed by Escrow Holder, within 3 (or ____) Days, shall pay to Escrow Holder or HOA or HOA management company or others any fee required by paragraphs 7, 10 or elsewhere in this Agreement.
   B. A Copy of this Agreement including any counter offer(s) and addenda shall be delivered to Escrow Holder within **3 Days After** Acceptance (or _____). Buyer and Seller authorize Escrow Holder to accept and rely on Copies and Signatures as defined in this Agreement as originals, to open escrow and for other purposes of escrow. The validity of this Agreement as between Buyer and Seller is not affected by whether or when Escrow Holder Signs this Agreement. Escrow Holder shall provide Seller's Statement of Information to Title company when received from Seller. If Seller delivers an affidavit to Escrow Holder to satisfy Seller's FIRPTA obligation under paragraph 10C, Escrow Holder shall deliver to Buyer a Qualified Substitute statement that complies with federal Law.
   C. Brokers are a party to the escrow for the sole purpose of compensation pursuant to paragraph 18A and paragraph D of the section titled Real Estate Brokers on page 10. Buyer and Seller irrevocably assign to Brokers compensation specified in paragraph 18A, and irrevocably instruct Escrow Holder to disburse those funds to Brokers at Close Of Escrow or pursuant to any

Buyer's Initials (_____)(_____)   Seller's Initials (_____)(_____)

RPA-CA REVISED 11/14 (PAGE 7 OF 10) Print Date
CALIFORNIA RESIDENTIAL PURCHASE AGREEMENT (RPA-CA PAGE 7 OF 10)

FIGURE 10.6 (continued): California Residential Purchase Agreement and Joint Escrow Instructions

Property Address: _____ Date: _____

other mutually executed cancellation agreement. Compensation instructions can be amended or revoked only with the written consent of Brokers. Buyer and Seller shall release and hold harmless Escrow Holder from any liability resulting from Escrow Holder's payment to Broker(s) of compensation pursuant to this Agreement.

D. Upon receipt, Escrow Holder shall provide Seller and Seller's Broker verification of Buyer's deposit of funds pursuant to paragraph 3A and 3B. Once Escrow Holder becomes aware of any of the following, Escrow Holder shall immediately notify all Brokers: (i) if Buyer's initial or any additional deposit or down payment is not made pursuant to this Agreement, or is not good at time of deposit with Escrow Holder; or (ii) if Buyer and Seller instruct Escrow Holder to cancel escrow.

E. A Copy of any amendment that affects any paragraph of this Agreement for which Escrow Holder is responsible shall be delivered to Escrow Holder within **3** Days after mutual execution of the amendment.

21. **REMEDIES FOR BUYER'S BREACH OF CONTRACT:**
A. **Any clause added by the Parties specifying a remedy (such as release or forfeiture of deposit or making a deposit non-refundable) for failure of Buyer to complete the purchase in violation of this Agreement shall be deemed invalid unless the clause independently satisfies the statutory liquidated damages requirements set forth in the Civil Code.**
B. **LIQUIDATED DAMAGES: If Buyer fails to complete this purchase because of Buyer's default, Seller shall retain, as liquidated damages, the deposit actually paid. If the Property is a dwelling with no more than four units, one of which Buyer intends to occupy, then the amount retained shall be no more than 3% of the purchase price. Any excess shall be returned to Buyer. Except as provided in paragraph 14G, release of funds will require mutual, Signed release instructions from both Buyer and Seller, judicial decision or arbitration award. AT THE TIME OF ANY INCREASED DEPOSIT BUYER AND SELLER SHALL SIGN A SEPARATE LIQUIDATED DAMAGES PROVISION INCORPORATING THE INCREASED DEPOSIT AS LIQUIDATED DAMAGES (C.A.R. FORM RID).**

Buyer's Initials _____/_____   Seller's Initials _____/_____

22. **DISPUTE RESOLUTION:**
A. **MEDIATION:** The Parties agree to mediate any dispute or claim arising between them out of this Agreement, or any resulting transaction, before resorting to arbitration or court action through the C.A.R. Real Estate Mediation Center for Consumers (**www.consumermediation.org**) or through any other mediation provider or service mutually agreed to by the Parties. The Parties **also agree to mediate any disputes or claims with Broker(s), who, in writing, agree to such mediation prior to, or within a reasonable time after, the dispute or claim is presented to the Broker.** Mediation fees, if any, shall be divided equally among the Parties involved. If, for any dispute or claim to which this paragraph applies, any Party (i) commences an action without first attempting to resolve the matter through mediation, or (ii) before commencement of an action, refuses to mediate after a request has been made, then that Party shall not be entitled to recover attorney fees, even if they would otherwise be available to that Party in any such action. THIS MEDIATION PROVISION APPLIES WHETHER OR NOT THE ARBITRATION PROVISION IS INITIALED. **Exclusions from this mediation agreement are specified in paragraph 22C.**
B. **ARBITRATION OF DISPUTES:**
The Parties agree that any dispute or claim in Law or equity arising between them out of this Agreement or any resulting transaction, which is not settled through mediation, shall be decided by neutral, binding arbitration. The Parties also agree to arbitrate any disputes or claims with Broker(s), who, in writing, agree to such arbitration prior to, or within a reasonable time after, the dispute or claim is presented to the Broker. The arbitrator shall be a retired judge or justice, or an attorney with at least 5 years of residential real estate Law experience, unless the parties mutually agree to a different arbitrator. The Parties shall have the right to discovery in accordance with Code of Civil Procedure §1283.05. In all other respects, the arbitration shall be conducted in accordance with Title 9 of Part 3 of the Code of Civil Procedure. Judgment upon the award of the arbitrator(s) may be entered into any court having jurisdiction. Enforcement of this agreement to arbitrate shall be governed by the Federal Arbitration Act. Exclusions from this arbitration agreement are specified in paragraph 22C.
"NOTICE: BY INITIALING IN THE SPACE BELOW YOU ARE AGREEING TO HAVE ANY DISPUTE ARISING OUT OF THE MATTERS INCLUDED IN THE 'ARBITRATION OF DISPUTES' PROVISION DECIDED BY NEUTRAL ARBITRATION AS PROVIDED BY CALIFORNIA LAW AND YOU ARE GIVING UP ANY RIGHTS YOU MIGHT POSSESS TO HAVE THE DISPUTE LITIGATED IN A COURT OR JURY TRIAL. BY INITIALING IN THE SPACE BELOW YOU ARE GIVING UP YOUR JUDICIAL RIGHTS TO DISCOVERY AND APPEAL, UNLESS THOSE RIGHTS ARE SPECIFICALLY INCLUDED IN THE 'ARBITRATION OF DISPUTES' PROVISION. IF YOU REFUSE TO SUBMIT TO ARBITRATION AFTER AGREEING TO THIS PROVISION, YOU MAY BE COMPELLED TO ARBITRATE UNDER THE AUTHORITY OF THE CALIFORNIA CODE OF CIVIL PROCEDURE. YOUR AGREEMENT TO THIS ARBITRATION PROVISION IS VOLUNTARY."
"WE HAVE READ AND UNDERSTAND THE FOREGOING AND AGREE TO SUBMIT DISPUTES ARISING OUT OF THE MATTERS INCLUDED IN THE 'ARBITRATION OF DISPUTES' PROVISION TO NEUTRAL ARBITRATION."

Buyer's Initials _____/_____   Seller's Initials _____/_____

C. **ADDITIONAL MEDIATION AND ARBITRATION TERMS:**
(1) **EXCLUSIONS:** The following matters are excluded from mediation and arbitration: (i) a judicial or non-judicial foreclosure or other action or proceeding to enforce a deed of trust, mortgage or installment land sale contract as defined in Civil Code §2985; (ii) an unlawful detainer action; and (iii) any matter that is within the jurisdiction of a probate, small claims or bankruptcy court.
(2) **PRESERVATION OF ACTIONS:** The following shall not constitute a waiver nor violation of the mediation and arbitration provisions: (i) the filing of a court action to preserve a statute of limitations; (ii) the filing of a court action to enable the recording of a notice of pending action, for order of attachment, receivership, injunction, or other provisional remedies; or (iii) the filing of a mechanic's lien.
(3) **BROKERS:** Brokers shall not be obligated nor compelled to mediate or arbitrate unless they agree to do so in writing. Any Broker(s) participating in mediation or arbitration shall not be deemed a party to this Agreement.

Buyer's Initials (_____)(_____)   Seller's Initials (_____)(_____)

RPA-CA REVISED 11/14 (PAGE 8 of 10)   Print Date

CALIFORNIA RESIDENTIAL PURCHASE AGREEMENT (RPA-CA PAGE 8 OF 10)

FIGURE 10.6 (continued):   **California Residential Purchase Agreement and Joint Escrow Instructions**

Property Address: _____   Date: _____

23. **SELECTION OF SERVICE PROVIDERS:** Brokers do not guarantee the performance of any vendors, service or product providers ("Providers"), whether referred by Broker or selected by Buyer, Seller or other person. Buyer and Seller may select ANY Providers of their own choosing.

24. **MULTIPLE LISTING SERVICE ("MLS"):** Brokers are authorized to report to the MLS a pending sale and, upon Close Of Escrow, the sales price and other terms of this transaction shall be provided to the MLS to be published and disseminated to persons and entities authorized to use the information on terms approved by the MLS.

25. **ATTORNEY FEES:** In any action, proceeding, or arbitration between Buyer and Seller arising out of this Agreement, the prevailing Buyer or Seller shall be entitled to reasonable attorney fees and costs from the non-prevailing Buyer or Seller, except as provided in paragraph 22A.

26. **ASSIGNMENT:** Buyer shall not assign all or any part of Buyer's interest in this Agreement without first having obtained the separate written consent of Seller to a specified assignee. Such consent shall not be unreasonably withheld. Any total or partial assignment shall not relieve Buyer of Buyer's obligations pursuant to this Agreement unless otherwise agreed in writing by Seller (C.A.R. Form AOAA).

27. **EQUAL HOUSING OPPORTUNITY:** The Property is sold in compliance with federal, state and local anti-discrimination Laws.

28. **TERMS AND CONDITIONS OF OFFER:**
This is an offer to purchase the Property on the above terms and conditions. The liquidated damages paragraph or the arbitration of disputes paragraph is incorporated in this Agreement if initialed by all Parties or if incorporated by mutual agreement in a counter offer or addendum. If at least one but not all Parties initial, a counter offer is required until agreement is reached. Seller has the right to continue to offer the Property for sale and to accept any other offer at any time prior to notification of Acceptance. The Parties have read and acknowledge receipt of a Copy of the offer and agree to the confirmation of agency relationships. If this offer is accepted and Buyer subsequently defaults, Buyer may be responsible for payment of Brokers' compensation. This Agreement and any supplement, addendum or modification, including any Copy, may be Signed in two or more counterparts, all of which shall constitute one and the same writing.

29. **TIME OF ESSENCE; ENTIRE CONTRACT; CHANGES:** Time is of the essence. All understandings between the Parties are incorporated in this Agreement. Its terms are intended by the Parties as a final, complete and exclusive expression of their Agreement with respect to its subject matter, and may not be contradicted by evidence of any prior agreement or contemporaneous oral agreement. If any provision of this Agreement is held to be ineffective or invalid, the remaining provisions will nevertheless be given full force and effect. Except as otherwise specified, this Agreement shall be interpreted and disputes shall be resolved in accordance with the Laws of the State of California. **Neither this Agreement nor any provision in it may be extended, amended, modified, altered or changed, except in writing Signed by Buyer and Seller.**

30. **DEFINITIONS:** As used in this Agreement:
   A. **"Acceptance"** means the time the offer or final counter offer is accepted in writing by a Party and is delivered to and personally received by the other Party or that Party's authorized agent in accordance with the terms of this offer or a final counter offer.
   B. **"Agreement"** means this document and any counter offers and any incorporated addenda, collectively forming the binding agreement between the Parties. Addenda are incorporated only when Signed by all Parties.
   C. **"C.A.R. Form"** means the most current version of the specific form referenced or another comparable form agreed to by the parties.
   D. **"Close Of Escrow"**, including **"COE"**, means the date the grant deed, or other evidence of transfer of title, is recorded.
   E. **"Copy"** means copy by any means including photocopy, NCR, facsimile and electronic.
   F. **"Days"** means calendar days. However, after Acceptance, the last **Day** for performance of any act required by this Agreement (including Close Of Escrow) shall not include any Saturday, Sunday, or legal holiday and shall instead be the next Day.
   G. **"Days After"** means the specified number of calendar days after the occurrence of the event specified, not counting the calendar date on which the specified event occurs, and ending at 11:59 PM on the final day.
   H. **"Days Prior"** means the specified number of calendar days before the occurrence of the event specified, not counting the calendar date on which the specified event is scheduled to occur.
   I. **"Deliver"**, **"Delivered"** or **"Delivery"**, unless otherwise specified in writing, means and shall be effective upon: personal receipt by Buyer or Seller or the individual Real Estate Licensee for that principal as specified in the section titled Real Estate Brokers on page 10, regardless of the method used (i.e., messenger, mail, email, fax, other).
   J. **"Electronic Copy"** or **"Electronic Signature"** means, as applicable, an electronic copy or signature complying with California Law. Buyer and Seller agree that electronic means will not be used by either Party to modify or alter the content or integrity of this Agreement without the knowledge and consent of the other Party.
   K. **"Law"** means any law, code, statute, ordinance, regulation, rule or order, which is adopted by a controlling city, county, state or federal legislative, judicial or executive body or agency.
   L. **"Repairs"** means any repairs (including pest control), alterations, replacements, modifications or retrofitting of the Property provided for under this Agreement.
   M. **"Signed"** means either a handwritten or electronic signature on an original document, Copy or any counterpart.

31. **EXPIRATION OF OFFER:** This offer shall be deemed revoked and the deposit, if any, shall be returned to Buyer unless the offer is Signed by Seller and a Copy of the Signed offer is personally received by Buyer, or by _____,
who is authorized to receive it, by 5:00 PM on the third Day after this offer is signed by Buyer (or by ☐ _____ ☐AM/☐PM,
on _____(date)).

☐ One or more Buyers is signing this Agreement in a representative capacity and not for him/herself as an individual. See attached Representative Capacity Signature Disclosure (C.A.R. Form RCSD) for additional terms.

Date _____   BUYER _____

(Print name) _____

Date _____   BUYER _____

(Print name) _____

☐ Additional Signature Addendum attached (C.A.R. Form ASA).

RPA-CA REVISED 11/14 (PAGE 9 of 10)   **Print Date**   Seller's Initials (_____)(_____)

CALIFORNIA RESIDENTIAL PURCHASE AGREEMENT (RPA-CA PAGE 9 OF 10)

FIGURE 10.6 (continued): **California Residential Purchase Agreement and Joint Escrow Instructions**

Property Address: _____ Date: _____

32. ACCEPTANCE OF OFFER: Seller warrants that Seller is the owner of the Property, or has the authority to execute this Agreement. Seller accepts the above offer and agrees to sell the Property on the above terms and conditions. Seller has read and acknowledges receipt of a Copy of this Agreement, and authorizes Broker to Deliver a Signed Copy to Buyer.

☐ (If checked) SELLER'S ACCEPTANCE IS **SUBJECT TO ATTACHED COUNTER OFFER (C.A.R. Form SCO or SMCO) DATED:**
_____.

☐ One or more Sellers is signing this Agreement in a representative capacity and not for him/herself as an individual. See attached Representative Capacity Signature Disclosure (C.A.R. Form RCSD) for additional terms.

Date _____ SELLER _____

(Print name) _____

Date _____ SELLER _____

(Print name) _____

☐ Additional Signature Addendum attached (C.A.R. Form ASA).

(____/____) **(Do not initial if making a counter offer.) CONFIRMATION OF ACCEPTANCE:** A Copy of Signed Acceptance was
(Initials) personally received by Buyer or Buyer's authorized agent on (date) _____ at _____
☐AM/☐PM. **A binding Agreement is created when a Copy of Signed Acceptance is personally received by Buyer or Buyer's authorized agent whether or not confirmed in this document. Completion of this confirmation is not legally required in order to create a binding Agreement; it is solely intended to evidence the date that Confirmation of Acceptance has occurred.**

REAL ESTATE BROKERS:
A. **Real Estate Brokers are not parties to the Agreement between Buyer and Seller.**
B. **Agency relationships are confirmed as stated in paragraph 2.**
C. If specified in paragraph 3A(2), Agent who submitted the offer for Buyer acknowledges receipt of deposit.
D. **COOPERATING BROKER COMPENSATION:** Listing Broker agrees to pay Cooperating Broker **(Selling Firm)** and Cooperating Broker agrees to accept, out of Listing Broker's proceeds in escrow, the amount specified in the MLS, provided Cooperating Broker is a Participant of the MLS in which the Property is offered for sale or a reciprocal MLS. If Listing Broker and Cooperating Broker are not both Participants of the MLS, or a reciprocal MLS, in which the Property is offered for sale, then compensation must be specified in a separate written agreement (C.A.R. Form CBC). Declaration of License and Tax (C.A.R. Form DLT) may be used to document that tax reporting will be required or that an exemption exists.

Real Estate Broker (Selling Firm) _____ CalBRE Lic. # _____
By _____ CalBRE Lic. # _____ Date _____
By _____ CalBRE Lic. # _____ Date _____
Address _____ City _____ State _____ Zip _____
Telephone _____ Fax _____ E-mail _____
Real Estate Broker (Listing Firm) _____ CalBRE Lic. # _____
By _____ CalBRE Lic. # _____ Date _____
By _____ CalBRE Lic. # _____ Date _____
Address _____ City _____ State _____ Zip _____
Telephone _____ Fax _____ E-mail _____

ESCROW HOLDER ACKNOWLEDGMENT:
Escrow Holder acknowledges receipt of a Copy of this Agreement, (if checked, ☐ a deposit in the amount of $ _____),
counter offer numbers _____ ☐ Seller's Statement of Information and _____
_____, and agrees to act as Escrow Holder subject to paragraph 20 of this Agreement, any supplemental escrow instructions and the terms of Escrow Holder's general provisions.

Escrow Holder is advised that the date of Confirmation of Acceptance of the Agreement as between Buyer and Seller is _____

Escrow Holder _____
By _____ Escrow # _____
Address _____ Date _____
Phone/Fax/E-mail _____
Escrow Holder has the following license number # _____
☐ Department of Business Oversight, ☐ Department of Insurance, ☐ Bureau of Real Estate.

PRESENTATION OF OFFER: (_____) Listing Broker presented this offer to Seller on _____ (date).
                          Broker or Designee Initials

REJECTION OF OFFER: (_____)(_____) No counter offer is being made. This offer was rejected by Seller on_____ (date).
                       Seller's Initials

©1991- 2014, California Association of REALTORS®, Inc. United States copyright law (Title 17 U.S. Code) forbids the unauthorized distribution, display and reproduction of this form, or any portion thereof, by photocopy machine or any other means, including facsimile or computerized formats.
THIS FORM HAS BEEN APPROVED BY THE CALIFORNIA ASSOCIATION OF REALTORS® (C.A.R.). NO REPRESENTATION IS MADE AS TO THE LEGAL VALIDITY OR ACCURACY OF ANY PROVISION IN ANY SPECIFIC TRANSACTION. A REAL ESTATE BROKER IS THE PERSON QUALIFIED TO ADVISE ON REAL ESTATE TRANSACTIONS. IF YOU DESIRE LEGAL OR TAX ADVICE, CONSULT AN APPROPRIATE PROFESSIONAL.

Buyer's Acknowledge that page 10 is part of this Agreement (_____)(_____)

Published and Distributed by:
REAL ESTATE BUSINESS SERVICES, INC.
a subsidiary of the CALIFORNIA ASSOCIATION OF REALTORS®
525 South Virgil Avenue, Los Angeles, California 90020

Reviewed by _____
Broker or Designee _____

RPA-CA REVISED 11/14 (PAGE 10 of 10) Print Date

CALIFORNIA RESIDENTIAL PURCHASE AGREEMENT (RPA-CA PAGE 10 OF 10)

Understanding the Purchase Agreement Form

Paragraph 1: Basic offer.   1A shows the buyer or buyers; 1B describes the property by address, legal description, and/or assessor's parcel number and further indicates the city or county where the property is located; 1C sets forth the purchase price; and 1D sets the time for close of escrow to complete the transaction.

Paragraph 2: Agency.

A.   This is acknowledgment by buyer and seller as to receipt of agency disclosure.

B.   The agency relations selected are confirmed.

C.   The possibility of multiple representations is explained.

Paragraph 3: Finance terms.   Buyer represents that funds will be good when deposited in escrow (cash, cashier's check, etc.).

Subparagraphs A through K under Financing are explained below.

A.   This provides for the initial earnest money deposit, its form, and if it is to be deposited (escrow or trust account) or held uncashed.

B.   Provision is made for increasing the earnest money (used in cases of low initial deposits).

C.   Can be checked if it is an all-cash offer without financial contingencies.

D.   Paragraph (1) states the requirements of the new first loan on which this offer is contingent. If the buyer cannot obtain the loan, the buyer is relieved of any purchase obligation. For this paragraph, consider setting the interest rate and points above current market interest, so that a minor fluctuation will not relieve the buyer from the purchase obligation. Paragraph (2) applies to conditions of any second loan. Paragraph (3) applies to terms if FHA or VA financing is sought.

E.   This provides for additional financing terms, such as seller financing, loan assumptions, balloon payments, et cetera.

F.   Provision is made for the balance of the purchase price to be deposited in escrow before closing.

G.   This paragraph shows the total purchase price. (**Note:** The down payment and loans assumed and/or new loans by lenders or seller should equal the purchase price.)

H.   This paragraph requires the buyers to verify that they have the down payment and closing costs.

I.   This paragraph provides, by checking, whether or not the agreement is to be contingent upon an appraisal equal to or greater than the purchase price.

J.   Loan terms (1) require providing evidence of prequalification or preapproval for the loan, (2) require the buyer to act diligently to obtain the loan, (3) provides for removal of loan contingency, or if checked, no loan contingency.

K.   Provides that the seller has relied upon buyer representation as to financing sought and failure to obtain alternative type of financing will not excuse the buyer.

Paragraph 4: Sale of buyer's property.   If checked, the sale is contingent upon the sale of the buyer's property.

Paragraph 5: Addendum and advisories.   Addendums and advisory notices to buyer are checked if they are to be included in the offer.

Paragraph 6: Other terms.   Space is provided for other terms of the offer.

Paragraph 7: Allocation of costs.

A.   Subparagraph A. Checking the appropriate box determines who is to pay which costs as to inspection reports and certificates.

B. Subparagraph B sets forth who is responsible. Compliance with government inclusion requirements and retrofit.

C. Subparagraph C determines responsibility for escrow fees, the escrow holder and time period to sign and return escrow provisions, as well as responsibility for title insurance.

D. Subparagraph D determines, by checking appropriate boxes, who shall be responsible for other costs and fees.

Paragraph 8: Items included and excluded.   This paragraph makes it clear that designated fixtures remain with the property, but it also provides for inclusion of other items in the sale, as well as exclusion of designated items from the sale. The agent should make certain that questionable items such as installed TVs, et cetera, are covered.

Paragraph 9: Closing and possession.

A. This paragraph states whether the buyer intends to occupy the premises as a principal residence. If the buyer intends the property to be a principal residence, then liquidated damages resulting from buyer default cannot exceed 3% of the purchase price. (See paragraph 21B.)

(If a buyer falsely indicates a property will be the principal residence for the purpose of obtaining a loan at a lower rate of interest, it would be fraud against the lender.)

B. This paragraph provides the date on which seller-occupied or vacant property will be turned over to the buyer.

C. Subparagraph C provides for conditions of the seller remaining in possession after close of escrow.

D. This paragraph provides that tenant-occupied property will be vacant before close of escrow unless agreed otherwise. If the property is not vacated, the seller could be in breach of contract. If the box allowing the tenant to remain in possession is checked, the buyer and the seller are to enter into a written occupancy agreement. If they do not reach an occupancy agreement, either the buyer or the seller may cancel the purchase agreement in writing.

E. This paragraph provides that the seller will assign to the buyer any assignable warranty rights.

F. This paragraph provides that keys, openers, et cetera, will be given to the buyer.

Paragraph 10: Statutory and other disclosures. This paragraph requires the seller to provide all required statutory and other disclosures, including lead paint, transfer disclosure statement, natural and environmental hazard disclosures and booklets, withholding as to FIRPTA, Megan's Law database, notice regarding gas and hazardous liquids, transmission lines, as well as condominium and planned development disclosures

Paragraph 11: Conditions of property. Unless otherwise indicated, property is sold in present condition, subject to buyer's inspection rights, and will be maintained in substantially the same condition.

A. The seller will disclose known material facts and defects.

B. The buyer has the right of inspection and may cancel the agreement or request corrective action based on defects discovered.

C. The buyer is strongly advised to conduct an investigation of the property.

Paragraph 12: Buyer's investigation of property and matters affecting property. This paragraph provides for the buyer's rights to inspection and provides for either the removal of the inspection contingency or cancellation of the agreement. Utilities must be on for the buyer's inspection. The buyer agrees to keep the property free from liens (pay for investigative work), repair any damage and costs associated with inspection, and protect the owner from any liability because of such investigations and inspections.

Paragraph 13: Title and vesting.

A. This paragraph provides that the buyer will receive a preliminary title report.

B. This paragraph indicates that title will be taken in present condition and subject to stated nonmonetary encumbrances.

C. This paragraph sets forth the seller's duty to disclose all matters known to the seller affecting title.

D. This paragraph provides that title will be transferred by a grant deed, and the buyer is notified to obtain professional advice as to the manner of taking title.

E. This paragraph provides that the buyer will receive a homeowners policy of title insurance.

Paragraph 14: Time periods; removal of contingencies; cancellation rights.
This paragraph sets forth all time periods for compliance and disclosures. Modification of time periods must be in writing. If the seller removes contingencies, this will be conclusive evidence of the buyer's election to proceed with the transaction. If the buyer and seller agree to cancellation of the agreement, release of the funds will require mutual signed agreement (with a civil penalty of up to $1,000 for refusal to sign the agreement if no good faith dispute exists).

In November 2014, the California Association of REALTORS® made a pretty significant change to the purchase contract. Previously in the event of a failed escrow, the release of the buyer's deposit could only be released after receiving mutually signed cancellation instructions. However, the current iteration of the purchase contract allows the escrow company to make a demand on a party for cancellation of the escrow. If the party fails to respond within 10 days, the escrow company is permitted to release the buyer's deposit. This is a massive shift from all previous versions of the purchase contract because it allows either the buyers or the sellers to tell escrow that they want to cancel a given transaction, and theoretically if the other party didn't respond for whatever reason for 10 days, the escrow company can unilaterally release funds without a subsequent signature.

Paragraph 15: Final verification of condition. This paragraph provides the buyer the right to conduct a final inspection before close of escrow to confirm that the property has been properly maintained and repairs have been made, and that the seller has complied with other contractual obligations.

Paragraph 16: Repairs. Seller repairs will be performed in accordance with governmental requirements in a skillful manner.

Paragraph 17: Prorations of property taxes and other items. This paragraph provides for proration of taxes and other items based on a 30-day month. Bonds will be assumed without buyer credit if not yet due.

Paragraph 18: Brokers. Parties agree to pay brokers as determined in a separate written agreement. Subparagraph B points out what the broker doesn't do and is not responsible for.

Paragraph 19: Representative capacity. If a party is acting as a representative, the party will so indicate and deliver supporting documentation to escrow.

Paragraph 20: Joint escrow instructions to escrow holder. This paragraph provides that designated paragraphs of the agreement are joint escrow instructions and that the agreement will be delivered to the escrow within a designated period. It makes clear that the broker is a party to the escrow only so far as those commission rights are concerned that have been irrevocably assigned to the broker.

Paragraph 21: Remedies for buyer's breach of contract. Any added remedy for buyer breach will be invalid unless the clause added satisfies the statutory liquidated damages requirement. For 1-4 residential units that buyer intends to occupy, the liquidated damages cannot exceed 3% of the sale price.

Paragraph 22: Dispute resolution. The parties agree to try to settle any dispute by mediation. By initialing, the parties agree to binding arbitration of any dispute not settled by mediation. (If it is not initialed, the parties could settle disputes through the courts.)

Disputes with brokers are subject to mediation and arbitration only if the brokers agree to such resolution.

Paragraph 23: Selection of service providers.   The broker does not guarantee performance of any service provider she may have referred to the buyer and/or seller.

Paragraph 24: Multiple listing service.   This paragraph gives the broker the right to report the sale terms to an MLS to be published. Without this authorization, release of information by an agent could breach the duty of confidentiality.

Paragraph 25: Attorney's fees.   In the event of a legal proceeding or arbitration, the prevailing party will be entitled to reasonable attorney's fees.

Paragraph 26: Assignment.   The buyer agrees not to assign any portion of this agreement to a named party without the written permission of seller. Permission will not be unreasonably withheld toward the buyer's obligation unless otherwise agreed.

Paragraph 27: Equal housing opportunity.   This paragraph states that the sale is being made in compliance with antidiscrimination laws.

Paragraph 28: Terms and conditions of offer.   This paragraph makes it clear it is an offer that includes initialed paragraphs and provides that should the buyer default after acceptance, the buyer may be responsible for the broker's commission.

Paragraph 29: Time of essence; entire contract; changes.   This is the complete agreement and may not be contradicted by prior agreements or contemporaneous oral agreements. It cannot be extended, modified, or changed except in writing signed by both buyer and seller.

Paragraph 30: Definitions.   This paragraph provides definitions of terms used.

Paragraph 31: Expiration of offer. This paragraph provides a definite termination time and date if the offer is not accepted by that time and date. The buyer's signature as to the offer is included in this paragraph.

Paragraph 32: Acceptance of offer. The seller warrants ownership and accepts the offer on terms indicated, or by checking the appropriate block indicates acceptance subject to attached counteroffer.

The buyer initials confirmation of receipt of acceptance.

There is a block for the broker to sign in which the broker agrees to cooperating broker compensation.

Another block is signed by the escrow holder acknowledging receipt of copy of the agreement.

SUMMARY

Selling is helping others meet their needs. Selling can give buyers the security of home ownership.

Selling involves elements such as persuasion, communication, discovery, and knowledge of the customer and knowledge of the product. Your strategy should be based on the type of prospect and the prospect's attitude toward purchasing in general and purchasing a special property in particular.

To close a sale you must appeal to buying motives, watch for buying signals, overcome any resistance that is raised, and attempt a trial close. Buying motives include survival, security, pride of ownership, love of family, health, desire for profit or gain, and desire for comfort and convenience.

If you understand buying signals, you know when to close. Timing can be essential. Treat objections as a natural part of a sale. Welcome the objection, concede before answering, rephrase the objection as a question, and meet the objection. You can forestall an obvious objection by bringing it up yourself and covering it.

You have a choice of six basic techniques with untold variations for closing:

1. An assumptive close asks a question that assumes the prospect will buy.

2. The positive choice gives the prospect a choice between positive actions.

3. The inducement technique contains a benefit for buying now.

4. The fear of loss or approval is based on a "last chance."

5. The narrative close uses third-party verification.

6. The ask-for-a-deposit close gets right to the heart of the matter.

Sales can be lost for many reasons. Generally, salespeople lose sales by talking when they should be listening and not knowing when they should be silent. Overeagerness, incomplete knowledge, too much pressure, appearing frightened, criticizing competitors, wandering from your purpose, displaying a negative attitude, and being argumentative or negative are all reasons why salespeople fail.

The estimated buyer's closing cost should be given to the buyer before the offer is complete. Buyers don't like to be surprised. Be realistic in estimating buyer costs.

The eight-page California Residential Purchase Agreement and Joint Escrow Instructions form is a complete agreement that you must fully understand before attempting to sell a property. The form is designed to aid you in explaining the agreement and in meeting your obligations.

CLASS DISCUSSION TOPICS

1. How would you overcome the following buyer objections?

   a. I wanted a house with a [pool] and this house doesn't have a [pool].

   b. I didn't want an older house.

   c. I don't like the location.

   d. The price is too high.

   e. The monthly assessments are way too high.

   f. The interest rate is too high; I better wait.

   g. The mortgage payments are more than my rent.

   h. The financing is too complicated.

   i. I'm worried about [my job/the economy].

   j. I want to sell my present home first.

   k. We want to think it over.

   l. I'd like to discuss it with [my accountant/lawyer/son-in-law].

2. Using another student to represent a buyer, demonstrate a closing (no more than three minutes).

3. Complete a Residential Purchase Agreement for the residential property in Unit 6, Class Discussion Topic 5, according to the following:

   Buyers: Orem and Melody Rosatta

   Deposit: Personal check for $15,000

   Purchase price: $500,000

   Financing contingency: Contingent on obtaining a new 80% fixed-rate loan at no more than 5¼% interest and no more than $8,000 in loan fees and discount points. Buyers will provide evidence that they are prequalified for a loan, meeting above terms within five days of acceptance.

   Appraisal contingency: Offer contingent on property appraisal for no less than purchase price (there are no other contingencies).

Closing: Within 60 days of acceptance. Possession at closing.

Occupancy: Buyers intend property as their permanent residence.

Fees and costs: Seller will pay transfer fees and title insurance. Escrow fees shall be split equally. Apex Escrow shall be the escrow for the transaction. Sewer and well costs are not applicable. Seller will pay for smoke detector and water heater bracing as required. All other costs are to be borne by seller. Seller will pay for a one-year home warranty, as well as a pest control inspection, and seller will pay for any corrective work indicated.

Condition: Seller will pay for inspections and reports set forth in paragraph 7 of the purchase contract.

Personal property included: Refrigerator, pool equipment, fireplace accessories, window coverings, portable steel garden building, and riding lawn mower.

Time periods specified in paragraph 14 are adequate.

4. Bring to class one current-events article dealing with some aspect of real estate practice for class discussion.

UNIT 10 QUIZ

1.   A good salesperson
     a.   uses technical terms whenever possible to impress buyers.
     b.   speaks fast so she can reach the closing.
     c.   approaches every customer in the same way.
     d.   does none of these.

2.   A salesperson appeals to buying motives. Which of the following is a buying motive?
     a.   Love of family
     b.   Comfort and convenience
     c.   Security
     d.   All of these

3.   Disadvantages of home ownership include
     a.   increase in expenses.
     b.   risk.
     c.   lack of liquidity.
     d.   all of these.

4.   Buying signals might include a buyer's
     a.   whispering with a spouse.
     b.   pacing off a room.
     c.   seeming reluctant to leave a property.
     d.   doing all of these.

5.   A prospective buyer says, "The price is too high." The *BEST* response is
     a.   "I think the price is fair."
     b.   "Why don't you offer less?"
     c.   "The comparable sales don't bear that out."
     d.   "Why do you feel that the price is too high?"

6. A professional salesperson knows that
    a. telling is more effective than asking.
    b. appealing to emotions should be avoided.
    c. in dealing with a cautious buyer, you should be assertive and push for a decision.
    d. none of these apply.

7. When you ask prospective buyers if they prefer June 1, July 1, or August 1 for possession, what type of closing technique are you using?
    a. Inducement
    b. Positive choice
    c. Fear of loss
    d. Narrative close

8. The paragraph in the purchase contract in which the buyer indicates an intention to occupy the property (applies to 1–4-unit residential properties) is important because it relates to
    a. liquidated damages.
    b. vesting of title.
    c. smoke detectors.
    d. home protection plans.

9. Who can modify an accepted offer to purchase?
    a. The selling broker
    b. The listing broker
    c. The listing broker and the seller
    d. The buyer and the seller by mutual agreement

10. In making a property inspection, the inspector hired by the buyer negligently damaged the air-conditioning unit. Who is responsible for the damage based on the California Residential Purchase Agreement and Joint Escrow Instructions?
    a. The seller
    b. The buyer
    c. The buyer's agent
    d. The seller's agent

UNIT ELEVEN

11

FROM OFFER TO CLOSING

LEARNING OBJECTIVES

When you have completed this unit, you will be able to

- describe the preparation required before presentation of the offer,

- explain how to deal with multiple offers and how to present offers to owners,

- understand your agency duties to your principal as to recommendations,

- demonstrate how ow to deal with objections,

- explain when and how to prepare a counteroffer and what to do when an offer is accepted, and

- explain the importance of checklists for closing.

KEY TERMS

acceptance	history of the sale	rent skimming
buyer's remorse	multiple offers	seller objections
cash-out scheme	price	subordination clause
closing	rejection	terms
counteroffer	release of contract	

THE OFFER TO PURCHASE

The offer to purchase is really the California Residential Purchase Agreement and Joint Escrow Instructions that was covered in Unit 10. When it is signed by the buyers, we customarily call it an *offer to purchase*. Keep in mind that selling real estate really involves the following three separate sales:

1. Selling the owner on a listing or the buyer on agency representation

2. Selling the buyer on an offer

3. Selling the seller on an acceptance

While two out of three might be a tremendous average in baseball, you have totally failed if the third sale is not completed.

A seller's agent must continue sales efforts until an offer has been accepted. To cease working to sell a property merely because an offer was received is not in the owners' best interest. It could be regarded as unethical conduct.

Preparing to Submit the Offer

After you receive an offer to purchase, preparation is normally necessary for your presentation of the offer to the owners.

> The third sale—acceptance of the offer—is the one that means success.

The appointment.   When you have a signed offer to purchase, notify the listing office immediately and deliver the offer to the listing office as soon as possible. Provide information you have about the buyers and whether they have qualified or been approved for a loan. If the offer is for less than the list price, you might want to include any data you have that justifies the price.

The listing agent has a fiduciary relationship with the owner. The listing agent should present the offer to the owner. There might be circumstances where the listing agent would want the selling agent present when making the offer. Keep in mind that a listing agent, who has sole agency duties to the seller, has different objectives than an agent whose sole agency is to the buyer. It is the listing agent's responsibility to make an appointment with the owners to present the offer to them.

Avoid giving any details about an offer to an owner until you can present the offer in its entirety.

It is a good idea to set up an appointment with the owner so as not to be questioned by the owner over the phone about price. You need to present the entire offer, not just the price. Revealing only one aspect of an offer, when not presented as part of the total package, could result in antagonistic owners rejecting an offer, an action that could be to their detriment.

When viewed as a whole, the offer at what an owner regards as too low a price might appear much more acceptable, or it could be the starting point for an acceptable counteroffer.

You want to be able to present the offer to all the owners at once. Whenever possible, schedule the presentation after small children have gone to bed, because any interruptions can make your job extremely difficult.

Should the owners contact you before you present the offer and ask you what the offer is, we suggest this answer:

> It wouldn't be fair to you or the buyers to condense the offer into a minute or two. This offer deserves careful consideration as well as explanation. You will want to see this offer.

If the owner persists, ask "Can you and [spouse or co-owner, if applicable] meet with me right now?"

Owners can't accept offers over the phone, so try to avoid presenting them over the phone.

Generally, you should not present an offer over the telephone. The sellers can't accept over the phone, but they can say no. A phone presentation also gives owners time to talk to others about the offer before your presentation to them. Unfortunately, friends tend to give uninformed advice they think the owners want to hear, such as "Oh! Your home is worth more than that!"

If you must present the offer by phone, you should also fax or email the offer. The offer cannot be accepted until a signed copy is transmitted electronically or placed in the mail.

If the listing agent does not have much experience, the agent's broker may want to be present.

Estimated seller's proceeds.   For an offer less than list price, prepare an Estimated Seller Proceeds form, based on the offer received. Show the owners what they will net from the offer. Use of this form shows the owners that you are being straightforward in your dealings with them. Your recommendations will bear more weight when it is clear to the owners that you are being totally aboveboard in your dealings.

Comparative market analysis.   If market values have been falling and the property has been on the market for several months, update the comparative market analysis (CMA) that you prepared when you took the listing. If a comparable used for the CMA has been sold, you want to be able to present the sale information.

Anticipate problems.   Role-playing exercises such as those discussed in Unit 1 can be an important part of your preparation. From analysis of the offer, you can anticipate the objections you will receive. Decide how you are going to help the owners overcome problem areas (if you believe it is in their best interests to accept the offer).

Some agents lose sight of their agency duties and give priority to their own interests over those of their principals. This is unethical conduct and cannot be tolerated. It might mean a commission now, but in the long run, it will have far greater negative impact on your reputation and future business.

Multiple offers.   When more than one offer has been received on a property, you must present the **multiple offers** together. If you know of another offer that has not yet been received, you have a duty to inform the owners of it. You even have a duty to inform owners of verbal offers, although they're not binding, nor can they be accepted.

Keep in mind that as a listing agent your first duty is to your seller, not to your firm or for your personal gain. Offers should be presented in a nonprejudicial manner so that owners can compare the offers and make their decision. With multiple offers, you might want to suggest obtaining loan preapproval on the prospective purchasers. The owners might otherwise accept an offer from a buyer who is unable to obtain financing and reject the offer from a prospective buyer who would have no difficulty obtaining the necessary loan.

A listing agent might want to encourage multiple offers so that the seller is able to take advantage of competition. The listing agent may want to obtain the seller's permission to inform all offerors of the fact that there are multiple offers. The agent could suggest to the owner that a deadline be set for improved offers. In a seller's market, this could be beneficial to the seller.

| Present multiple offers in an impartial manner. |

A selling agent wants the buyer to be successful in a competitive situation, as long as the successful purchase is in the best interests of the buyer. Price is important to the seller, as is the cleanest deal, which is the sale that will most likely avoid problems. Besides increasing price, even if above list price, sellers are likely to react favorably to an offer where the buyer pays all escrow fees and other closing costs. Therefore, it is important for the listing agent to prepare a seller's net sheet to show the seller the net from a successful sale, including any concessions to the buyer.

Setting the mood.   You should present the offer to the owners at your office or the owners' home. If at the home, a good place to present the offer is at the kitchen table (likely in the same location where you took the listing). This is a nonthreatening environment, and the listing and selling agent can physically be quite close to the owners. If presented in any other room, use a table such as a cocktail table and sit close together with direct eye contact with the owners.

To set a positive mood, mention some feature that played a part in the sale and that the owners can be proud of. For example:

> Frankly, I think the reason I have an offer on the house is because of your delightful garden. The buyers fell in love with your rose bushes.

> While [Mrs. Wilson] loves your light and bright decorating, [Mr. Wilson] was sold on your house because of the workroom in the garage. It's something he has always wanted.

This is also the time to confirm agency election and obtain the seller's signature on the confirmation, unless it is part of the purchase contract.

Stages of the presentation.   Professional presentations are well organized. One organization plan is a three-stage presentation, as follows:

1. A history of the property sales effort and any problems with the property

2. Information about the buyers—humanize the buyers so that they can be seen as people the sellers would like

3. The offer itself

As in a sale, agents should use a closing if they feel acceptance of the offer is in the best interest of the sellers.

History of the sale.   If the property has been on the market for several months or longer, go over the **history of the sale**.

Cover the following:

- The length of time on the market (in days)

- Previous listings or sale efforts (for sale by owner)

- Advertising (all types)

- The role of the multiple listing service

- Internet postings

- Agent caravans

- Open houses

- Showings

- Responses to showings—reasons why other buyers rejected the home (negative features or lack of features)

- Any other offers received

If the property was recently listed and you already have received an offer, it is possible the owners may feel that they must have set their sale price too low. These owners can become adamant about not giving one inch.

Consider the following approach:

[Mr. and Mrs. Finch], when you listed the property with me, I explained that offers are very often received within a few days of the property being placed on the market. When this happens, you are fortunate, and you're fortunate today. Real estate agents, as well as buyers, get excited over new listings, because they feel they're getting first chance at a home rather than it being shopworn merchandise that hundreds of buyers have rejected. In fact, the most active sale period for a listing is the first 30 days it is on the market. When it's on the market longer than that, it can become much harder work to locate a buyer. For this reason, it is important to avoid listing a property at a price that is too high because you will lose much of the momentum resulting from taking a new listing. Steer clear of the trap to "list high and then come down later."

Often, owners reject offers that they receive within days of the listing and then go for a long time without another offer. Do you know what happens then? In most cases, when they do get an offer, it is for less than they received earlier. I'm telling you this so you don't respond emotionally to this offer but rather receive it with reason.

About the buyers.   Whenever possible, paint a verbal picture of the buyers that will make the sellers feel they are likable people who will appreciate the home. For example:

> The buyers are the [Henleys], the young family who came here last Thursday and then again yesterday. [Tom Henley] is [chief of security] at the [Nesco Corporation] and [Mary Henley] is an [associate editor] for the [Daily News].
>
> Their daughter [, Tricia,] [age nine,] goes to [Sunnyvale School]. One of the reasons they like your home is that the children would not have to change schools. Their son [, Jeffrey,] is just four years old and is in preschool.

Note: Obtain the buyers' permission before you reveal any personal information about the buyers.

Keep in mind that a home sale is emotional, and although owners have logical reasons to sell, there is often emotional reluctance at the same time.

In addition to reassuring sellers that the prospective buyers are nice people, you also want their offer to appear reasonable. If the buyers also are interested in another property, and most buyers are, point this out. When they receive an offer, owners tend to forget that they're competing with many other sellers:

> The [Henleys] were undecided between your house and a three-bedroom, two-and-one-half-bath Spanish-style home off [Wedgewood Way]. That house has two and a half baths, while your home has two baths, and had concrete block walls, but I was able to convince the [Henleys] that your house met their total needs better because it doesn't require [Tricia] to change schools, and the workroom in the garage was just what [Tom] wanted for his woodworking. He carves duck decoys.

Cover all three steps:
1. History
2. Buyers
3. Offer

With this kind of comparison, you have shown the owners to be winners over the competition (the house off Wedgewood Way). The owners will feel their house is appreciated and that you have been working for them. Never use an imaginary competitive house. Remember, be honest. All you need to do is to tell the owners why they are winners.

The Offer

We recommend that you gain agreement on the little things before you hand the offer to the sellers. As an example, get agreement about the following:

- The occupancy date

- What stays with the house or goes

- Seller preparing a transfer disclosure statement

- Name of escrow and if costs are to be split

- Prorating of taxes

- Keys and openers to be turned over

- Other pertinent terms

Then hand copies of the offer to each owner. If everything else has been agreed upon, then the only obstacle to a sale is the price.

Some agents like to use a silent approach and wait for owners to react. If the offer is substantially in accordance with the listing, you could go through the offer paragraph by paragraph with the owners. Answer any questions they may have. When you are finished, ask them to initial clauses where appropriate and to approve the agreement by signing where you have indicated.

Justify the Offer

When an offer is less than the list price, you must be able to justify the offer, or you risk that the sellers will regard the buyers as arbitrary. Explain how or why the buyer decided on the offering price. When sellers and buyers have a high regard for each other, there is less likelihood of a sale's failing during escrow. An example of such an explanation is:

> You don't want the buyer to appear arbitrary as to price.

While the offer I have is less than the list price, I believe it is a fair offer. Even though I convinced the [Henleys] that your home met their needs better than [the house off Wedgewood Way], they didn't feel they should pay more than what they would have paid for the [Wedgewood Way] house.

Not only does this statement justify the price, it again emphasizes that the sellers are in competition with other sellers. In cases in which an offer is reasonable, acceptance rather than a counteroffer should be sought. By accepting, your sellers will be the winners over the owners of the competing house. Always be completely honest in justifying acceptance of an offer.

Agent Recommendations—Accept, Reject, or Counteroffer

It is unethical for a seller's agent to recommend to owners that an offer be accepted if the agent does not feel that the offer is in the best interests of the owners, considering the market, the property, and their needs. If an offer is clearly not in the owners' best interests, tell them. This is part of your fiduciary duty. The less sophisticated the owners, the greater is your duty to advise them. The name of the game is not "a commission by any means."

Owners' Responses to Offers

Keep in mind that owners have three choices when an offer is received:

1. Acceptance
2. Rejection
3. Counteroffer

It would be unusual if you were to recommend outright rejection. This recommendation likely would be made only in cases of clearly frivolous offers or offers in which the buyers are attempting to take unconscionable advantage of the sellers.

If an offer is fair, work for its acceptance rather than for a counteroffer. Many agents are too quick to suggest a counteroffer when it isn't necessarily in the owners' best interests. Some agents like to push for a counteroffer because it is relatively easy and avoids further confrontation with the owners. If you truly represent the owners, you have a duty to try to make them understand that a counteroffer rejects the offer and gives the buyers an out. Once an offer is rejected, the owners have lost their right to accept and form a contract. The offer is dead.

Until accepted, an offer can be withdrawn.

Explain **buyer's remorse**. Buyer's remorse is like a virus. Most buyers get it—some worse than others. They question their wisdom in having made the offer at the price they did and wonder whether it should have been made at all. They wonder if they should have spent more time looking. To some, a counteroffer is like a heaven-sent escape.

Even buyers who intend to accept a counteroffer frequently decide to spend one more day looking before they sign. All too often, they find something they like. A great many owners have lost advantageous deals because they tried to squeeze just a little more out of buyers. A counteroffer gives up the "bird in the hand."

It is not unethical conduct to use your persuasive skills to persuade an owner to accept an offer you believe is reasonable. In fact, it is the only truly ethical way to deal with the situation.

If owners want "to sleep on it" and you feel acceptance is in their best interests, you should consider a response such as this: "Let's take a moment to go over the sale again. You placed your home on the market because . . . Are your reasons for selling still valid?" Then continue with a logical summary of the benefits of the offer and go to a closing such as this one: "Don't you agree that accepting this offer now makes sense rather than allowing the buyers an opportunity to change their minds?" You could then hand them a pen.

Duties as a Buyer's Agent

If an agent does not represent the seller, then the agent has a duty to try to get his client's offer accepted. However, the agent must be absolutely honest about any facts presented to influence the seller. An agent must never aid the buyer in fraud. The buyer's agent should fully explain the offer to the seller's agent, especially any provision that is unusual or provides the buyer with a right to cancel the agreement. It is important that the seller understand that the agent represents the buyer as a buyer's agent.

Protecting the Seller

As the sellers' agent, you have a duty to protect them from fraudulent or "shady" practices. There are offers that on careful reading do not actually state what you expect them to.

If you are unsure of the meaning of an offer that has come through another agent, suggest the owners obtain legal help or reword the offer in a counter-offer. Be especially wary of any offer received on an offer form you are not familiar with. Some sharp operators use their own forms printed with a computer printer. They may even label the form with a designation number so it looks like a standard form. By submitting forms that contain what appear to be standard or "boilerplate" clauses, they could, for example, require that the sellers pay all the buyers' loan costs, as well as all closing costs.

Be wary of offers with low earnest money deposits coupled with lengthy escrow periods. The buyer may be using the purchase offer more as an option than as a purchase with the hope of reselling it before closing. You should ask for an increased down payment and either verification of funds or the buyers' loan preapproval.

Be particularly alert for any purchase in which it appears the buyer could be promoting a **cash-out scheme**. While there are a number of ways this can be done, the most popular is by use of a **subordination clause**. Where the property is owned free and clear or the sellers have substantial equity, the buyer offers a large cash amount and asks the sellers to carry the balance with a short-term trust deed. The catch is that the trust deed is a "subordinate" trust deed.

EXAMPLE Ina Cent owns her home free and clear. She wants to sell it for $400,000. After the home has been on the market for several months, Cent receives an offer from Joe Sharp. Sharp offers her full price for the home, with $100,000 down. He asks that she carry a subordinate trust deed for the $300,000 balance at 10% interest, all due and payable in one year. This offer looks terrific to Ina Cent, so she accepts the offer. Sharp arranges for a first trust deed at $250,000. Because the trust deed for $300,000 is subordinate, the lender is protected by the full value of the property (a $250,000 loan on a property having value of $400,000).

Even though Sharp's scheme would be apparent to a lender, there are lenders who will make the new loan but would likely charge high loan origination costs, as well as a high rate of interest. As far as the lender is concerned, Sharp has a$250,000 equity in the home. Sharp uses $100,000 for his down payment and has $150,000 left. He is a cash-out buyer.

The normal scenario is that Sharp would make no payments on the $250,000 first trust deed or the $300,000 subordinate (second) trust deed. The first trust deed would either foreclose and wipe out Ina Cent's equity or she would have to cure the first trust deed and foreclose on her second trust deed, leaving her in possession of her house but with a $250,000 trust deed against it. Joe Sharp, in the meantime, is spending his money.

Other buyers to be on the alert for are those who enter into a purchase with no investment. While many no-down-payment sales are legitimate, there have been horror cases. No-down buyers have rented the property, collecting rent without making payments on the trust deed obligation. This is called **rent skimming**. Rent skimming is illegal in California and subject to criminal penalties, but violations still occur. The definition of rent skimming has been expanded to cover collecting rents and deposits on property not owned or controlled by the renter. The penalty for renting a unit without the owner's permission is up to one year of imprisonment plus a $2,500 fine. While this form of rent skimming usually involves a party who rents out a vacant property, usually in foreclosure, a variation occurs when a buyer with low or no earnest money is given possession prior to closing. The buyer rents out the property, delays closing, and eventually the purchase fails. Other no-down buyers have harvested trees and sold personal property that was included in the sale but was not separately secured by a lien.

At the very least, you have a duty to warn the owners of negative possibilities. You also might suggest that a check be made of court dockets to determine whether such potential buyers have been defendants in lawsuits.

Be wary of offers in which buyers want to exchange personal property or real property. Again, many exchanges are valid transactions, but there also have been many sharp deals. Make certain the value of the property being received has been properly verified. Don't accept at face value appraisals provided by the buyers. Be particularly careful if a property profile indicates that buyers have only recently acquired the property. If a trust deed is being traded for property, be on guard if it is a new trust deed. It is important to determine the creditworthiness of the trustor and if the trustor has personal liability. Also, determine the value of the property. Some buyers have created trust deeds on nearly worthless property to use as trading material for valuable property.

A few years ago, sharp buyers were using uncut diamonds and colored gemstones as trading material. They also were including appraisals. Sellers who accepted the stones often found they had sold their properties for less than 10 cents on the dollar.

Because real estate involves large amounts of money, it can attract some very unscrupulous people. Many of these people are very intelligent and will devise elaborate schemes to get something for as close to nothing as possible. Some seminars have explained these unethical and often illegal schemes to attendees as a get-rich-quick answer to all their dreams. It is your duty as a real estate professional to look carefully at any deal that looks too good to be true. You have a fiduciary duty to protect your principal against the devious schemes of others. Of course, this points out why sellers should be represented by agents. (Even if you are a buyer's agent, you don't want to be an accomplice in an unethical and/or fraudulent scheme.)

Gaining an Acceptance

Many sellers will accept your recommendations for acceptance when those recommendations are logical and you have built up a relationship of trust with the owners. However, a home sale is not all logic. Emotions play a significant role in acceptance or rejection of a purchase offer. The primary **seller objections** concern price.

Price.   The most common objection to an offer is about **price**. The sellers might have counted on obtaining a specified price, and they feel that accepting less is a price cut. You can answer this objection by minimizing the difference. The goal of minimizing the difference is to make the difference—the unattained portion—appear small in relation to the whole:

> Buyers, not sellers, determine price. A price set by sellers is merely a wish unless they have a buyer. Right now, we have a buyer. While the offer is less than we had hoped, it is within [7%] of the comparative market

analysis, which places the offer in the realm of reasonableness. You are being offered [93%] of what you hoped for. You are only a signature away from a sale.

An excellent approach when sellers are adamant on a price is:

[Mr. and Mrs. Jones], if you did not own this house and you were given the opportunity to buy it right now, would you buy the house if it could be yours for [the price of the offer]?

The answer to such a question probably will be, "No, we don't need the house; that's why we are selling it!" You should now continue with the very logical:

Then why are you bidding on it? When you turn down an offer for [$489,000], you're really saying that the house is worth more to you than has been offered. You're an active bidder competing against this buyer. If you wouldn't pay [$489,000] for this house today, then you should be accepting an offer to sell it at [$489,000].

If the owners indicate that a reasonable offer is ridiculous, point out the following:

Right now I have a check for [$10,000]; now that's not ridiculous. I also have an offer for [$489,000]. It may be less than you had hoped for, but it is only [7%] less than the value established by our comparative market analysis. That to me is not ridiculous. It is a serious offer deserving serious consideration.

You will likely hear the "our friend said . . ." response. Basically, it is that someone they know who is "very knowledgeable" about real estate told them, "Don't take a dollar less than [$500,000] for your home." The way to deal with this invisible friend is:

[Mr. and Mrs. Jones], let us assume that you reject this offer, and that, despite my best efforts, months pass without another offer on your house. Let us also assume we finally obtain another offer at less than the present offer. Now assume you accept this offer. Will your friend make up your loss?

This shows that the owners alone bear the results of the decision and that it should not be made by anyone else. You can point out actual case histories that sellers can relate to. Chances are your broker can tell you many stories that follow this identical scenario.

When sellers are adamant about a set price and refuse an offer that almost gives them what they want, an approach you could raise is the following:

Right now, you are willing to wait until you get what you are asking. Suppose we are able to find a buyer willing to meet your price but it takes us three months to do so, acceptance of the offer before us will likely mean more dollars in your pockets than the full price in three months. Consider the costs of taxes, insurance, (utilities), maintenance, and the lost opportunity in not having ($_____) right now. Coupled with these costs are additional risks of future offers at even lower prices.

Put the difference in perspective; show it as a percentage.

The sellers may be thinking in terms of thousands of dollars less than they had hoped for; however, you must present the positive side of a reasonable offer. You can do this by showing the difference not in dollars but in a percentage:

Right now we have an offer giving you 93% of what you wanted to receive for your home. I think that's a pretty good offer.

The following "gambler" argument is also an excellent approach that uses percentages:

[Mr. and Mrs. Jones], you certainly are gamblers. By accepting the offer before us, you can tie the buyers to this agreement. You are proposing a counteroffer that will give you [7%] more than this offer. You are wagering [93%] against [7%]. To me those seem like pretty long odds. I know I wouldn't gamble [93 cents] to make [7 cents], and I don't think you should either.

THE COUNTEROFFER

A little more work on the offer might eliminate the need for a counteroffer.

If agents worked harder with buyers in formulating offers, the need for **counteroffers** would be diminished. Unfortunately, some agents accept unreasonable offers from potential purchasers without expending much effort to improve the offer. This allows prospective buyers to believe that a terrific bargain is possible. What the agent is hoping for isn't acceptance but a counteroffer that might be accepted. Unfortunately, it can be difficult to get a reasonable counteroffer accepted, once prospective buyers have been given these false hopes. Nevertheless, an unreasonable offer should be countered rather than rejected, because there is still the chance of a sale. Try to structure the counteroffer in such a manner that it will be met with acceptance.

What Is a Reasonable Offer?

What is a reasonable offer will vary, depending on the market. In a seller's market with many buyers and relatively few sellers, an offer of 10% below the CMA might be viewed as unreasonable. However, in a buyer's market with many sellers, such an offer might be regarded as reasonable. As a rule of thumb, a reasonable and acceptable offer falls within 10% of the value established by the CMA, again depending on the market.

If the listing agent does not feel acceptance of an offer is in the principal's best interest, the agent should advise against acceptance and make suggestions for a counteroffer that will serve the principal's interests. However, when an agent feels that the principal's best interests would be served by acceptance of an offer, the agent should strongly recommend acceptance and explain the reasons for the recommendation.

When all other efforts have failed to obtain acceptance of the offer in its present form, persuade the seller to make a counteroffer or a new offer in response to a potential buyer's offer. Any alteration to an offer, even a change in date or time of close, is considered a counteroffer. A counteroffer is a new offer where the seller becomes the offeror.

The following are the most common conditions desired by the seller when making a counteroffer:

- Increase in purchase price and/or cash deposit

- Safeguard provisions for the seller when the buyer's offer is conditional on sale of other property

- Limitations on the seller's warranties or demands that the buyer accept property as is

- Change of amount, terms, and conditions relating to loans to be carried

- Limitations on time allowed to obtain financing and the right of the seller to assist in locating a lender

- Limitation on the liability for termite work, repairs, and the like

- Change in date of possession and demand for free occupancy

- The seller's right to accept other offers until the counteroffer is accepted

The following *dos* and *don'ts* will help you prepare and present a legitimate counteroffer:

- *Do* start by amending the acceptance clause to incorporate reference to the counteroffer

- *Do* have the seller sign the printed acceptance clause as amended if a separate acceptance clause is not inserted in the provisions of the counteroffer

- *Don't* make changes in the contract simply for the sake of change

- *Don't* pressure your principal to agree when the other party wishes to have some particular right or remedy inserted

- *Do* make sure that the addendum is dated and proper reference is made to the contract of which it is a part

- *Don't* make piecemeal changes in important terms; instead, rewrite the whole paragraph in which the terms occur for better clarity

- *Do* number the items of the counteroffer and refer to the contract paragraph where possible

- *Don't* let disagreement concerning language terminate the sale

- *Do* use a simple checklist for all points to be included in the counteroffer when drafting it

- *Do* be sure that all changes are initialed or signed properly and that all parties receive copies of the final contract executed by both sides

If you recommend a counteroffer, we suggest using a separate counteroffer, such as form 101-A prepared by Professional Publishing (Figure 11.1). Do not make changes on the purchase contract. If you change the purchase contract and the buyers counter the counteroffer and the sellers then counter the counter-counteroffer, you have a form that becomes difficult to understand. Tracing the chronological order of the sale also becomes difficult. If you use separate dated forms, what was agreed to and when will be clear. You may wish to number each counteroffer for clarity as to what the final agreement is.

FIGURE 11.1:   Counter Offer

COUNTER OFFER

In response to the Offer concerning the property located at _____
_____ made by, _____ , Buyer,
dated _____ **the following Counter Offer is submitted:**

_____
_____
_____
_____
_____
_____
_____
_____
_____
_____
_____
_____
_____
_____
_____
_____
_____
_____

OTHER TERMS: All other terms to remain the same.
RIGHT TO ACCEPT OTHER OFFERS: Seller reserves the right to accept any other offer prior to Buyer's written
acceptance of this Counter Offer. Acceptance shall not be effective until a copy of this Counter Offer, dated and signed by
Buyer, is received by Seller or _____ , the Agent of the Seller.
EXPIRATION: This Counter Offer shall expire unless written acceptance is delivered to Seller or his or her Agent on or
before _____ ☐ a.m., ☐ p.m., on (date) _____ .

Seller _____ Date _____ Time _____

Seller _____ Date _____ Time _____

ACCEPTANCE

The undersigned Buyer accepts the above Counter Offer (if checked ☐, subject to the attached Counter to Counter Offer).

Buyer _____ Date _____ Time _____

Buyer _____ Date _____ Time _____

Receipt of acceptance is acknowledged.

Seller _____   Seller _____

Use a separate form for a counteroffer. Do not make changes on the purchase contract.

A counteroffer at full asking price isn't much of a counteroffer, even if the original price was fair or below market value. You must allow the buyers to receive some advantage from the negotiations. Many sales are lost because of stubborn buyers and sellers. Sellers refuse to give an inch, and buyers want to "save face" by gaining some concession. Many buyers will walk away from an advantageous purchase rather than pay the full price.

Unless care is exercised in negotiations, a psychological wall may be built between the buyer and the seller. Figure 11.2 shows the bricks of a psychological wall between two principals.

A good approach to use when sellers do not want to give buyers a concession on a counteroffer is the following:

> Why not split the difference? The offer is for [$430,000] and you want [$490,000]. Why not counter at [$460,000]?

In presenting the counteroffer to the buyers, you can make the sellers appear reasonable, because "splitting the difference" is often considered fair. Although there is no rational justification for splitting the difference, very often it is accepted.

There are often counters to counteroffers and counters to the counters to the counteroffers. You can feel like a messenger. Much of the running from seller to buyer could ordinarily have been avoided by pressing to improve the offer when originally prepared.

THE ACCEPTANCE

Acceptance of an offer must be unqualified; a *qualified acceptance* must be considered as a new offer or a counteroffer. The legal effect of any changes is to reject the original offer and bar its later acceptance.

Acceptance must be unqualified or it becomes a counteroffer.

Keep in mind that acceptance does not take place until the person making the offer is notified of the acceptance. Until that time, the offeror is free to revoke the offer. Notification of acceptance is the delivery of a signed copy of the acceptance to the offeror. The CAR Residential Purchase Agreement allows notification of acceptance to be to the buyer's agent (broker).

Placing the acceptance in the mail constitutes notification. We recommend that you notify buyers of the acceptance immediately on receiving it.

Leave a completed offer form with the buyers, and let them know the procedure to be followed, as well as when you will contact them again. Be certain to give the buyers assurances of value and that they have purchased a fine house. People need to feel that they have done the right thing.

FIGURE 11.2: Building a Psychological Wall Between Principals

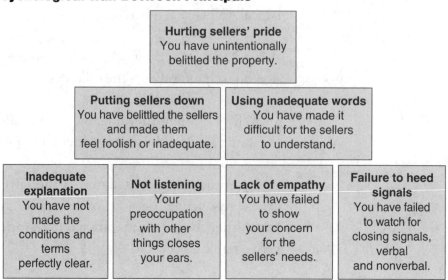

If buyers enjoy a home, they will not feel that they have overpaid, no matter what the price. On the other hand, if buyers are not happy in their home, even though they thought the home was a bargain—they overpaid. What really counts in the long run are the benefits, not the price tag.

Fax and Email Acceptance

There will be circumstances where you will be unable to present offers in person. In California, an electronic acceptance can be used. When you present an offer by fax, you should put your recommendations and your reasoning in a cover letter. If the offer is accepted by fax or a counteroffer is made, the seller should generate a transmission report reflecting the accurate transmission of the document.

Because email is considered an increasingly common means of modern communication, email acceptances of offers are now considered possible. The accepted offer can be an attachment to the email. Nevertheless, a signed copy of the acceptance should be placed in the mail to avoid any problems of delayed or claimed nonreceipt of electronic acceptance.

Advise the buyer

Advise the buyer to put off any large credit purchases until after closing. Buying a new car on credit for that new garage could mean the buyer is no longer qualified for the loan and will have a new car without a garage.

CHECKLIST FOR CLOSING

Your job isn't finished with the accepted offer. Because you don't receive compensation until the escrow closes, you must make certain the **closing** actually takes place. There are many things you must do to be sure no delays occur during closing. When there are delays, the likelihood of something happening to "kill" the sale tends to increase.

Because the individuals involved in the closing of a transaction may miss certain details and errors may creep in, it is your job to check frequently to uncover small problems before they become big ones. Check frequently to see if everything is moving according to schedule. Keep all parties fully informed of all events and conclusions. Remember, referrals depend on good follow-through. Some agents and teams have personal assistants that specialize in handling the required disclosures and paperwork of closing. They keep the lines of communication open with buyers, sellers, lenders, and escrow and prevent the occurrence of many problems.

Some agents tend to lose a great many deals during escrow. They like to blame it on bad luck, but they would be surprised how much luckier they could have been if they had worked just a little harder during escrow. There are a number of low-cost computer programs available to aid you in tracking the progress of escrows.

Closing Checklist

The following checklist contains some of the things you should be doing:

- Provide information or purchase contract to escrow so the escrow holder can prepare escrow instructions.
- Make certain all applicable disclosures discussed in Unit 3 or stated in the purchase contract are made.
- If the offer calls for a structural pest control inspection, make certain that it is ordered as soon as possible.
- If the offer provides for a professional home inspection, make certain that arrangements are made and that any problems be promptly resolved.
- Make certain that parties sign the escrow instructions as soon as they are available (if they are not part of the purchase contract), as well as the necessary transfer documentation.
- Keep in touch with the lender and make certain that this entity has everything needed to complete the loan.
- Communicate with both buyer and seller at least once each week. Let both know what is happening and what you are doing for them. If there are any problems, disclose them and work with both parties toward a solution.
- If there is a walk-through final inspection, you should be there. You don't want a nervous buyer and seller getting together without you.
- Make certain the seller has labeled all keys and left behind any applicable appliance manuals, warranties, matching paint, garage-door openers, et cetera. Also, be sure the property is in clean condition. If necessary, suggest that the seller have the carpet cleaned as soon as the house is vacated.
- Communicate with the escrow on a weekly basis. You want to know if a party has not done something or if there is a problem.
- Contact the lending officer on a regular basis to make certain things are running smoothly.
- After closing, thank both buyer and seller for their faith in you.

Some buyers will use their property inspection as the basis for another "bite at the apple" or a renegotiation of the price. They may seek disproportionate adjustment in price for real or perceived problems revealed by the inspection. You can point out to such buyers that they could be giving the seller the opportunity to get out of the contract and, if they really want the property, they should not take this risk.

Should the buyer or the seller, or both, be unable or unwilling to complete the purchase, you will want the buyer and the seller to agree, as soon as possible, as to the disposition of the deposit. By immediately addressing the problem, you will reduce the likelihood of legal action. A Cancellation of Agreement form is shown in Figure 11.3. This form calls for return of funds to parties depositing the funds, as well as a waiver of all rights pertaining to the agreement and who will pay required costs and fees incurred. A lawsuit means time spent testifying as a witness or, possibly, a defendant.

FIGURE 11.3: **Cancellation of Agreement**

CANCELLATION OF AGREEMENT
Release and Waiver of Rights with Distribution of Funds in Escrow

Prepared by: Agent _____   Phone _____
Broker _____   Email _____

DATE: _____, 20_____, at _____, California.
Items left blank or unchecked are not applicable.

FACTS:

1. This mutual cancellation and release agreement with waiver of rights pertains to the following agreement:
    ☐ Purchase agreement
    ☐ Exchange agreement
    ☐ _____
    1.1 dated _____, 20_____, at _____, California,
    1.2 entered into by _____, as the Buyer, and
    _____, as the Seller,
    1.3 whose real estate brokers (agents) are
    Buyer's Broker_____
    Seller's Broker_____,
    a. If an exchange is involved, the first and second parties to the exchange are here identified as Buyer and Seller, respectively.
    1.4 regarding real estate referred to as _____
    _____.
    1.5 Escrow Agent _____ Escrow Number _____

AGREEMENT:

2. Buyer and Seller hereby cancel and release each other and their agents from all claims and obligations, known or unknown, arising out of the above referenced agreement.

3. The real estate broker(s) and escrow agent(s) are hereby instructed to return all instruments and funds to the parties depositing them.

4. Costs and fees to be disbursed and charged to ☐ Seller, or ☐ Buyer.
    4.1 $_____ to _____
    4.2 $_____ to _____
    4.3 _____
    _____
    _____
    _____
    _____
    _____
    _____

5. The parties hereby waive any rights provided by Section 1542 of the California Civil Code, which provides: "A general release does not extend to claims which the creditor does not know or suspect to exist in his or her favor at the time of executing the release, which if known by him or her must have materially affected his or her settlement with the debtor."

I agree to the terms stated above.	I agree to the terms stated above.
☐ See attached Signature Page Addendum. [ft Form 251]	☐ See attached Signature Page Addendum. [ft Form 251]
Date: _____, 20_____	Date: _____, 20_____
Buyer's Name: _____	Seller's Name: _____
Signature: _____	Signature: _____
Buyer's Name: _____	Seller's Name: _____
Signature: _____	Signature: _____

FORM 181 03-11 ©2011 **first tuesday**, P.O. BOX 20069, Riverside, CA 92516 (800) 794-0494

©2015 RPI — Realty Publications, Inc., P.O. BOX 5707, RIVERSIDE, CA 92517

SUMMARY

It is important that the owners not know the details of any offer you have until you present it, so they can see the entire offer. Otherwise, they may build psychological walls that will make communication difficult. Before meeting with the owners, you should prepare a new Estimated Seller Proceeds form, and you might want to update the comparative market analysis.

Multiple offers should be presented in a fair and honest manner. A listing agent might encourage bidding by the offerees to raise the price.

Before you present the offer, set the mood by discussing what sold the buyers on the house. You also want the owners to sign the agency confirmation, if not covered in the offer form. The presentation process involves three stages:

1. The history of the sale

2. About the buyers

3. The offer itself

By covering the history of the sale, you will bring out the problems, if any, with the property that led other prospective buyers to reject the property. This helps deflate unrealistic expectations.

When you tell the owners about the buyers, make the buyers appear to be nice people that the sellers would like in their home. The buyers cannot appear to be arbitrary.

After covering the minor points, explain how the offer was arrived at. Recommend acceptance of a reasonable offer rather than advising a counteroffer. If the offer is not in the owners' best interests, however, recommend rejection or a counteroffer. If multiple offers are obtained, they should be presented in a nonprejudicial manner. Consider prequalifying buyers when multiple offers are received.

You must protect owners against fraud and sharp operators. Be on the alert for buyers who use their own forms, who want the sellers to carry a subordinate note, or who might otherwise be cash-out buyers. Also, be concerned if buyers are to obtain possession without any cash investment or if buyers want to exchange real or personal property for the owners' property. Don't place any value on appraisals provided by the buyers—verify everything. Be on the alert for buyers who recently acquired trust deeds or property and want to use them as trade property.

The most common objection raised by sellers to buyers' offers is price. It is in the owners' best interests to accept a reasonable offer rather than make a counteroffer that frees the buyers from the agreement. Counteroffers should consider benefits to both buyers and sellers and should be written on a separate form rather than added to the purchase contract. In this way, it will be easier to determine what exactly was agreed on and when.

Buyers can withdraw an offer anytime before acceptance. Acceptance does not take place until the accepted offer is mailed or delivered to the buyers.

Prepare a checklist of what must be done before closing.

Monitor the sale closely from acceptance to close of escrow while communicating with the buyers, the sellers, the escrow officer, and the loan officer on a regular basis. You must help the parties and make certain everything gets done; remember, a commission is not received until the closing.

CLASS DISCUSSION TOPICS

1. (If assigned by instructor) present a completed offer to an owner (another student). Your presentation will be either

   a. the history of the sale,

   b. information about the buyer, or

   c. the offer itself.

2. How would you handle the following objections of the seller to an offer?

   a. "That's $20,000 less than I paid."

   b. "Last year the house across the street from me sold for $10,000 more than this offer, and my house is nicer than their house."

   c. "If I have to cut my price, then you have to cut your commission or I won't accept the offer."

   d. "We would like to think it over."

   e. "The house is paid for. We can wait until we receive our price."

3. Bring to class one current-events article dealing with some aspect of real estate practice for class discussion.

UNIT 11 QUIZ

1. For listing agents, selling real estate involves three separate sales. Which is *NOT* one of them?
   a. Obtaining the listing
   b. Advertising for buyers
   c. Selling the buyer as to an offer
   d. Selling the seller on acceptance

2. You receive two offers on a property you have listed. One is from your own firm and the other, which was received an hour earlier, is from another firm. You should
   a. present the offers in the order received.
   b. present the highest-price offer first and, if not accepted, present the next offer.
   c. present the offers at the same time.
   d. always present your firm's offer before offers from other firms.

3. It would be MOST difficult to persuade an owner to accept a reasonable offer received
   a. 3 days after listing the property.
   b. 30 days after listing the property.
   c. 90 days after listing the property.
   d. 180 days after listing the property.

4. When presenting an offer on your listing for less than list price, it is good policy to
   a. immediately tell the seller what the offer is.
   b. not recommend acceptance or rejection.
   c. recommend that sellers counter or reject offers when acceptance is not in their best interest.
   d. have a number of your office staff present to intimidate the sellers.

5. Many buyers have second thoughts after placing an offer. This buyer apprehension is commonly known as
   a. feedback.
   b. the gambler syndrome.
   c. buyer's remorse.
   d. negative motivation.

6. Which statement regarding counteroffers is *NOT* true?
   a. A counteroffer serves as a rejection of an offer.
   b. If the counteroffer is not accepted, the owner has the option of accepting the original offer.
   c. A counteroffer turns the original offeree (the owner) into an offeror.
   d. Both a and c.

7. You should be particularly wary if an offer is received on your listing that contains the word(s)
   a. "subordination."
   b. "transfer disclosure."
   c. "time is of the essence."
   d. "liquidated damages."

8. Rent skimming is
   a. charging minorities an exorbitant rent.
   b. a property manager's failure to disclose all rents received.
   c. a buyer's failure to apply rents to loans that were assumed.
   d. a tenant making monthly rent payments every 40 days.

9. After two months, you receive an offer on one of your listings. Although for less than the listing amount, the offer is certainly reasonable based on the CMA. You should recommend to the owners that
   a. they counteroffer at a price halfway between list price and the offer to split the difference.
   b. the offer be rejected so that the offeror will raise the offer to the list price.
   c. they let the offer period expire without taking any action to make the offeror anxious.
   d. they accept the offer.

10. After an offer is accepted, the listing agent should
    a. keep track of escrow progress.
    b. make certain all papers are signed by the parties.
    c. make certain that conditions are being met.
    d. do all of these.

12

REAL ESTATE FINANCING

LEARNING OBJECTIVES

When you have completed this unit, you will be able to

- explain how the monetary policy of the Federal Reserve and the government's fiscal policy can affect the availability of funds for mortgage lending;

- describe the effect interest rates have on the real estate marketplace;

- explain the difference between primary and secondary financing and primary and secondary mortgage markets;

- explain the difference between conventional and government-involved financing;

- compare and contrast FHA, VA, and CalVet loans;

- describe different types of loans, including advantages and disadvantages of each; and

- explain the loan-qualifying process, the use of ratios and FICO scores, and the regulations that pertain to real estate finance.

KEY TERMS

adjustable-rate mortgage
adjustment period
affordability index
annual percentage rate (APR)
back-end ratio
blanket trust deed
California Housing Finance Agency loans
CalVet loans
closing the loan
commercial banks
computerized loan origination
conforming loans
construction loan
controlled business arrangement
conventional loans
convertible ARM
cosigner
credit union
direct endorsement
discount points
discount rate
Dodd-Frank
due-on-sale clause
Equal Credit Opportunity Act
Fair Credit Reporting Act
Fannie Mae
Farmer Mac
Federal Reserve
FHA-insured loan
FICO score

fixed-rate loan
Freddie Mac
front-end ratio
Ginnie Mae
hard money loans
hybrid loans
index rate
institutional lenders
insurance
interest-only loans
jumbo loans
life insurance company
Loan Estimate
margin
monetary policy
mortgage banker
mortgage broker
mortgage companies
mortgage loan broker
mortgage loan disclosure
mortgage warehousing
negative amortization
nonconforming loans
noninstitutional lenders
open market transactions
open-end trust deed
option ARM
origination points
packaged loan
participation loan
payment shock
pension fund
points
portfolio loans
predatory lending

primary financing
primary mortgage market
private mortgage
qualified mortgage
qualifying borrowers
real estate investment trust
release clause
renegotiable-rate mortgage
reserve requirements
reverse mortgage
SAFE
savings associations
secondary financing
secondary mortgage market
seller carryback financing
Service Members Civil Relief Act
statement
subprime lender
take-out loan
third-party originator
TILA-RESPA Integrated Disclosure (TRID) rule
Truth in Lending Act
Truth in Savings Act
VA-guaranteed loan
verification of employment
wraparound trust deed

FEDERAL RESERVE

The **Federal Reserve** is responsible for our **monetary policy**. It seeks to adjust the availability and cost of money so there is steady economic growth with minimum unemployment and inflation in check. The Federal Reserve has three basic controls:

1. **Discount rate.** By raising and lowering the discount rate charged to member banks to borrow funds, the Federal Reserve affects long-term rates charged by lenders. Lower rates fuel the economy, but higher rates are a contractionary economic policy.

2. **Reserve requirements.** By raising and lowering reserve requirements of banks, the amount of available funds to loan is regulated. Less funds for lending means higher interest based on supply and demand factors.

3. **Open market transactions.** The Federal Reserve can buy government securities on the open market to put money into the economy or to sell government securities to take money from the economy to slow growth.

INTEREST RATES AND THE REAL ESTATE MARKET

The health of the real estate industry is directly related to the cost of money or interest rates. Lower interest rates mean lower payments, which in turn means that more people become qualified for loans. With more buyers, we tend to have a seller's market and see real estate prices increase.

Real estate sales had been strong because of affordability brought about by low interest rates. Strong real estate sales also aided construction-related industries, as well as sales of furniture, appliances, and textiles for households.

When interest rates increase, real estate sales tend to decrease. (Sales are related inversely to interest rates.) Rising interest rates affect affordability.

LOAN POINTS

Points are percentages of the loan. They are charged to the borrower at the time the loan is made. One point would be 1% of the loan amount.

Points are either discount points or origination points.

Discount points are monies paid at the time of loan origination that allow the borrower a rate of interest less than originally offered by the lender. Therefore, discount points could be considered prepaid interest. As a rule of thumb, a lender considers eight points equivalent to 1% difference in a fixed rate loan. So a lender would want two points on a 6¼% loan if the lender wanted a 6½% yield.

Origination points are fees to cover administrative loan costs and lender compensation. As an example, a mortgage broker may want one point to make the loan even though the lender intends to sell the loan at face amount to another lender.

The **affordability index** from the National Association of REALTORS® measures the median family income necessary to support a mortgage for the median-priced home. The index is based on a 30-year fixed-rate mortgage with a 20% down payment at the current Freddie Mac mortgage rate. It is also based on the assumption that total monthly house payments, including taxes and insurance, cannot exceed 30% of gross household income. Because lenders allowed families to pay more than 30% of gross income and because of the variety of loan products offering lower payments, the affordability index best measures changes in housing affordability.

According to the California Association of REALTORS®, only 30% of California homebuyers can afford the median-priced home in California. In order to afford the median-priced house, a household would have to have income of $95,980 annually to make monthly payments of $2,400. A rapid rise in property values from 2012 to early 2016 has made housing less affordable.[1]

---

1   California Association of REALTORS®, "Growth in spring home prices leads to sizable drop in California housing affordability, C.A.R. reports," August 22, 2015, 2nd Qtr 2015 Housing Affordabiity report, news release, www.car.org/newsstand/newsreleases/2015releases/2q2015hai.

SOURCES OF FUNDS

Almost everyone is at some time a user, a buyer, or a seller of real estate. The average American spends more than 20% of his lifetime income on some form of real estate, either for rental or for purchase as an investment or as a residence. Because real estate is the largest purchase most people make in their lifetimes, few are prepared to pay cash. Thus, the completion of most real estate sales will depend on funds available in the money market at the time of the transaction.

Because most buyers are unable or unwilling to pay cash for real property, long-term financing in the form of a mortgage (or trust deed) loan is necessary. Understanding the use of real estate mortgage money requires an understanding of the sources of these funds. Money to finance real estate purchases is available through three primary money market areas: *directly* from someone or some institution that has accumulated this money, *indirectly* from a lending institution that loans money deposited in customers' accounts, or from investors who purchase loans or collateralized mortgage securities. You should be constantly aware of the status of the money market in your area, including policies of lenders, interest rates, points, and lending costs.

Different lenders offer variations in products (loans) and have different underwriting standards for different types of properties. An experienced agent will help clients select a lender and type of loan whose standards meet the property being purchased, as well as the specific client needs.

PRIMARY AND SECONDARY FINANCING

Primary financing refers to the first loan recorded against the property. Because interest rates are related to risk, primary financing generally has lower interest rates than other loans in which the security interest is secondary (i.e., second trust deeds).

Primary financing refers to first trust deeds, secondary financing to junior loans.

Any junior trust deed is **secondary financing**. Holders of a second trust deed bear a greater risk than holders of a first trust deed; therefore, second trust deeds customarily bear a higher rate of interest. In the event of default of the first trust deed, the holders of the second have to either cure the default and foreclose on the second trust deed or wait until the foreclosure and bid cash. If holders of the second trust deed fail to do either, they may lose their security.

PRIMARY AND SECONDARY MORTGAGE MARKETS

While primary financing refers to first trust deeds, the **primary mortgage market** refers to loans being made directly to borrowers, either first or second trust deeds. The **secondary mortgage market** refers to the resale of existing mortgages and trust deeds.

Four agencies—Fannie Mae (FNMA), Ginnie Mae (GNMA), and Freddie Mac (FHLMC), and Farmer Mac—are responsible for creating and establishing a viable secondary mortgage market. They buy loans originated by others and resell mortgage-backed securities. Their operations have created a national securities market for the sale of real estate debt instruments by the originators to second buyers. Selling the loans frees capital to create more real estate mortgages. The secondary market also minimizes the effects of regional cycles and redistributes the funds from cash-rich areas to cash-poor ones, thus stabilizing the money market.

Fannie Mae

Fannie Mae, formerly the Federal National Mortgage Association (FNMA), was established in 1938 to stimulate the secondary mortgage market by buying FHA-insured and VA-guaranteed mortgages made by private lenders. In 1968, Fannie Mae evolved into a private, profit-oriented corporation that markets its own securities and handles a variety of real estate loans. These loans are purchased (sometimes at a discount) and can be resold to other lenders or investors. Stabilizing the market gives lenders a sense of security and encourages them to make more loans. Because of loan problems, Fannie Mae is again under government conservatorship.

Freddie Mac

Freddie Mac, formerly the Federal Home Loan Mortgage Corporation (FHLMC), was founded with money provided by the 12 Federal Home Loan Banks when new mortgage loans could not be made because money was flowing out of the savings and loan associations (S&Ls). Freddie Mac created needed funds by floating its own securities backed by its own pool of mortgages and guaranteed by Ginnie Mae. This gave S&Ls a secondary market for selling their conventional mortgages. Freddie Mac buys loans that have been closed within one year at specified discount rates.

Both Fannie Mae and Freddie Mac ran into serious financial difficulties because of their purchases of high-risk loans.

Federal Takeover of Fannie Mae and Freddie Mac

In September 2008, the federal government placed a conservatorship over Freddie Mac and Fannie Mae. The conservatorship of these government-sponsored agencies was to be run by the Federal Housing Finance Agency (FHFA). Huge losses and concerns that the agencies could no longer raise capital to support the U.S. housing market necessitated the takeover. Both agencies are now operating at a profit, and there is political pressure to again place them under private control.

Ginnie Mae

Ginnie Mae, once the Government National Mortgage Association (GNMA), is presently a wholly government-owned agency, but privatization is being considered. Higher-risk—but important—programs, such as urban renewal, low-income housing, and other special-purpose government-backed programs, are financed through this agency. Ginnie Mae participates in the secondary mortgage market through its mortgage-backed securities programs. Qualified mortgage lenders and approved dealers can obtain additional capital for mortgages by pooling a group of homogeneous existing loans and pledging them as collateral. Ginnie Mae guarantees that holders of these securities will receive timely principal and interest payments.

Federal Agricultural Mortgage Corporation

Farmer Mac, the Federal Agricultural Mortgage Corporation, is a government-chartered, but now private, corporation that provides a secondary mortgage market for farm property and rural housing.

CONFORMING LOANS

> Conforming loans meet Fannie Mae and Freddie Mac purchase criteria.

A lender that makes a loan either keeps the loan in its portfolio or sells the loan in the secondary mortgage market. Loans that the lender keeps (does not sell) are called **portfolio loans**. Loans that the lender sells are called *nonportfolio loans*. **Conforming loans** are conventional loans that meet the underwriting standards for purchase by Fannie Mae or Freddie Mac. These loans are written for 15-year or 30-year terms and are not assumable. They have strict guidelines regarding down payments and maximum amounts. In 2015, a single-family loan had a limit to $417,000 to be eligible for purchase by Fannie Mae or Freddie Mac (this amount is revised on January 1 of each year) and is higher in some high-housing-cost areas. Because of the ready market for these loans, lenders are willing to make them and to purchase them on the secondary mortgage market. Because of their strict underwriting requirements, the interest rates for conforming loans are generally less than rates charged for **nonconforming loans**.

Loans for amounts of $417,000 and more are customarily called jumbo loans. Interest rates on **jumbo loans** are higher than rates for conforming loans.

LENDERS

All lenders are interested in the value of the property, the character of the borrower reflected in the FICO score, and the buyers' ability to make the payments.

Lenders can be divided into two groups: institutional lenders and noninstitutional lenders.

Institutional Lenders

Institutional lenders are subject to government regulations. These are major commercial banks, savings associations, and life insurance companies. (See Figure 12.1.)

Commercial banks. **Commercial banks** are familiarly known as the "department stores" of financial institutions because of the variety of operations in which they engage. A principal activity of commercial banks is lending money. Commercial banks prefer to make loans to their customers because this preference helps create depositors.

Banks often charge lower loan fees than other institutional lenders. They are quite versatile in the type of loans they may consider, but they seldom allow secondary financing at the time of providing a purchase-money loan.

Commercial banks have been a major source for construction loans. They like the shorter term and higher interest rates of these loans.

Banks have been expanding their home equity loans (second trust deeds). Some offer an open-end line of credit secured by the borrowers' home equity.

Banks in California

In California, banks are either federally chartered or state chartered and are regulated by federal and state laws, respectively. They tend to favor short-term loans and follow relatively conservative appraisal and lending practices. Their real estate loans generally are 80% or less of the appraised value of the property. Borrowers who are unable to put at least 20% down will likely be required to buy **private mortgage insurance** (PMI). A homeowner can request cancellation of the mortgage insurance when the homeowner's equity reaches 20%, payments are current, and there has not been more than one late payment in the prior year. The insurance must be canceled when the homeowner's equity reaches 22% (based on purchase price).

FIGURE 12.1:   Institutional Lenders

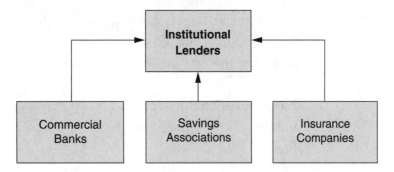

Many banks have also gone into the mortgage banking business. They make loans, which they then sell to other lenders or investors such as pension funds. They may continue to service loans that they sell.

Savings associations. Savings associations, also known as "thrifts" and originally known as savings and loan associations (S&Ls), formerly accounted for more home loans than any other source. After deregulation in the 1980s, they branched into other higher-yielding but higher-risk loans, which led to a great many S&L failures. Like banks, savings associations are state or federally chartered. They are allowed to loan up to 95% of the property's appraised value, although an 80% loan-to-value ratio (LTV) is most usual. The distinction between banks and savings associations has almost disappeared. Most California S&Ls have now become state- or federally chartered banks

Life insurance companies. The lending policies of **life insurance companies** are governed by the laws of the state in which the company is chartered, the laws of the state in which the loan originates, the policies of management, and the availability of loan funds.

Insurance companies supply many of the loans on properties for which huge loans are required (commercial properties, shopping centers, industrial properties, and hotels). In California, they make loans for up to 75% of the property's market value. Their commercial loans are commonly for 25 to 30 years. Insurance companies' interest rates often are lower than those of banks or savings associations. These loans seldom have due-on-sale clauses.

Insurance companies frequently demand an equity position as a limited partner as a condition of making a loan (**participation loan**). Many insurance companies were motivated by the benefit of an equity position coupled with the rapid depreciation allowed by the Tax Reform Act of 1981 to make large commercial loans. (Insurance company lending in the mid-1980s contributed to the overbuilding of shopping centers and office structures in many areas of the country.)

Noninstitutional lenders that make real estate loans include private individuals who use their own funds and real estate investment trusts. (See Figure 12.2.)

FIGURE 12.2:   **Noninstitutional Lenders**

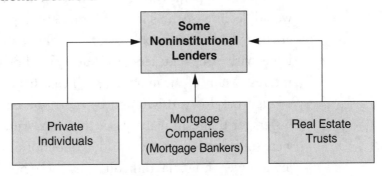

Mortgage Bankers or Mortgage Companies

Mortgage bankers can be licensed in California by either the Bureau of Real Estate or the Department of Corporations.

Mortgage bankers make loans using a line of credit from another lending institution and usually resell the loans on the secondary mortgage market. This resale of existing loans allows mortgage bankers to free up capital on their line of credit in order to make new loans. They usually have a close working relationship with one or more lenders and receive daily rate sheets. **Mortgage companies** are currently the largest single source of residential mortgage loan origination in California. You will see that the lender websites listed in the appendix are primarily mortgage bankers.

Mortgage companies make money on origination fees, as well as on loan servicing fees. Though they generally resell the loans that they originate, mortgage companies often continue to service these loans.

Mortgage companies might hold off selling mortgages that they originated if they believe that mortgage interest rates will drop. If they are right, mortgages made at higher rates could be sold at a premium above face value. The mortgage banker might borrow on this inventory of loans held for resale. This is known as **mortgage warehousing**.

Mortgage companies are careful in qualifying borrowers because loans that fail to conform to Fannie Mae and Freddie Mac purchase requirements are difficult to sell on the secondary mortgage market. Mortgage bankers will generally only make loans when they have a buyer for them. They seldom make loans that they do not intend to resell.

Mortgage companies are able to make many difficult loans that most banks would decline, such as loans for mixed-use properties or loans where buyers have had credit problems or low FICO scores. They might place such loans with **subprime lenders** that make difficult loans at a higher rate of interest. Many of the financial problems, beginning in 2008, were the result of high-risk loans originated by mortgage companies because there were buyers for them. In many cases the loans were used to back securities that were sold throughout the world. Nonperforming loans and foreclosure have led to severe financial difficulties by those holding those loans and/or their mortgage backed securities.

Mortgage Loan Broker

> Mortgage brokers are strictly middlemen who bring lenders and borrowers together.

According to the state's Mortgage Loan Brokerage Law, a **mortgage loan broker** is a person who acts for compensation in negotiating a new loan and is required to be licensed as a real estate broker or salesperson. No separate license is required. Real estate brokers who negotiate mortgage loans under the Mortgage Loan Brokerage Law are limited in the amount that they may charge as a commission for arranging the loan and for costs and expenses of making the loan. Loans on first trust deeds of $30,000 or more or on second trust deeds of $20,000 or more do not come within the purview of the law, but commissions and expenses are negotiable between the broker and the buyer.

Commission maximums under the law are as follows:

- First trust deeds (less than $30,000)—5% of the loan if less than three years; 10% if three years or more

- Second trust deeds (less than $20,000)—5% of the loan if less than two years; 10% if at least two years but less than three years; 15% if three years or more

If the loan comes under the purview of the law, the expenses of making the loan charged to the borrower (i.e., appraisal fees, escrow fees, title charges, notary fees, recording fees, and credit investigation fees) cannot exceed 5% of the principal amount of the loan. However, if 5% of the loan is less than $390, the broker may charge up to that amount. Regardless of the size of the loan, the buyer (borrower) cannot be charged more than $700 for costs and expenses. In no event may the maximum be charged if it exceeds the actual costs and expenses incurred.

Because mortgage loan brokers can arrange loans for noninstitutional as well as institutional lenders, they are often able to place loans that many direct lenders turn down because of perceived problems with the borrower or the loan security. These loans could require higher loan costs and/or a higher rate of interest. Mortgage loan brokers are required to provide a **mortgage loan disclosure statement** to borrowers (see Figure 12.3).

Because most loans arranged by mortgage loan brokers are first trust deeds of $30,000 or more or second trust deeds of $20,000 or more, the limitations on loan cost and commissions seldom become an issue. The lender can charge whatever the market will bear for loans above the amounts stated.

Mortgage loan brokers arrange a wide variety of loans. Because the mortgage loan broker is a middleman, the security for the loan must satisfy the *lender's criteria* for the loan. Mortgage loan brokers generally do not service the loans they arrange.

FIGURE 12.3: Mortgage Loan Disclosure Statement (Borrower)

MORTGAGE LOAN DISCLOSURE STATEMENT
(Traditional) (DRE 882)

Prepared by: Agent _____ Phone _____

Broker _____ Email _____

BORROWER'S NAME(S)

REAL PROPERTY COLLATERAL: THE INTENDED SECURITY FOR THIS PROPOSED LOAN WILL BE A DEED OF TRUST OR MORTGAGE ON (STREET ADDRESS OR LEGAL DESCRIPTION)

THIS MORTGAGE LOAN DISCLOSURE STATEMENT IS BEING PROVIDED BY THE FOLLOWING CALIFORNIA REAL ESTATE BROKER ACTING AS A MORTGAGE BROKER

INTENDED LENDER TO WHOM YOUR LOAN APPLICATION WILL BE DELIVERED (IF KNOWN)   ☐ Unknown

❖ For any federally related mortgage loans, HUD/RESPA laws require that a Good Faith Estimate (GFE) be provided. A RE 882 Mortgage Loan Disclosure Statement (MLDS) is required by California law and must also be provided.

❖ The information provided below reflects estimates of the charges you are likely to incur at the settlement of your loan. The fees , commissions, costs and expenses listed are estimates; the actual charges may be more or less. Your transaction may not involve a charge for every item listed and any additional items charged will be listed.

Item	Paid to Others	Paid to Broker
Items Payable in Connection with Loan		
Mortgage Broker Commission/Fee	▉▉▉▉▉▉	$
Lender's Loan Origination Fee	$	▉▉▉▉▉▉
Lender's Loan Discount Fee	$	▉▉▉▉▉▉
Appraisal Fee	$	$
Credit Report	$	$
Lender's Inspection Fee	$	$
Tax Service Fee	$	$
Processing Fee	$	$
Underwriting Fee	$	$
Wire Transfer Fee	$	$
Items Required by Lender to be Paid in Advance		
Interest for _____ days at $_____ per day	$ 0.00	$
Hazard Insurance Premiums	$	$
County Property Taxes	$	$
Mortgage Insurance Premiums	$	$
VA Funding Fee/FHA MIP/PMI	$	$
Other:_____	$	$
Reserves Deposited with Lender		
Hazard Insurance: _____ months at $_____ /mo.	$ 0	$
Co. Property Taxes: _____ months at $_____ /mo.	$ 0	$
Mortgage Insurance: _____ months at $_____ /mo.	$ 0	$
Other:_____	$	$
Title Charges		
Settlement or Closing/Escrow Fee	$	$
Document Preparation Fee	$	$
Notary Fee	$	$
Title Insurance	$	$
Other:_____	$	$

— — — — — — — — — — — — — — — — — *PAGE ONE OF FOUR — FORM 204 (DRE 882)* — — — — — — — — — — — — — — — — — —

FIGURE 12.3 (continued):   Mortgage Loan Disclosure Statement (Borrower)

— — — — — — — — — — — — — — — — — — — PAGE TWO OF FOUR — FORM 204 (DRE 882) — — — — — — — — — — — — — — — — — — —

**Government Recording and Transfer Charges**

Recording Fees $ _____ $ _____

City/County Tax/Stamps $ _____ $ _____

Other:_____ $ _____ $ _____

**Additional Settlement Charges**

Pest Inspection $ _____ $ _____

Credit Life, and/or Disabilty Insurance (See Note below)✳ $ _____ $ _____

Subtotals of Initial Fees, Commissions, Costs and Expenses $0.00 $0.00

Total of Initial Fees, Commissions, Costs and Expenses $ 0.00

**Compensation to Broker (Not Paid Out of Loan Proceeds)**

Yield Spread Premium, Service Release Premium or Other Rebate Received from Lender $ _____

Yield Spread Premium, Service Release Premium or Other Rebate Credited to Borrower $ _____

Total Amount of Compensation Retained by Broker $ _____

✳ **Note: The purchase of Credit Life and/or Disability Insurance is NOT required as a condition of making this proposed loan.**

ADDITIONAL REQUIRED CALIFORNIA DISCLOSURES

Proposed Loan Amount $ _____

Initial Commissions, Fees, Costs, and Expenses Summarized on Page 1 $ _____

Down Payment or Loan Payoffs/Creditors (List): $ _____

_____ $ _____

_____ $ _____

_____ $ _____

Subtotal of All Deductions $ _____

Estimated Cash at Closing ☐ **To You** ☐ **That You Must Pay** $ _____

GENERAL INFORMATION ABOUT LOAN	
PROPOSED INTEREST RATE: _____% ☐ FIXED RATE ☐ INITIAL VARIABLE RATE	Proposed Monthly Loan Payments: $_____ Principal & Interest (P&I) If the loan is a variable interest rate loan, the payment will vary. See loan documents for details. Total Number of Installments: _____

Loan Term: _____ Years _____ Months

BALLOON PAYMENT INFORMATION		
IS THIS LOAN SUBJECT TO A BALLOON PAYMENT? ☐ Yes ☐ No	DUE DATE OF FINAL BALLOON PAYMENT (ESTIMATED MONTH/DAY/YEAR)	AMOUNT OF BALLOON PAYMENT $

IF YES, THE FOLLOWING PARAGRAPH APPLIES:

NOTICE TO BORROWER: IF YOU DO NOT HAVE THE FUNDS TO PAY THE BALLOON PAYMENT WHEN IT COMES DUE, YOU MAY HAVE TO OBTAIN A NEW LOAN AGAINST YOUR PROPERTY TO MAKE THE BALLOON PAYMENT. IN THAT CASE, YOU MAY AGAIN HAVE TO PAY COMMISSIONS, FEES, AND EXPENSES FOR THE ARRANGING OF THE NEW LOAN. IN ADDITION, IF YOU ARE UNABLE TO MAKE THE MONTHLY PAYMENTS OR THE BALLOON PAYMENT, YOU MAY LOSE THE PROPERTY AND ALL OF YOUR EQUITY THROUGH FORECLOSURE. KEEP THIS IN MIND IN DECIDING UPON THE AMOUNT AND TERMS OF THIS LOAN.

PREPAYMENT INFORMATION		
PREPAYMENT PENALTY? ☐ Yes ☐ No	# OF YEARS THAT PREPAYMENT PENALTY IS IN EFFECT	MAXIMUM DOLLAR AMOUNT OF PENALTY

IS THERE A PREPAYMENT PENALTY FOR PAYING IN EXCESS OF 20% OF THE ORIGINAL OR UNPAID LOAN BALANCE?

☐ Yes ☐ No   If Yes, see loan documents for details.

TAXES AND INSURANCE	
IMPOUND ACCOUNT? ☐ Yes ☐ No **APPROXIMATE** AMOUNT THAT WILL BE COLLECTED MONTHLY $	IMPOUND ACCOUNT WILL INCLUDE County Property Taxes Mortgage Insurance Hazard Insurance Flood Insurance Other:_____ ☐ Yes ☐ No ☐ Yes ☐ No ☐ Yes ☐ No ☐ Yes ☐ No ☐ Yes ☐ No

— — — — — — — — — — — — — — — PAGE TWO OF FOUR — FORM 204 (DRE 882) — — — — — — — — — — — — — — —

FIGURE 12.3 (continued):   Mortgage Loan Disclosure Statement (Borrower)

— — — — — — — — — — — — — — — — — *PAGE THREE OF FOUR — FORM 204 (DRE 882)* — — — — — — — — — — — — — — — —

IF NO, PLAN FOR THESE PAYMENTS ACCORDINGLY	BORROWER MUST PLAN FOR PAYMENTS OF THE FOLLOWING ITEMS
→	County Property Taxes Mortgage Insurance Hazard Insurance Flood Insurance Other: _____ ☐ Yes ☐ No ☐ Yes ☐ No ☐ Yes ☐ No ☐ Yes ☐ No ☐ Yes ☐ No

Note: In a purchase transaction, county property taxes are calculated based on the sales price of the property and may require the payment of an additional (supplemental) tax bill issued by the county tax authority. The payment of county property taxes (including supplemental bills) may be paid by your lender if an impound/escrow account has been established.

If an impound/escrow account has not been established, the payment of all tax bills including any and all supplemental tax bills will be the responsibility of the borrower(s).

OTHER LIENS

LIENS CURRENTLY ON THIS PROPERTY FOR WHICH THE BORROWER IS OBLIGATED

Lienholder's Name	*Amount Owing*	*Priority*

LIST LIENS THAT WILL REMAIN OR ARE ANTICIPATED TO REMAIN ON THIS PROPERTY AFTER THE PROPOSED LOAN FOR WHICH YOU ARE APPLYING IS MADE OR ARRANGED (INCLUDING THE PROPOSED LOAN FOR WHICH YOU ARE APPLYING):

Lienholder's Name	*Amount Owing*	*Priority*

NOTICE TO BORROWER: BE SURE THAT YOU STATE THE AMOUNT OF ALL LIENS AS ACCURATELY AS POSSIBLE. IF YOU CONTRACT WITH THE BROKER TO ARRANGE THIS LOAN, BUT IT CANNOT BE ARRANGED BECAUSE YOU DID NOT STATE THESE LIENS CORRECTLY, YOU MAY BE LIABLE TO PAY COMMISSIONS, COSTS, FEES, AND EXPENSES EVEN THOUGH YOU DO NOT OBTAIN THE LOAN.

ARTICLE 7 COMPLIANCE

If this proposed loan is secured by a first deed of trust in a principal amount of less than $30,000 or secured by a junior lien in a principal amount of less than $20,000, the undersigned broker certifies that the loan will be made in compliance with Article 7 of Chapter 3 of the Real Estate Law.

WILL THIS LOAN BE MADE WHOLLY OR IN PART FROM BROKER CONTROLLED FUNDS AS DEFINED IN SECTION 10241(J) OF THE BUSINESS AND PROFESSIONS CODE?

☐ May   ☐ Will   ☐ Will Not

Note: If the broker indicates in the above statement that the loan "may" be made out of broker-controlled funds, the broker must inform the borrower prior to the close of escrow if the funds to be received by the borrower are in fact broker-controlled funds.

STATED INCOME

IS THIS LOAN BASED ON LIMITED OR NO DOCUMENTATION OF YOUR INCOME AND/OR ASSETS?

☐ Yes ☐ No   If Yes, be aware that this loan may have a higher interest rate or more points or fees than other products requiring documentation.

NOTICE TO BORROWER: THIS IS NOT A LOAN COMMITMENT

Do not sign this statement until you have read and understood all of the information in it. All parts of this form must be completed before you sign it. Borrower hereby acknowledges the receipt of a copy of this statement.

NAME OF BROKER	LICENSE ID NUMBER	BROKER'S REPRESENTATIVE	LICENSE ID NUMBER
	NMLS ID NUMBER		NMLS ID NUMBER

BROKER'S ADDRESS			

BROKER'S SIGNATURE	DATE	OR SIGNATURE OF REPRESENTATIVE	DATE
BORROWER'S SIGNATURE	DATE	BORROWER'S SIGNATURE	DATE

FIGURE 12.3 (continued):   Mortgage Loan Disclosure Statement (Borrower)

— — — — — — — — — — — — — — — *PAGE FOUR OF FOUR — FORM 204 (DRE 882)* — — — — — — — — — — — — — — —

Department of Real Estate license information telephone number: 877-373-4542, or check license status at www.dre.ca.gov

NMLS - http://mortgage.nationwidelicensingsystem.org/about/pages/nmlsconsumeraccess.aspx

The Real Estate Broker negotiating the loan shall retain on file for a period of three years a true and correct copy of this disclosure signed and dated by the borrower(s).

THE RE 855 MORTGAGE LOAN DISCLOSURE STATEMENT, NON-TRADITIONAL MORTGAGE MUST BE USED FOR NON-TRADITIONAL MORTGAGE LOANS OF RESIDENTIAL PROPERTY (1-4 UNITS).

Non-Traditional Mortgage Loans are loan products that allow the borrower to defer payments of principal or interest. If any of the payments are not full principal and interest payments, then it is considered a Non-Traditional Mortgage Loan.

FORM 204 (DRE 882)   3-11   ©2011 first tuesday, P.O. BOX 20069, RIVERSIDE, CA 92516 (800) 794-0494

©2015 RPI — Realty Publications, Inc., P.O. BOX 5707, RIVERSIDE, CA 92517

Scope of lending activity—real estate brokers.   There are three distinct areas of lending activity that a real estate broker can engage in:

> The mortgage broker brings together individual lenders and borrowers.

1. **Hard money makers and arrangers**—A **hard money loan** is a cash loan rather than an extension, such as seller financing. Articles V and VII of the real estate law primarily deal with hard money loans where the mortgage broker acts as an intermediary, bringing together lenders and borrowers. This activity is commonly known as *mortgage brokerage*, and the real estate licensee is acting as a **mortgage broker**.

   The loans are not made in the broker's name. They are made in the name of the lender. Most of the hard money loans are equity loans rather than purchase loans. Lenders are often private individuals.

2. **Third-party originators**—Third-party originators prepare loan applications for borrowers, which they submit to lenders. They may be agents of the borrower or the lender or dual agents of both borrower and lender. Out-of-state lenders that wish to invest directly in California mortgages frequently use third-party originators, as do pension plans and trusts. Thus, lenders that are not prepared to take loan applications in California can be direct lenders rather than having to purchase loans that were originated by others in the secondary mortgage market. They primarily deal in purchase-money loans.

Mortgage bankers are regulated by either the Bureau of Real Estate or the Department of Corporations.

3. **Mortgage bankers**—Not all mortgage bankers are real estate brokers. Some mortgage bankers are licensed under the California Residential Mortgage Lending Act, which is administered by the Department of Corporations. A mortgage banker must elect which license to operate under. Thus, we have two state agencies, the Bureau of Real Estate and the Department of Corporations, regulating the same type of activity, depending on which license the mortgage banker is operating under. (The broker makes loans while operating as a mortgage banker; however, the broker only arranges loans as a third party when operating as a mortgage broker.)

Real estate investment trusts. The **real estate investment trust** (REIT) was created in 1960 to encourage small investors to pool their resources with others to raise venture capital for real estate transactions. To qualify as a REIT, the trust must have at least 100 investors, and 90% of the trust's income must be distributed annually to its investors.

While a number of equity trusts invests solely in ownership of real property, there are many mortgage trusts that invest their money in mortgages, either directly or through a mortgage company. There also are hybrid trusts that invest in both equity ownership and mortgages.

Pension funds. At one time, **pension funds** invested primarily in stocks. However, they perceived mortgages to be safe yet high-return investments and they became important players in the mortgage market. They made loans on large projects. Pension funds generally purchased loans originated by mortgage companies or worked through mortgage brokers. They often take an equity position in large developments.

Credit unions. At one time, **credit unions** offered mostly low-dollar loans for consumer purchases. Credit unions have evolved to become major lenders. While they limit loans to members, they have expanded their loan activity. Unlike profit-oriented lenders, their loans are more community based. Besides home equity loans and home purchase loans, credit unions have expanded their community lender role to include construction and development loans. Credit unions in many ways now resemble commercial banks.

Seller Carryback Financing

When conventional financing is not available to a buyer in the amount required or is too costly, a seller often can be persuaded to carry back a first or second mortgage on property to facilitate a sale. If a seller does not need the cash and the purchaser will pay a rate of interest higher than that provided by a certificate of deposit, the seller is a likely candidate for carryback financing.

Generally, **seller carryback financing** is customized to the needs of the parties. Such loans are generally fixed-rate loans with payments based on a 30-year amortization but due and payable in five to seven years. Most sellers are not interested in having their money tied up for longer periods of time.

Because most loans now have due-on-sale clauses, seller carryback financing is limited to situations where the property is owned by the seller free of loans, where the lender will agree to a loan assumption, where the existing loan does not have a due-on-sale clause, or where the seller will hold a secondary loan after the buyer obtains primary financing.

SAFE Act

The Federal Secure and Fair Enforcement Mortgage Licensing Act (SAFE). SAFE was enacted for consumer protection and to reduce fraud. The act requires licensing for mortgage loan originators. Anyone who accepts compensation for taking a loan application, offers or negotiates terms of a 1–4-residential-unit mortgage loan, or who is compensated by a mortgage originator must have an **MLO endorsement** on their license. The endorsement requires education, testing, and reporting.

TYPES OF LOANS

While most 1–4-unit dwellings still are financed by conventional loans, the choice of a loan is no longer a foregone conclusion. Both buyers and sellers need to know what is currently available, which loan best suits their requirements, and even where to go for financing. With real estate firms allying themselves with financial institutions, even the players are changing every day.

CONVENTIONAL LOANS

By definition, a **conventional loan** is any loan that does not involve government participation. The advantages of conventional over government-backed loans are that conventional loans involve less red tape and shorter processing time. Government loans do not have equivalent flexibility. Buyers can obtain a larger loan amount, and because there are more sources for conventional loans, borrowers have the option of choosing a wide variety of fixed-rate or adjustable-rate loans.

Conventional loans have no government insurance or guarantee.

Disadvantages of conventional loans in comparison with government-backed loans can include higher down payments and prepayment penalties. Furthermore, private mortgage insurance (PMI) may be required if a purchaser has less than a 20% down payment.

How to Compare Loans

Borrowers should compare loans on the basis of the following:

- LTV (the percentage of the appraised value that the lender will lend determines down payment requirements; loan to value ratio)
- Interest rate and if it can be changed
- Loan costs and fees required
- Prepayment penalties
- Length of loan (longer-term loans result in lower monthly payments)
- Amount of fixed monthly payment
- Initial rate, adjustment period, caps, index, and margin of adjustable-rate loans

GOVERNMENT LOANS

Government Loans

There are several types of government-involved loans, including **FHA-insured loans**, **VA-guaranteed loans**, and **CalVet loans**. There are also California Housing Finance Agency loans. These types of loans are compared in Figure 12.4.

Federal Housing Administration (FHA)

The purposes of the Federal Housing Administration are stated in its pre-amble: to "encourage improvement in housing standards and conditions, to provide a system of mutual mortgage insurance, and for other purposes."

There are two divisions under which this protection is granted: Title I and Title II. In general, the following types of loans are available:

- Title I—loans for modernization, repairs, or alterations on existing homes

- Title II—loans for purchase or construction of residential structures

FIGURE 12.4:   Government Home Loan Programs

	FHA-Insured	VA-Guaranteed (GI)	CalVet
Who is eligible?	Anyone who qualifies	U.S. veterans	California residents who have met the veteran requirements
Who makes the loans?	Approved lending institutions	Approved lending institutions	Calif. Dept. of Veterans Affairs (mortgage brokers can originate loans)
Type of loan	Insure (up-front insurance premium may be financed)	Guaranteed (see Figure 12.5)	Land contract
Points and fees	Loan fee 1% plus mortgage insurance premium	Negotiable loan fees plus a funding fee (may be financed)	1.25% to 3% (may be financed)
Interest rates	May be negotiated	May be negotiated	Flexible rate based on cost of bonds. Can change annually.
What is the maximum you can pay for a home?	No limit	Loan cannot exceed appraisal	Cannot exceed the CalVet appraisal (certificate of reasonable value [CRV])
Maximum loan allowed	$625,000	No money down, to county limit; loan can't exceed the certificate of reasonable value (CRV)	125% of Fannie Mae maximum
Term	Usually 30 years	Maximum 30 years	30 years
Down payment	Approximately 3.5%	None required for loans up to county limit	0% to 5%
Secondary financing	Not allowed at time of sale, but can be placed later	Generally not allowed at time of sale, but can be placed later	Yes, but the 1st and 2nd cannot exceed 90% of the CalVet appraisal
Prepayment penalty	None	None	None
Assumability	Loans before Dec. 15, 1989, are assumable; subsequent loans assumable with FHA approval	Loans before Mar. 1, 1988, are assumable; subsequent loans require buyer to qualify	Assumable with prior CalVet approval

Section 203(b) of Title II accounts for most loans for 1–4-unit residences. FHA loans provide high LTVs based on appraisal.

The maximum FHA loan amount will vary by region, but the purchaser generally must have a minimum down payment of 3½%.

The down payment may come from a gift, but there is a ban on seller and nonprofit group assistance programs.

The *mortgage insurance premium* (MIP) must be paid at the time of loan origination. Based on the down payment, an MIP is also added to payments for the life of the loan.

Lenders may be authorized to make the underwriting decision that a loan qualifies for FHA insurance. This is known as **direct endorsement**, and it serves to speed up the loan processing time. Because of foreclosure problems, down payment requirements have increased for most other loans. As of January 1, 2009, FHA down payments were increased from 3% to 3.5%. Despite this increase, the low down payment requirement for FHA loans compared with other loans resulted in an increase in FHA loan applications.

A recent rule change allows borrowers who have gone through a foreclosure, bankruptcy, or other adverse events, and who have repaired their credit, to be eligible for an FHA-insured loan after one year. Previously, they had to wait at least three years before they would qualify for a new government-backed loan. To qualify for the shorter period, borrowers must show that their credit problems were caused by job loss or reduction in income beyond their control.

HUD (Department of Housing and Urban Development)

FHA loans are insured by HUD. The insurance protects the lender should the borrower default. Loans insured by HUD must be **qualified mortgages**. To be qualified, the loan must

- be for 30 years or less;
- limit points and fees to 3%;

■ have periodic payments without toxic features such as interest only, negative amortization, or balloon payments; and

■ have a debt-to-income ratio of no more than 43% of income.

Department of Veterans Affairs (VA)

The Servicemen's Readjustment Act of 1944 (GI Bill) was intended to help veterans to make the necessary readjustments to civilian life, particularly to assist them in the acquisition of homes. The VA does not make loans, but it guarantees a portion of the loan. Figure 12.5 explains the VA-guaranteed loan.

The largest VA loan on which no down payment is required is $729,750 in certain areas, but the VA has suspended zero down loans over $417,000. A 25% down payment is required on amounts over the county no-down-payment limit. VA loans can be used to

■ buy or build an owner-occupied home;

■ alter, repair, or improve real estate;

■ purchase a mobile home; and

■ refinance existing mortgage loans for dwellings owned and occupied by veterans.

To qualify for a VA-guaranteed loan, an individual must have had 181 days of active service. An appraiser approved by the VA checks the property.

The loan cannot exceed the appraisal known as the *certificate of reasonable value* (CRV). The certificate of reasonable value is based on a VA appraisal made for insurance purposes. (The loan amount is not regulated, but the guarantee is.)

FIGURE 12.5:   VA Guaranteed Loan (GI)

Loans	Guarantee
Up to 45,000	40% of loan
$45,000 to $144,000	Minimum guarantee of $22,500 Maximum guarantee is 40% of loan up to $36,000
More than $144,000	25% of loan up to a maximum of $60,000

CalVet loans.   Under the CalVet loan program (the California Farm and Home Purchase Program), California veterans can acquire a suitable farm or a single-family residence at a low financing cost. The State of California actually takes title to the property and sells it to the veteran under a land contract. Following are some features of the CalVet loan:

- CalVet loans can now be arranged through lenders approved to handle CalVet loans.

- CalVet loans are now processed with DVA guidelines. The loans are available to peacetime as well as wartime veterans and active-duty military. The maximum home loan amount is 125% of the maximum for a Fannie Mae conforming loan; the 2015 limit is $521,250.

- Depending on the type of CalVet loan, the down payment can range from 0 to 5%. The programs with no down payment have a limit of up to $521,250.

- 2015 CalVet loans start at 4.25% interest for a 30-year home loan (higher rate for mobile homes).

- CalVet loans have an origination fee of 1%.

- CalVet loans have a funding fee of 1.25% to 3.30%.

- Mortgage brokers who originate and process CalVet loans receive a $350 processing fee plus a 1% origination fee.

- The state raises the funds for CalVet loans by issuing tax-exempt bonds.

> With a CalVet loan, the veteran is buying under a land contract.

WEB LINK

For more information on CalVet loans, call 1-800-952-5626 or check the website at www.calvet.ca.gov/calvet-programs/home-loans/.

The California Housing Finance Agency (CalHFA).   CalHFA is California's self-supporting housing bank that offers fixed-rate conventional and interest-only financing at low rates, and down payment assistance for first-time homebuyers. CalHFA uses no appropriated taxpayer dollars for its programs but utilizes a tax-exempt bond program. Loans are for low-income and moderate-income buyers.

Programs of CalHFA include the following:

- Interest-only programs for the first 5 years of a 35-year fixed-rate mortgage

- Conventional 30-year fixed-rate mortgage

- Down-payment assistance programs for teachers in high-priority schools

- Down-payment assistance for designated high-cost counties

- Down-payment assistance for new homes based on school facility fees paid by the builder

- Down-payment assistance up to 3% to low-income buyers using FHA-insured loans

- Down-payment and closing-cost assistance in community revitalization areas

- Lower interest rates for lower-income disabled purchasers

- Lower interest rates for homebuyers receiving financial assistance from an approved government agency

CalHFA housing programs include mortgage insurance that makes home payments for up to six months if a borrower involuntarily loses her job. Eligibility requirements can be ascertained by visiting the website, www.calhfa.ca.gov.

WEB LINK

@

Because of state budgeting problems, in December 2008, CALHFA suspended its 30-year fixed-rate loan programs, as well as down payment assistance programs.

Other Types of Mortgages and Trust Deeds

Open-end trust deed.   An **open-end trust deed** allows the borrower to receive additional loan money up to an agreed amount, using the same trust deed or mortgage as security. (It is like having a credit card with a set limit.) A home equity line of credit is an example of an open-end loan.

Blanket trust deed. With a **blanket trust deed**, the borrower uses more than one parcel of property as security. This type of document should contain a **release clause** that allows the partial reconveyance of separate parcels of property on repayment of a portion of the loan.

Construction loan. This unamortized loan, usually for three years or less, is given until permanent financing is in place.

Take-out loan. This is permanent financing that takes out (replaces) short-term financing such as gap or construction loans.

Packaged loan. A loan that includes personal property, as well as real property.

Wraparound trust deed. A **wraparound trust deed** also is called an *all-inclusive trust deed*. There are times when it is almost impossible for buyers to refinance an existing loan on investment real estate to raise additional capital. With a wraparound mortgage the existing loan is not disturbed. The seller continues the payments on the existing mortgage or trust deed while giving the borrower a new, increased loan, usually at a higher interest rate. The new loan is for the amount due on the existing loan plus the amount of the seller's equity being financed.

Assume a property is being sold for $200,000 with $20,000 down. Also assume that there is a $90,000 trust deed against the property at 7% interest. If the buyer were willing to pay 9% interest, the seller could take advantage of this interest difference with a wraparound loan.

$$\left.\frac{\$90,000 \text{ loan} \quad 7\%}{\$90,000 \text{ loan} \quad 9\%}\right\} \$180,000 \text{ wraparound loan at } 9\%$$

In this case, the seller receives 9% on his equity plus a 2% differential on the 7% being paid on the existing loan. This really gives the seller 11% interest on the equity. In addition, because the seller continues to make the payments on the $90,000 loan, the seller knows that the payments are being made. If the seller had allowed the buyer to assume the existing loan, then the buyer, not the seller, would have taken advantage of the low financing.

To use a wraparound loan, the underlying loan must not have a **due-on-sale clause**. A due-on-sale clause, also known as an alienation clause, accelerates loan payments, making the entire loan amount due upon a sale. These clauses are enforceable by lenders. While a number of ways have been devised to get around the clauses, the methods basically are based on deception. Advocating use of such methods could subject you to liability and disciplinary action, as well as result in a buyer losing a property because of the inability to obtain a new loan. Because of possible problems, legal counsel should be sought before a wraparound loan is used.

Gap loan. These loans are usually short-term loans, such as loans between construction loans and the **take-out loan** (permanent financing) or by buyers who have found a new home but have not yet sold their prior residence. They are also called *swing loans* or *bridge loans*. They generally bear a relatively high rate of interest.

Fixed-rate loans. Lenders will make fixed-rate long-term amortized loans because they must in order to be competitive, but they generally prefer adjustable-rate or shorter-term loans. The reason is that they were hurt in the past by long-term **fixed-rate loans**.

In the late 1970s and early 1980s, many lenders, particularly S&Ls, had a great deal of capital invested in long-term fixed-rate loans. During this period, the United States had great inflation, and interest rates increased dramatically. Lenders had to pay higher interest rates on accounts to attract funds. In many cases, the average yield from their portfolios of loans was less than the average rate they were paying depositors for funds. While relatively short-lived, lenders had been burned and still worry that history could repeat itself.

To encourage borrowers to use other types of loans, lenders offer lower loan costs than for fixed-rate loans and even lower interest rates. With current low index rates, many adjustable-rate loans are pegged so low that lenders are again pushing fixed-rate loans.

15-year vs. 30-year fixed-rate loans. If a buyer is able to pay the additional monthly payment on a 15-year loan, significant savings are possible compared with a 30-year loan.

As an example, at 7½% interest, the monthly payment on a $100,000 loan for 15 years comes to $927.02. For a 30-year loan having the same rate of interest, the monthly payment is $699.22.

For the 30-year loan, total payments equal as follows:

$$12 \text{ (months)} \times 30 \text{ (years)} \times \$699.22 = \$251{,}719.20$$
$$\text{or interest of } \$151{,}719.20.$$

For a 15-year loan the total payments are as follows:

$$12 \text{ (months)} \times 15 \text{ (years)} \times \$927.02 = \$166{,}863.60$$
$$\text{or interest payments of } \$66{,}863.60.$$

The interest paid on the 30-year loan is more than twice the interest of the 15-year loan, and the payments are only $227.80 higher than the 30-year loan payments.

The savings are likely to be significantly greater than those shown in the example because 15-year loans usually have an interest rate from 0.375% to 0.75% lower than a similar 30-year loan. Lower interest rates are used because shorter-term loans are considered by lenders to present less risk.

40-year loans. To help offset higher home prices that have reduced housing affordability, some lenders may offer 40-year loans. While the payments are reduced by the longer amortization period, making payments for an extra 10 years might not be in the buyer's best long-term interest if the buyer can qualify and make the payments on a 30-year loan. As an example, for a 30-year loan for $300,000 at 6% interest, the monthly payment amounts to $1,798.68. For the same loan at 40 years, the payments would be $1,650.66, or $148.02 less than for the 30-year loan. However, total payments for the 30-year loan would be $647,524, but the 40-year loan total payments would be $792,316, or $144,792 greater. FHA will not insure a loan greater than 30 years.

Interest-only loans. In order to qualify buyers for home loans, many lenders formerly offered **interest-only loans**. These are also known as straight notes. The borrower makes payments of interest only for a set period of time, such as five years. At the end of the period, the borrower must make full amortized payments. As an example, interest only on a 6%, $300,000 loan would be $1,500 per month, which would be $300 less than an amortized payment.

80-20 loans.   For borrowers who didn't have a down payment, 80-20 loans were made before the mortgage meltdown. Eighty percent of the purchase price was made by a conventional lender. Because the loans are for only 80% of value, private mortgage insurance is not required. The balance of the purchase price, 20%, was covered with a second trust deed at a higher rate of interest. The second trust deed was also likely to have higher origination costs.

The 80-20 loans, as well as other low or no down payment loans, were a factor in buyers walking away from their homes when their loans exceeded the value of the homes. The resultant foreclosure sales were a factor in decreasing housing prices in 2008. Because of the foreclosure problems, lenders no longer make 80-20 loans.

Renegotiable-rate mortgages.   **Renegotiable-rate mortgages,** also known as rollover loans, usually have payments based on a 30-year amortization. However, they are only partially amortized. Generally, they are due in full in five or seven years. The lender will rewrite the loan at this time at the current interest rate, or the borrower can refinance with another lender.

Because the lender is not locked into the interest rate for a long period, lenders offer these loans for a lower interest rate than for the fixed 30-year rate. Frequently, the rate is about 1% less than fixed-rate loans. Lenders also might offer lower loan origination fees and costs.

Hybrid loans.   Lenders will offer combination fixed–adjustable-rate loans such as a 5–30, where the first 5 years are at a fixed rate and the balance of the loan (25 years) is at an adjustable rate. In order to sell borrowers on the **hybrid loan,** the fixed-rate portion of the loan has an interest rate less than that for a 30-year fixed-rate loan. This allows borrowers to qualify for the loan when they might not qualify for a 30-year fixed-rate loan.

Reverse mortgage (reverse annuity mortgage).   This unusual loan is not for home purchases. A **reverse mortgage** is a loan whereby the lender annuitizes the value of the owner's equity and makes monthly payments to the borrowers based on the equity and the age of the borrowers. The loan is not repaid until the borrowers die or the property is sold. Homeowners must be age 62 or older to qualify for a reverse mortgage.

A normal loan charges simple interest; that is, the interest for the previous month is paid with each payment and is charged on the principal balance only. A reverse mortgage, however, has compound interest (interest is charged on interest). Each month, the interest is greater than the previous month because more principal has been advanced; therefore, the principal balance has increased, and accrued interest also has been added to the principal and has increased the balance due.

Reverse mortgages have higher loan fees than most other loans. Several lenders have agreed to make settlements because of alleged unconscionable loan costs and fees for their reverse mortgages.

Piggyback loan. This is really two loans, first and second, made by a lender at the same time.

Adjustable-rate mortgage (ARM). In contrast to a fixed-rate loan, the interest rate in an **adjustable-rate mortgage** changes periodically, usually in relation to an index, with payments going up or down accordingly. Lenders usually charge lower initial interest rates for ARMs than for fixed-rate loans, which makes the ARM easier on the borrower's pocketbook than a fixed-rate loan for the same amount and also makes it easier for the borrower to qualify for the loan. In addition, it could mean that the borrower could qualify for a larger loan, because lenders sometimes qualify buyers on the basis of current income and the first year's payment. This means the buyer (borrower) could maintain a better lifestyle with an ARM. Moreover, an ARM might be less expensive over a long period than a fixed-rate loan. For example, interest rates may remain at current low rates.

Another advantage of an ARM is that it generally does not have prepayment penalties. Therefore, if the borrower expects to be reselling within a relatively short period, the absence of this penalty could give the ARM a significant advantage over loans requiring prepayment penalties.

To induce borrowers to choose an ARM, lenders may offer lower loan origination costs than for fixed-rate loans. Lower origination costs also make ARMs attractive to borrowers who intend to resell within a few years.

Against these advantages, the buyer must weigh the risk that an increase in interest rates will lead to higher monthly payments in the future. The trade-off with an ARM is that the borrower obtains a lower rate in exchange for assuming more risk. The borrower considering an ARM should envision a worst-case scenario with interest increasing to the set limit to fully understand the degree of risk involved.

Myriad ARMs variations are being offered by financial institutions today. It is important for both the borrower and the agent to learn to ask questions so that they can compare loans adequately. Here are four basic questions the buyer needs to consider:

1. Is my income likely to rise enough to cover higher mortgage payments if interest rates go up, or can I afford the higher payment?

2. Will I be taking on other sizable debts, such as a loan for a car or school tuition, in the near future?

3. How long do I plan to own this home? If I plan to sell soon, rising interest rates may not pose the problem they will if I plan to own the home for a long time.

4. Can my payments increase even if interest rates in general do not increase?

If the buyer can answer these questions satisfactorily, an ARM might be the loan of choice. However, the borrower still has to decide which ARM to take out, which entails obtaining the answers to many more questions.

When discussing an ARM with a borrower, the real estate agent needs to understand and be able to explain certain terms that do not apply to fixed-rate loans. These include *adjustment period, index rate, margin, interest rate cap, overall cap, payment cap, negative amortization, and conversion clause.* The remainder of this section defines these terms and explains the calculations that will enable a borrower to choose the proper ARM for the circumstances.

Adjustment period.   The **adjustment period** of an ARM is the period of time between one interest rate and monthly payment change and the next. (Some ARMs have two adjustments: one for the rate, the other for the payment.) This period is different for each ARM; it may occur once a month, every six months, once a year, or even every three years. A loan with an adjustment period of one year is called a *one-year* ARM, and the interest rate can change once each year. Lenders often have a longer adjustment period for the first adjustment. Different lenders use different adjustment periods. Because a single lender might offer four different types of ARMs, each with a different adjustment period, it is important for the borrower to read the loan documents and understand the adjustment period before the loan documents are cut or signed.

Index and margin.   Most lenders tie ARM interest-rate changes to changes of an **index rate**. The only requirements a lender must meet in selecting an interest index are as follows:

- The index control cannot be the lender.

- The index must be readily available to and verifiable by the public.

These indexes usually go up and down with the general movement of interest rates. If the index moves up, so does the interest rate on the loan, meaning the borrower will probably have to make higher monthly payments. If the index rate goes down, interest rate and monthly payments may go down as well.

Lenders base ARM rates on a variety of indexes; in fact, the index can be almost any interest rate the lender selects. Also, different lenders may offer a variety of ARMs, and each may have a different index and margin. Among the most common indexes are six-month, three-year, or five-year Treasury securities (T-bills); national or regional cost of funds to savings associations (11th district cost of funds of the Federal Home Loan Bank Board [FHLBB]); and the London InterBank Offering Rate (LIBOR). Borrowers and their agents should ask which index will be used and how often it changes. Also, find out how the index has behaved in the past and where it is published, so the borrower can trace it in the future.

The index rate plus the margin equals the interest rate.

To determine the interest rate on an ARM, lenders add to the index rate a few percentage points (two to three), called the **margin** (also *differential* or *spread*).

$$\text{index} \quad + \quad \text{margin} \quad = \quad \text{ARM interest rate}$$

Elastic, subject to change   Set figure   Limited by caps

The amount of the margin can differ from one lender to another, but it is always constant over the life of the loan. Loans that have lower loan-origination costs tend to have higher margins. Upward adjustments of the ARM interest rate are made at the lender's option, but downward adjustments are mandatory. Actual adjustments to the borrowers' mortgage interest rate can occur only on a predetermined time schedule (the adjustment period, as described). On each loan, the borrowers' terms, including initial rate, caps, index, margin, interest-rate-change frequency, and payment-change frequency, are stated in the note that accompanies the deed of trust. Terms will vary from lender to lender.

In comparing ARMs, look at both the index and the margin for each plan. Some indexes have higher average values, but they are usually used with lower margins. Be sure to discuss the margin with the lender.

In calculating an ARM payment, the first period is calculated in exactly the same way as a fixed-rate loan payment. After the first-period adjustment, it is as if the borrower were starting a new loan: calculations must be made to figure the loan balance and the number of payments left, and the new interest rate must be taken into account. Of course, because no one can anticipate accurately whether interest rates will increase or decrease, in analyzing various ARMs a borrower is considering, the agent can accurately calculate the loan payment for only the first period.

ARM discounts.   Some lenders offer initial ARM rates that are lower than the sum of the index and the margin. Such rates, called *discounted rates, introductory rates, tickler rates,* or *teaser rates,* are usually combined with loan fees (points) and with higher interest rates after the discount expires. Many lenders offer introductory rates that are significantly below market interest rates. The discount rates may expire after the first adjustment period (for example, after one month, six months, or one year). At the end of the introductory discount rate period, the ARM interest rate automatically increases to the contract interest rate (index plus margin). This can mean a substantial increase in the borrower's interest rate and monthly payment. If the index rate has moved upward, the interest rate and payment adjustment can be even higher. Even if the index rate has decreased, the borrower's interest rate and monthly payment will likely be adjusted upward at the end of the introductory period.

Many lenders use the first year's payment as the basis for qualifying a borrower for a loan. So even if a lender approves the loan based on the low introductory rate, it is the borrowers' responsibility to determine whether they will be able to afford payments in later years, when the discount expires and the rate is adjusted. With a discounted ARM, any savings made during the discounted period may be offset during the life of the loan or be included in the price of the home. In fact, this kind of loan subjects borrowers to greater risk, including that of **payment shock**, which may occur when the mortgage payment rises at the first adjustment.

Whenever the lender's advertised qualifying interest rate is lower than the lender's current ARM index rate plus margin, a below-market rate is being offered. Assume the current index rate is 5% and the margin 2%. That makes the ARM rate 7%. If the advertised qualifying introductory rate is 5%, the introductory rate is 2% below the market rate, making it a discounted rate. Any qualifying rate below 7% in this case is called an *introductory rate* or a *below-market rate*.

Many lenders describe the introductory rate in their documentation as follows: "There is no rate change in the first six months. Thereafter, the interest rate is established by adding a rate differential (margin) to the index provided in the note."

The **annual percentage rate (APR)** gives a more accurate picture of the cost of a loan and must be disclosed by law. The APR differs from the nominal interest rate in that the APR includes the interest as well as the costs associated with obtaining the loan. The APR represents a rate based on a buyer's net loan proceeds, which is the loan amount less the cost of credit. This is outlined in the RESPA letter sent within three days of application for a loan. When calculating the APR, lenders who offer below-market rates must account for the higher index rate that will be charged in the future.

A borrower who chooses an ARM impulsively because of a low initial rate could end up in difficult straits. Agents can help borrowers protect themselves from large increases by looking at a mortgage with certain features that are explained in the next sections. Remember that all loans are different and that many different types of ARMs exist. Agents can help borrowers shop around until they find the loan that will meet their needs with minimal risk.

Caps can limit payment increases and loan interest.

Caps on an ARM.   Most ARMs have caps that protect borrowers from increases in interest rates or monthly payments beyond an amount specified in the note. If loans have no interest rate or payment caps, borrowers might be exposed to unlimited upward adjustments in monthly payments, should interest rates rise.

Caps vary from lender to lender. The borrower needs to check with the lender to determine the cap rates in the loan under consideration. Two types of interest-rate caps are used:

1. A *periodic cap* limits the interest-rate increase or decrease from one adjustment period to the next. These caps are usually 1 percentage point to 2 percentage points or sometimes 7½% of the previous period's payment amount.

2. A *lifetime cap* or overall cap limits the interest-rate increase over the life of the loan. Assume the introductory rate is 4% and is below the market rate and at the first adjustment becomes 5%. The overall cap will be attached to the 5%; thus, a 5% cap could mean an interest rate as high as 10%.

An ARM usually has both a periodic and an overall interest rate cap. A drop in the index does not always lead to an immediate drop in monthly payments. In fact, with some ARMs that have interest rate caps, the monthly payment may increase, even though the index rate has stayed the same or declined. This may happen after an interest rate cap has been holding the interest rate below the sum of the index plus margin. When the next adjustment period comes along and the interest rate stays the same or declines, previous obligations are in arrears and must be paid; thus, the monthly payment will increase.

The rate on a loan can go up at any scheduled adjustment when the index plus margin is higher than the rate before the adjustment. As stated earlier, an ARM usually has an overall interest rate cap. Some ARMs have a stated cap, such as 15%; others specify a percentage over the initial rate, such as an overall interest rate cap of 5%. Again, caps vary from lender to lender and sometimes from loan to loan offered by the same lender. It is important for the borrowers to know what caps are available and what they are obtaining with a loan.

As previously stated, some ARMs include a payment cap that limits the monthly payment increase at the time of each adjustment, usually to a percentage of the previous payment. In other words, if the payment cap is 7½%, a payment of $1,000 could not increase or decrease by more than $75 in the next adjustment period.

Because payment caps limit only the amount of payment increases and not interest-rate increases, payments sometimes do not cover all the interest due on a loan. This is sometimes called **negative amortization** and means the mortgage balance is increasing. The interest shortage in the payment is automatically added to the loan, and interest may be charged on that amount. As of 2010, negative amortization loans were banned in California.

Option ARMs. Option ARMs are adjustable-rate loans where the borrower has the option of making the payments necessary to amortize the loan or to make a minimum payment that is less than the interest. The result is negative amortization, with the amount due on the principal increasing each month. At a stated future date, such as five years, the borrower must start making payments that will amortize the loan. The low minimum payment of the option ARM allowed borrowers to more easily qualify for a loan. The borrowers hoped that increases in income would allow full payments at the later date and that increased property value would offset the negative amortization. A major California bank indicated in 2005 that 87% of its ARMs were option ARMs. There have been a great many foreclosures in option ARMs when payments increased on homes whose value had decreased. Because of lender risks, option ARMs are likely a thing of the past. In October 2009, then-Governor Schwarzenegger signed emergency legislation banning new negative amortization residential loan originations in California.

Convertible ARMs. Borrowers whose financial circumstances may change at some time during the term of the loan may decide that they do not want to risk any further changes in the interest rate and payment amount; or interest rates may drop, and the borrower might want to lock in the lower rate. In such cases, a conversion clause becomes important. A **convertible ARM** clause is one that allows the borrower to convert the ARM to a fixed-rate loan at designated times. When the borrower converts, the new rate is generally set at the current market rate for fixed-rate loans plus at least 0.375 of 1% as a servicing premium.

Assumable ARMs.   Although most ARMs are assumable, lenders normally place conditions on the assumption of the loan. The lender may require that the new borrower supply credit information, complete a credit application, and meet the customary credit standards applied by the lender. In some cases, the lender may charge points or other fees when a loan is assumed.

Some lenders allow only one assumption. Other lenders allow assumption but adjust the overall cap or the margin to the rate in effect at the time of assumption. Some lenders allow assumptions with the original lifetime cap already in effect. Because conditions of assumption vary greatly among lenders, the documentation should be checked for this information.

Figure 12.6 contains a list of questions that a borrower should ask, and the agent or the lender should be able to answer, when the borrower is looking for an ARM.

Loan Costs

In comparing loans, you must also compare loan costs. Lenders break down loan costs so that consumers will understand exactly what they are paying for. No matter what the cost or fee is called, the bottom line is the total of all loan costs. For many loans, these costs can be added to the amount of the loan.

FIGURE 12.6:   ARM Checklist

❏   What is the initial (or qualifying) interest rate on the ARM?

❏   How long is this initial rate in effect? When is the first rate and/or payment adjustment?

❏   To what index is the ARM's interest rate tied?

❏   What is the current level of the index?

❏   What margin above the index is used to calculate the actual ARM rate?

❏   How can the index and the margin be used to calculate the mortgage rate initially and at the first adjustment?

❏   What will happen to the interest rate at the first adjustment, assuming the index rate stays the same?

❏   What is the annual percentage rate (APR) of the loan? How does this compare with the APR on other ARMs and that on a fixed-rate loan?

❏   How often is the interest rate on the mortgage adjusted? How often does the monthly payment change?

❏   Does the ARM have a periodic interest rate cap? If so, what is the limit on the increase in the ARM rate at each adjustment? If the index rate increases more than this limit, can the unused change in the index be carried over to the next adjustment period? Does the periodic interest rate cap apply to the first adjustment? Does the periodic rate cap apply to the rate decreases, as well as to any increases?

❏   Does the ARM have an overall cap rate? If so, what are the maximum and minimum rates?

❏   Does the ARM have a payment cap? If so, what is the maximum that the monthly payment can increase at each adjustment? Does the payment cap apply to the first payment adjustment?

❏   Can the borrower convert this ARM to a fixed-rate loan at any time? Does this ARM have an open-end credit feature? What other features does this ARM have?

❏   Is this ARM assumable? Is this assumption feature limited to one time only? What are the qualification features? Will the original caps still be in effect? If not, what are the new caps?

❏   Does the ARM have a loan-to-value ratio greater than 80%? If so, is private mortgage insurance required on the loan?

Calculating Loan Costs

■   An initial application fee

■   A flat fee in addition to loan points

■   Loan points

■   Loan escrow costs (if not a purchase-money loan)

■   Title insurance (if not a purchase-money loan)

■   Document fees

■   Private mortgage insurance

■   A number of charges developed by different lenders, such as processing fees, which are generally fees for miscellaneous lender services (These fees are often called garbage fees.)

CHOOSING AMONG LOAN CATEGORIES

Lenders offer a number of different basic loan classifications, with different lenders offering different variations. Because of differing loan provisions, interest rates, and loan costs, it becomes difficult for borrowers to decide which loan type and lender best meet their particular needs.

Borrowers will find that they must shop for loans the same way they shop for any other large purchase. There are significant variations in costs among lenders. In some cases, loan costs can be negotiated.

Borrowers who believe they will remain in a property for many years likely will want an overall lower interest rate and be willing to pay higher loan-origination costs (including discount points) to obtain that rate.

Borrowers who expect to remain in a property for only a few years likely will want a loan that can be prepaid without a penalty and that has low loan-origination costs. Such borrowers likely will be willing to pay a higher interest rate to obtain the lower origination costs. Generally, lower loan-origination fees mean a higher interest rate.

Borrowers who believe interest rates are about as low as they will go are likely to want a long-term fixed-rate mortgage. Borrowers who believe interest rates are likely to drop probably will want a loan without a prepayment penalty, a short-term loan that can be rewritten at a future interest rate, or an adjustable-rate loan that can be converted to a fixed-rate loan.

Borrowers who have very low down payments would be interested in loans having a high LTV, such as FHA-insured loans, VA-guaranteed loans, and loans with PMI. And if borrowers have a low income for loan-qualifying purposes, they likely will want an ARM with low initial payments, a longer-term loan, or an interest-only loan.

For many buyers, the deciding factor will be the additional improvement in lifestyle afforded by using an ARM. Usually an ARM allows borrowers to buy more home for their money than would be possible with a fixed-rate loan. Assume fixed-rate loans are at 6%, and ARMs have a lower interest rate. If the agent knows how much the buyer can afford for a monthly payment, the agent can calculate the loan amount for which the borrower can qualify. The easiest way to do this is simply to use an amortization table and check the qualifying rate to determine how large a loan that payment will support.

The real estate agent needs to understand the lending business and be willing to communicate with the lender when he does not know why a certain interest rate, point, loan fee, or PMI is required, or does not understand other conditions of the loan.

One of the fundamental misunderstandings about financing arises because real estate buyers and sellers do not realize that money is a commodity. Money is like a loaf of bread, a car, a home, or any other commodity, and it is bought and sold. When it is bought and sold, the lender expects to make a profit on the sale. Some like to compare loaning money to renting. The payment of interest is the cost of renting the money, and points are like first and last months' rent or the security deposit, but unlike security deposits, it is not refundable. Every lender needs to make a profit on the rental of money to stay in business.

If the lender reduces one cost to a borrower in one area, the lender generally will raise it in another area to compensate for the loss. As an example, a lender offering a lower interest rate may charge higher loan costs, as well as a larger prepayment penalty, than a lender offering the higher interest rate. Help your borrower choose the loan that offers the combination of features that best meets that borrower's specific needs.

Computerized Loan Origination

Computerized loan origination (CLO) is now possible on the internet. Various websites provide interest rates, points, and APRs for various types of loans. Agents can complete a loan application on the internet and in many cases have loan approval, subject to verifications, before the client leaves your office.

There are also several large multilender shopping sites for loans that allow a borrower to view loan offerings from a great many lenders on a competitive basis. These sites are updated daily.

A borrower can evaluate loan types, points, costs, and rates to make an informed decision and then be qualified by the selected lender, as well as complete the loan application, all on the internet. The result of competition is often lower loan costs for the borrower. Because of this advantage, many buyers' agents use these shopping sites.

The websites also avoid the possibility that the borrower is being charged an overage. An *overage* is a charge, typically points, by a mortgage banker that exceeds what a lender would charge.

Four of the major loan shopping websites are as follows:

WEB LINK

1. www.eloan.com

2. www.homesadvisor.com

3. www.quickenloans.com

4. www.bankrate.com

We suggest that you gain familiarity with these websites, as well as local mortgage companies, and the process of qualification and loan application. You should also be familiar with the other sites, including local market lenders that are used by your office.

When a real estate agent charges a fee to a borrower for CLO, a disclosure must be provided to the borrower in a format specified by RESPA. The disclosure must inform the borrower that the fee can be avoided by approaching lenders directly.

THE FINANCING PROCESS

The basic steps for obtaining real estate financing are much the same with any type of lender. Figure 12.7 illustrates the following five-step financing process:

1. Qualifying the borrower

2. Qualifying the property

3. Approving and processing the loan

4. Closing the loan

5. Servicing the loan

Qualifying the Borrower

In understanding lender requirements for **qualifying borrowers**, you should realize that lender requirements often are dictated by the secondary mortgage market. Unless a lender expects to hold on to a loan for the life of the loan, the lender wants the loan to meet the requirements of a holder in the secondary market, such as Fannie Mae.

FIGURE 12.7:   The Financing Process

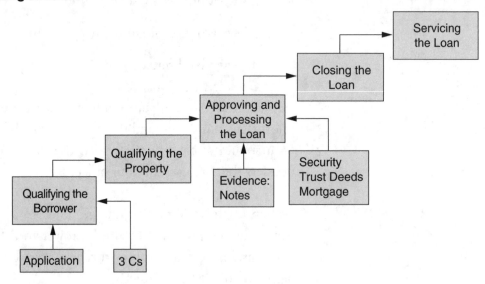

Unit 9 introduced you to lender qualifying requirements in prequalifying prospective purchasers. Lenders first ask prospective borrowers to complete an application form. Most applications are similar to the one in Figure 12.8, which asks for the borrower's employment record, credit references, and a financial statement of assets and liabilities. To verify the accuracy of the information, the loan officer checks with past employers, requests verification of deposits from the bank(s), and contacts references. The loan officer also may obtain a Dun & Bradstreet report (in case of commercial loans) and a credit report by an outside agency, so there is no question of the borrower's ability to repay the loan.

Most lenders use the "three Cs"—*character, capacity,* and *collateral*—as a screening device to determine whether the borrower meets the qualifications set by the lender.

Character.   With regard to prospective borrowers' character, lenders consider their attitude toward financial obligations as evidenced by their track record of borrowing and repaying loans evidenced by credit reports. Lenders also try to ascertain whether borrowers are honest in their dealings.

The desire to pay is very difficult to measure. There are methods used by a lender to determine the borrower's desire to make timely payments, such as **FICO score.** Fair Isaac Co. developed this scoring system used by most lenders. Following are the primary factors used for scoring:

- Late payments

- Negative credit information

- How long credit has been established

- Amount of credit used versus credit available

- Length of time at present residence

- Employment history

Credit scores range from about 300 to 850. Scores above 720 are regarded by lenders as being good and qualify for the lowest rate. Scores above 780 can result in ever lower loan costs as lenders compete for these borrowers.

Traditionally the cut-off point between prime and subprime mortgages was 620, but some mortgage companies now put the line at 680 to 700 with full documentation of an applicant's income and assets. Many lenders are no longer willing to take the risk of 620 FICO scores for nonconforming loans, (loans that are not to be sold to Freddie Mac or Fannie Mae).

FIGURE 12.8:   Uniform Residential Loan Application Form

Uniform Residential Loan Application

This application is designed to be completed by the applicant(s) with the Lender's assistance. Applicants should complete this form as "Borrower" or "Co-Borrower," as applicable. Co-Borrower information must also be provided (and the appropriate box checked) when ☐ the income or assets of a person other than the Borrower (including the Borrower's spouse) will be used as a basis for loan qualification or ☐ the income or assets of the Borrower's spouse or other person who has community property rights pursuant to state law will not be used as a basis for loan qualification, but his or her liabilities must be considered because the spouse or other person has community property rights pursuant to applicable law and Borrower resides in a community property state, the security property is located in a community property state, or the Borrower is relying on other property located in a community property state as a basis for repayment of the loan.

If this is an application for joint credit, Borrower and Co-Borrower each agree that we intend to apply for joint credit (sign below):

Borrower _____   Co-Borrower _____

I. TYPE OF MORTGAGE AND TERMS OF LOAN

Mortgage Applied for:	☐ VA ☑ Conventional ☐ Other (explain):		Agency Case Number	Lender Case Number
	☐ FHA ☐ USDA/Rural Housing Service			**Case #6**

Amount	Interest Rate	No. of Months	Amortization Type:	☑ Fixed Rate ☐ Other (explain):
$ **450,000.00**	**5.000** %	**360**		☐ GPM ☐ ARM (type):

II. PROPERTY INFORMATION AND PURPOSE OF LOAN

Subject Property Address (street, city, state & ZIP) **8709 Grosvenor ST, Silver Spring, MD 20910**	No. of Units **1**
Legal Description of Subject Property (attach description if necessary) **Other; Detached**	Year Built **0**

Purpose of Loan	☑ Purchase ☐ Construction ☐ Other (explain):	Property will be:
	☐ Refinance ☐ Construction-Permanent	☑ Primary Residence ☐ Secondary Residence ☐ Investment

Complete this line if construction or construction-permanent loan.

Year Lot Acquired	Original Cost	Amount Existing Liens	(a) Present Value of Lot	(b) Cost of Improvements	Total (a + b)
	$	$	$	$	$

Complete this line if this is a refinance loan.

Year Acquired	Original Cost	Amount Existing Liens	Purpose of Refinance	Describe Improvements ☐ made ☐ to be made
	$	$		Cost: $

Title will be held in what Name(s)	Manner in which Title will be held	Estate will be held in: ☑ Fee Simple ☐ Leasehold (show expiration date)

Source of Down Payment, Settlement Charges, and/or Subordinate Financing (explain)

III. BORROWER INFORMATION

Borrower	Co-Borrower
Borrower's Name (include Jr. or Sr. if applicable) **John Homeowner**	Co-Borrower's Name (include Jr. or Sr. if applicable) **Mary Homeowner**

Social Security Number **999-40-5000**	Home Phone (incl. area code)	DOB (mm/dd/yyyy)	Yrs. School	Social Security Number **500-22-2000**	Home Phone (incl. area code)	DOB (mm/dd/yyyy)	Yrs. School

☐ Married ☐ Unmarried (include ☐ Separated single, divorced, widowed)	Dependents (not listed by Co-Borrower) no. ages	☐ Married ☐ Unmarried (include ☐ Separated single, divorced, widowed)	Dependents (not listed by Borrower) no. ages

Present Address (street, city, state, ZIP) ☐ Own ☐ Rent **0** No. Yrs. **175 13th Street, Washington, DC, 20013**	Present Address (street, city, state, ZIP) ☐ Own ☐ Rent **0** No. Yrs. **175 13th Street, Washington, DC, 20013**
Mailing Address, if different from Present Address	Mailing Address, if different from Present Address

If residing at present address for less than two years, complete the following:

Former Address (street, city, state, ZIP) ☐ Own ☐ Rent ___ No. Yrs.	Former Address (street, city, state, ZIP) ☐ Own ☐ Rent ___ No. Yrs.

IV. EMPLOYMENT INFORMATION

Borrower	Co-Borrower
Name & Address of Employer ☐ Self Employed	Yrs. on this job **7.17**	Name & Address of Employer ☑ Self Employed	Yrs. on this job **12.42**
	Yrs. employed in this line of work/profession		Yrs. employed in this line of work/profession
Position/Title/Type of Business	Business Phone (incl. area code)	Position/Title/Type of Business	Business Phone (incl. area code)

If employed in current position for less than two years or if currently employed in more than one position, complete the following:

FIGURE 12.8 (continued): Uniform Residential Loan Application Form

Borrower		IV. EMPLOYMENT INFORMATION (cont'd)		Co-Borrower	
Name & Address of Employer	☐ Self Employed	Dates (from – to)	Name & Address of Employer ☐ Self Employed		Dates (from – to)
		Monthly Income $			Monthly Income $
Position/Title/Type of Business		Business Phone (incl. area code)	Position/Title/Type of Business		Business Phone (incl. area code)
Name & Address of Employer	☐ Self Employed	Dates (from – to)	Name & Address of Employer ☐ Self Employed		Dates (from – to)
		Monthly Income $			Monthly Income $
Position/Title/Type of Business		Business Phone (incl. area code)	Position/Title/Type of Business		Business Phone (incl. area code)

V. MONTHLY INCOME AND COMBINED HOUSING EXPENSE INFORMATION

Gross Monthly Income	Borrower	Co-Borrower	Total	Combined Monthly Housing Expense	Present	Proposed
Base Empl. Income*	$3,850.00	$4,300.00	$8,150.00	Rent	$2,500.00	
Overtime			$0.00	First Mortgage (P&I)		$2,415.70
Bonuses			$0.00	Other Financing (P&I)		
Commissions	$1,050.00		$1,050.00	Hazard Insurance		$65.00
Dividends/Interest			$0.00	Real Estate Taxes		$300.00
Net Rental Income	$0.00	$0.00	$0.00	Mortgage Insurance		$100.00
Other (before completing, see the notice in "describe other income," below)	0.00	0.00	0.00	Homeowner Assn. Dues Other:		
Total	$4,900.00	$4,300.00	$9,200.00	Total	$2,500.00	$2,880.70

*   Self Employed Borrower(s) may be required to provide additional documentation such as tax returns and financial statements.

Describe Other Income   *Notice:* Alimony, child support, or separate maintenance income need not be revealed if the Borrower (B) or Co-Borrower (C) does not choose to have it considered for repaying this loan.

B/C		Monthly Amount
		$

VI. ASSETS AND LIABILITIES

This Statement and any applicable supporting schedules may be completed jointly by both married and unmarried Co-Borrowers if their assets and liabilities are sufficiently joined so that the Statement can be meaningfully and fairly presented on a combined basis; otherwise, separate Statements and Schedules are required. If the Co-Borrower section was completed about a non-applicant spouse or other person, this Statement and supporting schedules must be completed about that spouse or other person also.

Completed ☐ Jointly ☑ Not Jointly

ASSETS Description	Cash or Market Value	Liabilities and Pledged Assets. List the creditor's name, address, and account number for all outstanding debts, including automobile loans, revolving charge accounts, real estate loans, alimony, child support, stock pledges, etc. Use continuation sheet, if necessary. Indicate by (*) those liabilities, which will be satisfied upon sale of real estate owned or upon refinancing of the subject property.		
Cash deposit toward purchase held by:	$0.00			
List checking and savings accounts below		LIABILITIES	Monthly Payment & Months Left to Pay	Unpaid Balance
Name and address of Bank, S&L, or Credit Union **Savings Account**		Name and address of Company	$ Payment/Months	$
Acct. no.	$18,500.00	Acct. no.		
Name and address of Bank, S&L, or Credit Union **Certificate of Deposit**		Name and address of Company	$ Payment/Months	$
Acct. no.	$40,000.00	Acct. no.		
Name and address of Bank, S&L, or Credit Union **Checking Account**		Name and address of Company	$ Payment/Months	$
Acct. no.	$2,800.00	Acct. no.		

Uniform Residential Loan Application
Freddie Mac Form 65 7/05 (rev. 6/09)

Page 2 of 5

Fannie Mae Form 1003 7/05 (rev.6/09)

FIGURE 12.8 (continued):   Uniform Residential Loan Application Form

VI. ASSETS AND LIABILITIES (cont'd)				
Name and address of Bank, S&L, or Credit Union **Money Market Fund**		Name and address of Company	$ Payment/Months	$
Acct. no.	$ 12,000.00	Acct. no.		
Stocks & Bonds (Company name/ number & description)	$0.00	Name and address of Company	$ Payment/Months	$
		Acct. no.		
Life insurance net cash value Face amount: $0.00	$0.00	Name and address of Company	$ Payment/Months	$
Subtotal Liquid Assets	$73,300.00			
Real estate owned (enter market value from schedule of real estate owned)	$0.00			
Vested interest in retirement fund	$0.00			
Net worth of business(es) owned (attach financial statement)	$0.00	Acct. no.		
Automobiles owned (make and year)	$0.00	Alimony/Child Support/Separate Maintenance Payments Owed to:	$0.00	
Other Assets (itemize)	$0.00	Job-Related Expense (child care, union dues, etc.)	$0.00	
		Total Monthly Payments	$0.00	
Total Assets a.	$73,300.00	Net Worth (a minus b) ▶	$73,300.00	**Total Liabilities b.** $0.00

Schedule of Real Estate Owned (If additional properties are owned, use continuation sheet.)

Property Address (enter S if sold, PS if pending sale or R if rental being held for income) ▼	Type of Property	Present Market Value	Amount of Mortgages & Liens	Gross Rental Income	Mortgage Payments	Insurance, Maintenance, Taxes & Misc.	Net Rental Income
		$	$	$	$	$	$
Totals		$0.00	$0.00	$ 0.00	$ 0.00	$0.00	$ 0.00

List any additional names under which credit has previously been received and indicate appropriate creditor name(s) and account number(s):

Alternate Name	Creditor Name	Account Number

VII. DETAILS OF TRANSACTION		
a.	Purchase price	$500,000.00
b.	Alterations, improvements, repairs	$0.00
c.	Land (if acquired separately)	$0.00
d.	Refinance (incl. debts to be paid off)	$0.00
e.	Estimated prepaid items	$0.00
f.	Estimated closing costs	$3,500.00
g.	PMI, MIP, Funding Fee	$0.00
h.	Discount (if Borrower will pay)	$0.00
i.	Total costs (add items a through h)	$503,500.00

VIII. DECLARATIONS	Borrower		Co-Borrower	
If you answer "Yes" to any questions a through i, please use continuation sheet for explanation.	Yes	No	Yes	No
a. Are there any outstanding judgments against you?	☐	☐	☐	☐
b. Have you been declared bankrupt within the past 7 years?	☐	☑	☐	☑
c. Have you had property foreclosed upon or given title or deed in lieu thereof in the last 7 years?	☐	☑	☐	☑
d. Are you a party to a lawsuit?	☐	☐	☐	☐
e. Have you directly or indirectly been obligated on any loan which resulted in foreclosure, transfer of title in lieu of foreclosure, or judgment?	☐	☐	☐	☐

(This would include such loans as home mortgage loans, SBA loans, home improvement loans, educational loans, manufactured (mobile) home loans, any mortgage, financial obligation, bond, or loan guarantee. If "Yes," provide details, including date, name, and address of Lender, FHA or VA case number, if any, and reasons for the action.)

FIGURE 12.8 (continued):   Uniform Residential Loan Application Form

VII. DETAILS OF TRANSACTION		VIII. DECLARATIONS				
		If you answer "Yes" to any questions a through i, please use continuation sheet for explanation.	Borrower		Co-Borrower	
			Yes	No	Yes	No
j. Subordinate financing	$0.00	f. Are you presently delinquent or in default on any Federal debt or any other loan, mortgage, financial obligation, bond, or loan guarantee?	☐	☐	☐	☐
k. Borrower's closing costs paid by Seller	$3,500.00	g. Are you obligated to pay alimony, child support, or separate maintenance?	☐	☐	☐	☐
		h. Is any part of the down payment borrowed?	☐	☐	☐	☐
l. Other Credits (explain)	$0.00	i. Are you a co-maker or endorser on a note?	☐	☐	☐	☐
m. Loan amount (exclude PMI, MIP, Funding Fee financed)	$450,000.00	j. Are you a U.S. citizen?	☑	☐	☑	☐
n. PMI, MIP, Funding Fee financed	$0.00	k. Are you a permanent resident alien?	☐	☑	☐	☑
o. Loan amount (add m & n)	$450,000.00	l. **Do you intend to occupy the property as your primary residence?** If "Yes," complete question m below.	☑	☐	☑	☐
p. Cash from/to Borrower (subtract j, k, l & o from i)	$50,000.00	m. Have you had an ownership interest in a property in the last three years?	☐	☑	☐	☑
		(1) What type of property did you own—principal residence (PR), second home (SH), or investment property (IP)?				
		(2) How did you hold title to the home— by yourself (S), jointly with your spouse (SP), or jointly with another person (O)?				

IX. ACKNOWLEDGEMENT AND AGREEMENT

Each of the undersigned specifically represents to Lender and to Lender's actual or potential agents, brokers, processors, attorneys, insurers, servicers, successors and assigns and agrees and acknowledges that: (1) the information provided in this application is true and correct as of the date set forth opposite my signature and that any intentional or negligent misrepresentation of this information contained in this application may result in civil liability, including monetary damages, to any person who may suffer any loss due to reliance upon any misrepresentation that I have made on this application, and/or in criminal penalties including, but not limited to, fine or imprisonment or both under the provisions of Title 18, United States Code, Sec. 1001, et seq.; (2) the loan requested pursuant to this application (the "Loan") will be secured by a mortgage or deed of trust on the property described in this application; (3) the property will not be used for any illegal or prohibited purpose or use; (4) all statements made in this application are made for the purpose of obtaining a residential mortgage loan; (5) the property will be occupied as indicated in this application; (6) the Lender, its servicers, successors or assigns may retain the original and/or an electronic record of this application, whether or not the Loan is approved; (7) the Lender and its agents, brokers, insurers, servicers, successors, and assigns may continuously rely on the information contained in the application, and I am obligated to amend and/or supplement the information provided in this application if any of the material facts that I have represented herein should change prior to closing of the Loan; (8) in the event that my payments on the Loan become delinquent, the Lender, its servicers, successors or assigns may, in addition to any other rights and remedies that it may have relating to such delinquency, report my name and account information to one or more consumer reporting agencies; (9) ownership of the Loan and/or administration of the Loan account may be transferred with such notice as may be required by law; (10) neither Lender nor its agents, brokers, insurers, servicers, successors or assigns has made any representation or warranty, express or implied, to me regarding the property or the condition or value of the property; and (11) my transmission of this application as an "electronic record" containing my "electronic signature," as those terms are defined in applicable federal and/or state laws (excluding audio and video recordings), or my facsimile transmission of this application containing a facsimile of my signature, shall be as effective, enforceable and valid as if a paper version of this application were delivered containing my original written signature.

Acknowledgement. Each of the undersigned hereby acknowledges that any owner of the Loan, its servicers, successors and assigns, may verify or reverify any information contained in this application or obtain any information or data relating to the Loan, for any legitimate business purpose through any source, including a source named in this application or a consumer reporting agency.

Borrower's Signature X	Date	Co-Borrower's Signature X	Date

X. INFORMATION FOR GOVERNMENT MONITORING PURPOSES

The following information is requested by the Federal Government for certain types of loans related to a dwelling in order to monitor the lender's compliance with equal credit opportunity, fair housing and home mortgage disclosure laws. You are not required to furnish this information, but are encouraged to do so. The law provides that a lender may not discriminate either on the basis of this information, or on whether you choose to furnish it. If you furnish the information, please provide both ethnicity and race. For race, you may check more than one designation. If you do not furnish ethnicity, race, or sex, under Federal regulations, this lender is required to note the information on the basis of visual observation and surname if you have made this application in person. If you do not wish to furnish the information, please check the box below. (Lender must review the above material to assure that the disclosures satisfy all requirements to which the lender is subject under applicable state law for the particular type of loan applied for.)

BORROWER ☐ I do not wish to furnish this information			**CO-BORROWER** ☐ I do not wish to furnish this information		
Ethnicity: ☐ Hispanic or Latino ☐ Not Hispanic or Latino			**Ethnicity:** ☐ Hispanic or Latino ☐ Not Hispanic or Latino		
Race: ☐ American Indian or Alaska Native ☐ Native Hawaiian or Other Pacific Islander	☐ Asian ☐ White	☐ Black or African American	**Race:** ☐ American Indian or Alaska Native ☐ Native Hawaiian or Other Pacific Islander	☐ Asian ☐ White	☐ Black or African American
Sex: ☐ Female ☐ Male			**Sex:** ☐ Female ☐ Male		

To be Completed by Loan Originator:
This information was provided:
☐ In a face-to-face interview
☐ In a telephone interview
☐ By the applicant and submitted by fax or mail
☐ By the applicant and submitted via e-mail or the Internet

Loan Originator's Signature X		Date
Loan Originator's Name (print or type)	Loan Originator Identifier	Loan Originator's Phone Number (including area code)
Loan Origination Company's Name	Loan Origination Company Identifier	Loan Origination Company's Address

Page 4 of 5

Uniform Residential Loan Application
Freddie Mac Form 65   7/05 (rev.6/09)   Fannie Mae Form 1003   7/05 (rev.6/09)

FIGURE 12.8 (continued): **Uniform Residential Loan Application Form**

CONTINUATION SHEET/RESIDENTIAL LOAN APPLICATION		
Use this continuation sheet if you need more space to complete the Residential Loan Application. Mark **B** f or Borrower or **C** for Co-Borrower.	Borrower: **John Homeowner**	Agency Case Number:
	Co-Borrower: **Mary Homeowner**	Lender Case Number: **Case #6**

I/We fully understand that it is a Federal crime punishable by fine or imprisonment, or both, to knowingly make any false statements concerning any of the above facts as applicable under the provisions of Title 18, United States Code, Section 1001, et seq.

Borrower's Signature X	Date	Co-Borrower's Signature X	Date

Uniform Residential Loan Application
Freddie Mac Form 65   7/05 (rev.6/09)

Fannie Mae Form 1003   7/05 (rev.6/09)

FIGURE 12.9: Qualifying Ratios

Front-End Rate

$$\frac{\text{PITI (Principal, Interest, Taxes, \& Insurance)}}{\text{Borrowers Monthly Gross Income}} = 0.28 \text{ or less}$$

Back-End Rate

$$\frac{\text{Total Loan Obligations}}{\text{Borrowers Monthly Gross Income}} = 0.36 \text{ or less}$$

Capacity. In considering borrowers' capacity, lenders want to know their ability to repay the debt. Capacity is strengthened by an occupation that ensures a steady income. The level of present debts and obligations also is a factor; too much debt may prevent a borrower from discharging a new obligation.

Lenders will consider second-job income if the applicant has a history of second-job income.

Lending institutions sometimes take overtime wages into consideration. Other lenders will consider both spouses' wages in computing the gross income of the borrower, even if only one spouse is applying for the loan. Occasionally, a lender will request a **cosigner**—a person with additional capital who agrees to share liability for the loan—to strengthen the borrower's application. Lenders also might reduce down payment requirements with a cosigner.

When a lender qualifies a borrower, the lender is attempting to answer two questions:

1. Can the borrower afford the payments?

2. Will the borrower make the payments on time? (This question refers to character.)

To determine whether the borrower has the capacity to make the monthly payments, the lender needs to answer these questions:

- Does the borrower earn enough to make the payments?

- Will the income be a steady source of income?

- Does the borrower have the down payment?

- Can the borrower make the payments on time?

The lender is going to verify the applicant's ability to make timely monthly payments and the applicant's employment history (steady stream of income). The lender will want to know the down payment on the property before determining the loan amount. This information is usually confirmed by the lender through the use of verifications of deposits and employment.

Once the lender knows the loan amount, it can calculate the *principal, interest, taxes, and insurance (PITI)* on it. This is the first step in the qualification process. These are qualifying programs available for your smartphone or computer.

> The important qualifying ratios are 28% and 36%.

To qualify the borrower, we examine two ratios (percentages). The **front-end ratio**, also called the *top ratio* (*mortgage payment ratio*), is the mortgage payment (PITI) divided by the borrower's gross income. Conforming loans require that the front-end ratio be approximately 28% or less. The reason it is called the top ratio is because it is at the top of the form (above the bottom ratio). The other ratio is the **back-end ratio**, or *bottom ratio* (*total obligation ratio*). This ratio should be approximately 36% or less to qualify for a conforming loan (see Figure 12.9). Nonconforming loans may have different values for these ratios. The preceding ratios (28% and 36%) are for loans that do not require PMI. For loans with PMI, the ratios might be top equals 33% and bottom equals 38%.

EXAMPLE Assume the buyers have a gross income of $4,000 per month and wish to buy a home where the principal, interest, and tax payments will amount to $1,100.

$$\frac{1,100 \, (PITI)}{4,000 \, (gross)} = 0.275 \text{ or } 27.5\%$$

The purchasers would meet the qualifying front-end ratio of 28% or less.

Assume the same purchasers have long-term debt payments of $900 per month, so PITI plus debt payments would mean a total monthly obligation of $2,000.

$$\frac{2,000 \, (total \, payments)}{4,000 \, (gross \, income)} = 0.5 \text{ or } 50\%$$

The buyers would not qualify for the loan. Although the buyers met the front-end ratio of 28% or less, they failed to meet the back-end ratio of 36% or less.

From the **verification of employment** and other financial information, the lender determines the borrower's gross income. Lenders require a signed statement from the borrower to permit a check with the borrower's employer to verify wages and length of employment. *Gross income* is defined as the income made by the borrower before taxes and deductions. For a married couple, the gross income for a loan is generally the total gross income of one spouse plus the total gross income of the other spouse. Employment usually must be verified for two years.

The lender also needs to determine the monthly long-term rotating credit bills owed by the borrower. These include car payments, credit cards, furniture payments, student loans, and other bank or credit union loans, including mortgage loans. If a credit bill will be paid in less than 10 months, it is not included.

Qualifying the Property

Collateral.   After the loan is granted, the lender has to rely for a long time on the value of the security for the loan for the safety of the investment, should the borrower default. For this reason, lenders consider it important to qualify the property, as well as the borrower.

> Collateral refers to the value of the security for the loan.

Because the underlying security for almost every property loan is the property itself, lenders require a careful valuation of the property, the *collateral*. The value depends on the property's location, age, architecture, physical condition, zoning, floor plan, and general appearance. The lender will have an appraisal done by the financial institution's appraiser or by an outside fee appraiser. Brokers who are familiar with lending policies of loan companies are in a good position to make accurate and helpful estimates.

After the S&Ls were deregulated in the 1980s, allowing them to make commercial loans, many made high-value loans at significantly higher interest rates than was possible for residential loans. Competition for many of these loans was intense, and S&Ls did not want to lose choice loan opportunities because of conservative appraisals. They encouraged more liberal appraisals, but appraisers who failed to cooperate found themselves shut out from lucrative business. In the mid-1980s, there was a collapse in the S&L industry with over 500 S&L bankruptcies and a government bailout. Instead of placing the blame on greed of the S&Ls, the blame was placed largely on the appraisers. In 1989, the federal government passed the Financial Institutions Reform, Recovery, and Enforcement Act (FIRREA). Part of the law created the Appraisal Foundation and required state-certified and state-licensed appraisers.

When an appraisal is less than the purchase price, it requires the seller to lower the price or the buyer to come up with a larger down payment because the amount of the loan will be reduced. The purchaser often does not have the resources for the large down payment. In addition, many offers include a contingency that the appraisal will be at least the amount of the purchase price. This provides an avenue of escape for the buyers.

A great many mortgage loan officers are paid by commission. They don't get paid when a loan cannot be funded. Appraisals seldom came in at less than the purchase price. Some appraisals were likely inflated by appraisers in order to gain referrals. This resulted in lenders having insufficient security in case of buyer default.

WEB LINK

@

The Dodd-Frank Wall Street Reform and Consumer Protection Act(Dodd-Frank) (15 USC 1639e) prohibits attempts by lenders or brokers to influence appraisal. (See www.law.cornell.edu/uscode/text/15/1639e.)

The act prohibits the following:

- Withholding or threatening to withhold payments

- Threat of withholding payment

- Promising benefits for higher appraisals

- Basing compensation on appraisal valuation

- Setting predetermined value for appraiser

- Removal of an appraiser from a list of appraisers without evidence of violation of Uniform Standards of Professional Appraisal Practice (USPAP)

- Ordering a second appraisal without evidence an appraisal was flawed

Some **subprime lenders** that specialize in high-risk borrowers made loans for the full appraisal amount, and even loans exceeding the appraisal if the risk factor was sufficiently offset by the higher interest rate.

While competition for loans led to low down and no down financing instruments, losses by lenders have tightened the controls so that few lenders are willing to make no-down-payment loans, even with interest premiums.

Approving and Processing the Loan

Processing involves drawing up loan papers, preparing disclosure forms regarding loan fees, and issuing instructions for the escrow and title companies. Loan papers include the *promissory note* (the evidence of the debt) and the security instruments (the *trust deed* or *mortgage*).

Closing the Loan

Closing the loan involves signing all the loan papers and preparing the closing statements. First-time buyers, especially, are often confused by the various fees involved. Real estate licensees play a vital role in making this transition period smooth.

Servicing the Loan

After the title has been transferred and the escrow closed, the loan-servicing portion of the transaction begins. This refers to the recordkeeping process once the loan has been placed. Some lenders do their own servicing, whereas others use outside sources. The goal of loan servicing is to see that the borrower makes timely payments so that the lender makes the expected yield on the loan, which keeps the cost of the entire package at a minimum.

REGULATION OF REAL ESTATE FINANCING

Because this is a real estate practices text, all references to the regulations governing real estate financing will, of necessity, be brief. For further information relating to this subject, consult a real estate finance book.

Truth in Lending Act

The *Truth in Lending Act* (*Regulation Z*) is a key portion of the federal Consumer Credit Protection Act passed in 1969. The Truth in Lending Act applies to banks, savings associations, credit unions, consumer finance companies, and residential mortgage brokers. This disclosure act requires that lenders reveal to customers, either by delivery or mailing, how much they're being charged for credit in terms of an annual percentage rate (APR). Customers can then make credit cost comparisons among various credit sources. The lender must wait at least seven days after disclosure to consummate the loan.

The act gives individuals seeking credit a right of rescission of the contract. This means that under certain circumstances a customer has the right to cancel a credit transaction up until midnight of the third day after signing. This right of rescission applies to loans that place a lien on the borrower's residence. The rescission rights do not apply to primary financing (first trust deed) to finance the purchase of the borrower's residence (purchase-money loan).

Truth in Savings Act

For savings-type accounts, banks must disclose all fees, costs, and yields (savings, checking, money market, and certificates of deposit). If there are any changes, free checking cannot be claimed. The yield must be expressed as the annual percentage yield (APY).

TILA-RESPA Integrated Disclosure (TRID) Rule

The regulations contained in the **TILA-RESPA Integrated Disclosure (TRID) rule** apply only to first loans on 1–4-unit residential properties. This is another disclosure act. Within three days of the date of the loan application, a lender must furnish the buyer with an itemized list of all closing costs that will be encountered in escrow. This must be a **Loan Estimate** provided to every person requesting credit. Each charge for each settlement service the buyer is likely to incur must be expressed as a dollar amount or range. The lender also must furnish a copy of a special information booklet prepared by the secretary of the Department of Housing and Urban Development (HUD). It must be delivered or placed in the mail to the applicant no later than three business days after the application is received.

The good-faith estimate required by RESPA has been combined with early truth-in-lending disclosures to include the following:

- Estimated monthly payment

- Estimated taxes, insurance, and assessments

- Estimated closing costs and cash required to close

- Services that cannot be shopped for

Figure 12.10 is a sample completed integrated loan estimate prepared by the Consumer Financial Protection Bureau, an independent agency of the U.S. government.

FIGURE 12.10: Loan Estimate

FICUS BANK
4321 Random Boulevard • Somecity, ST 12340

Save this Loan Estimate to compare with your Closing Disclosure.

Loan Estimate

DATE ISSUED	2/15/2013
APPLICANTS	Michael Jones and Mary Stone
	123 Anywhere Street
	Anytown, ST 12345
PROPERTY	456 Somewhere Avenue
	Anytown, ST 12345
SALE PRICE	$180,000

LOAN TERM	30 years
PURPOSE	Purchase
PRODUCT	Fixed Rate
LOAN TYPE	☒ Conventional ☐ FHA ☐ VA ☐ _____
LOAN ID #	123456789
RATE LOCK	☐ NO ☒ YES, until 4/16/2013 at 5:00 p.m. EDT

*Before closing, your interest rate, points, and lender credits can change unless you lock the interest rate. All other estimated closing costs expire on **3/4/2013** at 5:00 p.m. EDT*

Loan Terms		**Can this amount increase after closing?**
Loan Amount	$162,000	**NO**
Interest Rate	3.875%	**NO**
Monthly Principal & Interest *See Projected Payments below for your Estimated Total Monthly Payment*	$761.78	**NO**
		Does the loan have these features?
Prepayment Penalty		**YES** • **As high as $3,240** if you pay off the loan during the first 2 years
Balloon Payment		**NO**

Projected Payments		
Payment Calculation	**Years 1-7**	**Years 8-30**
Principal & Interest	$761.78	$761.78
Mortgage Insurance	+ 82	+ —
Estimated Escrow *Amount can increase over time*	+ 206	+ 206
Estimated Total Monthly Payment	$1,050	$968

Estimated Taxes, Insurance & Assessments *Amount can increase over time*	$206 a month	**This estimate includes** ☒ Property Taxes ☒ Homeowner's Insurance ☐ Other: *See Section G on page 2 for escrowed property costs. You must pay for other property costs separately.*	**In escrow?** YES YES

Costs at Closing		
Estimated Closing Costs	$8,054	Includes $5,672 in Loan Costs + $2,382 in Other Costs – $0 in Lender Credits. *See page 2 for details.*
Estimated Cash to Close	$16,054	Includes Closing Costs. *See Calculating Cash to Close on page 2 for details.*

Visit **www.consumerfinance.gov/mortgage-estimate** for general information and tools.

Figure 12.10 (continued):   Loan Estimate

Closing Cost Details

Loan Costs

A. Origination Charges	$1,802
.25 % of Loan Amount (Points)	$405
Application Fee	$300
Underwriting Fee	$1,097

B. Services You Cannot Shop For	$672
Appraisal Fee	$405
Credit Report Fee	$30
Flood Determination Fee	$20
Flood Monitoring Fee	$32
Tax Monitoring Fee	$75
Tax Status Research Fee	$110

C. Services You Can Shop For	$3,198
Pest Inspection Fee	$135
Survey Fee	$65
Title – Insurance Binder	$700
Title – Lender's Title Policy	$535
Title – Settlement Agent Fee	$502
Title – Title Search	$1,261

D. TOTAL LOAN COSTS (A + B + C)	$5,672

Other Costs

E. Taxes and Other Government Fees	$85
Recording Fees and Other Taxes	$85
Transfer Taxes	

F. Prepaids	$867
Homeowner's Insurance Premium (6 months)	$605
Mortgage Insurance Premium (months)	
Prepaid Interest ($17.44 per day for 15 days @ 3.875%)	$262
Property Taxes (months)	

G. Initial Escrow Payment at Closing	$413
Homeowner's Insurance $100.83 per month for 2 mo.	$202
Mortgage Insurance per month for mo.	
Property Taxes $105.30 per month for 2 mo.	$211

H. Other	$1,017
Title – Owner's Title Policy (optional)	$1,017

I. TOTAL OTHER COSTS (E + F + G + H)	$2,382

J. TOTAL CLOSING COSTS	$8,054
D + I	$8,054
Lender Credits	

Calculating Cash to Close

Total Closing Costs (J)	$8,054
Closing Costs Financed (Paid from your Loan Amount)	$0
Down Payment/Funds from Borrower	$18,000
Deposit	– $10,000
Funds for Borrower	$0
Seller Credits	$0
Adjustments and Other Credits	$0
Estimated Cash to Close	$16,054

Figure 12.10 (continued): **Loan Estimate**

Additional Information About This Loan

LENDER	Ficus Bank
NMLS/__ LICENSE ID	
LOAN OFFICER	Joe Smith
NMLS/__ LICENSE ID	12345
EMAIL	joesmith@ficusbank.com
PHONE	123-456-7890

MORTGAGE BROKER	
NMLS/__ LICENSE ID	
LOAN OFFICER	
NMLS/__ LICENSE ID	
EMAIL	
PHONE	

Comparisons

Use these measures to compare this loan with other loans.

In 5 Years	$56,582	Total you will have paid in principal, interest, mortgage insurance, and loan costs.
	$15,773	Principal you will have paid off.
Annual Percentage Rate (APR)	4.274%	Your costs over the loan term expressed as a rate. This is not your interest rate.
Total Interest Percentage (TIP)	69.45%	The total amount of interest that you will pay over the loan term as a percentage of your loan amount.

Other Considerations

Appraisal	We may order an appraisal to determine the property's value and charge you for this appraisal. We will promptly give you a copy of any appraisal, even if your loan does not close. You can pay for an additional appraisal for your own use at your own cost.
Assumption	If you sell or transfer this property to another person, we ☐ will allow, under certain conditions, this person to assume this loan on the original terms. ☒ will not allow assumption of this loan on the original terms.
Homeowner's Insurance	This loan requires homeowner's insurance on the property, which you may obtain from a company of your choice that we find acceptable.
Late Payment	If your payment is more than *15 days* late, we will charge a late fee of *5% of the monthly principal and interest payment*.
Refinance	Refinancing this loan will depend on your future financial situation, the property value, and market conditions. You may not be able to refinance this loan.
Servicing	We intend ☐ to service your loan. If so, you will make your payments to us. ☒ to transfer servicing of your loan.

Confirm Receipt

By signing, you are only confirming that you have received this form. You do not have to accept this loan because you have signed or received this form.

_____   _____   _____   _____
Applicant Signature   Date   Co-Applicant Signature   Date

LOAN ESTIMATE   PAGE 3 OF 3 • LOAN ID #123456789

A **controlled business arrangement** (CBA) is a situation where a broker offers "one-stop shopping" for a number of broker-controlled services, such as financing arrangements, home inspection, title insurance, property insurance, and escrow. These controlled businesses could be located within the broker's premises. RESPA permits such controlled business arrangements as long as the consumer is clearly informed of the relationship between the broker and the service providers and other providers are available. Fees may not be exchanged between the companies simply for referrals. A broker-controlled mortgage company must have its own employees and cannot contract out its services or it would violate RESPA provisions that prohibit kickbacks for referral services.

It's the position of the attorney general of California that a broker may not pay referral fees to a real estate salesperson for referral to broker-affiliated services.

Fair Credit Reporting Act

The **Fair Credit Reporting Act** affects credit reporting agencies and users of credit information. If a loan is rejected because of information disclosed in a credit report, the borrower must be notified and is entitled to know all the information the agency has in its file on the buyer, as well as the sources and the names of all creditors who received reports within the past six months.

Equal Credit Opportunity Act

The federal **Equal Credit Opportunity Act** prohibits lending discrimination based on an applicant's race, color, religion, national origin, marital status, age, and whether or not the source of income is a public assistance program or Social Security.

Helping Families Save Their Homes Act of 2009

Bankruptcy judges now have the authority to modify mortgages on principal residences. They can order a reduction in the loan interest rate and/or extend the payment period as long as 40 years.

California Homeowners Bill of Rights

The California Homeowner Protection Act set forth the California Homeowners Bill of Rights:

- Dual track foreclosure is not allowed. The foreclosure process cannot be advanced after the homeowners complete an application for loan modification and the application has been fully reviewed.

- Homeowners must have a single point of contact.

- Lenders must verify all documents filed.

- Borrowers can seek redress for material violations of the foreclosure process.

- Tenant lease rights must be honored; if not, a 90-day notice must be given.

- Homeowners can compel owners of foreclosed homes in areas to remedy code violations.

Home Affordable Modification Program (HAMP)

Provides for loan modification of loans guaranteed or insured by Fannie Mae, Freddie Mac, FHA, VA or USDA originated before 2009 if because of financial hardship the borrower cannot make loan payments.

Hope for Homeowners Program (Hope Act)

A HUD program to change variable rate FHA loans to fixed rate.

Service Members Civil Relief Act of 2003

This act applies to citizen military members called to active duty, not career military. The act provides the following:

- A maximum of 6% interest on credit obligations entered into before active duty. Interest above 6% must be forgiven.

- Foreclosures may be postponed by the court until 90 days after active service ceases.

- A court order is required for evictions when rent is $3,329.84 per month or less. (2015 – changes annually.)

- If transferred, service personnel may terminate any lease.

Predatory Lending

California law prohibits predatory lending. Loans made to homeowners by finance companies, real estate brokers, and residential mortgage lenders without considering the borrowers' ability to repay are considered **predatory lending**. Violations subject the lender to civil penalties. This law was enacted because some loans were made where the lenders actually wanted the borrowers to default in order to foreclose on the properties securing the loans.

Some loans had high loan costs that were added to the loan balance. When borrowers had trouble with repayment, they were encouraged to refinance to another loan with high loan costs that offered no economic benefit to the borrower and reduced the borrowers' equity.

Borrowers are protected in the following ways:

- Prepayment penalties for the first 36 months of a loan are strictly limited and not allowed thereafter.

- Loans with terms of five years or less must be amortized.

- Loans other than first trust deeds cannot include negative amortization, and even then it must be properly disclosed.

- Requiring payment advances from loan proceeds are prohibited.

- Interest rates cannot be increased as a result of default.

- The person originating the loan must reasonably believe the borrower will be able to repay the loan from resources other than the borrower's equity in the property.

- Payments made directly to contractors from proceeds of home improvement loans are prohibited. (Payments jointly to the homeowner and the contractor are allowed.)

■ Recommending that a consumer default on an existing loan or debt is prohibited.

■ Loans with call provisions allowing the lender to accelerate debt at its discretion are generally prohibited.

■ Refinancing that does not result in identifiable tangible benefits to the consumer is prohibited.

■ Steering or directing a consumer to a loan product with a higher-risk grade than the consumer would otherwise qualify for, or with a higher cost than the consumer would qualify for, is prohibited.

■ Structuring a loan as an open line of credit to avoid predatory lending restrictions is prohibited.

■ All consumer fraud is prohibited.

See Financial Code 4970-4979.8.

SUMMARY

The Federal Reserve is responsible for monetary policy and has control over the availability and cost of funds by controlling the discount rate charged member banks, by controlling the reserve requirements of banks, and by buying and selling government securities on the open market and controlling the supply of currency. The fiscal policy of the government to raise and lower taxes, as well as to spend, also affects the availability of funds.

While low interest rates increase housing affordability and can lead to a strong market, high rates have an opposite effect.

Whereas primary financing refers to first trust deeds and secondary financing refers to junior liens, the primary and secondary mortgage markets are far different. The primary mortgage market refers to lenders making loans direct to borrowers; the secondary mortgage market refers to the sale of existing loans.

Fannie Mae (the Federal National Mortgage Association) and Freddie Mac (the Federal Home Loan Mortgage Corporation) create a secondary mortgage market by buying FHA, VA, and conforming conventional loans. Conforming loans are loans that meet the standards established by Fannie Mae.

Institutional lenders such as banks, savings associations, and life insurance companies are major sources of primary real estate financing. Noninstitutional lenders include mortgage companies, which originate most real estate loans today. Mortgage companies (mortgage bankers) generally sell loans in the secondary market or act as loan correspondents for other lenders.

Mortgage loan brokers are real estate brokers who serve as middlemen for loans. These loans generally have a high loan cost and bear a higher rate of interest than do loans from institutional lenders. Mortgage loan brokers must provide a Mortgage Loan Disclosure Statement to borrowers. Other noninstitutional lenders include private individuals who use their own funds and real estate investment trusts.

Seller carryback financing is also a source of funding for real estate purchases.

Conventional loans are loans made without any government participation, guarantee, or insurance.

Government participation loans provide for lower down payment requirements and include FHA, VA, and CalVet loans.

The California Housing Finance Agency provides low rates and low down payment loans to first-time homebuyers.

Today, borrowers have a wide choice of types of loans and loan variations, including fixed-rate loans, renegotiable-rate mortgages, reverse mortgages, adjustable-rate mortgages, interest-only loans, 80-20 loans, and 40-year loans. The special features of the loans vary by lender. Buyers must analyze their needs and the important factors of down payment, loan costs, interest, assumability, convertibility, loan term, qualifying rate of interest, and so forth, as they pertain to the borrowers' needs.

The internet provides a convenient and efficient way to shop for loans, as well as to complete and submit loan applications.

The financing process involves qualifying the buyer, using front-end and back-end ratios and FICO scores, qualifying the property, approving and processing the loan, closing the loan, and servicing the loan.

The Truth in Lending Act and the Real Estate Settlement Procedures Act are federal regulations concerning lending activities. The Equal Credit Opportunity Act prohibits lender discrimination based on public assistance programs being the source of income.

The good-faith estimate of loan costs, formerly required by RESPA, has been combined with truth-in-lending disclosures for simplification purposes as mandated by Dodd-Frank.

Brokers and lenders are prohibited from seeking to influence appraisals.

Predatory lending practices are prohibited.

CLASS DISCUSSION TOPICS

1. Using a front-end (top) ratio of 33% and a back-end (bottom) ratio of 38%, qualify a buyer earning $100,000 per year for a 30-year loan of $400,000 with an 8% interest rate. Assume taxes at $5,000 per year and insurance at $1,000 per year. Assume the buyer is making payments on loans of $43,000, and the monthly payments are $2,080.

2. Obtain the ARM terms from three different lenders. Lay them out on paper, showing the differences. Which loan would be best suited for a person having what needs?

3. Discuss prequalification practices of local lenders.

4. Complete a loan application for a fictitious borrower, using realistic income, expense, debt, and savings figures. How large a conforming loan will this fictitious applicant qualify for?

5. Bring to class one current-events article dealing with some aspect of real estate practice.

UNIT 12 QUIZ

1. A loan covering more than one property would be a
   a. compound loan.
   b. blanket encumbrance.
   c. subordinated loan.
   d. reverse mortgage.

2. What type of mortgage has compound interest?
   a. Reverse mortgage
   b. Renegotiable-rate mortgage
   c. Adjustable-rate mortgage
   d. Straight mortgage

3. The difference between the interest rate of an index and the rate charged by a lender under an adjustable-rate mortgage is known as the
   a. discount.
   b. gap.
   c. margin.
   d. cap.

4. A lender who believes interest rates will be rising significantly will be *LEAST* interested in
   a. a hybrid mortgage.
   b. a 30-year fixed-rate mortgage.
   c. a 15-year fixed-rate mortgage.
   d. an adjustable-rate mortgage.

5. A danger that an adjustable-rate mortgage poses to a buyer is
   a. higher payments if interest rates increase.
   b. a longer payment period if interest rates increase.
   c. that the margin will increase.
   d. none of these.

6.   An adjustable-rate loan index is 6% at the time a loan is made. The margin for the loan is 2½%. With a 5% lifetime cap, the highest the interest rate could go is
   a.   6%.
   b.   8½%.
   c.   11%.
   d.   13½%.

7.   A convertible ARM is a loan that can be changed to
   a.   a shorter-term loan.
   b.   a fixed-rate loan.
   c.   another property.
   d.   another borrower.

8.   A buyer intends to sell a house within two years. The buyer would prefer
   a.   a loan with no prepayment penalty.
   b.   a loan with low initial loan costs.
   c.   an assumable loan.
   d.   all of these.

9.   Which loan type is MOST likely to meet all the criteria of question 8?
   a.   Renegotiable-rate mortgage
   b.   Adjustable-rate mortgage
   c.   Fixed-rate mortgage
   d.   Reverse mortgage

10.   An expansionary policy of the Federal Reserve would be to
   a.   lower taxes.
   b.   increase the discount rate.
   c.   buy government securities.
   d.   raise bank reserve requirements.

13

ESCROW AND TITLE INSURANCE

LEARNING OBJECTIVES

When you have completed this unit, you will be able to

- define *escrow* and explain the difference between northern and southern California escrows,

- describe the requirements of an escrow and an escrow's responsibility,

- explain the requirements of escrow licensing and laws governing the escrow,

- describe escrow procedures, and

- explain the role played by title insurance and the difference between standard and extended coverage policies.

KEY TERMS

abstract	deed of reconveyance	preliminary title report
ALTA policy	demand statement	proration
amend the escrow	escrow	rebate law
instructions	escrow agent	recurring costs
beneficiary statement	escrow instructions	special title insurance
closing costs	escrow officer	policies
Closing Disclosure	extended policy	standard policy
CLTA policy	good funds	title insurance
credits	impound account	title plant
debits	marketable title	

ESCROW

The word *escrow* is derived from the French word *escroue*, meaning scroll or roll of writing. An owner of real property executed an instrument in the form of a deed, conveying land to another party on the fulfillment of certain conditions. This instrument, the *escroue*, was given to a third person with instructions that it would take effect as a deed on the performance of an act or the occurrence of an event, such as payment of a designated sum of money. The term was taken in English as **escrow**, meaning "a deed, a bond, money, or a piece of property held in trust by a third party, to be turned over to the grantee only on fulfillment of a condition."

Escrow is the last step in a property transaction. The California Financial Code defines *escrow* as follows:

> Escrow means any transaction wherein one person for the purpose of effecting the sale, transfer, encumbering, or leasing of real or personal property to another person, delivers any written instrument, money, evidence of title to real or personal property or other things of value to a third person to be held by such third person until the happening of a specified event. The performance is then to be delivered by such third person to a grantee, grantor, promisee, promisor, obligee, obligor, bailee, or bailor, or any agent or employee or any of the latter.

This definition has been changed somewhat, and the activities of an escrow agent have been expanded considerably. In brief, an escrow agent is an impartial third party or "stakeholder who receives and disburses documents, money, and papers from every party involved in a transaction, such as a sale of real estate." The escrow operates as a neutral depository.

FIGURE 13.1: Escrow Responsibility

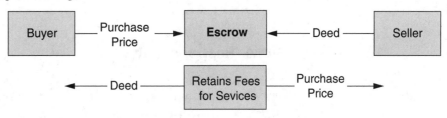

The escrow is an impartial stakeholder.

The business that conducts the escrow is considered the **escrow agent**. The individual who handles the escrow in the office of the escrow agent is the **escrow officer**.

Escrow Requirements

When the buyer offers a sum of money to the seller and the seller's acceptance is transmitted to the buyer, a binding contract is formed. Generally, this is the first requirement for a sales escrow. Escrow is created on the conditional delivery of transfer instruments and monies to a third party.

Although escrows are not generally required by law in California, they have become an almost indispensable mechanism in this state to protect the parties involved in exchanges, leases, and sales of securities, loans, business opportunity sales, mobile home sales, and primarily real property sales.

In some states, the listing real estate office handles escrow functions. In some states, attorneys are used for real estate closings. In some communities, the local lender handles the closing functions. However, closings are primarily handled by either third-party escrows or title companies in California.

Escrow Responsibility

The escrow agent holds all money and documents during the transaction. When conditions agreed upon by the buyer and the seller are met, the deed and the monies involved are disbursed concurrently to the appropriate parties. (See Figure 13.1.) Funds must be **good funds** before they can be disbursed. Good funds include cash, cashier's checks, and personal checks that have cleared.

Broker Responsibility

Once the escrow instructions have been signed, the escrow acts in a dual-agency capacity to carry out the instructions of the buyer and the seller. However, the broker still has agency duties.

The broker should track the escrow to make certain that the escrow is receiving what it requires, when it is required. If there are problems concerning the escrow, the broker should notify the parties and attempt to resolve these problems.

The broker also should monitor the loan application and keep in contact with the lender to avoid or resolve any problems or delays.

Parties to an Escrow

Buyers.   When buyers have performed in full (paid the purchase price), they are entitled to a deed transferring title, subject only to encumbrances agreed on by both parties. Buyers do not want to pay sellers until the buyers know they are certain of obtaining title to the property as agreed. While the title search is being conducted, the buyers' deposits are held in escrow.

Sellers.   Although sellers may have made a firm contract to sell their real property, they do not want to give up their title until they are certain of receiving their money. They therefore retain legal title to the property as security until they have the money in hand. The sellers' legal title usually is transferred by deed. The title is placed in escrow until buyers have produced the full purchase price for the property. If a seller dies before a transaction has been completed, that seller's right to the unpaid part of the purchase price may pass to the heirs. If a buyer dies, the heirs may be required to continue with the purchase. However, the loan may be affected owing to qualification.

Lenders. In lending money to buyers to complete a purchase, lenders, like buyers, do not want to commit their funds without assurance that titles to the properties in question are clear. Therefore, impartial third parties (escrow agents) hold money, deeds, and other documents until liens have been paid off and clear titles have been confirmed. Thereafter, it is the escrow agent's responsibility to see that the proper disbursements are made.

Brokers. Real estate agents, unless principals to the transaction, are not parties to the escrow. While the agent is not a party to the escrow, agents should understand escrow procedure so that they can both monitor the escrow to avoid delays and other problems and explain the escrow procedures to their clients and help them comply with escrow requirements. Once the escrow has been opened, the escrow may not make any changes to the escrow instructions based on orders of a real estate agent unless authorized to do so by the principals. However, the escrow instructions might provide for the payment of the commission out of escrow and stipulate that the broker's commission rights cannot be canceled. On a case-by-case basis, the broker can authorize that a commission be paid directly to a salesperson out of broker-entitled funds upon a closing.

| The broker is not a party to an escrow. |

Escrow Agents

In California, escrow companies licensed by the California Department of Corporations must be structured as corporations. This includes companies conducting escrows using the internet. Individuals cannot be licensed under the escrow law, but certain organizations and individuals are permitted to act as escrow agents without licensure. These include the following:

| Escrows are corporations under the jurisdiction of the Commissioner of Corporations. |

- Banks

- Attorneys (to act as an escrow, an attorney must have had a prior client relationship with a party to the escrow)

- Real estate brokers

- Title and trust companies

- Savings associations

In some northern California areas, escrow transactions are handled by title insurance companies; they usually process the escrow and issue the title insurance policy together. In southern California, escrow companies handle most escrow transactions with a title company issuing the title insurance separately. In some northern California areas, there are *separate* (*unilateral*) *escrow instructions* for each of the parties. In southern California, the parties sign *joint* (*bilateral*) *escrow instructions*. There are other regional deviations in the way escrows operate.

In Unit 10, you saw that the purchase agreement can be combined with joint escrow instructions such as the CAR form *California Residential Purchase Agreement and Joint Escrow Instructions*.

Selection of Escrow Holder

The parties to the escrow determine who shall be the escrow holder. In a real estate sales agreement, the buyer will customarily identify the escrow, and the seller, by acceptance of the agreement, agrees to the escrow selected.

Broker as Escrow

The real estate broker exemption from licensing as an escrow is applicable only when the broker represents the buyer or the seller or is a principal in the transaction. The escrow function is therefore incidental to the broker's business and the exemption cannot be a veil through which a primarily escrow business is conducted. The broker may charge for services. Many larger offices have escrow services as a separate profit center for their operations. A number of computer escrow programs are available to aid in this function. Check the website www.softprocorp.com to learn about one such program.

WEB LINK

A broker can act as an unlicensed escrow only if the broker is a principal or represents the buyer or the seller.

While brokers are exempt from the licensing requirements for their own transactions, this exemption applies only to brokers. Brokers cannot delegate escrow duties to others. The exemption is not available to any association of brokers for the purpose of conducting escrows for the group.

Real estate brokers cannot advertise that they conduct escrow business unless specifying that such services are only in connection with the real estate brokerage business. Brokers are also prohibited from using a fictitious or corporate name that contains the word *escrow*. While acting as an escrow, brokers must put aside agency relationships, as well as any special interests, and adopt the position of a neutral depository, the same as any other escrow.

Escrow funds held by a broker must be placed in a special trust account, subject to periodic inspection by the Commissioner of Corporations and, at the broker's own expense, subject to an independent annual audit.

A broker who conducts five or more escrows in a calendar year or conducts escrows totaling $1 million or more must file an annual report with the BRE as to the number of escrows conducted and the dollar amount. The report must be filed within 60 days of end of calendar year. Failure to report as required will result in a penalty of $50 per day for the first 30 days and then $100 per day thereafter, up to $10,000. Failure to pay the penalty can result in suspension or revocation of license (penalties go to the Consumer Recovery Account).

A broker can be licensed separately as an escrow and operate the escrow business in a controlled business arrangement. (See RESPA, Unit 12.)

Requirements for DOC Escrow Licensure

Any corporation applying for a Department of Corporations escrow license under the Escrow Act must

- pay an application fee;

- pass a background check;

- meet minimum financial requirements;

- meet minimum experience requirements (managers must have at least five years of responsible escrow experience);

- furnish a surety bond for $25,000 to $59,000;

- arrange for the fidelity bonding of responsible employees (minimum of $125,000 each);

- be a member of the Escrow Agents' Fidelity Corporation (EAFC);

- set up a trust fund for all monies deposited in escrow;

- keep accurate records, subject to audit at any time by the Commissioner of Corporations and the Bureau of Real Estate; and

- submit to an independent audit annually at its own expense.

Laws Governing Escrow

No escrow licensee may

■ disseminate misleading or deceptive statements referring to its supervision by the State of California;

■ describe either orally or in writing any transaction that is not included under the definition of escrow in the California Financial Code;

■ pay referral fees to anyone except a regular employee of its own escrow company;

■ solicit or accept escrow instructions or amended or supplemental instructions containing any blanks to be filled in after the instructions are signed; or

■ permit any person to make additions to, deletions from, or alterations of an escrow instruction unless it is signed or initialed by all signers of the original instructions.

Figure 13.2 summarizes legal requirements pertaining to the actions of escrow officers.

FIGURE 13.2:   Legal Requirements for Escrow Officers

Officers Must	Officers May Not
act according to issued written instructions.	make a transaction for another officer.
act as a neutral party at all times.	negotiate with the parties separately.
hold monies deposited by parties until disbursed.	suggest that terms or provisions be inserted in the escrow.
follow escrow instructions in every detail unless instructions are in violation of the law.	act as collection agencies to persuade a client to furnish funds.
give to parties only that information that concerns them.	notify parties that they have not ordered a certain document that may be necessary to close an escrow.
make sure that escrow does not close with an unverified check.	

Escrow Procedures

Before closing, the escrow is a dual agent. After closing, the escrow has separate agency duties.

Escrow is a limited agency relationship governed by the content of the escrow instructions, and the escrow holder acts only on specific written instructions of the principals as agent for both parties. When the escrow is closed, the escrow holder becomes agent for each principal with respect to those things in escrow to which the respective parties have become completely entitled. Oral instructions should not be accepted or acted on.

Certain procedures must be followed to fulfill the legal requirements for escrow procedures. The broker needs to provide certain information to the escrow agent. Buyers and sellers must be aware of the responsibilities each must assume in the escrow procedure.

Escrow is a many-faceted procedure and includes but is not limited to the following:

- Order preliminary title report

- Conveying preliminary title report to buyer

- Ordering beneficiary statement or payout demands

- Handle receipt and disbursement of all funds

- Facilitate handling, preparation, and signing of all documents

- Comply with all government regulations

- Act as communicator with parties to the escrow, as well as broker and lender

- Ensure that all conditions of escrow are met

- Satisfy lender conditions and that a clear title will be conveyed to buyer

- Accept fire insurance policy

- Make all payments and fees

- Inform parties when escrow is ready to proceed

- Prepare closing statement

- Authorize the release and recording of all documents and disbursement of funds

- Secure title insurance policy

These duties are in addition to maintaining the highest level of trust and maintaining the confidentiality of the escrow.

FIGURE 13.3:   Procedures of an Escrow

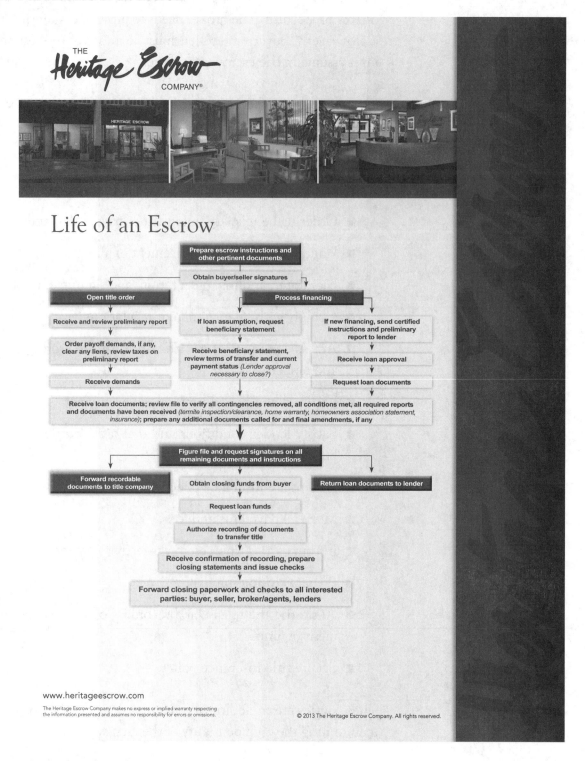

Reprinted with permission.

Advantages of an Escrow

If you decide to buy a television set, you make your purchase from an appliance store. You pay for it by giving cash or adding it to your credit account. You likely would not give a second thought to whether the store has a right to sell the set to you. You probably give no thought at all to whether you need written evidence of your right to own the appliance. It is a simple sales transaction. With the sale of real property, the procedure is much more complicated. The seller could sign a simple deed of conveyance and deliver it to the buyer in exchange for the purchase price. However, neither the buyer nor the seller should agree to such an arrangement, for these reasons:

1. Title to the property may be encumbered. The buyer needs someone to make a title search for the purpose of issuing a title insurance policy.

2. An accurate description of the property is necessary for legal purposes.

3. The seller and the buyer need an experienced person to prepare the instrument of conveyance for their signatures.

4. The buyer and the seller need assurance that their instructions have been carried out and that the deeds will be delivered and any monies transferred only when all terms of the contract have been met.

5. There are distinct advantages to escrow and the use of a neutral third party in the transaction.

6. Escrow provides a custodian of papers, instructions, funds, and documents until the transaction is closed.

7. It makes possible the handling of accounting details in a professional manner.

8. It ensures the validity of a binding contract between participating parties.

9. It is of value to the buyers, assuring them that their monies will not be transferred until the title is conditioned to the specifications of their contract or agreement.

10. It is of value to the sellers, assuring them that the monies have been paid and all other terms and conditions have been met.

Escrow instructions.   **Escrow instructions** are the written directions from the principals to the impartial third party, the escrow agent, to do all the necessary acts to carry out the escrow agreement of the principals. All principals in the escrow agreement (buyers, sellers, lenders, and borrowers) sign identical or conforming instructions that fully set out the understanding of the parties to the transactions. They deliver the signed instructions to the escrow agent.

Figure 10.6 in Unit 10 contains CAR Form RPA-CA, California Residential Purchase Agreement and Joint Escrow Instructions. The form provides that when the purchase offer is accepted, portions of the purchase agreement become the escrow instructions. The wide use of this form has significantly reduced the necessity of escrow instructions being prepared by the escrow holder or agent.

Communities vary in their escrow procedures. However, a title or escrow company would likely use preprinted forms for instructions, whereas a bank or other authorized agent may issue instructions by letter.

When both parties have signed the instructions, the parties are contractually bound to their agreement. If signed separate escrow instructions vary from the purchase agreement, the escrow instructions generally prevail because they most likely were the last agreement signed. In the absence of a purchase contract, the signed escrow instructions become the purchase contract.

> Amendments to the escrow instructions must be signed by all parties to the escrow.

Amending the escrow instructions.   Once both buyer and seller have signed the escrow instructions, the escrow is bound to carry out their agreement. If any changes are necessary, both buyer and seller must agree to **amend the escrow instructions**. Neither buyer nor seller can unilaterally modify the escrow agreement once it is signed.

Closing the escrow.   When the escrow agent has fulfilled all instructions from buyer, seller, and lender; when the remainder of the purchase price has been produced; and when a deed has been signed, the escrow arrangements are complete. The basic steps in closing escrow are as follows:

1. A statement showing the condition of the indebtedness and the unpaid balance of the current loan is requested from the beneficiary, the lender. By law the beneficiary must respond within 21 days of receipt of the request.

2. When the escrow agent has received all funds, documents, and instructions necessary to close the escrow, the escrow agent makes any necessary adjustments and prorations on a settlement sheet.

3. All instruments pertinent to the transaction are then sent to the title insurance company for recording. At this point, time becomes important.

4. The title search runs right up to the last minute of the escrow recording to ensure that nothing has been inserted in the record. If no changes have occurred, the deed and other instruments are recorded on the following morning. Thus, a title policy can be issued with the assurance that no intervening matters of record against the real property have occurred since the last search.

5. On the day the deed is recorded, the escrow agent disburses funds to the parties, according to their signed instructions. These include the following:

   a. Seller's lender—amount of loan(s) and cost(s) remaining at date of recording

   b. Listing and selling brokers' sales commissions

   c. Contractors—termite work, roof repairs, plumbing and/or electrical repairs, and so forth

   d. Other liens against the property

6. After recording, the escrow agent presents closing statements to the parties who should receive them.

7. The title insurance company endeavors to issue a policy of title insurance on the day of recordation.

8. Shortly thereafter, the recorded deed is sent from the county recorder to the customer.

Failed escrow.   If an escrow cannot be completed, the parties must agree to the release of funds (less costs and fees). If a party refuses to agree to the release of funds when there is not a good-faith dispute as to who is entitled to the funds, that party can be liable for treble damages but not less than $100 or more than $1,000 (CC1057.3(b)). A buyer's deposit may be released only if the parties agree. The matter is settled in arbitration or a judgment is rendered regarding the dispute.

Terms Used in Escrow Transactions

Recurring costs.   Impound account costs for taxes and insurance are called **recurring costs**.

Impound account.   When a real estate loan is made, monthly payments for taxes and fire insurance often are required. The lender estimates the funds needed for taxes and insurance, which vary from year to year. These funds are placed in a special reserve trust fund called an **impound account**. When the sale of the property is final and the loan is paid off, the seller is entitled to the unused portion of the impound account, as well as any interest earned.

Beneficiary statement. If an existing loan is to be paid or assumed by the buyer, the escrow agent will obtain a **beneficiary statement** showing the exact balance due from the one holding the deed of trust.

Demand statement. The **demand statement** indicates the amount due to the lender from escrow if the loan is to be paid off. It could include a prepayment penalty. (It is different from the beneficiary statement, which shows balance and condition of loan.)

Reconveyance. If the seller has a loan that is not being assumed by the buyer, the loan must be paid off to clear the title. The seller instructs the escrow agent to pay off the loan, for which the seller receives a **deed of reconveyance**. A *reconveyance fee* is charged the seller for this service. The sum due the lender is entered in the seller's escrow instructions as an estimate. The total figure will not be known until the final computations are made by the escrow officer at the time of closing.

Closing costs. The sum that the seller and the buyer have to pay beyond the purchase price is called the **closing costs**. Closing costs consist of fees charged for the mortgage loan, title insurance, escrow services, reconveyances, recording of documents, and transfer tax, among others. Amounts vary, depending on the particular locale involved and the price of the property. Figure 13.4 shows a sample of the customary seller's closing costs, but these costs vary regionally. Costs also vary, not only from area to area but also from institution to institution within an area. Some costs change with fluctuations in the economy. Figure 13.5 lists those items that are the buyer's responsibility.

As indicated in these lists, certain costs are customarily charged to the buyer and others to the seller. However, the two parties may agree to share some costs. Who pays closing costs is a negotiable item, unless required by a government-backed loan. Adapt this division of charges to your area. For actual fees, obtain copies of fee schedules from an escrow or title company in your area.

Prorations

The adjustment and distribution of costs to be shared by buyer and seller is called **proration**. Costs typically prorated include interest, taxes, insurance, and in the event that income property is involved, prepaid rents. Costs are prorated in escrow as of the closing of escrow or an agreed-upon date. Who is responsible for the day of closing may vary by local custom, although this can be changed by agreement. Generally, the buyer is responsible for the day of closing. Proration of taxes in California is generally based on a 30-day month and a 360-day year, known as a *banker's year*. In some other states, proration is based on the actual number of days. Mortgage interest is charged on a true per diem basis and is not rounded to a 30-day month.

Property taxes.   Property taxes are levied annually (July 1 to June 30 is the tax year) and are paid in two installments. Taxes often require proration. If, for example, the sellers had paid the first installment of a given year's taxes but completed the sale before that tax period was over, they would receive a credit for the remainder of that period's taxes. If, on the other hand, the sellers retained the property through part of the second tax period but had not yet paid taxes for that period, the amount due would be prorated between the sellers and the buyers, with the sellers having to pay for the portion of the tax period during which they still owned the property.

FIGURE 13.4: **Closing Costs Customarily Paid by the Seller**

Legal Closing

1. Owner's title policy
2. Escrow services (generally shared by buyer and seller)
3. Drawing deed
4. Obtaining reconveyance deed
5. Notary fees (typically, signing party pays to notarize)
6. Recording reconveyance
7. Documentary transfer tax (provided county and/or city has adopted this tax), $0.55 for each $500 or fractional part thereof (Check your local area for differences in rates and requirements for transfer taxes.)
8. Other agreed charges

Financial Closing

1. Mortgage discounts (points)
2. Appraisal charge for advance loan commitment
3. Structural pest control report or structural repair (if any needed). Typically, inspections are paid for by the buyer, and the structural pest report is provided by seller. Buyer and seller may negotiate who pays for inspection fees.
4. Interest on existing loan from last monthly payment to closing date
5. Beneficiary statement (balance on existing loan)
6. Loan payoff (first trust deed and/or any junior trust deed)
7. Prepayment penalty
8. Other agreed charges

Adjustments between Seller and Buyer (depend on closing or other date agreed on)

1. Pay any tax arrears in full
2. Pay any improvement assessment arrears (assessment may have to be paid in full)
3. Pay any other liens or judgments necessary to pass clear title
4. Pay broker's commission
5. Reimburse buyer for prepaid rents and deposits and adjust taxes, insurance, and interest as required
6. Occupancy adjustments

Source: *California Department of Real Estate Reference Book*, 1989–1990 Edition.

Insurance.   Fire insurance is normally paid for one year in advance. If the buyer assumes a fire insurance policy that has not yet expired, the seller is entitled to a prorated refund of the unused premium. (Assumption may not be allowed since insurance is a personal contract.)

Interest.   If a loan of record is being taken over by the buyer, interest will be prorated between buyer and seller. Because interest is normally paid in arrears, if a closing is set for the 15th of the month and the buyer assumes a loan with payments due on the 1st of the month, the seller owes the buyer for one-half-month's interest.

Rents.   Prepaid rents will be prorated in cases involving income-producing properties. Rents are generally prorated on an actual day basis (calendar year) using 365 or 366 days.

FIGURE 13.5: **Closing Costs Customarily Paid by the Buyer**

Legal Closing

1. Standard or owners policy in some areas (usually a negotiable charge)
2. ALTA policy and inspection fee, if ordered
3. Escrow services (generally shared by buyer and seller)
4. Drawing second mortgage (if used)
5. Notary fee (typically, signing party pays to notarize)
6. Recording deed (person receiving deed pays to record)
7. Other agreed charges

Financial Closing

1. Loan origination fee
2. Appraisal fee
3. Credit report
4. Drawing up note(s) and trust deed(s)
5. Notary fees
6. Recording trust deed
7. Tax agency fee
8. Termite inspection fee (if Section 2)
9. Interest on new loan (from date of closing until first monthly payment due)
10. Assumption fee
11. Other agreed charges
12. New fire insurance premium one year prepaid, if applicable
13. For new FHA-insured loan, mortgage insurance premium

Adjustments between Seller and Buyer (depend on closing or other date agreed on)

1. Reimburse seller for prepaid taxes
2. Reimburse seller for prepaid insurance
3. Reimburse seller for prepaid improvement assessment
4. Reimburse seller for prepaid impounds (in case buyer is assuming an existing loan)
5. Other occupancy adjustments

Reserves (Impounds) Limitations by Real Estate Settlement Procedures Act (RESPA)—Variations

1. Any variation from custom in closing a transaction should be agreed on in advance. Some times through sheer bargaining power one party can demand relief from and be relieved of all or some of the customary charges and offsets generally assessed. The financial aspects of each transaction differ and should always be negotiated by the parties.
2. Accruals: Unless agreed on in advance, interest-bearing debts are accrued up to date of settlement and constitute a charge against the seller.

Source: *California Department of Real Estate Reference Book*, 1989–1990 Edition.

Closing Disclosure

Procedure for closing disclosure.   Closing statements do not follow usual bookkeeping formulas. In a normal accounting situation, such as balancing a checkbook, all the credits (deposits to the account) are added. Then all the debits (checks written) are totaled and deducted from the credits, and the remainder is the balance.

At a closing, separate statements are issued for the buyer and the seller. Each settlement sheet includes **debits** (amounts owed) and **credits** (amounts entitled to receive). In contrast to usual accounting procedures, on the seller's settlement sheet all the credits to the seller are added (selling price of the property, prorations, etc.). Any debits owed by the seller are then totaled and deducted from the credits. The difference is entered as a cash credit (usually) to the seller, and the escrow agent forwards a check for this amount at the close of escrow.

On the buyer's settlement sheet, the buyer is charged (debited) with the purchase price of the property. The loans the buyer has obtained are credited to the buyer. Cash is credited, prorations may be debited or credited (as the case warrants), and escrow fees and closing costs are debited. The difference between the total debits and credits usually is required in cash by the escrow agent. The cash payment into escrow becomes an additional credit and forces the account to balance. Because of the forced balances, the totals on the buyers' and sellers' statements will be different from each other and from the purchase price.

Dodd-Frank simplified closing disclosure requirements of the Truth in Lending Act and RESPA. The Closing Disclosure includes a detailed accounting of the mortgage transaction, including a breakdown of closing costs paid by the buyer, the seller and others. The new closing form replaces the HUD-1 Settlement Statement. The Closing Disclosure form must be in the hands of the borrower at least three business days before closing. A copy must also be provided to the seller no later than the day of closing, Figure 13.6 is a completed sample Closing Disclosure prepared by the Consumer Financial Protection Bureau, an independent agency of the U.S. government.

If information on the closing statement becomes inaccurate before closing, a corrected statement must be provided at least one business day before closing. Material changes requiring corrections include

- changes in the type of loan,

- a difference in the APR, and

- addition of a prepayment penalty.

Broker's Added Responsibility

Despite the care taken in escrow, mistakes can be made. The real estate broker's final duties are to meet with the buyers or the sellers and explain the closing statement, to help them understand all charges and credits on the statement, and to verify that they have received the correct amount from escrow or paid the correct amount into escrow.

IRS reporting.   Cash payments of over $10,000 must be reported to the IRS on IRS Form 8300. Gross proceeds to the seller are reported on IRS Form 1099S.

When Is Escrow Complete?

Escrow is complete when the following actions have been taken:

- The escrow officer sends the deed and deeds of trust to the recorder's office to be recorded. This offers protection of the title to the buyer and of the lien to the lender. The broker's responsibility is to confirm the recordation and inform the clients.

- The escrow agent sends to the seller and the buyer the closing statements showing the disbursement of funds.

- The escrow agent forwards the title policy, assuring the buyer of marketable title, except for certain items; the agent sends the original copy to the buyer.

Liability of an Escrow

Escrow could be held liable for its negligence or breach of duty. However, escrow companies do not have any duty to warn a party of possible fraud or point out any detrimental fact or risk of a transaction. If, however, the escrow was a broker, the broker would have these disclosure obligations.

FIGURE 13.6:   Closing Disclosure

Closing Disclosure

This form is a statement of final loan terms and closing costs. Compare this document with your Loan Estimate.

Closing Information

Date Issued	4/15/2013
Closing Date	4/15/2013
Disbursement Date	4/15/2013
Settlement Agent	Epsilon Title Co.
File #	12-3456
Property	456 Somewhere Ave
	Anytown, ST 12345
Sale Price	$180,000

Transaction Information

Borrower	Michael Jones and Mary Stone
	123 Anywhere Street
	Anytown, ST 12345
Seller	Steve Cole and Amy Doe
	321 Somewhere Drive
	Anytown, ST 12345
Lender	Ficus Bank

Loan Information

Loan Term	30 years
Purpose	Purchase
Product	Fixed Rate
Loan Type	☒ Conventional ☐ FHA
	☐ VA ☐ _____
Loan ID #	123456789
MIC #	000654321

Loan Terms

		Can this amount increase after closing?
Loan Amount	$162,000	**NO**
Interest Rate	3.875%	**NO**
Monthly Principal & Interest *See Projected Payments below for your Estimated Total Monthly Payment*	$761.78	**NO**
		Does the loan have these features?
Prepayment Penalty		**YES** • **As high as $3,240** if you pay off the loan during the first 2 years
Balloon Payment		**NO**

Projected Payments

Payment Calculation	Years 1-7	Years 8-30
Principal & Interest	$761.78	$761.78
Mortgage Insurance	+ 82.35	+ —
Estimated Escrow *Amount can increase over time*	+ 206.13	+ 206.13
Estimated Total Monthly Payment	**$1,050.26**	**$967.91**

Estimated Taxes, Insurance & Assessments *Amount can increase over time* *See page 4 for details*	$356.13 a month	**This estimate includes** ☒ Property Taxes ☒ Homeowner's Insurance ☒ Other: Homeowner's Association Dues *See Escrow Account on page 4 for details. You must pay for other property costs separately.*	**In escrow?** YES YES NO

Costs at Closing

Closing Costs	$9,712.10	Includes $4,694.05 in Loan Costs + $5,018.05 in Other Costs – $0 in Lender Credits. *See page 2 for details.*
Cash to Close	$14,147.26	Includes Closing Costs. *See Calculating Cash to Close on page 3 for details.*

FIGURE 13.6 (continued): Closing Disclosure

Closing Cost Details

Loan Costs		Borrower-Paid		Seller-Paid		Paid by Others
		At Closing	Before Closing	At Closing	Before Closing	
A. Origination Charges		**$1,802.00**				
01 0.25 % of Loan Amount (Points)		$405.00				
02 Application Fee		$300.00				
03 Underwriting Fee		$1,097.00				
04						
05						
06						
07						
08						
B. Services Borrower Did Not Shop For		**$236.55**				
01 Appraisal Fee	to John Smith Appraisers Inc.					$405.00
02 Credit Report Fee	to Information Inc.		$29.80			
03 Flood Determination Fee	to Info Co.	$20.00				
04 Flood Monitoring Fee	to Info Co.	$31.75				
05 Tax Monitoring Fee	to Info Co.	$75.00				
06 Tax Status Research Fee	to Info Co.	$80.00				
07						
08						
09						
10						
C. Services Borrower Did Shop For		**$2,655.50**				
01 Pest Inspection Fee	to Pests Co.	$120.50				
02 Survey Fee	to Surveys Co.	$85.00				
03 Title – Insurance Binder	to Epsilon Title Co.	$650.00				
04 Title – Lender's Title Insurance	to Epsilon Title Co.	$500.00				
05 Title – Settlement Agent Fee	to Epsilon Title Co.	$500.00				
06 Title – Title Search	to Epsilon Title Co.	$800.00				
07						
08						
D. TOTAL LOAN COSTS (Borrower-Paid)		**$4,694.05**				
Loan Costs Subtotals (A + B + C)		$4,664.25	$29.80			

Other Costs		Borrower-Paid		Seller-Paid		Paid by Others
E. Taxes and Other Government Fees		**$85.00**				
01 Recording Fees	Deed: $40.00 Mortgage: $45.00	$85.00				
02 Transfer Tax	to Any State			$950.00		
F. Prepaids		**$2,120.80**				
01 Homeowner's Insurance Premium (12 mo.) to Insurance Co.		$1,209.96				
02 Mortgage Insurance Premium (mo.)						
03 Prepaid Interest ($17.44 per day from 4/15/13 to 5/1/13)		$279.04				
04 Property Taxes (6 mo.) to Any County USA		$631.80				
05						
G. Initial Escrow Payment at Closing		**$412.25**				
01 Homeowner's Insurance $100.83 per month for 2 mo.		$201.66				
02 Mortgage Insurance per month for mo.						
03 Property Taxes $105.30 per month for 2 mo.		$210.60				
04						
05						
06						
07						
08 Aggregate Adjustment		– 0.01				
H. Other		**$2,400.00**				
01 HOA Capital Contribution	to HOA Acre Inc.	$500.00				
02 HOA Processing Fee	to HOA Acre Inc.	$150.00				
03 Home Inspection Fee	to Engineers Inc.	$750.00			$750.00	
04 Home Warranty Fee	to XYZ Warranty Inc.			$450.00		
05 Real Estate Commission	to Alpha Real Estate Broker			$5,700.00		
06 Real Estate Commission	to Omega Real Estate Broker			$5,700.00		
07 Title – Owner's Title Insurance (optional) to Epsilon Title Co.		$1,000.00				
08						
I. TOTAL OTHER COSTS (Borrower-Paid)		**$5,018.05**				
Other Costs Subtotals (E + F + G + H)		$5,018.05				
J. TOTAL CLOSING COSTS (Borrower-Paid)		**$9,712.10**				
Closing Costs Subtotals (D + I)		$9,682.30	$29.80	$12,800.00	$750.00	$405.00
Lender Credits						

FIGURE 13.6 (continued): Closing Disclosure

Calculating Cash to Close

Use this table to see what has changed from your Loan Estimate.

	Loan Estimate	Final	Did this change?
Total Closing Costs (J)	$8,054.00	$9,712.10	YES • See **Total Loan Costs (D)** and **Total Other Costs (I)**
Closing Costs Paid Before Closing	$0	– $29.80	YES • You paid these Closing Costs **before closing**
Closing Costs Financed (Paid from your Loan Amount)	$0	$0	NO
Down Payment/Funds from Borrower	$18,000.00	$18,000.00	NO
Deposit	– $10,000.00	– $10,000.00	NO
Funds for Borrower	$0	$0	NO
Seller Credits	$0	– $2,500.00	YES • See Seller Credits in **Section L**
Adjustments and Other Credits	$0	– $1,035.04	YES • See details in **Sections K and L**
Cash to Close	$16,054.00	$14,147.26	

Summaries of Transactions

Use this table to see a summary of your transaction.

BORROWER'S TRANSACTION

K. Due from Borrower at Closing	$189,762.30
01 Sale Price of Property	$180,000.00
02 Sale Price of Any Personal Property Included in Sale	
03 Closing Costs Paid at Closing (J)	$9,682.30
04	
Adjustments	
05	
06	
07	
Adjustments for Items Paid by Seller in Advance	
08 City/Town Taxes to	
09 County Taxes to	
10 Assessments to	
11 HOA Dues 4/15/13 to 4/30/13	$80.00
12	
13	
14	
15	

L. Paid Already by or on Behalf of Borrower at Closing	$175,615.04
01 Deposit	$10,000.00
02 Loan Amount	$162,000.00
03 Existing Loan(s) Assumed or Taken Subject to	
04	
05 Seller Credit	$2,500.00
Other Credits	
06 Rebate from Epsilon Title Co.	$750.00
07	
Adjustments	
08	
09	
10	
11	
Adjustments for Items Unpaid by Seller	
12 City/Town Taxes 1/1/13 to 4/14/13	$365.04
13 County Taxes to	
14 Assessments to	
15	
16	
17	

CALCULATION	
Total Due from Borrower at Closing (K)	$189,762.30
Total Paid Already by or on Behalf of Borrower at Closing (L)	– $175,615.04
Cash to Close ☒ From ☐ To Borrower	**$14,147.26**

SELLER'S TRANSACTION

M. Due to Seller at Closing	$180,080.00
01 Sale Price of Property	$180,000.00
02 Sale Price of Any Personal Property Included in Sale	
03	
04	
05	
06	
07	
08	
Adjustments for Items Paid by Seller in Advance	
09 City/Town Taxes to	
10 County Taxes to	
11 Assessments to	
12 HOA Dues 4/15/13 to 4/30/13	$80.00
13	
14	
15	
16	

N. Due from Seller at Closing	$115,665.04
01 Excess Deposit	
02 Closing Costs Paid at Closing (J)	$12,800.00
03 Existing Loan(s) Assumed or Taken Subject to	
04 Payoff of First Mortgage Loan	$100,000.00
05 Payoff of Second Mortgage Loan	
06	
07	
08 Seller Credit	$2,500.00
09	
10	
11	
12	
13	
Adjustments for Items Unpaid by Seller	
14 City/Town Taxes 1/1/13 to 4/14/13	$365.04
15 County Taxes to	
16 Assessments to	
17	
18	
19	

CALCULATION	
Total Due to Seller at Closing (M)	$180,080.00
Total Due from Seller at Closing (N)	– $115,665.04
Cash ☐ From ☒ To Seller	**$64,414.96**

CLOSING DISCLOSURE

FIGURE 13.6 (continued):   Closing Disclosure

Additional Information About This Loan

Assumption

If you sell or transfer this property to another person, your lender

☐ will allow, under certain conditions, this person to assume this loan on the original terms.

☒ will not allow assumption of this loan on the original terms.

Demand Feature

Your loan

☐ has a demand feature, which permits your lender to require early repayment of the loan. You should review your note for details.

☒ does not have a demand feature.

Late Payment

If your payment is more than *15* days late, your lender will charge a late fee of *5% of the monthly principal and interest payment.*

Negative Amortization (Increase in Loan Amount)

Under your loan terms, you

☐ are scheduled to make monthly payments that do not pay all of the interest due that month. As a result, your loan amount will increase (negatively amortize), and your loan amount will likely become larger than your original loan amount. Increases in your loan amount lower the equity you have in this property.

☐ may have monthly payments that do not pay all of the interest due that month. If you do, your loan amount will increase (negatively amortize), and, as a result, your loan amount may become larger than your original loan amount. Increases in your loan amount lower the equity you have in this property.

☒ do not have a negative amortization feature.

Partial Payments

Your lender

☒ may accept payments that are less than the full amount due (partial payments) and apply them to your loan.

☐ may hold them in a separate account until you pay the rest of the payment, and then apply the full payment to your loan.

☐ does not accept any partial payments.

If this loan is sold, your new lender may have a different policy.

Security Interest

You are granting a security interest in

456 Somewhere Ave., Anytown, ST 12345

You may lose this property if you do not make your payments or satisfy other obligations for this loan.

Escrow Account

For now, your loan

☒ will have an escrow account (also called an "impound" or "trust" account) to pay the property costs listed below. Without an escrow account, you would pay them directly, possibly in one or two large payments a year. Your lender may be liable for penalties and interest for failing to make a payment.

Escrow		
Escrowed Property Costs over Year 1	$2,473.56	Estimated total amount over year 1 for your escrowed property costs: *Homeowner's Insurance Property Taxes*
Non-Escrowed Property Costs over Year 1	$1,800.00	Estimated total amount over year 1 for your non-escrowed property costs: *Homeowner's Association Dues* You may have other property costs.
Initial Escrow Payment	$412.25	A cushion for the escrow account you pay at closing. See Section G on page 2.
Monthly Escrow Payment	$206.13	The amount included in your total monthly payment.

☐ will not have an escrow account because ☐ you declined it ☐ your lender does not offer one. You must directly pay your property costs, such as taxes and homeowner's insurance. Contact your lender to ask if your loan can have an escrow account.

No Escrow		
Estimated Property Costs over Year 1		Estimated total amount over year 1. You must pay these costs directly, possibly in one or two large payments a year.
Escrow Waiver Fee		

In the future,

Your property costs may change and, as a result, your escrow payment may change. You may be able to cancel your escrow account, but if you do, you must pay your property costs directly. If you fail to pay your property taxes, your state or local government may (1) impose fines and penalties or (2) place a tax lien on this property. If you fail to pay any of your property costs, your lender may (1) add the amounts to your loan balance, (2) add an escrow account to your loan, or (3) require you to pay for property insurance that the lender buys on your behalf, which likely would cost more and provide fewer benefits than what you could buy on your own.

FIGURE 13.6 (continued):   Closing Disclosure

Loan Calculations

Total of Payments. Total you will have paid after you make all payments of principal, interest, mortgage insurance, and loan costs, as scheduled.	$285,803.36
Finance Charge. The dollar amount the loan will cost you.	$118,830.27
Amount Financed. The loan amount available after paying your upfront finance charge.	$162,000.00
Annual Percentage Rate (APR). Your costs over the loan term expressed as a rate. This is not your interest rate.	4.174%
Total Interest Percentage (TIP). The total amount of interest that you will pay over the loan term as a percentage of your loan amount.	69.46%

 Questions? If you have questions about the loan terms or costs on this form, use the contact information below. To get more information or make a complaint, contact the Consumer Financial Protection Bureau at **www.consumerfinance.gov/mortgage-closing**

Other Disclosures

Appraisal
If the property was appraised for your loan, your lender is required to give you a copy at no additional cost at least 3 days before closing. If you have not yet received it, please contact your lender at the information listed below.

Contract Details
See your note and security instrument for information about
• what happens if you fail to make your payments,
• what is a default on the loan,
• situations in which your lender can require early repayment of the loan, and
• the rules for making payments before they are due.

Liability after Foreclosure
If your lender forecloses on this property and the foreclosure does not cover the amount of unpaid balance on this loan,

☒ state law may protect you from liability for the unpaid balance. If you refinance or take on any additional debt on this property, you may lose this protection and have to pay any debt remaining even after foreclosure. You may want to consult a lawyer for more information.

☐ state law does not protect you from liability for the unpaid balance.

Refinance
Refinancing this loan will depend on your future financial situation, the property value, and market conditions. You may not be able to refinance this loan.

Tax Deductions
If you borrow more than this property is worth, the interest on the loan amount above this property's fair market value is not deductible from your federal income taxes. You should consult a tax advisor for more information.

Contact Information

	Lender	Mortgage Broker	Real Estate Broker (B)	Real Estate Broker (S)	Settlement Agent
Name	Ficus Bank		Omega Real Estate Broker Inc.	Alpha Real Estate Broker Co.	Epsilon Title Co.
Address	4321 Random Blvd. Somecity, ST 12340		789 Local Lane Sometown, ST 12345	987 Suburb Ct. Someplace, ST 12340	123 Commerce Pl. Somecity, ST 12344
NMLS ID					
ST License ID			Z765416	Z61456	Z61616
Contact	Joe Smith		Samuel Green	Joseph Cain	Sarah Arnold
Contact NMLS ID	12345				
Contact ST License ID			P16415	P51461	PT1234
Email	joesmith@ ficusbank.com		sam@omegare.biz	joe@alphare.biz	sarah@ epsilontitle.com
Phone	123-456-7890		123-555-1717	321-555-7171	987-555-4321

Confirm Receipt

By signing, you are only confirming that you have received this form. You do not have to accept this loan because you have signed or received this form.

_____   _____   _____   _____
Applicant Signature   Date   Co-Applicant Signature   Date

CLOSING DISCLOSURE

TITLE INSURANCE

In a number of states, **marketable title** is shown by an **abstract**. An *abstract of title* is a recorded history of a property. It includes a summary of every recorded document concerning the property. An attorney reads the abstract and gives an opinion of title based on what the abstract reveals. A problem with using abstracts to verify title is that the records of recordation do not reveal title defects, such as a forged instrument in the chain of title, unknown spousal interests, incapacity of a grantor, an illegal contract, or failure of delivery. These risks and more are covered by title insurance, which explains why the use of title insurance has been expanding.

Title insurance insures the ownership of real property (land, buildings, and minerals below the surface) against any unknown encumbrances and other items that may cloud the title. These are primarily claims that might be made by a third party against the property. Buyers are assured that a thorough search has been made of all public records affecting the property being purchased and that the buyers have a marketable title.

Title insurance is paid for once, at the time title passes from one owner to another, and it remains in effect until the property is sold again, at which time title passes to the new owner. If a property owner dies, title insurance continues to protect the owner's heirs.

If a buyer does not elect to buy title insurance protection, that buyer is not protected, even though a prior owner had title insurance.

Both the lender and the buyer should benefit from and have title insurance—the buyer to ensure clear title, and thus protect her investment, and the lender to protect his interest in the property.

For years, title insurance companies had similar rates. It is now possible to obtain title insurance at significant savings online. Entitle Direct, www.entitledirect.com, is one such company. It is rated "A Prime" by Demotech, Inc., which rates insurer financial stability.

The two basic types of policies are the California Land Title Association (CLTA) policy and the American Land Title Association (ALTA) policy.

In 1987, the title insurance industry issued a new set of policies with new coverages and exclusions.

Standard Policy

The policy usually used by the buyer in California is the **CLTA policy**. This policy is called a **standard policy**. The standard policy of title insurance covers matters of record, if not specifically excluded from coverage, as well as specified risks not of record, such as the following:

- Forgery

- Lack of capacity of a grantor

- Undisclosed spousal interests (a grantor who claimed to be single had a spouse with community property interests)

- Failure of delivery of a prior deed

- Federal estate tax liens

- Deeds of a corporation whose charter has expired

- Deeds of an agent whose capacity has terminated

Excluded from coverage by a standard policy of title insurance are the following:

- Defects known by the insured and not disclosed to the title insurer

- Zoning (although a special endorsement is possible that a current use is authorized by current zoning)

- Mining claims (filed in mining districts; legal descriptions are not required)

- Taxes and assessments that are not yet liens

- Easements and liens not a matter of record (such as prescriptive easements and rights to a mechanic's lien)

- Rights of parties in possession (unrecorded deeds, leases, options, etc.)

- Matters not a matter of record that would be disclosed by checking the property (such as encroachment)

- Matters that would be revealed by a correct survey

- Water rights

- Reservations in government patents

A title insurance policy may include an exception to a particular problem so that the policy will not cover a loss resulting from that problem.

A standard CLTA policy protects the buyer as to matters of record and specified risks.

Generally, in southern California the seller pays for the standard policy of title insurance. In some northern California communities, the buyer pays for this coverage. Any agreement of the parties as to who pays takes precedence over local custom. (In some areas of California, the escrow and title insurance functions are joined in a single firm, while in other areas the functions are separate.)

ALTA Policy

An **ALTA extended policy** is generally purchased for the benefit of the lender. The buyer pays for this lender protection. It insures that the lender has a valid and enforceable lien, subject to only the exclusions from coverage noted in the exception schedule of the policy. It insures the lender for the amount of the loan, not the purchase price of the property. There are three basic ALTA policies—one deals with homes described by lot, block, and tract; one deals with homes described by either the metes-and-bounds or government survey system; and one deals with construction loans.

While ALTA covers the United States, CLTA only covers California. An ALTA lender policy provides extended coverage to the lender, not the buyer.

The extended coverage lender policy protects the lender only, not the purchaser, from the risks covered. Buyers who desire extended protection must pay for that protection. An owner's policy that offers this extended protection is available. (Both CLTA and ALTA have homeowner extended coverage policies.)

In addition to the coverage offered by the standard policy, the extended coverage policy of title insurance includes the following:

- Unrecorded liens

- Off-record easements

- Rights of parties in physical possession, including tenants and buyers under unrecorded instruments

- Rights and claims that a correct survey or physical inspection would disclose

- Mining claims

- Water rights

- Lack of access

Insurers might require a survey before they issue an extended coverage policy of title insurance. The extended coverage policy does not cover the following:

- Matters known by the insured but not conveyed to the insurer

- Government regulations, such as zoning

- Liens placed by the insured

- Eminent domain

- Violations of the map act

The coverage of standard and extended coverage policies can be seen in Figure 13.7.

There are also special construction loan title insurance policies, policies that guarantee trustee sales, bankruptcy guarantees, boundary line agreement guarantees, and special policies for unimproved land. California Title Company publishes a summary of California endorsement to title policies. Information on the endorsements offered can be obtained from California Title Company at www.caltitle.com.

WEB LINK

@

FIGURE 13.7: **Owner's Title Insurance Policy**

Standard Coverage

1. Defects found in public records
2. Forged documents
3. Incompetent grantors
4. Incorrect marital statements
5. Improperly delivered deeds

Extended Coverage

Standard Coverage plus defects discoverable through:

1. Property inspection, including unrecorded rights of persons in possession
2. Examination of survey
3. Unrecorded liens not known of by policyholder

Not Covered by Either Policy

1. Defects and liens listed in policy
2. Defects known to buyer
3. Changes in land use brought about by zoning ordinances

The premiums paid reflect the work that goes into the issuance of a title policy, not the amount paid in claims. Typically, less than 5% of premium dollars is paid out by a title insurer in claims.

Preliminary Title Report

> The preliminary title report does not provide any insurance.

Before a policy of title insurance is issued, the issuer issues a **preliminary title report**. This report is designed to provide an interim response to an application for title insurance. It is also intended to facilitate the issuance of a particular type of policy. The preliminary report identifies the title to the estate or interest in the prescribed land. It also contains a list of the defects, liens, encumbrances, and restrictions that would be excluded from coverage if the requested policy were to be issued as of the date of the report.

Licensees often will obtain a copy of the preliminary report in order to discuss the matters set forth in it with their clients. Thus, a preliminary report provides the opportunity to seek the removal of items referenced in the report that are unacceptable to the prospective insured. Such arrangements can be made with the assistance of the escrow office.

With respect to preliminary reports, the title industry has been making a concerted effort to improve communications with agents representing sellers and buyers. The latest forms are distinguished from early versions in that the printed encumbrances and exclusions are set forth verbatim and not incorporated by reference. Consequently, the preliminary report now constitutes a more complete communication of the offer to issue a title insurance policy.

In fact, preliminary reports are just one of the steps in the risk elimination process. Risk elimination includes the maintenance and collection of title records (known as the **title plant**), the searching and examination of the records, and the underwriting standards of each title insurance company.

The preliminary report does not necessarily show the condition of the title; it merely reports the current vesting of title and the items the title company will exclude from coverage if the policy should be issued later. The elements of this definition are threefold:

1. A preliminary report is an offer.

2. It is *not* an abstract of title reporting a complete chain of title.

3. It is a statement of the terms and conditions of the offer to issue a title policy.

The title insurer customarily makes a last-minute check to ensure there are no new recordings concerning a property's title before issuing its policy of insurance.

Special Policies

There are a number of **special title insurance policies,** such as construction lender policies and policies for vendees (purchasers under real property sales contracts), policies insuring leasehold interest, and even policies for oil and gas interests. Special coverage policy amendments also can be purchased.

Policy Interpretation

Title insurance policies are interpreted in accordance with the reasonable expectations of the insured. In the event of ambiguities, they normally would be resolved against the insurer.

Rebate Law (RESPA)

Title insurance companies are precluded by law from providing kickbacks to brokers for referral of business. They must charge brokers the same as other customers and make a sincere effort to collect any premiums due. The **rebate law** extends to escrows, as well as to title insurers. Besides being grounds for disciplinary action, receiving a rebate from a title insurer is considered commercial bribery and could subject a licensee to up to one year in jail and a $10,000 fine for each transaction.

SUMMARY

An escrow is a third-party stakeholder who receives and disburses documents and funds in a real property transaction. The escrow is usually selected by the buyer and the seller in the purchase agreement. The escrow cannot be completed until all conditions are met. The escrow basically has agency duties to both buyer and seller. There may be duties to a lender as well. The broker is not a party to the escrow, and the escrow agent has no duty to obey instructions of the broker after the escrow instructions have been signed.

Escrows must be corporations and licensed as escrow. An exception is that a broker can act as an escrow without a license if the broker was a principal to the transaction or represented either the buyer or the seller. Aside from the broker, the lender, and attorney exemptions, an escrow must be a corporation and must meet strict licensing requirements.

An escrow is opened with the parties signing escrow instructions. A valid escrow consists of a signed agreement and conditional delivery of transfer documents to the escrow. The delivery is conditioned on the buyer's fully meeting obligations. Once escrow instructions have been signed by both buyer and seller, any change to the instructions requires the signatures of both buyer and seller.

When the escrow disburses funds and records the deed, the escrow is considered closed. A Closing Disclosure is issued by the escrow showing the debits and the credits of the transaction. Rents, taxes, interest, and insurance are likely to be prorated by the escrow. Proration is based on a 30-day month and a 360-day year. After escrow closes, the broker should make certain the client fully understands the disclosure statement.

Escrow companies are liable for their negligence, but they are not liable for failure to warn a party of possible fraud or to point out a detrimental fact or risk of a transaction.

An abstract shows only the recorded history of a property. A title opinion based on an abstract does not reveal defects such as forgery, lack of capacity, unknown spousal interests, and so forth. These and other risks are covered by a standard policy of title insurance, which also covers risks of record. Greater coverage for lenders can be obtained with an ALTA extended coverage policy. If buyers want this protection for themselves, they have to buy an extended coverage owners policy.

The preliminary title report is an offer to insure and does not give the buyer any protection unless a policy of title insurance is purchased. There are special title insurance policies for specific needs.

The rebate law prohibits title insurance carriers and escrows from rebating fees for referrals or otherwise providing special advantages or deals to brokers.

CLASS DISCUSSION TOPICS

1. Which offices and developments in your area handle their own escrows? Why?

2. In your area, are escrow instructions separate for buyer and seller or are the instructions a single agreement?

3. What are typical escrow costs for the sale of a $600,000 residence in your area?

4. What does it cost for a standard policy of title insurance for a $600,000 home in your area?

5. What does it cost for a $600,000 extended coverage policy of title insurance for lender protection?

6. What does it cost for a preliminary title report on a $600,000 home sale?

7. How does a preliminary title report differ from a property profile provided by a title insurer?

8. Bring to class one current-events article dealing with some aspect of real estate practice for class discussion.

UNIT 13 QUIZ

1. A broker can act as an escrow when the broker
    a. represents the buyer in the transaction.
    b. represents the seller in the transaction.
    c. is a principal in the transaction.
    d. is any of these.

2. An escrow company is prohibited from
    a. paying referral fees to anyone other than an employee of the escrow company.
    b. bonding employees.
    c. both of these.
    d. neither of these.

3. To determine the balance due on a loan, escrow requests
    a. a closing statement.
    b. a beneficiary statement.
    c. a reconveyance.
    d. an impound statement.

4. Which is a debit to the seller on a seller's closing statement?
    a. Selling price
    b. Prepaid taxes
    c. First trust deed to be assumed by buyer
    d. All of these

5. Which is a credit to the buyer on the buyer's closing statement?
    a. Purchase price
    b. Escrow costs
    c. Title insurance
    d. First trust deed assumed

6. An escrow company has a duty to
   a. warn parties if the escrow knows of possible fraud.
   b. suggest changes when one party is not being adequately protected.
   c. do both of these.
   d. do neither of these.

7. A standard policy of title insurance is used to show
   a. that there are no encumbrances against a property.
   b. that the seller has a marketable title.
   c. both of these.
   d. neither of these.

8. Which of the following is covered by the CLTA standard policy of title insurance?
   a. Easements not a matter of public record
   b. Rights of a party in possession
   c. Unknown spousal interests
   d. Encroachment

9. Which is *NOT* covered by an ALTA extended coverage policy of title insurance?
   a. Mining claims
   b. Liens placed by the insured
   c. Water rights
   d. Off-record easement

10. Title insurance companies may
    a. give rebates to brokers for referrals.
    b. give brokers preferential rates on their own purchases.
    c. charge brokers the same as others but make no effort to collect.
    d. do none of these.

TAXATION

LEARNING OBJECTIVES

When you have completed this unit, you will be able to

■ explain why taxes play an important role in real estate ownership and investment;

■ describe statutory exemptions on property taxation; and

■ understand tax shelters, probate, and living trusts.

KEY TERMS

acquisition
   indebtedness
adjusted basis
ad valorem taxes
basis
boot
capital gain
capital loss
deferred gain
depreciable basis
depreciation
entity rule
equity indebtedness
estate tax
excluded gain
Foreign Investment in
   Real Property Tax
   Act

home improvements
homeowner's
   exemption
installment sale
investment property
   rule
like-kind rule
living trust
no-choice rule
no-loss rule
original basis
primary personal
   residence
probate
Proposition 13
Proposition 58
Proposition 60
Proposition 90

realized gain
recognized gain
reverse exchange
sale-leaseback
special assessments
stepped-up basis
supplemental tax bill
tax-deferred exchange
1031 exchange
Urban Agriculture
   Incentive Zone Act
veteran's exemption
Williamson Act

REAL PROPERTY TAXES

Real Property Tax Calendar

> Real property taxes are based on value.

Real property taxes are **ad valorem taxes**. *Ad valorem* is a Latin expression that means "according to value." Real estate tax rates are a percentage of the property's "full cash value." The concept is not new; throughout history, people's wealth has been determined largely by the amount of real property they own. Landowners almost always have been taxed on the basis of their property holdings. Governments favor real estate taxation because it is the one form of taxation that cannot be evaded. If a taxpayer fails to pay taxes, the levying body can foreclose on its tax lien to satisfy the taxpayer's obligations. In the United States, property taxes are fully deductible on a homeowner's income tax return. However, special assessments for improvements generally are not considered a tax-deductible expense. They do, however, increase the cost basis.

The levying of real property taxes profoundly affects the real estate market. If taxes are high, potential customers may hesitate to involve themselves with such an expense by purchasing property. On the positive side, revenues from property taxes are a vital source of government income on the local level, enabling local government to provide for the health, education, safety, and welfare of the citizenry.

A basic understanding of real property taxes in California begins with knowing the chronological order for processing real property taxes.

Taxes are assessed and paid based on a fiscal year (July 1 through June 30). Taxes may be paid in two equal installments. The acronym *NDFA* (No Darn Fooling Around) is a memory tool for understanding the dates of these two payments:

N – November 1, first installment due

D – December 10, first installment becomes delinquent

F – February 1, second installment due

A – April 10, second installment becomes delinquent

Billing

If taxes are to be paid through a lending agency, the county sends a tax bill to that agency and a copy of it to the owner. The owner's copy states that it is for information only. If the owner is to pay the taxes, the original bill is sent directly to the owner for payment. The tax bill includes any special assessments. Unpaid taxes become delinquent, and a penalty is charged even if the taxpayer never received a notice of taxes due. It is the taxpayer's responsibility to make sure that tax payment deadlines are met.

Figure 14.1 shows a sample tax bill.

> ### Typical California Tax Bill
>
> A typical California tax bill includes the following information:
>
> - An identifying parcel number, with reference to the map page and property number or other description
> - A breakdown between land assessments and improvement assessments
> - Tax exemptions such as homeowner's exemption
> - A breakdown of the bonded indebtedness or special assessments
> - The full amount of the tax
> - Itemized or perhaps separate payment cards with the full tax equally divided into first and second installments

The supplemental tax bill covers the difference between the seller's assessed valuation and the new valuation based on the sales price.

Supplemental tax bill.   A recent homebuyer may come into an agent's office and say, "I paid my property tax, and a month later I received a new assessment for almost the same amount. How much are my taxes on this property?" Before the property is purchased, the agent should explain to buyers that in the first year of ownership, they will receive two or three tax bills: the regular tax bill and one or two **supplemental tax bills**. Supplemental tax bills are issued because property is reassessed as of the sale date. A change of ownership statement must be filed in the county assessor's office within 45 days of the transfer. The sale will generally trigger a reassessment.

Property taxes are billed and paid for the fiscal year of July 1 through June 30. When a buyer purchases a new home, it takes time to notify the tax collector's office of the sale of property and for the tax collector's office to issue the new property tax bill based on the new assessed value. The county assessor is directed to put new values on a supplemental assessment roll from the completion date of construction or the change of ownership date (for example, a sale). If the new value is higher than the current assessed value, a supplemental tax bill is sent to the property owner that reflects the higher valuation for the remainder of the tax year.

FIGURE 14.1:   Sample Tax Bill

RIVERSIDE COUNTY SECURED PROPERTY TAX BILL
For Fiscal Year July 1, 2015 through June 30, 2016

Offices in Riverside, Palm Desert and Temecula
Visit our website: www.countytreasurer.org

IMPORTANT INFORMATION ON REVERSE SIDE

DON KENT, TREASURER   058342
4080 Lemon St (1st Floor) Riverside, California
(P.O. Box 12005, Riverside, CA 92502-2205)

Telephone: (951) 955-3900
or, from area codes 951 and 760 only
toll free: 1 (877) RIVCOTX (748-2689)

Property Data   752250035-1 LOT 41 MB 275/097 TR 28926

Address Owner,   12345 ADAMS STREET PALM SPRINGS 92262
JANUARY 1, 2015   DOE, JOHN Q & MARY S

DOE, JOHN Q & MARY S
12345 ADAMS STREET
PALM SPRINGS, CA 92262-2515

ASSESSMENT NUMBER
752250035-1

Tax Rate Area	Bill Number
075-004	000473330

Q   09/18/2015
All questions about ownership, values or
exemptions must be directed to the
Riverside County Assessor at (951) 955-6200.

UNPAID PRIOR-YEAR TAXES
(See Item #6 on reverse)
NONE

Tax bill requested by	Loan Identification	Multiple Bills

CHARGES LEVIED BY TAXING AGENCIES (See Item #4 on reverse)		AMOUNT
1% TAX LIMIT PER PROP 13		3954.46
DESERT SANDS UNIFIED SCHOOL	(760) 771-8516	431.62
DESERT COMMUNITY COLLEGE	(760) 773-2513	82.52
COACHELLA VALLEY WATER DISTRICT	(760) 398-2661	395.44
COACHELLA VALLEY MOSQUITO & RIFA	(866) 807-6864@	6.06
AD COACHELLA VALLEY RC/PK 93-1	(866) 807-6864@	9.90
CVWD SEWER SERVICE CHARGE ID81	(760) 391-9600@	331.80

LAND	137,907
STRUCTURES	264,539
TRADE FIXTURES	
TREES & VINES	
BUSINESS PERSONAL PROPERTY	
FULL VALUE	402,446
EXEMPTIONS HOX	7,000
NET VALUE	395,446
TAX RATE PER $100 VALUE	1.23002
TAXES	$4,864.06
Special Assessments & Fixed Charges	$347.76
TOTAL AMOUNT If over $50,000, see Item #1 on reverse	$5,211.82

$2,605.91	$2,605.91
Add 10% penalty after 12/10/2015	Add 10% penalty plus cost after 04/10/2016
$2,605.91	$2,605.91

PLEASE KEEP TOP PORTION FOR YOUR RECORDS
(NO RECEIPTS WILL BE ISSUED - YOUR CANCELLED CHECK IS YOUR RECEIPT)

E X A M P L E   Mr. and Mrs. Newly Boute purchased a home on January 2 of this year for $300,000. Assume no bond issues or assessment other than the basic levy of 1%. The new property tax will be $3,000 (1% of $300,000). The old assessment on the home was $100,000. Therefore, the property tax on the home was $1,000 for the fiscal year from July 1 of last year to June 30 of this year. So, when the Boutes purchased their home, their tax bill for the second installment of the fiscal year would be $500 (half of $1,000) due February and delinquent April 10, which is the old bill. The Boutes should be paying $1,500 on the new tax bill (half of $3,000). Because they paid $500 on the old bill, they will have to pay a supplemental tax bill of $1,000 ($1,500 – $500). See the following chart.

	FISCAL YEAR	
	July 1 Last Year Jan. 1	This Year June 30
Old	$500	$ 500
Assessed Value		
$100,000 × 0.01 = $1,000		
Property Tax		
New		
Assessed value		
$300,000 × 0.01 × 0.5 = $3,000		
($1,500 for 6 months)		
Property tax (for only half a year)		$ 1,500
Since they paid $500		
Supplemental bill will be for $1,000		$ 1,000
Total paid for year		$ 1,500

Special Assessments

Cities, counties, and special districts may, by a two-thirds vote of the electors of the district, impose special taxes on such districts. These **special assessments** are levied for specified local improvements, such as streets, sewers, irrigation, drainage, flood control, and special lighting. This voter-approved bonded indebtedness varies from county to county and within each county.

Proposition 13

Proposition 13 was enacted in 1978. It states basically that newly acquired real estate or new construction will be assessed according to the fair market value (FMV) and taxed at a maximum tax rate of 1% (called the *basic* levy). In addition, the assessed values of properties acquired before 1978 will be reduced to the amount shown on the 1975 tax roll. Because different areas of a county have different bond issues or special assessments for that particular area, additional monies up to 1% are added to the basic levy (Proposition 13), causing the tax rate for these areas to range from 1% to more than 2%, depending on the area.

EXAMPLE   Your client, Mr. Bior, purchased a home this year for $300,000. Because of Proposition 13, the property taxes will be $3,000 ($300,000 × 0.01). Mr. Bior's area could have an additional assessment of 0.5%. Therefore, for his particular area, his property taxes could be $4,500 ($300,000 × 0.015).

Proposition 13 limits annual increases in assessed valuation to 2 percent.

One additional aspect of Proposition 13 is that the assessment value may be increased by up to 2% each year, as long as the Consumer Price Index (CPI) is not exceeded. The CPI measures inflation. This 2% increase in the assessed value represents the maximum amount the county assessor may increase the property's value each fiscal year.

EXAMPLE   Mr. Bior purchased a home for $300,000 and paid $4,500 ($300,000 × 0.015) in property taxes the first year. For the second year, the assessed value of the property will be $306,000 ($300,000 × 1.02). Presumably, the tax rate of 1.5% remains the same. Thus, Mr. Bior's property tax bill will be $4,590 ($306,000 × 0.015) for the second year. The property tax bill can be calculated in the same manner for each subsequent year of ownership.

One of the objectives of Proposition 13 is to keep property taxes as low as possible. According to Proposition 13, certain transfers of title (such as a sale) will cause a reassessment of the property, which will increase the property taxes. Transfers changing the form of ownership (changing from joint tenancy to community property), creation of revocable living trusts, and cosigners for loan qualification and transfers of a principal residence from parent to child or child to parent are exempt from reassessment.

Proposition 58

Proposition 58 allows transfers without reassessment to a spouse or children.

Proposition 58 provides that transfers of real property between spouses or domestic partners and transfers of the principal residence and the first $1,000,000 of other real property between parent and child are exempt from reassessment. The code defines a *child* as a natural child (any child born of the parents), any stepchild or spouse of that stepchild when the relationship of stepparent and stepchild exists, a son-in-law or daughter-in-

law of the parent(s), or a child who was adopted by the age of 18. (Note that Proposition 193 subsequently extended the exemption from reassessment to persons who inherit property from a grandparent when both parents of the grandchild are deceased. The grandchild can therefore keep the grand-parent's assessment for property taxes.)

To receive this exclusion, a claim must be filed with the county assessor. The claim must contain a written certification by the transferee made under penalty of perjury that the transferee is a parent or child of the trans-feror. This statement must also state whether the property is the transferor's principal residence. If the property is not the transferor's principal residence and the full cash value of the real property transferred (the taxable value on the roll just prior to the date of transfer) exceeds the allowable exclusion ($1,000,000), the eligible transferee must specify the amount and allocation of the exclusion on the claim. The $1,000,000 exemption can be doubled by both parents combining their $1,000,000 exemptions to transfer $2,000,000 in property to a child without an increase in tax assessment.

Proposition 60

Proposition 60 allows homeowners over 55 years of age to transfer their assessed valuation to a new residence in the same county.

The purpose of **Proposition 60** was to encourage older people to move to less-expensive housing without having to pay higher taxes because of reassessment on a new home. Proposition 60 provides that qualified homeowners aged 55 or over, as well as taxpayers who are severely and per-manently disabled, may transfer the current base-year value of their present principal residence to a replacement (that is, sell their old home and buy a new home), with the following conditions:

- Both properties must be in the same county.

- The transferor must be at least 55 years old as of the date of transfer (sale). (If married, only one spouse needs to be at least 55 but must reside in the residence; if co-owners, only one co-owner needs to be at least 55 and must reside in the residence.)

- The original residence must be eligible for a homeowner's exemption at the time of sale (transfer).

- The new home must be of equal or lesser value than the old residence.

Proposition 90

Proposition 90 extends Proposition 60 to participating counties.

Proposition 90 is an extension of Proposition 60. Proposition 60 limits the purchase of the new home to the same county. Proposition 90 allows the purchase of the new home in a different county in California. However, the county the homeowner is planning to move into may reject Proposition 90. The only counties that have accepted Proposition 90 are Alameda, Los Angeles, Orange, Santa Clara, San Diego, Riverside, San Bernardino, San Mateo, Eldorado and Ventura. To qualify, a homeowner must meet all the requirements for Proposition 60.

Change-in-Ownership Statement

Any person acquiring an interest in property subject to local taxation must notify the county assessor by filing a *change-in-ownership statement* within 45 days of the date of recording or, if the transfer is not recorded, within 45 days of the date of transfer. Failure to do so will result in a penalty. In practice, escrow typically handles this task.

Exemptions

Some of the numerous properties that are assessed are partially or wholly tax exempt. For example, many nonprofit charitable organizations, churches, all government, and several nonprofit educational institutions are entirely exempt. Other relief is available in various forms for homeowners, veterans, senior citizens, and renters.

Homeowner's exemption is $7,000 in valuation.

Homeowner's exemption. Each residential property that is owner-occupied is entitled to an annual tax **homeowner's exemption** of $7,000 from the "full cash value." The homeowner needs to apply only once for this homeowner's exemption if from year to year there is no change in the ownership of and residency on the property. A homeowner must have been the owner of record on or before January 1 (apply by February 15) and actually have occupied the property to claim this exemption for the upcoming tax year beginning July 1. A homeowner is allowed only one exemption at a time. Once this exemption has been filed, it remains in effect until terminated. The assessor must be notified of a termination, or an assessment plus 25% penalty may be made.

Veteran's exemption. California's war veterans may receive a $4,000 **veteran's exemption** on the full cash value of their homes. Because a person cannot take both the homeowner's and the veteran's exemptions, a person would not apply for the basic veteran's exemption if eligible for the higher homeowner's exemption. A totally disabled veteran or the veteran's surviving spouse may be eligible for a higher exemption. The exemption increases with inflation. In 2016, the exemption applies for disabled veterans on their personal residence property valued up to $191,266 and for disabled veterans who possess income limited to $57,258 or less.

Senior citizen's property tax postponement. Another form of relief is the *senior citizen's property tax postponement.* Homeowners who are at least 62 years old with household income of $35,500 or less and who have a 40% home equity may be eligible to have the State of California pay all or part of the real property tax on their home. Persons of any age who are blind or totally disabled and meet the income requirement are also eligible. The taxes are postponed and not repaid until the property is sold or the claimant no longer occupies the property. The program was discontinued because of budgetary problems but will be reinstated in 2016. Taxes are secured by a lien against the home in favor of the State of California.

Lower assessment for agriculture. The Urban Agricultural Incentive Zone Act provides tax incentives for urban farms from 0.1 acre to 3 acres. The Williamson Act allows local governments to tax land based upon agriculture use rather than land value if the owner contracts to keep it in agriculture use for a specified period.

Documentary transfer tax. Counties may adopt a documentary transfer tax of 55 cents for each $500 or fraction thereof of consideration. Cities in counties that have adopted the tax may add an additional tax. As an example, the City of Berkeley has a $15 per $1,000 property transfer tax, making the total city and county tax $16.10. Most cities with transfer taxes have set them at half the county rate or 55 cents per $500.

Parties can negotiate as to who pays the tax, but generally the seller pays in southern California and the buyer pays in northern California. In central California, it can be a combination of both.

The county recorder will not accept taxable conveyance for recording without a Documentary Transfer Tax Declaration. Documents subject to the tax must show the amount of tax paid on its face, it cannot be hidden.

INCOME TAXES

Real estate licensees should not advise a buyer or a seller as to income tax matters. Questions should be directed to an accountant or a tax attorney.

Today, income taxes play an important role in real estate owners' decisions, from buying or selling their personal residences to decisions involving the most exotic real investment properties. Because the tax laws are always changing, it is important for the real estate agent to stay abreast of them. Agents should advise buyers and sellers to seek professional advice from an accountant or tax attorney if the situation indicates a possible problem. Because of significant liability issues, the agent should refrain from providing tax advice.. We will discuss income taxes as they relate to business and investment property, as well as to a personal residence.

While rental income is taxed at regular tax rates, capital gains are taxed at preferential rates in order to encourage investments. A capital gain is the gain on the sale of a capital asset. Capital assets include real estate.

Capital Gains

Before the 1997 Taxpayer Relief Act, capital gains were taxed at a 28% maximum tax rate if the capital assets were held more than one year. The 1997 act reduced the rate to 20% for long-term capital gains.

The 2003 Jobs & Growth Tax Relief Reconciliation Act cut the long-term capital gains to a maximum of 15% for gains from the sale of assets held for more than 12 months. (Gains from the sale of assets held for one year or less are taxed as regular income.) Except for high-income taxpayers, who will have long-term capital gains taxed at 20%, the capital gains tax will remain at 15% for 2013.

In California, the state income tax on capital gains is the same as for other income (no special treatment).

For taxpayers in the 10% and 15% tax brackets, the long-term gain was cut to 5%. In 2008, the long-term capital gains tax for these lower income brackets was reduced to zero.

Under the American Taxpayer Relief Act of 2012, as of 2013, the capital gains rate has been permanently increased to 20% for single filers with incomes above $400,000 and married couples filing jointly with incomes exceeding $450,000.

In addition, there is a 3.8% Medicare surcharge applied to net investment income for taxpayers whose threshold income exceeds $200,000 for single filers and $250,000 for married couples filing jointly. Therefore, higher-income taxpayers could be paying 23.8% tax on capital gains, the 20% rate plus the surcharge.

Business and Investment Property

Property held for business and investment has some distinct differences in federal income tax treatment from property used as a personal residence. We will begin with the concept of depreciation.

Depreciation

The two most obvious and important characteristics of real estate investments are income and expenses. Real estate is one of those assets that benefit from a special accounting device for a special kind of expense called **depreciation**.

Land may not be depreciated.

Depreciation is a method of accounting for the wear that results from the use of a capital good. A capital good, such as a piece of equipment or a building, does not last forever. As it is used, it wears out or becomes obsolete; at some point, the owner must replace it or substantially repair it. Depreciation is used to reflect this replacement cost. The main reasons depreciation is allowed are to encourage investment in real estate and to reflect, in accounting terms, the real costs of property ownership. Only investment or income property may benefit from depreciation. Only improvements to land may be depreciated. Land is never depreciated.

For depreciation purposes, real estate can be divided into two categories:

1. Residential property

2. Nonresidential property

The depreciation period is 27½ years for residential property and 39 years for nonresidential property. Landing is never depreciated.

Residential property is where people live—for example, single-family residences, duplexes, triplexes, fourplexes, and multiunit apartments. A personal residence may not be depreciated. Nonresidential property is property that is not residential in nature—for example, industrial, commercial, office buildings, and other similar types of properties. Since January 1, 1987, all real property must use the straight-line method of depreciation where the value of the property is depreciated in equal annual amounts over the depreciable life of the property.

Generally, residential rental property must use a useful life of 27½ years and nonresidential property must use a useful life of 39 years. Either residential or nonresidential property may elect to use 40 years.

Basis

To explore the tax implications of investment properties, the agent must understand the concept of **basis** and know how to correctly compute the original basis, depreciable basis, and adjusted basis. The **original basis** (OB) is used to determine the depreciable basis and adjusted basis. The **depreciable basis** (DB) is used to determine the amount of allowable depreciation. The **adjusted basis** (AB), which changes as time progresses, is required to calculate the gain on the disposition of a property.

Original basis is purchase price plus buying expenses.

Original basis.   The *original basis* of a property is the sum of its *purchase price* (PP) and the *buying expenses* (BE) on acquisition (OB = PP + BE). When a client purchases a property, the escrow statement includes the sale price and a listing of other costs and expenses. These amounts can be classified into four basic groups:

1. Purchase price (PP)

2. Operating expenses (OE)

3. Buying expenses (BE) (nonrecurring closing costs associated with the purchase)

4. Nondeductible items (ND), such as impound accounts

Depreciable basis.   The *depreciable basis* is defined as the original basis minus the value of the land:

It is the cost basis of the improvements.

$$\text{depreciable basis} = \text{original basis} - \text{land value}$$

There are three methods for determining the value attributable to the land: the assessed value method, the appraisal method, and the contract method.

Assessed value method.   The county assessor's property tax statement now lists the full cash value of both the land and the improvements. The value of the improvements for depreciation purposes is thus the assessor's determination of the part of the purchase price that represents the value of the improvements.

Appraisal method.   The property owner may secure the services of a professional appraiser to appraise the building and the land. The appraisal method may give either a more or a less favorable ratio than the assessed value method. The taxpayer should compare the ratios from the two methods to verify which is more advantageous.

Contract method.   One other method of determining the percentage of improvements is the contract method. With this method, the buyer and the seller determine the relative values of the improvements and land and designate these values in the contract, deposit receipt, or escrow instructions. Note that the determination must be at arm's length and reasonable. Before using this method, we strongly suggest that the owner obtain professional help. The owner should be prepared to justify value in the event of an IRS audit.

Adjusted basis.   The *adjusted basis* of a property is the amount that the client has invested in the property for tax purposes. In other words, the adjusted basis is equal to original basis, plus capital improvements made, less all depreciation taken:

adjusted basis = original basis + improvements – depreciation

It is extremely important that the homeowner or investor understand the relationship between the basis and the final sales price of the property, because basis is the beginning point for calculating the amount of gain or loss on the sale. Calculation of the basis is affected by how the property originally was acquired.

- *Basis by purchase* is the price paid for the property, as described.

- *Basis by gift* is the donor's (gift giver's) adjusted basis plus the gift tax paid, not to exceed the fair market value at the time of the gift.

- *Basis by inheritance* generally is the fair market value at the time of the owner's death.

Computing gain.   The basis is the beginning point for computing the gain or the loss on the sale, but numerous adjustments to the basis always are made during the ownership period. Some of the costs that increase the basis are title insurance, appraisal fees, legal fees, cost of capital improvements, and sales costs on disposition. Accrued (past) depreciation is deducted from the basis. The result is the adjusted basis.

The gain (or loss) is the difference between the adjusted basis and the sales price. An example may clarify this:

$80,000	Purchase price
+ 800	Cost associated with purchase
+ 3,000	Capital improvements
$83,000	
– 12,500	Accumulated depreciation
$71,300	Adjusted cost basis
$100,000	Sales price
– 4,000	Sales cost
– 71,300	Adjusted cost basis
$24,700	Total gain

Computing Depreciation

To compute the depreciation, follow these six steps:

1. Compute the original basis

2. Determine allocation between land and building

3. Compute the depreciable basis

4. Determine whether the property is residential or nonresidential (If residential, you must use the 27½-year table for residential property. If nonresidential, you must use the 39-year table.)

5. Divide the depreciable basis by 27.5 (residential) or 39 (nonresidential).

6. This will give you the annual straight-line depreciation.

E X A M P L E

$\dfrac{\$100{,}000}{27.5 \text{ (residential)}}$ depreciable basis = $3,636.36 annual depreciation

$\dfrac{\$100{,}000}{39 \text{ (nonresidential)}}$ depreciable basis = $2,564.10 annual depreciation

For the year of the sale, the depreciation would be determined by multiplying the percentage shown in Figure 14.2 times the depreciable basis.

FIGURE 14.2:   Depreciation of Real Property

—General Depreciation System			Method: Straight Line				Recovery Period: 27.5 years				
The month in the 1st recovery year the property is placed in service:											
Year	1	2	3	4	5	6	7	8	9	10	11	12
1	3.485%	3.182%	2.879%	2.576%	2.273%	1.970%	1.667%	1.364%	1.061%	0.758%	0.455%	0.152%
2–27.5	3.636%	3.636%	3.636%	3.636%	3.636%	3.636%	3.636%	3.636%	3.636%	3.636%	3.636%	3.636%

The month in the 1st recovery year the property is placed in service:											
—General Depreciation System			Method: Straight Line				Recovery Period: 39 years				
1	2.461%	2.247%	2.033%	1.819%	1.605%	1.391%	1.177%	0.963%	0.749%	0.535%	0.321%	0.107%
2–39	2.564%	2.564%	2.564%	2.564%	2.564%	2.564%	2.564%	2.564%	2.564%	2.564%	2.564%	2.564%

Capital Gains Due to Depreciation

The capital gains tax rate for gains attributable to depreciation is the rate for regular income, with a maximum of 25%. As an example:

Property cost	$300,000
Depreciation taken	− 100,000
Adjusted cost basis	$200,000

If the property were sold at $500,000, there would be a $300,000 gain; $200,000 of the gain would be taxed at the 15% rate, but the $100,000 of the gain that is attributable to the depreciation that was taken would likely be taxed at the 25% rate.

Mortgage Foreclosure Debt Relief Act of 2007

A person relieved of debt receives an IRS Form 1099C from the lender. Because debt relief is considered taxable income, this amount is ordinarily taxed. However, the Mortgage Foreclosure Debt Relief Act of 2007 provides that debt forgiveness on the principal residence resulting from loan restructuring, short sale, or foreclosure be excluded from income. Although the act expired at the end of 2013, the IRS, as well as California, has ruled that a short sale of 1-4 residential units will not be taxed on unpaid debt.

1031 Exchanges

- The **1031 exchange** is part of federal tax law—Internal Revenue Code Section 1031 (the State of California has a similar code section). Section 1031 allows for exchange of personal property, as well as real property. Many of the concepts for 1031 **tax-deferred exchanges** come from court cases and IRS regulations and revenue rulings and from Section 1031.

Because of depreciation taken, as well as appreciation of property, many property owners do not want to sell and be required to pay the high taxes. An exchange allows the owner to delay taxes and thus have more money to invest in a new property. Because of refinancing, many owners are in a position where their equity is not sufficient to cover their tax liability. An exchange allows them to defer tax liability.

EXAMPLE   A woman owns a 10-unit apartment house she wants to dispose of, and she plans to buy a 20-unit apartment building. The 10-unit building would sell for $1,000,000, with selling costs of $50,000 and an adjusted basis of $275,000. Her taxable gain would be as follows:

Sales price	$1,000,000
Selling costs	− 50,000
Net sales price	$950,000
Adjusted basis	− 275,000
Taxable gain	$675,000

If the woman sells the property, she will have to pay federal and state taxes on the gain. She would be taxed at the 15% federal capital gains rate, possibly a 3.8% surcharge, a 25% rate for the portion of the gain attributable to depreciation, as well as having California regular tax liability on the gain. These taxes will have to be paid out of the proceeds from the sale. If she exchanged rather than sold, she would have her entire equity to invest in the new property and could defer any tax liability.

When a client becomes involved in a 1031 exchange, two questions must be answered:

1. Does the transaction qualify for a 1031 exchange?

2. What are the mathematics of the exchange?

    — How are equities balanced?

    — Who is giving or receiving boot? (Boot is unlike property that does not qualify for a tax-deferred exchange.)

    — Is the exchange partially or totally tax deferred, and what is the basis in the new property?

This section discusses the transactions that qualify for a 1031 tax-deferred exchange.

Tax-deferred exchanges involve at least three parties.   Most agents think of A exchanging with B. While this is essentially what happens, more often three parties are involved. The most widely used exchange is the *buy-sell exchange*, sometimes called a *three-corner exchange* or *three-legged exchange*. The three people involved are the exchanger (person wanting to exchange), the seller (a person who wants to sell property and doesn't want to retain any property), and the buyer (a person who wants the property of the exchanger).

In a three-legged exchange, the buyer offers to purchase the exchanger's property, but the buyer does not have any property to exchange. So the exchanger needs to find another property ("up-leg"), the property the exchanger wants to acquire. When the exchanger finds the up-leg, the buyer buys this property from the seller. Now the buyer has a property to exchange with the exchanger. Note that if the exchanger sold her property to the buyer and then bought the seller's property, this transaction would be a purchase and a sale. To satisfy the IRS, the buyer will buy the seller's property and exchange with the exchanger, and this is all done in escrow in a matter of minutes. A general rule of exchanging is that any person can be the center (hub) of the exchange except the person wanting the exchange. Sometimes this procedure is called the *flashing of mirrors*.

EXAMPLE Here is an example of improper escrow instructions. E wants to complete a 1031 tax-deferred exchange, and S and B agree to cooperate in completing the exchange. E will transfer his property to B, and S will transfer his property to E to complete the exchange. Here is the diagram for this transaction.

$$S \rightarrow E \rightarrow B$$

E is the hub of the exchange; hence, the exchange is invalid. If the escrow instructions were to read, "S will transfer his property to B, B will transfer S's property to E, and E will transfer his property to B," then the following diagram would apply:

$$E \overset{\leftarrow}{\rightarrow} B \leftarrow S$$

The latter would be a valid exchange.

When a client wants a 1031 tax-deferred listing, a statement that the client wants to make a 1031 tax-deferred exchange should be on the listing and in the multiple listing service. This statement helps convince the IRS that the client intends to make a 1031 exchange from the beginning of the transaction.

The buy-up rule. With the *buy-up rule*, to qualify for a totally tax-deferred exchange, the exchanger needs to trade up in value and put all equity dollars into the new property or properties.

Trade up means the new property must be equal to or greater in value than the old property. If the exchanger withdraws any cash, the cash withdrawn will be taxable. Withdrawing cash will not disallow the exchange—an exchange may be partial—but the client will not have a totally tax-deferred exchange.

EXAMPLE E wants to complete a 1031 tax-deferred exchange. The FMV of his property is $350,000; therefore, the property he is trading for must be valued at $350,000 or more. If E trades for property and $50,000 cash, he will pay taxes on $50,000 only, and the $300,000 he put into the new property will be deferred.

The entity rule. Three basic entities can hold property: individuals, partnerships, and corporations. The **entity rule** can be stated as follows: The way the exchanger holds property going into an exchange is the way the exchanger must hold the property coming out of the exchange. As an example, two partners cannot trade a partnership property for two properties, each of which would be separately owned by the partners.

The investment property rule. The **investment property rule** comes from Internal Revenue Code (IRC) Section 1031(a)(1):

> In general—no gain or loss shall be recognized on the exchange of property held for productive use in a trade or business or for investment if such property is exchanged solely for property of like kind which is to be held either for productive use in a trade or business or for investment.

Personal residence does not qualify for a tax deferred exchange.

Note: A personal residence is not held for productive use in a trade or business or for investment. Therefore, a person cannot have a tax-deferred exchange of his personal residence for business or investment property. (Like-kind property is discussed later in the unit.) By turning a personal residence into a rental or to a property for a trade or business, the former personal residence could be eligible for a tax deferred exchange.

Like-kind rule.   Exchanges of property must observe the **like-kind rule**. In exchanging, property is categorized as either personal or real property. Personal property and real property are not like kind.

For personal property, like-kind property must be exactly the same in character or have the same nature, and this sometimes is very difficult to determine.

For real property, like-kind property is simply any piece of real property exchanged for any other piece of real property:

What Is Real Property?

Real property includes the following:

- Vacant land (unimproved real estate)
- Improved real estate, such as farms, buildings, orchards, and so on
- Leases that have a remaining term at the time of the exchange of 30 years or more (the 30 years may include all options)
- Mineral and water rights (if they are considered real property by the state, they are included)

Source: Critchton 122 F.2d 181 (1941), Rules, 55-749 and 68-3331

Therefore, the general rule for real property is that any piece of real property may be exchanged for any other piece of real property (like-for-like), except for inventory and personal residences.

The no-choice rule.   If an exchange qualifies as an exchange, it must be treated as an exchange. If the real estate transaction was structured as an exchange, the gain must be deferred (postponed).

The no-loss rule.   In conjunction with the no-choice rule is a rule called the **no-loss rule**. If a real estate transaction qualifies as an exchange, a loss cannot be recognized. Losses must be deferred along with gains. The no-loss rule comes from IRC Section 1031(a)(1).

Money control.   An *accommodating party* is a third party who has control of buyers' money in a delayed exchange.

> To be a valid 1031 exchange, the exchanger cannot have control of the buyer's money.

At no time can the exchanger have control of the buyer's money. This point was emphasized by the *June P. Carlton* case. Carlton owned ranch land and wished to structure a 1031 exchange. The agreement was to sell property to General Development Corporation (GDC) if a suitable replacement property (up-leg) could be found. Two suitable parcels of land were found by Carlton: property belonging to Lyons and Fernandez (sellers). Carlton gave an option to GDC, and GDC advanced $50,000 to Carlton. Carlton thought that this would be a 1031 exchange.

The IRS argued, and the court agreed, that Carlton had sold the ranch land to General Development Corporation. Because Carlton had received $50,000 in her hands, the $50,000 did not go directly to the sellers, Lyons and Fernandez. One of the essences of an exchange is the transferring of property, and the mark of a sale is the receipt of cash. This case points out the extreme importance of proper procedure: the exchanger can never receive cash or even the right to cash. —*June P. Carlton v. Comm.* 385 F.2d 238 (5th Cir., 1967)

Delayed exchange. IRC Section 1031(a)(3) allows a delayed exchange with the following characteristics:

> For a deferred exchange, the property must be identified within 45 days and the exchange completed within 180 days of transfer of the exchanged property.

REQUIREMENT THAT PROPERTY BE IDENTIFIED WITHIN 45 DAYS AND THAT EXCHANGE BE COMPLETED NOT MORE THAN 180 DAYS AFTER TRANSFER OF EXCHANGED PROPERTY—For purposes of this subsection, any property received by the taxpayer shall be treated as property which is not like-kind property if—

(A)   such property is not identified as property to be received in the exchange on or before the day which is 45 days after the date on which the taxpayer transfers the property relinquished in the exchange, or

(B)   such property is received after the earlier of—

   (i)   the day which is 180 days after the date on which the tax-payer transfers the property relinquished in the exchange, or

   (ii)   the due date (determined with regard to extension) for the transferor's return of the tax imposed by this chapter for the taxable year in which the transfer of the relinquished property occurs.

Properties purchased and closed within the 45-day period qualify as an identification.

Reverse exchange.   In a **reverse exchange**, the replacement property is acquired before the property owner gives up her property. An exchange accommodation titleholder takes title to the property the exchanger wishes to acquire and holds the title until the sale of the exchange property can be arranged. This type of exchange removes the problem of acquiring property within a prescribed time period of the delayed exchange. However, the sale must be within 180 days.

WEB LINK

For information on reverse exchange, as well as other forms of exchanges, visit the Federation of Exchange Accommodators website at www.1031.org.

Boot.   Unlike property in an exchange is called **boot**. In many exchanges, some property will be given in an exchange that is boot. Boot is taxable to the person receiving it. It is important to understand that the property needs to qualify as like kind only to the person seeking the tax-deferred exchange.

Boot is defined as all other unlike properties: cash, paper (trust deeds or notes), and personal properties (cars, boats, planes, paintings, jewels, etc.).

> Boot is cash received, unlike property or debt relief.

Boot may be classified as cash boot or mortgage boot. *Cash boot* is a result of the balancing of equities, which must be done in every exchange. *Mortgage boot* is the difference between the loans on the conveyed property and the loans on the acquired property. This is also called *debt relief*. If the client assumes a mortgage larger than the one that he conveys, then he has paid mortgage boot. However, if he assumes a mortgage that is less than the one that he conveys, then he has received mortgage boot (debt relief).

E X A M P L E   If I traded my real property for your real property and $20,000, the $20,000 I received would be taxable boot. If you gave me your new car as part of the trade for my property, then the value of the car would be taxable boot.

Assume we traded properties without boot but your property was free and clear of debt while my property was mortgaged and you assumed the mortgage. I would be taxed on the amount of the mortgage (debt relief).

Installment Sales

By using an **installment sale**, the investor can spread the tax gain on a sale over two or more years. The following guidelines concern the use of the installment method of reporting deferred-payment sales:

> In an installment sale, the gain is taxed in the year it is received.

- The total tax to be paid in any one year may be reduced by spreading the payment amount, and thus the gain, over two or more tax years.

- The seller pays tax in future years with cheaper, inflated dollars.

- The seller does not pay the entire tax until after receiving the entire amount of the purchase price. A provision of the previous law stating that no more than 30% of the sales could be received in the taxable year of the sale to qualify for installment sales treatment has been eliminated.

- The installment sales method is automatic unless the taxpayer elects not to have the installment sale treatment apply.

Sale-Leaseback

Buyers and sellers can derive tax advantages through an arrangement in which property is sold with provisions for the seller to continue occupancy as a lessee. This form of transaction is called a **sale-leaseback**, *purchase-lease, sale-lease, lease-purchase,* or *leaseback.*

> In a sale-leaseback, the seller benefits from capital being freed and rent that is a fully tax-deductible expense.

With a sale-leaseback, seller/lessees gain the advantages of getting property exactly suited to their needs without tying up working capital in fixed assets. Often, more capital can be raised this way than by borrowing. In addition, because leases are not considered long-term liabilities, rent is totally tax deductible. Frequently, writing off total lease payments is better than depreciation, for the land portion of property cannot be depreciated. If a property has a significant mortgage, a sale-leaseback would remove debt from a balance sheet, which would present a positive impression to lenders and purchasers of the corporate stock.

Often, only the land is sold and leased back because rent on land is a deductible expense, and improvements can be written off with depreciation deductions.

For companies working under government contracts that pay cost plus a fixed fee, rent is an allowable expense item, but mortgage payments are not. This is why many aircraft, electronics, and other defense plants are leased rather than owned.

Buyer/lessors gain the advantage of obtaining a long-term carefree investment and appreciation in the value of the property, as well as having the convenience of a built-in tenant. Usually, the yield on a sale-leaseback is higher than on a mortgage.

The lease payments will pay off the original investment, and the lessor still will have title to the property. The investment will not be paid off prematurely (as mortgages often are through refinancing), so the investor will not have to go out seeking another good investment to replace the one prematurely paid off. In addition, the lease terms often give the lessor a claim against other assets of the lessee in the event of a default, which is better security protection than a trust deed affords.

Principal Residence

Real estate that constitutes a homeowner's personal residence receives special tax treatment. The term *personal residence* is generally understood to refer to the taxpayer's **primary personal residence**, the dwelling in which a taxpayer lives and which the taxpayer occupies most of the time. A taxpayer may have only one principal residence at a time, and it may be as follows:

- Single-family house

- Houseboat

- Mobile home

- Motor home

- Trailer

- Condominium

- Cooperative housing

If you live in one unit of a multiple-unit dwelling, that unit will be considered your principal residence.

Primary or secondary residence. The taxpayer's primary residence is the place occupied more often than any other. All other residences are termed *secondary residences*. One secondary residence will receive favorable income tax treatment, but unlike a primary residence, a secondary residence does not qualify for universal exclusion treatment.

Land. The term *residence* includes not only the improvements but also the land [Rev. Rul. 56 420, 1956 2 (CD 519)]. However, vacant land cannot be considered a personal residence. When a principal residence is located on a large tract of land, the question arises as to just how much of the land is included with the principal residence. There is no clear-cut answer to this question, but the courts have made the determination based on the use and the intent of the taxpayer rather than on the amount of land involved.

> The universal exclusion requires two years' occupancy and can be taken every two years.

Universal exclusion for gain on sale of principal residence. A seller of any age who has owned and used the home as a principal residence for at least two years of the five years before the sale can exclude from income up to $250,000 of gain ($500,000 for joint filers meeting conditions). In general, the exclusion can only be used once every two years.

Married couples filing jointly in the year of sale may exclude up to $500,000 of home-sale gain if either spouse owned the home for at least two of the five years before the sale. Both spouses must have used the home as a principal residence for at least two of the five years before the sale.

One spouse's inability to use the exclusion because of the once-every-two-years rule won't disqualify the other spouse from claiming the exclusion. However, the other spouse's exclusion cannot exceed $250,000.

E X A M P L E Mary sells her principal residence in December 2010 at a $100,000 gain. She is single at that time, and qualifies for and claims the home sale exclusion. She marries Abel in May 2011 and moves into the home that has been his principal residence for the 20 years of his bachelorhood. If Abel sells the home the following July, up to $250,000 of his profit is tax free.

The two-year occupancy need not be continuous. For example, a person could have occupied the property as a principal residence for 6 months and then rented it for a year but later moved back for an 18-month occupancy.

If the total occupancy is 24 months during a five-year period, then the occupancy requirement will have been fully met.

California has adopted the federal universal exclusion of $250,000/$500,000. If a sale gain meets the federal criteria for exclusion, it would also be excluded from California income taxation.

Tax Benefits

Taxpayers are eligible for certain income tax write-offs while they own their homes. The general rule for income tax purposes is that ownership transfers when the title is transferred (a deed given) or when the buyer is given the rights of possession (the benefits and burdens of ownership), whichever occurs first. To be eligible for these tax deductions, a taxpayer must be the legal owner or equitable owner of the home.

Note: When the property is purchased on a land contract, the owner has equitable title. According to tax law, a buyer who has possession of the property (equity) owns the property and receives all the tax deductions of the property.

During ownership, owners taking itemized deductions may write off real estate taxes and mortgage interest in the year they are paid. Note that paying monies into an impound account is not the same as paying them to the agency to which they are owed. Monies paid into an impound account are not deductible. Only the money paid from the impound account to the proper authority can be deducted.

| Home interest and property taxes are deductible. |

Home interest. Interest on a primary residence and second home will be treated as home mortgage interest on mortgage amounts of up to $1 million, whereas interest on additional secondary homes will be treated as personal interest. Personal interest does not qualify as a deductible expense.

For homes that qualify as either a primary home or a second home, the interest is called *home mortgage interest* or *qualified residence interest*. There are two types of home interest: acquisition indebtedness and home equity indebtedness (or equity indebtedness).

Acquisition indebtedness interest. Taxpayers may deduct interest on home acquisition debt of $1,000,000 or less (first and second home).

EXAMPLE A man purchased a home for $10,000,000 with a $9,000,000 purchase money loan. He is limited in his interest deductions to the interest on $1,000,000 only.

Home equity debt interest. Taxpayers may deduct interest on up to $100,000 of home equity debt (money borrowed on property to use for other purposes).

Home Improvements

Systematically recording amounts spent for **home improvements** and retaining any and all receipts are of great importance to the homeowner. Unfortunately, they are often neglected. Many homeowners are completely unaware of the ultimate tax implications of the home improvements or capital improvements that are added to their properties through the years. These improvements may be added to the homeowner's basis, making the adjusted basis greater and reducing the gain at the time of sale. The adjusted basis (AB) is equal to the original basis (OB) plus home improvements (HI):

$$AB = OB + HI$$

adjusted basis = original basis + home improvements

There is a great deal of misunderstanding about what items are classified as home improvements. The IRS defines improvements differently for homes than it does for rental property. Examples of home improvements include the following:

- Electrical wiring (new, replacement, rearrangement)

- Floors

- Heating units

- Partitions (including removal)

- Pipes and drainage (including replacement)

- Roof (new or reshingling over old shingles)

- Walls (plastering, strengthening)

- Room additions

- Patios

- Pools

- Fencing

- Landscaping (trees, shrubbery, grass seed, etc.)

- Sprinkler systems

Maintenance items are not home improvements. Some examples are as follows:

- Painting

- Papering

- Carpeting

- Drapes

- Furniture

- Replacement of built-in appliances (stoves, ovens, dishwashers, etc.)

Relief for "forced" sales.   A relief provision may apply to some taxpayers who sell their principal residence but fail to meet the once-every-two-years rule for use of the exclusion. If the taxpayer's failure to meet the rule occurs because the home must be sold due to a change in the place of employment, health status, or—to the extent provided by regulations—other unforeseen circumstances, then the taxpayer may be entitled to a partial exclusion. Under these circumstances, the excludable portion of the gain that would have been tax-free had the requirements been met is computed proportionately.

EXAMPLE   A woman sells her principal residence because she has a new job in another city. On the date of the sale, she has used and owned her principal residence for the past 18 months. She has never excluded gain from another home sale. If she had used her principal residence for two years, the entire amount of the gain ($250,000) would be excluded. Although the woman fails to meet the use and ownership requirements for the full exclusion, because the sale is forced by employment, she is entitled to a partial exclusion. The amount of gain excluded by this seller cannot exceed the amount determined by the following computation (computed using months; see the observation above): the woman occupied her home for 18 of the 24 months required for the full exclusion. Therefore, she is entitled to a 75% exclusion from her gain (18/24 = 0.75). As a result, the woman may exclude $187,500 (250,000 × 0.75 = $187,500) of her gain on the sale of her principal residence.

Capital loss.   A taxpayer may use a capital loss to offset a capital gain in the year of the loss. If a taxpayer lost $100,000 on one capital sale but made $100,000 on another capital sale in the same year, there would be no capital gain tax. If, however, the taxpayer made $50,000 on the profitable sale, the taxpayer would have a $50,000 loss carryover. The taxpayer can take $3,000 of the carryover loss and use it as a deduction against income each year. To take advantage of a capital loss, a taxpayer should consider selling another capital asset where a profit would be made in the same year as the property loss.

FIRPTA

Before 1985, a foreigner (a person who is neither a U.S. citizen nor a U.S. resident alien) could purchase property in this country and later sell it, and then move back to her homeland and not pay income taxes on the sale of the property. Because it is very difficult, if not impossible, to collect delinquent taxes from such an individual, the U.S. Congress passed the **Foreign Investment in Real Property Tax Act (FIRPTA)**. The State of California passed a similar law. To distinguish between federal and California law, the federal law will be called *FED-FIRPTA* and the state law *CAL-FIRPTA*.

Federal Withholding

FED-FIRPTA generally requires that a buyer withhold estimated taxes equal to 10% of the sale price in transactions involving real property in the United States sold or exchanged by a foreign person. In addition, CAL-FIRPTA requires that a buyer withhold estimated taxes equal to one-third of the amount required to be withheld under FED-FIRPTA (3-1/3% of the sales price). The 10% estimated withholding must be reported and paid to the Internal Revenue Service within 10 days after the close of escrow. If the buyer fails to withhold the estimated taxes, and the seller fails to pay taxes on the sale, the buyer is subject to a penalty equal to 10% of the purchase price or the seller's actual tax liability plus interest and penalties, whichever is less.

For personal residences, FED-FIRPTA applies only to sales prices of $300,000 or more. When a buyer signs a certification (Figure 14.3) stating that he plans to use the property as a personal residence and the purchase price is less than $300,000, the buyer is relieved of withholding estimated taxes.

All other property—investment, rental, commercial, land, and so forth—requires withholding when a foreign person sells the property. If a foreign person owns a five-unit apartment building and sells it for $600,000, $60,000 will have to be withheld for the federal government and $20,000 for the State of California.

If more than one person owns the property and some are U.S. citizens and some are foreign, the amount of withholding must be prorated on the basis of the capital invested. If a married couple own property and one spouse is a citizen and the other is not, withholding is prorated 50/50.

Withholding under section 1.1445(a) may be reduced or eliminated pursuant to a withholding certificate issued by the Internal Revenue Service in accordance with the rules of this section. (It usually takes six to eight weeks to receive the certificate from the IRS.)

EXAMPLE A foreign person is selling her personal residence to buy a new home of more value. Assuming that this transaction is not taxable, does the buyer of the old property need to withhold?

Yes. If the foreign person does not want the buyer to withhold, she will have to file for a withholding certificate from the IRS.

How is the buyer to know if the seller is a foreign person? The burden falls on the buyer, and there are only a few measures that will relieve the buyer of the obligation to withhold. In one such case, the seller must provide the buyer with an affidavit of nonforeign status. The seller also must provide a U.S. taxpayer identification number and state, under penalty of perjury, that he is not a foreign person.

As previously stated, California has adopted its own law covering real property sales by foreign persons who are defined as nonresidents of California.

California Withholding

As of 2003, buyers of property, other than the seller's personal residence, must withhold 31/3% of the net proceeds of the sale and remit them to the Franchise Tax Board at close of escrow. Besides the seller's personal residence, the following are other exclusions:

- Property sold for less than $100,000

- Property sold at a loss

- Property involved in a tax-deferred exchange

- Involuntary conversion (foreclosure sale)

TAX SHELTER

Because depreciation is shown as an expense for income tax purposes, it can reduce the tax liability of a real estate investor and could result in a paper loss, even though cash receipts exceed cash expenses.

Taxpayers can use real estate operating losses (passive losses) to offset real estate income without limit. Real estate losses also can be used, with limitations, to offset active income such as wages.

FIGURE 14.3: **Seller's Federal Residency Declarations**

FEDERAL RESIDENCY DECLARATIONS
Citizen Status (Internal Revenue Code §1445)

Prepared by: Agent_____   **Phone**_____
Broker_____   **Email**_____

NOTE: If the declarations differ for individual sellers, then each seller must fill out a separate form.

DATE: _____, 20_____, at _____, California.

Items left blank or unchecked are not applicable.

FACTS:

1. This declaration complies with Section 1445 of the United States Internal Revenue Code regarding Seller's status as a citizen or resident of the United States or otherwise, and is for reliance by Broker and any buyer.

   1.1 Seller _____
       U.S. Tax Identification Number (or Social Security Number) _____
   1.2 Seller _____
       U.S. Tax Identification Number (or Social Security Number) _____

2. Regarding the proposed sale of real estate referrred to as _____
   _____.

SELLER'S DECLARATIONS:

3. Seller hereby declares:

   3.1 ☐ I am a citizen of the United States of America;
   3.2 ☐ I am a resident alien of the United States of America; my resident status is established by the following:

   a. ☐ I have been declared a permanent legal resident of the United States by the U.S. Immigration and Naturalization Service. Resident Alien registration number
      _____, or;

   b. ☐ I have resided at least 31 days in the United States during the current calendar year, and my days of residence in the United States over the last three years are as follows:

Current calendar year . . . . _____ X 1	=	_____
Last calendar year . . . . _____ X 0.334	=	0.00
Second preceding year . . . . _____ X 0.167	=	0.00
TOTAL DAYS	=	0.00

   Since the total days equals or exceeds 183 days, I meet the substantial presence test of Internal Revenue Code §7701(b)(3).

   Exclusions:
   Residency does not include days during which Seller:
   - remained in the U.S. due to a medical condition which arose while he was visiting;
   - was in transit between two points outside the U.S.;
   - worked for an agency of a foreign government;
   - was a teacher, trainee, or student; or participated as a professional athlete

4. ☐ I am neither a United States citizen nor a resident alien as defined in item 3, above; and

   4.1 Unless I obtain a "qualifying statement" [IRC §1445(b)(4)], or other special permission from the Internal Revenue Service, I authorize Buyer of the above-referenced real estate to deduct and withhold 10% of the sales price for the federal government. I further authorize Escrow-holder to deduct these amounts from funds due me at close of escrow, and to deposit it as a tax deposit in an authorized commercial bank.

5. I consent to the reliance on this declaration of the Brokers, Agents, Escrow-holder, and Buyer in any transaction regarding this real estate.

6. **Note:** This transaction is exempt from IRC §1445 withholding if the sales price is $300,000 or less and Buyer will use the real estate as his residence.

BUYER'S ACKNOWLEDGMENT:

7. I have read and received a copy of this Seller's Residency Declaration.

8. ☐ I hereby declare I will use the real estate as my residence. If the final sales price is $300,000 or less, I consent to reliance on this declaration by Brokers, Agents, Escrow-holder and the nonresident alien Seller.

I declare under penalty of perjury that the foregoing is true and correct.	**I declare under penalty of perjury that the foregoing is true and correct.**
Date: _____, 20_____	Date: _____, 20_____
Seller: _____	Buyer: _____
Seller: _____	Buyer: _____

Taxpayers with an adjusted gross income of less than $100,000 can use real estate losses (which are considered passive losses) to shelter up to $25,000 of their active income. Taxpayers whose adjusted gross income is between $100,000 and $150,000 lose $1 of this $25,000 maximum for each $2 that their adjusted gross income exceeds $100,000.

Taxpayers with adjusted gross income less than $100,000 can shelter up to $25,000 of active income with passive losses.

If investors do not actively manage their property (active management includes hiring a property manager), then the taxpayer is precluded from sheltering active income. Because investors have no management responsibilities in investments such as limited partnerships, the investor cannot use such losses to shelter active income.

Real estate professionals can use passive losses from investment property to offset other income without any limitations if they meet specific criteria, which include devoting at least 750 hours during the tax year to property management activities.

Estate Tax

Death is a tax shelter in that it avoids capital gains tax on the increased value of assets of the deceased. However, the assets may be subject to an estate tax. For persons dying in 2015, the estate tax exclusion for an individual is $5.43 million (adjusted annually for inflation). The maximum estate tax rate is 40%.

Inherited property receives a stepped-up basis, meaning that the property is valued at the time of decedent's death. This means the asset is shielded from any capital gains based on appreciation in value that occurred before to the decedent's death.

If a decedent gifted property prior to death, then the recipient would retain the cost basis of the grantor and a subsequent sale could subject the grantee to substantial capital gain taxation.

California no longer has an estate tax, although several states do tax estates. Differences in estate taxation, as well as income tax rates, have caused some wealthy individuals to make economic decisions as to where their residence should be.

Federal Gift Tax

The federal gift tax is taxed to the donor. The annual exemption is $14,000 per donee. A married couple with three children could give each child $14,000 each year, making total gifts of $84,000 each year that are tax exempt.

PROBATE AND LIVING TRUSTS

Probate is the court-approved procedure to pay off the just debts of a deceased person and to distribute the assets according to a will or intestate succession. There are three reasons for probate avoidance:

- The cost of probate

- Reduction of possible estate taxation

- Time

In California, a $1,000,000 estate could be subject to a $23,000 attorney fee plus $23,000 for an executor fee, for a total of $46,000. There are also finding fees of approximately $400, as well as appraisal costs.

Probate may be avoided by use of a joint tenancy, community property, or a revocable living trust.

With a *living trust*, trustors transfer their property to their trust but retain absolute control and serve as trustee. Upon death, a successor trustee distributes the estate without probate expenses.

For larger estates, it is possible for married couples to double the size of their exemption. Assume a couple has an estate worth over $5,430,000 and the current exemption from estate taxation is $5,430,000. They could have two trusts, known as an A-B trust. If one spouse dies, the spouse could give $5,430,000, the exempt amount, to the trust for the benefit of the successors. The balance of the trust would go to the A portion of the trust for the benefit of the other spouse. Since estate taxes are not levied on gifts to a spouse, the first death is not subject to estate taxation. When the surviving spouse dies, that estate goes to the B trust, but the one portion that is subject to estate taxation would be the portion in excess of $5,000,000. The B trust, which is distributed to the successors (heirs), therefore, will have received a $10,860,000 exemption from estate taxation rather than $5,430,000.

SUMMARY

Real estate taxes are ad valorem taxes. Property is reassessed when sold, and property is taxed for the basic levy at a maximum rate of 1% of the fair market value (Proposition 13). The tax rate cannot increase more than 2% per year. Additional special assessments can be added, up to 1% of the fair market value. The homeowner's exemption is $7,000 from the assessed valuation. There is also a veteran's exemption of $4,000. In 2015, the exemption for a totally disabled veteran was $126,380.

Tax transfers between family members may be exempt from reassessment. For taxpayers older than 55, a sale and repurchase of a principal residence within the same county may allow the taxpayer to keep the old assessed valuation if the new purchase is at the same price as or less than the sales price of the old residence. For residents over 55 years of age, the transfer of assessed value can extend to other counties if the other county has agreed to it (Proposition 90).

For some senior citizens (low income or disabled), a postponement of taxes is possible until the claimant no longer occupies the property.

Capital gains are sale gains on the sale of capital assets. A long-term gain, over 12 months, is currently taxed at a maximum of 15%, except the rate is 20% for high-income taxpayers. There is also a 3.8% Medicare surcharge for high-income taxpayers.

Depreciation is a noncash expense for tax purposes that applies to improvements to income, business, and investment property. It is a return on the investment. Any gain on sale is taxed from the basis adjusted by adding buying expenses and capital improvements to the purchase price, then deducting the accumulated depreciation (adjusted cost basis). For residential property, a 27½-year life is used for depreciation purposes. For nonresidential property, a 39-year life is used.

A taxpayer can defer gains on the sale of business or investment property by use of a 1031 exchange. The property must be like-for-like (real property for real property), and the taxpayer would be taxed only on boot received. Boot is unlike property received, as well as debt relief. A delayed tax-deferred exchange is possible if the taxpayer identifies the property within 45 days of a transfer and closes escrow within 180 days of the transfer.

Installment sales allow a taxpayer to spread a gain over the years in which the gain is received. This could mean a lower tax rate.

A sale-leaseback allows a seller to gain operating capital, reduce debt, and have the 100% tax deduction of business rent.

Residential property owners have a tax advantage for interest payments on $1,000,000 in acquisition indebtedness (for primary and secondary residences), as well as up to $100,000 in equity indebtedness.

A homeowner's gain on the sale of a residence is determined by deducting the adjusted cost basis (cost plus improvements) and the selling expenses from the selling price. The Taxpayer Relief Act of 1997 made some significant changes to tax law regarding gains on the sale of real estate. These changes include a once-every-two-year exclusion from taxation for gains on the sale of a principal residence that has been occupied by the sellers for at least two years during the prior five-year period. This exclusion from taxation is as follows:

- Married couples, $500,000

- Single persons, $250,000

When a property is sold by a foreign national, it is the buyer's responsibility to withhold 10% of the price for federal income taxes and 31/3% for state income taxes, unless the transaction is exempt from such withholding. The state withholding applies to all nonresidents of California.

Depreciation is a paper expense that can be used to shelter up to $25,000 in active income from taxation (The maximum amount is reduced by $1 for every $2 in income over $100,000).

Death results in a stepped-up cost basis that is based on value at the time of the decedent's death. There is a federal estate tax but no California estate tax. By using a living trust, a couple can double the amount of their estate tax exemption.

CLASS DISCUSSION TOPICS

1. A buyer of an apartment building has $60,000 annual rent, total cash expenses of $52,000, and depreciation of $9,000. What are the investor's benefits, if any?

2. A person renting a home pays $1,200 per month in rent. The owner offers it for sale to the tenant at a price of $240,000. The tenant is offered a $200,000, 7%, 30-year loan; PITI payments will come to $1,650 per month.

3. Although the tenant has $40,000 for the down payment, she concludes that she cannot afford the house and will continue to rent it. Discuss the wisdom of her decision. What assumptions would be necessary to arrive at any conclusion?

4. Diagram a three-party exchange.

5. Compute the adjusted basis when the original basis was $137,500, improvements to the property totaled $31,650, and depreciation taken was $11,436.

6. Bring to class one current-events article dealing with some aspect of real estate practice for class discussion.

UNIT 14 QUIZ

1. The MOST difficult tax to avoid is the
   a. sales tax.
   b. real property tax.
   c. income tax.
   d. estate tax.

2. The months of November, December, February, and April relate to
   a. real property taxes.
   b. income taxes.
   c. estate taxes.
   d. sales taxes.

3. What did Proposition 13 provide for?
   a. It set a maximum tax rate.
   b. It set assessments for property acquired before 1978 back to the value on the 1975 tax roll.
   c. The tax can be increased 2% per year.
   d. All of these.

4. The proposition that allows a tax assessment for certain homeowners to be transferred from one county to another is Proposition
   a. 13.
   b. 58.
   c. 60.
   d. 90.

5. The homeowner's property tax exemption is
   a. $50,000 for a single person.
   b. $4,000 from assessed valuation.
   c. $7,000 from assessed valuation.
   d. the first $100,000 of assessed valuation.

6. Depreciation for a residential property uses
   a. the straight-line method.
   b. a 27½-year table.
   c. a 39-year table.
   d. both a and b.

7. To have a tax-deferred delayed exchange, which of the following is required?
   a. The exchange property must be identified within 45 days after the taxpayer relinquishes his property.
   b. The sale must be completed within 180 days after the taxpayer relinquishes his property.
   c. Both of these.
   d. Neither of these.

8. To have a 1031 tax-deferred exchange, you need all of the following *EXCEPT*
   a. like-for-like properties.
   b. to receive boot rather than pay it.
   c. a trade of investment real property for investment real property.
   d. to hold property after the exchange in the same manner as you held property going into the exchange.

9. Albert wants to exchange property with Baker. Which would be boot to Albert in the exchange?
   a. Cash given by Albert to balance equities
   b. Cash received by Albert to balance equities
   c. Acceptance of a greater debt by Albert
   d. Both a and c

10. A homeowner can receive preferential tax treatment by
    a. an interest deduction.
    b. use of the universal exclusion.
    c. a property tax deduction.
    d. all of these.

15

PROPERTY MANAGEMENT AND LEASING

LEARNING OBJECTIVES

When you have completed this unit, you will be able to

- describe the variety of positions, duties, and responsibilities available within the property management field;

- explain the different types of properties managed and how each affects the manager's activities;

- name the types of leases and their provisions;

- explain landlord and tenant responsibility; and

- describe how a tenant can be evicted.

KEY TERMS

Accredited Management Organization	estate at will	periodic tenancy
	estate for years	Protecting Tenants at
	exculpatory clause	Foreclosure Act of
Accredited Resident Manager	gross lease	2009
	habitability	recapture clause
assignment	Help Families Save	rent schedule
Certified Property Manager	Their Home Act	resident manager
	holdover clause	scheduled rent
condominium association	Institute of Real Estate Management	security deposit
		step-up lease
management	late charge	sublease
Costa-Hawkins Rental Housing Act	management agreement	30-day notice
		three-day notice
effective rent	net lease	trust ledger
estate at sufferance	percentage lease	unlawful detainer

THE PROPERTY MANAGEMENT FIELD

Property management is not a new field of specialization. In biblical days, owners employed "overseers" who supervised the running of estates. In colonial America, English companies that had land charters, such as the Virginia Company, employed managers to run their operations.

Most properties were managed by owners. The growth of the modern property management profession was facilitated by two factors:

1. The invention of the electric elevator and the use of structural steel, which allowed for highrise construction, starting in the late 1800s. Highrise construction allows a property owner to have more tenants with a smaller construction footprint. The large number of tenants creates a greater responsibility for a landlord. These huge structures generally were owned by large companies or groups of investors, who had to hire managers for their operations.

2. The Great Depression of the 1930s, which resulted in lenders accumulating vast inventories of property because of foreclosures. To maximize the income and protect the property, these lenders required property managers.

Professionalism

The number of people involved in property management increased rapidly. However, because many of these managers lacked reasonable qualifications due to limited knowledge and abilities, there were many failures within the property management field.

In 1933, to slow down this failure trend and to improve the professional standing of this management group, approximately 100 companies met and formed the **Institute of Real Estate Management (IREM)**, a subdivision of the National Association of REALTORS® (NAR). These companies certified that they would

- refrain from commingling their clients' funds with personal funds,

- bond all employees handling client funds, and

- disclose all fees, commissions, or other payments received as a result of activity relating to the client's property.

This move improved the situation, but after several years it became apparent that the companies were not meeting the standards set, mainly because of constant personnel changes.

In 1938, the IREM changed its policy and developed the designation **Certified Property Manager (CPM)** to certify individual managers rather than the companies that employed them. The concept has been successful. IREM's certification requirements are designed to ensure that managers have the general business and industry-specific experience necessary to maintain high standards within the profession. To earn the CPM designation, an individual must

- actively support the institute's rules and regulations;

- demonstrate honesty, integrity, and the ability to manage real estate, including at least three years' experience in a responsible real estate management position; and

- be a member of a local real estate board and a member of the National Association of REALTORS®.

IREM also has the designation **Accredited Resident Manager (ARM)** for residential managers. **Accredited Management Organization (AMO)** is a designation given by IREM to a company. To receive this designation, a company must

- have at least one CPM in charge,

- have property management as a primary activity,

- follow minimum standards and the rules of IREM, and

- renew its accreditation yearly.

There are several other professional property management organizations. They include the Real Estate Management Broker's Institute of the National Association of Real Estate Brokers, the Apartment Owners and Managers Association of America, the Building Owners and Managers Association International (BOMA), and the National Society of Professional Resident Managers. These organizations produce publications, conduct seminars, and award professional designations.

Kinds of Property Managers

There are three basic kinds of managers: licensee/property managers, individual property managers, and resident managers.

> A person working under direct supervision of a licensed property manager need not be licensed.

Licensee/property manager. A licensee/property manager is a licensee of a real estate office or agency that manages a number of properties for various owners. Such a manager may be a member of the firm who spends full time in management, may be self-employed as a managing agent, or may be one of several managers in the management department of a large real estate company. Persons working under the direct supervision of a licensed property manager need not be licensed to show property, accept preprinted rental applications, provide information on rental terms, and accept signed leases and deposits.

Individual property manager. An *individual property manager* manages a single property for the owner and may or may not possess a real estate license. This person usually is employed on a straight salary basis.

Resident manager.   A **resident manager**, as the title implies, lives on the property and may be employed by the owner or by a managing agent. The resident manager does not require a real estate license. A resident manager usually is qualified for this assignment by previous management experience or by special training. Personality is critical to success; specifically, the manager should exhibit the following:

- The merchandising ability to contact, show, and close the rental of a unit

- A high degree of self-confidence and willingness to take charge

- Accuracy in handling money, checks, bank deposits, and other bookkeeping duties

- Awareness of and sensitivity to the events occurring on and around the property

- Orderliness and legibility in keeping records and meticulousness in filing, cataloging, and making reports

- Computer skills, such as the ability to access and interpret data

- The ability to select residents on the basis of economic capability and credit references

- The diligence to maintain the property (The amount of maintenance will vary with the size of the property and the policies of management)

State law requires a resident manager for property containing 16 or more units and specifies that the resident manager must be a "responsible person." Mobile home parks having more than 50 units must have a resident manager.

Functions of a Property Manager

The author of the following statement is unknown, but the words give a splendid overview of the making of a property manager:

> *The past is his experience, and with its valuable ramifications, he is helped immeasurably to mold the plans for his future. During his years of experience, he has built and sold houses, appraised property, dealt in long-term commercial and industrial leases, made many complicated and intricate transactions, bought and sold hotels—in short, has had a long experience with the public, including businessmen, husbands and wives, doctors and lawyers, engineers and financiers, yes, with gamblers, beggars and thieves, mothers-in-law, fanatics, the feebleminded, strong and weak characters of every type and description, politicians too, and with this experience has automatically been turned out a well-rounded, socially conscious, alert, and aggressive person— in short, a skillful businessman, and when he has reached this point, he has automatically qualified for the job of property management.*

Depending on the complexity of the property, the property manager's duties and responsibilities are many and varied. Inherent in these duties is the dual role of an administrator for the owner and an advocate for the resident.

The property manager's responsibility is to understand and communicate with both parties. The astute property manager is in an ideal position to both represent the owner and work with the residents with procedures that are fair and equitable. The manager should recognize that the owner wants a fair return on investment and that the resident wants decent housing or space that is properly maintained.

Administrator for the owner.   As the administrator for the owner, the property manager must recognize that the owner is interested primarily in the following:

- The highest return from the property, realizing its highest and best use

- The enhancement or preservation of the physical value of the property

Specific duties of a property manager.   Under the property management system, the owner is relieved of all executive functions as well as of all details connected with the operation or physical upkeep of the property.

A conscientious manager realizes the following:

- Renters need to know what is expected of them and what they can expect from the owner. (This should be stated in writing.)

- Residents' questions should be handled properly and promptly.

- If any request is denied, the manager should state why and avoid pointless arguing.

- The owner, manager, and employees should guard against the attitude that all tenants are unreasonable. However, it would be disastrous to adopt the principle that the customer is always right. The resident is, of course, always entitled to fair and sympathetic treatment.

- The property manager must make certain that tenants' and prospective tenants' legal rights are protected.

As an agent, the property manager must show good faith and loyalty to her principal (the owner); perform her duties with skill, care, and due diligence; fully disclose all pertinent facts; avoid commingling funds; and refrain from personal profits without the principal's full knowledge and consent.

State-defined responsibilities.   In addition to the general responsibilities described here, the California Bureau of Real Estate has prepared a list of specific duties:

- Establish the rental schedule that will bring the highest yield consistent with good economics

- Merchandise the space and collect the rents

- Create and supervise maintenance schedules and repairs

- Supervise all purchasing

- Develop a policy for tenant-resident relations

- Develop employee policies and supervise employees' operations

- Maintain proper records and make regular reports to the owner

- Qualify and investigate prospective tenants' credit

- Prepare and execute leases

- Prepare decorating specifications and secure estimates

- Hire, instruct, and maintain satisfactory personnel to staff the building(s)

- Audit and pay bills

- Advertise and publicize vacancies through selected media and broker lists

- Plan alterations and modernizing programs

- Inspect vacant space frequently

- Keep abreast of economic conditions and posted competitive market conditions

- Pay insurance premiums and taxes and recommend tax appeals when warranted

Basic Responsibilities

The principal functions of a property manager can be summarized as seven basic responsibilities:

1. Marketing space by advertising and securing desirable tenants

2. Collecting rents

3. Handling tenant complaints and physically caring for the premises

4. Purchasing supplies and equipment and paying for repairs

5. Hiring needed employees and maintaining good public relations

6. Keeping proper records and preparing required reports

7. Making recommendations to the owner on matters of improvements, changes in use and insurance coverage, and operational changes requiring owner approval

Establishing rent schedules.   Rent schedules are the rents to be asked for and set forth in the lease. **Effective rent** is often less than **scheduled rent** if inducements are provided to the tenant, such as one month's free rent for a one-year lease. If the scheduled rent were $1,200 a month, the effective rent in this case would only be $1,100 per month ($1,200 × 11 months = $13,200 for the year or $1,100 per month). *Rent levels* usually are determined on the premise of scarcity and comparability of values in the area. How much rent is charged will affect the cost and time required to rent the unit, the length of each tenant's stay, decorating costs between tenants, and overall vacancy rate. To set up proper **rent schedules**, the manager must make a skilled and thorough analysis of the neighborhood. This analysis will include but not be limited to the following:

- The character of the immediate neighborhood

- The economic level and size of families

- Trends in population growth and occupants per unit

- Directional growth of the community and expansion and growth of local industries

- Availability of transportation, recreation, shopping, churches, and schools

- The condition of the housing market versus population growth trends

- Current area vacancy factors

- Similarly desirable rental units currently available

The objective of the analysis is to set up a rental schedule commensurate with the findings.

WEB LINK

@

There are internet sites that provide data on comparable properties. They are very helpful in setting rent schedules. Two such websites are www.rentometer.com and www.zilpy.com.

The objective of good property management is to achieve the combination of rent and vacancy that provides the owner with the greatest net. Conducting surveys and establishing rental schedules are very important. Statistics show that uncollected rent is worse than a vacancy, because the property suffers wear and tear from the occupant and the opportunity to place a desirable tenant in the unit is lost. In establishing rent levels, the property manager should realize that a vacant unit is not in competition with units already rented. The only competition is with other vacant units.

KNOWING THE LAW

The property manager must know the legal rights of tenants and legal procedures to take in notices and evictions. The manager must be aware of federal and state antidiscrimination statutes. The manager must also understand what actions could be construed as sexual harassment. Knowledge of local and state building health and safety codes, as well as any rent control restrictions, is also necessary as they relate to management duties.

The Occupational Safety and Health Act (OSHA) is important to property managers who are hiring seven or more employees. The law requires compliance with safety standards, recordkeeping, and reporting. It covers equipment condition, maintenance, and safety precautions. The maximum penalty OSHA can assess for a single violation is $7,000. The amount of $70,000 can be assessed for repeated or willful violations. California has passed its own Cal OSHA provisions.

TYPES OF PROPERTY MANAGED

Properties requiring management include office buildings, apartment buildings and other residential properties, commercial structures, shopping centers, distribution centers, public buildings, recreation centers, hotels, motels, industrial facilities, restaurants, and theaters. Recently, other properties have joined the list and are rapidly gaining in importance and popularity. These include the following:

- Condominium associations
- Industrial parks
- Mobile home parks
- Miniwarehouses
- Marinas
- Airports

A few of these are described in more detail in this section.

Professional Qualifications of a Property Manager

What kind of person is qualified to be not only a human relations specialist but also a detail manager? Such a person must be able to play the following roles:

■ Merchandising specialist. The property manager must be able to advertise and to sell prospective tenants on the merits of a building.

■ Leasing expert. Being well informed on all types of leases assists a manager in determining the most beneficial lease for a particular client.

■ Accounting specialist. The law requires that certain records be kept and reports made.

■ Maintenance supervisor. Preventive and corrective maintenance will prevent expensive repairs at some future date.

■ Purchasing supervisor. The manager must keep up with all current technological advances in building in order to be able to recommend needed replacements for obsolete installations.

■ Credit specialist. Credit ratings are extremely important. Knowing whether a tenant can live up to the terms of a lease is vital.

■ Insurance adviser. Understanding the various types of policies available and the extent of coverage can save both the owner and the tenant time and money.

■ Tax interpreter. A manager must be well versed in property taxes and their effect on the property being managed. The manager should be cognizant of the relationship of depreciation to the income and profit of the property.

■ Psychology expert. This capacity is crucial to day-to-day communication.

■ Budget manager. A property manager must be able to maintain and operate within the budget established for the property.

Residential Properties

Residential properties are by far the most numerous of the properties subject to professional management. There are approximately 133 million occupied housing units in the United States (Census Bureau 2013 estimate).

The housing market is stratified, meaning that the marketplace behaves differently based on price range. There may be a high vacancy rate at one rental range and a severe housing shortage at another range. Nevertheless, a general nationwide housing shortage has resulted in a rapid rise in rental rates. Three million new housing starts each year would be required merely to replace end-of-the-line units that should be demolished.

Residential property managers should be familiar with local rent control ordinances to make certain that rents and rent increases charged are not in violation of the law. Rent control restrictions vary significantly by community.

Allowable rental increases are also subject to different restrictions. Under the **Costa-Hawkins Rental Housing Act**, landlords who are subject to rent control are free to establish new base rents for new tenants, as well as for sublessees and assignees when landlord consent is required for the sublease or assignment.

Residential managers also must fully understand their obligations under state and federal fair housing legislation, as well as under the Real Estate Commissioner's Regulations dealing with fair housing. (See Unit 2 for specific requirements.)

Residential managers of lower-priced units should be familiar with Section 8 housing. This is a rental program under which all or part of a low-income tenant's rent is paid through the county. County administrators must inspect the property for eligibility, and tenants must meet stated criteria and be approved by the county.

Condominiums. Individual ownership of condominiums generally involves property management. Condominiums and cooperatives are similar from the standpoint of management duties.

A growing segment in the property management field is **condominium association management**. This type of management is often heavy on the accounting aspects. The duties of the condominium association manager likely would include the following:

- Collecting fees and assessments from members

- Issuing financial statements to the association

- Ensuring that homeowners associations provide members an annual financial statement and the Assessment and Reserve Funding Disclosure Summary form, which spells out current assessments, additional scheduled assessments reserve account balance, and obligations

- Contracting for or hiring for all maintenance and repairs

- Enforcing covenants, conditions, and restrictions (CC&Rs)

- Handling tenant interpersonal disputes and/or complaints

- Filing tax returns (if applicable), as well as handling workers' compensation, unemployment compensation, insurance, and so forth

- Seeing that the property is insured as to damage and owner liability

- Making suggestions to the board of directors

- Attending directors' meetings

In condominium associations, property managers don't make policy; they merely carry out policy as directed by the board of directors and the covenants, conditions, and restrictions in each deed. A condominium association manager must understand that different board members have different personal agendas. For example, some members may be primarily focused on security, while others are interested in keeping assessments to a minimum. A property manager must avoid becoming involved in the politics of the homeowners association and must focus on the instructions of the board. However, the manager does have a duty to make informed recommendations to the board.

A number of computer programs designed for condominium association management provide financial records, spreadsheets, work orders, and even much of the routine correspondence of the association.

Mobile home parks.   Management of a mobile home park is a specialty field involving the following:

- Park development

- Public amenities

- Enforcement of park rules

- Approval of lease assignments on sale of units

The tenant in a mobile home park is entitled to a 12-month lease on request.

In parks where the individual lots are owned by the mobile-unit owners, the mobile home park management duties become similar to the duties of a condominium association manager. However, the park manager should be aware that the laws governing evictions from rental space parks are much more restrictive for park owners than for other residential landlords. The park manager must give tenants a 12-month lease on request at current rent and must furnish tenants with an annual copy of the current California Civil Code covering mobile home parks, so that tenants understand their rights and responsibilities. The management of a mobile home park cannot require a homeowner to use a specific broker when replacing a unit in a rental park.

Multifamily units. Residential property bought for investment is the most common professionally managed property. Statistics indicate that multiple-family units account for approximately 30% of residential housing in the United States.

The more problems a property has, the more it needs professional management. Because properties that have had a troubled history can take a great deal of a property manager's time, the manager's fee scale is generally higher for such properties.

Public housing. Ownership of public housing is important to property management. The largest single landlord in the United States is the collective 3,300 public housing authorities. More than 1.2 million units are controlled by public housing authorities. A great many property managers are employed by federal, state, and local housing authorities.

Traditionally, management of public housing has almost exclusively concentrated on the physical and financial aspects of the projects. Management is beginning to realize the importance of social aspects of public housing management.

Single-family homes. Besides homes purchased for rental, there are many instances requiring single-family home management for absentee owners. In resort areas, many owners use property management to care for their properties and, in some cases, to handle short-term rentals. Property management might also be required for property in probate and for lenders who have foreclosed. Generally, because single-family units require more management time per unit than multifamily units, management charges tend to reflect this greater effort.

Office Buildings

Office buildings are the major commercial property. Office space requirements, as well as available inventory, are directly related to the local economy. The larger users of office space, such as banks, savings associations, and insurance companies, often build for their own use but also provide a large amount of excess of space for leasing purposes.

Overbuilding of office structures intensified the need for professional management because owners didn't want to give any advantage to other owners: Competition for lessees can be heated.

Most areas of California now have a glut of office space. In such areas, concessions are necessary to attract tenants. In some instances, property managers agree to assume a tenant's current lease to encourage the tenant to take a larger space under a long-term lease. The agent then has the job of marketing the "trade-in" space.

Specialized offices, such as medical or legal offices, have special problems.

Merchandising office space.   Rental or lease of office space can be tied to the following criteria:

- Appearance of surroundings

- Transportation facilities

- Prestige and image of area

- Proximity to clients

- Building appearance

- Lobby appearance

- Elevator appearance and condition

- Corridor appearance

- Office interiors

- Tenant services offered

- Management

- Other tenants

Advertising is an essential part of conducting an aggressive leasing campaign for office space. Such publicity ideas as the following can be most helpful:

- Groundbreaking ceremonies

- Signs

- Brochures

- Newspaper ads

- Website (referenced in ads and brochures)

- Mailing lists of professional groups, including attorneys, doctors, and CPAs

- Personal solicitation

- Use of a model office

- Communication with other leasing agents

- Making technical data readily available, including floor plans, available space, and space arrangements

Maintenance. The manager of an office building must handle maintenance or service problems unique to this type of operation. This job includes such activities as the following:

- Servicing all operating equipment and public facilities, such as lobbies, lights, and washrooms

- Maintaining elevators, which are indispensable in a highrise (usually involves an elevator maintenance contract)

- Cleaning (usually done at night)

- Other routine maintenance, including window cleaning, waste removal, light bulb replacement, heating, ventilation, and air-conditioning

- Preparing and updating a maintenance operations manual that shows a list of all equipment with the vital information concerning each piece of equipment

- Compliance with health and fire codes, as well as the Americans with Disabilities Act.

Protection.   Protection of the premises is a management function. It includes such vital items as these:

- Key control

- Alarm systems

- Lighting

- Security guard employment

- Fire-prevention techniques

Retail Space

Management of retail space requires many of the same skills and concerns as office management. In multiunit commercial properties, the manager should consider the effect a prospective tenant will have on the business of other tenants. Managers will often seek out particular tenants or businesses in order to contribute to the overall operation of the property.

Industrial Management

Industrial management is rather specialized because of the skills required. Industrial managers must have knowledge in many areas, including the following:

- Fire-suppression systems (sprinklers) and water capacity and pressure for various uses

- Floor and ceiling load capacities

- Hazardous and toxic substances (use and storage), as well as underground tanks

- Air- and water-quality control

- Loading dock requirements

- Electrical capacity and three-phase wiring

- Reading blueprints for modification

- Specific zoning regarding uses allowed

- Special insurance requirements

- Security and security systems

- Large cooling, heating, and ventilation systems

Industrial managers might manage specific property or an entire industrial park. The industrial property manager's duties primarily relate to renting, but they also involve common area maintenance and protecting the property and the owners from liability.

SECURITY

Security is of prime importance to lessors and lessees for all types of property. It applies to personal security of tenants, employees, and guests as well as security for the lessee's property.

Because no property can be absolutely safe, a property manager should never indicate to tenants that a property is safe or secure. This could be seen by the court as a warranty as to safety. Nevertheless, your best efforts should be used to make the premises as safe as is reasonably possible.

A property manager should consider, as applicable to a property, the following:

- *Emergency evacuation plan*—In light of 9/11, such a plan is extremely important for large structures. Evacuation plans for earthquakes are also very important in California.

- *Properly marked exits*—This may require going beyond bare legal requirements.

- *Appropriate landscaping*—Remove any trees or shrubbery around entrances and walkways that could conceal a person.

- *Exterior lighting*—Take special care in entryways, walkways, and parking areas. Perimeter areas could be lighted by motion sensor lighting. Having well-lit property is a cost-effective way to reduce crime.

- *Interior lighting*—Light all hallways and public areas (use fluorescent and LED bulbs that are unlikely to be removed). Battery-operated emergency lighting that is kept charged by the electrical service but goes on when service is cut should be considered.

- *Circuit breaker box*—This should be locked or in a locked room.

- *Exterior and unit doors*—All should be solid core rather than hollow core. Steel doors should be considered. Apartment doors should have peepholes and a security chain with screws at least 2½ inches long.

- *Door locks*—Do not use key-in-knob locks; they are easy to pry off. Do not use mortised locks because they create a very weak spot in the door. Use a dead bolt and a strike plate held in place by screws three inches or longer. The more tumblers a lock has, the harder it is to pick.

- *Window locks*—Use security latches on windows. Tenants must be able to easily open windows in an emergency.

These are just a few of the security measures you should consider. Hiring security consultants who can analyze your property could be dollars well spent.

Liability of Manager

Managers have been held liable for failure to comply with health and safety ordinances, as well as for building code violations. If funds are not available for compliance, it would be in the manager's best interest to give up management.

Managing for Foreign Owners

Property managers who remit rent payments to a foreign owner must withhold 30%, unless exempt by tax treaty. Failure to comply can result in manager liability for 30% of gross rent plus penalties and interest.

MANAGEMENT AGREEMENT

It makes no difference whether the property involved is an office building, a residential property, or a shopping center; the responsibilities assumed by the manager are so important that they warrant a written agreement. The **management agreement** formalizes the relationship between the owner and the manager and points out the rights, and duties of each party. The forms used for this purpose may vary, but regardless of the property involved, certain basic points must be included:

- Identification of the parties

- Sufficient identification of the property

- The contract period, including the beginning and the termination dates

- Management's and owner's responsibilities

- Management fees—the amount, when it is to be paid, and the manner of payment

- Provision for management accounting, including records to be kept and reports to be made

Management fees can cover one or a combination of the following:

- Flat fees

- Minimum fee

- Minimum plus percentage of the gross (very common compensation)

- Leasing fee (flat fee or a percentage of the lease rental; generally a higher percentage for the first year and a lower percentage for subsequent years)

- Additional fees or percentages for special services, such as drafting leases, supervising repairs, remodeling, handling evictions, overseeing contracts, and collecting delinquent accounts of former tenants

In addition, management contracts provide for reimbursement of costs, which may or may not include such items as advertising. Generally, the more management problems a property has, the higher the management fee percentage. Larger properties tend to be managed at lower percentages.

Figure 15.1 is the Property Management Agreement Form 590 prepared by RPI — Realty Publications, Inc., This excellent form is self-explanatory.

> Management fees are usually a percentage of the gross, not the net.

FIGURE 15.1:   **Property Management Agreement**

PROPERTY MANAGEMENT AGREEMENT

NOTE: This form is used by a licensed broker or their agent when entering into an employment to act as a property manager for an owner's rental property, to document the employment and set forth the rights, responsibilities and expectations of the property manager and the landlord, including authorized activities, performance standards and expense limitations.

DATE: _____, 20_____, at _____, California.
Items left blank or unchecked are not applicable.

1. RETAINER PERIOD:

1.1   Owner hereby retains and grants Broker the exclusive right to lease, rent, operate and maintain the property as Property Manager, commencing _____, 20_____, and continuing for one year and thereafter until terminated.

2. RECEIPT OF SECURITY DEPOSITS:

2.1   Owner hands $_____ to Broker for deposit into the trust account towards Owner's security deposit obligation to Tenants.

3. RECEIPT OF CASH RESERVE:

3.1   Owner hands $_____ to Broker as a deposit towards Owner's obligation under the agreement.

3.2   Owner to maintain a minimum cash reserve, in addition to any security deposits, in the amount of $_____. On request from Broker, Owner will advance additional funds to maintain this minimum balance.

3.3   The cash reserve may be used to pay costs diligently incurred by Broker or due Broker in fulfilling Broker's obligations.

4. BROKERAGE FEE:

NOTICE: The amount or rate of real estate fees is not fixed by law. They are set by each Broker individually and are negotiable between Owner and Broker.

4.1   Broker compensation to be:

a.   _____% of all rents collected and deposited by Broker during the month, except for any first month's rent for which a Broker fee is paid under §4.1 b as follows,

b.   _____% of the first month's rent collected and deposited under ☐ rental agreements, and ☐ leases,

c.   All sums remaining from credit check fees in excess of credit report expenses, and

d.   ☐ Late payment charges and returned check charges paid by a tenant.

5. TRUST ACCOUNT:

5.1   Broker will place Owner's deposit for costs and security deposits into
☐ Broker's trust account, or ☐ separate trust account for Owner, maintained with
_____ at their _____ branch

a.   This account will be ☐ non-interest bearing, or ☐ interest bearing.

5.2   All funds received by Broker for the account of Owner will be placed in the trust account.

5.3   Amounts to pay and satisfy the obligations incurred by Broker may be disbursed from the account after payment is due.

5.4   On termination of this agreement, Broker will return to Owner all remaining trust funds belonging to Owner.

6. PERIODIC ACCOUNTING:

6.1   Within ten days after each calendar ☐ month, or ☐ quarter, and on termination of this agreement, Broker will deliver to Owner a Statement of Account for all receipts and expenditures, together with a check to Owner for any funds in excess of minimum reserves under §3.2.

6.2   Amounts to compensate Broker under §4 may be withdrawn from the trust account.

6.3   Each Statement of Account delivered by Broker will include no less than the following information for the period:

a.   Amount of security deposits received or refunded.

b.   Amount of rent or receipts, itemized by unit.

c.   An itemized description of disbursements.

d.   End of month balance of the income, expense and security deposit trust accounts.

6.4   ☐ Broker to reserve and disburse from the trust account any property and employee taxes, special assessments, insurance premiums, loan payments and other payments required to be made by the owner.

6.5   Advertising costs incurred to locate new tenants to be paid ☐ by Owner, or ☐ by Broker.

FIGURE 15.1 (continue):   **Property Management Agreement**

7. TITLE CONDITION AND LOANS:

7.1   The property is referred to as _____
_____
_____
_____.

7.2   Owner's interest in the property is:
    ☐ Fee simple, ☐ _____

7.3   Loan payments are to be timely disbursed by Broker to:

    a.   Lender _____
         Address _____
_____
_____
         Phone   _____
         Payment of $_____, due on the _____ day and delinquent on the _____ day of each month.

    b.   Lender _____
         Address _____
_____
_____
         Phone   _____
         Payment of $_____, due on the _____ day and delinquent on the _____ day of each month.

8. BROKER AGREES TO:

8.1   Use diligence in the performance of this employment.

8.2   Continuously maintain a California real estate broker's license.

8.3   Collect all rents, security deposits or other charges and expenses due Owner, and timely refund tenants' security deposits, less allowable deductions and including any interest due tenants.

8.4   Prepare and place advertisements for prospective tenants.

8.5   Show property to prospective tenants, obtain credit reports and confirm creditworthiness of tenants before executing rental or lease agreements.

8.6   Execute, renegotiate or cancel rental or lease agreements with tenants.
    No lease to exceed _____ months.

8.7   Serve rent collection and other notices, file unlawful detainer and money damage actions, recover possession of premises or settle with delinquent tenants.

8.8   Inspect the property monthly and each unit when tenants vacate.

8.9   Maintain and periodically confirm the inventory of personal property on premises.

8.10   Evaluate rental and lease agreements periodically for income, expense and provision updates.

8.11   Contract for utilities, services and equipment to operate and maintain the property and safeguard the tenants.

8.12   Contract for any repairs, maintenance or improvements needed to rent or lease the property.
    a.   Owner to approve all repairs in excess of $_____.

8.13   Obligate Owner to no unauthorized agreement or liability.

8.14   Protect and enhance the goodwill of Owner's rental business and keep confidential and secure any knowledge of Owner's business activities acquired during this employment.

8.15   Hire, supervise and discharge ☐ a resident manager, and ☐ an assistant resident manager.

8.16   Inspect and take any action necessary to comply with federal, state, county or municipal safety and building codes affecting the property.

8.17   Notify Owner of any potential hazards to the tenants or property, and Owner to respond within seven (7) days. Should an emergency situation arise placing the tenants or property in jeopardy, Broker may immediately remedy the situation without further authority from Owner.

9. OWNER AGREES TO:

9.1   Hand Broker all keys and entry codes to the property, and copies of rental and lease agreements with existing tenants.

9.2   Hand Broker (if Broker is to disburse) loan payment coupons/envelopes, property tax bills, insurance premium billings and _____.

9.3   Indemnify Broker for the expense of any legal action arising out of Broker's proper performance of this agreement.

FIGURE 15.1 (continue):   Property Management Agreement

9.4   Provide public liability, property damage and workers' compensation insurance sufficient in amount to protect Broker and Owner, naming Broker as an additional insured.

9.5   Owner's insurance agent is _____

10.   TERMINATION:

10.1   This agreement will continue until terminated by mutual written agreement or until either party, for legally justifiable cause, serves a written Notice of Termination. [See **RPI** Form 590-2]

10.2   Owner may terminate this agreement at any time during the initial one-year term by paying Broker a fee equal to three times Broker's management fee earned during the month preceding termination.

10.3   On termination, Owner will assume the obligation of any contract entered into by Broker under this agreement.

11.   GENERAL PROVISIONS:

11.1   Broker is authorized to place a For Rent/Lease sign on the property and publish and disseminate property information.

11.2   Owner authorizes Broker to cooperate with other brokers and divide with them any compensation due.

11.3   The authorized agent-for-service is ☐ Broker, ☐ Owner, ☐ _____

11.4   Broker may have or will contract to represent Owners of comparable properties or represent Tenants seeking comparable properties during the retainer period. Thus, a conflict of interest exists to the extent Broker's time is required to fulfill the fiduciary duty owed to others he now does or will represent.

11.5   Before any party to this agreement files an action on a dispute arising out of this agreement which remains unresolved after 30 days of informal negotiations, the parties agree to enter into non-binding mediation administered by a neutral dispute resolution organization and undertake a good faith effort during mediation to settle the dispute.

11.6   The prevailing party in any action on a dispute will be entitled to attorney fees and costs, unless they file an action without first offering to enter into mediation to resolve the dispute.

11.7   If this agreement authorizes Property Manager to execute and negotiate lease terms greater than one year, Landlord acknowledges receipt of the Agency Law Disclosure. [See **RPI** Form 305]

11.8   ☐ See attached addendum(s) for additional terms. [See **RPI** Form 250]

11.9   _____
_____
_____

Broker:

I agree to render services on the terms stated above.

☐ See attached Signature Page Addendum. [**RPI** Form 251]

Date: _____, 20____

Broker's Name: _____

Broker's CalBRE #: _____

Agent: _____

Agent's CalBRE #: _____

Signature: _____

Address: _____
_____

Phone: _____ Cell: _____

Email: _____

Owner:

I agree to employ Broker on the terms stated above.

☐ See attached Signature Page Addendum. [**RPI** Form 251]

Date: _____, 20____

Owner: _____

Signature: _____

Owner: _____

Signature: _____

Address: _____
_____

Phone: _____ Cell: _____

Email: _____

FORM 590   11-15   ©2015 **RPI — Realty Publications, Inc.**, P.O. BOX 5707, RIVERSIDE, CA 92517

ACCOUNTING RECORDS

Although the number of bookkeeping records needed depends on the type of property managed and the volume of business involved, the selection and maintenance of an adequate trust fund accounting system is essential in property management because of the fiduciary nature of the business. The responsibility for trust fund records is placed with the property management broker. The trust fund requirements set forth in Unit 3 are applicable to property managers and must be complied with. It is further recommended that an outside accountant be employed to review and audit the accounting system.

Reasons for Accounting Records

There are a number of basic reasons for keeping orderly records in property management:

- The law states that a separate record must be kept for each managed property.

- The fiduciary relationship between the owner and the manager dictates full disclosure.

- Contractual relationships call for an accounting of all funds.

- Records are needed for income tax purposes.

- It may be necessary to satisfy third parties who have an interest in the property.

- Accurate records serve as controls in evaluating income and expenses, analyzing costs, and preparing budgets.

- Records provide the broker with a source of information when inquiries are made or problems arise.

In the days before computers, property managers relied on file systems for each property, with file cards for each tenant. The only time the manager really understood the operating conditions of a property was when the monthly account was tabulated to show income received and disbursements. Computer programs now provide property managers with instant access to property data on one property, on a group of properties, or even on one tenant. These programs have reduced the paperwork of property management.

Computer programs for property management range in cost from only a few hundred dollars to around $10,000. Most computer companies offer free demonstration disks so you can see what a program can do. The following are just a few of the firms offering programs that are likely to meet your property management needs:

- Yardi   www.yardi.com
- AppFolio   www.appfolio.com
- Buildium   www.buildium.com

WEB LINK

@

An unusual program is the Yield Star Price Optimizer (www.realpage .com/yieldstar/price-optimizer-difference/). It allows property managers to update pricing based on real-time information as to leasing and availability of units. According to Camden Property Trust, one of the nation's largest residential REITs, it allows higher rents faster than competitors in a rising market and faster adjustments in a down market.

Today, to operate a property management firm without computer assistance would be like running a brokerage office without the internet. It is possible, but it is not very efficient.

Some Property Management Tasks That Can Be Performed by Computer

- Trust journals
- Security deposit registries
- Monthly, quarterly, semiannual, and annual financial reports
- Accounts payable ledger
- Accounts receivable ledger
- Operating account deposits
- Tenant registries
- Vacancies
- Rental analysis
- Rental summary
- Rent increase calendar
- Automatic billing
- Late charges
- Late-charge reports
- Late letters
- Notices and unlawful detainer
- Market rent variances
- Rent receipts
- Property fees
- Payment histories
- Owner's checks and/or billing
- Owner's ledger

- Owner's income/loss
- Bad-check report
- Tenant data
- Check registry
- Check writing
- Insurance register
- Lease expiration register
- Mortgage check register
- Comparative lease analysis
- Inactive property files
- Repair orders
- Lease abstracts
- Vendor lists
- Vendor history (by vendor)
- Insurance expiration data
- Tickler files (scheduling payments)
- Association fees
- Owner's 1099s
- Hold-back (reserves) register
- Checkbook reconciliation
- Budgets (monthly and annual)
- Maintenance history
- Repetitive correspondence

Trust Ledger

Section 2830 of the commissioner's regulations requires that a **trust ledger** for property management accounts be established. As rents come in, they are posted to the owner's account. Also recorded in the trust ledger is the money paid out on behalf of the owner. This includes any repair costs, payments of encumbrances, and payments for utilities or commissions. These expenses are charged against the income of the property, and the manager sends a statement to the owner at the end of each month. Again, trust records today generally are kept using computer software.

IRS Reporting

Any person who receives rental income must provide IRS Form 1099 for all service providers of $600 or more.

LEASEHOLD ESTATES

One of the responsibilities of a property manager involves leasing the property or acting as a consultant when drawing up the terms of the lease.

A leasehold estate arises when an owner or a property manager acting as the owner's agent grants a tenant the right to occupy the owner's property for a specified period for a consideration. The *lessor* is the owner and the *lessee* is the tenant.

Basic Types of Leasehold Estates

There are four basic types of leasehold estates, based on the length and nature of their duration: the estate for years, the estate from period to period, the estate at sufferance, and the estate at will.

> An estate for years has a definite termination date.

Estate for years.   An estate that continues for a definite fixed period of time is an **estate for years**. The lease may be for any specified length of time, even for less than a year, measured in days, weeks, or months. Professional property managers will generally insist on an estate for years.

Estate from period to period.   An estate from period to period is commonly called a **periodic tenancy**. The lease continues from period to period (either year to year, month to month, or week to week), as designated. The most common periodic tenancy is month to month.

A periodic tenancy can be ended by a notice for the length of the rent-paying period but for no more than 30 days (60 days for mobile homes). However, if a residential tenant has lived on the premises for at least 12 months, a landlord must provide a 60-day notice to terminate the tenancy.

If a tenant is under a rental agreement with a government agency, in certain Section 8 housing situations, a 90-day notice must be given to terminate.

The lessor can change lease terms on a periodic tenancy by providing a tenant a 30-day written notice; however, if the rent is increased more than 10% during a 12-month period, then a 60-day notice is required.

Estate at sufferance. An **estate at sufferance** is created when a tenant obtains possession of property legally but then remains on the property without the owner's consent, such as a holdover tenant after the expiration of the leasehold interest. A tenant at sufferance would need to be evicted from the property and cannot simply be ejected as a trespasser would. If the lessor accepts rent, the estate then becomes a periodic tenancy based on the rent-paying period.

Estate at will. An **estate at will** has no specified time limit. Possession is given with permission, but no agreement is made as to rent. As an example, possession is given to a prospective tenant before the lease terms are agreed to. In California, such an estate requires a **30-day notice** to terminate.

Types of Leases

The three basic lease forms the property manager will be expected to work with are the gross lease, the net lease, and the percentage lease.

Gross lease. Under a **gross lease**, the tenant pays a fixed rental and the owner pays all other expenses for the property. Most residential leases and small commercial leases on office buildings are gross leases. As an example, the typical month-to-month lease is for a gross amount.

To keep a tenant on a gross lease from holding over at the end of the term, the lease might include a **holdover clause**, which materially raises the rent when the lease period expires. This encourages the tenant to either sign a new lease or vacate the premises.

Net lease means the owner gets a net amount and property expenses are paid by the tenant. Payments are similar to an annuity.

Net lease. Under the terms of a **net lease**, besides a basic rent, building expenses are passed on to the tenant. There are three types of net leases:

- Single net lease—The tenant pays the taxes and the base rent.

- Double net lease—The tenant pays for the insurance, as well as taxes and base rent.

- Triple net lease—In addition to taxes, insurance, and base rent, the tenant is responsible for all property maintenance and repairs.

The term *net lease* is generally used in reference to a triple net lease.

Net leases are generally long-term leases and often are found in sale-lease-backs and where buildings are constructed for a particular tenant. The buyer (investor) wants a stated return. To keep the same relative purchasing power, the lessor on a net lease generally wants the net amount tied to an inflationary index, such as the Consumer Price Index.

Percentage lease. A **percentage lease** generally provides for a stated percentage of the gross receipts of a business to be paid as rent. Generally, the percentage lease is tied in with a minimum rent and a covenant to remain in business. The percentage lease also might include hours of operation and a prohibition against the lessee's conducting offsite "warehouse" sales.

Percentage leases are typically used in shopping centers, where each business aids other businesses. Shopping center leases may have a requirement that a separate percentage of the gross be used for cooperative advertising in newspaper supplements or on radio or TV.

In addition, a percentage lease may include a **recapture clause**, which provides that should a tenant not obtain a desired gross, then the lessor has the right to terminate the lease.

Leases may combine features; for example, a basic gross lease plus a percentage of the gross. What can be done with leases is limited only by the imagination of the parties.

Figure 15.2 shows typical percentages charged for different businesses having percentage leases. In determining the percentage of gross sales that must be paid by the lessee, the greater the tenant's markup, the higher the percentage on the lease (e.g., 50% on a parking lot rental and 2% on a supermarket rental). Percentages will vary based on vacancy factors, alternative locations, quality of goods sold, traffic count, et cetera.

A tenant having a higher percentage markup on sales should be able to pay a higher percentage of sales as rent.

Various professional associations publish average percentages currently being charged for different types of businesses. Lessors, of course, want the maximum percentage possible that will still allow the business to remain a viable entity. Typically, a percentage lease will include an audit provision that allows a landlord the ability to periodically audit the books of a tenant to determine whether they are reporting all their income to the landlord.

Step-up lease. A **step-up lease** has a fixed rent like a gross lease, but it provides for increases at set periods. Increases may be predetermined or according to a definite formula. For example, a 10-year lease at $2,000 per month could provide for a $100 monthly increase in rent every two years, so that the rent would be $2,400 for the last two years of the lease. As an alternative, the lease could provide that the rent increase would be made annually based on the percentage increase in the consumer price index.

RESIDENTIAL LEASING

Most rentals are residential, and most property managers are primarily involved in residential leases. The property manager has a duty to the owner to use care in the selection of tenants. The most important decision any property manager makes is, *Who do I rent to?* A tenant who has no desire to pay rent or is destructive, or both, is worse than having no tenant at all. As protection, property managers should not allow occupancy to a prospective tenant until that person is cleared as being a desirable tenant for the property and the deposit and rent checks have cleared.

FIGURE 15.2: Typical Lease Percentages Charged

Type of Business	Percentage of Gross Sales
Liquor stores	1.5–5
Card and gift	3–6
Drugstores	2.5–4
Jewelry	7 and up
Pet stores	5–8
Restaurants	4–7
Grocer and supermarkets	1–2

Rental Application

Figure 15.3 is an Application to Rent by RPI — Realty Publications, Inc. You can see that the application requires personal information, as well as financial data and employment information.

Many lessors also require a copy of the prospective lessee's last pay stub, which serves to verify income. As a minimum, the lessor should verify the present employment and length of employment with the present employer, as well as check with present or prior landlords regarding any problems they may have had. Keep in mind that you must similarly check all tenants, or you could be in violation of one or more of the fair housing laws.

It is also a good practice to see and make a copy of the prospective tenant's driver's license. This will show you that the applicant is who he claims to be, as well as provide you with a previous address.

Although the civil rights law prohibits discrimination for reasons of race, sex, age, national origin, and so forth (Unit 2), there are valid reasons for discrimination. You can discriminate against a tenant who has had problems with other tenants at a previous rental, was late in making payments, broke rules, damaged the property, left owing rent, or generally has had a poor work or credit history. You don't have to accept a problem tenant. It is a lot easier to refuse a rental than it is to rectify a mistake once it is made.

Lease Provisions

A landlord may charge a nonrefundable screening fee.

You are allowed to charge a nonrefundable screening fee of up to a certain maximum amount. The maximum fee is adjusted each year based on changes in the Consumer Price Index since January 1, 1998, when the fee was $35. The change is indexed for inflation. (The fee is adjusted annually to reflect the cost of living index.) This fee is to cover the costs of obtaining and gathering information to make an acceptance or rejection decision regarding a tenant. The fee is adjusted annually for inflation (Civil Code 1950.6).

Civil Code Section 2924.85, requires rental applicants be given notice that an owner has received a notice of default and that there is a pending foreclosure.

Even though you are renting on a month-to-month basis, you should nevertheless use a written rental agreement that clearly sets forth lessor and lessee duties and obligations. If you have apartment rules or regulations, they should be attached to the lease or rental agreement and signed by the tenant.

Don't try to draft a lease or use sections from a number of leases for a "cut and paste" lease. You could be personally liable for errors or omissions, and it also could be considered the unauthorized practice of law. If a simple form lease, such as the short term Residential Lease Agreement published by RPI—Realty , (Figure 15.4), is not appropriate, consult an attorney. You will note that the lease form provides for some of the disclosures covered in Unit 3. When the appropriate block is checked, this form can be used for a month-to-month rental or a lease with a definite termination date.

If a lease is negotiated in Spanish, Chinese, Tagalog, Vietnamese, or Korean, the lease (as well as other contracts) must include a translation in the language in which it was negotiated.

Name of parties.   Any lease should include the full names of all parties. If any person is younger than 18, you ordinarily would need a cosigner unless the underage party qualifies as an emancipated minor by reason of marriage, is an active military service member, or has been declared emancipated by a court. In signing the lease, the parties should sign "jointly and severally," so it is clear that each signer is liable for the entire rent and you can go to one or to all tenants for the rent.

FIGURE 15.3:   Application to Rent

APPLICATION TO RENT

Prepared by: Agent _____   **Phone** _____
Broker _____   **Email** _____

DATE: _____, 20_____, at _____, California.
THIS CREDIT APPLICATION is for payment of monthly rent in the amount of $_____.
Property address: _____
Received from Applicant(s) $_____, ☐ cash, or ☐ check, for a consumer credit report which is
   a non-refundable cost and not a deposit.
Received from Applicant(s) $_____, ☐ cash, or ☐ check, as a deposit toward the first month's rent on
   Landlord's acceptance of the applicant's creditworthiness.
Applicant(s):
Applicant One _____ Date of Birth ____/____/_____
                                           (Name)
      Social Sec. # _____ Drivers Lic. # _____ State___
      Phone _____ Cell _____ Email _____
Applicant Two _____ Date of Birth ____/____/_____
                                           (Name)
      Social Sec. # _____ Drivers Lic. # _____ State___
      Phone _____ Cell _____ Email _____
Additional Occupant(s): Name _____
                          Name _____
Rental History: Have you ever been party to an eviction? ☐ Yes ☐ No   Filed bankruptcy? ☐ Yes ☐ No
Present Address _____
      City _____ Zip _____
      Length of Residency _____ Monthly Rent $_____
      Landlord/Agent _____ DRE # _____
      Address _____
      Phone _____ Cell _____ Email _____
      Reason for Moving _____ Moving Date ____/____/_____
Previous Address _____
      City _____ Zip _____
      Length of Residence _____ Monthly Rent $_____
      Landlord/Agent _____ DRE # _____
      Address _____
      Phone _____ Cell _____ Email _____
Employment:
Applicant One
      Employer _____
      Address _____
      Phone _____ Cell _____ Email _____
      Length of Employment _____ Position _____ Wages _____
      Pay Period _____ Union _____
      Previous Employer _____
      Address _____
      Phone _____ Cell _____ Email _____
Applicant Two
      Employer _____
      Address _____
      Phone _____ Cell _____ Email _____
      Length of Employment _____ Position _____ Wages _____
      Pay Period _____ Union _____

— — — — — — — — — — — — — *PAGE ONE OF TWO — FORM 553* — — — — — — — — — — — — —

FIGURE 15.3 (continued): **Application to Rent**

— — — — — — — — — — — — — — PAGE TWO OF TWO — FORM 553 — — — — — — — — — — — — — — —

Previous Employer _____

Address _____

Phone _____ Cell _____ Email _____

Additional Income Amount $_____ Source _____

Recipient _____

General Credit Information:

Automobile One: Make _____

    Year _____ Model _____ Lic. #/State _____

    Lender _____

Automobile Two: Make _____

    Year _____ Model _____ Lic. #/State _____

    Lender _____

Bank/branch _____

    Check Acc. # _____ Savings Acc. # _____

Bank/branch _____

    Check Acc. # _____ Savings Acc. # _____

Credit References:

    1. _____

    Address _____

    Account # _____ Balance due $_____ Phone _____

    2. _____

    Address _____

    Account # _____ Balance due $_____ Phone _____

Personal Reference _____

    Address _____

    Phone _____ Cell _____ Email _____

Personal Reference _____

    Address _____

    Phone _____ Cell _____ Email _____

Nearest Relative (name/relationship) _____

    Address _____

    Phone _____ Cell _____ Email _____

Emergency Contact (name/relationship) _____

    Address _____

    Phone _____ Cell _____ Email _____

I/We declare all information given in this application is true and correct. I/We authorize your credit reporting agency to obtain and verify a complete consumer report and supply the information obtained to you. This information is not privileged.

Date: _____, 20_____

Name: _____

Signature: _____
                 (Applicant 1)

Name: _____

Signature: _____
                 (Applicant 2)

> **I acknowledge receipt of this credit application and accompanying payment.**
>
> Landlord: _____
>
> Signature: _____
>
> Phone: _____
>
> Email: _____

FORM 553   02-14   © 2014 **first tuesday**, P.O. Box 5707, RIVERSIDE, CA 92517 (800) 794-0494

©2015 RPI — Realty Publications, Inc., P.O. BOX 5707, RIVERSIDE, CA 92517

FIGURE 15.4:   Residential Lease Agreement

THIS FORM FOR USE IN CALIFORNIA ONLY

Real Estate Forms Since 1966

RESIDENTIAL LEASE-RENTAL AGREEMENT AND DEPOSIT RECEIPT

AGENCY RELATIONSHIP CONFIRMATION. The following agency relationship is hereby confirmed for this transaction and supersedes any prior agency election (If no agency relationship insert "NONE"):

LISTING AGENT: _____ is the agent of (check one):
(Print Firm Name)
☐ **the Owner exclusively; or** ☐ **both the Tenant and the Owner.**

LEASING AGENT: _____ (if not the same as the Listing Agent) is the agent of (check one):
(Print Firm Name)
☐ **the Tenant exclusively; or** ☐ **the Owner exclusively; or** ☐ **both the Tenant and the Owner.**

Note: This confirmation DOES NOT take the place of the AGENCY DISCLOSURE form (such as P.P. Form 110.42 CAL) required by law if the term exceeds one year.

RECEIVED FROM _____, hereinafter referred to as Tenant, the sum of $_____ (_____ dollars), evidenced by _____, as a deposit. Upon acceptance of this Agreement, the Owner of the premises, will apply the deposit as follows:

	TOTAL	RECEIVED	BALANCE DUE PRIOR TO OCCUPANCY
Rent for the period from _____ to _____ .	$_____	$_____	$_____
Security deposit (not applicable toward last month's rent)	$_____	$_____	$_____
Other _____	$_____	$_____	$_____
TOTAL	$_____	$_____	$_____

In the event this Agreement is not accepted by the Owner, **within** _____ **days**, the total deposit received will be refunded.

Tenant offers to rent from the Owner the premises situated in the City of _____, County of _____, State of California, commonly known as _____ _____,

upon the following **terms and conditions:**

1. **TERM.** The term will commence on _____, and continue **(check one of the two following alternatives):**
   ☐ LEASE until _____, for a total rent of $_____ (_____ _____ dollars).
   ☐ RENTAL on a month-to-month basis, until either party terminates this Agreement by giving the other party written notice as required by law.

2. **RENT.** Rent will be $_____, per month, payable in advance by personal check, cashier's check, cash or money order, on the _____ day of each calendar month to Owner or his or her authorized agent, by mail or personal delivery to the following address: _____ or at such other place as may be designated by Owner in writing from time to time. Payment by personal delivery may be made (check one): ☐ Monday through Friday, 9:00 a.m. to 5:00 p.m., or ☐ at the following times: _____ _____. In the event rent is not received by Owner in full **within** ____ **days** after due date, Tenant agrees that it would be impracticable or extremely difficult to fix the actual damages to Owner caused by that failure, and Tenant agrees to pay a **late charge** of $_____. Tenant further agrees to pay $ 25.00 for each dishonored bank check. All late fees and returned check fees will be considered additional rent. The late charge period is not a grace period, and Owner is entitled to make written demand for any rent if not paid when due and to collect interest thereon. Any unpaid balance including late charges, will bear interest at 10% per annum, or the maximum rate allowed by law, whichever is less.

3. **MULTIPLE OCCUPANCY.** It is expressly understood that this Agreement is between the Owner and each signatory jointly and severally. Each signatory will be responsible for timely payment of rent and performance of all other provisions of this Agreement.

4. **UTILITIES.** Tenant will be responsible for the payment of all utilities and services, except: _____ _____, which will be paid by Owner.

5. **USE.** The premises will be used exclusively as a residence for no more than _____ persons. Guests staying more than a total of _____ days in a calendar year without written consent of Owner will constitute a violation of this Agreement. Tenant shall park operable automobiles in assigned spaces only. Trailers, boats, campers, and inoperable vehicles are not allowed without the written consent of Owner. Tenant may not repair motor vehicles on the leased premises.

6. **ANIMALS.** No animals will be brought on the premises without the prior consent of the Owner; except _____.

7. **RULES AND REGULATIONS.** In the event that the premises is a portion of a building containing more than one unit, or is located in a common interest development, Tenant agrees to abide by all applicable rules, whether adopted before or after the date of this Agreement, including rules with respect to noise, odors, disposal of refuse, animals, parking, and use of common areas. Tenant will

Tenant [_____] [_____] [_____] [_____] has read this page.

CAUTION: The copyright laws of the United States forbid the unauthorized reproduction of this form by any means including scanning or computerized formats.
Page 1 of 4
FORM 105.1 CAL (10-2012) COPYRIGHT BY PROFESSIONAL PUBLISHING LLC, NOVATO, CA

PROFESSIONAL PUBLISHING

Form generated by: TrueForms™   www.TrueForms.com   800-499-9612

FIGURE 15.4 (continue): **Residential Lease Agreement**

Property Address _____

pay any penalties , including attorney fees, imposed by homeowners' association for violations by tenant or tenant's guests.

8. **ORDINANCES AND STATUTES.** Tenant will comply with all statutes, ordinances, and requirements of all municipal, state and federal authorities now in force, or which may later be in force, regarding the use of the premises. Tenant will not use the premises for any unlawful purpose including, but not limited to, using, storing or selling prohibited drugs. If the premises are located in a rent control area, the Tenant should contact the Rent and Arbitration Board for his or her legal rights.

9. **ASSIGNMENT AND SUBLETTING.** Tenant will not assign this Agreement or sublet any portion of the premises without prior written consent of the Owner.

10. **MAINTENANCE, REPAIRS, OR ALTERATIONS.** Tenant acknowledges that, unless the Owner is notified immediately upon occupancy, the premises, including the furniture, furnishings and appliances, including all electrical, gas and plumbing fixtures, are in good working order and repair. Tenant will keep the premises in a clean and sanitary condition, and will immediately notify Owner of any damage to the premises or its contents, or any inoperable equipment or appliances. Tenant will surrender the premises, at termination, in as good condition as received, normal wear and tear excepted. Tenant will be responsible for any damage, repairs or replacements, caused by Tenant's negligence and that of the tenant's family, invitees, and guests, except ordinary wear and tear. **Verification of the working order (using the "test" button) and the maintenance of both the smoke detector(s) and carbon monoxide detector(s) is the responsibility of the Tenant.** Tenant will not commit any waste upon the premises, or any nuisance or act which may disturb the quiet enjoyment of any neighbors. Tenant will not paint, paper or otherwise redecorate or make alterations to the premises without the prior written consent of the Owner. Tenant will irrigate and maintain any surrounding grounds, including lawns and shrubbery, if they are for the Tenant's exclusive use. **It is understood that Owner's insurance does not cover Tenant's personal property.**

11. **INVENTORY.** Any furnishings and/or equipment to be furnished by Owner will be listed in a special inventory. The inventory will be signed by both Tenant and Owner concurrently with this Lease. Tenant will keep the furnishings and equipment in good condition and repair, and will be responsible for any damage to them other than normal wear and tear. Tenant acknowledges receipt of _____ sets of keys, _____ garage door openers, other: _____

12. **DAMAGES TO PREMISES.** If the premises are damaged by fire, earthquake or other casualty which renders the premises totally or partially uninhabitable, either party will have the right to terminate this Agreement as of the date on which the damage occurs. Written notice of termination will be given to the other party **within fifteen (15) days after occurrence** of such damage. Should such damage or destruction occur as the result of the negligence of Tenant, or his or her invitees, then only the Owner will have the right to terminate. Should this right be exercised by either Owner or Tenant, rent for the current month will be prorated between the parties as of the date the damage occurred. Any prepaid rent and unused security deposit will be refunded to Tenant. If this Agreement is not terminated, Owner will promptly repair the premises and there will be a proportionate reduction of rent until the premises are repaired and ready for Tenant's occupancy. The proportionate reduction will be based on the extent which repairs interfere with Tenant's reasonable use of the premises.

13. **ENTRY AND INSPECTION.** Owner and owners agents will have the right to enter the premises: (a) in case of emergency; (b) to make necessary or agreed repairs, decorations, alterations, improvements, supply necessary or agreed services, inspect the condition of the property, show the premises to prospective or actual purchasers, lenders, tenants, workers, or contractors; (c) when tenant has abandoned or surrendered the premises. Except under (a) and (c), entry may be made only during normal business hours, and with at least 24 hours prior written notice to Tenant including the date, approximate time, and purpose of entry.

    If the purpose of the entry is to exhibit the dwelling unit to prospective or actual purchasers, the notice may be given orally, in person or by telephone, if the owner or his or her agent has notified the tenant in writing within 120 days of the oral notice that the property is for sale. At the time of entry, the Owner or agent shall leave written evidence of the entry inside the unit.

14. **INDEMNIFICATION.** Owner will not be liable for any damage or injury to Tenant, or any other person, or to any property, occurring on the premises, or in common areas, unless such damage is the legal result of the negligence or willful misconduct of Owner, his or her agents, or employees. Tenant agrees to hold Owner harmless from any claims for damages, no matter how caused, except for injury or damages caused by negligence or willful misconduct of Owner, his or her agents or employees.

15. **PHYSICAL POSSESSION.** If Owner is unable to deliver possession of the premises at the commencement date set forth above, Owner will not be liable for any damage caused, nor will this Agreement be void or voidable, but Tenant will not be liable for any rent until possession is delivered. Tenant may terminate this Agreement if possession is not delivered **within _____ days** of the commencement of the term in Item 1.

16. **DEFAULT.** If Tenant fails to pay rent when due, or perform any provision of this Agreement, after not less than **three (3) days written notice** of such default given in the manner required by law, the Owner, at his or her option, may terminate all rights of Tenant, unless Tenant, within said time, cures such default. If Tenant abandons or vacates the property while in default of the payment of rent, Owner may consider any property left on the premises to be abandoned and may dispose of the same in any manner allowed by law. In the event the Owner reasonably believes that such abandoned property has no value, it may be discarded. All property on the premises will be subject to a lien for the benefit of Owner securing the payment of all sums due, to the maximum extent allowed by law.

    In the event of a default by Tenant, Owner may elect to: (a) continue the lease in effect and enforce all his rights and remedies, including the right to recover the rent as it becomes due, provided that Owner's consent to assignment or subletting by the Tenant will not be unreasonably withheld; or (b) at any time, terminate all of Tenant's rights and recover from Tenant all damages he or she may incur by reason of the breach of the lease, including the cost of recovering the premises, and including the worth at the time of such termination, or at the time of an award if suit be instituted to enforce this provision, of the amount by which the unpaid rent for the balance of the term exceeds the amount of such rental loss which the Tenant proves could be reasonably avoided.

Tenant [_____] [_____] [_____] [_____] **has read this page.**

Page 2 of 4
FORM 105.2 CAL (10-2012) COPYRIGHT BY PROFESSIONAL PUBLISHING LLC, NOVATO, CA

Form generated by: TrueForms™   www.TrueForms.com   800-499-9612

PROFESSIONAL PUBLISHING

FIGURE 15.4 (continue): **Residential Lease Agreement**

Property Address _____

17. **SECURITY.** The security deposit will secure the performance of Tenant's obligations. Owner may, but will not be obligated to, apply all portions of said deposit on account of Tenant's obligations. Any balance remaining will be returned to Tenant, together with an accounting of any disbursements, **21 calendar days** after the Tenant has vacated the premises, or earlier if required by law. Tenant will not have the right to apply the security deposit in payment of the last month's rent. No interest will be paid to Tenant on account of the security deposit, unless required by local ordinance.

18. **WAIVER.** Failure of Owner to enforce any provision of this Agreement will not be deemed a waiver. The acceptance of rent by Owner will not waive his or her right to enforce any provision of this Agreement.

19. **NOTICES.** Unless otherwise provided, any notice which either party may give or is required to give, must be in writing, may be given personally or by mailing the same, postage prepaid, to Tenant at the premises or to Owner or Owner's authorized agent at the address shown in the signature block or at such other places as may be designated by the parties from time to time. Notice will be deemed effective three (3) days after mailing, or on personal delivery, or when receipt is acknowledged in writing.

20. **HOLDING OVER.** Any holding over after expiration of this Agreement will be (check one):
☐ with the consent of Owner, a month-to-month tenancy at a monthly rent equal to the rent for the month immediately preceding the expiration date, or such other amount as agreed upon by Owner and Tenant. The monthly rent shall be payable in advance and the occupancy subject to all of the other terms and conditions set forth in this Agreement, until either party terminates the tenancy by giving the other party **thirty (30) days (or longer if required by law) written notice**; or
☐ the property is subject to a local rent control ordinance and the holding over will be a month-to-month tenancy with the rent and termination provisions as mandated by the ordinance.

21. **TIME.** Time is of the essence of this Agreement.

22. **ATTORNEY'S FEES.** In any action or proceeding involving a dispute between Tenant and Owner arising out of the execution of this Agreement, whether for tort or for breach of contract, and whether or not brought to trial or final judgment, the prevailing party will be entitled to receive from the other party a reasonable attorney fee, expert witness fees, and costs to be determined by the court or arbitrator(s).

23. **SUBROGATION.** To the maximum extent permitted by insurance policies which may be owned by the parties, Lessor and Lessee waive any and all rights of subrogation against each other which might otherwise exist.

24. **FAIR HOUSING.** Owner and Tenant understand that the state and federal housing laws prohibit discrimination in the sale, rental, appraisal, financing or advertising of housing on the basis of race, color, religion, sex, sexual orientation, marital status, national origin, ancestry, familial status, source of income, age, mental or physical disability, immigration or citizenship status. In addition, California Civil Code §1940.3 prohibits a landlord from making any inquiry regarding the immigration or citizenship status of any tenant or prospective tenant.

25. **SMOKING RESTRICTIONS.** Check box: Landlord ☐ does allow smoking, as follows: ☐ in the unit and/or ☐ on the premises, including exterior and common areas. Landlord ☐ does NOT allow smoking in the unit but does allow smoking in exterior areas, but ☐ not including common areas. This applies to tobacco and all other substances. If smoking is further regulated by local laws, tenant agrees to comply. Tenant will inform guests of any smoking restrictions to insure their cooperation.

26. **ADDITIONAL TERMS AND CONDITIONS.**
_____
_____
_____
_____
_____
_____
_____
_____
_____

27. ☐ This unit is subject to rent control and the agency responsible to adjudicate claims is: _____

28. **ENTIRE AGREEMENT.** The foregoing constitutes the entire agreement between the parties and may be modified only in writing signed by all parties. This Agreement and any modifications, including any photocopy or facsimile, may be signed in one or more counterparts, each of which will be deemed an original and all of which taken together will constitute one and the same instrument. The following addenda, if checked, have been made a part of this Agreement before the parties' execution:
☐ Addendum _____ : Lead-Based Paint Disclosure (Required by Law for Rental Property Built Prior to 1978)
☐ Addendum _____ : Regarding Mold Contamination and Agreement to Maintain Premises
☐ Addendum _____ : _____
☐ Addendum _____ : _____

NOTICE: Pursuant to Section 290.46 of the Penal Code, information about specified registered sex offenders is made available to the public via an Internet Web site maintained by the Department of Justice at http://www.meganslaw.ca.gov. Depending on an offender's criminal history, this information will include either the address at which the offender resides or the community of residence and ZIP Code in which he or she resides.

Tenant [_____] [_____] [_____] [_____] has read this page.

Page 3 of 4
FORM 105.3 CAL (10-2012) COPYRIGHT BY PROFESSIONAL PUBLISHING LLC, NOVATO, CA

PROFESSIONAL PUBLISHING

Form generated by: TrueForms™   www.TrueForms.com   800-499-9612

FIGURE 15.4 (continue): **Residential Lease Agreement**

Property Address _____

Tenant _____
(Signature)

_____
(Please Print Name)

Date _____ Telephone _____

Address _____

_____

Email _____

Tenant _____
(Signature)

_____
(Please Print Name)

Date _____ Telephone _____

Address _____

_____

Email _____

Tenant _____
(Signature)

_____
(Please Print Name)

Date _____ Telephone _____

Address _____

_____

Email _____

Tenant _____
(Signature)

_____
(Please Print Name)

Date _____ Telephone _____

Address _____

_____

Email _____

The undersigned Owner accepts the foregoing offer and agrees to lease the premises on the terms and conditions set forth above.

Owner _____
(Signature of Owner or Authorized Agent)

_____
(Please Print Name)

Date _____

Telephone _____ Fax _____

Address _____

_____

Email _____

Owner _____
(Signature)

_____
(Please Print Name)

Date _____

Telephone _____ Fax _____

Address _____

_____

Email _____

Receipt for deposit acknowledged by _____ Date _____

Tenant acknowledges receipt of a copy of the accepted lease on (date) _____

[_____] [_____] [_____] [_____]
initials

CAUTION: The copyright laws of the United States forbid the unauthorized reproduction of this form by any means including scanning or computerized formats.

Page 4 of 4
FORM 105.4 CAL (10-2012) COPYRIGHT BY PROFESSIONAL PUBLISHING LLC, NOVATO, CA

PROFESSIONAL PUBLISHING

Form generated by: TrueForms™   www.TrueForms.com   800-499-9612

Reprinted with permission, Professional Publishing. Endorsement not implied.

Description of premises.   The premises should be described in such a manner that there is no ambiguity. If a parking space or a garage is included, it should be specified.

Dates.   An estate for years must have a beginning date and an ending date. A periodic tenancy would have a beginning date and length of period.

Rent and late charge.   The rent amount or rental formula should be clearly stated, as well as where and when the rent is due. Landlords may not require rent payments be made in cash unless the tenant has previously attempted to pay rent with a check drawn on insufficient funds or has instructed a bank to stop payment on a rent check. Consider late charges for late payments. Keep in mind that if the late charge is too high, a court could determine it to be a penalty and declare it unenforceable.

Pets.   Pet agreements are common in residential leases. Lessors may require an additional deposit and also charge additional rent or limit the size and type of pet allowed. Pet deposits are refundable except for damage amounts. All security deposits cannot exceed California limits.

Water beds.   Common water-bed agreements require the tenant to have a liner on any water bed and to pay for a policy of water-bed insurance, should the water bed cause damage to the premises.

Inspection.   Some leases provide for pre-tenancy walk-through inspections. Deficiencies should be noted on a form provided for this purpose, which should be signed by tenant and landlord. (See Figure 15.5.)

Cleaning and security deposits.   A controversial item in leases and rental agreements is the **security deposit**. The security deposit functions as a form of insurance for the landlord in case the rental premises are left damaged or dirty or rent is owed. According to the law, the amount of the security deposit that may be demanded or received is limited to an amount equal to two months' rent, in the case of unfurnished residential property, and to three months' rent for furnished residential property. Nonrefundable deposits, such as *cleaning deposits*, are not allowed.

FIGURE 15.5: Condition of Premises Addendum

CONDITION OF PREMISES ADDENDUM

Prepared by: Agent _____ Phone _____
Broker _____ Email _____

DATE: _____, 20_____, at _____, California.

Items left blank or unchecked are not applicable.

FACTS:

1. This is an addendum to the following agreement:

   ☐ Lease agreement
   ☐ Rental agreement
   ☐ Occupancy agreement
   1.1 ☐ of same date, or dated _____, 20_____, at _____, California,
   1.2 entered into by _____, as the Landlord, and
   1.3 _____, as the Tenant,
   1.4 regarding real estate referred to as _____
   _____.

AGREEMENT:

2. Landlord and Tenant have jointly inspected the premises and common areas and agree the premises and unchecked items such as fixtures, appliances and furnishings are in a satisfactory and sanitary condition.
3. Check only those items which are unsatisfactory and state why in "REMARKS."

4. EXTERIOR/COMMON AREAS:

☐ Garage/parking lot	☐ Garbage facilities	☐ Storage area	☐ TV antenna
☐ Pool/spa	☐ Satellite dish	☐ Patio/decks	☐ CATV hookup
☐ Stairs/railings	☐ Garage door opener(s)	☐ Hallway/lobby	☐ Laundry area
☐ Fencing	☐ Roof	☐ Exterior lighting	☐ Eaves/gutters
☐ Sprinklers/hose	☐ Mailbox	☐ Walkways	☐ _____

5. ENTRY:

☐ Door	☐ # of keys _____	☐ Doorbell/knocker	☐ Closet
☐ Intercom/security	☐ Shelves	☐ Locks	☐ _____

6. KITCHEN:

☐ Range	☐ Trash compactor	☐ Oven	☐ Water purifier
☐ Refrigerator	☐ Counters/laminate	☐ Garbage disposal	☐ Cabinets/drawers
☐ Exhaust fan(s)	☐ Pantry/shelves	☐ Dishwasher	☐ Tile/linoleum
☐ Microwave	☐ Sink/faucets		

7. BATHROOM:

☐ Sink	☐ Tile/linoleum	☐ Faucets/hardware	☐ Closets/shelves
☐ Toilet	☐ Exhaust fan(s)	☐ Shower	☐ Shower enclosure
☐ Tub	☐ Medicine cabinet		

8. ELECTRICAL:

☐ Outlets	☐ Lighting	☐ Switchplates	☐ Thermostat
☐ Fixtures	☐ Furnace	☐ Smoke detectors	☐ Ventilation
☐ Air conditioning	☐ _____		

9. PLUMBING:

☐ Water heater	☐ Washer	☐ Hot/cold water	☐ Dryer
☐ Gas hookups	☐ _____		

— — — — — — — — — — — *PAGE ONE OF TWO — FORM 560* — — — — — — — — — — —

©2015 RPI — Realty Publications, Inc., P.O. BOX 5707, RIVERSIDE, CA 92517

FIGURE 15.5 (continued):   Condition of Premises Addendum

— — — — — — — — — — — — — — — — PAGE TWO OF TWO — FORM 560 — — — — — — — — — — — — — — — — — —

10. INTERIOR:

☐ Wall coverings   ☐ Floor coverings   ☐ Ceilings   ☐ Walls

☐ Draperies   ☐ Rods/tracks   ☐ Glass doors   ☐ Windows

☐ Doorknobs   ☐ Fireplace   ☐ Wood doors   ☐ Paint

☐ Floors   ☐ Baseboards/trim   ☐ Hardware/fittings   ☐ Shades

☐ Closets   ☐ Screens   ☐ Sills/jambs   ☐ Kickplates/stops

☐ Chimney/flue

11. REMARKS:

_____

_____

_____

_____

_____

_____

_____

_____

_____

_____

_____

_____

_____

_____

_____

_____

_____

12. REPAIRS PROMISED:

12.1   _____

_____

Completion date _____

12.2   _____

_____

Completion date _____

I agree to the terms stated above.	**I accept the premises as stated above.**
☐ See attached Signature Page Addendum. [ft Form 251]	☐ See attached Signature Page Addendum. [ft Form 251]
Date: _____, 20_____	Date: _____, 20_____
Landlord/Manager: _____	Tenant: _____
Signature: _____	Signature: _____
Address: _____	Tenant: _____
_____	Signature: _____
Phone: _____Cell: _____	Address: _____
Fax: _____	_____
Email: _____	Phone: _____Cell: _____
	Fax: _____
	Email: _____

FORM 560   03-11   ©2011 **first tuesday**, P.O. BOX 20069, RIVERSIDE, CA 92516 (800) 794-0494

©2015 RPI — Realty Publications, Inc., P.O. BOX 5707, RIVERSIDE, CA 92517

Landlords must notify a departing tenant of the tenant's right to be present at a pre-vacancy inspection of the tenant's rental unit. The purpose is to allow the tenant to correct any deficiencies noted.

Nonrefundable tenant deposits are forbidden.

At the termination of the tenancy, the landlord is permitted to retain only that portion of the security deposit reasonably necessary to remedy tenant defaults. The landlord must notify the lessee in writing as to the retention of any portion of the security deposit unless the expenses were less than $125. Copies of receipts for labor and material must be included for amounts deductible from the security deposit. If the landlord must return any portion of the deposit to the tenant, it must be returned within three weeks after tenancy is terminated (60 days for nonresidential tenants). The bad-faith failure to return the security deposit will subject the landlord to actual damages plus a penalty of up to two times the amount of the security deposit. If the landlord defaults on this obligation, the tenant may initiate legal action through an attorney or small-claims court or file a complaint with the Consumer Protection Bureau.

Lease-option arrangement. With a lease-option, usually used when loans are not easily available or the lessor lacks the required down payment, the purchaser leases the property desired with an option to purchase at a later date. A portion of the amount paid as rent usually will be applied against the purchase price. (Options also can be for lease extensions.)

Exculpatory clauses are invalid for residential leases.

Exculpatory clause (hold-harmless clause). Leases frequently contain an **exculpatory clause**, whereby the tenant agrees to relieve the landlord from all liability for injury or property damage resulting from the condition of the property or the negligence of the owner. Many residential leases contain these clauses, but the clauses are invalid for residential leases. Even though the tenant has agreed, the tenant has not given up her rights under the law.

Right of entry. A lease may provide the landlord the right to check the property for specific purposes. In the absence of any agreement, the landlord can enter residential property only under the following circumstances:

■ An emergency requires entry.

■ The tenant consents to an entry.

- The entry is during normal business hours after a reasonable notice (24 hours is considered reasonable) to make necessary or agreed repairs, alterations, or improvements, or to show the property to prospective or actual purchasers, mortgagees, tenants, workers, or contractors; landlord can enter without a 24-hour notice to make repairs requested by the tenant.

- The tenant has abandoned or surrendered the premises.

- The landlord has obtained a court order to enter.

Landlord Disclosures

Residential landlords in California must make the following disclosures to tenants:

- Existence of registered sexual offender database (Megan's Law)

- Presence of known lead-based paint

- Pesticides used

- Any asbestos discovered on property

- Known carcinogenic material (if landlord has 10 or more employees)

- Methamphetamines contamination

- Application for demolition permit

- That the building is within one mile of a closed military base where explosives were stored

- If a previous tenant died on the premises within the past three years

- If the unit is in a condominium conversion project

Landlord's Responsibilities

A residential lease has an **implied warranty of habitability**. This duty does not extend to cases in which the problem is one of tenant cleanliness. The landlord must assume at least that the

- plumbing is in proper working order;

- the heat, lights, and wiring work and are safe;

- the floors, stairways, and railings are in good condition;

- when rented, the premises are clean and free of pests;

- areas under lessor control are maintained; and

- the roof does not leak and no doors or windows are broken.

If a landlord demands or collects rent for an untenable dwelling, the lessor is liable for actual damages sustained by the tenant and special damages of not less than $100 or more than $5,000. The tenant can also raise the defense of habitability against any eviction action.

Tenant's Responsibilities

If a landlord fails to take corrective action within a reasonable time of notice when a repair is the landlord's responsibility, the tenant has the following four options:

1. The tenant may abandon the property and not be held liable for back rents or an unfulfilled lease.

2. The tenant may refer the problem to a mediator, an arbitrator, or in serious circumstances, the small-claims court.

3. The tenant may notify the owner in writing of an emergency situation that must be taken care of. If the owner does not respond, the tenant may call in a professional repairman and offset the cost of repair with up to one month's rent on the next rent check. However, tenants may do this only twice in each year of tenancy.

4. The tenant can remain in possession and pay a reduced rent based on reduction of usefulness of the premises when the landlord fails to maintain a habitable dwelling.

The tenant cannot be prohibited from installing a satellite dish within the area under tenant control.

The landlord must allow the installation of a electric vehicle charging station, as long as station meets minimum standards.

The landlord must allow tenant agriculture in potable containers that meet minimum standards.

The California Civil Code states that the tenant is obligated to do the following:

- Keep the living unit clean and sanitary

- Dispose of garbage and other waste sanitarily

- Use all utility fixtures properly, keeping them clean and sanitary

- Avoid defacing or damaging property

- Use property only for its intended lawful purpose

- Pay rent on time

- Abide by rules and regulations

- Give 30-day notice when vacating (month-to-month lease)

- Return door and mailbox keys when vacating

- Leave the unit in a clean condition when vacating

Assignment vs. Sublease

Provided that the terms of the lease do not prohibit such activity, a tenant has the right to assign or sublet her interest in the property.

> In an assignment, the assignee is a tenant of the landlord. In a sublease, the sublessee is the tenant of the sublessor.

Assignment transfers the entire leasehold rights to a third party. The third party, the assignee, pays rent directly to the original lessor. While the assignee becomes primarily liable on the lease, the original lessee retains secondary liability (if assignee defaults).

A **sublease** of property transfers only a part of the tenant's interest. The sublessee pays rent to the original lessee, who in turn is responsible to the lessor. The original lessee is said to have a *sandwich lease*.

The lease should clearly indicate if it may be assigned or subleased. Lessors frequently provide that assignment or subleasing be allowed only with the approval of the lessor; however, this approval must not be unreasonably withheld.

Some leases provide that if the premises are sublet at a rent higher than the lessee is paying the lessor, the higher portion will be split between the lessor and the lessee. This encourages tenants to try to sublet for a maximum amount and also allows the lessor to share in the increased rent. (See Figure 15.6 for the difference between assignments and subleases.)

Airbnb Inc., www.airbnb.com, allows apartment dwellers to market rental units or rooms through a global website. They can rent a room or their unit on short-term rental, often overnight, much as a hotel room. Airbnb violates many leases in that leases usually require landlord approval to sublease. Therefore, these unauthorized rentals could be cause for eviction. Because Airbnb takes a percentage of the rent, many large apartment owners now want a cut of the revenue ($340 million revenue reported by Airbnb in the third quarter of 2015). Airbnb has indicated they are negotiating with landlords for a sharing arrangement to legitimize their rental operation. Some cities are concerned that Airbnb will turn many apartments into hotels, which will deplete the stock of affordable housing.

TERMINATION OF LEASE

A tenancy for a specified period, as in an estate for years, requires no notice for termination because the date has already been specified. Other than by expiration of the lease term, termination may be made by the following:

- The tenant for violation of the landlord's duty to place the tenant in quiet possession

- The tenant, if a victim of domestic violence

- The tenant for the landlord's failure to repair

- The tenant on eviction by the landlord

- Either party on destruction of the premises

- The landlord on use of the premises for unauthorized purposes or on abandonment of the premises by the tenant

- Either party on breach of a condition of the lease

- The tenant for the landlord's breach of the implied warranty of habitability

Landlords cannot terminate or refuse to renew a lease because the tenant was the victim of domestic violence. Protection is waived if the victim allows the perpetrator to visit the property. The landlord must rekey at the tenant's request within 24 hours of written proof that a court protection order is in effect.

A residential landlord can prohibit smoking of tobacco products in the premises if it's stated in the lease. For existing tenants, a notice of change of terms of tenancy must first be given.

FIGURE 15.6:   Assignment vs. Subletting

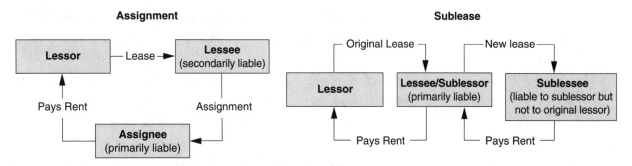

Protecting Tenants at Foreclosure Act of 2009

Before this act, foreclosure of a prior lien would nullify a residential tenant lease. Now the lease survives foreclosure and the tenant is allowed to remain in possession until the lease term expires. However, if the buyer at foreclosure intends to occupy the property, the lease may be terminated with 90 days' notice.

In case of a month-to-month lease, the tenant is entitled to 90 days' notice to vacate.

Tenants in foreclosed properties must be given notice of their rights.

Evictions and Unlawful Detainer

A landlord may evict tenants and bring an **unlawful detainer** action against them for failure to pay rent when due, violation of provisions contained in the lease or rental agreement, or failure to vacate the premises after termination of 30-day or 60-day written notice. The process of removing a tenant for being behind in rent follows:

1. The landlord serves the tenant with a **three-day notice** to quit or pay rent.

2. If the tenant fails to heed the notice, the landlord files an unlawful detainer action in court.

3. If the landlord wins, the court awards the landlord a judgment. The landlord then asks for a writ of possession authorizing the sheriff to evict the tenant.

4. The sheriff sends the tenant an eviction notice. If the tenant fails to leave, the sheriff then physically removes the tenant.

Because of drug-related crime, the legislature has authorized several city attorney and prosecutor offices to bring unlawful detainer actions to abate drug-related nuisances (the landlord will be charged fees and costs).

Property managers frequently bring action against tenants and former tenants in small-claims courts for back rent or for damages to the premises. Attorneys are not allowed in small-claims courts. The maximum amount of the suit is $5,000 by a business ($10,000 for individuals). The procedure is simple and informal:

1. Determine the full legal name and address of the person(s) you are suing.

    This will help you decide where you must file your claim.

2. Visit the clerk of the small-claims court and fill out the form after paying a small fee.

3. Arrange for the order to be served on the defendant (but not by yourself). The clerk will mail it for a fee, or you may authorize someone to serve it personally.

4. While waiting for the trial, gather all important documents and have them ready. Contact all potential witnesses and arrange for them to come with you to the trial, or obtain a subpoena from the clerk for any witness who will not come voluntarily. If you need an

interpreter, find out if one is available at small-claims court; otherwise, bring your own.

5. Come to the court building early and ask the clerk where your case is being heard. When you reach the courtroom, check the calendar to see that your case is listed.

6. When your case is called, give your testimony, presenting only the facts.

   Be brief. Submit all papers and documents you think will help your case.

7. If you win, ask the defendant for the money awarded you in the judgment.

8. If you have difficulties in collecting your money, ask the clerk to assist you.

9. As plaintiff, you are not allowed to appeal if you lose (unless you must pay as the result of a counterclaim).

A landlord cannot decrease services, increase rent, or evict a tenant within 180 days after the tenant exercises a right protected under the law, including the following:

- Complaining to the landlord about the habitability of the premises

- Complaining to a public agency about defects

- Lawfully organizing a tenant association

Tenants cannot waive their rights against retaliatory eviction.

Prohibition of retaliatory eviction is a defense against eviction. If a landlord is shown to have acted maliciously, the tenant will be entitled to actual damages plus $100 to $2,000 in punitive damages.

Retaliatory Eviction Menace

The landlord is subject to $2,000 in damages for threatening a residential tenant to vacate by force or by other menacing conduct.

SUMMARY

Property management, an ancient field of real estate specialization, is on the cutting edge of technology today. Property management has made rapid strides in professionalism, and besides the Institute of Real Estate Management (IREM), there are a number of other professional organizations.

Real estate managers fall into the following three general categories:

1. Licensee/property manager, who generally works out of a property management office handling numerous properties

2. Individual property manager, who handles just one property and who usually is an employee of an owner

3. Resident property managers

Property managers' duties vary with the type of property, but basically the manager has two main duties:

1. Strive for that rent/vacancy combination that will maximize the net earnings

2. Protect the property

To accomplish these duties, a property manager needs expertise in a variety of fields, from marketing to maintenance. The property manager, as a professional, has a duty to advise the owner in the operation of the property.

While most property management is residential, residential is broken down into specialized areas, such as mobile home parks and condominium associations. Property management also can involve commercial and industrial property and even public buildings, marinas, and so forth.

Commercial and industrial property management requires special lease knowledge, as well as technical knowledge of buildings and tenant requirements.

The property manager has a management contract similar to a sale listing that provides for a management fee and a leasing fee. Fees are based on complexity of the management and the rent received. The manager is responsible for trust records and owner accounting. Many other accounting records can also aid a property manager. Computer software is available to fulfill almost all needs of the property manager.

Leases are gross, net, percentage, or a combination of all three. Generally, net and percentage leases are found in connection with commercial rentals. To protect the owner in residential leasing, a rental application allows the owner to check out a tenant before committing to the tenant. Leases should be used for all tenancies, even month-to-month agreements, because they spell out rights and obligations of the parties.

In a lease assignment, all of the tenants' interests are transferred. In a sublease, the sublessor remains on the lease and the sublessee is the tenant's tenant.

Leases may be terminated for a number of reasons. If a tenant has breached a lease, the owner can sue for damages. The owner also may evict a tenant for breach of a material provision of the lease or if the tenant fails to leave after proper notice.

Residential landlords have disclosure requirements that relate to health and safety.

Residential landlord responsibilities include keeping the plumbing and other systems in operating order and keeping the structure safe and tight from the elements and free of pests. Residential tenant duties include keeping the unit clean; disposing of garbage properly; avoiding damaging the premises, systems, or appliances; paying rent on time; and leaving the unit clean when vacating.

A landlord may not evict a tenant (retaliatory eviction) because the tenant complained to the landlord or a public agency about the condition of the premises, or because the tenant lawfully organized a tenant group.

The Protecting Tenants at Foreclosure Act of 2009 allows residential tenants to remain in possession until the end of their lease. Month-to-month tenants are entitled to a 90-day notice to vacate.

CLASS DISCUSSION TOPICS

1. A particular percentage lease provides that after a tenant reaches a specific gross annual amount, the percentage decreases. Why was this written into the lease?

2. Identify property in your geographic area that you feel needs professional property management. Why?

3. Which offices in your area have separate property management departments?

4. Which properties in your area do you think would require the greatest management effort? Why?

5. Identify a nonresidential property in your community that has been vacant for a long time. What type of tenant would the property be suited for, and how would you market the property?

6. Do you know of any property where you feel the security is inadequate? If so, why? What could be done to provide better security?

7. Bring to class one current-events article dealing with some aspect of real estate practice for class discussion.

UNIT 15 QUIZ

1. The term *CPM* refers to
    a. California Property Manager.
    b. Certified Property Manager.
    c. Certified Professional Manager.
    d. none of these.

2. Which of the following statements regarding a property manager's compensation is *TRUE*?
    a. Compensation is generally a percentage of the gross.
    b. As the income of properties managed increases, the percentage fee charged tends to increase.
    c. Both of these.
    d. Neither of these.

3. Property managers can be protected against receiving no fees when managing a vacant property they are unable to rent by a
    a. holdover clause.
    b. recapture clause.
    c. minimum fee.
    d. separate leasing fee.

4. A lease for 30 months would be described as
    a. an estate at sufferance.
    b. an estate at will.
    c. an estate for years.
    d. a periodic tenancy.

5. A lease under which the tenant is to pay $500 per month for three years is a
    a. gross lease.
    b. net lease.
    c. percentage lease.
    d. month-to-month lease.

6. A lease that contains a minimum rent and a covenant to remain in business is
   a. a percentage lease.
   b. a net lease.
   c. a gross lease.
   d. none of these.

7. Which business would likely pay the highest percentage on a percentage lease?
   a. Parking lot
   b. Supermarket
   c. Clothing store
   d. Restaurant

8. Which business is likely to pay the lowest percentage on a percentage lease?
   a. Sporting goods store
   b. Music shop
   c. Supermarket
   d. Clothing store

9. A valid two-year lease need NOT
   a. have parties capable of contracting.
   b. contain a legal description of the property.
   c. contain the amount of rent and manner of payment.
   d. be a written agreement.

10. Which statement regarding security deposits is TRUE?
    a. Nonrefundable cleaning deposits are not allowed.
    b. Deposits for furnished rentals can't exceed three months' rent.
    c. Security deposits for unfurnished rentals can't exceed two months' rent.
    d. All of these.

INTERNET SITES FOR REAL ESTATE PROFESSIONALS

The following is a partial listing of thousands of real estate–related sites. Neither the authors nor the publisher recommend any particular sites, but we have included these for your own evaluation.

APARTMENTS FOR RENT

www.apartments.com
www.apartment finder.com
www.apartment list.com
www.homeaway.com
www.homes.com (plus mortgage center)
www.nestigator.com
www.onradpad.com
www.trulia.com
www.move.com/apartments/
www.nestigaor.com
www.rent.com
www.homeaway.com
www.rentals.com

ASSOCIATIONS

Association of Real Estate License Law Officials
www.arello.org
Building Owners and Managers Association
www.boma.org
California Association of REALTORS®
www.car.org
California Community Colleges Real Estate Education Center
http://cccreec.org

California Real Estate Education Association
www.creea.org
Federation of Exchange Accommodators
www.1031.org
Institute of Real Estate Management
www.irem.org
International Association of Home Staging Professionals
www.iahsp.com
NAR Code of Ethics
www.realtor.org/code-of-ethics/
National Apartment Association
www.naahq.org
National Association of Real Estate Brokers
www.nareb.com
National Association of Real Estate Investment Trusts (REITs)
www.reit.com/nareit
National Association of REALTORS®
www.realtor.org
Real Estate Educators Association
www.reea.org
Real Estate Staging Association
www.realestatestagingassociation.com

BOOKS

www.dearborn.com/products/bookstore/
www.nolo.com

CAN-SPAM (EMAIL SOLICITATIONS)

www.ftc.gov/tips-advice/business-center/guidance/
can-spam-act-compliance-guide-business

CHOOSING A BROKER

www.homegain.com (Homeowners post their property and desired form of representation and brokers send their proposals. This site also includes homeowner and homebuyer information.)

CREDIT REPORTS

www.annualcreditreport.com

DO-NOT-CALL REGISTRY

www.donotcall.gov

DO-IT-YOURSELF FORMS

www.legalzoom.com

ENVIRONMENTAL LAW

http://resources.ca.gov/ceqa/ (an information site developed by the California Natural Resources Agency that includes a database containing California environmental law with links to federal law)

ENVIRONMENTAL PROTECTION AGENCY SITE

www.epa.gov

FORMS

California Association of REALTORS® (CAR)
www.car.org/legal/standard-forms/
First Tuesday
www.firsttuesday.us

GOVERNMENT-RELATED SITES

California Bureau of Real Estate
www.bre.ca.gov
California Department of Fair Employment and Housing
www.dfeh.ca.gov
California Department of Finance
www.dof.ca.gov
California Department of Housing and Community Development
www.hcd.ca.gov
California Department of Justice
www.meganslaw.ca.gov (listing of names, addresses and zip codes
of registered sex offenders)
California Office of Real Estate Appraisers
www.orea.ca.gov
Consumer Price Index
www.bls.gov/cpi/
Department of Housing and Urban Development (HUD)
www.hud.gov
Department of Veterans Affairs
www.va.gov
Environmental Protection Agency
www.epa.gov
Fair Housing (HUD)
www.hud.gov/fairhousing/
Fannie Mae
www.fanniemae.com
Farmer Mac
www.farmermac.com
Federal Reserve Bank of San Francisco
www.frbsf.org
Freddie Mac
www.freddiemac.com
Ginnie Mae
www.ginniemae.gov
Government websites (search engine)
www.usa.gov
National Flood Insurance Program
www.fema.gov/national-flood-insurance-program/

FORECLOSURES

www.realtytrac.com

FOR SALE BY OWNER

www.craigslist.com
www.forsalebyowner.com
www.owners.com
www.FSBO.com
www.homepoint.com
www.homesbyowner.com

HOME PRICES (VALUE)

www.realtytrac.com (recent home prices by area)
www.homes.com/homeprices/
www.zillow.com

LISTINGS OF PROPERTY FOR SALE

www.ca-homes.com
www.californiarealestate.com
www.century21.com www.coldwellbanker.com
www.coldwellbankerpreviews.com www.craigslist.org
www.era.com www.forsalebyowner.com
www.homefinder.com
www.homes.com
www.homeseekers.com
https://homes.yahoo.com
www.househunt.com
http://newhomes.move.com
www.oodle.com
www.owners.com
www.realtor.com

www.realtyexecutives.com
www.remax.com www.trulia.com
www.zillow.com

Note: Most of the listed sites also provide for loan prequalification and application.

LOANS

www.bankofamerica.com
www.bankrate.com
www.eloan.com
www.greenlightloans.com
www.lendingtree.com
www.loantek.com
www.mortgageloan.com
www.quickenloans.com
www.wellsfargo.com

MORTGAGE CALCULATIONS

www.homefair.com
www.interest.com
www.mortgage-calc.com

PROFESSIONAL INFORMATION

Federation of Exchange Accommodators
www.1031.org
Inman News
www.inman.com
The Real Estate Library
www.relibrary.com
The Real Estate Professional magazine
www.therealestatepro.com
RealtyNow
www.realtynow.com

RealtyTimes
www.realtytimes.com
RISMedia (Real Estate Magazine)
www.rismedia.com

REAL ESTATE ATTORNEYS

www.lawyers.com
www.martindale.cm
http://real-estate-law.freeadvice.com/real-estate-law/

RENTAL COMPARABLES

www.rentometer.com

VIRTUAL HOME TOURS

www.abirdseye.com
www.easypano.com
www.ipix.com
www.paradym.com
www.spotlighthometours.com/

GLOSSARY

abstract of title. A summary or digest of all recorded transfers, conveyances, legal proceedings, and any other facts relied on as evidence of title to show continuity of ownership and indicate any possible impairments to title.

acceleration clause. A provision in a real estate financing instrument that allows the lender to declare the remaining indebtedness due and payable on the occurrence of certain conditions, such as the sale of the property or the borrower's default in payment.

acceptance. Indication by the person to whom an offer is made (the offeree) of agreement to the terms of the offer. If the offer requires a writing, the acceptance also must be in writing.

accession. The process of manufactured or natural improvement or addition to property.

accommodating party. Third party who has control of funds in delayed exchange.

accretion. Accession by natural forces, such as alluvion.

acknowledgment. A formal declaration made before an authorized person by a person who has executed a written instrument, stating that the execution of the instrument is the person's own act.

acquisition cost. For FHA-insured loans, the price to procure property, including purchase price and all nonrecurring closing costs, including discount points, FHA application fee, service charge and credit report, FHA appraisal, escrow, document preparation, title insurance, termite inspection, reconveyance, and recording fees.

acre. A measure of land equaling 160 square rods, 4,840 square yards or 43,560 square feet, or a tract about 208.71 feet square.

action for declaratory relief. Legal proceeding brought to determine the respective rights of the parties before a controversy arises.

action to quiet title. A court proceeding brought to establish title to real property.

actual age. The number of years since completion of a building; also called *historical* or *chronological age.*

actual authority. The authority agents have because it is specified in the agency agreement or that the agents believes they have because of an unintentional or careless act of the principal.

administrator/administratrix. Personal representative of the estate of a decedent, appointed by the probate court. *See also* **executor/executrix.**

ad valorem. A Latin phrase meaning "according to value," used to describe a tax charged in relation to the value of the property taxed.

adverse possession. A method of acquiring title to real property by occupying the property against the interests of the true owner and fulfilling other statutory requirements.

affordability index. An NAR index that measures the ability of median family income to support a mortgage for the median-priced home. An index of 100 means that the median income is equal to the amount necessary to afford the median-priced home.

after-acquired title. If title is acquired by a grantor only after a conveyance to a grantee, the deed to the grantee becomes effective at the time the grantor actually receives title.

agency. The relationship between a principal and the agent of the principal that arises out of a contract, whether express or implied, written or oral, by which the agent is employed by the principal to do certain acts dealing with a third party.

agent. One who acts for and with authority from another person, called the principal; a special agent is appointed to carry out a particular act or transaction, and any other agent is a general agent.

air rights. The real property right to the reasonable use of the airspace above the surface of the land.

alienation. The transferring of property to another.

all-inclusive trust deed. *See* **wraparound mortgage or trust deed.**

alluvion. Alluvium; the increase of soil along the bank of a body of water by natural forces.

Americans with Disabilities Act. Federal law prohibiting discrimination that would deny the equal enjoyment of goods, services, facilities, and accommodations in any existing place of public accommodation, based on an individual's physical or mental disabilities. .

amortization. The payment of a financial obligation in installments; recovery over a period of time of cost or value. An amortized loan includes both principal and interest in approximately equal payments, usually due monthly, resulting in complete payment of the amount borrowed, with interest, by the end of the loan term. A loan has negative amortization when the loan payments do not cover all the interest due, which then is added to the remaining loan balance.

annual percentage rate (APR). The relative cost of credit as determined in accordance with Regulation Z of the Board of Governors of the Federal Reserve System for implementing the federal Truth in Lending Act.

anticipation, principle of. Expectation that property will offer future benefits, which tends to increase present value.

apparent authority. Authority to act as an agent that someone appears to have but does not actually have, which will place no obligation on the party the agent claims to represent if that party is in no way responsible for the representation.

appraisal. An estimate of a property's monetary value on the open market; an estimate of a property's type and condition, its utility for a given purpose, or its highest and best use.

appropriation, right of. *See* **right of appropriation.**

appurtenance. Anything affixed (attached) to or used with land for its benefit and that is transferred with the land.

APR. *See* **annual percentage rate.**

area. Measure of the floor or ground space within the perimeter of a building or land parcel.

arm's-length transaction. A transaction in which neither party acts under duress and both have full knowledge of the property's assets and defects, the property involved has been on the market a reasonable length of time, there are no unusual circumstances, and the price represents the normal consideration for the property sold without extraordinary financing.

assessed valuation. A valuation placed on a piece of property by a public authority as a basis for levying taxes on that property.

assessor. The official responsible for determining assessed values.

assumption. An undertaking or adoption of a debt or an obligation resting primarily on another person.

attachment. The process by which the real or personal property of a party to a lawsuit is seized and retained in the custody of the court; intended to compel an appearance before the court or to furnish security for a debt or costs arising out of the litigation.

attorney-in-fact. An agent who has been granted a power of attorney by a principal.

avulsion. The tearing or washing away of land along the bank of a body of water by natural forces.

balance, principle of. The combination of land uses that results in the highest property values overall.

balloon payment. An installment payment on a promissory note—usually the final payment—that is significantly larger than the other installment payments.

bankruptcy. A federal court proceeding in which the court takes possession of the assets of an insolvent debtor and sells the nonexempt assets to pay off creditors on a pro rata basis; title to the debtor's assets is held by a trustee in bankruptcy.

base lines. Imaginary lines that run east-west and intersect meridians that run north-south to form the starting point for land measurement using the rectangular survey system of land description.

basis. Cost basis is the dollar amount assigned to property at the time of acquisition under provisions of the Internal Revenue Code for the purpose of determining gain, loss, and depreciation in calculating the income tax to be paid on the sale or exchange of the property; adjusted cost basis is derived after the application of certain additions, such as for improvements, and deductions, such as for depreciation.

beneficiary. One on whose behalf a trustee holds property conveyed by a trustor; the lender under a deed of trust.

bequest. Transfer of property, particularly personal property, called a *legacy*, by will. *See also* **devise**.

bill of sale. Written instrument that conveys title to personal property.

blanket mortgage. A loan covering more than one property.

blind ad. An ad that fails to indicate that the advertiser is an agent.

blockbusting. The practice on the part of unscrupulous speculators or real estate agents of inducing panic selling of homes at prices below market value, especially by exploiting the prejudices of property owners in neighborhoods in which the racial makeup is changing or appears to be on the verge of changing.

bond. An obligation; a real estate bond is a written obligation issued on security of a mortgage or trust deed.

book value. The current value for accounting purposes of an asset expressed as original cost plus capital additions minus accumulated depreciation.

breach. The failure of a duty imposed by law or by contract, either by omission or commission.

building code. Standards for building, planning, and construction established by state law and local ordinance.

bundle of rights. The legal rights of ownership of real property, including the rights of possession, use, disposition, and exclusion of others from the property.

Bureau of Real Estate. California agency that administers the real estate law, including the licensing of real estate brokers and salespeople; headed by the real estate commissioner, who is appointed by the governor and presides over the Real Estate Advisory Commission (whose 10 members are appointed by and serve at the commissioner's discretion).

business opportunity. The assets of an existing business enterprise, including its goodwill.

buyer's market. Real estate marketplace that has more sellers than buyers.

CalVet loan. Home or farm loan procured through the California Veterans Farm and Home Purchase Program.

capital assets. Assets of a permanent nature used in the production of income, such as land, buildings, machinery, and equipment; usually distinguishable under income tax law from "inventory," assets held for sale to customers in the ordinary course of the taxpayer's trade or business.

capital gain. The amount by which the net resale proceeds of a capital item exceed the adjusted cost basis of the item.

capitalization rate. The rate of interest that is considered a reasonable return on an investment, used in the process of determining value based on net operating income; the yield necessary to attract investment.

capitalization recapture. The return of an investment; an amortization rate based on the right of the investor to get back the purchase price at the end of the term of ownership or over the productive life of the improvements; computed by straight-line depreciation, by using Inwood tables or Hoskold tables. (Students should refer to a real estate appraisal text for further explanation.)

cash flow. The net income generated by a property before depreciation and other noncash expenses.

CC&Rs. Covenants, conditions, and restrictions; limitations on land use imposed by deed, usually when land is subdivided, as a means of regulating building construction, density, and use for the benefit of other property owners; may be referred to simply as *restrictions*.

certificate of reasonable value. Property appraisal required for a VA-guaranteed loan.

certificate of redemption. Issued by the county tax collector when all past due amounts have been paid.

certificate of sale. Document received by the buyer at an execution or a judicial foreclosure sale; replaced by a sheriff's deed if the debtor fails to redeem the property during the statutory redemption period.

certificate of title. Statement of a property's owner of record as well as any existing encumbrances.

chain of title. The history of the conveyances and encumbrances affecting the present owner's title to property, as far back as records are available.

change, principle of. Effect on property value of constantly varying physical, economic, social, and political forces.

chattel mortgage. Use of personal property to secure or guarantee a promissory note.

chattel real. An estate related to real estate, such as a lease of real property.

chattels. Personal property; any property that is not real property.

Civil Rights Act of 1866. The first U.S. civil rights act. It applied to race only and had no exceptions.

Civil Rights Act of 1968. This comprehensive act is known as the Fair Housing Act.

closing. The completion of a real estate transaction, at which point required documents are transmitted and funds are transferred.

Closing Disclosure. New form mandated by the TILA-RESPA rule that helps consumers to understand all the costs of the transaction. It must be provided to consumers three business days before closing.

cloud on the title. Any claim, condition, or encumbrance that impairs title to real property.

coastal zone. An area of about 1,800 square miles that runs the length of the state from the sea inland about 1,000 yards, with wider spots in coastal estuarine, habitat, and recreational areas; any development or improvement of land within the coastal zone must meet local requirements for coastal conservation and preservation of resources, as authorized by the Coastal Zone Conservation Act.

codicil. Written amendment to a will, made with the same legal formalities.

color of title. A claim of possession to real property based on a document erroneously appearing to convey title to the claimant.

commingling. Mixing broker and principal funds.

commission. An agent's compensation for performing the duties of the agency; in real estate practice, typically a percentage of the selling price of property, rentals, or other property value.

common law. The body of law from England based on custom, usage, and court decisions.

community apartment project. A form of subdivision in which the owner has an individual interest in the land and exclusive right of occupancy of an apartment on the land.

community property. All property acquired by husband and wife during marriage except that qualifying as separate property.

community redevelopment agency (CRA). An agency authorized by state law but formed by a local governing body to provide low-and moderate-income housing and employ low-income persons by rehabilitating existing structures and/or bringing new development.

competition, principle of. Business profits encourage competition, which ultimately may reduce profits for any one business.

comparative market analysis. Informal estimate of market value performed by a real estate agent for either seller or buyer, utilizing the sales history of nearby properties; usually expressed as a range of values that includes the probable market value of the subject property.

compound interest. Interest paid on original principal and also on the accrued and unpaid interest that has accumulated as the debt matures.

concurrent ownership. Ownership of property by more than one person, not necessarily in equal shares.

condemnation. *See* **eminent domain**.

condition. A qualification of an estate granted that can be imposed only in a conveyance; it can be a condition precedent or a condition subsequent. *See also* **CC&Rs**.

condition precedent. A qualification of a contract or transfer of property providing that unless and until the performance of a certain act, the contract or transfer will not take effect.

condition subsequent. A stipulation in a contract or transfer of property that already has taken effect that will extinguish the contract or defeat the property transfer.

condominium. A subdivision providing an exclusive ownership (fee) interest in the airspace of a particular portion of real property, as well as an interest in common in a portion of that property.

conforming loan. Loan that meets Fannie Mae and Freddie Mac purchase criteria.

conformity, principle of. Holds that property values are maximized when buildings are similar in design, construction, and age, particularly in residential neighborhoods.

consideration. Anything of value given or promised by a party to induce another to enter into a contract; may be a benefit conferred on one party or a detriment suffered by the other.

constructive eviction. Interference by the landlord in a tenant's legitimate use of leased property, such as by making unwarranted alterations to the property.

contract. A written or oral agreement to do or not to do certain things. There may be an express agreement of the parties, or a contract may be implied by their conduct. A unilateral contract imposes an obligation on only one of the parties, whereas both parties to a bilateral contract have an obligation to perform. A contract is executory when a contract obligation is to be performed in the future, and executed when all obligations have been performed and the contract transaction has been completed. A real estate contract must be a signed writing made by competent parties, for valuable consideration, with an offer by one party that is accepted by the other.

contribution, principle of. A component part of a property is valued in proportion to its contribution to the value of the entire property, regardless of its separate actual cost.

conventional loan. A loan secured by a mortgage or trust deed that is made without governmental underwriting (FHA-insured or VA-guaranteed).

cooperative apartment. *See* stock cooperative.

corporation. A legal entity that acts through its board of directors and officers, generally without liability on the part of the person or persons owning it. A domestic corporation is one chartered in California—any other corporation is a foreign corporation in California.

correction lines. Guide meridians running every 24 miles east and west of a meridian, and standard parallels running every 24 miles north and south of a base line, used to correct inaccuracies in the rectangular survey system of land description caused by the earth's curvature.

Costa-Hawkins Rental Housing Act. Statute that allows landlords of rent-controlled property to set new base rents for new tenants.

cost approach. Appraisal method in which site value is added to the present reproduction or replacement cost of all property improvements, less depreciation, to determine market value.

covenant. An agreement or a promise to do or not to do a particular act, usually imposed by deed. *See also* CC&Rs.

covenant of quiet enjoyment. Promise of a landlord, implied by law, not to interfere in the possession or use of leased property by the tenant.

covenant to repair. Express or legally implied obligation of the landlord to make necessary repairs to leased premises.

declaration of homestead. *See* homestead.

dedication. The giving of land by its owner for a public use, and the acceptance of the land for such use by the appropriate government officials.

deed. Written instrument that, when properly executed and delivered, conveys title to real property from a grantor to a grantee.

deed in lieu of foreclosure. A deed to real property accepted by a lender from a defaulting borrower to avoid the necessity of foreclosure proceedings by the lender.

deed of trust. *See* trust deed.

defendant. A person against whom legal action is initiated for the purpose of obtaining criminal sanctions (in a case involving violation of a penal statute) or damages or other appropriate judicial relief (in a civil case).

deficiency judgment. A judgment given by a court when the value of security pledged for a loan is insufficient to pay off the debt of the defaulting borrower.

demand statement. Statement requested by escrow as to amount due lender at close of escrow to pay off loan and any charges.

depreciation. Decrease in value of an asset that is allowed in computing property value for tax purposes; in appraising, a loss in the value of a property improvement from any cause; depreciation is *curable* when it can be remedied by a repair or an addition to the property, and it is incurable when there is no easy or economic way to cure the loss. *See also* **physical deterioration**, **functional obsolescence**, and **external obsolescence**.

designated agent. In some states one agent in an office can be the seller's agent and another agent in the same office can be the buyer's agent.

devise. Transfer of title to property by will. *See also* **bequest**.

devisee. Person receiving title to property by will. *See also* **legatee**.

devisor. One who wills property to another.

direct endorsement. A lender who is authorized to determine if a loan qualifies for FHA insurance.

discount points. *See* **points**.

discount rate. Interest rate charged member banks by Federal Reserve Banks.

documentary transfer tax. A tax applied on all transfers of real property located in a county where the county is authorized by the state to collect; notice of payment is entered on the face of the deed or on a separate paper filed with the deed.

Dodd-Frank Act. The Dodd-Frank Wall Street Reform and Consumer Protection Act signed into law in 2010.

dominant tenement. *See* **easement**.

donee. One who receives a gift.

donor. One who makes a gift.

dual agency. An agency relationship in which the agent represents two principals in their dealings with each other.

due-on-sale clause. An acceleration clause in a real estate financing instrument granting the lender the right to demand full payment of the remaining indebtedness on a sale of the property.

easement. The right to a specific use of or the right to travel over the land of another. The land being used or traveled over is the servient tenement; the land that is benefited by the use is the dominant tenement. An easement appurtenant is a property interest that belongs to the owner of the dominant tenement and is transferred with the land; an easement in gross is a personal right that usually is not transferable by its owner.

easement by prescription. Acquiring a specific use of or the right to travel over the land of another by statutory requirements similar to those for adverse possession.

economic life. The period of time over which an improved property will yield a return on investment over and above the return attributable solely to the land.

economic obsolescence. *See* **external obsolescence.**

economic rent. The reasonable rental expectancy if the property were available for renting at the time of its valuation.

effective gross income. Property income from all sources, less allowance for vacancy and collection losses.

effective rent. Scheduled rent adjusted for rental incentives given.

elder abuse law. Requirement that realty agents and others report elder financial abuse, fraud, or undue influence.

emblements. Crops produced annually by labor and industry, as distinguished from crops that grow naturally on the land.

eminent domain. The right of the government to acquire title to property for public use by condemnation; the property owner receives compensation—generally fair market value. *See also* **inverse condemnation.**

encroachment. The unlawful intrusion of a property improvement onto adjacent property.

encumbrance. Anything that affects or limits the fee simple title to or affects the condition or use of real estate.

environmental impact report (EIR). Evaluation of effects on the environment of a proposed development; may be required by local government.

environmental obsolescence. *See* **external obsolescence.**

e-PRO certification. NAR professional designation of an internet professional.

Equal Credit Opportunity Act. Act that prohibits lender discrimination against a borrower based on the fact that the source of income is public assistance.

Equator Platform. A system for obtaining short sale approval.

equity of redemption. The right to redeem property during the fore-closure period, or during a statutorily prescribed time following a foreclosure sale.

escalator clause. Provision in a lease agreement for an increase in pay-ments based on an increase in an index, such as the Consumer Price Index.

escheat. The reverting of property to the state when there are no heirs capable of inheriting.

escrow. The deposit of instruments and/or funds (with instructions) with a neutral third party to carry out the provisions of an agreement or a contract.

escrow agent. Escrow holder; the neutral third-party company holding funds or something of value in trust for another or others.

escrow offices. The employee of the escrow agent who handles the escrow.

estate. The interest held by the owner of property.

estate at sufferance. The occupancy of a tenant after the lease term expires.

estate at will. A tenancy in which the tenant's time of possession is indefinite.

estate for years. A tenancy for a fixed term.

estate from period to period. Periodic tenancy; a tenancy for a fixed term, automatically renewed for the same term unless the owner or the tenant gives the other written notice of intention to terminate the tenancy.

eviction. Dispossession by process of law.

exchange. A means of trading equities in two or more real properties, treated as a single transaction through a single escrow.

exclusive-agency listing. A listing agreement employing a broker as sole agent for a seller of real property under the terms of which the broker is entitled to compensation if the property is sold through any other broker, but not if a sale is negotiated by the owner without the services of an agent.

exclusive-authorization-and-right-to-sell listing. A listing agree-ment employing a broker as agent for a seller of real property under the terms of which the broker is entitled to compensation if the listed property is sold during the duration of the listing, whether by the list-ing agent, another agent, or the owner acting without the services of an agent.

executor/executrix. Personal representative of the estate of a decedent, named in the decedent's will. *See also* **administrator/administratrix.**

express agreement. An agreement established by a deliberate act of the parties that both parties acknowledge as their intention.

external obsolescence. Economic or environmental obsolescence; loss in value due to outside causes, such as changes in nearby land use.

Fair Employment and Housing Act. *See* **Rumford Act.**

Fannie Mae (Federal National Mortgage Association). Now a private corporation dealing in the secondary mortgage market.

Farmer Mac (Federal Agricultural Mortgage Corporation). Now a private corporation providing a secondary mortgage market for farms and rural housing.

fee simple absolute. A fee simple estate with no restrictions on its use.

fee simple defeasible. An interest in land, such as a fee simple conditional or fee simple with special limitation, that may result in the estate of ownership being defeated.

fee simple estate. The greatest interest in real property one can own, including the right to use the property at present and for an indeterminate period in the future.

fee simple qualified. A fee simple estate with some restrictions on the right of possession.

feng shui. Laws governing orientation and spatial relationship in regard to the flow of energy.

fiduciary. A person in a position of trust and confidence who owes a certain loyalty to another, such as an agent to a principal.

final subdivision map. *See* **tentative subdivision map.**

fiscal year. A business or an accounting year as distinguished from a calendar year.

fixture. Anything permanently attached to land or improvements so as to become real property.

foreclosure. Sale of real property by mortgagee, trustee, or other lienholder on default by the borrower. *See also* **judicial foreclosure action.**

form appraisal report. A short report, typically two pages plus addenda, using a preprinted form to summarize the data contributing to an appraiser's conclusion of value.

fraud. The intentional and successful use of any cunning, deception, collusion, or artifice to circumvent, cheat, or deceive another person, so that the other person acts on it to the loss of property and legal injury; actual fraud is a deliberate misrepresentation or a representation made in reckless disregard of its truth or falsity, the suppression of truth, a promise made without the intention to perform it or any other act intended to deceive; constructive fraud is any misrepresentation made without fraudulent intent (the deliberate intent to deceive). Fraud is affirmative when it is a deliberate statement of a material fact that the speaker knows to be false and on which the speaker intends another person to rely, to the speaker's detriment. Fraud is negative when it is a deliberate concealment of something that should be revealed.

Freddie Mac (Federal Home Loan Mortgage Corporation). Now a private secondary mortgage corporation.

freehold estate. An estate in land in which ownership is for an indeterminate length of time, as in a fee simple or life estate.

front foot. Property measured by the front linear foot on its street line, each front foot extending the depth of the lot.

functional obsolescence. Loss in value due to adverse factors within a structure that affect its marketability, such as its design, layout, or utility.

general partnership. An association of two or more persons to carry on a business as co-owners for profit.

general plan. Master plan; includes a statement of policy of the development and land uses within a city or county and a program to implement that policy.

gift deed. A deed for which the only consideration is "love and affection."

Ginnie Mae (Government National Mortgage Association). A government corporation that provides assistance to federally related housing projects. Funds are raised by selling securities backed by pools of mortgages.

goodwill. An intangible but salable asset of a business derived from the expectation of continued public patronage.

grant deed. A limited warranty deed using a granting clause—the word *grant* or words to that effect—assuring the grantee that the estate being conveyed is free from encumbrances placed on the property by the present owner (the grantor) and that the grantor has not previously conveyed the property to anyone else.

grantee. A person to whom property is transferred by grant.

grantor. A person conveying property to another by grant.

gross income. Total property income from all sources before any expenses are deducted.

gross income multiplier. Gross rent multiplier; a number derived by dividing the sales price of a comparable property by the income it produces, which then is multiplied by the gross income produced by the subject property to derive an estimate of value.

gross lease. Provides for the tenant to pay a fixed rental over the lease term, with the landlord paying all expenses of ownership, such as taxes, assessments, and insurance.

ground lease. An agreement for the use of land only, sometimes secured by improvements placed on the land by the user.

ground rent. Earnings of improved property credited to earnings of the ground itself after allowance is made for earnings of improvements.

guarantee of title. Guarantee of title as determined from examination of the public records and described in the guarantee document.

guide meridians. *See* **correction lines**.

hard money loans. Cash loans made by individual investors.

highest and best use. In appraising real estate, the most profitable, physically possible, and legally permissible use for the property under consideration.

holder in due course. Someone who takes a negotiable instrument for value, in good faith and without notice of any defense against its enforcement that might be made by any person.

holdover tenancy. Possession of property by a tenant who remains in possession after the expiration or termination of the lease term.

holographic will. A will written entirely in the testator's handwriting, signed and dated by the testator.

homestead. A statutory exemption of real property used as a home from the claims of certain creditors and judgments up to a specified amount; requires a declaration of homestead to be completed and filed in the county recorder's office.

implied warranties. Warranties by grantor to grantee that will be implied by law, even if not mentioned in the deed; the grantor warrants that he has not already conveyed the property and that there are no encumbrances on the property brought about by the grantor or any person who might claim title from the grantor.

income capitalization approach. Appraisal method in which the actual or likely net operating income of property is divided by its expected rate of return (capitalization rate) to arrive at an estimate of market value. *See also* **capitalization rate**.

independent contractor. A person employed by another who has almost complete freedom to accomplish the purposes of the employment.

index method. Way of estimating building reproduction cost by multiplying the original cost of the subject building by a factor that represents the percentage change in construction costs, generally from the time of construction to the time of valuation.

inherent authority. The authority of an agent to perform activities that are not specifically mentioned in the agency agreement but are necessary or customary to carry out an authorized act.

injunction. A writ or an order issued by a court to restrain one or more parties to a suit or proceeding from doing an act deemed to be inequitable or unjust in regard to the rights of some other party or parties in the suit or proceeding.

installment sales contract. *See* **sales contract.**

institutional lenders. A financial intermediary or depository, such as a savings association, commercial bank, or life insurance company, that pools the money of its depositors and then invests funds in various ways, including trust deeds and mortgage loans.

interest. A portion, share, or right in something; partial ownership; the charge in dollars for the use of money for a period of time.

interest rate. The percentage of a sum of money borrowed that is charged for its use.

interim loan. A short-term temporary loan used until permanent financing is available, typically during building construction.

interpleader. A court proceeding that may be brought by someone, such as an escrow agent, who holds property for another, for the purpose of deciding who among the claimants is legally entitled to the property.

intestate succession. Statutory method of distribution of property that belonged to someone who died intestate (without having made a valid will).

inverse condemnation. A legal action brought by the owner of land when government puts nearby land to a use that diminishes the value of the owner's property.

joint tenancy. Ownership of property by two or more co-owners, each of whom has an equal share and the right of survivorship.

joint venture. Two or more individuals or firms joining together on a single project as partners, typically with a lender contributing the necessary funds and the other partner(s) contributing their expertise.

judgment. The final determination of a court of competent jurisdiction of a matter presented to it; may include an award of money damages.

judicial foreclosure action. Proceeding in which a mortgagee, a trustee, or another lienholder on property requests a court-supervised sale of the property to cover the unpaid balance of a delinquent debt.

land. The earth's surface, including substances beneath the surface extending downward to the center of the earth and the airspace above the surface for an indefinite distance upward.

land contract. *See* **sales contract.**

landlord. Lessor; one who leases property to another.

lateral support. The support that the soil of an adjoining owner gives to a neighbor's land.

lease. A contract between a property owner, called *lessor* or *landlord*, and another, called *lessee* or *tenant*, conveying and setting forth the conditions of occupancy and use of the property by the tenant.

leaseback. *See* sale-leaseback.

leasehold estate. A tenant's right to occupy real estate during the term of the lease; a personal property interest.

legacy. Property, usually personal property, transferred by will.

legal description. A land description used to define a parcel of land to the exclusion of all others that is acceptable by a court of law.

legatee. Person who receives property, called a legacy, by bequest. *See also* devisee.

letter of opinion. A letter from appraiser to client presenting only the appraiser's conclusion of value, with no supporting data.

leverage. Use of debt financing to purchase an investment, thus maximizing the return per dollar of equity invested; enables a purchaser to obtain possession for little or no initial cash outlay and relatively small periodic payments on the debt incurred.

lien. An encumbrance that makes property security for the payment of a debt or discharge of an obligation; a voluntary lien is one agreed to by the property owner, such as a deed of trust; an involuntary lien exists by operation of law to create a burden on property for certain unpaid debts, such as a tax lien.

life estate. An interest in real property conveying the right to possession and use for a term measured by the life or lives of one or more persons, most often the holder of the life estate.

limited equity housing cooperative. A stock cooperative financed by the California Housing Finance Agency.

limited partnership. Partnership of one or more general partners, who run the business and are liable as partners, and limited partners, investors who do not run the business and are liable only up to the amount invested.

liquidated damages. An amount agreed on by the parties to be full damages if a certain event occurs.

listing agreement. Authorization by the owner of property, acting as principal, for a real estate broker to act as the agent of the principal in finding a person to buy, lease, or rent property; may be used to employ a real estate broker to act as agent for a person seeking property to buy, lease, or rent.

Loan Estimate. New form mandated by the TILA-RESPA rule that helps consumers to understand the key features, costs, and risks of a mortgage loan. It must be provided to consumers no later than three business days after they submit a loan application.

lot and block system. Subdivision system; method of legal description of land using parcel maps identified by tract, block, and lot numbers.

marker. *See* **metes and bounds.**

marketable title. Title that a reasonably prudent purchaser, acting with full knowledge of the facts and their legal significance, would be willing and ought to accept.

market comparison approach. *See* **sales comparison approach.**

market data approach. *See* **sales comparison approach.**

market value. The most probable price a property would bring in an arm's-length transaction under normal conditions on the open market. *See also* **arm's-length transaction.**

material fact. A fact that would be likely to affect the judgment of a person to whom it is known, such as information concerning the poor physical condition of a building that is for sale.

mechanic's lien. A statutory lien against real property in favor of persons who have performed work or furnished materials for the improvement of the property.

Mello-Roos bonds. Improvement bonds that place offsite improvement costs on the home purchaser rather than on the developer.

meridians. Imaginary lines that run north to south and intersect base lines that run east to west to form the starting point for land measurement using the rectangular survey system of land description.

metes and bounds. Method of legal description of land using distances (called metes) measured from a point of beginning and using natural or artificial boundaries (called bounds), as well as single objects (called monuments or markers) as points of reference.

minor. A person younger than 18 years of age.

mobile home. A structure transportable in one or more sections, designed and equipped to contain no more than two dwelling units, to be used with or without a foundation system; does not include a recreational vehicle.

mobile home park. Any area or tract of land where two or more mobile home lots are rented, leased, or held out for rent or lease.

monument. *See* **metes and bounds**.

mortgage. A legal instrument by which property is pledged by a borrower, the mortgagor, as security for the payment of a debt or an obligation owed to a lender, the mortgagee.

Mortgage Loan Disclosure Statement. The statement on a form approved by the real estate commissioner that is required by law to be furnished by a mortgage loan broker to the prospective borrower of a loan of a statutorily prescribed amount before the borrower becomes obligated to complete the loan.

multiple listing clause. Clause in a listing agreement, usually part of an exclusive authorization and right-to-sell listing, taken by a member of a multiple listing service, providing that members of the multiple listing service will have the opportunity to find a ready, willing, and able buyer for the listed property.

multiple listing service (MLS). An organization of real estate agents providing for a pooling of listings and the sharing of commissions on transactions involving more than one agent.

narrative appraisal report. The longest and most thorough appraisal report, containing a summary of all factual materials, techniques, and appraisal methods used in setting forth the appraiser's conclusion of value.

negotiable instrument. An instrument, such as a promissory note, that is capable of being assigned or transferred in the ordinary course of business.

net listing. A listing agreement providing that the agent may retain as compensation for services all sums received over and above a net price to the owner.

net, net, net lease. *See* **triple net lease**.

net operating income. Profit; the money remaining after expenses are deducted from income.

niche marketing. Specialization in an area, type of property, and/or category of buyer.

nonexclusive listing. *See* **open listing.**

notice. Knowledge of a fact; actual notice is express or implied knowledge of a fact; constructive notice is knowledge of a fact that is imputed to a person by law because of the person's actual notice of circumstances and the inquiry that a prudent person would have been expected to make; legal notice is information required to be given by law.

novation. The substitution or exchange of a new obligation or contract for an old one by mutual agreement of the parties.

null and void. Of no legal validity or effect.

observed condition method. Breakdown method; depreciation computed by estimating the loss in value caused by every item of depreciation, whether curable or incurable.

one hundred percent commission. An office where salespersons pay broker fees but keep commissions earned.

open listing. Nonexclusive listing; the nonexclusive right to secure a purchaser, given by a property owner to a real estate agent; more than one agent may be given such authorization, and only the first to procure a ready, willing, and able buyer— or an offer acceptable to the seller—will be entitled to compensation.

opinion of title. An attorney's written evaluation of the condition of the title to a parcel of land after examination of the abstract of title.

option. A right given for a consideration to purchase or lease property on specified terms within a specified time, with no obligation on the part of the person receiving the right to exercise it.

option ARM. Adjustable-rate mortgage where the buyer has the option of making a minimum payment.

overriding trust deed. *See* **wraparound mortgage** or **trust deed.**

ownership in severalty. Separate ownership; ownership of property by one person only.

participation loan. A loan where the lender takes an equity position in the property, as well as interest for the loan.

partition action. Court proceeding by which co-owners may force a division of the property or its sale, with co-owners reimbursed for their individual shares.

partnership. *See* **general partnership.**

percentage lease. Provides for rent as a percentage of the tenant's gross income, usually with a minimum base amount; the percentage may decrease as the tenant's income increases.

personal property. All property that is not real property.

physical deterioration. Loss in value brought about by wear and tear, disintegration, use and action of the elements.

piggyback loan. A second mortgage taken out at the same time as the first mortgage to reduce down payment requirements and/or avoid the need for private mortgage insurance.

plaintiff. The person who sues in a court action.

planned unit development (PUD). A land-use design that provides intensive utilization of the land through a combination of private and common areas with prearranged sharing of responsibilities for the common areas; individual lots are owned in fee with joint ownership of open areas; primarily residential but may include commercial and/or industrial uses.

planning commission. An agency of local government charged with planning the development, redevelopment, or preservation of an area.

plottage. Assemblage; an appraisal term for the increased value of two or more adjoining lots when they are placed under single ownership and available for use as a larger single lot.

pocket listing. A listing not provided to other brokers.

points. One point represents one percentage point of a loan amount; may be charged by lenders at the time of loan funding to increase the loan's effective interest rate.

police power. The right of government to enact laws and enforce them to benefit the public health, safety, and general welfare.

power of attorney. A written instrument authorizing an agent to act in the capacity of the principal; a general power of attorney provides authority to carry out all of the business dealings of the principal; a special power of attorney provides authority to carry out a specific act or acts.

power of sale. The power that may be given by a promissory note to a trustee, a mortgagee, or another lienholder to sell secured property without judicial proceedings if the borrower defaults.

predatory lending. Making loans without regard to payment ability of borrower in order to obtain the security by foreclosure.

primary mortgage market. Composed of lenders that deal directly with borrowers. *See also* **secondary mortgage market.**

prime rate. Interest rate that banks charge their most favorably rated commercial borrowers.

principal. The employer of an agent; one of the parties to a transaction; the amount of money borrowed.

private mortgage insurance (PMI). Mortgage guaranty insurance available to conventional lenders on the high-risk portion of a loan, with payment included in the borrower's loan installments.

probate. Court proceeding by which the property of a decedent is distributed according to the decedent's will or, if the decedent died intestate (without a will), according to the state law of intestate succession.

procuring cause. The cause originating a series of events that lead directly to the intended objective; in a real estate transaction, the procuring cause is the real estate agent who first procures a ready, willing, and able buyer.

progression, principle of. The worth of a less-valuable building tends to be enhanced by proximity to buildings of greater value.

promissory note. A written promise to repay a loan under stipulated terms; establishes personal liability for payment by the person making the note.

property management. A branch of the real estate business involving the marketing, operation, maintenance, and other day-to-day requirements of rental properties by an individual or a firm acting as agent of the owner.

proration. Adjustment of interest, taxes, insurance, and other costs of property ownership on a pro rata basis as of the closing or agreed-upon date; usually apportions those costs based on seller's and buyer's respective periods of ownership.

puffing. Exaggerating the attributes or benefits of property as an inducement to purchase.

purchase money mortgage or trust deed. Trust deed or mortgage given as part or all of the purchase consideration for real property.

qualified mortgage. Loans that meet standards for HUD insurance.

quantity survey method. Way of estimating building reproduction cost by making a thorough itemization of all construction costs, both direct (material and labor) and indirect (permits, overhead, profit), then totaling those costs.

quiet title. *See* **action to quiet title.**

quitclaim deed. A deed that conveys any interest the grantor may have in the property at the time of the execution of the deed, without any warranty of title or interest.

ranges. In the rectangular survey system of land description, townships running east and west of a meridian.

ratification. The adoption or approval of an act by the person on whose behalf it was performed, as when a principal ratifies conduct of an agent that was not previously authorized.

ready, willing, and able buyer. A buyer who wants and is prepared to purchase property, including being able to finance the purchase, at the agreed price and terms.

real estate. Real property; land; includes the surface of the earth, the substances beneath the surface, the airspace above the surface, fixtures, and anything incidental or appurtenant to the land.

real estate board. A local organization whose members consist primarily of real estate brokers and salespeople.

real estate broker. A person employed for a fee by another to carry on any of the activities listed in the real estate law definition of a broker.

Real Estate Education and Research Fund. California fund financed by a fixed portion of real estate license fees, designed to encourage research in land use and real estate development.

real estate investment trust (REIT). Way for investors to pool funds for investments in real estate and mortgages, with profits taxed to individual investors rather than to the corporation.

real estate salesperson. A person licensed under the provisions of the real estate law to act under the control and supervision of a real estate broker in carrying on any of the activities listed in the license law.

real estate syndicate. An organization of real estate investors, typically in the form of a limited partnership.

real property. *See* real estate.

reconciliation. In appraising, the final step, in which the estimates of value reached by each of the three appraisal approaches (sales comparison, cost, and income capitalization) are weighed in light of the type of property being appraised, the purpose of the appraisal, and other factors, to arrive at a final conclusion of value.

reconveyance deed. Instrument by which the trustee returns title to the trustor after the debt underlying a deed of trust is paid.

recovery account. State fund financed by real estate license fees and intended to help compensate victims of real estate licensee fraud, misrepresentation, deceit, or conversion of trust funds, when a court-ordered judgment cannot be collected.

rectangular survey system. Section and township system; U.S. government survey system; method of legal description of land using areas called townships measured from meridians and base lines.

recurring costs. Impound costs for taxes and insurance.

red flag. A physical indication of a possible problem with a property.

redlining. An illegal lending policy of denying real estate loans on properties in older, changing urban areas (usually with large minority populations) because of alleged higher lending risks, without due consideration of the individual loan applicant.

reformation. An action to correct a mistake in a contract, a deed, or another document.

regression, principle of. A building's value will decline if the buildings around it have a lower value.

release. Removal of part of a contract obligation, for consideration, by the party to whom the obligation is owed; removal of part of a property from a lien on payment of part of the debt owed.

reliction. The increase of a landowner's property by the receding of an adjacent body of water.

remainder. The right of future possession and use that will go to someone other than the grantor upon termination of a life estate.

rent. The consideration paid for possession and use of leased property.

rent control. A regulation imposed by a local governing body as a means of protecting tenants from relatively high rent increases over the occupancy period of a lease; if a law provides for vacancy decontrol, when a unit becomes vacant, there is no restriction on the rent set for a new tenant.

REO's. Foreclosure real estate owned by lender.

repair and deduct. Tenant's remedy when landlord is on notice of and fails to make necessary repairs to leased premises; a tenant may spend up to one month's rent on repairs, but no more than twice in any 12-month period.

replacement cost. The cost of a new building using modern construction techniques, design, and materials but having the same utility as the subject property.

reproduction cost. The cost of a new building of exactly the same design and materials as the subject property.

rescission. The cancellation of a contract and restoration of the parties to the same position they held before the contract was formed.

restraint on alienation. An illegal condition that would prohibit a property owner from transferring title to real estate.

restriction. A limitation on the use of real property; public restrictions imposed by government include zoning ordinances; private restrictions imposed by deed may require the grantee to do or refrain from doing something. *See also* **CC&Rs**.

reverse exchange. Delayed exchange where the property desired is acquired prior to sale of exchanger's property.

reverse mortgage. Mortgage where the borrower receives payments and does not repay loan until the property is sold or the borrower dies.

reversion. The right of future possession and use retained by the grantor of a life estate.

right of appropriation. Right of government to take, impound, or divert water flowing on the public domain from its natural course for some beneficial purpose.

right of entry. The right of the landlord to enter leased premises in certain circumstances.

right of survivorship. The right of surviving cotenants to share equally in the interest of a deceased cotenant; the last surviving cotenant is sole owner of the property.

riparian rights. The right of a landowner whose property borders a lake, river, or stream to the use and enjoyment of the water adjacent to or flowing over the property, provided the use does not injure other riparian landowners.

Rumford Act. California's fair housing law. Also called the Fair Employment and Housing Act.

safety clause. A clause that protects the broker's commission when a sale is consummated after a listing expires to a buyer procured by the broker.

sale-leaseback. A transaction in which, at the time of sale, the seller retains occupancy by concurrently agreeing to lease the property from the purchaser.

sales comparison approach. Market comparison approach; market data approach; appraisal method in which the sales prices of properties that are comparable in construction and location to the subject property are analyzed and adjusted to reflect differences between the comparables and the subject.

sales contract. Land contract; installment sales contract; a contract used in a sale of real property whereby the seller retains title to the property until all or a prescribed part of the purchase price has been paid, but no earlier than one year from the date of possession.

salvage value. In computing depreciation for tax purposes under all but the declining balance method, the reasonably anticipated fair market value of the property at the end of its useful life.

sandwich lease. A leasehold interest between the primary lease and the operating lease.

satisfaction. Discharge of an obligation before the end of its term by payment of the total debt owed.

scheduled rent. Rent charged, not adjusted for rental incentives.

secondary financing. A loan secured by a second (or subsequent) mortgage or trust deed on real property.

secondary mortgage market. Investment opportunities involving real property securities, other than direct loans from lender to borrower; loans may be bought, sold, or pooled to form the basis for mortgage-backed securities.

section. A standard land area of one mile square, containing 640 acres, used in the rectangular survey system of land description.

section and township system. *See* **rectangular survey system**.

security deposit. An amount paid at the start of a lease term and retained by the landlord until the tenant vacates the premises, all or part of which may be kept by the landlord at that time to cover costs of any default in rent payments or reasonable costs of repairs or cleaning necessitated by the tenant's use of the premises.

security instrument. A written document executed by a debtor that pledges the described property as the lender's assurance that the underlying debt will be repaid.

seller's market. Real estate market with more buyers than sellers.

separate property. Property owned by a married person other than community property, including property owned before marriage, property acquired by gift or inheritance, income from separate property, and property acquired with the proceeds of separate property.

servient tenement. *See* **easement**.

set-back ordinance. An ordinance requiring improvements built on property to be a specified distance from the property line, street or curb.

severalty, ownership in. *See* **ownership in severalty**.

sheriff's deed. Deed given to the purchaser at a court-ordered sale to satisfy a judgment, without warranties.

short sale. A sale for less than is owed on a loan where the lender agrees to accept sale proceeds to extinguish the debt.

sick building syndrome. Illness attributed to a sealed structure; believed related to ventilation.

simple interest. Interest computed on the principal amount of a loan only. *See* **compound interest**.

sinking fund. Fund set aside from the income from property that, with accrued interest, eventually will pay for replacement of the improvements.

sole proprietor. Only owner of a business.

special limitation. A limiting condition specified in a transfer of fee simple ownership that, if not complied with, will immediately and automatically extinguish the estate and return title to the grantor.

special studies zone. One of the areas, typically within a quarter-mile or more of an active earthquake fault, requiring a geologic report for any new project involving improvements or structures initiated after May 4, 1975; the report may be waived by the city or county if the state geologist approves.

special warranty deed. A deed in which the grantor warrants or guarantees the title only against defects arising during the grantor's ownership of the property and not against defects existing before the time of the grantor's ownership.

specific performance. Action to compel a breaching party to adhere to a contract obligation, such as an action to compel the sale of land as an alternative to money damages.

specific plan. Formulated after adoption of a general plan by a city or a county to give further details of community development, including projected population density and building construction requirements.

square-foot method. Way of finding reproduction cost by multiplying the current cost per square foot of a comparable building by the number of square feet in the subject building.

staging. Preparing a home for sale showings.

standard parallels. *See* **correction lines**.

statute of frauds. A state law requiring that certain contracts be in writing and signed before they will be enforceable, such as a contract for the sale of real estate.

statute of limitations. Law that stipulates the specific time period during which a legal action must be brought following the act that gives rise to it.

statutory warranty deed. A short-term warranty deed that warrants by inference that the seller is the undisputed owner, has the right to convey the property, and will defend the title if necessary; if the seller does not do so, the new owner can defend against said claims and sue the former owner.

steering. The illegal act of directing prospective homebuyers to or from a particular residential area on the basis of the homebuyer's race or national origin.

step-up lease. Lease with set rent that provides for periodic rent increases.

stock cooperative. A form of subdivision, typically of an apartment building, in which each owner in the stock cooperative is a shareholder in a corporation that holds title to the property, each shareholder being entitled to use, rent, or sell a specific apartment unit. *See also* **limited equity housing cooperative**.

straight-line method. Depreciation computed at a constant rate over the estimated useful life of the improvement.

straight note. A note in which a borrower repays the principal in a lump sum at maturity, with interest due in installments or at maturity.

subdivision. The division of real property into separate parcels or lots for the purpose of sale, lease, or financing.

subdivision public report. Issued by the real estate commissioner after a subdivision developer has met the requirements of the Subdivided Lands Law; provides details of the project and financing, and a copy must be given to all prospective purchasers; sales may begin on the basis of an approved preliminary public report, but no sales can be closed or transactions completed until the final public report is received.

subject to. When a grantee takes title to real property "subject to" a mortgage or a trust deed, the grantee is not responsible to the holder of the promissory note for the payment of any portion of the amount due, and the original maker of the note retains primary responsibility for the underlying debt or obligation.

sublease. A lease given by a lessee (tenant).

subordination agreement. An agreement by the holder of an encumbrance against real property to permit that claim to take an inferior position to other encumbrances against the property.

subprime lender. A lender who will take loans that are considered too risky by other lenders. Subprime loans bear a higher rate of interest.

substitution, principle of. Market value tends to be set by the present or recent cost of acquiring an equally desirable and valuable property, comparable in construction and/or utility.

supply and demand, principle of. Takes into account the effect on market value of the relationship between the number of properties on the market at a given time and the number of potential buyers.

survey. The process by which a parcel of land is measured and its area ascertained.

syndicate, real estate. *See* real estate syndicate.

take-out loan. The loan arranged by the owner or builder developer for a buyer; the permanent financing that pays off and replaces the interim loan used during construction.

tax deed. Deed issued by the county tax collector when property is sold at public auction because of nonpayment of taxes.

tenancy in common. Co-ownership of property in equal or unequal shares by two or more persons, each holding an undivided interest without right of survivorship.

tenancy in partnership. The ownership by two or more persons, acting as partners, of property held for partnership purposes.

tenant. Lessee under a lease; one who has the legal right to possession and use of property belonging to another.

tentative subdivision map. The initial or tentative map required of subdividers by the Subdivision Map Act, submitted to the local planning commission, which notes its approval or disapproval; a final map embodying any changes requested by the planning commission also must be submitted.

testator. A person who makes a will.

third-party originator. A party who prepares loan applications for borrowers and submits the loan package to lenders.

tiers. In the rectangular survey system of land description, townships running north and south of a base line.

time-share estate. A right of occupancy in a time-share project (subdivision) coupled with an estate in the real property.

time-share project. A form of subdivision of real property into rights to the recurrent, exclusive use or occupancy of a lot, parcel, unit, or segment of the property on an annual or other periodic basis, for a specified period.

time-share use. A license or contractual or membership right of occupancy in a time-share project that is not coupled with an estate in the real property.

title insurance. Insurance to protect a real property owner or a lender up to a specified amount against certain types of loss affecting title or marketability.

tort. Any wrongful act, other than a breach of contract, for which a civil action may be brought by the person wronged.

township. A standard land area of six miles square, divided into 36 sections of one mile square each, used in the rectangular survey system of land description.

toxic mold. Usually a greenish black mold that causes respiratory problems. It usually grows on material with a high cellulose content.

trade fixtures. Articles of personal property that are annexed by a business tenant to real property that are necessary to the carrying on of a trade and are removable by the tenant.

triple net lease. Guarantees a specified net income to the landlord, with the tenant paying that amount, plus all operating and other property expenses, such as taxes, assessments, and insurance.

trust account. An account separate from a broker's own funds (business and personal) in which the broker is required by law to deposit all funds collected for clients before disbursement.

trust deed. A deed issued by a borrower of funds (the trustor) conveying title to a trustee on behalf of a lender, the beneficiary of the trust; the trust deed authorizes the trustee to sell the property to pay the remaining indebtedness to the beneficiary if the trustor defaults on the underlying obligation.

trustee. One who holds property conveyed by a trustor on behalf of (in trust for) the beneficiary, to secure the performance of an obligation.

trustee in bankruptcy. *See* bankruptcy.

trustee's deed. Deed given to the purchaser at a foreclosure sale by the trustee acting under a deed of trust.

trustor. One who conveys property to a trustee to hold on behalf of (in trust for) a beneficiary to secure the performance of an obligation; borrower under a deed of trust.

Truth in Lending Act. Federal act requiring loan term disclosures, as well as advertising disclosures.

undue influence. Use of a fiduciary or confidential relationship to obtain a fraudulent or an unfair advantage over another person because of that's person's weakness of mind, distress, or necessity.

Uniform Commercial Code. Establishes a unified and comprehensive method for regulation of security transactions in personal property, superseding the existing statutes on chattel mortgages, conditional sales, trust receipts, assignments of accounts receivable, and others in this field.

unit-in-place method. Way of estimating building reproduction cost by adding the construction cost per unit of measure of each of the component parts of the subject property; each unit cost includes material, labor, overhead, and builder's profit.

unlawful detainer. The legal action that may be brought to evict a tenant who is in unlawful possession of leased premises.

Unruh Act. California's antidiscrimination act that applies to businesses.

upside-down loan. A loan that exceeds the fair market value of a property.

useful life. The period of years in which a property improvement may be used for its originally intended purpose.

U.S. government survey system. *See* **rectangular survey system**.

usury. The charging of a rate of interest on a loan that is greater than the rate permitted by law.

vacancy decontrol. *See* **rent control**.

vacancy factor. The percentage of a building's space that is unrented over a given period.

value in use. The subjective value of property to its present owner, as opposed to market value, which should be objective.

vicarious liability. A principal is liable for wrongful and negligent acts of the agent within the scope of the agency.

void. To have no force or effect; that which is unenforceable.

voidable. That which can be adjudged void but is not void unless action is taken to make it so.

waiver. The giving up of a right or privilege voluntarily.

warranties, implied. *See* **implied warranties**.

warranty deed. A deed that expressly warrants that the grantor has good title; the grantor thus agrees to defend the premises against the lawful claims of third persons.

warranty of habitability. Legally implied obligation of a landlord to meet minimal housing and building standards.

will. A written, legal declaration of a person called a *testator*, expressing the testator's desires for the disposition of the testator's property after death.

wraparound mortgage or trust deed. Overriding or all-inclusive trust deed; a financing device in which a lender assumes payments on an existing mortgage or trust deed and takes from the borrower a junior mortgage or trust deed with a face value in an amount equal to the amount outstanding on the old instrument and the additional amount of money borrowed.

writ of execution. Court order directing the sheriff or another officer to satisfy a money judgment out of the debtor's property, including real estate not exempt from execution.

writ of possession. Order issued by the court directing the sheriff or the marshal to take all legal steps necessary to remove the occupant(s) from the specified premises.

yield. Profit; return; the interest earned by an investor on an investment or by a bank on the money it has loaned.

zoning. An act of city or county government specifying the possible uses of property in a particular area.

ANSWER KEY

Unit 1

1. **(b)** The real estate marketplace could best be described as being stratified based on price. Demand and supply could vary in different price ranges. p. 8

2. **(a)** Most real estate agents are primarily involved in residential property sales because most properties sold are residential. p. 14

3. **(b)** Real estate salespersons will be treated by the IRS as independent contractors if: the salesperson's reimbursement is based solely on sales, not hours worked; there is a written contract stating that the salesperson shall be treated as an independent contractor for tax purposes; and the salesperson is licensed as a real estate agent. Merely representing oneself as an independent contractor would be a violation of disclosure requirements and is not considered to be an IRS criteria. p. 17

4. **(b)** A broker is ordinarily liable to salespersons for workers' compensation which covers work-related injuries. p. 21

5. **(c)** When choosing a broker, a new licensee should remember that training is more important than commission split for new licensees. p. 26

6. **(d)** The best way to learn is to use the ideas you observe or read about. By using ideas, they become yours. p. 34

7. **(d)** Role-playing situations are only limited by imagination and can be verbalized or nonverbalized. They can also involve more than one person. p. 36

8. **(c)** Exact goals are measurable, such as setting a number of calls you plan to make or appointment for showings to make. p. 39

9. **(c)** It is important to make goals attainable, based on what you want, and exact. Goals should also be shared so you are accountable for making them. When no one knows the goals, it is easier to abandon them. p. 39

10. **(d)** Proper daily planning should: increase "A" Time activities, and place more emphasis on probabilities than possibilities. p. 40

Unit 2

1. **(a)** If a group of brokers agree to not allow another broker to show any of their listings, this is called a group boycott and is prohibited by the Sherman Act. p. 81

2. **(b)** What is legal but unethical is likely to become illegal. p. 63

3. **(d)** All of the following phrases indicate a discriminatory preference: "Christian family," "Prefer working married couple," and "Just two blocks to St. Michael's." p. 71

4. **(b)** If an employer widens the doorway to a restroom to allow wheelchair access, this is considered reasonable accommodation for handicapped and complies with the Americans with Disabilities Act (ADA). p. 73

5. **(d)** The Civil Rights Act of 1866 covers racial discrimination and originally gave rights to former slaves. p. 68

6. **(d)** If a broker specifically shows prospective buyers homes based on racial make-up, this is illegal, unethical, and known as steering. It is specifically prohibited by Civil Rights Act of 1968. p. 71

7. **(c)** A broker can only refuse to show a property to a prospective buyer if the development has an age exemption because all occupants are 55 years of age or older. This is an exception to Fair Housing Act. p. 72

8. **(d)** A landlord cannot refuse to rent to protected classes. p. 72

9. **(a)** The state act that specifically prohibits discrimination in business establishments is the Unruh Act. p. 76

10. **(d)** Placing trust funds in the personal care of a bonded employee is a violation of the law. pp. 82–83

Unit 3

1. **(d)** In a real estate transaction, the agent has a fiduciary duty to their principal, must disclose any known detrimental information to a buyer (even if representing the seller), and must disclose any material facts to their principal. pp. 107–109

2. **(b)** Agency disclosure applies to commercial and residential units and listing agent can only be seller's agent or dual agent. pp. 112–113

3. **(d)** The confirmation of agency must be in writing, the three steps of the disclosure process are disclose, elect, and confirm, and the selling agent must confirm the agency prior to the buyer making an offer. pp. 116–117

4. **(b)** A seller of a 4-unit apartment building must provide a Real Estate Transfer Disclosure Statement. pp. 118–120

5. **(c)** An agent's duty of inspection and disclosure covers a visual inspection only of readily accessible areas. p. 124

6. **(a)** Earthquake safety disclosure only applies to 1–4-unit residential properties. p. 129

7. **(a)** The buyer must sign to acknowledge receipt of a booklet relating to environmental hazards. There is also a booklet Residential Guide to Earthquake Safety for which the buyer also signs a receipt. pp. 129–130

8. **(b)** Brownfields is a term used to describe contaminated soil. p. 137

9. **(c)** The purpose of the Subdivided Lands Law is to protect purchasers from fraud. p. 141

10. **(a)** The right of rescission is provided by law for purchase agreements involving time-shares and undivided interest subdivisions. pp. 153–154

Unit 4

1. **(b)** The CAN-SPAM Act puts control on unsolicited misleading emails. p. 193

2. **(c)** Unlicensed party is limited to introduction and may not engage in any sales activities. p. 209

3. **(d)** Direct mail solicitation for listings is more effective if you indicate you will be contacting them. This forces the recipient to think about your call. You must consider the do-not-call register. p. 214

4. **(d)** Under do-not-call regulations, it would be proper to make a call for survey purposes or as an agent of a prospective buyer. p. 190

5. **(d)** Owners of single housing units would often rather sell than rent. p. 198

6. **(d)** A notice of vacancy is not a legal action. Notices of eviction, foreclosure, and probate are all legal notices and can provide good leads for listings. pp. 199–200

7. **(d)** A high vacancy rate, tenant evictions, and code violations are all indications that an owner might be interested in selling an income property. pp. 199–200

8. **(b)** Endless chain refers to obtaining additional prospects from every lead. p. 207

9. **(d)** The real estate term farming refers to working or prospecting a geographic are or special interest area for buyers and sellers. p. 213

10. **(d)** A nongeographic farm would be specialization in mobile homes, income property, or lots. p. 215

Unit 5

1. **(c)** A comparative market analysis (CMA) shows comparable sale prices and is used to estimate value for listing purposes. p. 222

2. **(c)** The most important portion of your analysis is the prices of comparable properties that have sold since it shows the reality of the marketplace. p. 223

3. **(c)** For data used on the CMA, the older the data, the less reliable and sales prices that seem unusually high or low are often the result of market imperfections. p. 223

4. **(c)** Owners must be made to realize that the higher they price their home over fair market value, the longer it will take to sell and the lower the likelihood of a sale during the listing period. The agent is not doing the seller a favor by taking a listing over market value. pp. 224–225

5. **(c)** A recommended list price below what the CMA indicates is in an owner's best interest when the seller must sell quickly. pp. 224–225

6. **(d)** What a seller receives in hand from a sale is the seller's net proceeds. p. 231

7. **(b)** The principal reason owners try to sell their homes without an agent is to save the commission. Even when not specifically stated, it is frequently the reason an owner wants to try to sell without an agent. p. 235

8. **(d)** Your listing presentation book material should be organized to follow your listing presentation, should not be used in lieu of a verbal presentation, and can be helpful in selling an owner on the concept of listing in general and listing with your firm in particular. p. 231

9. **(d)** When selling the benefits of listing with a small office, the best approach would be to emphasize that you specialize in a small number of select properties. p. 244

10. **(d)** The shorter time to sell is positive while a percentage of success indicates a percentage of failure. pp. 252–254

Unit 6

1. **(d)** A valid exclusive listing requires a lawful purpose, mutual consent, and consideration. p. 263

2. **(d)** A verbal listing is unenforceable. p. 263

3. **(b)** If an open listing is sold by any other party, the listing broker is not entitled to any compensation. This makes it least attractive to a broker and the least likely to be advertised. pp. 264–265

4. **(c)** A listing under which the owner can sell the listed property without paying a commission but the agent is nevertheless an exclusive agent is an exclusive agency listing. p. 272

5. **(b)** Would be entitled to commission if there was a valid listing. p. 272

6. **(d)** An exclusive-right-to-sell listing likely includes an agency relationship disclosure, an attorney fee provision, and an arbitration agreement. p. 266

7. **(d)** In an exclusive-right-to-sell listing, escrow does not have to close for an agent to be entitled to a commission. Additionally, it must have a termination date for the agent to collect a commission, and the agent must give the owner a copy of the listing when the owner signs. It is not true that the agent is precluded from working with other agents to sell the property. p. 266

8. **(c)** The type of listing that has the greatest likelihood of resulting in a sale is an exclusive-right-to-sell listing as it has the best outcome for the agent's work. p. 266

9. **(d)** If an owner tells you that another agent told them that they could get far more for the property than your CMA indicated, your best response would be to state that your CMA covers all recent comparables and clearly shows the market value. Asking to see the CMA prepared by the other agent would be a good idea. p. 285

10. **(d)** By taking a listing at a low fee that will result in a less than normal fee for any cooperating brokers you are not benefiting your office, the selling office, or the owner. p. 288

Unit 7

1. **(b)** The most likely reason why an expired listing was not extended with the original listing office is dissatisfaction with communications. p. 300

2. **(a)** Agent advice to owners on showing their home could include cleaning instructions, landscaping instructions, and repair instructions. However, having the owners present for an open house would probably not be encouraged because buyers are less likely to feel at ease and will not openly discuss their feelings when owners are present. p. 301

3. **(a)** If there has been little or no interest in a property, the agent should convey this information to the sellers. pp. 300, 307

4. **(c)** Standard system used by many lenders. p. 332

5. **(b)** It is good to get neighborhood information from owners to give your listings a competitive advantage. p. 334

6. **(c)** An owner should understand that a list price above the CMA is merely a hope unsupported by fact. Adjusting a price gives nothing away because there is no buyer, and without a buyer there is only an offering price. pp. 312–313

7. **(c)** Placing a rider strip on your listing to show positive features not readily seen such as "4 bedrooms". p. 314

8. **(b)** A property brief should not be used as a substitute for other types of advertising. They are, however, great for a handout at open houses, a handout at caravans, and as a mailing piece in response to enquiries. pp. 318–319

9. **(a)** A broker open house is of greatest value when it is in a large market because many agents may miss the caravan. p. 326

10. **(d)** Advantages of open houses include pleasing owners because they indicate activity, they locate buyers for other properties, and they can obtain leads for listings. They also assist in marketing the property that is open for inspection. p. 327

Unit 8

1. **(b)** The AIDA approach includes: attention, interest, desire, and action. p. 343

2. **(d)** Personal advertising includes name tags, calling cards, blogs and car signs. pp. 346–347

3. **(b)** The term logo refers to an identifying design or symbol. p. 347

4. **(c)** Blind ads fail to include broker identification. p. 351

5. **(b)** The most cost-effective advertising medium for selling a home would be the internet. p. 362

6. **(a)** Classified ads are different from most other forms of real estate advertising because they are actually sought out by the reader. pp. 351–352

7. **(d)** Real estate professionals know that ads that tell about the problems of the property are often very effective, attracting bargain hunters, flippers, and do-it-yourself buyers. p. 352

8. **(c)** An advertiser with an extremely low advertising budget would most likely avoid billboards. Press releases, For Sale signs, and the internet are relatively low- or no-cost. pp. 358–359

9. **(d)** Capital letters are not easier to read than lowercase letters. However, it is true that readers' eyes tend to move from upper left to lower right, one large picture is generally more effective than several smaller ones, and short words are easier to read than long ones. p. 357

10. **(c)** In preparing display ads, a good advertiser should use no more than two typefaces per ad. p. 357

Unit 9

1. **(d)** Callers from a For Sale sign are likely to be satisfied with the area and with the general exterior appearance, or they would not have called. pp. 383–384

2. **(c)** In general, callers from signs are more likely to end up buying homes that cost less than the home they called about and callers from ads are more likely to end up buying homes that cost more than the home they called about. pp. 383–384

3. **(d)** There is duty to attempt to best meet needs of buyers. pp. 394–395

4. **(d)** In showing property, you should adjust to needs of purchaser and show properties based on needs. pp. 394–395

5. **(d)** The qualifying period includes discovering the buyers' motivation, needs, and interests, as well as a down payment they can make and the amount they can finance. p. 397

6. **(a)** The front-end qualifying ratio is the ratio of gross housing cost to gross income. p. 397

7. **(b)** The back-end qualifying ratio refers to the ratio of total housing expense plus long-term debt to gross income. p. 397

8. **(c)** You need information to sell and open-end questions elicit information. p. 394

9. **(d)** All reduce likelihood of becoming a victim. p. 393

10. **(c)** If another agent is showing a home when you arrive for a showing, you should wait inconspicuously until the other agent completes the showing and leaves. p. 418

Unit 10

1. **(d)** A good salesperson does not use technical terms to impress buyers, does not speak fast to reach closing, and does not approach each customer in the same way. pp. 427–428

2. **(d)** A love of family, comfort and convenience, and security are all buying motives. pp. 432–436

3. **(d)** Disadvantages of home ownership include increase in expenses, risk, and a lack of liquidity. p. 438

4. **(d)** Buying signals could include whispering with a spouse, pacing off a room, or seeming reluctant to leave a property. pp. 437–438

5. **(d)** Asking a question is the best response to, "The price is too high." "Why?" would have been the appropriate first question. pp. 438–439

6. **(d)** A professional salesperson knows that it is more effective to ask than tell, it is good to appeal to emotions, and it is not recommended to be assertive with a cautious buyer. pp. 438–442

7. **(b)** When asking a prospective buyer whether he would prefer one of a range of dates, you are using the positive choice closing technique. p. 444

8. **(a)** The paragraph in the purchase contract referring to the intent to occupy is important because it relates to liquidated damages. p. 465

9. **(d)** The buyer and seller by mutual agreement can modify an accepted offer to purchase. p. 467

10. **(b)** The buyer is responsible for the damage to the air conditioning unit based on the California Residential Purchase Agreement and Joint Escrow Instructions. p. 468

Unit 11

1. **(b)** The three separate sales involved in selling real estate are: obtaining the listing, obtaining the offer, and gaining acceptance of the offer. p. 478

2. **(c)** When you receive two offers on a listed property, you should present the offers at the same time and in a nonprejudicial manner, no matter the source of the offers. pp. 480–481

3. **(a)** It would be most difficult to persuade an owner to accept a reasonable offer received three days after listing the property. p. 483

4. **(c)** When presenting an offer on your listing for less than list price, it is good policy to recommend that the sellers counter or reject offers when acceptance is not in their best interest. pp. 495–496

5. **(c)** The common buyer apprehension felt after placing an offer is known as buyer's remorse. p. 487

6. **(b)** Once a counteroffer is not accepted, the owner does not have the option of accepting the original offer. Question asks, "Not True." p. 493

7. **(a)** If an offer received on your listing contains the word "subordination," you should be wary. p. 488

8. **(c)** Rent skimming is a buyer's failure to apply rents to loans that were assumed. p. 489

9. **(d)** If a reasonable, but lower than listing price, offer is received, you should recommend to the owners that they accept the offer. p. 487

10. **(d)** After an offer is accepted, the listing agent should keep track of the escrow progress, make certain all papers are signed by the parties, and make certain that conditions are being met. pp. 499–500

Unit 12

1. **(b)** A loan covering more than one property would be a blanket encumbrance. p. 532

2. **(a)** A reverse mortgage has compound interest. p. 536

3. **(c)** The difference between the interest rate of an index and the rate charged by the lender under an ARM is known as the margin. p. 539

4. **(b)** A lender who believes that interest rates will rise significantly will be least interested in a 30-year fixed-rate mortgage, although a borrower might prefer it. pp. 533–534

5. **(a)** A danger that ARMs pose to buyers is the threat of higher payments if interest rates increase. p. 537

6. **(d)** With an adjustable-rate loan index at 6% at the time the loan is made, a margin for the loan at 2-1/2%, and a 5% lifetime cap, the highest the interest rate could go is 13-1/2%. p. 538

7. **(b)** A convertible ARM is a loan that can be changed to a fixed-rate loan. p. 543

8. **(d)** A buyer who intends to sell a house within two years would prefer a loan with no prepayment penalty, a loan with low initial loan costs, and an assumable loan. pp. 545–546

9. **(b)** An adjustable-rate mortgage is most likely to meet all the criteria of a buyer who intends to sell a house within two years (no prepayment penalty, low initial loan costs, and assumable). p. 545–546

10. **(c)** An expansionary policy of the Federal Reserve would be to buy government securities putting more money into the economy. p. 509

Unit 13

1. **(d)** A broker can act as an escrow when the broker is a principal or represents the buyer or seller in the transaction. pp. 578–579

2. **(a)** An escrow company is prohibited from paying referral fees to anyone other than an employee of the escrow company. p. 580

3. **(b)** To determine the balance due on a loan, escrow requires a beneficiary statement. p. 586

4. **(c)** First trust deed to be assumed by the buyer is a debit to the seller on the seller's closing statement. p. 588

5. **(d)** First trust deed assumed is a credit to the buyer on the buyer's closing statement. Purchase price, escrow costs, and title insurance are debits. p. 588

6. **(d)** An escrow company does not have a duty to warn parties of possible fraud or suggest changes when one party is not being adequately protected. p. 592

7. **(b)** A standard policy of title insurance is used to show that the seller has marketable title. It ensures against undisclosed encumbrances. pp. 599–600

8. **(c)** Unknown spousal interests are covered by the CLTA standard policy of title insurance. p. 599

9. **(b)** Liens placed by the insured are not covered by an ALTA extended policy of title insurance. However, mining claims, water rights, and off-record easements are. pp. 600–601

10. **(d)** Title insurance companies do not give rebates to brokers for referrals, do not give brokers preferred rates on their own purchases, and cannot charge brokers the same as others but make no effort to collect. p. 604

Unit 14

1. **(b)** The most difficult tax to avoid is the real property tax because it cannot be hidden. p. 610

2. **(a)** The months of November, December, February, and April relate to real property taxes. p. 611

3. **(d)** Proposition 13 provided for a maximum tax rate, it set assessments for property acquired before 1978 back to the value on the 1975 tax roll, and allowed for a 2% per year tax increase. pp. 614–615

4. **(d)** Proposition 90 provided for a tax assessment for certain homeowners to be transferred from one county to another. p. 617

5. **(c)** The homeowner's property tax exemption is $7,000 from assessed value. p. 617

6. **(d)** Depreciation for a residential property uses the straight-line method and a 27-1/2-year table. p. 624

7. **(c)** To have a tax-deferred delayed exchange, the exchange property must be identified within 45 days and must be completed within 180 days of the taxpayer relinquishing their property. p. 630

8. **(b)** To have a 1031 tax-deferred exchange, you need to have like-for-like properties, have a trade of investment real property for investment real property, and must hold property after the exchange in the same manner as you held property going into the exchange. pp. 625–630

9. **(b)** If Albert wants to exchange property with Baker, cash received by Albert to balance equities would be boot to Albert in the exchange. Debt relief would also be boot. p. 631

10. **(d)** A homeowner can receive preferential tax treatment by an interest deduction, use of the universal exclusion, and a property tax deduction. pp. 634–635

Unit 15

1. **(b)** The term CPM refers to Certified Property Manager of IREM. p. 651

2. **(a)** Compensation is generally a percentage of the gross. Percentage is lower for higher income properties. p. 668

3. **(c)** A property manager can be protected against receiving no fees when managing a vacant property they are unable to rent by a minimum fee. p. 668

4. **(c)** A lease for 30 months would be described as an estate for years because it is a definite fixed period. p. 675

5. **(a)** A lease under which the tenant is to pay $500 per month for three years is a gross, or flat, lease (fixed rent). p. 676

6. **(a)** A lease that contains a minimum rent and a covenant to remain in business is a percentage lease. p. 677

7. **(a)** A parking lot would likely pay the highest percentage on a percentage lease. p. 678

8. **(c)** A supermarket would likely pay the lowest percentage on a percentage lease. p. 678

9. **(b)** A valid two-year lease need not contain a legal description of the property. pp. 680, 687–690

10. **(d)** Regarding security deposits, the following is true: nonrefundable cleaning deposits are not allowed, deposits for furnished rentals cannot exceed three months' rent, and security deposits for unfurnished rentals cannot exceed two months' rent. p. 687

INDEX

Notes

Notes

Notes

Notes

Notes

Notes

Notes

Notes

Notes

Notes

Notes

Notes

Notes